The GALE
ENCYCLOPEDIA
of SCIENCE

The GALE ENCYCLOPEDIA of SCIENCE

VOLUME 4
Lacewings – Phenyl group

Bridget Travers,
Editor

Gale Research

An ITP Information/Reference Group Company

Changing the Way the World Learns

NEW YORK • LONDON • BONN • BOSTON • DETROIT
MADRID • MELBOURNE • MEXICO CITY • PARIS
SINGAPORE • TOKYO • TORONTO • WASHINGTON
ALBANY NY • BELMONT CA • CINCINNATI OH

The GALE ENCYCLOPEDIA of SCIENCE

Bridget Travers, *Editor*

Sheila M. Dow, *Coordinating Editor (Advisors)*
James Edwards, *Coordinating Editor (Databases)*
Paul Lewon, *Coordinating Editor (Illustrations)*
Jacqueline Longe, *Coordinating Editor (Contributors)*
Donna Olendorf, *Coordinating Editor (Submissions, Indexing)*

Christine B. Jeryan, Kyung-Sun Lim, Kimberley A. McGrath, Robyn V. Young, *Contributing Editors*

Kristine M. Binkley, Zoran Minderovic, *Associate Editors*

Nicole Beatty, Pamela Proffett, Carley Wellman, *Assistant Editors*

Linda R. Andres, Shelly Andrews, Dawn R. Barry, Ned Burels, Melissa Doig, David Oblender, *Contributors*

Marlene S. Hurst, *Permissions Manager*
Margaret A. Chamberlain, *Permissions Specialist*
Susan Brohman, *Permissions Associate*

Victoria B. Cariappa, *Research Manager*
Maureen Richards, *Research Specialist*

Mary Beth Trimper, *Production Director*
Evi Seoud, Assistant *Production Manager*
Shanna Heilveil, *Production Assistant*

Cynthia Baldwin, *Product Design Manager*
Mary Krzewinski, *Art Director*
Barbara Yarrow, *Graphic Services Manager*
Randy Bassett, *Image Database Supervisor*
Robert Duncan, *Digital Imaging Specialist*
Pamela A. Hayes, *Photography Coordinator*

Benita L. Spight, Manager, *Data Entry Services*
Gwendolyn S. Tucker, *Data Entry Supervisor*
Beverly Jendrowski, *Senior Data Entry Associate*
Francis L. Monroe, *Data Entry Associate*

Jeffrey Muhr, Roger M. Valade, III, *Editorial Technical Services Associates*

Indexing provided by the Electronic Scriptorium

Gale encyclopedia of science / Bridget E. Travers, editor.
    p.   cm.
    Includes bibliographical references and index.
    Summary: Contains 2,000 entries ranging from short definitions to major overviews of concepts in all areas of science.
    ISBN 0–08103–9841–9 (alk. paper)
    1. Science--Encyclopedias, Juvenile.   [1. Science--Encyclopedias.]   I. Travers, Bridget.
    Q121.G35 1995
503--dc20   95-25402
                                                          CIP
                                                          AC

CONTENTS

ORGANIZATION OF THE ENCYCLOPEDIA

The Gale Encyclopedia of Science has been designed with ease of use and ready reference in mind.

- Entries are **alphabetically arranged** in a single sequence, rather than by scientific field.

- Length of entries varies from **short definitions** of one or two paragraphs to longer, more **detailed entries** on complex subjects.

- Longer entries are arranged so that an **overview** of the subject appears first, followed by a detailed discussion conveniently arranged under subheadings.

- A list of **key terms** are provided where appropriate to define unfamiliar terms or concepts.

- Longer entries conclude with a **further reading** section, which points readers to other helpful sources.

- The **contributor's name** appears at the end of longer entries. His or her affiliation can be found in the "Contributors" section at the front of each volume.

- **"See-also" references** appear at the end of entries to point readers to related entries.

- **Cross-references** placed throughout the encyclopedia direct readers to where information on subjects without their own entries can be found.

- A comprehensive **general index** guides readers to all topics and persons mentioned in the book.

ADVISORY BOARD

A number of experts in the library and scientific communities provided invaluable assistance in the formulation of this encyclopedia. Our advisory board performed a myriad of duties, from defining the scope of coverage to reviewing individual entries for accuracy and accessibility. We would therefore like to express our appreciation to them:

Academic Advisors

Bryan Bunch
Adjunct Instructor
Department of Mathematics
Pace University

David Campbell
Head
Department of Physics
University of Illinois at Urbana
    Champaign

Neil Cumberlidge
Professor
Department of Biology
Northern Michigan University

Bill Freedman
Professor
Department of Biology and
    School for Resource and Environmental Studies
Dalhousie University

Clayton Harris
Assistant Professor
Department of Geography and
    Geology
Middle Tennessee State University

William S. Pretzer
Curator
Henry Ford Museum and Greenfield Village
Dearborn, Michigan

Theodore Snow
Fellow and Director
Center for Astrophysics and
    Space Research
University of Colorado at Boulder

Robert Wolke
Professor emeritus
Department of Chemistry
University of Pittsburgh

Richard Addison Wood
Meteorlogical Consultant
Tucson, Arizona

Librarian Advisors

Donna Miller
Director
Craig-Moffet County Library
Craig, Colorado

Judy Williams
Media Center
Greenwich High School
Greenwich, Connecticut

Carol Wishmeyer
Science and Technology Department
Detroit Public Library
Detroit, Michigan

CONTRIBUTORS

Nasrine Adibe
Professor Emeritus
Department of Education
Long Island University
Westbury, New York

Mary D. Albanese
Department of English
University of Alaska
Juneau, Alaska

James L. Anderson
Soil Science Department
University of Minnesota
St. Paul, Minnesota

Susan Andrew
Teaching Assistant
University of Maryland
Washington, D.C.

John Appel
Director
Fundación Museo de Ciencia y
  Tecnología
Popayán, Colombia

David Ball
Assistant Professor
Department of Chemistry
Cleveland State University
Cleveland, Ohio

Dana M. Barry
Editor and Technical Writer

Center for Advanced Materials
  Processing
Clarkston University
Potsdam, New York

Puja Batra
Department of Zoology
Michigan State University
East Lansing, Michigan

Donald Beaty
Professor Emeritus
College of San Mateo
San Mateo, California

Eugene C. Beckham
Department of Mathematics and
  Science
Northwood Institute
Midland, Michigan

Martin Beech
Research Associate
Department of Astronomy
University of Western Ontario
London, Ontario

Massimo D. Bezoari
Associate Professor
Department of Chemistry
Huntingdon College
Montgomery, Alabama

John M. Bishop III
Translator
New York, New York

T. Parker Bishop
Professor
Middle Grades and Secondary
  Education
Georgia Southern University
Statesboro, Georgia

Carolyn Black
Professor
Incarnate Word College
San Antonio, Texas

Larry Blaser
Science Writer
Lebanon, Tennessee

Jean F. Blashfield
Science Writer
Walworth, Wisconsin

Richard L. Branham Jr.
Director
Centro Rigional de
  Investigaciones Científicas y
  Tecnológicas
Mendoza, Argentina

Patricia Braus
Editor
American Demographics
Rochester, New York

David L. Brock
Biology Instructor
St. Louis, Missouri

Leona B. Bronstein
Chemistry Teacher (retired)
East Lansing High School
Okemos, Michigan

Brandon R. Brown
Graduate Research Assistant
Oregon State University
Corvallis, Oregon

Lenonard C. Bruno
Senior Science Specialist
Library of Congress
Chevy Chase, Maryland

Scott Christian Cahall
Researcher
World Precision Instruments, Inc.
Bradenton, Florida

G. Lynn Carlson
Senior Lecturer
School of Science and
  Technology
University of Wisconsin—
  Parkside
Kenosha, Wisconsin

James J. Carroll
Center for Quantum Mechanics
The University of Texas at Dallas
Dallas, Texas

Steven B. Carroll
Assistant Professor
Division of Biology
Northeast Missouri State
  University
Kirksville, Missouri

Rosalyn Carson-DeWitt
Physician and Medical Writer
Durham, North Carolina

Yvonne Carts-Powell
Editor
Laser Focus World
Belmont, Massachustts

Chris Cavette
Technical Writer
Fremont, California

Kenneth B. Chiacchia
Medical Editor

University of Pittsburgh Medical
  Center
Pittsburgh, Pennsylvania

M. L. Cohen
Science Writer
Chicago, Illinois

Robert Cohen
Reporter
KPFA Radio News
Berkeley, California

Sally Cole-Misch
Assistant Director
International Joint Commission
Detroit, Michigan

George W. Collins II
Professor Emeritus
Case Western Reserve
Chesterland, Ohio

Jeffrey R. Corney
Science Writer
Thermopolis, Wyoming

Tom Crawford
Assistant Director
Division of Publication and
  Development
University of Pittsburgh Medical
  Center
Pittsburgh, Pennsylvania

Pamela Crowe
Medical and Science Writer
Oxon, England

Clinton Crowley
On-site Geologist
Selman and Associates
Fort Worth, Texas

Edward Cruetz
Physicist
Rancho Santa Fe, California

Frederick Culp
Chairman
Department of Physics
Tenneesse Technical
Cookeville, Tennessee

Neil Cumberlidge
Professor

Department of Biology
Northern Michigan University
Marquette, Michigan

Mary Ann Cunningham
Environmental Writer
St. Paul, Minnesota

Les C. Cwynar
Associate Professor
Department of Biology
University of New Brunswick
Fredericton, New Brunswick

Paul Cypher
Provisional Interpreter
Lake Erie Metropark
Trenton, Michigan

Stanley J. Czyzak
Professor Emeritus
Ohio State University
Columbus, Ohio

Rosi Dagit
Conservation Biologist
Topanga-Las Virgenes Resource
  Conservation District
Topanga, California

David Dalby
President
Bruce Tool Company, Inc.
Taylors, South Carolina

Lou D'Amore
Chemistry Teacher
Father Redmund High School
Toronto, Ontario

Douglas Darnowski
Postdoctoral Fellow
Department of Plant Biology
Cornell University
Ithaca, New York

Sreela Datta
Associate Writer
Aztec Publications
Northville, Michigan

Sarah K. Dean
Science Writer
Philadelphia, Pennsylvania

Sarah de Forest
Research Assistant
Theoretical Physical Chemistry
 Lab
University of Pittsburgh
Pittsburgh, Pennsylvania

Louise Dickerson
Medical and Science Writer
Greenbelt, Maryland

Marie Doorey
Editorial Assistant
Illinois Masonic Medical Center
Chicago, Illinois

Herndon G. Dowling
Professor Emeritus
Department of Biology
New York University
New York, New York

Marion Dresner
Natural Resources Educator
Berkeley, California

John Henry Dreyfuss
Science Writer
Brooklyn, New York

Roy Dubisch
Professor Emeritus
Department of Mathematics
New York University
New York, New York

Russel Dubisch
Department of Physics
Sienna College
Loudonville, New York

Carolyn Duckworth
Science Writer
Missoula, Montana

Peter A. Ensminger
Research Associate
Cornell University
Syracuse, New York

Bernice Essenfeld
Biology Writer
Warren, New Jersey

Mary Eubanks

Instructor of Biology
The North Carolina School of
 Science and Mathematics
Durham, North Carolina

Kathryn M. C. Evans
Science Writer
Madison, Wisconsin

William G. Fastie
Department of Astronomy and
 Physics
Bloomberg Center
Baltimore, Maryland

Barbara Finkelstein
Science Writer
Riverdale, New York

Mary Finley
Supervisor of Science Curriculum
 (retired)
Pittsburgh Secondary Schools
Clairton, Pennsylvania

Gaston Fischer
Institut de Géologie
Université de Neuchâtel
Peseux, Switzerland

Sara G. B. Fishman
Professor
Quinsigamond Community
 College
Worcester, Massachusetts

David Fontes
Senior Instructor
Lloyd Center for Environmental
 Studies
Westport, Maryland

Barry Wayne Fox
Extension Specialist,
 Marine/Aquatic Education
Virginia State University
Petersburg, Virginia

Ed Fox
Charlotte Latin School
Charlotte, North Carolina

Kenneth L. Frazier
Science Teacher (retired)
North Olmstead High School

North Olmstead, Ohio

Bill Freedman
Professor
Department of Biology and
 School For Resource and
 Environmental Studies
Dalhousie University
Halifax, Nova Scotia

T. A. Freeman
Consulting Archaeologist
Quail Valley, California

Elaine Friebele
Science Writer
Cheverly, Maryland

Randall Frost
Documentation Engineering
Pleasanton, California

Robert Gardner
Science Education Consultant
North Eastham, Massachusetts

Gretchen M. Gillis
Senior Geologist
Maxus Exploration
Dallas, Texas

Kathryn Glynn
Audiologist
Portland, Oregon

Natalie Goldstein
Educational Environmental
 Writing
Phoenicia, New York

David Gorish
TARDEC
U.S. Army
Warren, Michigan

Louis Gotlib
South Granville High School
Durham, North Carolina

Hans G. Graetzer
Professor
Department of Physics
South Dakota State University
Brookings, South Dakota

Jim Guinn
Assistant Professor
Department of Physics
Berea College
Berea, Kentucky

Steve Gutterman
Psychology Research Assistant
University of Michigan
Ann Arbor, Michigan

Johanna Haaxma-Jurek
Educator
Nataki Tabibah Schoolhouse of
   Detroit
Detroit, Michigan

Monica H. Halka
Research Associate
Department of Physics and
   Astronomy
University of Tennessee
Knoxville, Tennessee

Jeffrey C. Hall
Astronomer
Lowell Observatory
Flagstaff, Arizona

C. S. Hammen
Professor Emeritus
Department of Zoology
University of Rhode Island

Beth Hanson
Editor
The Amicus Journal
Brooklyn, New York

Clay Harris
Associate Professor
Department of Geography and
   Geology
Middle Tennessee State
   University
Murfreesboro, Tennessee

Catherine Hinga Haustein
Associate Professor
Department of Chemistry
Central College
Pella, Iowa

Dean Allen Haycock
Science Writer
Salem, New York

Paul A. Heckert
Professor
Department of Chemistry and
   Physics
Western Carolina University
Cullowhee, North Carolina

Darrel B. Hoff
Department of Physics
Luther College
Calmar, Iowa

Dennis Holley
Science Educator
Shelton, Nebraska

Leonard Darr Holmes
Department of Physical Science
Pembroke State University
Pembroke, North Carolina

Rita Hoots
Instructor of Biology, Anatomy,
   Chemistry
Yuba College
Woodland, California

Selma Hughes
Department of Psychology and
   Special Education
East Texas State University
Mesquite, Texas

Mara W. Cohen Ioannides
Science Writer
Springfield, Missouri

Zafer Iqbal
Allied Signal Inc.
Morristown, New Jersey

Sophie Jakowska
Pathobiologist, Environmental
   Educator
Santo Domingo, Dominican
   Republic

Richard A. Jeryan
Senior Technical Specialist
Ford Motor Company
Dearborn, Michigan

Stephen R. Johnson
Biology Writer
Richmond, Virginia

Kathleen A. Jones
School of Medicine
Southern Illinois University
Carbondale, Illinois

Harold M. Kaplan
Professor
School of Medicine
Southern Illinois University
Carbondale, Illinois

Anthony Kelly
Science Writer
Pittsburgh, Pennsylvania

Amy Kenyon-Campbell
Ecology, Evolution and
   Organismal Biology Program
University of Michigan
Ann Arbor, Michigan

Eileen M. Korenic
Institute of Optics
University of Rochester
Rochester, New York

Jennifer Kramer
Science Writer
Kearny, New Jersey

Pang-Jen Kung
Los Alamos National Laboratory
Los Alamos, New Mexico

Marc Kusinitz
Assistant Director Media
   Relations
John Hopkins Medical Instituition
Towsen, Maryland

Arthur M. Last
Head
Department of Chemistry
University College of the Fraser
   Valley
Abbotsford, British Columbia

Nathan Lavenda
Zoologist
Skokie, Illinios

Jennifer LeBlanc
Environmental Consultant
London, Ontario

Benedict A. Leerburger
Science Writer
Scarsdale, New York

Betsy A. Leonard
Education Facilitator
Reuben H. Fleet Space Theater
  and Science Center
San Diego, California

Scott Lewis
Science Writer
Chicago, Illinois

Frank Lewotsky
Aerospace Engineer (retired)
Nipomo, California

Karen Lewotsky
Cartographer
Portland, Oregon

Kristin Lewotsky
Editor
Laser Focus World
Nashua, New Hamphire

Stephen K. Lewotsky
Architect
Grants Pass, Oregon

Sarah Lee Lippincott
Professor Emeritus
Swarthmore College
Swarthmore, Pennsylvania

David Lunney
Research Scientist
Centre de Spectrométrie
  Nucléaire et de Spectrométrie de
  Masse
Orsay, France

Steven MacKenzie
Ecologist
Spring Lake, Michigan

J. R. Maddocks
Consulting Scientist
DeSoto, Texas

Gail B. C. Marsella
Technical Writer
Allentown, Pennsylvania

Karen Marshall
Research Associate
Council of State Governments
  and Centers for Environment
  and Safety
Lexington, Kentucky

Liz Marshall
Science Writer
Columbus, Ohio

James Marti
Research Scientist
Department of Mechanical
  Engineering
University of Minnesota
Minneapolis, Minnesota

Elaine L. Martin
Science Writer
Pensacola, Florida

Lilyan Mastrolla
Professor Emeritus
San Juan Unified School
Sacramento, California

Iain A. McIntyre
Manager
Electro-optic Department
Energy Compression Research
  Corporation
Vista, California

G. H. Miller
Director
Studies on Smoking
Edinboro, Pennsylvania

J. Gordon Miller
Botanist
Corvallis, Oregon

Christine Miner Minderovic
Nuclear Medicine Technologist
Franklin Medical Consulters
Ann Arbor, Michigan

David Mintzer
Professor Emeritus
Department of Mechanical

Engineering
Northwestern University
Evanston, Illinois

Christine Molinari
Science Editor
University of Chicago Press
Chicago, Illinois

Frank Mooney
Professor Emeritus
Fingerlake Community College
Canandaigua, New York

Partick Moore
Department of English
University of Arkansas at Little
  Rock
Little Rock, Arkansas

Robbin Moran
Department of Systematic Botany
Institute of Biological Sciences
University of Aarhus
Risskou, Denmark

J. Paul Moulton
Department of Mathematics
Episcopal Academy
Glenside, Pennsylvania

Otto H. Muller
Geology Department
Alfred University
Alfred, New York

Angie Mullig
Publication and Development
University of Pittsburgh Medical
  Center
Trafford, Pennsylvania

David R. Murray
Senior Associate
Sydney University
Sydney, New South Wales
Australia

Sutharchana Murugan
Scientist Three Boehringer
  Mannheim Corp.
Indianapolis, Indiana

Muthena Naseri
Moorpark College

Moorpark, California

David Newton
Science Writer and Educator
Ashland, Oregon

F. C. Nicholson
Science Writer
Lynn, Massachusetts

James O'Connell
Department of Physical Sciences
Frederick Community College
Gaithersburg, Maryland

Dónal P. O'Mathúna
Associate Professor
Mount Carmel College of
  Nursing
Columbus, Ohio

Marjorie Pannell
Managing Editor, Scientific
  Publications
Field Museum of Natural History
Chicago, Illinois

Gordon A. Parker
Lecturer
Department of Natural Sciences
University of Michigan—
  Dearborn
Dearborn, Michigan

David Petechuk
Science Writer
Ben Avon, Pennsylvania

John R. Phillips
Department of Chemistry
Purdue University, Calumet
Hammond, Indiana

Kay Marie Porterfield
Science Writer
Englewood, Colorado

Paul Poskozim
Chair
Department of Chemistry, Earth
  Science and Physics
Northeastern Illinois University
Chicago, Illinois

Andrew Poss
Senior Research Chemist
Allied Signal Inc.
Buffalo, New York

Satyam Priyadarshy
Department of Chemistry
University of Pittsburgh
Pittsburgh, Pennsylvania

Patricia V. Racenis
Science Writer
Livonia, Michigan

Cynthia Twohy Ragni
Atmospheric Scientist
National Center for Atmospheric
  Research
Westminster, Colorado

Jordan P. Richman
Science Writer
Phoenix, Arizona

Kitty Richman
Science Writer
Phoenix, Arizona

Vita Richman
Science Writer
Phoenix, Arizona

Michael G. Roepel
Researcher
Department of Chemistry
University of Pittsburgh
Pittsburgh, Pennsylvania

Perry Romanowski
Science Writer
Chicago, Illinois

Nancy Ross-Flanigan
Science Writer
Belleville, Michigan

Gordon Rutter
Royal Botanic Gardens
Edinburgh, Great Britain

Elena V. Ryzhov
Polytechnic Institute
Troy, New York

David Sahnow
Associate Research Scientist

John Hopkins University
Baltimore, Maryland

Peter Salmansohn
Educational Consultant
New York State Parks
Cold Spring, New York

Peter K. Schoch
Instructor
Department of Physics and
  Computer Science
Sussex County Community
  College
Augusta, New Jersey

Patricia G. Schroeder
Instructor
Science, Healthcare, and Math
  Division
Johnson County Community
  College
Overland Park, Kansas

Randy Schueller
Science Writer
Chicago, Illinois

Kathleen Scogna
Science Writer
Baltimore, Maryland

William Shapbell Jr.
Launch and Flight Systems
  Manager
Kennedy Space Center, Florida

Anwar Yuna Shiekh
International Centre for
  Theoretical Physics
Trieste, Italy

Raul A. Simon
Chile Departmento de Física
Universidad de Tarapacá
Arica, Chile

Michael G. Slaughter
Science Specialist
Ingham ISD
East Lansing, Michigan

Billy W. Sloope
Professor Emeritus
Department of Physics

Virginia Commonwealth
University
Richmond, Virginia

Douglas Smith
Science Writer
Milton, Massachusetts

Lesley L. Smith
Department of Physics and
Astronomy
University of Kansas
Lawrence, Kansas

Kathryn D. Snavely
U.S. General Accounting Office
Policy Analyst, Air Quality Issues
Raleigh, North Carolina

Charles H. Southwick
Professor
Environmental, Population, and
Organismic Biology
University of Colorado at
Boulder
Boulder, Colorado

John Spizzirri
Science Writer
Chicago, Illinois

Frieda A. Stahl
Professor Emeritus
Department of Physics
California State University, Los
Angeles
Los Angeles, California

Robert L. Stearns
Department of Physics
Vassar College
Poughkeepsie, New York

Ilana Steinhorn
Science Writer
Boalsburg, Pennsylvania

David Stone
Conservation Advisory Services
Gai Soleil
Chemin Des Clyettes
Le Muids, Switzerland

Eric R. Swanson
Associate Professor

Department of Earth and Physical
Sciences
University of Texas
San Antonio, Texas

Cheryl Taylor
Science Educator
Kailua, Hawaii

Nicholas C. Thomas
Department of Physical Sciences
Auburn University at
Montgomery
Montgomery, Alabama

W. A. Thomasson
Science and Medical Writer
Oak Park, Illinois

Marie L. Thompson
Science Writer
Ben Avon, Pennsylvania

Melvin Tracy
Science Educator
Appleton, Wisconsin

Karen Trentelman
Research Associate
Archaeometric Laboratory
University of Toronto
Toronto, Ontario

Robert K. Tyson
Senior Scientist
W. J. Schafer Assoc.
Jupiter, Florida

James Van Allen
Professor Emeritus
Department of Physics and
Astronomy
University of Iowa
Iowa City, Iowa

Julia M. Van Denack
Biology Instructor
Silver Lake College
Manitowoc, Wisconsin

Kurt Vandervoort
Department of Chemistry and
Physics
West Carolina University
Cullowhee, North Carolina

Chester Vander Zee
Naturalist, Science Educator
Volga, South Dakota

Jeanette Vass
Department of Chemistry
Cuyahoga Community College
Timberlake, Ohio

R. A. Virkar
Chair
Department of Biological
Sciences
Kean College
Iselin, New Jersey

Kurt C. Wagner
Instructor
South Carolina Governor's
School for Science and
Technology
Hartsville, South Carolina

Cynthia Washam
Science Writer
Jensen Beach, Florida

Joseph D. Wassersug
Physician
Boca Raton, Florida

Tom Watson
Environmental Writer
Seattle, Washington

Jeffrey Weld
Instructor, Science Department
Chair
Pella High School
Pella, Iowa

Frederick R. West
Astronomer
Hanover, Pennsylvania

Glenn Whiteside
Science Writer
Wichita, Kansas

John C. Whitmer
Professor
Department of Chemistry
Western Washington University
Bellingham, Washington

CONTRIBUTORS

Donald H. Williams
Department of Chemistry
Hope College
Holland, Michigan

Robert L. Wolke
Professor Emeritus
Department of Chemistry
University of Pittsburgh
Pittsburgh, Pennsylvania

Jim Zurasky
Optical Physicist
Nichols Research Corporation
Huntsville, Alabama

ACKNOWLEDGEMENTS

Photographs appearing in the *Gale Encyclopedia of Science* were received from the following sources:

© Account Phototake/Phototake: **Genetic disorders**; © James Allem, Stock Market: **Gazelles**; © A. W. Ambler, National Audubon Society Collection/Photo Researchers, Inc.: **Goats, Newts, Sedimentary rock**; © Toni Angermayer, National Audubon Society Collection/Photo Researchers, Inc.: **Hamsters**; © Mark Antman/Phototake: **Textiles**; AP/Wide World Photos: **Elements, formation of**; © Archiv, National Audubon Society Collection/Photo Researchers, Inc.: **Astrolabe**; © Bachman, National Audubon Society Collection/Photo Researchers, Inc.: **Wombats**; © Bill Bachman, National Audubon Society Collection/Photo Researchers, Inc.: **Grasslands**; Baiyer River Sanctuary, New Guinea © Tom McHugh, National Audubon Society Collection/Photo Researchers, Inc.; © M. Baret/RAPHU, National Audubon Society Collection/Photo Researchers, Inc.: **Biotechnology**; Jen and Des Bartlett, National Audubon Society Collection/Photo Researchers, Inc.: **Sea lions**; © Jen and Des Bartlett, National Aububon Society Collection/Photo Researchers, Inc.: **Cicadas, Langurs and leaf monkeys, Aardvark, Bandicoots, Grebes, Lorises, Monitor lizards, Opossums, Pipefish, Sea horses, Secretary bird, Spiny anteaters**; © Bat Conservation Int'l: **Bats**; © John Bavosi, National Audubon Society Collection/ Photo Researchers, Inc.: **Hernia**; Tom Bean: **Archaeology**; © Tom Bean, Stock Market: **Volcano**; © James Bell, National Audubon Society Collection/Photo Researchers, Inc.: **Buds and budding**; © Pierre Berger, National Audubon Society Collection/Photo Researchers, Inc.: **Beech family**; © J. Bernholc et al, North Carolina State University/Science Photo Library, National Audubon Society Collection/Photo Researchers, Inc.: **Buckminsterfullerene**; © The Bettmann Archive: **Chemical warfare, Photography**; © Art Bileten, National Audubon Society Collection/Photo Researchers, Inc.: **North America**; © Biophoto Associates, National Audubon Society Collection/Photo Researchers, Inc.: **Acne, Chromosome, Tropical diseases, Spina bifida**; © Wesley Bocxe, National Audubon Society Collection/Photo Researchers, Inc.: **Oil spills**; © Mark Boulton, National Audubon Society Collection/Photo Researchers, Inc.: **Bustards, Erosion**; © Malcolm Boulton, National Audubon Society Collection/Photo Researchers, Inc.: **Porcupines, Baboons**; © Mark N. Boulton, National Audubon Society Collection/Photo Researchers, Inc.: **Yak**; © Dr. Tony Brain/Science Photo Library, National Audubon Society Collection/Photo Researchers, Inc.: **Aerobic**; © Thomas H. Brakefield, Stock Market: **Cats**; © Tom Brakefield, Stock Market: **Wolverine**; © 1980 Ken Brate, National Audubon Society Collection/Photo Researchers, Inc.: **Citrus trees**; Andrea Brizzi, Stock Market: **Sewage treatment**; © S. Brookens, Stock Market: **Mynah birds**; © John R. Brownlie, National Audubon Society Collection/Photo Researchers, Inc.: **Lyrebirds**; © Dr. Jeremy Brugess/Science Photo Library, National Audubon Society Collection/ Photo Researchers, Inc.: **Leaf, Chloroplast, Aphids, Battery**; © John Buitenkant 1993, National Audubon Society Collection/Photo Researchers, Inc.: **Buttercup**; © 1994, Michele Burgess/Bikderberg, Stock Market: **Elephant**; © Michele Burgess, Stock Market: **Flightless birds**; © Jane Burton, National Audubon Society Collection/Photo Researchers, Inc.: **Pangolins**; © Diana Calder/Bikderberg, Stock Market: **Barometer**; © Scott Camazinr, National Audubon Society Collection/Photo Researchers, Inc.: **AIDS**; © Tardos Camesi/Bikderberg, Stock

ACKNOWLEDGEMENTS

Market: **Transformer**; © John Cancalosi: **Numbat**; © Robert Caputo, National Audubon Society Collection/Photo Researchers, Inc.: **Hyena**; © Alan D. Carey, National Audubon Society Collection/Photo Researchers, Inc.: **Captive breeding and reintroduction, Coffee plant**; © Carolina Biological Supply Company/Phototake: **Chemoreception, Microscopy, Plant, Cashew family, Yeast**; © Tom Carrill/Phototake: **Pollution control**; © Tom Carroll/Phototake: **Air pollution, Bridges, Freeway**; © CBC/CBC/Phototake: **Petrels and shearwaters**; © Jean-Loup Charmet, National Audubon Society Collection/Photo Researchers, Inc.: **Anesthesia, Rabies**; © Ann Chawatsky/Phototake: **Burn**; © Ron Church, National Audubon Society Collection/Photo Researchers, Inc.: **Barracuda**; © Geoffrey Clifford,Stock Market: **Fractal**; © CNRI/ Science Photo Library, Nationa Audubon Society Collection/Photo Researchers, Inc.: **Influenza**; © CNRI/Phototake: **Leprosy**; © CNRI/Science Photo Library, National Audubon Society Collection/ Photo Researchers, Inc.: **Enterobacteria**; © Pedro Coll, Stock Market: **Cave, Machine tools**; © Holt Confer/Phototake: **Cranes**; © Judd Cooney/Phototake: **Weasels**; © Tony Craddock, National Audubon Society Collection/Photo Researchers, Inc.: **Microwave communication**; © Allan D. Cruickshank, National Audubon Society Collection/Photo Researchers, Inc.: **Cuckoos, Gila monster**; © Russell D. Curtis, National Audubon Society Collection/ Photo Researchers, Inc.: **Sleep disorders**; © Tim Davis, National Audubon Society Collection/Photo Researchers, Inc.: **Colobus monkeys, Finches**; © John Deeks, National Audubon Society Collection/Photo Researchers, Inc.: **Clouds**; © E.R. Degginger, National Audubon Society Collection/Photo Researchers, Inc.: **Tundra**; © Nigel Dennis, National Audubon Society Collection/Photo Researchers, Inc.: **Flamingos**; © Jack Dermid, National Audubon Society Collection/Photo Researchers, Inc.: **Dune**; © Jack Dermid 1979, National Audubon Society Collection/Photo Researchers, Inc.: **Bromeliad family**; © Jack Dermid, National Audubon Society Collection/Photo Researchers, Inc.: **Puffer fish**; © 1992 Alan L. Detrick, National Audubon Society Collection/Photo Researchers, Inc.: **Amaranth family**; © Mike Devlin, National Audubon Society Collection/Photo Researchers, Inc.: **Prosthetics**; © Richard Dibon-Smith, National Audubon Society Collection/Photo Researchers, Inc.: **Sheep**; © Gregory G. Dimijian 1990, National Audubon Society Collection/Photo Researchers, Inc.: **Coca**; © Thomas Dimock, Stock Market: **Crabs**; © Martin Dohrn, National Audubon Society Collection/Photo Researchers, Inc.: **Interference, Skeletal system**; © Martin Dohrn/Science Photo Library, National Audubon Society Collection/Photo Researchers, Inc.: **Wave motion**; © Dopamine-CNRI, National Audubon Society Collection/Photo Researchers, Inc.: **Ulcers**; © A. B. Dowsett/Science Photo Library, National Audubon Society Collection/ Photo Researchers, Inc.: **Virus**; © John Dudak/Phototake: **Arrowroot, Composite family**; © Richard Duncan,National Audubon Society Collection/Photo Researchers, Inc.: **Geometry**; © Hermann Eisenbeiss, National Audubon Society Collection/Photo Researchers, Inc.: **Surface tension**; © Thomas Ernsting, Stock Market: **Metric system**; © Thomas Ernsting/Bikderberg, Stock Market: **Virtual reality**; © 1992 Robert Essel/Bikderberg, Stock Market: **Electricity**; © Robert Essel, Stock Market: **Moose**; © Kenneth Eward/BioGrafx, National Audubon Society Collection/Photo Researchers, Inc.: **Atom**; © Dr. Brian Eyden, National Audubon Society Collection/Photo Researchers, Inc.: **Cancer**; © Douglas Faulkner, National Audubon Society Collection/Photo Researchers, Inc.: **Manatee, Coral reef**; © Fawcett, National Audubon Society Collection/ Photo Researchers, Inc.: **Cell**; © Fawcett/Phillips, National Audubon Society Collection/Photo Researchers, Inc.: **Flagella**; © Kenneth W. Fink, National Audubon Society Collection/Photo Researchers, Inc.: **Turacos**; © Cecil Fox/Science Source, National Audubon Society Collection/Photo Researchers, Inc.: **Alzheimer's disease**; © Carl Frank, National Audubon Society Collection/Photo Researchers, Inc.: **Rivers**; © Stephen Frink, Stock Market: **Squirrel fish**; © Petit Fromat/Nestle, National Audubon Society Collection/Photo Researchers, Inc.: **Embryo and embryonic development**; © G.R. Gainer, Stock Market: **Spiral**; Gale Research Inc.: **Jet engine**; © Gordon Garrado/Science Photo Library, National Audubon Society Collection/Photo Researchers, Inc.: **Thunderstorm**; © Frederica Georgia, National Audubon Society Collection/Photo Researchers, Inc.: **Hydrothermal vents**; © Ormond Gigli, Stock Market: **Frigate birds**; © 1989 Ned Gillette, Stock Market: **Mass wasting**; © A. Glauberman, National Audubon Society Collection/Photo Researchers, Inc.: **Cigarette smoke**; © F. Gohier 1982, National Audubon Society Collection/Photo Researchers, Inc.: **Amaryllis family**; © Francois Gohier, National Audubon Society Collection/Photo Researchers, Inc.: **Stromatolites**; © Spencer Grant, National Audubon Society Collection/Photo Researchers, Inc.: **Robotics**; © Stephen Green-Armytage, Stock Market:

Boas; © Al Greene and Associates, National Audubon Society Collection/Photo Researchers, Inc.: **Coast and beach**; © Barry Griffiths, National Audubon Society Collection/Photo Researchers, Inc.; © Tommaso Guicciardini/Science Photo Library, National Audubon Society Collection/Photo Researchers, Inc.: **Gravity**; © Dan Guravich 1987, National Audubon Society Collection/Photo Researchers, Inc.: **Atmospheric optical phenomena**; © Dan Guravich, National Audubon Society Collection/Photo Researchers, Inc.: **Alluvial systems**; © A. Gurmankin 1987/Phototake: **Begonia**; © Clem Haagner, National Audubon Society Collection/Photo Researchers, Inc.: **Giraffes and okapi**; © Hugh M. Halliday, National Audubon Society Collection/Photo Researchers, Inc.: **Shrikes**; © David Halpern, National Audubon Society Collection/Photo Researchers, Inc.: **Oil drilling**; © Chris Hamilton, Stock Market: **Waterwheel**; © Craig Hammell/Bikderberg, Stock Market: **Caliper**; © Hammond Incorporated, Maplewood, New Jersey.: **Bar code**; © 1993 Brownie Harris, Stock Market : **Antenna**; © Brownie Harris, Stock Market: **Turbine**; © Adam Hart-Davis/Science Photo Library, National Audubon Society Collection/Photo Researchers, Inc.: **Electrostatic devices**; © Adam Hart-Davis, National Audubon Society Collection/Photo Researchers, Inc.: **Thermometer, Integrated circuit**; © Anne Heimann, Stock Market: **Horseshoe crabs**; © Robert C. Hermes,National Audubon Society Collection/Photo Researchers, Inc.: **Mayflies**; © John Heseltine, National Audubon Society Collection/Photo Researchers, Inc.: **Geodesic dome**; © Andrew Holbrooke, Stock Market: **Landfill, Prosthetics**; © Holt Studios International, National Audubon Society Collection/Photo Researchers, Inc.: **Cashew family**; © Eric Hosking, F.R.P.S., National Audubon Society Collection/Photo Researchers, Inc.: **Auks**; © Eric Hosking, National Audubon Society Collection/Photo Researchers, Inc.: **Kingfishers, Loons, Mice, Stilts and avocets**; © John Howard, National Audubon Society Collection/Photo Researchers, Inc.: **Electromagnetic Field**; Robert J. Huffman/Field Mark Publications.: **Anoles, Anteaters, Armadillos, Bison, Blackbirds, Butterflies, Cactus, Capybaras, Carnivorous plants, Carnivorous plants, Composting, Cormorants, Cranes, Crayfish, Crows and jays, Deer, Ducks, Eagles, Falcons, Fossil and fossilization, Frogs, Fungi, Geese, Goats, Gulls, Hawks, Herons (2 photos), Horsetails, Ibises, Iguanas, Juniper, Koalas, Mockingbirds and thrashers, Moths (2 photos), Nuclear fission, Nuthatches, Oaks, Owls (2 photos), Parrots, Peafowl, Peccaries, Pelican, Pheasants, Pigeons and doves, Prairie dog, Praying mantis, Quail, Recycling, Rhinoceros, Sandpipers, Seals, Sparrows and buntings, Squirrels, Starfish, Swallows and martins, Swans, Terns, Thistle, Thrushes, Turkeys, Turtles, Tyrant flycatchers, Warblers, Waste management, Wetlands, Wrens, Zebras**; IBM Almaden: **Compact disc**; © Institut Pastuer/Phototake: **Immune system**; © Bruce Iverson/Science Photo Library, National Audubon Society Collection/Photo Researchers, Inc.: **Electric motor**; © Jacana, National Audubon Society Collection/Photo Reasearchers, Inc.: **Tuna**; © Y. Lanceau Jacana, National Audubon Society Collection/Photo Researchers, Inc.: **Carp**; JLM Visuals: **Acid rain, Africa, Agricultural machines, Agronomy, Alternative energy sources, Animal breeding, Antarctica, Arachnids, Astroblemes, Australia, Barrier Islands, Bitterns, Blue revolution, Brick, Bridges, Buoyancy, Principle of, Camels, Carnivore, Chameleons, Coal, Cotton, Crop rotation, Cycads, Deposit, Desert, Dinosaur, Disturbance, ecological, Dogwood tree, Dust devil, Earthquake, Endangered species, Europe, Fault, Ferns, Ferrets, Flax, Flooding, Fold, Fossil and fossilization, Freshwater, Gerbils, Ginger, Ginkgo, Glaciers, Goatsuckers, Gourd family, Grasses, Grasshoppers, Groundwater, Heath family, Hornbills, Horse chestnut, Ice ages, Igneous rocks, Introduced species, Iris family, Irrigation, Karst topography, Lagomorphs, Lake, Land use, Legumes, Lice, Lichens, Liverwort, Lobsters, Mangrove tree, Marmots, Mass wasting, Milkweeds, Mint family, Mistletoe, Mulberry family, Muskoxen, Mutation, Myrtle family, Nightshade, Octopus, Olive family, Orchid family, Oviparous, Paleobotany, Palms, Pandas, Penguins, Peninsula, Petroleum, Pigs, Pike, Plate tectonics, Pollination, Poppies, Prairie chicken, Pythons, Radio astronomy, Rushes, Savanna, Saxifrage family, Scavenger, Scorpionfish, Sculpins, Sea anemones, Sea level, Sedges, Sediment and sedimentation, Segmented worms, Sequoia, Shrimp, Silk cotton family, Skinks, Snails, Species, Spiderwort family, Storks, Swamp cypress family, Symbiosis, Tea plant, Terracing, Territoriality, Thermal expansion, Tides (2 photos), Trains and railroads, Turbulence, Vireos, Volcano, Vultures, Walnut family, Waterlilies, Wheat, Woodpeckers**; © Mark A. Johnson, Stock Market: **Jellyfish**; © Verna Johnston 1972, National Audubon Society Collection/Photo Researchers, Inc.: **Amaryllis family**; © Verna R. Johnston, National Audubon Society Collection/Photo

Researchers, Inc.: **Gophers**; © Darrell Jones, Stock Market: **Marlins**; © Chris Jones Photo, Stock Market: **Mining**; © Chris Jones, Stock Market: **Mass Production**; © Joyce Photographics, National Audubon Society Collection /Photo Researchers, Inc.: **Soil, Eutrophication**; © Robert Jureit, Stock Market: **Desert**; © John Kaprielian, National Audubon Society Collection/Photo Researchers, Inc.: **Buckwheat**; © Ed Kashi/Phototake: **CAD/CAM/CIM**; © Ted Keane, National Audubon Society Collection/Photo Researchers, Inc.: **Arum family**; © Michael A. Keller 1989, Stock Market: **Nutrition**; © Tom Kelly/Phototake : **Submarine**; © Karl W. Kenyon, National Audubon Society Collection/Photo Researchers, Inc.: **Otters**; © Paolo Koch, National Audubon Society Collection/Photo Researchers, Inc.: **Ore**; © Carl Koford, National Audubon Society Collection/Photo Researchers, Inc.: **Condors**; © Stephen J. Krasemann, National Audubon Society Collection/Photo Researchers, Inc.: **Prescribed burn**; © Charles Krebs, Stock Market: **Dating techniques, Walruses**; © J. Kubec A. NR.m, Stock Market: **Glass**; © Dr. Dennis Kunkel/Phototake: **Membrane, Natural fibers**; © Dennis Kunkel/Phototake : **Blood**; Dennis Kunkel (2) /Phototake: **Mites**; © Maurice & Sally Landre, National Audubon Society Collection/Photo Researchers, Inc.: **Bromeliad family**; © Lawrence Livermore National Laboratory/Science Photo Library, National Audubon Society Collection/Photo Researchers, Inc.: **States of matter**; © Lawrence Berkeley Laboratory/Science Photo Library, National Audubon Society Collection/Photo Researchers, Inc.: **Cyclotron, Particle detectors**; © Francis Leroy, Biocosmos/Science Photo Library, National Audubon Society Collection/Photo Researchers, Inc.: **Hydrothermal vents**; © Tom & Pat Lesson, National Audubon Society Collection/Photo Researchers, Inc.: **Old-growth forests**; © Yoav Levy/Phototake: **Acupuncture, Motion, Machines, simple, Phases of matter, Superconductor, Viscosity, Water pollution**; © Dr. Andrejs Liepins, National Audubon Society Collection/Photo Researchers, Inc.: **Hodgkin's disease**; © Norman Lightfoot, National Audubon Society Collection/Photo Researchers, Inc.: **Albinism**; © Suen-O Linoblad,National Audubon Society Collection/Photo Researchers, Inc.: **Eland**; © R. Ian Lloyd, Stock Market: **Island**; © Paul Logsdon/Phototake: **Contour plowing**; Courtesy of Jacqueline Longe.: **Ultrasonics**; © Dr. Kari Lounatimaa/ Science Photo Library, National Audubon Society Collection/Photo Researchers, Inc.: **Asexual reproduction**; © Alexander Lowry, National Audubon Society Collection/Photo Researchers, Inc.: **Hazardous wastes**; © Renee Lynn, National Audubon Society Collection/Photo Researchers, Inc.: **Capuchins**; © John Madere, Stock Market: **Mass transportation**; © Dr. P. Marazzi, National Audubon Society Collection/Photo Researchers, Inc.: **Edema**; © Andrew J. Martinez, National Audubon Society Collection/Photo Researchers, Inc.: **Flatfish**; © Bob Masini/Phototake: **Radial keratotomy**; © Karl H. Maslowski, National Audubon Society Collection/Photo Researchers, Inc.: **Caribou, Weaver finches**; © Don Mason, Stock Market: **Bats**; © Cynthia Matthews, Stock Market: **Birth**; © C. G. Maxwell, National Audubon Society Collection/Photo Researchers, Inc.: **Cattails**; © Henry Mayer, National Audubon Society Collection/Photo Researchers, Inc.: **Beech family**; © Fred McConnaughey, National Audubon Society Collection/Photo Researchers, Inc.: **Boxfish, Cuttlefish, Mackerel**; © Tom McHugh/Science Source, National Audubon Society Collection/Photo Researchers, Inc.: **Fossil and fossilization**; © Tom McHugh, National Audubon Society Collection/Photo Researchers, Inc.: **Bowerbirds, Canines, Elapid snakes, Elephant shrew, Gibbons and siamangs, Gorillas, Mole-rats, Skates, Sturgeons, Vipers, Salamanders**; © Will and Deni McIntyre, National Audubon Society Collection/Photo Researchers, Inc.: **Canal, Dyslexia, Amniocentesis, Lock**; © Eamonn McNulty, National Audubon Society Collection/Photo Researchers, Inc.: **Pacemaker**; © Dilip Mehia/Contact Giza, Stock Market: **Pyramid**; © Anthony Mercieca Photo, National Audubon Society Collection/Photo Researchers, Inc.: **Bluebirds**; © Astrid & Hanns-Frieder Michler/Science Photo Library, National Audubon Society Collection/Photo Researchers, Inc.: **Precipitation**; © 1983 Lawrence Midgale, National Audubon Society Collection/Photo Researchers, Inc.: **Composite family**; Courtesy of J. Gordon Miller.: **Horses**; © Mobil Solar Energy Corporation/Phototake: **Photovoltaic cell**; © Viviane Moos, Stock Market: **Perpendicular, Smog**; © Moredun Animal Health LTD, National Audubon Society Collection/Photo Researchers, Inc.: **Thrombosis**; © Hank Morgan, National Audubon Society Collection/Photo Researchers, Inc.: **In vitro fertilization**; © Hank Morgan, National Audubon Society Collection/Photo Researchers, Inc.: **Radiation detectors**; © Roy Morsch, Stock Market: **Bioluminescence, Seeds, Toucans**; © Roy Morsch/Bikderberg, Stock Market: **Dams**; © John Moss, National Audubon Society Collection/Photo Researchers, Inc.: **Aqueduct**; © Prof. P. Motta/Dept. of Anatomy/University La Sapienza,

Rome/Science Photo Library, National Audubon Society Collection/Photo Researchers, Inc.: **Connective tissue, Skeletal system, Osteoporosis**; © Prof. P. Motta/G. Macchiarelli/University La Sapienza, Rome/Science Photo Library, National Audubon Society Collection/ Photo Researchers, Inc.: **Heart**; © Mug Shots, Stock Market: **Electrocardiogram**; © Joe Munroe, National Audubon Society Collection/Photo Researchers, Inc.: **Amaranth family, Starlings**; © Dr. Gopal Murti, National Audubon Society Collection/Photo Researchers, Inc.: **Sickle cell anemia**; © S. Nagendra, National Audubon Society Collection/Photo Researchers, Inc.: **Spider monkeys**; © NASA/Science Photo Library, National Audubon Society Collection/Photo Researchers, Inc.: **Radar**; © NASA, National Audubon Society Collection/Photo Researchers, Inc.: **Satellite**; NASA: **Aircraft (2 photos), Airship, Balloon, Black Hole, Comets, Constellation, Dark Matter, Earth, Jupiter (3 photos), Mars (3 photos), Mercury (2 photos), Meteors and meteorites, Moon (3 photos), Neptune (2 photos), Planetary nebulae, Pluto, Rockets and missiles, Saturn (2 photos), Saturn, Solar flare, Solar system, Space Shuttle, Spacecraft, manned, Sun (2 photos), Sunspots, Telephone, Tropical cyclone, Uranus (2 photos), Venus (2 photos)**; © National Aububon Society Collection/Photo Researchers, Inc.: **Monoculture, Aye-ayes, Bass, Chinchilla, Crocodiles, Fossa, Lemur, Plastics, Pneumonia**; © Tom Nebbia, Stock Market: **Drought**; © Nelson-Bohart & Associates/Phototake: **Metamorphosis**; © Ray Nelson/Phototake: **Amplifier**; © Joseph Nettis, National Audubon Society Collection/Photo Researchers, Inc.: **Computerized axial tomography**; © Mark Newman/Phototake: **Glaciers**; © Newman Laboratory of Nuclear Studies, Cornell University, National Audubon Society Collection/Photo Researchers, Inc.: **Subatomic particles**; © NIH, National Audubon Society Collection/Photo Researchers, Inc.: **Artificial heart and heart valve**; © Novosti Press Agency, National Audubon Society Collection/Photo Researchers, Inc.: **Nuclear fusion, Spacecraft, manned**; © Richard Nowitz/Phototake: **Engraving and etching**; © Gregory Ochocki, National Audubon Society Collection/Photo Researchers, Inc.: **Ocean sunfish**; © John Olson , Stock Market : **Brewing, Metal production**; © Omikron, National Audubon Society Collection/Photo Researchers, Inc.: **Lampreys and hagfishes, Squid**; © Omikron, National Audubon Society Collection/Photo Researchers, Inc.: **Tarsiers**; © Stan Osolinski 1993, Stock Market: **Predator**; © Stan Osolinski 1992, Stock Market: **Evolution**; © 1992 Gabe Palmer/Bikderberg, Stock Market: **Sextant**; © David Parker, ESA/National Audubon Society Collection/Photo Researchers, Inc.: **Rockets and missiles**; © David Parker/Science Photo Library, National Audubon Society Collection/Photo Researchers, Inc.: **Oscilloscope**; © David Parker, National Audubon Society Collection/Photo Researchers, Inc.: **Computer, digital**; © Claudia Parks, Stock Market: **Coast and beach**; © David Parler, National Audubon Society Collection/Photo Researchers Inc.: **Particle detector**; © Pekka Parviatnen, National Audubon Society Collection/Photo Researchers, Inc.: **Auroras**; © Alfred Pasieka/Science Photo Library, National Audubon Society Collection/Photo Researchers, Inc.: **Magnetism**; © Bryan F. Peterson, Stock Market: **Natural Gas**; © David M. Phillips/The Population Council/Science Source, National Audubon Society Collection/Photo Researchers, Inc.: **Fertilization**; © Mark D. Phillips, National Audubon Society Collection/Photo Researchers, Inc.: **Monkeys**; © Phototake: **Oryx**; Phototake (CN) /Phototake: **Abscess**; © Photri, Stock Market: **Explosives**; © 1973 Photri/Bikderberg, Stock Market: **Tornado**; © Roy Pinney, National Audubon Society Collection/Photo Researchers, Inc.: **Arum family**; © Philippe Plailly, National Audubon Society Collection/Photo Researchers, Inc.: **Hologram and holography, Microscopy, Gene therapy**; © Philippe Plailly/Eurelious/Science Photo Library, National Audubon Society Collection/Photo Researchers, Inc.: **Microscopy**; © Philippe Plailly/Eurelios, National Audubon Society Collection/Photo Researchers, Inc.: **Electrostatic devices**; © Rod Planck, National Audubon Society Collection/Photo Researchers, Inc.: **Mosquitoes**; © Planet Earth: **Coelacanth, Crocodiles, Orang-utan, Tapirs**; © 1986 David Pollack/Bikderberg, Stock Market: **Concrete**; © J. Polleross, Stock Market: **Emission**; © Marco Polo/Phototake: **Slash-and-burn agriculture**; © Cecilia Posada/Phototake: **Assembly line**; © Masud Quraishy, National Audubon Society Collection/Photo Researchers, Inc.: **Cats**; © E. Hanumantha Rao, National Audubon Society Collection/Photo Researchers, Inc.: **Bee-eaters**; © Rapho, National Audubon Society Collection/Photo Researchers, Inc.: **Dik-diks**; © G. Carleton Ray, National Audubon Society Collection/Photo Researchers, Inc.: **Sharks**; © Hans Reinhard/Okapia 1990, National Audubon Society Collection/Photo Researchers, Inc.: **Carrot family**; © H. Reinhard/Okapia, National Audubon Society Collection/Photo Researchers, Inc.: **Buzzards**; © Roger Ressmeyer/Starlight/for the W. M. Keck Observatory, courtesy of California Associate for Research and Astronomy.: **Telescope**; © Chris Rogers/Bikderberg, Stock Market: **Laser**; © Otto Rogge, Stock Market: **Precious metals**; © Frank Rossotto, Stock Market: **Temperature regulation**; © Martin M. Rotker/Phototake: **Adrenals, Aneurism**; Neasaphus Rowalewkii: **Fossil and fossilization**; © Royal Greenwhich Observatory, National Audubon Society Collection/Photo Researchers, Inc.: **Atomic clocks**; © Royal Observatory, Edinburgh/AATB/Science Photo Library, National Audubon Society Collection/Photo Researchers, Inc.: **Star cluster**; © Royal Observatory, Edinburgh/National Audubon Society Collection/Photo Researchers, Inc.: **Telescope**; © Ronald Royer/Science Photo Library, National Audubon Society Collection/Photo Researchers, Inc.: **Star**; © Leonard Lee Rue III, National Audubon Society Collection/Photo Researchers, Inc.: **Groundhog, Kangaroos and wallabies, Mongooses, Muskrat, Coatis, Rats, Rusts and smuts, Seals**; © Leonard Lee Rue, National Audubon Society Collection/Photo Researchers, Inc.: **Camels**; © Leonard Lee Rue, National Audubon Society Collection/Photo Researchers, Inc.: **Shrews**; © Len Rue Jr., National Audubon Society Collection/Photo Researchers, Inc.: **Badgers**; © S.I.U.,National Audubon Society Collection/Photo Researchers, Inc.: **Lithotripsy**; © 1994 Ron Sanford, Stock Market: **Behavior**; © Nancy Sanford, Stock Market: **Mink**; © Ron Sanford, Stock Market: **Beavers, Raccoons**; © Science Photo Library, National Audubon Society Collection/Photo Researchers, Inc.: **Arthritis, Gangrene, Artificial fibers**; Science Photo Library: **Binary star, Galaxy, Halley's comet, Milky Way, Paleontology, Star formation**; Science Source: **Eclipses, Quasar**; © Secchi-Lecague/Roussel-UCLAF/CNRI/Science Photo Library, National Audubon Society Collection/Photo Researchers, Inc.: **Neuron**; © Nancy Sefton, National Audubon Society Collection/Photo Researchers, Inc.: **Sponges**; © Dr. Gary Settles/Science Source, National Audubon Society Collection/Photo Researchers, Inc.: **Aerodynamics**; James Lee Sikkema: **Elm , Gesnerias, Grapes, Holly family, Lilac, Lily family, Lily family, Maples, Mustard family, Nightshade, Pines, Rose family, Spruce, Spurge family, Swamp cypress family, Willow family**; © Lee D. Simon, National Audubon Society Collection/Photo Researchers, Inc.: **Bacteriophage**; © James R. Simon, National Audubon Society Collection/Photo Researchers, Inc.: **Sloths**; © Ben Simon, Stock Market: **Elephant;** © SIU, National Audubon Society Collection/Photo Researchers, Inc.: **Frostbite**; © SIU, National Audubon Society Collection/ Photo Researchers, Inc.: **Birth**; © Prof. D. Skobeltzn, National Audubon Society Collection/Photo Researchers, Inc.: **Cosmic rays**; © Howard Sochurek, Stock Market: **Gene**; © Dr. M.F. Soper, National Audubon Society Collection/Photo Researchers, Inc.: **Plovers**; Courtesy of Charles H. Southwick: **Macaques, Rhesus monkeys**; © James T. Spencer, National Audubon Society Collection/Photo Researchers, Inc.: **True eels**; © Hugh Spencer, National Audubon Society Collection/Photo Researchers, Inc.: **Spore**; © Spielman/CNRI/Phototake: **Lyme disease**; © St Bartholomew's Hospital, National Audubon Society Collection/Photo Researchers, Inc.: **Bubonic Plague**; © Alvin E. Staffan, National Audubon Society Collection/Photo Researchers, Inc.: **Walkingsticks**; © S. Stammers, National Audubon Society Collection/Photo Researchers, Inc.: **Interferons**; © Peter Steiner, Stock Market: **LED**; © Tom Stewart, Stock Market: **Icebergs**; © David Stoeklein, Stock Market: **Partridges**; © Streinhart Aquarium, National Audubon Society Collection/Photo Researchers, Inc.: **Geckos**; © Mary M. Thacher, National Audubon Society Collection/Photo Researchers, Inc.: **Genets**; © Mary M. Thatcher, National Audubon Society Collection/Photo Researchers, Inc.: **Carrot family**; © Asa C. Thoresen, National Audubon Society Collection/Photo Researchers, Inc.: **Slash-and-burn agriculture**; Geoff Tompkincon, National Audubon Society Collection/Photo Researchers, Inc.: **Surgery**; © Geoff Tompkinson, National Audubon Society Collection/Photo Researchers, Inc.: **Cryogenics**; © Tom Tracy, National Audubon Society Collection/Photo Researchers, Inc.: **Refrigeration**; © Alexander Tsiaras, National Audubon Society Collection/Photo Researchers, Inc.: **Cauterization, Transplant, surgical**; © George Turner, National Audubon Society Collection/Photo Researchers, Inc.: **Cattle family;** © U.S. Fish & Wildlife Service: **Canines, Kangaroo rats, Toads, Turtles**; © Akira Uchiyama, National Audubon Society Collection/Photo Researchers, Inc.: **Saiga antelope**; © Howard Earl Uible, National Audubon Society Collection/Photo Researchers, Inc.: **Marmosets and tamarins**; © Howard E. Uible, National Audubon Society Collection/Photo Researchers, Inc.: **Tenrecs**; © R. Van Nosstrand, National Audubon Society Collection/Photo Researchers, Inc.: **Gibbons and siamang**; © G. Van Heijst and J. Flor, National Audubon Society Collection/Photo Researchers, Inc.: **Chaos**; © Irene Vandermolen, National Audubon Society Collection/Photo Researchers, Inc.: **Banana**; © K. G. Vock/Okapia, National Audubon Society Collection/Photo

Researchers, Inc.: **Birch family**; © Ken Wagner/Phototake: **Herbicides, Agrochemicals**; © Susan Woog Wagner, National Audubon Society Collection/Photo Researchers, Inc.: **Down's syndrome**; © M. I. Walker/Science Photo Library, National Audubon Society Collection/Photo Researchers, Inc.: **Copepods**; © Kennan Ward, Stock Market: **Chimpanzees, Salmon**; Bill Wassman: **Dinosaur**; © C. James Webb/Phototake: **Smallpox**; C. James Webb/Phototake: **Elephantiasis**; © Ulrike Welsch, National Audubon Society Collection/Photo Researchers, Inc.: **Deforestation**; © Jerome Wexler 1981, National Audubon Society Collection/Photo Researchers, Inc.: **Carnivorous plants**; © Herbert Wexler, National Audubon Society Collection/Photo Researchers, Inc.: **Livestock;** © Jeanne White, National Audubon Society Collection/Photo Researchers, Inc.: **Hippopotamuses, Dragonflies**; © George Whiteley, National Audubon Society Collection/Photo Researchers, Inc.: **Horticulture**; © Mark Wilson, National Audubon Society Collection/Photo Researchers, Inc.: **Falcons**; © Charles D. Winters, National Audubon Society Collection/Photo Researchers, Inc.: **Centrifuge**; © Anthony Wolff/Phototake: **Boobies and Gannets**; Illustrations reprinted by permission of Robert L. Wolke.: **Air pollution (2 illustrations), Aluminum, Amino acid, Atom, Barbiturates, Calorimetry, Carbon (3 illustrations), Chemical bond (3 illustrations), Chemical compound (2 illustrations), Crystal, Deoxyribonucleic Acid (DNA), Earth's interior, Electrolysis, Electrolyte, Electromagnetic spectrum, Ester, Fatty acids, Gases, properties of (4 illustrations), Hydrocarbon (3 illustrations), Metric system, Metabolism, Molecule, Nuclear fission (2 illustrations), Plastics, Radiation, Soap, Solution, States of matter (2 illustrations), Water, X rays**; © David Woods, Stock Market: **Cockatoos**; © Norbert Wu, Stock Market: **Courtship, Rays**; © Zefa Germany, Stock Market: **Codfishes, Forests, Hummingbirds, Mole, Rain forest**; © 1994 Zefa Germany, Stock Market: **Bears, Mimicry, Pollination**.

Line art illustrations provided by Hans and Cassady of Westerville, Ohio.

L

Lacebugs see **True bugs**

Lacewings

Lacewings are insects in the order Neuroptera, sub-order Planipennia. Lacewings are named after the fine, complex, cross–branched venation of their four wings, which presents a beautiful, lacelike pattern. Lacewings are rather poor, fluttery fliers. When at rest, they hold their wings tentlike over their back.

Lacewings have a complete metamorphosis, with four life history stages: egg, larva, pupa, and adult. The eggs of lacewings are laid on vegetation, and occur singly at the end of a long stalk. The aquatic larvae are predators of other invertebrates. The larvae of some species of lacewings cover themselves with organic debris as a form of protective camouflage.

Adult lacewings are commonly found in vegetation, usually in the vicinity of surface waters such as streams and ponds. At night, lacewings are often attracted to lights in large numbers. Adult lacewings are terrestrial, and most species are predators of other insects. Some species are important predators of aphids (family Aphididae, order Homoptera) and other soft–bodied insects, and they can be beneficial by helping to prevent those sap–sucking insects from maintaining populations that are injurious to economically important plants.

The most abundant lacewings in North America are the greenish–colored, common, or green lacewings (family Chrysopidae), sometimes known as aphid–lions because of their voracious feeding on herbivorous insects. These lacewings can be quite abundant in herbaceous vegetation near aquatic habitats, and when handled they may give off an unpleasant–smelling odor. *Chrysopa californica* is a western species that has been mass–reared and used as a biological control of certain species of mealybugs (family Coccoidea, order Homoptera) in agriculture. The brown lacewings (family Hemerobiidae) are another relatively common group, while the pleasing lacewings (Dilaridae), beaded lacewings (Berothidae), ithonid lacewings (Ithonidae), and giant lacewings (Polystoechotidae) are relatively rare groups.

Lactic acid

Lactic acid is a colorless, water–soluble liquid that freezes, or solidifies, at 62° F (18° C)—just slightly below normal room temperature. It is scientifically known as alpha–hydroxypropanoic acid and has the chemical formula $C_3H_6O_3$; the structural formula is shown below:

$$
\begin{array}{c}
\text{H} - \text{COOH} \\
| \\
\text{HO} - \text{C} - \text{H} \\
| \\
\text{H} - \text{C} - \text{H} \\
| \\
\text{H}
\end{array}
$$

The "hydroxy" portion of the name tells chemists that there is an alcohol (OH) group in the molecule, and the "alpha" part of the name means that the alcohol is attached to the carbon atom adjacent to the acid (COOH) group. The "prop" portion of the name indicates that there are three carbon atoms. Lactic acid can also be called 2–hydroxypropanoic acid. Each of the two isomers rotates polarized light in a different direction: the L–isomer rotates light to the left, and the D–isomer rotates light to the right. Like most acids, lactic acid has a sour taste. It is found in sour milk, molasses, and many fruits. The lactic acid found in milk is usually a mixture of both isomers. It is used commercially in the textile and dairy industries. Lactic acid is the by–product of anaerobic respiration, and is largely responsible for the aches in sore muscles after a vigorous workout.

Lactic acid in foods

Lactic acid is found throughout nature—from fruits to molasses, although most people's experience with lactic acid is in sour milk. Lactic acid in milk is the product of the fermentation of lactose (milk sugar) by the bacteria *lactobacillus bulgaris* and *lactobacillus acidi lacti*. In the manufacture of yogurt, this reaction is carefully controlled to ensure the production of yogurt and not spoiled milk. The lactic acid in molasses is the product of the digestion of sugars by other species of bacteria.

Lactic acid in human metabolism

Lactic acid is the product of anaerobic respiration, the burning of stored sugars without sufficient oxygen by cells. Anaerobic respiration is much less efficient than aerobic respiration, for which there is enough oxygen to fully utilize the stored sugar energy. Essentially, anaerobic respiration causes the halving of glucose molecules $(C_6H_{12}O_6)$ into lactic acid molecules $(C_3H_6O_3)$. The lactic acid builds up in muscles, accounting for the soreness in overworked muscles. This build-up of lactic acid may also lead to cramps. One advantage of anaerobic respiration is that it can take place very quickly and in short bursts, as opposed to aerobic respiration, which is designed for slower and more steady use of muscles. Eventually the build-up of lactic acid is carried away in the bloodstream and the lactic acid is converted to carbon dioxide (CO_2) gas and water vapor, both of which are exhaled. If lactic acid levels in the bloodstream rise faster than the body's natural pH buffers—combinations of acids, salts, and bases that maintain a constant pH level—can neutralize them, a state known as lactic acidosis may exist. Lactic acidosis rarely happens in healthy people. It is more likely the result of the body's inability to obtain sufficient oxygen (as in heart attacks or carbon monoxide or cyanide poisoning) or from other diseases such as diabetes.

The ability of the body to metabolize, or break down, lactic acid is decreased significantly by alcohol, which impairs the liver's ability to carry out normal metabolic reactions. Thus, alcoholics often have sore muscles from lactic acid build up that was not caused by exercise. Lactic acid can also lead to a build-up of uric acid crystals in the joints, since lactic acid reduces

KEY TERMS

Buffers—Combinations of acids, bases, and salts that neutralize changes in pH.

Humectant—A moisturizing agent, often used in cosmetics.

Isomers—Different arrangements of the atoms of the same chemical formula, resulting in different molecules with different properties.

Mordant—A chemical that helps fabrics accept dyes more readily.

Polarized light—Light that vibrates in a single plane, as opposed to ordinary light that vibrates in all planes.

the elimination of uric acid and related compounds. This build-up can lead to gout, a very painful disease.

Uses of lactic acid

Lactic acid is used as a humectant, or moisturizer, in some cosmetics and as a mordant, a chemical that helps fabrics accept dyes, in textiles. It is also used in making pickles and sauerkraut, foods for which a sour taste is desired. Lactic acid is used in the dairy industry not only in making yogurt but in making cheese as well. It is also used in tanning leather. Lactic acid is important in the pharmaceutical industry as a starting material for other substances and is involved in the manufacturing of lacquers and inks. A related compound that is made from lactic acid is calcium stearoyl–2–lactylate, which is used as a food preservative.

See also Acids and bases; Metabolic disorders; Metabolism.

Further Reading:

"Babies Fuss Over Post–Exercise Milk." *Science News*. vol. 142, July 18, 1992, p. 47.

Chase, Marilyn. "High Lactic Acid Found in Patients with Huntington's." *The Wall Street Journal*. Oct 27, 1992, p. B12.

Drake, Geoff. "The Lactate Shuttle—Contrary to What You've Heard, Lactic Acid is Your Friend." *Bicycling*. vol. 33, August 1992, p. 36.

Roberts, Marjorie. "Keeping Yogurt Honest—Its Reputation as a Health Food May Not Always be Deserved." *U.S. News and World Report*. vol. 109, November 5, 1990, p. 76.

"Some Babies Turn Up their Noses at Breast Milk After Mom Exercises." *Environmental Nutrition*. vol. 16, June, 1993, p. 3.

Louis Gotlib

Lactose see **Carbohydrates**

Lady's slipper see **Orchid family**

Ladybugs see **Beetles**

Lagomorphs

Lagomorphs are herbivorous mammals such as rabbits, hares, and pikas, in the order Lagomorpha. Because they exploit similar ecological niches, lagomorphs and rodents (order Rodentia) are rather similar in many aspects of their morphology and behavior. However, these orders are also different in important respects, and each represents an ancient evolutionary lineage.

One distinguishing feature of the lagomorphs is the two pairs of upper incisor teeth, one set being relatively small and located behind the larger pair. These incisors grow throughout the life of lagomorphs, and are completely covered with enamel; the larger pair has rather deep, vertical grooves. The incisors are used for clipping vegetation, and they are separated from the high–crowned cheek teeth, used for grinding food, by a rather wide gap, technically known as a diastema.

In addition, lagomorphs have five toes on the forefeet and four on the hind, a dense, short fur, covering a thin, fragile skin that tears rather easily. The tail of these animals is short or absent. All lagomorphs are herbivores. Their major food is succulent leaves and herbaceous stems of a wide range of plant species. However, twigs and buds are also eaten, especially by northern species during the winter. Lagomorphs have a specialized enlarged portion of the large intestine known as the caecum, which acts as a fermentation chamber for the digestion of the cellulose in their bulky food of herbage and woody shoots.

Families of lagomorphs

The 60 species of lagomorphs are included in two families. The Leporidae consists of rabbits and hares, familiar animals that have long ears and large hind feet.

The Ochotonidae or pikas have relatively short ears and small hind feet.

Rabbits and hares are well–known animals to most people. The natural distribution of this group of animals is extensive, occurring worldwide except for Madagascar, Australia, New Zealand, and various Pacific islands. However, humans have deliberately introduced rabbits to these other places, in particular the European rabbit (*Oryctolagus cuniculus*) and the European hare (*Lepus europaeus*). Both of these species typically become pests in their introduced habitats, where their abundance is not well controlled by predators.

Rabbits and hares have long ears, and large, strong, hind legs with big feet, structures that are well adapted to leaping, or to more leisurely hopping. Most species are either crepuscular, meaning they are most active around dawn and dusk, or they are nocturnal, being active at night. The young of rabbits are born naked and blind in an underground burrow, while baby hares are born fully furred, with their eyes open in a surface nest. Young rabbits are initially quite helpless, while baby hares are relatively independent and can run soon after birth.

Rabbits and hares produce two types of fecal pellets. One type is soft and green, consists of partially digested food, and is produced at night. These soft pellets are refected, or re–ingested by the animal, and are swallowed without chewing. Eating its own droppings (coprophagy) allows for a twice–through process of digestion and assimilation of nutrients from the cecum, which is sited after the stomach and small intestine. This is similar in some respects to the habit of ruminant animals of regurgitating their cud, which is chewed again, and then re–swallowed. The other type of fecal pellet of rabbits and hares is brown and drier, is not eaten again, and is produced during the day.

Pikas or conies are small animals in the genus *Ochotona* that live in two disjunct parts of the world – in central Asia and Japan, and in western North America. This is an unusual distribution, and it suggests that the pikas probably migrated to North America from Asia via the Bering land bridge, exposed when sea levels were lowered during the Pleistocene glaciation, which ended about fifteen thousand years ago. The two populations of pikas became separated when sea levels rose again, and eventually evolved in isolation into distinct species.

Pikas have short ears and small feet, and they lack an external tail, although close examination of their skeletons reveals a vestigial tail structure. The color of the pelage of pikas varies from blackish to cinnamon-brown. Pikas are diurnal, or active during the day. Their

A black-tailed jackrabbit.

habitat is alpine tundra, where these animals typically live in rocky piles, or bouldery talus at the base of cliffs.

Rabbits and hares of North America

North America is home to 15 species of rabbits and hares. All of these are rather abundant within their range. These medium–sized herbivores are important sources of food for many species of predatory birds and mammals, and they are also commonly hunted by people.

The most familiar native rabbit in much of North America is the eastern cottontail (*Sylvilagus floridanus*), a relatively small species that typically weighs about 2.4–3.3 lbs (1.1–1.5 kg), with females being slightly larger than males. The common name of this rabbit comes from its tail, which is white underneath and is held erect when running. The eastern cottontail is common in shrubby thickets in the vicinity of forest, orchards, and meadows. This rabbit is abundant across southeastern North America, extending into Mexico. The eastern cottontail has significantly expanded its range during the past century, probably because of improved habitat that has resulted from various human influences, especially the conversion of closed forests into certain types of agricultural and forestry ecosystems.

The cottontail rabbit is active all year, eating foliage of a wide range of plants when available, and buds and twigs of woody plants during the winter. Cottontails begin to mate during the winter, and the females (does) bear their first litters of two to seven young in the springtime, and may have three or more litters per year. This sort of explosive reproductive potential is typical of rabbits and hares, and it is not surprising that so many predators depend on these fertile animals as food.

Other common rabbits of North America include the mountain cottontail (*S. nuttalli*) of mountainous regions of the west, the desert cottontail (*S. auduboni*) of arid regions of the southwest, the brush rabbit (*S. bachmani*) of Oregon and California, and the swamp and marsh rabbits (*S. aquaticus* and *S. palustris*, respectively) of wet habitats in the southeast. The latter two species take readily to the water, and swim well. All of these rabbits are abundant, and are hunted over much of their range.

The most widespread hare in North America is the snowshoe or varying hare (*Lepus americana*), which occurs from the low–arctic tundra, through much of the northern United States. This species is dark brown during the summer, but is a camouflaged white in winter. This species goes through more–or–less cyclic variations of abundance in northern parts of its range, which are tracked by the populations of some of its predators, such as lynx (*Lynx rufus*).

The arctic hare (*L. arcticus*) occurs throughout the northern tundra regions of North America, extending as far as the limits of land on the northern islands of Canada and Greenland. The white–tail jackrabbit (*L. townsendii*) occurs in semi–desert and dry prairies of central–western North America, while the black–tail jackrabbit (*L. californicus*) is more southwestern in its distribution. The European hare (*L. europaeus*) has been introduced to parts of the eastern United States and Canada, and is the largest lagomorph in North America, weighing as much as 10 lbs (4.5 kg).

The American pika

The American pika (*Ochotona princeps*) occurs through much of the Rocky Mountains, from southern Alaska, through British Columbia, and the northwestern United States. The American pika is about 7.5–7.9 in (19–20 cm) long, and weighs 6.1–8.2 oz (175–235 g).

Pikas are active during the day. When they are not foraging, they spend much of their time surveying their alpine domain for danger, usually from the top of a prominent rock. When a potential predator is seen to approach, the pika emits loud bleats, which warn other animals of the danger. However, as with many types of warning calls of small mammals and birds, it is very difficult to locate the source of the bleating noise, so the pika is not readily revealing its location. If a human sits quietly nearby, most pikas will carefully approach to appraise the nature of the intruder.

Pikas do not hibernate, remaining active under the alpine snowpack. They store fodder for their long winters, as large haystacks of dried forage, each about 1/4 m^3 in volume, and typically located beneath an overhanging rock that provides shelter from the weather.

Pikas are prey for a wide range of alpine predators, including the golden eagle, buteo hawks, foxes, and mustellids such as weasels. Pikas are especially vulnerable to predators when they are foraging in alpine meadows, beyond the immediate safety of the rocks and crevices in which these animals typically find shelter and protection. However, some smaller predators, such as the ermine (*Mustela erminea*), can follow pikas through their pathways and tunnels among the rocks.

Economic importance

Wild rabbits and hares of all species are a favorite class of small game hunted by many people for the pot and as sport. These animals are rather fecund and their populations can be quite productive, and they can therefore be harvested in large numbers. Millions of these animals are shot and snared each year in North America. They are mostly hunted for their meat, because the skins of these animals are fragile and tear easily, and therefore the fur has little commercial value.

The populations of rabbits and hares have increased greatly in many areas, because of human activities that have resulted in the elimination of lagomorph predators and in substantial improvements in the quality of the habitat of these animals. Most rabbits and hares of forested regions are early– and mid–successional species. Consequently, these animals benefit from many types of forest disturbances associated with human activities, such as the harvesting of trees in forestry, and some types of agricultural developments. Rabbits and hares are also typically abundant on agricultural or residential lands that have been abandoned, and are in a shrubby stage of the succession back to forest.

Rabbits and hares often do significant damage in gardens, by eating vegetables, and by damaging shrubs of various species, sometimes killing them by eating the bark at the base of these woody plants. This damage can be controlled using fencing, or by protecting the bases of the shrubs with chemical repellants or metal collars. Hares can do considerable damage in forestry plantations, by clipping small seedlings of conifers or other planted trees.

The domestic rabbit has been developed through cultural selection from the old–world or European rabbit (*Oryctolagus cuniculus*). This rabbit often lives colonially and digs extensive systems of underground tunnels and dens, known as warrens, the largest of which can cover more than one hectare. The old–world rabbit was originally native to southwestern Europe and northwestern Africa. However, this rabbit is now much more widespread in the wild, because it has been introduced throughout most of western Europe and Britain, the Americas, Australasia, and many other places. The European rabbit often causes severe damage in its introduced habitats by developing large, feral populations that overgraze the vegetation. A deadly disease known as myxomatosis has been introduced in Australia and other countries to try to reduce the population of this invasive rabbit. Although this pathogen generally achieves initial reductions in the abundance of rabbits, the surviving animals are relatively resistant to the dis-

KEY TERMS

Cultural selection—Selection by humans of individual animals having some desirable, genetically based traits, leading to evolution at the population level. This selective breeding eventually results in the development of distinctive varieties of domesticated species of plants and animals. See entry on evolution.

Lagomorphs—A widespread mammalian order, consisting of two families, the pikas or Ochotonidae, and the rabbits and hares or Leporidae.

Myxomatosis—An infectious, usually fatal viral disease of rabbits. Myxomatosis is sometimes introduced by humans to control the populations of rabbits when they become pests. Symptoms of the disease include swelling of the mucous membranes, and the development of skin tumors.

Refection—The habit of rabbits and hares of re–ingesting their soft, green fecal pellets. Refection allows for a twice–through passage of food, which contributes to more efficient digestion and absorption of nutrients.

Succession—A process of ecological change, in which there is a progressive replacement of younger biotic communities with others over time. Succession is usually initiated by disturbance of a pre–existing ecosystem, followed by recovery. See entry on succession.

ease, so that longer–term control is not generally realized.

Because of selective breeding, domestic rabbits are now available in a wide range of genetically based varieties, which differ in size, shape, color, length of fur, and other characteristics. Many domestic rabbits are raised specifically for food, others are used as laboratory animals, and many others are kept as pets.

Further Reading:
Banfield, A.W.F. *The Mammals of Canada.* Toronto, Ont.: University of Toronto Press, 1974.
McBride, G. *Rabbits and Hares.* U.K.: Whittet Press, 1988.
Thompson, H.V. and C.M. King. *The European Rabbit. History and Biology of a Successful Colonizer.* Oxford, U.K.: Oxford University Press, 1994.

Bill Freedman

Lake

Lakes are inland bodies of water—millions of which are scattered over the Earth's surface. Lakes are classified on the basis of origin, age, salinity, fertility, and water circulation. Lakes can be formed by glaciers, tectonic plate movements, river and wind currents, and volcanic or meteorite activity. Lakes can also be a phase of evolution in the aging process of a bay or estuary. Some lakes are only seasonal, drying up during parts of the year. As a lake reaches old age, it can become a marsh, bog, or swamp. Young lakes have clear water with less organic matter, while older lakes have murkier water and higher levels of organic matter as well as nitrogen, phosphorous, and detritus or decaying matter. Salinity is a measure of the dissolved ionic components in lake water. High salinity lakes, salt lakes, have high levels of precipitates and less organic matter, whereas freshwater or low salinity lakes have fewer precipitates and more organic matter. Lake shape, climate, and salinity each effect water movement within a lake, contributing to an individual lake's annual circulation patterns. Most lakes exchange surface water with bottom water at least once during the year, but multiple factors influence this complex process. Life within any given lake is determined by multiple factors as well and is of considerable interest to fishermen and marine biologists. Lakes are used for several purposes other than for the food they contribute to the food chain: they are used for recreation and enhance scenic beauty. The study of fresh water, including lakes and ponds, is called limnology.

Origins

Although several geological phenomenon account for the formation of numerous lakes on Earth, most lakes were formed as a result of glacier activity. Earth's glacial ice formed and extended into what is now Canada, the northernmost United States, and northern Europe. As the heavy, thick ice pushed along, it scoured out top soil, creating crevices in the former landscape. Glacial growth peaked about 20,000 years ago, after which time the ice slowly began to melt. As the ice melted, the glaciers retreated, but the basins formed by glaciers remained and filled with water from the melting glaciers. Lake basins formed at the edge of glaciers were generally not as deep as basins underneath glaciers. The shallower lakes are called ice–block or depression lakes; the lakes formed under glaciers (some more than a mile high) are called ice–scour lakes.

Movements of earth, water, and wind can also form lakes. Rock deformations of the earth's crust occur as folds, tilts, or sinking, usually along fault lines. Depres-

Kettle lakes like this one in Dundee, Wisconsin, are formed when blocks of ice buried by moving glaciers melt and leave a depression.

sions created can fill with water, forming lakes such as Lake Baikal in Siberia. It may seem peculiar to state that water forms lakes also, but water currents and land erosion by water form specific types of lakes: oxbow and solution lakes. Oxbow lakes are created as windy rivers change course. Windy rivers such as the Mississippi meander, carrying water through twists and turns; when they change direction at a particular twist or turn in the river, a loop can become separate from the main water flow. As deposits build up and separate the loop from the river, an oxbow lake such as Lake Whittington in Mississippi forms. Solution lakes result from ground water eroding the bedrock above it, creating a sinkhole. Sinkholes are the predominant type in Florida and on the Yucatan Peninsula. Wind can also create lake basins called blowouts; such lakes usually occur in coastal or arid areas. Blowouts created by sand shifted in arid regions are typical of lakes in northern Texas, New Mexico, southern Africa, and parts of Australia.

A few lakes result from meteors or volcanic activity. Gases at high pressure under crests of volcanic lava can explode, forming basins that collect water. Volcanic basins up to a mile in diameter are called craters, and those with diameters greater than a mile are called calderas. Crater Lake in Oregon is a caldera 1,932 ft (590 m) deep, 20 ft (6 m) in length, and 16 ft (5 m) in width. This makes it the seventh deepest lake in the world. The largest well–documented meteorite–formed lake in the world is Chubb Lake in Quebec. Lake Chubb is 823 ft (250 m) deep inside a crater 10,990 ft (3,350 m) wide.

Dams made by streams, beavers, and humans have also created lakes. Natural dams can be formed as a stream deposits debris at the point that it enters a river; the accumulated material can close off the stream, creating a lake. Man–made lakes have many characteristics in common with natural lakes, although water level can be less consistent in man–made lakes.

Age

Lake formation (or birth) and evolution (or aging) are natural periods of lake existence as they are for all living things. Some lakes have a short lifespan of 100–1,000 years, although many lakes will exist for 10,000 years or longer, but there are lakes that only exist in damper seasons of the year. Because people who study lakes have considerably shorter life spans, the chemical, physical, and life–supporting properties of water are used to classify lake age. As water tends to support life, lakes are often assessed based on what life they can and do support: their fertility. The deposits in lake basins have strata, or layers, that reveal details about a lake's history. And a lake's present fertility is related to water stratification by regions of similar temperature and light penetration.

Fertility is governed by a number of biological and chemical factors. The photosynthetic plankton that grow on a lake's surface are eaten by zooplankton; these plankton make up the primary link in the lake's food chain. Photo plankton contribute to a lake's fertility as a food source and as an oxygen source through photosynthesis. Plankton are consumed by aquatic invertebrates which are, in turn, eaten by small and larger fish.

Minerals such as phosphorous and oxygen are also required for life to flourish. Phosphorous levels can vary over a range of parts per billion (ppb). Most fish require an oxygen concentration of at least 5 parts per million (ppm). Oxygen concentration is primarily due to photosynthesis in lake plants and surface wind agitation. Some oxygen can also come from tributary streams.

Lakes are classified as oligotrophic, mesotrophic, or eutrophic depending on age and whether they have little, some, or a lot of life, respectively. Oligotrophic lakes are the youngest and, usually, least fertile lakes; they tend to be deep with sparse aquatic vegetation and few fish. Mesotrophic lakes are middle–aged lakes that are less deep and more fertile than oligotrophic lakes. And eutrophic lakes (the oldest lakes) are most fertile and even more shallow than mesotrophic lakes. Eutrophic lakes eventually reach the point where demand for oxygen exceeds the oxygen supply. Eutrophic lakes have many aquatic life forms that eventually die and decompose; decomposition uses up oxygen that could have supported additional life. Decomposing material, detritus, collects on the lake's benthos (basin bottom), making the lake shallower. As oxygen becomes sparse, lakes approach senescence, full maturity to death.

Salinity, wind, temperature, and light

One can focus on almost any characteristic of water in a lake and see that the particular factor influences and is influenced by other characteristics of the same water. A profile of any given lake must take several of these factors into account. For example, salinity and temperature are two factors that seriously inhibit or pro-

mote life. High salinity does not favor most life other than some algal and shrimp growth. The Dead Sea, which has a salinity seven times that of seawater, has very low fertility. Temperature effects fertility both directly and indirectly. Most fish species prefer certain temperatures. While largemouth bass flourish at 75° F (24°C), trout prefer 50°F (10°C). Indirectly, temperature affects fertility by playing a large part in determining oxygen capacity of water. Warmer water holds less oxygen than colder water. Water at 45°F (7°C) can hold up to 12 ppm of oxygen; while 75°F (24°C) water can only hold a maximum of 8.5 ppm of oxygen.

Salinity remains relatively constant in some lakes, while it tends to increase significantly in others. A lake that has outflow, such as a runoff stream, keeps within a normal salinity range for that lake. But lakes that have no runoff lose water over time to evaporation, and a higher salinity results.

Wind plays an important role in water circulation, wave action, and surface temperature. On a warm, windy day, the surface water may be considerably warmer than the water beneath it. Since wind is directional and effects surface water more readily than lower water, it pushes warm water in the direction of the wind. The result can be a dramatic temperature difference between opposing shores of the same lake. The downwind shore may be as much as 30°F (-1.1°C) warmer than the upwind shore. Strong winds can also create choppy waves that effectively decrease light penetrance.

Sunlight can only penetrate water to a limited depth. Both murky and choppy water decrease light penetrance. Submerged regions receiving light throughout are called euphotic. Since light is required by plants for photosynthesis, which produces oxygen, cloudy water generally has less oxygen. However, plants vary in how much light they require for growth. Some aquatic plants, such as hydrilla, can grow on the lake's littoral zone (part of the lake that slopes from the shore toward the benthos) 50 ft (15 m) under clear water. Other plants, like cattails, maidencane, wild rice, and lily pads grow in 3 ft (1 m) or less of water closer to shore.

Water circulation

Water circulation is the mixing of water in a lake. Water mixes at the surface, within the top layer, the epilimnion, and among layers. The bottom layer of water is called the hypolimnion, and the water between the hypolimnion and epilimnion makes up the metalimnion. The metalimnion is also called the thermocline, because a drastic temperature change occurs the lower one goes in it. Mixing is facilitated by wind at the epilimnion and is possible due to water density variation between layers. When layers mix and change places, a lake is said to turn over. Turnover occurs when water in an upper layer is heavier, or denser than the layer of water underneath it. Lakes that turn over once a year are said to be monomictic. Lakes that turn over twice a year, once in spring and once in fall, are called dimictic. Lakes that turn over at least once a year are called holomictic. Some lakes do not fully turn over at all due to high salt content; the high salt lower layer prevents hypolimnic turnover in these meromictic lakes.

The most controlling factors in lake circulation are changes and differences in water temperature; however, salinity, wind, and lake shape each have a role in circulation as well. Bowl–shaped lakes tend to turn over more easily than oxbow lakes. Water temperature determines water density which, in turn, accounts for turnover. Water is at its minimum density in the form of ice. Warmer water is less dense than cooler water until cold water reaches $39.2°F$ $(4°C)$, when it gets lighter. Deeper water is generally both denser and colder than shallower water—other than ice.

In fall, the surface is cooled in proximity to the surrounding air. As this surface water cools, it sinks, mixing throughout the epilimnion. The epilimnion continues to cool and eventually matches the metalimnion in temperature. Wind mixes these two water layers, which then cool to temperatures lower than the hypolimnion temperature. Then the hypolimnion water mixes in with the rest of the water and rises to surface. If hypolimnion water was oxygen–depleted, then it will obtain more oxygen at the surface during the winter. During winter, the hypolimnion is warmer than the epilimnion—unless the entire lake freezes. This process is called fall turnover.

In spring, the ice warms, melts, and mixes within the epilimnion. As the entire epilimnion warms, it becomes denser than the hypolimnion, the whole lake turns over, and mixing takes place. This is spring turnover. As summer progresses, the metalimnion warms and the three temperature layers are apparent until fall. If snow has piled high onto the surface over the winter and blocked photosynthesis, then much lake life may die, resulting in a phenomenon called winterkill.

Tremendous variability exists in turnover patterns and date of onset. Polar lakes warm later in spring and cool sooner in fall than similar lakes in tropical regions. Ice may only melt away from some lakes for two months a year, resulting in slow fish growth compared to warmer climates. High altitude lakes also warm later and cool sooner than equivalent low altitude lakes.

KEY TERMS

Eutrophic—Older, fertile lakes with thick basin deposits and several life forms.

Mesotrophic—Middle–aged lakes with intermediate levels of basin deposits and numbers of life forms.

Oligotrophic—Young lakes with the least amount of basin detritus and numbers of life forms.

Turnover—The mixing and flip–flopping of thermal layers within a lake that results in nutrient mixing within the lake.

Tropical, high altitude lakes lose heat continuously, do not develop layers, and overturn continually, whereas sub–tropical, low altitude lakes that never freeze only layer in summer and turn over in winter.

Lake threats

Aside from the natural aging process, major threats to the longevity of lake fertility include pollution (including acid rain), eutrophication, and shoreline overdevelopment. Acid rain is formed by sulfates and nitrates emitted from coal–burning industries and automobile exhaust pipes. These chemicals combine with moisture and sunlight and are converted into sulfuric and nitric acid that enter lakes via precipitation. Acid rain has a pH of four and half, contrasting with the normal rain pH value of 5.6. Since a single digit pH difference (say, from eight to nine) represents a 10–fold change in acidity, acid rain is more than 10 times more acidic than normal rain. Freshwater life generally prefers alkaline (basic, non–acidic) conditions, but lake fertility is usually fairly functional down to a pH of six. However, when pH drops to five and below, as the effects of acid rain accumulate, life forms are severely effected. Plants, plankton, insects, and fish all gradually disappear. Young and old organisms die first, followed by the young and middle–aged adults. Many bacteria even die. Other chemical pollutants include fertilizers and pesticides that drain into lakes through soil and enter through streams. Pesticides are toxic to fish, while fertilizers can cause eutrophication.

Eutrophication is the abundance of nutrients for fertile growth. It is a natural phenomenon in mature lakes. However, chemical pollutants, including phosphorous and nitrogen compounds, can artificially propel lakes to this state where the demand by aquatic animals on lake oxygen is great. Man–made eutrophication threatens to deplete lake oxygen which can kill most of a lake's fish. Some eutrophigenic lakes are now aerated by man to increase available oxygen.

Shore overdevelopment disrupts natural habitats and increases pollution. Shorelines that are built up with dirt to support construction of buildings can crush wet, rocky areas that some lake species use for spawning. In addition, shoreline plant life is sometimes removed to create sandy, recreational areas, and the influx of people usually increases pollution.

See also Basin; Ecosystem; Eutrophication; Freshwater; Ice ages; Rivers.

Further Reading:

Cvancara, A. *At the Water's Edge.* New York: John Wiley & Sons, 1989.

Sternberg, D. *Fishing Natural Lakes.* R. R. Donnelley & Sons Company, 1991.

Louise Dickerson

A lamprey hanging within a waterfall.

Lampreys and hagfishes

Lampreys and hagfishes are unusual, jaw–less fish that comprise the order Cyclostomata, so named because of the circular shape of the mouth. The 41 species of lampreys are in the super family Petromyzontoidea, while the approximately 35 species of hagfishes and slime hags are in the super family Myxinoidea.

Lampreys and hagfishes totally lack the scales typical of fish, and are covered with a slimy mucous. These animals have an elongated, eel–like shape, and do not have any paired fins on their sides. Lampreys and hagfishes have gill pouches for respiratory ventilation, connected to the external environment by numerous holes or slits. These animals have a simple, cartilaginous skeleton. However, lampreys and hagfishes are divergent in various anatomical characteristics, and each represents an ancient and distinct evolutionary lineage.

Lampreys and hagfishes are living representatives of an ancient order of jawless, fish–like animals that comprise the class Agnatha. Almost all of these jawless vertebrates became extinct by the end of the Devonian period about 365 million years ago. This dieback probably occurred because of competition from and predation by the more efficient, jawed fishes that evolved at that time. The ancestors of lampreys and hagfishes survived. These distinctive creatures first appear in the fossil record during the Carboniferous period (365–290 million years ago), and are considered to be relatively recently evolved, jawless fish. The lack of scales and paired fins in lampreys and hagfishes are traits that evolved secondarily, and are atypical of their class, Agnatha.

Lampreys

Adult lampreys have relatively large dorsal and ventral fins on the latter half of their bodies, and have a well–developed visual sense. These animals have a circular mouth that can be used to attach sucker–like to the body of a fish. Parasitic species of lamprey then rasp a hole in the body wall of their victim, using rows of keratinized, epidermal structures that function like teeth, and a tongue that can protrude beyond the mouth. The lamprey then feeds on the ground–up tissues and bloody discharges of its prey. If the victim is a large fish, it will generally survive the lamprey attack, and perhaps several attacks during its lifetime. However, the victim is seriously weakened, and may fail to reproduce, or may eventually succumb to environmental stresses that a more vigorous animal could tolerate. Because lampreys do not usually kill their victims directly, they are generally considered to be parasites, rather than predators.

Lampreys also use their disk–mouths to hold onto rocks to stabilize themselves in moving water, and to move pebbles while digging their nests in a stream. The name of the common genus of lampreys, *Petromyzon*, translates as "stone sucker" from the Greek.

Lampreys can pump water directly into and out of their seven gill cavities through separate gill slits. This ability allows lampreys to ventilate water over their gills, even though their mouth may be actively being used for feeding or sucking on rocks.

Most species of lampreys are anadromous, spending their adult life at sea or in a large lake, and swimming upstream in rivers to their breeding sites in gravelly substrates. The larvae of lampreys, known as an ammocoete larvae, look very unlike the adult and were once believed to be a different species. The ammocoete larvae live in muddy sediment, and are a filter–feeder on suspended aquatic debris and algae. The larval stages can last for more than four years, finally transforming into the adult stage, when they reenter the oceans on lakes.

Hagfishes

Hagfishes are entirely marine animals, living in burrows dug into the sediment of the sea floor of the temperate waters of the continental shelves. Hagfishes have degenerate, non–functional eyes, and appear to rely mostly on short, sensory tentacles around their mouths for detecting their food. Hagfishes have a single nostril, through which water is taken in and used to ventilate the gas–exchange surfaces of their gill pouches before being discharged back to the ambient environment through individual gill slits. Hagfishes have four distinct blood–pumping regions in their circulatory systems, which represent four functional hearts.

Hagfishes have a single, elongated gonad, the front part of which develops into an ovary in females, and the back part into a testis in males. In 1864, the Copenhagen Academy of Sciences offered a prize for the first zoologist to describe the method by which hagfish eggs get fertilized. This prize has yet to be claimed!

Hagfishes feed largely on invertebrates, especially polychaete worms. They also feed on dead fish, which they enter through the mouth, and then eat from the inside out. Hatchlings of hagfishes resemble the adults, and therefore are not, strictly speaking, larvae.

Hagfishes are extremely slimy creatures. Their mucous may protect them from some types of predators, but it can also represent a problem to the hagfish, by potentially plugging its nostril. Hagfishes periodically de–slime themselves by literally tying themselves into a tight knot, which is skillfully slid along the body, pushing a slime–ball ahead of itself. This unusual,

---

KEY TERMS

Anadromous—Refers to fish that migrate from salt water to fresh water, in order to breed.

---

knotty behavior is also used by hagfishes to escape from predators, and to tear into the flesh of dead fish.

Interactions with humans

Hagfishes are sometimes a minor nuisance to marine fishermen, because they may swim into deep–set nets and eat some of the catch. Hagfishes are extremely messy and unpleasant to remove from nets, because of the copious, thick, sticky slime that covers their bodies.

The sea lamprey (*Petromyzon marinus*) is an important parasite of economically important species of fish in the Great Lakes and North America. This species was probably native to Lake Ontario, but it spread to the other Great Lakes after the construction of the Welland Canal in 1829 allowed the sea lamprey to get around Niagara Falls, which had been an insurmountable barrier to its movement up–river. The sea lamprey was similarly able to colonize Lake Champlain after a transportation canal was built to link that large waterbody to the sea. The sea lamprey now occurs in all the Great Lakes and in other large lakes in North America, where it parasitizes all of the larger species of fish and greatly reduces their productivity. The lake trout (*Salvelinus namaycush*) was virtually eliminated from some lakes by the sea lamprey, and probably would have been extirpated if not for the release of young trout raised in hatcheries.

The deleterious effects of the sea lamprey are now controlled to a significant degree by the treatment of its spawning streams with a larvicidal chemical (TFM, or 3–trifluoromethyl–4–nitrophenol) that is applied to the water, killing the ammocoetes. However, TFM cannot be applied to all of the breeding habitats of the sea lamprey, and this parasite continues to cause important damage to commercial and sport fisheries, especially on the Great Lakes.

Further Reading:

Carroll, R.L. *Vertebrate Paleontology and Evolution.* New York: Freeman, 1988.

Harris, C.L. *Concepts in Zoology.* New York: Harper-Collins, 1992.

Bill Freedman

Lamp shells

Lamp shells, or brachiopods, are a group of marine species classified in the phylum Brachiopoda. In appearance, lamp shells bear a close resemblance to bivalve molluscs, as they have a hard, calcareous outer shell which comprises two valves and a structure similar to the mantle of a mollusc. At one time, lamp shells were actually classified together with molluscs, but have since been placed in a separate phylum on the basis of their internal structure and lifestyle. One of the reasons for this has been that bivalve molluscs such as clams have a left and right shell, while those of a brachiopod represent dorsal and ventral surfaces, with the latter frequently being larger. The gape (or opening) of the brachiopod shell is at the anterior end and the hinge is at the opposite, posterior end. The two shells can be opened and closed by means of muscles. The shells are secreted by two folds of skin, which enclose the main part of the body, which is usually crowded into the hind part of the shell.

Brachiopods first appeared during the Cambrian period, some 500 million years ago. Since then, they have undergone many changes, and more than 30,000 species are thought to have occurred. Many of the larger forms are now extinct, but living species of the genus *Lingula* are thought to closely resemble some of these ancient forms. In total, some 280 living species have been described.

All lamp shells are exclusively marine, living in shallow waters. Although fossil species were widely distributed, and often apparently at considerable depths, modern–day species are largely restricted to cold water. The vast majority of lamp shells are sessile animals. Two major groupings have been defined within this phylum. In the first—articulate brachiopods—the shells are either fixed directly to a hard substrate or are attached to rocks by a short piece of connective tissue known as the pedicle, which arises from the posterior end of the shell. This arrangement allows the lamp shell a little, albeit limited, degree of motion. The shells of these species can only open a short distance. The second group—inarticulate brachiopods—are free–moving species of the genus *Lingula* that have specialized muscular pedicles which are used for burrowing through sand and other soft sediments. (The shape of these animals, which is thought to resemble the shape of former Roman oil lamps, has led to the common name for these animals.) In these species the shells, which are often more flattened than in other species, are held together by muscles, and the shell can open quite widely. This adaptation also enables the shell to rest on the surface while feeding, with the stalk firmly secured in the substrate beneath. If the animal is threatened and needs to conceal itself, the muscular stalk constricts, drawing the closed shell deep within the substrate.

Lamp shells feed by means of a special organ known as a lophophore, a feature only seen in a few other groups of marine and freshwater animals, chiefly the entoprocts and ectoprocts. This structure, which occupies much of the space in the anterior portion of the shell, resembles a circle of small tentacles surrounding the mouth. Each tentacle bears large numbers of tiny cilia which, when they beat, create a water current that draws water and suspended food particles in and down toward the mouth. Once trapped in the lophophore, tiny plankton are passed along special grooves that lead to the mouth and, from there, to a stomach and intestine. The water current also maintains a steady supply of oxygen to the animal.

Most lamp shells are dioecious, producing either male or female gametes. In the majority of species, when the gonads have ripened, the gametes are released into the coelom and pass through the nephridia to the sea. Fertilization takes place outside the body. Some species, however, brood their young by retaining their eggs and awaiting the arrival of male gametes with the incoming flow of water. The fertilized eggs develop into free–swimming larvae that are capable of feeding. Further development of the larvae depends on the species: in most articulate brachiopods, larvae undergo a transformation of the body shape and structure before settling, while the larvae of inarticulate brachiopods already resembles the final adult stage apart from its diminutive size. As the shell develops in the latter species, the larvae are encouraged to settle on the seabed.

See also Brachiopods.

David Stone

Landfill

The term "sanitary landfill" was first used in the 1930s to refer to the *compacting* of solid waste materials. Initially adopted by New York City and Fresno, California, the sanitary landfill used heavy earth–moving equipment to compress waste materials and then cover them with soil. The practice of covering solid waste was evident in Greek civilization over 2,000 years ago, but the Greeks did it without compacting.

Today, the sanitary landfill is the major method of disposing of waste materials in North America and other developed countries, even though considerable efforts are being made to find alternative methods, such as recycling and composting. In addition, landfills are being engineered to recover the methane gas that they generate during decomposition, and some older landfills are being mined for useful products.

About 70% of materials that are routinely disposed of in landfills could be recycled instead. More than 30% of bulk municipal garbage collections consists of paper that could be remanufactured into other paper products. Other materials like plastic, metal, and glass can also be reused in manufacturing, which can greatly reduce the amount of waste materials disposed in landfills, as well as preserving sources of nonrenewable raw materials.

Composting is frequently cited as an alternative to the landfill process. Some municipalities have initiated programs to collect grass clippings, leaves, food wastes, and other material suitable for preparation into compost for use in gardens. Other significant efforts involve the use of composted sewage sludge for soil application on farms, yards, and golf courses. The special collection of hazardous chemical wastes has also been initiated in communities that either recycle them or dispose of them more safely than in a landfill. Paper, glass, and plastic are the items most frequently targeted for recycling in municipal programs to ease the problem of dwindling sites for landfill disposal.

Another alternative to landfill disposal for many areas has been the incineration of solid wastes. This method is often criticized because it has the potential of polluting the air, and the residual ash still has to be buried in a secure landfill. Dumping in the ocean has also come under attack by environmentalists who cite pollution of marine ecosystems and destruction of recreational beaches as reasons against ocean dumping.

All efforts to recycle and compost are designed to ease the burden of continuously finding and operating sanitary landfills. Space is not the only problem municipalities face in disposing of solid wastes in landfills. Pollution of the groundwater is another important factor.

Sanitary landfill

Sanitary landfills involve well–designed engineering methods to protect the environment from contamination by solid or liquid wastes. A necessary condition in designing a sanitary landfill is the availability of vacant land that is accessible to the community being served and has the capacity to handle several years of waste material. In addition, cover soil must be available. Of course, the location must also be acceptable to the local community. For instance, a landfill that is too close to housing would usually be considered unacceptable because of the associated odors and pests, although methods have been developed to control such problems.

The three basic procedures that are carried out in sanitary landfills are: spreading the solid waste materials in layers; compacting the wastes as much as possible; and covering the material with dirt at the end of each day. This method reduces the breeding of rats and insects at the landfill, reduces the threat of spontaneous fires, prevents uncontrolled settling of the materials, and uses the available land efficiently. Another important consideration for landfill design is the use of the site after it is filled. Some sites have become parks, housing projects, or are used for agriculture. Under pressure from government, environmentalists, and the public, and with diminishing natural and financial resources available to them, municipalities are now planning their landfills carefully to avoid some of the later costs of clean–up or containment.

Method types

Trench and area methods, along with combinations of both, are used in the operation of landfills. Both methods operate on the principle of a "cell," which in landfills comprises the compacted waste and soil covering for each day. The trench method is good in areas where there is relatively little waste, low groundwater, and the soil is over 6 ft (1.8 m) deep. The area method is usually used to dispose of large amounts of solid waste.

In the trench method, a channel with a typical depth of 15 ft (4.6 m) is dug, and the excavated soil is later used as a cover over the waste. Grading in the trench method must accommodate the drain-off of rain water. Another consideration is the type of subsurface soil that exists under the top soil. Clay is a good source of soil because it is nonporous. Weather and the amount of time the landfill will be in use are additional considerations.

In the area method, the solid wastes and cover materials are compacted on top of the ground. This method can be used on flat ground, in abandoned strip mines, gullies, ravines, valleys, or any other suitable land. This method is useful when it is not possible to create a landfill below ground.

A combination method is the progressive slope or ramp method, where the depositing, covering, and compacting are performed on a slope. The covering soil is

Fresh Kills Landfill on Staten Island, New York.

excavated in front of the daily cell. Where there is no cover material at the site, it is then brought in.

Decomposition

A landfill has three stages of decomposition. The first one is an aerobic phase. The solid wastes that are biodegradable react with the oxygen in the landfill and begin to form carbon dioxide and water. Temperature during this stage of decomposition in the landfill rises about 30°F (16.7°C) higher than the surrounding air. A weak acid forms within the water and some of the minerals are then dissolved. The next stage is the anaerobic one in which microorganisms that do not need oxygen break down the wastes into hydrogen, ammonia, carbon dioxide, and inorganic acids.

In the third stage of decomposition in a landfill, methane gas is produced. Sufficient amounts of water and warm temperatures have to be present in the landfill for the microorganisms to form the gas. About half of the gas produced during this stage will be carbon dioxide, but the other half will be methane. Systems of controlling the production of methane gas are either passive or active. In a passive system the gas is vented into the atmosphere naturally, and may include venting trenches, cutoff walls, or gas vents to direct the gas. An active system employs a mechanical method to remove the methane gas and can include recovery wells, gas collection lines, a gas burner, or a burner stack. Both active and passive systems have monitoring devices to prevent explosions or fires.

Operating principles

While landfills may outwardly appear simple, they need to operate carefully and follow specific guidelines that include where to start filling, wind direction, the type of equipment used, method of filling, roadways to and within the landfill, the angle of slope of each daily cell, controlling contact of the waste with groundwater, and the handling of equipment at the landfill site.

Considerations have to be made regarding the soil that is used as a daily cover, which is usually 6 in (15.2 cm) thick, an intermediate cover of 1 ft(30.5 cm), and a final cover of 2 ft (61 cm). The compacting of the solid waste and soil has to be considered as well, so that the biological processes of decomposition can take place properly.

Shredding of solid wastes is one method of saving space at landfills. Another method is baling of wastes. The advantages to shredding are twofold. The material can be compacted to a greater density, thereby extending the life of the landfill, and it can be compacted more quickly as well. Less cover is required and there is also less danger of spontaneous fire. Landfills using shredded materials produce more organic decomposition than those disposing of unshredded solid wastes. The advantages of baling are an increase in landfill life because of an increase in waste density. Hauling times are reduced, as are litter, dust, odor, fires, traffic, noise, earth moving, and land settling. Less heavy equipment is needed for the cover operation and the amount of time it takes for the land to stabilize is reduced.

Alternatives to landfills

In the 1960s, Dr. Frederick Pohland of the University of Pittsburgh developed the concept of treating landfills as biodigesters by installing trickling filters in them to hasten the decomposition process. An additional method of hastening the decomposition of solid waste is to recirculate the leachate throughout the landfill. Pohland maintained that the biological processes taking place in a landfill could be controlled and scheduled to release gases that could then be used for energy sources. Accelerating decomposition in landfills can greatly reduce the time it takes to reclaim old landfills, which on its own can take as long as 40 years.

A United States federal regulation, Subtitle D, that became effective in October 1993 required the installation of a leachate collection system in new landfills in this country. The Environmental Protection Agency (EPA) has studied leachate recirculation and selected two landfill sites to carry out their research. They are located in Alachua County, Florida, and in Monroe County, New York. Additionally, there are more than 200 landfills across the country involved in leachate recirculation. In Yolo County, California, the landfill releases 1.4 million cubic feet of gas a day and is used to generate electricity. The EPA does require a special liner in projects that recirculate leachate.

Landfill mining of is another process that is used to reclaim the materials of the landfill for other purposes. More than 65% of the product from a landfill is usable soil. Small percentages of other materials, such as rock, metal, wood, aluminum, glass, plastic, polystyrene, and other items, can also be extracted from a landfill that is ready to be closed. The soil can be used as daily cover at other landfills and for grading roads and other construction projects. This process can only take place in landfills that are free of toxic wastes. Other landfill mining projects use the material to turn waste into energy.

Recycling

As a method of reducing the costs of solid waste disposal in landfills and of solving the problem of finding suitable landfill sites, many communities have initiated recycling programs. Some programs are carried out by segregating and collecting the recyclables separately from the materials destined for the landfill. There are also many drop–off programs for specific items such as bottles, plastics, cans, and newspapers.

Some communities require individual households to separate glass, plastic, and paper, while other programs have installed systems to separate the items at a plant and then sell them to manufacturers. Several things, besides saving space in landfills, are then accomplished with recycling programs. One is a cost benefit to the municipality and another is a decrease in the exploitation of natural resources, such as trees, metals, and petroleum.

Composting

The composting of organic materials for reuse in gardening and in agriculture can help alleviate the problem of using land to dispose of waste material. Plant and food substances are biodegradable, which means they are capable of decomposing through the agency of bacteria, fungi, and other living organisms. Temperature and sunlight play a role in the decomposition of biodegradable substances as well. When substances are not biodegradable they may remain in the environment and may be capable of polluting the soil and water of an area if they are toxic. Some biodegradable pollutants may also be capable of causing harm to the environment.

Substances that in the past were freely disposed of by dumping are now being considered by many municipalities for recycling as compost, such as weeds, leaves, and cut grass. Many communities throughout the country encourage people to compost plant material and use it as humus in their gardens. Since plant material is biodegradable this is a significant way to reduce solid waste problems for towns and cities.

Long–term care and end uses of landfills

Recycling programs range from home chemical collection in Dade County, Florida, to a beverage container recycling program in Washington, D.C. Organizations in Baltimore, Maryland, accepted a challenge to triple paper recycling. A major paper company now uses recycled paper to produce copier and printing

KEY TERMS

. . . .

Aerobic—Requiring oxygen for respiration.

Anaerobic—The condition where there is little or no oxygen present.

Baling—Compacting solid waste under heavy pressure to form a compressed bundle.

Biodegradable—Able to decompose naturally through the agency of bacteria, fungi, and other microorganisms.

Biodigester—A landfill that uses methods to hasten the decomposition of its solid waste materials.

Compacting—The practice of compressing solid waste to take up less space.

Humus—Composted organic material.

Leachate—Excess rainwater draining from a landfill.

Shredding—The milling of solid wastes before disposal in the landfill.

paper. An incineration project in Broward County, Florida, produces electricity for Florida Power & Light. Baltimore and Sanger, California, have city composting programs. In Sanger, the green waste is collected weekly and composted in windrows. Four to six months later the compost is available for gardeners free of charge. Liquid sludge is being used on farmland and golf courses as a water resource. A foam packaging firm in Michigan developed a recycling program for polystyrene foam, which can be recycled over and over again, never needing to be discarded in a landfill.

Because of the potential environmental impact of landfill sites that have been closed, special care is involved in the closure of a site. The two considerations are the need to limit long–term maintenance and leaving the site in an environmentally sound condition. The consequences of closing a site that is later deemed hazardous could threaten a community with heavy costs for clean–ups. When a landfill is closed, a primary step is to landscape and cover the area with vegetation, usually a grass. In addition, monitoring systems need to be kept in place for groundwater, venting of methane gas needs to be maintained, and collection of leachate needs to continue.

Among the planning and closing steps for a landfill are a topographic plan, site drainage plan, engineering procedures for a new site, vegetative cover, fences, and

signs. The uses to which closed landfills have been put are varied. Efforts to limit what goes into the landfill reflect particular concerns of different communities across the country. They include industrial parks, airport runways, recreational parks, ski slopes, ball fields, golf courses, playgrounds, and many others. When it has been determined that the bearing capacity of the landfill surface is adequate, buildings can also be erected. The antiquated view of landfills as "garbage dumps" has given way to a science to engineer the establishment, maintenance, closure, and re–use of the area for the community.

See also Biodegradable; Composting; Hazardous wastes; Incineration; Leaching; Recycling; Waste management.

Further Reading:

"Composting: Nature's Recycling Program." *Consumer Reports* (February 1994): 112.

Forster, Christopher F. *Environmental Biotechnology.* New York: John Wiley & Sons, 1987.

Ladesich, Jim. "Composting Comes of Age." *American City & County* (July 1993): 1012.

Magnuson, Anne. "Garbage: Gold at the End of the Rainbow." *American City & County* (July 1993): 48.

Robinson, William D. *The Solid Waste Handbook.* New York: John Wiley & Sons, 1986.

"Solid Waste Management." *American City & County* (July 1993): 3, 13.

Vita Richman

Landform

A landform is a natural sculpture of the surface of the earth. Most landforms are produced by the actions of weathering and erosion, carving away material from higher elevations and depositing it down lower. Different kinds of rock erode at a variety of rates under particular climatic conditions. As softer rock is worn away the more resistant rock is exposed, producing another series of landforms. Other landforms develop from volcanic activity or movements along faults during earthquakes. Study of landforms reveals much about the deformation, stresses, and strains which have affected the rocks to date at Earth's surface.

Erosion and deposition

Nature's sculpting tools are the agents of weathering, mass wasting, and erosion. Weathering breaks down bedrock into transportable fragments, mass wasting moves the fragments down hill, and erosion transports them in a number of different ways. Each process can produce characteristic landforms.

Rivers

The ability of water to move sediment depends on its velocity, which is related to the slope of its bed. When it is moving rapidly it can transport a great deal, but if it slows down it deposits its load. High in the mountains the gradient is steep and erosion dominates. Rivers actively cut downward, and mass wasting adjusts the walls to a "V" shape. These valleys intersect in a branching network as tributaries merge to form fewer, larger streams. As the water moves downstream the slope of its bed decreases and eventually a steady state develops where there is little down cutting. Here the slopes continue to retreat until a gentle, rolling topography evolves. Further downstream the slope of the bed is even less, and deposition begins to dominate. Here the river deposits much of its load during times of flooding, and modifies these deposits the rest of the time. One distinctive landform resulting from this is the meander. As the river winds back and forth across its flood plain it erodes on the outside of each sinuous curve, the cut bank, and deposits material on the inside, the point bar. Eventually the river flows into a standing body of water, either a lake or the sea, and slows down even more, depositing its sediment in deltas. These landforms emerge if the level of the lake or sea goes down.

Glaciers

A glacier is a flowing mass of solid ice. It erodes the sides of its valley, not just the bottom, resulting in distinctive "U" shaped valleys. The rate at which it erodes is proportional to its depth, because a thicker pile of ice bears down harder on the rocks below. When a glacial tributary joins a larger glacier, the tops of both will usually flow to be at nearly the same elevation, but the bottoms will not be. This difference results in "hanging valleys", which often display magnificent waterfalls as Yosemite Falls and Bridal Veil Falls in Yosemite Valley, after the ice has melted away. A glacier can transport material at any velocity, but only while it is frozen. Where it melts, its sediments pile up into hills called moraines. Sometimes rivers flow beneath the ice, leaving sinuous mounds of sediments called eskers. Other deposits of sediment washed off the top of the glacier form steep sided hills called kames. If the glacier advances again and runs over any of these deposits, it can modify them into streamlined hills called drumlins.

Wind

Moving air can only transport sand and dust, and does not erode solid rock very effectively. Its characteristic landforms, sand dunes, occur in many sizes and shapes. Most have a gentle slope on the windward side, where sand is being eroded away, and a steeper leeward side, where sand is deposited. Movement of sand from one side to the other may result in the migration of the sand dune in the direction the wind is blowing. As with water, transport capability varies with velocity, so sand dunes often develop where the wind slows down. This is the case at Great Sand Dunes National Monument, Colorado, and Death Valley National Park, California, where spectacular, but localized, dune fields occur.

Chemical dissolution and precipitation

Although erosion and deposition are most easily observed where solid sediment is being moved about, invisible chemical reactions also produce landforms. As water moves through the soil it becomes acidic, in part because of the addition of carbon dioxide produced by the decay of organic matter. This weak acid is able to dissolve some kinds of rock, particularly limestone, giving us spectacular underground caverns, such as the Carlsbad Caverns of New Mexico. If such caves develop near the surface they often collapse, and a landform called a sinkhole develops above the cave–ins.

After passing through limestones, the water often becomes saturated with calcium carbonate. If it comes to the surface in springs, the calcium carbonate may precipitate to build up mounds of travertine, such as those in Saratoga Springs, New York. Similar travertine deposits can develop in arid climates when evaporation brings about the precipitation of calcium carbonate. Sometimes these form a series of little dams holding back pools of water, such as at Mooney Falls in the Grand Canyon, Arizona.

Differential weathering and erosion

As erosion progresses, by whatever means, some rock units will be more resistant than others. These will be left exposed at higher elevations, and may protect underlying rock. Depending on the orientation and shape of the resistant unit, and the agents of erosion acting on it, various landforms may develop.

Although easily attacked in humid regions, limestone is a resistant rock in arid areas. Its crystalline structure gives it strength, much like solid lava. Where nearly horizontal, both of these rock types are found capping, and protecting, softer rocks beneath them in much of the American southwest. When erosion breaches the resistant unit, it may cut down through the soft rock below very rapidly, leaving isolated islands of resistant cap rock. As this continues, the protection these cap rocks provide preserves tall, nearly vertical landforms called buttes, if they are small, or mesas if they are larger. Monument Valley, near the four corners of Utah, Arizona, New Mexico, and Colorado has dozens of spectacular examples.

If a resistant unit dips at a moderate angle, it will often hold up an asymmetric hill. A small one is called a hogback, and a bigger one, usually on the scale of counties, is a cuesta. Rivers, cutting down through such layers, leave a notch as they cut. If a river continues to flow through such a notch it is called a water gap; if not, it is called a wind gap. Delaware Water Gap; between New Jersey and Pennsylvania, is a classic example. Sometimes people get the wrong idea about how these form, figuring that the hill was there first, and then the river cut through it. Usually, however, the main river cuts the resistant rock and the softer rock on either side of it at the same time. Tributaries to the main river, however, erode the soft rocks down to near the elevation of the river, while the more resistant rocks remain higher on either side.

A resistant unit may also be nearly vertical, because sometimes it is formed that way. Molten rock can flow into vertical cracks deep beneath the surface, and then solidify into resistant igneous rock bodies called dikes. When surrounding rocks weather away, the resistant rocks can form vertical walls extending many miles. The Spanish Peaks of south central Colorado have classic swarms of such dikes dominating the topography.

Vertical walls can form from resistant sedimentary units which have been rotated into a vertical orientation. Rock climbers work out at Seneca Rocks, in West Virginia, the remains of a resistant sandstone unit which is now vertical.

Tectonic landforms

If nothing countered weathering and erosion, the continents would be reduced to sea level in a few million years. Tectonic processes, driven by the gradual movements of giant global plates, raise the elevations of parts of the continents, producing their own landforms.

Volcanism

Volcanism produces a number of landforms. First, of course, are volcanoes themselves. These may be steep sided cinder cones, gently sloping shield volca-noes constructed of lava flows, or a combination of the two, called composite volcanoes, or strato–volcanoes. Cinders and ash fall out of the air and accumulate in steep-sided piles, but these are easily washed away by agents of erosion so they are rarely very large. Solidified lava flows are much more resistant to erosion, but because the lava flows downhill easily before it cools, their slopes are usually very gentle. The composite volcanoes have layers of ash, giving them substantial slopes, protected from erosion by layers of lava. Many of the most famous volcanoes, such as Mt. Fuji, are composite.

Like any fluid, molten lava flows downhill, moving down valleys and off ridges. Frequently it will cool and solidify in the valleys, forming a rock which is very resistant to weathering and erosion. As time goes by, the surrounding softer rocks may be eroded away, leaving the lava flows at a higher elevation, protecting the rock beneath them from erosion. In this way "inverted topography" is developed, where those areas which were lowest become the most elevated.

Faults and earthquakes

As the plates move about, bending and twisting within them produces fractures called faults. Where these reach the surface they can produce scarps—sharp changes in elevation—if movement on the fault had a vertical component. Scarps can be very small, or the size of whole mountain ranges. If a typical mountain range is cut by a fault with large vertical movement, many ridges may be beveled off along the same plane, giving rise to what is often called a faceted mountain range. One classic example is the Grand Teton range in Wyoming.

If the fault movement is horizontal, such as on the San Andreas fault, the grinding up of the rock in the vicinity of the fault may make it susceptible to weathering and erosion. This can result in long, linear valleys such as those in much of southern California. These valleys, if filled with water, become sag ponds, such as the San Andreas Lake. Dry valley floors are often among the flattest terrain, making them prime locations for building municipal facilities. As the reason for their existence has become understood, however, the wisdom of such construction has been called into question.

Joint sets

Sometimes sets of fractures develop where the surface of the earth is stretched. Such fractures have no displacement along them, and are called joints. Weathering, particularly in arid regions, may exploit these joints, leaving a series of vertical slabs of rock. Contin-

KEY TERMS

Deposition—Accumulation of sediments at the end of their transport by erosion.

Erosion—Movement of material caused by the flow of ice, water, or air, and the modification of the surface of the earth (by forming or deepening valleys, for example) produced by such transport.

Fault—A fracture in the crust of the earth across which there has been significant displacement, which may be the site of earthquakes.

Joint—A fracture in bedrock across which there has not been significant displacement, but which forms as a result of extensional stresses.

Weathering—Biological, chemical, and mechanical attack on rock which breaks it up and alters it at or near the surface of the Earth.

ued weathering of these slabs can result in the formation of arches, such as those at Arches National Monument, in Utah.

Tectonic control of landforms

In addition to producing its own distinctive landforms, deformation of the Earth's crust is influential in controlling what landforms result from differential weathering and erosion. During major mountain building episodes huge volumes of rock are compressed, folded into complex three-dimensional forms, and sometimes metamorphosed into different kinds of rocks. Later, when these folded layers are exposed to the agents of weathering and erosion, the more resistant units become ridges which outline the folds and deformation. Often resistant units offer better protection at the bottom of the fold than they do at the top, resulting in landforms with higher elevations over what were the troughs in the folds, and lower elevations over what were the crests. Much of the valley and ridge areas of Pennsylvania and adjacent states have this kind of landform.

See also Erosion; Karst topography; Mass wasting; Topology.

Further Reading:

Chorley, Richard J., Antony J. Dunn and Robert P. Beckinsale. *The History Of The Study Of Landforms; or, The Development Of Geomorphology*, London: Methuen; New York: Wiley, 1964–91.

Cooke, Ron, Andrew Warren and Andrew Goudie. *Desert Geomorphology*. London: UCL Press, 1993.

Ollier, Cliff. *Ancient Landforms*. New York: Belhaven Press, 1991.

Press, Frank, and Raymond Siever. *Understanding Earth*. New York: W.H. Freeman and Co., 1994.

Otto H. Muller

Landslide see **Mass wasting**

Lanthanum see **Lanthanides**

Land use

Land use is a geographical concept that refers to the ways in which parcels of land are utilized by people and society. Land–use planning is an activity that examines the factors that influence the nature and dynamics of land usage and develops ways to optimize those variables to achieve larger social, economic, and ecological benefits.

Uses of the land

Particular areas of land can be utilized by humans in diverse ways. These can include residential, institutional, business, industrial, agricultural, forestry, park, and other relatively natural land uses. Each of these broader categories can be further subdivided, based on the nature and intensity of the activities that are undertaken.

Residential land uses, for example, can involve single–family dwellings on large or small lots, or aggregations of multiple–unit dwellings of various sorts. The most intensive residential land–uses are associated with clusters of apartment buildings, which can support extremely large densities of human populations.

Institutional land uses are mostly associated with land that is occupied by public buildings such as schools, universities, government office buildings, art galleries, and museums. These facilities are most commonly located in urban or suburban areas. Business land uses are rather similar in many respects, and are mostly associated with land that is appropriated to retail facilities of various types, and with office buildings.

Industrial land uses are extremely varied, depending on the nature of the industry being considered. Urban–industrial land usage generally refers to the siting of factories or petroleum refineries, and of utilities such as electricity generating stations, and water– and sewage–treatment facilities. Industrial land use in rural areas can include mines, smelters, and mills for the production of ores and metals; mines and wellfields for the production of fossil fuels such as coal, oil, and natural gas; and large water–holding reservoirs for the production of hydroelectricity.

Land uses for agriculture and forestry are also types of industrial land uses, in this case involved with the production of food or tree–fiber as renewable resources. The nature of agricultural land uses depends on the types of crops and agronomic systems, which can vary from intensively managed monocultures, to more organic systems involving annual or perennial crops and little use of fertilizers or pesticides. Similarly, the intensity of land use in forestry varies from systems involving clear–cutting and the establishment of short–rotation plantations, to selection–harvesting systems with long–spaced interventions.

Some land uses associated with parks and golf courses also represent intensive modifications of the natural landscape. The management practices required to maintain these lawn–dominated ecosystems are similar to those utilized in some types of monocultural agricultural systems. Other types of parks, however, are little changed from the natural state of the land, and they may only involve the development of a few access roads, unpaved trails, and interpretation facilities.

The last major category of land use is really a nonuse, and involves designation of an area as an ecological or wilderness reserve. In most cases, this sort of land–use designation precludes the exploitation of natural resources by mining, forestry, or agriculture, and usually by hunting and fishing as well. However, scientific research and recreational activities that do not require extensive facilities, such as hiking and canoeing, may be permitted in many areas designated for natural land use.

Land–use conflicts, planning, and regulation

Land–use planning is an important activity of many geographers and planners. Land–use planning is usually pursued at the larger spatial scale, for example, by local or regional municipalities, counties, and states or provinces. The goal of land–use planning is to ensure that uses of the land are appropriate and sustainable, and do not cause unacceptable social or economic disruptions, or serious environmental degradations of the site or landscape.

The Incas used terraces to make optimal use of the limited land areas available for cultivation. These terraces are found near Machu Picchu, Peru.

Of course, land–use planning cannot achieve this goal by itself. There must also be a political will to implement appropriate land–use plans through regulation and zoning of the activities of people, businesses, and government itself. Achievement of a successful and sustainable pattern of use of the land requires planning, regulation, and monitoring, as well as effective resolution of unanticipated conflicts as they arise.

One of the most useful tools available to land–use planners is known as geographic information systems, or GIS. GIS is a computer–based system for the storage, retrieval, analysis, and portrayal of data on the uses, characteristics, and ecological dynamics of areas of land. Examples of spatial information that GIS is extremely useful in analyzing, portraying, and overlaying include data on topography, landforms, surface waters, environmental chemistry, wildlife populations, ecological communities, floodplains, political boundaries, etc. Because of its powerful capabilities, GIS has proven to be an almost revolutionary tool for planners, who can use this computerized system to describe both existing and future land–use characteristics, and to effectively model the potential implications of various land–use scenarios.

Urban and suburban land–use planning generally focuses on designing an appropriate mixture of residential, retail, business, institutional, industrial, and recreational land uses and activities. Attention must be paid to the delivery of utilities such as water, electricity, telephone lines, and sewerage services to all of these user groups, while also ensuring that there is an appropriate network of transportation facilities, and that unacceptable conflicts do not occur among user groups.

Unfortunately, many cities and larger urban–suburban regions have developed without paying appropriate attention to planning and regulating the various sorts of uses of the land, and tremendous problems have subsequently occurred. These diverse predicaments include such problems as large numbers of people living beside heavily polluted industries, terrible traffic jams due to little coordination of the development of residential facilities and employment opportunities, and large numbers of people having inadequate access to clean water and other elements of a healthy life–support system.

Land–use planning in rural areas must also focus on identifying and avoiding unacceptable environmental damages and conflicts among resource users. For example, in planning agricultural land use, it is critical to consider land capability and whether particular agricultural systems might cause excessive erosion, resulting in degradation of the agricultural resource, and unacceptable damage to nearby aquatic ecosystems.

In addition, land that is used for agriculture, forestry, hydroelectric reservoirs, or mining is not available for other uses, and this can have great implications for regional economies and their sustainability. Therefore, wherever possible, it is desirable to have a balanced mixture of appropriate land–uses and activities on the landscape.

It is also critical that rural land–use planning accommodate the need to preserve some areas as natural, self–maintaining ecosystems, so that unacceptable damages to biodiversity resources are not caused. This is also a consideration in urban land–use planning, although the opportunities to accommodate natural, ecological values are more limited in urban areas.

See also Ecological economics; Ecology; Human ecology.

KEY TERMS

· ·

Geographic information systems (GIS)—A computer–based system for the storage, analysis, and portrayal of spatial data related to geography, ecology, and environmental science.

Landscape—An extensive area of terrain, encompassing many discrete ecological communities.

Further Reading:

Coppock, J.T. *Land Use*. New York: Pergamon Press, 1978.
Freedman, B. *Environmental Ecology, 2nd ed.* San Diego, CA: Academic Press, 1994.
Wright, W.R. *Cases and Materials on Land Use*. St. Paul, MN: West Pub., 1991.

Bill Freedman

Langurs and leaf monkeys

Langurs belong to the primate family Cercopitecidae, of which 13 species are represented in the genus *Semnopithecus*. This represents one of the largest and most diverse groups of colobine monkeys in Asia, with most species restricted to the south and southeast. Many species are distinguished by their vocalizations and the color of their fur, which ranges from a silver–grey in the common or Hanuman langur (*Semnopithecus entellus*), to the glossy black fur of the Ebony leaf monkey (*S. auratus*) from Vietnam and Indonesia, a glistening orange coloration and black face in the golden leaf monkey (*S. geei*), and a ruby face in the elegantly patterned purple–faced leaf monkey (*S. vetulus*) of Sri Lanka, which has a brownish coat and a distinct white–yellow throat patch. Many species have raised brow crests which are used to express messages such as anger or pleasure to other members of the same species.

These monkeys are extremely agile animals with long limbs and tails, which are not prehensile like those of South American monkeys. Most species measure from 16–32 in (40–80 cm), with a tail length that can reach up to 43 in (108 cm) in the Hanuman langur. Body weight ranges from 11–53 lbs (5–24 kg), with most species weighing around 13–18 lbs (6–8 kg). They are mostly arboreal, leaf–eating species, but some may spend a lot of time foraging on the ground. Most of

A spectacled langur (*Presbytis obscurus*) in Asia.

The social behavior of langurs and leaf moneys varies considerably according to species as well as to age, sex, and ecological conditions. In Hanuman langurs for example, one of the best–studied species, each troop has its leaders and subordinate animals, but the roles are often not clearly defined. Most breeding groups consist of a single adult male. The core of the troop, which may number up to 70 animals, is composed of many related adult females. Females rarely leave the troop. Males, in contrast, leave shortly before they reach sexual maturity, at about three years of age—before they are able to threaten the dominant male of the troop and/or mate with females within their natal troop. Solitary males usually join bands of other nomadic males and may wander over large areas each year in search of breeding females and the opportunity to establish their own troops. Nomadic males therefore pose a constant threat to the dominant male: aggressive encounters and chases are common in such attempts to take over a territory and breeding females. If an intruding male is successful in his bid, the former leader will be evicted and the newcomer then takes over the troop and breeds with the females. Often such males will kill any young offspring sired by the former male, and by doing so, the females will come into breeding condition again relatively quickly and allow this new male to increase his breeding potential.

Not all langur or leaf monkey troops are as large as those of the Hanuman langur. Troop size in the purple–faced, hooded–black (*S. johnii*) and capped (*S. pileatus*) leaf monkeys, for example, is often just six to nine animals, while most other species have a range of 10–18 individuals. In addition to size, the composition and role of troop members also varies considerably. Some species may have more than one breeding male in the troop and, in the case of territorial species, the role of defending the home range may fall primarily to adult males or to all members of the troop. The size of individual territories varies enormously according to local habitat and food conditions, as well as the size of the troop. Large troops of Hanuman langurs, for example, may have a home range of more than 1,000 ha, but this is an extreme case. More often, leaf monkeys and langurs occupy home ranges from 10–200 ha, of which only part may be actively defended from other monkeys.

Young langurs learn to recognize their own mothers shortly after birth, which is important in a society where many curious arms reach out to touch and hold a newborn infant. Although the mother tries to remain apart from the rest of the troop with her infant, young monkeys will be given to temporary female babysitters to hold and groom. Mothers may even suckle offspring

these monkeys, however, are opportunistic feeders and will consume insects, fungi, and fruit when the opportunity arises. Many species also eat small amounts of soil—probably for its mineral content. Some species, such as the Hanuman langur eat sap and gum and even large quantities of certain fruit with high strychnine content that could kill other species.

Leaf monkeys have large stomachs that are divided into a number of sacs, like those of ruminants such as cattle and deer. The upper section is larger than, and separated from, the lower, more acidic, section. The upper part is where the fermentation of green foliage takes place with assistance from anaerobic bacteria. These bacteria allow the monkeys to break down cellulose (a major component of all leaves) and overcome the many toxins in the leaves, enabling them to feed from a wide range of trees, many of which are inedible to other monkeys. This not only enables leaf monkeys to feed off a wider selection of food items than other monkeys, but also guarantees them a more efficient digestion of low–quality leaves than any other primate. The slow fermentation and digestive processes also allow for a higher absorption rate of materials as they pass through the intestines.

that are not their own. When they are weaned, young langurs usually retain some association with their mothers, even though she may by now have additional offspring. Young females, in particular, often assist the mother with bringing up her young.

Although langurs and leaf monkeys are all versatile animals and display a wide range of feeding habits, the populations of many species have been seriously reduced in recent decades as a result of habitat loss and destruction. Many of southeast Asia's tropical forests have been seriously affected by logging and subsequent clearance by agricultural settlers. Newly built logging roads have opened up the interior of many forests, allowing greater access to remote regions. As a result of new and spreading settlements along these roads, hunting wild animals for food and their glossy fur, particularly vocal and visible species such as leaf monkeys and langurs, has increased significantly in some areas. Some species, such as Hanuman's langur, are pests on agricultural crops when the crops have been planted up to the forest fringes. Although this species is considered sacred by Hindus in part of its range, this does not prevent its destruction in others.

See also Rumination.

Lantern fish

Light plays a vital role in the life of all oceans. At the simplest level, it provides one of the basic requirements for photosynthesis and promotes development of a food chain. Some species of fish that live in the darker reaches of the oceans also rely on light for survival. Some of these species, such as lantern fish, have even developed their own artificial means of generating light.

Lantern fish are so called on account of the special light–producing organs that are found in their skin. Each light organ, known as a photophore, is connected to the animal's nervous system which, perhaps together with some form of hormonal control, dictates the flashing sequence of these organs. In addition to a series of rows of light–producing organs along their sides (the pattern and number of which varies according to species), some lantern fish, such as those of the genus *Diaphus*, also have larger organs both in front of and underneath the eyes, rather like a miner's lamp. The former organs give off a twinkling effect as the animals swim, while the latter are far more powerful, effectively lighting up the area immediately ahead of the fish.

Some species even have light organs on their tails; the purpose of these is probably to act as false lures to potential predators. The eyes themselves are large with large lenses and pupils and highly sensitive retinas, suggesting that vision is an important sense for these species.

Lantern fish (family Myctophidae) are one of the most important groups of midwater fishes, with some 250–300 species known. Most are small fish, measuring from 0.8–10.4 in (2–15 cm) in length. They are commonly found in large schools. Living at depths between 655–3,280 ft (200–1,000 m), these species undergo nightly migrations to the surface to feed, descending once again to the depths during the day. One explanation for this behavior is that vast quantities of tiny plankton rise to the surface of the ocean at night; species that feed on this rich food source, such as the lantern fish, therefore gain from having a condensed source of food at such times. Lantern fish also take advantage of the fact that they are not alone in harvesting the plankton; other small species such as amphipods and krill are also consumed at such times. By retreating to the gloomy depths during the day, they may also reduce the risk of predation from larger species.

The lantern fish is able to control the intensity and frequency of its flashing lights, and it is likely that the intermittent flashing serves a dual purpose. Many smaller organisms such as krill and copepods are attracted to sources of light and, by responding to the flashes of a lantern fish, unwittingly offer themselves as a meal. Recognition and warning are two other possible functions of the flashing lights. Light–producing organs are commonly found in species inhabiting the darkest regions of the sea, where the dark water can present a problem when trying to find a mate. By detecting and responding to a certain fixed frequency of light flashes, however, a lantern fish may find a mate more easily.

See also Fish.

Lanthanides

The lanthanides are a series of 14 metallic elements that appear at the bottom of the periodic table. Lanthanum, the element preceding the lanthanides in the periodic table, is usually also included in a discussion of the lanthanides since all 15 elements have very similar properties. When first discovered and isolated, the lanthanides were called the rare earth elements. Many uses have been found for these elements and their compounds despite their expense.

Discovery of the lanthanides

Although once called the rare earths, most lanthanides are not particularly rare in the earth's crust. Today, with the exception of promethium, the lanthanides are known to have abundances comparable to many other elements. The 15 elements, together with their chemical symbols, are lanthanum (La), cerium (Ce), praseodymium (Pr), neodymium (Nd), promethium (Pm), samarium (Sm), europium (Eu), gadolinium (Gd), terbium (Tb), dysprosium (Dy), holmium (Ho), erbium (Er), thulium (Tm), ytterbium (Yb), and lutetium (Lu). Thulium, one of the scarcest lanthanides, has an abundance in the earth's crust of 0.2 parts per million (ppm), and is more abundant than arsenic or mercury. The most abundant is cerium (46 ppm), which is more abundant than tin. Promethium, which is radioactive, is found only in trace amounts in uranium ores. Small amounts have been isolated from the spent fuel of nuclear reactors. The lanthanide elements, cerium through lutetium, have corresponding atomic numbers of 58 through 71.

The discovery of the lanthanides spanned more than a century of work, beginning in the late 1700s. In 1794, the Finnish chemist Johan Gadolin (1760–1852) studied ytterbia, which he believed was a new element. More than a decade later, the English chemist Sir Humphrey Davy (1778–1829) showed that ytterbia was a compound, composed of oxygen and a metal, rather than an element. Because many of the lanthanides occur together in the same minerals, and due to their similar properties, separation of the lanthanides proved a challenge to 19th century chemists. This often led to confusion, since it was difficult to distinguish one element from another or from its mineral precursor. The mid–19th century invention of the spectroscope, an instrument that measures light emission and absorption from heated substances, assisted with unravelling lanthanide identification. With this instrument it is possible to analyze light from the Sun and the stars, and we now know that lanthanides are present in other parts of our solar system and even beyond it.

Properties of the lanthanides

Like many metals, the lanthanides have a bright silvery appearance. Five of the elements (La, Ce, Pr, Nd, Eu) are very reactive and when exposed to air react with oxygen to form an oxide coating that tarnishes the surface. For this reason these metals are stored under mineral oil. The remainder of the lanthanides are not as reactive, and some (Gd, Lu) retain their silvery metallic appearance for a long time. When contaminated with nonmetals, such as oxygen or nitrogen, the lanthanides become brittle. They will also corrode more easily if contaminated with other metals, such as calcium. Their melting points, which range from about 1,508°F (820°C) (Yb) to about 3,020°F (1,660°C) (Lu), are also sensitive to contamination. The lanthanides form alloys with many other metals, and these alloys exhibit a wide range of physical properties.

The lanthanides react slowly with cold water (more rapidly with hot water) to form hydrogen gas, and readily burn in air to form oxides. Oxides are substances in which a metal and oxygen have chemically combined to form a compound. For example, samarium and oxygen combine to form the compound samarium oxide. Yttrium has a natural protective oxide coating, making it much more resistant. The lanthanides form compounds with many nonmetals, such as hydrogen, fluorine, phosphorous, sulfur, and chlorine, and heating may be required to induce these reactions.

The arrangement of electrons in an atom (the electron configuration) influences the atom's reactivity with other substances. In particular, it is the outer or valence electrons—those furthest away from the center of the atom—that are most involved in reactions since these are exposed to the surrounding environment. All the lanthanides, from cerium to lutetium, have a similar arrangement of their outer electrons. This explains why they are all found in nature together and why they all react similarly. When they react with other elements to form compounds, most lanthanides lose three of their outer electrons to form tripositive ions. For most compounds of the lanthanides, this is the most stable ion. Some lanthanides form ions with a positive two or four charge, but these are usually not as stable. A comparison of the sizes of the lanthanide atoms, and their ions, reveals a progressive decrease in going from lanthanum to lutetium and is referred to as the lanthanide contraction. Compounds containing positive and negative ions are called ionic compounds. Most ionic lanthanide compounds are soluble in water. Compounds of lanthanides with the element fluorine (lanthanide fluorides), however, are insoluble. Adding fluoride ions to a solution of tripositive lanthanide ions can generally be used as a characteristic test for the presence of the lanthanides. Likewise, lanthanide oxalates (oxalate is the negative ion $C_2O_4^{-2}$) have low solubility.

Isolation and production

The lanthanides occur naturally in many minerals but are most concentrated in monazite, a heavy dark sand, found in Brazil, India, Australia, South Africa, and the United States. The composition of monazite varies depending on its location, but generally contains about 50% of lanthanide compounds by weight. Like any group of elements that have similar properties and that occur in nature together, the separation and purification of the lanthanides requires considerable effort. Consequently, commercial production of the lanthanides tends to be expensive.

To separate the lanthanides from other elements occurring with them, they are chemically combined with specific substances to form lanthanide compounds with low solubility (oxalates and fluorides, for example). A process known as ion exchange is then used to separate the lanthanides from each other. In this process, a solution of the lanthanides in ionic, soluble form is passed down a long column containing a resin. The lanthanide ions "stick" to the resin with various strengths based on their ion size. The lanthanum ion, being smallest, binds most tightly to the resin, whereas the largest ion, lutetium, binds the weakest. The lanthanides are then washed out of the ion exchange column with various solutions, emerging one at a time, and so are separated. Each is then mixed with acid, precipitated as the oxalate compound, and then heated to form the oxide. A number of methods have been used to obtain the lanthanides in metallic form. For example, the oxides can be converted to fluorides or chlorides which are then reduced with calcium to metallic form.

Uses of lanthanides

Although the lanthanide elements, alloys, and compounds have many uses, less expensive alternatives functioning just as efficiently are used where possible. But despite their cost, the unique properties of the lanthanides do sometimes favor their use over cheaper substances, and millions of tons of lanthanides, in metallic, alloy, and compound form, are produced annually. One of the earliest uses involved an alloy of cerium and iron, called Auer metal, which produced a brilliant spark when struck. This has been widely used as a "flint" in cigarette and gas lighters. Auer metal is one of a series of mixed lanthanide alloys called misch metals that have a variety of metallurgical applications. These alloys are composed of varying amounts of the lanthanide metals, mostly cerium and smaller amounts of others such as lanthanum, neodymium, and praseodymium. They have been used to impart strength, hardness, and inertness to structural materials. They have also been used to remove oxygen and sulfur impurities from systems.

As catalysts (substances that speed up chemical reactions), the lanthanides are widely used in the oil refining industry since they speed up the conversion of crude petroleum into widely used consumer products such as gasoline. The color television industry also makes extensive use of europium and yttrium oxides to produce the red colors on television screens. Other lanthanide compounds are used in street lights, searchlights, and in the high–intensity lighting in sports stadiums. The ceramics industry uses lanthanide oxides to color ceramics and glasses. Optical lenses made with lanthanum oxide are used in cameras and binoculars. Others (Pr, Nd) are used in glass, such as in television screens, to reduce glare. Cerium oxide has been used to polish glass. The lanthanides have a variety of nuclear applications. Because they absorb neutrons, they have been used in control rods used to regulate nuclear reactors. They have also been used as shielding materials, and as structural components in reactors. Some lanthanides have unusual magnetic properties. For instance, cobalt–samarium magnets are very strong permanent magnets.

See also Element, chemical; Ion exchange; Metal; Periodic table.

Further Reading:

Cotton, S. *Lanthanides and Actinides*. New York: Oxford University Press, 1991.
Emsley, J. *The Elements*. New York: Oxford University Press, 1989.
Heiserman, D.L. *Exploring Chemical Elements and Their Compounds*. Blue Ridge Summit, Penn.: TAB Books, 1992.
Lide, D.R., ed. *CRC Handbook of Chemistry and Physics*, 74th ed., Boca Raton, Fla.: CRC Press, 1991.

Larch see **Pines**

Large intestine see **Digestive system**

Larks

Larks are 75 species of small, terrestrial songbirds that make up the family Alaudidae. Larks breed on all of the continents except Antarctica. Their usual habitats are all open areas and typically include prairies, savannas, alpine and arctic tundras, heathlands, and some types of agricultural fields.

Larks have long, pointed wings, a notched tail, and rather long legs and toes, with the hind, backward–pointing toe having an unusually long claw. The beak is rather small and pointed. The colors of larks are rather cryptic, usually involving brownish hues, often with streaky patterns, and sometimes with black and yellow markings. The sexes are similar in size and coloration.

Larks feed on a variety of insects and other invertebrates and on plant seeds. Many species migrate to warmer climates during their non–breeding season, and they often occur in flocks at that time.

Male larks are pleasing, melodious singers, often performing that activity while flying or hovering in the air. Larks lay two to six eggs in a cup–shaped nest woven of grass fibers and located on the ground, usually beside a sheltering, grassy tussock or rock. The female incubates the eggs, and her mate feeds her on the nest. Both parents share in the rearing of their young.

The only species native to North America is the horned lark (*Eremophila alpestris*), which breeds in open habitats over much of the continent and south into Central America. This species winters in the southern parts of its breeding range.

In addition, a small population of skylarks (*Alauda arvensis*), a species native to Eurasia and Africa, has been introduced to southern Vancouver Island. This bird was introduced by European immigrants, who longed for the beautiful, warbling, song–flights of skylarks, so familiar in their memories of the European countryside. Unlike other birds introduced for this sort of reason, such as the starling and house sparrow, the skylark did not become an invasive pest.

Many other species of larks occur in Eurasia, Australasia, and especially Africa, where 80% of the species occur. The largest genus is that of the bush larks (*Mirafra* spp.), with 23 species. The singing bush lark (*M. javanica*) is very widespread, occurring in savannas and grasslands from East Africa, across Asia, through Southeast Asia, to Australia. The largest species is the 9 in (23 cm) hoopoe lark (*Alaemon alaudipes*), which occurs in deserts of North Africa and Central Asia.

Laryngitis

Laryngitis is an inflammation of the larynx. Located at the upper end of the trachea, or windpipe, the larynx contains the vocal chords that are used to form sounds. Because the larynx plays such an important role in speech, it is sometimes called the "voice box."

When the larynx becomes inflamed in laryngitis, it swells and reddens. The major symptom of laryngitis is hoarseness. Other symptoms include cough, a sore throat, and noisy breathing.

Laryngitis can be caused by infections of the upper respiratory tract, and is either acute or chronic. Acute infectious laryngitis strikes quickly and lasts a short time. The laryngitis that accompanies the common cold, the flu, or a bacterial infection as in strep throat, are all examples of acute laryngitis. Chronic infectious laryngitis is more serious and long lasting. Chronic infectious laryngitis can result from infection by the tuberculosis bacterium or by various yeasts or other fungi.

Although it is relatively rare, one form of acute infectious laryngitis can be fatal. The cause of this deadly laryngitis is a bacterium called *Haemophilius influensae*. In this infection, the larynx and the tissues surrounding it swell to such a degree that the windpipe becomes blocked. If untreated, the affected person can suffocate. This infection is extremely dangerous because the symptoms progress quickly, especially in children. A child with a cold or flu that leads to laryngitis should be watched carefully for signs of obstructed breathing.

Laryngitis can result from causes other than infections. Raising the voice for long periods of time has been known to cause laryngitis. Smoking has been linked to chronic laryngitis. A condition called gastrointestinal reflux can also lead to chronic laryngitis. In this condition, stomach acid is forced upward, "refluxed," into the esophagus or food tube. If this acid is forced high enough, it can spill over into the windpipe, which can irritate the larynx and eventually cause laryngitis. Doctors treat this kind of laryngitis with antacids that neutralize the stomach acid.

Most of us will experience a bout of acute laryngitis in our lifetimes. Whether brought on by a cold or flu or simply talking too much, the cure is the same: rest the voice and drink lots of fluids. Gargling with warm salt water can also be soothing. Sprays that numb the throat are not recommended because they tend to dry out delicate tissues.

Larynx see **Respiratory system**

Laser

The laser is a device which uses the principle of stimulated emission to produce light. The qualities of the light generated by a laser are significantly different from that generated by a conventional source, like an incandescent light bulb or fluorescent light tube. These major differences include: a) divergence; the laser generally emits a pencil thin beam of light whose divergent angle is closely related to the wavelength and limiting aperture size; b) bandwidth; the light emitted by the laser generally consists of a very narrow range of wavelengths, or color; c) intensity; the output from a laser is typically orders of magnitude higher in intensity (measured in Watts per square meter) than a conventional light source; and d) coherence; the output from a laser is generally coherent; that is, the light will be able to form clear interference patterns.

Background and history

In the 1950s, there was a push by scientists to develop sources of coherent electromagnetic radiation at wavelengths shorter than vacuum tubes could provide. Charles Townes and co–workers at Columbia University, New York, developed the ammonia *maser* (microwave amplification by stimulated emission of radiation) in 1954, a device which produced coherent microwaves. In 1958, Townes and Art Schawlow published the principles of a maser operating in the visible region of the electromagnetic spectrum. The first successful demonstration of a laser followed in 1960 by Theodore Maiman of Hughes Laboratories, who operated a pulsed ruby laser which generated several kW of optical power. In the following few years, several different laser systems were demonstrated in gases (helium neon mixture, carbon dioxide, argon, krypton) and solids (uranium, samarium, neodymium, nickel, cobalt, and vanadium ions implanted in electrically insulating crystalline hosts). Since that time, laser action has been demonstrated in many different materials, involving all four states of matter (solid, liquid, gas, and plasma), covering the range of wavelengths from x–rays to submillimeter waves. Only a few types of laser find widespread use because of issues such as efficiency, ease of use, reliability, and cost.

How it works

The laser consists of the following components: 1) the pump, which is the source of energy to drive the laser; 2) the active medium, which is where the stored energy is converted into the laser light through the process of stimulated emission; and 3) the optical cavity, which is usually made up of a pair of mirrors, one whose reflectivity at the wavelength of the laser is as close to 100% as possible and the other with a reflectiv-ity less than 100%, through which the output beam propagates.

Stimulated emission

Stimulated emission is a process similar to absorption, but operates in the opposite direction. In absorption, an incoming photon is absorbed by an atom, leaving the atom in an excited state and annihilating the photon in the process. In stimulated emission, an incoming photon stimulates an excited atom to give up its stored energy in the form of a photon which is identical in wavelength, direction, polarization, and phase to the first photon. If the excited atom is unable to produce a photon which matches the incoming photon, then stimulated emission cannot take place. As a photon passes through a collection of excited atoms also referred to as the active medium, it can stimulate the generation of many trillions of photons, or more, through a snow-balling effect. The active medium can thus be regarded as an amplifier which takes in a small signal (one photon, say) and delivers a large signal (many photons, all identical to the first) at the output. In this case, the amplifier gain is provided by stimulated emission; hence the term laser—Light Amplification by Stimulated Emission of Radiation.

To illustrate laser operation, consider the well–known helium neon (HeNe) laser, which is found in supermarket scanners. The active medium is a mixture of helium and neon gases, enclosed in a glass tube a few inches long, with an electrode and a mirror at each end. Energy is deposited in the gas mixture by running a discharge through it, in much the same way that a neon sign is lit. The conditions in the HeNe laser have been optimized so that the maximum number of neon atoms are in the correct state to emit light at the familiar red wavelength, 633 nm.

Oscillation

It is well known in electronics that an amplifier will start to oscillate if used in conjunction with sufficient feedback. The same is true in the optical case: feedback can be provided to the active medium by placing mirrors at either end, an arrangement which is known as an optical cavity. With the mirrors reflecting light back along the same axis, any signal which starts spontaneously within the laser can be amplified by repeated round trips through the cavity, resulting in the generation of a strong light beam. The output is directed along the axis between the two mirrors, resulting in the highly directional output which is characteristic of lasers.

The beam of a mode locked, frequency doubled Nd YLF laser is reflected off mirrors and through filters at Colorado State University.

Pulsed operation

Lasers can generate short pulses of light using two processes which are unique to lasers and cannot be used by conventional light sources. The first is called Q–switching. In this method a shutter in the cavity prevents feedback from occurring, which prevents the laser from oscillating and so the excited atoms do not experience stimulated emission. Once a large population of excited atoms has been formed and the active medium has a very high gain, the shutter is opened very quickly, resulting in the generation of a short, high-power light pulse. This is like filling a bucket slowly with water from a faucet which only delivers a trickle. Once the bucket has been filled, it can be turned upside down and emptied very quickly, in a short–lived torrent. The Q–switched laser stores the energy accumulated at low power and dumps it out of the active medium in the form of a very short light pulse. Typical Q–switched

lasers generate pulses a few nanoseconds in duration, commonly with energies in the 10–500 mJ regime, resulting in peak optical powers of 1–100 MW.

The second method of generating pulses is termed mode–locking. This makes use of the coherent nature of the light produced by the laser and the fact that most lasers generate not just a single wavelength, but a group of closely spaced wavelengths (modes). A high amplitude pulse is generated when the peaks of all the modes add constructively but, since the modes have slightly different frequencies, they quickly march out of step with one another and the high amplitude pulse is quickly terminated. The constructive interference occurs only once every round trip through the cavity. Mode–locking generates pulses much shorter in duration than does Q–switching, typically picoseconds (10^{-12} s) or femtoseconds (10^{-15} s). Lasers have directly generated pulses as short as 11 fs.

Different laser types

There are many different types of lasers, reflecting the many forms of matter in which stimulated emission may occur.

Helium neon laser (HeNe)

The HeNe was one of the first lasers developed and the most widely used until the semiconductor diode laser took over. As described above, it is a discharge–pumped gas laser, which generally produces an output measuring a few mW in power. The gas discharge dynamics are such that it is very difficult to produce powers much higher than this. The standard HeNe emits at 633 nm, but it can also be made to operate at other wavelengths, including 1,150 nm (infra–red).

Semiconductor laser diode

The most commonly found laser is the semiconductor laser diode, which is used to generate the light used to read compact discs. Unlike all other types of lasers, pumping is achieved simply by running a current through a semiconductor junction diode: this simplicity, the small size afforded by semiconducting devices, the high efficiency (higher than 50% of electrical power in to optical power out), plus the ability to modulate, or encode, the output by simply modulating the electrical current, give the laser diode many attractive features for several applications, such as communications and optical data retrieval. Stimulated emission takes place when large numbers of free conduction band electrons recombine with holes in the valence band, emitting photons equal in energy to the band gap of the semiconductor. The only suitable semiconductors are the so–called "direct gap" materials, such as gallium arsenide and indium phosphide. By using alloys of different compositions, the laser band–gap can be engineered to produce light over a wide range of wavelengths (650 nm–1,550 nm). Silicon, having an indirect gap, is not used for diode lasers.

Diode lasers are typically very small (the laser chip, with wires running into it, is mounted on a copper block only 6 mm wide): the cavity is formed by cleaved crystal facets between 100 microns and 1 mm apart and the emitting volume has a cross–section of about 1 micron high by 1 to 200 microns wide. A diode laser can produce power in the range 1 mW to 1 W, depending on the size of the active volume. Standard semiconductor processing techniques can be used to form arrays of individual lasers in order to generate higher powers: an array with an emitting area of 1 cm x 1 cm can produce several kW of optical power.

Nd:YAG

The Nd:YAG (neodymium ions embedded in an yttrium aluminum garnet crytalline host) laser is the most common of the family of lasers usually referred to as "solid state" lasers, where the active species is distributed throughout a solid, usually crystalline, material, although glass can also be used as a host. Like all other solid state lasers, the Nd:YAG laser is optically pumped, i.e., the excitation process is the absorption of pump light. The most popular pumps are gas flash lamps or diode lasers.

Like most solid state lasers, the Nd:YAG laser can emit at several different wavelengths in the infra–red, the strongest of these lines being at 1,064 nm. The Nd:YAG laser finds many applications because it can produce pulses over a wide range of duration: it can operate continuously, or produce pulses in the millisecond/microsecond, few nanosecond, and few picosecond regimes, with average output powers typically in the range from 0.01 W to 10 W. It is also flexible in that the output from a Nd:YAG laser can be efficiently converted from the fundamental wavelength to 532 nm, green, using a nonlinear technique known as frequency doubling. Both the fundamental and the frequency doubled light find wide application in materials processing cutting, trimming, welding, marking, and laser surgery.

Carbon Dioxide

Like the HeNe laser, the carbon dioxide (CO_2) laser is a gas laser powered by an electrical discharge. However, the photon generated by stimulated emission arises from a vibrational transition within the molecule, rather than an electronic transition within an atom. As a result, the photon energy is much less than the laser systems described so far, and the wavelength is correspondingly longer at 10.6 µm. The CO_2 laser is one of the most efficient laser sources, having an efficiency in excess of 10%. Since the gas can flow through the discharge tube, the gas can easily take away excess heat and the laser can be cooled very effectively; this allows the CO_2 laser to operate at high average powers up to around 10 kW.

Applications

When it was first invented, the laser was called "a solution looking for a problem" because few good applications could be found for it. This is no longer the case, and the laser has found its way into many uses in every day life. The major application areas for the laser are in communications, materials processing, optical data storage, surgery, military uses, and scientific research.

Communications (diode lasers)

It is a well known theory in communications that the rate of information transfer which can be transmitted by a signal is limited to the frequency bandwidth of the signal. Since the frequency of light is several orders of magnitude times higher than the frequency of microwaves, a single light beam can carry thousands of times the information which can be carried by a copper wire. It is therefore of great advantage to operate communication systems using optical frequencies. In addition, low–loss optical fiber is lighter, more compact, and less expensive than the more traditional copper wire. Transcontinental and transoceanic optical fiber systems have been installed for telephone systems, using directly modulated laser diodes, operating at 1.55 |8-25|m, for generating the signals. Sometimes, if the distance is great enough, the signal will need to be amplified because it has been attenuated simply by passing through many kms of fiber. The optical amplifier is a piece of fiber which is doped with erbium and is pumped with a diode laser, which is spliced into the fiber link.

Materials Processing (CO_2 and Nd:YAG)

Since a laser beam can be focused down to a very small spot of light which can be absorbed very well at the surface of a material (be it metal, plastic, textile, etc.), the material can reach very high temperatures up to 9,032°F (5,000 °C) and melt or even vaporize. Lasers are used for cutting, welding, heat-treating surfaces to harden them, and marking. The major advantage in laser processing is in problems where traditional methods of manufacture have difficulty, such as drilling long thin holes in metal, cutting arbitrary shapes quickly, and making very small markings on components.

Optical data storage (laser diodes)

The fact that a laser beam can be focused down to a very small spot has been used by the information industry and implemented in the form of the compact disc. The area needed to store a bit of information on a disc surface is smaller when optical reading is used than when magnetic reading is used. Much more information can be stored on a compact disc (several Gbytes) than on an equivalent magnetic disc (several hundred Mbytes). This represents a savings in space and cost, which has opened up new markets for optical data storage–music CDS, CD–ROM, and optical storage libraries for large computer systems.

KEY TERMS

Absorption—The destruction of a photon when its energy is used by an atom to jump from a lower energy level to a higher level.

Coherent light — A light beam where the phase difference between any two points on a line perpendicular to the direction of propagation is constant with time.

Optical Cavity—An optical structure formed by at least two mirrors in which a light beam can be made to circulate in such a way that it retraces the same path every round trip.

Phase—The term phase is used when comparing two or more optical waves. If the waves are at the same point in their cycle at the same moment in time, they are said to be "in phase."

Photon—The particle associated with light. A photon is emitted by an atom when the atom undergoes a shift in internal energy from a high state to a lower state: the excess energy is carried off by the photon.

Stimulated emission — A process of emitting light in which one photon stimulates the generation of a second photon which is identical in all respects to the first.

Surgery (Nd:YAG, CO_2)

Using laser beams whose wavelength is absorbed strongly, surgeons can cut and remove tissue with great precision by vaporizing it, with little damage to the surrounding tissue. The CO_2 laser is also useful in cauterizing exposed blood vessels, avoiding excessive bleeding in the procedure. The laser is routinely used in many types of surgery and is increasingly used in new applications. For instance, lasers are being used in non–invasive surgical techniques, such as angioplasty (removing plaque from artery walls) and lithotripsy (the destruction of kidney stones in the bladder), where the laser light is fed into the body via an optical fiber: the small opening required for the fiber results in reduced scarring and shorter healing times. Ultraviolet lasers are beginning to be used for photo refractive keratectomy, the sculpting of the outer layer of the eye, in order to correct for vision disorders.

See also Atomic clocks; Compact disks; Fiber Optics; Hologram and holography; Laser surgery; Maser; Optical data storage; Semiconductor.

Further Reading:

Hecht, Jeff. *Laser Pioneers*, New York: Academic Press, 1992.

Hecht, Jeff. *Understanding Lasers*, New York: IEEE Press, 1994.

Laurence, Clifford L. *The Laser Book*, New York: Prentice Hall, 1986.

Stevens, Lawrence. *Laser Basics*, New York: Prentice Hall, 1985

Verdeyen, Joseph. *Laser Electronics*, New York: Prentice Hall, 1994

Iain A. McIntyre

Laser surgery

Laser surgery is a technique that harnesses the power of light in the form of lasers to perform a variety of surgical procedures. Most laser surgery relies on the intense heat of the laser beam to destroy or vaporize tissue. However, laser surgery can also incorporate the nonthermal effects of laser light, like creating shock waves and breaking atomic bonds. Laser surgery has many benefits over standard surgical procedures that require an incision with a scalpel. Laser surgery involves less chance for infection, less blood loss, and reduced swelling and scarring. Many of these benefits can be attributed to the highly selective precision of laser light, which can hone in on its target, whether it be an organ or a cell, without damaging surrounding tissue. There are several types of lasers currently used for surgical procedures ranging from ophthalmic (or eye) surgery to destroying tumors.

History of laser surgery

The power of light, specifically in the form of solar radiation, had been pondered and studied by scientists and physicians since the days of Socrates. However, it was not until 1946 that this power was first harnessed for medical use when Ger Meyer–Schwickerath harnessed the magnified power of the sun for eye surgery on detached retinas (the back part of the eyes that is sensitive to light) and tumors—nearly 15 years before the invention of the laser.

In 1960, Theodore Maiman, a 33–year–old engineer for the Hughes Research Laboratory, generated the first laser beam by using a ruby crystal. Medical scientists were quick to realize and develop the potential of laser light surgery. In 1961, animal testing for laser surgery had already begun at the New York University School of Medicine, where Milton Zaret experimented with laser light to make lesions on (or cause damage to) the eyes. In 1963, Chris Szeng performed the first laser surgery on humans at the Palo Alto Medical Research Foundation in California. His technique to treat retinal diseases marked the beginning of a revolution in ophthalmic surgery.

As laser technology continued to advance over the following decades, its use spread to include a wide range of surgical approaches for a variety of diseases. One of the major advances in laser surgery was made in 1983 by R. Rox Anderson and John A. Parrish at Harvard University. They proposed that extremely short exposure to laser light lasting less than one–thousandth of second would reduce the possibility of the laser spreading to and damaging other tissue, which can occur in certain laser surgery procedures. Eventual application of this technique proved that short–pulse waves of laser light would prevent scarring of surrounding tissue. (A pulse is a rhythmical beat or sensation instead of a constant one, like the pulse of blood through the veins.)

How lasers work

The word laser stands for Light Amplification by Stimulated Emission of Radiation. Simply put, by harnessing light, a basic form of energy, the laser becomes a powerful but precise tool.

The basis for laser energy lies in the ability to stimulate an atom, molecule, or ion into a higher energy state using focused light waves (usually through crystals). These atoms remain in this higher state only momentarily before returning to their original or ground state (the original stable energy state of atoms and molecules). As the atoms return to the ground state, a small amount of energy is released in the form of *photons*, a basic unit of light energy. These photons are trapped between mirrors and begin to collide, creating more energy with each collision. Finally, the photons burst through one end of the laser as a fine stream of concentrated light. Unlike an electric bulb or sunlight, which haphazardly emits light in various wavelengths and directions, laser light is a coherent radiation energy that is released in the same wavelengths and in one direction.

One of the reasons lasers are so conducive to surgery is that the wavelengths produced by the laser can be matched to a specific target's ability to absorb the light (known as its *absorption band*). Since different tissues and cells have various absorption bands, the laser will only damage the tissue whose absorption band matches the particular laser light wavelength. One of the reasons laser surgery advanced so rapidly in ophthalmic surgery is that the retina has a dark brown melanin pigment that absorbs the light of the argon laser. As a result, in addition to being quick and effective, lasers are safer because they do not affect surrounding eye tissue, which have different absorption bands.

Thermal and nonthermal lasers

There are two basic types of lasers used for surgery: thermal and nonthermal lasers. Thermal (or heat) lasers, which were the first laser–based surgical tools, work by producing an intense heat in a precise targeted area, causing the tissue, for example, to vaporize or shrink. This approach is also used in the more conventional surgical approach of cutting out tissue.

The Argon laser is a thermal laser that produces a green light easily absorbed by the retina. This laser can also produce a blue light used to treat red birthmarks, known as port–wine stains. The laser surgery works by destroying the over abundance of blood vessels that lie beneath the skin and cause red discoloring.

The thermal CO_2 (carbon dioxide) laser is the most commonly used laser for surgery. The laser light is produced by a mixture of carbon dioxide, helium, and nitrogen. Unlike the short wavelength lasers, the CO_2 laser produces a longer wavelength of light which is more suitable to procedures requiring deep incisions. Called a continuous–wave laser, the advantage lies in the fact that the heat used to cut the tissue lasts just long enough to spread to nearby capillaries (tiny blood vessels that connect arteries and veins). The residual, or left over, heat both sterilizes and seals the capillaries, thus reducing the chances of infection and bleeding. Continuous–wave lasers have also been used on the end of minute optical fibers (called a *laparoscope*) that are passed through a small hole in the abdomen into the gallbladder. The laser is then directed to cut the diseased sections of the gallbladder, which is then removed.

Unlike the CO_2 laser, the *eribium YAG* (yttrium–aluminum–garnet) *laser* is a short–pulse laser, with each pulse lasting only 200 microseconds. This laser light is made with a YAG crystal and eribium, a rare metal, and is typically used for *ablation*, or removal of bone or fibroids (fibrous tissues or tumors).

The *xenon chloride eximer laser* is an ultraviolet laser that can also vaporize bone without damaging surrounding tissue. The ultraviolet laser is a nonthermal laser, meaning it does not use the heat generating qualities of laser light to work. Instead, this laser cuts or vaporizes tissue, even bone, by breaking molecular bonds through a process called *molecular photodissociation*. This approach, which allows the surgeon to remove precise amounts of tissue in very small increments, is especially suitable for eye surgery, like reshaping the cornea (transparent tissue on the outer eye) for better vision.

Another laser surgery technique is to produce shock waves with short–pulsed lasers like the neodymimum YAG laser. By focusing an intense light beam on specific tissue, a tremendous amount of energy or heat is absorbed and produces a shock wave that tears apart the tissue. This approach has been used to treat cataracts and has the potential for destroying kidneystones and gallstones.

Benefits and risks of laser surgery

The two greatest benefits of laser surgery are the reduced risk of infection and blood loss. Infections with laser surgery are less likely because, unlike scalpels and other "physical tools," lasers do their work with beams of light which can not carry the microbes that cause infection. Laser light also sterilizes tissue that it passes through.

Laser light reduces blood loss during surgery for two reasons. First, laser surgery often requires little or no surgical cutting to get to the diseased area, relying instead on the laser light to pass harmlessly through other tissues that are obstructing the target. Second, lasers used to treat a specific tissue or cell mass also work in a cauterizing fashion to sterilize and seal surrounding blood vessels with the heat that they produce.

Part of the mystique of surgery stems from the steely nerves that are required to perform delicate operations where the slightest slip can cause irreparable damage. With a precisely guided laser beam, surgeons have to worry less about harming surrounding tissue. In addition, many procedures using laser surgery require no incision at all, which can eliminate the need for an anesthetic and the associated expenses and risks involved. If an incision is needed, it is usually very small and causes little damage to surrounding tissue.

However, despite laser surgery's rapid growth and many benefits, some fear that it has been over hyped. There are many surgical procedures that are extremely safe and less expensive than laser surgery and should be continued. Despite the accuracy of lasers, there are still risks like burning or other damage to surrounding tissues and organs. Although laser surgery is regulated by the Food and Drug Administrations's Center for Devices and Radiological Health, some people are concerned that laser surgery may move beyond generally accepted uses or may be used by people without regard to the potential problems. One area of concern is the use of lasers for cosmetic types of surgeries, like face lifts and the removal of varicose veins.

The future of laser surgery

Some laser surgery techniques under investigation are not "surgical" procedures in the strict sense of the term. In other words, they do not work by directly damaging or cutting the tissue but rather, affect chemical reactions in cells. This ability of lasers is being investigated to treat cancer. The idea is to apply a laser wavelength that is absorbed by *porphyrin*, a brownish–red blood pigment, found in cancer tissue. An Argon laser is used in combination with a red dye laser that sets off a chemical process in this pigment, reducing the size of the tumor or destroying it entirely. The technique is known as *photodynamic therapy*.

In addition to treatment of diseases like lung, bladder, and esophageal cancer, photodynamic therapy promises to provide new diagnostic tools for detecting these cancers in their early stages. First, a special dye that is attracted by cancerous tissue is injected into the patient. Next, a krypton laser, which emits a blue–violet light, is used to make the dye become fluorescent, thus revealing the exact size and location of the cancerous tissue. Dyes and lasers are also being developed to study specific cells in the body to determine and possibly correct genetic deficiencies in the cell's DNA, which carries the genetic or hereditary code of life.

Although lasers are often referred to as "scalpels of light," another new approach uses the laser more like a tweezer than a knife. In effect, the lasers' enormously powerful photon light beams enable scientists to hold, rotate, and move cells around. This technique may have applications for genetic engineering, which requires precise tools to manipulate the minute chromosomes, DNA, and genes which determine how a particular cell functions.

The future of laser surgery lies in learning more about the many biological mechanisms involved in laser light's interaction with cells and organs. One outgrowth for these investigations will be an increasing use of lasers to stimulate chemical reactions and cell functions through photodynamic therapy. In the meantime, an estimated 650,000–plus laser surgeries treating human ailments from head to toe are performed in the United States each year.

See also Cauterization; Laser; Surgery.

KEY TERMS

Absorption band—The measurement in terms of wavelengths in which a tissue will absorb the energy of laser light.

Molecular photodissociation—A process by which laser light breaks down molecular bonds.

Nonthermal lasers—Lasers that do not use the intense heat of lasers but rely on other qualities of laser light, such as its ability to break molecular bonds.

Photodynamic therapy—The use of laser light to initiate certain chemical processes in tumor cells that can lead to cell destruction.

Thermal lasers—Lasers that rely on the intense heat of lasers to perform specific functions, like cutting or vaporizing tissue.

Wavelength—A measurement used in physics to indicate distance in terms of a wave's direction and progression from one wave to the next.

Further Reading:

Berkman Sue. "Laser Surgery: What Doctors Can Do Now." *Good Housekeeping* (November 1991): 237–238.

Berns, Michael W. "Laser Surgery." *Scientific American* (June 1991): 84–90.

Merewood, Anne. "The Latest On Laser Surgery." *Cosmopolitan* (April 1992): 194–196.

David Petechuk

Lathe see **Machine tools**

Laughing-thrushes see **Babblers**

Laurel family

The laurels are a family of flowering plants known to botanists as the Lauraceae. Lauraceae contains about 45 genera and 2,000 species, and is the most diverse family in the order Laurales. Most species grow in the tropical forests of Southeast Asia and Central and South America.

The best known species is *Laurus nobilis*, a Mediterranean shrub used by the ancient Greeks to decorate the head of victors in the Pythian games, which led to modern phrases such as "poet laureate" and "Nobel laureate." Additional well–known species include avocado, California laurel, sassafras, and cinnamon tree. American gardeners often refer to *Kalmia latifolia* as "mountain laurel," and to *Rhododendron maximum* as "great laurel," despite the fact that both of these shrubs are in the Ericaceae family, and are unrelated to the "true" laurels of the Lauraceae.

Characteristics of the Lauraceae

The flowers of most species in this family are small, yellow, and aromatic. Some species have bisexual flowers containing both male and female organs. Some species have unisexual flowers, with each flower having either male organs or female organs. Some species are polygamous, in that individuals have some flowers which are bisexual, and others that are unisexual.

The flowers of most species have six sepals, arranged in two cycles. Sepals are the outermost whorl of a flower, typically leaf–like in appearance. The stamens, or male organs, of laurel flowers occur in three or four cycles, with three stamens in each. The flowers usually have a single pistil, or female organ, which contains a single ovule that develops into a seed after fertilization. The fruit of most species is aromatic, and is classified as a drupe, in that is has a fleshy outer layer and a hard inner layer with a single seed.

The leaves, stems, and roots of most species in the laurel family are aromatic. The leaves are typically alternate, rather than opposite, to one another on the stem. The leaves are simple in that they consist of a single blade. The California laurel (*Umbellularia californica*) and most tropical species in the Lauraceae have persistent leaves, which remain attached to the plant after they are no longer functional. Other species such as sassafras (*Sassafras albidum*) and spice bush (*Lindera benzoin*) have seasonally deciduous leaves, which fall off in the autumn, after they become nonfunctional.

Important species

The avocado (*Persea americana*), also known as the alligator pear, is one of the best known and most economically important species of the laurel family. Avocado is native to tropical regions of the Caribbean, Mexico, and South America. Many different races and varieties are cultivated in southern France, South Africa, Mexico, California, and Florida for their green edible fruits, which are eaten raw or used to make guacamole, a staple of Mexican cuisine.

The avocado fruit can be green or brown in color, depending on the variety, and is rich in oil. The avocado fruit is a drupe with a single large seed in the center. The early Spanish explorers, who observed cultivation of avocados by the Aztecs, thought that the fruit resembled a testicle, and that a man could increase his sexual potency by eating avocados. This belief was based on the "doctrine of signatures," which holds that a plant part that resembles a bodily organ would affect the function of that organ. We now know that the doctrine of signatures has no scientific basis.

The California laurel (*Umbellularia californica*) is a woody plant which grows from southern California to southern Oregon, and is the only species of this family native to the western United States. It has evergreen, aromatic, elliptical leaves. Under optimal conditions, it grows as a tree and reaches 150 ft (15 m) or so in height, and is shrub–like in appearance. The wood of the California laurel is fine textured, and is sometimes used to manufacture veneer, furniture, and wooden novelties.

There are three species in the genus *Sassafras*. One is from Taiwan, another from China, and one (*Sassafras albidum*) is a tree native to the eastern United States. Foresters classify the American sassafras as intolerant because it does not grow well under a closed forest canopy. Indeed, the American sassafras commonly grows in open fields and at the edge of forests. Its leaves are variable in shape, and can be elliptical, two–lobed, or three–lobed. The leaves turn characteristic red in the autumn. Leaves, roots, and twigs are all highly aromatic. Some biologists have suggested that the leaves of *Sassafras* are allelopathic, in that they chemically inhibit the growth of nearby plants, thus reducing competition. Sassafras tea is made by removing and boiling the bark from the roots. Sassafras oil is used in the manufacture of certain aromatic bath oils.

All species in the *Cinnamon* genus are aromatic, and most are native to Southeast Asia. Cinnamon is a well–known spice which comes from *Cinnamonum zeylanicum*, a tree native to Sri Lanka but now cultivated throughout Asia, the Caribbean, and South America. Commercial cinnamon comes from the bark of young twigs, which is stripped off, dried in the sun, and later powdered or used whole.

Another species in this genus, *Cinnamon camphora*, is the source of camphor. This tree is native to Southeast Asia. Camphor is an aromatic compound derived from the bark and wood of the camphor tree and is used as a medicine to relieve gas pains in the digestive tract, in ointments, and as an insect repellent.

KEY TERMS

. . . .

Bisexual—Flowers which have functional male and female organs.

Drupe—Fruits which have a fleshy outer layer and a hard inner layer.

Pistil—Female reproductive organ of a flower, which contains ovules that develop into seeds after fertilization by pollen.

Polygamous—Plants that have some unisexual and some bisexual flowers.

Sepal—External whorl of a flower, which is typically leaf–like and green.

Stamen—Male reproductive organ of a flower that produces pollen.

Unisexual—Flowers which have male or female organs, but not both.

Further Reading:

Audubon Society and staff. *Familiar Trees of North America: Eastern Region*. New York: Knopf, 1987.

Audubon Society and staff. *Familiar Trees of North America: Western Region*. New York: Knopf, 1987.

Heywood, V. H. *Flowering Plants of the World*. Oxford: Oxford University Press, 1993.

Peter A. Ensminger

Lava see **Magma**

Lawrencium see **Element, transuranium**

Laws of motion

What makes a bird fly? A person run? A judo expert flip a heavier opponent? The Earth orbit the Sun? These and any other motions are governed by three deceptively simple laws first stated by Isaac Newton in the seventeenth century. These three laws of motion when coupled with Newton's law of gravity form the basis for explaining both the motions we see on the Earth and the motions of the heavenly bodies.

History

In the sixteenth century, Copernicus suggested that the Earth and other planets orbited the Sun, but his model contained no physics. It did not say why the planets should orbit the Sun. After Galileo was censured by the Catholic Church and forced to recant his belief in the Copernican model, he realized that to ultimately win the Copernican model needed a physical basis. Galileo therefore started to quietly develop the new physics needed to explain planetary motions. Isaac Newton, who was born the year Galileo died, built on the foundation laid by Galileo. The resulting edifice, Newton's Laws, was a grand synthesis that for the first time explained motions both on the Earth and in the heavens with a unified set of laws.

Newton's three laws

Slide a block of wood across a level uncarpeted floor and notice its behavior. The block continues to move as long as you apply a force. When the force stops, the block stops moving. The block will continue to slide for a while after you stop applying a force. Your pushing is not the only force acting on the block. There is also a frictional force opposing the motion. The block sliding across the floor stops because this frictional force acts on it. The block on an icy surface takes longer to stop because there is less frictional force. If you could slide the block across a surface with absolutely no friction, it would never stop. The block would keep moving until some outside force, such as the wall of the room, stopped it. A block on a level surface, without application of forces will not move unless something applies an outside force; it will remain there at rest forever.

The first of Newton's laws states an object will continue its motion at a constant velocity until an outside force acts on it. The block has a tendency to continue in its state of motion, whatever that state might be, until some force changes that state of motion. This tendency to continue in a state of motion is called the object's inertia. An object at rest simply has a constant velocity of zero, so it needs an outside force to start moving. The physicist's definition of velocity includes both speed and direction, so any deviation from straight line motion is a change in velocity and will require an outside force. The inertia of any object will cause it to continue to move at a constant (in a straight line) velocity (or stay at rest) until an outside force acts on it.

A block will slide more easily than, for instance, a refrigerator because it has less mass. Newton's first law says that a force is needed to change the velocity of an object; the second law tells us how much force. Any change in velocity (speed up, slow down, or change direction) is an acceleration. For the common case where the mass does not change, Newton's second law states that the force required is equal to the accelerated mass times the acceleration (Force = Mass × Acceleration). It's harder to slide the refrigerator than the block across the floor because the greater mass requires a greater force to accelerate it from rest. A force in the same direction as the velocity increases the velocity; in the opposite direction, decreases it. A force perpendicular to the velocity changes the direction of motion. Occasionally the accelerated mass changes. In this case, the force is equal to the rate at which the momentum changes with time.

Newton's third law states that for every action there is an equal and opposite reaction. The action and reaction are equal and opposite forces forming an action reaction pair. If you are sitting in a chair, the Earth's gravity pulls you down. The reaction is that you pull the Earth up with exactly the same amount of force. The action reaction pair is: you on the Earth, the Earth on you. The reaction is NOT as is often thought the floor or chair holding you up. Not all equal and opposite forces form an action reaction pair.

Newton's three laws of motion revolutionized physics. For the first time the same simple set of laws explained a wide variety of apparently unrelated types of motion both on the Earth and in the heavens. Not until the 20th century were these laws surpassed by quantum mechanics and relativity for the special cases of subatomic particles, motion near the speed of light and strong gravitational fields.

See also Force; Gravity and gravitation; Mass; Motion; Quantum mechanics; Relativity, general; Velocity.

Further Reading:

Cutnell, John D. and Johnson, Kenneth W. *Physics, 3rd ed.* New York: Wiley, 1995.

Epstein, Lewis C. and Hewitt, Paul G. *Thinking Physics.* San Francisco: Insight Press, 1981.

Feynman, Richard P., Leighton, Robert B., and Sands, Matthew. *The Feynman Lectures on Physics.* Reading, MA: Addison–Wesley, 1963. (Vol I, Chapters 9 & 10).

Ostdiek, Vern J. and Bord, Donald J. *Inquiry into Physics, 2nd ed.* St. Paul: West Publishing, 1991.

Paul A. Heckert

LCD

LCD is short for liquid crystal display. LCDs are devices that use liquid crystals to create images. Liquid crystal images are being used in watch faces, laptop computer screens, camcorder viewers, virtual reality helmet displays, and television screens.

The two main LCDs are passive and active. In passive LCDs, once the image has been made, it cannot be changed. In active LCDs, the image can be manipulated even over short periods of time by using electricity. Most LCDs are of the active type.

The most common way to build an active LCD is by sandwiching liquid crystals between two clear plate electrodes. Electrodes are able to conduct electrical current. When electrical current is applied to the electrodes, the liquid crystal molecules change orientation. The orientation of liquid crystal molecules controls the amount, color and direction of vibration of the light that passes through them. As the electrical current is turned on and off, the liquid crystal alternates between being transparent (able to see through) and opaque (scatters so much light that you can't see through).

The most popular version of this liquid crystal sandwich is the twisted nematic, or TN, cell. In the TN cell, the liquid crystal is placed between the electrodes. Then one of the electrodes is twisted in–plane by 90°F (32°C). The electrode sandwich is then placed between polarizers. These polarizers control which direction of light vibration can pass through the whole system. In a TN cell, the polarizers are arranged so that light that can get though the first one is vibrating in the wrong direction to get through the second one unless the liquid crystal helps it. When the electrical current is off, light is vibrating in the same direction as the liquid crystals are lying. The twisted liquid crystal guides the light, rotating it by 90 degrees, until it reaches the next polarizer and can pass though. When the electrical current is

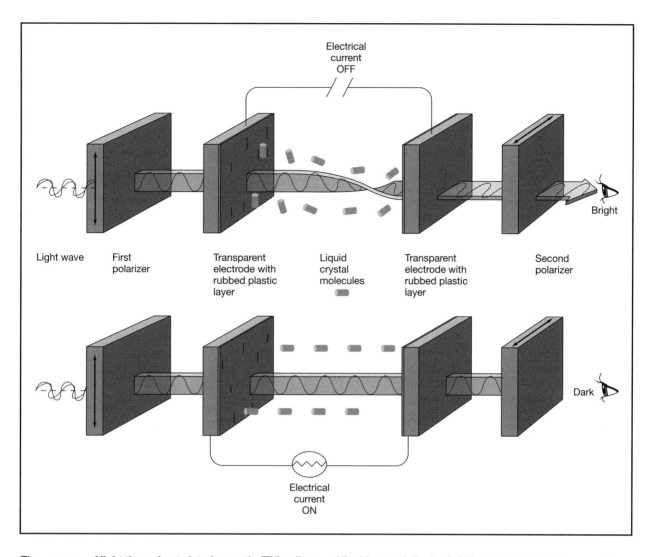

The passage of light through a twisted nematic (TN) cell type of liquid crystal display (LCD) when the current to the electrodes is off (top) and when it is on (bottom).

turned on, the liquid crystal molecules are reoriented. The light is not guided through from one polarizer to the next. You see a dark spot where this happens. If these sandwiches are made very small and are individually controlled, each sandwich becomes a picture element or pixel. This is a common way to build LCD watch faces. The dark digits are made up of pixels where the electrical current supplied by the watch battery is preventing the liquid crystal molecules from guiding light to your eye.

The pixels can be made extremely small. If there are many of them, small enough so that your eye can not tell them apart, your eye then blends all the pixels into an image. An LCD television may have more than 300,000 pixels in a picture. The more pixels, the more detailed the image can be.

Although liquid crystals may be used in their pure form, current research is focused on mixing liquid crystals with other materials such as polymers. This allows the liquid crystal to be dispersed as droplets. Because the droplets are small, they require less energy to re–orient. They are also very efficient at scattering light which can make displays brighter and useful over wider viewing angles.

See also LED; Liquid crystals.

Leaching

Leaching usually refers to the movement of dissolved substances with water percolating through soil.

Sometimes, leaching may also refer to the movement of soluble chemicals out of biological tissues, as when rainfall causes potassium and other ions to be lost by foliage.

Leaching occurs naturally in all soils, as long as the rate of water input through precipitation is greater than water losses by evapotranspiration. In such cases, water must leave the site by downward movement, ultimately being deposited to deep groundwater, or emerging through springs to flow into surface waters such as streams, rivers, and lakes. As the subterranean water moves in response to gradients of gravitational potential, it carries dissolved substances of many kinds.

Leaching is a highly influential soil-forming process. In places where the climate is relatively cool and wet, and the vegetation is dominated by conifers and heaths, the soil–forming process known as podsolization is important. In large part, podsolization occurs through the dissolving of iron, aluminum, calcium, organic matter, and other chemicals from surface soils, and the downward leaching of these substances to lower soil depths, where they are deposited. Some solubilized materials may also be altogether lost from the soil, ending up in deep groundwater or in surface water. A different soil–forming process known as laterization occurs under the warm and humid climatic conditions of many tropical rain forests, where aluminum and iron remain in place in the surface soil, while silicate is dissolved and leached downward.

The ability of water to solubilize particular substances is influenced to a substantial degree by the chemical nature of the solution. For example, highly acidic solutions have a relatively great ability to dissolve many compounds, especially those of metals. Aluminum (Al), for instance, is an abundant metallic constituent of soils, typically present in concentrations of 7–10%, but occurring as aluminum compounds that are highly insoluble, so they cannot leach with percolating water. However, under highly acidic conditions some of the aluminum is solubilized as positively charged ions (or cations), particularly as Al^{3+} and $AlOH^{2+}$. These soluble ions of aluminum are highly toxic to terrestrial plants and animals, and if they are leached to surface waters in large quantities they can also cause biological damage there. Aluminum ions are also solubilized from soils by highly alkaline solutions, in which they occur mostly as the anion $Al(OH)^-$. A large salt concentration in soil, characterized by an abundance of dissolved ions, causes some ions to become more soluble through an osmotic extraction, also pre–disposing them more readily to leaching.

Soils can become acidified by various human activities, including emissions of air pollutants that cause acidic precipitation, certain types of agricultural fertilization, harvesting of biomass, and the mining of coal and sulfide minerals. Acidification by all of these activities causes toxicity of soil and surface waters through the solubilization of aluminum and other metals, while also degrading the fertility and acid–neutralization capacity of soil by causing the leaching of basic cations, especially calcium, magnesium, and potassium.

Another environmental problem associated with leaching concerns terrestrial ecosystems that are losing large quantities of dissolved nitrogen, as highly soluble nitrate. Soils have little capability to bind nitrate, so this anion leaches easily whenever it is present in soil water in a large concentration. This condition often occurs when disturbance, fertilization, or atmospheric depositions of nitrate and/or ammonium result in an availability of nitrate that is greater than the biological demand by plants and microorganisms, so this chemical can leach at relatively high rates. Terrestrial ecosystems of this character are said to be "nitrogen–saturated." Some negative environmental effects are potentially associated with severe nitrogen saturation, including an increased acidification and toxicity of soil and water through leaching of aluminum and basic cations (these positively charged ions move in companion with the negatively charged nitrate), nutrient loading to aquatic systems, potentially contributing to increased productivity there, and possibly pre–disposing trees to suffer decline and die back. If the nitrogen saturation is not excessive, however, the growth of trees and other vegetation may be improved by the relatively fertile conditions.

See also Hydrology; Landfill; Soil.

Bill Freedman

Lead

A metallic element with atomic number 82. Symbol Pb, atomic weight 207.19, specific gravity 11.35, melting point 621.32°F (327.4°C), boiling point 3,191°F (1,755°C).

Lead is in column IVA of the Periodic table. It has four naturally occurring stable isotopes, lead–204, lead–206, lead–207, and lead–208. The last three of these are all end products of one or another radioactive family.

Lead is one of the first elements known to human societies. It is described in some of the oldest books of the Old Testament and was widely used by some early civilizations. Examples of objects containing lead from 5th millennium Egyptian cultures have been found. The Greeks and Romans also used lead for the manufacture of a variety of tools and containers. Some experts claim that one reason for the decline of the Roman civilization was the extensive use of lead in the empire's water supply system. Lead is now known to have a variety of serious effects on the human nervous system, including diminished mental capacity.

Lead was originally known by its Latin name of plumbum, from which its modern chemical symbol is derived. The Latin name is still preserved also in the common names for lead compounds, as in plumbic and plumbous chlorides.

General properties

Lead is a heavy, ductile, soft, grayish solid. It can be cast and fabricated easily and has the unusual ability to absorb sound and other forms of vibration. Although it is dissolved by dilute nitric acid, it tends to be resistant to other forms of acid solutions.

By far the most important use of lead is in storage batteries, with the production of antiknock gasolines, pigments, ammunition, solder, and plumbing materials following. In the last half century, evidence about the toxic effects of lead has accumulated to the point where its presence in the environment is considered to be a serious hazard for humans, especially for young children.

Where it comes from

Lead is thought to be the 36th most abundant element in the Earth's crust, with a concentration of about 13 parts per million. This makes the element more common than other heavy metals such as thallium or uranium, but much less abundant than less well known elements such as niobium, neodymium, lanthanum, and gallium.

The most important ore of lead is galena, lead sulfide (PbS). Anglesite (lead sulfate; $PbSO_4$) and cerussite ($PbCO_3$) are also economically important. Both are formed by the weathering of galena.

Over half of the lead produced in the world comes from just four regions and nations: the United States, Russia, other members of the former Soviet Union, Australia, and Canada. In the United States, about 90% of all lead comes from seven mines in Missouri, with the rest originating from mines in Colorado, Idaho, and Utah.

How the metal is obtained

The raw material from which lead metal is produced is either a naturally occurring ore or, more commonly today, lead products returned for recycling. In the United States, more than half of all lead produced comes from recycled materials, especially recycled storage batteries. After initial treatment, the major steps by which lead is obtained from either ore or recycled material are very similar.

In the case of a naturally occurring ore of lead, the first step is usually to concentrate the ore and separate it from other metallic ores. This step often involves the froth flotation process in which the mixture of ores is finely ground and then added to a water mixture that contains one or more other materials, such as hydrocarbons, sodium cyanide, copper sulfate, or pine oil. Air is then pumped through the ore/water/secondary material mixture, producing a frothy mixture containing many small bubbles.

The added material causes secondary ores such as ores of copper or zinc either to adhere or not adhere to the bubbles in the froth, allowing their separation from lead ores which respond in the opposite manner to the secondary material. The use of copper sulfate in the flotation process, for example, aids in the separation of zinc ores from lead ores.

After separation, lead sulfide is heated in a limited supply of air to convert it to lead oxide. The lead oxide is then mixed with coke (carbon) and a flux such as limestone in a blast furnace. Within the blast furnace, coke burns to form carbon monoxide which, in turn, reacts with lead oxide to form metallic lead and carbon dioxide.

In a variation of this procedure, the lead oxide can be mixed with lead sulfide and heated. The reaction that takes place results in the formation of lead metal and sulfur dioxide gas.

The lead produced by either of these methods is still impure, containing small amounts of copper, tin, arsenic, antimony, and other metals. Each metallic impurity is then removed by some additional step. In the case of copper, for example, the impure lead is heated to a temperature just above its melting point. At this temperature, copper is still a solid. Any copper mixed with the lead floats on top of the lead, and can be scraped off.

How we use it

Metallic lead is sometimes used in a pure or nearly pure form, usually because of its high density and ability to be bent and shaped. The metal is an efficient absorber of radiation and, for that reason, is commonly used as a shield for X–rays, nuclear radiation, and other forms of radiation.

Far more commonly, however, lead is alloyed with one or more other elements to produce a product with special properties of interest for some specific application. More than half of all the lead used in the United States, for example, goes to the production of lead storage batteries. The positive plates, made of lead(IV) oxide, and the negative plates, made of spongy lead, are both made from an alloy containing 91% lead and 9% antimony. Over 80% of this lead is now recovered and recycled as a source of lead metal.

At one time, very large amounts of lead were used in the production of tetraethyl lead, a compound that reduces the amount of knocking in an internal combustion engine. The problem with tetraethyl lead, however, is that it tends to break down within an engine, releasing free lead to the environment. Because of the health hazards that lead poses for humans and other animals, tetraethyl lead has been banned for use as a gasoline additive.

Because of its chemical inertness, lead has also been popular as a covering for underground cables, such as buried cables that carry telephone messages, and for pipes through which liquids are transported. For many years, lead was the material of choice in the construction of water pipes since it was inert to most chemicals occurring in nature and easily shaped. With the recognition of lead's threat to humans, however, many of these applications have been discontinued.

Alloys of lead are also popular for the manufacture of solders. Ordinary plumber's solder, for example, contains about two parts of lead to one part of tin. This alloy has a melting point of about 527°F (275°C).

Lead compounds were once widely used also for paints. They were in great demand because they covered surfaces well and were available in a number of vivid colors. Among these were lead chromate (yellow), lead molybdate (reddish–orange), lead(II) oxide (canary yellow), red lead oxide (Pb_3O_4; red), and white lead, a complex lead carbonate/lead hydroxide mixture. As with other lead compounds, however, the potential health hazards of the element have greatly reduced the availability of lead–based paints.

Chemistry and compounds

Lead is a reactive metal, but its reactivity is somewhat inhibited by the formation of an outer skin of protective compounds. For example, when a freshly cut piece of lead metal is exposed to the air, it quickly reacts with oxygen to form a thin outer layer of lead oxide. This outer layer then prevents further reaction between the metal and oxygen and other constituents of the air. A similar phenomenon occurs when lead metal is placed into water. Compounds present in water react with lead to form an outer skin of lead carbonate, lead silicate, or similar compounds that protect the metal from further attack. This property helps to explain the long popularity of lead for the lining of pipes designed to carry many different kinds of liquids.

From its position in a table of electrode potentials, one would expect lead to replace hydrogen from acids. But the difference in electrode potentials between the two elements is so small (0.126 volts), that lead reacts with most acids only very slowly indeed. The element does tend to react with oxygen–containing acids more readily, but only because of oxidation that may take place at the same time.

One application that takes advantage of this property is the use of lead to line containers that hold concentrated sulfuric acid. As long as those containers are kept at temperatures below 140°F (60°C), there is essentially no reaction between the acid and metal lining.

When lead does take part in a chemical reaction, it demonstrates one of two oxidation states, 4+ and 2+. Compounds of the former class are known as lead(IV) or plumbic compounds, while those of the latter class are lead(II) or plumbous compounds. Like aluminum, lead is amphoteric and will react with strong bases. The products of such reactions are known as plumbates and plumbites.

Biological effects

Throughout most of human history, lead was used for a wide variety of applications with little or no appreciation of the serious health hazards it poses. Today, physiologists understand that the human body is able to excrete about 2 milligrams of lead efficiently each day, but that quantities in excess of that can cause serious health problems.

Children are especially at risk for lead poisoning. Their bodies do not metabolize lead as quickly as do those of adults, so a given concentration of lead in the blood will have more serious consequences for a child than for an adult.

KEY TERMS

Ductile—Capable of being drawn or stretched into a thin wire.

Flux—In the conversion of ores to metals, a substance used to remove impurities from a blast furnace or other kind of processing system.

Froth flotation—A system for separating a desired ore from other kinds of ores by pumping air through a mixture of water and one or more other substances.

Hemoglobin—A complex iron–containing compound that transports oxygen from the lungs to the body's cells.

Isotopes—Two or more forms of an element that differ from each other in their atomic weights.

At relatively low concentrations, lead produces relatively modest or short–term effects, including elevation of blood pressure, reduction in the synthesis of hemoglobin, and decreased ability to utilize vitamin D and calcium. With increased blood concentrations of lead, however, these problems become more severe. Impairment of the central nervous system can occur, with decreased mental functioning and hearing damage as two possible results. At very high lead concentrations, a person can fall into a coma and, eventually, die.

With the recognition of these problems, governmental agencies have continually restricted the number of applications in which lead can be used. Unfortunately, its widespread use in previous years means that many children (especially) and adults are still at risk for lead poisoning. As an example, children not uncommonly pick off and then eat chips of paint from the walls of old buildings. Since many of these paints were made with compounds of lead, those children are then exposed to the harmful effects of the element.

See also Alloy; Element, chemical; Metallurgy

Further Reading:

Greenwood, N. N., and A. Earnshaw. *Chemistry of the Elements*. Oxford: Pergamon Press, 1990.

Hawley, Gessner G., ed. *The Condensed Chemical Dictionary*, 9th edition. New York: Van Nostrand Reinhold 1977.

Howe, H. E., "Lead," in *Kirk–Othmer Encyclopedia of Chemical Technology*. New York: John Wiley & Sons, 1981.

Joesten, Melvin D., David O. Johnston, John T. Netterville, and James L. Wood. *World of Chemistry*. Philadelphia: Saunders, 1991.

Newton, David E. *The Chemical Elements*. New York: Franklin Watts, 1994.

David E. Newton

Leaf

A leaf is a plant organ which is an outgrowth of the stem, and has three main parts: the blade, a flattened terminal portion; the petiole, a basal stalk which connects the blade to the stem: and the stipules, small appendages at the base of the petiole. However, the leaves of many species lack one or more of these three parts.

Leaves function in photosynthesis, or the biological conversion of light energy into chemical energy; in transpiration, or the transport of water from the plant by evaporation; and in cellular respiration, the oxidation of foods, and consequent synthesis of high–energy molecules.

There is great variety of leaf size and shape among different species of plants. Duckweeds are tiny aquatic plants with leaves that are less than 1 millimeter in diameter, the smallest of any species of vascular plant. Certain species of palm tees have the largest known leaves, more than 230 ft (70 m) in length.

Morphology

All leaves can be classified as simple or compound. A simple leaf has a single blade, whereas a compound leaf consists of two or more separate blades, each of which is termed as leaflet. Compound leaves may be palmately compound, in which the separate leaflets originate from one point on the petiole, or pinnately compound, in which the leaflets originate from different points along a central stalk which extends from the petiole.

Blade

The size and shape of the blade are often characteristic of a species, and are useful in species identification. However, the leaf blades of some species, such as those of Oaks (*Quercus*), exhibit great variation in size and shape, sometimes even when on the same tree. Botanists use a large vocabulary of specialized terms to describe the leaf outline, margin, apex, base, and vestiture (surface covering). For example, Pine (*Pinus*) leaves are considered acicular, meaning they are shaped like a needle; Aspen (*Populus*) leaves are considered ovate, meaning they resemble a two–dimensional projection of an egg; May apple (*Podophyllum*) leaves are considered peltate, meaning they are shaped like a shield, and are attached to the stalk on the lower leaf surface.

Venation

Venation is the pattern of veins in the blade of a leaf. The veins consist of vascular tissues which are important for the transport of food and water. Leaf veins connect the blade to the petiole, and lead from the petiole to the stem. The two primary vascular tissues in leaf veins are xylem, which is important for transport of water and soluble ions into the leaf, and phloem, which is important for transport of carbohydrates (made by photosynthesis) from the leaf to the rest of the plant.

The venation pattern of a leaf is classified as reticulated, parallel, or dichotomous. In reticulated venation, the veins are arranged in a net–like pattern, in that they are all interconnected like the strands of a net. Reticulated venation is the most common venation pattern, and occurs in the leaves of nearly all dicotyledonous Angiosperms, whose embryos have two cotyledons (seed leaves) as in flowering plants such as Maple, Oak, and Rose. In parallel venation, the veins are all smaller in size and parallel or nearly parallel to one another, although a series of smaller veins connects the large veins. Parallel venation occurs in the leaves of nearly all monocotyledonous Angiosperms, whose embryos have one cotyledon, as in flowering plants such as lilies and grasses. In dichotomous venation, the veins branch off from one another like the branches of a tree. This is the rarest venation pattern, and occurs in the leaves of some ferns and in the conifer tree, *Ginkgo biloba*.

Anatomy

Although the leaves of different plants vary in their overall shape, most leaves are rather similar in their internal anatomy. Leaves generally consist of epidermal tissue on the upper and lower surfaces, vascular tissues in the veins, and less–differentiated mesophyll, or throughout the body. Some plant species have a special type of photosynthesis, known as C–4 photosynthesis, and their leaves have a unique internal anatomy. These highly specialized leaves are not considered here.

Epidermis

Epidermal cells are on the upper and lower surfaces of a leaf. They have two features which prevent evaporative water loss: they are packed densely together and they are covered by a cuticle, a waxy layer secreted by the cells. The epidermis usually consists of a single layer of cells, although the specialized leaves of some desert plants have epidermal layers which are several cells thick. Epidermal cells often have large vacuoles which contain flavonoid pigments. Flavonoids generally absorb ultraviolet radiation, and may act as a sort of natural sunscreen for the internal layers of the leaf, by filtering out harmful ultraviolet radiation from the sun.

The leaf epidermis has small pores, called stomata, which open up for photosynthetic gas exchange and transpiration. Stomata are scattered throughout the epidermis, but are typically more numerous on the lower leaf surface. Each individual stoma (pore) is surrounded by a pair of specialized epidermal cells, called guard cells. In most species, the guard cells close their stomata during the night to prevent transpirational water loss, and open their stomata during the day so they can take up carbon dioxide for photosynthesis, and give off oxygen as a waste product.

Mesophile

Mesophile cells constitute the main body of a leaf, occurring between the upper and lower epidermis. Typically, the leaves of temperate–zone plants have two layers of mesophile cells, the palisade mesophile on the adaxial (upper) side, and the spongy mesophile on the abaxial (lower) side. The palisade mesophile is a layer of densely packed, columnar cells which contain many chloroplasts. This layer is responsible for most of the photosynthesis of leaves. The spongy mesophile is composed of large, often odd–shaped, photosynthetic cells separated from one another by large, intercellular spaces. The intercellular spaces apparently facilitate the exchange of photosynthetic gases.

Veins

Veins penetrate the mesophile layers of a leaf. Veins consist of vascular tissue, xylem, and phloem, and connect the vascular tissue of the stem to the photosynthetic cells of the mesophile, via the petiole. Xylem cells mainly transport water and minerals from the roots to the leaves, and phloem cells mainly transport carbohydrates made by photosynthesis in the leaves to the rest of the plant. Typically, the xylem cells are on the upper side of the leaf vein, and the phloem cells are on the lower side.

Phyllotaxy

Phyllotaxy is the arrangement of leaves on a stem. As a stem grows at its apex, new leaf buds form along the stem by a highly controlled developmental process. Depending on the species, the leaf origins on the stem may be opposite (in which leaves arise in pairs on opposite sides of the stem), whorled (three or more leaves

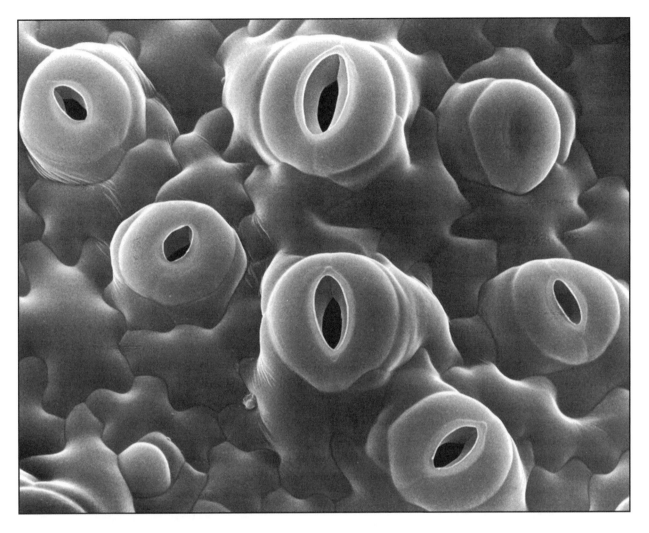

A scanning electron micrograph (SEM) of open stomata on the surface of a tobacco leaf (*Nicotiana tabacum*). Stomata are breathing pores scattered over the leaf surface, and sometimes stem, that regulate the exchange of gases between the leaf's interior and the atmosphere. Stomatal closure is a natural response to darkness or drought as a means of conserving water. Each pore is controlled by the turgor of two guard cells (sides seen beneath pore's opening) on either side of it. When they are full of water the pore is open; when they lose turgor, the pore closes.

arise from the same locus on the stem), or alternate (leaves are arranged in a helix along the stem).

Most species have alternate leaves. This pattern is often called spiral phyllotaxy because a spiral is formed when an imaginary line is drawn which connects progressively older leaf origins on the stem. The divergence angle of successive leaves determines the developmental spiral of leaves and homologous plant organs, such as the individual florets of a sunflower, and has been intensively studied by botanists and mathematicians since the mid–1800's. Interestingly, the angle between successive leaves on a stem is often about 137.5 degrees, known as the Fibonaci angle.

Two major theories have been proposed to explain spiral phyllotaxy: available space theory and repulsion theory. Both propose that the siting of leaf nodes is determined by the position of existing leaf nodes. While the two are often portrayed as competing theories, they are not in fact mutually exclusive. Available space theory says that the physical space among existing leaf nodes determines where new leaves originate. Repulsion theory says that synthesis of a chemical growth inhibitor(s) at the apex and older leaf nodes determines where the concentration of the growth inhibitor(s) is below a certain threshold.

Evolution

About 380 million years ago, plants with vascular tissue first evolved a special type of leaf, referred to as a micarophyll. A micarophyll typically has a single midvein, and arises from a stem which does not have leaf gaps, in regions of parenchyma (i.e, specialized) tissue where the vascular strand leads into the leaf base. The microphyll may have originated as an outgrowth of a vascularized stem, or by evolutionary simplification of a complex branch system. The leaves of certain modern plants in the Lycopodophyta (Lycopods) and Sphenophyta (Horsetails) are classified as microphyllis. Although the microphylls of these modern plants are quite small, some of their fossilized relatives had very large microphylls.

About 350 million years ago, plants first evolved megaphylls, the leaf type of modern seed plants and ferns. A megaphyll typically has a complex venation pattern, and arises from a stem which has leaf gaps, or regions of parenchyma tissue where the vascular strand leads into the leaf base. One theory proposes that megaphylls, as well as other plant organs, evolved by modification of branch systems. In other words, megaphylls may have evolved by the flattening of a three–dimensional branch system, and connection of the flattened branches with a cellular webbing.

Many botanists believe that the four different whorls of a flower (sepals, petals, stamens, and carpels) originated by evolutionary modification of the megaphylls of a free–sporing plant. Shortly after the evolutionary origin of the Angiosperms (flowering plants), there was a major division between the monocots (plants whose embryos have one cotyledon) and dicots (plants whose embryos have two cotyledons). The leaves of modern monocots, such as grasses and lilies, tend to be narrow and have parallel venation; the leaves of dicots tend to be wide, and have reticulated venation.

Many modern plants have evolved complex and highly specialized leaves. For example, the insect–eating organs of carnivorous plants, such as Venus Flytrap, Sundew, Pitcher Plant, and Bladderwort, are all highly specialized leaves. *Dischidia rafflesiana*, a tropical epiphyte, has among the most specialized leaves of any plant. Its leaves are tubular in shape and they collect forest debris and rain water, providing a habitat for the colonies of ants which live inside. As the ants die, their bodies dissolve and special roots of the plant absorb the nutrients that are released, providing nourishment for the plant.

See also Photosynthesis; Respiration; Transpiration.

Further Reading:
Attenborough, D. *The Private Life of Plants.* Princeton University Press, 1995.

Galston, A.W. *Life Processes of Plants: Mechanisms for Survival.* W.H. Freeman Press, 1993.
Kaufman, P.B. et al. *Plants: Their Biology and Importance.* Harp College Press, 1990.
Wilkins, M. *Plant Watching.* Facts on File Inc., 1988.

Peter A. Ensiminger

Leaf-footed bugs see **True bugs**

Leafhoppers

Leafhoppers are a species of insects in the family Cicadellidae, order Homoptera, a group that also includes the cicadas, whiteflies, aphids, and scale insects. There are about 20,000 species of leafhoppers, including about 2,500 species in North America.

Leafhoppers are leaf–feeding herbivores that use their sucking mouthparts to pierce the tissues of plants and feed on their juices, in some cases causing economically important damage to crop species. Leafhoppers have relatively specific feeding habits, and they only occur on particular species of plants, or closely related groups. Some species of leafhoppers emit "honeydew" from their anus. Honeydew is a solution rich in sugars, similar to that emitted by the closely related aphids.

Leafhoppers are rather small insects, the largest being no more than 0.5 in (13 mm) in body length, but most species only being a few millimeters long. Leafhoppers have short, bristle–like antennae, and a double row of spines running along the tibia of their hind legs. Leafhoppers have wings, which are held tent–like back over the thorax and abdomen when the insect is not flying. Most species are beautifully marked with stark color patterns that can be seen upon close viewing, especially on their somewhat thickened fore–wings, and sometimes their head and thorax. The tropical species *Cardioscarta pulchella* is brilliantly colored with red, black, and white hues, and is commonly used as a model in Central American folk art.

Leafhoppers have three stages in their life–cycle: egg, nymph, and adult. Most species only produce one or two generations per year, overwintering as either adults or eggs.

Some leafhoppers use rather weak, species–specific sounds to communicate with each other. These leafhoppers produce their noises using structures known as tymbals, which are anatomically similar to the much–louder sound–producing organs of cicadas.

A few species of leafhoppers are migratory in North America. The beet leafhopper (*Circulifer tenellus*), for example, maintains permanent populations in the southern parts of its range, but migrates northward as the weather and availability of food become favorable during the growing season. When climatic conditions deteriorate again at the end of summer, beet leafhoppers may migrate south, although these individuals are not of the same generation as the animals that made the earlier, northward migration.

Some species of leafhoppers cause important damage to crop plants. The potato leafhopper (*Empoasca fabae*) causes damage to potato and bean leaves by plugging the vascular tissues, causing the death of foliage. Other species of leafhoppers cause injuries to leaves at their feeding sites, or they damage foliage by removing excessive quantities of sugars and chloro-plasts. Some species of leafhoppers are the vectors of infectious diseases of crop plants. The beet leafhopper, for example, is responsible for spreading curly top, a disease of sugarbeets, spinach, beans, squash, and some other vegetables.

See also Cicadas.

Least common denominator

A common denominator for a set of fractions is simply the same (common) lower symbol (denominator). In practice the common denominator is chosen to be a number that is divisible by all of the denominators in an addition or subtraction problem. Thus for the fractions 2/3, 1/10, and 7/15, a common denominator is 30. Other common denominators are 60, 90, etc. The smallest of the common denominators is 30 and so it is called the least common denominator.

Similarly, the algebraic fractions $x/2(x+2)(x-3)$ and $3x/(x+2)(x-1)$ have the common denominator of $2(x+2)(x-3)(x-1)$ as well as $4(x+2)(x-3)(x-1)(x^2+4)$, etc. The polynomial of the least degree and with the smallest numerical coefficient is the least common denominator. Thus $2(x+2)(x-3)(x-1)$ is the least common denominator.

The most common use of the least common denominator (or L.C.D.) is in the addition of fractions. Thus, for example, to add 2/3, 1/10, and 7/15, we use the L.C.D. of 30 to write

2/3 + 1/10 + 7/15 as 2x10/3x10 + 1x3/10x3 + 7x2/15x2 which gives us 20/30 + 3/30 + 14/30 or 37/30

Similarly, we have

$$x/2(x+1)(x-3) + 3x/(x+2)(x-1) =$$
$$x(x-1)/2(x+1)(x-3)(x-1) + 6x(x-3)/2(x+2)(x-1)(x-3) =$$
$$[x(x-1)+6x(x-3)]/2(x+1)(x-3)(x-1)$$

Roy Dubisch

Le Châtelier's principle see **Equilibrium, chemical**

Lecithin

Lecithin is a phospholipid which consists of glycerol, two fatty acids, a phosphate group and choline, $HOCH_2CH_2N(CH_3)_3^+$.

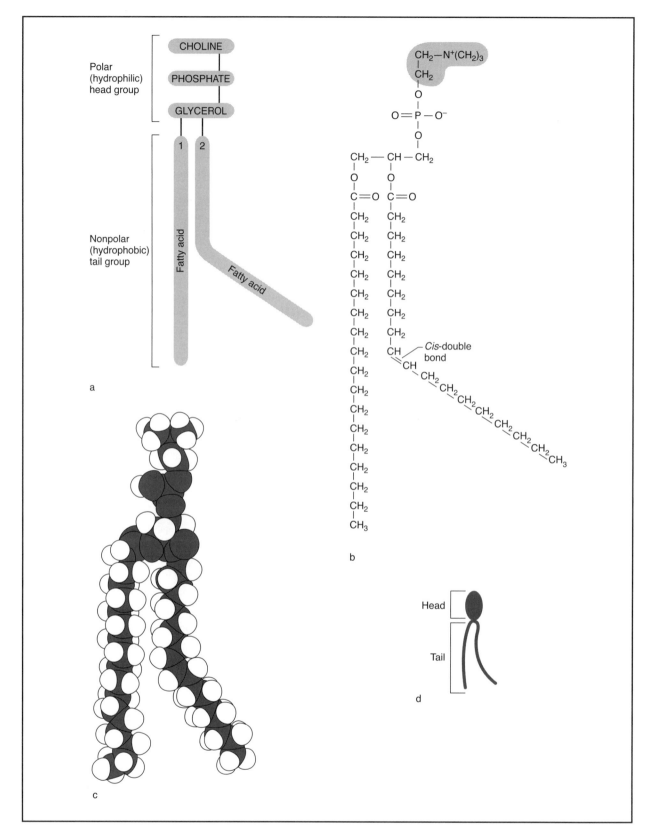

Figure 1. The structure of lecithin represented schematically (A), as a formula (B), as a model (C), and symbolically (D). Such phospholipid bilayers are thought to constitute the basic structure of cell membranes.

Lecithin was first found in eggs in 1846, so its name was coined from the Greek word for egg yolk, *lekithos*. Though lecithin is its common name, chemists refer to it as phosphatidylcholine. It is a yellow–brown fatty substance. In contrast to fats, which function as fuel molecules, lecithin serves a structural role in cell membranes. It is found in all cells. Without lecithin and other membrane phospholipids, cells would be unable to maintain their structure and probably would dissolve back into their surroundings. Lecithin is apparently vital for life in mammals, because no hereditary diseases in its biosynthesis are known. (A genetic defect involving a vital substance is lethal to the organism and therefore cannot be passed on.)

The lecithin we purchase in a store is actually a mixture of lecithin and other phospholipids as well as fatty (soy bean) oil. The fatty acid components in lecithin can vary, depending on the number of carbon atoms they contain and whether they are saturated or unsaturated. The nature of the fatty acid components in a lecithin molecule greatly influence its role. For example, a lecithin molecule in which both fatty acids are saturated aids oxygen uptake in the lungs. Another "species" of lecithin, which contains two unsaturated fatty acids is involved in the transport of cholesterol in the blood.

Structure and properties

The structure of lecithin is illustrated in Figure 1. Glycerol, which contains three carbon atoms, serves as the backbone of the lecithin molecule. The two fatty acids are linked to glycerol at carbon atoms 1 and 2 and the phosphate group is linked to carbon atom 3. Choline is, in turn, linked to the phosphate group. Typically, though not always, the fatty acid attached to carbon 1 of glycerol is saturated, while that attached to carbon 2 is unsaturated.

To get a crude idea of the structure of the lecithin molecule, imagine a balloon with two long paper streamers attached to it. The balloon or "head" region corresponds to the polar portion of the molecule, the negatively–charged phosphate group and the positively–charged choline, which readily dissolve in water. The streamers or "tails" represent the nonpolar part, the long chain of 12 to 18 carbon atoms in the two fatty acids, which are insoluble in water. As a result of the nature of its head and tail groups, lecithin molecules tend to disperse themselves in water with their nonpolar tails back–to–back to form bilayers, or double layers, in which the polar heads project outward into the water. This arrangement sequesters, or conceals, the nonpolar tails away from the water, forming a structural barrier to

the passage of polar and ionic molecules as shown in Figure 2.

Dietary and commercial sources

Because lecithin is found in all living organisms, it is readily available in foods. Egg yolks, liver, peanuts, corn, spinach, and whole grains are good dietary sources. Soy beans are by far the most important commercial source of lecithin, because they are an excellent source, and because such huge amounts are produced. Commercial lecithin is widely used to process food products, including baking mixes, candy, chewing gum, chocolate, ice cream, macaroni and noodles, margarine, whipped toppings, and so on. It is generally used as an emulsifier, a substance that can bring water and oil together. However, the amounts used as a food additive in such products are not enough to be a good dietary source of lecithin.

Role in health and disease

Lecithin is the most abundant membrane phospholipid in our cells. A study involving cells with a temperature–sensitive genetic defect in lecithin biosynthesis illustrates how essential it is for cell survival. When grown above a certain temperature, these cells were unable to make lecithin. Under these conditions the cells began to burst open and eventually died.

Several studies suggest that lecithin is involved in cell signaling, the process by which one cell initiates changes in another. For example, a hormone, neurotransmitter, or growth factor secreted by one cell communicates with another by altering its cell membrane in some way, usually by activating an enzyme which breaks down phospholipid in the membrane. The breakdown products interact with an enzyme which sets into motion a domino effect of changes in cell growth, metabolism, function, and so on. Disruptions in this process may give rise to certain diseases. Some recent evidence suggests that lecithin deficiency may interfere with cell signaling and so may be a factor in the development of liver and colon cancer.

Lecithin plays an important role in the transport of fats and cholesterol from the liver to sites where they can be either used or stored. Since fats do not dissolve in water solutions like blood plasma, they are transported in spherical particles called lipoproteins. These particles can mix with water solutions because the water–friendly proteins, cholesterol and phospholipids are on the outside surface. The nonpolar fats associated with them make up the core, which is unexposed to water. Because lecithin is required for lipoprotein syn-

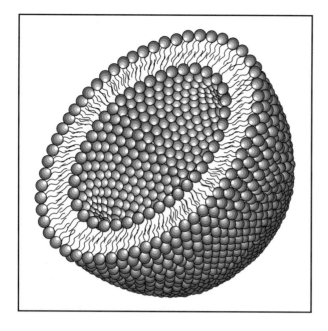

Figure 2.

thesis, a lecithin deficiency results in fats accumulating in the liver and leads to liver damage. Lecithin deficiency also leads to increased amounts of cholesterol in the blood and atherosclerosis, a disease in which narrowing of the arteries is caused primarily by the deposit of fats from the bloodstream.

Lecithin is the primary source of choline, the precursor of the neurotransmitter acetylcholine. Recent findings suggest a relationship between the lack of availability of lecithin to nerve cells which produce acetylcholine, and the progress of Alzheimer's disease.

Commercial importance

Commercial lecithin is actually a mixture of lecithin, other related phospholipids and oil. Due to its ability to break up fat and oil globules and its antioxidant properties, lecithin extracted from soy beans is important commercially for processing food and other products. In food it aids in the mixing of vegetable oils, butters, and other fatty ingredients so that they are uniformly distributed throughout the product. Without lecithin these ingredients tend to separate out. A familiar example is the separation of fat out of chocolate, leaving a light oily film on the surface. Lecithin stabilizes oils against oxidation during processing, resulting in better flavor and longer shelf life. Lecithin is also used in the manufacture of paints, dyes, inks, leather goods, plastics, cosmetics, textiles, and pharmaceutical products, among others.

See also Cell; Molecule.

Further Reading:

Bretscher, Mark S. "The Molecules of the Cell Membrane." *Scientific American*, (October 1985): 100–08.

Canty, David J., and Steven H. Zeisel. "Lecithin and Choline in Human Health and Disease." *Nutrition Reviews* 52, (1994): 327.

Delaney, Lisa, and Cemela London. "Dictionary of Healing Techniques and Remedies—part 35." *Prevention* 44, (February 1992): 135.

Patricia V. Racenis

LED

A LED (light–emitting diode) converts electrical energy to light by means of a *semiconductor*, made of a solid material, such as silicon, whose electrical conductivity when hot is as great as that of metals and very low when cold. LEDs were commonly referred to early in their history as solid–state lamps. The light produced by LEDs is known as *electroluminescence*, distinguishing it from *incandescence*, which is characteristic of light bulbs.

Semiconductors for LEDs are made from slices of crystal so thin that their *lattice*, or most basic physical structure, can be easily traversed. This crystal is alloyed with materials of opposing charges, one on each side. The negative side of the semiconductor is electron rich, and the positive side is electron poor. The positive–negative junction formed by the alloyed crystal is known as a *depletion layer*, which is relatively inactive. The crystal is then subjected to *doping*, a process of destabilizing

Red clover (*Trifolium pratense*).

The fruits of legumes are dry or fleshy, multi–seeded structures known as legumes or pods. The fruits and seeds of some legume species are highly nutritious because of their large concentrations of protein. The seeds of some species, however, contain toxic alkaloids and can be poisonous.

About one–half of the species of legumes have bumpy nodules present on their roots which house symbiotic (or mutualistic) bacteria that have the ability to metabolically fix atmospheric nitrogen gas into ammonia which can be utilized by the plant as a nutrient for the synthesis of proteins. The bacteria responsible for nitrogen fixation in legumes are in the genus *Rhizobium* with separate strains or species associated with each species of symbiotic legume. The *Rhizobium* bacteria have the ability to synthesize a chemical known as nitrogenase which is an enzyme that can cleave the very strong triple bond of nitrogen gas (N_2) so that ammonia (NH_3) is produced. Because nitrogen gas is otherwise inert to biological reactions, while ammonia (as ammonium ion, NH_4^+) is a chemical that plants can easily utilize in their nutrition, nitrogen fixation is an extremely useful function. Legumes that have symbiotic *Rhizobium* living in their root nodules may have important ecological advantages in competition with other types of plants, especially if they are growing in otherwise nitrogen–poor habitats.

Native legumes of North America

Many species in the legume family are indigenous to the natural plant communities of North America. Numerous other species of legumes have been introduced by humans from Eurasia, Africa, and elsewhere and are now naturalized in suitable habitats in North America. The introduced plants are mostly species that are grown in agriculture or horticulture and were able to escape from cultivation and establish wild populations.

Native species of legumes are among the most beautiful and engaging wildflowers of North America. Some of the most interesting and attractive groups of native legumes include the wild lupines (such as *Lupinus perennis*), false blue indigo (*Baptisia australis*), wild indigo (*B. tinctoria*), tick–trefoils (*Desmodium* spp.), bush–clovers (*Lespedeza* spp.), beach pea (*Lathyrus maritimus*) and marsh pea (*L. palustris*), milk–vetches (*Astragalus* spp.), and loco–weeds (*Oxytropis* spp.).

Some North American examples of tree–sized legumes that occur in temperate climates include the black locust (*Robinia pseudoacacia*), yellow–wood (*Cladrastis lutea*), redbud (*Cercis canadensis*), honey locust (*Gleditsia triacanthos*), and Kentucky coffee tree (*Gymnocladus dioica*). These are all native to parts of the eastern United States but are cultivated as ornamentals more widely, sometimes escaping into roadside and secondary–forest habitats.

Other native species of legumes occur in subtropical habitats in the southern United States. These include the eastern coralbean (*Erythrina herbacea*) of the southeastern states, Bahama lysiloma (*Lysiloma bahamensis*), and fish–poison tree (*Piscidia piscipula*) of southern Florida. Subtropical legumes in the southwestern states include cattail acacia (*Acacia greggii*), sweet acacia (*A. farnesiana*), and other acacias, along with species of leadtrees (*Leucaena* spp.) and blackbeads (*Pithecellobium* spp.).

Legumes in agriculture

Some species of legumes are very important as foods for humans and domestic livestock. The seeds of legumes are typically highly nutritious and rich in protein, carbohydrates, oils, fiber, and other nutrients. However, the protein–rich nature of legume seeds, a consequence of their nitrogen–fixing symbiosis, is perhaps their most important attribute as a food for animals. Numerous species of legumes are grown in agriculture, and it is likely that there are other species of legumes of potential agricultural importance that have not yet been discovered, especially in the tropics.

One of the most important agricultural legumes is the peanut or ground–nut (*Arachis hypogaea*), originally native to Brazil but now cultivated much more widely. After the above–ground flowers of the peanut are pollinated, their supporting stem turns and forces its way into the ground where the flowers then develop into their familiar, shelled fruits. Peanuts can be eaten raw or roasted, pulverized into peanut butter, or baked into cakes and cookies. Peanuts are also used to manufacture an edible oil. Sometimes a fungus known as *Aspergillus flavus* will infest stored peanuts. This fungus will excrete a potent toxic known as aflatoxin which can cause liver damage and perhaps lead to the development of cancers. In addition, some people develop an extreme allergy to peanuts, and these hypersensitive individuals can be killed by inadvertently eating any food containing peanuts.

Another very important species of legume is the soybean (*Glycine max*), originally native to Southeast Asia. This species can be eaten cooked or as fresh sprouts, or it can be processed into a protein–rich material known as tofu, another substance known as soy flour, or into a nutritious drink known as soy–milk. Soybeans are important ingredients in some of the meat substitutes that have recently been developed such as vegetarian hot dogs. Soybeans are also pressed to produce edible oils.

The seeds of many other species of legumes are also eaten. These include the chick pea (*Cicer arietinum*), lentil (*Lens esculenta*), common pea (*Pisum sativum*), broad or faba bean (*Vicia faba*), cow pea (*Vigna sinensis*), common bean (*P. vulgaris*), mung bean (*Phaseolus aureus*), Lima bean (*P. lunatus*), and scarlet runner bean (*P. multiflorus*). The entire pod of the carob (*Ceratonia siliqua*) can be eaten and is similar to a candy because of the naturally large concentration of sugar that it contains.

The licorice (*Glycyrrhiza glabra*) is a perennial herb that is native to southern Europe and Asia and is now cultivated more widely. The rhizome of licorice is mostly used in the preparation of candy and to much smaller degrees to prepare medicinals, shoe polish, and to flavor tobacco.

Some species of legumes are important in agriculture as nitrogen–rich forages for domestic livestock. Species of forage legumes that are commonly cultivated in North America include alfalfa or lucerne (*Medicago sativa*), sweet clovers (*Melilotus officinalis* and *M. alba*), birds–foot trefoil (*Lotus corniculatus*), vetches (*Vicia cracca* and other species), and various species of clovers, including red clover (*Trifolium pratense*), white clover (*T. repens*), hop–clovers (*T. agrarium* and *T. procumbens*), and alsike clover (*T. hybridum*). Legumes are also used as a so–called "green manure" or soil conditioner which is grown and then ploughed into the ground to improve the soil quality in terms of organic matter and fixed nitrogen.

Other economic products obtained from legumes

Many tree–sized species in the legume family are valuable for their hard, durable timber. North American species are relatively minor in this respect, although the Kentucky coffee tree, black locust, and honey locust are used as lumber to some degree.

Some leguminous species of tropical hardwoods are highly prized for fine woodworking. Purpleheart (*Peltogyne paniculata*) is a very hard, durable, and strong wood found in northern South America which is a brownish color when first sawn but turns a spectacular purple after being exposed to the atmosphere for a while. This tropical hardwood is used to manufacture fine furniture and as a decorative inlay into other woods. Rosewoods also have hard, dark–purple woods that are widely sought after to manufacture fine furniture and other goods. Examples include Brazilian rosewood (*Dalbergia nigra*) and Asian rosewoods (*D. latifolia* and *D. sissoo*).

Various species of trees in the genus *Acacia* are also important sources of lumber, for example, *A. melanoxylan* and *A. visco* in Australia. Species of *Albizia* are also important timber trees.

The seeds of the mesquite (*Prosopis juliflora*) of the southwestern United States and Mexico are used as animal feed, while the wood is burned to manufacture a flavor–enhancing charcoal. Mesquite flavorings have become quite popular in recent years, and many foods are now seasoned with this plant, including potato and corn chips.

Sunhemp is a fiber obtained from *Crotalaria juncea*, a legume native to south Asia. This is an annual plant, grown mostly in the Indian subcontinent and used to manufacture twine, ropes, bags, and canvas.

Gums are plant compounds that are used as adhesives, to manufacture paints and candies, to prepare paper, and to manufacture certain medicines. Important gums are made from extracts of certain legume species including gum tragacanth from *Astragalus gummifer*, gum Arabic from *Acacia senegal* and *A. stenocarpa*, and tragasol from the carob (*Ceratonia siliqua*).

The barks of some species of acacias are sometimes used as sources of tannins, chemicals that are mostly used to manufacture leather from animal skins. Species used for this purpose include *Acacia dealbata*, *A. decurrens*, and *A pycnantha*, all native to Australia but also cultivated elsewhere.

Some important dyes are extracted from species in the legume family. One of the world's most important, natural dyes is indigo, extracted from the foliage of the indigo (*Indigofera tinctoria*) of south Asia and to a lesser degree from American indigo (*I. suffruticosa*) of tropical South America. Indigos are still cultivated widely for their dark–blue dye, although similar chemicals have been synthesized and are now widely available.

Other important natural dyes are obtained from the heartwood of several species of leguminous trees. Logwood (*Haematoxylon campechianum*) is a small, thorny tree native to Central America that is an important source of a dye known as *hematoxylin*, which has a deep, purple–red color, and can also be manufactured into a persistent black dye. The brazilette (*H. brasiletto*) is a source of a natural red dye as are brazilwood (*Caesalpina brasiliensis*) and sappanwood (*C. sappan*) of south Asia.

Derris or rotenone is a poisonous alkaloid that has long been used by indigenous peoples of Southeast Asia as arrow and fish poisons. Rotenone is now used widely as a rodenticide to kill small mammals and as an insecticide to kill pest insects. This chemical is mostly extracted from the plants *Derris elliptica* and *D. malaccensis*.

Shellac is now a relatively minor product, but until recently it was widely used for finishing wood and for manufacturing products such as phonograph records and electrical insulators. Shellac is derived from a sticky substance that is secreted by an Asian insect, *Tachardia lacca*. However, several species in the legume family are cultivated as hosts for the insect, including the pigeon pea (*Cajanus cajan*) and babul tree (*Acacia arabica*).

Legumes in horticulture

Some species of legumes are important in horticulture where they are typically grown for their beautiful flowers and sometimes as foliage plants. The scotch broom (*Cytisus scoparius*) is a green–stemmed, bushy shrub with attractive, yellow flowers. Gorse (*Ulex europaeus*) is also a shrub with spiny branches and bright yellow flowers. These shrubs are widely used in horticulture in temperate climates as are the North American trees, redbud, Kentucky coffee tree, and black and honey locust. Some non–native species that are used in horticulture in temperate climates of North America include species of laburnum such as Scotch laburnum (*Laburnum alpinum*) and common laburnum (*L. anagyroides*).

Many other leguminous trees and shrubs are grown as ornamentals in subtropical and tropical climates. Species cultivated in southern parts of the United States

KEY TERMS

Bilateral symmetry—In reference to flower shape, this indicates that a vertical sectioning of the flower will produce two halves with symmetric features.

Compound leaf—A leaf in which the blade is separated into several or many smaller units, called leaflets, arranged along a central petiole or stalk known as a rachis.

Cultivar—A cultivated variety of a species.

Legume—This is a type of fruit, also known as a pod, which is developed from a single ovary but contains multiple seeds and opens along a single seam when ripe.

Nitrogenase—An enzyme synthesized by *Rhizobium* and some other microorganisms that is capable of cleaving the triple bond of nitrogen gas (N_2), generating ammonia (NH_3), a type of fixed nitrogen that plants can utilize in their nutrition.

Nitrogen fixation—The conversion of atmospheric nitrogen gas (N_2) to ammonia or an oxide of nitrogen. This process can occur biologically through action of the microbial enzyme, nitrogenase, or inorganically at high temperature and pressure.

Rhizome—This is a modified stem that grows horizontally in the soil and from which roots and upward–growing shoots develop at the stem nodes.

Tendril—A spirally winding, clinging organ that is used by climbing plants to attach to their supporting substrate. In the legume family, tendrils are derived from modified leaflets.

Weed—This refers to any plant that is judged to interfere with some human purpose, usually by hindering the growth of crop plants, by poisoning livestock, or by degrading visual aesthetics as in the case of weeds in lawns.

include the royal poinciana (*Delonix regia*) of Madagascar, the paradise poinciana (*D. gilliesii*) of South America, the tamarind (*Tamarindus indica*) of south Asia, and the silktree (*Albizia julibrissin*) and woman's tongue (*A. lebbek*) of south Asia.

Various species of garden lupines (*Lupinus*) are grown for their attractive, tall spikes of colorful flowers. Commonly grown species include *L. polyphyllus* and *L. nootkatensis* whose flowers are naturally colored blue but also occur in white, pink, red, and other floral cultivars.

Other legumes that are commonly grown in gardens include the Japanese wisteria (*Wisteria floribunda*), Chinese wisteria (*W. sinensis*), and related species. The sweet pea (*Lathyrus odoratus*) is also commonly grown as an attractive, climbing plant.

Legumes as weeds

Some species of legumes that are cultivated in agriculture or horticulture have become naturalized in semi–natural and natural habitats, and some of these are locally considered to be invasive weeds. Examples of these species include Scotch broom, gorse, garden lupines, vetches, and some other species. These are rarely considered important enough as weeds to be the specific targets of control programs.

One exception, however, is the kudzu vine (*Pueraria lobata*), native to Japan and introduced to the southeastern United States as a forage plant and for use in controlling erosion. This species is considered to be a serious, invasive weed in some places. Control methods for the kudzu include the use of herbicides and the excavation of its large, underground, roots.

A few species of legumes have foliage or seeds that can be extremely toxic to humans and domestic animals, and these may be actively controlled to reduce the risks of poisoning. The best North American examples of toxic legumes that are sometimes considered to be pests because they can poison livestock on rangelands are the locoweeds (*Oxytropis* spp., and to a lesser degree, *Astragalus* spp.). The precatory pea or rosary bean (*Abrus precatorius*) grows wild in subtropical and tropical climates and was introduced as an ornamental plant to south Florida where it is now naturalized. This species has small (less than 0.4 in (1 cm) long), very attractive, crimson–red seeds, with one jet–black spot at one end, but these are so toxic that a single one can kill a person if chewed. Precatory peas are sometimes used to make beautiful seed–necklaces, but these can be deadly in the hands of children.

See also Nitrogen fixation.

Further Reading:

Duke, J. A. *Handbook of Legumes of World Economic Importance*. New York: Plenum Press, 1981.
Hvass, E. *Plants That Serve and Feed Us.* New York: Hippocrene Books, 1975.
Klein, R. M. *The Green World: An Introduction to Plants and People.* New York: Harper and Row, 1987.
Woodland, D. W. *Contemporary Plant Systematics.* Englewood Cliffs, NJ: Prentice–Hall, 1991.

Bill Freedman

Lemmings

Lemmings are small mouselike rodents in the family Cricetidae, which also includes the voles, gerbils, hamsters, and the American rats and mice. Lemmings occur in open, northern habitats, especially in alpine and arctic tundra of North America and Eurasia. Lemmings are herbivores, feeding on sedges, grasses, berries, roots, and lichens. Lemmings are ecologically important in their habitat, in part because they are the major food of many species of predators.

Lemmings are highly fecund animals. When conditions are appropriate to their survival, some species of lemmings can become extremely abundant, an event that population ecologists refer to as an "irruption." When this happens, it seems that lemmings are everywhere, and indeed they are — they literally run over your feet in meadows, and may invade northern towns. Under these conditions the lemmings are driven to make short–distance migrations in search of food and new habitat.

Northern European legends about lemmings include references to mass migrations by these animals, in some cases including large numbers approaching seacliffs, jumping fearlessly into the ocean, and then swimming out toward the horizon until they become exhausted, and drown. These stories about mass migrations of lemmings are quite remarkable, but they may be somewhat embellished. There is no doubt, however, the some species of lemmings can periodically attain extraordinarily large populations, which then crash to smaller abundances, on about a three–to–five–year periodicity.

The true lemmings are four species in the genus *Lemmus*. The brown lemming (*Lemmus sibiricus*) occurs in alpine and arctic tundras of northern North America, and in Siberia. The Norway lemming (*Lemmus lemmus*) is most famous for its periodic irruptions. When these animals are abundant, they can literally eat most of the available food, causing their own starvation and that of other herbivores, including reindeer (*Rangifer tarandus*).

The collared or Arctic lemming (*Dicrostonyx torquatus*) is a widespread species of the Arctic tundra, occurring in both North America and Eurasia. Collared lemmings sometimes irrupt in abundance, and when this happens they are the focus of hunting of all predators, even those as large as wolves and bears. This species has a white pelage in the winter, but is brown during the brief, arctic summer.

The bog lemmings are North American species of moist habitats, especially *Sphagnum* bogs. The southern bog lemming (*Synaptomys cooperi*) occurs in the northeastern United States and southeastern Canada, while the northern bog lemming (*S. borealis*) ranges through most of forested Canada and Alaska.

See also Rodents.

Bill Freedman

Lemurs

Lemurs are primitive primates, or prosimians, found only on the island of Madagascar and adjacent small islands off the coast of Africa. Although lemurs, lorises, and tarsiers are all prosimians, or "pre–monkeys," only the lemurs and lorises have the typical prosimian snout that, like a dog's, remains moist. This wet snout, called a rhinarium, means that scent is important to lemurs. Most lemurs, like other prosimians, also possess two built–in tools for grooming. The toilet claw is a claw located on the second toe of the hind foot (all other digits have nails), which is used for picking through fur and eating. They also have a group of lower teeth (incisors) that combine into a horizontal tool called a dental comb, also used for grooming. All lemurs are nocturnal in habit.

Lemurs are classified in four families: the typical lemurs (Lemuridae), the dwarf and mouse lemurs (Cheirogaleidae), the indrids (Indriidae, including indri, sifaka, and avahi), and the aye–aye, the lone member of Daubentoniidae.

The common name lemur means "ghost." It was given to these elusive creatures by the eighteenth century Swedish scientist Carolus Linnaeus. Attracted by their large, bright eyes and strange calls, he thought they resembled the wandering spirits of the dead called *lemures* in Latin. He gave the name to many prosimi-

ans, but today the term lemur is used only for the prosimians of Madagascar and the Comoro Islands.

The lemurs of Madagascar were cut off from the mainstream of primate evolution at least 50 million years ago. In Madagascar, they evolved to occupy many ecological niches that, on the continent of Africa, were occupied by monkeys or apes. About 40 different species of lemurs evolved. Some, perhaps as large as the great apes, are known now only by their fossils.

Lemurs have flat nails instead of claws on both hands and feet. Most have 36 teeth, though the indrids have 30 and the ring–tailed lemur has 32. Many lemurs exhibit profound differences in weight and activity from one season to the next. For example, the male's scrotum, which holds the testicles, may enlarge as much as eight times as summer, and the mating season, approaches.

Mouse and dwarf lemurs

The smallest lemurs are called mouse and dwarf lemurs, family Cheirogaleidae. The smallest, the lesser mouse lemur, *(Microcebus murinus)* is about 5 in (12.5 cm) in length with an equally long tail. It weighs less than 2 oz (57 g). The brown lesser mouse lemur *(M. rufus)* is approximately the same size. Coquerel's mouse lemur *(Mirza coquereli)*, the largest species in this group, is about twice that long. It is also one of the rarest lemurs because its deciduous forest is drying up or being destroyed by logging.

These little, large–eyed lemurs have long hind legs, useful for leaping. The lesser mouse lemur hops like a frog when on the ground. The females have three pairs of nipples, while true lemurs have only a single pair. They bear two or three tiny young (only about 5 g each) after a gestation period of about 60 days in the smaller species and 89 days in the larger.

Mouse lemurs survive the dry season, when food is scarce, by living off nourishment stored in their fat tails. Mouse lemur females share a spherical leaf nest with each other and their young, while males usually curl up by themselves. They all hunt at night as solitary individuals, eating primarily insects and some leaves, usually those bearing ant secretions. As they move around, they communicate with each other by high–pitched calls.

Mouse lemurs are active, busy creatures, while the dwarf lemurs *(Cheirogaleus)* are rather sluggish all year. Dwarf lemurs are true hibernators, and are active only in the rainy season. The fat–tailed dwarf lemur *(C. medius)* stores plenty of fat at the base of its tail for use during its six–month hibernation. Dwarf lemurs are

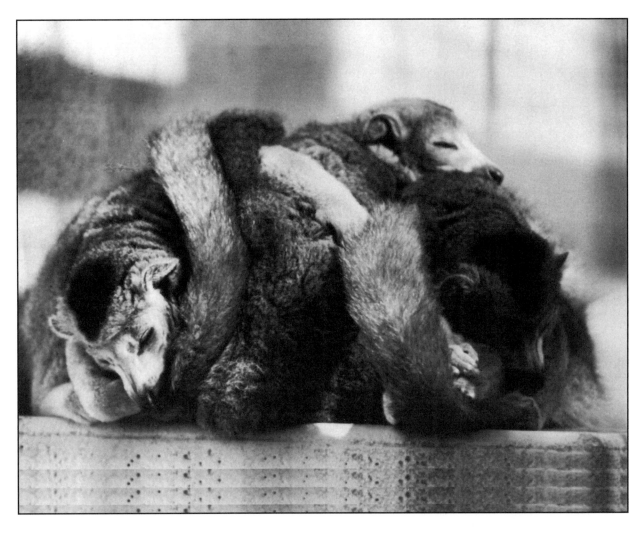

Sleeping crowned lemurs (*Eulemur [Lemur] coronatus*).

incapable of leaping from branch to branch, and they live in areas where the tree branches are closer together. Only the greater dwarf lemur *(C. major)* resides in wet rain forest; the other three species live in the drier forests.

The hairy–eared dwarf lemur *(Allocebus trichotis)* was long thought to be extinct but was rediscovered in 1965. Virtually nothing is known about it. The fork–marked dwarf lemur *(Phaner furcifer)* has a dark stripe on its back which curves over the head and links up with the dark eye rings that mark all mouse and dwarf lemurs. Unlike *Cheirogaleus*, it is a great leaper, achieving distances of up to 33 ft (10 m) in a single bound.

True lemurs

The true, or typical, lemurs (Lemuridae) are diurnal primates and thus have smaller eyes than the mouse and dwarf lemurs. Their eyes are golden yellow. Their bodies are about the size of a cat's, but their tails are considerably longer. These lemurs eat fruit, leaves, and some insects. Their social groups vary in size from two to more than 20, and the females tend to dominate the males. The females also are responsible for defense of the group. The females usually bear to only a single offspring after a gestation period of about 18 weeks. The young lemur rides on its mother's back for several months.

The fluffy black–and–white striped tail of the ring–tailed lemur *(Lemur catta)* is present in both males and females, though most lemurs exhibit sexual dimorphism, or different coloring in males and females. When moving, the ring–tailed lemur holds its dramatic tail up in a gentle curve. It also waves it to disperse the chemical released by its scent glands, which are located on its forearms. These glands have tiny spurs that can slash the bark of trees, leaving the slash scented with their territory–marking odor. The ring–tailed male also uses this scent in a strange kind of combat. When two aggressive males confront each other, each rubs its long tail on its forearm scent gland, turns, and waves its smelly tail. Apparently, one of the "combatants" finds itself overwhelmed and gives in.

The ring–tailed lemur is about 15 in (38 cm) long, with an 18– or 20–in (46–51 cm) tail, and weighs about 6–7 lb (2.7–3.2 kg). Though ring–tailed lemurs spend most of their time on the ground (they are probably the only lemur that does this), they climb trees in their open forest in the early morning to reach the sunlight, which warms them after chilly nights. Because they spend much of their time walking on the ground, they have smooth, leathery palms and soles.

Only the male black lemur *(L. macaco)* is completely black. Females have white ruffs around the black face and a white chest. The rest of the female's body is reddish brown. The mongoose lemur *(L. mongoz)* exhibits similar sexual dimorphism. Although both males and females are gray–brown in color, the females have white cheeks and neck, while the males have red cheeks. The widely occurring brown lemur *(L. fulvus)* is a stay–at–home, rarely moving more than 300 ft (90 m) from its territory, which consists of only a few trees. Within this territory it tends to remain near the tops of the trees. It may be active day or night.

The largest of the true lemurs is the ruffed lemur *(Varecia variegata)* of eastern Madagascar. It may be 4 ft (1.2 m) long from head to tail and weigh up to 6.5 lb (3 kg). Basically a black animal, the long, shaggy fur of its ruff may be white or reddish. Its back and part of its legs are also white. Strangely, unlike the other true lemurs, the ruffed lemur has a fairly short gestation period (about 100 days compared to 120–135 days), and the offspring (often twins) are born too weak to hang onto their mother. She places them in a small fur–lined nest for at least three weeks.

The genus of so–called gentle lemurs (which are probably no more gentle than other lemurs), *Hapalemur*, prefers a watery habitat as well as forests. These lemurs live among the reeds located by lakes, and are sometimes good swimmers. They eat the soft heart, or pith, of the reeds, and they also like sugarcane. The gentle lemurs are more thickset than most lemurs. The broad–nosed gentle lemur *(H. simus)* occurs in only three tiny populations and may be close to extinction. The gray gentle lemur *(H. griseus)* is more widespread but still endangered.

The sportive lemur *(Lepilemur mustelinus)* received its name because, when threatened, it turns and raises its arms as if preparing to box. In its dry habitat, this lemur eats primarily prickly succulent plants that have so little nourishment, it eats its own feces in order to further digest the food. Unlike most lemurs, the sportive lemur lives a semi–solitary life, with one male in a territory encompassing the smaller territories of several separated females. It is also the only true lemur to have 32 teeth as an adult instead of 36. Recent genetic studies have shown that the sportive lemurs, also called weasel lemurs, of different areas in Madagascar may actually be different enough from each other to represent seven different species in a separate family (Lepilemuridae).

Indris or leaping lemurs

Family Indriidae includes the woolly lemur or avahi, the indri, and two sifakas. These prosimians have only 30 teeth instead of the 36 found in most other lemurs. When on the ground, these primates tend to walk or leap upright.

The indri *(Indri indri)* is the largest prosimian. Its name comes from a misunderstanding. Early explorers thought the natives were naming the animal when they said, "indri, indri." Instead, they were exclaiming, "There it is" or "Look at that." The indri is quite heavy, weighing more than 13 lb (6 kg) with a head and body 27 in (69 cm) long. Unlike most prosimians, its tail is insignificant. It is black and cream in color, with an alert, humorous face. The cream color on its rump continues on down the back of its legs. However, some individuals do not have clear color differentiations. Indris live in groups that continually sing (actually closer to a "howl") together, a sound that echoes through the tropical rain forest. They are protected, which is fortunate because they do not breed frequently. A female gives birth only once in two or three years.

The sifakas *(Propithecus)* are soft, fluffy, and fairly large, at least 40 in (102 cm) in length including their long tail. Their whitish color is highlighted by a dark face and crown. Their name is an interpretation of the sound they commonly make. Sifakas mostly cling to vertical tree trunks and have legs and feet specially adapted for that position. Their legs are longer than their arms, and the big toe is especially long and strong for grasping. The diademed sifaka *(P. diadema)* of eastern Madagascar is quite rare and has not been studied to any extent; attempts to keep it in captivity have failed. The more common Verreaux's sifakas *(P. verreauxi)* are territorial animals that mark their territories using glands located on the throat. The single offspring is carried on the mother's stomach for several months before moving onto her back.

The woolly lemur, or avahi *(Avahi laniger)*, is the smallest member of this family, being only about 12 in (30 cm) long, plus an equally long tail, and weighing about 1.5 lb (0.7 kg). Basically colored gray–brown, it has lighter rings around its eyes. Its major food comes from the mango tree, from which it eats leaves, buds, and bark. Unlike the other indrids, the avahi is nocturnal, and its social groups include only two or three individuals.

Aye–Aye, a superfamily of its own

The aye–aye *(Daubentonia madagascariensis)* is placed in a family, Daubentoniidae, and even a superfamily, by itself. It was given its friendly little name by European discoverer, Pierre Sonnerat, from the sound it makes. Looking rather like a squirrel with large eyes, it is about 3 ft (91 cm) long including its bushy tail. It has short white fur beneath dark brown and white–tipped coarser fur. One of the prime reasons it is placed in a family by itself is that it has only 18 teeth. And, instead of a dental comb, it has front incisors that, like a rodent's, grow continuously.

Seen head–on, the aye–aye's face looks triangular, made so by its large pointed ears and sharply pointed nose and chin. The aye–aye's long grasping hands and feet have extra–long middle fingers with hooked claws. This flexible digit is used as a probe to clean insects from its fur and to scrape insect larvae, especially beetle grubs, from holes in wood. It also uses the claw on this long middle finger as a cup for drinking and for scooping coconut meat out of the shell. Aye–ayes lacks the toilet claw of other lemurs. Aye–aye females apparently breed only every other year or so. They are the only primates that have nipples located on the abdomen instead of on the chest.

A larger aye–aye *(D. robusta)* became extinct probably less than 1,000 years ago. *D. madagascariensis* was thought to be extinct after 1930, but was rediscovered in 1957 in the eastern rain forest. The aye–aye was once considered to be one of the most endangered mammals in Madagascar, but scientists now speculate that it is elusive rather than very rare. The species is found in several protected areas in Madagascar and an uninhabited island, Nosy Mangabe, is a protected reserve for this species. In the 1960s nine aye–ayes were captured and taken to this island, where they have established a small population.

Threats to lemur survival

At least 14 species of Madagascar lemurs have become extinct since humans moved to the island about

---

KEY TERMS

Dental comb—A group of lower incisor teeth on most prosimians that have moved together into a horizontal position to form a grooming tool.

Diurnal—Active in or related to daytime.

Grooming claw—A claw located on the second hind toe of many prosimians, used for grooming the fur.

Nocturnal—Active in or related to nighttime.

Rhinarium—The rough–skinned end of the snout, usually wet in prosimians, indicating that smell is important to them.

Sexual dimorphism—Two forms in a species, based on sex. Some male and female monkeys of the same species have quite different coloration.

2,000 years ago. The remainder are all in danger of extinction as the human population continues to expand, requiring space, food, and firewood. Those species that eat a wider variety of food than others will be more likely to survive as their habitat diminishes.

Lemurs are protected by Malagasy law, but they are still often hunted as a delicacy. Some lemurs are killed for superstitious reasons, but others are protected for the same reasons. For example, some tribes believe the indri takes on the souls of their ancestors, therefore they are opposed to killing these lemurs. On the other hand, some tribes regard the presence of an aye–aye near a village as a signal of coming death and they quickly kill it.

Although all lemurs need protecting, not all of them can be bred in captivity. Successful captive breeding programs have been established for the black lemur and the ruffed lemur with the hope of returning them to Madagascar. Indris and aye–ayes, on the other hand, have proved very difficult to maintain, let alone breed, in captivity.

See also Lorises; Primates; Prosimians; Tarsiers.

Further Reading:

Bromley, Lynn. *Monkeys, Apes and Other Primates.* Santa Barbara, CA: Bellerophon Books, 1981.

Durrell, Gerald. *The Aye–Aye and I.* New York: Viking Press, 1992.

Harcourt, Caroline, and Jane Thornback. *Lemurs of Madagascar and the Comoros.* Gland, Switzerland: IUCN—The World Conservation Union, 1990.

Kerrod, Robin. *Mammals: Primates, Insect–Eaters and Baleen Whales.* New York: Facts on File, 1988.

Mittermeier, R., et al., eds. *Lemurs of Madagascar: An Action Plan for Their Conservation: 1993–1999.* Gland, Switzerland: IUCN—The World Conservation Union, 1992.

Napier, J. R., and P. H. Napier. *The Natural History of the Primates.* Cambridge, MA: The MIT Press, 1985.

Peterson, Dale. *The Deluge and the Ark: A Journey into Primate Worlds.* Boston: Houghton Mifflin, 1989.

Preston–Mafham, Rod and Ken. *Primates of the World.* New York: Facts on File, 1992.

Jean F. Blashfield

Lemon tree see **Citrus trees**

Lens

In the field of optics, a lens is a device used for focusing or defocusing a beam of light. It is commonly formed from a disk–shaped blank of transparent material, such as glass, plastic, or fused quartz; both sides are ground and polished, with at least one surface being polished with a curve. The word lens is derived from the Latin word for lentil, since the shape of a lens resembles the curved surface of a lentil bean.

Lenses are important in everyday life. Eyes have lenses that can be adjusted by the ciliary muscles surrounding the lens to provide a clear image of objects far away or up close. The ability of the lens to change its focal length diminishes with age, often requiring correction with external lenses (glasses or contact lenses). Lenses are also used in optical instruments such as cameras, telescopes, binoculars, microscopes, and lighthouse assemblies. Lenses come in many differing shapes, with each surface being flat, concave, or convex.

Focusing, or convergence, occurs because the lens refracts light, as is shown in figure 1a: parallel rays enter the convex lens from the left and, since light travels more slowly through the lens than through air, the rays are bent toward the optical axis that runs through the center of the lens. The rays come together at a point in space that is separated from the lens by the focal length (f). Calculating f for a simple spherical lens (which has a curved surface with a spherical shape) is done using the simple formula

$$\frac{1}{f} = (n-1) \left(\frac{1}{r1} + \frac{1}{r2} \right)$$

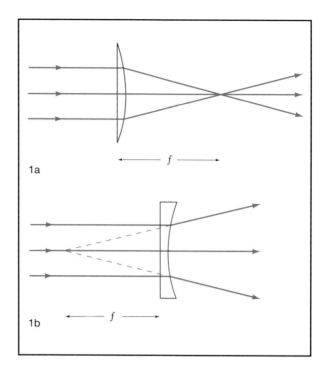

1a

1b

Figure 1.

where n is the refractive index of the glass, and $r1$ and $r2$ are the radii of curvature of the first and second surfaces respectively. The radius value is positive if the surface is concave and negative if convex. From this formula, it is apparent that reducing the radius of curvature of one or both surfaces will shorten the focal length. Flat surfaces have an infinite radius of curvature and therefore do not contribute to focusing. Figure 1b shows the effect of concave surfaces on the focusing of light: the parallel rays entering the lens are bent away from the optical axis and are said to diverge. In this case the lens is called a negative lens. Note that divergence of the rays is such that they seem to emanate from a point that is one focal length behind the lens.

Lenses are important because they can be used to form an image of an object. There are two types of images that may be formed. The first is the real image, which is formed on the side of a lens away from the object and can be projected onto viewing screen. The second is a virtual image, which is formed on the object side of the lens and cannot be projected on a screen; however, the virtual image can be viewed by looking into the lens, as with a microscope. The size, position, magnification, and type of image formed by a positive lens depend on the position of the object relative to the focal length. When the object is located two focal lengths away from the lens, the image is real, inverted, and the same size as the object (figure 2a). If an object is moved further away, the image becomes smaller (fig-

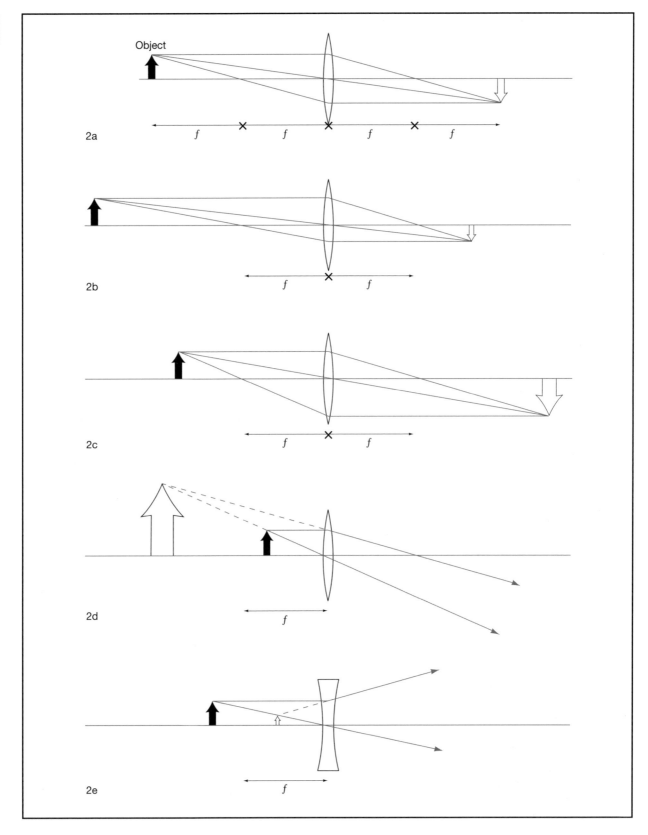

Figure 2.

ure 2b). If the object is moved closer, then the image becomes larger (figure 2c) until the separation is one focal length. If the object is placed less than one focal distance away from the lens, then a virtual, magnified, upright image is formed (figure 2d). Negative lenses always form a virtual image which is smaller than the object (figure 2e). The position of the image is calculated using the simple equation

$$\frac{1}{o} + \frac{1}{i} = \frac{1}{f}$$

where o is the distance between the object and the lens and I is the location of the image. A negative value of I indicated that the image is virtual.

Single lenses may cause several types of aberration, such as chromatic or spherical aberration, which tend to distort an image. For instance, chromatic aberration occurs because the refractive index depends on the wavelength, and so the lens has a different focal length for different wavelengths. Since the human eye detects light over a large range of wavelengths, chromatic aberration causes the colors of the image to separate and blur. This distortion can be corrected using a compound lens (an achromatic pair), in which the chromatic aberration of the first lens is compensated for by the second. A compound lens is usually a pair of lenses glued together in which the two inner surfaces have the same radius of curvature. Spherical aberration, a distortion caused by the spherical shape of the lens, can be reduced by using special combinations of spherical lenses or by using a lens with a different profile. For instance, a lens with a parabolic profile is used instead of a spherical lens to focus a laser beam on a very fine point.

The f–number of a lens is given by the ratio of the focal length of the lens to the aperture, the opening through which light passes. A lens with a large aperture has a small f–number and therefore lets more light through than a smaller diameter lens. Aberrations become increasingly noticeable as the f–number decreases; thus the design of a low f–number lens system is more complex because there are more aberrations in the system that must be reduced. The recent introduction of computers to lens system design has helped produce new systems that perform better than systems designed using the older design techniques.

Many optical instruments require the use of several lenses, firmly held together and relative to one another; such assemblies are called lens systems. The simplest lens system is the telescope, which consists of two lenses, a large diameter objective that gathers as much light as possible, and a smaller eyepiece that aligns the rays of light in order to allow the eye to see the image. The magnification of the telescope is equal to the ratio

KEY TERMS

Aberration—A distortion or defect in an image formed by a lens.

Magnification—The ratio between the size of an image seen using an optical instrument and the size of the image seen with the naked eye. A magnification of 10 means that the image is 10 times larger than it would have been if seen unaided.

Optical axis—An imaginary line running through the center of an optical system, to which all optical elements are aligned.

Parabolic lens—A lens where the curved surface, or surfaces, can be described by a parabola which is rotated in space. The parabolic lens is used to reduce spherical aberration.

Refraction—The deviation of a beam of light when it passes from one medium to another.

Refractive index—A dimensionless number, given by the ratio of the velocity of light within a vacuum to the velocity of light within a medium, which indicates the degree of refraction seen at an interface between two media.

Spherical lens—A lens where the curved surface is part of a spherical surface. This is the simplest type of lens to manufacture.

of the focal lengths of these two lenses. More complex lens systems can be found in the field of photography, either as camera lenses or in enlarging machines. A camera lens is essentially a positive lens that produces a real image at the film plane; however, because of aberrations and the need for different magnifications, most camera lens systems have multiple elements. Wide–angle lenses have an angle–of–view of 90°–140° (180° for fisheye lenses) and show considerable distortion, particularly around the edges. Standard camera lenses have an angle–of–view of 50°–60° and telephoto lenses have and angle–of–view of 20°–40°. Both of these lenses show less distortion. The telephoto lens is designed to give a long effective focal length (in the range of 85mm–300mm) without the bulk of a long focal length lens; for example, a 200mm telephoto lens system uses several lenses to produce the 200 mm effect without being four times as long as a 50mm system. Zoom lenses contain elements that can be moved relative to the others in order to change the focal length of the combination, and so a single lens system can take the place of many. However, since the zoom lens system is not optimized for any set focal length, the image is often not as good as that provided by a fixed focal length lens.

The term lens can also be applied to devices that control the divergence of beams other than light beams. For instance, a magnetic lens is used to focus beams of charged particles (such as electrons and protons) and can be found in particle accelerators and television tubes.

Further Reading:

Hecht, Jeff. *Optics: Light for a New Age.* New York: Scribner, 1987.

Kingslake, Rudolph. *A History of the Photographic Lens.* New York: Academic Press, 1989.

Smithson, Greg. *Light and You.* Chicago: Physics Press, 1991.

Sobel, Michael. *Light.* Chicago: University of Chicago Press, 1987.

Iain A. McIntyre

Lens see **Eye; Vision**

Leopard see **Cats**

Leprosy

Leprosy, also called Hansen's disease, affects 10–12 million people worldwide. Caused by an unusual bacterium called *Mycobacterium leprae*, leprosy primarily affects humans. Leprosy is found in tropical areas, such as Africa, South and Southeast Asia, and Central and South America. In the United States, cases of leprosy have been reported in areas of Texas, California, Louisiana, Florida, and Hawaii. Leprosy can take many forms, but the most familiar form is characterized by skin lesions and nerve damage. Although leprosy is curable with various antibiotics, it remains a devastating illness because of its potential to cause deformity, especially in the facial features. Fortunately, antibiotic regimens are available to treat and eventually cure leprosy, and two different leprosy vaccines are being tested for efficacy in locations worldwide.

The cause of leprosy

M. leprae is an unusual bacterium for several reasons. The bacterium divides very slowly; in some tests, researchers have noted a dividing time of once every twelve days. This differs from the dividing time of most bacteria, which is once every few hours. *M. leprae* can-

not be grown on culture media, and is notoriously difficult to culture within living animals. Because of these culturing difficulties, researchers have not been able to investigate these bacteria as closely as they have other, more easily cultured, bacteria. Questions remain unanswered about *M. leprae*; for instance, researchers are still unclear about how the bacteria are transmitted from one person to another, and are not sure about the role an individual's genetic make up plays in the progression of the disease.

Because *M. leprae* almost exclusively infects humans, animal models for studying leprosy are few. Surprisingly, a few species of armadillo can also be infected with *M. leprae*. Recently, however, wild armadillos have been appearing with a naturally occurring form of leprosy. If the disease spreads in the armadillo population, researchers will not be able to use these animals for leprosy studies, since study animals must be completely free of the disease as well as the bacteria that cause it. Mice have also been used to study leprosy, but laboratory conditions, such as temperature, must be carefully controlled in order to sustain the infection in mice.

Scientists have been able to determine some facts about *M. leprae* from their experiments. *M. leprae* is temperature–sensitive; it favors temperatures slightly below normal human body temperature. Because of this predilection, *M. leprae* infects superficial body tissues such as the skin, bones, and cartilage, and does not usually penetrate to deeper organs and tissues. *M. leprae* is an intracellular pathogen; it crosses host cell membranes and lives within these cells. Once inside the host cell, the bacterium reproduces. The time required by these slow–growing bacteria to reproduce themselves inside host cells can be anywhere from a few weeks to as much as 40 years. Eventually, the bacteria lyse (burst open) the host cell, and new bacteria are released that can infect other host cells.

Researchers believe that the bacteria are transmitted via the respiratory tract. *M. leprae* exists in the nasal secretions and in the material secreted by skin lesions of infected individuals. *M. leprae* has also been found in the breast milk of infected nursing mothers. *M. leprae* may be transmitted by breathing in the bacteria, through breaks in the skin, or perhaps through breast–feeding.

The leprosy continuum

Leprosy exists in several different forms, although the infectious agent for all of these forms is *M. leprae*. Host factors such as genetic make up, individual immunity, geography, ethnicity, and socioeconomic circum-

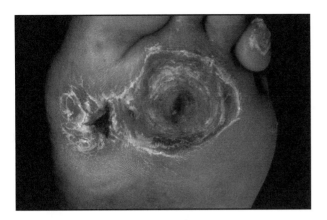

Leprosy.

stances determine which form of leprosy is contracted by a person exposed to *M. leprae*. Interestingly, most people who come in contact with the bacterium—about three–fourths—never develop leprosy, or develop only a small lesion on the trunk or extremity that heals spontaneously. Most people, then, are not susceptible to *M. leprae,* and their immune systems function effectively to neutralize the bacteria. But one–fourth of those exposed to *M. leprae* come down with the disease, which may manifest itself in various ways.

Five forms of leprosy are recognized, and a person may progress from one form to another. The least serious form is tuberculoid leprosy. In this form, the skin lesions and nerve damage are minor. Tuberculoid leprosy is evidence that the body's cellular immune response—the part of the immune system that seeks out and destroys infected cells—is working at a high level of efficiency. Tuberculoid leprosy is easily cured with antibiotics.

If tuberculoid leprosy is not treated promptly, or if a person has a less vigorous cellular immune response to the *M. leprae* bacteria, the disease may progress to a borderline leprosy, which is characterized by more numerous skins lesions and more serious nerve damage. The most severe form of leprosy is lepromatous leprosy. In this form of leprosy, the skin lesions are numerous and cause the skin to fold, especially the skin on the face. This folding of facial skin leads to the leonine (lion–like) features typical of lepromatous leprosy. Nerve damage is extensive, and people with lepromatous leprosy may lose the feeling in their extremities, such as the fingers and toes. Contrary to popular belief, the fingers and toes of people with this form of leprosy do not spontaneously drop off. Rather, because patients can not feel pain because of nerve damage, the extremities can become easily injured. Sometimes these

injuries are severe, and fingers and toes are cut off by sharp objects which the patient cannot even detect.

Lepromatous leprosy occurs in people who exhibit an efficient antibody response to *M. leprae* but an inefficient cellular immune response. The antibody arm of the immune system is not useful in neutralizing intracellular pathogens such as *M. leprae*; therefore, people who initially react to invasion by *M. leprae* by making antibodies may be at risk for developing more severe forms of leprosy. Researchers are not sure what determines whether a person will react with a cellular response or an antibody response; current evidence suggests that the cellular immune response may be controlled by a special gene. If a person has this gene, he or she will probably develop the less severe tuberculoid leprosy if exposed to *M. leprae*.

Treatment of leprosy

Treatments for leprosy have improved considerably over the past 40 years. In fact, some experts believe that the drug regimens being tested in various trials throughout the world (including the United States) may eradicate leprosy completely by the year 2000. Beginning in the 1950s, an antibiotic called dapsone was used to treat leprosy, offering the first hope of a cure for persons with the disease. Dapsone's main disadvantage was that the patient had to take the medication daily throughout his or her lifetime. In addition, the *M. leprae* in some patients underwent genetic mutations that rendered it resistant to the antibiotic. In the 1960s, the problem of resistance was tackled with the advent of multidrug therapy. Bacteria are less likely to become resistant to several drugs given in combination. The new multidrug treatment time was also considerably shorter—typically about four years. Currently, researchers are experimenting with a new drug combination which includes an antibiotic called oflaxicin. Oflaxicin is a powerful inhibitor of certain bacterial enzymes that are involved in DNA coiling. Without these enzymes, the *M. leprae* cannot copy the DNA properly and the bacteria die. The treatment time for this current regimen is about four weeks—the shortest time so far.

One risk of treatment, however, is that antigens—the proteins on the surface of *M. leprae* that initiate the host immune response—are released from the dying bacteria. In some people, when the antigens combine with antibodies to *M. leprae* in the bloodstream, a reaction called erythema nodosum leprosum may occur, resulting in new lesions and peripheral nerve damage. Some leprosy experts are experimenting with the drug thalidomide to treat this reaction, with good results. But because thalidomide causes severe birth defects, women of childbearing age must be carefully monitored while taking the drug.

A leprosy vaccine?

A promising development in the treatment and management of leprosy is the preliminary success shown by two different vaccines. One vaccine being tested in Venezuela combines a vaccine originally developed against tuberculosis, called Bacille Calmette–Guerin (BCG), and heat–killed *M. leprae* cultured from infected armadillos. The other vaccine uses a relative of *M. leprae* called *M. avium*. The advantage of this vaccine, currently being tested in India, is that *M. avium* is easy to culture on media and is thus cheaper than the Venezuelan vaccine. Both vaccines have performed well in their clinical trials, leading many to hope that a vaccine against leprosy might be available as early as 1995.

See also Antibiotics; Antibody and antigen; Bacteria; Immune system; Vaccine.

Further Reading:
Cohen, Jon. "Vaccines Get a New Twist." *Science* 264: (22 April 1994): 503–5.
Gunby, Phil. "Can Leprosy Be Neutralized by the Year 2000?" *Journal of the American Medical Association* 267 (6 May 1992): 2289.
Joklik, Wolfgang K., et al. *Zinsser Microbiology.* 20th edition. Norwalk, Conn.: Appleton and Lange, 1992.
Mastro, Timothy D., et al. "Imported Leprosy in the United States, 1978 through 1988: An Epidemic Without Sec-

ondary Transmission." *American Journal of Public Health* 82 (August 1992): 1127–30.
Randall, Teri. "Thalidomide's Back in the News, but in More Favorable Circumstances." *Journal of the American Medical Association* 263: (16 March 1990): 1467–68.
Ulrich, Marian, et al. "Leprosy in Women: Characteristics and Repercussions." *Social Science and Medicine* 37, No. 4 (August 1993): 445–56.

Kathleen Scogna

Leptons see **Subatomic particles**

Lettuce see **Composite family**

Leukocytes see **Blood**

Lever see **Machines, simple**

Leyden jar see **Electrostatic devices**

Lice

Lice are small, wingless, biting or sucking insects, many of which are ecto–parasites. There are about 3,000 species of lice in the orders Mallophaga and Anopleura. The Anopleura are sucking lice, which are parasites of mammals, and which feed only on blood. The Mallophaga are chewing or biting lice, and are primarily pests of birds, feeding on skin and feathers.

Most species of lice are specific to one or a few related species of host animals, and lice cannot survive away from their appropriate hosts. Lice are generally spread from host to host by direct body contact, or through shared clothing or bedding (in the case of human lice).

Both orders of lice have direct development, in which the eggs hatch into nymphs that look like miniature versions of the adult. Lice have a flattened body and poorly developed eyes, or no eyes at all.

Most lice commonly occur in the fur or feathers of their warm–blooded hosts. These lice have specialized, hook–like appendages on their relatively short legs for securing these parasitic insects onto the body of their hosts.

Lice on humans

Three species of lice occur as parasites on humans. These lice are blood suckers, and they can be disconcertingly abundant under unsanitary conditions. The

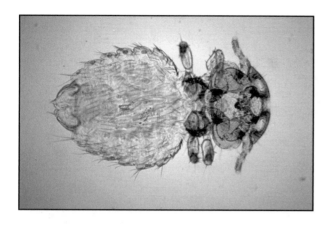

A chewing louse.

human louse, *Pediculus humanus*, occurs as two races, which feed on different parts of the body. The head louse, *capitis* race, occurs in the hairs of the head, to which it attaches its whitish eggs, also known as "nits." The body louse *corporis* race, also known as the "cootie," feeds on the human body, and hides and lays its eggs in clothing. Bites from human lice are irritating, and they can become infected. Human lice are also important as vectors of some deadly diseases, such as typhus, relapsing fever, and trench fever, which are transmitted to humans through scratching the bodies or feces of infected lice into the skin.

The crab louse *Phthirus pubis* is another parasite of humans, which occurs in the coarser hair of the underarms and genital area.

Lice infestations of humans are still commonly treated by dusting the body with an insecticide such as DDT, which is still the preferred chemical for this relatively restricted usage. Clothing may also be washed in an insecticidal solution, and living areas must be fumigated with an insecticide or steam. The eggs of head lice are relatively resistant to many chemical treatments, and they may have to be removed using a fine–toothed comb, and then killed by crushing between the fingernails. This meticulous, pest–control procedure is sometimes known as "nit–picking."

Lice on other animals

Poultry lice include the chicken shaft louse, *Menopon gallinae*, the chicken body louse, *Menacanthus stramineus*, the chicken head louse, *Cuclotogaster heterographa*, and the large turkey louse, *Chelopistes meleagridis*. These pests feed by chewing the skin or feathers of poultry, causing the birds discomfort and aggravation, and sometimes resulting in unfeathered patches of skin. As a result, the birds lay

relatively few eggs, grow poorly, and are susceptible to stress–induced diseases. Young chickens can be killed by louse infestations, while adults may develop a droopy–wing symptom.

Wild birds have a different type of lice, such as the loose, *Esthiopterum crassicorne*, which is a parasite of the blue–winged teal, *Anas discors*, a native species of duck.

The cow–biting louse, *Bovicola bovis*, chews on the skin and hair of cattle, causing great discomfort to these animals. The horse–biting louse, *B. equi,* and dog–biting louse, *Trichodectes canis*, are other examples of chewing lice that infect mammals.

Most lice that parasitize agricultural mammals are the anopleuran, blood sucking kinds. The short–nosed cattle louse, *Haematopinus eurysternus*, can occur in infestations serious enough to make animals weak and anemic from blood loss. Related lice include the pig louse, *H. suis*, and horse–sucking louse, *H. asini*. The sheep–sucking body louse, *Linognathus ovillus*, long–nosed cattle louse, *L. vituli*, and dog–sucking louse, *L. setusus* are other pests of domestic animals.

See also Parasites.

Lichens

Lichens are an intimate symbiosis, in which two species live together as a type of composite organism. Lichens are an obligate mutualism between a fungus mycobiont and an alga or blue–green bacterium phycobiont.

Each lichen mutualism is highly distinctive, and can be identified on the basis of its size, shape, color, and biochemistry. Even though lichens are not true "species" in the conventional meaning of the word, lichenologists have developed systematic and taxonomic treatments of these mutualisms.

The fungal partner in the lichen mutualism gains important benefits through access to photosynthetic products of the alga or blue–green bacterium. The phycobiont profits from the availability of a relatively moist and protected habitat, and greater access to inorganic nutrients.

Lichen biology

The most common fungi in lichens are usually species of Ascomycetes, or a few Basidiomycetes. The

British soldiers (*Cladonia cristatella*), a species of lichen.

usual algal partners are either species of green algae *Chlorophyta* or blue–green bacteria of the family Cyanophyceae. In general, the fungal partner cannot live without its phycobiont, but the algae is often capable of living freely in moist soil or water. The largest lichens can form a thallus up to 3 ft (1 m) long, although most lichens are smaller than a few inches or centimeters in length. Lichens can be very colorful, ranging from bright reds and oranges, to yellows and greens, and white, gray, and black hues.

Most lichens grow very slowly. Lichens in which the phycobiont is a blue–green bacterium have the ability to fix nitrogen gas into ammonia. Some lichens can commonly reach ages of many centuries, especially species living in highly stressful environments, such as alpine or arctic tundra.

Lichens can grow on diverse types of substrates. Some species grow directly on rocks, some on bare soil, and others on the bark of tree trunks and branches. Lichens often grow under exposed conditions that are frequently subjected to periods of drought, and sometimes to extremes of hot and cold. Lichen species vary greatly in their tolerance of severe environmental con-

ditions. Lichens generally respond to environmental extremes by becoming dormant, and then quickly becoming metabolically active again when they experience more benign conditions.

Lichens are customarily divided into three growth forms, although this taxonomy is one of convenience, and is not ultimately founded on systematic relationships. Crustose lichens form a thallus that is closely appressed to the surface upon which they are growing. Foliose lichens are only joined to their substrate by a portion of their thallus, and they are somewhat leaf–like in appearance. Fruticose lichens rise above their substrate, and are much branched and bushy in appearance.

Most lichens regenerate asexually as lichen symbioses, and not by separate reproduction of their mycobiont and phycobiont. Reproduction is most commonly accomplished by small, specialized fragments of thallus known as soredia, consisting of fungal tissue enclosing a small number of algal cells. The soredia generally originate within the parent thallus, then grow out through the surface of the thallus, and detach as small bits of tissue that are dispersed by the wind or rain. If the dispersing soredium is fortunate enough to lodge in a favorable microenvironment, it develops into a new thallus, genetically identical to the parent.

Uses of lichens

Because they are capable of colonizing bare rocks and other mineral substrates, lichens are important in soil formation during some ecological successions. For example, lichens are among the first organisms to colonize sites as they are released from glacial ice. In such situations lichens can be important in the initial stages of nitrogen accumulation and soil development during post–glacial primary succession.

Lichens are an important forage for some species of animals. The best known example of this relationship involves the northern species of deer known as caribou or reindeer (*Rangifer tarandus)* and the so–called reindeer lichens (*Cladina* spp.) that are one of their most important foods, especially during winter.

Some species of lichens are very sensitive to air pollutants. Consequently, urban environments are often highly impoverished in lichen species. Some ecologists have developed schemes by which the intensity of air pollution can be reliably assayed or monitored using the biological responses of lichens and their communities. Monitoring of air quality using lichens can be based on the health and productivity of these organisms in places variously stressed by toxic pollution. Alternatively, the chemical composition of lichens may be assayed, because their tissues can effectively take up and retain sulfur and metals from the atmosphere.

Some lichens are useful as a source of natural dyes. Pigments of some of the more colorful lichens, especially the orange, red, and brown ones, can be extracted by boiling and used to dye wool and other fibers. Other chemicals extracted from lichens include litmus, which was a commonly used acid–base indicator prior to the invention of the pH meter.

Some of the reindeer lichens, especially *Cladina alpestris,* are shaped like miniature shrubs and trees. Consequently, these plants are sometimes collected, dried, and dyed, and are used in "landscaping" the layouts for miniature railroads and architectural models.

In addition, lichens add significantly to the aesthetics of the ecosystems in which they occur. The lovely orange and yellow colors of *Caloplaca* and *Xanthoria* lichens add much to the ambience of rocky seashores and tundras. And the intricate webs of filamentous *Usnea* lichens hanging in profusion from tree branches give a mysterious aspect to humid forests. These and other, less charismatic lichens are integral components of their natural ecosystems. These lichens are intrinsi-

KEY TERMS

· ·

Mutualism—A mutually beneficial relationship between species.

Symbiosis—A biological relationship in which different species interact in some meaningful way.

Thallus—A simple, undifferentiated biomass of fungi, algae, and lichens.

cally important for this reason, as well as for the relatively minor benefits that they provide to humans.

See also Algae; Fungi; Indicator species; Mutualism; Symbiosis.

Further Reading:
Ahmadjian, V. *The Lichen Symbiosis.* New York: Wiley, 1993.
Richardson, D. H. S. *Pollution Monitoring With Lichens.* United Kingdom: Richmond, 1992.

Bill Freedman

Life history

Life history is an ecological term that refers to the significant features of the life cycle of organisms and their relationships with environmental conditions. Life cycle refers to the sequence of discrete developmental stages of an organism from their origin as gametes to their eventual death. Life cycle also refers to the stages through which generations of organisms pass from their own origin through to their production of gametes toward establishment of the succeeding generation.

Most ecological studies of life history focus on strategies that influence survival and reproduction at the levels of individuals, populations, or species. Studies of this sort are relevant to the notion of adaptation or the complex of biological and ecological traits that enhance the persistence and reproductive success of organisms. In this sense, life histories represent unique biological solutions to the opportunities and difficulties provided by the ecosystems and environments in which organisms live. Each solution involves a complex of life–history traits involving allocations of limited resources of energy, biomass, and time among various competing attributes that may have significant effects on survival and reproduction.

Many adaptational tradeoffs are associated with alternative life–history possibilities. For example, for any given expenditure of energy on reproduction, organisms could potentially produce large numbers of relatively small offspring or smaller numbers of larger offspring. Depending on the ecological circumstances, each of these life–history alternatives has potential benefits and potential detriments.

For instance, the production of large numbers of offspring is beneficial to the relatively short–lived species of plants that are common in recently disturbed habitats. These so–called ruderal plants are only successful for a few years following disturbance, after which they are eliminated from the vegetation by more competitive species. Consequently, the ruderals have to colonize newly disturbed sites on the landscape for the species to survive over the longer term. Because colonization is a very risky business, the chances of evolutionary success of individuals and of persistence at the metapopulation level, that is, of various populations on the landscape, are enhanced if mature plants produce large numbers of small seeds having physical characteristics that enhance dispersal. These include an aerodynamic shape as in dandelions and willows, a tendency to stick to the fur of mammals like burs and ticks, and an ability to pass unharmed through the gut of a large animal after being eaten with the fleshy fruit like cherries and elderberries. In contrast, plants that inhabit relatively mature and stable ecosystems such as forests may be better served by producing relatively few but large, well–provisioned seeds such as acorns and walnuts that are better suited to perennating the species population in predictable, local habitats.

A major sector of activity in ecology is composed of diverse studies directed toward quantifying the benefits and tradeoffs of life–history characteristics and understanding the survival, reproductive, and evolutionary costs and benefits to individuals, populations, and the species as a whole. This type of ecological research has its own intrinsic interest and importance. However, these life–history studies also allow ecologists to develop deeper insights into the relationships between species and their environments. This knowledge may eventually be important in allowing humans to develop sensible methods of utilizing the ecological resources that sustain them and their societies.

See also Adaptation; Competition; Ecosystem; Evolution; Extinction.

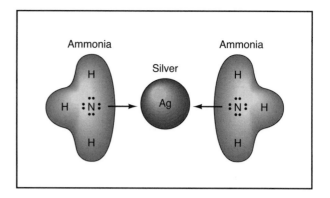

Figure 1. Two ligands (ammonia) each donate a pair of electrons to bond with a silver ion. (N = nitrogen, H = hydrogen, Ag = silver.)

Ligand

In inorganic chemistry, ligands are molecules or electrically charged atoms (ions) which are bonded to metal atoms or ions. The ligand changes the metal's ability to dissolve in or react with its surroundings. In biochemistry, ligands are defined as molecules, usually protein, that change the biological activity of other molecules by bonding with them. The inorganic meaning is more common, and will be the subject of this article.

Structure and bonding

The bonding atoms of ligands are usually non-metal elements such as oxygen, nitrogen, or chlorine. Whether alone or in molecules such as water or ammonia, these atoms have pairs of electrons that are not involved in chemical bonds. The electron pairs can enter the space around the metal atom and bond with it (Fig. 1).

Thus, the metal and ligand are joined by a covalent bond, consisting of two electrons shared between them. However, both electrons are provided by the ligand itself.

Metal atoms or ions usually bond to two, four or six ligands. These are arranged with geometric symmetry around the central metal atom. The metal together with its ligands are called a coordination compound. If the structure has an overall electrical charge it is called a complex ion.

Because of their shapes, there can be different coordination compounds having exactly the same atoms and bonds, but arranged differently. Such molecules are called geometric isomers (See Fig. 3).

The different arrangement causes differences in physical properties such as color and melting tempera-

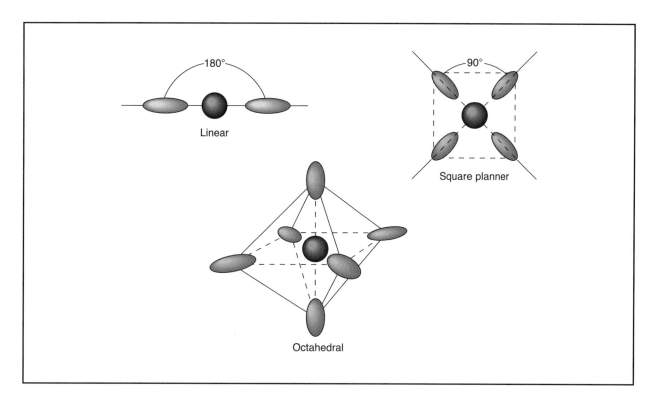

Figure 2. Geometric symmetry of ligands around metal.

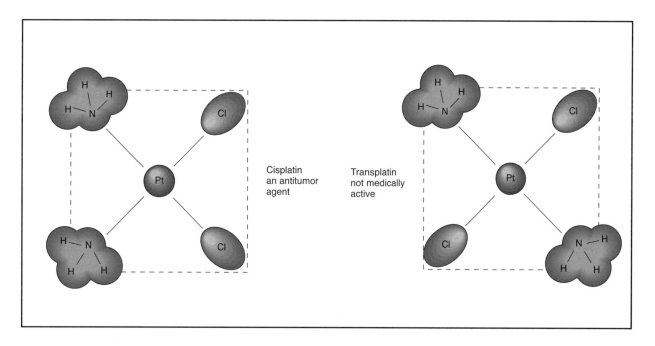

Figure 3. Geometric isomers have the same formulas but different symmetry and different properties.

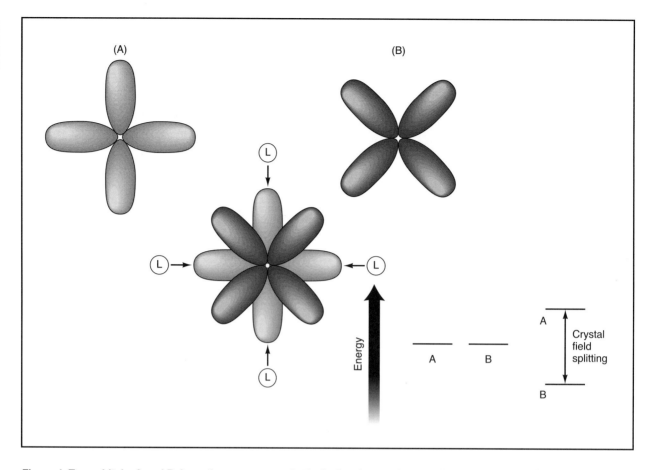

Figure 4. Two orbitals, A and B, have the same energy in the isolated atom. Ligands (L) approach closer to A than to B, hence the energy of A rises and B falls.

ture. Geometric isomers also differ in their chemical reactions, especially when these occur in living organisms. That is because the molecules which make up living things are themselves usually geometric isomers with very specific shapes. Reactions only occur between molecules whose shapes match each other, like a key fitted to a lock.

An example of a biologically active geometric isomer is cisplatin, a coordination compound used in medicine to suppress tumors. The molecule consists of a platinum atom surrounded by two ammonia molecules and two chlorine atoms. The four ligands lie at the corners of a square, with ligands of the same kind as neighbors (Fig. 2).

The isomer transplatin, in which they are diagonally opposite each other, has no affect on tumors.

Compounds of metals with ligands are often brightly colored. This results from repulsion between the electrons of the ligand and those of the metal atom itself. The atom's electrons are also geometrically arranged around its nucleus. They occupy regions

called orbitals. In an isolated metal atom, groups of similar orbitals have the same energy. But when ligands bond to the atom, they approach some orbitals more closely than others. Electrons in the closer orbital are repelled more strongly. They must have more energy to occupy those orbitals. The energy difference is called "crystal field splitting" (Fig 4.).

The metal's electrons can move to a higher energy orbital by absorbing energy from visible light. Therefore, such compounds appear colored.

Chelating agents

Some ligands can form more than one bond to a single metal atom. These are called chelating agents. The name comes from the Greek word *chele*, meaning "claw." The ligands surround the metal atom and hold it as if in a claw. Because they hold metals so strongly, chelates are also referred to as "metal scavengers." They effectively remove metal atoms and prevent them from reacting with anything else.

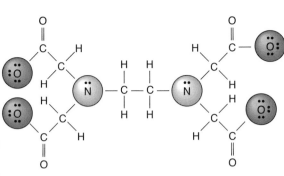

a. EDTA, ethylenediaminetetraacetate, a chelate. The six shaded atoms can each donate a pair of electrons (represented by dots) to bond to a single metal atom. (C=carbon, N=nitrogen, O=oxygen, H=hydrogen)

b. A single molecule of EDTA bound to lead (Pb). The ligands are shown in bold, and the shape of the plane is suggested with shading.

Figure 5. Ethylenediaminetetraacetic acid (EDTA) is one of the best–known chelating agents.

One of the best–known chelating agents is ethylenediaminetetraacetic acid, or EDTA. It contains 32 atoms, six of which can bond to a single metal atom (Fig. 5).

EDTA is a common food preservative. Foods contain ions of iron, zinc, magnesium, and other metals. These are natural components of food substances, but they hasten the chemical reactions which cause flavor and color to deteriorate. EDTA added to foods forms strong, stable bonds to the metal ions, blocking their chemical activity. EDTA is also used to treat lead poisoning in human beings. The EDTA–lead complex is safely excreted in body waste.

Metal–ligand bonds in biological chemistry

The porphyrin ring is a chelate that plays several different roles in the chemistry of living things (Fig. 6).

Bound to magnesium, it forms chlorophyll, the green pigment which is central to photosynthesis in plants. Bound to iron, it forms cytochrome molecules, which assist in the transfer of energy throughout living cells. Hemoglobin, which gives blood its red color and carries oxygen to body cells, is also an iron–porphyrin molecule. Iron can form six bonds to ligands, and the porphyrin ring uses only four bonds. Of the remaining two, one holds a protein molecule, and the other holds the oxygen molecule which will be delivered to the cells.

Other uses

Inorganic salts, which contain metal ions, do not dissolve in organic solvents such as benzene. However, by surrounding the metal ion with a chelate called a "crown ether" the desired solution can be made. The mining industry uses cyanide ions to dissolve gold out of the quartz rocks in which it is often found. The cyanide ligands are removed in subsequent chemical steps.

Further Reading:
Benarde, Melvin A. *The Chemicals We Eat.* New York: American Heritage Press, 1971.

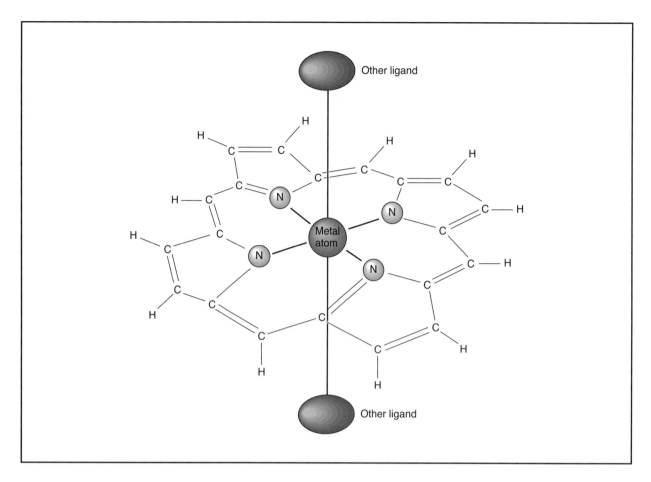

Figure 6. The porphyrin molecule surrounds the metal, bonding to it by nitrogen atoms at the four corners of a square. Other ligands may bond above and below the plane of the square. (N = nitrogen, C = carbon, H = hydrogen)

"Molecular Architecture." Unit 9 of *The World of Chemistry*. Videotape Series. University of Maryland at College Park. Gilbert Castellan, Nava Ben–Zvi and Isidore Adler, project co–directors. The Annenberg/CPB Project, 1990.

Newton, David E. *Consumer Chemistry Projects for Young Scientists*. New York: Franklin Watts, 1991.

Schmidt, Karen F. "Mirror–Image Molecules." *Science News* 143 (29 May 1993): 348–350.

Sara G. B. Fishman

Light

Light can be narrowly defined as the visible portion of the electromagnetic spectrum. A broader definition would include infrared, ultraviolet, and x–ray wavelengths, which are not visible to the eye. The nature of light has been the subject of controversy for thousands of years. Even today, while scientists know how light behaves, they do not always know why light behaves as it does.

The Greeks were the first to theorize about the nature of light. Led by the scientists Euclid and Hero (first century A.D.), they came to recognize that light traveled in a straight line. However, they believed that vision worked by intromission—that is, that light rays originated at the eye and traveled to the object being seen. Despite this erroneous hypothesis, the Greeks were able to successfully study the phenomena of reflection and refraction and derive the laws governing them. In reflection, they learned that the angles of incidence and reflection were approximately equal; in refraction, they saw that a beam of light would bend as it entered a denser medium (such as water or glass) and bend back the same amount as it exited.

The next contributor to the embryonic science of optics was the Arab mathematician and physicist Alhazen (965–1039), who is sometimes called the greatest scientist of the Middle Ages. Experimenting around the year 1000, he showed that light comes from a source (the Sun) and reflects from an object to the eyes, thus allowing the object to be seen. He also studied mirrors and lenses and further refined the laws of reflection and refraction.

By the 12th century, scientists felt they had solved the riddles of light and color. The English philosopher Francis Bacon (1561–1626) contended that light was a disturbance in an invisible medium which could be detected by the eye; subsequently, color was caused by objects "staining" the light as it passed. More productive research into the behavior of light was sparked by the new class of realistic painters, who strove to better understand perspective and shading by studying light and its properties.

In the early 1600s, the refracting telescope was perfected by Galileo and Johannes Kepler, providing a reliable example of the laws of refraction. These laws were further refined by Willebrord Snel, whose name is most often associated with the equations for determining the refraction of light. By the mid–1600s, enough was known about the behavior of light to allow for the formulation of a wide range of theories.

The renowned English physicist and mathematician Isaac Newton was intrigued by the so–called "phenomenon of colors"—the ability of a prism to produce colors from white light. It had been generally accepted that white was a single color, and that a prism could somehow combine white light with others to form a multicolored mixture. Newton, however, doubted this assumption. He used a second prism to recombine the rainbow spectrum back into a beam of white light; this showed that white light must be a combination of colors, not the other way around.

Newton performed his experiments in 1666 and announced them shortly thereafter, subscribing to the corpuscular (or particulate) theory of light. According to this theory, light travels as a stream of particles that originate from a bright source and are absorbed by the eye. Aided by Newton's reputation, the corpuscular theory soon became accepted throughout Great Britain and in parts of Europe.

In the European scientific community, many scientists believed that light, like sound, traveled in waves. This group of scientists was most successfully represented by the Dutch physicist Christiaan Huygens, who challenged Newton's corpuscular theory. He argued that a wave theory could best explain the appearance of a spectrum as well as the phenomena of reflection and refraction.

Newton immediately attacked the wave theory. Using some complex calculations, he showed that particles, too, would obey the laws of reflection and refraction. He also pointed out that, if truly a wave form, light should be able to bend around corners, just as sound does; instead it cast a sharp shadow, further supporting the corpuscular theory.

In 1660, however, Francesco Grimaldi examined a beam of light passing through a narrow slit. As it exited and was projected upon a screen, faint fringes could be seen near the edge. This seemed to indicate that light did bend slightly around corners; the effect, called diffraction, was adopted by Huygens and other theorists as further proof of the wave nature of light.

One piece of the wave theory remained unexplained. At that time, all known waves moved through some kind of medium—for example, sound waves moved through air and kinetic waves moved through water. Huygens and his allies had not been able to show just what medium light waves moved through; instead, they contended that an invisible substance called ether filled the universe and allowed the passage of light. This unproven explanation did not earn further support for the wave theory, and the Newtonian view of light prevailed for more than a century.

The first real challenge to Newton's corpuscular theory came in 1801, when English physicist Thomas Young discovered interference in light. He passed a beam of light through two closely spaced pinholes and onto a screen. If light were truly particulate, Young argued, the holes would emit two distinct streams that would appear on the screen as two bright points. What was projected on the screen instead was a series of bright and dark lines—an interference pattern typical of how waves would behave under similar conditions.

If light is a wave, then every point on that wave is potentially a new wave source. As the light passes through the pinholes it exits as two new wave fronts, which spread out as they travel. Because the holes are placed close together, the two waves interact. In some places the two waves combine (constructive interference), whereas in others they cancel each other out (destructive interference), thus producing the pattern of bright and dark lines. Such interference had previously been observed in both water waves and sound waves and seemed to indicate that light, too, moved in waves.

The corpuscular view did not die easily. Many scientists had allied themselves with the Newtonian theory and were unwilling to risk their reputations to support an antiquated wave theory. Also, English scientists were not pleased to see one of their countrymen challenge the theories of Newton; Young, therefore, earned little favor in his homeland.

Throughout Europe, however, support for the wave nature of light continued to grow. In France, Etienne–Louis Malus (1775–1826) and Augustin Jean Fresnel (1788–1827) experimented with polarized light, an effect that could only occur if light acted as a transverse wave (a wave which oscillated at right angles to its path of travel). In Germany, Joseph von Fraunhofer (1787–1826) was constructing instruments to better examine the phenomenon of diffraction and succeeded in identifying within the Sun's spectrum 574 dark lines corresponding to different wavelengths.

In 1850 two French scientists, Jéan Foucault and Armand Fizeau, independently conducted an experiment that would strike a serious blow to the corpuscular theory of light. An instructor of theirs, Dominique-Françios Arago, had suggested that they attempt to measure the speed of light as it traveled through both air and water. If light were particulate it should move faster in water; if, on the other hand, it were a wave it should move faster in air. The two scientists performed their experiments, and each came to the same conclusion: light traveled more quickly through air and was slowed by water.

Even as more and more scientists subscribed to the wave theory, one question remained unanswered: through what medium did light travel? The existence of ether had never been proven—in fact, the very idea of it seemed ridiculous to most scientists. In 1872, James Clerk Maxwell suggested that waves composed of electric and magnetic fields could propagate in a vacuum, independent of any medium. This hypothesis was later proven by Heinrich Rudolph Hertz, who showed that such waves would also obey all the laws of reflection, refraction, and diffraction. It became generally accepted that light acted as an electromagnetic wave.

Hertz, however, had also discovered the photoelectric effect, by which certain metals would produce an electrical potential when exposed to light. As scientists studied the photoelectric effect, it became clear that a wave theory could not account for this behavior; in fact, the effect seemed to indicate the presence of particles. For the first time in more than a century there was new support for Newton's corpuscular theory of light.

The photoelectric effect was explained by Albert Einstein in 1905 using the principles of quantum physics developed by Max Planck. Einstein claimed that light was quantized—that is, it appeared in "bundles" of energy. While these bundles traveled in waves,

certain reactions (like the photoelectric effect) revealed their particulate nature. This theory was further supported in 1923 by Arthur Holly Compton, who showed that the bundles of light—which he called photons—would sometimes strike electrons during scattering, causing their wavelengths to change.

By employing the quantum theories of Planck and Einstein, Compton was able to describe light as both a particle and a wave, depending upon the way it was tested. While this may seem paradoxical, it remains an acceptable model for explaining the phenomena associated with light and is the dominant theory of our time.

See also Interference; Photoelectric effect; Photon; Wave motion.

Further Reading:
Born, Max and Emil Wolf. *Principles of Optics*. New York, NY: Pergamon Press, 1980.
Hecht, Eugene. *Optics*. Reading, MA: Addison–Wesley Publishing Company, 1987.

Lightning see **Thunderstorm**
Lightning bugs see **Beetles**

Light–year

A light–year is the distance that light (or any other form of electromagnetic radiation, such as radio waves) travels in a vacuum in one year. Since light travels at a velocity of 186,171.1 mi/s (299,792.5 km/s), one light-year equals 5,878,489,000,000 miles (9,460,530,000,000 km). The light–year is a convenient unit of measurement to use when discussing distances to the stars in the Milky Way galaxy and throughout the observable universe. When discussing distances within our solar system, the astronomical unit (the mean distance between Earth and the Sun) is commonly used. One light–year equals 63,239.7 astronomical units.

Since the distances between Earth and even the nearest stars are so enormous, a light–year can also be thought of as a measurement of time. Sirius, for example, is 8.57 light–years away. This means that when an observer on Earth looks at Sirius, they see light that left Sirius 8.57 years ago. The observer is therefore looking backward in time, seeing the star in the condition it was in more than eight years ago.

Alpha Centauri, the closest star to Earth, is 4.35 light–years distant. Among other stars, Barnard's star is 5.98 light–years away, 61 Cygni is 11.3 light–years away, and Antares is 400 light–years away. The center of the Milky Way galaxy is 27,000 light–years away, while the most distant clusters of galaxies are roughly estimated to be one million light–years away.

See also Astronomical unit.

Frederick R. West

Lilac

Lilacs (*Syringa* spp.) are about 10 species of shrubs and small trees in the olive family (Oleaceae). Lilacs are native to Eurasia but have been widely planted elsewhere as ornamental shrubs.

The common lilac (*Syringa vulgaris*) is the most familiar species to most people. The common lilac has shiny green wedge–shaped leaves without teeth on the margins which are arranged alternately on the twigs. This and other species of lilacs develop large numbers of spike–like inflorescences in the early springtime before the leaves have developed. These flowers are rich in nectar and fragrance and are pollinated by insects.

The common lilac is originally native to southeastern Europe and adjacent parts of southwestern Asia and is the oldest and most widespread species in cultivation. Other species include the Persian lilac (*S. persica*), the Chinese lilac (*S. oblata*), and the Japanese lilac (*S. japonica*). However, hundreds of horticultural hybrids have been bred by crossing the flowers of various species of lilacs. If the hybrids are considered to have desirable attributes in terms of flower shape or color, fragrance, or tolerance of local or regional environmental conditions, it may be given a distinctive name and is subsequently propagated by rooting vegetative shoots, known as cuttings.

Lilacs have been widely planted as horticultural species in Eurasia, North America, and elsewhere that a suitable, temperate climate occurs. Lilacs are utilized in this way because they are relatively easy to grow, and they develop spectacular displays of white, lavender, or purple flowers in the early springtime while also perfuming the air with their fragrance. Lilac flowers contain fragrant oils that are sometimes used to flavor candy or cake or to manufacture perfume.

A lilac in bloom.

Lilacs sometimes escape from cultivation and becomes a locally invasive pest that may displace native shrubs from early successional or roadside habitats.

See also Olive family.

Lily family (Liliaceae)

Lilies are the classic representatives of the monocotyledons—those plants with only one seed leaf. Lilies, are mostly perennial, erect herbs arising from a bulb. Some climb, a few are woody, but most arise from underground stems or other structures. The leaves vary in number from one to many, and are arranged on the stem alternately or in whorls. The leaves are flat, linear to lance–shaped, without teeth along the margins, often widen into a papery sheath where they attach to the stem, lack stalks, and are typically parallel veined.

Some species of lilies are famous for their magnificent flowers, which are often trumpet or funnel shaped, nodding, and heavily scented. Lily flowers are bisexual, radially symmetrical, and their parts are usually in some multiple of three (four in *Maianthemum*), with no distinction in the appearance of petals and sepals. There are usually six main segments to the showy part of the flower, which are attached to the base of the ovary. Flowers may occur singly at the top of a leafless stem (tulip), as several flowers arranged on a spike (as in Lily–of–the–Valley, *Convallaria majalis*), or in various other arrangements of many flowers, including the umbels of onions (*Allium* spp.). Lily flowers are insect pollinated. The fruits of lilies are either capsules or berries. The capsules are divided into three compartments, which contain many flat, round seeds that are often stacked like coins.

There are about 240 genera and 4,000 species in the Liliaceae. Lilies are a diverse group and recent taxonomists have tended to split the group into four main families: Liliaceae, the lilies proper; Convallariaceae, lily–of–the–valley and Solomon's seals; Melanthaceae, or bunchflowers; and Smilaceae, the catbriers or greenbriers. In this article, the Liliaceae is considered in the broadest sense, including all of these four groups.

Lilies are widely distributed, primarily in the Northern Hemisphere, with a major center of distribution in the southwest and from Himalayan Asia to China, where they commonly are spring–flowering plants of steppes and mountain meadows. In North America, many familiar woodland plants of the springtime are members of the lily family, such as the trilliums and wake–robins of the genus *Trillium*, bellworts or merrybells (*Uvularia*), dog–tooth violets (*Erythronium*) with their characteristic mottled brown leaves, wild lily of the valley (*Maianthemum canadense*), and Solomon's seals (*Polygonatum*). Species of *Smilax,* which are mostly perennial herbs or shrubs occurring in tropical and subtropical regions, also occur in North America. Smilaxes are unusual among the monocotyledonous plants in producing tendrils, which are slender twining structures, used to climb and hold onto other plants.

Lilies are highly prized as house and garden ornamentals, and many of the most beautiful of these belong to the genus *Lilium,* the namesake of the family. Lilies have long held a fascination for people. The Madonna lily (*L. candidum*), which is native to the region of Greece to Syria, was depicted by early civilizations on pottery and mosaics. The most commonly grown greenhouse lily is the Easter or trumpet lily (*L. longiflorum*). Lilies have long been associated with Easter. During the Renaissance, European painters used white lilies to symbolize the Annunciation of the Virgin, that is, the

Greigii tulips.

announcement by the angel Gabriel to Mary that she would conceive a Son. The uniform, bright white color of many lilies symbolizes purity in some cultures. However, lilies also come in a variety of other colors. Flowers are purple in *L. martagon* of central Europe to China, yellow in *L. canadense* of eastern North America and *L. croceum* of central to southern Europe, orange in *L. japonicum* of Japan and *L. tigrinum* of east Asia, and rose in *L. pardinarium*. Many lilies have enchanting fragrances that are sometimes extracted for use in perfumes.

Tulips are also members of the lily family, in its broadest sense. Tulips are native to the Northern Hemisphere, with the greatest diversity of species occurring in the western and central parts of Asia. The name tulip derives from a Turkish word for turban, referring to the shape of the flower. Most horticultural varieties descend primarily from multiple crosses between two species, *Tulipa gesneriana* and *T. suaveolens* of western Asia. These are usually sold under the name *T. gesneriana,* although other species are increasingly involved in the development of new varieties.

The Turks were the first to cultivate the tulip and they introduced it into Europe, exactly when is not known, although the first reference to the tulip in a European publication was made in 1559. Tulips gradually increased in popularity until the early seventeenth century, when tulip mania swept Holland. There was a hysterical rush to raise and breed new and rarer varieties of tulips. Speculators invested the equivalent of thousands of dollars for a single bulb, and some people sold their houses to invest in the tulip market. In 1630 one bulb of a rare variety sold for the equivalent of $10,000. Tulip mania reached its peaked between 1634–1637, forcing the Dutch government to step in and regulate the industry. The Netherlands remains the single largest pro-

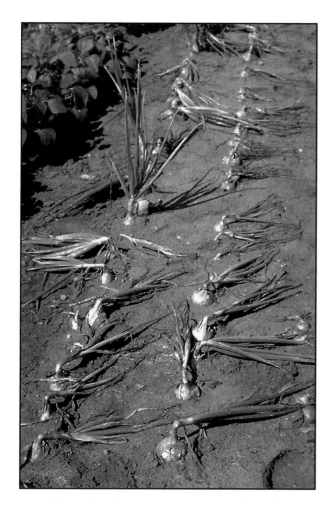

Yellow Spanish onions.

ducer of tulip bulbs, although Japan and the state of Washington are now important producers.

The economically important genus *Allium* is widely cultivated for its strong odor and flavor. Plants are characterized by a bulb, that is actually a giant bud surrounding a short stem. The leaves of the bud are extremely fleshy and tightly overlapping. The concentric lines seen in an onion cut crosswise are the margins of fleshy leaves. The outermost leaves are not fleshy but papery, forming the skin of the onion. Various members of this genus are cultivated: the common onion (*A. cepa*), garlic (*A. sativum*), leeks (*A. porum*), shallots (*A. ascalonicum*), and chives (*A. schoenoprasum*). Texas, New York, and California are the major onion producing regions in North America.

A number of other members of the lily family are of economic importance for a variety of reasons. A large number of lilies other than those described above are also important ornamentals. Fritallarias are popular ornamentals, with few to many leaves arranged either alternately or in whorls on the stem, and large, showy, bell–like flowers that are usually nodding. Many species of *Fritallaria* are of ornamental interest because the flowers are one basic color, checkered with another color. *Fritallaria meleagris* from central and southern Europe is purplish with white checkering, and *F. aurea* from Turkey is yellow and checkered. In the wild, many of the fritillarias appear to be pollinated by queen wasps.

Lily–of–the–valley (*Carvallaria magolus*) is a small perennial native of Europe, that has become naturalized in parts of eastern North America, and is frequently planted for its beautifully scented spike of flowers that are commonly used in wedding bouquets and for perfumes. Other commonly grown ornamental lilies are hyacinths, grape hyacinths, and scillas.

The young shoots of asparagus (*Asparagus officinalis*) are an important cash crop, and *A. plumosus* is the asparagus fern (though not a fern) used by florists as lacy greenery in bouquets.

Wild sarsaparilla (*Avalia nudicaulis*) has long been an ingredient of soft drinks, and aloe (*Aloe vera*) once provided needles for early phonographs, and remains important today as a salve in the treatment of burns and in cosmetics. Meadow saffron or (*Colchicum autumnale*) was used to treat gout (a painful disease of inflamed joints), and is still much used in research. Cochicine is extracted from the plant and used to prevent spindle formation during mitosis, so that replicated chromosomes do not split apart. This produces a polyploid, that is, a double (or more) of the normal chromosome number.

Dragon's blood, the resin of *Dracaena,* the dragon tree, was once collected and used as a finish for the great Italian violins of the eighteenh century.

Many lilies are poisonous. Lily of the valley is mildly poisonous, enough to be on the United States list of poisonous plants. Death camases (*Zygadenus* spp.) are extremely poisononous species. *Zygadenus elegans* is an attractive plant with a wand–like cluster of star–shaped flowers. It has an onion–like bulb, that unfortunately resembles the bulb of edible camases, which are in the genus *Camassia*. *Zagadenus venenosus* is a common cause of cattle poisoning in the western United States. Lilies known as squills are also quite toxic; the red bulbs of *Urginea maritima* are a valuable heart stimulant, but the white bulbs have been used as rodent killers. *Scilla,* another squill, also contains glucosides that have been used as rodenticides. Some greenhouse workers who handle tulips develop a severe dermatitis called tulip finger, which causes reddening and swelling of the finger in association with itchy and

KEY TERMS

. . . .

Seed leaves—The first leaves produced by a young plant while still within a seed.

Umbel—An arrangement of flowers, whereby each flower stalk arises from the same level of the stem, as in onions.

burning sensations, and in the worst cases results in scaly, eczematous skin.

Further Reading:

Dahlgren, R. M. T., H. T. Clifford, and P. F. Yeo. *The Families of the Monocotyledons: Structure, Evolution, and Taxonomy.* Berlin: Springer–Verlag, 1985.

Taylor, N. *Taylor's Encyclopedia of Gardening.* 4th ed. New York: Houghton Mifflin, 1961.

Les C. Cwynar

Lily–of–the–valley see **Lily family**

Limbic system see **Brain**

Lime see **Calcium oxide**

Limestone see **Calcium carbonate**

Lime tree see **Citrus family**

Liming and acidifying agents see **Agrochemicals**

Limit

In mathematics the concept of limit formally expresses the notion of arbitrary closeness. That is, a limit is a value that a variable quantity approaches as closely as one desires. The operations of differentiation and integration from calculus are both based on the theory of limits. The theory of limits is based on a particular property of the real numbers; namely that between any two real numbers, no matter how close together they are, there is always another one. Between any two real numbers there are always infinitely many more.

Nearness is key to understanding limits: only after nearness is defined does a limit acquire an exact meaning. Relevantly, a neighborhood of points near any given point comprise a neighborhood. Neighborhoods are definitive components of infinite limits of a sequence.

History

Archimedes of Syracuse first developed the idea of limits to measure curved figures and the volume of a sphere in the third century B.C. By carving these figures into small pieces that can be approximated, then increasing the number of pieces, the limit of the sum of pieces can give the desired quantity. Archimedes' thesis, *The Method*, was lost until 1906, when mathematicians discovered that Archimedes came close to discovering infinitesimal calculus.

As Archimedes' work was unknown until the 20th century, others developed the modern mathematical concept of limits. Englishman Sir Issac Newton and German Gottfried Wilhelm von Leibniz independently developed the general principles of calculus (of which the theory of limits is an important part) in the 17th century.

Limit of a sequence

The ancient Greek philosopher Zeno may have been one of the first mathematicians to ponder the limit of a sequence and wonder how it related to the world around him. Zeno argued that all motion was impossible because in order to move a distance l it is first necessary to travel half the distance, then half the remaining distance, then half of that remaining distance and so on. Thus, he argued, the distance l can never be fully traversed.

Consider the sequence 1, 1/2, 1/4, 1/8,...$(1/2)^n$ when n gets very large. Since $(1/2)^n$ equals 1/2 multiplied by itself n times, $(1/2)^n$ gets very small when n is allowed to become infinitely large. The sequence is said to converge, meaning numbers that are very far along in the sequence (corresponding to large n) get very close together and very close to a single value called the limit.

A sequence of numbers converges to a given number if the differences between the terms of the sequence and the given number form an infinitesimal sequence. For this sequence $(1/2)^n$ gets arbitrarily close to 0, so 0 is the limit of the sequence. The numbers in the sequence never quite reach the limit, but they never go past it either.

If an infinite sequence diverges, the running total of the terms eventually turns away from any specific value, so a divergent sequence has no limiting sum.

Limit of a function

Consider an arbitrary function, y=f(x). (A function is a set of ordered pairs for which the first and second elements of each pair are related to one another in a fixed way. When the elements of the ordered pairs are real numbers, the relationship is usually expressed in the form of an equation.) Suppose that successive values of x are chosen to match those of a converging sequence such as the sequence S from the previous example. The question arises as to what the values of the function do, that is, what happens to successive values of y. In fact, whenever the values of x form a sequence the values f(x) also form a sequence. If this sequence is a converging sequence then the limit of that sequence is called the limit of the function. More generally when the value of a function f(x) approaches a definite value L as the independent variable x gets close to a real number p then L is called the limit of the function. This is written formally as:

$$\lim_{x \to p} f(x) = L$$

and reads "The limit of f of x, as x approaches p, equals L." It does not depend on what particular sequence of numbers is chosen to represent x; it is only necessary that the sequence converge to a limit. The limit may depend on whether the sequence is increasing or decreasing. That is the limit, as x approaches p from above may be different from the limit as x approaches p from below. In some cases one or the other of these limits may even fail to exist. In any case since the value of x is approaching the finite value p the difference (p–x) is approaching zero. It is this definition of limit that provides a foundation for development of the derivative and the integral in calculus.

There is a second type of functional limit: the limit as the value of the independent variable approaches infinity. While a sequence that approaches infinity is said to diverge, there are cases for which applying the defining rule of a function to a diverging sequence results in creation of a converging sequence. The function defined by the equation y = 1/x is such a function. If a finite limit exists for the function when the independent variable approaches infinity it is written formally as:

$$\lim_{x \to \infty} f(x) = L$$

and reads "The limit of f of x, as x approaches infinity, equals L." It is interesting to note that the function defined by y = 1/x has no limit when x approaches 0 but has the limit L = 0 when x approaches ∞.

KEY TERMS

Converge—To converge is to approach a limit that has a finite value.

Interval—An interval is a subset of the real numbers corresponding to a segment of the real number line and is defined by its endpoints. If the interval contains its endpoints then is said to be closed; if not it is referred to as open.

Real Number—The set of numbers containing the integers and all the decimals including both the repeating and nonrepeating decimals.

Sequence—A series of numbers for which each successive number is related to the previous one in a fixed way as the infinite series consisting of 1, 1/2, 1/4, 1/8, $(1/2)^n$.

Applications

The limit concept is essential to understanding the real number system and its distinguishing characteristics. In one sense real numbers can be defined as the numbers that are the limits of convergent sequences of rational numbers. One application of the concept of limits is on the derivative. The derivative is a rate of flow or change, and can be computed based on some limits concepts. Limits are also key to calculating intergrals (expressions of areas). The integral calculates the entire area of a region by summing up an infinite number of small pieces of it. Limits are also part of the iterative process. An iteration is repeatedly performing a routine, using the output of one step as the input of the next step. Each output is an iterate. Some successful iterates can get as close as desired to a theoretically exact value.

See also Calculus; Integral; Real number.

Further Reading:

Abbot, P. and M. E. Wardle. *Teach Yourself Calculus*. Lincolnwood: NTC Publishing, 1992.

Allen, G.D., C. Chui, and B. Perry. *Elements of Calculus*, 2nd ed. Pacific Grove: Brooks/Cole Publishing Co., 1989.

Gowar, Norman. *An Invitation to Mathematics*. New York: Oxford University Press, 1979.

McLaughlin, William I. "Resolving Zeno's Paradoxes." *Scientific American*. 271 (1994): 84–89.

Silverman, Richard A. *Essential Calculus With Applications*. New York: Dover, 1989.

Thomas, George B., Jr. and Ross L Finney. *Elements of Calculus and Analytic Geometry,* 6th ed. Reading: Addison Wesley, 1989.

J. R. Maddocks

Limiting factor

Limiting factors are environmental influences that constrain the productivity of organisms, populations, or communities and thereby prevent them from achieving their full biological potential which could be realized under optimal conditions. Limiting factors can be single elements or a group of related factors.

The environment of organisms must be suitable in many respects. Environmental factors must satisfy minimum and maximum criteria for life. For example, temperature cannot be too cold or hot, and the availability of nutrients cannot be too small or too large. The minimal criteria for metabolically essential environmental factors represent the least availability that will sustain organisms or ecological processes, while the maxima represent toxicity or other biological damages. The minimum and maximum levels of environmental factors bound a relatively broad range within which there are optimal levels at which factors exert no constraints on biological productivity.

The principle of limiting factors is an ecological generalization that suggests that, at any given time in a particular ecosystem, productivity is constrained by a single, metabolically essential factor that is present in least supply relative to the potential biological demand. This limiting factor could be climatic, as is the case of sub–optimal conditions of temperature, windspeed, or moisture. Or the factor could involve an insufficient supply of a particular nutrient, or an excessive, toxic availability of another chemical. In this sense, the limiting factor represents a type of ecological stress which if alleviated will result in greater productivity and development of the ecosystem.

The potential limitations by particular environmental factors are best studied by doing experiments, preferably in the field. For example, limitations of tundra vegetation by climatic factors such as cool temperatures have been studied by enclosing small areas of intact vegetation within greenhouses. Limitations by particular nutrients such as phosphate or nitrate have been studied by fertilization experiments in which nutrients are added alone or in combination with others. Limitations by toxic environmental factors can sometimes be studied by transplanting organisms into cleaner environments, for example, away from a place that is polluted by sulfur dioxide. If these sorts of experiments are properly designed and the organisms do not respond to manipulation of a particular environmental characteristic, then it was not the limiting environmental factor.

The principle of limiting factors can be illustrated by reference to the productivity of phytoplankton in lakes, that is, the community of unicellular algae that live in the water column. In most freshwater lakes algal productivity is limited by the availability of inorganic phosphorus in the form of the ion phosphate. When experimentally fertilized with phosphate, most lake waters will respond by a large increase in productivity. (This will also happen if the lake receives phosphate through sewage inputs or agricultural runoff). In contrast, if the lake water is fertilized with other important nutrients such as nitrate, ammonium, potassium, or inorganic carbon, there will be no increase in productivity, indicating that these are not primary limiting nutrients. However, if the lake water is first well fertilized with phosphate, its productivity will then respond to nitrate addition, indicating that this source of inorganic nitrogen is the secondary limiting factor.

See also Ecological productivity; Ecosystem; Eutrophication; Stress, ecological.

Limpets

Limpets are a common mollusk of the class Gastropoda. Its shell is generally low, flat, oval, and more bilaterally symmetrical than coiled (like a snail's), and it covers the entire soft body, so that the living animal inside is rarely visible. Limpets adhere strongly to rocks by means of a broad muscular foot. It is important for their survival that they are not dislodged easily, since their shell structure does not permit withdrawal into the shell.

The Atlantic plate limpet is *Tectura testudinalis; testudinal* means resembling a tortoise shell. The common European limpet is *Patella vulgata;* the patella in human anatomy is the kneecap; *patelliform* means saucer–shaped, like a kneecap or limpet shell.

Limpets are prosobranch snails of the Order Archaeogastropoda, which allies them with the slit shells, abalones, top shells, and nerites. They are sufficiently varied that they are assigned to several families. Species of *Tectura* and a number of Pacific coast species of the genus *Lottia* are classified as Family Lottiidae. *Patella* is in the Family Patellidae. The small white *Acmaea mitra* of the Pacific coast and a few deep–sea limpets are in the Family Acmaeidae.

Quite different from the families named above are the key–hole limpets, Family Fissurellidae. A common species is *Diodora cayenensis,* which ranges from New Jersey to Brazil. Members of the Fissurellidae family have an opening near the apex of the shell, giving the appearance of a miniature volcano and permitting the outflow of fecal matter and water that has already passed over the gills. The hole begins as a slit in the embryonic shell, and becomes closed as the mantle deposits more shell during growth to adult size.

Limpets are intertidal herbivores, and they do not often feed when exposed to the open air. Some species have a radula, a horny edge on the shell with projections resembling teeth, that helps tear up the animal's food and bring it to its mouth. The food then passes through a simple stomach, where it is exposed to enzymes from paired digestive glands, and then into a long, coiled intestine, where it is turned into feces. Some limpets are not stationary, but make forays of up to 5 ft (1.5 m) at night or at high tide, then return to their original position, which is sometimes marked by a "home scar" on the rock surface. The "brain" of limpets consists of a relatively small number of neurons, and it is not clear how they find their way home.

Like other archaeogastropods, male and female limpets look much the same, and can be distinguished only by the color of the gonads and microscopic examination of their sex cells, or gametes. The majority of smaller animals are males and the larger animals are females, so it is probable that individual males, as they age, become females. During reproduction, eggs and sperm are released into the water at the same time. After several days, 10 for *Patella,* the new larvae settle on some solid substratum, and grow into adults. The larvae of *Lottia strigatella* prefer to settle on boulders where adults of the same species are established, even though other species may be present. This is known as *gregarious settlement.*

The largest limpet is *Lottia gigantea,* a Mexican species 4–8 in (10–20 cm) long. Most species of limpets are 0.4–1 in (1–2.5 cm) long. Some species have been estimated to live 15 years. The larger species are consumed, cooked or raw, in various parts of the world, but limpets are not known to support a commercial fishery.

Further Reading:

Abbott, R.T. *Seashells of the northern hemisphere.* New York: Gallery Books, 1991.

C.S. Hammen

Linden see **Basswood**

Linear accelerator see **Accelerators**

Linear algebra

The study of Linear Algebra includes the topics of vector algebra, matrix algebra, and the theory of vector spaces. Linear Algebra originated as the study of linear equations, including the solution of simultaneous linear equations. An equation is linear if no variable in it is multiplied by itself or any other variable. Thus, the equation $3x + 2y + z = 0$ is a linear equation in three variables. The equation $x^3 + 6y + z + 5 = 0$ is not linear, because the variable x is raised to the power 3 (multiplied together three times); it is a cubic equation. The equation $5x - xy + 6z = 7$ is not a linear equation either, because the product of two variables (xy) appears in it. Thus linear equations are always degree 1.

Two important concepts emerge in Linear Algebra to help facilitate the expression and solution of systems of simultaneous linear equations. They are the vector and the matrix. Vectors correspond to directed line segments. They have both magnitude (length) and direction. Matrices are rectangular arrays of numbers. They are used in dealing with the coefficients of simultaneous equations. Using vector and matrix notation, a system of linear equations can be written, in the form of a single equation, as a matrix times a vector.

Linear Algebra has a wide variety of applications. It is useful in solving network problems, such as calculating current flow in various branches of complicated electronic circuits, or analyzing traffic flow patterns on city streets and interstate highways. Linear algebra is also the basis of a process called linear programming, widely used in business to solve a variety of problems that often contain a very large number of variables.

Historical background

The collection of theorems and ideas that comprise Linear Algebra have come together over some four centuries, beginning in the mid 1600's. The name Linear Algebra, however, is relatively recent. It derives from the fact that the graph of a linear equation is a straight line. In fact the beginnings of Linear Algebra are rooted in the early attempts of 16th and 17th century mathematicians to develop generalized methods for solving systems of linear equations. As early as 1693, Gottfried Leibniz put forth the notion of matrices and their determinants, and in 1750, Gabriel Cramer published his rule (it bears his name today) for solving n equations in n unknowns.

The concept of a vector, however, was originally introduced in physics applications to describe quantities having both magnitude and direction, such as force and velocity. Later, the concept was blended with many of the other notions of linear algebra when mathematicians realized that vectors and one column (or one row) matrices are mathematically identical.

Finally, the theory of vector spaces grew out of work on the algebra of vectors.

Fundamental principles

An equation is only true for certain values of the variables called solutions, or roots, of the equation. When it is desired that certain values of the variables make two or more equations true simultaneously (at the same time), the equations are called simultaneous equations and the values that make them true are called solutions to the system of simultaneous equations.

The graph of a linear equation, in a rectangular coordinate system, is a straight line, hence the term linear. The graph of simultaneous linear equations is a set of lines, one corresponding to each equation. The solution to a simultaneous system of equations, if it exists, is the set of numbers that correspond to the location in space where all the lines intersect in a single point.

Vectors

Since the solution to a system of simultaneous equations, as pointed out earlier, corresponds to the point in space where their graphs intersect in a single point, and since vectors represent points in space, the solution to a set of simultaneous equations is a vector. Thus, all the variables in a system of equations can be represented by a single variable, namely a vector.

Matrices

A matrix is a rectangular array of numbers, and is often used to represent the coefficients of a set of simultaneous equations. Two or more equations are simultaneous if each time a variable appears in any of the equa-

tions, it represents the same quantity. For example, suppose the following relationship exists between the ages of a brother and two sisters: Jack is three years older than his sister Mary, and eleven years older than his sister Nancy, who is half as old as Mary. There are three separate statements here, each of which can be translated into mathematical notation, as follows:

Let: j = Jack's age, m = Mary's age, n = Nancy's age.
Then: $j = m + 3$ (1)
$j = n + 11$ (2)
$2n = m$ (3)

This is a system of three simultaneous equations in three unknowns. Each unknown age is represented by a variable. Each time a particular variable appears in an equation, it stands for the same quantity. In order to see how the concept of a matrix enters, rewrite the above equations, using the standard rules of algebra, as:

$1j - 1m - 0n = 3$ (1')
$1j + 0m - 1n = 11$ (2')
$0j - 1m + 2n = 0.$ (3')

Since a matrix is a rectangular array of numbers, the coefficients of equations (1'), (2'), and (3') can be written in the form of a matrix, A, called the matrix of coefficients, by letting each column contain the coefficients of a given variable (j, m, and n from left to right) and each row contain the coefficients of a single equation (equations (1'), (2'), and (3') from top to bottom. That is,

$$A = \begin{matrix} 1 & -1 & 0 \\ 1 & 0 & -1, \\ 0 & -1 & 2 \end{matrix}$$

Matrix multiplication is carried out by multiplying each row in the left matrix times each column in the right matrix. Thinking of the left matrix as containing a number of "row vectors" and the right matrix as containing a number of "column vectors," matrix multiplication consists of a series of vector dot products. Row 1 times column 1 produces a term in row 1 column 1 of the product matrix, row 2 times column 1 produces a term in row 2 column 1 of the product matrix, and so on, until each row has been multiplied by each column. The product matrix has the same number of rows as the left matrix and the same number of columns as the right matrix. In order that two matrices be compatible for multiplication, the right must have the same number of rows as the left has columns. The matrix with 1s on the diagonal (The diagonal of a matrix begins in the upper left corner and ends in the lower right corner) and all other elements zero, is the identity element for multiplication of matrices, usually denoted by I. Thus the inverse of a matrix A is the matrix A^{-1} such that $AA^{-1} = I$. Not every matrix has an inverse, however, if a square matrix has an inverse, then $A^{-1}A = AA^{-1} = I$. That is, multiplication of a square matrix by its inverse is commutative.

Just as a matrix can be thought of as a collection of vectors, a vector can be thought of as a one–column, or one–row, matrix. Thus, multiplication of a vector by a matrix is accomplished using the rules of matrix multiplication. For example, let the variables in the previous example be represented by the vector j = (j,m,n). Then the product of the coefficient matrix, A, times the vector, j, results in a three–row, one–column matrix, containing terms that correspond to the left hand side of each of equations (1'), (2'), and (3').

$$\begin{bmatrix} 1 & -1 & 0 \\ 1 & 0 & -1 \\ 0 & -1 & 2 \end{bmatrix} \begin{bmatrix} j \\ m \\ n \end{bmatrix} = \begin{bmatrix} 1j - 1m + 0n \\ 1j + 0m - 1n \\ 0j - 1m + 2n \end{bmatrix}$$

Finally, by expressing the constants on the right hand side of those equations as a constant column vector, c, the three equations can be written as the single matrix equation: Aj = c. This equation can be solved using the inverse of the matrix A. That is, multiplying both sides of the equation by the inverse of A provides the solution: $j = A^{-1}c$. The general method for finding the inverse of a matrix and hence the solution to a system of equations is given by Cramer's rule.

Applications

Applications of Linear Algebra have grown rapidly since the introduction of the computer. Finding the inverse of a matrix, especially one that has hundreds or thousands of rows and columns, is a task easily performed by computer in a relatively short time. Virtually any problem that can be translated into the language of linear mathematics can be solved, provided a solution exists. Linear Algebra is applied to problems in transportation and communication to route traffic and information; it is used in the fields of biology, sociology, and ecology to analyze and understand huge amounts of data; it is used daily by the business and economics community to maximize profits and optimize purchasing and manufacturing procedures; and it is vital to the understanding of physics, chemistry, and all types of engineering.

See also Algebra; Matrix; Solution of equation; Vector.

KEY TERMS

Linear equation—A linear equation is one in which no product of variables appears. The graph of a linear equation is a straight line, hence the term linear.

Matrix—A matrix is a rectangular array of numbers, such as a table, having I rows and j columns.

Simultaneous equations—When the solution to an equation satisfies two or more equations at the same time, the equations are called simultaneous equations.

Variable—A variable is a quantity that is allowed to have a changing value, or that represents an unknown quantity.

Vector—A vector is a directed line segment, thus it has both magnitude (given by its length) and direction.

Further Reading:

Garfunkel, Soloman A., ed. *For All Practical Purposes, Introduction to Contemporary Mathematics*. New York: W. H. Freeman, 1988.

Kenschaft, Patricia Clark. *Linear Mathematics, A Practical Approach*. New York: Worth Publishers, Inc., 1978.

McKeague, Charles P. *Intermediate Algebra*, 5th edition. Fort Worth: Saunders College Publishing, 1995.

Swokowski, Earl W. *Pre Calculus, Functions, and Graphs*, 6th. ed. Boston: PWS–KENT Publishing Co., 1990.

Thomas, George B., Jr. and Ross L Finney. *Elements of Calculus and Analytic Geometry*, 6th ed. Reading, MA: Addison Wesley, 1989.

J. R. Maddocks

Line, Equations of

There are many different ways of writing the equation of a line in a coordinate plane. They all stem from the form $ax + by + c = 0$. Thus $2x + 3y - 5 = 0$ is an equation of a line, with $a = 2, b = 3, and c = -5$.

When the equation is written in the form $y = mx + b$ we have slope–intercept form: m is the slope of the line and b is the y–intercept. The equation $2x + 3y - 5 = 0$ becomes

$$y = \frac{-2}{3}x + \frac{5}{3}$$

So the line has slope –2/3 and a y–intercept 5/3.

When the equation is written in the form

$$\frac{x}{a} + \frac{y}{b} = 1$$

we have the intercept form: a is the *x–intercept* and b is the *y–intercept*. The equation 2x + 3y –5 =0 becomes

$$\frac{x}{(5/2)} + \frac{y}{(5/3)} = 1$$

with x–intercept 5/2 and y–intercept 5/3.

When the equation is written in the form

$$y-y_1 = \frac{y_2-y}{x_2-x_1}(x-x_1)$$

where (x_1, y_1) and (x_2, y_2) are points on the line, we have the two point form. If we choose the two points (1, 1) and (–2, 3) that lie on the line 2x + 3y–5 = 0, we have

$$y-1 = \frac{3-1}{-2-1}(x-1) = \frac{2}{3}(x-1)$$

When the equation is written in the form $y–y_1 = m(x–x_1)$ where (x_1, y_1) is a point on the line, we have the point–slope form. If we choose (–2, 3) as the point that lies on the line 2x + 3y = 0, we have y – 3 = –2/3 (x + 2).

In three space, a line is defined as the intersection of two non–parallel planes, such as 2x + y + 4z = 0 and x + 3y + 2z = 0. Standard equations of a line in three space are the two–point form:

$$\frac{x-x_1}{x_2-x_1} = \frac{y-y_1}{y_2-y_1} = \frac{z-z_1}{z_2-z_1}$$

where (x_1,y_1,z_1) and (x_2,y_2,z_2) are points on the line; and the parameter form: $x = x_1 + lt$, $y = y_1 + mt$, $z = z_1 + nt$ where the parameter t is the directed distance from a fixed point (x_1,y_1,z_1) on the plane to any other point (x,y,z) of the plane, and l, m, and n are any constants.

Further Reading:
Aufmann, Richard N. and Vernon C. Baker. *Intermediate Algebra: An Applied Approach*, 4th edition. Houghton Mifflin, 1995.
Ellis, Robert, and Denny Gulich. *Precalculus,* 4th edition. Harcourt, Brace, Jovanovich, 1992.

Lion see **Cats**

Lipid

Lipids are a class of natural, organic compounds in plants and animals, defined by a specific way they behave: they are soluble in non–polar solvents. That is, lipids are not soluble in water but dissolve in solvents like gasoline, ether, carbon tetrachloride, or oil. The vast majority of lipids are colorless and mostly fats and oils.

Lipids comprise one of the three broad classifications into which nourishing substances can be broken. Lipids, proteins, and carbohydrates are the three very general classifications. Fiber may be filling but is not called nourishment. Lipids are rich in energy, supplying twice the caloric value per unit weight than carbohydrates or proteins. Seeds contain lipids as energy storage substances to get the plant started.

Lipids are derived from living systems of plants, animals, or humans. In the example vitamins that follows, attention is focused on the behavior and not the exact nature nor structure of the vitamins in the example.

Substances that are lipids are sometimes also called fat–soluble. For example, this designation is frequently applied to those vitamins in our food that a human can store in body fat. This is contrasted with the vitamins that are not lipid–like, but are instead water soluble. Excesses of the water soluble vitamins are passed in one's urine and must be replaced frequently. The fat soluble, lipid-like vitamins do not need to be taken daily. (The common known fat–soluble vitamins are Vitamins A, D, E, and K.)

Typical lipids

Besides the lipid vitamins that are fat–soluble, hormones, waxes, oils, and many very important substances are also examples of lipids. These examples bear little similarity to one another in terms of their chemical formulations. Lipids also vary greatly in their molecular structure. Most lipid molecules are not electrically charged, nor is either end of the compound the least bit electrically polarized. They are non–polar compounds, electrically neutral throughout.

Because there is no structural definition of lipids, the exact definition of a lipid is a bit vague and a few scientists seeking a broad definition will include almost any organic compound that is not water soluble. Many of these can be volatile because their molecules are small. Most scientists do not include mineral oils nor waxes obtained from petroleum or paraffin. Instead interest is focused on substances related to living plant and animal biochemistry. And these substances are comprised of large molecules that are non–volatile.

Many lipids are essential to good human health. Some of them serve as chemical messengers in the body. Others serve as ways to store chemical energy. There is a good reason that babies are born with "baby fat." Seeds contain lipids for the storage of energy. People living in Arctic zones seek fatty foods in their diet.

Fat is a poor conductor of heat so lipids can also function as an insulator. Their functions are as varied as their structures. But because they are all fat soluble, they all share in the ability to approach and even enter a body cell.

Lipids and cell membranes

Body cells have a membrane that is quite complicated but to a first approximation it can be represented by a double layer of lipids or lipids attached to proteins. Thus the behavior of lipids and lipid–like molecules becomes very important in understanding how a substance may or may not enter a cell. Many biochemical processes that occur in our bodies are becoming better understood as scientists learn more about the lipid–like layer around cells.

Another insight to be gained by understanding the lipid layer around a cell membrane deals with problems associated with pesticides or other lipid–like molecules that get into places other than those intended. The problems arise because many pesticides are lipid–like and may change the way the cell membrane behaves.

Lipids that are found associated with proteins go by the term lipoproteins. Lipids attached to sugars or carbohydrates are called glycolipids. There are also lipids attached to alcohols and some to phosphoric acids. The attachment with other compounds greatly alters the behavior of a lipid, often making one end of the molecule water soluble. Such new substances are bipolar and can become involved in aqueous chemistry. This is important because it allows lipids to move out of one's intestine and into the blood stream. In the digestion process, lipids are made water soluble by either being broken down into smaller parts or becoming bipolar through association with another substance. The breaking down is usually done via two different processes. One is called hydrolysis, which means chemical reaction with water, and the other is called saponification.

Metabolism of lipids

The processes by which a lipid is broken down or by which it is built are quite complicated. The liver can convert fats into blood sugar, or glucose. Very specific and very effective enzymes are involved in the many steps of the processes. As a group, these enzymes are

KEY TERMS

Enzyme—A protein material that serves to promote and ease biochemical reactions in plants and animals.

Metabolism—The process by which food material is broken down and used in the construction of new material.

Molecule—The smallest unit of a compound having the properties of the compound. A molecule is made up of more than one atom. Water, H_2O, is a molecule composed of three atoms.

Organic—Substances associated with living systems is the old, but common definition. Now chemists apply it to most compounds that contain carbon atoms, especially rings or chains of carbon atoms.

Polar/non–polar—Characterized by having opposite ends, as a magnet has a north and south pole. When applied to compounds it means that one end of the molecule, or individual part that comprises the compound, has an abundance of electrical charge and the other end has a shortage of electrical charge. Something that is non–polar is electrically neutral throughout the molecule. The compound has no positive or negative end.

Proteins—Important nitrogen containing organic compounds that are most easily identified as the building material of a body, meat, skin, and finger nails.

Solubility—When one substance dissolves in another and becomes homogeneous with it, we say that the substance is soluble. Precisely, the solute is dissolved in the solvent and becomes a solution.

Volatile—Easily evaporated, the ability of a solid or a liquid to be turned into a gas or vapor. Volatile substances are usually made of small molecules.

called lipases. There is one group of lipids that are not easily broken down. These non–saponifiable lipids are the steroids and carotenoids. Carotenoids are red or yellow pigments found cells involved in photosynthesis.

Further Reading:
Gebo, Sue. *What's Left to Eat?* New York: McGraw Hill, 1992.
Holme, David J. and Hazel Peck. *Analytical Biochemistry.* Essex, England: Burnt Mill, Harlow, 1993.

Sullivan, Darryl, and Donald E. Carpenter, eds. *Methods of Analysis for Nutritional Labeling.* Arlington, VA: AOAC International, 1993.

Donald H. Williams

Liquid see **States of matter**

Liquid crystals

Liquid crystals are pure substances in a state of matter that shows properties of both liquids and solids over a specific temperature range. At temperatures lower than this range, the liquid crystals are only like solids. They do not flow and their molecules maintain a regular arrangement. At temperatures above this range, the liquid crystals behave only like liquids. They can flow and the molecules have no special arrangement. Within the temperature range, different for every liquid crystal, liquid crystals are able to flow but they still keep their molecules in a specific arrangement.

The molecules of liquid crystals are usually much longer than they are wide. You can think of them like pencils. When light waves pass through these molecules, the speed of the light depends on whether it is traveling along the short direction or along the long direction. Depending on the specific liquid crystal, one direction will be faster than the other. Imagine the light wave as a wiggling rope. The direction of wiggle or vibration is called the polarization of the light wave. When the light wave emerges from the liquid crystal, the direction of polarization may have been changed due to the difference in light speed along different directions. Our eyes can not detect the direction of light polarization but a device called a polarizer can. Many of the first liquid crystals discovered were chemically made from cholesterol and showed this twisting effect. Cholesterol itself is not a liquid crystal, but any liquid crystal that shows this spiral, even if it not made from cholesterol, is still called cholesteric.

The cholesteric class of liquid crystals shows some color effects that do not require a polarizer to see. The twist of the spiral structure is very regularly spaced, almost like the steps of a spiral staircase. When white light falls on this spiral, most of it passes through. But white light is actually composed of many different colors of light waves. Light waves of different colors have different lengths. The length of a wave, called the

KEY TERMS

Light speed—How fast light gets from one place to another. The speed of light depends on the material through which it must travel.

Light wave—A way of picturing the energy in light as a wiggling rope.

Molecule—A combination of atoms. Molecules are the smallest units of compounds.

Polarization—The direction of vibration or "wiggle" of a light wave.

Polarizer—A device that allows only one direction of light vibration to pass through it.

State of matter—The condition of being a gas, liquid, or solid.

Wavelength—The distance from one point on a light wave to the next identical point.

wavelength, is measured from one point of the wave to another identical point. If the light wave is just the right length to match the regular spacing of the spiral, it will be reflected instead. So depending on the size of the helix spacing, only certain colors will be reflected. One way to control the size of the helix spacing is by choosing liquid crystals that twist a lot or a little from one layer to the next. Another way is by controlling the temperature. When a cholesteric helix is warmed, the layers twist a little more. This means that the regular spacing of the "stairs" of the spiral is closer. The light waves that are reflected will be the short light waves which are blue in color. When the cholesteric is cooled, there is less twisting and a longer spacing, so longer light waves are reflected. Long light waves are red. This is the mechanism that makes liquid crystal thermometers work – you see red when the liquid crystals in the thermometer are cool, then yellow, green, and blue as they are warmed.

The most important use of liquid crystals is in displays because the molecules of a liquid crystal can control the amount, color, and direction of vibration of the light that passes through them. This means that by controlling the arrangement of the molecules, an image in light can be produced and manipulated. Liquid crystal displays, or LCDs, are used in watch faces, laptop computer screens, camcorder viewers, virtual reality helmet displays, and even television screens.

Current research in liquid crystals is focused on mixing liquid crystals with other materials like polymers. Scientists hope to make mixtures for liquid crystal displays so that these displays can show more detail, more color, and change image faster, but use less energy.

Further Reading:

Collings, Peter J. *Liquid Crystals: Nature's Delicate Phase of Matter.* Princeton University Press, 1990.

Chandrasekhar, S. *Liquid Crystals*, 2nd. ed., Cambridge University Press, 1992.

De Gennes, P.G., and J. Prost. *The Physics of Liquid Crystals*, 2nd. ed., Oxford Science Publications, 1993.

Eileen M. Korenic

Liter see **Metric system**

Lithification see **Sedimentary rock**

Lithium

Lithium has been the treatment of choice for manic–depressive illness for several decades. Lithium is a trace element found in plants, mineral rocks, and in the human body. Today, the major source of medical lithium is mines in North Carolina. Lithium is classified as an antimonic medication because of its ability to reverse mania, a mood disorder characterized by extreme excitement and activity. In addition, lithium is also effective in reversing deep depression, the other mood extreme of manic–depressive illness, and in decreasing the frequency of manic and depressive cycles in patients. Manic–depressive illness is now generally referred to as bipolar disorder, a term preferred in the psychiatric community.

While there has been a great deal of success in treating manic–depressive patients with lithium and returning them to a normal life, researchers are not exactly sure how it works. It is a non–addictive and non–sedating medication, but its use must be carefully monitored for possibly dangerous side effects. For some patients suffering from some symptoms of schizophrenia, lithium may be used in combination with other medications. Lithium is also used to treat people who suffer from unipolar depression.

Before lithium was in general use for the treatment of bipolar disorder, as many as one in five patients with this condition committed suicide. Many who suffered from this illness were never able to live normal, productive lives. Lithium therapy now allows many people with bipolar disorder to participate in ordinary everyday life. Seventy to eighty percent of bipolar patients respond well to lithium treatment without any serious side effects.

History of use

The use of lithium for medicinal purposes can be traced back 1,800 years to the Greek physician Galen, who treated patients with mania by having them bathe in alkaline springs and drink the water, which probably contained lithium. In 1817, the Swedish chemist, August Arfwedson, described the element lithium, which he named from the Greek word that means stone. It is the lightest of the alkali (soluble salt) metals. In the 1840s, lithium was mixed with carbonate or citrate to form a salt and was used to treat gout, epilepsy, diabetes, cancer, and sleeplessness. None of these treatments were effective, but interest in lithium as a medicine continued. In the 1940s, lithium chloride was administered as a salt substitute for patients requiring low–salt diets. This proved to be dangerous because an insufficient amount of sodium in the body causes lithium to build up. Too much lithium can cause poisoning and even death if the levels become too high.

John Cade

The story of lithium parallels other stories in medical history where the medicinal value of a substance is discovered accidently. In 1949, John Cade, an Australian psychiatrist, decided to experiment with lithium on guinea pigs. He theorized that uric acid was a cause of manic behavior. Since he needed to keep the uric acid soluble, he used lithium salts as an agent in the solution. The guinea pigs did not become manic as he expected, but instead they responded by becoming extremely calm.

When Cade used the lithium treatment on 10 manic patients, he reported remarkable improvement in the patients' condition. One patient who had been in a manic state for five years was able to leave the hospital after a three–month treatment and resume a normal life. Cade reported his results in the *Medical Journal of Australia*, but his findings did not have an impact on the medical community at that time.

When Cade carried out his experiments, reports of lithium poisonings were widespread in the United States. It was not until the work of Mogens Schou, who campaigned for recognition of lithium as a treatment for manic–depressive illness, that acceptance of lithium began. In the United States, however, it did not gain full FDA approval until 1974, although trials were conducted during the 1960s.

Administration

The dosage of lithium must be regulated on an individual basis. The level of concentration in the blood must be approximately between 0.8–1.4 milli–equivalents per liter of blood. For this reason blood samples must be taken regularly when a person is receiving lithium treatment. When the concentration of lithium is too low, the desired results will not be obtained and if it is too high, there may be adverse side effects.

Initially, the dose given is very low, then a blood sample is taken, and the dosage is increased gradually until the desired concentration is reached. When therapy is initiated, blood samples are taken every three or four days, then once a week, progressing to every two weeks, once a month, then perhaps every three or four months. In order to maintain the desired level, the medication is usually taken periodically throughout the day, depending upon the dosage. Slow–release and sustained–release tablets and capsules have been developed that make the administration of lithium medication easier. It is sometimes taken in liquid form as well.

Precautions

Lithium is absorbed quickly into the bloodstream and carried to all tissues of the body and brain. It is excreted through the kidneys. Because sodium is also passed out through the kidneys and affects lithium secretion, a normal sodium balance is necessary to maintain a lithium balance as well. If there is an insufficient amount of sodium in the body, the lithium builds up and can become toxic.

Besides avoiding a low–salt diet, patients receiving lithium therapy for bipolar disorder are cautioned to drink alcohol in moderation and to discuss all over–the–counter and prescription medicine with their psychiatrists, since some antibiotics and anti–inflammatory agents like ibuprofen can increase lithium levels in the bloodstream. The use of lithium during pregnancy presents certain risks. Electroconvulsive therapy (ECT) is sometimes recommended for pregnant patients who have been taking lithium as treatment for bipolar disorder. Older persons on lithium and low–salt diets must also be cautious.

Possible side effects of lithium therapy are stomach ache, nausea, vomiting, diarrhea, hand tremors, thirst, fatigue, and muscle weakness. Some patients report weight gain while on lithium and a thyroid condition may develop, but can be easily treated with thyroid replacement hormones.

By and large, lithium treatment has been a "miracle drug" for patients suffering from bipolar disorder. Many remain in treatment for extended periods of time without any harmful side effects, and most importantly, are able to lead normal and productive lives without hospitalization.

See also Antipsychotic drugs; Manic depression.

Further Reading:

Bohn, John. *Lithium and Manic Depression.* Madison, WI: University of Wisconsin, 1990.

Goodwin, Frederick K., and Kay Redfield Jamison. *Manic–Depressive Illness.* New York: Oxford University Press, 1990.

Jamison, Kay Redfield. *Touched with Fire.* New York: Free Press, 1993.

Papolos, Demitri F., and Janice Papolos. *Overcoming Depression.* New York: Harper & Row, 1987.

Schou, Mogens. *Lithium Treatment of Manic–Depressive Illness.* 5th rev. ed. New York: Basel, 1993.

Vita Richman

KEY TERMS

Electroconvulsive therapy—A form of treatment for depression in which an electric current is passed through the brain to produce convulsions.

Manic–depressive illness—Bipolar disorder, a condition where the patient exhibits both an excited state called mania and a depressed state.

Schizophrenia—A mental illness characterized by thought disorder, distancing from reality, and sometimes delusions and hallucinations.

Unipolar depression—A mental illness in which the patient suffers from depression only.

Lithography

Lithography is a method of printing an image by applying patterned layers of color to paper with a series of etched metal or stone plates. This is the process used to print many newspapers and multi–colored lithographs. It is also the general name for the techniques used to fabricate integrated circuits (ICs).

Lithography in printing

The concept of lithography was developed by German Aloys Senefelder in 1796. He used a stone slab with printed grease marks and dampened it with water. When a coating of ink was applied to the stone, it adhered to the grease marks and washed away from the wet areas. The ink was then transferred to paper by pressing the stone against it.

Senefelder's method was perfected over time. Metal plates were soon used in place of stone slabs. Several chemical solutions that repelled water and adhered to ink better than grease could were experimented with. Lithography was used with several different color inks to create color pictures, called lithographs, which were made famous by Currier and Ives.

Photolithography

The invention of photography in the 20th century spurred the development of a new lithographic process called *photolithography*. In this method, the printer shines a bright light through a photo negative onto a thin plate coated with light–sensitive chemicals. The areas of the plate struck by the light harden into a reproduced image, serving the same function as the grease design in early lithography. Today, lithographic processes are the most widely–used printing methods.

Lithography and integrated circuits

The same lithographic concepts used to reprint text and pictures on paper can be used to manufacture integrated circuits. In this case, a polymer resist is used to repel the subsequently applied layers of metal conductors, semiconductor materials, and dielectric insulators which are the "ink."

An integrated circuit is a tiny version of a conventional electrical circuit. Thin films of various materials act as insulators between conductive material and the silicon metal substrate, or protect existing layers from implantation of other atoms. These devices are built by coating a silicon wafer with patterned layers of material, designed to allow the insulators or protective barriers to be applied, or to leave holes in the barrier layer permitting electrical contact. Sophisticated circuits may require 20 or more layers. Small features and narrow lines must be precisely placed, and the absence of material in a given spot is as critical as the presence of it somewhere else.

There are several ways lithography is used to make integrated circuits, including visible and ultraviolet lithography (forms of photolithography), electron beam

---

KEY TERMS
. . . .

Negative photoresist—A type of photosensitve polymer that leaves a barrier only where exposed to light.

Photolithography—A method of integrated circuit fabrication that uses a light–sensitive polymer to pattern a silicon wafer with other materials.

Photoresist—Photosensitive polymer that is used to pattern silicon wafers during integrated circuit fabrication.

Positive photoresist—A type of photosensitive polymer that leaves a barrier only where not exposed to light.

Reticle—A photomask used to print patterns on silicon wafers, typically made of chrome–patterned transparent glass.

Stepper—A lithographic system that exposes the wafer one small section at a time before 'stepping' to the next location.

Substrate—The foundation material on which integrated circuits are built; usually made of silicon.

Wafer—A very thin disk of silicon metal on which integrated circuits are built.

---

patterning, ion beam patterning, and x–ray lithography. The most common method is photolithography, which is well suited to high volume production of consumer electronics.

Making integrated circuits

In the manufacture of integrated circuits, the silicon wafer that acts as the base and a light–sensitive polymer material, called *photoresist*, are used to create the pattern of the circuit's layers. Negative photoresists harden when exposed to light, adhering to the base through the developing process. Positive photoresists degrade when they are exposed to light and developed, leaving a depression. The coated wafer is then dried 10–30 minutes in an oven at 176–194°F (80–90°C).

After photoresist is applied to the silicon wafer, it is selectively exposed to light with the aid of a *reticle*. A reticle consists of a layer of patterned chrome on transparent glass; gaps in the chrome permit light to reach the resist–covered wafer. Exposure takes place in a device, called a *stepper*, that shines light on the wafer through the transparent regions of the reticle. Only a small region of the wafer is exposed at a time. Then the wafer is moved, or *stepped*, forward and a new segment is exposed. After exposure, the wafer is put into developing solution where the positive and unexposed photoresists are removed. It is hard–baked at temperatures between 248 and 356°F (120–180°C).

After the photoresist is in place, a layer of conducting, semiconducting, or insulating metal solution is applied to the wafer and adheres in the pattern opposite to the photoresist. The application and removal of photoresist and metal solutions is repeated 10–20 times in the manufacture of a single integrated circuit. In addition to the number of steps needed to make the circuit, the complexity of the task is increased by the necessity for precision in the manufacturing process. For instance, some circuits use printed features as small as 0.35 micron. A human hair, on the other hand, is about 100 microns in diameter.

See also Integrated circuit; Photography; Printing.

Further Reading:

Jaeger, Richard. *Introduction to Microelectronic Fabrication.* New York, NY: Addison–Wesley, 1988.
Glendinning, William, and John Helbert, eds. *Handbook of VLSI Microlithography.* Park Ridge, NJ: Noyes Publications, 1991.

Kristin Lewotsky

Lithosphere

The word lithosphere is derived from the word "sphere," combined with the Greek word "lithos" which means rock. The lithosphere is the solid outer section of the Earth which includes the earth's crust (the "skin" of rock on the outer layer of planet Earth), as well as the underlying cool, dense, and fairly rigid upper part of the upper mantle. The lithosphere extends from the surface of the earth to a depth of about 44–62 m (70–100 km). This relatively cool and rigid section of the earth is believed to "float" on top of the warmer, non–rigid, and partially melted material directly below.

The Earth is made up of several layers. The outermost layer is called the earth's crust. The thickness of earth's crust varies. Under the oceans the crust is only about 3–5 m (5–10 km) thick. Under the continents, however, the crust thickens to about 22 m (35 km) and reaches depths of up to 37 m (60 km) under some mountain ranges. Beneath the crust is a layer of rock material that is also solid, rigid, and relatively cool, but

is believed to be made up of denser material. This layer is called the upper part of the upper mantle, and varies in depth from about 31 m (50 km) to 62 m (100 km) below the Earth's surface. The combination of the crust and this upper part of the upper mantle, which are both comprised of relatively cool and rigid rock material, is called the lithosphere.

Below the lithosphere, the temperature is believed to reach 1,832°F (1,000°C) which is warm enough to allow rock material to flow if pressurized. Seismic evidence suggests that there is also some molten material at this depth (perhaps about 10%). This zone which lies directly below the lithosphere is called the asthenosphere, from the Greek word "asthenes," meaning "weak." The lithosphere, including both the solid portion of the upper mantle and the Earth's crust, is carried "piggyback" on top of the weaker, less rigid asthenosphere, which seems to be in continual motion. This motion creates stress in the rigid rock layers above it, and the slabs or plates of the lithosphere are forced to jostle against each other, much like ice cubes floating in a bowl of swirling water. This motion of the lithospheric plates is known as plate tectonics, and is responsible for many of the movements that we see on the earth's surface today including earthquakes, certain types of volcanic activity, and continental drift.

See also Earth's interior; Magma.

Lithotripsy

Lithotripsy, extracorporeal shock wave (ESWL) is the first non–invasive (not requiring surgical opening of the body) treatment for eliminating kidney stones by breaking them into sand–like particles, usually by means of high pressure waves generated in water. The particles are then eliminated from the body during urination.

The ESWL machine, called a lithotripter, generates shock waves in a reservoir of water outside the body, then focuses them with a reflecting device so they pass through the water and into the body, striking individual stones. Waves are disturbances that travel from one point to another without transporting the material of the medium itself. Rather, there is successive compression and expansion of adjacent areas of the fluid. This can be visualized by imagining a cork bobbing up and down in water as a wave passes by. There is no net movement of water that can carry the cork along, only the passage of the disturbance itself. A shock wave is a compression

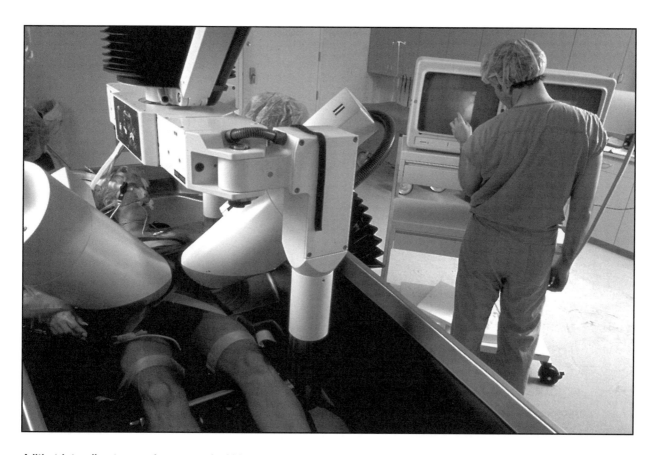

A lithotripter directs sound waves at the kidney stones of a patient, causing the stones to break and dissolve.

wave (wave formed by compression of a fluid) that is fully developed, of very large amplitude, and travels through the medium at the speed of sound.

History

The concept of using shock waves to fragment stones had its origin in research done in Germany during the 1960s. Researchers found that the pitting of aircraft wings following supersonic flight was caused by collision of the airplane wing with rain drops. ESWL was introduced into the United States in 1984.

The use of sound waves to destroy kidney stones is based on the destructive force generated when a shock wave in fluid suddenly hits a substance that has different properties, such as a kidney stone. The shock waves pass efficiently through fluid mediums and can be focused so they strike small objects.

Lithotripsy and kidney stones

Kidney stones are formed from deposits of salt and mineral crystals on the inner surface of the kidneys or in the bladder. Often this occurs when the urine is per-

sistently either acidic or alkaline. Most kidney stones contain large amounts of calcium. They vary in size and may remain inside the kidney or dislodge and pass into the ureter, the tube that carries urine from the kidney to the bladder.

If stones remain inside the kidney they may cause damage directly, or obstruct the flow of urine. Such an obstruction causes a buildup of pressure inside the kidney and interferes with the function of this organ, a condition called hydronephrosis. In turn, this can cause bacterial buildup in the stagnant urine, a condition called acute bacterial pyelonephritis.

Most kidney stones produce no symptoms and are only discovered during a routine x–ray examination, although some stones may cause blood in the urine. Usually, however, people discover they have kidney stones when they are stricken with terrible pain along their side or back, which occurs when the stone moves down the ureter.

Formerly, the two major forms of treatment were to wait for stones to pass through the bladder in the urine, or to remove it, usually by major abdominal surgery.

Later, endoscopes—long light tubes used for looking inside the body—were used to locate stones, which were then grasped or crushed with basketlike devices on the end of tubes inserted under the guidance of endoscopes. But stone formation often recurs, and repeated surgery greatly increases the risk of permanent kidney damage or loss of the kidney. More recently, ESWL has become the common method of treating kidney stones.

How it works

A lithotripter generates shock waves by means of electrical or spark discharges within a spherical or ellipsoidal reflector submerged in water. Some waves propagate directly away from the curved surface of the reflector (primary shock waves). Others strike and bounce off the inner wall of the reflector (reflected shock waves).

In order to focus the shock waves so they pass into the body and strike kidney stones, physicians must first locate the stones by means of fluoroscopy or ultrasound.

During the treatment, there are a series of clicks that correspond to the shock waves passing through the water and body tissue to break up the stone. Treatment takes about one to two hours.

Many lithotripters require patients to be lowered into a water bath. Shock waves travel through the water and into the body. The procedure restricted the positioning of the patient so that only stones in the upper urinary tract were accessible to shock waves.

More recent lithotripters do not require patients to be lowered into a bath or to lie on a bed of water. Rather, the water is located inside the shock wave generator under the table on which the patient lies. This keeps the patient and water apart, permitting doctors to more easily position patients on the table to treat kidney stones, and increases the ability of physicians to target and destroy them.

ESWL does not damage the kidney, so the physician can repeat the procedure if necessary. Most patients can return home the same day of treatment.

In some patients, a stone may be able to be seen only after a narrow tube called a stent is placed in the ureter. The patient is first put under anesthesia. Then the physician inserts a thin, narrow light tube called a cystoscope into the urethra to help guide placement of the stent. The stent is removed after treatment.

Following treatment, the patient may feel an ache in the lower back, and may have some discomfort passing the remains of the stones. In addition, there is often blood in the urine.

The treatment is not recommended for everyone. For example, women who are pregnant and individuals who already have urinary tract infections should not undergo ESWL.

See also Bacteria; Fiber optics; Urology.

Marc Kusinitz

Liver see **Digestive system**

Liverwort

The liverworts are one of three classes in the plant phylum Bryophyta. The other two classes are mosses and hornworts. Liverworts are small, green, terrestrial plants. They do not have true roots, stems, or leaves. Instead, they have an above ground leaf–like structure, known as a thallus, and an underground structure, known as a rhizoid. Most liverworts are found in moist environments and they tend to be less resistant to desiccation than their relatives, the mosses. Many liverwort species are found in temperate North America, but most species grow in the tropics.

General characteristics

Like mosses and higher plants, liverworts use chlorophyll–a, chlorophyll–b, and carotenoids as photosynthetic pigments and store their food reserves as starch. As in mosses and higher plants, their cell walls are composed of cellulose.

Like mosses and hornworts, liverworts are restricted to moist environments for two principal reasons. First, they lack a vascular system for efficient transport of water and food. Second, their sperm cells must swim through water to reach the egg cells.

The thalli of most liverworts have dorsiventral morphology. In other words, they have distinct front and back sides. In this respect, liverwort thalli are similar to the leaves of higher plants.

The name "liverwort" is centuries old and was given to these plants because their thalli are liver–shaped. In earlier times, people believed in the "doctrine of signatures." This dictated that a plant part which resembles a bodily organ can be used to treat diseases of that organ. Thus, liverworts were used to treat diseases of the liver. Western science has long since discredited the "doctrine of signatures," although it is still

Common liverwort (*Marchantia polymorpha*).

advocated by various "New Age" and other pseudoscientific movements.

Life cycle

The general features of the liverwort life cycle are the same as that of mosses. Both have a characteristic alternation of generations in which the multicellular diploid sporophyte is dependent on the green and "leafy" haploid gametophyte. As with mosses, the gametophyte of liverworts is the form most commonly seen in nature.

In most species, a haploid liverwort spore germinates and gives rise to a single–celled protonema, a small filamentous cell. In general, the haploid gametophyte develops from the protonema. In most liverworts, the gametophyte is procumbent, although in some species it is erect. Typically, the gametophyte has a subterranean rhizoid, a specialized single–celled structure which anchors the liverwort to its substrate and takes up nutrients from the soil.

Male and female reproductive organs, the antheridia and archegonia, grow from the gametophyte. These arise directly from the thallus or are borne on stalks. About 80% of the liverwort species are dioecious (male and female on separate plants) and the other 20% are monoecious (male and female on the same plant). Each archegonium produces a single egg; each antheridium produces many motile sperm cells, each with two flagella. The sperm cells must swim through water to reach the archegonium. Then, the sperm fertilizes the egg to form a diploid cell. This eventually develops into a multicellular diploid sporophyte.

The sporophyte of liverworts, like that of mosses, has a terminal capsule borne on a stalk, known as a seta. As the sporophyte develops, haploid spores form inside the capsule. In general, the sporophytes of liverworts are smaller and simpler in morphology than those of mosses. Another difference is that the liverwort seta elongates after capsule maturation, whereas the moss seta elongates before capsule maturation.

Spore dispersal

Liverworts have a characteristic method of spore dispersal. Inside the sporophyte capsule, spores are attached to specialized cells known as elaters. The elater is tubular in shape and has one or more cell wall thickenings which are helically oriented along the long axis of the cell. These helical thickenings are hydroscopic, in that they readily absorb water.

As the liverwort capsule dries, it opens up. Then the helical cell wall thickenings of the elater dry out and the elater changes its shape. As this happens, the elater releases the bound spores which are then dispersed by wind.

Asexual reproduction

Like mosses, many species of liverworts reproduce by making gemmae. Gemmae are small circular or spherical reproductive structures which are borne inside gemmae cups. The gemmae cups form on top of the thallus. Gemmae formation is an important form of asexual reproduction in many species of liverworts and mosses.

Evolution

There are only a few fossils of liverworts and mosses and there are no fossils of hornworts. This is because the soft tissue of these bryophytes does not fossilize well. The oldest known liverwort fossil is from the late Devonian period, about 350 million years ago. Most botanists believe that they originated long before this.

Some botanists have proposed that there are over 10,000 species of liverworts in the world. A more realistic estimate is about 6,000 species. The number of species may have been overestimated in the past because the morphology of many species is plastic, in that it differs in different environments. This makes identification of liverwort species very difficult, typically more difficult than that of higher plants.

Interestingly, even though liverworts originated several hundred million years before the flowering plants, there are several hundred thousand species of flowering plants but only about 6,000 species of liverworts. The reason for this may be that liverworts rely upon the inefficient mechanism of water-transported sperm for sexual reproduction. Thus, it has been pro-

KEY TERMS

. . . .

Diploid—Nucleus or cell containing two copies of each chromosome, generated by fusion of two haploid nuclei.

Elater—Specialized tubular cells with helically oriented cell wall thickenings to which liverwort spores are attached.

Gametophyte—Haploid gamete–producing generation in a plant's life cycle.

Gemma—Multicellular asexual reproductive structure of mosses and liverworts.

Haploid—Nucleus or cell containing one copy of each chromosome.

Meiosis—Division of the cell's nucleus in which the number of chromosomes is reduced by half, typically from the diploid to the haploid.

Sporophyte—Diploid spore–producing generation in a plant's life cycle.

Thallus—A single plant body lacking distinct stem, leaves, and roots.

posed that most species of liverworts rely upon asexual gemmae as a means of reproduction. Asexual reproduction tends to reduce genetic diversity. Since genetic diversity is needed for new species to evolve, the liverworts and other bryophytes may have evolved into a sort of evolutionary dead end.

See also Asexual reproduction; Bryophyte; Moss; Spore.

Further Reading:

Greenaway, T. *Mosses and Liverworts.* Raintree Steck–Verlag, 1992.
Margulis, L. and Schwartz, K.V. *Five Kingdoms.* W.H. Freeman and Company, 1988.

Peter A. Ensminger

Livestock

Livestock is a collective term for domesticated animals that are kept, mostly for the production of meat, milk, wool, or other products. The most common species are cattle, pigs, sheep, goats, horses, and chickens. The term is not used in reference to animals that are kept as pets or companions.

Livestock are domesticated species, which have been genetically modified over time through the artificial selection of desirable traits by humans, with a view to increasing the docility of the animals, their size and productivity, their quality as agricultural products, and other culturally desired features. Some species of livestock no longer occur in their original, non–domesticated, free–living form, and they are totally dependent on humans for their continued existence. However, humans are also substantially dependent on their livestock for sustenance and other purposes. Consequently, the symbiotic relationship between humans and their domestic livestock could be termed a mutualism, that is, a mutually beneficial relationship between two species.

Some of the domesticated species of livestock have become enormously abundant in cultivation. The world's population of sheep and goats has been estimated at about 1.7 billion, while there are some 1.3 billion cows, 0.85 billion pigs, 0.12 billion horses, and 0.16 billion camels and water buffalo. Some smaller species of livestock are even more abundant, including an estimated 10–11–billion fowl, mostly chickens. In comparison, the total population of humans is about 5.8 billion individuals. The populations of species of both livestock and humans are growing quite rapidly, in the case of humans at about 1.7% per year or 93 million people per year.

Cows

Cows are large animals in the family Bovidae that are kept as sources of meat, hides, and milk. Cows are grazing animals, eating grasses and other types of herbaceous plants.

The domestic cow or ox (*Bos taurus*) is a massive animal with a heavy body, a short neck with a dewlap hanging beneath, two hollow horns, and a long, tufted tail. The natural tendency of these animals is to live in herds of mature females and their calves, led by a mature bull. One calf is usually born after a nine–month gestation, and these feed on their mother's milk for six months, after which they are weaned.

Some races of domestic cattle may be descended in part from the golden ox or aurochs (*Bos primigenius*) of Europe, which became extinct in the wild in the seventeenth century. Domestic cows are also partly descended from the zebu (*B. indicus*) and the Indian ox (*B. namadicus*).

Domestic chickens.

The zebu, brahman, or oriental domestic cow is a tropical species of cow with a distinctive, fatty–humped back, and a pronounced dewlap. Relatively minor, domesticated species are the gayal (*Bos frontinalis*) of southern Asia, and the banteng (*B. sondaicus*) of Southeast Asia.

The domestic cow, however, is by far the most abundant cow in agriculture. This species can be used as a draft animal, in which case they are referred to as oxen. These animals are very strong and are capable of hauling heavy loads or plowing soil. There are various races of domestic cows, which vary in the length and shape of their horns, body size and shape, body color, and other characteristics. The black-and-white blotched holstein is a familiar variety, as is the uniformly light-brown jersey.

In modern North American agriculture, beef cattle are commonly born and initially raised on rangelands.

They are then herded together and transported to feedlots closer to their markets, where they are fed nutritious foods, and gain a great deal of weight prior to being slaughtered at a central facility. The carcass is dissected into various products, ranging from high–value steaks and roasts, to lower grades of meat that are ground into a composite product, known as hamburger. Especially fatty meats, internal organs, blood, and other tissues are generally used to manufacture sausages and hot dogs. The hide is used to make leather. Remarkably little of the carcass is wasted.

Veal is a specialty meat that is produced from young animals that are kept in very close confinement for their entire lives. The highest–quality, epicurean veal is pale–colored and very tender. To achieve this product grade, veal calves are tethered and confined closely so they cannot move very much, and they are fed a diet that is highly deficient in iron, which helps to lighten the color of their flesh. They are also removed from their mothers before they are fully weaned, because a milk diet also promotes the development of a less tender, red–colored flesh.

Dairy cattle are raised for their milk, which is a nutritious fluid rich in sugar, protein, and fat. Dairy cattle are usually kept under relatively confined conditions, although when the weather is suitable they are usually allowed to forage in local pastures. Cow milk can be drunk directly by humans (after pasteurization to kill bacterial pathogens that may be present), or used to manufacture butter, cream, cheese, or other foods. When their milk production starts to decline significantly as they age, dairy cows are typically slaughtered for their meat.

Sheep and goats

Domestic sheep and goats are horned species of livestock that are commonly raised around the world.

The domestic sheep (*Ovis aries*) is an ancient domesticated species, probably native to southern Europe, the Middle East, and North Africa. However, the domestic sheep has been widely kept as livestock for thousands of years, and its exact lineage is not known. Sheep are very hardy animals in alpine, boreal, and temperate climates, and they are most commonly cultivated for their wool, meat (known as mutton), hides, and milk. Sheep are usually kept in relatively open pastures, where they forage on grasses and other herbaceous plants.

Many varieties of sheep have been bred to suit particular climates, or to yield particular types of products. Probably the most widely–cultivated variety is the Merino sheep, which is commonly raised for its fine wool, and is well suited to relatively dry climates. This variety is the most common sheep raised in Australia, which is the world's leading producer of sheep and their products.

The domestic goat (*Capra hircus*) is descended from wild goats of the mountains of Asia Minor. The domestic goat is a very hardy animal, capable of finding forage in seemingly barren and arid places, and is resistant to many types of diseases. Goats are primarily raised for their meat, milk, and hides.

There are numerous varieties of domesticated goats. The Swiss or alpine goat is a common breed which is often raised for its milk, which can be consumed directly, or used to make butter or cheese. The Kashmir and angora goats are long–haired varieties that

are raised for their long "wool," which can be woven into warm, soft garments.

The yak (*Poephagus grunniens*) is a sheep–like animal that is kept as livestock on highland plateaus of the Himalayas of Asia. This animal is a source of an extremely fine wool, as well as hides, meat, and milk. The related musk-ox (*Ovibos moschatus*) is a minor species of livestock that is in the initial stages of domestication for its extremely light and fine wool and its gamey meat.

Pigs

The domestic pig or boar (*Sus scrofa*) is derived from the wild boar of Eurasia. The pig is an ancient domesticate, and has been cultivated for thousands of years, from the tropics to the temperate zone. Pigs are raised mostly as a source of meat. Pigs are an extremely productive type of livestock because they have large litters (as many as 12 babies at a time), and they are quite efficient in converting their feed into body growth.

There are many varieties of pigs, adapted for various climates, cultural conditions, and uses. The white Yorkshire is a commonly cultivated, light–colored, rapidly growing variety, with erect ears.

Horse and donkey

The domestic horse (*Equus caballus*) is descended from the wild horse of the steppes of Eurasia. Horses are mostly used for riding and as draft animals, and they are also eaten in many countries.

There are many varieties of horses. The Arabian horse has been bred for great speed, and is the most common type of riding and racing horse. Although quite fleet, this breed does not have great endurance, and cannot maintain a fast pace for very long. Other horses, such as the hackney and the American standard, have been bred to haul lightweight carriages and racing harnesses. Horses bred for use as draft animals to pull large wagons or plows are much larger, and include the Clydesdale, Percheron, and Belgian breeds.

The domestic donkey (*Equus asinus*) is derived from the wild ass of Africa. This animal is mostly used for riding and as a beast of burden, but it is also eaten and used as a source of milk. The mule is a hybrid cross between a male donkey and a female horse, and is highly prized as a draft and riding animal. However, mules are infertile, and the only way to produce them is to keep crossing horses and donkeys.

Camels and llamas

The dromedary, or Arabian one–humped camel (*Camelus dromedarius*) is a species native to the deserts of either or both Asia and northern Africa, although today it only occurs in domestication. This species has a single, large, fatty hump on its back, and it can tolerate extremely dry conditions. Dromedaries are used as pack and riding animals, and as sources of meat, milk, and hides.

The bactrian camel (*Camelus bactrianus*) is a species native to central Asia, where some wild herds still roam the desert. The bactrian camel is distinguished by the two, large, fatty humps on its back, and its shaggy pelage. This animal is commonly kept for riding and carrying cargo, and as a source of meat, milk, and leather.

The llamas are closely related to the camels, but they are smaller and do not have humps. Llamas are found in the highland plateaus and pampas of South America. There are two wild species, the guanaco or huanaco (*Llama huanacos*) and the vicuna (*L. vicugna*). The domesticated llama is believed to have been derived from the guanaco. These animals are ridden and used as beasts of burden, and they also produce other useful products. A variety known as the alpaca produces an especially fine, highly prized wool.

Buffaloes

The water buffalo (*Bubalus bubalis*), also known as the old–world buffalo or domestic buffalo, is a common species of livestock in tropical countries. The water buffalo is commonly used as a draft animal, particularly for plowing wet fields, for example, in the cultivation of paddy rice. This species is also utilized for its meat, and for milk.

The bison or American buffalo (*Bison bison*) is also kept as livestock, although this is a relatively recent phenomenon, and the species is not as yet intensively domesticated. Bison are generally reared on ranches, and are utilized mostly for their meat and hide.

Deer

The reindeer (*Rangifer tarandus*) has long been herded by northern peoples of Eurasia, such as the Lapps of Scandinavia. This animal is mostly raised for its meat, milk, and hides. In recent years, a strong market has developed for the antlers of reindeer, especially when they are still covered with fur, that is, are "in velvet." These antlers are sold to countries in eastern Asia,

especially China and Korea, where they are powdered and used as an ingredient in traditional medicines.

Various other species of deer are being increasingly kept as livestock, often on so–called "game ranches." Most commonly kept in this way are the American elk or wapiti (*Cervus canadensis*) and the Eurasian red deer (*C. elaphus*). Both of these species of deer can be considered as being in the early stages of domestication, and they may be more important as livestock in the future.

Rabbits

The domestic rabbit (*Oryctolagus cuniculus*) has been derived from the old–world or European rabbit. The domestic rabbit is mostly raised as a source of meat, and for its fur, although the latter is of relatively poor quality.

Fowl

By far, the most abundant species of cultivated fowl is the chicken (*Gallus gallus*), derived from the red jungle fowl of the tropical forests of south and southeastern Asia. The chicken has been domesticated for thousands of years, and may today be the world's most abundant bird, albeit in cultivation. Billions of chickens are eaten each year by people around the world, as are even larger numbers of chicken eggs.

Several species of ducks have been domesticated for agricultural purposes. The most commonly cultivated duck is derived from the mallard (*Anas platyrhynchos*), which was domesticated in China about two thousand years ago. Domesticated mallards are usually white in color, and are sometimes called Peking ducks. The muscovy duck (*Cairina moschata*) is less common, and was domesticated by South Americans prior to the European colonization of the Americas.

Two commonly raised species of domesticated goose are derived from the greyleg goose (*Anser anser*) of Eurasia. This goose may have been domesticated about four thousand years ago, and it now occurs in various agricultural races, most of which are white in color. A less common, domesticated species is the swan goose (*A. cygnoides*).

The common turkey (*Meleagris gallopavo*), native to North America and Mexico, was first domesticated by indigenous peoples of Mexico, long before the Spanish conquest. Domestic turkeys are typically white, although some varieties are black. Domestic turkeys are raised for their meat, and for this reason have been selected to have large breast muscles.

Other birds raised as food include the domestic pigeon (*Columba livia*), and the domestic Guinea fowl (*Numida meleagris*), among others.

The welfare of livestock

In modern times, livestock is raised using various systems of husbandry, which can vary greatly in their intensity of management. The oldest, and most simple systems commonly involve animals that are locally free–ranging, and are penned in large fenced areas, or return to their designated shelters in each evening. Whenever these animals are required as food, for milking, or to sell for cash, individual or small numbers of animals are killed or taken to the market, while the breeding nucleus remains conserved. Raising livestock in these relatively simple ways is common in subsistence agricultural systems, especially as practiced in poorer regions of the world.

Of course, systems used in modern, industrial agriculture involve much more intensive management of livestock than is practiced by subsistence farmers. Animals raised on so–called "factory farms" are typically bred with great attention to breeding lineages, commonly using artificial insemination to control the stud line, and embryo implantation to control the maternal lineage.

Industrial farms also keep their animals indoors much or all of the time, usually under quite crowded conditions. The animals are fed a carefully designed diet that is designed to optimize their growth rates. The disposal of sewage wastes is a major problem on factory farms, and animals commonly are kept in rather unsanitary, crowded conditions, standing in fecal materials and urine. Along with the social stresses of crowding, this makes the livestock susceptible to diseases and infections. Close attention must be paid to the health of the animals on industrial farms, and regular inoculations and treatments with antibiotics may be required.

The intensively managed systems by which livestock are raised in industrial agriculture are criticized by ethicists, who complain about the morality of forcing animals such as cows, pigs, and chickens to live under unnatural and difficult conditions.

Serious environmental damage is also associated with many types of industrial husbandry of livestock. For example, serious ecological damage may be caused by the disposal of sewage and other wastes, and by the use of pesticides and other cultural practices to grow

the enormous quantities of fodder required as food by the livestock.

The ethical and environmental dimensions of modern systems of raising livestock are increasingly becoming important issues in the debate concerning the relationships of humans with other species, and with ecosystems more broadly.

KEY TERMS

Domestication—The breeding of an animal or plant species to develop varieties that are compatible with living with humans, either under cultivation, or as pets.

Draft animal—A large animal that is used to pull a load, often hitched to a wheeled vehicle, or used to plow a field.

Husbandry—The science of propagating and raising domestic animals, especially in agriculture.

Mutualism—A mutually beneficial relationship between species.

Sentience—This refers to the ability of an animal to sense aspects of its environment, and to have a conscious awareness.

Symbiosis—An intimate biological relationship, in which different species interact in some meaningful way.

Further Reading:

Blatz , C.V., ed. *Ethics in Agriculture*. Bozeman Idaho: Idaho University Press, 1991.

Cole, D.J.A. and G.C. Brander. *Bioindustrial Ecosystems*. New York: Elsevier, 1986.

Curtis, S. *Environmental Management in Animal Agriculture*. Ames Iowa: Iowa State University Press, 1994.

Francis, C.A., C.B. Flora, and L.D. King, eds. *Sustainable Agriculture in the Humid Tropics*. New York: Wiley and Sons, 1990.

Grzimek, B., ed. *Grzimek's Encyclopedia of Mammals*. London: McGraw Hill, 1990.

Paradiso, J.L., ed. *Mammals of the World, 2nd ed.* Baltimaore, Maryland: John Hopkins Press, 1968.

Wilson, D.E. and D. Reeder (comp.). *Mammal Species of the World*. Washington, DC: Smithsonian Institution Press, 1993.

Bill Freedman

Llamas see **Camels**

Lobsters

Lobsters are large crustaceans in the order Decapoda, which also includes about 10,000 species of crayfish, crabs, and shrimps. Decapods are characterized by having their carapace fused with their thoracic segments to form a gill chamber above the places where the legs join the body, and the first three of their eight pairs of thoracic legs being modified into grasping, clawlike structures known as maxillipeds.

There are two major groups of lobsters: the typical lobsters, in the infra order Astacidea, and the spiny lobsters, in the infra order Palinura.

The true lobsters, and the closely related crayfish, have their three pairs of maxillipeds developed as chelae, or large pincer-like claws used for catching and handling food. The first pair of claws is especially large. These animals also have well-developed uropods, a paired appendage that arises from the last segment of the body, and forms a major part of the tail fan. The spiny lobsters are not chelate (that is, they do not have large foreclaws), and their third maxilliped resembles a leg.

Biology and ecology of lobsters

The exoskeleton of living lobsters is greenish-black in color, but turns red if the animals are boiled in water or steamed, as when they are prepared as a meal for humans. Like many crustaceans, lobsters do not have a terminal moult — they appear to keep growing until they die an accidental death, are predated, or develop a fatal disease. The largest of the typical lobsters can exceed 44 lb (20 kg) in weight, more than half of which is made up of their enormous foreclaws.

Both groups of lobsters are scavengers of dead animals of all types, detecting the presence of food of this type using their well–developed sense of smell. Both types of lobsters, but particularly the typical lobsters, are also predators of a diverse range of other invertebrates, including cannibalism of other lobsters. The typical lobsters are very effective predators, because of their large, powerful claws, which can crush and cut even seemingly well–protected prey.

Lobsters are most active at night. During the day they typically hide in burrows or cavities in rock piles, which they enter by backing in. Lobsters can crawl in all directions, but when they are foraging they mostly proceed in a forward direction. Smaller lobsters can swim jerkily, by rapidly back–flipping their tail fan.

An American lobster.

Lobster reproduction

Typical male lobsters will deposit packets of sperm on the underside of the female. The female will later use the sperm to fertilize her eggs as they are laid. The female can store the sperm for as long as several months, waiting for the egg–laying season, which typically occurs during July and August. Females breed every two years.

Female lobsters carry their eggs (known as "berries") beneath their abdomen, attached to structures called spinnerets. The number of eggs is related to the size of the female, and typically it will carry about 5,000 eggs for a 10 in (25 cm) long female, and 40,000 for a 14 in (36 cm) long animal. However, one 17 in (43 cm) long female had 63,000 eggs, and another slightly larger one had 97,000.

The egg masses are periodically waved on their spinnerets to ensure their access to clean, well–oxygenated water. Female lobsters carry their eggs for 10–11 months. Hatchling lobsters are planktonic and commonly disperse quite widely with water currents. After their fifth molt, when they are about 1 in (2.5 cm) long, the young lobsters go to the bottom and begin the relatively sedentary existence that they have for the rest of their lives. Lobsters are extremely vulnerable to the vagaries of drift and predation when they are in their planktonic stage, and when they are sedentary but small. This is the reason for the enormous reproductive output of these animals.

Species of lobsters

There are several species of typical lobsters, and a larger number of spiny lobsters. The economically important species native to North American waters are briefly described below.

The northern or East Coast lobster (*Homarus americanus*) is an abundant and widespread species of the Atlantic coast of North America, ranging as far north as Labrador, Canada to as far south as Virginia, in the United States. This species occurs most abundantly on rocky bottoms, and it ranges over the entire continental shelf, and even in some of the deeper waters of the continental slope. Individual animals can reach quite large, formidable sizes. Some humungous animals caught in relatively deep places on the continental slope have exceeded 3 ft (1 m) in length and 44 lb (20 kg) in weight. These venerable individuals are probably more than 100 years old.

The European lobster (*Homarus vulgaris*) is a closely related species, occurring in temperate waters of western Europe. This species is considerably smaller than the American lobster.

The Norwegian lobster or scampi *(Nephrops norvegicus)* is an even smaller lobster that ranges from the Norwegian coast to the Adriatic coast in the eastern Mediterranean Sea.

There are two species of spiny lobsters in North America. The West Coast spiny lobster (*Panulirus interruptus*) occurs on the west coast, and the Caribbean spiny lobster (*P. argus*) occurs in the Caribbean Sea, off the Florida Coast, and in the Gulf of Mexico. These warm–water species do not have the huge, crushing, and tearing claws of the *Homarus* typical lobsters, but they have a needle–sharp, spiny carapace, and very long antennae.

Lobsters and people

Lobsters are commonly captured as a food for humans, and their "fishery" is economically important in places where these crustaceans are abundant. For example, lobsters caught in the waters off New England in the United States or eastern Canada are more likely to be eaten in an expensive restaurant in New York, London, Paris, or Hong Kong, than in a local eatery. Lobsters are so valuable that they are routinely shipped by air freight across the world to wealthy markets — entire jets may be chartered at certain times of year—for example, around Christmas—when there is great demand for these animals in France and elsewhere in western Europe.

Lobsters are most commonly caught using traps of various sorts. In general, the traps are baited with a piece of fish, and there are several entrance holes through which hungry lobsters can enter the trap, but cannot exit. Alternatively, lobsters are sometimes caught by scuba divers, or by snorkeling in shallow, warm waters.

However, it is quite easy to over–harvest lobsters, resulting in the degradation of the resource, and a loss of economic opportunity. Fortunately, systems have been developed to limit the rate of harvesting of lobster populations, so that harvests can be sustained over the longer term. These systems require monitoring of stock sizes, and setting and implementing appropriate catch limits by regulating the numbers and sizes of animals that can be taken each year.

Recent research has also been targeted to working out systems by which lobsters can be cultivated. Lobster "ranching" would likely involve capturing pregnant females, and growing their young offspring in captivity, to be harvested when they reach a marketable size.

Domestication of lobsters is more complex, and would involve keeping carefully selected breeding stock, and periodically spawning these mature animals to produce progeny that could be reared under conditions optimized for their growth. Eventually, controlled breeding could lead to the development of breeding stock that was genetically optimized for docility, growth rates, ease of spawning, resistance to disease, and other desirable traits.

So far, however, cultivation systems for lobsters are not well developed, and virtually all harvesting is done from wild stocks of these animals.

Ships in the Miraflores locks on the Panama canal.

Further Reading:

Bliss, D.E. *Shrimps, Lobsters, and Crabs.* Washington, DC: Columbia University Press, 1990.

Herrick, F.H. 1909. *Natural History of the American lobster.* Bulletin of the Bureau of Fisheries, 29 (1909): 148–408.

Schram, D.F. *The Crustacea.* Oxford, United Kingdom: Oxford University Press, 1986.

Waddy, S.L. and D.E. Aiken. *Cold–Water Aquaculture in Canada.* A.D. Boghen (ed.). Moncton, New Brunswick: Institute for Research on Regional Development, 1995.

Bill Freedman

Lock

A lock or water lock is an enclosed, rectangular chamber with gates at each end, within which water is raised or lowered to allow boats or ships to overcome differences in water level. Locks have a history of over 2,000 years, and although they are most often used by boats on canals, they also are used to transport massive ships between seas. All locks operate on the simple buoyancy principle that any vessel, no matter what size, will float atop a large enough volume of water. By raising or lowering the level of a body of water, the vessel itself goes up or down accordingly. Locks are used to connect two bodies of water that are at different ground levels as well as to "walk" a vessel up or down a river's more turbulent parts. This is done by a series of connecting or "staircase" locks. Locks contributed significantly to the Industrial Revolution by making possible the interconnection of canals and rivers, thus broadening commerce. They still play a major role in today's industrial society.

History

The ancestor of the modern lock is the *flash lock*, also called a navigation weir or stanch. It originated in China and is believed to have been used as early as 50 B.C. The flash lock was a navigable gap in a masonry dam or weir that could be opened or closed by a single wooden gate. Opening the gate or sluice very quickly would release a sudden surge of water that was supposed to assist a vessel downstream through shallow water. This was often very dangerous. Using the flash lock to go upstream was usually safe but extremely slow since the gap in the dam was used to winch or drag a vessel through.

At some point, what now seems to be a very obvious improvement was made, and a second gate was added to the flash lock, thus giving birth to the *pound lock*. The first known example of a pound lock (whose dual gates "impound" or capture the water) is in China in 984 A.D. Supposedly built by Chiao Wei–Yo on the West River section of the Grand Canal near Huai–yin, it consisted of two flash locks about 250 ft (76.2 m) apart. By raising or lowering guillotine gates at each end, water was captured or released. The space between the two gates thus acted as an equalizing chamber that elevated or lowered a vessel to meet the next water level. This new method was entirely controllable and had none of the hazards and surges of the old flash lock.

Although a primitive form of lock was used in Belgium as early as 1180, the first pound lock in Europe was built at Vreeswijk, Holland in 1373. Like its Chinese ancestor, it also had guillotine or up–and–down gates. The pound lock system spread quickly throughout Europe during the next century and was eventually replaced by an improved system that formed the basis of the modern lock system. During the 15th century, the multi–talented Italian artist, Leonardo da Vinci

(1452–1519), served the Duke of Milan as engineer and devised an improved form of pound lock whose gates formed a V–shape when closed. In 1487, da Vinci built six locks with gates of this type. These gates turned on hinges, like doors, and when closed they formed a vee shape pointing upstream—thus giving them their name of *miter gates*. da Vinci realized that one great advantage of miter gates is that they were self–sealing by the pressure of the water (since they point upstream). Also when there is a difference in water level between one side and the other, the pressure holding the gates together is at its greatest. Most of the great canals of Europe use locks. In France, the Briare Canal, completed in 1642, included 40 locks, one series of which was a staircase of six locks that handled a fall of 65 ft (20 m). The famous Canal du Midi that leads to the Mediterranean was finished in 1692 and used 26 locks to surmount the 206–foot (61 m) difference from Garonne to Toulouse. It then descended 620 ft (189 m) through 74 locks. The first lock in England was built in 1566, but it was not until 1783 that a lock was completed in North America at Lake St. Francis in Canada.

Construction and operation

The earliest locks were built entirely of wood, with stone and then brick becoming standard materials. The gates themselves were always wooden, with some lasting as long as 50 years. Filling or emptying these early locks was often accomplished by hand–operated sluices built in the gates. On later and larger locks, it was found that conduits or culverts built into the lock wall itself were not only more efficient but let the water enter in a smoother, more controlled manner. Nearly all locks operate in the following manner: (1) A vessel going downstream to shallower water enters a lock with the front gate closed. (2) The rear gate is then closed and the water level in the lock is lowered by opening a valve. The vessel goes down as the water escapes. (3) When the water level inside the lock is as low as that downstream, the front gate is opened and the vessel continues on its way. To go upstream, the process is reversed, with the water level being raised inside the lock. What the operators always strive for is to fill or empty the lock in the fastest time possible with a minimum of turbulence. In modern locks, concrete and steel have replaced wood and brick, and hydraulic power or electricity is used to open and close the gates and side sluices. Movable gates are the most important part of a lock, and they must be strong enough to withstand the water pressure arising from the often great difference in water levels. They are mostly a variation of da Vinci's miter gates, except now they usually are designed to be stored inside the lock's wall recesses.

KEY TERMS

Flash lock—A simple wooden gate that was placed across a moving body of water to hold it back until it had become deep; the sudden withdrawal of which would cause a "flash" of water downstream that would carry a boat over the shallows below.

Guillotine gate—An early wooden gate on a lock that was operated by being raised or lowered.

Miter gate—An improved type of lock gate that turns on hinges, like a door, and meets to form a vee pointing upstream.

Pound lock—A name for an early form of two-gate lock in which a chamber is enclosed at either end by vertically–rising gates and into which water is admitted or released to change its water level and allow a vessel to do the same.

Staircase lock—Two or more locks sharing a common gate that form a series of water steps and allow a vessel to negotiate a steep rise.

Probably the best known locks in the world are those used in the Panama Canal—the most–used canal in the world. Completed in 1914, the Panama Canal is an interoceanic waterway 51 miles (82 km) long that connects the Atlantic and Pacific Oceans through the Isthmus of Panama. It has three major sets of locks, each of which is built in tandem to allow vessels to move in either direction, like a separated, two–way street. Each lock gate has two leaves, 65 ft (20 m) wide by 7ft (2 m) thick, set on hinges. The gates range in height from 47–82 ft (14–25 m), and are powered by large motors built in the lock walls. The chambers are 1,000 ft (305 m) long, 110 ft (33.6 m) wide, and 41 ft (12.5 m) deep. Most large vessels are towed through the locks. As with all locks today, they are operated from a control tower and use visual signals and radio communications. Any future major changes or improvements in the canal or its locks must consider the fact that ocean–going vessels are simply becoming too large to pass through. The future may see the construction of a sea–level canal 10 miles (16 km) west of the existing canal. If so, it, like the Suez Canal, will contain no locks of any kind.

See also Canal.

Further Reading:

De Bono, Edward. *Eureka! An Illustrated History of Inventions From the Wheel to the Computer.* London: Thames and Hudson, 1974.

Paget–Tomlinson, Edward. *The Illustrated History of Canal & River Navigations.* Sheffield, England: Sheffield Academic Press, 1993.

Leonard C. Bruno

Lock and key

A lock is a mechanical device for securing a door, chest, or other receptacle so that it can only be opened by an authorized person. Most locks are opened by a key which is placed in the lock and turned. Combination locks do not use a key but rather have a cylinder that is turned to certain stops. Today, many hotels use special plastic cards with magnetic strips as keys which cause a door to open electronically when inserted in a slot near the doorknob.

History

The lock originated in the Near East, and the earliest known lock to be operated by a key was the Egyptian lock. Possibly 4,000 years old, this large wooden lock was found in the ruins of the palace of Khorsabad near Nineveh, the ancient capital of Assyria. The Egyptian lock is also known as the pin–tumbler type, and it evolved as a practical solution to the problem of how to open a barred door from the outside. The first and simplest locks were probably just a bar of wood or a bolt across a door. To open it from the outside, a hand–size opening was made in the door. This evolved into a much smaller hole into which a long wooden or metal prodder was inserted to lift up the bar or bolt. The Egyptians improved this device by putting wooden pegs in the lock that fell into holes in a bolt, which meant that the bolt could not be moved until the pegs were lifted out. This was done by giving the long wooden key some corresponding pins that lifted out the pegs from the holes in the bolt so it could be drawn back. These locks were up to 2 ft (61 cm) long and their keys were long, wooden bars resembling a toothpick. It was this invention of tumblers — small, movable wooden pegs that fell by their own weight into the bolt — that would eventually form the basis of modern type of locks.

The ancient Romans built the first metal locks, and their iron locks and bronze keys are easily recognizable even today. They improved the Egyptian model by adding wards — projections or obstructions inside the lock — that the key must bypass in order to work. Besides these warded locks, the Romans also invented the portable padlock with a U–shaped bolt which is known to have been invented independently by the Chinese. Some Roman locks used springs to hold the tumblers in place, and the Romans made locks small enough that they could wear tiny keys on their fingers like rings. In medieval times, locks and keys changed little in design, with most of the effort directed at making them more elaborate and beautiful. It was during this time that lock–making became a skilled trade, and although there were some design changes, like a pivoted tumbler and more complicated wards, medieval locks are characterized mainly by their high degree of lavish embellishment. Despite this high level of medieval craftsmanship, these medieval locks did not provide a great deal of security against the determined and skilled thief, and even with especially elaborate warding systems, they were still relatively easy to pick or open.

Modern locks

The modern age of the lock and key is usually said to have begun in 1778 in England when Robert Barron first patented his double–acting tumbler lock. Also called the multiple tumbler, this ingenious design was a major advance in lock security and established the principle of all lever locks. Barron's new lock had two tumblers, which are really levers, that had to be raised to exactly the right height for the lock to open. Unless a properly notched key was used to raise each tumbler, the lock would not open. His lock could still be picked by a determined individual however, and in 1818 Jeremiah Chubb was able to improve Barron's lock by adding a "convict–defying detector." This was a spring or a special lever that was activated if any tumbler was raised too high. The lock would then jam, both preventing the bolt from releasing and showing the owner that the lock had been tampered with. Real lock security was not achieved however until English engineer Joseph Bramah (1748–1814) first introduced his pick–proof lock in 1784, after Barron's lock but before Chubb. Bramah's lock was exhibited in his shop window with a sign offering a substantial sum to anyone who could pick it. The offer outlived Bramah whose lock remained unopened for over 50 years until a skilled American mechanic finally picked it open after 51 hours of effort. Bramah's 4 in (10 cm), hand made, iron padlock was impervious because of its extreme complexity, and he soon found that he could not produce enough locks to meet the growing demand by using traditional methods. His locks used a notched diaphragm plate and a number of spring–loaded radial slides that were pushed down by a notched key until they matched the notches on the diaphragm. Producing such precision instruments on a large scale necessitated precision machine tools, and with the help of English engineer Henry Maudslay (1771–1831), Bramah produced a series of machines that were among the first machine tools designed for mass production. Thus the simple lock and key were at the forefront of a revolution in manufacturing, heralding the standardization and interchangeability of parts and division of labor that would characterize modern methods of mass production.

By the mid–19th century, the lock industry was in full flower and was attempting to meet the growing demands of an economy spurred by the Industrial Revolution. In 1861, the American inventor Linus Yale, Jr. (1821–1868) produced the Yale cylinder lock which was based on the pin–tumbler mechanism of the ancient Egyptians. This type of lock is still the most common type used today, and it uses a small, flat key whose serrated edges raise five pins in the cylinder to proper heights and make it possible to turn the cylinder. Varying the lengths of these five pins combined with other slight internal changes, allowed for millions of possible combinations, meaning that practically no two notched keys are alike. In an odd twist on conventional wisdom, it could be said that Yale took advantage of mass production methods to manufacture unidentical articles, since he made each set of lock and key slightly different from the one before it. While still not infallible, Yale cylinder locks are quite difficult to pick and offer reasonable security under ordinary circumstances. This style of lock and key is the most familiar and the most generally used to secure the outside doors of buildings and automobiles.

Keyless combination locks have been known since the 16th century. They contain a series of rings or tumblers threaded on a spindle which must be turned from the outside in such a way that all the rings line up. These rings usually have numbers or letters on them, and if a lock has three rings with 100 numbers on each, there are approximately one million possible combinations, only one of which will open the lock. Combination locks have no keyholes in which to pry or insert explosives, and they became popular for safes and vaults. They are often used in conjunction with time–lock devices, preventing a safe or door from being opened during certain hours even if the correct combination is used.

Altogether, today's mechanical locks are variations of the three basic types of locks: the early Bramah lever, the Yale cylinder, and the combination lock. Sometimes a single lock may combine some features of each, such as a Finnish combination lock whose rings must be

KEY TERMS

Combination Lock — One which is operated by a rotating dial by which certain numbers or letters in a particular order, after a given number of turns in the prescribed direction, are brought opposite the setting mark, after which the lock can be opened.

Cylinder — The part of a cylinder lock that provides the security. It consists of a short cylindrical plug containing the key hole and mechanism, adjustable by the key.

Spindle — The shaft of a knob or handle usually square which passes through the follower to enable the handle, when turned, to operate the spring bolt.

Tumbler — A part to retain the bolt or provide security in certain locks. In England, this part is called a "lever."

Ward — A fixed projection in a lock to prevent a key from entering or turning, unless it is properly shaped.

moved to the proper position by a the turn of a key. In the United States in the 1970s, electronic locks that worked on the same principle as the touch–tone phone became popular. When the correct sequence of spring–loaded buttons was pushed, the door would open. This system used no keys, proved to be as tamper–proof as any traditional combination lock, and allowed the touch–tone sequence to be changed at any time. Magnetism has also been used to operate a Yale–type lock. These locks had keys with no serrations but rather contained several small magnets. Insertion of the key allowed its magnets to repel magnetized spring–loaded pins inside the lock which were raised to open it. The newest lock and key systems do not use anything recognizable as a traditional lock or key. Increasingly, today's hotels are switching to special plastic cards with magnetic strips on them. Like a key, they are inserted but only momentarily into a slot usually just above the doorknob. Often a small green light flickers after withdrawal, and the door opens if the doorknob is turned. These cards open the door using electronic systems.

Locks and keys may change considerably over time, but the universal human need to keep other people away from one's possessions will remain as important to future generations as it did to the ancient Egyptians.

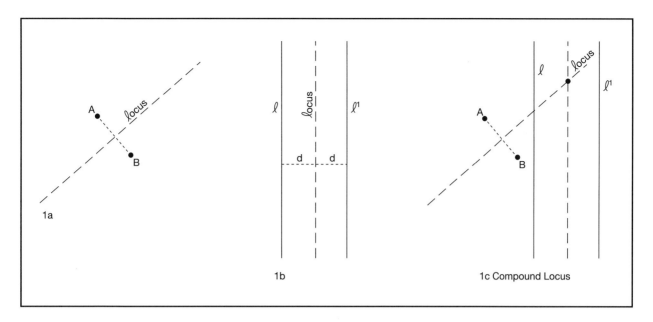

1a

1b

1c Compound Locus

Figure 1.

Further Reading:

Eras, Vincent J. M. *Locks and Keys Throughout the Ages.* Schiedam: Interbook International, 1975.

Hennessy, Thomas F. *Early Locks and Lockmakers of America.* Des Plaines, IL: Nickerson & Collins Pub. Co., 1976.

Hobbs, A. C. *The Construction of Locks.* West Orange, New Jersey: A. Saifer, 1982.

Roper, C. A. *The Complete Book of Locks & Locksmithing.* Blue Ridge Summit, PA: G/L Tab Books, 1990.

Leonard C. Bruno

Lockjaw see **Tetanus**

Locus

A locus is a set of points that contains all the points, and only the points, that satisfy the condition, or conditions, required to describe a geometric figure. The word *locus* is Latin for place or location. A locus may also be defined as the path traced out by a point in motion, as it moves according to a stated set of conditions, since all the points on the path satisfy the stated conditions. Thus, the phrases "locus of a point" and "locus of points" are often interchangeable. A locus may be rather simple and appear to be obvious from the stated condition. Examples of loci (plural for locus) include points, lines, and surfaces. The locus of points in a plane that are equidistant from two given points is the straight line that is perpendicular to and passes through the center of the line segment connecting the two points (see figure 1a).

The locus of points in a plane that are equidistant from each of two parallel lines is a third line parallel to and centered between the two parallel lines (see figure 1b). The locus of points in a plane that are all the same distance r from a single point a circle with radius r. Given the same condition, not confined to a plane but to three–dimensional space, the locus is the surface of a sphere with radius r. However, not every set of conditions leads to an immediately recognizable geometric object.

To find a locus, given a stated set of conditions, first find a number of points that satisfy the conditions. Then, "guess" at the locus by fitting a smooth line, or lines, through the points. Give an accurate description of the guess, then prove that it is correct. To prove that a guess is correct, it is necessary to prove that the points of the locus and the points of the guess coincide. That is, the figure guessed must contain all the points of the locus and no points that are not in the locus. Thus, it is necessary to show that (1) every point of the figure is in the locus and (2) every point in the locus is a point of the figure, or every point not on the figure is not in the locus.

Compound loci

In some cases, a locus may be defined by more that one distinct set of conditions. In this case the locus is

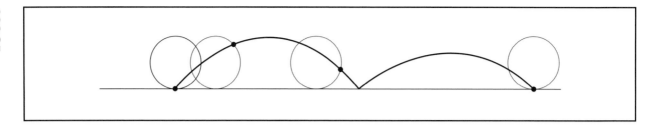

Figure 2.

called a compound locus, and corresponds to the intersection of two or more loci. For example, the locus of points that are equidistant from two given points and also equidistant from two given parallel lines (see figure 1c), is a single point. That point lies at the intersection of two lines, one line containing those points equidistant from the two points, and one line containing all those points equidistant from the parallel lines.

Applications

There are many other interesting loci, for example the cycloid (see figure 2).

The cycloid is the locus of a point on a circle as the circle rolls in a straight line along a flat surface. The cycloid is the path that a falling body takes on a windy day in order to reach the ground in the shortest possible time. Some interesting loci can be described by using the moving point definition of locus. For example, consider the simple mechanism in figure 3.

It has a pencil at point A, pivots at points B and C and point D is able to slide toward and away from point C. When point D slides back and forth, the pencil moves up and down drawing a line perpendicular to the

base (a line through C and D). More complicated devices are capable of tracing figures while simultaneously enlarging or reducing them.

See also Circle; Plane.

Further Reading:

Fuller, Gordon, and Dalton Tarwater. *Analytic Geometry.* 6th ed. Reading, MA: Addison Wesley, 1986.
Gowar, Norman. *An Invitation to Mathematics.* New York: Oxford University Press, 1979.
Smith, Stanley A., Charles W. Nelson, Roberta K. Koss, Mervin L. Keedy, and Marvin L. Bittinger. *Addison Wesley Informal Geometry.* Reading, MA: Addison Wesley, 1992.
Thomas, George B., Jr., and Ross L. Finney. *Elements of Calculus and Analytic Geometry.* 6th ed. Reading, MA: Addison Wesley, 1989.

J. R. Maddocks

Locusts see **Grasshoppers**

Lodestone see **Magnetism**

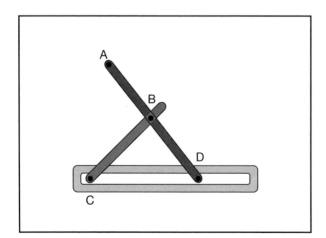

Figure 3.

KEY TERMS

Conic section—A conic section is a figure that results from the intersection of a right circular cone with a plane . The conic sections are the circle, ellipse, parabola, and hyperbola.

Line—A line is a collection of points. A line has length, but no width or thickness.

Plane—A plane is also a collection of points. It has length and width, but no thickness.

Point—In geometric terms a point is a location. It has no size associated with it, no length, width, or thickness.

Right circular cone—The surface that results from rotating two intersecting lines in a circle about an axis that is at a right angle to the circle of rotation.

TABLE 1. MAJOR LAWS OF LOGARITHMS

I $\log_b (xy) = \log_b x + \log_b y$	$b^n \bullet b^m = b^{n+m}$
II $\log_b (x/y) = \log_b x - \log_b y$	$b^n / b^m = b^{n-m}$
III $\log_b x^y = y \bullet \log_b x$	$(b^n)^m = b^{(nm)}$
IV $\log_b x = (\log_b a)(\log_a x)$	If $x = b^r$; $b = a^p$, then $x = a^{pr}$
V $\log_b b^n = n$	If $b^n = b^m$, then $n = m$
VI $\log 1 = 0$ (any base)	$b^0 = 1$

Logarithms

A logarithm is an exponent. The logarithm (to the base 10) of 100 is 2 because $10^2 = 100$. This can be abbreviated $\log_{10} 100 = 2$.

Because logarithms are exponents, they have an intimate connection with exponential functions and with the laws of exponents.

The basic relationship is $b^x = y$ if and only if $x = \log_b y$ Since $2^3 = 8$, $\log_2 8 = 3$. Since, according to a table of logarithms, $\log_{10} 2 = .301$, $10^{.301} = 2$.

The major laws of logarithms and the exponential laws from which they are derived are as follows:

In all these rules, the bases a and b and the arguments x and y are limited to positive numbers. The exponents m, n, p, and r and the logarithms can be positive, negative, or zero.

Because logarithms depend on the base that is being used, the base must be clearly identified. It is usually shown as a subscript. There are two exceptions. When the base is 10, the logarithm can be written without a subscript. Thus log 1000 means $\log_{10} 1000$. Logarithms with 10 as a base are called "common" or "Briggsian." The other exception is when the base is the number e (which equals 2.718282...). Such logarithms are written ln x and are called "natural" or "Napierian" logarithms.

In order to use logarithms one must be able to evaluate them. The simplest way to do this is to use a "scientific" calculator. Such a calculator will ordinarily have two keys, one marked "LOG," which will give the common logarithm of the entered number, and the other "LN," which will give the natural logarithm.

Lacking such a calculator, one can turn to the tables of common logarithms which are to be found in various handbooks or as appendices to various statistical and mathematical texts. In using such tables one must know that they contain logarithms in the range 0 to 1 only.

These are the logarithms of numbers in the range 1 to 10. If one is seeking the logarithm of a number, say 112 or .0035, outside that range, some accommodation must be made.

The easiest way to do this is to write the number in scientific notation:

$$112 = 1.12 \times 10^2$$
$$.0035 = 3.5 \times 10^{-3}$$

Then, using law I

$$\log 112 = \log 1.12 + \log 10^2$$
$$\log .0035 = \log 3.5 + \log 10^{-3}$$

Log 1.12 and log 3.5 can be found in the table. They are .0492 and .5441 respectively. Log 10^2 and log 10^{-3} are simply 2 and –3 according to law V: therefore

$$\log 112 = .0492 + 2 = 2.0492$$
$$\log .0035 = .5442 - 3 = -2.4559$$

The two parts of the resulting logarithms are called the "mantissa" and the "characteristic." The mantissa is the decimal part, and the characteristic, the integral part. Since tables of logarithms show positive mantissas only, a logarithm such as –5.8111 must be converted to .1889 – 6 before a table can be used to find the "antilogarithm," which is the name given to the number whose logarithm it is. A calculator will show the antilogarithm without such a conversion.

Tables for natural logarithms also exist. Since for natural logarithms, there is no easy way of determining the characteristic, the table will show both characteristic and mantissa. It will also cover a greater range of numbers, perhaps 0 to 1000 or more. An alternative is a table of common logarithms, converting them to natural logarithms with the formula (from law IV) $\ln x = 2.30285 \bullet \log x$

Logarithms are used for a variety of purposes. One significant use—the use for which they were first invented—is to simplify calculations. Laws I and II enable one to multiply or divide numbers by adding or subtracting their logarithms. When numbers have a

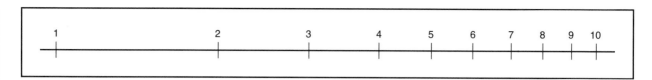

Logarithmic scale.

large number of digits, adding or subtracting is usually easier. Law III enables one to raise a number to a power by multiplying its logarithm. This is a much simpler operation than doing the exponentiation, especially if the exponent is not 0, 1, or 2.

At one time logarithms were widely used for computation. Astronomers relied on them for the extensive computations their work requires. Engineers did a majority of their computations with slide rules, which are mechanical devices for adding and subtracting logarithms or, using log–log scales, for multiplying them. Modern electronic calculators have displaced slide rules and tables for computational purposes—they are quicker and far more precise—but an understanding of the properties of logarithms remains a valuable tool for anyone who uses numbers extensively.

If one draws a scale on which logarithms go up by uniform steps, the antilogarithms will crowd closer and closer together as their size increases.

They do this in a very systematic way. On a logarithmic scale, as this is called, equal intervals correspond to equal ratios. The interval between 1 and 2, for example, is the same length as the interval between 4 and 8.

Logarithmic scales are used for many purposes. The pH scale used to measure acidity and the decibel scale used to measure loudness are both logarithmic scales (that is, they are the logarithms of the acidity and loudness). As such, they stretch out the scale where the acidity or loudness is weak (and small variations noticeable) and compress it where it is strong (where big variations are needed for a noticeable effect). Another example of the advantage of a logarithmic scale can be seen in a scale which a sociologist might construct. If he were to draw an ordinary graph of family incomes, an increase of a dollar an hour in the minimum wage would seem to be of the same importance as a dollar–an–hour increase in the income of a corporation executive earning a half million dollars a year. Yet such an increase would be of far greater importance to the family whose earner or earners were working at the minimum–wage level. A logarithmic scale, where equal intervals reflect equal ratios rather than equal differences, would show this.

Logarithmic functions also show up as the inverses of exponential functions. If $P = ke^t$, where k is a constant, represents population as a function of time, then $t = K + \ln P$, where $K = -\ln k$, also a constant, represents time as a function of population. A demographer wanting to know how long it would take for the population to grow to a certain size would find the logarithmic form of the relationship the more useful one.

Because of this relationship logarithms are also used to solve exponental equations, such as $3 - = 2x$ as or $4e\ k = 15$.

The invention of logarithms is attributed to John Napier, a Scottish mathematician who lived from 1550 to 1617. The logarithms he invented, however, were not the simple logarithms we use today (his logarithms were not what are now called "Napierian"), Shortly after Napier published his work, Briggs, an English mathematician met with him and together they worked out logarithms that much more closely resemble the common logarithms that we use today. Neither Napier nor Briggs related logarithms to exponents, however. They were invented before exponents were in use.

See also E (number); Exponent.

Further Reading:

Eves, Howard. *An Introduction to the History of Mathematics.* New York: Holt, Rinehart and Winston, 1976.
Finney, Thomas, Demana, and Waits. *Calculus: Graphical, Numerical, Algebraic.* Reading Mass.: Addison Wesley Publishing Co., 1994.

KEY TERMS

Characteristic—The integral part of a logarithm.

Logarithm—An exponent. If $a = b^c$, c is the logarithm to the base b of a.

Logarithmic function—A function of the form $y = K + \log_b x$.

Logarithmic scale—A scale in which the logarithms of the numbers are uniformly spaced.

Mantissa—The decimal part of a logarithm.

Hodgman, Charles D., Editor. C. R. C. Standard Mathematical Tables. Cleveland: Chemical Rubber Publishing Co, 1959.

Turnbull, Herbert Westren. "The Great Mathematicians" in *The World of Mathematics*, Newman, James R., Editor. New York: Simon and Schuster, 1956.

J. Paul Moulton

Long–legged jumping marsupials see
Marsupial rats and mice

The arctic loon or black-throated diver (*Gavia arctica*).

Loons

Loons are the only surviving members of an ancient order of birds, the Gaviiformes, which has a fossil record extending back to the Lower Cretaceous, more than 100 million years ago. Loons comprise their own family, the Gaviidae, which consists of 12 extinct and 5 surviving (extant) species. All of the extant species of loons live in the Northern Hemisphere, where they breed on lakes and ponds, from the northern part of the temperate zone to the high Arctic, and winter on marine waters, near the shore, mostly in temperate or low–subarctic climates. All of the loons have, to varying degrees, a Holarctic distribution, meaning that they occur throughout most of the Northern Hemisphere, in both Eurasia and North America. In Eurasia loons are called divers.

All loons have a heavy, waterproof plumage, generally blackish or grayish above and white below. During the breeding season, the above–water plumage can be strikingly marked in a species–specific fashion, but the sexes are not distinct. During winter, the plumage is much more plainly countershaded (that is, dark above and white below). Loons are strong, direct flyers, and are capable of daily long–distance trips between feeding and nesting habitats, as well as of longer seasonal migrations during which they may travel more than 3,100 mi (5,000 km). However, because they are heavy birds with relatively small wings, loons must run briefly over the surface of the water in order to gain enough speed to become airborne (with the exception of the relatively small, red–throated loon, which can take off directly). During the feather molt, loons cannot fly at all. Usually, for safety, the molt is carried out on large bodies of water.

Loons are excellent swimmers, propelling themselves with large webbed feet, located relatively far to the rear of the body in order to make swimming more efficient. To some degree, loons use their wings while swimming, but underwater the wings are used mostly for steering. Because of the rearward placement of their legs, loons are very clumsy and almost immobile on land. Consequently, their nests are placed close to the shoreline, preferably on an island or islet, and not elevated much above the surface of the water. Loons typically lay two eggs in a crude nest—essentially a scrape—and both sexes participate in incubation and rearing of the young. Loon hatchlings can swim almost immediately, but it takes almost two months before they are capable of flying. While they are small, the babies often roost within the back feathers of a parent. Loons typically mature at three years of age. Immature birds stay on salt water until they are ready to breed.

Loons mostly eat small fish, which they seize underwater with their bills. Loons may also consume frogs and larger species of aquatic crustaceans and insects, especially if they are breeding on fishless ponds. However, in such situations loons may also travel from the breeding pond to the ocean or to a larger lake with fish in search of food.

Loons are known for their extraordinarily haunting and resonant calls and wails, which may be heard while they are flying or while they are on the water. In addition, they often engage in spectacular courtship and territorial displays while running over the water, sometimes while calling. Loons do not call during winter.

The red–throated loon (or red–throated diver, *Gavia stellata*) has a wide, Holarctic distribution, breeding on Arctic and subarctic lakes and ponds in both Eurasia and North America, as far north as the limit of land on the high Arctic islands and Greenland.

It is the smallest loon, and the only one capable of taking off directly from water and from land. Consequently, the red–throated loon can breed on smaller ponds than any other species of loon.

The Arctic loon (black–throated diver, *G. arctica*) is found in eastern Eurasia and western Alaska, and is closely related to the Pacific loon (*G. pacifica*), which occurs in northern North America. In fact, until recently these were considered to be a single, holarctic species, under *G. arctica*.

Common loons (great northern diver, *G. immer*) breed in subarctic and northern temperate regions of North America, as far south as the Great Lakes region. The common and yellow–billed loons tend to replace each other geographically and ecologically, with little overlap in their distributions. Yellow–billed loons (white–billed diver, *G. adamsii*) are more common in Eurasia, especially Siberia, and in northwestern North America.

In the past, loons have been killed by humans in some areas because they were viewed as important competitors for fish. Loons have sometimes been hunted for their feathers and skins, but are rarely eaten because of the strong, fishy taste of their flesh. Today, loons are threatened by oil spills in their oceanic wintering habitat, by deforestation and other habitat damage in the surroundings and edges of breeding lakes, by cottage development and motorboats, and by the effects of acid rain. Acid rain can acidify lakes and ponds in the northern breeding ranges of loons, causing these bodies of waters to lose their fish populations and exposing the birds to toxic elements such as mercury, cadmium, and aluminum.

Further Reading:

Godfrey, W. E. *The Birds of Canada.* Toronto: University of Toronto Press, 1986.

Harrison, C. J. O., ed. *Bird Families of the World.* New York: H. N. Abrams, 1978.

McIntyre, J. W. *The Common Loon: Spirit of the Northern Lakes.* Minneapolis: University of Minnesota Press, 1988.

Bill Freedman

Loran

LORAN (Long Range Navigation) is a radio–based navigational aid first used during World War II to locate ships and planes with greater accuracy than could be achieved with conventional techniques. LORAN determines location by comparing accurately–synchronized powerful radio pulses originating from different reference transmitter sites. Pulses from nearby transmitters arrive earlier than pulses from distant transmitters since radio signals travel at a constant speed.

At least three different LORAN signals must be received to determine latitude and longitude. In practice, the distance to more than the minimum three LORAN signals increases accuracy.

The first LORAN systems were in use before computers were sophisticated enough to perform the complex calculations needed to process the timing comparisons. Early LORAN installations required highly-skilled operators to interpret the radio pulses. A half century later technical innovations eliminated the need for much of the skill once required to use LORAN for navigation.

LORAN has evolved through three distinct phases, LORAN A, LORAN B, and the present version, LORAN C. The A and B versions were designed for navigational assistance over relatively (short distances). LORAN A and LORAN B transmissions operated in a range of frequencies just slightly higher than the standard AM broadcast band in the United States. The present version, LORAN C, is assigned to 100 kHz, a frequency well below the AM standard broadcast band. 100 kHz, a frequency where long–distance radio propagation is very dependable. In contrast to LORAN A and LORAN B, LORAN C is reliable over distances of many hundreds of miles.

The principle of LORAN

The phenomenal accuracy of LORAN is possible because radio signals travel at a constant known speed. Each coordinated LORAN transmitter sends out a continuous succession of sharp radio pulses. If the LORAN receiver is equidistant from two transmitters, the pulses will be coincident. If the pulses from one station are received earlier than the pulses from the other station, the difference in the time of arrival of the two pulses contains information about the difference in distance to the two transmitters.

Radio signals travel a distance of almost exactly 984 feet (300 m) a microsecond. If a LORAN receiver measures a 100–microsecond time delay between pulses from two identified transmitters, the receiver is somewhere along a line corresponding to all the locations that are 9,843 feet (30,000 m) closer to the station transmitting the pulses received first than to the other transmitter site. That is, the receiver is not necessarily located 9,843 feet from the closest station, but it is 9,843 feet closer to this station than to the other station. If pulses from a different pair of stations is measured, with at least one signal source not involved in the first measurement, the difference in the distance to these new transmitter sites can be determined similarly. If this second comparison reveals that one of these transmitter sites is 16,405 feet (50,000 m) closer than the other, the LORAN receiver will be along a different line where the difference in distance equals 16,405 feet. The coordinates of the point where these two lines cross satisfy both measurement pairs. A third pair of signals must be measured to remove a final ambiguity.

Interpreting LORAN measurements

Early LORAN operation required the use of a previously–prepared map, covered with curved lines that corresponded to various distance differences from sets of received signal sources. The early LORAN devices indicated which map lines to use, the operator found the point on the map where the lines intersected to learn the location.

The latest versions of LORAN C receivers no longer require the use of a special map to determine location. These updated units contain a more sophisticated computer that calculates longitude and latitude directly, displaying in a format that does not need interpretation.

The LORAN C receiver automatically tunes first one then another and another of as many LORAN signals that can be received well enough to provide good data. After a short calculation delay the latitude and longitude is displayed.

As an illustration of the great locating accuracy achieved by LORAN C systems, commercial fishers sometimes use LORAN C when looking for buoys marking submerged crab traps left unattended in the open ocean.

Sources of LORAN measurement error

There is a limit to the accuracy with which the relative timing of radio pulses can be measured. For greater precision, pulses need to have a very steep wavefront. That is, they must start very quickly. Pulses with steep wavefronts must have a high harmonic content, and this means that the transmitted signals will have sideband components far to either side of the assigned frequency. The LORAN signals must be confined within a fairly–narrow band of frequencies to avoid interference with other services, and this limitation blurs the defini-

<table><tr><td colspan="2">KEY TERMS</td></tr></table>

100 kHz—100,000 Hz, radio–frequency with a 3–kilometer wavelength.

AM—Amplitude Modulation.

Coincident—Events timed to have a constant time difference.

GPS—Global Positioning Satellite.

Latitude—Number of degrees north or south of the earth's equator.

Longitude—Number of degrees east or west of the earth's prime meridian.

Microsecond—One-millionth part of a second.

Pulse—Signal that rises to a peak abruptly, with a steep waterfront.

Synchronized—Occurring with the same frequency.

tion of the start of each pulse. The result is a compromise in the accuracy of measurements of pulse timing.

There is less variation in the radio–signal propagation path taken by LORAN C signals at 100 kHz, but there are path variations that cannot be measured. The effect is to further reduce the quality of the information available to the LORAN computer. These effects are small, but they nevertheless set a limit on the available precision of navigation information that can be obtained from LORAN techniques.

After LORAN C

A relatively–new development in electronically-supported navigation systems, the Global Position Satellite system, seems destined to replace LORAN C. During the years from 1978 through 1995 the United States launched more than two dozen specialized navigational satellites that each orbit the earth twice every day. These satellites transmit data that permits even portable handheld receivers and decoders to display latitude and longitude with great accuracy. The Global Positioning Satellite system provides better information than can be achieved using LORAN so it seems likely that the GPS system will soon render the LORAN system obsolete. LORAN will somebody be found only in the history of electronics–based navigational systems but it will have served the world well for better than a half century.

Further Reading:

The 1995 ARRL Handbook, The American Radio Relay League. 1995.

Now You're Talking, The American Radio Relay League. 1994.

Jacobs, George and Theodore J. Cohen. *The Shortwave Propagation Handbook.* Cowan Publishing Corp., 1970.

Stix, Gary, "Aging Airways," *Scientific American,* (May 1994).

Walker, Paul F., "Precision–guided Weapons," *Scientific American,* (August 1981).

Donald Beaty

Lorises

The loris or bushbaby family, Lorisidae, includes 14 species of Asian and African primates. Loris is a Dutch word for clown, given to these amusing creatures by European seaman who first saw them. With the lemurs, these attractive little primates make up the group called prosimians, or "pre–monkeys." All lemurs are found on the big island of Madagascar; other members of the loris family can be found elsewhere. Unlike the lemurs, the lorisids have no or little tail.

The family is divided into two subfamilies—the Lorisinae, including the slow–moving pottos and lorises, and the Galaginae, the quick–moving galagos. The galagos, or bushbabies, are limited to Africa, but the lorises and the pottos have expanded into India and southeast Asia.

All of these tree–living primates are nocturnal, active in nighttime. This fact keeps them from competing with the monkeys with which they share their habitat. Therefore, the monkeys are asleep when the lorisids are active. Like other prosimians, they have a reflective layer, called the tapetum lucidum, in back of the retina of the eye. This allows them to see when there is very little light. It also makes their eyes shine in the dark, like a cat's eye.

Like the lemurs, but not like the related tarsiers, lorisids have rhinariums, which are rough–skinned, moist noses indicating that scent is very important in their lives. They mark their paths for other lorises as they move throughout their range by wetting their hands and feet in urine. They apparently prefer to stay alone in their territories except during breeding season.

Lorisids have front bottom teeth that point forward, forming a dental comb used in grooming and feeding. Underneath the tongue is a hard structure with points that are used to clean the dental comb. Lorisids can also groom their soft fur with the toilet claw. This is a special claw located on the second toe. All other fingers and toes bear flat nails. This does not mean that they have trouble climbing, however. Their feet bear a single opposable big, or first, toe that allows them to grasp branches tightly. This grasping ability allows the lorisids to hang securely upside down, dangling from their hind feet while they eat with their hands, or perhaps just being playful. The lorisids diet includes fruit, insects, and the oozing gum of trees.

Lorisids range in size from the tiny dwarf bushbaby *(Galago demidovii)* at 2.1 oz (60 g) to the plump potto *(Perodicticus potto),* which may reach more than 2 lb (1 kg). Though it is not known how long these primates live in the wild, they have been known to reach 12, even 14 years in captivity.

Lorises, slow and not so slow

Lorises move in very deliberate fashion, with none of the free–wheeling abandon of many other primates. Moving among the branches of trees at night is serious business. They make sure that one hand is well anchored before moving the next one. They also make the movements with incredible smoothness, disturbing nothing around them. This keeps them from being seen by predators as they move through the dense tree tops. They can remain absolutely motionless for many hours at a time, a technique that is very effective in staying alive. They also have to remain silent, otherwise their high–pitched twitter can reveal their presence.

A loris's opposable thumb is even more specialized than the thumbs of most primates. It has moved almost exactly opposite the last three fingers, and the first finger has almost disappeared. This arrangement is handy for a tight grip on the high branches in the forest canopies in which they live. Lorises are generally solitary creatures, though they may hunt in pairs or family groups.

The slender loris *(Loris tardigradus)* of southern India and Sri Lanka has round eyes that look larger than they are because they are set in pear–shaped patches of dark fur on their lighter–colored triangular faces. This primate is called the slender loris because its body is much thinner than the well–rounded slow loris. It has comparatively long arms and legs.

The two species called slow lorises are indeed slow, moving very carefully and deliberately among the trees. They are plumper than the slender loris. The somewhat larger slow lorises *(N. coucang)* of Southeast Asian islands Java and Borneo has a dark strip up its back and a white patch on its head and upper back. The

A slender loris (*Loris tardigradus*) in Asia.

slow loris is rapidly disappearing wherever its forest habitat is being disturbed, although it is legally protected throughout most of the countries where it lives. The pygmy slow loris (*Nycticebus pygmaeus*) of Vietnam and Laos is only about 7.5 in (19 cm) long. It is round and woolly with large, close–set eyes. It is sometimes regarded as a subspecies of slow loris.

The larger potto *(Perodicticus potto)* lives in Guinea, Zaire, and Kenya. It may weigh more than 2 lb (1 kg). Its tail is visible beyond its silky fur, unlike the slow loris's, which is not long enough to show. Also, the potto has three or four unusual skin–covered bony spines behind its neck. When threatened, the potto clings tightly to its branch, tucks in its head, and turns these spines to the attacker, which can be taken by surprise because they are hidden in the pott's dense fur. If not left alone because of its spines, a potto can curl its head under its body and give a ferocious bite. In their homelands, pottos are famed for the strength of their grip.

Pottos generally live solitary lives, but the male in an area inhabited by several females keeps track of their readiness to mate by following their urine trails. After a period of getting acquainted, they may mate while hanging upside down from a branch. They have a longer gestation period than most prosimians, 193 days. This produces a baby mature enough to cling to the moving mother almost immediately after birth.

Closely related to the potto, but inhabiting the shrubs of the forests of Gabon, Congo, and Zaire instead of the high canopy is the angwantibo, also called the golden potto *(Arctocebus calabarensis)*. The angwantibo is much smaller than the potto, about 10 in (25 cm), as opposed to about 14 in (36 cm), and it lacks the tail and the neck spines. Even from birth the golden potto exhibits its skill in clinging upside down. The mother "parks" her infant upside down on a branch while she goes about her nocturnal eating. When she returns, she anchors herself around the baby, also upside down. The baby releases itself from the branch and clings right side up to her stomach. A mother angwantibo continues to nurse one infant until just before the next one is born.

Galagos or bushbabies

Unlike the other lorisids, galagos or bushbabies as they are called because of their infant-like mewing sound and sheer cuteness, reside in the lower levels of the forest. The Galaginae are known for the swiftness of their movements, which lets them capture flying insects as they zip past in midair. The commotion they make while leaping may be deliberate in that it sends disturbed insects into flight. Many jumps have been spotted as long as 15 ft (4.6 m).

Unlike most bushbabies, Allen's bushbaby, *Galago alleni,* eats on the ground, where it listens for rustling insects with large, mobile ears. The ears of a galago are so important that they can fold, like an accordion, when the little animal is moving through prickly or otherwise dangerous leaves.

Galagos have longer legs compared to arms than any other primate. This allows them to make vertical leaps, from tree to tree, farther than most other primates. The tips of the fingers are broadened into soft pads that help them cling to branches. Their bushy tails are used to balance them during leaping. Galagos, like the other lorisids, mark their trails through the forest with urine, which they deposit directly into the bottom of one foot while standing on the other. When they hunt at night, they communicate with a variety of sounds. Then, at dawn, they gather and locate a communal sleeping hole, where they spend the daytime hours.

Mother bushbabies usually give birth to twins, which she carries in her mouth for the first two weeks. When she leaves to eat, she parks them securely on a wide branch. A female galago, her infants, and older female offspring occupy a specific territory which they

KEY TERMS

Binocular—Using two eyes set so that their fields of vision overlap, giving the ability to perceive depth.

Dental comb—A formation of lower incisor teeth that have moved close together and horizontally to make a grooming tool.

Diurnal—Active in or related to daytime.

Opposable—If a thumb or big toe, positioned opposite the other digits, thus providing a good grip on a branch.

Rhinarium—The rough–skinned end of the snout, usually wet in prosimians, indicating that smell is important to them.

Tapetum lucidum—The special layer behind the retina of the eye of most nocturnal animals that reflects light in such a way as to amplify available light.

into sharp points for use in climbing tall tree trunks to reach gum–producing parts of the trees. As is common in prosimians, only the second toe still bears a toilet claw. These animals are reddish in color, fading to a gray underneath. They do not curl up in holes in trees or build nests.

The main protection that lorisids have from direct harm by humans is that they are so difficult to see. Thus they are not hunted as larger monkeys are. However, their forest habitat is readily degraded.

Further Reading:

Kerrod, Robin. *Mammals: Primates, Insect–Eaters and Baleen Whales.* Encyclopedia of the Animal World series. New York: Facts on File, 1988.

Napier, J.R., and Napier, P. H. *The Natural History of the Primates.* Cambridge, MA: The MIT Press, 1985.

Napier, Prue. *Monkeys and Apes.* A Grosset All–Color guide. New York: Grosset & Dunlap, 1972.

Peterson, Dale. *The Deluge and the Ark: A Journey into Primate Worlds.* Boston: Houghton Mifflin, 1989.

Preston–Mafham, Rod and Ken. *Primates of the World.* New York: Facts on File, 1992.

Jean F. Blashfield

Lou Gehrig's disease see **Neuromuscular diseases**

LSD see **Hallucinogen**

Luffa see **Gourd family**

Lumber see **Forestry**

protect from outsider females. Several of these female enclaves may be located within the much larger territory of one dominant male. However, that male may lose his harem to another male the following year if he cannot put up a fierce enough fight.

Some authorities place all galagos in one genus, *Galago.* Others give most of them separate genera, as shown here. The smallest galago, called the dwarf or Demidoff's galago *(Galagoides demidovii),* of East and West Africa is very much like the mouse lemur. It weighs only 2 oz (57 g). The largest is the fat–tailed galago *(Galago crassicaudatus),* which is about the size of a small cat with a very bushy tail. This species is found mostly in Africa south of the Sahara.

The lesser bushbaby *(G. senegalensis)* of the African rain forests is about 15 in (38 cm) long, including 9 in(23–cm) tail, and weighs about .66 lb (250 g). It has the amazing ability to leap straight up to a height of almost 7 ft (2.13 m). On the ground, they leap like kangaroos, using both hind legs in one movement. The greater bushbaby, *Otolemur crassicaudatus,* lives in equatorial Africa in more open land than the other bushbabies. At almost 30 in (76 cm) and weighing almost 4 lb, it is much larger.

The forest canopy of the rain forest of Gabon and Cameroon between the Niger and Zaire rivers is the habitat of the two species of strange little needle–nailed galagos *(Euoticus elegantulus).* Their nails are modified

Luminescence

Light generation by a process other than by heating is luminescence. For example, an incandescent light bulb, in which the filament is heated until it is literally white–hot, is not luminescent; a fluorescent light tube (which is cool to the touch) is luminescent. Luminescence is generated as part of a process in which a atoms or molecules with electrons excited into higher energy states shed energy by emitting visible light.

People have observed luminescence in nature for centuries. In the early 20th century, Marie Curie, in her doctoral thesis, mentioned that calcium fluoride glows when exposed to the radioactive material, radium. In the past 50 years, the use of luminescent devices, such as fluorescent lights and television screens, have become widespread.

Fluorescence and phosphorescence

Luminescence can be divided into categories by duration (fluorescence or phosphorescence) or by the mechanism that creates the light. By definition, fluorescent things stop emitting light very soon (about 10 ns) after the exciting energy is cut off. Phosphoresce continues for longer than fluorescence. Glow–in–the–dark stickers and watch hands that glow are examples of phosphorescence. A less obvious but more exact definition of the difference is that the amount of time phosphorescence continues after the material has been excited may change with temperature, but in fluorescence, this decay time does not change. Also, phosphorescence tends to occur at longer wavelengths than fluorescence.

Fluorescent dyes are included in many clothing detergents to make the clothes appear brighter. Because most organic materials fluoresce when excited by ultraviolet light, fluorescent spectroscopy is used to study organic molecules and atoms by the "fingerprint" of their light emissions: the wavelengths, lifetime, polarization, and brightness of their fluorescence.

A common uses of phosphors (phosphorescent materials) is in televisions and computer monitors: small dots of red, green, and blue phosphors are grouped together on the inner surface of a cathode–ray tube. When electrons generated in the back of the tube hit the phosphors, they absorb the energy and then emit light.

Processes that create luminescence

Other types of luminescence are defined by the source of the energy that causes the light emission. These include chemiluminescence, bioluminescence, electroluminescence, sonoluminescence, triboluminescence, and thermoluminescence.

Chemical reactions provide the energy to generate photons in chemiluminescence. These chemical reactions often involve oxygen.

Cyalume sticks are chemiluminescent: when you bend the flexible tube enough to break the barrier that separates two substances, the tube glows for several hours until the chemical reactions are completed. A method called enhanced chemiluminescent detection, developed by researchers in Paris, offers a non–radioactive way of keeping track of genes and is being used in the international Human Genome Mapping Project.

Bioluminescence is a subset of chemiluminescence in which the chemical change occurs in living things, such as fireflies. Such reactions are very efficient. They occur when a substance called a luciferin is oxidized with the aid of a catalyst called a luciferase.

Electroluminescent devices glow when a current is applied, although not because of chemical changes. In neon lamps, current causes electroluminescence of the gas in the tube. Another fun example of this is the pickle trick: if electrical contacts are connected to either end of a cucumber pickled in brine, then current passing through the ionized pickling salts glows. (It also smells very bad.) Many flat–panel displays, such as in laptop computers, are made of electroluminescent materials. (Although the most common type uses a fluorescent light to backlight a liquid–crystal mask.)

Luminescence because of electron bombardment or an electrical field is related to electroluminescence. In fluorescent lamps, current ionizes the gas in the tube, and the ions activate a fluorescent coating on the inside of the lamps. The television example mentioned above is a case of cathodoluminescence, in which the phosphor is activated by a stream of electrons.

In sonoluminescence, the light is produced from energy provided by sound waves. This mechanism is fairly unusual. Recent research into sonoluminescence suggests that in some situations, sound may be concentrated to produce extremely high energies in small areas. This energy is dispelled as light, but it may be possible to harness that energy for other uses.

In triboluminescence, friction is responsible for the light. A famous example of this is the flash of light sometimes produced by crunching wintergreen flavor Life–Savers. (Don't confuse this with sparks given off by hitting flint and steel together. Those sparks, which can ignite a fire, are incandescent bits of metal.)

Thermoluminescence

Thermoluminescence uses heat to release already–excited ions in a solid. When subjected to ultraviolet light, X–rays, or gamma rays (all of which are energetic enough to separate electrons from atoms, thus forming ions), some electrons or ions become trapped in excited states. They are prevented from decaying back to a ground state because quantum mechanics forbids the transition. Heating allows the ion to rise to a higher state that can drop back to ground state by emitting light.

Thermoluminescence can be used to measure how much radiation a material has been subjected to. It is used for dosimeters by people working around X–rays or radioactivity who need to know how much ionizing

KEY TERMS

Cathode ray tube or CRT—A display device that includes an electron gun to produce a stream of electrons, magnets to direct the electrons to specific spots on the opposite end of the tube, and phosphors on the receiving end that absorb the electrons and glow briefly.

Decay time—The length of time between when energy is introduced into a molecular system and when the system returns to equilibrium.

Fluorescence—Luminescence that stops within 10^{-5} seconds after the energy source is removed.

Incandescence—Light created by heating. Incandescence is not a luminescent process.

Phosphor—A material that absorbs energy over some period of time, then gives off light for a longer period. Commonly used in CRTs.

Wavelength—A characteristic of electromagnetic radiation, which can be described as periodic waves with a specific length between two points having the same phase. Visible light wavelengths range from about 670 nm (red) to 330 nm (violet). The shorter the wavelength, the higher the energy of the electromagnetic radiation.

made from porous silicon. If the chemical theory is correct, then the luminescent period is probably inherently short–lived and the material would not make good reusable devices. Although no one has published reports that definitely debunk one theory, the chemical theory is most popular at the moment because of the instability of porous silicon devices.

See also Fluorescence; Phosphorescence.

Further Reading:

Barkan, Joanne. *Creatures that glow.* New York: Doubleday, 1991.

Becker, Ralph. *Theory and Interpretation of Fluorescence & Phosphorescence.* New York: Wiley Interscience, 1969.

Canham, L. T. Applied Physics Letters. (1990) 57:1046.

Gundermann, K.–D. and McCapra, F. *Chemiluminescence in organic chemistry.* New York: Springer–Verlag, 1987.

Horowitz, Yigal S., ed. *Thermoluminescence and thermoluminescent dosimetry, Vol I and II.* Boca Raton, FL: CRC Press Inc., 1984.

Horsburgh, P. *Living light: exploring bioluminescence.* New York: J. Messner Publishing, 1978.

Iyer, S. S. and Xie, Y.–H. "Light Emission from Silicon." *Science* 260 (2 April, 1993):40–46.

Stepanov, B. I. *Theory of Luminescence.* London: Iliffe Books Ltd., 1968.

Yvonne Carts–Powell

radiation they have been exposed to. Thermoluminescence is also used for radioactive dating of pottery shards and for finding radioactive minerals.

Porous silicon

In the early 1990s, L. T. Canham at the Royal Signal and Radar Establishment in England reported luminescence from porous silicon. This generated great interest, because if the luminescence could be controlled, then light–emitting devices could be integrated with silicon microelectronics. Although silicon photodetectors had been made, the material had not been known to emit light before. This could lead the way to relatively inexpensive optical computers, signal–processing devices, and optical communications devices.

Debate about what process creates the light is divided: those who believe the light is emitted as part of a quantum confinement effect and those who believe that the light is the product of a chemical reaction between the silicon and oxygen. If the quantum confinement theory proves correct and the effect can be prolonged, then useful light–emitting devices could be

Lungfish

Bony fish are divided into two major groups: ray–finned and fleshy–finned fish. The fleshy–finned fish are further subdivided into two orders: the lungfish, or Dipnoi, and the lobe–finned fish, or Crossopterygii. Although crossopterygian fish are the group that is thought to be close to the ancestors of the land vertebrates, lungfish also display many of these characteristics. In the early stages of development, lungfish resemble a frog–like amphibian, providing evidence of close association with land forms. However, despite the critical presence of lungs, other features, such as the fusion of the teeth into bony plates, and the solid union of the jaw with the skull (which does not occur in early amphibians) make such a direct link with amphibians unlikely.

Lungfish have changed little over the past 400 million years, and so might be regarded as living fossils. Three living genera of lungfish are recognized today: *Neoceratodus* in the Mary and Burnett Rivers of south-

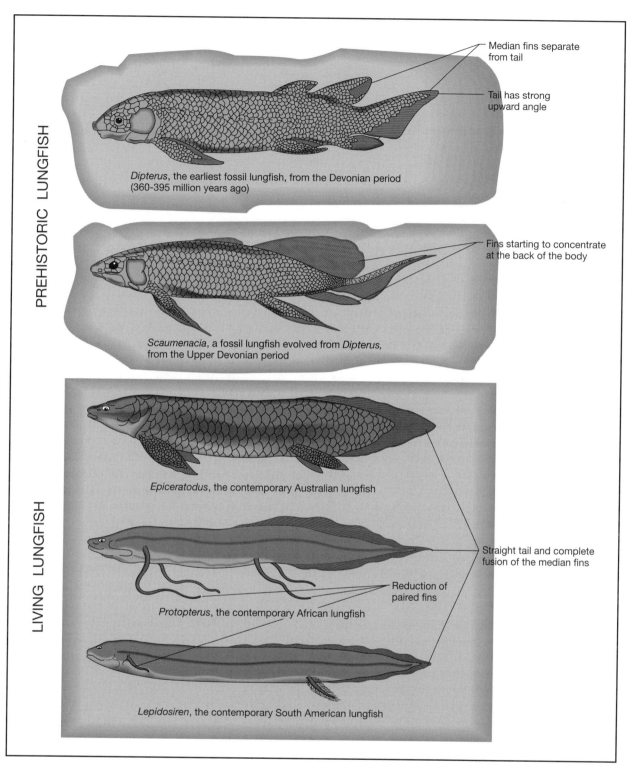

PREHISTORIC LUNGFISH

Median fins separate from tail

Tail has strong upward angle

Dipterus, the earliest fossil lungfish, from the Devonian period (360-395 million years ago)

Fins starting to concentrate at the back of the body

Scaumenacia, a fossil lungfish evolved from *Dipterus*, from the Upper Devonian period

LIVING LUNGFISH

Epiceratodus, the contemporary Australian lungfish

Straight tail and complete fusion of the median fins

Reduction of paired fins

Protopterus, the contemporary African lungfish

Lepidosiren, the contemporary South American lungfish

The evolution of lungfish.

east Queensland, Australia; *Lepidosiren* in the Paraná and Amazon River systems of South America; and *Protopterus* in sub–Saharan Africa ranging from the Nile in Sudan southward to Senegal in West Africa to the Zambezi River system in southern Africa.

African and South American lungfish

African and South American lungfish can easily be distinguished by their appearance, but they also share many similar characters. In fact, some zoogeographers have used the close link between these two lungfishes to provide supporting evidence of an early land connection between South America and Africa. Lungfish are eel–like, with a long, narrow, tubular body and small scales well embedded in the body of the fish. Both the pectoral and pelvic fins of lungfish are elongated and somewhat threadlike. In *Lepidosiren* the pelvic fins are modified to function as accessory respiratory organs, with feathery margins receiving an increased blood supply—they function like a pair of gills. The primary respiratory organs of *Lepidosiren* are a pair of lungs with a single opening on the floor of the mouth. These lungs have furrowed walls and receive a full supply of blood. The young of both species have long, feathery, external gills located behind the head which are lost in the South American lungfish at 1.6 in (4 cm) in length, and at 5.9 in (15 cm) in the African lungfish. Both South American and African species reach a length of 3.3–6.6 ft (1–2 m).

When lungfish are in water, they breathe air by rising to the surface and sticking the tips of their nasal opening and mouth out of the water, so as to empty their lungs and take in fresh air. In most fish, the nostrils are pouchlike. However, the jaw construction of the lungfish is modified so that there is a opening from the nasal sac to the inside of the mouth. This internal nostril allows the fish to breathe air at the surface without opening its mouth and swallowing water. Because lungfish breathe by lungs instead of gills, air is essential for their survival; if lungfish are forced to remain underwater, they will drown.

Lungfish live in areas with temporary water bodies, such as shallow swamps, the stagnant backwaters of river courses, and small creeks. These areas are prone to dry out during the dry season. As the water recedes, lungfish burrow into the mud, forming a hollow at the end of the tunnel. The lungfish curl up, tail over head, keeping the nostrils clear of dust and dirt, and secreting a mucous cocoon. Air enters the burrow through a small hole at the top of the dried mud. Lungfish are able to remain in a period of aestivation (dormancy) for the duration of the dry season and have been known to sur-vive as long as four years, although usually a year is all that is necessary. During the aestivation period, lungfish experience a drop in their metabolism and obtain adequate nutrition from the stored fat in their tail. Breeding takes place in the wet season following the reestablishment of the water bodies they inhabit. The male of the South American lungfish guards the eggs during the period of incubation and hatching.

Australian lungfish

The Australian lungfish is the most primitive of the modern lungfish and has changed little over the past several million years. The body is long, slim, and has very large scales, and broad, flipper–like pectoral and pelvic fins. A dorsal fin is lacking. The tail of the Australian lungfish is most unusual, and consists of a rim of fin material around the rear end of the body.

The Australian lungfish has four big teeth which look as though they have grown together into fan–shaped crushing plates somewhat resembling a rooster's comb. Prior to the discovery of the first Australian lungfish around 1869, large teeth of this type had only been found in the fossil record. These teeth are an efficient adaptation for shearing and crushing. *Neoceratodus* is a carnivorous fish, feeding on small mollusks, crustaceans, and other aquatic invertebrates. Its paddle–like fins are unsuitable for crawling; however, the lungfish can stand on these appendages, using them like legs underwater. The Australian lungfish has a single lung located above the gut which is slightly less developed than the lungs of the African and South American species.

Also known as the Burnett salmon, the Australian lungfish inhabits rivers that generally remain as permanent watercourses and do not dry out periodically, although the dissolved oxygen content does vary considerably. This lungfish uses its gills more than the other two types of lungfishes and, in well-oxygenated water, does not need to return to the surface for air. However, this species is less tolerant of poor water quality and can efficiently use its lung to breathe fresh air from the atmosphere when necessary. The Australian lungfish does not aestivate in a cocoon of mud like the African lungfish. Instead the Australian lungfish spawns in shallow water in the fall, laying its eggs on water plants. The native Australians call this lungfish *dyelleh* .

See also Bony fishes.

Further Reading:

Burton, Maurice, ed. *The New Larousse Encyclopedia of Animal Life*. New York: Bonanza Books, 1984.

Ley, Willy. *The Lungfish and the Unicorn: An Excursion into Romantic Zoology.* New York: Modern Age Books, 1941.

Mason, George F. *Animal Tails.* New York: William Morrow & Company, 1958.

Betsy A. Leonard

Lyme disease

Lyme disease (also called Lyme borreliosis) is a debilitating, chronic disease transmitted to humans by hard–shelled ticks. The most noticeable initial symptom of Lyme disease is a characteristic red rash, called an erythema chronicum, that extends outward from the site of the tick bite. If the disease is not treated early with antibiotics, the infected person will continue to experience intermittent episodes of arthritis and fever, as well as neurological symptoms.

The bacterium that causes Lyme disease, *Borrelia burgdorferi*, was identified and characterized in 1981. Although cases of Lyme disease had been reported as early as 1969, the disease came to prominence in 1975 after several rural children in Lyme, Connecticut, were stricken with the illness. Lyme disease continues to be a threat in tick–infested areas of the United States and Europe, such as woods and heavy brush. Because the disease must be caught early for effective treatment, successful recovery from Lyme disease depends on recognizing and treating the initial stages of the disease.

Characteristics and transmission

Borrelia burgdorferi is a type of spiral–shaped, flexible bacterium called a spirochete. Unlike many other bacteria, spirochetes are able to move quickly through many types of materials, by either rotating on their helical axes or by propelling forward in a straight line. This characteristic allows the bacteria to spread quickly in the human body and affect organs such as the brain and heart.

The preferred hosts of *B. burgdorferi* are wild deer that roam the rural areas of the United States and Europe. A secondary host of the bacteria are hard–shelled ticks that bite the deer and ingest the bacteria along with the deer's blood. Several species of hard–shelled ticks carry the bacteria: *Ixodes pacificus* on the west coast; *Ixodes dammini* the east coast and in the midwest; *Ixodes ricinus* in Europe; and *Amblyomma americanum*, the "Lone Star" tick, found in Texas and other southwestern states. Areas where these ticks live, therefore, are major foci of infection. In the United States, these foci include northern California, the midwest (especially Minnesota and Wisconsin), and the northeast coast from Virginia to Massachusetts. However, Lyme disease has been reported in about 30 states, as well as in Europe and Asia.

Adult ticks seldom bite humans. The young ticks, called nymphs, prefer deer mice for hosts, but will also bite humans. Nymphs are numerous in the spring and summer months. The incidence of Lyme disease is high during these months, and tapers off as colder weather sets in.

Signs and symptoms of Lyme disease

The first symptoms appear anywhere from 3–32 days after a bite from an infected tick. In this initial stage of the disease, the site of the tick bite becomes red and swollen, and a papule develops at the site. A red rash—the hallmark of Lyme disease—extends outward from the site in a circular pattern, with the papule at the center. The rash has sharply demarcated borders and may develop into bands, which gives the rash the look of a bull's–eye. The rash can be quite large, may fade and then return, or may develop on other parts of the body. Symptoms such as fever, malaise, headache, and a stiff neck may accompany the rash.

In the second stage of the disease, the bacteria begin to migrate from the tick bite site to other parts of the body. Only 5–15% of patients develop symptoms

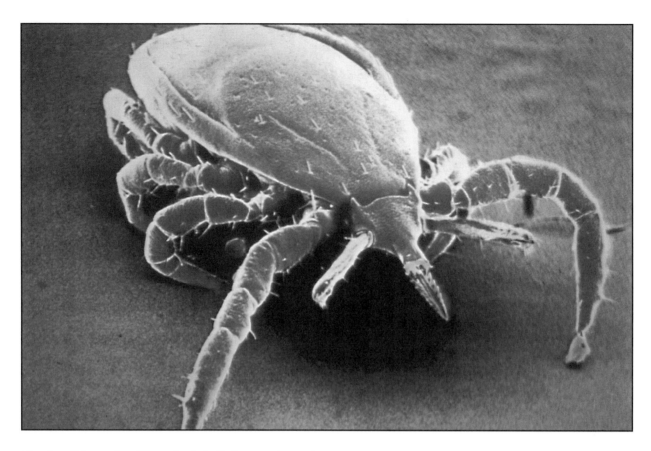

The deer tick, carrier of the spirochete that causes Lyme disease.

during this stage. Symptoms include cardiac problems, such as irregular heartbeat, and neurological problems, including facial palsy, headache, and even brain infection. These symptoms appear within a few months of the onset of the disease.

Weeks to months after the tick bite, the third stage of the disease sets in. The infected person develops arthritis; the large joints of the body, such as the knees, swell and become inflamed. The arthritis occurs in episodes and is not long–lasting. These episodes are intermittent and end without any lasting damage to the joint. Often the arthritic episodes are accompanied by flu–like symptoms, such as fever and fatigue. Other complications of the third stage of Lyme disease include serious neurological symptoms. Patients may become disoriented and experience mood, memory, and sleep disturbances. Many of the neurological symptoms resemble Alzheimer's disease. Patients may also experience loss of feeling in the arms and legs, as nerves become infected and inflamed.

Treatment

Lyme disease is treated with antibiotics. However, treatment must begin early in order to prevent progres-

sion to the later stages of the disease. If treated during the second stage of the disease, 50% of patients continue to have signs and symptoms. Treatment during the later stages of the disease is usually insufficient, because the bacteria have spread to other parts of the body. Both antibiotics and symptomatic relief are prescribed for second and third stage Lyme disease.

Prevention

Prevention centers around avoiding tick bites. Some experts recommend that in areas infested with hard–shelled ticks, particularly in states where Lyme disease is endemic, people avoid woods and heavy brush. When venturing into these areas, people should wear light–colored clothing (so that ticks can be easily seen), tuck pants legs into boots or socks, and spray clothing with insect repellant. Frequent body checks for ticks should also be performed. If a tick is found, it should be removed with tweezers. Early removal of ticks effectively prevents Lyme disease. Only 1–3% of people who find and remove a tick become infected with the bacteria. Another way to lower the risk for Lyme disease is to clear away leaves and brush from around houses and gardens.

KEY TERMS

. . . .

Chronic—Long–lasting.

Host—An organism that provides food for a parasitic organism.

Spirochete—A type of coiled, flexible, motile bacteria.

If a person contracts Lyme disease, early detection and treatment are keys to successful recovery. People who live in areas where Lyme disease is common should be familiar with the signs and symptoms of the disease, and should seek prompt medical help if infected.

See also Arthritis.

Further Reading:

Axford, John S. and David H. E. Rees, eds. *Lyme Borreliosis.* New York: Plenum Press, 1994.

Castleman, Michael. "Seasons of the Tick." *Sierra* 79 (July–August 1994): 36.

Kantor, Fred S. "Disarming Lyme Disease." *Scientific American* 271 (September 1994): 34.

Lord, Mary. "The Latest on Lyme Disease." *U.S. News and World Report* 115 (16 July 1993): 61.

Pfister, Hans–Walter, et al. "Clinical Management of Lyme Borreliosis." *The Lancet* 343 (23 April 1994): 1017.

Weber, Klausinaalter, et al. "Lyme Borreliosis: Basic Science and Clinical Aspects." *The Lancet* 343 (23 April 1994): 1013.

Kathleen Scogna

Lymphatic system

The lymphatic system is the body's network of organs, ducts, and tissues that filter harmful substances out of the fluid that surrounds body tissues. Lymphatic organs include the bone marrow, thymus, spleen, appendix, tonsils, adenoids, lymph nodes, and Peyer's patches (in the small intestine). The thymus and bone marrow are called primary lymphatic organs, because lymphocytes are produced in them. The other lymphatic organs are called secondary lymphatic organs.

Lymphocytes are a type of white blood cell (wbc), which is highly concentrated in lymphatic fluid. This clear fluid, also called lymph, travels through the lymphatic vessels, which connect the lymphatic organs. The terminal lymphatic vessels feed into the thoracic duct that returns body fluids to the heart prior to blood reoxygenation. The reincorporated fluid originates in the bloodstream, bathes organs and tissues, and is returned to the bloodstream after passing through lymphatic filters that function as part of the body's defense system against infection and cancer.

Lymph nodes, primarily clustered in the neck, armpits, and pelvic area, are the system's battle stations against infection. Lymph nodes are connected to one another by lymphatic vessels. It is in the nodes and other secondary organs where wbcs engulf and destroy debris to prevent them from reentering the bloodstream. Of the other two major secondary lymphatic organs, the spleen removes dead red blood cells (rbcs), and Peyer's patches remove intestinal antigens (foreign or harmful substances in the body).

Lymphocytes

Lymphocytes are the lymphatic system's foot soldiers. These cells identify enemy particles and attempt to destroy them. Lymphocytes fall into two general categories: T lymphocytes (T cells) and B lymphocytes (B cells). T cells form in the thymus (in the chest), and B cells form in the bone marrow of the long, thick bones of the thigh, arm, spine, or pelvis. While T cells primarily attack viral antigens, B cells attack bacterial antigens. Both T and B cells travel in lymph, through lymphatic vessels, and into lymph nodes.

T cells are further divided into three primary classes: helper T cells (T–H cells), cytotoxic T cells (ctx T cells), and T suppressor T cells. T–H cells augment B cell responses to bacterial antigens. Ctx T cells attack viral antigens and some early cancer cells. And suppressor T cells halt immune cell functions, allowing the body to rest.

B cells produce antibodies. According to their basic immunoglobulin type, antibodies are subdivided into five classes (IgM, IgD, IgG, IgE, and IgA). B cell antibodies recognize specific bacterial invaders and destroy them. Certain antibodies are more concentrated in areas of the body where they are most needed. For example, IgA–producing B cells are most concentrated in the Peyer's patches where they sample intestinal contents for potential antigens that could signal an infectious invasion of food–born bacteria.

Lymph nodes

Lymph nodes are pockets of lymph that orchestrate the removal of foreign material (including bacteria, viruses, and cancerous cells) from the lymph. They vary in size from microscopic to about 1 in (.394 cm) in diameter. Some nodes cluster at key sites where the limbs join the torso. Lymph nodes are named after their locations in the body. The nodes at the arm are called axial and brachial, those under the jaw are called subclavian, and those in the groin are called inguinal. Fibrous connective tissue covers the lymphatic tissue inside the lymph node.

Each node, also called a lymph gland, has both arterial blood supply and venous drainage. Lymphocytes drain out of the arteries into the node interior, usually through a high endothelial venule that facilitates their entry. This venule (small vein) derives its name from the higher-than-usual tightly joined endothelial cells that line it.

Before they can enter the lymph node, lymphocytes are carefully selected from other blood cells. They are recognized and distinguished by a lymphocyte-cell-surface protein called E–selectin. Receptors on the endothelial cells bind the E–selectin positive lymphocytes and slowly roll them toward a gap between adjacent cells. Then the lymphocyte is fed through this area much the way film is fed into a camera. The lymphocytes emerge on the interior of the node.

The internal lymph node tissue is separated into lobes. The lobe end at the center of the node is called the medulla, whereas the wider lobe end toward the perimeter of the node is called the cortex. The lobe area just next to the cortex is called the paracortex. Surrounding the lobes is an area called the medullary sinus. T cells are concentrated in the paracortex, whereas B cells primarily are concentrated in the cortex in structures called primary follicles. Lymphocytes first travel to the medullary sinus before migrating to the cortical and paracortical regions.

In addition to lymphocytes, several other kinds of antigen–fighting wbcs are contained within the nodes. Macrophages destroy and devour foreign antigens under direction from lymphocytes. Within the cortex, a large wbc called an interdigitating dendritic cell actually gathers the foreign antigen and presents it to the T cells that, in turn, trigger the antigen's destruction. This system is carefully controlled to avoid destroying host cells. Within the paracortex, follicular dendritic cells present antigens to B cells in a region of the follicles called the germinal centers. Within germinal centers, memory B cells are formed that are specifically primed to launch an attack against an antigen if it is encountered again. Like seasoned soldiers who know how to fight a particular enemy, memory B cells are molecularly armed to combat a known antigen.

Foreign antigens are constantly being destroyed; however, when a particularly strong infection occurs, the lymph nodes will sometimes swell with the influx of backup troops (more wbcs) sent in to help fight a particular molecular attacker. Eventually, the lymphocytes leave the node through the efferent lymphatic vessel.

Lymphatic vessels

Lymphatic vessels infiltrate tissues that are bathed in fluid released from blood into those tissues. Pockets of fluid collect in the tissues, and increased pressure allows the fluid to seep into the lymphatic vessels. Whereas blood vessels return deoxygenated blood to the heart to be pumped to the lungs for oxygen, lymphatic vessels return fluid that has leaked out of the capillaries into various tissues. However, before this lymphatic fluid is rejoined with venous fluid at the thoracic duct, it is filtered through the lymph nodes to remove infectious agents.

Lymphatic vessels are made up of single–cell epithelial layers that drain fluid away from tissue. Smooth muscles controlled by the autonomic nervous system direct the fluid away from tissues toward the lymph nodes and, eventually, the heart. The vessels contain one–way valves that close behind fluid traveling back to the heart so that lymphatic fluid cannot go backward. Lymphatic fluid is usually returned to the circulation within 24 hours. When the lymphatic vessels become clogged, stopped up, or blocked, severe edema (bloating due to water retention) can result in a condition known as lymphedema.

Other lymphatic organs

Of the remaining lymphatic system components, the thymus, bone marrow, spleen, and Peyer's patches have fairly unique roles. Both the bone marrow and thymus introduce "virgin" lymphocyte to the lymphatic system. The spleen filters old rbcs from the blood and fights infections with lymphocytes and monocytes (cells that engulf and devour antigens). And the Peyer's patches are lymph tissue pockets under raised intestinal projections that examine intestinal contents for foreign antigens. Although the spleen's role is important, the human body is capable of functioning without it if it becomes injured or diseased.

Although the thymus is critical for T cell development in children, it begins to shrink as they progress toward adulthood and thereafter plays an increasingly reduced role. T cells are "educated" in the thymus to recognize "self" versus "nonself" (foreign) antigens. Without the ability to recognize self–antigens, T cells would target a person's own tissues in a very destructive manner. The thymus is also responsible for fostering maturation of T cells into their various subclasses. T cells function in a cell-mediated way such that they only recognize antigens presented to them by other cells; hence, T cell immunity is called cell–mediated immunity.

Both T cells (before branching off to develop in the thymus) and B cells originate in the pluripotential stem cells of the bone marrow or the fetal liver. Pluripotential stem cells are the body's cellular sculpting clay. They can be shaped into any cell—including lymphocytes, rbcs, macrophages, and numerous other blood constituents—and become increasingly specialized as they reach maturity. The B cells can generate an infinite number of antibodies in response to a multitude of foreign antigens. This amazing diversity arises from the many combinations of antibody components that can be rearranged to recognize individual antigens. Once a B cell identifies a particular enemy, it undergoes a process called clonal expansion. During this process, it makes many clones (copies) of itself in order to fight several invaders of a single type. This highly sophisticated molecular process destroys infections wherever they arise in the body.

One specialized form of antibody, IgA, detects antigens in the gastrointestinal tract at Peyer's patches. IgA contained within small projections, called lamina propriae, that extend into the small intestine test the intestinal lining for pathogens. The IgA binds to the foreign antigen, returns to exit the patch at its efferent lymphatic vessel, and travels to a mesenteric lymph node that gears up to fight the invader. IgA antibodies are also passed to nursing babies in their mothers' milk, because newborns do not synthesize IgAs until later.

Lymphatic diseases

Although lymph nodes commonly enlarge to fight infection, an overwhelming infection can leave a lymph node and travel through the lymphatic system to other nodes and even to other body tissues. Cancer can spread very easily through the lymph system, but different cancers vary in how soon they attack the nodes. Lymphedema, fluid accumulation, can occur when the movement of fluid in a lymphatic region is blocked. Although lymphedema is rare, limbs are the most commonly affected areas.

The unregulated growth of cells and tissues of the lymphatic system can lead to lymphoma, or lymph cancer. Lymphomas are classified into two types, Hodgkin's or non–Hodgkin's, both of which can be malignant. Hodgkin's disease is marked by enlargement

of lymph nodes, usually those in the neck. Symptoms of Hodgkin's include chronic fatigue, depressed immune function, weight loss, night sweats, and pain after drinking alcohol. Hodgkin's is diagnosed by lymph node biopsy, with identification confirmed by the presence of Reed–Sternberg cells, large multinucleated cells. Hodgkin's is further categorized as lymphocyte predominant, nodular sclerosis, mixed cellularity, or lymphocyte–depleted on the basis of the cell populations present in the biopsy sample. Hodgkin's can be successfully treated and cured with radiation or chemotherapy if it is caught in its early stages. Although the cause of Hodgkin's is unknown, males, Caucasians, people of higher socioeconomic status, the well–educated, and people with certain blood types are more prone to develop it. Hodgkin's most often affects people in their 20s or 70s for unknown reasons. People who work with certain chemicals, such as benzene and rubber products, also seem to be more prone to develop the disease.

Non–Hodgkin's lymphoma is also diagnosed through lymph tissue biopsy. Several lymphomas have been identified, but have little in common. Burkitt's lymphoma, prevalent among Central African children, is characterized by enlargement of the lymph nodes under the jaw. In contrast with most lymphomas whose causes are unclear, Burkitt's lymphoma has been linked to infection with the Epstein–Barr virus. Mycosis fungoides is a rare T cell lymphoma that affects the skin.

Non–Hodgkin's lymphomas are further classified as lymphocytic or histiocytic. Lymphocytic lymphomas may be poorly differentiated (according to the extent to which they have evolved from the pluri potential stem cell); they may also be nodular (concentrated) or diffuse.

Symptoms for most lymphomas are similar. Many patients experience enlargement of the liver and spleen as well as the lymph nodes. Some patients have bloody stools or vomit blood. Tiredness, itching, weight loss, fever, and general immunosuppression may also be present. The symptoms may abate and intensify over several months before a diagnosis is made. Sometimes, a bone marrow biopsy is also performed. Treatment includes radiation or chemotherapy with effectiveness varying according to severity of the lymphoma at the time of diagnosis. Bone marrow transplants have been effective against some advanced-stage lymphomas. The "cure" rate for non-Hodgkin's lymphomas is generally poorer than for Hodgkin's lymphomas.

See also Antibody and antigen; Hodgkin's disease; Immune system; Infection.

Further Reading:

Alberts, B., D. Bray, J. Lewis, M. Raff, K. Roberts, and J. Watson, eds. *Molecular Biology of the Cell, 3d ed*. New York: Garland Publishing, 1994.

Rhoads, R., and R. Pflanzer, eds. *Physiology*, 2d ed. New York: Saunders College Publishing, 1992.

Louise Dickerson

Lymph nodes see **Lymphatic system**

Lynx see **Cats**

Lyrebirds

Lyrebirds are so named for the male's magnificent tail which spreads in fanlike display, resembling a lyre, an ancient Greek stringed instrument. The male's body is little longer than 12 in (30.5 cm), but the tail may longer than 16 in (40.5 cm). The only two species of lyrebird in the world are indigenous to a strip of rugged, hilly bushland along the east coast of the Australian states Victoria, New South Wales, and Queensland. The superb lyrebird (*Menura superba*) and Prince Albert lyrebird (*Menura alberti*) belong to the genus *Menura* (from the Greek meaning "mighty tail") of the suborder Oscines and the order Passeriformes (perching birds), the largest and most diverse bird order in the world. Lyrebirds have one of the most beautiful singing voices in the entire bird kingdom. But apart from their songs and unique calls, they are excellent mimics, copying perfectly not only the songs of other birds, but all types of environmental noises like chain saws, lawn mowers, tractors, human voices, and whistles.

A male superb lyre bird (*Menura superba*) in Australia. Here the bird is in the rainforest foliage though it is generally seen on the floor of the rainforest where it finds its food.

Identification and behavior

Both species have a reddish brown back, pale grey underbody, and a russet slash down the throat. Their huge feet have four long, unwebbed, clawed toes—three pointing forward and one backward. The legs are designed so that, as the bird squats, the tendons draw tight, curling the toes around the branch, holding the bird secure even while asleep. The superb lyrebird is the larger of the two species, with a more elegant tail. Females are smaller than males, their tails shorter, and they lack lyre feathers.

Normally, as with the peacock, the male's tail trails behind the body. However, when courting a mate he performs an artistic dance, spreading his tail like a fan, raising it, then swooping it over his back until his entire body and head disappear beneath a magnificent mass of silvery–plumed feathers. As he dances, he may hop from foot to foot or prance forward, sideways, and backward in a repetitive pattern, all the time singing gloriously and slipping in some mimicry. The superb male performs his dances on mounds of soft earth about 3 ft (1 m) in diameter and several inches high. Scratching, raking, and tramping with his clawed feet, he creates a clearing, forming this mound in the middle. Up to a dozen mounds may be found in one male's territory, but each male seems to have one or two favorites which he uses frequently. The Prince Albert lyrebird does not build mounds, but displays from the ground or sometimes from a log.

Often, the female does not even see the male's fascinating dance, although sometimes the superb female ventures briefly onto the mound where the male approaches her, covering her with his tail which he vibrates rapidly while singing beautifully. Sometimes their beaks may touch, but soon she leaves, scurrying off into the bush.

Reproduction

An unusual phenomenon in the bird kingdom, lyrebirds nest in winter, laying their solitary egg in June or July. The female is the nest–builder, egg–incubator, and caregiver to the hatched chicks. She constructs a bulky home from twigs, dried bracken fern, moss, leaves, and bark over a framework of thin, flexible roots and pliable bark, leaving a single side entrance, lining the entire inside with soft underfeathers which she plucks from her own body. She may snuggle her nest in a hollow on a rocky ledge, in the cavity of a tall stump, or among tree roots. In locations where humans and domestic animals pose a threat, nests may be found high in a tree between forking branches.

The egg of the superb lyrebird may vary from a light grey to a deep purplish brown with grey streaks and spots. The Prince Albert lyrebird's egg is usually grey with darker grey spots. Chicks hatch naked with their eyes closed, and stay in the nest until they are well–feathered. Their mother continues to feed them for some time after they leave the nest, which is about six weeks after hatching. Chicks in high nests take up to two weeks longer to leave the nest, allowing time for their wings to develop. Even as adults, lyrebirds are not strong flyers, jumping and flapping from ground to branch and gliding from their sleeping place high in a tree back to the ground, where they spend most of their time scratching up underbrush and digging into decaying logs in search of insects, worms, grubs, and snails. Except in national parks, these shy, wary little birds are seldom sighted, but their loud, clear voices can be heard at considerable distances. During the summer (December through February), their singing and miming is mostly confined to daybreak and dusk. As autumn approaches, they can be heard throughout the day, particularly the male, as he begins building new display mounds and repairing old ones for his upcoming courting period.

Further Reading:

Cayley, Neville W. *What Bird Is That? A Guide to the Birds of Australia.* Sydney: Angus & Robertson, 1969.

Hill, Robin. *Australian Birds.* New York: Funk & Wagnalls, 1967.

Marie L. Thompson

Lysosome see **Cell**

Macaques

Macaques are medium to large-sized monkeys native to Asia and Africa belonging to the genus *Macaca,* Family Cercopithecidae, Order Primates. Macaques are usually various shades of brown, gray or black in fur color, although golden and white color phases occur rarely. Approximately 20 species are known. Locomotion is mainly quadrupedal, and most species are terrestrial in habit, although they take readily to trees, and a few species are primarily arboreal. Body weights range from 8-40 lb (3.5 kg-18 kg) for adult males, and from 5-36 lb (2.5-16.5 kg) for females; thus they vary from the size of a small dog, such as a beagle, to a moderate-sized border collie or dalmatian. Tails in different species vary from small stub-like tails in the Barbary macaques, or Sulawesi macaques, to long graceful tails 2 ft (70 cm) in length.

The most famous macaques are the rhesus monkey of India, Nepal, and China; the Japanese monkey of Japan; the crab-eating or long-tailed macaques of Thailand, Malaysia, the Philippines, and Indonesia. All of these play an important part in the cultural history of their countries, and all are well represented in folktales, dance, drama, and religious beliefs. Also well-known in popular literature is the "Barbary ape," properly called the Barbary macaque in North Africa and Gibraltar, and the "Celebes Ape," properly called the Celebes macaque, of Sulawesi, Indonesia. Both species were incorrectly called "apes" because their small stub-tails make them appear tailless, and in the case of the Celebes macaques, their black coats give them the appearance of small chimpanzees.

Macaques have the widest geographic and ecological ranges of any nonhuman primates. Their geographic range includes Morocco and Algeria in northwest Africa, home of *Macaca sylvana,* the Barbary macaque, to the broad expanses of Asia from Afghanistan to northern China, Japan, Taiwan, Philippines, southeast Asia, and Indonesia as far east as Sulawesi and the Molucca Islands. No other group of nonhuman primates has such an extensive geographic range.

Ecologically, macaques live in a great variety of habitats from tropical rain forests of southeast Asia, to the agricultural plains of northern India, the deserts of Rajasthan, the arid mountains of Pakistan and Afghanistan, and even temperate snow-capped mountains of Japan, northern China, Nepal, and Morocco. Several species are also conspicuous commensal inhabitants of villages, temples, towns and cities in Asia, especially the rhesus monkey in India and Nepal, the Japanese monkey, and the crab-eating monkey of southeast Asia and Indonesia. One species alone, the rhesus monkey, *Macaca mulatta,* is both a close commensal associate of human populations in the crowded cities of India, and an inhabitant of cool pine forests in northern India.

The widespread ecological and geographic distribution of the macaques is a reflection of their great adaptability to different climates and habitats. Many species of macaques can tolerate wide temperature regimes, thrive on a great variety of natural or agricultural foodstuffs, and live in very different landscape settings from the mangrove forests of the Gangetic delta, to the steep slopes of the Himalaya mountains. They readily adapt to people, can survive well in urban environments if allowed to steal food, but they can also exist without humans in completely natural habitats.

In food habits, macaques are mainly vegetarian, although some species have been observed to feed on insects for a small part of their diet. In forest habitats, macaques are known to consume parts of more than 100 species of plants, primarily fruits, but also buds, young leaves, twigs, bark, and occasionally flowers, and even roots. In agricultural habitats, where macaques live in close association with people, they are notable crop raiders, feeding on field crops such as wheat, rice, and sugar cane, and on garden crops such as tomatoes, melons, bananas, papayas, and mangos. In commensal habitats such as towns, villages, temples, and roadsides, they also feed extensively on direct food handouts from people — food such as peanuts, rice, grams (a type of legume like a soybean), and even prepared foods including chapatis. In India, one study showed that a roadside group of rhesus monkeys in a populated portion of the Gangetic Basin east of New Delhi obtained 83% of its food from people, 10% from agricultural field crops, and only 7% from natural vegetation. In contrast, a forest-dwelling group near Dehra Dun obtained virtually all of its food from natural forest vegetation. Other forest-dwelling species such as the lion-tailed macaque of south India, *Macaca silenus,* obtain all of their food from natural vegetation, as do most of the Sulawesi macaques such as *Macaca nigra* and *Macaca tonkeana.* The latter, however, have taken to crop raiding recently as homesteaders and farmlands invade their natural forest habitats.

Macaques are intensely social animals, living in established social groups of just a few to several hundred individuals. A typical social group of macaques has 20-50 individuals of both sexes and all ages, consisting normally of approximately 15% adult males, 35% adult females, 20% infants, less than one year of age, and 30% juveniles 1-3 or 4 years of age. However, there is great variation in group sizes and structures.

The macaques living in temperate environments such as northern India, China, and Japan, have mating seasons, usually in the late fall (September-December), with most births occurring in the spring and early summer (late March-July). Gestation periods average around 160 days, varying from 145-186 days. Usually only one young is born at a time. Twins are rare. In different species and different populations, 30-90% of the adult females give birth to one young per year. Infant macaques are carefully cared for, nursed, and protected by the mother for many months, and weaning usually occurs 9-12 months after birth when the next infant is born. Infants are bright-eyed and active but remain in close contact with the mother for several weeks. After 6-8 weeks, they begin to explore on their own, leaving their mother briefly, beginning to play with other infants in games of wrestling and chasing. They return to their mother, however, when she shows signs of moving. They ride with her wherever she goes, at first clinging to her belly, but after several months, they often ride on her back.

After one year of age, macaques pass from infant dependency on their mother to a juvenile status, where they associate more frequently with other juveniles. This is the period of most active rough and tumble play. They become sexually mature at 3-5 years of age. Females normally stay within the social group to which they were

Rhesus monkeys, a mother and infant.

born, whereas young adult males often disperse and try to enter other social groups. This can be a time of aggressive activity, and not all males successfully enter new groups. Some may become solitary, and continue attempts to join social groups for many years. If successful adulthood is reached within a social group, macaques have a normal longevity of 20-25 or even 30 years.

The reproductive potential of some species, such as the rhesus monkey, enables populations to grow at rates of 10-15% per year if all environmental conditions are favorable. Other species, especially the forest dwelling lion-tailed macaque and some of the Sulawesi macaques, however, have much lower reproductive rates, and their populations are actually endangered.

Macaques have been subjects of great scientific interest for many years in both field and laboratory studies. Field studies have focused on their fascinating ecology, behavior, and adaptations to a wide range of habitats. Laboratory studies of behavior have involved research on intelligence, learning, social development, and communication. In research at the University of Wisconsin, and Cambridge University, England, for example, it has been shown that the maternal-infant bond is essential for normal behavioral development. Without proper mothering, young macaques fail to develop all the social and communicative skills for successful life in a social group. Some of these social deficits may be relieved with adequate peer group experience, but in any case, the overwhelming importance of the social environment is evident. Adult males do not participate in infant care, except in a few species and occasional individuals. The Barbary macaque is notable for adult males taking an active role in carrying and holding infants, and even in rhesus macaques, where infant care is normally the sole province of the mother, occasionally an adult male will show interest in holding infants. This is rare, however. Usually, fatherhood is not readily recognizable—mating behavior of most macaques is promiscuous, and a female may mate with more than one male in an estrous cycle.

Macaques have a number of basic similarities in anatomy and physiology to human beings, and for this reason they have been used extensively in biomedical research, vaccine development, and pharmaceutical testing. The rhesus monkey was the primary subject, for example, in research, development, and testing of polio vaccines and in discovering principles of human blood antigens such as the Rh factor. Rhesus have also been valuable as research subjects in cardiovascular diseases, cancer, immunology, toxicology, orthopedics, cerebral palsy, and a variety of infectious diseases. *Macaca nigra* has been important in diabetes research, and *Macaca nemestrina* in research on retroviruses and AIDS. The use of primates in biomedical research is a controversial subject, strongly opposed by animal rights groups, but generally supported as necessary and beneficial by most biomedical scientists, providing adequate safeguards are taken to assure humane treatment and proper care.

The extensive uses of macaques in biomedical research, along with habitat loss and other ecological pressures, have severely depleted the numbers of some species. Certain conservation measures have resulted in some recoveries of declining populations, however, especially of rhesus and Japanese monkeys. The rarer species of macaques, including the lion-tailed, Barbary, Formosan, Tibetan, and Celebes macaques, are seriously endangered, however, mainly because of habitat losses. Strong action on conservation protection is needed on these species, as well as on many other non-human primates.

Whenever groups of macaques are displayed in zoos they form popular exhibits with their active patterns of social interaction: grooming, maternal care, infant and juvenile play, and occasionally, adult conflict and aggression. We can often see reflections of our own personalities in their behavior. In Asia, these similarities have been encoded into rich cultural attachments, especially in Hinduism, Buddhism, and the religions of China, where macaques play an important role in religious traditions and folklore. In both India and China, for example, macaques and other primates enjoy the status of gods capable of defeating evil and restoring justice to human life. Throughout the world, macaques enrich our lives in many practical and intangible ways.

See also Monkeys; Primates; Rhesus monkeys.

Further Reading:

Lindburg, D.G. , ed. *The Macaques — Studies in Ecology, Behavior and Evolution.* New York: Van Nostrand Reinhold Co., 1980.

Napier, J.R. and P.H. *The Natural History of the Primates.* Cambridge, MA: MIT Press, 1985.

Southwick, Fa, and J., and C. eds. *Ecology and Behavior of Food-Enhanced Primate Groups.* New York: Alan R. Liss, Inc., 1988.

Charles H. Southwick

Machines, simple

A simple machine is a device for doing work that has only one part. Most authorities list six kinds of simple machines: levers, pulleys, wheels and axles, inclined planes, wedges, and screws. One can argue, however, that these six machines are not entirely different from each other. Pulleys and wheels and axles, for example, are really special kinds of levers, and wedges and screws are special kinds of inclined planes.

Levers

A lever is a simple machine that consists of a rigid bar supported at one point, known as the fulcrum. A force called the effort force is applied at one point on the lever in order to move an object, known as the resistance force, located at some other point on the lever. A common example of the lever is the crow bar used to move a heavy object such as a rock. To use the crow bar, one end is placed under the bar, which is supported at some point (the fulcrum) close to the rock. A person then applies a force at the opposite end of the crow bar to lift the rock. A lever of the type described here is a first-class lever because the fulcrum is placed between the applied force (the effort force) and the object to be moved (the resistance force).

The effectiveness of the lever as a machine depends on two factors: the forces applied at each end and the distance of each force from the fulcrum. The farther a person stands from the fulcrum, the more his or her force on the lever is magnified. Suppose that the rock to be lifted is only one foot from the fulcrum and the person trying to life the rock stands 2 yd (1.8m) from the fulcrum. Then, the person's force is magnified by a factor of six. If he or she pushes down with a force of 30 lb (13.5 kg), the object that is lifted can be as heavy as 180 (6 x 30) lb (81 kg).

Two other types of levers exist. In one, called a second-class lever, the resistance force lies between the effort force and the fulcrum. A nutcracker is an example of a second-class lever. The fulcrum in the nutcracker is at one end, where the two metal rods of the device are hinged together. The effort force is applied at the opposite ends of the rods, and the resistance force, the nuts to be cracked open, lies in the middle.

In a third-class lever, the effort force lies between the resistance force and the fulcrum. Some kinds of garden tools are examples of third-class levers. When you use a shovel, for example, you hold one end steady to act as the fulcrum, and you use your other hand to pull up on a load of dirt. The second hand is the effort force, and the dirt being picked up is the resistance force. The effort applied by your second hand lies between the resistance force (the dirt) and the fulcrum (your first hand).

Mechanical advantage

The term mechanical advantage is used to described how effectively a simple machine works. Mechanical advantage is defined as the resistance force moved divided by the effort force used. In the lever example above, for example, a person pushing with a force of 30 lb (13.5 kg) was able to move an object that weighed 180 lb (81 kg). So the mechanical advantage of the lever in that example was 180 lb divided by 30 lb, or 6.

The mechanical advantage described here is really the theoretical mechanical advantage of a machine. In actual practice, the mechanical advantage is always less than what a person might calculate. The main reason for this difference is resistance. When a person does work with a machine, there is always some resistance to that work. For example, you can calculate the theoretical mechanical advantage of a screw (a kind of simple machine) that is being forced into a piece of wood by a screwdriver. The actual mechanical advantage is much less than what is calculated because friction must be overcome in driving the screw into the wood.

Sometimes the mechanical advantage of a machine is less than one. That is, a person has to put in more

A lever being used.

force than the machine can move. Class three levers are examples of such machines. A person exerts more force on a class three lever than the lever can move. The purpose of a class three lever, therefore, is not to magnify the amount of force that can be moved, but to magnify the distance the force is being moved.

As an example of this kind of lever, imagine a person who is fishing with a long fishing rod. The person will exert a much larger force to take a fish out of the water than the fish itself weighs. The advantage of the fishing pole, however, is that it moves the fish a large distance, from the water to the boat or the shore.

Pulleys

A pulley is a simple machine consisting of a grooved wheel through which a rope runs. The pulley can be thought of as a kind of lever if one thinks of the grooved wheel as the fulcrum of the lever. Then the effort force is the force applied on one end of the pulley rope, and the resistance force is the weight that is lifted at the opposite end of the pulley rope.

In the simplest form of a pulley, the grooved wheel is attached to some immovable object, such as a ceiling or beam. When a person pulls down on one end of the pulley rope, an object at the opposite end of the rope is raised. In a fixed pulley of this design, the mechanical advantage is one. That is, a person can lift a weight equal to the force applied. The advantage of the pulley is one of direction. An object can be made to move upward or downward with such a pulley. Venetian blinds are a simple example of the fixed pulley.

In a movable pulley, one end of the pulley rope is attached to a stationary object (such as a ceiling or beam), and the grooved wheel is free to move along the rope. When a person lifts on the free end of the rope, the grooved wheel and any attached weight slides upward on the rope. The mechanical advantage of this kind of pulley is two. That is, a person can lift twice as much weight as the force applied on the free end of the pulley rope.

More complex pulley systems can also be designed. For example, one grooved wheel can be attached to a stationary object, and a second movable pulley can be attached to the pulley rope. When a person pulls on the free end of the pulley rope, a weight attached to the movable pulley can be moved upward with a mechanical advantage of two. In general, in more complicated pulley systems, the mechanical advantage of the pulley is equal to the number of ropes that hold up the weight to be lifted. Combinations of fixed and movable pulleys are also known as a block and tackle. Some blocks and tackles have mechanical advantages high enough to allow a single person to lift weights as heavy as that of an automobile.

Wheel and axle

A second variation of the lever is the simple machine known as a wheel and axle. A wheel and axle consists of two circular pieces of different sizes attached to each other. The larger circular piece is the wheel in the system, and the smaller circular piece is the axle. One of the circular pieces can be considered as the effort arm of the lever and the second, the resistance arm. The place at which the two are joined is the fulcrum of the system.

Some examples of the wheel and axle include a door knob, a screwdriver, an egg beater, a water wheel, the steering wheel of an automobile, and the crank used to raise a bucket of water from a well. When the wheel in a wheel and axle machine is turned, so is the axle, and vice versa. For example, when you turn the handle of a screwdriver, the edge that fits into the screw head turns at the same time.

The mechanical advantage of a wheel and axle machine can be found by dividing the radius of the wheel by the radius of the axle. For example, suppose that the crank on a water well turns through a radius of 2 ft (61 cm) and the radius of the axle around which the rope is wrapped is 4 in (10 cm). Then the mechanical advantage of this wheel and axle system is 2 ft divided by 4 in, or 6.

Inclined planes

An inclined plane is any sloping surface. Many people have used an inclined plane at one time or another when they tried to push a wheelbarrow or a dolly up a sloping board into a truck. One major differ-

ence between an inclined plane and a lever is that motion always takes place with the latter, but not with the former.

The primary advantage of using an inclined plane is that it takes less effort to push an object up an inclined plane than it does to lift the same object through the same vertical difference. Just compare how difficult it might be to lift a can that weighs 10 lb (4.5 kg) straight up into a truck compared to how difficult it would be to push the same can up a sloping board into the truck.

The mechanical advantage of an inclined plane can be found by dividing the length of the plane by its height. In the preceding example, suppose that the sloping board is 10 ft (3 m) long and 2 ft (61 cm) high. Then the mechanical advantage of the inclined plane would be 10 ÷ 2, or 5. A person could move the ten pound weight into the truck using a force only one-fifth as great as if the can were lifted directly into the truck.

Wedges

A wedge is an inclined plane that can be moved. Chisels, knives, hatches, carpenter's planes, and axes are all examples of a wedge. Wedges can have only one sloping plane, as in a carpenter's plane, or they can have two, as in a knife blade. The mechanical advantage of the wedge is calculated in the same way as with an inclined plane by dividing the length of the wedge by its width at the thickest edge.

Screws

A screw can be considered to be an inclined plane that has been wrapped around some central axis. You can see this relationship by making an inclined plane out of paper and then wrapping the paper around a pencil. The spiral shaped form that you make is a screw.

Screws can be used in two major ways. First, they can be used to hold things together. Some simple examples include wood and metal screws and the screws on jars and bottles and their tops. Screws can also be used to apply force on objects. The screws found in vises, presses, clamps, monkey wrenches, brace and bits, and corkscrews are some examples of this application.

The screw acts as a simple machine when an effort force is applied to the larger circumference of the screw. For example, a person might apply the effort force to a wood screw by turning a screwdriver. That force is then transmitted down the spiral part of the screw called the thread to the tip of the screw. The movement of the screw tip into the wood is the resistance force in this machine. Each complete turn of the screwdriver produces a movement of only one thread of the screw tip

KEY TERMS

Compound machine—A machine consisting of two or more simple machines.

Effort force—The force applied to a machine.

Friction—A force that acts at the boundary between two touching surfaces in opposition to some applied force.

Mechanical advantage—A mathematical measure of the amount by which a machine magnifies the force put into the machine.

Resistance force—The force exerted by a machine.

into the wood. This distance between two adjacent threads is called the pitch.

The mechanical advantage of a screw can be found by dividing the circumference of the screw by its pitch. For example, suppose that a carpenter is working with screws whose heads have a circumference of 1 in (2.54 cm) and a pitch of 1/8 in (.33 cm). Then the mechanical advantage of these screws is 1 ÷ 1/8, or 8. The carpenter magnifies his or her efforts by a factor of 8 in driving the screw into a piece of wood.

Compound machines

In many instances, the combination of two or more simple machines achieves results that cannot be achieved by a simple machine alone. Such combinations are known as compound machines. An example of a compound machine is the common garden hoe. The handle of the hoe is a lever, while the blade that cuts into the ground is a wedge. Machines with many simple machines combined with each other — such as typewriters, bicycles, and automobiles — are sometimes referred to as complex machines.

Further Reading:

Bains, Rae. *Simple Machines*. Mahwah, NJ: Troll Associates, 1985.

Hurd, Paul DeHart, and John C. Mayfield. *Everyday Problems in Science*. Glenview, IL: Scott, Foresman and Company, 1976.

James, Elizabeth. *The Simple Facts of Simple Machines*. New York: Lothrop.

O'Brien, Robert, and the Editors of LIFE. *Machines*. New York: Time Incorporated, 1964.

Sharp, Elizabeth N. *Simple Machines and How They Work*. New York: Random House, 1959.

David E. Newton

Machine tools

A machine tool is an electrically-powered tool which is used to remove material, usually metal, at a controlled rate to achieve a desired shape or finish. A machine tool typically holds the workpiece and a cutting tool, and moves either the workpiece or tool or both to provide a means of machining the material to the desired shape. Machining, another term for metalcutting, is performed by shaving away the metal in small pieces called chips. An average machining operation can reduce the original workpiece weight by approximately 50%. The modern machine tool is a precision piece of equipment designed to cut metal and produce thousands of parts to an accuracy of millionths of an inch, which is approximately equal to 1/300 of the thickness of a human hair. Machine tools range from very small bench mounted devices to large complex machines weighing hundreds of tons. The major operations performed by machine tools are milling, turning, boring, planing, shaping, drilling, power sawing, and grinding.

Milling machines

Milling machines comprise one of the largest categories of machine tools with many different varieties and configurations available. A milling machine is considered essential equipment in any machine shop because of its wide variety of machining operations and its high metal removal rates. The workpiece, mounted on a movable machine table, is fed against one or more multiple-tooth rotating tools called milling cutters, or mills. The workpiece is usually held in vises, special holding fixtures, or clamped directly to the machine table and fed at right angles to the axis of the milling cutter to produce flat, recessed, or contoured surfaces.

Classifications

Milling machines can generally be classified according to the orientation of the spindle, either vertical or horizontal. Vertical milling machines can also have what is called "multiaxis" capability where the vertical axis can tilt and swivel to enable the machining of closed angles and contoured surfaces. Vertical milling machines are extremely versatile and can machine horizontal surfaces, vertical surfaces, angular surfaces, shoulders, grooves, fillets, keyways, T-slots, dovetails, and precision holes.

Horizontal milling machines are available in plain and universal types. Plain milling machines have tables which are fixed at right angles to the knee. Universal milling machines have a table which can be pivoted in a

A lathe turns an object on a horizontal axis so it can be cut with a fixed tool.

horizontal plane. This allows the machine table to be swiveled to different angles for milling helical grooves.

The universal milling machine is widely used by maintenance machinists and toolmakers because of its versatility. Computer numerically controlled (CNC) mills or "machining centers" are available in vertical and horizontal configurations and come with automatic tool changers which can store many different tools in "carousels."

The major components of a typical milling machine include the following: base, column, knee, elevating screw, saddle, machine table, ram, head, and spindle. The base is the heavy foundation member of the machine which can also be used as a reservoir for coolant or cutting lubricant often used in machining operations. The base is a massive casting which helps to absorb and dampen vibration from the machining process. The column, which is either cast with the base or keyed and bolted on, supports the functioning members of the machine. Horizontal "ways" on top of the column support the ram and head while vertical "ways" on the column front face support the knee, saddle, and machine table. The knee moves along the vertical ways of the column and is the basic work-supporting member. The knee is equipped with ways on top to allow horizontal movement of the saddle to and from the column face. The elevating screw provides additional support for the knee and allows the knee to be raised and lowered. The saddle mounts on the ways of the knee and has horizontal ways at right angles to the knee ways to support the machine table. The machine table moves longitudinally on the ways of the saddle and supports the workpiece. Combined movements of the knee, saddle, and machine table allow for precise positioning and feeding of the workpiece left and right, in and out, and up and down. This is called "3-axis" movement (X=left

and right movement, Y= in and out movement, and Z= up and down movement). A rotary table can be added to a 3-axis mill to give it 4-axis capabilities (typically rotation is about the longitudinal or X-axis), while 5-axis mills are able to tilt and swivel about the vertical axis. The ram is mounted on the horizontal ways at the top of the column and supports the head and provides horizontal movement and positioning of the head at varying distances from the column face. The head includes the motor, stepped pulley and belt drive (or in the case of heavier duty mills, the gear drive), and the spindle. The head assembly provides for rotation of the spindle and spindle feeding along the vertical axis using a quill. The spindle contains the toolholding mount and drives the cutter.

Turning centers or lathes

Lathes are considered to be one of the oldest machine tools in existence. Lathes were typically foot-powered until water and steam power were harnessed. One of the first machines driven by Watt's steam engine was a lathe which is how it came to be known as an "engine lathe." The lathe operates by holding the workpiece in a rotating holder, usually a chuck or collet, and then a single-point cutting tool is fed into the workpiece. If the tool is fed along the axis of rotation of the workpiece, it is considered to be a "turning" operation and any desired cylindrical contour can be made. If the cylindrical contour is produced on the inside of the workpiece, the operation is called "boring." In addition to turning and boring, the lathe is also used for threading, tapping, facing, tapering, drilling, reaming, polishing, and knurling. Some typical parts a lathe may produce are pins, bolts, screws, shafts, discs, pulleys, and gear blanks. Different attachments allow a lathe to perform milling, grinding, and broaching operations. With the right combination of attachments, it is said that the lathe is the only machine tool capable of reproducing itself. The size of a lathe is given in terms of the maximum "swing" and length of bed. The swing refers to the maximum diameter of work which can be rotated in the lathe. The length of the lathe bed refers to the maximum length of the lathe ways, not the maximum distance between centers of the chuck and tailstock. Many different varieties of lathes are available ranging from the small precision lathe used for making watch parts to the extremely large lathes used in producing mill rolls and rocket casings.

Lathes can generally be classified in one of the following 5 basic groups: engine lathes, speed lathes, turret lathes, vertical lathes, and automatics. The engine lathe, sometimes referred to as a "geared-head" lathe, is the most commonly found lathe model. Speed lathes are used where the workpiece is polished or formed (e.g. spinning) rather than cut. Turret lathes have a "turret" tool changer which rotates to permit a number of different tools to be used in a certain sequence. Vertical lathes have a vertical axis of workpiece rotation rather than horizontal. Automatic lathes consist of high production turning machines such as screw machines and single or multiple spindle chucking and bar fed machines. All of the five basic lathe groups can also be found in a computer numerically controlled version, sometimes called a "turning center."

The main components of a typical engine lathe include the following: bed, headstock, feedbox, tailstock, and carriage. The bed is the base of the lathe which supports the other components. The precision ways are the part of the bed on which the carriage travels. The bed is a massive casting in order to absorb and dampen vibration from the machining process. The headstock is mounted rigidly on the bed and houses all the gearing and mechanism for the spindle drive and power takeoff source for the feedbox. Controls for selecting and changing spindle speeds are also part of the headstock. The feedbox, which may be an integral part of the headstock or a separate unit, drives both the feed rod and the lead screw for the feed rate or thread lead required. A direct mechanical connection with the spindle drive is required to provide the proper relationship for feeding or threading operations. The lead screw is a precision part and is usually only used for threading operations to avoid unnecessary wear. Most engine lathes incorporate a feed rod which is used to drive the carriage for operations other than threading. The headstock spindle supports a faceplate, chuck, or collet, which in turn holds and drives the workpiece. There are four types of standard spindles, all identified by the type of nose: threaded nose, camlock, taper nose key drive, or flanged nose. The threaded nose spindle is usually only found on smaller and less expensive lathes. The camlock type allows faster changing of faceplates or chucks. The taper nose key drive type provides greater support to the workpiece while the flanged spindle nose permits mounting of special chucks or power operated equipment and can be found on turret lathes and automatics. The tailstock is mounted on the bedways and may be positioned and clamped to support work for turning. It may also use a tool mounted in place of the tailstock center so that boring, drilling, or reaming can be done. The tailstock must be perfectly aligned with the headstock spindle in order to produce good parts. The carriage is the tool platform of the machine and supports and feeds the cutting tool over the work. The carriage consists of the cross slide which

bridges the ways to support the compound and tool post, or toolholder and the apron. The lead screw and the feed rod pass through the apron and transmit feeding power to the carriage. The main controls for positioning and feeding the tool are also located on the apron.

Boring machines

Boring machines are similar in construction to milling machines except they are generally more massive and built lower to the floor, use different tooling, and feed differently along the axis of the spindle. Boring machines are typically located in very clean, climate controlled environments and are massive for extra rigidity and vibration damping to ensure close tolerance hole sizes and locations, one example being automobile engine piston bores.

Jig boring machines are primarily intended for toolroom use and are used to produce precision dies, jigs, and gages which are used to ensure the accuracy and interchangeability of high volume production parts. There are three common designs of jig boring machines in use, the open-sided or C-frame, adjustable-rail, and fixed-bridge construction. Variations of the jig boring machine include jig grinders, which are used to realign holes after hardening, and the horizontal jig boring and milling machine, which is utilized for general production operations.

The base of the jig bore machine supports a saddle which moves in and out from the operator to the column. A table moves right or left on the saddle to complement the saddle movement. A massive column supports the spindle housing which adjusts to the work location by moving up and down the column ways. The spindle moves inside a quill which is supported by the housing or spindlehead. The quill also moves up and down inside the housing to give a telescoping mechanism which adds rigidity to the spindle. The spindle, quill, and housing are manufactured under very careful and exacting conditions to eliminate any lost motion. The housing is usually made of Invar cast iron to minimize errors due to thermal expansion. Stability of the housing is extremely critical because any expansion would change the tool location relative to the column. The spindle is hardened, ground, and lapped. Preloaded ball bearings also help to eliminate lost motion of the tool and its driving mechanism. Spindle speeds range from 30-1500 rpm on an average machine. A digital readout (DRO) system is used to provide a continuous numerical readout of the table position. Jig boring machines may also be computer numerically controlled (CNC). CNC control permits many additional jobs that would be impossible with a manually operated machine. One example would be to produce precise, irregularly curved forms to be generated on cams or master templates without operator involvement.

Planers

Planers remove metal in a series of straight cuts by reciprocating (moving back and forth) the workpiece as the single-point tool feeds. The fixed tool is rigidly supported while the workpiece moves on precision ways for the full length of the cut thus ensuring maximum accuracy. The rigidity of the tool allows the use of powerful motors, up to 150 hp, which permits higher production speeds and the use of multiple tooling with extremely heavy cuts and feeds. Planers are typically big machines used for handling the largest and heaviest work that can be supported on the machine table, as much as 75 tons (68 tonnes). Planers may be fitted with hydraulic tracing attachments to enable them to cut curved surfaces.

There are two distinct types of planers, the single-housing, or open-side planer, and the double-housing planer. Double-housing planers are the most widely used and provide the greatest tool support rigidity. The major components of a double-housing planer are the bed, table, housings, arch, cross rail, and heads (side and rail). The bed is the foundation to which the housings are attached. The bed is provided with precision ways over its entire length and supports the reciprocating table. The table supports the workpiece and reciprocates along the ways of the bed. The table is slightly less than half the length of the bed and its travel determines the dimensional capacity of the machine in length of stroke. The housings are rigid box-type columns placed on each side of the bed and table. They are heavily braced and ribbed to absorb the large cutting forces encountered in planing. The arch joins the housings at the top for greater rigidity of construction and also houses the drive mechanism for tool feeding. The cross rail is a rigid horizontal beam mounted above and across the table on the vertical ways of the columns. It supports the rail heads and provides for horizontal feeding of the cutting tools. The heads carry the cutting tools and are equipped with "clapper" blocks that lift the tools clear of the work on the return stroke of the table. Single-housing or open-side planers support the cross rail from a single column. This permits wide workpieces to overhang the table on the open side if necessary.

Planers require many strokes of the workpiece to complete a cutting operation. Horizontal and vertical mills are much more efficient at metal removal than planers and have replaced planers for production work.

Shapers

Shapers utilize a reciprocating single-point tool with the workpiece clamped on the machine table. The workpiece position and feeding are controlled to produce the desired shape or surface as the tool passes back and forth along a fixed path taking a series of straight cuts. Horizontal shapers are used for machining flat surfaces which may be horizontal, vertical, or angular. Vertical shapers or slotters are used for machining slots, keyways, and splines. Shapers may be fitted with hydraulic tracing attachments to enable them to cut curved surfaces. The size of a shaper is designated by the maximum length of stroke or cut it can take.

There are many different types of shapers but the most common is the horizontal plain shaper which consists of a bed, column, cross rail, table, ram, and the head. The bed is the rigid base of the machine which supports the column and sometimes an outrigger table support which is used to increase the rigidity of the workpiece mounting. The column houses the motor and drive mechanisms and is equipped with two sets of precision ways which support the ram and cross rail. The cross rail is a horizontal member which travels vertically on the ways of the column to be adjusted and clamped in place in the desired position. The cross rail supports the table on precision ways. The table supports the workpiece and feeds along the cross rail. The ram is the tool driving member and reciprocates on precision ways on top of the column. The length of stroke, rate of reciprocation, and overhang at the extreme end of the ram travel are all adjustable. The head, which is mounted on the forward end of the ram, supports the toolholder and provides for vertical feeding or swiveling of the tool 30° either way from vertical.

Shapers require many strokes of the tool to complete a cutting operation. Horizontal and vertical mills are much more efficient at metal removal than shapers and have replaced shapers for production work.

Drilling machines

Drilled holes are required in the manufacture of almost every product and drilling is one of the most common machining operations. Drilling machines are similar in construction to milling machines except they are used exclusively for making holes.

All drilling machines are characterized by a rotating cutting tool which advances along its axis into a stationary workpiece producing a hole. Six common operations which can be performed on a drill press are drilling, reaming, boring, counterboring, countersinking, and tapping. Drilling machine capacity is determined by the size of the largest workpiece over which the spindle can be centered, the maximum clearance under the spindle, and the maximum drill diameter which can be fed at a practical feed rate through mild steel. The five major classifications of drilling machines are uprights, radials, horizontals, turret drills, and multiple-spindle machines. Each classification represents a family of machines which is further subdivided.

Upright drills comprise the largest group and are characterized by a single vertical spindle rotating in a fixed position and supported in a modified C-frame structure. The major components of the upright drill include the base, column, spindle, motor, head, table, feed mechanism, and quill.

Radial drills are designed to accommodate large work. These machines are arranged so that the spindle can be positioned to drill anywhere within reach of the machine by means of movement provided by the head, the arm, and the rotation of the arm about the column. Some types of radials and portable horizontal machines allow the entire machine to be moved to the workpiece.

Horizontal drills are characterized by the position of the spindle. Way-type and spindle-feed horizontals are self-contained units consisting of motor drive, gearing, and spindle which may be mounted at any predetermined drill angle and are used extensively to meet high production needs.

Turret drilling machines provide a number of tools mounted in a turret designed to handle a sequence of operations. The turret drilling machine is also available as a computer numerically controlled machine.

Multiple-spindle drilling machines include those designed with fixed spindles for single-purpose production and those where the spindles are adjustable, either by means of universal joints or by traversing along a worm or spiral drive in a straight line. Multiple-spindle drilling machines are primarily used for high production rate workpieces.

Sawing machines

Sawing machines are primarily used to part material such as rough cutting excess material away before machining or cutting curved patterns in sheetmetal. Sawing machines substitute mechanical or hydraulic powered motion for arm motion to achieve the speed necessary for production operations. The cutoff operation is usually one of the first requirements in any production process before any machining, welding, or forg-ing is done. The saw blade has individual teeth which "track" through the workpiece, each tooth deepening the cut made by the preceding tooth in the direction of feed. The saw or work may be fed and by controlling the direction of feed, either straight or curved cuts can be made. The width of the cut (also known as "kerf") is approximately equal to the thickness of the saw blade and because of this saw blades are made as thin as possible but with adequate tool strength and rigidity.

There are three common types of sawing machines, reciprocating or hack saws, band saws, and circular saws. These machines all perform the same operation but vary in capability, capacity, and application. Power hacksaws use a reciprocating stroke where on the cutting stroke the saw blade teeth are forced into the metal either by gravity or hydraulic pressure while on the return stroke the pressure is automatically removed to prolong saw blade life. Most of the machines come equipped with a chip tray and a cabinet base which contains the coolant reservoir and its circulating pump. Heavy duty power hacksaws come with automatic bar feeds where the stock is loaded on a carriage which automatically moves forward the necessary distance when the cutting is finished. Hydraulic pressure automatically operates the vise jaws, gauges the material, and raises and lowers the saw blade. After being set up for cutting material to a specified length, the power hacksaw will operate automatically without need for an operator until all the material loaded on the carriage has been cut. Horizontal band saws are one of the most widely used sawing machines for cutoff operations. These band saws range from small manually operated machines to large, fully automatic production machines. Vertical band saws are also used but are primarily manually controlled machines used in tool rooms and shops for maintenance and low production work.

Band saws have several advantages over other kinds of cutoff machines. The saw blade cutting width or kerf is 1/16 in (.16 cm) compared to 1/8 in (.33 cm) for power hacksaws and abrasive disc circular saws, and 1/4 in (.64 cm) for cold saws. This can represent a sizable savings especially when cutting large or expensive material. The thinner saw blades also require less power to cut through material making them more economical to operate. Because bandsaws have endless blades (band saw blades are welded together to create an endless loop) which cut continuously, the cutting rates are much higher.

Two of the most popular circular saws are the cold saw and the abrasive disc cutoff saw. Cold saws are low rpm circular saws for metal cutting. These saws range in size from hand-operated bench-top models with 8 in (20 cm) blades to fully automatic machines with blades of 3 in (7.6 cm) diameter and larger. Light duty manual or automatic machines are sometimes equipped with a swivel head which enables cuts to be made at different angles. These saws are mostly used for cutting structural shapes such as I-beams, angles, and channel sections because the circular blades can complete their cuts with less travel than straight blades. Heavy duty machines are available with bar feeds and can be used for cutting solid bars up to 10 in (25 cm). Material larger than this size would require excessively large blade diameters, which must be more than double the cutting capacity, which would become too costly along with the machine necessary to drive them. Different speed ranges are provided for cutting metals of different hardness and toughness, and built-in coolant systems help produce better finishes and prolong blade life.

Abrasive cutoff saws utilize an abrasive disc to separate material by using a grinding action. Abrasive cutoff saws are built for either manual operation or with power feeds, with either fixed or oscillating wheel heads. Oscillating wheel heads are used when cutting thick sections of tough materials such as titanium, nickel-based superalloys, and other high alloy steels. Sizes range from small bench-top machines with 8 in (20 cm) wheels to bigger machines with 20 in (50 cm) or larger wheels. Abrasive cutoff saws are very useful for rapidly cutting small sizes of bar stock, tubing, and structural shapes and also for cutting tough or hardened materials that cannot be cut efficiently with other types of saws.

Grinding machines

There are many different types of grinding machines available which are used to obtain very close tolerances and fine finishes. Grinding machines are used for grinding flat surfaces, external and cylindrical surfaces, tapered surfaces, and irregular surfaces. Production parts are typically ground to tolerances of plus or minus .0001 in and special parts for precision instruments are ground to plus or minus .000020 in (20 microinches). All grinding machines utilize a rotating abrasive wheel or moving belt in contact with a workpiece to remove metal. Various combinations of wheel feed, either along or normal to the axis of wheel rotation, and also rotary or linear workpiece motion, are provided by the different types of grinding machines. To produce shapes of cylindrical section, workpiece and wheel both rotate on parallel axes while one or the other is fed along its own axis of rotation. Contact between workpiece and wheel is on the outside diameter of the wheel and the work is mounted between centers, chucked, or rotated without centers by a back-up wheel

(this is called "centerless" grinding). To produce flat surfaces, the workpiece is mounted on a table and traversed along a line parallel to the surface to be ground or rotated about an axis at right angles to the surface to be ground. The axis of grinding wheel rotation can either be parallel or perpendicular to the surface to be ground, applying either the side or face of the wheel. Complex shapes are routinely ground such as thread forms, cam contours, gear teeth, and cutting tool edges. The same basic devices that control motion between the cutting tool and workpiece in other machine tools are also used in grinding machines such as lead screws, cams, special fixtures and tracer mechanisms. Grinding machines have limitations as to how fast and how much material can be removed but modern manufacturing, with the help of more accurate castings and forgings, is utilizing grinders more and more for both sizing and finishing operations. Some finished parts are produced by grinding only.

The major types of grinding machines available are cylindrical grinders, internal and chucking grinders, universal grinders, centerless grinders, surface grinders, face grinders, disc grinders, and tool and cutter grinders.

See also Industrial Revolution.

Further Reading:

Habicht, Frank H. *Modern Machine Tools.* Princeton, New Jersey: D. Van Nostrand Company, Inc., 1963.

Kalpakjian, Serope. *Manufacturing Processes for Engineering Materials.* New York: Addison-Wesley Publishing Company, 1991.

Neely, John E., and Richard E. Kibbe. *Modern Materials and Manufacturing Processes.* New York: John Wiley & Sons, 1987.

Repp, Victor E., and Willard J. McCarthy. *Machine Tool Technology.* Mission Hills, CA: Glencoe Publishing Company, 1984.

Society of Manufacturing Engineers (SME). *Tool and Manufacturing Engineers Handbook, Desk Edition.* Dearborn, MI: Society of Manufacturing Engineers, 1989.

Vickers, G.W. *Numerically Controlled Machine Tools.* Great Britain: Ellis Horwood Limited, 1990.

Glenn G. Whiteside

Machine vision

Machine vision, also referred to as computer or robot vision, is a term which describes the many techniques by which machines visually sense the physical world. These techniques, which are used primarily for monitoring industrial manufacturing, are becoming increasing popular as today's manufacturing environments become more automated and quality control standards increase. Whether the task is to sort and assemble a group of machined parts, to determine if a label has been placed properly on a soda bottle, or to check for microscopic defects in an automotive door panel, machine vision plays an essential role.

The human vision model

Machine vision systems tend to mimic the human vision system. An optical sensor and electronic main processor typically act as the eyes and brain and, as in humans, they work together to interpret visual information. Also like their human counterparts, the sensor and processor are each somewhat responsible for filtering out the useless information within the scene before it is analyzed. This reduces the overall processing requirements and is what allows humans and well-designed machine vision systems to make decisions based on visual information very quickly.

Filtering the information within a scene begins with matching the vision system to its industrial requirements. Just as humans can adjust to a variety of situations by dilating their pupils or by tuning themselves to look for a particular shape or color, machine

vision systems must also be somewhat flexible. Typically, however, the most efficient system is one which is designed with only limited applications in mind. For this reason, machine vision designers have developed a variety of application-specific techniques and systems to meet the speed and accuracy standards that modern industry demands.

One-dimensional methods

The simplest type of vision system is one which senses only along a line. These one-dimensional sensors function best when used to simply detect the presence or absence of an object, and generally make no attempt at interpretation beyond that. Typically, these are used in applications such as automated assembly line counters, where perhaps the number of bottles passing by a particular point needs to be monitored. The light passing from one side of a conveyor belt to a detector on the other side is occluded when a bottle passes by. This break in the light signal is then recorded electronically and another unit is added to the total count.

Along with the simplicity of this system, unfortunately, comes its limited applicability. This system (like most other one-dimensional scanners) is not very good at distinguishing between different objects. Two different-shaped bottles, for example, can not be identified from one another. Perhaps even a pickle jar, a hand, or a large flying insect may trigger this system to record the break in light as another bottle. Although they tend to be inexpensive, the limited abilities of one-dimensional vision systems make them popular choices for only very specific, well-controlled applications. For the more sophisticated sensing requirements of most vision applications, two-dimensional techniques need to be employed.

Two-dimensional methods

The most common type of machine vision system is one which is responsible for examining situations two-dimensionally. These two-dimensional systems view a scene in much the same way that a person views a photograph. Cues such as shapes, shadows, textures, glares, and colors within the scene allow this type of vision system to be very good at making decisions based on what essentially amounts to a flat picture.

Shape

Like humans, most machine vision systems are designed to use shape as the defining characteristic for an object. For these systems, then, it is important to make an object's shape as easy to isolate as possible.

Both proper illumination of the object and efficient computer processing of the image of that object are necessary.

Illuminating from behind is the most straightforward optical way to make an object's shape stand out. The resulting silhouette effect is the same as that which occurs when a moth is seen flying in front of a bright light. To an observer a few feet away, the moth's colors pale, and the contrast between the moth and the background is enhanced so that its shape and size become its only discernable characteristics. For a machine vision system, an image of this silhouette is much easier to process than a conventional image.

Oftentimes, unfortunately, optical techniques alone do not make an object's shape stand out clearly enough. For this majority of cases, computer software-based techniques are generally employed. These routines perform mathematical operations on the electronic image of the scene to convert it into an image which is easier to interpret. Commonly used software routines can enhance the contrast of an image, trace out the edges of objects within an image, and group objects within an image.

Surface texture

Another defining characteristic for an object is its surface reflectivity. This cue is most often used for distinguishing between objects made from different materials and for distinguishing between objects of the same material but with different surface finish (such as painted or unpainted objects.)

At the extremes, an object is considered either a specular reflector or a diffuse reflector. If it is specular, it tends to act like a mirror, with most of the light bouncing off at the same angle with which it struck the surface (with respect to a surface normal.) This is the case for a finely polished piece of metal, a smooth pool of water, or even oily skin to some extent. If, on the other hand, the surface is diffuse, light is reflected more or less evenly in all directions. This effect is caused by roughness or very slight surface irregularities, and is the reason objects made from materials like wood or cloth generally appear softer in tone and can be distinguished from those made from metal.

Color

Often an object's color or color pattern can serve as its identifying feature. Every object has a color signature which is determined by its material and its surface coating. Spectroscopic—or color sensing—machine vision systems are cued to make decisions based on this feature and typically operate in one of two ways. Both

techniques illuminate an object with white light, but one looks at the light reflected by the object while the other looks at the light transmitted through the object for identification.

The simplest color sensing systems are responsible for monitoring only one color across a scene. These are typically used in quality control applications such as monitoring of paints, to ensure consistency between batches made at different times. More sophisticated color sensors look at the color distribution across a two-dimensional image. These systems are capable of complex analysis and can be used for checking multi-colored labels or for identifying multi-colored objects by their color patterns.

Three-dimensional methods

The most advanced machine vision systems typically involve acquisition and interpretation of three-dimensional information. These systems often require more sophisticated illumination and processing techniques than one- and two-dimensional systems, but their results can be riveting. These scanners can characterize an object's shape three-dimensionally to tolerances of far less than a millimeter. This allows them to do things such as identify three-dimensional object orientation (important for assembly applications), check for subtle surface deformations in high precision machined parts, and generate detailed surface maps used by computer-controlled machining systems to create clones of the scanned object.

Triangulation techniques

The simplest way to extract three-dimensional information from a scene is to do it one point at a time, using a method known as point triangulation. The working principle behind this method is based on simple trigonometry. A right triangle is formed between a laser, a video camera, and the laser's spot on the object. Measurement of the camera-to-laser distance and the camera-to-laser projection angle allows for easy determination of the camera-to-object distance (for a particular object point.) This range gives the third dimension, and can be determined for every object point by scanning the laser beam across the surface.

This is a very powerful technique and is used quite commonly for three-dimensional scanning because of its straightforwardness. The problem for this type of system, though, is that it has a relatively slow scan speed. A typical image may contain over a quarter of a million points. Recording only a fraction of these points, one at a time, tends to be quite time-consuming. And, like taking a long exposure photograph of a moving as the TV lines. Moiré scanners typically operate by projecting a set of lines onto an object and then viewing that object through a transparency containing another set of lines. The resulting moiré pattern is an array of curves which trace-out paths of equal object height, much like elevation lines on a topographical map. This image can then be used directly to check for surface features or combined with a few others and processed to give a true three-dimensional plot of the object.

Further Reading:

Braggins, Don. "3-D Inspection and Measurement: Solid Choices for Industrial Vision." *Advanced Imaging.* (October 1994): 36-39.

Harding, Kevin G. "Current State-of-the-Art of Contouring Techniques in Manufacturing." *Journal of Laser Applications.* (Summer/Fall 1990): 41-47.

Lake, Don. "Lighting and Imaging, Part 2: Making It All Work Right." *Advanced Imaging.* (June 1994): 66-69.

Weiss, Stephanie A. "Photonics Drives Auto Manufacturing." *Photonics Spectra.* (April 1994): 76-85.

Scott Christian Cahall

ing car, the three-dimensional image can be blurred for all but the most stationary objects. To help overcome this problem, a technique known as line scanning is often used. Line scanning, or line triangulation, is a simple extension of point triangulation. In this case, however, the projected light is a line and an entire strip of the surface is scanned at a time. Although the computational algorithms are somewhat more complex for this method, the time required to scan an object is substantially less.

Structured illumination and moiré techniques

A further increase in image-capture speed can be achieved through the use of more sophisticated illumination. This illumination can take on many forms, but is typically an array of dots or a set of projected lines. An image of the structured illumination shown on an object can then be processed in much the same way as triangulation data, but a full frame at a time. It generally only takes a handful of these full-frame images to describe a surface three-dimensionally, making structured illumination techniques extremely fast.

One particularly interesting type of three-dimensional scanner which uses structured illumination is based on a phenomenon known as the moiré effect. The moiré effect is a fascinating visual display which often occurs when two periodic patterns are overlaid. It can easily be seen in everyday experiences such as overlapping window curtains or on television when a character wears a shirt with stripes that have nearly the same spac-

Mach number

The Mach number is used in fluid mechanics and is especially useful in studies involving supersonic aerodynamics. It is named after Ernst Mach (1838-1916), the Austrian physicist and philosopher who pioneered the study of supersonic projectiles. The Mach number is the ratio of the velocity of a fluid to the velocity of sound in that same fluid. In the case of a body moving through a fluid, the Mach number is the velocity of the body relative to the fluid divided by the velocity of sound in the fluid. The velocity of sound varies with temperature and also varies from one fluid to another. At sea level, for example, the velocity of sound in air at 59°F (15°C) is about 760 mph (340 m/second). At an elevation of 40,000 ft (12,200 m), however, the temperature is about -70°F (-57°C), and the velocity of sound in air is only 660 mph (295 m/second). Thus, an airplane flying at 760 mph at sea level would have a Mach number of 1.0, while at an elevation of 40,000 ft it would have a higher Mach number of almost 1.2.

One of the principal uses of the Mach number is to define the behavior of fluid flows. For example, pressure disturbances in a fluid, as might be caused by an object such as an airplane wing moving through air, radiate at the speed of sound within the fluid. When the

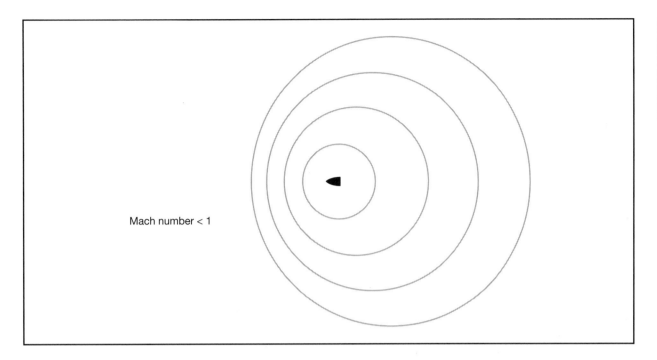

Figure 1.

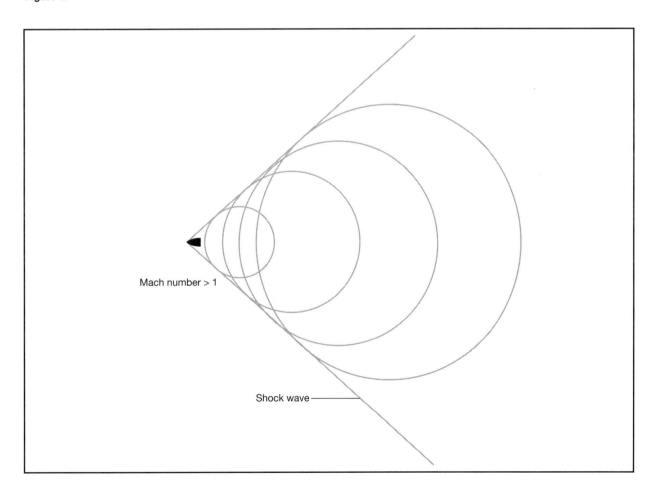

Figure 2.

Mach number of an object is less than 1, the object is moving slower than the speed of sound. In that case the pressure disturbances can move ahead of the object as shown in Figure 1.

This produces gradual pressure and density differences around the object which result in a certain kind of fluid flow behavior. However, when the Mach number is greater than 1, the object is moving faster than the speed of sound. When this happens the pressure disturbances cannot move out of the way fast enough, and very abrupt density and pressure changes, known as shock waves, appear. This results in a very different fluid flow behavior. These shock waves are shown in Figure 2 and are the cause of the "sonic boom" sometimes heard when an airplane exceeds the speed of sound.

Scientists now categorize four kinds of fluid flow behavior based on the Mach number. Flows with Mach numbers less than 0.8 are called subsonic, 0.8 to 1.2 are called transonic, 1.2 to 5.0 are called supersonic, and above 5.0 are called hypersonic. For each type of flow there is a different fluid behavior. Aircraft designers have to take these differences into account when designing planes that take off and climb to altitude at speeds in the subsonic region, then pass through the transonic region, and cruise at speeds in the supersonic region.

See also Fluid mechanics; Velocity.

Mackerel

The Atlantic mackerel, *Somber scombrus*, supports one of the most important commercial fisheries and supports a significant sport fishing interest. The fish is a close relative of the tuna. The attraction of mackerel as sport fish is due primarily to the streamlined body, forked tail, pointed head, and high-speed swimming. An unusual characteristic of the mackerel is that it does not possess a swim-bladder. Mackerel are found in large schools in the Atlantic Ocean from the New England coast to the Carolinas, and in the Eastern Atlantic south to Spain.

The average size of mackerel is less than a pound (1/2 kg) although some fish weighing 2 lb (1 kg) are found in deeper water. Mackerel feed on pilchards, herrings, small schooling fish, and small crustaceans such as shrimp.

At spawning time female mackerels lay up to 500,000 eggs, which float due to the presence of oil droplets. Spawning occurs in the mid Atlantic states in

KEY TERMS

Caudal peduncle—The area immediately posterior to the anal fin and extending to the base of the caudal or tail fin.

Dorsal fin—A fin on the back of the fish.

Keel—A raised prominence or ridge often associated with the caudal peduncle.

Lateral line—A line of pores opening on the side of the fish which has been shown to be sensitive to pressure changes.

Lunate—A term which refers to the shape of the tail fin. This form resembles the early phase of the moon (lunar).

Pectoral fin—One of paired fins located at the proximate shoulder of the fish and which corresponds to the forelegs of air-breathing vertebrates on land.

Swim bladder or air bladder—An elongated membranous pouch filled with gases and which aids the fish to remain buoyant.

the latter half of May and throughout June, and a few weeks later further north. The eggs hatch in about 96-120 hours, the lower the temperature the longer it takes for them to hatch.

The Atlantic mackerel can be distinguished from other species of mackerels by the pattern of up to 24 wavy black lines along the sides of its body above the lateral line. The chub mackerel, *S. japonicus*, is smaller than the Atlantic mackerel but closely resembles it in its behavior and physical characteristics but has fewer, fainter black markings than the Atlantic mackerel.

The Pacific mackerel is the only mackerel found on the west coast of North America and is the same species (*S. scombrus*) as is found in the Atlantic Ocean. Pacific mackerels are found from Chile to Alaska and along the coasts of Japan and the mainland coast of Asia.

The kingfish of king mackerel, *Scomberomorus cavalla* ranges widely in size from under 10 lb (5 kg) to more than 20 lb (10 kg). Some specimens caught in nets have been reported to weigh 100 lb (50 kg) and to exceed 5 ft (1.5 m) in length. The king mackerel has a blue-green back and silver sides, and a lateral line that is positioned high near the head and quickly descends below the second dorsal fin. King mackerel are found in great numbers in the Caribbean in the spring time migrating up the Atlantic coast with some entering the Gulf of Mexico.

A painted mackerel (*Scomberomorus regalis*) at Benwood wreck, Key Largo, Florida. The fishes of the *Scomberomorus* genus are the Spanish mackerels, or seerfishes.

The Spanish mackerel (*S. maculatus*) is a close relative of the King mackerel but grows only up to 12 lb (6 kg), the average being under 2 lb (1 kg). In warm offshore and inshore waters, the Spanish mackerel is subjected to heavy commercial and sport fishing.

The sierra, *S. sierra*, is very similar to the Spanish mackerel (some taxonomists consider them to be the same species) and is found in warm waters from Baja California to South America.

The cero, *S. regalis,* is found together with the Spanish and with king mackerels, and is characterized by rows of yellow or brown spots along its sides. The frigate mackerel, *Auxis thazard*, closely resembles the tuna because it has a lunate tail rather than the forked tail typical of mackerels.

See also Tuna.

Further Reading:

Dickson Hoese, H., and R. H. Moore. *Fishes of the Gulf of Mexico, Texas, Louisiana, and Adjacent Waters*, 1977.
Kennedy, M. *The Sea Angler's Fishes*, London: Hutchinson & Co. (Publishers) Ltd., 1954.
Migdalski, E. C. and G. S. Fichter. *The Fresh & Salt Water Fishes of the World.* New York: Greenwich House, 1982.

Nathan Lavenda

Madtoms see **Catfish**

Maggot see **True flies**

Magic square

Magic square is an unusual numerical configuration containing consecutive integers in arrangements so that the sum of numbers in any row, column, or diagonal are identical. Such squares were known approximately 4,000 years ago in China.

The basic magic square is a square containing consecutive integers starting with number 1.

Three of the basic magic squares are shown in Table 1.

TABLE 1. THREE BASIC MAGIC SQUARES

2	9	4
7	5	3
6	1	8

12	7	9	6
13	2	16	3
8	11	5	10
1	14	4	15

9	2	25	18	11
3	21	19	12	10
22	20	13	6	4
16	14	7	5	23
15	8	1	24	17

Other magic squares can be constructed by starting with one of the basic squares shown above and adding the same whole integers to each integer; equals added to equals, the sums are equivalent. Likewise subtracting the same value from each integer can result in other magic squares. In a similar manner, multiplication or division can be used to create other magic squares.

A general equation for constructing basic magic squares is shown below:

$$X = \tfrac{1}{2}n\,(\,n^2 + 1\,)$$

where X equals the sum of integers in any row, column, or diagonal, and n equals the number of rows.

Jeanette Vass

MAGLEV

MAGLEV stands for magnetically levitated transportation. This transportation consists of high speed electric trains that travel levitated above guideways. The technology incorporates two types of magnetic levitation: levitation due to attractive forces between magnets and steel rails, and levitation due to repulsive forces between magnets and induced magnetic fields in aluminum rails. Presently, there are prototype MAGLEV trains in the testing stage in Germany and Japan. Also, there are proposals to use MAGLEV trains at several locations in the United States.

Attractive magnetic levitation

Attractive magnetic levitation can be produced by suspending a magnet slightly below a material that it is attracted to, for example steel. The force of gravity that pulls down on the magnet is balanced by the magnetic force that pulls up on the magnet. This principle is used for levitating MAGLEV trains. Magnets are attached to the underside of the train and wrap underneath steel rails on the guideway. This type of levitation would be almost impossible to perform with simple permanent magnets, however. As you can demonstrate for yourself, the magnet will either stick, if too close, or will fall to the ground, if too far from the steel. Finding exactly the right distance for levitation is extremely difficult.

For this reason, the magnets used in MAGLEV trains are electromagnets rather than permanent magnets. An electromagnet is a coil of wire wound in the shape of a cylinder that carries an electric current. A magnetic field is produced in the coil that is proportional to the electric current. By using electromagnets, it is possible to vary the magnetic attraction by varying the electric current. The optimum levitation position is controlled through an electronic feedback circuit. The electronic feedback circuit monitors the position of the train and compensates for any deviation in this position by adjusting the current in the electromagnets. A distance of about 0.4 in (1 cm) is maintained between the rails and the train. Electronic feedback is the same principle used in antilock braking systems (ABS), available on many automobiles. A feedback circuit monitors the movement of the tires and adjusts the brake pressure to avoid skidding.

Repulsive magnetic levitation

The second method of magnetic levitation involves repulsive forces. Magnets mounted on the train induce electric currents in aluminum rails lying below the train. These induced currents, known as eddy currents, produce a magnetic field that is directed opposite to the field produced by the magnets on the train. The net effect is a repulsive force similar to the force between the north poles of two bar magnets.

It is possible to demonstrate this levitation effect by dropping a strong cylindrical magnet down the center of a copper pipe. As the magnet falls, it induces eddy currents in the copper that tend to suspend the magnet.

Rather than falling at its normal rate, the magnet will slowly "float" to the bottom of the pipe.

To induce eddy currents in the aluminum rails, it is necessary that the magnetic field be changing rather than constant. This requirement is met only after the train is moving, when the magnets on the train produce a changing magnetic field as they pass the sections of stationary rail. The train must begin moving, therefore, on wheels until enough speed is achieved to induce the eddy currents needed for the repulsive lift force. (Compare this to an airplane speeding down the runway before take-off.)

The magnetic fields required for repulsive levitation are generally greater than those needed for attractive levitation. For this reason, superconducting magnets, which are electromagnets made from superconductors, are employed. Superconductors are materials that carry electric current without any dissipation in heat energy, as long as they are kept at low temperatures. Without heat dissipation, these magnets are much smaller in size, carry larger currents and produce higher magnetic fields then conventional electromagnets. With superconducting magnets, trains are operated at levitation heights of about 4 in (10 cm) above the rails. This high levitation distance, as opposed to 0.4 in (1 cm) for trains suspended through attractive levitation, allows for greater tolerances in guideway construction and correspondingly lower costs.

Propulsion

Once the train is levitated, there must be some way to propel it. This is achieved with a series of electromagnets situated along the guideways on either side of the train. An alternating current is employed in these electromagnets, which periodically changes the orientation of the magnetic field in each magnet. At one instant, the north pole is pointing upward, at the next instant the south pole is pointing upward. The electromagnets on the train keep a constant magnetic field orientation, however. The alternating current in the guideway magnets is synchronized to produce north and south poles which will alternately pull and push the magnets on the train. It is similar to the action of pushing a person on a swing. The pushing is synchronized to always occur at the instant when the person begins their downward descent.

On a levitated train, friction between the rails is eliminated and air resistance becomes the primary force impeding motion. Because there is no metal to metal contact like that found in conventional non-levitating trains, noise is substantially reduced. Speeds of up to 300 miles per hour (483 kph) can be achieved. To slow

down, the procedure for speeding up can be reversed and an alternating current in the guideway magnets is synchronized to impede motion.

History

The concept of magnetically levitated transportation goes back to 1909 when the American rocket scientist Robert Goddard (1882-1945), for whom the Goddard Space Flight Center is named, proposed a transportation system with vehicles suspended and propelled by magnetic forces. In 1912, a French engineer working in America, Emile Bachelet, built a small model train which he levitated using electromagnets and aluminum rails, similar to the repulsive magnetic levitation designs of today. At that time, superconducting magnets were not invented and, consequently, Bachelet would not have been able to levitate a full scale train.

It wasn't until the 1960s when research on MAGLEV resumed. This was made possible by the development of superconducting magnets and modern electronics. James Powell and Gordon Danby from Brookhaven National Laboratory developed theoretical designs for maglev trains using repulsive magnetic levitation. By the early 1970s, a few groups in United States began tests on reduced scale models. At Stanford Research Institute, a half-ton vehicle was suspended and tested along a 328 ft (100 m) guideway. At Massachusetts Institute of Technology, Henry Kolm and Richard Thornton tested a 1/25th scale model on a circular shaped guideway which allowed the vehicle to bank as it circled corners.

In the past 20 years, England, Canada, United States, Japan, and Germany have conducted research on maglev. The most extensive research has been conducted in Japan and Germany. The main focus of Japanese research has been on the magnetic repulsion levitation design, while the main focus of German research has been on the magnetic attraction levitation design. Maglev trains have been used at exhibitions in Japan and Canada where they carried over one million people on a short track. In Berlin, Germany, over two million people have ridden on a slow speed (~50 miles per hour, or 80 kph) MAGLEV that served as transportation for urban airport traffic.

After extensive testing, it appears that MAGLEV is a feasible means of transportation. There are proposals to use MAGLEV transportation at several locations in the United States, including a 13-mi (21-km) system between Orlando, Florida, and the entrance to Disney World, a 19-mi (31-km) system connecting downtown

Pittsburgh with its airport, and a 275-mi (442-km) system between Las Vegas, Nevada, and Anaheim, California. Future government funding decisions will determine whether these transportation systems will be implemented.

See also Electromagnetism; Magnetic levitation; Trains and railroads.

Further Reading:

Moon, Francis. *Superconducting Levitation*. New York: John Wiley and Sons, 1994.
Moore, Taylor. "High-Speed Rail Heading Down the Track." *EPRI Journal* 19 (1994): 24-32.
Stix, Gary. "Air Trains." *Scientific American* 267 (1992): 102-113.
Vranich, Joseph. *Super Trains*. New York: St. Martin's Press, 1991.

Kurt Vandervoort

Magma

In geology, magma refers to molten rock deep within the Earth that consists of liquids, gases, and particles of rocks and crystals. Magma has been observed in the form of hot lava and the various rocks made from the solidification of magma. Geologists have created magmas (artificial melts) in the laboratory to learn more about the physical conditions in which magma originated and its composition. Magma is the source of igneous rocks; it can intrude or force itself into surrounding rock where it cools and eventually hardens. These rocks are called intrusive igneous rocks. If magma rises all the way to Earth's surface it will extrude (push out), flowing or erupting out at the surface as lava, forming extrusive igneous rock (also called volcanic rock). Magma and the rocks it creates have similar chemical compositions.

Magma is generated within Earth's mantle, the thick layer between Earth's crust and outer core. Rock found deep within the crust is extremely hot, soft, and pliable, but rock does not become liquid until much deeper in the upper mantle. Pockets, or chambers of magma, can originate at various depths within the Earth. The composition of the magma varies and indicates the source materials and depth from which they originated. Silicon dioxide (SiO_2) is the predominant ingredient in magma. Other ingredients include aluminum oxide, iron, magnesium, calcium, sodium, potassium, titanium, manganese, phosphorus, and water.

There are three basic types of magma, each having a characteristic origin and composition: basaltic (the most common, originating in the lower crust/upper mantle), rhyolitic (originates in the oceanic crust), and andesitic (most originate is the continental crust). New magma is formed by rocks melting when they sink deep into the mantle at subduction zones. The chemical composition, temperature, and the amount of dissolved liquids and gases determine the viscosity of magma. The more fluid a lava mixture is, the lower the viscosity. As magma or a lava flow cools, the mixture becomes more viscous, making it move slowly. Magmas having a higher silica (SiO_2) content are very viscous and move very slowly.

Magma has the tendency to rise because it weighs less than surrounding hard rock (liquids are less dense than solids) and because of the pressure caused by extreme temperature. The pressure is reduced as magma rises toward the surface. Dissolved gases come out of solution and form bubbles. The bubbles expand, making the magma even less dense, causing the magma to rise faster. The magma exerts a great deal of pressure on weak spots and fills up any cracks produced by the continual shifting of the Earth's crust. On its way up toward the surface, magma can melt adjacent rock, which provides a suitable environment for the development of metamorphic rocks. When magma erupts as lava, its gases are released at the surface into the atmosphere or can be trapped in the molten rock and cause "air bubbles" in rock. The gases can also create violent explosions, throwing debris for miles around.

See also Igneous rocks; Rocks; Volcano.

Further Reading:
Skinner, Brian J. & Porter, Stephen C. *Physical Geology.* John Wiley & Sons, Inc., 1987.
Menard, H.W. *Geology, Resources, and Society.* W.H. Freeman and Co., 1975.

Magnesium see **Alkaline earth metals**

Magnesium sulfate

Magnesium sulfate ($MgSO_4$) is a white powder, commonly known as Epsom salts. It is easily dissolved in water, making it a source of magnesium that can be readily absorbed by living things. It is used in manufacturing mother-of-pearl, in dyeing calico, in tanning leather, in manufacturing fertilizer, and in treating and preventing seizures during pregnancy. Magnesium sulfate is also used to treat constipation. It has recently been noticed that many people with diabetes have abnormally low levels of magnesium ions in their blood.

Physical and chemical properties of magnesium sulfate

Magnesium sulfate is obtained from the mineral epsomite, a white solid. It can also be prepared commercially by the reaction of magnesium carbonate ($MgCO_3$) with sulfuric acid (H_2SO_4). Magnesium sulfate is usually found in the form magnesium sulfate heptahydrate ($MgSO_4 . 7 H_2O$). The "hepta" prefix refers to the seven water molecules that are loosely attached to each magnesium sulfate molecule. Magnesium sulfate is very soluble in water. At room temperature about 1.5 lb (700 g) of $MgSO_4$ can be dissolved in a quart (1 l) of water. When dissolved in water, magnesium sulfate ionizes (or separates into ions) into magnesium (Mg^{+2}) ions, and sulfate (SO_4^{-2}) ions. Solutions of magnesium sulfate have a neutral pH. Magnesium sulfate is used in many industrial processes and in the manufacturing of fertilizers. Magnesium is essential for plant growth because each chlorophyll molecule contains a magnesium atom. Without this magnesium atom in the center of the chlorophyll molecule, plants would be unable to use the energy from sunlight for growth.

KEY TERMS

. . . .

Eclampsia—A condition of pregnancy marked by high blood pressure, swelling of body tissues, and convulsions.

Edema—Swelling of body tissue.

Magnesium sulfate and medicine

Magnesium sulfate is used to prevent the convulsions and seizures that can occur during pregnancy, in a condition known as *eclampsia*. Eclampsia is characterized by high blood pressure, edema (swelling of tissues, notably in the arms and legs), and convulsions. Magnesium sulfate is used to prevent and reduce the severity of convulsions and to reduce some of the excess body fluids. Magnesium sulfate is used as a purgative (laxative). It is thought to work by preventing the intestines from taking up or absorbing water from their contents, thus stimulating more frequent bowel movements. It has also been used to treat some heavy metal poisoning (notably barium, which is in the same family of the periodic table) and works by helping the body to rid itself of the contents of the digestive tract more rapidly. Magnesium sulfate is used to treat conditions of low blood levels of magnesium. It is used over other compounds containing magnesium because of its greater solubility and thus more rapid uptake by the body.

Recent research has shown that there is a link between diabetes and lower blood levels of magnesium. This does not necessarily mean that low blood levels of magnesium cause diabetes, but may simply mean that magnesium is lost more rapidly due to the frequent urination of people with diabetes.

See also Alkaline earth metals; Diabetes mellitus; Ionization.

Further Reading:
Fackelman, K. "Magnesium Eases Diabetics Blood Pressure," *Science News* 138 (22 September 1990): 189.
"Magnesium Supplementation in the Treatment of Diabetes." *Saturday Evening Post* 264, (September-October 1994): 66.
Malesky, G. "Magnesium for Moms to Be." *Prevention* 41 (January 1989): 8.
Owens, Mona, W. "Keeping an Eye on Magnesium." *American Journal of Nursing* 93, (February 1993): 66.

Louis Gotlib

Magnet see **Magnetism**

Magnetic field see **Electromagnetic field**

Magnetic levitation

Magnetic levitation is the phenomenon in which two magnetic objects are repelled from each other in a vertical direction. The phenomenon, also known as MAGLEV, has long been recognized as having some important commercial applications. The most significant of these is the construction of MAGLEV trains which are propelled a few inches above a track at very high rates of speed.

Principle of operation

Imagine that two bar magnets are suspended one above the other with like poles (two north poles or two south poles) directly above and below each other. Any effort to bring these two magnets into contact with each other will have to overcome the force of repulsion that exists between two like magnetic poles. The strength of that force of repulsion depends, among other things, on the strength of the magnetic field between the two bar magnets. The stronger the magnet field, the stronger the force of repulsion.

If one were to repeat this experiment using a very small, very light bar magnet as the upper member of the pair, one could imagine that the force of repulsion would be sufficient to hold the smaller magnet suspended — levitated — in air. This example illustrates the principle that the force of repulsion between the two magnets is able to keep the upper object suspended in air.

In fact, the force of repulsion between two bar magnets would be too small to produce the effect described here. In actual experiments with magnetic levitation, the phenomenon is produced by magnetic fields obtained from electromagnets. For example, imagine that a metal ring is fitted loosely around a cylindrical metal core attached to an external source of electrical current. When current flows through the core, it sets up a magnetic field within the core. That magnetic field, in turn, sets up a current in the metal ring which produces its own magnetic field. According to Lenz's Law, the two magnetic fields thus produced — one in the metal core and one in the metal ring — have opposing polarities. The effect one observes in such an experiment is that the metal ring rises upward along the metal core as the two parts of the system are repelled by each other. If the current is increased to a sufficient level, the ring can actually be caused to fly upward off the core. Alternatively, the current can be adjusted so that the ring can be held in suspension at any given height with relation to the core.

MAGLEV vehicles

Credit for foreseeing the applications of magnetic levitation in the construction of vehicles is usually given to rocket pioneer Robert Goddard. In 1907, Goddard published a story in which he described a vehicle that traveled by means of the principle of magnetic levitation. The first working model of such a vehicle was constructed in 1912 by the French engineer Emile Bachelet. Bachelet's vehicle was propelled by the repulsive forces set up between copper electromagnets suspended above an aluminum track. Bachelet's model proved to be a dead end, however, because the amount of electrical energy needed to create suspension was much too great to produce economically.

In fact, that problem was the primary reason that MAGLEV vehicles remained a dream until very recently. In order to lift an object weighing many tons, a very strong force of repulsion between vehicle and track must be created. The force of repulsion, in turn, can be produced only by means of very powerful electromagnets. The weight of such magnets and the electrical energy needed to operate them placed the idea of MAGLEV vehicles out of the realm of real-life technology for many decades.

Superconducting magnets

For many years, scientists have been aware of at least one obvious way of dealing with these practical problems — superconducting magnets. Superconductivity is the tendency of a conducting material (such as copper) to carry an electrical current with virtually no resistance. Although superconductivity had been discovered as early as 1911, its application to real-life inventions had always been limited by the fact that it was observable only at temperatures close to absolute zero. A MAGLEV vehicle that made use of superconducting magnets would, therefore, be much more efficient than one using traditional electromagnets. But the superconducting model would also have to be designed so as to operate at very low temperatures (close to -450° F [-268° C]).

Still, by the 1960s, researchers had begun to design and build prototype MAGLEV vehicles powered by superconducting electromagnets. Most such vehicles operated on a common principle. Superconducting coils are suspended beneath the body of the MAGLEV vehicle itself. As current begins to flow through these coils, a magnetic field is created. That magnetic field, as in the example noted earlier, sets up a magnetic field in the metal track beneath the vehicle. The force of repulsion between the two magnetic fields forces the train upward and keeps it suspended a few inches above the track. As the electrical current in the superconducting coils increases, so do the opposing magnetic fields and the force of repulsion between them.

Of course, the vehicle must not only be lifted above the track, but it must also be moved in a forward (or backward) direction. This propulsive force is provided by an electric current that flows through guideway coils in the track. As the current changes in the coils, so does the strength of the magnetic field. As a result, the MAGLEV vehicle is alternatively pushed and pulled by the changing magnetic field in the coils. The speed of the train can be controlled by the electrical current passing through the coils.

A MAGLEV train begins operation like any other railway train, with its wheels resting on the track. As electrical current begins to flow through its superconducting coils, the train is pushed forward on the track and then gradually lifted off it. At maximum speed, most trains are designed to travel a few inches above the track and at speeds of 250 mi (402 km) per hour or more.

Disadvantages of MAGLEV vehicles

Magnetic levitation as a means of transportation is not without its problems. For example, initial plans call for the construction of MAGLEV tracks in the United States adjacent to the nation's interstate highway system. But passengers traveling in a 250-mile-per-hour MAGLEV train will feel much stronger gravitational forces in rounding an interstate curve than will passengers in a car moving at 65 mi (105 km) per hour. Also, initial tests suggest that MAGLEV vehicles may produce a high level of noise when they operate at top speed. Tests have shown that sound levels of 100 decibels at a distance of 80 ft (24 m) from the guideway may be possible. Such levels of sound are, however, unacceptably high for any inhabited area.

Prospects for MAGLEV vehicles

The new age of MAGLEV technology can be traced to the early 1960s. During that period, many observers saw MAGLEV vehicles as a way of solving a number of problems confronting the United States and other developed nations. For example, they offered an apparently efficient way of moving large numbers of people quickly and efficiently through and around urban areas. They could be powered with almost any form of energy from which electricity could be made, not just with coal or petroleum. By 1970, then, a number of model MAGLEV vehicles had been constructed.

That research has been vigorously continued in a number of nations, including Japan, Great Britain, Germany, and France. All of these nations have developed a number of prototype vehicles that may soon move into commercial operation. For example, Japanese engineers have designed a 27-mile (43.5 km) test line through the Yamanashi Prefecture that would carry up to 10,000 passengers per hour in 14-car trains traveling at 310 mi (499 km) per hour. Some German models have used a somewhat different form of magnetic levitation. The German's Transrapid 07 has nonsuperconducting magnets attached to the vehicle body and suspended beneath the guide rail. The magnets are attracted (rather than repelled) upward to the rail, lifting the train to within an inch of the guide rail.

In contrast to this kind of progress, however, the United States had by 1975 virtually abandoned research on magnetic levitation. That decision, made by the Office of Management and Budget, had been made on the belief that MAGLEV transportation would not be an economically feasible alternative in this country in the foreseeable future.

That attitude underwent a dramatic reversal in the early 1990s, largely as the result of the interest of one politician, Senator Daniel Patrick Moynihan of New York. Moynihan had become convinced that MAGLEV vehicles were the means by which the nation's interurban transportation problems could be solved. And, as chairman of the Senate subcommittee responsible for the U.S. highway system, Moynihan was in a position to put his beliefs into practice. In 1989, Moynihan inserted into the highway bill a special provision for the development of new MAGLEV technology, the Magnetic Levitation Prototype Development Program, with a budget of $750 million. Given this seed money, many experts once more have high hopes for the eventual development of a commercial MAGLEV vehicles program in the United States.

See also Electromagnetism; MAGLEV; Trains and railroads.

Further Reading:

"High-Speed Ground Transportation Oversight." Hearing before the Subcommittee on Surface Transportation of the Committee on Commerce, Science, and Transportation, United States Senate, One Hundred Second Congress, Second Session 6 August 1992.

"High-Speed Rail Transportation." Hearing before the Subcommittee on Transportation and Hazardous Materials of the Committee on Energy and Commerce, House of Representatives, One Hundred Third Congress, First Session, 29 April 1993.

Rhodes, R. G., and B. E. Mulhall, *Magnetic Levitation for Rail Transport*. Oxford: Clarendon Press, 1981.

Rossing, Thomas D., and John R. Hull, "Magnetic Levitation," *The Physics Teacher*, December 1991, pages 552 - 562.

Singer, Sanford S., "Advanced Transportation Systems," in Frank N. Magill, *Magill's Survey of Science: Applied Science Series*, Volume 6. Pasadena, CA: Salem Press, 1993, pages 2724 - 2730.

Stix, Gary, "Air Trains," *Scientific American*, August 1992, pages 102 - 113.

David E. Newton

Magnetic pole see **Magnetism**

Magnetic recording/ audiocassette

Audiocassette tape recorders are widely used to record and play back music or speech. Information is stored on a narrow ribbon of plastic tape that has one side coated with a magnetic material, such as iron oxide. An electromagnet aligns individual magnetic particles in a pattern that corresponds to the loudness and frequency of incoming sounds. In order to play back the recorded information, the magnetic tape moves past a pickup coil that generates an electrical output signal. After being amplified, this signal causes a speaker to vibrate which produces sound waves for the listener. A tape recording can be erased by using a rapidly changing magnetic field that scrambles previously recorded patterns of particle alignment.

The discovery of electromagnetism

Before 1820, magnetism and electricity were two completely separate fields of science. Magnetism was associated with the attraction of magnets for iron objects and the use of a compass needle to locate north and south. Electricity was of practical interest in connection with the hazards of lightning. Some scientists experimented with static electricity in the laboratory by rubbing a wool cloth against glass, but no useful applications came about.

In 1821, a Danish physics teacher named Hans Christian Oersted made a remarkable discovery while doing a demonstration for his class. He had made a crude chemical battery by placing strips of copper and zinc into an acid solution. By connecting the two metal terminals with a wire, he provided a path for electric current to flow. A magnetic compass was lying on the table nearby. To his great surprise, Oersted noticed that the compass needle would deflect whenever current flowed through the wire. Apparently, the electric current created a magnetic field around the wire. His discovery was the beginning of electromagnetism, a joining of these two sciences.

Other scientists followed up on Oersted's discovery. For example, it was found that a much stronger magnetic field could be produced by winding the electric wire into a coil. Also, an iron core at the center of the coil intensified its magnetic field even more. Joseph Henry, an American inventor who later became head of the Smithsonian Institution in Washington, D. C., made an electromagnet that was powerful enough to support a load weighing 2,000 lb (908 kg).

Recording on tape with an electromagnet

Information becomes stored on magnetic tape as it passes by the so-called "recording head," which is a small electromagnet. There must be a narrow gap in this electromagnet so that its magnetic field will extend over the nearby section of tape.

The signal coming from the audio input is an alternating, back-and-forth current. An audio sound with a frequency of 1,000 cycles per second, for example, reverses its electric current direction every one-thousandth of a second. When the current is reversed, the North and South poles of the recording head electromagnet are interchanged. Consequently, the nearby magnetic particles embedded in the tape will become reoriented in the opposite direction.

When a loud sound is being recorded, the current to the electromagnet is large and its magnetic field will be relatively strong. Therefore a large number of magnetic particles in the tape will become aligned. A soft sound produces a weak field, so only a small fraction of magnetic particles will be affected.

For audiocassette players, the tape is designed to move at a standard speed of 1 7/8 in (4.8 cm) per second. During one cycle of a 1,000 cycle note, the tape moves only about l/500th of an inch (0.005 cm), which

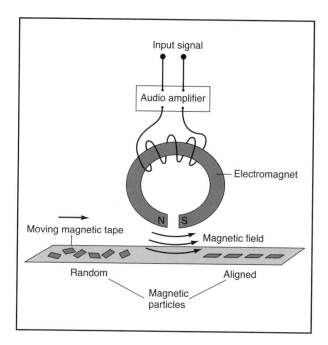

Figure 1. Recording head.

is a distance smaller than the diameter of the period at the end of this sentence. Several magnetic particles in a row must fit into such a short distance on the tape.

The human ear normally can hear sounds up to about 15,000 cycles per second. To record such a high frequency without distortion requires extremely tiny magnetic particles. The magnetic material must be easy to align and should retain its pattern of orientation indefinitely. Better quality audio tapes use very fine grains of chromium dioxide instead of iron oxide. Inexpensive tapes are adequate for recording the spoken voice because its frequency range is much less than for music.

An audiocassette has a built-in erase head to remove previously recorded information. The tape has to be blank before it can be used again to make a new recording. The erase head normally is an electromagnet that operates at an ultrasonic frequency, much higher than the human ear can hear. It effectively randomizes the alignment of magnetic particles. Audiocassettes are designed so that the tape passes by an erase head just before the recording head. Sometimes musicians at a recording studio want to record a second sound track over the first one. In that case the erase head has to be deactivated, so the original sound is not lost.

Operation of the playback head

How can the information, which was stored in a pattern of magnetically aligned particles on tape, be converted back into sound waves? The magnetic pattern

must be transformed into an electric current, which then can be amplified and cause a speaker to vibrate.

The operation of the playback is based on a discovery made in the 1830s by an English physicist, Michael Faraday. He knew about Oersted's earlier observation that magnetism is created by an electric current. Faraday wondered if the opposite process might occur, where an electric current could be created from magnetism. By experimenting with magnets and coils of wire, he was able to show that a moving magnet did create a small current in a coil. His discovery was called electromagnetic induction because current was "induced" in the coil by the moving magnet. The induction principle, combining magnetism and motion, is the basis for the operation of the generators that produce electricity at power plants.

The tape of an audiocassette has a weak magnetic field around it that varies from point to point depending on the orientation of its magnetic particles. The playback head contains a coil of wire. When the magnetized tape moves past the coil, Faraday's condition for inducing a current in the coil is fulfilled. The induced current will alternate in direction depending on the orientation of the magnetic particles as they pass by the playback head. The magnetic pattern originally recorded on the tape is transformed into a precisely corresponding electrical signal.

The electric current from the playback head is amplified and sent to an audio speaker, which vibrates in synchronism with the varying current. The back-and-forth motion of the speaker creates pressure waves in the air. This causes the listener's ear drums to vibrate, producing the sensation of sound.

When someone wants to listen to a previously recorded tape, only the playback head is activated. However, to record new information on a tape requires two operations: the erase head must be activated, followed by the recording head. It is possible to activate all three heads, so that the first one erases, the second one records and the third one plays back what has just been recorded.

Motor drive for constant tape speed

In an audiocassette player, the tape must move from the supply reel to the take-up reel at constant speed. Otherwise the sound becomes distorted. It would not work to pull the tape along simply by rotating the take-up reel, because each successive revolution would pull a longer section of tape past the heads, causing the tape speed to increase.

To obtain a constant tape speed, a motor is used to turn a small metal cylinder, called a capstan, at constant

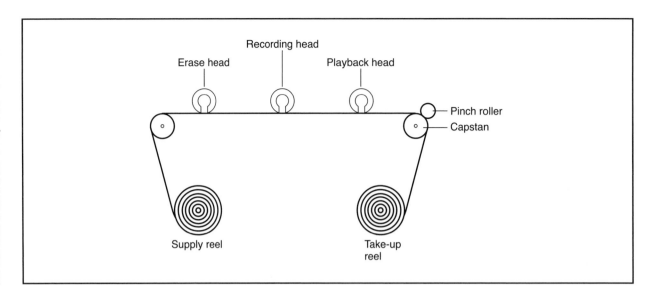

Figure 2. Cassette and heads.

speed. When the tape player is switched on, a roller presses the tape against the rotating capstan. The tape is pinched between the roller and capstan, forcing it to move toward the take-up reel at constant speed, as desired.

The main problem with this tape drive mechanism is that it may generate a background hum in the output sound. One can listen for hum by playing a tape that is blank and turning the volume control up to maximum. This provides a helpful comparison test when trying out several models in an audio store for possible purchase.

History of magnetic recording

The first working model of a magnetic recording device was demonstrated in 1898 by a Danish engineer named Valdemar Poulson. He used the mouthpiece from a telephone to convert speech into an electric current. The current went to an electromagnet which recorded the signal on a thin steel wire. The wire moved past the electromagnet very rapidly, a hundred times faster than modern cassette tapes. Recordings could only be very brief and the wires were awkward to handle. A competing technology, the phonograph, had been invented by Thomas A. Edison a few years earlier. It was easier to operate and was already quite popular by 1900, so magnetic recording attracted little interest at the time.

A step forward in magnetic recording was to replace the wire with a thin steel ribbon. A further advance was the development of paper tape with a layer of iron oxide adhering to one side, which was introduced in Germany in 1930. A few years later, plastic tape replaced the paper.

Commercial recording studios and radio stations greatly preferred tapes over phonograph records because they were suitable for editing. For example, if an otherwise excellent musical performance had minor flaws such as a cough or a note out of tune, the tape could be cut and spliced to remove the offending segment. For home use, only phonograph records were available at this time. Records could be mass-produced cheaply by making a master disk and pressing copies from it, while duplicating tapes was a lengthy process.

The invention of the transistor in 1947 revolutionized the communication industry. The subsequent development of microelectronics and a cartridge tape system led to commercialization of audio cassettes for the mass market in the 1960s. Magnetic tapes were designed to have two sound tracks, one to play in the forward direction and the second one when the tape was reversed. Then stereo sound, using two speakers, came into vogue. Four separate sound tracks were needed now, two tracks in each direction.

A further development in ultra-high fidelity music recordings was the introduction of digital audio tape (DAT) in the 1990s. Each second of sound is subdivided into 48,000 time intervals. The sound intensity during each interval is measured and recorded numerically on the tape in a binary, two-valued code. Each magnetic particle on the tape is like a tiny compass needle, pointing either forward or back, so a binary numerical system is appropriate. For playback, the digital information must be decoded before being sent to the speakers.

DATs can not be played on ordinary tape players. The digital cassettes are smaller in size, although they

KEY TERMS

Capstan—A rotating metal rod, driven by an electric motor, that pulls the cassette tape along at constant speed.

Digital audio tape (DAT)—A high fidelity technology developed in the 1990s, where information is stored on magnetic tape in binary code.

Electromagnet—A coil of wire surrounding an iron core that becomes magnetized when electric current flows through the wire.

Erase head—An electromagnet operating at an ultrasonic frequency to scramble previously recorded information on a tape.

Iron oxide—Tiny, needle-shaped particles that can be easily magnetized, coating one side of the plastic cassette tape.

Playback head—A small coil that senses the varying magnetic field of the moving tape and converts it into an electrical signal that can be amplified.

Recording head—An electromagnet that aligns the magnetic particles of the cassette tape while it moves by.

play for a longer time. They are fragile and must be handled carefully. Digital recordings have the advantage that background noise and distortion are virtually eliminated. The sound quality of DAT's is often compared to being present in the concert hall.

See also Electromagnetism.

Further Reading:

Brophy, Michael. *Michael Faraday.* Pioneers of Science Series. Watts, Franklin, 1991.

Davidson, Homer L. *Troubleshooting and Repairing Audio and Video Cassette Players and Recorders.* TAB Books, 1992.

Horn, Delton T. *Creative Sound Recording on a Budget.* TAB Books, 1987.

Jorgenson, Finn. *The Complete Handbook of Magnetic Recording. 3rd ed.* TAB Books, 1988.

Shamos, Morris H. "Electromagnetism - Hans Christian Oersted," in *Great Experiments in Physics.* Dover Publications, 1987.

Hans G. Graetzer

Magnetic resonance imaging (MRI) see **Nuclear magnetic resonance**

Magnetic survey methods see **Subsurface detection**

Magnetism

Magnetism is a force generated in matter by the motion of electrons within its atoms. Magnetism and electricity represent different aspects of the force of electromagnetism, which is one part of Nature's fundamental electroweak force. The region in space that is penetrated by the imaginary lines of magnetic force describes a magnetic field. The strength of the magnetic field is determined by the number of lines of force per unit area of space. Magnetic fields are created on a large scale either by the passage of an electric current through magnetic metals or by magnetized materials called magnets. The elemental metals—iron, cobalt, nickel, and their solid solutions or alloys with related metallic elements—are typical materials that respond strongly to magnetic fields. Unlike the all-pervasive fundamental force field of gravity, the magnetic force field within a magnetized body, such as a bar magnet, is polarized—that is, the field is strongest and of opposite signs at the two extremities or poles of the magnet.

History of magnetism

The history of magnetism dates back to earlier than 600 B.C., but it is only in the twentieth century that scientists have begun to understand it, and develop technologies based on this understanding. Magnetism was most probably first observed in a form of the mineral magnetite called lodestone, which consists of iron oxide—a chemical compound of iron and oxygen. The ancient Greeks were the first known to have used this mineral, which they called a magnet because of its ability to attract other pieces of the same material and iron.

The Englishman William Gilbert (1540-1603) was the first to investigate the phenomenon of magnetism systematically using scientific methods. He also discovered that the Earth is itself a weak magnet. Early theoretical investigations into the nature of the Earth's magnetism were carried out by the German Carl Friedrich Gauss (1777-1855). Quantitative studies of magnetic phenomena initiated in the eighteenth century by Frenchman Charles Coulomb (1736-1806), who established the inverse square law of force, which states that the attractive force between two magnetized objects is directly proportional to the product of their individual fields and inversely proportional to the square of the distance between them. Danish physicist Hans Christian Oersted (1777-1851) first suggested a link between electricity and magnetism. Experiments involving the effects of magnetic and electric fields on one another were then conducted by Frenchman Andre Marie Ampere (1775-1836) and Englishman Michael Faraday (1791-1869), but it was the Scotsman, James Clerk Maxwell (1831-1879), who provided the theoretical foundation to the physics of electromagnetism in the nineteenth century by showing that electricity and magnetism represent different aspects of the same fundamental force field. Then, in the late 1960s American Steven Weinberg (1933-) and Pakistani Abdus Salam (1926-), performed yet another act of theoretical synthesis of the fundamental forces by showing that electromagnetism is one part of the electroweak force. The modern understanding of magnetic phenomena in condensed matter originates from the work of two Frenchmen: Pierre Curie (1859-1906), the husband and scientific collaborator of Madame Marie Curie (1867-1934), and Pierre Weiss (1865-1940). Curie examined the effect of temperature on magnetic materials and observed that magnetism disappeared suddenly above a certain critical temperature in materials like iron. Weiss proposed a theory of magnetism based on an internal molecular field proportional to the average magnetization that spontaneously align the electronic micromagnets in magnetic matter. The present day understanding of magnetism based on the theory of the motion and interactions of electrons in atoms (called quantum electrodynamics) stems from the work and theoretical models of two Germans, Ernest Ising (1900-) and Werner Heisenberg (1901-1976). Werner Heisenberg was also one of the founding fathers of modern quantum mechanics.

Origin of magnetism

Magnetism arises from two types of motions of electrons in atoms—one is the motion of the electrons in an orbit around the nucleus, similar to the motion of the planets in our solar system around the sun, and the other is the spin of the electrons around its axis, analogous to the rotation of the Earth about its own axis. The orbital and the spin motion independently impart a magnetic moment on each electron causing each of them to behave as a tiny magnet. The magnetic moment of a magnet is defined by the rotational force experienced by it in a magnetic field of unit strength acting perpendicular to its magnetic axis. In a large fraction of the elements, the magnetic moment of the electrons cancel out because of the Pauli exclusion principle, which states that each electronic orbit can be occupied by only two electrons of opposite spin. However, a number of so-called transition metal atoms, such as

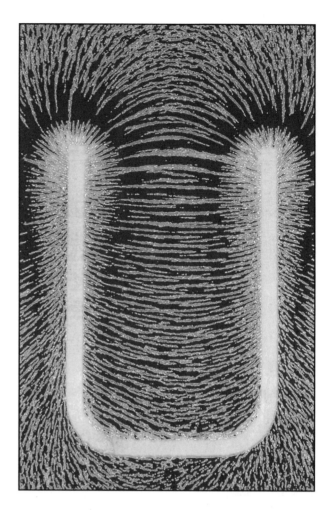

A computer graphic of a horseshoe magnet with iron filings aligned around it.

iron, cobalt, and nickel, have magnetic moments that are not cancelled; these elements are, therefore, common examples of magnetic materials. In these transition metal elements the magnetic moment arises only from the spin of the electrons. In the rare earth elements (that begin with lanthanum in the sixth row of the Periodic Table of Elements), however, the effect of the orbital motion of the electrons is not cancelled, and hence both spin and orbital motion contribute to the magnetic moment. Examples of some magnetic rare earth elements are: cerium, neodymium, samarium, and europium. In addition to metals and alloys of transition and rare earth elements, magnetic moments are also observed in a wide variety of chemical compounds involving these elements. Among the common magnetic compounds are the metal oxides, which are chemically bonded compositions of metals with oxygen.

The Earth's geomagnetic field is the result of electric currents produced by the slow convective motion of its liquid core in accordance with a basic law of electromagnetism which states that a magnetic field is generated by the passage of an electric current. According to this model, the Earth's core should be electrically conductive enough to allow generation and transport of an electric current. The geomagnetic field generated will be dipolar in character, similar to the magnetic field in a conventional magnet, with lines of magnetic force lying in approximate planes passing through the geomagnetic axis. The principle of the compass needle used by the ancient mariners involves the alignment of a magnetized needle along the Earth's magnetic axis with the imaginary south pole of the needle pointing towards the magnetic north pole of the Earth. The magnetic north pole of the Earth is inclined at an angle of 11 degrees away from its geographical north pole.

Types of magnetism

Five basic types of magnetism have been observed and classified on the basis of the magnetic behavior of materials in response to magnetic fields at different temperatures. These types of magnetism are: ferromagnetism, ferrimagnetism, antiferromagnetism, paramagnetism, and diamagnetism.

Ferromagnetism and ferrimagnetism occur when the magnetic moments in a magnetic material line up spontaneously at a temperature below the so-called Curie temperature, to produce net magnetization. The magnetic moments are aligned at random at temperatures above the Curie point, but become ordered, typically in a vertical or, in special cases, in a spiral (helical) array, below this temperature. In a ferromagnet magnetic moments of equal magnitude arrange themselves in parallel to each other. In a ferrimagnet, on the other hand, the moments are unequal in magnitude and order in an antiparallel arrangement. When the moments are equal in magnitude and ordering occurs at a temperature called the Neel temperature in an antiparallel array to give no net magnetization, the phenomenon is referred to as antiferromagnetism. These transitions from disorder to order represent classic examples of phase transitions. Another example of a phase transition is the freezing of the disordered molecules of water at a critical temperature of 32°F (0°C) to form the ordered structure of ice. The magnetic moments—referred to as spins—are localized on the tiny electronic magnets within the atoms of the solid. Mathematically, the electronic spins are equal to the angular momentum (the rotational velocity times the moment of inertia) of the rotating electrons. The spins in a ferromagnetic or a ferrimagnetic single crystal undergo spontaneous alignment to form a macroscopic (large scale) magnetized object. Most magnetic solids, however, are not single crystals, but consist of single crystal domains separated by domain walls. The spins align within a domain below the Curie temperature, independently of any external magnetic field, but the domains have to be aligned in a magnetic field in order to produce a macroscopic magnetized object. This process is effected by the rotation of the direction of the spins in the domain wall under the influence of the magnetic field, resulting in a displacement of the wall and the eventual creation of a single large domain with the same spin orientation.

Paramagnetism is a weak form of magnetism observed in substances which display a positive response to an applied magnetic field. This response is described by its magnetic susceptibility per unit volume, which is a dimensionless quantity defined by the ratio of the magnetic moment to the magnetic field intensity. Paramagnetism is observed, for example, in atoms and molecules with an odd number of electrons, since here the net magnetic moment cannot be zero. Diamagnetism is associated with materials that have a negative magnetic susceptibility. It occurs in nonmagnetic substances like graphite, copper, silver and gold, and in the superconducting state of certain elemental and compound metals. The negative magnetic susceptibility in these materials is the result of a current induced in the electron orbits of the atoms by the applied magnetic field. The electron current then induces a magnetic moment of opposite sign to that of the applied field. The net result of these interactions is that the material is shielded from penetration by the applied magnetic field.

Measurement of magnetic field

The magnetic field or flux density is measured in metric units of a gauss (G) and the corresponding international system unit of a tesla (T). The magnetic field strength is measured in metric units of oersteds (Oe) and international units of amperes per meter (A/m). Instruments called gaussmeters and magnetometers are used to measure the magnitude of magnetic fields.

One form of the gaussmeter that is used commonly in the laboratory consists of a current carrying semiconducting element called the Hall probe, which is placed perpendicular to the magnetic field being measured. As a consequence of the so-called Hall effect, a voltage perpendicular to the field and to the current is generated in the probe. This induced voltage is proportional to the magnetic field being measured and can be simply measured using a voltmeter.

Magnetometers are extremely sensitive magnetic field detectors. In one commonly used form the magnetic force is detected by means of a sensitive electronic balance. In this instrument the magnetic substance is placed on one arm of a balance, which in turn is placed in a magnetic field. The magnetic force on the sample is then determined by the weight required to balance the force generated by the magnetic field. The most sensitive magnetometer in a modern physics laboratory utilizes a magnetic sensing element called the SQUID (which stands for Superconducting QUantum Interference Device). A SQUID consists of an extremely thin electrically resistive junction (called a Josephson junction) between two superconductors. Superconductors are materials which undergo a transition at low temperatures to a state of zero electrical resistance and nearly complete exclusion of magnetic fields. In its direct current mode of operation, a SQUID is first cooled down to its superconducting state, and then a current is passed through it while the voltage across the junction is monitored. When the junction senses a magnetic field, the flow of current is altered due to an interference phenomenon at the quantum level between two electron wave fronts through the junction, resulting in a change in voltage. Interference is a phenomenon that occurs generally due to the mixing of two wave fronts; the waves add up in some regions and cancel out in others depending on the location of the crest and trough of each wave in space. For example, the interference between the sound waves from two simultaneously played musical instruments tuned at somewhat different frequencies results in the occurrence of beats or modulations in the sound intensity.

A variation of the SQUID magnetometer is the SQUID gradiometer which measures differences in magnetic fields at different positions. Using this type of instrument magnetic field variations in the femtotesla (10^{-15} tesla) range can be detected. Devices of this type have been used to map the tiny magnetic signals from the human brain.

Applications of magnetism

Electromagnets are utilized as key components of transformers in power supplies that convert electrical energy from a wall outlet into direct current energy for a wide range of electronic devices, and in motors and generators. High field superconducting magnets (where superconducting coils generate the magnetic field) provide the magnetic field in MRI (magnetic resonance imaging) devices that are now used extensively in hospitals and medical centers.

Magnetic materials that are difficult to demagnetize are used to construct permanent magnets. Permanent magnet applications are in loudspeakers, earphones, electric meters, and small motors. A loudspeaker consists of a wire carrying an alternating current. When the wire is in

the magnetic field of the permanent magnet it experiences a force that generates a sound wave by alternate compression and rarefaction of the surrounding air when the alternating frequency of the current is in the audible range.

The more esoteric applications of magnetism are in the area of magnetic recording and storage devices in computers, and in audio and video systems. Magnetic storage devices work on the principle of two stable magnetic states represented by the 0 and 1 in the binary number system. Floppy disks have dozens of tracks on which data can be digitally written in or stored by means of a write-head and then accessed or read by means of a read-head. A write-head provides a strong local magnetic field to the region through which the storage track of the disk is passed. The read-head senses stray magnetic flux from the storage track of the disk as it passes over the head. Another example of digital magnetic storage and reading is the magnetic strip on the back of plastic debit and credit cards. The magnetic strip contains identification data which can be accessed through, for example, an automatic teller machine.

Some current research trends in magnetism

Ideally pure magnetic systems have provided the most extensively investigated models of the large scale collective behavior of atoms and electrons that occur in the vicinity of the critical point of phase transitions. More recent studies have unearthed fascinating effects caused by the intentional introduction of impurities and defects into random locations in the atomic lattice of a magnetic material. For example, these random magnetic systems display transitions to states of order that have no counterparts in pure systems, because pure systems are, by necessity, always close to thermodynamic equilibrium or stability. For these reasons there is now intense interest and research activity in disordered systems, and random magnets provide ideal model systems for such investigations.

An area of intense current activity centers around the search for a likely magnetic pairing force in the high temperature ceramic superconductors that were discovered in 1987 by the German-Swiss team of Georg Bednorz and Karl Alexander Muller. A superconductor achieves a zero resistance state by means of a force field that pairs up the conducting electrons within its atoms. The new ceramic materials are antiferromagnets in their undoped state, but on doping start to superconduct at temperatures that are over 182°F (100°C) warmer than conventional pure metal and alloy superconductors.

The effects of extremely high magnetic fields on the properties of condensed matter continues to be an area of high interest. New research areas, such as the search and study of magnetism in organic matter, and the study of diamagnetism and novel magnetic effects in the recently synthesized nanometer-sized (a nanometer is equal to 10^{-9} meter) carbon tubes, are of increasing interest to physicists and material scientists.

See also Electromagnetism; Electron.

Further Reading:

Chikazumi, S. *Physics of Magnetism,* John Wiley and Sons, Ltd., 1984.
J. Clarke, "SQUIDs." *Scientific American*, (August, 1994): 46-53.
Cox, D.L. and M.B. Maple, "Electronic Pairing in Exotic Superconductors." *Physics Today* (1995): 32-40.
"Materials Science in High Magnetic Fields." *Materials Research Society Bulletin*, 27 (1993).
R.G. Newton, *What Makes Nature Tick?* Harvard University Press, 1993.

Zafar Iqbal

Magnetosphere

The magnetosphere is a comet-shaped region of Earth's outer atmosphere in which the behavior of charged particles is strongly influenced by magnetic and ionic phenomena. The term was first introduced by the British astronomer Thomas Gold in 1959 although speculation about the existence of such a region goes back to the early 1930s in the studies of Sydney Chapman and V.C.A. Ferraro.

The magnetosphere exists because of the interaction between Earth's own magnetic field and the solar wind, a rapidly moving plasma consisting of protons and electrons expelled from the sun's surface. The magnetosphere's distinctive shape is a consequence of the fact that the solar wind is deflected by Earth's magnetic field in a manner somewhat similar to the way in which a rock deflects the flow of a stream of water.

The forward (sun-facing) edge of the magnetosphere is located at a distance of about ten Earth radii (about 40,365 mi/65,000 km) from the Earth's surface. At this distance, the pressure of particles escaping from Earth's atmosphere is equal to the pressure of the solar wind. An equilibrium layer with a thickness of about 62 miles (100 km) in this region is known as the magnetopause. The magnetopause completely surrounds the magnetosphere like a thin envelope. Forward of the magnetopause in the direction of the sun is the magnetosheath, a region in which Earth's magnetic field is highly turbulent.

The magnetosphere extends much farther from Earth on the side away from the Sun (the "night" sides) because both the solar wind and particles escaping from Earth's atmosphere are moving in the same direction. It appears that the magnetopause in this direction may be located at a distance of a few thousand Earth radii.

The internal structure of the magnetopause is highly complex. The reason for this complexity is that three distinct factors—the solar wind, Earth's magnetic

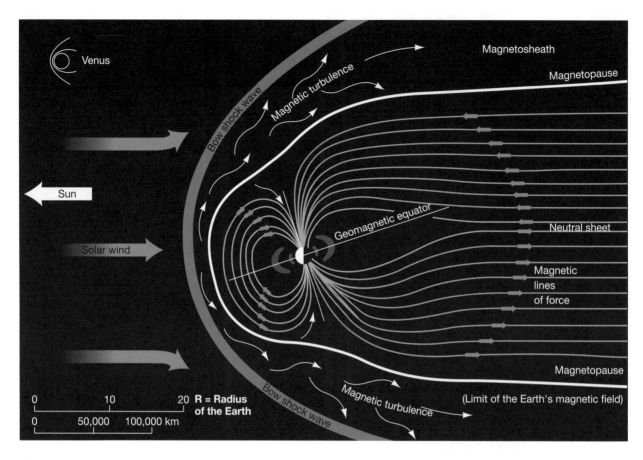

The Earth's magnetosphere.

field, and the Sun's magnetic field—are constantly interacting with each other. This interaction causes the development of distinct regions within the magnetosphere. For example, the night side of the magnetosphere appears to be subdivided into two regions by a thin layer of plasma called the plasma sheet.

Certain familiar astronomical phenomena are related to the magnetosphere. For example, particles excited by the interaction between the solar wind and the magnetosphere may eventually collide with and ionize particles in the upper atmosphere. When these ionized particles return to their ground state, they give off energy that may appear in the form of auroras (aurora australis, aurora borealis, or aurora australis).

See also Atmosphere, composition and structure of; Solar wind.

Magnolia

Magnolias are species of trees and woody shrubs that comprise the family Magnoliaceae. This is an ancient and relatively primitive group of dicotyledonous plants with fossil materials known from as early as the Upper Cretaceous. The magnolia family contains about 220 species in 12 genera, including the true magnolias (*Magnolia* spp.), with about 100 species.

Magnolias have seasonally deciduous or evergreen, oval-shaped, toothless leaves, arranged alternately on their twigs and branches. The flowers are bisexual, containing both male and female elements with three or more sepals and six or more showy petals. There are numerous stamens, arranged in a spiral fashion on the lower part of the elongate floral axis with numerous pistils spirally arranged above. The fruits are numerous, bright red or brown, and they hang with thread-like attachments from a semi-woody, cone-like structure derived from the floral axis.

Magnolias occur in warm-temperate and subtropical climates of the Northern Hemisphere, particularly in southeastern North America and most diversely, eastern Asia.

The most widespread, tree-sized species in eastern North America is the cucumber tree (*Magnolia acuminata*) with greenish flower petals and extending over much of the eastern United States and extreme southern Ontario. The southern magnolia (*M. grandiflora*), sweetbay (*M. virginiana*), and umbrella magnolia (*M. tripetala*) are more southern in their distributions and have white-petalled flowers. Species with relatively restricted southern distributions include the big-leaf magnolia (*M. macrophylla*), Ashe magnolia (*M. ashei*), Fraser magnolia (*M. fraseri*), and pyramid magnolia (*M. pyramidata*).

Magnolias are often cultivated as attractive trees and shrubs around homes and in parks. The native species most commonly used in horticulture is *Magnolia grandiflora*, which is one of the famous shade trees of the southeastern United States. Although it is a less showy species than the southern magnolia, *Magnolia acuminata* is also commonly planted, especially in more northern regions. Asiatic species that commonly occur in horticulture include the star magnolia (*Magnolia stellata*), kobus magnolia (*M. kobus*), and saucer magnolia (*M. soulangeana*).

The tulip-tree (*Liriodendron tulipifera*) is another member of the magnolia family with a relatively wide distribution in southeastern North America. This species is commercially important for its straight, clear lumber, and as an ornamental tree.

Bill Freedman

Mahogany

Mahogany (*Swietenia mahogani*) is a member of the family Meliaceae, which contains about 500 other species of trees and shrubs native to tropical forests in the Americas, Africa, and Asia. Other common names for this species are the Spanish or West Indies mahogany. Various species of trees have also been given the name "mahogany," but the true mahogany is *Swietenia mahogani*. Mahogany is one of the most valuable of the tropical hardwoods, because of its desirable qualities for the crafting of fine furniture.

Mahogany is native to tropical forests of the West Indies, Mexico, and Central America. Until rather recently, mahogany was especially abundant in forests in Honduras. However, the quantity of mahogany has been greatly reduced throughout its range by extensive logging.

Mahogany is also indigenous to extreme southern Florida, where it occurs in some of the hardwood "islands" in the sawgrass of Everglades National Park, known locally as hammocks. However, mahogany reaches the northern limits of its range in southern Florida, and is rather sparce in that region. Because of its great value as lumber, mahogany has also been planted in suitable tropical climates beyond its native range.

Biology of mahogany

Mahogany grows as tall as about 66-98 feet (20-30 m), and can achieve a diameter of more than 24 in (60 cm), exclusive of the large, basal buttresses that the tree usually develops. Mahogany is a slow-growing tree, and it usually occurs in closed forests.

The wood of mahogany is very hard, heavy, and strong, and has a rich, red-brown color, with an attractive, crooked grain. Mahogany wood is among the world's most prized and hardest-wearing timbers, and it is principally used to manufacture fine furniture. The bark of mahogany is a dark brown color and rather scaly.

The dark-green colored leaves of mahogany are arranged in an alternate fashion on the twigs. Mahogany leaves are compound, meaning that six to eight oval-shaped, leathery leaflets arise from a single petiole. The entire leaf has a length of 4-7 in (10-18 cm). Mahogany leaves are "evergreen," that is, they are not shed all at once at some particular season.

The flowers of mahogany are small, only 0.08-0.12 in (2-3 mm), with five greenish or whitish petals, and occurring in open clusters as a loose inflorescence. The flowers secrete nectar, and are pollinated by insects. The fruits of mahogany are a reddish-brown capsule, which when ripe split along five seams to shed the 0.78 in (2 cm) long seeds.

Uses of mahogany

The wood of mahogany is one of the world's most outstanding materials for the manufacturing of fine furniture. Mahogany wood is valued because it is durable and can be carved with intricate details. It has a deep, rich color, attractive grain, stains beautifully and glues solidly onto manufactured products.

Mahogany was first imported to Europe in 1724, and it soon became famous because of the gracefully ornate furniture that Chippendale, an English cabinet maker, began to make from the wood.

The most valuable raw product produced from mahogany wood is solid lumber, which can then be manufactured into expensive furniture and cabinets. However, solid mahogany is a very expensive material, and is becoming increasingly difficult to obtain. As a result, much mahogany is now used to manufacture a veneer product, in which a core of inferior wood is covered with a thin layer of mahogany. This composite material is glued together, and combines many of the desirable qualities of mahogany, especially its beautiful grain and color, with the cost savings associated with the use of other, relatively inexpensive species of trees.

Some related species

Some other species in the family Meliaceae are of commercial importance as sources of lumber, or as ornamental plants in horticulture.

The Spanish or cigar-box cedar (*Cedrela odorata*) of Central and South America has a hard, durable, richly colored wood that is used as a substitute for the true mahogany in fine cabinetry and furniture, as is the crabwood (*Carapa guianensis*), with a broadly similar range. The African mahogany (*Khaya senegalensis*) grows in tropical forests on the west coast of Africa and is one of the many African species in the genera Entandrophragma and Lovoa which are substituted for the wood of the true mahogany. Some tropical hardwoods in other plant families are also used as substitutes for mahogany, for example, the Columbian mahogany (*Cariniana pyriformis*) family Lecythidaceae.

The Chinaberry (*Melia azedarach*) is native to southern Asia, but is grown as an ornamental plant in parts of the southern United States. The compound leaves of the Chinaberry can be longer than fifty centimeters 19.7 in (50 cm), and its purplish flowers are attractive and fragrant.

Both species *Azadirachta* and *Melia* are used to manufacture botanical insecticides. Seeds of the trees

Carapa guianensis and *C. moluccensis* are used to manufacture a minor product known as carapa fat, a thick white or yellow oil used in oil lamps, and sometimes as an insect repellant.

Further Reading:

Hvass, E. *Plants That Feed and Serve Us.* New York: Hippocrene Books, 1975.

Woodland, D.W. *Contemporary Plant Systematics.* New Jersey: Prentice-Hall, 1991.

Bill Freedman

Maidenhair fern

These are a group of ferns found in tropical and warm temperate regions. They are characterized by having delicate, fan-shaped fronds, arising from a thin black midrib, with small green leaflets. Maidenhair fern belong to the genus *Adiantum*, and some species are popular as house plants. In North America there are three common species, the northern maidenhair fern (*A. pedatum*), the southern maidenhair fern (*A. capillus-veneris*), and the western maidenhair fern (*A. aleuticum*). They can grow up to 3 ft (1 m) tall and are generally found in clumps.

The leaflets are covered in a thick waxy epidermis with strong water-repellent properties (the Greek translation of *Adiantum* means unmoistened). The maidenhair ferns have been used as ingredients of medicinal shampoo, and also as hair restorer. In the sixteenth century they were also used to relieve asthma, snake bites, coughs, and as a stimulant.

The southern maidenhair fern tends to be found on shady, moist slopes with calcium-rich soil in the Southeastern and Gulf states and the Rockies as far north as Utah and west to California. Northern maidenhair fern occurs most abundantly in Virginia, though scattered collections are known from other coastal areas, as well as from woodlands within North and South Carolina and Georgia, and as far north as Ontario. Western maidenhair is also known as Five Finger Maidenhair, due to the appearance of the leaves at the ends of the stalks, and it is native to western North America. Species of maidenhair ferns can also be found in Europe, around the Mediterranean and in Japan.

The maidenhair tree or ginkgo (*Ginkgo biloba*) is said to be named after this group of ferns because of the similarity of leaf shape. However, the ginkgo is a conifer tree, and is not related to the maidenhair ferns.

See also Ferns.

Maize see **Grasses**

Malaria

Malaria has been described as the world's greatest public health problem. Transmitted by the bite of the *Anopheles* mosquito, malaria is a disease caused by one of several strains of the *Plasmodium* protozoan, a one-celled parasite. The disease results in 1-3 million deaths annually, primarily in developing countries; hundreds of millions are struck by it each year. Malaria has essentially been eradicated in North America, Europe, and Russia, although infected travelers and immigrants can reintroduce the disease if they are bitten by a mosquito. Malaria is on the increase worldwide, and it presents a major burden for tropical communities and travelers, particularly in areas where the parasite has evolved resistance to drugs used to treat it.

Origin of the disease

Alphonse Laveran, a French Army physician working in North Africa in the 1880s, was the first to observe evidence of malarial parasites in human blood. Its mode of transmission was not understood, however, until Ronald Ross, a medical officer in India, found the organisms within the bodies of *Anopheles* mosquitos. We now know that malaria is caused by four species of parasitic protozoa: *Plasmodium vivax, P. ovale, P. malariae,* and *P. falciparum.* These organisms have complex life cycles, involving several different developmental stages, and both a human and a mosquito host. Present as infective sporozoites in the salivary glands of the mosquito, they are transferred by the mosquito's bite to the human blood stream, where they travel to the liver. There, each sporozoite divides into thousands of merozoites, which emerge into the blood once again and begin invading the host's red blood cells. This event triggers the onset of disease symptoms. The merozoites consume proteins necessary for proper red blood cell function, including hemoglobin; in so doing, they mature into the trophozoite phase and reproduce by division. As a result, many more merozoites are released into the blood when the host cell finally ruptures. In *P. vivax* and *P. ovale* infection, some sporozoites may delay their development in the liver, lingering there in a dormant phase, to emerge later and cause the characteristic recurrence of symptoms.

The cycle of red blood cell invasion and parasite multiplication repeats itself numerous times during a bout of malaria. If the affected person is bitten by a mosquito, the insect takes up merozoites, which reproduce sexually within its gut. The cycle completes itself as the larval parasites pass through the gut wall and make their way to the mosquito's salivary glands, from where they may again be transferred to a human host as sporozoites.

Symptoms

Malaria is easily misdiagnosed because it resembles many other diseases. Early symptoms include malaise, fatigue, headache, nausea and vomiting, and muscular aches; after several hours, the characteristic high fever and chills occur. The body's principal defenses are fever, which destroys many pathogens, and filtration of infected red blood cells in the spleen. Neither of these mechanisms is completely effective in ridding the body of the parasite, however.

P. falciparum is the most dangerous of the four strains, as it can kill a healthy adult in 48 hours. This type is so dangerous because the parasitized red blood cells become sequestered in the deep vascular beds of the brain—hence the name "cerebral malaria" for infection with this strain. The sequestration happens because parasite-derived proteins on the surface of infected red blood cells make them stick to each other and to the cells lining the host's tiny venules and capillaries (two types of small veins), especially in the brain and heart. This has the effect of keeping the parasite away from the host's natural defense system. It also means that the progress of the disease can be hidden from a health practitioner who draws blood from a peripheral body region (for example, the arm); such a blood sample won't reveal the true extent of the infection. Delirium, convulsions, and coma are features of falciparum malaria, which is associated with a 20% mortality rate in adults.

Treatment and control

The connection between swampy areas and fever was made centuries ago, and the name malaria comes from the popular belief that the illness was caused by bad air (Italian, *mal aria*). During the sixteenth century, people discovered that the disease could be treated using quinine, a compound derived from the bark of the tropical *Cinchona* tree. Currently, the synthetic agent chloroquine is the most widely used antimalarial drug; it can clear non-resistant parasites from the blood in two to three days.

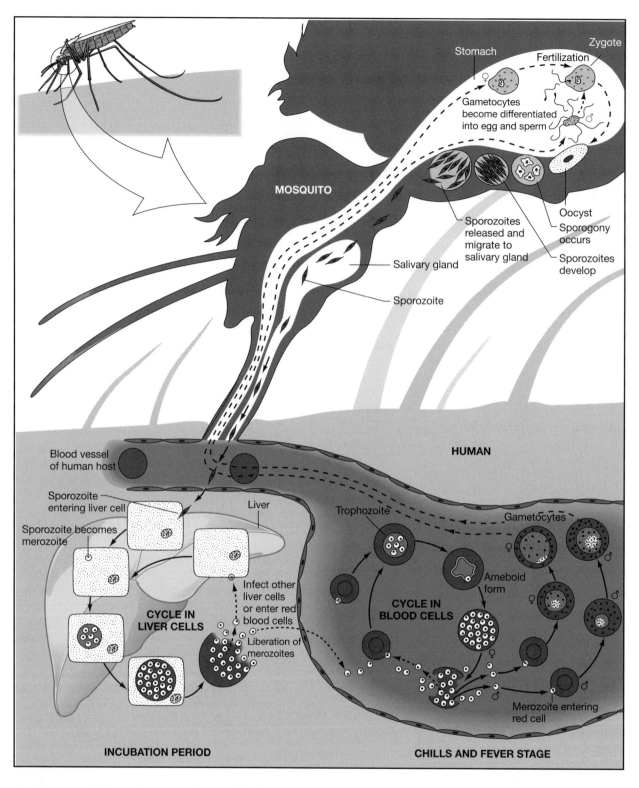

The life cycle of *Plasmodium vivax,* the parasite that causes malaria.

Chloroquine is often used together with the drug primaquine for malaria prophylaxis—that is, as protection for people who are at risk of becoming infected while visiting or working in malarial regions. Chloroquine attacks parasites that are circulating in the blood; primaquine is necessary to eradicate any dormant parasites from the liver. Malaria prophylaxis begins one week before entering a malarial area and continues for several weeks after returning to unaffected areas, because of the complex nature of the parasite's life cycle and the potential for relapse.

Unfortunately, chloroquine-resistant strains of falciparum malaria are on the increase worldwide. For this resistant parasite, the drug mefloquine is the preferred method of prophylaxis and treatment, although resistance to this drug may emerge rapidly, and resistant strains have been found in areas where the drug has never been used.

Efforts at preventing the disease have been directed at draining swampy areas and spraying for mosquitos in areas where they breed. A DDT-spraying campaign undertaken in India was effective for several years, until the mosquitos evolved resistance to the insecticide used against them and rebounded with a vengeance. Avoiding being bitten may be the best defense, and people in malarial areas are advised to avoid the outdoors during peak mosquito feeding times (dusk to dawn), to make use of window screens, and to sleep under nets treated with insecticide.

In areas where malaria is endemic and ever-present, many individuals appear to be immune to the disease. In some African populations, for example, the genetic trait causing sickle-cell anemia is directly connected with malaria immunity: a person possessing two sickle-cell genes will be afflicted with anemia, but a person with only one such gene will be malaria-resistant. Even where malaria is endemic, however, immunity from disease manifestations is not the same thing as freedom from infection; many individuals will host parasites within their bodies for months and years, although they show no symptoms. This phenomenon would seem to suggest that a vaccine could be developed, if the mechanism of host immunity could be identified. Thus far, however, the complexity of the immune response and the diversity of the parasite's evasive mechanisms have prevented researchers from clinically assessing immunity. Evidently, each of the protozoan's developmental stages bears different antigens, the molecules that trigger the development of immunity in the host. What is more, these factors are different for each of the four strains of the parasite. This explains why no individual is immune to all four malarial strains.

KEY TERMS

Antigen—A molecular factor that the body identifies as foreign and toward which it marshals an immune response.

Merozoite—The motile, infective stage of protozoa, which in malaria is responsible for disease symptoms.

Parasite—An organism that lives on or within a host organism, to the detriment of the host.

Protozoan—Microscopic, single-celled, eukaryotic organism, classified in the kingdom Protista.

Sporozoite—Protozoan developmental stage, during which the malaria parasite is transferred from mosquito to human host.

Trophozoite—The amoeboid, vegetative stage of some protozoa, including the malarial parasite.

The human battle with malaria is ongoing. Even as we seek ways to eliminate the organism that causes this dangerous disease, we can marvel at its remarkable adaptability and resilience. The efforts of immunologists, parasitologists, and health professionals in many countries will be needed to win the struggle against this insidious and elusive parasite.

See also Mosquitoes; Quinine.

Further Reading:
Beaver, P.C. and R.J. Jung. *Animal Agents and Vectors of Human Disease.* Philadelphia: Lea and Febiger, 1985.
Oaks, S.C. Jr., C.S. Carpenter, and C.S. Oaks. *Malaria: Obstacles and Opportunities.* Washington: National Academy Press, 1991.
Schmidt, G.D. and L.S. Roberts. *Foundations of Parasitology.* St. Louis: Times Mirror/Mosby, 1985.
Schroeder, Dirk G. *Staying Healthy in Asia, Africa, and Latin America.* Chico, CA: Moon Publications, Inc., 1993.

Susan Andrew

Mallards see **Ducks**

Malleus see **Ear**

Malnutrition

Malnutrition is a dietary condition marked by the depletion of the individual's nutritional reserves and energy resources. It is caused either by an insufficient intake of food or the reliance on a limited diet that fails to deliver vital nutrients to the body. The single most important factor in creating malnourishment is poverty, especially for those who live in poorly developed countries either in Asia or Africa or other parts of the economically underdeveloped world. Those who are most at risk of malnutrition where conditions of poverty exist are infants, children, pregnant woman, and the elderly.

Even in countries with high standards of living, like the United States, there is evidence of malnutrition caused by hunger among the poor. Estimates of as much as, if not more than, twenty million Americans go hungry periodically within the month. Throughout the world the death toll from malnutrition caused by hunger ranges from 40,000-50,000 people a day, while 450 million to 1.3 billion face the prospect of starvation from their limited food supplies.

The elderly who are in nursing homes or hospitals who are suffering from long term illness or chronic metabolic disorder are also at risk of malnutrition. Professional caregivers have procedures to monitor the nutritional condition of these patients. Malnutrition is also experienced by those suffering from a condition called anorexia nervosa, a psychosomatic disorder marked by intentional food denial that leads to starvation. Malnutrition leads to nutritional deficiency diseases caused by the lack of energy-producing foods for caloric intake, protein, vitamins and minerals.

Nutrient deficiency diseases

Nutrient deficiency diseases occur as a consequence of either the lack or absence of those nutrients which are essential for growth and health. Lack of food leading to either malnutrition or starvation gives rise to these diseases. Another cause for a deficiency disease may be due to a structural or biological imbalance in the individual's metabolic system.

There are more than fifty known nutrients in food. Nutrients enable body tissues to grow and maintain themselves. They contribute to the energy requirements of the individual organism and they regulate the processes of the body. Carbohydrates, fats, and proteins provide the body with energy. The energy-producing component of food is measured in calories. Aside from the water and fiber content of food, which are also important for their role in nutrition, the nutrients that serve functions other than energy production can be classified into four different groups: vitamins, fats, proteins, and minerals. These are referred to as essential nutrients because they are necessary for proper body function and survival.

Protein-energy malnutrition (PEM)

Proteins play a key role in the development of body tiswsues. They contain amino acids, which, once metabolized, provide the necessary components for the production of other proteins that also aid in the restructuring and maintenance of numerous bodily tissues and complex functions.

Protein deficiency, in most cases, can be attributed to situations of undernourishment and malnutrition. Such nutrient deficiency is more prevalent in (though not limited to) lesser developed regions of the world. Among children in these areas, it is quite extensive.

The terms undernourishment (inadequate caloric intake) and malnourishment (a deficiency of one or even all nutrients) are so closely related, the term protein-energy malnutrition (PEM) has become widely accepted in generally discussing the problems as one. However, once the symptoms of PEM have persisted, they can evolve into two specific, more severe syndromes: kwashiorkor and marasmus.

There are two types of protein: fibrous and globular. Fibrous protein is insoluble and goes into making the structural tissues of the body. Globular protein forms amino acids that become enzymes and hormones and other vital parts of cellular functioning within the body.

Kwashiorkor and marasmus

Kwashiorkor, taken from an African word, generally affects children from infancy to three years old and is the result of a poor weaning diet. The diet, which is mainly sugar and water or a starchy gruel, is high in carbohydrates and lacks protein or has a poor quality of protein. The weaning diet for these young children leads to other nutrient deficiency diseases as well.

The main symptom of kwashiorkor is edema; other symptoms may include loss of hair and skin pigmentation, scaliness of the skin, diarrhea, and anemia. Other repeated infections (viral, bacterial, parasitic) can strike during the illness. Left untreated, kwashiorkor can be fatal. Marasmus is a more severe condition characterized by: a low body weight (relative to age), wasting of muscle tissue, and diarrhea. Oftentimes, there may be a converging of symptoms which would be described as marasmic kwashiorkor.

In cases of severe PEM it is necessary to hospitalize the child and to administer antibiotics to prevent infections which accompany the condition. Diets rich in protein should be continued after hospitalization, using skimmed milk powder for an energy basis. Legumes (beans) and fish meal are also good sources for protein.

Social and political problems have to be managed to allow relief workers to help and to provide an ongoing source of food preparations that can be consumed for adequate nourishment by those in need. It is also important to keep other diseases and infections down through the use of safe drinking water and sanitation.

Scurvy

Scurvy is one of the oldest deficiency diseases recorded and the first one to be cured by adding a vitamin to the diet. It was a common malady of sailors during the age of exploration of the New World. Vasco da Gama is supposed to have lost half of his crew to scurvy in his journey around the Cape of Good Hope at the end of the fifteenth century and Richard Hawkins reported that he lost ten thousand sailors from the disease a century later.

The main symptom of scurvy is hemorrhaging. Hemorrhage marks appear as spots under the skin or bruises given the medical terms of petechiae and ecchymoses respectively. The gums are swollen and usually become infected (gingivitis). Bleeding can take place in the membranes covering the large bones as well as in the membranes of the heart and brain. Wounds heal slowly and the bleeding in or around vital organs can be fatal. The disease is slow to develop and is early manifested by fatigue, irritability, and depression. In the advanced stages of the disease laboratory tests will show an absence of the vitamin needed to protect against the disease, vitamin C.

In 1747 a British naval physician, James Lind, in a response to a an outbreak of scurvy aboard an English ship that was cruising in the English channel conducted a controlled experiment. He took twelve of the sailors who had developed scurvy and divided them up into six groups and then gave each group different medicines for the condition. Some were given nutmeg, cider, seawater, and vinegar while others were given lemons or oranges. He found that the two groups given the oranges and lemons completely recovered in about a week after the trial.

Lind's *Treatise of the Scurvy,* published in 1753, is the first example of a controlled clinical trial experiment. In his treatise, Lind gave a thorough review of other authors who had written on scurvy along with a careful clinical description of the condition. It was not until the end of the eighteenth century that the British navy finally had its sailors drink a daily portion of lime or lemon juice to prevent scurvy. The American slang term for the English, "limeys," originated from that practice.

Vitamin C (ascorbic acid) is necessary for collagen formation, which is the protein component of connective tissue, strong blood vessels, healthy skin and gums, formation of red blood cells, wound healing, and the absorption of iron. In addition to scurvy, other scurvy-like conditions can develop from a deficiency of vitamin C, such as adult acne, easy bruising, sore gums, and hemorrhages around bones. Good sources for vitamin C are citrus fruit, broccoli, strawberries, cantaloupe, and other fruits and vegetables.

In the modern world, individuals who are on diets which lack diverse food choices still are susceptible to developing scurvy. Infants who depend on processed cow's milk and are not given vitamin supplementation are at risk for the disease. Food faddists and those who follow a diet of just cereals, bread, and milk, without any citrus fruits, like oranges or grapefruits, become at risk.

Beriberi

The attempt to discover the causes for beriberi is part of the history for the discovery of vitamins. Christian Eijkman (1858-1930) was a Dutch physician who was a member of a government commission sent to the East Indies in the 1880s to study the disease beriberi, which was prevalent in southeast Asia.

There are three forms of this disease: infantile beriberi, wet beriberi, and dry beriberi. In infantile beriberi, the mother who nurses the child may not manifest the disease, but the deficiency occurs through the breast feeding and the child usually dies after the fifth month. In the childhood and adult versions of the disease there is a preliminary condition of fatigue, loss of appetite, and a numb tingling feeling in the legs. This condition can then lead to either wet or dry beriberi.

In wet beriberi there is an accumulation of fluid throughout the body and a rapid heart rate that can lead to sudden death. In dry beriberi there is no fluid swelling, but there is a loss of sensation and a weakness in the legs. The patient first needs to walk with the aid of a stick and then becomes bed-ridden to become an easy prey to an infectious disease.

The Dutch commission on beriberi decided that the disease was caused by some type of infection; Eijkman, however, continued his research. In his laboratory he noticed that some of the fowl he was experimenting with developed paralysis and polyneuritis which were symptoms similar to the dry form of beriberi. The director of the hospital had forbidden Eijkman to feed these birds table scraps, which consisted mainly of polished rice. He therefore began to feed them with whole rice, after which he noticed that they regained their movement and there was no recurrence of paralysis.

The idea that the birds had some form of beriberi was rejected by Eijkman's colleagues. His explanation for the cure was that the polished rice had some toxin in it which the unpolished rice did not have. This explanation was rejected by a fellow researcher, Gerrit Grijns (1865-1944), who also stayed on to study the disease after the work of the original commission concluded. He found that when the chickens were taken off the rice diet completely and fed with meat instead, they did not develop the characteristic paralysis; but if the meat was overcooked, then the condition would reappear.

Vitamin B₁ (thiamine) prevents the disease or symptoms of beriberi. Food sources for this vitamin are (well- but not overcooked) meats, wheat germ, whole grain and enriched bread, legumes, peanuts, peanut butter, and nuts.

Today, beriberi is still prevalent in Japan, Indonesia, China, Malaysia, India, Burma, the Philippines, Brazil, Thailand, and Vietnam. In the United States and other western societies, it usually occurs in a milder form and is associated with other diseases. It accompanies malnutrition, alcoholism, pregnant women who have a poor diet, prison inmates where there is poor nutritional planning, geriatric hospitals, or other such institutions.

Mineral deficiency diseases

There are about twenty-five mineral elements in the body, usually appearing in the form of simple salts. Those which appear in large amounts are called macrominerals while those that are in small or trace amounts are microminerals. Some that are essential are calcium, phosphorous, cobalt, copper, fluorine, iodine, iron, and sodium. Chromium and tin may be essential and aluminum, lead, and mercury are among those that are not essential. Calcium, in conjunction with phosphorous and vitamin D, is needed for preventing rickets and for preventing other bone diseases such as osteoporosis (loss of bone tissue), which is part of several other complex factors in causing that disease.

Goiter

Iodine is necessary for the proper functioning of the thyroid gland which controls the body's basal metabolism rate through its production of two hormones: thyroxine and triiodinethyronine. Without a sufficient amount of iodine in the diet, the gland begins to enlarge its cells in its efforts to produce the hormone, thus producing a goiter which is a swelling around the neck. Globally, certain regions lack iodine in the soil

---

KEY TERMS

. . . .

Ascorbic acid—Another name for vitamin C.

Calorie—A measure of energy. The amount of energy required to raise one gram of water one centigrade.

Collagen—The protein that holds the body together found in bones, tendons, and connective tissues.

Fibrous protein—protein used to make new body tissue as opposed to globular protein which from which the body produces hormones and enzymes.

Gingivitis—Inflammation of the gums—a symptom of scurvy.

Hemorrhage—The medical term for bleeding—a symptom of scurvy.

Legumes—The general name for beans which are a good vegetable source for proteins.

Marasmus—Wasting away of muscle and skin in children suffering from calorie deficiency.

PEM—Protein-energy malnutrition. The general name for a wide range of conditions that occur as a result of both energy and protein deficiency.

Psychosomatic disorder—A physical disorder involving both the body and mind.

---

and that could lead to cretinism, the arrested physical and mental development of an infant passed on from the lack of iodine in the mothers diet.

Anemia

Iron is necessary for hemoglobin and enzyme formation. An iron deficiency can lead to anemia, a lack of oxygen in the blood, leading to fatigue and other complications. Good food sources for iron are liver, lean meats, legumes, dried fruits, and green leafy vegetables.

Other diseases

Other diseases caused by malnutrition throughout the present-day world are pellagra, rickets, tetany (a calcium deficiency that causes muscular spasms), osteomalacia (an adult form of rickets), osteoporosis (an age-related bone disorder), and xerophthalmia (a vitamin A deficiency that affects the eyes and causes blindness).

See also Nutrient deficiency diseases; Nutrients; Nutrition.

Further Reading:

Eschleman, Marian M. *Nutrition & Diet Therapy*. New York: Lippincott, 1991.

Guthrie, Helen A. *Introductory Nutrition*. Boston: Mosby College Publishing, 1989.

Hendler, Sheldon S. *The Doctor's Vitamin and Mineral Encyclopedia*. New York: Simon and Shuster, 1990.

Williams, Sue R. *Nutrition and Diet Therapy*. Boston: Mosby College Publishing, 1989.

Yudkin, John. *The Penguin Encyclopedia of Nutrition*. New York: Viking, 1985.

Jordan P. Richman

Mambas see **Elapid snakes; Snakes**

Mammals

The more than 4,000 species of living mammals belong to the vertebrate class Mammalia. This diverse group of animals has certain common features: all have four legs, bodies covered by hair, a high and constant body temperature, a muscular diaphragm used in respiration, a lower jaw consisting of a single bone, a left systemic aortic arch leaving the left ventricle of the heart, and three bones in the middle ear. In addition, all female mammals have milk-producing glands. There are three living subclasses of mammals: the Monotremata (egg-laying mammals), the Marsupialia (pouched mammals), and the Placentalia (placental mammals).

Mammals range in size from bats, some of which weigh less than 1 oz (28.4 g), to the blue whale, which weighs more than 200,000 lb (90,800 kg). Mammals are found in cold arctic climates, in hot deserts, and in every terrain in between. Marine mammals, such as whales and seals, spend most of their time in the ocean. While mammals are not as numerous and diverse as, for example, birds or insects, mammals have a tremendous impact on the environment, particularly due to the use of Earth's natural resources by one species of mammal: humans.

Species of mammals have developed varying adaptations in response to the different environments in which they live. Mammals in cold climates have insulating layers—a thick coat of fur, or a thick layer of fat (blubber)—that help retain body heat and keep the animal's body temperature constant. Some mammals that live in deserts survive by special adaptations in their kidneys and sweat glands, as well as by their ability to avoid heat by behavioral means. Other adaptations for survival in extreme climates include hibernation (a state of winter dormancy) or estivation (summer dormancy). These responses make it possible for the animal to conserve energy when food supplies become scarce.

The care of the young (parental care) is notable among mammals. Born at an average of 10% of its mother's weight, mammalian young grow rapidly. The protection the young receive from one or both parents during the early stages of their lives enables mammals to maintain a strong survival rate in the animal kingdom.

The subclass Placentalia contains the majority of living mammals. The embryo of placentals develops in the mother's uterus, is nourished by blood from the placenta, and is retained until it reaches an advanced state of development. The Marsupialia are found in Australia and in North and South America. Their young develop inside the uterus of the mother, usually with a placenta connected to a yolk sac. Young marsupials are born in a very undeveloped state and are sheltered in a pouch (the marsupium) which contains the nipples of the milk glands. Kangaroos, wallabies, and most Australian mammals are marsupials, as is the opossum of the New World. The Monotremata of Australia include the duck-billed platypus and two species of spiny anteaters. Monotremes lay eggs, but have hair and secrete milk like other mammals.

See also Marsupials; Monotremes.

Manakins

Manakins are 53 species of small, tropical birds that comprise the family Pipridae, occurring from southern Mexico to Paraguay. Manakins are species that dwell in mature, tropical forests.

Manakins are squat, compact birds, with short, rounded wings and a short tail. However, in some species the tail of the male is greatly lengthened by the occurrence of long, thin extensions, sometimes longer than the rest of the body. Manakins have a short beak, slightly hooked at the tip. Manakins are skilled and maneuverable fliers.

Male manakins of most species are very brightly colored, with brilliant patterns of red, yellow, blue, or white on a background of black or dark grey. Female manakins are much less brilliant, and are typically olive-green in color.

Manakins are highly active birds. They commonly fly-catch insects, which are a major component of their diet. Manakins even utilize aerial sallies to pluck fruit, another of their important foods.

Manakins are famous for their elaborate courtship rituals, which are among the most complex of any of the birds. The most celebrated courtships involves species in which the males display at leks, or communal assembly areas where males gather to display to each other and to females as they arrive seeking a potential mate.

Individual males of the white bearded manakins (*Manacus* spp.) clear a small, approximately 3 ft (1 sq m) area of the forest floor of leaves, twigs, and other litter, as do other males. In this way a large lek of as many as 70 courts can develop, over an area as wide as 98 ft (30 m). These courts are the places where the individual male birds perform their pre-nuptial displays to females that arrive from far and wide, to choose their beaux from the many males on hopeful display.

The actual displays vary greatly among the species of manakins, but they generally involve quick, ritualized movements. Those of the golden-headed manakins (*Pipra* spp.) are relatively well known, and include quick slidings along a horizontal branch, fleet turn-arounds on the branch, and rapid flutterings of the wings, which produce sharp, snappy noises. The males also execute rapid flights over a distance of less than 98 ft (30 m), somehow making ripping noises with the wings. These displays are carried out even in the absence of an attending female, but they are especially intense when the male knows that a potential mate is nearby, and watching, and hopefully choosing.

Bill Freedman

Manatee

Manatees, dugongs, or sea cows are large, passive herbivorous aquatic mammals in the order Sirenia. There are four species and one species which is recently extinct. Regrettably, all species of sirenians are either endangered, or are significantly threatened by humans and their activities.

Sirenians are charismatic animals with a gentle nature, but are by no means handsome animals. Considering this, it is difficult to imagine how sightings of dugongs could have been the basis of mariners' fables of mermaids.

Biology of sirenians

Sirenians are large animals, weighing as much as almost 1,544 lb (700 kg), with a body length of up to 14.8 ft (4.5 m) and a large head and small mouth. Sirenians have paddle-shaped forelimbs, no hindlimbs and a broad flattened tail. Their bones are heavy and dense for maintaining a near-neutral buoyancy, so that these animals can easily stay submerged while feeding. Sirenians have thick, nearly hairless skin. There are stiff hairs (vibrissae) around the mouth which are tactile sensors for detecting food in turbid waters. The teeth of sirenians are reduced and specialized for processing vegetation and one sirenian, Steller's sea cow, (*Hydrodamalis stelleri*) completely lacks teeth. The nostrils open on the top of the flat-faced muzzle, and can be closed when the animal is submerged. Sirenians have small eyes and poor vision, but they have a good sense of hearing.

Manatees (genus *Trichechus*) have an evenly rounded tail while dugongs (genus *Dugong*) have a deeply notched tail. The upper lip of manatees is deeply cleft, and male dugongs have a pair of incisor teeth.

Sirenians eat a wide range of marine plants, such as turtlegrasses, seagrasses, kelps, and other large species of algae.

Sirenians can occur in groups of up to twenty individuals, but they are more commonly seen in smaller groups, and are often solitary. These animals give birth to a single offspring after a gestation period of about eleven months. The young are carefully nurtured by their mother.

Species of sirenians

The American or northern manatee (*Trichechus manatus*) occurs in coastal waters of northeastern South America, the Caribbean, Florida, and west to Texas and the Gulf Coast of Mexico. In the southeastern United States these animals will congregate in the relatively warm, thermal plumes of electric generating stations during the cooler months of winter. The Amazonian or Brazilian manatee (*T. inunguis*) is a freshwater species found in parts of the Amazon and Orinoco Rivers of South America. The African manatee (*T. senegalensis*) lives in freshwater rivers and large lakes, and in shallow, marine coastal waters of western Africa.

The dugong (*Dugong dugon*) inhabits the shallow, coastal, tropical waters of the Red Sea, East Africa, Asia, and northern Australia. Dugongs can be 3-10 ft (1-3 m) long, weigh up to 662 lb (300 kg), and occur in pairs or small groups in marine habitats, although some dugongs occasionally venture into estuaries.

Steller's sea cow (*Hydrodamalis stelleri*) has been extinct since the mid-eighteenth century and was the only sirenian to occur in cold waters. This was a rela-

A young manatee in the Crystal River, Florida.

tively large animal, achieving a body length of up to 24.6 ft (7.5 m) and a weight of about four tonnes. The range of Steller's sea cow was the Bering Sea, where it fed on kelp and other marine algae.

People and sirenians

Because of their enormous capacity to consume aquatic vegetation, manatees have occasionally been used to reduce the abundance of aquatic plants in inland waterways. This can be a substantial, local benefit, because canals, slow-moving rivers, and other important transportation corridors can be choked by dense growths of aquatic plants.

Because sirenians occur in shallow waters and are slow moving, they are extremely vulnerable to predation by humans. As a result, sirenians have long been hunted by aboriginal peoples for their meat, hides, and fat, which can be rendered into oil. Some cultures believe that body parts of sirenians can be used as folk medicines for the treatment of certain diseases.

Manatees and dugongs often suffer injuries from motorboats. If the operator of a motorboat is not aware of a partially or shallowly submerged sirenian, the boat's propeller can cause serious, even lethal, injuries. Many of the adult animals in the endangered populations of manatees in Florida have healed propeller wounds on their bodies. Go-slow zones are often posted in waters where manatees live, but this by no means eliminates the threat of injuries in part because there speed restrictions are not always vigorously enforced.

All four sirenians are threatened or endangered species largely because of hunting, habitat loss, and pollution.

The now extinct Steller's sea cow, formerly occurred in the Bering Sea, and was first discovered by explorers employed by the Russian Czar in 1741. This vulnerable, inoffensive animal was hunted for its hide and oil, and since its population was already small it was became extinct by 1768, after only 26 years of commercial hunting.

Further Reading:

Dietz, T. *The Call of the Siren: Manatees and Dugongs.* London: Fulcrum Press, 1992.

Grzimek, B. (ed.). *Grzimek's Encyclopedia of Mammals.* London: McGraw Hill, 1990.

Paradiso, J.L. (ed.). *Mammals of the World,* 2nd ed. Baltimore: Johns Hopkins Press, 1968.

Reynold, J. and D. Odell. *Manatees and Dugongs.* New York: Facts on File,1994.

Ridgeway, S.H. and R.J. Harrison (eds.). *Handbook of Marine Mammals. Vol. 3. The Sirenians and Baleen Whales.* San Diego: Academic Press, 1985.

Wilson, D.E. and D. Reeder (comp.). *Mammal Species of the World.* Washington D.C.: Smithsonian Institution Press, 1993.

Zeiler, W. *Introducing the Manatee.* Miami: Florida University Press, 1992.

Bill Freedman

Mandrill see **Baboons**

Manganese see **Element, chemical**

Mango see **cashew family**

Mangrove tree

Mangroves are trees in the family Rhizophoraceae, occurring in tropical and sub-tropical environments as swampy forests fringing muddy, tidal, marine shores. Mangrove forests are generally the first type of woody ecosystem that is encountered when a low-lying tropical shore is approached from the ocean.

Mangrove forests comprise a biome, that is, a distinctive ecosystem that occurs in appropriate habitats worldwide. Compared with other tropical forests, the mangrove ecosystem is rather poor in species. The richest mangrove forests occur closest to the equator, especially in the western Pacific Ocean. The number of mangrove species diminishes with increasing latitude in both hemispheres, with black mangrove (*Avicennia* spp.) generally being the last species to drop out, reaching about 32°N in Bermuda and 38°S in northern Australia.

Mangrove trees are well adapted to growing in saline water, having glands on their leaves for excreting their excess of absorbed salt, and evergreen foliage to aid in the retention of scarce nutrients. Some species have aerial roots that aid in transporting oxygen to their below-ground tissues, and seeds that are specialized for establishing in tidal muds.

Species of mangrove trees

The family Rhizophoraceae contains about 100 species of woody plants, all of which are tropical or subtropical in distribution. The most important of the tree-sized species are in the genera *Avicennia*, *Bruguiera*, *Ceriops*, and *Rhizophora*.

The red mangrove (*Rhizophora mangle*) is abundant in mangrove forests of south Florida, the Caribbean, and Central and South America. This species has distinctive, round, stilt-roots, which emerge from aerial parts of the stem and then curve downwards to set into the sediment. The red mangrove also retains its ripe seeds on its branches, where they germinate aerially, extending a radicle up to 10 in (25 cm) long. This sort of germination system is known as vivipary, and is analogous in some respects to the bearing of live young by animals. The germinated seedlings eventually detach from the parent tree, and may plop upright into the mud and establish a new plant, or they may float for a while until they become lodged in sediment after a longer-range dispersal from the parent. The established seedlings of red mangrove send out prop-roots, which quickly become firmly anchored and help to accrete mud around the plant. Young plants of this sort are abundant along the leading edge of developing stands of red mangrove, with older, larger trees occurring further into the stand. The individual stands often occur as discrete mangrove "islands," which may eventually coalesce as an extensive forest.

The black mangrove (*Avicennia nitida*) is also abundant in mangrove forests of Florida, the Caribbean, and Latin America. This species has radially spreading, underground roots from which emerge numerous, vertically growing pneumatophores, or extensions of the roots that emerge from the mud. The pneumatophores are exposed to the atmosphere during low tide, and are useful in conducting oxygen to the underwater tissues of the plant, which grow in an anaerobic environment. Black mangroves often do not reproduce well beneath their own closed canopy, and when their stands senesce and die back the site may convert into a relatively open community dominated by plants of salt marshes and protected mudflats.

Red mangroves in Florida.

Ecology of mangrove forests

The mangrove environment is stressful to most plants, largely because of the large salt concentrations in water, which are physiologically difficult for most species to deal with. However, mangrove trees can tolerate this stress, and as a result they are able to assemble into forests under these environmental conditions, although these are relatively species-poor ecosystems in comparison with other types of tropical forests.

The mangrove ecosystem is periodically subject to catastrophic disturbances, usually associated with severe windstorms such as hurricanes. These can be energetic enough to uproot and kill mature trees, and to initiate ecological recovery through primary succession. Species of *Rhizophora* are often the primary mangrove colonist, followed by *Avicennia* and other secondary species as the ecosystem begins to stabilize and mature.

The patterns of successional dynamics of mangrove forest are related to the environmental tolerances of the species, and often result in distinct zonations of community types within this ecosystem. Usually the succession culminates in a mature forest of mangrove species. However, in some cases succession in the mangrove ecosystem can sufficiently reduce the influence of tidal waters to allow relatively fresh-water conditions to develop. Under these circumstances succession can result in the development of a relatively species-rich forest that is lacking in mangrove species, because these are not very competitive under the less-stressful conditions of fresh water.

Mangrove forests are very effective at binding coastal muds and helping to prevent their erosion. This contributes to the development of a stable substrate that enhances the rate of ecosystem development, and allows the forest to resist tidal and other disturbances and thereby form a relatively stable ecosystem.

Mangrove forests provide critical nursery habitat for various commercially important species of tropical fish and invertebrates, such as shrimps. These coastal wetlands also provide important habitat for a wide range of non-economic species of wildlife.

Mangroves and humans

Mangrove forests are commercially important in some places. Lumber can be manufactured from all of

KEY TERMS

· ·

Biome—A geographically extensive ecosystem, usually characterized by its dominant life forms.

Ecotourism—Ecology-based tourism, focused primarily on natural or cultural resources.

Mangrove—A coastal, tropical, wet forest growing on muddy substrate, and dominated by species of mangrove trees in the family Rhizophoraceae.

Pneumatophores—Exposed roots of some marsh plants that are useful in conducting oxygen to the plant's underwater tissues.

Radicle—Embryonic root.

Senesce—To age.

the mangrove trees, but the most durable wood is that of *Ceriops*. Where it is abundant, *Rhizophora* may also be harvested to manufacture lumber or pulp. In some places, mangroves trees are harvested and used to manufacture charcoal. The bark of mangroves is rich in tannins, and has been used for the commercial production of these chemicals, which are utilized to tan animals skins into leather. Mangrove forests are also commonly harvested for local use as firewood.

Ecotourism is a less consumptive use of the mangrove ecosystem. In large part this recreational use is based on the fact that many species of large, colorful birds can be abundant in mangrove forests and their integrated, open-water wetlands and shores. These include species of herons, ibises, pelicans, gulls, terns, osprey, and shorebirds.

Mangrove forests in many parts of the world are under intense pressure from various types of human stressors. This is partly associated with overly intensive harvesting of natural resources from mangrove forests. In addition, in many regions mangrove forests are being lost to various types of coastal developments, which convert these natural ecosystems into agriculture, plantations, tourism developments, or aquaculture facilities, especially for the culturing of shrimp. In some places, mangrove forests are also being degraded through pollution associated with agricultural runoff, sewage dumping from residential areas, and aquatic industrial emissions of various types.

Further Reading:

Stafford-Deitsch, J. *Mangroves.* London: Immel, 1994.

Walter, H. *Vegetation of the Earth.* New York: Springer-Verlag, 1978.

Bill Freedman

Mania

Mania is a mood disturbance marked by an abnormal degree of elation or irritability along with a number of other symptoms including restlessness, inflated self confidence, a marked decrease in the need for sleep, rapid and loud speech that is difficult to interrupt, racing thoughts, high distractibility, and a marked increase in certain goal-directed activities. Over time, manic episodes are usually preceded or followed by periods of major depression, and diagnostically mania is seen as a component of bipolar or manic-depressive, disorder. In bipolar disorders individuals experience alternating manic and depressive symptoms. Mania then is not currently considered a separate psychiatric disorder.

Symptoms

The primary symptom of a manic episode is a marked disturbance of mood in which the individual is extremely elated or irritable for at least one week unless hospitalization is necessary. The individual's mood may be unusually cheerful or good, and while this may not seem unusual to those who don't know the individual, to those who do, it is usually seen as excessive and strange. The person's mood may also be one of extreme irritability, especially when their desires and goals are interfered with. It also quite common for the person to switch rapidly between irritability and elation. In addition to the mood disturbance the individual will usually show three or four of the following symptoms.

In a manic episode the need for less sleep is almost always seen, so that the individual may rise hours earlier than normal yet still be full of energy. Indeed, they may not sleep for days but feel no fatigue. Another common symptom is overly high self-confidence. The individual may attempt complex and difficult tasks for which they have no experience or knowledge, such as sailing around the world or climbing Mount Everest. They may also have grandiose delusions (false beliefs that do not seem possible) about themselves. Rapid and loud speech that is difficult to interrupt is also a common symptom. Speech will often show a pressured quality as if the person is compelled to speak, so that individuals may talk a lot. They may even talk for hours without stopping.

Extremely rapid or racing thoughts are often present in a manic episode. This may be seen in very rapid speech in which the individual switches topics very rapidly, and in extreme cases speech may become so disorganized that it is incomprehensible. A person having a manic episode will often plan and participate in an excessive amount of goal-directed behaviors, such as sexual, professional, or political, religious activities. They may, for example, volunteer in numerous school or work related committees without regard to whether they can fulfill these obligations. Often a person having a manic episode does not believe there is anything wrong with them and they resist treatment. Taken together, these symptoms often lead to reckless behaviors the individual would not normally engage in that are likely to have negative consequences. For instance, the individual may make unnecessary purchases which they cannot afford, or make unwise investments. In order for a diagnosis of manic episode to be made, an individual's interpersonal, professional, or school functioning must be noticeably impaired or they must require hospitalization because of these symptoms.

Course

Manic episodes can last from a few weeks to two to three months in length, and they are often preceded by stressful life events. While the average age for a first manic episode is in the early 20s, some occur in the teenage years. Those who have their first episode in their teens often have a history of behavior problems. Sometimes mania is not seen until after age 50.

Over 90% of individuals who have one manic episode will have additional episodes. And approximately 60-70% of manic episodes occur just before or after periods of major depression. While this may paint a rather bleak picture, it should be noted that some experts hold that while up to 40% of those with bipolar disorder will experience repeating cycles, they rarely experience long-term physical or mental impairment. And most people with bipolar disorder have periods with almost no symptoms in which they essentially function normally.

Causality

Most researchers believe bipolar disorders have a biological basis. And this stance is supported by findings that close relatives of those with bipolar disorder are significantly more likely to develop affective disorders than are relatives of people with no history of psychiatric illness. Theories of the underlying biological mechanisms have centered on concentrations of various neurotransmitters in the nerve connections of the brain. Because

neurotransmitter interactions are subtle, complex, and obviously hard to observe, the strongest supportive and disconfirming evidence for the roles of specific neurotransmitters comes from the differential efficacy of various drug treatments. And the fact that patients diagnosed with bipolar disorder respond differently to various drugs indicates there may be more than one type of bipolar disorder with different biological bases.

Treatment

Lithium carbonate is the predominant drug treatment for manic episodes. Carbamazepine has been used to successfully treat those who cannot tolerate or do not respond to lithium. Various antipsychotic and antidepressant medications have also proven useful. Electroconvulsive shock therapy has shown some effectiveness in the treatment of mania and it may be indicated for patients who cannot take lithium or antipsychotics, though its use remains controversial. For treating some types of depression, psychotherapy has been found to be effective, its efficacy in treating manic states however is still unclear, as there have been few studies assessing this. This may be due to the general difficulty of treating someone in a manic state. In general, however, it seems that after a manic episode most people may benefit from supportive psychotherapy as they often experience a lowering of their confidence and self esteem.

Current research

Currently, the *Diagnostic and Statistical Manual of Mental Disorders,* 4th edition (DSM-IV) has no separate diagnostic disorder called mania or manic disorder. The DSM-IV is the official psychiatric classification system for medical and legal uses in the United States. Over the years, psychiatrists and psychologists have questioned whether mania is experienced without depressive episodes and thus whether it is a disorder distinct from bipolar disorder. Some recent research looking at this indicates that it the concept of mania as a distinct disorder merits further investigation. Neuroimaging techniques allowing visualization of the functioning brain have enabled further distinctions between psychiatric disorders based on underlying differences in brain structure, and hold promise for research in bipolar disorder and mania.

See also Manic depression.

Further Reading:

American Psychiatric Association. *Diagnostic and Statistical Manual of Mental Disorders*, 4th ed. Washington, DC: American Psychiatric Association, 1994.

KEY TERMS

Antipsychotic drugs—These drugs, also called neuroleptics, seem to block the uptake of dopamine in the brain. They help to reduce psychotic symptoms across a number of mental illnesses.

Bipolar disorder—A psychiatric disorder in which individuals experience alternating states of mania and depression, it is often referred to as manic-depressive disorder.

Delusions—False beliefs that seem to be beyond the bounds of possibility, they are usually absurd and bizarre, and resist disconfirming evidence.

Electroconvulsive shock therapy (ECT)—Administration of a low dose electric current to the head in conjunction with muscle relaxants. A treatment method whose underlying action is still not fully understood, it has proven effective in relieving symptoms of some severe psychiatric disorders for which no other treatment has been effective, for example, severe depression.

Neuroimaging techniques—High technology methods that enable visualization of the brain without surgery such as computed tomography (CT), and magnetic resonance imaging (MRI).

Neurotransmitters—Biochemical substances that transmit nerve impulses between nerve cells.

Psychotherapy—A broad term that usually refers to interpersonal verbal treatment of disease or disorder that addresses psychological and social factors.

Andreason, N.C., and D.W. Black. *Introductory Textbook of Psychiatry*. Washington, D.C.: American Psychiatric Press, Inc. 1991.

Kaplan, H.I., and B.J. Sadock. *Comprehensive Textbook of Psychiatry*, 6th ed. Baltimore, MD: Williams and Wilkins, 1995.

Marie Doorey

Manic depression

Manic-depressive illness, clinically called bipolar disorder, is a major mental illness belonging to the category of illnesses designated as mood disorders. It is estimated that as many as twenty million Americans may suffer from this illness and that one in every five families will be confronted with a family member who may experience a manic episode or an episode of clinical depression. As the term bipolar suggests, there are two extreme moods in manic depression: one is depression and the other is mania, where behavior and irritability or anger become extreme.

Mood disorders are characterized by emotional changes that take place when a person suffers from manic depression. The mood may be one of an emotional high where a person has excessive energy, may feel exuberant, creative, and ready to take on the world. This is characteristic of a manic episode. The person may feel that he or she needs little sleep and may even get only three or four hours of sleep during the manic episode. People in this mode of the illness may have racing thoughts, may have auditory hallucinations, and may suffer from delusions of grandeur. The person often exhibits a great deal of irritability and can become quite argumentative.

The other side of manic-depressive illness is a state of depression during which the person feels that everything is hopeless. The mood in the depressed state is flat. The person may have a poor appetite, may sleep too much or too little, feel tired, lose interest in otherwise pleasurable activities, experience difficulty in concentrating, may feel worthless or extremely guilty, and may have thoughts of suicide.

Diagnosis

Like the range of colors seen in a prism, manic depression or bipolar disorder has a spectrum from which psychiatrists make their diagnosis. One of the factors they examine is whether the person is in a depressed, manic, or hypomanic state. A hypomanic state is one in which a person experiences a more controlled mania. The person may become excessively active and feel elated, but does not become disorganized or delusional. People with these symptoms may be cyclothymic, that is they exhibit periods of depression and mania, but for shorter and less intense durations.

Cyclothymia, however, tends to be a chronic condition that the patient can experience throughout their lifetime. It usually begins during adolescence. Manic-depressive illness usually appears in late adolescence or early adulthood.

In bipolar disorder, the person who experiences periods of depression that alternate with periods of mania is said to have bipolar disorder I, while the person who suffers mild hypomanic periods alternating with periods of depression is classified as having bipolar disorder II. In both illnesses, episodes are limited in time, lasting from several weeks to several months, although depression can last for more than a year without going into remission. If manic depression, bipolar disorder, is not treated, however, recurrences tend to become more severe over time.

Emil Kraepelin

Since the 1950s, the psychiatric community has had the benefit of antimanic and antidepressant medications to treat manic-depressive illnesses. These medications were developed using the work of Emil Kraepelin, a German physician who wrote about mental illness in the late nineteenth century and early part of the twentieth century. Kraepelin had carefully noted distinguishing symptoms among mental patients and had followed the course of the various illnesses in many of them. He was the first to distinguish what he called dementia praecox, now called schizophrenia, and was able to differentiate this illness from manic depression.

During the 1950s and 1960s, a group at Washington University in St. Louis applied Kraepelin's method and began a classification system that led to the publication of the first *Diagnostic and Statistical Manual of Mental Disorders (DSM)*, which was published in 1952. In 1994, the *DSM-IV* was published. The DSM presents a standard set of definitions for psychiatric illnesses. It also presents the symptoms and the number of them that must be present to diagnosis a particular psychiatric illness, such as manic depression.

Another problem facing the diagnosis of depression or mania is the fact that other medical conditions can cause similar symptoms. Among them are illnesses such as thyroid diseases, infectious diseases (the flu), cancers of the central nervous system, neurological disorders (multiple sclerosis), blood diseases, and even some reactions to metal toxicity.

Treatments for manic-depressive illness

Lithium has been the treatment of choice for manic-depressive illness for several decades. Lithium is a trace element found in plants and in mineral rocks. While there has been a great deal of success in treating manic-depressive patients with lithium and returning them to a normal life, researchers are not exactly sure how it works. It is a nonaddictive and nonsedating medication, but it must be carefully monitored for possibly dangerous side effects.

More recently, newer medicines have been used to treat bipolar manic depression disorder. Carbamazepine and valproate are two anticonvulsants that are also

---

KEY TERMS
. . . .

Bipolar I disorder—A manic-depressive illness characterized by one or more manic episodes, along with a depressive episode.

Bipolar II disorder—A manic-depressive illness characterized by a depressive episode and a hypomanic episode.

Cyclothymic disorder—An illness in which there are many hypomanic episodes and many periods of depression during a period of time lasting at least two years.

Depression—A mood disorder where the predominant symptoms are apathy, hopelessness, sleeping too little or too much, loss of pleasure, self-blame, and possibly suicidal thoughts.

Hypomania—A condition in which a person is in an elevated mood and exhibits manic behavior that is not as severe as full-blown mania.

Mania—A condition in which the person's mood is elevated, is hyperactive, and has racing thoughts.

Mood disorder—An illness that is characterized by a disturbance of mood, which may be depressed or elevated and must be of a significant duration.

---

being used to treat manic depression. They have been particularly useful with patients who do not respond to lithium. These medications also have to be monitored for proper dosages.

The psychiatric community generally favors a combined treatment of medicine, along with an educational program for the patient and family, and psychological counseling to help the patient adjust to the medication and learn how to deal with the illness.

See also Depression; Lithium; Mania.

Further Reading:

Amchin, Jess. *Psychiatric Diagnosis: A Biopsychosocial Approach Using DSM-III-R.* Washington, D.C.: Psychiatric Press, 1991.

Diagnostic and Statistical Manual of Mental Disorders, DSM-IV. Washington, D.C.: American Psychiatric Association, 1994.

Goodwin, Frederick K. and Kay Redfield Jamison. *Manic-Depressive Illness.* New York: Oxford University Press, 1990.

Jamison, Kay Redfield. *Touched with Fire.* New York: Free Press, 1993.

Papolos, Demitri F. and Janice Papolos. *Overcoming Depression*. New York: Harper & Row, 1987.

Vita Richman

Manucodes see **Birds of paradise**

Many-body problem

The many-body problem involves describing a large number of interacting particles in a detailed way and, specifically, in a way that predicts their future behavior. In all of physics, there are few issues stated so simply, but the many-body problem is responsible for as many headaches as any other. In fact, the problem has not been completely solved, and it may never be. As with relations between people, interactions between particles, or bodies, become increasingly complex when more than one get involved. The many-body problem is not concerned with the bodies in and of themselves, for these can be successfully described; the central issue and the real difficulty lie in the effects that these particles have on one another. One body moving through space is easily understood and its future is predictable. When many bodies are involved, however, keeping track of their interactions quickly becomes nightmarish.

A simple many-body example appears in certain lotteries where a tumbler of numbered ping-pong balls determines winning numbers. Say there are one hundred such balls in a large, rotatable drum. Even if the exact position of each ball is know in the beginning, it is virtually impossible to predict which number will sit on top after the drum rotates a few dozen times. The ping-pong balls are obviously interacting. When they collide, they bounce from one another, changing directions. It is these interactions that make for such a wild, umpredictable scene inside the drum and leave the lottery with a practically random result.

Fundamental particles (such as electrons) make for a much more challenging instance of the many-body problem because their interactions are more varied and complicated than those of ping-pong balls. Physicists can take on quite a few ping-pong balls before running into trouble, but they have their hands full when they consider only two fundamental particles.

Many-body literature has turned increasingly to the use of Feynman diagrams in the last thirty years. These diagrams, introduced by the late Richard P. Feynmam, give physicists an elegant pictorial shorthand for complicated mathematical expressions. They involve a simple set of symbols (dots, arrows, various lines) and a short but rigid list of rules. Many-body physicists can carry on entire conversations and arguments using nothing more than these quick sketches.

Brandon Broron

Map

A map, or mapping, is a rule, often expressed as an equation, that specifies a particular element of one set for each element of another set. To help understand the notion of map, it is useful to picture the two sets schematically, and map one onto the other, by drawing connecting arrows from members of the first set to the appropriate members of the second set. For instance, let the set mapped from be well-known cities in Texas, specifically, let A = {Abilene, Amarillo, Dallas, Del Rio, El Paso, Houston, Lubbock, Pecos, San Antonio}. We will map this onto the set containing whole numbers of miles. The rule is that each city maps onto its distance from Abilene. The map (see Figure 1) can be shown as a diagram in which an arrow points from each city to the appropriate distance.

A relation is a set of ordered pairs for which the first and second elements of each ordered pair are associated or related. A function, in turn, is a relation for which every first element of an ordered pair is associated with one, and only one, second element. Thus, no two ordered pairs of a function have the same first element. However, there may be more than one ordered pair with the same second element. The set, or collection, of all the first elements of the ordered pairs is called the domain of the function. The set of all second elements of the ordered pairs is called the range of the function. A function is a set, so it can be defined by writing down all the ordered pairs that it contains. This is not always easy, however, because the list may be very lengthy, even infinite (that is, it may go on forever). When the list of ordered pairs is too long to be written down conveniently, or when the rule that associates the first and second elements of each ordered pair is so complicated that it is not easily guessed by looking at the pairs, then it is common practice to define the function by writing down the defining rule. Such a rule is called a map, or mapping, which, as the name suggests, provides directions for superimposing each member of a function's domain onto a corresponding member of its range. In this sense, a map is a function. The words map and function are often used interchangeably.

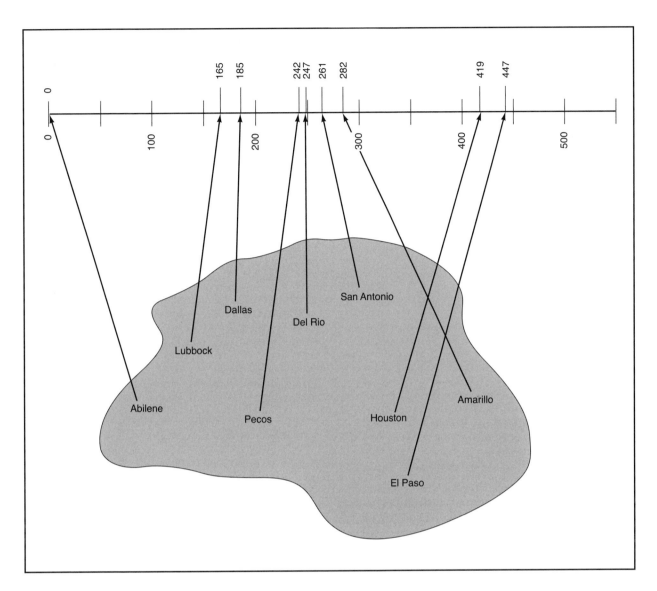

Figure 1.

In addition, because each member of the domain is associated with one and only one member of the range, mathematicians also say that a function maps its domain onto its range, and refer to members of the range as values of the function.

The concept of map or mapping is useful in visualizing more abstract functions, and helps to remind us that a function is a set of ordered pairs for which a well defined relation exists between the first and second elements of each pair. The concept of map is also useful in defining what is meant by composition of functions. Given three sets A, B, and C, suppose that A is the domain of a function f, and that B is the range of f. Further, suppose that B is also the domain of a second function g, and that C is the range of g. Let the symbol o represent the operation of composition which is defined to be the process of mapping A onto B and then mapping B onto C. The result is equivalent to mapping A directly onto C by a third function, call it h. This is written g o f = h, and read "the composition of f and g equals h."

Further Reading:

Christian, Robert R. *Introduction to Logic and Sets*. Waltham, MA: Blaisdell Publishing Co., 1965.

Gowar, Norman. *An Invitation to Mathematics*. New York: Oxford University Press, 1979.

Kyle, James. *Mathematics Unraveled*. Blue Ridge Summit, PA: Tab Book, 1976.

Peterson, Ivars. *Islands of Truth, A Mathematical Mystery Cruise*. New York: W. H. Freeman, 1990.

J. R. Maddocks

Maples

The maples are about 150 species of angiosperm trees and shrubs in the genus *Acer*, family Aceraceae. Most maples occur in temperate forests of the Northern Hemisphere.

Maples are characterized by the shape of their leaves, which in most species are broadly palmate with a three-or five-lobed outline, and are arranged in an opposite fashion on their branches. Maples have seasonally deciduous foliage, which is shed in the autumn. The leaves of many species of maples develop beautiful yellow, orange, or red colors in the autumn, prior to being shed for the winter. Maple flowers appear early in the springtime, and consist of non-showy, rather inconspicuous inflorescences. The flowers of some species produce nectar and are insect-pollinated, while other species shed their pollen to the air and are wind-pollinated. Maples have distinctive, winged seeds known as samaras, which are arranged in opposite pairs.

Maples of North America

About twelve tree-sized species of maples grow naturally in North America, along with other shrub-sized species. Other, non-native species of maples have been widely introduced to North America as attractive, ornamental plants.

The most widespread native species is sugar or rock maple (*Acer saccharum*), a prominent tree in temperate forests of eastern Canada and the northeastern United States. Sugar maple is extremely tolerant of shade, and is a major component of mature and older-growth angiosperm forests on rich, well-drained sites within its range. Sugar maple grows as tall as 115 ft (35 m), can achieve a diameter of more than 3 ft (1 m), and

can live to be older than four centuries. The roughly five-lobed leaves of sugar maple turn a beautiful, orange-yellow color in the autumn, when the green color of chlorophyll fades, exposing the yellow and orange pigments in the leaves. Sugar maple is the national tree of Canada, and a stylized leaf of this species is featured prominently on the Canadian flag.

Black maple (*A. nigrum*) is rather similar in appearance to sugar maple, but its leaves have a more three-lobed appearance. Florida maple (*A. barbatum*) replaces the sugar maple in southeastern North America.

Red maple (*A. rubrum*) is another widely distributed species, occurring over much of eastern North America, from northern Ontario to southern Florida. The habitat of red maple is highly varied, ranging from flooded swamps to dry hills and rocky slopes. The foliage of this species turns a brilliant scarlet in the autumn. The natural distribution of the silver maple (*A. saccharinum*) is largely restricted to swamps and floodplains.

There are fewer species of maples in western North America. The bigleaf maple (*A. macrophyllum*) has leaves that can be 12 in (30 cm) in diameter, turning a yellow-brown in the autumn. Vine maple (*A. circinatum*) has scarlet leaves in the fall.

The box-elder or Manitoba maple (*A. negundo*) is the only species of maple that has a compound leaf, consisting of three to seven leaflets. This fast-growing species is common in moist sites near water, and is an urban weed in many areas.

Lumber from maples

Some species of maples have a hard, durable wood that can be used for making furniture, cabinets, interior trim, hardwood flooring, and other products that require strength and an ability to take a smooth finish. In North America, sugar and black maples are most commonly used for these purposes, and are known to carpenters as "hard" maples. Unusual and attractive grains known as curly and bird's-eye are especially desirable for the making of furniture. Lumber is also made from red, silver, and bigleaf maples, but the wood of these "soft" maples is not considered to be of as high a quality as that of sugar and black maples.

Various species of maples are grown as horticultural plants in urban areas, in parks, around homes, and along country roads. Sugar, black, and silver maples are native species that are commonly grown along rural and urban roadsides. Some non-native species of maples are also commonly used in horticulture, especially Norway maple (*Acer platanoides*), sycamore maple (*A. pseudo-*

A sugar maple (*Acer saccharum*) on a road near Grandville, Michigan.

platanus), English maple (*A. campestre*), and Japanese maple (*A. palmatum*).

Maple syrup

In the early springtime, when there is still snow on the ground, various species of temperate angiosperm trees transport large quantities of sap from their roots to their branches, where energy is needed to develop the new season's crop of twigs, flowers, and leaves. The sapflow of sugar and black maples is especially voluminous, and these species are most commonly tapped for their sweet sap, which typically contains about 6% sucrose. The sap of maples is commonly collected by drilling holes into the base of the tree, inserting a tap into each, and collecting the drippings in small pails. More recently, low-head suction systems have been developed, in which sap is collected from large numbers of tapped trees, using a system of inter-connected hoses that drain to a central location. After the sap is collected, it is condensed by evaporation, often using wood-stoked fires and large, flat boiling pans.

The final product is usually maple syrup — about 10.5 gal (40 l) of raw sap is required to make 1 qt (1 l)of maple syrup. Sometimes, the syrup is further evaporated to crystallize a maple sugar. The grade of the maple syrup, and its value in the marketplace, is determined by its color. A light, amber syrup is more desirable than one that is rendered a darker brown by high-temperature caramelization of the maple sugar. Syrups with a delicate flavor are also considered to be better quality than those with a more pronounced flavor.

Maple sugaring is especially common in rural areas of southeastern Canada and New England. Many urban people in those regions love to go out into the country

to participate in sugar-maple festivals, considered to be an indispensable rite of spring.

Further Reading:

Brockman, C.F. *Trees of North America.* New York: Golden Press, 1968.
Fowells, H.A. *Silvics of Forest Trees of the United States.* Washington D.C.: U.S. Department of Agriculture, 1965.
Hosie, R.C. *Native Trees of Canada.* Ottawa: Canada Communications Group, 1985.
Klein, R.M. *The Green World. An Introduction to Plants and People.* New York: Harper and Row, 1987.
Petrides, G.A. *A Field Guide to the Trees and Shrubs of North America.* New York: Houghton Mifflin, 1986.
Woodland, D.W. *Contemporary Plant Systematics.* New Jersey: Prentice-Hall, 1991.

Bill Freedman

Marfan's syndrome

Marfan's syndrome is an inherited disease affecting the connective tissue within the body. This syndrome causes a variety of skeletal deformities, problems with the eye, and problems with the cardiovascular system (heart and blood vessels).

Physical characteristics of Marfan's syndrome patients

Typically a person with Marfan's syndrome appears quite tall and thin particularly when compared with other members of the same family. Some historians believe that tall, lanky Abraham Lincoln may have had Marfan's syndrome. The patient's fingers are generally long and thin (arachnodactyly). The patient's chest wall may protrude out or be sunken in while the spine often has an abnormal curvature.

A variety of eye abnormalities usually accompany Marfan's syndrome. Extreme near-sightedness and dislocation of the lens are the most common problems. Muscles are often smaller than normal. Hernias (protrusions of internal organs through weak areas in muscle) are frequent in Marfan's patients.

The most serious and potentially life-threatening complications of Marfan's syndrome lie in the heart and blood vessels. The mitral valve (the gateway out of the heart for all the blood entering the body's circulation) is frequently abnormal resulting in a heart murmur. The wall of the aorta (the major artery leaving the heart) is prone to stretching (dilatation) and becomes increasingly weak, leading to bulging (called an aneurysm) and possible rupture. Such a rupture would lead to a severe hemorrhage (bleeding into the body) and almost certain death.

Inheritance and biochemical causes of Marfan's

Marfan's syndrome is known to be a *dominant* genetic disorder (inheriting only one defective gene will lead to the syndrome). Twenty percent of all Marfan's patients have no family history of Marfan's; these patients are believed to undergo a spontaneous genetic mutation leading to the syndrome. Marfan's syndrome is said to have variable expression, meaning that a variable number of the classic signs of Marfan's syndrome may occur in any patient.

The biochemical problem leading to Marfan's syndrome has not been well defined. The current belief is that the affected gene results in an abnormality of a protein called *microfibrillin* which is responsible for certain structural characteristics of connective tissue in the body.

Diagnosis

There are no laboratory tests to aid in the diagnosis of Marfan's syndrome so diagnosis relies on the identification of some cluster of the classic signs of Marfan's occurring in a particular patient. A doctor's level of sus-

---

KEY TERMS

Aorta—The major blood vessel leaving the heart and carrying blood to numerous other smaller vessels which branch off and deliver blood to the entire body.

Connective tissue—A biochemically distinct group of the body's tissues, which provide structural support for other body tissues. Examples of connective tissue include bone and cartilage.

Mitral valve—A one way gateway for blood leaving the heart, located at the aorta.

---

picion would be higher in a family where other members have Marfan's syndrome. Diagnosis is important so that the cardiovascular system (especially the aorta) can be regularly and carefully evaluated in order to avoid a ruptured aneurysm.

Treatment

There is no treatment of Marfan's syndrome that can reverse the overall connective tissue defects. Each manifestation of the syndrome is addressed individually (braces and physical therapy for the spinal curvature, occasional lens removal for the lens dislocations). For females who have grown quite tall, and have cosmetic concerns about any further height, hormonal medications can be given to initiate an early puberty so that growth stops sooner and adult height is more normal.

The most important problems to follow closely are those affecting the heart and aorta. Some medications seem to be somewhat useful in slowing the stretching of the aorta, although surgical replacement of part of the aorta oris or of the defective mitral valve is sometimes necessary.

Outcome

Careful monitoring of Marfan's patients, along with advice to avoid stress (physical, emotional, and the stress of pregnancy) has helped to increase the expected life span of such patients well beyond the age of 30 or 40, which was once the typical age of death.

Further Reading:

Andreoli, Thomas E., et al. *Cecil Essentials of Medicine.* Philadelphia: W.B. Saunders Company, 1993.

Berkow, Robert and Andrew J. Fletcher. *The Merck Manual of Diagnosis and Therapy.* Rahway, NJ: Merck Research Laboratories, 1992.

Isselbacher, Kurt J., et al. *Harrison's Principles of Internal Medicine*. New York: McGraw Hill, 1994.

Rosalyn Carson-DeWitt

Marijuana

Marijuana is the common name for the hemp plant *Cannabis sativa*. Hemp grows in tropical as well as temperate climates. The dried ground leaves, flowers, and stems of the plant have a long history for their use as drugs. It has been cultivated in different regions of the world throughout centuries for its fiber to produce linen, rope, canvas, and oil. It has also been used as a medicine to relieve symptoms of illness and as a euphoric to induce states of intoxication or elation. Throughout its long history, parts of the plants have been smoked, eaten, chewed, or brewed for its pharmacological effects on human biochemistry.

There are over 400 chemicals in cannabis. By the mid-1960s the main psychoactive chemical was identified as tetrahydrocannabinol, commonly referred to as THC. Since then, other psychoactive compounds have been isolated from the plant and are being studied for their biochemical effects.

The origin of the word *marijuana* is not known but it appears to be the Spanish name for Maria and Juana (Mary and Jane). The drug slang for marijuana includes such names as Mary Jane, pot, grass, tea, reefer (as a cigarette), and weed. In India it is called *ghanja*, *dagga* in South Africa, and *Kef* in Morocco. The potency of the psychoactive cannabinoids found in a marijuana plant varies depending on the locale from which the plant was derived and its genetic makeup.

History

Reference to the hemp plant (cannabis) appears as early as 2700 B.C. in a Chinese manuscript. European explorers arriving to the New World first observed the plant in 1545. It was considered to be such a useful crop that early Jamestown settlers in 1607 began its cultivation and later in Virginia farmers were fined for not growing hemp; in 1617, it was introduced into England. From the seventeenth to the mid-twentieth century marijuana was considered as a household drug useful for treating such maladies as headaches, menstrual cramps, and toothaches. From 1913-38 a stronger variety of the marijuana plant was cultivated by American drug companies for use in their drug products. It was called *Cannabis americana*.

The Jazz Age

Prior to 1910, the growth and trade of marijuana (and hashish—a resinous substance produced by the flowering parts of the plant) was fairly limited. However, following the conclusion of the Mexican Revolution, trafficking of the drug opened up, making growth and transport of the drug easier and more profitable. The business expanded to reach the ports of New Orleans where it was sold on the black market, alongside other strains of the plant, to sailors passing through, as well as local residents. It wasn't long before the trend of marijuana use began to overshadow the historic applications of cannabis as a medicine.

The drug soon became popular (especially its stronger derivitives—hashish, charas, ghanja, and bhang) among musicians who maintained that smoking marijuana gave them the inspiration they needed to play their music. These musicians glamorized the use of marijuana. Some claimed it gave them contemplative vision and a feeling of overwhelming freedom and verve; others not only used the drug themselves, but sold it to a variety of customers. As the entertainers went on the road, so did their drugs. Eventually, use of marajuana, alcohol, and other mind-altering drugs spread and soon became prevalent in major cities worldwide, such as Chicago, New York, London, and Paris.

Many of the musicians and entertainers of the Jazz Age who used drugs and alcohol relied heavily on gangland kings for their "gigs" (jobs). Frequently, these gangsters were able to provide (for a fee) a variety of drugs and bootleg alcohol for the performers and their staffs.

Prohibition

In the 1920s, as a result of the amendment prohibiting the use of alcoholic beverages (Prohibition), marijuana use as a psychoactive drug began to grow. Even after the repeal of Prohibition in 1933, marijuana was widely used as were morphine, heroin, and cocaine. In 1937, 46 states banned the use of marijuana along with other narcotic drugs. The popular perception, however, was that marijuana was not as addictive as narcotics. It is classified today as a drug that alters mood, perception, and image, rather than as a narcotic drug.

By the 1960s it was widely used by the young from all social classes. It is estimated that by the 1970s as many as 43 million Americans had used marijuana. The presence of more potent strains of marijuana has widened the debate between the drug enforcement dose increases, other effects take place such as an altered sense of time and sensory awareness, difficulty in balancing and remembering from one moment to another (short-term memory). Conversation and thoughts become incomplete, and exaggerated laughter may take place with increased doses. At higher doses, severe psychological disturbances can take place such as paranoia, hallucinations, panic attacks, and the acting out of delusions.

The cardiovascular system is affected by an increased heart rate and dilation of eye blood vessels. Difficulty in coordinating body movements and pains in the chest may be other effects of the drug. Less is known about marijuana's effects on the lungs than cigarette smoking, but the evidence points to long-term damage similar to the effects of tobacco smoking.

The FDA in 1985 gave approval for the use of two psychoactive chemicals from marijuana to prevent nausea and vomiting after chemotherapy in cancer treatment. Other proposed medical uses of marijuana are for the treatment of glaucoma, as a bronchodilator, as an antidepressant, and for several other types of medical treatment drugs.

See also Addiction.

Further Reading:
Bakalar, James B. "The War on Drugs: a Peace Proposal." *The New England Journal of Medicine* (Feb 3 1994): 357-61.

Grinspoon, Lester and James B. Bakalar. *The Forbidden Medicine*. New Haven: Yale University Press, 1993.

Shapiro, Harry. *Waiting for the Man*. New York: William Morrow, 1988.

Stimmel, Barry. *The Facts About Drug Use*. New York: Haworth Medical Press, 1991.

Jordan P. Richman

authorities and the advocates of decriminalizing marijuana use because it is, they believe, not in the same class as the more addictive drugs. Others see marijuana as a "gateway" drug to the harder drugs and therefore believe rigid laws against its use and distribution should remain in effect.

Effects

Marijuana affects both the cardiovascular and central nervous systems. At low doses there tends to be a sense of well-being, drowsiness, and relaxation. As the

Marlins

Belonging to the Order Perciformes and the Suborder Scomproidei, marlins are large fish with elongated, bill-like snouts, fairly high dorsal fins, and streamlined bodies. Marlins are among the fastest of all fish in the world and are highly valued by sporting fisherman.

Taxonomy

The Order Perciformes is the largest and most diverse of all fish orders, encompassing around 8,000 species. Distributed worldwide, fish of this order exist

A marlin leaping.

in both marine and freshwater and represent fish with very diverse sizes, habitats, and behaviors. This order is broken into 150 families and 1,370 genera.

The Suborder Scomproidei is divided into two families: the Xiphiidae and the Istiophoridae. These two families have been separate since the early Eocene period. The Xiphiidae family contains only one species and one genus, the broadbill swordfish (*Xiphias gladius*). The swordfish is distinguished from members of the Istiophoridae family by lack of pelvic fins and its long, flattened bill. Marlins belong to the family known as Istiophoridae. Members of this family —commonly referred to as "billfish"— have elongated, rounded snouts, called "bills" and live in tropical and subtropical seas. The Istiophoridae Family includes three genera and about 10 species. The three genera are: *Istiophorus* (sailfishes); *Tetrapturus* (spearfishes); and *Makaira* (marlins). The *Makaira* genus contains two species of marlin: the Blue Marlin and the Black Marlin. Marlins are different from the other two genera because their dorsal fins do not measure in height as much as their bodies measure in depth. As with other fish in their family, their dorsal fins are long with many rays, and their tails have two sets of side keels.

Speed

Marlins are one of the sea's swiftest fish and greatest leapers. While the sailfish are commonly regarded as the fastest swimming fish, the Blue Marlin offers strong competition. The Blue Marlin is one of the few fish species that can swim fast enough to eat tuna species on a regular basis. In fact, marlins can attain speeds of up to 50 mph (80 kph). Furthermore, when they are hooked, they struggle heroically, sometimes jumping more than 40 times.

The marlins' speed make them fierce predators. Rushing a school of fish, marlins strike with their bills first, wounding and killing many fish unlucky enough to be in their paths. Once the slaughter is finished, they returning to feast on the dead and wounded.

Species

There are four species of fish with the common name "marlin." Interestingly, these fish are classified into two separate genera. In the strictest sense, marlins belong to the genus *Makaira*. Examples of marlins in this genus are the Blue Marlin (*Makaira nigricans*) and the Black Marlin (*Makaira indica*). However, there are two species of fish with the common name "marlin" that are classified in the *Tetrapturus* genus; obviously these marlins have much in common with the previously mentioned spearfish. These fish are the Striped Marlin (*Tetrapturus audax*) and the White Marlin (*Tetrapterus albidus*).

Blue Marlins are either blue or gray-blue, and their shading gets lighter toward their bellies, which are silver. These marlins measure between 10-15 (3-4.6 m). There weight varies widely; in fact, some reports say that they usually weigh 200-400 lb (91-181 kg); however, it is fairly common for Blue Marlins to weigh over 1,800 lb (800 kg). These fish have streamlined bodies with crescent shaped tails that are found in many high speed species of fish. They live in tropical and temperate seas throughout the world. For example, they are found in temperate seas from in the eastern Atlantic ranging from northern Spain south to South Africa and in the western Atlantic as far north as Massachusetts and as far south as Uruguay. They swim in open seas and make regular seasonal migrations to the equator in the winter and away from it in the summer. They prefer to swim in surface waters. They are a highly prized sporting fish.

The Black Marlin is the largest of all of the billfish. It reaches 16 ft (5 m) and can weigh more than 1,500 lb (681 kg). Its pectoral fins are rigid and do not fold into its body. It lives near the surface of warm, open seas from southern California to Chile.

The Striped Marlin is similar in appearance to the Blue Marlin, having an elongated bill and a streamlined body. The Striped Marlin lives in the Indian and Pacific Oceans and is more likely to inhabit temperate waters, such as from Oregon to Chile. It lives in the open seas but sometimes will swim in the inshore waters. What makes this fish different from the Blue Marlin is that it is marked with dark blue or white vertical bars on its sides. Additionally, this fish has pelvic fins that are much longer than its pectoral fins and it has a higher dorsal fin. Striped Marlins spawn from May to August in the Northern Pacific. It grows to about 10 ft (3 m) long and eats fish and various species of deep water and surface squid. It is a highly specialized sportfish and also an excellent food fish.

The White Marlin usually weighs about 50 lb (23 kg) but can measure as much as 10 ft (3 m) in length and weigh as much as 180 lb (82 kg). This migratory fish is found in the eastern part of the Atlantic Ocean—south of Portugal and into the southwestern Mediterranean—and in the western Atlantic—from Nova Scotia south to Brazil. It has also been seen in the Gulf of Mexico and the Caribbean. These marlins are bluish-green, brown, or gray on top and silver underneath.

KEY TERMS

Dorsal fin—The fin located on the back.

Pectoral fin—The uppermost of paired fins, usually located on the sides; this fin follows the gill openings.

Pelvic fin—The fin usually located and to the rear of the pectoral fin.

Marlins are among the most popular sporting fish in the world; however, their numbers are decreasing because of intense commercial overfishing and exploitation.

Further Reading:

Audubon Society: Field Guide to North American Fishes, Whales, and Dolphins. New York: Alfred A. Knopf, Inc. 1983.

Grzimek, H.C. Bernard, Dr., ed. *Grzimek's Animal Life Encyclopedia.* New York: Van Nostrand Reinhold Company, 1975.

Lythgoe, John and Gillian. *Fishes of the Sea.* Cambridge, Massachusetts: Blandford Press, 1991, pp, 154-183.

Nelson, Joseph S. *Fishes of the World.* 3rd edition. New York: John Wiley & Sons, Inc., 1994.

Webb, J.E. *Guide to Living Fishes.* Macmillan Publishing, 1991.

Kathryn Snavely

Marmosets and tamarins

Marmosets and tamarins are South and Central American primates of the Amazon Basin. Their family, Callitrichidae, includes 18 species that have been described as "near" monkeys. All are endangered or threatened.

The two groups of small, furry near-monkeys are very similar, but the marmosets (mostly in genus *Callithrix*) and the tamarins (the 11 species of genus *Saguinus*) are located in different regions, overlapping at only one area near the mouth of the Amazon River. In that area, they do not interbreed.

True marmosets have elongated lower incisor teeth, which look like extra canine teeth. Tamarins and marmosets also differ in the shape of the lower jaw. The

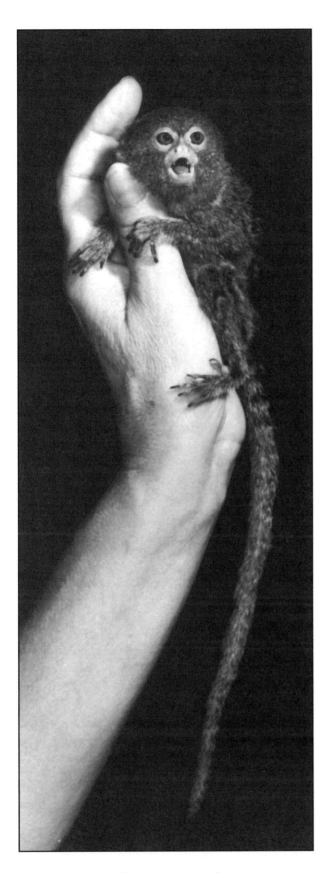

A pygmy marmoset (*Cebuella pygmaea*).

marmosets' jaws are V-shaped and pointed, making their faces pointed. The tamarins' are rounded into a U-shape. In addition, the marmosets have lower canine teeth about the same length as their incisors. They are sometimes called short-tusked marmosets. The tamarins, on the other hand, have canine teeth longer than their incisors and are often called long-tusked marmosets.

All marmosets and tamarins feed on the gum of trees, which they obtain by scraping the bark with their teeth. All other primates that eat gum or sap are content to let insects dig the holes. These near-monkeys also eat fruit, flowers, and small insects.

Most marmosets and tamarins have a head-and-body length that varies between 7-12 in (17-30 cm) plus a tail perhaps 3 in (7.5 cm) longer than that. The tail is not prehensile, or grasping. Unlike many other monkeys, marmosets and tamarins do not have an opposable thumb. Their sharp curved claws are adequate for allowing these lightweight monkeys to hold onto trees. Only the great toe bears a nail instead of a claw.

Their faces have little or no fur, but there can be large tufts of dense fur coming from their foreheads. Most also have tufts of long hair around or from the ears, though the silvery marmoset, *Callithrix argentata,* has bare ears.

These primates are active in the daytime and thus do not have the large eyes of prosimians. They sleep in tree holes or tangles of liana vines during the night.

Tamarins and marmosets live in groups of up to 40 individuals, though about 12-15 is more usual. Within the group they spend a great deal of time grooming each other. Such a large group can create a great amount of noise and commotion in the trees.

After a 140-145 day gestation period, a female (usually only one in a group at a time) produces one, two, or three young. The newborn ones are quite large in comparison to the mother, though they are helpless. They ride on a parent's (usually the father's) back until they are about 7 weeks old. They become sexually mature at 12-18 months. Unusual for mammals, the young of one generation are allowed to stay around the family even after they have reached sexual maturity and after a new family is born to the parents. But they do not produce their own offspring until after they leave the family unit. They are helpful around the family, often relieving the male of carrying his new offspring. The male usually turns the young over to the female for short feeding period every few hours.

Marmosets

There are at least three species of true marmosets or titis (though this name can confuse them with titi monkeys) in genus *Callithrix*. Some scientists regard several of the subspecies as separate species. These marmoset species do not share habitat with each other. This may be because each species relies on the sap of specific types of trees. Marmosets have light-colored, almost white, genitals, which the males may flash when an invader enters their territory.

The black-tailed or silvery marmoset is *C. argentata.* It has naked pink ears, and its face is also hairless. It is found in two widely separate areas of the Amazon Basin. One is east toward the ocean. The other is located more toward the west, near the beginning of the Andes Mountains. The marmosets in this area may be threatened by the expansion of farming into Amazonas.

The common, or white-headed, marmoset is *C. jacchus*. It has a white face and ear tufts that are lighter than its primary coloring of a splotchy gray and brown mixture. Its tail has rings. It lives in many pockets scattered across the eastern bulge of South America. The subspecies differ primarily in the color of their ear tufts. Several of them are in danger as their habitat is harmed.

The close-to-extinct tassel-ear, or santorem, marmoset, *C. humeralifer,* lives throughout central Brazil, though its habitat may also be threatened by the building of highways. Its ear tufts are longer, long enough to be called tassels. The western subspecies is mostly whitish, while the eastern is darker, with silvery ear tassels.

Tamarins

Tamarins are found north of the marmosets, thus north of the Amazon River and primarily west of the Madiera River. They are a little larger than marmosets, averaging about 9 in (23 cm) with a 14 in (36 cm) tail. They have a greater variety of color than the marmosets, occurring in black, brown, and red, and they often have dramatic white crests or moustaches. They communicate with high-pitched sounds that have been referred to as "trilling." Tamarins live primarily on fruit but may eat insects. They are especially fond of grasshoppers, which they obtain by dropping to the forest floor.

Some tamarins have naked faces and others have hairy faces. Their hair gives them a very distinct look. The emperor tamarin *(S. imperator),* for example, has a black head with flowing white moustaches that apparently reminded someone of the Emperor Franz Joseph of Austria. It lives in parts of Peru, Bolivia, and western Brazil. Unlike most members of this family, the emperor tamarin willingly shares part of its territory with a relative, the saddleback tamarin, *S. fuscicollis,* which has three distinct zones of variable color on its back.

In the shared territory of Peru, the two species apparently each gain some benefit from their association. Naturalists are not yet certain of what the benefit is, but they speculate that it has to do with increased communication about food supplies. The saddleback tamarin of Colombia eats resin from trees. The resin is not digested; instead, it turns into lumps in the stomach. This species has a speckled back, contrasting with reddish underparts and rump. It has white eyebrows.

The naked-faced tamarins are not truly naked-faced, except for the pied, or bare-faced, tamarin *(S. bicolor)* of northern Brazil, which has a bare black face which contrasts dramatically with the white upper half of its body. The lower half is rust-red. This species is endangered. Other bare-faced tamarins, such as the cottontop, actually have fine hair covering the face. The pinché, or cottontop tamarin *(S. oedipus),* of Colombia has a startling, long white crown to its black head as well as white chest and arms. A subspecies called Geoffroy's tamarin *(S. O. geoffroyi)* lives as far north as Panama. Deforestation is harming their habitat. Cottontops apparently live in smaller groups than other tamarins.

The odd ones out

There are two marmosets and one tamarin that do not belong to the more common genera. The tamarin and one marmoset are in separate genera. The second marmoset is in a completely separate family.

The golden lion tamarin *(Leontopithecus rosalia rosalia)* has long, dark golden-orange hair. It is in a separate genus from the other tamarins primarily because of its skull shape and its long, narrow hands and feet. Because the hair on its head appears to be cleanly combed back, this tamarin has sometimes been called the Liszt monkey, after the composer who wore his hair swept back. The golden lion has considerably longer arms and a shorter gestation period than other tamarins. It has a head-and-body length of about 11 in (27.5 cm) long, plus a tail more than twice as long.

The golden lion tamarin neared extinction as its low-altitude rain forest along the Atlantic Ocean was cut down. Also, it was for many decades popular as a captive pet. By 1980, the population was estimated at below 100 animals. However, it has been successfully bred in captivity and is being returned to the wild in Poço d'Anta Biological Reserve, which was established just to protect this animal. Its future depends on whether the owners of the remaining forest near Rio de Janeiro are willing to keep it from being built up as major cities approach. Most of the detail of habitat requirements of marmosets and tamarins was learned from the intense study made of the golden lion tamarins' habitat to keep it from extinction.

Two other subspecies of *L. rosalia* are the golden-rumped, or black, lion tamarin *(L. r. chrysopygus)* and the golden-headed, or gold-and-black, lion tamarin *(L. r. chrysomelas).* Each has a very tiny range and is in serious danger of extinction. These subspecies are also being bred in captivity.

The pygmy marmoset is *Cebuella pygmaea.* The smallest New World primate, it is only 5 in (13 cm) in head and body plus an 8 in (20 cm) tail, which is banded in shades of black and tan. Its tan body color is often referred to as "agouti" because it matches the South American rodent called the agouti. Its hands and feet may have an orange hue. This little furry creature feeds on the sap of trees, which it gets by gouging the bark with its sharp lower canine teeth. It roams in a range of not much more than an acre, which must supply a comfortable sleeping tree plus several trees that give off sap. It can gallop along the low tree branches which it prefers. The father takes care of the young except when they need to be fed. The twins ride on his back until they are grown. Fortunately, the pygmy marmoset is quite adaptable and does not appear to be harmed unduly when its forest is degraded.

Related to the tamarins and marmosets is a separate family containing only Goeldi's marmoset, *Callimico goeldii.* Black with long hair, its only color is a slight white tip to its full tail. It does not live in the heavy rain forests as the tamarins do. Instead, it likes open, second-growth forests. It also 36 teeth like the New World monkeys (Cebidae) instead of 32 like the marmosets and tamarins. It also has a considerably longer gestation period of 150-165 days and gives birth to only one young at a time, instead of twins. The mother cares for the newborn for about two weeks, and then the father takes over. Quite rare, Goeldi's marmoset lives only on some small rivers in the Amazon basin. It is being protected in Manu National Park in Peru.

Further Reading:

Kerrod, Robin. *Mammals: Primates, Insect-Eaters and Baleen Whales.* Encyclopedia of the Animal World series. New York: Facts on File, 1988.

Napier, J.R. and P. H. *The Natural History of the Primates.* Cambridge, MA: The MIT Press, 1985.

Napier, Prue. *Monkeys and Apes.* A Grosset All-Color guide. New York: Grosset & Dunlap, 1972.

Peterson, Dale. *The Deluge and the Ark: A Journey into Primate Worlds.* Boston: Houghton Mifflin, 1989.

Preston-Mafham, Rod and Ken. *Primates of the World.* New York: Facts on File, 1992.

Jean F. Blashfield

Marmots

Marmots are species of medium-sized robust, short-legged burrowing herbivorous rodents in the genus *Marmota*, family Sciuridae, order Rodentia. Marmots are closely related to the ground squirrels and gophers. Marmots live in burrows that they dig themselves, or sometimes in the deep crevices of rock piles and talus slopes beneath cliffs. Most species of marmots occur in alpine or arctic tundra or in open forests of North America, Europe, and Asia. The woodchuck or groundhog of North America is also a familiar species of marmot found in agricultural landscapes within its range.

Marmots have a plump, sturdy body, with a broad head, and small but erect ears. The legs and tail of marmots are short, and their fingers and toes have strong claws, and are useful tools for digging burrows. Marmots commonly line their subterranean dens with dried grasses and other haylike materials. Marmots are rather slow, waddling animals, and they do not like to venture very far from the protection of their burrows and dens. Marmots can climb rock faces and piles quite well. The pelage of marmots is short but thick, and is commonly brown or blackish colored.

Marmots often sit up on their haunches, and in this position they survey their domain for dangerous predators. Marmots are rather vocal animals, emitting loud, harsh squeaks and squeals as warnings whenever they perceive a potential predator to be nearby. As soon as any marmot hears the squeak of another marmot, it dashes back to the protection of its burrow. Marmots also squeak when communicating with each other, or if they are injured. Marmots are loosely social animals, sometimes living in open colonies with as many as tens of animals living in a communal maze of interconnected burrows.

Marmots are herbivores, eating the above-ground tissues and tubers of a wide range of herbaceous plants, as well as buds, flowers, leaves, and young shoots of shrubs. They store food in their dens, some of which is consumed during the wintertime.

Marmots gain weight through the growing season, and are very fat when they go into hibernation at the onset of winter. The hibernation occurs in dens that are thickly hay-lined for insulation, and the entrance to their den is plugged with hay or dirt at this time. Some alpine populations of marmots migrate to traditional winter-den sites lower in altitude than their summer range. Marmots typically winter in tightly huddling family groups. Marmots may occasionally waken from their deep sleep to feed, sometimes outside if the day is relatively warm and sunny.

A hoary marmot in Mount Rainier National Park, Washington.

Various animals are predators of marmots, including golden eagles, hawks, foxes, and coyotes. Humans are also predators of marmots in some parts of their range, using the animals as a source of meat, and sometimes as a source of medicinal oils.

North American marmots

The most familiar marmot to most North Americans is the woodchuck or groundhog (*Marmota monax*), a widespread and common species of open woodlands, prairies, roadsides, and the edges of cultivated fields. The woodchuck is a relatively large, reddish or brownish, black-footed marmot, with animals typically weighing about 7-13 lb (3-6 kg), although one captive animal achieved a most-fatty weight of 37 lb (17 kg) in the late autumn. Woodchucks dig their burrow complexes in well-drained soil, generally on the highest ground available to them.

The hoary marmot (*M. caligata*) is a species of alpine tundra and open montane forests of the mountains of northwestern North America, also occurring in the northern tundra of Alaska, Yukon, and the western Northwest Territories. There are various subspecies of hoary marmots, including the small dark-brown Van-

couver Island marmot (*M. c. vancouverensis*), the Olympic marmot (*M. c. olympus*) of northwestern Washington state, and the Kamchatkan marmot (*M. c. camtscharica*) of the mountains of far-eastern Siberia.

The yellow-bellied marmot (*M. flaviventris*) is a yellow-brown species of alpine and open montane habitats in the western United States.

Marmots elsewhere

The alpine marmot (*Marmota marmota*) occurs in the Alps of northern Italy, southeastern France, and Switzerland. The habitat of this species is alpine tundra and meadows, where it lives in rock piles and in burrows. This species is subjected to a sport hunt, the male animals being referred to as bears, and the females as cats. The meat of these marmots is eaten, and their fat is a highly regarded folk medicine in some parts of its European range.

The bobak marmot (*M. bobak*) occurs rather widely in high-altitude grasslands and alpine tundra of the Himalayan Mountains of central Asia. This species is hunted as food and for its fat throughout much of its range. The long-tailed marmot (*M. caudata*) occurs in a restricted, alpine range in Pakistan and Afghanistan.

See also Groundhog; Rodents.

Further Reading:

Banfield, A. W. F. *The Mammals of Canada*. Toronto: University of Toronto Press, 1974.

Barash, D. *Marmots. Social Behavior and Ecology*. Stanford, CA: Stanford University Press, 1989.

Hall, E.R. *The Mammals of North America*. 2nd ed. New York: Wiley & Sons, 1981.

Paradiso, J. L. ed. *Mammals of the World*. 2nd ed. Baltimore: John Hopkins Press, 1968.

Wilson, D. E. and D. Reeder (comp.). *Mammal Species of the World*. Washington, D.C.: Smithsonian Institution Press, 1993.

Bill Freedman

Marrow see **Blood; Circulatory system; Skeletal system**

Mars

Mars is the fourth planet from the center of the solar system, orbiting the Sun once every 687 days at a mean distance of 141 million miles (227 million km). Called the "red planet" for its distinct orange-red color, Mars has been the object of intense interest for over a century. Popularly regarded as a possible source of life, Mars proved to be barren when the *Viking* spacecraft landed on it in 1976 and found no evidence of living organisms. Despite the lack of life, Mars has numerous earthlike features. There are large, extinct volcanoes dotting its surface. Eroded channels indicate that water once flowed freely across the Martian surface, while the ice caps covering its poles look very much like Earth's polar regions. The thin Martian atmosphere is made mainly of carbon dioxide. Although Mars is by all appearances a dead world, the variety of features on its surface suggests a complex and fascinating past.

The red planet

There are three planets other than Earth in the inner solar system. The innermost is Mercury: tiny, barren, and hard to observe as it is located near the Sun. Next comes Venus, the planet nearest in size and mass to Earth, but swathed in clouds; a bland, featureless ball through the small telescope. Mars, half again as far from the Sun as Earth, is different. Features are distinguishable on its surface, and it sometimes shows polar ice caps that look much like Earth's.

A photograph of the Martian surface taken by one of the Viking landers. The layer of morning frost that can be seen in the photo is less than one one-thousandth of an inch thick.

Early observations of Mars by Giovanni Schiaparelli showed the existence of what Schiaparelli called *canali*, meaning channels. The existence of somewhat linear, light and dark channel-like features on Mars is affirmed by many other scientists, but the Italian word *canali* quickly acquired its popular and inaccurate meaning: canals. Water can cut a channel, but only intelligent life can build a canal.

The excitement of this discovery spurred a man named Percival Lowell in 1894 to leave his Boston home for Flagstaff, Arizona, where he founded the observatory that bears his name. Lowell spent the rest of his life studying Mars through the 24 in (61 cm) refracting telescope on Mars Hill above Flagstaff, and became convinced that intelligent life existed on the red planet. Lowell's drawings became increasingly complex as he observed and reobserved the planet, and he devoted himself to convincing the public that Mars was indeed inhabited.

Although Lowell Observatory soon became the site of fundamental advances in astronomy, such as the 1930 discovery of the outermost planet, Pluto, Percival Lowell was wrong about Mars. In 1976 two unmanned spacecraft, *Viking 1* and *Viking 2,* landed at different points on Mars's northern hemisphere. They carried experiments designed to test the Martian soil for the presence of microorganisms and ultimately found nothing. The expedition had initially looked promising as one experiment yielded reactions suggestive of life forms, but further analysis revealed that the reactions were not biological. The Martian terrain bears an eerie resemblance to some of the desert landscapes not so far from the hill where Lowell spent so many nights at his telescope. However, Mars seems to be like all the other places in the solar system but our own—a dead world.

Physical properties of Mars

The "red planet" is so named because of the color of its surface, which indeed is strikingly red. Simply put, Mars has rusted: iron oxides are responsible for its orange hue.

Mars is smaller than Earth. Its diameter of about 2,111 mi (3,400 km) is a little over half that of Earth, and it is only 10% as massive as our planet. Mars has seasons because the tilt of its axis relative to the plane of its orbit is nearly the same as Earth's. It rotates on its axis once every 24 hours and 40 minutes, so a Martian day is just a little longer than one of ours. The Sun would appear small in the Martian sky because Mars is half as far from the Sun as the Earth, and its year is 687 (Earth) days long.

Mars has two tiny satellites, Phobos and Deimos. Deimos is only 3.7 mi (6 km) across—marathon runners would go all the way around the little world! (Marathon runners would also fly off the world if they took too vigorous a step, for the gravity of such a tiny body is extremely weak.)

Mars's gravity is weaker than Earth's, and the planet has been unable to retain much of an atmosphere. The Martian atmosphere is less than 1% as dense as Earth's, and is made mostly of carbon dioxide, with trace amounts of nitrogen and argon.

The atmospheric carbon dioxide is the source of Mars's polar ice caps. Atmospheres act like giant insulators for planets, preventing heat from radiating away to space. Mars's thin atmosphere holds very little heat: a blazing summer day on Mars might get up to the freezing point of water 32°F (0°C/273 K), but at night the temperature plummets well back below 0°F (-18°C). At the poles, temperatures drop well below 200 K (-73°C), sufficiently cold for the carbon dioxide in the atmosphere to freeze. Mars's polar ice caps are consist of frozen carbon dioxide with an underlayer of ice.

Although there is no life on Mars, the planet's surface does have some very Earthlike features. There are enormous volcanoes, the largest of which, Olympus Mons, is almost the size of the entire state of Arizona. Elsewhere are long, eroded channels telling us that at some time in the past water flowed freely on the Martian surface.

The history of Mars

The surface features of Mars show that the planet has had an exciting history. Long ago, the planet was volcanically active. Early in the planet's history, it probably had crustal plates moving about as is the case on

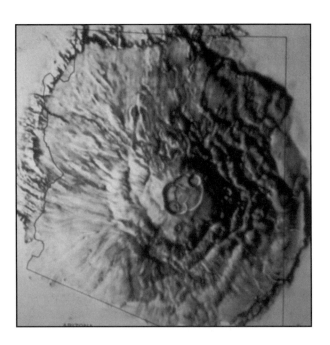

The largest volcano on Mars, Olympus Mons, is much larger than the largest volcano on Earth. Olympus Mons is over 15.5 miles (25 km) tall, three times as tall as Mt. Everest, and has a base the size of the state of Arizona. This photo shows how large Olympus Mons is compared to Arizona.

Earth, but as Mars cooled and its crust thickened, the tectonic activity ceased. The enormous size of Olympus Mons supports this idea. The crust slides over a hot spot and lava coming up forms a series of mountains. On Mars, with no plate motion, the lava simply piles up in one spot. There are several volcanoes on Mars larger than any on Earth, suggesting the planet has a thick, inactive crust.

The eroded channels on Mars's surface show that the planet once had running water. Water boils at progressively lower temperatures as one goes to higher altitudes because the atmospheric pressure is lower. At lower pressures it is easier for molecules to escape the surface of a liquid. On Mars today, water would boil immediately even at the low Martian temperatures, because the atmospheric pressure is so low. This suggests that the Martian atmosphere was once much denser than it is now. Otherwise, water could never have flowed on the planet's surface.

Some of the eroded channels on Mars resemble terrestrial riverbeds, but some show evidence of a violent past. They seem to have been formed by enormous flash floods, perhaps caused when a Martian lake broke through a collapsing natural feature such as a rock wall and cascaded across the land. Several such incidents are documented in the geologic record on Earth.

Mars, as seen from space by *Viking 1*. The planet is slightly more than one-tenth as massive as the Earth.

Many scientists theorize that Mars's atmosphere thinned, and, as the planet cooled, the water boiled away. Some of the water may still remain on the planet, permanently frozen in the ice caps or in the soil. Much of it was probably lost when the Sun's ultraviolet radiation dissociated the water molecules into their hydrogen and oxygen atoms.

Although Martian tectonic activity has ceased and the atmosphere has largely dissipated, storms still rage across its surface. The Viking orbiters observed giant dust storms sweeping across the Martian land. The largest of these storms can sweep dust particles around the entire planet, rushing past the streambeds, ancient craters, volcanoes, and canyons, obscuring everything in their path. One of the greatest dust storms ever observed on Mars occurred in 1971, when the entire planet was shrouded just as one of the earliest Mars orbiters, *Mariner 9*, arrived to take pictures. No pictures could be obtained until the end of the storm in 1972.

A requiem for Percival Lowell

It is apparent that Percival Lowell was, as far as we know, wrong about Mars. Perhaps in the past, simple life did develop on Mars. When water flowed across its surface, the planet necessarily had a thicker atmosphere and was also much warmer than today. It might have even been pleasant by our standards. This gentler age on Mars has passed, however, leaving today a cold, dry, almost airless world. If there is life on Mars, the *Viking* explorers did not find it.

But future missions will be designed to search for fossil microorganisms in the soil, particularly in the former lake and riverbeds, to see whether life might have gained a toehold before the atmosphere was dissipated and the water dried up. To many it seems inevitable that manned exploration of the solar system will occur. How soon is a subject of debate, but Mars is a good target for exploration because it is nearby and its surface is well mapped. The Apollo missions to the Moon have taught us the steps necessary to land manned spacecraft on another world, and to survive its inhospitable climate. Someday, perhaps in the next generation, or perhaps not until the one after that, there will be life on Mars—human life.

See also Planet; Planetary atmospheres; Solar system.

KEY TERMS

. . . .

Deimos—The smaller of Mars's two satellites, only 3.7 mi (6 km) across its smaller dimension.

Olympus Mons—The largest Martian volcano, nearly 373 mi (600 km) across at its base. The existence of such large volcanoes suggests that Mars has a tick, tectonically inactive crust.

Phobos—The larger of Mars's two satellites.

Polar caps—The deposits of frozen carbon dioxide at Mars's poles. The ice caps advance and recede with the changing Martian seasons, and bear a strong resemblance to Earth's polar regions.

Valles Marineris—The giant Martian canyon, located in a place of numerous rifts and faults in the Martian crust. This canyon would stretch across the entire continental United States.

Further Reading:

Bullock, M. A., "The Soil of Mars," *Mercury*, (Sept/Oct 1994): 10.

Beatty, J., and A. Chaikin. *The New Solar System*. Cambridge: Cambridge, 1991.

Chaikin, A. "Four Faces of Mars," *Sky & Telescope*, (Jul 1992): 18.

Haberle, R. M., "The Climate of Mars," *Scientific American*, (Aug 1978): 6.

Jeffrey C. Hall

Marsh see **Wetlands**

Marsupial cats

Marsupial cats are native carnivores of Australia, in the family Dasyuridae. Like all marsupials, the young of marsupial cats are born when they are still in an embryonic state, and they migrate to a belly pouch (or marsupium) on the female, where they fix onto a nipple and suckle until they are almost fully grown and independent.

Marsupial cats fill the ecological roles that are played by weasels, cats, foxes, and other medium-sized placental predators on other continents. The marsupial cats are typically about 3 ft (1 m) long (or less), with a similar length of body and tail. Marsupial cats are predators of small mammals, birds, and reptiles, which are killed by biting with their sharp canine teeth. Marsupial cats are intelligent and are fierce predators. Most species are nocturnal hunters.

The eastern Australian native cat, tiger cat, or quoll (*Dasyurus quoll*) is a medium-sized predator, with a grayish-brown or blackish pelage, marked with bright white spots.

The western Australian native cat or western Australian quoll (*Dasyurinus geoffroyi*) only occurs in remnants of its formerly extensive range of open-forest habitats, having been widely extirpated by introduced diseases and predators, hunters, and other factors.

The little northern native cats are *Satanellus hallucatus* of northern Australia, and *S. albopunctatus* of New Guinea. These animals have a light-brown, spotted pelage, and occur in rocky areas and open forests.

The tiger cat, or large spotted-tailed native cat (*Dasyurops maculatus*) is a native predator of dense forests of eastern Australia and Tasmania. This animal can reach a length of about 47 in (120 cm), of which almost one-half is comprised of its tail. Sometimes, individual animals will wreak havoc in situations where prey is confined in a relatively small space, for example, in a chicken coop.

See also Marsupials.

Bill Freedman

Marsupial rats and mice

Marsupial "rats" and "mice" are a diverse group of about 40 species of small, native carnivores of Australia, Tasmania, and New Guinea, in the family Dasyuridae. The young of marsupial rats and mice, as with those of all marsupials, are born while still in a tiny, embryonic stage of development. The almost helpless babies migrate to the belly of their mother, where they fix on a nipple and suckle until they are ready to lead an independent life. Unusual among the marsupials, the females of some species of marsupial rats and mice do not have a belly pouch (or marsupium) that encloses their nipples and protects their young. Other species do have a permanent pouch, or they have one that develops only during the breeding season.

Marsupial rats and mice are small mammals with a uniformly dark, brownish coat, often with a whitish belly, and they have a superficial resemblance to placental rats and mice. Most species are nocturnal predators that feed on insects and other small prey. The larger species, such as marsupial rats, feed on smaller marsupials, birds, and reptiles, and on introduced rodents. In a sense, marsupial mice fill the ecological roles played by the smallest placental predators on other continents, for example, shrews, while the marsupial rats are ecologically similar to larger small predators, such as weasels.

The brush-tailed marsupial mice or brush-tailed tuans (*Phascogale* spp.) are two species that occur in extreme southern Australia. The broad-footed marsupial mice (*Antechinus* spp.) are 10 species that occur in Australia, Tasmania, and New Guinea. The fat-skulled marsupial mice (*Planigale* spp.) are three species that live in Australia and New Guinea. The crested-tailed marsupial mouse (*Dasycercus cristicauda*) occurs in dry habitats of central Australia. The narrow-footed marsupial mice or pouched mice (*Sminthopsis* spp.) are about 10 species that occur in various types of habitats in Australia, Tasmania, and New Guinea. The long-legged jumping marsupials or jerboa marsupial mice (*Antechinomys* spp.) are two rare species of sandy deserts and savannas of Australia.

See also Marsupials.

Bill Freedman

Marsupials

Marsupials belong to the order Marsupalia, one of three subclasses of mammals (Metatheria). Marsupials are named for the *marsupium*, which means pouch in Latin; most female marsupials carry their young in pouches. The order Marsupalia includes eight families, 75 genera, and 250 species. Marsupials are divided into two groups based on the number and shape of the incisor teeth. One group has numerous small incisors (the Polyprotodontia) and includes the carnivorous and insectivorous marsupial mice and American opossum. The second group has a few, large incisors (Diprotodontia) and includes the herbivorous marsupials such as kangaroos and wallabies. The majority of species of marsupials, such as kangaroos, wallabies,

koalas, bandicoots, wombats, and Tasmanian devils inhabit the Australasian region (Australia, New Guinea, and the surrounding islands) to the east of Lombok in Indonesia, which marks the boundary between the Australian and Asian fauna. Approximately one-third of the species, most of which are opossums, are native to the Americas. Marsupials live underground (i.e. marsupial moles), on land (kangaroos), in trees (tree kangaroos and koalas), and in water (yapok), and inhabit rain forests, deserts, and temperate regions. Many species are nocturnal, while others are active by day. Marsupials may be herbivorous, carnivorous, insectivorous, or a combination of the three. Marsupials range in size from mouse-size to as large as adult humans.

All marsupials are born partially developed, and are small, blind, hairless; they have well-developed front legs with sharp claws and poorly developed hind legs. Immediately after birth, marsupial embryos crawl out of the birth canal using their front claws into the marsupium (pouch) where they attach themselves to a milk-secreting teat (nipple) for nourishment. The young marsupials are so helpless that they cannot suck milk right away. Contractions of muscles around the teat periodically squirt milk into the mouths of the attached embryos. The marsupial pouch helps keep the young attached to a teat. Newborn marsupials, born to species without pouches, stay attached by holding on to their mothers with their claws, and are aided by a swollen teat, which fills the baby's mouth, and makes it difficult for the young to detach. Female marsupials carry their young everywhere they go. When the young can no longer fit in the pouch or become too large for the mother to carry around, they detach and begin to live independently.

The oldest known fossils of marsupials date from the upper Cretaceous period (65 to 100 million years ago). Marsupials were once a dominant group with a wide distribution, and in the past were well represented in South America. The opossums of the Americas are extremely adaptable and some species have increased in number. The marsupial fauna of Australasia remained intact due to the isolation of this area from the rest of the world for millions of years, but many species are currently on the endangered list. Encroaching agriculture, urban sprawl, and the introduction of placental mammals have put some species of marsupial in danger of extinction. A century ago, the skins of large kangaroos were in great demand. Kangaroo hides have been used for leather and their meat used for human consumption, and for petfoods. Some species of kangaroo considered by farmers to be pests have been slaughtered in great numbers. Today, conservation groups, wild animal refuges and sanctuaries, and cooperation from ranchers and farmers are helping to keep the current populations of marsupials protected.

See also Anteaters; Bandicoots; Kangaroos and wallabies; Koalas; Marsupial cats; Marsupial rats and mice; Numbat; Opossums; Phalangers; Tasmanian devil; Wombats.

Further Reading:

Encyclopedia of Endangered Species. Detroit: Gale Research Inc., 1994.
Lavine, Sigmund A. *Wonders of Marsupials.* New York: Dodd, Mead & Company, 1978.
Lyne, Gordon. *Marsupials and Monotremes of Australia.* New York: Taplinger, 1967.
Morcombe, Michael. *Australian Marsupials and Other Native Animals.* New York: Charles Scribner's Sons, 1972.

Christine Miner Minderovic

Marten, sable, and fisher

Marten, sable, and fisher are species of medium-sized carnivores in the family Mustelidae, which also includes the weasels, otters, badgers, minks, skunks, and wolverine. Marten, sable, and fisher are generally solitary animals, living in forests of the Northern Hemisphere. All of these species have highly valuable fur, and are trapped intensively.

The American pine marten (*Martes americana*) ranges widely in conifer-dominated and mixedwood forests of North America. The closely related pine marten (*M. martes*) occurs in similar habitats in northern Europe and Asia, as does the Japanese marten (*M. melampus*) of Japan. The fisher (*M. pennanti*) of North America is a larger species, as are the beech marten (*M. foina*) of Eurasia, the sable (*M. zibellina*) of northern Asia, and the Himalayan marten (*M. flavigula*) of mountainous regions of southern Asia.

All of these species are excellent climbers, but they also forage on the ground. These animals are efficient predators, feeding largely on squirrels, rabbits, hares, smaller mammals, grouse, partridge, and pheasant.

All of the martens, sable, and fishers have a dense, lustrous fur, which is greatly prized by furriers. These animals have been relentlessly trapped for centuries, and they have become widely endangered or extirpated from much of their natural ranges.

Sable is the source of one of the world's most desirable furs. The original range of sable in northern Europe and Asia was larger than 20 million sq mi (52 million sq km), but by the mid-1700s the species had been widely extirpated by trapping, and survived in only a few refugia. Fortunately, the sable has greatly increased its range and abundance in recent decades, because of protection in some areas, and management of trapping pressures elsewhere, along with the release of thousands of captive-bred animals into suitable habitats in Russia.

American marten and fisher have extensive ranges in North America. Both species suffered many regional extirpations because of intensive trapping over much of their range. These species are also at risk from habitat losses associated with forestry and agriculture, because over much of their range they are significantly dependent on old growth, coniferous forests. Fortunately, both of these species are now protected, and have been reintroduced to some parts of their range from which they had been extirpated. The populations of marten and fisher are increasing in some areas, although their conservation status requires close monitoring and attention.

Bill Freedman

Martins see **Swallows and martins**

Maser

Maser is an acronym for Microwave Amplification by Stimulated Emission of Radiation. Microwaves correspond to that portion of the electromagnetic spectrum where the radiation has wavelengths between .039-12 in (1 mm-30 cm), i.e., between the far infrared and radio frequencies.

Crystals can be used as amplifiers of microwave radiation and as sources of radiation having a single wavelength and frequency. A maser amplifies the intensity of microwaves by taking advantage of a principle that was first discovered by the American physicist and Nobel Laureate, Charles Townes.

According to quantum mechanics, electrons exist in discrete energy states. In the case of a two level system, the electrons can populate one of two energy states. There will be a certain probability of finding an atom's electron in the lower energy state, and another probability of finding an atom's electron in the lower energy state, and another probability of finding an atom's electron in the higher energy state.

When an electron drops from the higher energy state to the lower one, it emits energy. Similarly, an electron must absorb energy to be promoted from the lower energy state to the higher one. The net energy emitted by electrons traversing the two energy states thus depends on the energy difference between the two states and on the difference in populations of the two energy states.

Under conditions of thermal equilibrium, the number of atoms having electrons in the lower energy state will exceed the number having electrons in the higher energy state. If electrons are pumped into the higher energy state by exciting them with excess energy, a higher rate of energy emission will result as the electrons try to restore thermal equilibrium by returning to the lower energy state.

The central problem of the maser is to obtain a suitable excess population in the upper state, thereby stimulating the emission of microwave radiation having a single wavelength and frequency. Such radiation is said to be coherent. In practice, masing action is accomplished in various ways. Good low noise amplifiers at microwave frequencies have been made using ruby masers. These amplifiers have found application in radio astronomy and space communication.

A laser (acronym for Light Amplification by Stimulated Emission of Radiation) amplifies light in a different region of the electromagnetic spectrum by the same method that the maser amplifies microwaves.

See also Laser.

Mass

Newton defined the mass of an object as the quantity of matter it possessed. A small rock, for example, has a mass—a fixed, unchanging quantity of matter. If you were to take that rock along with you on a trip to the moon, it would have the same quantity of matter—the same mass—that it had on earth. Its weight, however, would be less on the moon. The rock's weight on earth was the pull that the earth's gravity exerted on it. On the moon, its weight, as measured with a spring scale, will be less because the moon does not pull on it as strongly as the earth.

Defining the mass of an object as the quantity of matter it possesses is not a very good scientific defini-

tion. A better one can be found in Newton's second law of motion. If a constant force is applied to an object on a frictionless, horizontal surface, the object accelerates—its velocity increases uniformly with time. If a force twice as large is applied to the same object, its acceleration doubles as well. The object's acceleration is proportional to the force applied to it. We might write: $F \propto a$ where F is the force applied to the object and a is the acceleration of the object while the force acts. The symbol $\propto$ means that the two quantities, force and acceleration, are proportional; that is, if the force doubles the acceleration doubles.

Additional experiments show that force and acceleration are always proportional for any object; however, the same force applied to a baseball and a bowling ball will provide the bowling ball with a much smaller acceleration than the baseball. To convert the proportionality $F \propto a$ to an equation requires a proportionality constant so that we may write proportionality constant x $a = F$.

If the proportionality constant is to reflect the difference between the baseball and the bowling ball, we might write proportionality constant $= f(F,a)$, or $m = f(F,a)$.

Here, m is defined as the inertial mass of the object. It shows that a bowling ball requires a much bigger force than a baseball to produce the same acceleration.

Mass then can be defined as a ratio of force to acceleration. We define one kilogram to be an inertial mass that accelerates at one meter per second per second when a force of one newton is applied to it. If the same force (one newton) is applied to a two kilogram mass, its acceleration is only 0.5 meter per second per second.

If two objects acquire the same acceleration when the same force is applied to them, they have the same inertial mass. It makes no difference whether one is made of lead and the other of aluminum, their inertial masses are identical.

It is a common practice to measure mass on an equal arm balance. Two masses that balance are said to have the same gravitational mass because the gravitational pull on each of them is the same. Measuring inertial and gravitational masses are very different procedures. Inertial masses can be measured anywhere and are totally independent of gravity. Gravitational masses can be determined only in a gravitational field and there is no acceleration. Are the two kinds of masses related? Experiments have shown to within one part in ten billion, that two objects with the same gravitational mass have the same inertial mass.

See also Acceleration; Density; Force; Matter; Newton's laws of motion.

Further Reading:

Haber-Schaim et. al. *PSSC Physics*, 7th ed. Dubuque, Iowa: Kendall/Hunt, 1991. pp. 45-48.

Rogers, Eric M. *Physics for the Inquiring Mind.* Princeton, N.J.: Princeton University Press, 1960. pp. 105-134.

Sears, Zemansky, Young. *College Physics.* 6th ed., Reading, Mass.: Addison-Wesley, 1985. pp. 59-64.

White, Harvey. *Modern College Physics.* Princeton, N.J.: D. Van Nostrand, 1956. pp. 460-463.

Robert Gardner

Mass number

The mass number of an atom is the total number of protons plus neutrons in its nucleus.

Different isotopes of the same element have different mass numbers because their nuclei contain different numbers of neutrons. In the written symbol for a particular isotope, the mass number is written at the upper left of the symbol for the element, as in $^{238}_{92}U$, where 92 is the atomic number of uranium (U) and 238 is the mass number of this particular isotope. The symbol is read "uranium-238."

The mass number is always a whole number — just a count of the particles. It differs from the exact mass of the atom in atomic mass units, amu, which is often known and expressed to six decimal places. (One amu is exactly one-twelfth of the mass of an atom of carbon-12, ^{12}C, and is equal to approximately 1.66×10^{-24} gram.)

There are two reasons why the mass number of an atom is different from its exact mass. First, neutrons and protons don't happen to weigh exactly one amu apiece; the proton actually weighs 1.0072765 amu and the neutron weighs 1.0086650 amu. Second, when neutrons and protons are bound together as an atomic nucleus, the nucleus has less mass than the sum of the masses of the neutrons and protons. The difference in mass, when expressed in energy units according to Einstein's formula $E=mc^2$, is called the binding energy of the nucleus.

To understand this strange-sounding situation, we can think of the binding energy as the strength of the "glue" that holds the protons and neutrons together as a nucleus. It is, therefore, the amount of energy that would be required to break the "glue" and pull the nucleus apart into its individual neutrons and protons. But if energy must be added to an object in order to pull it apart, and if energy and mass are equivalent, then we could say that mass had to be added to pull it apart. The separated particles will therefore have more mass than when they were bound together as a nucleus.

See also Isotope; Neutron; Periodic table; Proton.

Robert L. Wolke

Mass production

Mass production is an entire system of manufacturing products that uses specialized labor, machinery, the smooth and logical flow of materials, and an assembly line to turn out large volumes of the same product at the lowest possible cost. The fullest expression of mass production was probably found at the Ford Motor Company in the early years of the twentieth century, when hundreds of thousands of Model Ts were produced a year, all exactly the same.

Predecessors to mass production

The principals of mass production grew out of manufacturing techniques that were already widespread in the United States. Called "the American system" or the "uniformity system," these techniques called for goods made of interchangeable parts. This meant that the cost of parts went down, but it was expensive to set up an interchangeable parts system.

Initially the uniformity system was most important in the manufacture of military equipment and clocks, both of which were built from many small parts that had to be made carefully. The United States government wanted to build weapons of high quality cheaply and swiftly, and make the parts uniform so that they could be quickly repaired during a battle. The process began at the end of the 1700s. At that time, while two rifles might look the same, any given part from one probably would not fit into the other. Guns were instead made one at a time by skilled craftsmen.

Guns required parts to be made with great accuracy. The federal government financed the initial attempts to use interchangeable parts. Eli Whitney, the inventor of the cotton gin, began the task around 1798. The parts of his muskets became more standardized but they were not really interchangeable. New equipment was invented that made parts with greater precision, and a system was created to ensure interchangeability. Patterns were used to make the parts, and a series of standardized tools were then used to measure them. Inspectors were sent to different arms factories. As a result, by mid-century the parts made at one factory fit into a gun made at another. Previously, the parts made by one worker would not fit into a gun made by the person next to him.

Around 1800, clocks still were made one at a time by hand. As a result, they were so expensive that few people owned one. The demand for clocks increased as more people lived in cities and had tight work schedules. To make clocks more cheaply, manufacturers began using power machinery and dividing labor so that workers specialized in a few tasks. Patterns were used to make parts interchangeable. Using these techniques, over 80,000 wooden clocks were made in Connecticut in 1836—twice as many as were owned in all of the United States in 1800. Division of labor was further refined so that by the 1850s, 60 workers had a part in making each clock. At the same time, fewer skilled workers were required because more work was done by machine, and this saved money. The price of a clock dropped from $10 in 1800, to $1.50 about 60 years later.

The techniques used to manufacture clocks and guns spread to other industries. The industrial revolution was underway and an increasing number of products were in demand by business and individuals. The uniformity system was used in varying degrees to make sewing machines, bicycles and mechanized farm equipment. In each case, some fitting had to be done by specialists. No one had looked at the process as a whole and broken it down into small tasks arranged in the most efficient order possible.

Such ideas were in the air, however. In the 1880s and 1890s management theorist Frederick W. Taylor studied the motion of people at work. He believed that production could be made more efficient by seeing where time and motion were wasted, then designing better work methods.

Mass production begins at Ford

The various threads of mass production came together at the Ford Motor Co. in Highland Park, Michigan, from 1908 to 1915. Cars were a relatively new invention and were still too expensive for the average person. Many were too heavy or low powered to be practical. Henry Ford set out to produce a light, strong car for a reasonable price. His Model T, released in 1908, was designed to meet these goals. Ford's top

Mass production of chocolate-covered doughnuts.

engineers and mechanics had backgrounds in the uniformity system, making sewing machines and farm equipment. From the beginning, they adopted interchangeability of parts as a core idea.

After studying how to make cars in the most logical, simple way possible, Ford built a Model T factory between 1908 and 1910 which favored the sequential assembly of parts. Machine tools, which made the parts of the car, were designed to perform one specialized operation. One machine tool did nothing but drill 45 holes into the side of an engine block. The machine tools were placed at the point in the assembly sequence where they were used; previous manufacturers usually had grouped machine tools together by category.

By 1913, a finished Model T rolled out of the factory every 40 seconds. Production went from 14,000 in 1909 to 189,000 in 1913, while the price of a Model T dropped from $950 to $550. Contemporary observers were amazed by this level of productivity, but a final innovation was coming.

The assembly line

Initially groups of workers at Ford moved down a line of parts and sub-assemblies, each worker carrying out a specific task. But some workers and groups were faster or slower than others, and they often got in each other's way. So Ford and his technicians decided to move the work instead of the workers. If engines in need of assembly were moved by a conveyor belt, the speed of work would become standardized to the speed the conveyor belt moved.

The concept of the assembly line came from many places, including slaughterhouses, where they operated in reverse. An animal carcass, hung on a hook, would slide down an overhead rail, while different workers removed various cuts of meat. No one had applied this idea to manufacturing, however.

After months of experimenting with various lengths and rates of speed for the assembly line, Ford switched its factory to assembly line production in 1913. The amount of time required to built a car plummeted to about a third of what it had been, and production skyrocketed, reaching 585,000 Model Ts in 1916. Because the assembly line was so demanding on workers, many left. To avoid constantly hiring and training new workers, Ford began paying them $5 a day—a good wage at the time.

The spread and limits of mass production

Ford became the toast of the nation. Manufacturers of many types quickly became interested in Ford's methods. The company's manufacturing process was initially known as Fordism, before being called mass production in the 1920s. Soon other car manufacturers, as well as manufacturers ranging from household appliances to radios, were using variations on Ford's methods. Ford's system call for making one unchanging product. Each copy of a product was exactly the same, and customers didn't have any choices about the cars they wanted to buy. For the first 12 years of its production, the Model T was only available in black. However, by the time the 15 millionth Model T had been built in 1927, the basic design was 20 years old and the market was saturated. No one wanted to buy any more Model Ts and its sales were falling fast.

When one of Ford's rivals, General Motors, designed and expanded its own mass production system during the 1920s, it built it with a greater amount of flexibility. GM used general purpose machine tools that could be adapted quickly to design changes. It also built the parts that went into its cars at a variety of locations, rather than all in the same factory as at Ford. When GM switched from a four-cylinder engine to a six-cylinder engine, the company first perfected the equipment at a small experimental plant. It was then able to switch over the main engine plant in Flint, Michigan, to six-cylinder production in a mere three weeks. Other parts of GM's business continued with no interruption at all.

In contrast, when Ford switched from the dying Model T to the Model A in 1927, the entire factory had to be shut down for six months. Ford had become so good at producing one product, and had become so specialized, that the change to a new product threw the company into chaos. After this demonstration of the shortcomings of doing everything in one factory, Ford too became less centralized. Mass production clearly had needed more flexibility; now it had it.

Mass production and advertising

Mass production calls for mass consumption. Thus mass production helped create the modern advertising industry as manufacturers sought to make consumers buy their products. But what if everyone already had bought a car? Partly to give customers more choices, partly to give those who already owned a car a reason to buy another, in the 1920s GM began creating a new version of its cars each year. In the 1930s, Ford followed. While mass-production purists like Henry Ford felt this was a marketing gimmick more appropriate for clothes than cars, most consumers were happy to finally have more choice in what they bought. Further, the Model T had been designed purely to function well. Many found it ugly. The Model A was considered far more visually appealing. Industrial design became important in winning customers. Just because hundreds of thousands of copies of a product were made did not mean it had to be visually uninteresting.

Supporters and detractors of mass production

As the idea of mass production became popular, manufacturers and industrialists of every kind looked for new areas in which to apply its methods. Henry Ford tried with mixed success to grow and process soybeans using mass production methods, turning them into products ranging from food to plastics and fabrics. Foster Gunnison considered himself the "Henry Ford of housing" because he built pre-fabricated houses on an assembly line beginning in the 1930s. Many furniture makers also tried mass production methods, but they did not work well for houses or furniture. Tastes for these kind of commodities were highly personal, and once bought, they were held onto for a long time. Henry

Ford and others believed that mass production would save the world and move into every facet of life, but it became clear that it was not suitable for building everything.

Many people were suspicious of mass production. It arose at a time when many people were leaving small towns and farms to work in the more anonymous environment of the big city. Many saw mass production as a reflection of this loss of individuality. Some critics saw it as a cause as well. In a mass production economy, everyone bought products that were exactly the same. And the workers who made these products were, in the view of these critics, little more than slaves to machines, doing the same thing all day, everyday. Mass production was seen by some as a symbol of all that was wrong with the world. It was criticized by Aldous Huxley in his 1932 novel, "Brave New World," and by filmmakers like Charlie Chaplin in "Modern Times," from 1936.

The defenders of mass production retorted that the high wages paid by mass-production factories meant that workers could afford more products themselves. They pointed out that mass production created a great number of useful things that more people could afford. Therefore, they said, it improved people's lives.

For most people, the doubts about mass production, which intensified during the Great Depression, were swept away by World War II. Mass production created incredible volumes of equipment for the war effort. Most manufacturers switched production to war materiel. Many car factories retooled, and began to make airplane or tank engines. Using mass production methods, some factories turned out tens-of-thousands of guns per month, more than the entire country produced in a year before beginning the uniformity system. Meanwhile the cost of building some weapons dropped to as little as 20% of the pre-war cost.

The interchangability of parts had become a basic law of manufacturing. During the war smaller factories often made just one part, which was combined at a second factory with parts from many other factories. At the same time, part sizes were getting more specific. The holes in engine blocks often had to be precise to within thousandths of an inch. The engineering and production advances were unprecedented, but as the war demonstrated, mass production also made mass destruction possible.

Mass production today

Mass production has become far more sophisticated than at its inception. To increase productivity,

managers have focused on planning and scheduling. Actual production has become a carefully managed flow of parts, materials and employees. Sales and marketing have become part of production, enabling management to know how many copies of a product to make.

One of the most important innovations is "just in time" production. Invented in Japan, the process requires detailed, predictable transportation and manufacturing schedules. Materials required for production arrive just in time to be used, while products are manufactured just in time to be shipped to their destination. This process cuts down on costly storage in warehouses, and prevents obsolete products from building up.

The emergence of computers has played an important role in planning and keeping complicated schedules that may involve thousands of people and parts. Computers help figure out production flow as well, keeping track of how much time different tasks take on the factory floor, and how much space they require.

In some ways, mass production has become so sophisticated that it is no longer true mass production. Many products come with a variety of options, and the customer can choose whatever combination of options he or she desires. When buying a computer from some manufacturers, for example, a customer can specify the size and make of the hard drive, how much memory they want and other details. Many theorists see a time in the near future when clothes are customized too. People would have their measurements taken, and when they order clothes, the clothes would be cut to their precise size by lasers at the clothes factory. The product would be created by specialized labor with the aid of machines, each shirt or pair of pants would be made using the same process, but by virtually any definition, this no longer would be mass production.

See also Assembly line; Industrial Revolution; Machine tools.

Further Reading:

Hindle, Brooke, and Lubar, Steven, *Engines of Change.* Washington, D.C.: Smithsonian Press, 1986.

Scott M. Lewis

Mass spectrometry

Mass spectrometry is an instrumental method of obtaining structure and mass information about either molecules or atoms by generating ionized particles and then accelerating them in a curved path through a magnetic field. Heavier particles are more difficult for the magnetic field to deflect around the curve, and thus travel in a straighter path than lighter particles. Consequently, by the time the particles reach the detector, a mixture of ions will have separated into groups by mass (or more specifically the mass-to-charge ratio of the individually weighted ions.)

The ions are produced from neutral molecules and atoms by stressing them with some form of energy to knock off electrons. In the case of molecules, fragmentation as well as ionization usually occurs. Each type of molecule breaks up in a characteristic manner, so a skilled observer can interpret a mass spectrum much like an archaeologist can reconstruct an entire skeleton from bone fragments. A mass spectrum can help establish values for ionization energy (the amount of energy it takes to remove an electron from a neutral atom or molecule) and molecular or atomic mass for unknown substances. The extremely high sensitivity of mass spectrometry makes it indispensable for analyzing trace quantities of substances, so it is widely used in environmental, pharmaceutical, forensic, flavor, and fragrance analysis. The petroleum industry has used mass spectrometry for decades to analyze hydrocarbons.

The basic principle underlying mass spectrometry was formulated by J. J. Thomson (the discoverer of the electron) early in the century. Working with cathode ray tubes, he was able to separate two types of particles, each with a slightly different mass, from a beam of neon ions, thereby proving the existence of isotopes. (Isotopes are atoms of the same element that have slightly different atomic masses due to the presence of differing numbers of neutrons in the nucleus.) The first mass spectrometers were built in 1919 by F. W. Aston and A. J. Dempster.

There are five major parts to a mass spectrometer: the inlet, the ionization chamber, the mass analyzer, the detector, and the electronic readout device. The sample to be analyzed enters the instrument through the inlet, usually as a gas, although a solid can be analyzed if it is sufficiently volatile to give off at least some gaseous molecules. In the ionization chamber, the sample is ionized and fragmented. This can be accomplished in many ways—electron bombardment, chemical ionization, laser ionization, electric field ionization—and the choice is usually based on how much the analyst wants the molecule to fragment. A milder ionization (lower electric field strength, less vigorous chemical reaction) will leave many more molecules intact, whereas a stronger ionization will produce more fragments. In the mass analyzer, the particles are separated into groups by mass, and then the detector measures the mass-to-charge ratio for each group of fragments. Finally, a readout device—usually a computer—records the data.

Mass spectrometers are often used in combination with other instruments. Since a mass spectrometer is an identification instrument, it is often paired with a separation instrument like a chromatograph. Sometimes two mass spectrometers are paired, so that a mild ionization method can be followed by a more vigorous ionization of the individual fragments.

See also Spectroscopy.

Mass transportation

Mass transportation is any kind of transportation system in which large numbers of people are carried within a single vehicle or combination of vehicles. Airplanes, railways, buses, trolleys, light rail systems, and subways are examples of mass transportation systems. The term mass transit is commonly used as a synonym for mass transportation.

In many parts of the world, mass transit systems are an important component of a nation's transportation system. Where people are too poor to buy automobiles, they depend on bicycles or animals or mass transit systems such as bus lines to travel within a city and from city to city. During the twentieth century, however, the

A New York city subway train above ground in Brooklyn.

role of mass transit systems in developed nations such as the United States has declined dramatically. The primary means of transportation has become the private automobile which typically carries only one or two passengers at a time.

Advantages of mass transportation

Mass transit systems have a number of obvious advantages over private means of conveyance, such as the automobile. In the first place, they are a far more efficient way of moving people than is the private automobile. For example, a subway system operating on two tracks 36 ft (11 m) wide can transport 80,000 passengers per hour. In comparison, an 8-lane freeway 125 ft (38 m) wide can carry only 20,000 passengers per hour. The cost of operating an inter-city bus line typically runs about 2¢ per vehicle mile, about one-tenth the comparable average for a private automobile.

Mass transit systems also take up much less space than do the highways needed for the movement of automobile traffic. Most urban landscapes today are a vivid testimony to the amount of space required for our automobile-dominated transportation system. Streets, high-ways, bridges, overpasses, and parking lots occupy as much as a third of the land available in some urban areas.

Mass transit systems are also more environmentally "friendly" than is the private automobile. A single bus filled with 80 people uses only slightly more fuel than does a single private automobile, yet is capable of carrying many times more passengers. The amount of air pollution produced per passenger, therefore, is much less.

Disadvantages of mass transportation

The desirable features of mass transit systems are balanced by a number of serious drawbacks. In the first place, such systems are economically feasible only in areas that have relatively large populations. As the number of inhabitants per square mile decreases, the efficiency of a mass transportation system also decreases.

Mass transit systems are also very expensive to build and to operate. This factor becomes more important when cities decide to install mass transit systems long after development has already taken place and disruption of existing structures is a serious problem.

Since mass transit systems seldom receive the government assistance provided to highway construction, consumers often have to pay a higher fraction of the costs of using mass transportation.

People complain about mass transportation systems also because they can be crowded, uncomfortable, dirty, and unreliable. Again, with limited budgets, mass transit systems are seldom able to maintain equipment and schedules to the extent that riders can rightly demand.

Finally, mass transportation systems are simply not as convenient as the automobile. A person can step into her or his car and drive virtually anywhere with a minimum of inconvenience. No mass transportation system can approach this level of ease.

Patterns in mass transportation use

The popularity of mass transportation systems varies inversely with the availability of the private automobile. Over the past century, as cars have become less expensive, consumers have opted for private transportation over subways, buses, trolleys, light rail systems, and other forms of mass transit. Between 1915 and 1980, automobile ownership increased 20 times faster than did population growth in the United States.

Probably the most significant shift in this pattern occurred during and just after World War II when automobiles were expensive and difficult to obtain by the private consumer. Mass transit usage reached record highs during the 1940s and 1950s. As prosperity returned to the nation, however, private cars once again became more popular as a means of transportation. In the two decades between 1950 and 1970, riders on all forms of public mass transit dropped from 19.5 billion to about 6.7 billion.

That decrease was reversed briefly in the early 1970s as a result of the oil embargo instituted by the Organization of Petroleum Exporting Countries (OPEC) in 1973. Americans suddenly became aware of the nation's dependence on other nations for our oil and natural gas, and there was a renewed interest in reviving the nation's nearly moribund public transportation systems. It was about this time (1972) that the first of the country's new mass transit systems, Bay Area Rapid Transit (BART), opened in the San Francisco Bay Area. BART was followed in the next two decades by new subway, bus, and trolley systems in Washington, D.C., San Jose and San Diego California, Atlanta, Baltimore, Dallas, Los Angeles, and other urban areas.

At about the same time, the U.S. Congress gave the nation's intercity passenger rail system, Amtrak, a new lease on life. Amtrak proved to be a huge success among intercity passengers, but the federal government has never maintained the consistent support of the system it showed during the aftermath of the OPEC crisis.

The surge of interest in mass transit that began in the 1970s has never produced the massive shift to mass transit for which so many people hoped. For more than four decades, the automobile and commercial airlines have accounted for more than 96% of all intercity travel. Buses and railroads carry the remaining intercity passengers.

Travel in urban areas reflect similar patterns. After intensive efforts to increase ridership on public transportation systems, most city and suburban dwellers still rely on their own cars for transportation. In Los Angeles, for example, the city's upgraded bus system and new light rail system are now used by no more than about 2% of the local population.

The uphill battle faced by proponents of mass transportation is understandable. The automotive industry (along with energy companies that sell gasoline) have been successful in convincing Americans of the pre-eminent value of the private automobile. The federal government has contributed to this philosophy with enormous investments in new streets, highways, and interstates. Currently, the United States government spends about six times as many dollars per person on new highway construction as it does on the support of all mass transit systems. In some states, this ratio may be as high as 60 to 1.

Alternative forms of mass transportation

Some critics have suggested that new forms of mass transportation be developed that will preserve the special advantages of this form of transit while avoiding some of its disadvantages. For example, many cities and companies have set up van pools for their employees. People who live close to each other are picked up in small vans and brought to and from work as a group. Other cities have experimented with dial-a-ride programs in which citizens (often elderly citizens) can call to request transportation in a mini-van from one point to another within the city.

Many cities have attempted to increase the use of mass transit systems by discouraging the use of automobiles. For example, they have imposed high taxes on parking within the city and have raised tolls on bridges and tunnels leading to the city.

Efforts to improve existing mass transit systems, the development of new subway, trolley, and bus lines, the introduction of alternative forms of mass transportation, and attempts to discourage automobile use have had limited successes in specific parts of the United States. On a national level, however, they have had only a limited impact on the way in which citizens choose to move about within a city and from city to city.

See also Trains and railroads.

Further Reading:

Meyer, John R., and Jose A. Gomez-Ibañez. *Autos, Transit, and Cities*. Cambridge, MA: Harvard University Press, 1981.

Miller, G. Tyler, Jr. *Living in the Environment: An Introduction to Environmental Science*, 4th edition. Belmont, CA: Wadsworth Publishing Company, 1985: 220 - 225.

Owen, Wilfred. *Transportation in Cities*. Washington, D.C.: Brookings Institution, 1976.

Reische, Diana, ed. *Problems of Mass Transportation*. New York: The H. W. Wilson Company, 1970.

David E. Newton

Mass wasting

Mass wasting, or mass movement, is the process that moves Earth materials down a slope, under the influence of gravity. Mass wasting processes range from violent landslides to imperceptibly slow creep. Mass wasting decreases the steepness of slopes, leaving them more stable. While ice formation or water infiltration in sediments or rocks may aid mass wasting, the driving force is gravity. All mass wasting is a product of one or more of the following mass wasting processes: flow, fall, slide, or slump.

Mass wasting processes

The four processes of mass wasting are distinguished based on the nature of the movement that they

An avalanche.

produce. Flow involves the rapid downslope movement of a chaotic mass of material. Varying amounts of water may be involved. A mud flow, for example, contains a large amount of water and involves the movement of very fine-grained Earth materials. Fall involves very rapid downslope movement of Earth materials as they descend (free fall) from a cliff. Ignoring wind resistance, falling materials move at 32 ft/sec (9.8 m/sec) — the fastest rate possible in a natural system. Slides result when a mass of material moves downslope, as a fairly coherent mass, along a planar surface. Slumps are similar to slides but occur along a curved (concave-upward) surface and move somewhat more slowly.

Moving mountains to the sea

Consider a chunk of rock currently attached to a jagged outcrop high on a mountain. It will move to the sea as a result of three processes: weathering, mass wasting, and erosion.

On warm days, water from melting snow trickles into a crack which has begun to form between this chunk and the rest of the mountain. Frigid nights make this water freeze again, and its expansion will widen and extend the crack. This and other mechanical, biological, and chemical processes (such as the growth of roots, and the dissolution of the more soluble components of rock) break apart bedrock into transportable fragments. This is called weathering.

Once the crack extends through it and the chunk has been completely separated from the rest of the mountain, it will fall and join the pile of rocks, called talus, beneath it that broke off the mountain previously. This pile of rocks is called a talus pile. This movement is an example of mass wasting, known as a rockfall. As the rocks in the talus pile slip and slide, adjusting to the weight of the overlying rocks, the base of the talus pile extends outward and eventually all the rocks making up the pile will move down slope a little bit to replace those below that also moved downslope. This type of mass movement is known as rock creep, and a talus pile that is experiencing rock creep is called a rock glacier.

In the valley at the bottom of this mountain, there may be a river or a glacier removing material from the base of the talus slope and transporting it away. Removal and transport by a flowing medium (rivers, glaciers, wind) is termed erosion.

These processes occur in many other situations. A river erodes by cutting a valley through layers of rock, transporting that material using flowing water. This erosion would result in deep canyons with vertical walls if the erosion by the river were the only factor. But very high, vertical walls leave huge masses of rock unsupported except by the cohesive strength of the material of which they are made. At some point, the stresses produced by gravity will exceed the strength of the rock and an avalanche (another type of mass movement) will result. This will move some of the material down the slope into the river where erosion will carry it away.

Erosion and mass wasting work together by transporting material away. Erosion produces and steepens slopes, which are then reduced by mass wasting.

Mass wasting in loose aggregates

The steepness of a natural slope depends on the size and shape of the material making up the slope and environmental factors, principally water content. Most people learn about this early in life, playing in a sandbox or on the beach. If you dump dry sand from a bucket it forms a conical hill. The more sand you dump the larger the hill gets, but the slope of the hill stays the same. If you stop dumping sand and start to dig into the bottom of the hill, sand will avalanche down into the hole you are trying to make. Loose, dry sand flows easily and will quickly re-establish its preferred slope whenever you do anything to steepen it. The flow of sand is a simple example of mass wasting.

As you probably know, if sand is moist, the slope of a sand pile can be higher. A sand castle can have vertical walls when it is built of moist sand in the morning, but as the afternoon wears on and the sand dries out, it crumbles and collapses (mass wastes) until a stable slope forms. This is because the water makes the sand more cohesive. With the proper moisture content, there will be both water and air between most of the grains of sand. The boundary between the water and the air has surface tension — the same surface tension that supports water striders or pulls liquids up a capillary tube. In moist sand, surface tension holds the grains together like a weak cement.

However, if sand becomes saturated with water (that is, its pores become completely water-filled as they are in quick sand), then the sand will flow in a process known as lateral spreading. Water-saturated sand flows because the weight of the sand is supported (at least temporarily) by the water, and so the grains are not continuously in contact. Apparently then, the slope of a pile of sand is dependant on water content, and either too little or too much water lowers the stable slope. This illustrates how slope stability is a function of water content.

The steepest slope that a material can have is called the angle of repose. Any loose pile of sediment grains has an angle of repose. As grain size increases, the angle of repose also increases. Talus slopes high on mountain sides may consist of large, angular boulders and can have slopes of up to 45°, whereas fine sand has an angle of repose of 34°. This is the slope that you can see inside a sand-filled hour glass. In nature, however, slopes less than the angle of repose are common because of wind activity and similar environmental processes.

A typical sand dune has a gentle slope on the windward side where erosion by the wind is responsible for the slope. On the leeward side, where sand falls freely, it usually maintains a slope close to the angle of repose. This permits you to run up the windward side where the sand has been tightly packed by the wind, then jump off the crest, land on the leeward slope where you cause, and become part of, a sand avalanche down that slope!

So far we discussed loose deposits of particles on land, but similar conditions exist if they are under water, although stable slopes are much gentler. When

A landslide in California.

sudden mass wasting events occur under water, large quantities of material may end up being suspended in the water producing turbidity currents which complicate the picture. Such currents occur because a mass of water with sediment suspended in it is denser than the clear water surrounding it, so it sinks, moving down the slope, eroding as it goes. Still, the initial adjustment of the slope was not the result of these currents, so the mechanism that produces turbidity currents is an example of mass wasting.

Mass wasting in rocks and soils

Most slopes in nature are on materials that are not loose collections of grains. They occur on bedrock or on soils which are bound together by organic material, etc. Yet many of the principles used to explain mass wasting in aggregates still apply. Instead of mass wasting taking place as an avalanche, however, it results from a portion of the slope breaking off and sliding down the hill. We usually call these events landslides, or avalanches, if they are large and damaging, or slumps if they are smaller.

If the gravitational forces acting on a mass of material are greater than its strength, a fracture will develop, separating the mass from the rest of the slope. Usually this fracture will be nearly vertical near the top of the break, curving to a much lower angle near the bottom of the break. Such events can be triggered by an increase in the driving forces (for example, the weight of the slope), a decrease in the strength of the material, or both.

When people build on slopes they often add to the gravitational forces by constructing very heavy things, such as houses and swimming pools. A period of heavy rain can add a lot of weight to a slope, too. Rain may also change the strength of the material making up the slope. As we have seen, saturated soil with no surface tension is much weaker than moist soil. But there is another effect that occurs even in solid rock.

Even very solid rocks contain pores, and many of these pores are interconnected. It is through such pores that water and oil move toward wells. Below the water table, all the pores are filled with water with no surface tension to eliminate. So it might seem that rock down there would not be affected by rainfall at the surface. As the rains come, however, the water table rises, and the additional water increases the pressure in the fluids in the pores below. This increase in pore pressure pushes adjacent rock surfaces apart, reducing the friction between them, which lowers the strength of the rock and makes it easier for fractures to develop. Elevated pore pressures are implicated in many dramatic mass wasting events.

When southern California gets heavy rains, the TV news cameras record beautiful homes moving down slope in a landslide or mud flow to become rubble at the bottom. Such dramatic examples of mass wasting are impressive, but represent only a fraction of what is all around us everyday.

Soil creep

When mass wasting by flow occurs so slowly that it cannot be observed, it is called creep. Most vegetated slopes in humid climates are subject to soil creep, and there are many indicators that it occurs. Poles and fence posts often tip away from a slope a few years after they are emplaced. Trees growing on a slope usually have trunks with sharp curves at their bases. Older trees are bent more than younger ones. All this occurs because the upper layers of soil and weathered rock move gradually down the slope while deeper layers remain relatively fixed. This tips inanimate objects such as power poles. It would tip trees, too, except that they grow toward the sun, keeping the trunk growing vertically, and so a bend develops.

This gradual downslope movement requires years to result in significant transport, but because it occurs over a great portion of the surface of the Earth it is responsible for most mass wasting.

Influence of climate

Rivers in the desert regions of the southwestern states form canyons with fairly steep walls, and the buttes and mesas in those regions also have very steep walls. The topography of the eastern states is much more subdued, dominated by rolling hills and gentle slopes. How does rainfall control this contrast in landscape? Weathering needs water for freezing and thawing, chemical reactions, and growth of roots. Less water means the rate of weathering will be reduced. Also, rainfall affects erosion by water. Less water means the rate at which rivers cut valleys will be reduced. If these were the only factors, however, only the rates would vary; arid regions would weather and erode more slowly than humid ones.

Much of the difference in landscape results from variations in mass wasting. Very steep slopes on dry rock with little or no pore pressure are much more stable than similar slopes on wet rock with high pore pressures. Water adds to the weight trying to break the rock and increases the pore pressure which weakens the rock. Hence the height of a vertical slope which can exist in dry rock is much greater than that in wet rock. Arid climates also have less vegetation to stabilize sediment at the base of a slope, so it is likely to be washed away during the infrequent storms.

What can we do about mass wasting?

In a natural setting, mass wasting presents little threat. Most slopes are relatively stable most of the time. However, when people modify slopes — their gravitational loads, or their water content — they may become unstable and fail. Engineers can study the stresses acting on a slope, test the material of which it is made, make some assumptions about behavior with higher pore pressure, etc., and predict how likely that slope is to fail if the additional load of a house were added to it. This study might conclude that the slope would still be stable, and so the house might be constructed. Later, after it has changed hands a few times, a new owner might decide to put in a swimming pool. A neighbor in the property just downhill, might decide to cut into the slope in order to widen a driveway, or a neighbor just uphill might inadvertently introduce large amounts of water into the ground while trying to maintain a gracious green lawn. Any one of these actions could bring the slope close to where it is unstable. A period of heavy rain could provide the final impetus, and a sudden mass wasting event could occur. To avoid such problems, property owners on such slopes must have their freedoms restricted. One way to accomplish this is to prohibit certain activities through zoning, deed restrictions, or insurance requirements. A less satisfactory means is by threat of litigation.

See also Erosion; Weathering.

Further Reading:

Cooke, Ronald U. *Geomorphological Hazards in Los Angeles: A Study of Slope and Sediment Problems in a Metropolitan County.* London; Boston: Allen & Unwin, 1984.

KEY TERMS

Angle of repose—The slope made by a pile of loose material, such as the sand in an hour glass.

Avalanche—A mass movement in which a chaotic mass of rock and/or soil very rapidly flows down slope along a discrete surface; an avalanche is a type of flow.

Creep—A mass movement that involves gradual downslope movement (flow), too slow to be observed directly, but apparent in many long term observations.

Erosion—Removal, transport, and deposition (accumulation) of weathered Earth materials by wind, water, or ice.

Flow—A mass movement process in which a chaotic mass of Earth material moves down slope; rates of flow are a function of fluid content of the mass and the grain size — the higher the fluid content and finer the particles, the faster the flow.

Landslide—A mass movement in which a fairly coherent mass of rock and/or soil rapidly moves down slope along a discrete plane; sometimes used to include all types of moderately rapid mass movements involving flows, falls, or slides.

Lateral spreading—Mass wasting of water saturated sediments; lateral spreading involves the flow of fine-grained sediments (clay, silt, or sand).

Pore pressure—The pressure of fluids contained within the pores of a rock, which influences the strength of the rock and is often a factor in dramatic landslides or mudslides.

Rock creep—Very slow mass movement of large rock fragments (pebbles, cobbles, and boulders) in response to the weight of overlying rocks.

Rock fall—Very rapid mass wasting of large rock fragments that have fallen from an exposed cliff.

Slide—A mass movement process in which a fairly coherent mass of rock and/or soil rapidly moves down slope over a discrete surface.

Slumps—A mass movement process in which a fairly coherent mass of rock and/or soil moves down slope over a discrete surface, but curved (concave-upward) surface. Slumps occur much faster than creep but slower than slides.

Talus—Large rock fragments that accumulate at the base of a steep slope, transported there by mass wasting.

Weathering—Biological, chemical, and mechanical attack on rock which breaks it up and alters it at or near the surface of the Earth.

Costa, John E. and Gerald F. Wieczorek, ed. *Debris Flows/ Avalanches: Process, Recognition, and Mitigation.* Boulder, CO: Geological Society of America, 1987.

Haneberg, William C. and Scott A. Anderson, ed. *Clay And Shale Slope Instability.* Boulder, CO: Geological Society of America, 1995.

Press, Frank, and Raymond Siever. *Understanding Earth.* New York: W.H. Freeman and Co., 1994.

Small, R.J. and M.J. Clark *Slopes And Weathering.* Cambridge; New York: Cambridge University Press, 1982.

Otto H. Muller

Mathematics

Mathematics, in the very broadest sense, is the systematic study of relationships in the physical world and relationships between symbols which need not pertain to the real world. In relation to the world, mathematics is the language of science. It operates within the laws and constraints of science as it examines physical phenomena. Unlike science, however, mathematics has no constraints. So in relation to symbols, mathematics can be considered a pure mental activity which is capable of generating new concepts within the mind unrelated to anything which presently exists.

Mathematics has many utilitarian uses and was developed for these purposes originally. Agriculture and farming required knowledge of geometry for making things. Astronomy and navigation required knowledge of trigonometry, while most everyday activities required knowledge of number and measurement for keeping account of transactions. Pythagorus (who preceded Euclid) considered number to be everything since it expresses the relationship between a multiplicity of natural phenomena from sounds in music to patterns in flowers, and relationships between man-made objects, from architecture to games.

It is often erroneously considered by students that arithmetic is an inferior part of mathematics concerned with computation and calculation. Mathematics is assumed to be the superior activity involved with reasoning and abstract ideas. In fact, arithmetic is said by mathematicians to be the Queen of Mathematics since number theory is one of the most abstract parts of mathematics. Number theory can be studied for its own sake rather than for its usefulness in science and technology.

It was mentioned earlier that we need numbers for keeping account of transactions. Numerical statements of fact in any area of inquiry are known as statistics. Statistical methods of mathematical processes used to summarize numerical data and help in their interpretation. For example, instead of listing everyone's test scores on an examination and comparing them to last year's scores, it is more expedient to calculate average scores as a measure of class progress.

Although mathematics is famous for the certainty of its results, statistical methods lead us into areas of uncertainty. For example, in the previous paragraph the "average" we calculate is subject to a degree of error. We recognize this and have ways of calculating the probability that the true score lies within a certain range of values. Probability is that part of mathematics that enables mathematicians to calculate the likelihood of an event happening in the future. Probability is the mathematical engine that drives statistics. It enables us to infer the behavior of a whole population from a small sample.

All branches of mathematics are interrelated, as may be seen from the school curriculum. Mathematics is the study of quantitative relationships. When such relationships are expressed in terms of number, that branch of mathematics is called arithmetic. When relationships are expressed in letters and numbers, with similar rules to arithmetic, the subject is known as algebra. Trigonometry studies relationships between angles. Geometry is concerned with size, shape, area, and volume of objects and position in space.

Calculus deals with the relationship between changing quantities. In differential calculus, the problem is to find the rate at which a known but varying quantity changes. The problem in integral calculus is the reverse of this: to find a quantity when the rate at which it is changing is known. Mathematics is the name for the broad area which is comprised of all these subject areas, and many others not included in the school curriculum, e.g., non-Euclidean geometry.

Understanding of quantitative relationships develops in the pre-school period as children learn concepts such as "greater than," "less than," and "equal to." Understanding concepts in mathematics is more important than memorizing rules. "Coming to grips" with time for example, means more than telling time on a watch or clock. It means having some idea of how long it takes to complete tasks, how to budget time, and so forth. Quantitative reasoning is a part of everyday life, yet mathematics tends to be seen as unrelated to daily living. The extent to which mathematics does pervade all aspects of life is astonishing. All the major advances in electricity and magnetism, thermodynamics, and so forth, were dependent on mathematics. Exploration of space and most of the technological discoveries of the twentieth century have been made through the application of mathematics.

Logicians and philosophers are concerned with mathematics for its own sake. They are interested in pure thought and mathematics as a system of reasoning, unrelated to the physical structure of the world. The correspondence between language and mathematics pursued by this branch of study led to information theory and its outgrowths, cybernetics, and operations research. It could also lead into areas of study which cannot be imagined at this time. Mathematics is an incomparable field of study, whose possibilities are limitless.

See also Arithmetic; Calculus; Geometry; Number theory; Trigonometry.

Further Reading:

Adler, Irving. *Mathematics*. New York: Doubleday, 1992.
Motz, Lloyd, and Jefferson Hane Weaver. *The Story of Mathematics*. New York: Plenum Press, 1993.
Slavin, Steven. *All the Math You'll Ever Need*. New York: Wiley, 1989.

Selma Hughes

Matrix

A matrix is a rectangular array of numbers or number-like elements:

$$\begin{pmatrix} 1 & 1 \\ 2 & 0 \end{pmatrix} \quad \begin{pmatrix} a_{11} & a_{12} \\ a_{21} & a_{22} \\ a_{31} & a_{32} \end{pmatrix}$$

In the example on the left, 1 1 and 2 0 are its rows; 1 2 and 1 0, its columns. In the example on the right there are three rows and two columns, making it a 3 x 2

matrix. When subscripted variables are used to represent the elements, the first subscript names the row,; the second, the column: $a_{row, column}$. For example, a_{21} is in the second row and first column, but a_{12} is in the first row, second column. Except when there is danger of confusion, the subscripts need not be separated by a comma. Some authors enclose a matrix in brackets: other authors use parentheses, as above.

Matrices can also be represented with single letters A, I, or with a single subscripted variable (a_{ij}) with variable subscripts. This latter form is useful in statements such as ($a_{ij} = b_{ij}$) if and only if $a_{ij} = b_{ij}$ for all i, j which says symbolically that two matrices are equal when their corresponding elements are equal.

Under limited circumstances matrices can be added, subtracted, and multiplied. Two matrices can be added or subtracted only if they are the same size. Then (a_{ij}) $\pm$ (b_{ij}) = ($a_{ij} \pm b_{ij}$) which says that the sum or difference of two matrices is the matrix formed by adding or subtracting the corresponding elements.

$$\begin{pmatrix} 1 & 2 & 1 \\ 0 & 4 & 7 \end{pmatrix} + \begin{pmatrix} -3 & 1 & 4 \\ -1 & 2 & 2 \end{pmatrix} = \begin{pmatrix} -2 & 3 & 5 \\ -1 & 6 & 9 \end{pmatrix}$$

These rules for adding and subtracting matrices give matrix addition the same properties as ordinary addition and subtraction. It is closed (among matrices of the same size), commutative, and associative. There is an additive identity (the matrix consisting entirely of zeros) and an additive inverse:

$$-(a_{ij}) = (-a_{ij})$$

This latter definition allows one to subtract a matrix by adding its opposite:

$$A - B = A + (-B)$$

Multiplication is much trickier. For multiplication to be possible, the matrix on the left must have as many columns as the matrix on the right has rows. That is, one can multiply an m x n matrix by an n x q matrix but not an m x n matrix by an p x q matrix if p is not equal to n. The product of an m x n matrix and an n x q matrix will be an m x q matrix.

Multiplication is best explained with an example:

$$\begin{pmatrix} 1 & 3 \\ 2 & 1 \end{pmatrix} \begin{pmatrix} 5 & 2 & 1 \\ 0 & -1 & 2 \end{pmatrix} = \begin{pmatrix} 5 & -1 & 7 \\ 10 & 3 & 4 \end{pmatrix}$$

The 5 in the product comes from (1) (5) + (3) (0). The -1 comes from (1) (2) + (3) (-1). The 7 comes from (1) (1) + (3) (2). In the second row of the product, 10 = (2) (5) + (2) (0); 3 = (2) (2) + (1) (-1); and 4 = (2) (1) + (1) (2).

Each row in the matrix on the left has been "multiplied" by each column in the matrix on the right. We say "multiplied" because each row on the left is a two-number row, and each column on the right is a two-number column. These numbers have been paired off, multiplied, and added. This kind of "multiplication" is somewhat more complicated than the ordinary sort. Those who are familiar with vectors will recognize this as forming the dot product of each row of the matrix on the left with each column on the right.

Multiplication is associative, but not communicative. That is (AB)C = A(BC) but, in general, AB ≠ BA.

In the example above, multiplication is not even possible if the 2 x 3 matrix is placed on the left.

There is a multiplicative identity, I. It is a square matrix of an appropriate size. It has 1's down the main diagonal and 0's elsewhere.

$$\begin{pmatrix} 1 & 0 \\ 0 & 1 \end{pmatrix} \begin{pmatrix} 5 & 2 & 1 \\ 0 & -1 & 2 \end{pmatrix} = \begin{pmatrix} 5 & 2 & 1 \\ 0 & -1 & 2 \end{pmatrix}$$

or

$$\begin{pmatrix} 5 & 2 & 1 \\ 0 & -1 & 2 \end{pmatrix} \begin{pmatrix} 1 & 0 & 0 \\ 0 & 1 & 0 \\ 0 & 0 & 1 \end{pmatrix} = \begin{pmatrix} 5 & 2 & 1 \\ 0 & -1 & 2 \end{pmatrix}$$

A matrix may or may not have a multiplicative inverse, which is a matrix A^{-1} such that $A^{-1}A = I$

Since

$$\begin{pmatrix} 1 & -1 \\ 1 & 2 \end{pmatrix} \begin{pmatrix} \frac{2}{3} & \frac{1}{3} \\ -\frac{1}{3} & \frac{1}{3} \end{pmatrix} = \begin{pmatrix} 1 & 0 \\ 0 & 1 \end{pmatrix}$$

the two matrices on the left side of the equation are multiplicative inverses of each other.

An example of a matrix which does not have an inverse is

$$\begin{pmatrix} 1 & 1 \\ 2 & 2 \end{pmatrix}$$

This can be seen by trying to solve the matrix equation

$$\begin{pmatrix} 1 & 1 \\ 2 & 2 \end{pmatrix} \begin{pmatrix} a & b \\ c & d \end{pmatrix} = \begin{pmatrix} 1 & 0 \\ 0 & 1 \end{pmatrix}$$

Using the row-by-column rule for multiplying gives

$$a + c = 1$$
$$2a + 2c = 0$$

which is impossible.

Typically one limits the concept of an inverse to matrices which are square. Without this limitation a matrix such as

$$\begin{pmatrix} 1 & 0 & 1 \\ 1 & 1 & 2 \end{pmatrix}$$

would have no left inverse at all and an infinitude of right inverses. Working only with square matrices, it is possible to show that a matrix and its inverse commute, that is, that any left inverse is also a right inverse. It is also possible to show that any inverse is unique.

Matrices are used in many ways. The following examples show three of those ways.

A matrix can be used to solve systems of linear equations. If

$$A = \begin{pmatrix} 1 & -1 \\ 1 & 2 \end{pmatrix} \quad X = \begin{pmatrix} x \\ y \end{pmatrix} \quad \text{and } B = \begin{pmatrix} 9 \\ 3 \end{pmatrix}$$

then the matrix equation AX = B represents the system

$$x - y = 9$$
$$x + 2y = 3$$

If one multiplies both sides of the matrix equation by the inverse of A (computed above) $A^{-1}AX = A^{-1}B$ then $X = A^{-1}B$.

Writing these matrices in expanded form

$$\begin{pmatrix} x \\ y \end{pmatrix} = \begin{pmatrix} \frac{2}{3} & \frac{1}{3} \\ -\frac{1}{3} & \frac{1}{3} \end{pmatrix} \begin{pmatrix} 9 \\ 3 \end{pmatrix}$$

and multiplying

$$\begin{pmatrix} x \\ y \end{pmatrix} = \begin{pmatrix} 7 \\ -2 \end{pmatrix}$$

or x = 7, y = -2,

For such a small system of equations, using matrices is rather inefficient. For systems with a large number of unknowns and equations, using matrices is very efficient, especially if one turns the work over to a computer. Computers love matrices.

Two-by-two matrices can be used to represent complex numbers:

$$a + bi \longleftrightarrow \begin{pmatrix} a & b \\ -b & a \end{pmatrix}$$

They behave like complex numbers, and they sneak around the sometimes disturbing property

$$i^2 = -1: \begin{pmatrix} 0 & -1 \\ -1 & 0 \end{pmatrix} \begin{pmatrix} 0 & 1 \\ -1 & 0 \end{pmatrix} = \begin{pmatrix} -1 & 0 \\ 0 & -1 \end{pmatrix}$$

Matrices can be used for enciphering messages. If the message were "OUT OF WATER," it would first be converted to numbers using a = 1, b = 2, etc. to become 15 21 20 15 6 23 1 20 5 18. These numbers would then be broken into pairs, and each pair, treated as a 2 x 1 matrix, would then be multiplied by a secret enciphering matrix:

$$\begin{pmatrix} 5 & 2 \\ 7 & 3 \end{pmatrix} \begin{pmatrix} 15 \\ 21 \end{pmatrix} = \begin{pmatrix} 117 \\ 168 \end{pmatrix} = \begin{pmatrix} 13 \\ 12 \end{pmatrix}$$

where 117 and 168 are reduced to numbers 26 or below by subtracting 26 as many times as needed. When this is done for the entire message, the numbers are converted back to letters, ML..., and the enciphered message is sent.

The recipient goes through the same steps, but uses a secret deciphering matrix:

$$\begin{pmatrix} 3 & 24 \\ 19 & 5 \end{pmatrix} \begin{pmatrix} 13 \\ 12 \end{pmatrix} = \begin{pmatrix} 327 \\ 307 \end{pmatrix} = \begin{pmatrix} 15 \\ 21 \end{pmatrix}$$

which can be converted back to "OU...."

This works because the product of the enciphering and the deciphering matrices is, after reducing the numbers by subtracting 26s, the identity matrix:

$$\begin{pmatrix} 5 & 2 \\ 7 & 3 \end{pmatrix} \begin{pmatrix} 3 & 24 \\ 19 & 5 \end{pmatrix} = \begin{pmatrix} 53 & 130 \\ 78 & 183 \end{pmatrix} = \begin{pmatrix} 1 & 0 \\ 0 & 1 \end{pmatrix}$$

Multiplying the message first by the enciphering matrix, then by the deciphering is equivalent to multiplying it by the identity matrix. Therefore the original message is restored.

A two-by-two enciphering matrix doesn't conceal the message very well. A skilled crytanalyst could crack a long message or series of short ones very easily. (This one, by itself, would be too short for the cryptanalyst to do any of the statistical analyses needed for cracking it.) If the enciphering and deciphering matrices were bigger, say ten-by-ten, the encipherment would be pretty secure.

Further Reading:

Birkhoff, Garrett, and Saunders Mac Lane, *A Survey of Modern Algebra.* New York: The Macmillan Co., 1947.

Kolman, Bernard, *Introductory Linear Algebra with Applications.* New York: Macmillan Publishing Co., 1980.

Pettofrezzo, Anthony, *Matrices and Transformations.* New York: Dover Publications, 1966.

Sinkov, Abraham, *Elementary Crytanlysis.* Washington, D.C.: The Mathematical Association of America, 1968.

J. Paul Moulton

Matter

Matter is anything that takes up space and has mass (or weight which is the influence of gravity on mass.) It is distinguished from energy, which causes objects to move or change, but which has no volume or mass of its own. Matter and energy interact, and under certain circumstances behave similarly, but for the most part remain separate phenomena. They are, however, interconvertible according to Einstein's equation $E=mc^2$, where E is the amount of energy that is equivalent to an amount of mass m, and c is a constant: the speed of light in a vacuum.

In 1804, the English scientist John Dalton formulated the atomic theory, which set out some fundamental characteristics of matter, and which is still used today. According to this theory, matter is composed of extremely small particles called atoms, which can be neither created nor destroyed. Atoms can, however, attach themselves (bond) to each other in various arrangements to form molecules. A material composed entirely of atoms of one type is an element, and different elements are made of different atoms. A material composed entirely of molecules of one type is a compound, and different compounds are made of different molecules. Pure elements and pure compounds are often referred to collectively as pure substances, as opposed to a mixture in which atoms or molecules of more than one type are jumbled together in no particular arrangement.

Elements and compounds can undergo chemical processes (reactions), which rearrange, break, or form bonds between atoms. Substances can also change by physical processes, which may alter the observable characteristics of the substance, but do not rearrange the internal structures of any molecules. The chemical compound water, for example, can be split into the element hydrogen and oxygen by electricity. That is a chemical reaction, because bonds in the water molecules break, and new bonds form. Water can also freeze into ice, or boil into vapor. Those are both physical processes because the water molecules do not change their internal bonding.

At the Earth's surface, matter exists in one of three physical states (or phases)—solid, liquid, or gas—categorized by the extent of attraction between the molecules or atoms of the substance. (Other intermediate states are possible under more extreme conditions.) Solids have a very orderly, rigid arrangement of their atoms or molecules, with strong forces holding the atoms or molecules together. Gas molecules or atoms, on the other hand, have almost no intermolecular forces holding them together. Liquids have intermediate properties; their molecules or atoms have some attractive force for each other, but are not fixed in place like those of a solid.

See also Atom; Element, chemical; Mass.

Maxima and minima

The terms maxima and minima refer to extreme values of a function, that is, the maximum and minimum values that the function attains. Maximum means upper bound or largest possible quantity. The absolute maximum of a function is the largest number contained in the range of the function. That is, if f(a) is greater than or equal to f(x), for all x in the domain of the function, then f(a) is the absolute maximum. For example, the function $f(x) = -16x^2 + 32x + 6$ has a maximum value of 22 occurring at x = 1. Every value of x produces a value of the function that is less than or equal to 22, hence, 22 is an absolute maximum. In terms of its graph, the absolute maximum of a function is the value of the function that corresponds to the highest point on the graph. Conversely, minimum means lower bound or least possible quantity. The absolute minimum of a function is the smallest number in its range and corresponds to the value of the function at the lowest point of its graph. If f(a) is less than or equal to f(x), for all x in the domain of the function, then f(a) is an absolute minimum. As an example, $f(x) = 32x^2 - 32x - 6$ has an absolute minimum of -22, because every value of x produces a value greater than or equal to -22.

In some cases, a function will have no absolute maximum or minimum. For instance the function $f(x) = 1/x$ has no absolute maximum value, nor does $f(x) = -1/x$ have an absolute minimum. In still other cases, functions may have relative (or local) maxima and minima. Relative means relative to local or nearby values of the function. The terms relative maxima and relative minima refer to the largest, or least, value that a function takes on over some small portion or interval of its domain. Thus, if f(b) is greater than or equal to f(b±h) for small values of h, then f(b) is a local maximum; if f(b) is less than or equal to f(b±h), then f(b) is a relative minimum. For example, the function $f(x) = x^4 - 12x^3 - 58x^2 + 180x + 225$ (see figure 1) has two relative minima (points A and C), one of which is also the absolute minimum (point C) of the function. It also has a relative maximum (point B), but no absolute maximum.

Finding the maxima and minima, both absolute and relative, of various functions represents an important class of problems solvable by use of differential calculus. The theory behind finding maximum and minimum values of a function is based on the fact that the derivative of a function is equal to the slope of the tangent. When the values of a function increase as the value of the independent variable increases, the lines that are tangent to the graph of the function have positive slope, and the function is said to be increasing. Conversely, when the values of the function decrease with increasing values of the independent variable, the tangent lines have negative slope, and the function is said to be decreasing. Precisely at the point where the function changes from increasing to decreasing or from decreasing to increasing, the tangent line is horizontal (has slope 0), and the derivative is zero. (With reference to figure 1, the function is decreasing to the left of point A, as well as between points B and C, and increasing between points A and B and to the right of point C). In order to find maximum and minimum points, first find the values of the independent variable for which the derivative of the function is zero, then substitute them in the original function to obtain the corresponding maximum or minimum values of the function. Second, inspect the behavior of the derivative to the left and right of each point. If the derivative is negative on the left and positive on the right, the point is a minimum. If the derivative is positive on the left and negative on the right, the point is a maximum. Equivalently, find the second derivative at each value of the independent variable that corresponds to a maximum or minimum; if the second derivative is positive, the point is a minimum, if the second derivative is negative the point is a maximum.

A wide variety of problems can be solved by finding maximum or minimum values of functions. For example, suppose it is desired to maximize the area of a rectangle inscribed in a semicircle (see figure 2). The area of the rectangle is given by A = 2xy. The semicircle

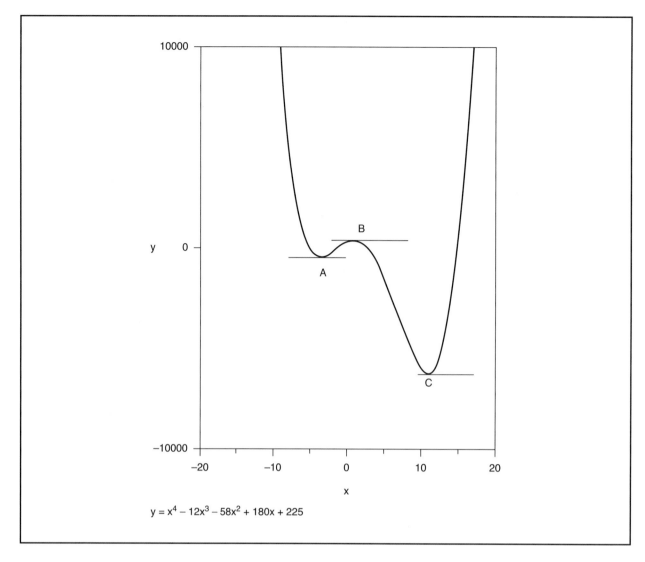

$$y = x^4 - 12x^3 - 58x^2 + 180x + 225$$

Figure 1.

is given by $x^2 + y^2 = r^2$, for $y \geq 0$, where r is the radius. To simplify the mathematics, note that A and A^2 are both maximum for the same values of x and y, which occurs when the corner of the rectangle intersects the semicircle, that is, when $y^2 = r^2 - x^2$. Thus, we must find a maximum value of the function $A^2 = 4x^2(r^2 - x^2) = 4r^2x^2 - 4x^4$. The required condition is that the derivative be equal to zero, that is, $d(A^2)/dx = 8r^2x - 16x^3 = 0$. This occurs when $x = 0$ or when $x = 1/2(r\sqrt{2})$. Clearly the area is a maximum when $x = 1/2(r\sqrt{2})$. Substitution of this value into the equation of the semicircle gives $y = 1/2(r\sqrt{2})$, that is, $y = x$. Thus, the maximum area of a rectangle inscribed in a semicircle is $A = 2xy = r^2$.

Applications

There are numerous practical applications in which it is desired to find the maximum or minimum value of a particular quantity. Such applications exist in economics, business, and engineering. Many can be solved using the methods of differential calculus described above. For example, in any manufacturing business it is usually possible to express profit as a function of the number of units sold. Finding a maximum for this function represents a straightforward way of maximizing profits. In other cases, the shape of a container may be determined by minimizing the amount of material required to manufacture it. The design of piping systems is often based on minimizing pressure drop which in turn minimizes required pump sizes and reduces cost. The shapes of steel beams are based on maximizing strength.

Finding maxima or minima also has important applications in linear algebra and game theory. For example, linear programming consists of maximizing

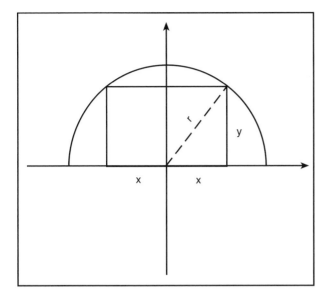

Figure 2.

(or minimizing) a particular quantity while requiring that certain constraints be imposed on other quantities. The quantity to be maximized (or minimized), as well as each of the constraints, is represented by an equation or inequality. The resulting system of equations or inequalities, usually linear, often contains hundreds or thousands of variables. The idea is to find the maximum value of a particular variable that represents a solution to the whole system. A practical example might be minimizing the cost of producing an automobile given certain known constraints on the cost of each part, and the time spent by each laborer, all of which may be interdependent. Regardless of the application, though, the key step in any maxima or minima problem is expressing the problem in mathematical terms.

Further Reading:

Abbot, P. and M. E. Wardle. *Teach Yourself Calculus*. Lincolnwood (Chicago) IL: NTC Publishing, 1992.

Allen, G.D., C. Chui, and B. Perry. *Elements of Calculus*, 2nd ed. Pacific Grove, California: Brooks/Cole Publishing Co., 1989.

Kenschaft, Patricia Clark. *Linear Mathematics: A Practical Approach*. New York: Worth Publishers, Inc., 1978.

Paulos, John Allen. *Beyond Numeracy, Ruminations of a Numbers Man*. New York: Alfred A Knopf, 1991.

Silverman, Richard A. *Essential Calculus With Applications*. New York: Dover, 1989.

Thomas, George B., Jr. and Ross L Finney. *Elements of Calculus and Analytic Geometry,* 6th ed. Reading MA: Addison Wesley, 1989.

J. R. Maddocks

Mayflies

Mayflies, or shadflies, are aquatic insects in the order Ephemeroptera. There are several thousand species of mayflies, distributed among 20 families. Mayflies have a relatively protracted nymphal stage, which occurs in freshwater habitats. The adults are a short-lived stage during which dense aggregations of animals engage in a frenzied procreation, needed to perennate the species in its local habitats.

Biology of mayflies

Mayflies have a simple metamorphosis, with three life-history stages: egg, nymph (or naiad), and adult. The nymphal stages are numerous and relatively protracted, generally lasting for at least one year. Mayfly nymphs occur in aquatic habitats, and account for most of the lifespan of mayflies. Some species have as many as 28 nymphal molts. The last, pre-adult stage occurs when a nymph rises to the water surface, molts, and develops into a winged form called a subimago, which flies a short distance, and usually rests on vegetation. Within a day or so, the subimago molts into the terrestrial, sexually mature adult stage, which is generally found in close proximity to the aquatic nymphal habitat. Mayflies are the only insects that have an additional molt after they have developed functional wings.

Mayflies have soft, elongate bodies, with two or (most commonly) three, distinctive, thread-like appendages projecting from the end of their abdomen. Adult mayflies have short antennae and many-veined, roughly triangular, membranous wings. The wings are

Bottom: the subimago stage of the mayfly. Center: an adult mayfly. Top: an adult crawling out of the subimago skin.

held erect and together over the body when the animal is at rest, and cannot be folded up as in most other orders of insects. The aquatic mayfly nymphs have distinctive, leaf-shaped appendages on the sides of their abdomen that serve as gills for the exchange of respiratory gases.

Larval mayflies are aquatic in fresh waters, and have mouthparts adapted for feeding on algae and other relatively soft, organic materials. Most mayflies are herbivores or detritivores, but a few species are carnivores of other aquatic invertebrates. Because they do not feed, adult mayflies have only vestigial mouthparts. Mayflies have large, compound eyes, and in many species the males are larger than the females, and have forelegs adapted for grasping the female during the nuptial (mating) flight. In most species the forewings are relatively large, while the hindwings may be absent, or are reduced in size compared with the forewings.

Adult mayflies do not feed and are short-lived, only living for a few hours or several days. This fact is reflected in the Latin root of the scientific name of this group of insects, Ephemeroptera, which refers to the highly ephemeral nature of the adult stage. The sole purpose of adult mayflies is procreation. To achieve this goal, adults of particular species emerge synchronously within a brief period of time. Adult mayflies sometimes occur in spectacularly large aggregations, in which the animals mate and deposit their eggs to water in frenzied swarms, and then die soon afterwards. Most of the mayflies in the swarm are males. The females fly briefly into the swarm, find a mate, and they couple then leave to copulate and lay their eggs.

Ecological and economic importance of mayflies

Sometimes, the mass emergences of adult mayflies can involve extremely large numbers of animals. During the brief times when mayflies are very abundant, some people may view them as a nuisance, because the insects seem to be flying everywhere and can be bothersome because of this, or because their bodies accumulate abundantly on beaches, streets, window screens, and in other places. Rarely, the accumulated biomass of mayfly bodies can represent a traffic hazard, by making roads rather slippery. However, this is quite a rare event, and in general mayflies should not be thought of as a nuisance. Mayflies are rarely abundant enough to be a bother. Almost always, mayflies are a harmless part of the natural world.

Mayfly nymphs are an important component of many freshwater ecosystems. Grazing by mayflies is important in preventing the build-up of a large biomass of aquatic algae and detritus, and in nutrient cycling. Because mayflies can be quite abundant in many habitats, they are an important food for many species of predators.

Mayfly species are rather particular in their choice of habitat, and in their tolerance of environmental conditions, such as the temperature and chemistry of water. Because of their specific habitat requirements, mayfly species are often studied by aquatic ecologists as indicators of water quality, for example, in studies of pollution. A famous study involving mayflies was conducted in Lake Erie during the 1950s and early 1960s. Lake Erie was badly polluted at that time, especially by organic debris associated with sewage and algal growths, the decomposition of which consumed most of the oxygen in the waters of deeper parts of the lake. The development of anoxic conditions resulted in mass die-offs of nymphs of the mayflies *Hexagenia rigida* and *H. limbata*, which were previously extremely abundant. The virtual collapse of the populations of mayflies in Lake Erie was widely reported in the popular press, which interpreted the phenomenon as an indication that the great lake was "dead," and had been rendered as such by pollution caused by humans. Today, the waters of Lake Erie are much cleaner, and its populations of mayflies have recovered somewhat.

KEY TERMS

Indicator—In environmental science, an indicator is a surrogate measurement that is known to be related to an important aspect of environmental quality. Mayfly species, for example, are often studied as indicators of water pollution.

Simple metamorphosis—A developmental series in insects having three life-history stages: egg, nymph, and adult.

Both nymphal and adult mayflies are a very important food for economically important sportfish, such as trout and salmon. Many sport fishers are highly skilled at tying mayfly "flies" as lures for use in fishing. The more realistically the lure portrays the species of mayfly that the trout or salmon are interested in feeding upon in a particular stream at a particular time, the greater is the fisher's success in catching fish.

See also Indicator species; Stoneflies.

Further Reading:

Arnett, R. H. *American Insects. A Handbook of the Insects of America North of Mexico.* Gainesville, FL: Sandhill Crane Pub., 1993.

Borror, D. J., C. J. Triplehorn, and N. Johnson. *An Introduction to the Study of Insects.* New York: Saunders, 1989.

Campbell, I. C., ed. *Mayflies and Stoneflies. Life Histories and Biology.* New York: Kluwer, 1990.

Freedman, B. *Environmental Ecology.* 2nd ed. San Diego: Academic Press, 1995.

Merritt, R. W., and K. W. Cummins. 1984. *An Introduction to the Aquatic Insects of North America.* New York: Kendall-Hunt, 1984.

Peckarsky, B. L., et al. *Freshwater Macroinvertebrates of Northeastern North America.* Ithaca, NY: Cornell University Press, 1990.

Swan, L. A., and C. S. Papp. *The Common Insects of North America.* New York: Harper & Row, 1975.

Bill Freedman

Mealybugs see **Scale insects**

Mean

The mean of a set of numbers, x_1, x_2,...x_n is defined to be $(x_1 + x_2 ...+ x_n) \div n$. Thus the mean of 2, 3, 7, and 5 is $(2 + 3 + 7 + 5) \div 4 = 17 \div 4$.

The mean is also known as the average. It is one of the measures of central tendency, the others being the mode and median.

See also Median; Mode.

Measles see **Childhood diseases**

Median

The median is a measure of central tendency, like an average. It is a way of describing a group of items or characteristics instead of mentioning all of them. If the items are arranged in ascending order of magnitude, the median is the value of the middle item.

If there is an odd number of items in the group, the median can be found precisely. For example, assume that 27 test scores are arranged from the lowest to the highest; the median score is the value of the 14th item. If there is an even number of items, the median has to be estimated. It is the value that lies between the value of the two middle items. For example, assume 26 scores arranged from the lowest to the highest, the median score lies between the value of the 13th and 14th items.

What is the advantage of using the median? First, it is easier to calculate than the average or the arithmetic mean and may be found more or less by inspection. The more important reason however for using the median is that it is not influenced by extreme values and so may be a better measure than the average or arithmetic mean.

For example, assume that we want to know the average income in a neighborhood where most of the people live below the poverty level, but there are two large houses where the occupants are millionaires. The arithmetic mean would average out all the incomes and give the erroneous impression that the neighborhood was middle class. The median would not be affected by the extreme values.

The median is very good for descriptive statistics since it enables us to make statements that half the observations lie above it and half below it. From the example in the previous paragraph we could say "half the people in the neighborhood had incomes below $12,850 and half had incomes above this figure." The median often represents a real value as distinct from a calculated value which does not exist. The disadvantage of the median is that it does not lend itself to further statistical manipulation like the arithmetic mean.

See also Mean; Mode.

Further Reading:
Gonick, Larry, & Smith, Woolcott. *The Carlton Guide to Statistics.* New York: Harper Perennial, 1993.
Hayslett, H. T. *Statistics Made Simple.* New York: Doubleday, 1968.

Selma Hughes

Medulla see **Brain**

Megapodes see **Moundbuilders**

Meiosis

Meiosis, also known as reduction division, consists of two successive cell divisions in diploid cells. The two cell divisions are similar to mitosis, but differ in that the chromosomes are duplicated only once, not twice. The end result of meiosis is four daughter cells, each of them haploid. Since meiosis only occurs in the sex organs (gonads), the daughter cells are the gametes (spermatozoa or ova), which contain hereditary material. By halving the number of chromosomes in the sex cells, meiosis assures that the fusion of maternal and paternal gametes at fertilization will result in offspring with the same chromosome number as the parents. In other words, meiosis compensates for chromosomes doubling at fertilization. The two successive nuclear divisions are termed as meiosis I and meiosis II. Each is further divided into four phases (prophase, metaphase, anaphase, and telophase) with an intermediate phase (interphase) preceding each nuclear division.

Events of meiosis

The events that take place during meiosis are similar in many ways to the process of mitosis, in which one cell divides to form two clones (exact copies) of itself. It is important to note that the purpose and final products of mitosis and meiosis are very different.

Meiosis I

Meiosis I is preceded by an interphase period in which the DNA replicates (makes an exact duplicate of itself), resulting in two exact copies of each chromosome that are firmly attached at one point, the centromere. Each copy is a sister chromatid, and the pair are still considered as only one chromosome. The first

phase of meiosis I, prophase I, begins as the chromosomes come together in homologous pairs in a process known as synapsis. Homologous chromosomes, or homologues, consist of two chromosomes that carry genetic information for the same traits, although that information may hold different messages (e.g., when two chromosomes carry a message for eye color, but one codes for blue eyes while the other codes for brown). The fertilized eggs (zygotes) of all sexually reproducing organisms receive their chromosomes in pairs, one from the mother and one from the father. During synapsis, adjacent chromatids from homologous chromosomes "cross over" one another at random points and join at spots called chiasmata. These connections hold the pair together as a tetrad (a set of four chromatids, two from each homologue). At the chiasmata, the connected chromatids randomly exchange bits of genetic information so that each contains a mixture of maternal and paternal genes. This "shuffling" of the DNA produces a tetrad, in which each of the chromatids is different from the others, and a gamete that is different from others produced by the same parent. Crossing over does, in fact, explain why each person is a unique individual, different even from those in the immediate family. Prophase I is also marked by the appearance of spindle fibers (strands of microtubules) extending from the poles or ends of the cell as the nuclear membrane disappears. These spindle fibers attach to the chromosomes during metaphase I as the tetrads line up along the middle or equator of the cell. A spindle fiber from one pole attaches to one chromosome while a fiber from the opposite pole attaches to its homologue. Anaphase I is characterized by the separation of the homologues, as chromosomes are drawn to the opposite poles. The sister chromatids are still intact, but the homologous chromosomes are pulled apart at the chiasmata. Telophase I begins as the chromosomes reach the poles and a nuclear membrane forms around each set. Cytokinesis occurs as the cytoplasm and organelles are divided in half and the one parent cell is split into two new daughter cells. Each daughter cell is now haploid (n), meaning it has half the number of chromosomes of the original parent cell (which is diploid—2n). These chromosomes in the daughter cells still exist as sister chromatids, but there is only one chromosome from each original homologous pair.

Meiosis II

The phases of meiosis II are similar to those of meiosis I, but there are some important differences. The time between the two nuclear divisions (interphase II) lacks replication of DNA (as in interphase I). As the two daughter cells produced in meiosis I enter meiosis II, their chromosomes are in the form of sister chromatids. No crossing over occurs in prophase II because there are no homologues to synapse. During metaphase II, the spindle fibers from the opposite poles attach to the sister chromatids (instead of the homologues as before). The chromatids are then pulled apart during anaphase II. As the centromeres separate, the two single chromosomes are drawn to the opposite poles. The end result of meiosis II is that by the end of telophase II, there are four haploid daughter cells (in the sperm or ova) with each chromosome now represented by a single copy. The distribution of chromatids during meiosis is a matter of chance, which results in the concept of the law of independent assortment in genetics.

Control of meiosis

The events of meiosis are controlled by a protein enzyme complex known collectively as maturation promoting factor (MPF). These enzymes interact with one another and with cell organelles to cause the breakdown and reconstruction of the nuclear membrane, the formation of the spindle fibers, and the final division of the cell itself. MPF appears to work in a cycle, with the proteins slowly accumulating during interphase, and then rapidly degrading during the later stages of meiosis. In effect, the rate of synthesis of these proteins controls the frequency and rate of meiosis in all sexually reproducing organisms from the simplest to the most complex.

Human gamete formation

Meiosis occurs in humans, giving rise to the haploid gametes, the sperm and egg cells. In males, the process of gamete production is known as spermatogenesis, where each dividing cell in the testes produces four functional sperm cells, all approximately the same size. Each is propelled by a primitive but highly efficient flagellum (tail). In contrast, in females, oogenesis produces only one surviving egg cell from each original parent cell. During cytokinesis, the cytoplasm and organelles are concentrated into only one of the four daughter cells—the one which will eventually become the female ovum or egg. The other three smaller cells, called polar bodies, die and are reabsorbed shortly after formation. The process of oogenesis may seem inefficient, but by donating all the cytoplasm and organelles to only one of the four gametes, the female increases the egg's chance for survival, should it become fertilized.

Mistakes during meiosis

The process of meiosis does not work perfectly every time, and mistakes in the formation of gametes are

---

KEY TERMS

Chiasmata—Points at which adjacent chromosomes overlap and connect.

Crossing over—In meiosis, a process in which adjacent chromosomes exchange pieces of genetic information.

Cytokinesis—The division of a cell's cytoplasm following the division of the nucleus.

Diploid—Having two sets of chromosomes, twice the number of chromosomes in the germ cell.

Haploid—Having a single set of unpaired chromosomes.

Homologues—Chromosomes carrying the same type of genetic information.

Nondisjunction—The failure of a chromosome pair to separate and go to different cells following cell division.

Sister chromatids—Two copies of the same chromosome produced by DNA replication.

Synapsis—Process in which homologues orient themselves side by side.

Tetrad—A set of four chromatids all belonging to the same homologues.

---

a major cause of genetic disease in humans. Under normal conditions, the four chromatids of a tetrad will separate completely, with one chromatid going into each of the four daughter cells. In a disorder known as nondisjunction, chromatids do not separate and one of the resulting gametes receives an extra copy of the same chromosome. The most common example of this mistake in meiosis is the genetic defect known as Down's syndrome, in which a person receives an extra copy of chromosome 21 from one of the parents. Another fairly common form of nondisjunction occurs when the sex chromosomes (XX, XY) do not divide properly, resulting in individuals with Klinefelter syndrome or Turner syndrome. Other mistakes that can occur during meiosis include translocation, in which part of one chromosome becomes attached to another, and deletion, in which part of one chromosome is lost entirely. The severity of the effects of these disorders depends entirely on the size of the chromosome fragment involved and the genetic information contained in it. Modern technology can detect these genetic abnormalities early in the development of the fetus, but at present, little can be done to correct or even treat the diseases resulting from them.

See also Cell; Chromosome; Deoxyribonucleic acid; Gamete; Gene; Genetic disorders; Mitosis.

Further Reading:

Edwards, Gabrielle I. *Biology the Easy Way.* 2nd ed. New York: Barrons Educational Service, Inc., 1990.

Hartl, Daniel L. *Genetics.* 3rd ed. Boston: Jones and Bartlett, 1994.

Haseltine, Florence P., and Susan Heyner. *Meiosis II: Contemporary Approaches to the Study of Meiosis.* Washington, D.C.: AAAS Press, 1993.

Jenkins, John B. *Human Genetics.* 2nd ed. New York: Harper & Row, 1990.

John, Bernard. *Meiosis.* New York: Cambridge University Press, 1990.

Murray, Andrew W., and Marc W. Kirschner. "What Controls the Cell Cycle." *Scientific American* (March 1991).

Cheryl Taylor

Meissner effect see **Superconductor**

Melanin see **Integumentary system**

Melon see **Gourd family**

Membrane

Cell membranes or plasma membranes surround cells, separating the cytoplasm and organelles on the inside from the extracellular fluid on the outside. Several cell organelles (mitochondria, endoplasmic reticulum, and Golgi bodies) are also bounded by membranes. The membrane allows a cell or organelle to maintain a constant internal environment, usually one that is quite different from the medium surrounding it. This is accomplished by the semipermeable nature of the membrane that regulates the passage of all substances going through it.

The detailed chemical composition of a membrane varies, depending on its location and the functions it performs. However, all membranes do have the same basic structure. The majority of the membrane is composed of two layers of phospholipid molecules lined up side by side with their fatty acid "tails" facing inward. The outer edges of the membrane are hydrophilic (soluble in water), while the interior area is hydrophobic (insoluble in water). Because of this dual chemical nature of the phospholipid bilayer, the entire membrane surface is permeable to gases (such as oxygen and carbon dioxide), to small, uncharged polar molecules (such as water and ammonia), and to nonpolar molecules (such as lipids). However, the membrane is impermeable to charged molecules (such as ions and proteins) and to larger, uncharged polar molecules.

Embedded within and spanning the phospholipid bilayer are various transport proteins that serve as "gates," selectively allowing charged molecules and ions and larger molecules to pass through the membrane. These transport proteins channel molecules by a variety of methods, including facilitated diffusion (movement with the concentration gradient, using no ATP energy) and active transport (movement against the concentration gradient, using ATP energy).

The plasma membrane that forms the boundary of a cell has several other molecules in addition to the basic membrane structure. These include integral proteins, cholesterol, glycoproteins, and glycolipids. The phospholipid bilayer with its biochemical inclusions is known as the fluid mosaic model of membrane structure. Some membrane proteins serve as receptors for hormones, transferring the signal to the interior of the cell (via G proteins) without allowing the "messenger" molecule to enter, thus protecting the integrity of the cell. Other carbohydrate molecules attached to the exterior of the plasma membrane act as "markers," identifying the cell as a particular type.

Cystic fibrosis—a fatal, hereditary disease characterized by a heavy mucus buildup in the lungs—is caused by a defective plasma membrane protein. In persons with cystic fibrosis this transport protein, known as the sodium-potassium pump, abnormally transports sodium ions across the membrane without carrying the chloride ions that usually accompany them. Research is currently underway to correct through genetic engineering the faulty gene that codes for the plasma membrane protein.

See also Cell; Diffusion; Nucleus, cellular; Osmosis (cellular).

Memory

Memory refers to the mental systems and processes involved in storing and recalling information about stimuli that are no longer present, as well as to all of the information that is stored. Memory is essential to healthy human functioning, and it can be said that every mental process involves some aspect of memory. Indeed, the ancient Greek philosopher Cicero once described memory as "the treasury and guardian of all things."

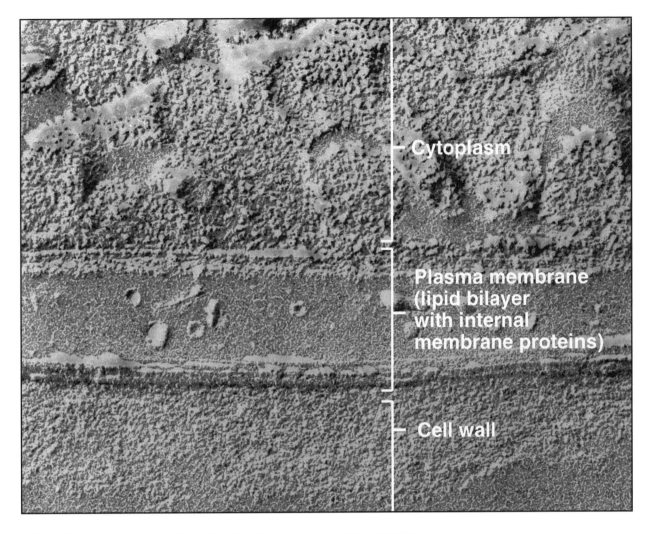

A freeze fracture image across the cell wall and membrane of a blue-green alga.

The human brain has evolved an enormous capacity for remembering, and in the course of life, people gather and store vast amounts of information. Memories of past experiences are necessary to understand new experiences, and to decide how to behave in unfamiliar situations. Without memory every person or situation we encountered would be strange and unfamiliar, and we could never learn from past experience. In fact, we would not be able to learn anything at all, since all learning requires remembering the material learned. Memory is also essential to a sense of self or identity, as memories of our past experiences, thoughts, and feelings inform us as to what we have done, who we have been, and who we are now. Memory can hold information ranging from how to put pants on, to the composition of the stars.

History

People have sought to understand the nature of memory since at least the time of the ancient Greek philosopher Plato, who is usually credited with the earliest serious discussion of it. He believed memory was like a blank slate on which accurate impressions of the world were made and preserved indefinitely. Plato distinguished two aspects of memory—the power to retain or keep information, and the power of recollection, or remembering information that is already present in memory. Plato's ideas are still active today as many contemporary psychological theories of memory contain these same beliefs.

During the Middle Ages, prior to when books were widespread, memory served as the vehicle through which history and knowledge were passed between people and generations. It seems having a good memory was greatly prized during the Middle Ages, and the improvement of memory skills was an important topic. A distinction was made between natural and artificial memory where natural memory was the memory abilities we were born with. They could not be trained and were thought to operate in a spontaneous, instinctive manner. On the other hand, artificial memory abilities were held to be trainable, and numerous systems were developed to improve them. As the printed word spread and the individual's memories became less essential in the transmission of knowledge the importance accorded to memory by society apparently diminished. During the 1800s, educators also focused on training and exercising the memory. Memory was seen by many as being like a muscle that required exercise to remain fit. Thus memorization was thought to strengthen one's current memory system as well as future memorization skills, and rote memorization (memorizing information for no purpose other than to memorize it) was advocated for students. This view came under great criticism as the 1800s ended, and eventually the advocacy of rote memorization within the school system faded. Indeed, more recent research indicates that memorization for memorization's sake does not improve overall memory abilities in any observable way.

During the late 1800s the medical profession became interested in disorders of memory such as aphasia (a complete or partial impairment of the ability to understand or use words), and amnesia (generally, a partial or total loss of memory). The medical profession naturally focused on physiological and biological factors, and one of their most important findings was that aphasia was caused by lesions in the brain. This finding was of immense importance as it demonstrated for the first time that physiological and psychological functioning are connected.

Sigmund Freud, an Austrian physician who began his career in the 1890s, focused on psychological disorders that he felt were caused by memory disturbances. Freud felt mental illness occurs when unpleasant childhood memories are repressed, or kept from consciousness. His highly influential theory of psychoanalysis is in fact based on the concept that memories can be repressed, and he developed psychoanalytic therapy to uncover those memories and cure the patient.

The German psychologist, Hermann Ebbinghaus, carried out the first controlled experiments on memory in 1885, and in so doing set a pattern for modern experimental research on memory. Ebbinghaus developed many methods of studying memory that are still in use today. For example, he developed lists of nonsense syllables (one syllable groups of letters that have no meaning, e.g. "treb," "fug," or "duj"), that individuals would be asked to memorize. Ebbinghaus used nonsense syllables in an attempt to avoid the effects of previous learning, and associations the individual might have to meaningful words. Ebbinghaus would vary different aspects of the experiments to test different aspects of memory. For instance, he varied the lists by length to see how the number of syllables affected recall, and he would vary the amount of time between memorization and recall to see how the amount of time lapsed between learning and recall affected the amount of material recalled or forgotten.

Theories of basic memory processes

It is important to note that Ebbinghaus was working within the philosophical/psychological framework of associationism. With roots stretching back to Aristotle, associationism asserts that higher order mental processes, such as creativity or language, are produced by the combination of simpler mental processes, such as the mental association of objects, ideas, or experiences due to their similarity. Memory is said to be made up of associations between elements based on their similarity, contrast, or occurrence together in time or space. This implies a rather passive or inactive mind and memory, where the individual and their memory receives impressions and basically categorizes them according to their straightforward, objective characteristics. Remembering is simply reproducing these impressions and associations. Within this framework, when asked to remember and describe a rose, a person might "search" their memory for a specific representation of a rose or a specific experience with a rose, and use this to describe one.

This is in contrast to reconstructive theories of memory as proposed for example by William James in 1890, and by Sir Frederic Charles Bartlett in 1932. Within these theories, memory is seen as an active reconstruction and organization of past experiences that influences how new information is interpreted and organized, as well as how and what information is remembered. In contrast to associative theories, reconstructive theories of memory hold that abstract principles about new experiences and information are what is stored, not exact reproductions of the experiences themselves. During recall, specific memories are often reconstructed according to these general principles, they are not always reproductions of experience. Thus memory processes take an active role in what and how information is remembered. Within this framework, a person asked to remember and describe a rose might first access their general knowledge of plants, then flowers, then their knowledge of roses in general, and using this information, build or construct a description of a rose. In recent years, reconstructive theories of memory have gained favor as many psychologists believe that most mental processes, such as language and perception, are too complex to be explained by the combination of simple associative connections and reproductive memory. We will now turn to the more comprehensive prevailing theories of memory and its operation.

Models of memory operation

Since memory and memory formation cannot be observed directly, various models have been put forth by memory researchers in an effort to clearly and simply describe how memory operates. In the early 1900s, psychologists proposed that memory was like a filing cabinet in that everything was categorized neatly and logically. In order to retrieve information, one simply and logically located the correct file folder. Later, as telephone systems were expanded, memory was likened to a telephone operator's switchboard with information coming in from many directions to a central source that sorted the information and decided on the appropriate output. With the development of the digital computer in the 1950s, psychologists began describing memory in terms of a computer model and focused on how the mind and memory might process information like computers do. This model has been highly influential, and since the 1950s researchers using this model have focused on the input and sequencing of information processing.

Three information processing systems

Most researchers divide memory's information processing operations into the stages of acquisition, consolidation, storage, and retrieval. Acquisition refers to the process the brain and the sensory organs use to bring information into the memory system. Consolidation is the process of organizing information to facilitate its storage in long-term memory. Storage describes the forming of a potentially permanent representation of information in the brain. Retrieval is the process of bringing stored information to consciousness. These processes are thought to occur within three largely accepted divisions of the memory processing system that are distinguished by the length of time information can be held, the amount of information that can be held, and the different processes that occur in each. The three stages are called sensory memory, short-term memory, and long-term memory. It should be noted that these systems are not presumed to occupy specific physical spaces within the brain. They are, more accurately, hypothesized systems distinguished by their varying characteristics.

Sensory memory

Sensory memory, or sensory register, notes or registers sensory stimuli as they are experienced. It consists of representations of the outside world as experienced through the senses such as touch, sight, or smell. It holds information for approximately one to two seconds. If, for instance, you glance at the ocean and turn away, the image of the ocean will be lost in one to two seconds unless the image is quickly transferred into the short-term memory system. The contents of sensory memory are constantly changing as new stimuli are perceived. Information that does not fade from sensory memory enters short-term memory.

Short-term memory

Short-term memory is thought to process information by actively repeating, grouping, and summarizing it to aid its storage in long-term memory. Information is thought to last within short-term memory for only a short period of time before it is either passed into long-term memory or discarded. For information to be transferred into long-term memory, it must be rehearsed or repeated.

Generally, short-term memory can hold five to nine units of information for between twenty seconds to one minute in length. It holds information for as long as its actively thought about, or until new information basically forces it out. Unless we repeat the information and purposely try to retain it, most, or all of it, will be lost. A good example of this process can be seen when you look up a new phone number, and repeat it to yourself as you dial it. After dialing it, within a few seconds you will usually forget it. Yet if you do this repeatedly (repetition or rehearsal), like for a friend with a new phone number, it will eventually enter long-term memory.

These "units" of information can represent single pieces of information, such as an individual's name, or the units can be single pieces of information that represent a number of different pieces of information, as in the last name of a family representing all of the family's members. The process of using a single item to represent a number of items is called chunking, and researchers have found that short-term memory's information holding capacity can be greatly enhanced with this process.

It seems there are many factors that determine what information enters long-term memory, two of the strongest being repetition and intense emotion. If something is repeated often enough, such as multiplication tables, it will enter long-term memory. And it is hard to forget intensely emotional experiences such as being involved in a serious car accident or falling in love.

Long-term memory

Long-term memory has been the focus of most research and theory on the memory system. It holds all the information that has managed to pass through the sensory and short-term memory systems. In contrast to both of those systems, long-term memory is thought to be able to hold potentially unlimited amounts of information for an indefinite period of time, possibly for a lifetime. It is thought to hold all of the memories of our life, as well as our knowledge of the world in general. In long-term memory one might find memories as diverse as the first person you ever had a crush on, knowledge of how to ride a bike or cook scrambled eggs, the names of the five great lakes of North America, or a second language. Indeed, long-term memory is often compared to an encyclopedia in terms of the amount and range of information it holds.

Long-term memory then stores and operates on very diverse types of information, and there are many theories as to how the different types of information are represented and organized within it. Research shows that long-term memory operates according to a number of different systems, and researchers disagree as to exactly how it should be divided up. Yet there are some very influential theoretical divisions of long-term memory that are now widely accepted. These are the divisions between procedural memory, episodic memory, and semantic memory.

Divisions of Long-Term Memory

Procedural memory

Procedural memory is, as its name implies, knowledge of the steps necessary to perform certain procedures or activities. It is the knowledge of how to ride a bike or swim, how to cook spaghetti and meatballs, and even how to walk and run. Procedural learning is the acquisition of skills, such as learning how to operate a computer. How well something is learned is reflected in improved performance of the skill. It seems well-learned knowledge stored in the procedural memory system can be used without conscious awareness of the steps being performed. For instance, in walking or driving a car, one rarely has to stop and think about what step comes next, and attention can be paid to other activities.

Often the information stored in procedural memory is difficult for the individual to articulate even though it is obvious from their smooth performance of the activity that they know it well. Procedural memories seem to last for a very long time, if not for a lifetime, and they are often very hard to change. Thus if one learns how to do something in a certain way, such as swim or play tennis, it can be very hard to change one's technique later.

Episodic memory

Episodic memory is the conscious recollection or remembering of specific experiences from a person's life. These memories often include the time and place of the experience, as well as a representation of the role the individual remembering played in it. An example of an episodic memory would be recalling the first time you operated a computer including where and with whom. This is in contrast with semantic memory which would involve your general knowledge of how to operate a computer. Episodic memories seem to be more affected by the passage of time than are procedural or semantic memories such that if the event is not recalled and thought of relatively often, details of the event, if not the event itself, seems to fade or be forgotten over time.

Semantic memory

Semantic memory is all the easily articulated stored knowledge you have of the world in general that does not refer to specific events in your life. Examples of semantic memory involve factual knowledge such as knowing a car has four wheels, that a United States senator is elected to a term of four years, that the earth revolves around the sun, or that giving a smile increases the odds of receiving a smile. Whereas procedural knowledge is knowing "how," semantic memory is knowing "that." Like procedural memory, semantic memory seems to last for a long time. It differs from procedural memory however, in that the knowledge can usually be articulated quite easily.

Exactly how the immense amount of information we acquire throughout life is stored or organized in semantic memory is still an active area of research. Most experts believe that, in general, information is stored in networks of related concepts. The more similar various concepts are, the more closely associated they will be in memory. Research in semantic memory does in fact indicate that it is organized such that when a certain idea is activated or brought to mind, related or similar items will be identified faster. For instance, if one is discussing roses, knowledge of other flowers and plants will be recalled faster and with more ease.

Mental representations in semantic memory

Two specific types of mental representations hypothesized to be used by the semantic memory system to organize information are schemas and categories. Schemas are ordered frameworks or outlines of world knowledge that help us organize and interpret new information. They are like a maps or blueprints into which new related information will be fitted. Knowledge of your home town or city, with its streets, various buildings, and neighborhoods is an example of a schema.

Research shows that new information relating to knowledge one already has will be remembered better than information about a topic one has little or no knowledge of. Thus, if two people are given directions to a party, the individual who knows the layout of their city or town pretty well will tend to remember the directions to the party better than a person who has little or no knowledge of the city's layout. This is presumably because the person with the pre-existing knowledge is able to fit the new information into their older knowledge, and thus form a stronger link in memory.

Schemas also help to reconstruct, or try to remember, information that may have been forgotten. For example, if a friend brings up something that happened one time you both went out to eat dinner a few months ago and you don't remember it clearly, you might ask for more information, and then use your schema for the usual sequence of events in eating out to try to remember or reconstruct what happened. The accuracy of reconstructions is open to question.

Categories are another representational form of thought used by semantic memory to organize information. Categories are sets of objects, experiences, or ideas, that are grouped together because they are similar to one another in some respect. For example, apartments, houses, huts, and igloos, might be grouped under the category of dwellings. Like schemas, categories help us make sense of, and organize, the multitudinous aspects of the world.

Relations among memory systems in long-term memory

While it is thought that the procedural, episodic, and semantic memory systems operate relatively independently, it is obvious that they also interact and work together. For instance, one's procedural knowledge of how to ride a bike or operate a computer will be linked with one's semantic knowledge of how bikes and computers work in general. Moreover, episodic memories of, for instance, one's first date, will add to one's semantic knowledge of dating in general, and possibly one's procedural knowledge of how to best have a good time on a date.

Research methods

Most research on long-term memory is highly specialized, focusing on particular types of information storage and the various retrieval processes associated with them. In the research laboratory memory is most often assessed by recognition, recall, or relearning tasks.

In recognition tasks, research subjects are commonly shown lists of words or groups of visual stimuli, such as pictures of faces. After a period of time subjects are then presented with new lists or groups of visual stimuli in which some of the original material is embedded or mixed in. They are then asked to indicate which items they recognize from the original material. In order to assess different aspects of memory, researchers may vary the amount of material presented, how long they let the subject study it, how much time passes between presentation of the original and altered material, and any number of other variables. Recognition is often quite accurate, especially if the subject is asked only if they have seen an item before. An example of a recognition task in which the subject is asked to choose a correct answer from among incorrect ones is a multiple-choice test.

In recall tasks, subjects are asked to reproduce material that was previously learned. The material may consist of lists of words, stories, or visual stimuli. They may be asked to report the material in exactly the same way it was presented, or to report as much of the material as they can remember in any order at all (this is called "free recall"). In "cued recall" the subject is given clues to aid their recall. Giving clues can improve recall greatly. As in recognition tasks, many variables, such as the amount of material, and time between learning and testing, can be manipulated to test different aspects of memory. An essay test is an example of a recall task.

In relearning studies, the time it takes to learn material initially is compared to the time it takes to learn the same material a second time after it is forgotten. Findings consistently show relearning time is much less than original learning time. The difference between the two learning times is called the "savings score." The high savings scores found across almost all relearning studies indicates that once something is learned, it is never really forgotten completely. It seems some of the original learning remains, although how much and in what form remains unclear.

Reminding and forgetting

Reminding is an aspect of memory that indicates ideas are organized in long-term memory by similarity, whereby when people think of something, they are often reminded of a similar thing. Remindings are usually of information that is similar in content, or of earlier experiences that are similar to the current situation. The most widely accepted explanation of the reminding process is spreading activation which assumes memory is made up of networks of concepts that are connected due to similarity. When a concept from a network of concepts is used, that concept is presumably energized or activated in some way. This activation, if strong enough, spreads along the associative pathways connecting the activated concept to other related concepts and in turn activates the related concepts.

The spreading or activation process is seen as being largely automatic. It can, however, be controlled to a certain extent. In this way we can concentrate on current goals without being constantly distracted by related but largely irrelevant ideas.

Forgetting is the inability to recognize, recall, or reproduce information which was previously known or learned. Different theories within psychology propose various processes for how forgetting occurs. Traditional, associative learning theories believe forgetting is the decay of associative bonds through disuse, or not thinking of something. Associative theories also believe forgetting is caused by interference. Material will be retained to the extent that it was well-learned, unless previously or newly learned information interferes. Interference is the confusion or substitution of one item in memory with another. There are two types of interference: retroactive interference, when old information is harder to remember because new information gets in the way; and proactive interference, when new information is harder to learn because it is similar to old information. Interference theory holds that material is rarely lost or forgotten, it is simply unavailable or inaccessible.

Psychoanalytic theory, as discussed earlier, sees forgetting as the result of repression. Freud felt a good deal of forgetting happens because the forgotten material is associated with unpleasant experiences that produce anxiety which automatically evokes the defense mechanism of repression. Memories then are never truly lost, but are irretrievable due to repression.

The contemporary cognitive approach proposes that each of the three stages of information processing forgets or loses information for different reasons. In both the sensory and short-term memory systems, information is lost through decay of their underlying neural connections. Information is never really forgotten in long-term memory. It is assumed to be there but cannot be accessed due to a failure in retrieval.

It should be noted that there is no way to definitively discover whether information is retained for life or ever truly lost from memory. This is because even if someone cannot recall something that does not mean it is not present in memory. It may instead be inaccessible due to repression, interference, or retrieval failure. Moreover, it is often impossible to assess the accuracy of someone's individual memories as there are no available corroborative witnesses.

Memory disorders

The two main memory disorders are amnesia and aphasia. Amnesia is a partial or total loss of memory caused by emotional trauma, disease, or brain injury (usually due to head trauma, surgical accidents, or chronic alcohol abuse). Memory loss can occur for events just prior to the amnesia-causing incident (retrograde amnesia), or for events occurring after the incident (anterograde amnesia). In severe cases of anterograde amnesia, the person may be unable to form new memories, although recall of material learned before amnesia's onset is usually unaffected. Many cases of amnesia (even severe) are temporary, so that the person recovers their memory.

Aphasias are a complete or partial impairment of the ability to understand or use words which are caused by lesions in the brain. There are numerous varieties of aphasia, and diagnostic classification systems are constantly being revised.

Physiological basis

In recent decades, research on the physiological basis of human memory in the brain has intensified. Much has been learned about how information in memory is organized in the brain, and the roles various parts of the brain play in memory from research with those with amnesia or aphasia. In fact, detailed studies of individuals with unusual patterns of brain damage have produced much of our current knowledge about the physiological basis of human memory. It seems that numerous brain structures are involved in memory processing and various subtypes of memory. For instance, the ventromedial frontal region of the brain (an area in the lower front portion) seems to link memory and emotions, and the basal ganglia (a set of neural cell bodies set deep in the base of the cerebral hemispheres) are involved in learning new motor skills. Indeed, some researchers would argue that in a broad sense, one could say the entire brain is involved with some aspect of memory.

Current research/future developments

As in many other fields of psychology, research into underlying biological (physiological, genetic, hormonal) factors in mental phenomena is thriving. Continual advances since the 1970s in brain-imaging techniques that allow non-intrusive visualization of the brain at work have contributed immensely to this area of research. Improvement in brain imaging techniques

KEY TERMS

. . . .

Associationism—A philosophical/psychological stance holding that mental associations are the building blocks of complex mental processes such as language and memory.

Brain imaging techniques—High technology techniques allowing non-intrusive visualization of the brain, these include computed tomography, positron emission tomography, and functional magnetic resonance imaging.

Category—A set of objects, experiences, or ideas, grouped together because of their similarity, they aid the organization of information in memory.

Episodic memory—Memory system holding conscious recollections of events from a person's life that often include time, place, and a representation of oneself.

Long-term memory—Part of memory system capable of holding large amounts of information for an indefinite period of time, possibly for a lifetime.

Memory—All of the information retained by an individual, and the mental systems and processes involved in storing and recalling information.

Procedural memory—Memory system holding often hard to articulate knowledge of how to perform certain procedures or activities.

Reconstructive memory—Type of memory thought to store experiences by abstract principles, which are then used to reconstruct memories during recall.

Schema—A structured framework of world knowledge that helps organize and interpret new information, as well as reconstruct information that may have been forgotten.

Semantic memory—Memory system holding all the easily articulated knowledge of the world an individual has that does not refer to particular events in their life.

Sensory memory—Part of the memory system that registers experience through the senses, holding onto information for one to two seconds before it is lost or transferred to short-term memory.

Short-term memory—Part of the memory system that repeats and organizes information to aid its storage in long-term memory, it is able to hold only limited amounts of information for short periods of time before it is either lost, or transferred to long-term memory.

such as computed tomography, positron emission tomography, and functional magnetic resonance imaging, as well as development of new techniques, will probably lead to more discoveries about the basis of memory and other mental functions in the brain.

See also Amnesia; Aphasia; Brain.

Further Reading:

Gregg, V.H. *Introduction to Human Memory.* New York: Routledge, 1986.

Lutz, J. *Introduction to Learning and Memory.* Pacific Grove, CA: Brooks-Cole, 1994.

McGaugh, J.L., N.M. Weinberger, and G. Lynch, eds. *Brain Organization and Memory: Cells, Systems and Circuits.* New York: Oxford University Press, 1992.

Morris, P.E., and Conway, M.E., eds. *The Psychology of Memory*, Vols. 1-3. New York: New York University Press, 1993.

Marie Doorey

Mendelevium see **Element, transuranium**

Mendelian laws of inheritance

The foundations of the modern science of genetics were laid by Gregor Mendel, an Austrian monk, who carried out experiments on the inheritance of characters between generations. Mendel worked on inheritance in sweet-peas, and selected characters that bred true; that is, the characters did not blend into one another in the next generation. Characteristics chosen for study by Mendel included flower color (such as red versus white), plant height (tall versus dwarf), seed coat (smooth-coated seeds versus wrinkled seeds), pod length (long pods versus short pods), and so on. Mendal eventually formulated the three laws of genetics, known today as the Mendelian laws of inheritance. These are the law of segregation, the law of independent assortment, and the law of dominance. Mendel's work went unnoticed for nearly two decades after his death in 1887, but was eventually recognized widely by the scientific community.

Mendel's laws

His database

In order to understand Mendel's three laws of inheritance, it is necessary to review the plant breeding

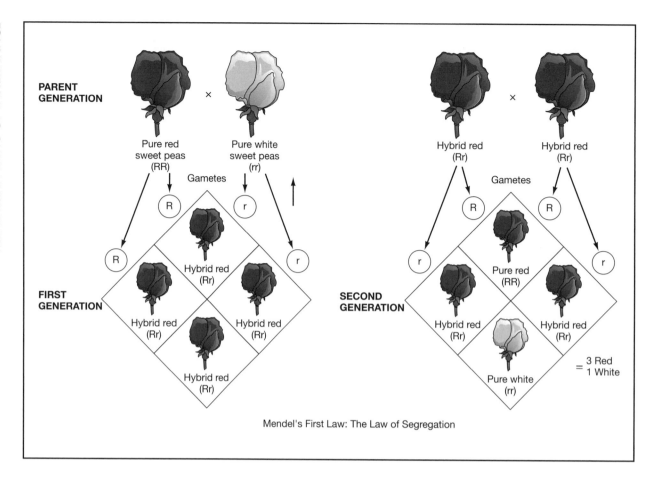

PARENT GENERATION

Pure red sweet peas (RR)   ×   Pure white sweet peas (rr)

Gametes

R   r

R   r

FIRST GENERATION

Hybrid red (Rr)

Hybrid red (Rr)   Hybrid red (Rr)

Hybrid red (Rr)

SECOND GENERATION

Hybrid red (Rr)   ×   Hybrid red (Rr)

Gametes

R   R

r   r

Pure red (RR)

Hybrid red (Rr)   Hybrid red (Rr)

Pure white (rr)

= 3 Red
1 White

Mendel's First Law: The Law of Segregation

experiments which inspired the laws. Two of the three laws involve dihybrid crosses where two different sets of traits are studied together. For example, if tall (controlled by two dominant alleles, TT), red-flowering (controlled by two dominant alleles, RR) sweet-peas are pollinated by dwarf (controlled by two recessive alleles, tt), white-flowering (controlled by two recessive alleles) plants, the pollen and ova will contain either TR or tr, which represent only a single allele of each set of genes. When fertilization takes place, the resulting first filial generation (F1) will all have progeny of the same outward appearance (phenotype); they will all be tall, red-flowering (TtRr) sweet-peas. The progeny of the first filial generation (the F2 generation) are also all tall, red-flowering plants, because R, the allele for red and T, the allele for tall are dominant to r and t, which are known as recessive alleles. Since sweet-peas are self-pollinating and each plant now produces gametes of four different genotypes, namely TR, Tr, tR, and tr. When the seeds resulting from the random combination of gametes with one of these genotypes, the second filial generation (F2) will have four different phenotypes: tall with red flowers, tall with white flowers, dwarf with red flowers, and dwarf with white flowers, in the proportion 9:3:3:1.

Mendel found that sweet peas with the same phenotype (purple flowers) had different genotypes which were only expressed in subsequent generations. Purple flowers were produced when the alleles contained at least one allele for purple flowers, which is dominant over the allele for white flowers. White flowers were produced when either both alleles (coded for white flowers the condition) which is the homozygous recessive allele.

Mendel's three laws of inheritance:

1) During Mendel's time neither the existence of genes nor their structure and function were understood. Indeed, chromosomes remained unknown for several years after Mendel's death. Mendel's experimental plants had factors that occurred in pairs. These factors have only one member of a pair in the gametes (pollen and ova).

2) Mendel described the three laws of inheritance that described the passage of genes from one generation to the next. The second Mendelian law is the law of independent assortment, which describes the chance distribution of alleles to the gametes (ova or spermatozoa). If an individual has two pairs of alleles, Aa and

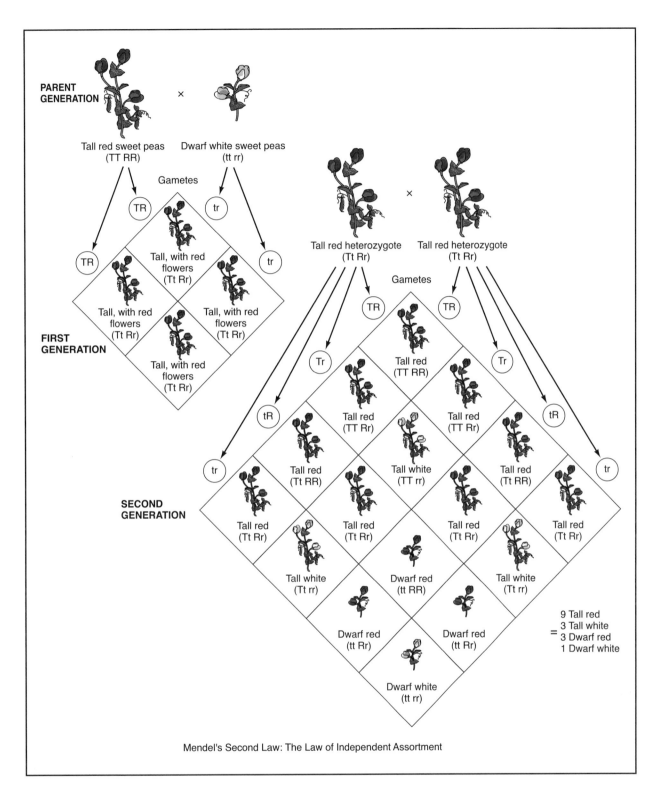

PARENT GENERATION

Tall red sweet peas (TT RR) × Dwarf white sweet peas (tt rr)

Gametes

TR   tr

FIRST GENERATION

TR

Tall, with red flowers (Tt Rr)

TR   Tall, with red flowers (Tt Rr)   tr

Tall, with red flowers (Tt Rr)

Tall, with red flowers (Tt Rr)

Tall red heterozygote (Tt Rr) × Tall red heterozygote (Tt Rr)

Gametes

TR   TR

Tr   Tall red (TT RR)   Tr

tR   Tall red (TT Rr)   Tall red (TT Rr)   tR

tr   Tall red (Tt RR)   Tall white (TT rr)   Tall red (Tt RR)   tr

SECOND GENERATION

Tall red (Tt Rr)   Tall red (Tt Rr)   Tall red (Tt Rr)   Tall red (Tt Rr)

Tall white (Tt rr)   Dwarf red (tt RR)   Tall white (Tt rr)

Dwarf red (tt Rr)   Dwarf red (tt Rr)

Dwarf white (tt rr)

= 9 Tall red
   3 Tall white
   3 Dwarf red
   1 Dwarf white

Mendel's Second Law: The Law of Independent Assortment

Bb, its gametes will contain equal numbers of the four possible combinations (AB, Ab, aB, ab), with one member from each pair. Independent assortment applies only to genes lying on different chromosomes, and does not-apply to linked genes on the same chromosomes. The F2 generation shows a ratio of nine tall red-flowers three dwarf red-flowering, three tall white-flowering, and one dwarf, white-flowering. A monohybrid cross, which involves a single character, such as plant height produces 12 tall plants and four dwarf plants, in a typical 3:1 ratio. Each pair of alleles making up a gene, whether controlling plant height or flower color

KEY TERMS
. . . .

Allele—A member making up a gene pair; the two alleles may have identical or different effects on the offspring.

Dihybrid cross—A breeding experiment in which two different sets of traits are observed together, such as body size and coat color.

Dominant—An allele whose effects in the phenotype are expressed even when paired with a different, recessive allele.

Gamete—The reproductive cells, either an egg cell or a sperm atozoan cell.

Genotype—The combination of alleles present in an organism.

Heterozygous—A condition in progeny, in which the two alleles in a given gene set are different-one being dominant, the other recessive.

Homozygous—A condition in progeny in which the two alleles of a given set are similar—either both dominant or both recessive.

Meiosis—Reduction division of reproductive cells producing gametes in which the number of chromosomes is reduced to one-half the original number.

Recessive—An allele of a pair whose effects in the progeny are concealed by a dominant allele in the pair. The opposite of dominant.

behaves though each pair were the only gene present for each pair segregates independently of other characters.

3) The third Mendelian law of inheritance, the law of dominance, states that heredity factors (genes) work together as sets usually as pairs of alleles. The total number of different alleles represents some of the variation available to species. Frequently, in heterozygotes (with one dominant and one recessive allele) only the dominant allele of the gene is expressed in the phenotype, the recessive allele being concealed and is not expressed. This gave rise to Mendels second law of inheritance known as the law of dominance.

Mendel's first law of inheritance is the law of segregation. This states that genes segregate during gamete formation into their different alleles. The two members of a pair of alleles separate (segregate) into two different gametes, and exert their influence in the offspring as one of a new pair of alleles. Segregation is the result of the separate carriage of genes on chromosomes, which are not altered or blended by forming pairs. A gene for red flowers in the sweet-pea does not become diluted from having been paired with the gene for white flowers. It is passed to subsequent generations unaltered in the gametes.

See also Chromosome; Gamete; Gene.

Further Reading:

Grange, J., et al. *Genetic manipulations.* Blackwell, 1991.
Strickberger, Monroe W. *Genetics.* New York: Macmillan Co.,
Wellington, E.N. *Genetic Interaction Among Microorganisms and the Natural Environment.* Pergamon Press, 1992.

Lawrence S. Dillon

Meningitis

Meningitis is a potentially fatal inflammation of the meninges, the thin, membranous covering of the brain and the spinal cord. Meningitis is most commonly caused by infection (by bacteria, viruses, or fungi), although it can also be caused by bleeding into the meninges, cancer, or diseases of the immune system.

Anatomical considerations

The meninges are three separate membranes, layered together, which serve to encase the brain and spinal cord. The dura is the toughest, outermost layer, and is closely attached to the inside of the skull. The middle layer, the arachnoid, is important in the normal flow of the cerebrospinal fluid (CSF), a lubricating fluid which bathes both the brain and the spinal cord. The innermost layer, the pia, helps direct brain blood vessels into the brain. The space between the arachnoid and the pia contains CSF, which serves to help insulate the brain from trauma. Through this space course many blood vessels.

CSF, produced within specialized chambers deep inside the brain, flows over the surface of the brain and spinal cord. This fluid serves to cushion these relatively delicate structures, as well as supplying important nutrients for brain cells. CSF is reabsorbed by blood vessels which are located within the meninges.

Because the brain is enclosed in the hard, bony case of the skull, any disease process which produces swelling will ultimately prove destructive to the brain.

The skull cannot expand at all, so when swollen brain tissue pushes up against the skull's hard bone, the brain tissue becomes damaged and may ultimately die. Furthermore, swelling on the right side of the brain will not only cause pressure and damage to that side of the brain, but by taking up precious space within the tight confines of the skull, the left side of the brain will also be pushed up against the hard surface of the skull, causing reciprocal damage to that side of the brain as well.

The cells of the brain require a very well-regulated environment for optimal function. Careful balance of oxygen, carbon dioxide, glucose (sugar), sodium, calcium, potassium, and other substances must be maintained in order to avoid damage to the relatively unforgiving brain tissue.

The cells lining the brain's capillaries (tiny blood vessels) are specifically designed to prevent many substances from passing into brain tissue. This is commonly referred to as the blood-brain barrier. The blood-brain barrier prevents various toxins (substances which could be poisonous to brain tissue), as well as many agents of infection, from crossing from the blood stream into the brain tissue. While this barrier obviously is an important protective feature for the brain, it also serves to complicate therapy in the case of an infection, by making it difficult for medications to pass out of the blood and into the brain tissue where the infection resides.

Infectious causes of meningitis

The most common infectious causes of meningitis vary according to an individual host's age, habits and living environment, and health status. In newborns, the most common agents of meningitis are those which are contracted from the newborn's mother, including Group B streptococci (becoming an increasingly common infecting organism in the newborn period), *Escherichia coli*, and *Listeria moncytogenes*. Older children are more frequently infected by *Haemophilus influenzae*, *Neisseria meningitidis*, and *Streptococcus pneumoniae*, while adults are infected by *S. pneumoniae* and *N. meningitidis*. *N. meningitidis* is the only organism which can cause epidemics of meningitis. These have occurred in particular when a child in a crowded day-care situation or a military recruit in a crowded training camp has fallen ill with *N. meningitidis* meningitis.

Viral causes of meningitis include the herpes simplex viruses, mumps and measles viruses (against which most children are protected due to mass immunization programs), the virus which causes chicken pox,

the rabies virus, and a number of viruses which are acquired through the bite of infected mosquitoes. Patients with AIDS (Acquired Immunodeficiency Syndrome) are more susceptible to certain infectious causes of meningitis, including by certain fungal agents, as well as by the agent which causes tuberculosis. Patients who have had their spleens removed, or whose spleens are no longer functional (as in the case of patients with sickle cell disease) are more susceptible to certain infections, including those caused by *N. meningitidis* and *S. pneumoniae*.

How the infectious agents of meningitis gain access to the meninges

The majority of meningitis infections are acquired by blood-borne spread. An individual may have another type of infection (of the lungs, throat, or tissues of the heart) caused by an organism which can also cause meningitis. The organism multiplies, finds its way into the blood stream, and is delivered in sufficient quantities to invade past the blood-brain barrier.

Direct spread occurs when an already resident infectious agent spreads from infected tissue next to or very near the meninges, for example from an ear or sinus infection. Patients who suffer from skull fractures provide openings to the sinuses, nasal passages, and middle ears. Organisms which frequently live in the human respiratory system can then pass through these openings to reach the meninges and cause infection. Similarly, patients who undergo surgical procedures or who have had foreign bodies surgically placed within their skulls (such as tubes to drain abnormal amounts of accumulated CSF) have an increased risk of the organisms causing meningitis being introduced to the meninges.

The least common method by which the organisms causing meningitis are transmitted, but one of the most interesting, is called intraneural spread. This involves an organism spreading along a nerve, and using that nerve as a kind of ladder into the skull where the organism can multiply and cause meningitis. Herpes simplex virus is known to use this type of spread, as is the rabies virus.

Symptoms of meningitis

The most classic symptoms of meningitis (particularly of bacterial meningitis) include fever, headache, vomiting, photophobia (sensitivity to light), irritability, lethargy (severe fatigue), and stiff neck. The disease progresses with seizures, confusion, and eventually coma.

A very young infant may not show the classic signs of meningitis. Early in infancy, a baby's immune system is not yet developed enough to mount a fever in response to infection, so fever may be absent. Some infants with meningitis have seizures as their only identifiable symptom.

How meningitis damages the brain

Damage due to meningitis occurs from a variety of phenomena. The action of infectious agents on the brain tissue is one direct cause of damage. Other types of damage may be due to mechanical effects of swelling of brain tissue, and compression against the bony surface of the skull. Swelling of the meninges may interfere with the normal absorption of CSF by blood vessels, causing accumulation of CSF and damage due to resulting pressure on the brain. Interference with the brain's carefully regulated chemical environment may cause damaging amounts of normally present substances (carbon dioxide, potassium) to accumulate. Inflammation may cause the blood-brain barrier to become less effective at preventing the passage of toxic substances into brain tissue.

Long term complications of meningitis

The most frequent long term effects of meningitis include deafness and blindness, due to compression of specific nerves and brain areas responsible for the senses of hearing and sight. Some patients develop permanent seizure disorders, requiring life-time treatment with anti-seizure medications. Scarring of the meninges may result in obstruction of the normal flow of CSF, causing abnormal accumulation of CSF. This may be a chronic problem for some patients, requiring the installation of tubes to regularly drain the accumulation.

Diagnosis

A number of techniques are used when examining a patient suspected of having meningitis to verify the diagnosis. Certain manipulations of the head (lowering the head, chin towards chest, for example) are difficult to perform and painful for a patient with meningitis.

The most important test used to diagnosis meningitis is the lumbar puncture (commonly called a spinal tap). Lumbar puncture (LP) involves the insertion of a thin needle into a space between the vertebrae in the lower back, and the withdrawal of a small amount of CSF. The CSF is then examined under a microscope. Normal CSF contains set percentages of glucose and protein. These percentages will vary with bacterial, viral, or other causes of meningitis. For example, bacterial meningitis causes a greatly lower than normal percentage of glucose to be present in CSF, as the bacteria are essentially "eating" the host's glucose, and using it for their own nutrition and energy production. Normal CSF should contain no white blood cells (infection fighting cells), so the presence of white blood cells in CSF is another indication of meningitis. Some of the withdrawn CSF is also put into special lab dishes to allow growth of the infecting organism, which can then be identified more easily.

In a few rare instances, lumbar puncture cannot be performed, because the amount of swelling within the skull is so great that the intracranial pressure (pressure within the skull) is extremely high. This pressure is always measured immediately upon insertion of the LP needle. If it is found to be very high, no fluid is withdrawn, because withdrawal of fluid could cause herniation of the brain stem. Herniation of the brain stem occurs when the part of the brain connecting to the spinal cord is thrust through the opening at the base of the skull into the spinal canal. Such herniation will cause compression of those structures within the brain stem which control the most vital functions of the body (breathing, heart beat, consciousness). Death or permanent debilitation follows herniation of the brain stem.

Treatment

Antibiotic medications (forms of penicillins and cephalosporins, for example) are the most important element of treatment against bacterial agents of meningitis. Because of the effectiveness of the blood-brain barrier in preventing passage of substances into the brain, medications must be delivered directly into the patient's veins (intravenous or IV) at very high doses. Antiviral medications (acyclovir) may be helpful in the case of viral meningitis, and antifungal medications are available as well.

Other treatment for meningitis involves decreasing inflammation (with steroid preparations) and paying careful attention to the balance of fluids, glucose, sodium, potassium, oxygen, and carbon dioxide in the patient's system. Patients who develop seizures will require medications to halt the seizures and prevent their return.

Prevention

A series of vaccines against *Haemophilus influenzae*, started at two months of age, has greatly reduced the incidence of that form of meningitis. Vaccines also exist against *Neisseria meningitidis* and *Streptococcus*

KEY TERMS

. . . .

Blood-brain barrier—An arrangement of cells within the blood vessels of the brain which prevents the passage of toxic substances, including infectious agents, from the blood and into the brain.

Cerebrospinal fluid (also called CSF)—Fluid made in chambers within the brain and which then flows over the surface of the brain and spinal cord, providing nutrition to cells of the nervous system, as well as cushioning.

Lumbar puncture (also called LP)—A medical test in which a very narrow needle is inserted into a specific space between the vertebrae of the lower back in order to draw off and examine a sample of CSF.

Meninges—The three layer membranous covering of the brain and spinal cord, composed of the dura, arachnoid, and pia. Provides protection for the brain, as well as housing many blood vessels.

pneumoniae bacteria, but these vaccines are only recommended for those people who have particular susceptibility to those organisms, due to certain immune deficiencies, lack of a spleen, or sickle cell anemia.

Because *N. meningitidis* is known to cause epidemics of disease, close contacts of patients with such meningitis (other children in day care with the patient, other military personnel within the same training camp, and people living within the patient's household), are treated with Rifampin. This generally prevents spread of the disease.

Mothers with certain risk factors may be treated with antibiotics during labor, to prevent the passage of certain organisms which may cause meningitis in the newborn (particularly Group B streptococcus).

Further Reading:

Andreoli, Thomas E., et al. *Cecil Essentials of Medicine.* Philadelphia: W. B. Saunders Company, 1993.
Berkow, Robert, and Andrew J. Fletcher. *The Merck Manual of Diagnosis and Therapy.* Rahway, NJ: Merck Research Laboratories, 1992.
Isselbacher, Kurt J., et al. *Harrison's Principles of Internal Medicine.* New York: McGraw Hill, 1994.
Krugman, Saul, et al. *Infectious Diseases of Children.* St. Louis: Mosby-Year Book, Inc., 1992.
Sherris, John C., et al. *Medical Microbiology.* Norwalk, CT: Appleton & Lange, 1994.

Rosalyn Carson-DeWitt

Menopause

Menopause is the stage in the female life cycle during which menstrual cycles stop. On average, menopause occurs at age 51, and generally takes from five to seven years from start to finish. For years, the menopausal stage was rarely talked about in public. Beginning in the 1960s, physicians began treating menopause aggressively as a medical problem, using estrogen hormones. Contemporary debate focuses on the wisdom of long-term estrogen use and the search for the best way to address problems linked to menopause.

A nineteenth-century term

Menopause has always been a part of natural life for women, and the history of medicine is littered with references to the period when women stop bearing children. The Greek philosopher Aristotle noted that women stop giving birth after the age of 50. But little was written about ways to ease women through the symptoms of menopause, which include hot flashes, night sweats, insomnia, and dryness in the urogenital area.

Occasional historical references to what we now call menopause and therapy for the condition can be found, such as the reference to hot flashes and other menopausal symptoms in the 1628 book, *The Anatomy of Melancholy* by Robert Burton. A 1675 account described a cooling diet for menopause, according to Greer. And in 1701, physician Thomas Sydenham described the tendency of women ages 45-50 to develop "Hysterick Fits," and suggested blood letting as therapy.

But the term menopause was not used until 1816, when a medical syndrome called "la Ménépause" was described in a French journal by C. P. L. de Gardanne. By 1839, the first book entirely about menopause was written by Frenchman C. F. Menville. The book explained symptoms of menopause as a response to the death of the womb.

Menopause was described clearly in 1899 in an article entitled "Epochal Insanities," under the heading "Climacteric Insanity." The article described symptoms of menopause and invited physicians to treat it as a syndrome in need of attention, Greer observed. Women in the late nineteenth century were often advised to rest as a way of combating menopausal symptoms. By the early twentieth century, menopause was seen as "the death of the woman in the woman."

Contemporary research has shown that menopause is not linked to mental illness or the death of the womb. The average woman of 51 can expect several more decades of life, making menopause more a stage of life than a death sentence.

The many symptoms noted by early observers of menopause stem from profound hormonal changes which occur when women experience menopause. During menopause, hormonal activity changes as the body's needs are altered and production of natural estrogen and progesterone is reduced. The most obvious of these changes is the end of the monthly menstrual cycle, a process which occurs gradually. When this process ends, women can no longer bear children and ovulation of eggs no longer occurs.

Various studies suggest that while a majority of women experience some menopausal symptoms, fewer than half have severe problems with the process.

A new era

The 1923 isolation of estrogen, the female sex hormone manufactured in both sexes, lead to a new era for menopausal women. Estrogens were first tried as an aid to menopausal women in the 1930s, but negative side affects cut short the effort. By the 1960s, a palatable estrogen supplement was developed. The substance was heavily promoted as a medication to keep menopausal women "feminine forever" (also the title of a 1965 book by Robert A. Wilson promoting estrogen therapy). Estrogen was promoted as a cure for hot flashes, urogenital dryness, and even mental illness.

However, in 1975, studies emerged linking estrogen with an elevated risk of endometrial cancer, and use of estrogen supplements dropped. Use of estrogens dropped considerably until researchers explored using estrogen with progesterone as a combined therapy. This combination is thought to reduce the risk of endometrial cancer.

Since the early 1980s, the use of synthetic hormones for menopause has climbed dramatically. In 1980, 12 million prescriptions were written for estrogen supplements. By 1993, a total of 48 million prescriptions were written. As estrogen has become used more widely, various benefits and risks have become apparent. Researchers have reported an elevated risk of breast cancer among women who use estrogen supplements for long periods of time, although such studies are controversial. Negative side effects of the estrogen-progesterone combination are commonly reported. These include headaches, depression, and bloating. One sign of the distaste with which many women view the estrogen-progesterone combination is that the average use of estrogen replacement prescriptions is nine months.

On the positive side, estrogen supplements have been shown to reduced the risk among women of heart disease, the leading cause of death among men and women and a far more likely cause of death than endometrial cancer. Research suggests that estrogen lowers total cholesterol and relaxes blood vessels, making the heart's job easier. Studies have also shown that estrogen supplements cut the risk of osteoporosis, a disease in which bones become brittle and easily broken. Several small studies suggest that estrogen may also increase short-term memory.

Better studies needed

Virtually millions of women must decide how best to approach the symptoms of menopause and life after menopause every year. There were 473 million women 50 or over in the world in 1990. But relatively little research has been conducted concerning the long-term health consequences of estrogen or estrogen and progesterone therapy in women or about other ways to address menopausal symptoms. There has never been a large-scale, long term study of estrogen and progesterone supplements which included scientifically selected individuals for control group and treatment groups. This means that the results of much current research is suspect.

The United States government is currently conducting a study with nine years of follow-up which will examine the effect of hormone replacement therapy on the prevention of heart disease and osteoporosis. The study is expected to enroll 63,000 women ages 50-79, and will include scientifically selected control and treatment groups.

Other research must also be conducted concerning alternative therapy for menopause and a variety of issues linked to health risk and the duration of hormone therapy use. In 1994, the World Health Organization scientific group announced a series of recommendations for research concerning physical and psychological aspects of menopause.

Menopause remains a time of life shrouded in scientific mystery. This stems from the paucity of ambitious studies concerning health options for menopausal

KEY TERMS

. . . .

Endometrium—Inner membrane of the uterus.

Estrogen—Female sex hormones, responsible for development of sex characteristics and for preparation of environment for the early embryo.

Progesterone—Hormone which plays a critical role in preparing the body for a developing embryo.

Osteoporosis—A disease which occurs primarily in women in which the mass of the bones is reduced, making it easier for fractures to occur.

women. As more research is conducted, the increasing availability of information should ease the transition for women entering this stage of life.

Further Reading:

Ehrenreich, Barbara and Deirdre English. *For Her Own Good.* New York: Doubleday, 1989.

Fackelmann, Kathleen. "Forever Smart. Does Estrogen Enhance Memory?" *Science News.* Vol. 147. 74-75.

Greer, Germaine. *The Change.* New York: Alfred A. Knopf, 1992.

Sheehy, Gail. *The Silent Passage: Menopause.* New York: Random House, 1992.

Te Velde, Egbert R.; Van Leusden, Huub AIM. "Hormonal treatment for the Climacteric: Alleviation of Symptoms and Prevention of Postmenopausal Disease." *The Lancet.* vol. 343, March 12, 1994. 654-657.

"WHO Scientific Group Formulates New Research Agenda on Menopause." *Public Health Reports.* Vol. 109, No. 5. September-October 1994. 715.

Patricia Braus

Menstrual cycle

The menstrual cycle technically refers to the cyclic changes that take place in the lining of the human uterus over the course of approximately 28 days in adult females. These cycle changes are associated with cyclic changes in the ovaries and in the brain and ovarian hormones. The term "menstrual" comes from the Latin word *menses*, meaning month. The purpose of the cyclic changes is to prepare the uterine lining, called the endometrium, to receive a fertilized egg (the zygote). In response to hormone levels, the endometrium thickens as a result of increases in the cells and blood vessels. If fertilized action does not occur, the uterine lining breaks down. The blood, mucus, and pieces of tissue of the thickened endometrial lining are sloughed off through the cervix of the uterus and out of the vagina, in a process called menstruation.

The first phase of the menstrual cycle in the uterus is the proliferative phase, which is followed by the secretory phase, and then by menstruation. Cyclic changes in hormonal levels control and orchestrate the events of the menstrual cycle.

Proliferative phase

During the proliferative phase in the uterus, the wall of the endometrium begins to thicken. This phase of the uterus begins at the end of menstruation and lasts until ovulation, when the egg is ejected from the ovary. Follicle-stimulating hormone (FSH), secreted by the anterior pituitary gland in the brain, targets the ovaries and triggers the maturation process of up to 25 follicles. Each month, only one egg is brought to maturity and is ejected from the Graafian follicle. About 24 hours before ovulation, the pituitary gland releases a surge of a second hormone, luteinizing hormone (LH), which stimulates the release of the egg out of the ovary and into the Fallopian tube.

During the proliferative phase in the uterus, the hormone estrogen is released from the maturing Graafian follicles in the ovaries. Estrogen stimulates the proliferation of cells in the endometrium of the uterus. Estrogen also plays a role in regulating the release of FSH and LH from the pituitary gland. The increasing levels of estrogen in the bloodstream stimulate the secretion of FSH and LH from the anterior pituitary. The increased levels of FSH and LH in turn further increase estrogen secretion from the follicles in the ovaries.

Secretory phase

During the secretory phase of the uterus, the hormone progesterone is produced by the ovaries. Progesterone (as well as estrogen) is secreted by the corpus luteum, (which means *yellow body*), which develops from the Graafian follicle. Progesterone secreted by the corpus luteum stimulates the further build-up of the cells in the endometrium of the uterus. Progesterone also stimulates the glands in the uterus to secrete substances that maintain the endometrium and keep it from breaking down. For this reason, this phase of the menstrual cycle is called the secretory phase.

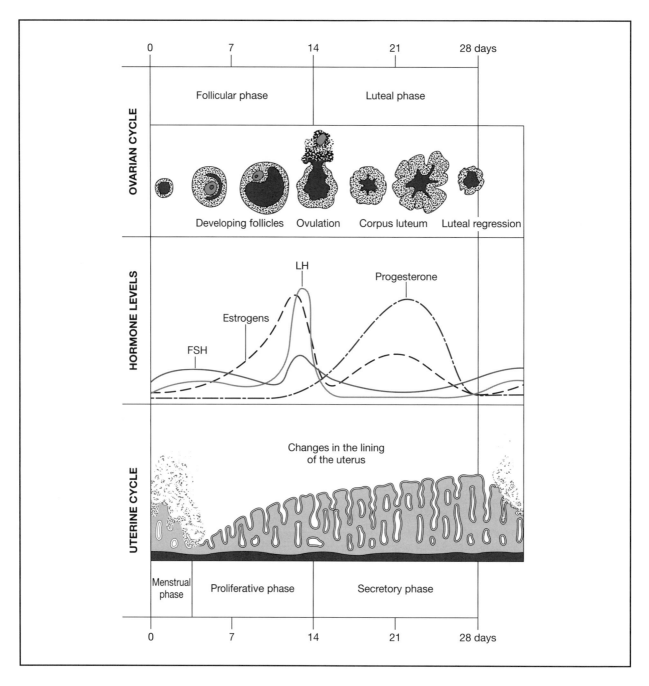

The menstrual cycle.

The presence of estrogen and progesterone in the blood inhibit the production of FSH and LH from the pituitary, and the levels of FSH and LH begin to fall.

If the egg that has been ovulated into the Fallopian tube is fertilized by spermatozoa, the developing zygote implants in the thickened endometrium of the uterus approximately seven days after ovulation. This stimulates the endometrium to secrete a human chorionic gonadotropic hormone (HCG). HCG maintains the corpus luteum in the ovary, so that it continues to secrete progesterone. HCG is secreted throughout pregnancy and keeps blood progesterone levels high, so that the endometrium continues to thicken, eventually forming the placenta. Without a high level of progesterone, the endometrium begins to break down. In a pregnancy, the breakdown of the endometrium would result in a miscarriage.

If fertilization does not occur, the corpus luteum shrinks and blood progesterone levels drop, at about day 22 in a 28 day cycle. Without progesterone, the endometrium degenerates, and is expelled through the cervix and out through the vagina.

Menstruation

The expulsion of tissue and blood from the uterus lasts from three to eight days, with much variation among women. Some women experience painful cramps during menstruation, which are the result of uterine contractions that expel the endometrium. Hormones known as prostaglandins are produced by uterine cells during menstruation, and the excessive production of prostaglandins is associated with stronger uterine contractions and more intense cramps. Menstrual cramps can be treated by drugs that inhibit the production of prostaglandins in uterine cells. Aspirin, ibuprofin, and naproxin sodium are all effective anti-prostaglandin drugs. It is important to take these medications at the onset of the menstrual flow, otherwise prostaglandin production can proceed for several hours unchecked, and the drugs will not be effective in reducing pain.

Some women also experience premenstrual syndrome (PMS), a condition occurring some time in the secretory phase prior to menstruation. Symptoms of PMS include mood changes, water retention and bloating, increase in appetite and cravings, cramps, breast pain, and headaches. Researchers are not sure what causes PMS, but the sharp drop in progesterone that occurs at about day 22 may be involved in triggering these physical and emotional symptoms. While no cure for PMS exists, experts recommend that women who experience PMS reduce their salt intake, take more exercise, and maintain a healthy diet during this time. The B vitamins may also be effective in reducing PMS symptoms. Some women have found relief in taking the medications prescribed for menstrual cramps, while lowering caffeine intake can be useful in reducing premenstrual breast pain.

Girls begin menstruating at the onset of puberty, at about the age of 12 or 13, although the onset of menstruation may be earlier or later, depending on the amount of body fat. The first menstrual period is called the menarche; during the first few cycles, ovulation may be absent.

Menopause is the cessation of the menstrual cycle, when ovulation and menstruation cease. The cessation of menstruation is gradual and is preceded by menstrual cycles in which ovulation does not occur. The menstrual cycle becomes irregular before finally stopping completely. The onset of menopause is individually variable, occurring between the ages of 45 to the late fifties.

KEY TERMS

Cervix—The opening of the uterus.

Corpus luteum—"Yellow body;" the "empty" follicle from which the egg is ovulated; secretes progesterone.

Endometrium—The lining of the uterus.

Estrogen—A female reproductive hormone secreted by the follicles.

Follicle—The structure in which eggs develop within the ovary.

Follicle-stimulating hormone—Hormone secreted by the anterior pituitary that stimulates the maturation of follicles.

Graafian follicles—Maturing ovarian follicles.

Human chorionic gonadotropin—Hormone secreted by the embryo that maintains the corpus luteum.

Luteinizing hormone—Hormone that acts with LH to stimulate the maturation of follicles.

Menarche—First menstrual period.

Menopause—Cessation of the menstrual cycle.

Menstruation—Sloughing off the lining of the uterus.

Ovary—Female reproductive organ that contains the eggs.

Ovulation—Process in which an egg is ejected from an ovarian follicle.

Progesterone—Hormone secreted by the corpus luteum; maintains the endometrium.

Prostaglandines—Complex fatty acids occurring in most human tissues.

Uterus—Female reproductive organ in which an embryo grows and develops.

Vagina—Passage from the uterus to outside the body.

Further Reading:

Ferin, Michel, et al. *The Menstrual Cycle: Physiology, Reproductive Disorders, and Infertility.* New York: Oxford University Press, 1993.

Mestel, Rosie. "Are Periods a Protection Against Men?" *New Scientist* 140, no. 1893 (2 October 1993): 8.

Quadagno, David, et al. "The Menstrual Cycle: Does It Affect Athletic Performance?" *The Physician and Sportsmedicine* 19, no. 3 (March 1991): 121.

Segal, Marion. "A Balanced Look at the Menstrual Cycle." *FDA Consumer* 27, no. 1 (December 1993): 32.

Sloane, Ethel. *Biology of Women*. 3d ed. Albany, NY: Delmar, 1993.

Kathleen Scogna

Mercurous chloride

Mercurous chloride (mercury [I] chloride), Hg_2Cl_2, is a white powder that is nearly insoluble in water. It is also called calomel. Mercurous chloride reacts with ammonia to produce a black solid, and this reaction has been widely used in the identification of dissolved mercury ions in water sources. Mercurous chloride finds uses as a purgative (laxative), and in the preparation of insecticides and medicines. It has also been used to treat infections of intestinal worms and as a fungicide (a substance which is used to kill fungi and prevent fungal growth) in agriculture.

Mercurous chloride has been most often used as a treatment for intestinal worms. In the past, large doses were often used to stimulate the intestines and remove blockages, although it is rarely used in medicine today due to the toxicity of mercury. When it is used as a laxative, if the treatment fails to work, large doses of other laxatives and water must be used to insure that no mercury is allowed to accumulate in the body. Mercury toxicity often results in severe neurological damage (vapors of mercury are far more dangerous than solid mercury compounds, although all mercury compounds are considered highly poisonous). Because of the extremely low solubility of mercurous chloride in water, very little is usually absorbed by the body, making it safer than most people would expect.

In laboratories, calomel electrodes are commonly found in pH meters and this is how mercurous chloride is widely used today.

See also Mercury.

Mercury (element)

Mercury is a metallic chemical element identified by the symbol Hg on the periodic table. It is silver in color and, unlike other metals, is liquid at room temperature. The ancient name for mercury was quicksilver, meaning "living" silver. This name reflected mercury's lustrous silver color and its unusually lively behavior: when it is poured onto a smooth surface, it forms beads that roll rapidly around. The element's modern name comes from Mercury (or Mercurius), the fleet-footed messenger of the gods in Roman mythology.

No one knows exactly when mercury was discovered, but many ancient civilizations were familiar with this element. As long ago as Roman times, people had learned to extract mercury from ore and used it to purify gold and silver. Ore containing gold or silver would be crushed and treated with mercury, which rejects impurities, to form a mercury alloy, called an amalgam. When the amalgam is heated, the mercury vaporizes, leaving pure gold or silver.

Mercury's presence in the Earth's crust is relatively low compared to other elements. However, mercury is not considered rare because it is found in large, highly concentrated deposits. Nearly all mercury exists in the form of a red ore called cinnabar, which is composed of mercury and sulfur. Sometimes shiny globules of mercury appear among outcrops of cinnabar, which is probably why mercury was discovered so long ago. The metal is relatively easy to extract from the ore by applying heat and a filtration process. First the ore is heated in an oxygen furnace. The mercury is released as fumes and those fumes condense into soot on a water-cooled metal condenser. The mercury is then removed from the soot by a filter system and purified in a vacuum. Much of the world's mercury has traditionally been mined in Spain and Italy, though several other countries also produce commercial quantities.

Properties of mercury

Mercury's atomic number is 80 and its atomic weight is 200.59. It has a boiling point of 673°F (352.5°C) and a melting point of -38°F (-70°C). Mercury is stable (it does not react) in air and water, as well as in acids and alkalis. The surface tension of mercury is six times higher than that of water. Because of this, even when mercury is in liquid form, it does not wet the surfaces it contacts.

Like some other metals, mercury exhibits unusual behavior at extremely low temperatures. In 1911, Dutch physicist Heike Kamerlingh Onnes discovered the phenomenon of superconductivity by freezing mercury to only a few degrees above absolute zero. At that temperature, mercury loses all of its natural resistance to the flow of electricity and becomes superconductive.

Mercury is uniquely suited for measuring temperatures. When heated or cooled, mercury expands or contracts at a rate that is more constant than most other substances. Also, it has a wide range of temperatures between its boiling and freezing points. In 1714, German-Dutch physicist Gabriel Daniel Fahrenheit developed the mercury thermometer. (Previous fluid thermometers had used alcohol or alcohol-water mixtures.) With mercury as the measuring fluid, temperatures could be recorded well above water's boiling point and below its freezing point. Using mercury also allowed the degrees to be marked more accurately in finer subdivisions.

Toxicity

Mercury and all of its compounds are extremely poisonous, and mercury is one of the few substances known to have no natural function in the human body. Classified as a heavy metal, mercury is difficult for the body to eliminate. This means that even small amounts can act as a cumulative poison, collecting over a long period of time until they reach dangerous levels. Humans can absorb mercury through any mucous membrane and through the skin. Its vapor can be inhaled, and mercury can be ingested in foods such as fish, eggs, meat, and grain. In the body, mercury primarily affects the nervous system, liver, and kidneys. Mercury poisoning symptoms include tremors, tunnel vision, loss of balance, slurred speech, and unpredictable emotions. The phrase "mad as a hatter" owes it origin to symptoms of mercury poisoning that afflicted hatmakers in the 1800s, when a mercury compound was used to prepare beaver fur and felt materials.

The toxic qualities of mercury have been known for hundreds of years. In the seventeenth century, Swiss toxicologist Johann-Jakob Wepfer studied the characteristics of mercury poisoning. In the early 1920s, German chemist Alfred Stock discovered that he had been suffering from undiagnosed mercury poisoning for most of his adult life. His case was probably caused by years of exposure to mercury vapors in poorly ventilated laboratories. Stock analyzed the pathology of mercury poisoning and devised techniques for detecting very small amounts of mercury. Often using himself as an experimental subject, Stock traced mercury's path through the body and its accumulation in various organs. He published numerous articles warning of mercury's dangers and suggesting safety precautions.

Until recently, scientists thought that inorganic mercury was relatively harmless, so industrial wastes containing it were routinely discharged into large bodies of water. Then in the 1950s, more than 100 people in Japan were poisoned by fish containing mercury; 43 people died, dozens more were horribly crippled, and babies born after the outbreak developed irreversible damage. It was found that inorganic mercury in industrial wastes had been converted to a much more harmful organic form—methyl mercury. As this substance works its way up the food chain, its quantities accumulate to dangerous levels in larger fish. Today, the dumping of mercury-containing wastes has been largely banned, and many of its industrial uses have been halted. However, mercury is still used in electrical switches and relays, fluorescent lamps, and electrolytic cells for manufacturing chlorine. Tiny amounts are also present in dental fillings.

Mercury (planet)

Mercury is the closest planet to the Sun. It is a small world only slightly larger than Earth's Moon. Next to the planet Pluto, Mercury is one of the least explored planets within our solar system.

Basic properties

Mercury orbits the Sun at a mean distance of 0.387 Astronomical Units. The high eccentricity of the planet's orbit ($e = 0.206$), however, dictates that it can be as far as 0.467 AU away from the Sun, and as close as 0.307 AU. The high eccentricity attributed to Mercury's orbit is the second largest in the solar system, only the planet Pluto has a more eccentric orbit.

(Eccentricity in astronomy indicates that an orbit is not absolutely circular. The value of $e = 1$ indicates an orbit shaped as a parabola. An ellipsis is less than one, and a circle has zero eccentricity.)

Constrained as it is in an orbit close to the Sun, Mercury is not an easy planet for naked-eye observers to locate. The greatest separation between the planet and the Sun, as seen from Earth, is 28° and consequently the planet is never visible against a truly dark sky. Even at its greatest angular separation from the Sun, Mercury will either set within two hours of sunset, or rise no earlier than two hours before the Sun. None the less, Mercury has been known since the most ancient of times, with observations of the planet being reported as far back as several centuries B.C. The Greek Philosopher Plato refers to the distinctive yellow color of Mercury in Book X of his *Republic*.

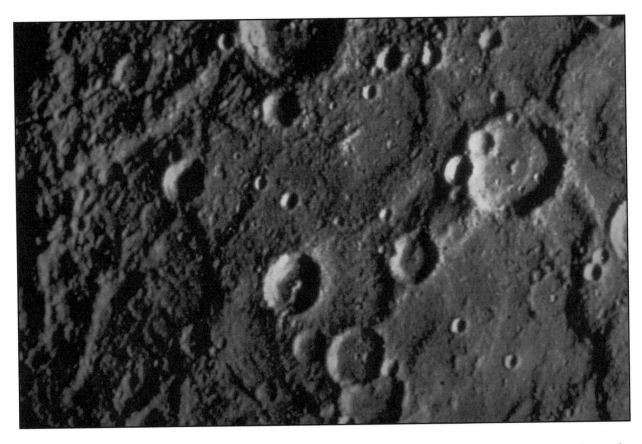

This expanse of the surface of Mercury is about 217 mi (350 km) across. These inter-crater plains, located near the south pole, are traversed by numerous ridges and scarps. The crustal fracturing on Mercury is as large in scale as that on Earth.

The sidereal period, or the time it takes Mercury to orbit the Sun, is 87.969 days. The planet's synodic period, which is the time required for Mercury to return to the same relative position with respect to the Sun and Earth, is 116 days. As seen from Earth, Mercury undergoes a change of phase as it moves around the Sun. These phase changes were first observed in the early seventeenth century by the Polish astronomer Johannes Hewelcke (1611-1687), who is perhaps better known today through his latinized name, Hevelius. Zero phase occurs when Earth, the Sun, and Mercury are directly in line, with Mercury on the opposite side of the Sun to Earth. At this phase, Mercury is said to be at superior conjunction. Half phase occurs when Earth, the Sun, and Mercury are once again in a line, but this time with Mercury being on the same side of the Sun as the Earth. Mercury is said to be a inferior conjunction when it exhibits and half phase. While moving from inferior to superior conjunction Mercury passes through a quarter phase, during which the disk of the planet is half illuminated as seen from the Earth. Mercury also passes through its greatest western elongation when moving form inferior to superior conjunction. Likewise, in moving from superior to inferior conjunction Mercury passes through greatest eastern elongation, and exhibits a second quarter phase, or half-disk illumination.

Because Mercury's orbit is quite elongated, so that its distance from the sun varies significantly, the maximum angular separation between Mercury and the Sun, as seen from the Earth, can vary from a minimum of 18 to maximum of 28°. The largest angular separation of 28° occurs when Mercury is at either greatest western, or greatest eastern elongation and near its aphelion (its greatest distance from the Sun). Irrespective of whether the planet is at aphelion or not, the best time to view Mercury in the evening is when the planet is near greatest eastern elongation. Since the synodic period of Mercury is about 116 days, the planet will be favorably placed for evening viewing three times each year. Similar conditions apply for viewing Mercury before sunrise.

The inclination of Mercury's orbit to that of the ecliptic plane (the plane of Earth's orbit about the Sun) is 7.0°. This slight orbital tilt dictates that when Mercury is at inferior conjunction it is only rarely silhouetted against the Sun's disk as seen from Earth. On those

Bright rayed craters and large craters, called basins, are prominent in this view of Mercury. Since, unlike Earth and Mars, Mercury has no atmosphere, its landscape is not continuously shaped by erosion and deposition. Although the exterior of Mercury resembles that of the moon, the interior of the planet is probably more similar to that of Earth.

struct a map of Mercurian features, he found that the shape and relative position of the fuzzy surface features that his telescope could reveal did not change greatly with time. Schiaparelli subsequently reasoned that his observations could be best explained if Mercury kept the same face pointed toward the Sun at all times.

If a planet or a satellite spins on its axis at exactly the same rate that it moves around in its orbit, then it is said to be in synchronous rotation. Our Moon, for example, is in synchronous rotation about Earth, and consequently we always see the same lunar features. Synchronous rotation arises through gravitational inter-actions, and mathematicians have been able to show that once the spin of an object has been synchronized it remains so in a stable fashion. An alternative way of saying that an object spins in a synchronous manner is to say that is satisfies a 1-to-1 spin-orbit coupling.

Astronomers believed that Mercury was in a 1-to-1 spin-orbit coupling with the Sun until the mid-1960s. The first hint that Mercury might not be in synchronous rotation about the Sun was revealed through Earth-based radar measurements. By analyzing the Doppler shift in the returned radar signals, astronomers were able to show that Mercury did not rotate fast enough to be in a 1-to-1 spin-orbit coupling with the Sun. Rather they found that Mercury's rotation rate is 58.646 days. Since Mercury orbits the Sun once every 87.969 days, the radar measurements indicated that the planet is in a 3-to-2 spin-orbit coupling with the Sun. That is, Mercury spins three times about its axis for every two orbits that it completes about the Sun. The Mercurian day, that is the time from sunrise to sunset is therefore 88 terrestrial days long.

Surface features

Mercury is a small planet. From Earth its greatest angular diameter is just 4/1000th of a degree. This angular size translates to a physical diameter of 3,030 mi (4,879 km), making Mercury about 1/3 the size of Earth, or about 1.5 times larger than the Moon.

Mariner 10 is the only spacecraft to have pho-tographed the surface of Mercury. Completing a total of three close encounters with the planet, in March and September 1974, and March 1975, the space probe was able to record details over about 50% of Mercury's crater strewn surface. The remaining half of Mercury's surface has never been photographed.

Mercury's surface is very similar to that of the Moon. There are, however, some important differences in features. Mercury has, for example, relatively fewer craters larger than 15.5-31 mi (25-50 km) in diameter.

rare occasions when Earth, Mercury, and the Sun are in perfect alignment, however, a solar transit of Mercury can take place, and a terrestrial observer will see Mer-cury move in front of, and across the Sun's disk. A tran-sit of Mercury can only occur when the planet is at infe-rior conjunction during the months of May and November. During these months Earth is near the line along which the orbit of Mercury intersects the ecliptic plane—this is the line of nodes for Mercury's orbit. Approximately a dozen solar transits of Mercury occur each century, and the final transit of this century will take place on 15 November 1999.

Mercury's rotation rate

When, in the mid-1880s, the Italian astronomer Giovanni Schiaparelli (1835-1910) attempted to con-

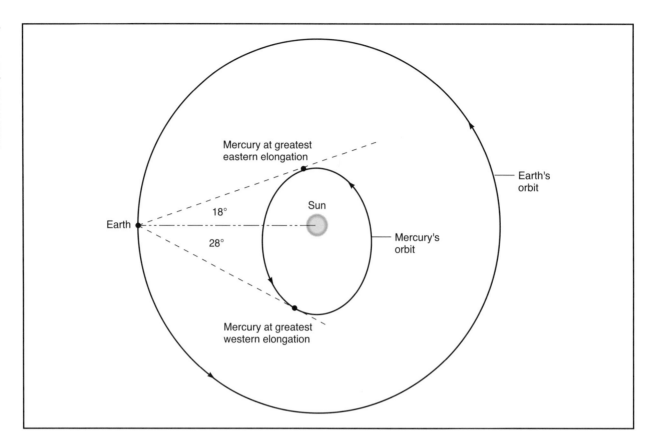

Figure 1. As seen from Earth the angle between the Sun and Mercury, when Mercury is at greatest eastern or greatest western elongation, can be as large as 28° if Mercury is near aphelion, and as small as 18° if Mercury is near perihelion.

There are no extensive highland regions on Mercury, but, unlike the Moon, it does exhibit many scalloped cliffs, or lobate scarps that can run for several hundred kilometers and be as much as 0.6 mi (1 km) high. Only one lunar-like *mare*, the so called Caloris Basin, has been discovered on Mercury. Sporting a relatively flat but wrinkled floor, and being surrounded by a ring of 1.24 mile-(2 km) high mountains, the Caloris Basin, with a diameter of about 807.5 mi (1,300 km), is the largest Mercurian feature.

The prominent scarp features recorded on Mercury by *Mariner 10* are unique to the planet. The scarps are interesting from a geological standpoint, because they run cross other surface markings, such as craters. This suggests that the scarps were formed through the shrinkage of the planets outer mantle. The rises of the observed scarp features suggests that since Mercury formed it has shrunk by about 2 mi (3 km) in radius. The shrinkage of the outer crust is caused by slow cooling of the planet.

The International Astronomical Union has established a guide to the naming of planetary features, and for Mercury the convention is that craters are named after artists, musicians, painters and authors; plains are given names corresponding to Mercury in various languages; scarps are named after famous ships of scientific discovery, and valleys are named after radio telescopes.

Polar ice

Perhaps one of the most unexpected Mercurian features to be discovered in recent times was that of water-ice at the planet's poles. The discovery of water ice on Mercury was made in 1991 by bouncing powerful radar signals off the planet's surface. The discovery of water ice on Mercury was surprising, since it was believed that the high daytime temperatures caused by the planet's proximity of the planet to the Sun would lead to the rapidly evaporation of any ices that might chance to form.

The polar regions of Mercury can be seen from Earth with powerful radars, because of the relatively large inclination (7°) that the planet's orbit presents to the ecliptic. These same polar regions, however, are never fully illuminated by the Sun, and it appears that water ice has managed to collect in the permanently-shadowed regions of many polar crater rims. It is not

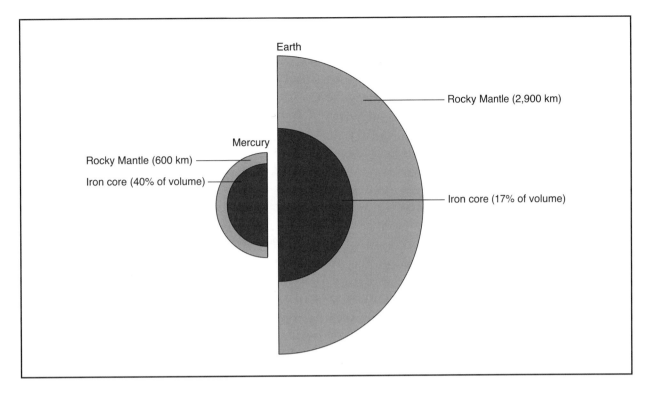

Earth

Rocky Mantle (2,900 km)

Mercury

Rocky Mantle (600 km)

Iron core (40% of volume)

Iron core (17% of volume)

Figure 2. A comparison of the internal structures of Mercury and Earth.

clear where the ice seen at Mercury's poles comes from, but it has been suggested that comet crashes may be one source.

Internal structure

Mercury has no natural satellites and consequently it is not an easy task to determine the planet's mass. By carefully recording the acceleration of the *Mariner 10* space probe during its close encounters with planet, however, NASA scientists were able to determine a Mercurian mass equivalent to 1/6,023,600 that of the Sun. This mass, of about 3.3×10^{23} kg, is some 6% that of the Earth's mass.

Some idea of Mercury's internal structure can be gained from the knowledge of its mass and radius. These two terms indicate that Mercury has a bulk density of 5,430 g/cm³. This density is only slightly smaller than that of Earth, suggesting by analogy that Mercury has a large nickel-iron alloy core, and a thin rocky mantle. The nickel-iron core probably accounts for about 40% Mercury's volume.

Mercury's relatively large nickel-iron core and thin crustal mantle suggests that the planet may have undergone a catastrophic collision during its final stages of formation. A glancing blow from a large planetesimal

may have caused most of the planet's initial mantle to be ejected into space, leaving behind a planet with a relatively large core.

Instruments carried on-board *Mariner 10* detected a weak Mercurian magnetic field. The magnetic field strength is about 1% that of Earth's. Even though Mercury's magnetic field is very weak, it was a surprise to scientists that is displayed one at all. It is presently believed that planetary magnetic fields are created by the so-called dynamo effect. It is thought that the dynamo effect should operate in those planets that have hot, and electrically conducting, liquid inner cores, that rotate reasonably quickly. Mercury is not thought to satisfy any of the conditions necessary for a planetary dynamo to operate, and consequently the observed magnetic field suggests that the standard picture of Mercury's internal structure needs revising, or that another, presently unknown, mechanism exists through which planets can generate magnetic fields.

Mercury's weak magnetic field is strong enough to force charged particles in the solar wind to flow around the planet. The cavity that consequently exists about the planet is called a magnetosphere, and its existence prevents solar wind material (mainly protons and electrons) impacting directly on the planet's surface.

Mercury's atmosphere

The mid-day surface temperature on Mercury rises to about 700K (803°F; 427°C), while the mid-nighttime temperature falls to 100K (-343°F; -173°C). This temperature variation, the largest experienced by any planet in the solar system, is due to the fact that Mercury has essentially no insulating atmosphere.

The main reason that Mercury does not have a distinctive atmosphere is that it is small and because it is close to the Sun. Mercury's small radius indicates that it has a low escape velocity, just 2.5 mi (4.2 km)/sec. *Mariner 10* did detect a very thin atmosphere of hydrogen and helium on Mercury. It is believed, however, that Mercury's wispy atmosphere is composed of atoms that have been temporarily captured from the solar wind. Ground-based observations have found that a sodium and potassium atmosphere exists on the daylight side of Mercury. These atoms are probably released through the interaction of ultraviolet radiation with surface rocks.

See also Doppler effect; Planet; Solar system.

Further Reading:

Moore, Patrick. *The Guinness Book of Astronomy.* Enfield, England: Guinness Books, 1988.

Strom, Robert. "Mercury: The Forgotten Planet." *Sky and Telescope* (September 1990): 256-60.

———. *Mercury: The Elusive Planet.* Washington, D.C.: Smithsonian Institution Press, 1987.

Vilas, Faith, Clark R. Chapman, and M. S. Matthews, eds. *Mercury.* Tucson: University of Arizona Press, 1988.

Martin Beech

Mergansers see **Ducks**

Mesons see **Subatomic particles**

Mesoscopic systems

The prefix "meso" means "in between" or "intermediate." Mesoscopic systems are those that are larger than atoms and yet very much smaller than the large-scale everyday objects that we can see and touch. They are a thousand to a hundred thousand times smaller than the diameter of a human hair and they range in size from several hundred nanometers or billionths of a meter. That is why materials composed of mesoscopic parts are also known as nanostructures and the technology based on these systems is referred to as nanotechnology. Since one nanometer is less than the width of ten atoms in a row, mesoscopic systems are made up of less than a thousand atoms. Mesoscopic or nanoscale systems behave very differently from large-scale objects and they often have unusual physical and chemical properties. This makes them extremely interesting to scientists and engineers who hope that, by manipulating systems on the nanoscale, they can make computers, sensors and other devices that have exactly the properties they want.

There are many examples of mesoscopic systems in nature. The molecules in our bodies that break down the foods in our stomachs and intestines, and the molecules that carry oxygen from the lungs to other parts of the body, are nothing but nanoscale machines. Artificial nanostructures, however, have been studied and fabricated only in the last few decades. Multilayered nanostructures, made up of thin mesoscopic layers of different materials, have been investigated since the 1970s and have been used in devices such as high-efficiency lasers and light-emitting diodes. More recently, re-

---

KEY TERMS

....

Astronomical Unit—The average distance between the Sun and Earth. One astronomical unit, symbol AU, is equivalent to 92.9 million mi (149.6 million km).

Doppler effect—the apparent change in the wavelength of a signal due to the relative motion between the source and observer.

Dynamo effect—A model for the generation of planetary magnetic fields: The circulation of hot, conducting fluids within a planet's liquid core leads to the generation of a magnetic field.

Escape velocity—The speed that an object must have in order to escape the gravitational pull of another body.

Lobate scarp—A long, near vertical was of rock running across a flat plain.

Mantle—The outer layers of a planets interior-core, usually composed of silicate rock.

Planetesimals—Asteroid-sized bodies that accumulated to form protoplanets.

Solar wind—A stream of charged and neutral particles that emanates from the Sun and moves into the solar system.

Synchronous rotation—Any object that spins on its axis at the same rate that it moves along in its orbit is said to be in synchronous rotation. Also called to 1-to-1 spin-orbit coupling.

---

searchers have begun studying and synthesizing atom clusters which are balls and tubes made up of ten to a thousand atoms. These clusters are sometimes put together to create new materials with novel properties. The properties depend on the size of the cluster. Copper, assembled from nanoscale clusters five to seven nanometers in diameter, is five times harder than ordinary copper. Brittle ceramics become ductile when they are synthesized from clusters with sizes less than fifteen nanometers. Cadmium selenide clusters of different sizes appear to have different colors.

Mesoscopic systems, particularly multilayered materials, are created and studied by a variety of well-established methods. One way of producing thin layers is to deposit atoms, from a chemical vapor or a beam of molecules, on to a base of some other material in an airless evacuated chamber. This is somewhat like spraying a thin layer of paint on a wall. Clusters of atoms are produced by chemical methods. An important tool in making and studying mesoscopic systems is the scanning tunneling microscope or STM. The STM creates an image of a surface at the atomic level by measuring the current which flows as the needle of the STM touches each atom. The STM can actually pick up individual atoms and move them around. In 1990, a group of researchers created a stir by writing "IBM" with thirty five precisely placed Xenon atoms on the surface of a Nickel crystal.

The study of mesoscopic systems provides scientists with a picture of how the behavior of a material changes as it grows from a few atoms to large visible and tangible objects. This information will be useful in fabricating minuscule machines when nanotechnology finally becomes a reality in the coming decades. The first steps are already being taken. Researchers have used the STM to create a 'switch', that could be used in computers, with a single atom which moves back and forth rapidly between two positions. Biologists are trying to manipulate large organic molecules such as proteins which could be used in the future for tasks such as the repair of damaged organs. Including wide-ranging applications in the computer industry, the possibilities of nanotechnology seem endless. Independent researcher Eric Drexler predicts that sometime in the future we may have minute machines that will repair clogged arteries, libraries that will fit into our pockets, and clothing that will change shape, color, and texture according to our needs.

See also Nanotechnology.

Further Reading:

Drexler, K. Eric, Chris Peterson, and Gayle Pergamit. *Unbounding the Future.* New York: William Morrow and Company, 1991.

KEY TERMS

· ·

Nanometer—A billionth of a meter.

Nanostructures—Materials made up of layers or clusters that are several to several hundred nanometers in size.

Nanotechnology—Technology of the future that will use components made up of less than a thousand atoms.

Scanning tunneling microscope (STM)—A device used to create images of surfaces at the atomic level.

Langreth, Robert. "Why Scientists are Thinking Small." *Popular Science* (April 1993): 71.

Langreth, Robert. "Molecular Marvels." *Popular Science* (May 1993): 91

Siegel, Richard W. "Exploring Mesoscopia: The Bold New World of Nanostructures." *Physics Today* (October 1993): 64.

Sreela Datta

Mesozoa

The phylum Mesozoa comprises a small group of parasitic animals which are related to flatworms—a widely dispersed group of free-living and parasitic organisms. Some 50 species have been identified in this phylum to date, all of which are exclusively marine in their life style. Relatively few detailed studies have been conducted on the behaviour and life cycles of these species and their taxonomic affiliations are also uncertain.

Mesozoans are all tiny organisms which have a very simple structure: the body wall consists of a thin outer membrane that is dotted with large numbers of small cilia. When they beat, they provide a means of locomotion through the host animal's body fluids. The vast bulk of the mesozoan body consists of egg and sperm cells. There are no specialized feeding organs, and nutrients and waste products pass directly across the cell wall.

Mesozoans are parasites of a wide range of marine invertebrates, including flatworms, roundworms, molluscs, and echinoderms. Two main groupings have been recognized: the order Orthonectida, which are free-living within their hosts, and the Dicyemida, which have specialized cells on the body wall that serve to attach them to the walls of the kidneys in species such as octopus and squid.

In most species, fertilized eggs are released inside the host organism and may either remain in the host system or pass out of the body with waste materials. The precise mechanisms of host detection and determination are not known. As free-swimming larvae, some juvenile mesozoans may enter other species such as fish or crustaceans prior to being ingested by their final hosts.

See also Parasites.

Metabolic disorders

Metabolic disorders are diseases caused by errors in metabolism. The term "metabolism" refers to the sum of the chemical reactions in the body. Metabolic problems can be traced to numerous metabolic pathways found in cells throughout the body.

Metabolic reactions are categorized into two types, anabolic and catabolic. Anabolic reactions construct complex molecules from simple molecules, usually while using up energy that becomes stored in chemical bonds. Catabolic reactions break down complex molecules into multiple simple molecules, usually while releasing energy.

Most metabolic pathways have several chemical steps each of which is catalyzed by a specific enzyme. Enzymes facilitate a chemical reaction by lowering the amount of energy required to initiate the reaction. In this function enzymes can be compared to a bridge joining two sides of a river. If the bridge was not present, someone would have to walk farther along the shore to get to a crossing point; the bridge decreases the amount of time and energy needed to get to the other side. Enzymes are so important to normal metabolic functions that the absence of an enzyme can prolong a reaction or prevent it from occurring. The molecules that are converted by an enzyme are called substrates. When an enzymatic step in a metabolic pathway causes the buildup of these substrates, then the accumulated molecules can be toxic and lead to a metabolic disorder. Some metabolic disorders are barely detectable, whereas others are life-threatening.

Most metabolic disorders are caused by genetic mutations present as inborn errors of metabolism. But some metabolic disorders are caused by dysfunctions of the endocrine system.

Inborn metabolic disorders

Although most metabolic disorders are also genetic disorders, not all genetic disorders are metabolic. About 1 in 1,000 babies is born with a genetically based inborn error of metabolism (IEM). There are about 200 known IEMs that range in their severity of mental and physical symptoms. Most symptoms are apparent at or soon after birth. The more severe IEM's may cause failure to thrive or develop properly, abnormally small or large body parts, bone deformities, or general lethargy. Most hereditary metabolic disorders are inherited in a recessive fashion-meaning that a copy of the defective gene was inherited from both parents. For this reason, individual IEMs tend to be rare, most occurring at a frequency of about 1 in every 10,000 births. Some of the best understood IEMs include alkaptonuria, phenylketonuria (PKU), thalassemias, porphyrias, Tay-Sachs disease, Hurler's syndrome, Gaucher's disease, abetalipoproteinemia, and galactosemia.

Alkaptonuria was the first condition known to be caused by a metabolic enzyme deficiency. In 1902, Sir Archibald Garrod studied newborns whose urine turned black shortly after urination. The black color was due to oxidation in the urine of homogenistic acid, which accumulates because of a deficiency of the enzyme homogentisate dioxygenase. Fortunately, the urine discoloration is not detrimental to people with this IEM; however, alkaptonurics do tend to develop arthritis later in life.

PKU is a serious IEM caused by a liver enzyme deficiency. In PKU, phenylalanine hydroxylase, the enzyme that converts phenylalanine to tyrosine, is defective. Several different mutations are responsible for altering or reducing the activity of the phenylalanine hydroxylase gene. Because PKU patients cannot make the pigment melanin, 90% of PKU patients are blond-haired with blue eyes. Other clinical features include seizures, a mousy body odor, and eczema. Left untreated, accumulated phenylalanine can cause severe mental retardation. If detected early enough, however, PKU can be controlled by restricting the intake of foods rich in phenylalanine, such as meat and milk. For this reason, are routinely screened for this disorder. The benefits of early detection of PKU to prevent mental retardation are enormous in terms of both health and cost.

Thalassemias are a group of metabolic disorders that affect hemoglobin synthesis. They can be caused by mutations in several locations in either the alpha or beta hemoglobin genes. The most severe thalassemia,

Cooley's anemia, is a recessively transmitted disorder caused by the mutant beta hemoglobin gene. These children appear normal at birth, but symptoms of vomiting, paling complexion, poor sleeping, and anorexia appear from 3-18 months of age. Death usually occurs before age eight. Children who inherit a mutated alpha hemoglobin gene from both parents are either stillborn or die shortly after birth.

Porphyrias are characterized by the dysfunctional metabolism of various pigments in several tissues particularly the liver and bone marrow cells. Afflicted individuals are highly sensitive to light and are usually quite mentally disturbed. Avoiding sunlight can reduce the symptoms. Unlike most other IEM's, porphyrias are dominantly inherited traits. King George III of England suffered from porphyria although, at the time, he was diagnosed as having manic depression by some and madness by others. This disorder has been well documented in the descendants of Mary Queen of Scots. Because of its link to the royal houses of Stuart, Hanover, and Prussia, it has been called the "Royal Malady."

Other IEMs include Tay-Sachs disease, Hurler's syndrome, and Gaucher's disease. Tay-Sachs is a disease that occurs in one out of about 3,600 pregnancies in Jews of Eastern European descent. Although the disease is usually not detectable until about six months after birth, it is usually apparent by one year of age. Tay-Sachs is triggered by abnormal brain chemistry due to a deficiency of hexosaminidase A, which is required for the catabolism of a class of fats, the sphingolipids. These lipids accumulate in the brain and cause severe problems including blindness, deafness, apathy, and death usually before age of five years. Hurler's syndrome is also usually detected between 6-12 months of age and is caused by a defect in or loss of the enzyme alpha L-iduronidase. Without this enzyme, Hurler's patients accumulate high levels of mucopolysaccharides. Hurler's victims have skeletal abnormalities including short stature, enlarged tongue and liver, distended stomachs, blindness and deafness, and cardiac abnormalities. Children with Hurler's usually die before age 10. Gaucher's disease is a rare disorder that also involves fat metabolism and leads to enlargement of the spleen and liver. Childhood mortality is high for those afflicted with Gaucher's but people who survive childhood can live many years into adulthood. The Gaucher defective gene is carried by about one in 600 Jews of Eastern European descent.

Abetalipoproteinemia is a rare IEM which also involves lipid dysfunction. Also called Bassen-Kornzweig syndrome, it is characterized by extremely low cholesterol due to deficient or absent beta lipoproteins, which are an important component of the cholesterol molecular complex. Symptoms include growth retardation, neurological dysfunction, retinal pigment degeneration, and upper intestinal malabsorption.

Galactosemia is a metabolic disorder marked by the inability to metabolize lactose, the primary sugar in milk. At an early evolutionary stage, most humans lost the ability to digest large quantities of milk after about age six. However, adults in Northern European populations developed the ability to digest milk sugar because of its prevalence in their diets. In adulthood people of other ancestries are more susceptible to this condition, sometimes called lactose intolerance. If present and untreated in infancy, galactosemia can lead to mental retardation.

Endocrine metabolic disorders

Endocrine metabolic disorders (EMDs) are caused by the overproduction or underproduction of a specific hormone. While most EMDs are the result of an imbalance without a genetic root, congenital adrenal hyperplasia (CAH) is genetically based. CAH is a malfunction of steroid hormone synthesis in the adrenals caused by a defective enzyme, 21 hydroxylase. The enzyme triggers an overproduction of testosterone which can masculinize females. CAH can be stabilized by cortisol treatment, allowing patients to have normal life spans. Some of the most studied EMDs include Cushing's syndrome, diabetes mellitus, hypothydroidism, and hyperthyrodism.

Cushing's syndrome is caused by the hypersecretion of cortisol by cells in the adrenal cortex. Hypersecretion can be due to overstimulation of cortisol-releasing mechanisms by excess ACTH, a pituitary hormone. Cushing's can result from pituitary or adrenal tumors. It is further characterized by obesity, a rounded face, muscle weakness, a tendency to bruise easily, and numerous other complications.

Diabetes mellitus (DM) is a metabolic carbohydrate disorder that results from either insufficient insulin (type 1 DM) or the body's inability to recognize available insulin (type 2 DM). DM is a multifactorially inherited disorder; this means that although people can inherit a propensity toward this condition, environment and diet can trigger onset of the actual disease. People who suffer from DM experience abnormally high blood glucose levels, excessive thirst and urine output, weight loss, and fatigue. DM can lead to lipid metabolism disorders as well. Ironically, one of the triggering symptoms of DM is obesity. Type 1 DM, called insulin-dependent diabetes, because it requires routine insulin injections, usually appears before age 35. Type 2 DM, called non-insulin dependent diabetes because it can be regulated by diet, weight control, and oral medication, usually does not appear until after age 40 years. Some women develop gestational diabetes, a temporary form of DM that appears during pregnancy and requires special prenatal care. Physicians routinely check the glucose levels of pregnant women at around 26 gestational weeks. Gestational diabetes usually disappears after delivery.

Hypothyrodism and hyperthyroidism can both be due to a number of causes, one of which is metabolic dysfunction. Hypothyroidism is caused by undersecretion, of thyroid hormones. In one form of childhood hypothyroidism, children born with abnormally small thyroids produce insufficient levels of the thyroid hormones T3 and T4, which are important for metabolically directed bone development. If detected in the first 6 months of life, this disorder can be treated with synthetic thyroid hormones such that its effects can be avoided. The most severe early onset hypothyroidisms are characterized by Cretinism, a type of dwarfism, and mental retardation. Adult hypothyroidism is called myxedema. Myxedema symptoms include slowed speech, yellowed skin, and generally slowed body functions. Myxedema can also be treated with synthetic T4, but if left untreated, can lead to coma.

Hyperthyroidism, caused by oversecretion of thyroid hormones, is marked by an overall rapid metabolism including a rapid pulse, high body temperature, and agitation. The most common form of hyperthyroidism in children and adults is Grave's disease. Grave's disease, which clinically distinguished by the appearance of an enlarged thyroid, or goiter, that grows at the front of the neck. Grave's disease is thought to be a malfunction of the immunological functions involving the thyroid.

Screening and future treatment

While the outlook for curing most metabolic disorders appears bleak, two powerful tools are available, genetic screening and genetic engineering. Most genetic metabolic disorders can be detected through prenatal testing, a service that helps people determine the likelihood of conceiving a child affected by a particular disorder. People who test positive as carriers have one copy of the recessively inherited gene linked to the disorder.

Genetic therapy is already being used to treat an enzyme deficiency known as adenosine deaminase deficiency (ADA). Children with ADA have severe immune system problems and considerably shortened life expectancies. Treatment of ADA involves gene replacement in which a normal copy of the ADA gene is replaced in cells that are then injected into the patient. Gene replacement has proven effective in helping patients lead normal lives. Research on gene therapy for other genetic disorders is ongoing.

KEY TERMS

Anabolism—The construction of complex molecules from simpler molecules by a metabolic process that usually requires energy input.

Catabolism—The break down of complex molecules into simpler molecules by a metabolic process that usually releases energy stored in the chemical bonds of the complex molecules.

Further Reading:

Modell, B., and M. Modell. *Towards a Healthy Baby: Congenital Disorders and the New Genetics in Primary Care.* New York: Oxford University Press, 1992.

Rhoads, R., and R. Pflanzer, eds. *Physiology,* 2nd ed. New York: Saunders College Publishing, 1992.

Louise Dickerson

Metabolism

Metabolism refers to the highly integrated network of chemical reactions by which living cells grow and sustain themselves. This network is composed of two major types of pathways: anabolism and catabolism. Anabolism uses energy stored in the form of adenosine triphosphate (ATP) to build larger molecules from smaller molecules. Catabolic reactions degrade larger molecules in order to produce ATP and raw materials for anabolic reactions.

Together, these two general metabolic networks have three major functions: (1) to extract energy from nutrients or solar energy; (2) to synthesize the building blocks that make up the large molecules of life: proteins, fats, carbohydrates, nucleic acids, and combinations of these substances; and (3) to synthesize and degrade molecules required for special functions in the cell.

These reactions are controlled by enzymes, protein catalysts that increase the speed of chemical reactions in

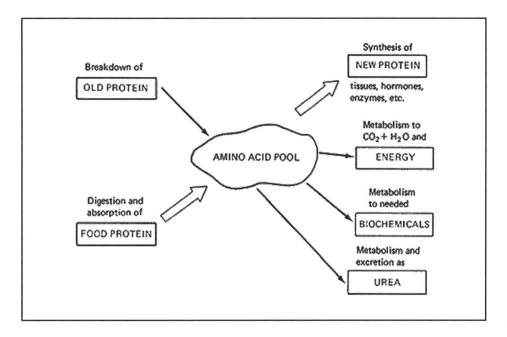

The amino acid pool.

the cell without themselves being changed. Each enzyme catalyzes a specific chemical reaction by acting on a specific substrate, or raw material. Each reaction is just one of a in a sequence of catalytic steps known as metabolic pathways. These sequences may be composed of up to 20 enzymes, each one creating a product that becomes the substrate—or raw material—for the subsequent enzyme. Often, an additional molecule called a coenzyme, is required for the enzyme to function. For example, some coenzymes accept an electron that is released from the substrate during the enzymatic reaction. Most of the water-soluble vitamins of the B complex serve as coenzymes; riboflavin (Vitamin B_2) for example, is a precursor of the coenzyme flavine adenine dinucleotide, while pantothenate is a component of coenzyme A, an important intermediate metabolite.

The series of products created by the sequential enzymatic steps of anabolism or catabolism are called metabolic intermediates, or metabolites. Each step represents a small change in the molecule, usually the removal, transfer, or addition of a specific atom, molecule or group of atoms that serves as a functional group, such as the amino groups ($-NH_2$) of proteins.

Most such metabolic pathways are linear, that is, they begin with a specific substrate and end with a specific product. However, some pathways, such as the Krebs cycle, are cyclic. Often, metabolic pathways also have branches that feed into or out of them. The specific sequences of intermediates in the pathways of cell metabolism are called intermediary metabolism.

Among the many hundreds of chemical reactions there are only a few that are central to the activity of the cell, and these pathways are identical in most forms of life.

All reactions of metabolism, however, are part of the overall goal of the organism to maintain its internal orderliness, whether that organism is a single celled protozoan or a human. Organisms maintain this orderliness by removing energy from nutrients or sunlight and returning to their environment an equal amount of energy in a less useful form, mostly heat. This heat becomes dissipated throughout the rest of the organism's environment.

According to the first law of thermodynamics, in any physical or chemical change, the total amount of energy in the universe remains constant, that is, energy cannot be created or destroyed. Thus, when the energy stored in nutrient molecules is released and captured in the form of ATP, some energy is lost as heat. But the total amount of energy is unchanged.

The second law of thermodynamics states that physical and chemical changes proceed in such a direction that useful energy undergoes irreversible degradation into a randomized form—entropy. The dissipation of energy during metabolism represents an increase in the randomness, or disorder, of the organism's environment. Because this disorder is irreversible, it provides the driving force and direction to all metabolic enzymatic reactions.

Even in the simplest cells, such as bacteria, there are at least a thousand such reactions. Regardless of the number, all cellular reactions can be classified as one of two types of metabolism: anabolism and catabolism. These reactions, while opposite in nature, are linked through the common bond of energy. Anabolism, or biosynthesis, is the synthetic phase of metabolism during which small building block molecules, or precursors, are built into large molecular components of cells, such as carbohydrates and proteins.

Catabolic reactions are used to capture and save energy from nutrients, as well as to degrade larger molecules into smaller, molecular raw materials for reuse by the cell. The energy is stored in the form of energy-rich ATP, which powers the reactions of anabolism. The useful energy of ATP is stored in the form of a high-energy bond between the second and third phosphate groups of ATP. The cell makes ATP by adding a phosphate group to the molecule adenosine diphosphate (ADP). Therefore, ATP is the major chemical link between the energy-yielding reactions of catabolism, and the energy-requiring reactions of anabolism.

In some cases, energy is also conserved as energy-rich hydrogen atoms in the coenzyme nicotinamide adenine dinucleotide phosphate in the reduced form of NADPH. The NADPH can then be used as a source of high-energy hydrogen atoms during certain biosynthetic reactions of anabolism.

In addition to the obvious difference in the direction of their metabolic goals, anabolism and catabolism differ in other significant ways. For example, the various degradative pathways of catabolism are convergent. That is, many hundreds of different proteins, polysaccharides and lipids are broken down into relatively few catabolic end products. The hundreds of anabolic pathways, however, are divergent. That is, the cell uses relatively few biosynthetic precursor molecules to synthesize a vast number of different proteins, polysaccharides and lipids.

The opposing pathways of anabolism and catabolism may also use different reaction intermediates or different enzymatic reactions in some of the steps. For example, there are 11 enzymatic steps in the breakdown of glucose into pyruvic acid in the liver. But the liver uses only nine of those same steps in the synthesis of glucose, replacing the other two steps with a different set of enzyme-catalyzed reactions. This occurs because the pathway to degradation of glucose releases energy, while the anabolic process of glucose synthesis requires energy. The two different reactions of anabolism are required to overcome the energy barrier that would otherwise prevent the synthesis of glucose.

Another reason for having slightly different pathways is that the corresponding anabolic and catabolic routes must be independently regulated. Otherwise, if the two phases of metabolism shared the exact pathway (only in reverse) a slowdown in the anabolic pathway would slow catabolism, and vice versa.

In addition to regulating the direction of metabolic pathways, cells, especially those in multicellular organisms, also exert control at three different levels: allosteric enzymes, hormones, and enzyme concentration.

Allosteric enzymes in metabolic pathways change their activity in response to molecules that either stimulate or inhibit their catalytic activity. While the end product of an enzyme cascade is used up, the cascade continues to synthesize that product. The result is a steady-state condition in which the product is used up as it is produced and there is no significant accumulation of product. However, when the product accumulates above the steady-state level for any reason, that is, in excess of the cell's needs, the end product acts as an inhibitor of the first enzyme of the sequence. This is called allosteric inhibition, and is a type of feedback inhibition.

A classic example of allosteric inhibition is the case of the enzymatic conversion of L-threonine into L-isoleucine by bacteria. The first of five enzymes, threonine dehydratase is inhibited by the end product, isoleucine. This inhibition is very specific, and is accomplished only by isoleucine, which binds to a site on the enzyme molecule called the regulatory, or allosteric, site. This site is different from the active site of the enzyme, which is the site of the catalytic action of the enzyme on the substrate, or molecule being acted on by the enzyme.

Moreover, some allosteric enzymes may be stimulated by modulator molecules. These molecules are not the end product of a series of reactions, but rather may be the substrate molecule itself. These enzymes have two or more substrate binding sites, which serve a dual function as both catalytic sites and regulatory sites. Such allosteric enzymes respond to excessive concentrations of substrates that must be removed. Furthermore, some enzymes have two or more modulators that may be opposite in effect and have their own specific allosteric site. When occupied, one site may speed up the catalytic reaction, while the other may slow it down. ADP and AMP (adenosine monophosphate) stimulate certain metabolic pathway enzymes, for example, while ATP inhibits the same allosteric enzymes.

The activity of allosteric enzymes in one pathway may also be modulated by intermediate or final products from other pathways. Such cross-reaction is an important way in which the rates of different enzyme systems can be coordinate with each other.

Hormone control of metabolism is regulated by chemical messengers secreted into the blood by different endocrine glands. These messengers, called hormones, travel to other tissues or organs, where they may stimulate or inhibit specific metabolic pathways.

A classic example of hormonal control of metabolism is the hormone adrenaline, which is secreted by the medulla of the adrenal gland and carried by the blood to the liver. In the liver adrenaline stimulates the breakdown of glycogen to glucose, increasing the blood sugar level. In the skeletal muscles, adrenaline stimulates the breakdown of glycogen to lactate ATP.

Adrenaline exerts its effect by binding to a receptor site on the cell surfaces of liver and muscle cells, where it initiates a series of signals that ultimately causes an inactive form of the enzyme glycogen phosphorylase to become active. This enzyme is the first in a sequence that leads to the breakdown of glycogen to glucose and other products.

Finally, the concentration of the enzymes themselves exert a profound influence on the rate of metabolic activity. For example, the ability of the liver to turn enzymes on and off—a process called enzyme induction—assures that adequate amounts of needed enzymes are available, while inhibiting the cell from wasting its energy and other resources on making enzymes that are not needed.

For example, in the presence of a high-carbohydrate, low-protein diet, the liver enzymes that degrade amino acids are present in low concentrations. In the presence of a high-protein diet, however, the liver produces increased amounts of enzymes needed for degrading these molecules.

The basis of both anabolic and catabolic pathways is the reactions of reduction and oxidation. Oxidation refers to the combination of an atom or molecule with oxygen, or the loss from it of hydrogen or of one or more electrons. Reduction, the opposite of oxidation, is the gain of one or more electrons by an atom or molecule. The nature of these reactions requires them to occur together; i.e., oxidation always occurs in conjunction with reduction. The term "redox" refers to this coupling of reduction and oxidation.

Redox reactions form the basis of metabolism and are the basis of oxidative phosphorylation, the process by which electrons from organic substances such as glucose are transferred from organic compounds such as glucose to electron carriers (usually coenzymes), and

then are passed through a series of different electron carriers to molecules of oxygen molecules. The transfer of electrons in oxidative phosphorylation occurs along the electron transport chain. During this process, called aerobic respiration, energy is released, some of which is used to make ATP from ADP. The major electron carriers are the coenzymes nicotinamide adenine dinucleotide (NADH) or flavin adenine dinucleotide ($FADH_2$). Oxidative phosphorylation is the major source of ATP in aerobic organisms, from bacteria to humans.

Some anaerobic bacteria, however, also carry out respiration, but use other inorganic molecules, such as nitrate (NO_3^-) or sulfate (SO_4^{2-}) ions as the final electron acceptors. In this form of respiration, called anaerobic respiration, nitrate is reduced to nitrite ion (NO_2^-), nitrous oxide (N_2O) or nitrogen gas (N_2), and sulfate is reduced to form hydrogen sulfide (H_2S).

Much of the metabolic activity of cells consists largely of central metabolic pathways that transform large amounts of proteins, fats and carbohydrates. Foremost among these pathways are glycolysis, which can occur in either aerobic or anaerobic conditions, and the Krebs cycle, which is coupled to the electron transport chain, which accepts electrons removed from reduced coenzymes of glycolysis and the Krebs cycle. The final electron acceptor of the chain is usually oxygen, but some bacteria use specific, oxidized ions as the final acceptor in anaerobic conditions.

As vital as these reactions are, there are other metabolic pathways in which the flow of substrates and products is much smaller, yet the products quite important. These pathways constitute secondary metabolism, which produces specialized molecules needed by the cell or by tissues or organs in small quantities. Such molecules may be coenzymes, hormones, nucleotides, toxins, or antibiotics.

The process of extracting energy by the central metabolic pathways that break down fats, polysaccharides and proteins, and conserving it as ATP, occurs in three stages in aerobic organisms. In anaerobic organisms, only one stage is present. In each case, the first step is glycolysis.

Glycolysis is a ubiquitous central pathway of glucose metabolism among living things, from bacteria to plants and humans. The glycolytic series of reactions converts glucose into the molecule pyruvate, with the production of ATP. This pathway is controlled by both the concentration of substrates entering glycolysis as well as by feedback inhibition of the pathway's allosteric enzymes.

Glucose, a hexose (6-carbon) sugar, enters the pathway through phosphorylation of the number six carbon by the enzyme hexokinase. In this reaction, ATP relinquishes one of its phosphates, becoming ADP, while glucose is converted to glucose-6-phosphate. When the need for further oxidation of glucose-6-phosphate by the cell decreases, the concentration of this metabolite increases, as serves as a feedback inhibitor of the allosteric enzyme hexokinase. In the liver, however, glucose-6-phosphate is converted to glycogen, a storage form of glucose. Thus a buildup of glucose-6-phosphate is normal for liver, and feedback inhibition would interfere with this vital pathway. However, to produce glucose-6-phosphate, the liver uses the enzyme glucokinase, which is not inhibited by an increase in the concentration of glucose-6-phosphate.

In the liver and muscle cells, another enzyme, glycogen phosphorylase, breaks down glycogen into glucose molecules, which then enter glycolysis.

Two other allosteric enzyme regulatory reactions also help to regulate glycolysis: the conversion of fructose 6-phosphate to fructose 1,6-diphosphate by phosphofructokinase and the conversion of phosphoenolpyruvate to pyruvate by pyruvate kinase.

The first stage of glycolysis prepares the glucose molecule for the second stage, during which energy is conserved in the form of ATP. As part of the preparatory state, however, two ATP molecules are consumed.

At the fourth step of glycolysis, the doubly phosphorylated molecule (fructose 1,6-diphosphate) is cleaved into two 3-carbon molecules, dihyroxyacetone phosphate and glyceraldehyde 3-phosphate. These 3-carbon molecules are readily converted from one to another, however it is only glyceraldehyde 3-phosphate that undergoes five further changes during the energy conserving stage. In the first step of this second stage, a molecule of the coenzyme NAD^+ is reduced to NADH. During oxidative phosphorylation, the NADH will be oxidized, giving up its electrons to the electron transport system.

At step 7 and 10 of glycolysis, ADP is phosphorylated to ATP, using phosphate groups added to the original 6-carbon molecule in the preparatory stage. Since this phosphorylation of ADP occurs by enzymatic removal of a phosphate group from each of two substrates of glycolysis, this process is called substrate level phosphorylation of ADP. It differs markedly from the phosphorylation of ADP that occurs in the more complex oxidative phosphorylation processes in the electron transport chain. Since two 3-carbon molecules derived from the original 6-carbon hexose undergo this process, two molecules of ATP are formed from glucose during this stage, for a net overall gain of two ATP (two ATP having been used in the preparatory stage).

Aerobic organisms use glycolysis as the first stage in the complete degradation of glucose to carbon dioxide and water. During this process, the pyruvate formed by glycolysis is oxidized to acetyl-Coenzyme A (Acetyl CoA), with the loss of its carboxyl group as carbon dioxide.

The fate of pyruvate formed by glycolysis differs among species, and within the same species depending on the level of oxygen available for further oxidation of the products of glycolysis.

Under aerobic conditions, or in the case of bacteria using a non-oxygen final electron acceptor, acetyl-CoA, enters the Krebs cycle by combining with citric acid. The Krebs cycle continues the oxidation process, extracting electrons as it does so. These electrons are carried by coenzymes (NADH and FADH) to the electron transport chain, where the final reactions of oxidation produce ATP.

During these reactions, the acetyl group is oxidized completely to carbon dioxide and water by the citric acid cycle. This final oxidative degradation requires oxygen as the final electron acceptor in the electron transport chain.

Organisms that lack the enzyme systems necessary for oxidative phosphorylation also use glycolysis to produce pyruvate and a small amount of ATP. But pyruvate is then converted into lactate, ethanol or other organic alcohols or acids. This process is called fermentation, and does not produce more ATP. The NADH produced during the energy-conserving stage of fermentation is used during the synthesis of other molecules.

Thus, glycolysis is the major central pathway of glucose catabolism in virtually all organisms.

While the main function of glycolysis is to produce ATP, there are minor catabolic pathways that produce specialized products for cells. One, the pentose phosphate pathway produces NADPH and the sugar ribose 5-phosphate. NADPH is used to reduce substrates in the synthesis of fatty acids, and ribose 5-phosphate is used in the synthesis of nucleic acids.

Another secondary pathway for glucose in animal tissues produces D-glucuronate, which is important in detoxifying and excreting foreign organic compounds and in synthesizing vitamin C.

Most of the energy conservation achieved by the oxidative phosphorylation of glucose occurs during the Krebs cycle. Pyruvate is first converted to acetyl CoA, in an enzymatic step the converts one of its carbons into carbon dioxide, and NAD^+ is reduced to NADH. Acetyl CoA enters the 8-step Krebs cycle by combining with the 4-carbon oxaloacetic acid to form the 6-carbon citric acid. During the next 7 steps, three molecules of NAD^+ and one molecule of FAD^+ are reduced, one ATP is formed by substrate level phosphorylation, and two carbons are oxidized to CO_2.

The reduced coenzymes produced during conversion of pyruvic acid to acetyl CoA and the Krebs cycle are oxidized along the electron transport chain. As the electrons released by the coenzymes pass through the stepwise chain of redox reactions, there is a stepwise release of energy that is ultimately used to phosphorylate molecules of ADP to ATP. The energy is converted into a gradient of protons established across the membrane of the bacterial cell or of the organelle of the eucaryotic cells. The energy of the proton flow back into the cell or organelle is used by the enzyme ATP synthetase to phosphorylate ADP molecules.

$FADH_2$ releases its electrons at a lower level along the chain than does NADH. The electrons of the former coenzyme thus pass along fewer electron acceptors than NADH, and this difference is reflected in the number of ATP molecules produced by the sequential transfer of each coenzymes electrons along the chain. The oxidation of each NADH produces three ATP, while the oxidation of $FADH_2$ produces two.

The total number of ATP produced by glycolysis and metabolism is 38, which includes a net of two from glycolysis (substrate level phosphorylation), 30 from the oxidation of 10 NADH molecules, four from oxidation of two $FADH_2$ molecules, and two from substrate level phosphorylation in the Krebs cycle.

In addition to their role in the catabolism of glucose, glycolysis and the Krebs cycle also participate in the breakdown of proteins and fats. Proteins are initially degraded into constituent amino acids, which may be converted to pyruvic acid or acetyl CoA before being passed into the Krebs cycle; or they may enter the Krebs cycle directly after being converted into one of the metabolites of this metabolic pathway.

Lipids are first hydrolyzed into glycerol and fatty acids, glycerol being converted to the glyceraldehyde 3-phosphate metabolite of glycolysis, while fatty acids are degraded to acetyl CoA, which then enters the Krebs cycle.

Although metabolic pathways in both single-celled and multicellular organisms have much in common, especially in the case of certain central metabolic pathways, they may occur in different locations.

In the simplest organisms, the prokaryotes, metabolic pathways are not contained in compartments separated by internal membranes. Rather, glycolysis takes place in the cytosol, while the electron transport chain and lipid synthesis occurs in the cell membrane. Proteins are made on ribosomes in the cytosol.

In eucaryotic cells, glycolysis, gluconeogenesis and fatty acid synthesis takes place in the cytosol, while the Krebs cycle is isolated within mitochondria; glycogen is made in glycogen granules, lipid is synthesized in the endoplasmic reticulum and lysosomes carry on a variety of hydrolytic activities. As in procaryotic cells, ribosomes in the cytosol are the site of protein synthesis.

The metabolic pathways discussed to this point oxidize organic matter to produce ATP. These organic compounds are made by plants and some microorganisms by photosynthesis, which takes place in organelles called chloroplasts. Using this process, these organisms synthesize organic compounds by converting the energy of sunlight into chemical energy, which is then used to convert CO_2 from the atmosphere to more reduced carbon compounds, particularly sugars.

Further Reading:

Alberts, Bruce, et al. *Molecular Biology of The Cell.* 2nd ed. New York: Garland Publishing, 1989.

Tortora, Gerard J., and Sandra R. Grabowski. *Principles of Anatomy and Physiology.* 7th ed. New York: Harper-Collins College Publishers, 1993.

Marc Kusinitz

Metal

A material is called a metal based on the way it reacts to other elements. Metallic elements characteristically form positive ions when their compounds are in solution. Their oxides form hydroxides rather than acids with water. Nearly three-fourths of the elements in each group of the periodic table are metals except for the Group 17 (halogen) and Group 18 (noble gas) elements. Most metals form crystalline solids, and most are good conductors of electricity; most have rather high chemical reactivities. Many metals are quite hard, with high physical strength. When polished, metals tend to be good reflectors of light.

Metals easily form alloys with other metals. The presence of even a small amount of another element in a metal severely affects its properties, as in the case of carbon in iron. Mercury, cesium, and gallium exist as liquids at room temperature.

The behavior of metals as atoms or ions deeply affects the electrochemical reactions they undergo, and similarly affects the metabolism of plants and animals. Iron, copper, cobalt, potassium, and sodium are examples of metals that are essential to biological function. Some metals such as cadmium, mercury, lead, barium, chromium, and beryllium are highly toxic.

Crystallography of metals

Metals usually differ from nonmetals by their excellent thermal and electrical conductivities, and by their great mechanical strengths and ductilities. These properties follow directly from the nonlocalized electronic bonds in these materials. The electrons in metals are mobile; in a true metal, there are no underlying directed bonds.

With the exception of manganese and uranium, all true metals have one of the following crystal structures: body-centered cubic (sodium, potassium, molybdenum), iron face-centered cubic (copper, silver, gold), iron close-packed hexagonal (beryllium, magnesium, zirconium).

The origins of metallic behavior may be understood by considering the first and simplest of these three structures. There are eight nearest neighbors in a body-centered cubic structure. The number of next nearest atoms is six. The one valence electron of a body-centered cubic element like sodium clearly cannot furnish 14 or even eight covalent bonds with its neighbors. Thus, the single valence electron is shared.

The elements on the left-hand side of the periodic table readily pool their valence electrons, as they have low ionization potentials. Their large de-localization energies result in net binding. As one moves to the right of Group 1 in the periodic table, the metallic properties of the elements become weaker, and the tendency to form covalent bonds increases. As a result, thermal and electrical conductivities diminish, densities decrease, and the materials become hard, but brittle.

Carbon in Group 14, for example, does not allow its valence electrons to escape, but readily shares them with four neighbors. Graphitic carbon is made up of well separated layer planes with high conductivities along the planes but weak conductivities at right angles to these planes; consequently graphite is a two dimensional metal. In diamond, the electron bonds are tetrahedral and highly directed; this has the effect of making diamond brittle. Silicon, germanium, and grey tin also have diamond-like structures, and their bonding is largely covalent.

Survey of the periodic table

The first element of the periodic table, hydrogen, is a nonmetal. In the case of the alkali metals of Group 1, however, one finds that lithium, sodium, potassium, rubidium, cesium, and francium all exhibit to a high degree typically metallic properties. Each of these atoms has one electron in the outermost energy level. The energies required to pull off these single valence electrons are relatively small; on the other hand, the energies required to pull off a second electron are many times higher.

Group 2 of the periodic table includes the elements beryllium, magnesium, calcium, strontium, and radium. These elements are known as the alkaline earth metals. In each of the Group 2 elements, there are two electrons in the outer-most energy level. Going down the group from beryllium to radium, one finds decreasing ionization potentials with increasing ionic radius. In general, the larger atoms hold their electrons less tightly than do the smaller atoms. Although the first two electrons are removed relatively easy, removal of a third electron from the Group 2 elements requires very high energies.

Groups 3 through 12 in the periodic table are known as the transition elements. The most characteristic property of the transition elements is that they are all metals. This is because the outermost electron shells of these elements contain very few electrons. Unlike the Group 1 and 2 elements, the transition metals tend to be hard, brittle, and fairly high melting. The difference is due in part to the relatively small size of the transition element radii, and partly to the existence of some covalent bonding between the ions.

The Group 13 elements have the same relationship to the alkaline-earth elements that the alkaline-earth elements have to the alkali metals, that is, the group properties are modified by the presence of a third valence electron. The elements of Group 13 are boron, aluminum, gallium, indium, and thallium. Except for boron, which may be classified as a semimetal, these elements tend to show metallic properties.

Group 14 elements include carbon, silicon, germanium, tin, and lead. As already noted, carbon forms a solid of complex structure that does not exhibit metallic properties. The second and third members of the group, silicon and germanium, cannot be classified as metals either; they are only semimetals.

In Group 15, there is a complete change of properties from nonmetallic to metallic in going down the group. The lighter members, nitrogen and phosphorous, are typically nonmetals. The middle members, arsenic and antimony, are semimetals . The heaviest member, bismuth, is a metal.

The Group 16 elements include oxygen, sulfur, selenium, tellurium, and polonium. As would be expected from their location on the far right of the periodic table, the Group 16 elements have high ionization potentials, and metallic properties are difficult to observe. However, in going down the group, electrons are less tightly held; so there is some suggestion of metallic behavior in the heavier Group 16 elements.

The Group 17 elements, i.e., fluorine, chlorine, bromine, iodine, and astatine, all have high electronegativities and consequently show practically no metallic properties. Iodine, however, does show some metallic characteristics. Astatine may have some metallic properties, but it is a short-lived radioactive element, and measurements of its properties are difficult to carry out.

The Group 18 elements, or noble gases, consist of six gases: helium, neon, argon, krypton, xenon, and radon. The noble gases are nonmetals.

See also Alloy; Electrical conductivity; Element, chemical; Metallurgy; Periodic table.

Randall Frost

Metal fatigue

Metal fatigue is the process by which a material is slowly damaged by stresses and strains that are less than those needed to actually break the material apart. For example, a steel wire might be used to suspend weights that are less than the amount needed to cause the wire to break apart (its tensile strength). Over time, however, those weights might slowly cause defects to develop in the steel. These defects might occur as scratches, notches, particle formation, or other abnormalities. At some point, these defects may become so

great that the steel wire actually breaks apart even though its tensile strength had never been exceeded.

The process of metal fatigue varies considerably from one material to another. In some cases, defects show up almost as soon as stresses and strains are applied to the material and grow very slowly until total failure occurs. In other cases, there is no apparent damage in the material until failure almost occurs. Then, in the very last stages, defects appear and develop very rapidly prior to complete failure.

The amount of stress or strain needed to bring about metal fatigue in a material — the fatigue limit or fatigue strength of the material — depends on a number of factors. First is the material itself. In general, the fatigue limit of many materials tends to be about one quarter to three quarters of the tensile strength of the material itself. Another factor is the magnitude of the stress or strain exerted on the material. The greater the stress or strain, the sooner metal fatigue is likely to occur. Finally, environmental factors are involved in metal fatigue. A piece of metal submerged in a salt water solution, for example, is likely to exhibit metal fatigue sooner than the same piece of metal tested in air. Similarly, materials that have undergone some oxidation tend to experience metal fatigue sooner than unoxidized materials.

See also Metal production; Welding.

Metallurgy

Metallurgy is the science and technology of metals. As indicated in Table 1, the recorded history of metal working goes back over 6,000 years. Chemical or extractive metallurgy is concerned with the extraction of metals from ores and with the refining of metals. Physical metallurgy is concerned with the physical and mechanical properties of metals as affected by composition, mechanical working, and heat treatment.

Chemical or extractive metallurgy

Metalliferous ores that are taken directly from the mine are seldom suitable for metal smelting. These ores must first undergo removal or separation of waste matter to increase the concentration of the desired mineral. These processes include sorting, crushing and grinding, sizing, and separation by magnetics, electrical conductivity, specific gravity, etc.

Flotation is a widely used separation technique that takes advantage of the fact that some mineral components attract water (hydrophilicity) and others repel it (hydrophobicity). Finely divided air is introduced into a mixture of solid minerals and water. Air bubbles adhere to the hydrophobic particles, causing them to rise to the surface. These components are skimmed off. The hydrophilic components remain behind in the pulp. The sulfides of heavy metals are readily floatable, so flotation is an important method for concentrating copper, lead, and zinc ores.

Other methods of treating impure metals include magnetic separation and electrolytic refining. In magnetic separation, the magnetic components of an ore are separated from the nonmagnetic residual material. In electrolytic refining, the metal is cast into plates which serve as electrodes in electrolytic tanks. The electric current causes the metal to dissolve, and the pure metal is deposited at the electrode of opposite polarity to the plates.

The ores or concentrates of heavy metals such as copper, lead, zinc, and nickel (but not iron and tin) consist for the most part as sulfides of those metals. Removal of the sulphur is accomplished by a process called roasting. Roasting is a heat treatment carried out in an oxidizing atmosphere that produces a metal oxide and sulphur dioxide gas, which is usually processed to sulfuric acid. Arsenic and antimony are also removed by roasting. Roasting produces a powder, which may be agglomerated by sintering.

Physical metallurgy

Casting

INGOT CASTING. Steel and nonferrous-metal ingots that will be further worked are usually cast into ingot molds made of cast iron. In 1875, Sir Henry Bessemer patented a method of continuous casting in which a metal would be cast between two water-cooled rollers and pulled out in the form of a single plate. If it had been practicable, this method would have had the advantage of introducing no intermediate stages between the molten metal and the semifinished product. It was not until shortly before World War II that a modification of this technique proved feasible with aluminum. It was later used to cast copper, and is still under development as a tool for casting iron and steel.

MOLDS. Most metallic objects begin their history by being cast in a mold. Mold casting consists of introducing molten metal into a cavity or mold having the desired form and allowing it to solidify. The molding material affects the ease and cost of making the mold, the permanency of the mold, the rate of

production, the rate of cooling of the molten metal, the surface roughness, the dimensional tolerances, and the mechanical strength of the molded piece.

Casting techniques that use a mold only once include the following:

Sand-mold casting, which is the oldest process known and is still used for the largest tonnage of castings. A pattern, slightly larger than the desired part to allow for shrinkage, is placed in a flask and molding sand is rammed around it. The pattern is then removed, and the mold is prepared for pouring. The sand used may include bonding agents such as fire clay, bentonite, cereal or liquid binders, and moisture to promote cohesion. Dry sand molds are dried thoroughly before pouring; green sand molds are poured without drying. The type of sand grain, binder, and moisture used depend on the desired results.

Shell mold casting, which uses molds that are thin shells of sand bonded with a thermosetting phenolic resin. The shell is removed from the pattern and baked at 300-400°F (147-202° C) to completely set the resins. Finally the shells are assembled to complete the mold.

Plaster of paris casting, which gives better surface finishes, dimensional accuracy, finer detail, and a more solid structure than sand castings, but it is more expensive. The plaster mold is made by mixing plaster of Paris with water, then pouring it around the pattern and allowing it to partially set. The pattern is then removed. Separate parts of the mold assembly are baked separately to complete setting and to drive off moisture.

Precision casting, which differs from sand-mold casting in that the mold consists of a single part. Precision molds are used in the casting of metals and alloys that are difficult to machine. (Cast metals usually require little or no finishing treatment.) Such castings are frequently used in precision engineering, clockmaking, and the manufacture of metal ornaments.

In lost wax casting, the most widely used precision casting method, a model is made of the desired product. The model is used to produce a permanent plaster or glue mold. Wax parts are then made from the mold. The casting mold is produced by pouring a specially bonded sand around the wax pattern and allowing it to harden. The mold is inverted, placed in an oven and baked. The baking hardens the mold and melts the wax, which escapes.

When a large number of parts is needed or when better surface or dimensional control is required, a permanent metal mold may be used. Semipermanent molds consist of metal and sand molds. Metal molds, however, are unsuitable for large castings or for alloys having high melting temperatures. Permanent casting techniques include the following:

Chill casting, which is used to obtain more uniform cooling rates. Thick sections can be made to solidify by chilling them with a metal mold or with pieces of metal close to the section. Thin pieces can be preheated or made from material having poor thermal conductivity.

Pressure die casting, which permits economical production of intricate castings at a rapid rate. In this process molten metal is forced into a mold under considerable pressure. The pressure is maintained until solidification is complete.

Centrifugal casting, which involves pouring a molten metal into a revolving mold. Centrifugal action forces the metal tightly against the mold. The metal solidifies with an outer surface that conforms to the mold's shape and surface of revolution on the inside.

The metal for casting may come from reduced ore, from an open hearth or other remelting furnace, from electroreduction processing, or from remelting and alloying. To obtain a perfect casting, the liquid metal must completely fill every part of the mold before solidifying. Vacuum melting, although expensive, permits higher casting temperatures, better fluidity, and lower surface tension conditions.

As the metal solidifies, impurities that were soluble in the liquid metal become concentrated in the last parts to solidify. This would normally give rise to non-uniform impurity distributions throughout the cast piece. Reservoirs are therefore often incorporated into the casting process to trap the impurities.

Powder metallurgy

In powder metallurgy, articles are produced by agglomeration of fine metallic powder. This technique is used where other methods of shaping such as casting, forging, and machining are impractical. The materials used in powder metallurgy usually consist of a mixture of metallic and nonmetallic powders. The are cold pressed to initially adhere the particles. Then they are heated in compacts in a nonoxidizing atmosphere (sintering) to obtain final cohesion. In isostatic pressing, the powder is pressed in a closed flexible container of rubber or plastic under liquid pressure.

Mechanical working

Mechanical working of a metal is plastic deformation performed to change dimensions, properties, and/or surface conditions. Plastic deformation below the recrystallization temperature is called cold working. Plastic deformation above the recrystallization temperature, but below the melting or burning point, is called hot working.

Cold working produces a good surface finish, close dimensional tolerance, and does not result in weight loss during working. It produces considerable increase in strength and hardness, and reduces ductility. By repeatedly cycling a material through stages of annealing and cold working, a very strong material can be produced.

Hot working is actually a combination of working and annealing that involves deforming the metal above the recrystallization temperature. Ductility is restored during recrystallization, and grain growth during or immediately following recrystallization.

Effects of hot working a metal piece may include: densifying the metal; refining the grain structure; introducing homogeneity into the metal; introducing a preferential orientation into the metal.

FORGING. One of the most important properties of metals is their malleability, i.e., their ability to be mechanically deformed by forging, rolling, extrusion, etc., without rupture and without significant resistance to deformation. If metals can be mechanically deformed when cold, the material is said to be ductile. In the course of such deformation, most metals undergo work hardening (strain hardening). Metals that undergo work hardening are processed at room temperature. Those that are first heated above certain temperatures to make them malleable are hot formed. Forging is an important hot-forming process. In the process, the metal flows in the direction of least resistance. The most important forged metals are steel and steel alloys.

COLD EXTRUSION. In cold extrusion, the metal is made to flow while cold by the application of high pressure. The process is used with any cold workable material, e.g., tin, zinc, copper and its alloys, aluminum and its alloys, and low-carbon soft-annealed steels.

HOT EXTRUSION. Hot extrusion is a hot-working process that makes use of the deformability of heated metallic materials to shape them. The process is sited for producing barlike and tubular objects. Most metals and alloys can be extruded.

CUTTING AND MACHINING. Forging and extrusion do not involve the removal of metal by means of cutting tools. Many important shaping processes are based on cutting operations. Cutting tools are made of special steels (tool steels), hard metals, oxide ceramics, and diamond.

WELDING. Welding is the joining of metals by the application of heat and/or pressure, with or without the addition of a filler metal. Welding is used to form joints and connections, or to protect components against corrosion or wear by the application of an armoring layer of a more resistant metal.

In pressure welding, the parts to be joined are locally heated at the place where the joint is to be formed. The parts are then pressed together in the plastic state so that they are joined. Usually no filler is employed. Cold pressure welding makes use of high pressure, without the aid of heat, to unite parts. Ultrasonic and explosion welding are variations of this technique.

In fusion welding, metals are heated to the temperature at which they melt, and are then joined without hammering or the application of pressure. Although the joint can be formed without using a filler material, a filler is usually employed. The source of heat may be gas, electricity, chemical reactions, etc. Gas welding uses a flame produced by burning acetylene in oxygen or sometimes another fuel gas. This is a widely employed method of welding iron, steel, cast iron, and copper. The flame is applied to the edges of the joint and to a wire of filler material, which is melted and runs into the joint.

SOLDERING. Soldering is the process of joining metal parts by means of a molten filler metal (solder) whose melting point is lower than that of the metals to be joined. The metals to be joined are wetted by the solder without themselves being melted (as in the case of welding). Unlike the case of welding, two different metals can be joined by soldering.

There are two types of solders: soft and hard. Soft solders usually consist of a mixture of lead and tin; and the heat required to melt them is supplied by a soldering iron. Hard solders include brass (copper-zinc alloys) solders, silver solders, copper solders, nickel-silver solders, and solders for light alloys; the heat to melt them is usually supplied by a blow torch.

METAL FORMING. Sheet metal can be formed into a wide variety of hollow shapes and sections. The equipment required to work sheet metal ranges from simple hand tools to highly automated machinery. The process usually begins with basic shearing operations such as cutting, slitting, and perforating. This is followed by shaping operations, i.e., folding and bending.

KEY TERMS

Annealing—Heating to and holding at a suitable temperature and then cooling at a suitable rate to obtain the desired mechanical, physical, or other properties.

Cold working—Deforming metal plastically at a temperature lower than the recrystallization temperature.

Ductility—The ability of a material to deform plastically without fracturing.

Fracture stress—The maximum principal true stress at fracture.

Metal—An opaque lustrous elemental chemical substance that is a good conductor of heat and electricity, and when polished a good reflector of light.

Metalliferous—Containing or yielding metal.

Sintering—The bonding of adjacent surfaces of particles in a mass of metal powders by heating.

Yield strength—The stress at which a material exhibits a specified deviation from the proportionality of stress to strain.

Metallic coatings

GALVANIZING. Zinc plays an important role in protecting iron and steel from corrosion. The process of applying the zinc coating is called galvanizing. In hot-dip galvanizing, the zinc coating is applied by dipping the object to be coated into a bath of molten zinc; the zinc combines with the iron to form a coating of iron-and-zinc crystals. Other galvanizing techniques include electrogalvanizing, metallizing, and sherardizing (forming intermetallic compounds of iron and zinc on a steel surface by heating in the presence of zinc dust below the dust's melting point).

METALLIZING. Metallizing is a process for applying protective coatings to iron and steel. It consists of spraying particles of molten metal to the surface to be treated, and can be used with most common metals including aluminum, copper, lead, nickel, tin, zinc, and various alloys. Coatings of lead, aluminum, silver or stainless steel are sometimes used for protection against corrosion in the chemical and food industries. Steel or hard alloy coatings are used as wearing surfaces. In the electronics industries, metallic coatings are applied to nonmetallic materials to make them electrically conductive.

TABLE 1. HISTORY OF METALLURGY

Date	Technology developed
Prior to 4000 B.C.	Gold, copper, and meteoritic iron used occasionally without melting. Hammered into shape. Copper first annealed about 4000 B.C.
4000 to 3000 B.C.	Reduction of oxidized ores of copper and lead. Bronzes produced by intentionally mixing copper and tin ores (about 3500 B.C.). Permanent molding of stone and metal. Soldering with copper-gold and lead-tin alloys.
3000 to 2000 B.C.	Most jewelry techniques known before 2500 B.C.
2000 to 1000 B.C.	Bellows used in furnaces by 1800 B.C. Wrought iron important by 1600 B.C. Steel produced by carburization in hearth.
1000 to 1 B.C.	Cast iron known in China. Iron and steel welded into composite tools and weapons. Stamping of coins by 700 B.C.
1 to 1000 A.D.	Zinc smelted in China and India.
1380	Blast furnaces used to carburize and melt iron.
≈ 1440	Type metals for printing. The earliest type metals were tin-based. These were later displaced by lead-antimony in the 1600s.
1509	First cast iron cannon produced.
1627	Brass known to have been produced from copper and metallic zinc.
1718	Tables of metal affinities published.
1783	Phlogistron theory of metals disproved by Lavoisier. Phlogistron was a hypothetical substance thought to be a volatile constituent of all combustible substances released as flame in combustion.
1841	Objects shaped by powder metallurgy.
1875	Bessemer process for making steel developed.
1882	Manganese steel developed.
1886	Electrolytic aluminum produced.
1892	Carbonyl nickel process developed.
1898	Heat treatment of high speed steels, i.e., alloy steels that remain hard and tough at red heat.

ELECTROPLATING. Electroplating is the process of producing a metallic coating on a surface by electro-deposition involving an electric current. In electroplating, the coating material is deposited from an aqueous acid or alkaline solution (electrolyte) onto the metal surface to be coated. Such coatings may have protective and/or decorative functions.

See also Metal; Metal production; Minerals; Ore; Welding.

Further Reading:

The Way Things Work, vol. 2. New York, NY: Simon and Schuster, 1971.
Lyman, Taylor. *Metals Handbook.* Metals Park, OH: American Society for Metals, 1961.
Smith, Charles O. *The Science of Engineering Materials.* Englewood Cliffs, NJ: Prentice-Hall, Inc, 1969.

Randall Frost

Metal production

The term metal production refers to all of the processes involved in the conversion of a raw material, such as a metallic ore, to a final form in which the metal can be used for some commercial or industrial purpose. In some instances, metal production involves relatively few steps since the metal already occurs in an elemental form in nature. Such is the case with gold, silver, platinum, and other so-called noble metals. These metals normally occur in nature uncombined with other elements and can therefore be put to some commercial use with comparatively little additional treatment.

In the majority of cases, however, metals occur in nature as compounds, such as the oxide or the sulfide, and must first be converted to their elemental state. They may then be treated in a wide variety of ways in order to make them usable for specific practical applications.

Mining

The first step in metal production always involves some form of mining. Mining refers to the process of removing the metal in its free or combined state from the Earth's surface. The two most common forms of mining are surface and sub-surface mining. In the former case, the metal or its ore can be removed from the upper few meters of the Earth's surface. Much of the world's copper, for example, is obtained from huge open-pit mines

may range in depth to as much as nearly a 0.6 mi (1 km) and in width to as much as more than 2.25 mi (3.5 km). Sub-surface mining is used to collect metallic ores that lie at greater depths below the Earth's surface.

A few metals can be obtained from seawater rather than or in addition to being taken from the Earth's crust. Magnesium is one example. Every cubic mile of seawater contains about six million tons of magnesium, primarily in the form of magnesium chloride. The magnesium is first precipitated out of seawater as magnesium hydroxide using lime (calcium hydroxide). The magnesium hydroxide is then converted back to magnesium chloride, now a pure compound rather than the complex mixture that comes from the sea. Finally, magnesium metal is obtained from the magnesium chloride by passing an electric current through a water solution of the compound.

Purification

In most cases, metals and their ores occur in the ground as part of complex mixtures that also contain rocks, sand, clay, silt and other impurities. The first step in producing the metal for commercial use, therefore, is to separate the ore from waste materials with which it occurs. The term ore is used to describe a compound of a metal that contains enough of that metal to make it economically practical to extract the metal from the compound.

One example of the way in which an ore can be purified is the froth flotation method used with ores of copper, zinc, and some other metals. In this method, impure ore taken from the ground is first ground into a powder and then mixed with water and a frothing agent such as pine oil. Then a stream of air is blown through the mixture, causing it to bubble and froth. In the frothing process, impurities such as sand and rock are wetted by the water and sink to the bottom of the container. The metal ore does not adsorb water but does adsorb the pine oil. The oil-coated ore floats to the top of the mixture, where it can be skimmed off.

Reduction

Metals always occur in their oxidized state in ores, often as the oxide or sulfide of the metal. In order to convert an ore to its elemental state, therefore, it must be reduced. Reduction is a chemical reaction that is the opposite of oxidation. Metals can be reduced in a variety of different ways.

With ores of iron, for example, reduction can be accomplished by reacting oxides of iron with carbon and carbon monoxide. One of the common devices used for

A steel worker sampling the quality of "hot steel" during production.

this purpose is the blast furnace. The blast furnace is a tall cylindrical vessel into which is fed iron ore (consisting of oxides of iron), coke (nearly pure carbon) and limestone. The temperature in the blast furnace is then raised to more than 1,832° F (1,000° C). At this temperature, carbon reacts with oxygen to form carbon monoxide which, in turn, reacts with oxides of iron to form pure iron metal. The limestone in the original mixture added to the blast furnace reacts with and removes silicon dioxide (sand), an impurity commonly found with iron ore.

Some metallic oxides do not readily yield to chemical reduction reactions like those in the blast furnace process described above. The reduction of aluminum oxide to aluminum metal is an example. Until 1886, no economically satisfactory method for carrying out this process had been discovered. Then a young college chemistry student, Charles Martin Hall, invented an electrical method for reducing aluminum oxide.

In the first step in this process, aluminum oxide is separated from other oxides (such as oxides of iron) with which it also occurs by the Bayer process. In the Bayer process, the naturally occurring oxide mixture is added to sodium hydroxide, which dissolves out aluminum oxide, leaving other oxides behind. The aluminum oxide is then dissolved in a mineral known as cryolite (sodium aluminum fluoride) and placed in an electrolytic cell. When electric current passes through the cell, molten aluminum metal is formed, sinks to the bottom of the cell, and can be drawn off from the cell.

In some instances, an ore is treated to change its chemical state before being reduced. The most common ores of zinc, for example, are the sulfides. These compounds are first roasted in an excess of air, converting zinc sulfide to zinc oxide. The zinc oxide is then reduced either by reacting it with coke (as in the case of iron) or by electrolyzing it (as in the case of aluminum).

Alloys

Pure metals themselves are often not satisfactory for many practical applications. For example, pure gold is too soft for most uses and is combined with other metals to form harder, more resistant mixtures. Mixtures that contain two or more metals are known as alloys. Perhaps the best known and most widely used of all alloys is steel.

The term steel refers to a number of different substances that contain iron as their major component along with one or more other elements. Stainless steel, as an example, contains about 18% chromium, 10% nickel, and small amounts of manganese, carbon, phosphorus, sulfur, and silicon, along with iron. When niobium is added to a steel alloy, the final product has unusually great strength. The addition of cobalt produces a form of steel that withstands the high temperatures of jet engines and gas turbines, and silicon steels are used in making electrical equipment.

In the final stages of metal production, the finished product is formed into some shape that can be used in other industries to make final products. Thus, steel can be purchased in the form of flat sheets, rings, wire rope and thread, slabs, cylinders, and other shapes.

See also Alloy; Metal; Metallurgy; Mining; Steel.

Further Reading:

Engh, T. Abel. *Principles of Metal Refining.* New York: Oxford University Press, 1992.
Hurd, Paul S. *Metallic Minerals: An Introduction to Metallurgy.* New York: Holt, Rinehart and Winston, 1968.
McDivitt, James M., and Gerald Manners. *Minerals & Men: An Exploration of the World of Minerals and Metals.* Washington, DC: Resources for the Future, 1974.
Metals & Minerals, 2 vols. New York: Gordon Press, 1992.
Patterson, James W., and Roberto Passino, eds. *Metals Speciation, Separation and Recovery*, Vol. II. Boca Raton, FL: Lewis Publications, 1990.

David E. Newton

Metamorphic rock

Metamorphic rock is rock that has changed from one type of rock into another. The word metamorphic (from Greek) means "of changing form." Metamorphic rock is produced from either igneous rock (rock formed from the cooling and hardening of magma) or sedimentary rock (rock formed from compressed and solidified layers of organic or inorganic matter). Most of Earth's crust is made up of metamorphic rock. Igneous and sedimentary rocks become metamorphic rock as a result of intense heat from magma and pressure from tectonic shifting. Although the rock becomes extremely hot and under a great deal of pressure it does not melt. If the rock melted, the process would result in igneous, not metamorphic rock. "Metamorphism" of rock causes the texture and/or mineral composition to change. New textures are formed from a process called recrystallization. New minerals (which are simply various combinations of elements) are created when elements recombine.

There are two basic types of metamorphic rock: regional and thermal. Regional metamorphic rock, found mainly in mountainous regions, is formed mainly by pressure, as opposed to heat. Different amounts of pressure produce different types of rock. The greater the pressure, the more drastic the change. Also, the deeper the rock the higher the temperature, which adds to the potential for diverse changes. For example, a pile of mud can turn into shale (a fine-grained sedimentary rock) with relatively low pressure, about 3 mi (5 km) down into the earth. With more pressure and some heat, shale can transform into slate and mica. Metamorphic rock found closer to Earth's surface, or produced by low pressure, characteristically splits or flakes into layers of varying thickness. This is called foliation. Slate is often used as roofing tiles and paving stones. With lots of pressure and increasing heat, rock called schist forms. Schist, which is a medium grained regional metamorphic rock also has a tendency to split in layers, is subjected to high temperatures and often contains crystals, such as garnets. Gneiss (pronounced "nice") is formed by a higher pressure and temperature than schist. These rocks are coarse grained and, although layered as schist is, do not split easily. Essentially, metamorphic rocks are made of the same minerals as the original rock or "parent" rock but the various minerals have been rearranged to make a new rock. Thermal metamorphic rock, also called contact metamorphic rock, is formed not only by considerable pressure but, more importantly, by intense heat. Imagine molten rock pushing up into Earth's crust. The incredible pressure fills any empty space, every nook and cranny, with molten rock. This intense heat causes the surrounding rock to completely recrystallize. During recrystallization, the chemical composition "regroups" to form a new rock. An example of this type of thermal metamorphic rock is marble, which is actually limestone whose calcite has recrystallized. Sandstone made mostly of quartz fragments recrystallizes into quartzite. Thermal metamorphic rocks are not as common or plentiful as regional metamorphic rocks. Sometimes a metamorphic rock can become metamorphosed. This is known as polymetamorphism.

See also Metamorphism; Rocks.

Further Reading:

Dixon, Dougal, *The Practical Geologist.* New York: Simon & Schuster, Inc., 1992.
Eyewitness: Rocks & Minerals. New York: Alfred A. Knopf, 1988.
Grolier's Academic American Encyclopedia, 1993.
Hay, E. and A. McAlester. *Physical Geology* 2nd Ed. Prentice-Hall, 1984.

Christine Miner Minderovic

Metamorphism

Metamorphism is the process by which the structure and mineral content of rocks transform in response to changes in temperature, pressure, fluid content (gas or water), or a combination of these. Because the minerals that make up rocks are stable only within certain ranges of temperature and pressure, large changes in these conditions cause minerals to change chemically or to change shape, or both. Minerals that form during metamorphism include spectacular varieties of garnet, mica, amphibole, and serpentine, to name a few. Metamorphism produces characteristic textures in metamorphic rocks, the type of rocks that have undergone metamorphism, such as alignment of elongate crystals or differentiation of different minerals into layers. Distinctive minerals and textures are keys to distinguishing

rocks that have experienced metamorphism from unmetamorphosed sedimentary and igneous rocks.

Metamorphism has captured the interest of geologists for many years. James Dana, a noted American geologist, wrote about the alteration of rocks by metamorphism in his *Manual of Geology*, first published in 1862. By the 1920, the Finnish geologist Pentii Eskola began to note differences in the degree of metamorphism of rocks in different areas on the basis of the different groups of minerals that typically occur together in metamorphic rocks.

The minerals that typically occur in distinctive groups in metamorphic rocks are known as metamorphic facies. Metamorphic facies reflect different conditions during metamorphism. For example, ongoing metamorphism of shale at continuously increasing temperature and pressure initially produces slate, then phyllite, schist, and gneiss. As the pressure and temperature change, the structures and minerals in rocks change to forms that are stable in those conditions. Thus, by studying the minerals present in an area, scientists can estimate the pressure and temperature at which metamorphism occurred.

Matching metamorphic rocks to their unmetamorphosed precursors is not always easy. However, some metamorphic rocks typically form from certain precursor rocks. For example, marble is a metamorphic rock that forms during metamorphism of limestone, a sedimentary rock. Metamorphism of other sedimentary rock, such as shale, can produce slate. Sandstone metamorphoses into quartzite. Granite, an igneous rock, can become gneiss during metamorphism.

Products of metamorphism occur worldwide. Familiar examples include slate roofs and marble floors, garnet jewelry, and asbestos insulation made from serpentine and amphibole minerals. Because of their unusual minerals and structures, as well as their association with majestic mountain ranges, metamorphic rocks are among the most beautiful.

Types of metamorphism

Scientists recognize several types of metamorphism: regional metamorphism, contact metamorphism, dynamic metamorphism, and hydrothermal metamorphism. These occur between the low-temperature process of diagenesis (temperature above 392°F or 200°C and pressure greater than 1,000 bars) and the high temperatures at which rocks melt and later cool to form igneous rocks (approximately 1,112-1,472°F or 600-800°C in temperature and more than 10,000 bars pressure).

Regional metamorphism, the wide-scale alteration of rocks during major tectonic events, can produce spectacular textures and structures in rocks, including folds of layers of rocks, folds of individual minerals (mica, for example), and rotated garnet crystals. Examples of regional metamorphism abound, from Acadia National Park in Maine and the Appalachian Mountains in the eastern part of the United States, to the Llano Uplift of central Texas, and the Precambrian rocks of the Grand Canyon. The Alps of Europe and the Himalayas of Asia also show effects of regional metamorphism.

Contact metamorphism, or thermal metamorphism, occurs when heat from igneous intrusions, melted rocks that move upward through the Earth, come in contact with cooler rocks above. The cooler rocks do not melt, but recrystallize as a result of heating. The Palisades sill, an igneous intrusion, produced contact metamorphism in the rocks into which it intruded, and is well exposed beneath the George Washington Bridge near New York City.

Dynamic metamorphism occurs along faults that have zones of intense pressure. Rocks along faults grind past each other during faulting. The finely ground rock in the fault can recrystallize under pressure, especially if friction along the fault produces heat or if hot fluids move through the fault.

Hydrothermal metamorphism requires the presence of hot fluids derived from igneous rock nearby. The fluids react with minerals in the surrounding rock to produce different minerals. The metamorphic mineral serpentine forms when dense igneous rocks, such as those in the oceanic crust, metamorphose in the presence of hot fluids to form less dense metamorphic rock called serpentinite.

Current research in metamorphism

Current research in the field of metamorphism ranges from studies of the chemical composition of single crystals within metamorphic rocks (garnet, for example) to the mysteries of metamorphic rocks that form at extremely high pressure, presumably deep within the Earth, and now exist at the surface of the Earth without changes in the minerals in the rocks as the pressure decreased during uplift to the surface. The effects of fluids on metamorphism continue to attract the attention of researchers.

Studies of the ratios of unstable isotopes (for example, uranium, rubidium, strontium, and argon) allow scientists to determine the times at which rocks metamorphosed. Such data are valuable in studies of

KEY TERMS

Diagenesis—Compaction, cementation, and other processes that transform sediments into sedimentary rock at low temperatures.

Intrusion—Movement of melted rock into solid rock. The heat from the melted material can cause contact metamorphism of the solid rock.

Isotopes—Forms of an element that have the same number of protons and electrons, but different numbers of neutrons. Uranium has three naturally-occurring isotopes, uranium-238, uranium-235, and uranium-234.

Metamorphic facies—A group of metamorphic minerals typically found together. Different metamorphic facies form at different temperatures and pressures.

Mineral—A naturally-occurring substance with a distinct chemical composition and structure. Quartz, magnetite, calcite, and garnet are minerals.

Regional metamorphism—Widespread change in temperature and pressure that alters rock, usually associated with tectonic events.

Rock—An aggregate of minerals or organic matter. Debris from coral reefs can form the rock limestone. A combination of quartz, feldspar, mica, and amphibole is typical in a metamorphic rock.

Tectonic event—Episode of movement or deformation of the large plates of oceanic and continental crust that cover the Earth. Mountain-building and regional metamorphism can result from tectonic events.

regional metamorphism, particularly in areas that have experienced multiple episodes of metamorphism.

Economically important metamorphic minerals such as serpentine can affect health. In the past few years, asbestos removal has had significant impact on the cost of operating schools and other public buildings. In the confusion over illness associated with asbestos made from the amphibole mineral crocidolite, citizens demanded the removal of all asbestos, unaware that a less-hazardous form of asbestos, the serpentine mineral chrysotile, also was removed at great expense.

Research in the field of metamorphism continues to include traditional geological activities such as preparing maps of surface exposures of metamorphic rocks from field studies, observing thin slices of metamorphic rocks using microscopes, and assessing the time, temperature, and pressure at which metamorphism occurs. New technology, particularly lasers and x-ray tomography, allow scientists to examine rocks and single crystals in sufficient detail to understand how crystals grow during metamorphism and at what temperatures and pressures they grow.

See also Asbestos; Metamorphic rock; Minerals; Rocks.

Further Reading:

Abelson, Phillip H. "The Asbestos Removal Fiasco." *Science* 247 (1990): 1017.

Lang, Helen M. "Metamorphic Petrology." *Geotimes* 40 (1995): 44-45.

Gretchen M. Gillis

Metamorphosis

Metamorphosis is the transition in overall body pattern which occurs during the life history of some animals following birth or hatching. Two well-known examples are the development of caterpillars into butterflies and tadpoles into frogs.

Metamorphosis is considered an indirect form of development, in that a metamorphic animal passes through morphologically distinct stages before reaching the adult form. In contrast, humans and many other animals undergo direct development, in that the young and old resemble one another, except in size and sexual maturity. Metamorphosis occurs in at least 17 phyla of the animal kingdom, including Porifera (sponges), Cnidaria (jellyfish and others), Platyhelminthes (flat worms), Mollusca (mollusks), Annelida (segmented worms), Arthropoda (insects and others), Echinodermata (sea urchins and others), and Chordata (vertebrates and others). Although the term "metamorphosis" is generally not applied to plants, many plants have a developmental life cycle, called the alternation of generations, which is also characterized by a dramatic change in overall body pattern.

General features

In general, cells in the different parts of a multicellular organism all have the same genes, although only some of these genes are expressed (translated into proteins) in any given cell. At the molecular level, highly regulated temporal and spatial changes in gene expression causes metamorphosis in all animals. Thus, in the case of a butterfly, a very simple model of metamorphosis is that one family of genes is expressed in the larva (caterpillar), a second family of genes in the pupa, and a third family of genes in the imago (adult). Such a model provides a framework for studies of metamorphosis, although there is clearly much more to metamorphosis than implied by this simple model.

Metamorphosis is associated with adaptive changes in the way an organism interacts with its environment, and this may be why it evolved independently in so many different phyla of the animal kingdom. For example, adult amphibians (Chordata phylum) often eat very different foods than their larvae. Thus, adults and larvae do not compete for food, a limiting resource in many environments. A second example of the adaptive significance of metamorphosis is in barnacles (Arthropoda phylum). Adult barnacles are sessile, but the larvae are free-swimming. Thus, the dispersal of larvae gives adults the opportunity to colonize new habitats, where the local environment might be more favorable.

Environmental cues often trigger hormonal changes in an animal that lead to metamorphosis. For example, many insects enter a dormant stage of development during the winter and often will not metamorphose unless exposed to low temperatures. Light is another important environmental cue which triggers metamorphosis. In one well known case, the length of the light period in a light-dark cycle controls metamorphosis of fruit fly pupae into adults.

Insects

Some of the best known cases of metamorphosis occur in insects, a class of the Arthropoda phylum. There are about a half million known species of insects, and great diversity in the way different insects develop. According to one classification scheme based on metamorphosis, insects are classified as Ametabola, Hemimetabola, or Holometabola.

The Ametabola do not undergo metamorphosis. This is an evolutionary primitive condition and is exemplified by insects such as the bristletails and springtails. During development, these insects increase in size, but do not undergo distinct changes in form. In general, the Ametabola do not have wings.

The Hemimetabola undergo gradual metamorphosis. This is exemplified by insects such as the dragonflies, termites, roaches, and grasshoppers. In the

The transformation from larva to adult that a butterfly undergoes during pupation is an example of metamorphosis.

Hemimetabola, a form called the nymph hatches from the egg. Nymphs lack wings, but have compound eyes and otherwise resemble the adult form, except they are smaller. The wings of the Hemimetabola grow gradually during a series of molts, developmental periods in which the cuticular exoskeleton is shed, allowing for growth.

The Holometabola undergo complete metamorphosis. This is exemplified by insects such as moths, butterflies, wasps, and flies. In the Holometabola, a worm-like larva with short legs, no wings, and simple eyes, hatches from the egg. As in the Hemimetabola, the larva increases in size through a series of molts. Eventually, the larva develops into a pupa inside a cocoon. The pupa is often considered a resting stage and can often survive in unfavorable environments. Eventually, the pupa metamorphoses into an adult. In this process, the pupa resorbs larval organs and uses them as nutrients while special groups of cells, called imaginal discs, form and reshape the insect. The adult typically has wings, compound eyes, legs, antennae, and sexual organs.

Hormones

Hormones have an important role in insect metamorphosis. In many species, two classes of hormones, molting hormones (made by the prothoracic glands) and juvenile hormones (made by the corpora allata) act together to control metamorphosis. Each regulates the expression of different genes, so that a change in their relative concentrations causes metamorphosis, the development of different body patterns.

The two well known molting hormones are ecdysone and 20-hydroxyecdysone. These control the molting of larvae prior to metamorphosis and their level remains relatively constant during development. There are three known juvenile hormones. These gradually decrease in concentration during the many stages of larval molting. When their concentration falls below a critical level, the larva transforms into a pupa. Then, production of juvenile hormones ceases and the pupa metamorphoses into an adult.

Interestingly, the leaves of some trees, such as hemlock, make a chemical similar to the juvenile hormones of insects. When larvae (caterpillars) feed on these leaves, they cannot metamorphose into the adult form. Apparently, this is a chemical defense mechanism which some trees use to prevent leaf-feeding insects from reaching sexual maturity.

Amphibians

Metamorphosis has also been extensively studied in amphibians, a class of vertebrates which includes frogs, toads, and salamanders. "Amphibian" means dual (amphi-) life form (-bian) and refers to the typical life history of these animals, in which an aquatic larva metamorphoses into a terrestrial adult. The reptiles, such as turtles, lizards, and snakes, is another class of vertebrates whose species superficially resemble adult amphibians, but do not undergo metamorphosis.

Metamorphosis differs in the many different amphibian species. In frog development, the eggs hatch and give rise to tadpoles, small aquatic larvae which have external gills and are mainly vegetarian. As the tadpole grows, internal gills and limbs form. Several significant changes occur during metamorphosis into the adult, including growth of a large mouth and tongue, loss of gills, formation of lungs, growth of the front legs, and resorption of the tail. Numerous biochemical changes accompany these morphological changes, such as synthesis of a new visual pigment in the eyes and a new oxygen-binding hemoglobin protein in the blood. The adult is mainly insectivorous and partly terrestrial.

Interestingly, the sexually mature adults of some amphibians, such as the axolotl, have a larval morphology. The retention of larval or juvenile characteristics in adulthood is defined as neoteny. Neoteny is apparently caused by a genetic mechanism which uncouples development of body cells and the development of the sexual organs. Although neoteny is most apparent in amphibians, because they are normally metamorphic, changes in developmental timing may underlie the evolution of many species, including humans.

Hormones

As in insects, a complex interaction of hormones in the amphibian larva precipitates metamorphosis. Ultimately, two major classes of hormones act together to control amphibian metamorphosis: the thyroid hormones (made by the thyroid gland) and prolactin (made by the pituitary gland). Thyroid hormones function somewhat like the molting hormones of insects, in that an increase of their concentration relative to prolactin leads to metamorphosis of the larva into the adult. Prolactin functions somewhat like the juvenile hormones of insects, in that it tempers the action of the thyroid hormones. In most species, thyroid hormones increase dramatically in concentration during metamorphosis and this stimulates resorption of certain larval organs and differentiation of new adult organs.

Developmental biologists often investigate amphibian metamorphosis by experimentally manipulating hormone levels. For example, injection of thyroxine into a young larva can induce metamorphosis, although the injection must be at an appropriate stage of larval development and injection of high levels can lead to developmental abnormalities. If the thyroid gland is removed from a larva, it will not metamorphose into the adult form; moreover, a larva without a thyroid will metamorphose into an adult if thyroid tissue is implanted.

The relative ease with which these and other experimental manipulations of hormone levels can alter metamorphosis indicates that hormones have a profound effect on development. It also indicates that the endocrine system is relatively malleable. These two features suggest that natural selection may dramatically affect the course of animal evolution by altering the endocrine system.

See also Amphibians; Insects.

Further Reading:

Chu, H. F. and L.K. Cutkomp. *How to Know the Immature Insects.* William C. Brown, 1992.
Fox, H. *Amphibian Morphogenesis.* Humana Press, 1984.
Friedlander, C. P. *The Biology of Insects.* Universe Publications, Inc., 1977.

KEY TERMS

. . . .

Alternation of generations—General feature of the life cycle of many plants, characterized by the occurrence of multiple reproductive forms which often have very different overall body patterns.

Gene—Segment of nucleic acid which determines a heritable characteristic of an organism.

Gene expression—Molecular process in which a gene is transcribed into a specific RNA (ribonucleic acid), which is then translated into a specific protein.

Hormone—Chemical regulator of physiology, growth, or development which is typically synthesized in one region of the body and active in another and is typically active in low concentrations.

Imago—Adult form of an insect which develops from a larva and often has wings.

Larva—Immature form (worm-like in insects; fish-like in amphibians) of a metamorphic animal which develops from the embryo and differs radically from the adult.

Molting—Shedding of the outer layer of an animal, such as the cuticle during growth of insect larvae.

Neoteny—Retention of larval or juvenile characteristics in a sexually mature adult.

Minelli, G. *Amphibians.* Facts on File, Inc., 1987.
O'Toole, C. *The Encyclopedia of Insects.* Facts on File, Inc., 1986.
Quiri, P. R. *Metamorphosis.* Franklin Watts, Inc., 1991.

Peter A. Ensminger

Meteors and meteorites

The word meteor is derived from the Greek *meteron,* meaning something high up. Today, however, the term is used to describe the light phenomena produced by the entry of a meteoroid into Earth's atmosphere. A meteoroid is defined to be any solid object moving in interplanetary space that is much larger than an atom or a molecule, but smaller than a few meters in diameter. A visual meteor, or shooting star, is produced whenever a sand-grain-sized meteoroid is vaporized in Earth's upper atmosphere. If a meteoroid survives its passage through the atmosphere, without being fully vaporized and falls to the ground, it is a called a meteorite.

Visual meteors

Upon entering Earth's upper atmosphere, a meteoroid begins to collide with an ever increasing number of air molecules. These collisions will both slow the meteoroid down and heat its surface layers. At the same time that the meteoroid is being decelerated, that energy is transferred from the meteoroid to the surrounding air. Some of the meteoroid's lost energy is transformed into light; it is this light that we observe as a meteor. As the meteoroid continues its journey through the atmosphere, its surface layers become so hot that vaporization begins. Continued heating causes more and more surface mass loss in a process known as ablation, and ultimately the meteoroid is completely vaporized.

The amount of surface heating that a meteoroid experiences is proportional to its surface area, and consequently very small meteoroids are not fully vaporized in the atmosphere. The size limit below which vaporization is no longer important is about 0.01 mm. The smallest of meteoroids can safely pass through Earth's atmosphere without much physical alteration, and they may be collected as micrometeorites at Earth's surface. It is estimated that 22,000 tons (20,000 metric tons) of micrometeoritic material falls to Earth every year.

Visual meteors (shooting stars) are produced through the vaporization of millimeter-sized meteoroids. The speed with which meteoroids enter Earth's atmosphere varies from a minimum of 7 mi/sec (11 km/sec) to a maximum of 45 mi/sec (72 km/sec). The meteoroid ablation process typically begins at heights between 62-71 mi (100-115 km) above the Earth's surface, and the whole meteoroid is usually vaporized by the time it has descended to a height of 43.5 miles (70 km).

Astronomers have found that the visually observed meteors are derived from two meteoroid populations; a continuously active, but sporadic, background and a number of specific sources called meteoroid streams.

Sporadic meteors

On any clear night of the year an observer can expect to see about 10-12 sporadic meteors per hour. Sporadic meteors can appear from any part of the sky, and about 500,000 sporadic meteoroids enter the Earth's atmosphere every day.

Meteor activity is often described in terms of the number of meteors observed per hour. The observed

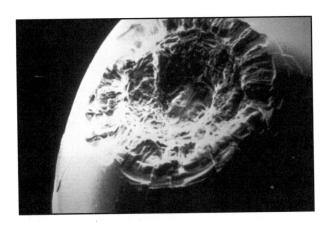

Meteorites vary greatly in size and so do the craters they make. This tiny crater is the result of a micro-meteor impact on lunar rock. This image, as viewed, is several hundred times the crater's actual size.

hourly rate of meteors will be dependent upon the prevalent "seeing" conditions, and factors such as the presence of a full Moon, local light pollution, and clouds will reduce the meteor count and hence lower the observed hourly rate. Astronomers often quote a corrected hourly rate which describes the number of meteors that an observer would see, each hour, if the observing conditions were perfect.

Observations have shown that the corrected hourly rate of sporadic meteors varies in a periodic fashion during the course of a day. On a typical clear night the hourly rate of sporadic meteors is at a minimum of about six meteors per hour at 6 P.M. in the evening. The hourly rate climbs steadily during the night until it reaches a maximum of about 16 meteors per hour around 4 A.M. This daily variation in the hourly rate of sporadic meteors is due to the change of an observer's position relative to the direction in which Earth is moving in its orbit about the Sun. In the evening, a sporadic meteoroid has to catch up with Earth if it is to enter the atmosphere and be seen. This is because at about 6 P.M. local time an observer will be on that part of Earth's surface which is trailing in the direction of Earth's motion. In the early morning, however, the observer will be on the leading portion of Earth's surface, and consequently Earth will tend to "sweep up" all the meteoroids in its path. An observer will typically see two to three times more sporadic meteors per hour in the early morning than in the early evening; and will see them at high speeds relative to Earth.

Meteor showers

Meteor showers occur when Earth passes through the tube-like structure of meteoroids left in the wake of

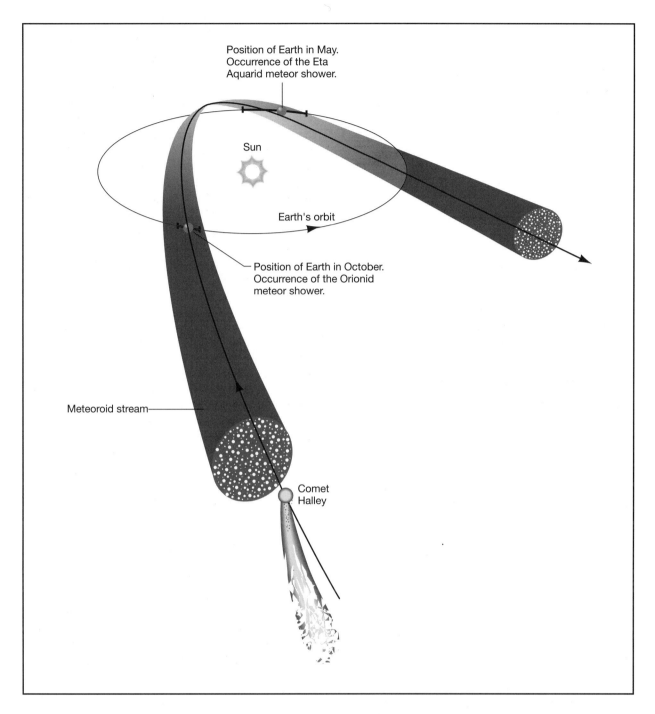

Position of Earth in May.
Occurrence of the Eta
Aquarid meteor shower.

Sun

Earth's orbit

Position of Earth in October.
Occurrence of the Orionid
meteor shower.

Meteoroid stream

Comet
Halley

Figure 1.

a comet. Such meteoroid tubes, or as they are more commonly called meteoroid streams, are formed after a comet has made many repeated passages by the Sun. Meteoroid streams are composed of silicate (i.e. rocky) grains that were once embedded in the surface ices of a parent comet. Grains are released from a cometary nucleus whenever solar heating causes the surface ices to sublimate. New grains are injected into the meteoroid stream each time the comet passes close by the Sun. The individual dust grains (technically meteoroids once they have left the comet) move along orbits that are similar to that of the parent comet. Gradually, over the course of several hundreds of years, the meteoroids form a diffuse shell of material around the whole orbit of the parent comet. Provided that the stream meteoroids are distributed in a reasonably uniform manner, a

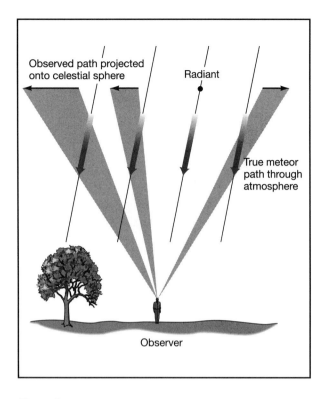

Figure 2.

meteor shower will be seen each year when the Earth passes through the stream (Fig. 1).

The shower occurs at the same time each year because the position at which the meteoroid stream intersects Earth's orbit does not vary much from one year to the next. There are long-term variations, however, and the days during which a shower is active will change eventually.

When Earth passes through a meteoroid stream, the meteoroids are moving through space along nearly parallel paths. Upon entering Earth's atmosphere, however, a perspective effect causes the shower meteors to apparently originate from a small region of the sky, this region is called the radiant (Fig. 2).

The radiant is typically just a few degrees across when projected onto the night sky. A meteor shower is usually, but not always, named after the constellation in which the radiant falls on the night of the shower maximum. The Orionid meteor shower, for example, is so named because on the night of the shower maximum (October 21st) the stream radiant is located in the constellation of Orion. Some meteor showers are named after bright stars. The Eta Aquarid meteor shower, for example, is so named because on the night of the shower maximum (May 3rd) the radiant is close to the seventh brightest star in the constellation of Aquarius

(by convention the brightest stars in a constellation are labeled after the Greek alphabet, and accordingly, the seventh letter in the Greek alphabet is eta).

Probably the best known meteor shower is the one known as the Perseid shower. This shower reaches its peak on the night of August 12th each year, but meteors can be observed from the stream for several weeks on either side of the maximum. The shower's radiant first appears in the constellation of Andromedia in mid-July, and by late August it has moved into the constellation of Camelopardalis. The radiant is in the constellation of Perseus on the night of the shower maximum. The steady eastward drift of the radiant across the night sky is due to the motion of Earth through the Perseid meteoroid stream. The nearly constant year to year activity associated with the Perseid meteor shower indicates that the stream must be very old. Essentially the Earth encounters about the same number of Perseid meteoroids each year even though it is sampling different segments of the stream. Since 1988, however, higher than normal meteor rates have been observed about twelve hours before the time of the traditional shower maximum (August 12th). This short-lived period (approximately half an hour) of high activity is caused by new meteoroids which were ejected from the streams parent comet, Comet Swift-Tuttle, in 1862. Comet Swift-Tuttle last rounded the Sun in late 1992, and it is expected that higher than normal meteor rates will be visible half-a-day before the time of the "traditional" Perseid maximum for the next few decades.

Meteorites

If a meteoroid is to survive its passage through the Earth's atmosphere, to become a meteorite, it must be both large and dense. If these physical conditions are not met it is more than likely the meteoroid, as it ploughs through Earth's atmosphere, will either crumble into many small fragments, or that it will be completely vaporized before it hits Earth's surface. Most of the meteoroids that produce meteorites are believed to be asteroidal in origin. In essence they are the small, fragmentary chips thrown off when two minor planets (asteroids) collide. Meteorites are very valuable therefore for being samples of asteroidal material that has landed on Earth. A few very rare meteorite samples are believed to have come from the planet Mars and the Moon. It is believed that these rare meteorite specimens characterize material that was ejected from the surfaces of Mars and the Moon during the formation of large impact craters.

Accurate orbits are presently known for just four recovered meteorites (the Pribram meteorite which fell

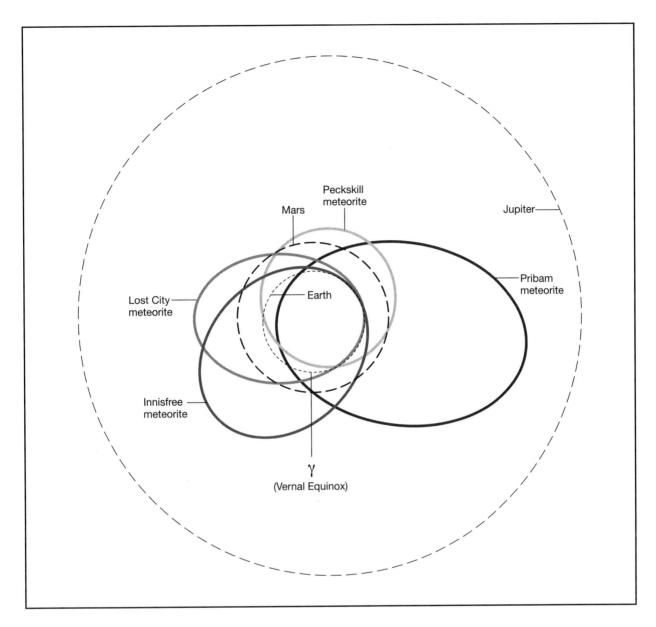

Figure 3.

in the Czech Republic in 1959; the Lost City meteorite which fell in Oklahoma in 1970; the Innisfree meteorite which fell in Alberta, Canada, in 1977, and the Peekskill meteorite which fell in New York State in 1992). All four of these meteorites have orbits that extend to the main asteroid belt between the planets Mars and Jupiter (Fig. 3).

Meteorites are superficially described as being either falls or finds. A meteorite fall is scientifically more useful than a find because the exact time that it hit Earth's surface is known. Finds, on the other hand, are simply that—meteorites that have been found by chance. The largest meteorite find to date is that of the

66 ton (60 metric ton) Hoba meteorite in South Africa. Meteorites are either named after the specific geographic location in which they fall, or after the nearest postal station to the site of the fall.

An analysis of meteorite fall statistics suggests that about 30,000 meteorites of mass greater than 3.5 oz (100 g) fall to Earth each year. Of these meteorites the majority weigh just a few hundred grams, only a few (about 5,000) weigh more than 2.2 lb (1 kg), and fewer still (about 700) weigh more than 22 lb (10 kg). In general the number of meteoroids hitting the Earth's atmosphere increases with decreasing meteoroid mass: milligram meteoroids, for example, are about a million times more common than meteoroids weighing a kilogram.

Classification

Meteorites are classified according to the amount of silicate and metallic nickel-iron that they contain. Three main meteorite types are recognized; these are the irons, the stones, and the stony-irons. The iron meteorites consist almost entirely of nickel-iron, while the stone meteorites are mostly silicates. The stony-iron meteorites contain both nickel-iron and silicates. The stony meteorites are further divided into chondrites and achondrites. The term chondrite (pronounced "kondrite") is applied if the meteorite is composed of many small, rounded fragments (called chondrules) bound together in a silicate matrix. If no chondrules are present then the meteorite is an achondrite. Most (about 85%) of the stony meteorites are chondrites. Meteorite fall statistics indicates that about 96% of meteorites are stony, 3% are irons and 1% are stony-irons.

Risk assessment

Even though many thousands of meteorites fall to Earth each year it is rare to hear of one hitting a human being. The chances of a human fatality resulting from the fall of a meteorite have been calculated as one death, somewhere in the world, every 52 years. Thankfully no human deaths from falling meteorites have been reported this century. A woman in Sylacauga, Alabama, was injured, however, by a 8.6 lb (3.9 kg) meteorite that crashed through the roof of her house in 1954. Another close call occurred in August of 1991 when a small meteorite plunged to the ground just a few meters away from two boys in Noblesville, Indiana.

In contrast to the situation with human beings, meteorite damage to buildings is much more common—the larger an object is the more likely it will be hit by a meteorite. A farm building, for example, was struck by a meteorite fragment in St. Robert, Quebec in June of 1994. Likewise, in August 1992 a small village in Uganda was showered by at least 50 meteorite fragments. Two of the meteorites smashed through the roof of the local railway station, one meteorite pierced the roof of a cotton factory, and another fragment hit an oil storage facility. Perhaps one of the more spectacular incidents of meteorite-sustained damage in recent times is that of the Peekskill meteorite which fell in October of 1992 and hit a parked car.

See also Astroblemes; Comets; Minor planets (asteroids).

Further Reading:

Bone, Neil. *Meteors.* Cambridge: Sky Publishing Corp., 1993.

Henbest, Nigel. "Dust in Space." *New Scientist Magazine,* 18 May, 1991, pp. 1-4.

Maurette, Michel. *Hunting for Stars.* New York: McGraw-Hill Inc., 1993.

Todd, Robert. *Thunder Stones and Shooting Stars: The Meaning of Meteorites.* Cambridge: Harvard University Press, 1986.

Martin Beech

Meter see **Metric system**

Methamphetamine see **Amphetamines**

Methane see **Hydrocarbon**

Methanol see **Alcohol**

Methyl group

Methyl group is the name given to the portion of an organic molecule that is derived from methane by removal of a hydrogen atom ($-CH_3$). A methyl group can be abbreviated in chemical structures as -Me. The methyl group is one of the alkyl groups defined by dropping the -ane ending from the parent compound and replacing it with -yl. The methyl group is derived from the parent alkane, methane (HCH_3) by removing one of the hydrogens. Methane has the molecular formula CH_4. It is composed of a central carbon atom bonded to four hydrogen atoms (C-H). The term, methyl is a blend of the Greek words for wine, *methy*, and wood, *hyle* and was first used in reference to wood alcohol or methyl alcohol (CH_3OH). The methyl group consists of a single carbon atom unit that is connected to a longer chain of carbon atoms or possibly a benzene ring.

Methane was originally called "marsh gas" because it was first isolated from the gas bubbling out of marshes. Methane is produced by certain microorganisms that grow in an oxygen-free environment such as sewage and mud. Natural gas is composed primarily of methane. When natural gas is mixed with steam and heated to a high temperature in the presence of a metal catalyst, synthetic gas composed of carbon monoxide (CO) and hydrogen (H_2) is produced.

Synthetic gas is used industrially to make methanol (CH_3OH). Methanol is an alcohol composed of a central carbon atom bonded to three hydrogens (C-H) and a hydroxyl group (-OH). It is used to make formaldehyde, methyl tert-butyl ether (MTBE) and other industrially important chemicals. Formaldehyde is a principal component of the resins that hold boards, such as plywood and particle board, together. Methyl tert-butyl ether (MTBE) is added to gasoline to increase its octane rating and to make it burn cleaner.

See also Alkyl group; Natural gas.

Metric system

The metric system of measurement is an internationally agreed-upon set of units for expressing the amounts of various quantities such as length, mass, time, temperature, and so on.

Whenever we measure something, from the weight of a sack of potatoes to the distance to the moon, we must express the result as a number of specific units: for example, pounds and miles in the English system of measurement (although even England no longer uses that system), or kilograms and kilometers in the metric system. As of 1994, every nation in the world has adopted the metric system, with only four exceptions: the United States, Brunei, Burma and Yemen.

The metric system that is in common use around the world is only a portion of the broader International

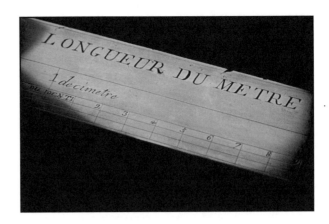

The first provisional standard scale of a meter. Made of copper in 1793, the scale is housed in the Archives Nationales de France, Paris.

System of Units, a comprehensive set of measuring units for almost every measurable physical quantity from the ordinary, such as time and distance, to the highly technical, such as the properties of energy, electricity and radiation. The International System of Units grew out of the 9th General [International] Conference on Weights and Measures, held in 1948. The 11th General Conference on Weights and Measures, held in 1960, refined the system and adopted the French name *Système International d'Unités*, abbreviated as SI.

Because of its convenience and consistency, scientists have used the metric system of units for more than 200 years. Originally, the metric system was based on only three fundamental units: the meter for length, the kilogram for mass, and the second for time. Today, there are more than 50 officially recognized SI units for various scientific quantities.

Measuring units in folklore and history

In the biblical story of Noah, the ark was supposed to be 300 cubits long and 30 cubits high. Like all early units of size, the cubit was based on the always-handy human body, and was most likely the length of a man's forearm from elbow to fingertip. You could measure a board, for example, by laying your forearm down successively along its length. In the Middle Ages, the inch is reputed to have been the length of a medieval king's first thumb joint. The yard was once defined as the distance between the nose of England's King Henry I and the tip of his outstretched middle finger. The origin of the foot as a unit of measurement is obvious.

In Renaissance Italy, Leonardo da Vinci used what he called a *braccio*, or arm, in laying out his works. It was equal to two *palmi*, or palms. But arms and palms,

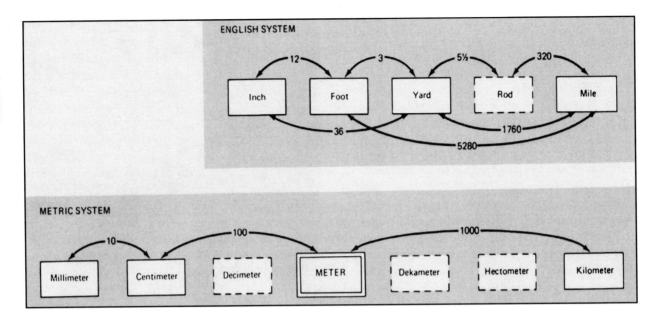

Conversions among English and metric units.

of course, will differ. In Florence, the engineers used a *braccio* that was 23 inches long, while the surveyors' *braccio* averaged only 21.7 inches. The foot, or *piede*, was about 17 inches in Milan, but only about 12 inches in Rome.

Eventually, ancient "rules of thumb" gave way to more carefully defined units. The Metric System was adopted in France in 1799 and the British Imperial System of units was established in 1824. In 1893, the English units used in the United States were redefined in terms of their metric equivalents: the yard was defined as 0.9144 meter, and so on. But English units continue to be used in the United States to this day, even though the Omnibus Trade and Competitiveness Act of 1988 stated that "it is the declared policy of the United States...to designate the metric system of measurement as the preferred system of weights and measures for United States trade and commerce."

English vs. metric units

Why do scientists and everybody else in the world except the United States and three tiny, non-industrialized nations believe that the metric system is superior to the English system? There are four main reasons.

(1) English units are based on silly standards. When that medieval king's thumb became regrettably unavailable for further consultation, the standard for the inch was changed to the length of three grains of barley, placed side by side—not much of an improvement. Metric units, on the other hand, are based on nature, not on the whims of humans.

(2) The standards behind the English units aren't reproducible. Arms, hands, and grains of barley will obviously vary in size; the size of a 3-foot yard depends on whose feet are in question. But metric units are based on standards that are precisely reproducible, time after time.

(3) There are simply too many English units. We have buckets, butts, chains, cords, drams, ells, fathoms, firkins, gills, grains, hands, knots, leagues, three different kinds of miles, four kinds of ounces, and five kinds of tons, to name just a few. There are literally hundreds more. For measuring volume or bulk alone, the English system (now more accurately called the American system) uses ounces, pints, quarts, gallons, barrels and bushels, among many others. In the metric system, on the other hand, there is only one basic unit for each type of quantity.

(4) Any measuring unit, in whatever system, will be too big for some applications and too large for others, so we must have a variety of sizes. People would not appreciate having their waist measurements in miles or their weights in tons. That's why we have inches and pounds. The problem, though, is that in the American system the conversion factors between various-sized units—12 inches per foot, 3 feet per yard, 1760 yards per mile—have no rhyme or reason to them. They're completely arbitrary. Metric units, on the other hand, have conversion factors that are all powers of ten. That is, the metric system is a decimal system, just like dollars and cents. In fact, our entire system of numbers is decimal, based on tens, not threes or twelves. There-

fore, converting a unit from one size to another in the metric system is just a matter of moving the decimal point.

The metric units

The SI starts by defining seven basic units: one each for length, mass, time, electric current, temperature, amount of substance and luminous intensity. ("Amount of substance" refers to the number of elementary particles in a sample of matter. Luminous intensity has to do with the brightness of a light source.) But only four of these seven basic quantities are in everyday use by non-scientists: length, mass, time and temperature. Their defined SI units are the meter for length, the kilogram for mass, the second for time and the degree Celsius for temperature. (The other three basic units are the ampere for electric current, the mole for amount of substance and the candela for luminous intensity.)

Almost all other units can be derived from the basic seven. For example, area is a product of two lengths: meters squared, or square meters. Velocity or speed is a combination of a length and a time: kilometers per hour.

The meter was originally defined in terms of the earth's size; it was supposed to be one ten-millionth of the distance from the equator to the North Pole, going straight through Paris. But because the earth is subject to geological movements, this distance can't be depended upon to remain the same forever. The modern meter, therefore, is defined in terms of how far light will travel in a given amount of time when traveling at—naturally—the speed of light. The speed of light in a vacuum is considered to be a fundamental constant of nature that will never change, no matter how the continents drift. The standard meter turns out to be 39.3701 inches.

The kilogram is the metric unit of mass, not weight. Mass is the fundamental measure of the amount of matter in an object. The mass of a baseball won't change if you hit it from the earth to the moon, but it will weigh less—have less weight—when it lands on the moon because the moon's smaller gravitational force is pulling it down less strongly. Astronauts can be weightless in space, but they can lose mass only by dieting. As long as we don't leave the earth, though, we can speak loosely about mass and weight as if they were the same thing. So you can feel free to "weigh" yourself (not "mass" yourself) in kilograms. Unfortunately, no absolutely unchangeable standard of mass has yet been found to standardize the kilogram on. The kilogram is therefore defined as the mass of a certain bar of plat-

inum-iridium alloy that has been kept (very carefully) since 1889 at the International Bureau of Weights and Measures in Sèvres, France. The kilogram turns out to be 2.2046 pounds.

The metric unit of time is the same old second that we've always used, except that it is now defined in a super-accurate way. It no longer depends on the wobbly rotation of our eccentric old planet (1/86,400th of a day), because Mother Earth is slowing down; her days keep getting a little longer as she grows older. So the second is now defined in terms of the vibrations of a certain kind of atom known as cesium-133. One second is defined as the amount of time it takes for a cesium-133 atom to vibrate in a particular way 9,192,631,770 times. This may sound like a strange definition, but it is a superbly accurate way of fixing the standard size of the second, because the vibrations of atoms depend only on the nature of the atoms themselves, and cesium atoms will presumably continue to behave exactly like cesium atoms forever. The exact number of cesium vibrations was chosen to come out as close as possible to what was previously the most accurate value of the second.

The metric unit of temperature is the degree Celsius (°C), which replaces the English system's degree Fahrenheit (°F). In the scientists' SI, the fundamental unit of temperature is actually the Kelvin (K). But the kelvin and the degree Celsius are exactly the same size: 1.8 times as large as the degree Fahrenheit. You can't convert between Celsius and Fahrenheit simply by multiplying or dividing by 1.8, however, because the scales start at different places. That is, their zero-degree marks have been set at different temperatures. For conversions and other characteristics of the temperature scales.

Bigger and smaller metric units

Because the meter (1.0936 yards) is much too big for measuring an atom and much too small for measuring the distance between two cities, we need a variety of smaller and larger units of length. But instead of inventing different-sized units with completely different names, as the English-American system does, we can create a metric unit of almost any desired size by attaching a prefix to the name of the unit. For example, since kilo- is a Greek form meaning a thousand, a kilometer (kil-OM-et-er) is a thousand meters. Similarly, a kilogram is a thousand grams. The complete set of prefixes that are used in the metric system to convert any unit into larger or smaller ones. For example, a gigagram is a billion grams or 10^9 grams; a nanosecond is one billionth of a second or 10^{-9} second.

Further Reading:

"The International System of Units (SI)." *United States Department of Commerce, National Institute of Standards and Technology, Special Publication,* 330 (1991).

"Interpretation of the SI for the United States and Metric Conversion Policy for Federal Agencies." *United States Department of Commerce, National Institute of Standards and Technology, Special Publication,* 814 (1991).

Robert L. Wolke

KEY TERMS

Kelvin—The International System (SI) unit of temperature. It is the same size as the degree Celsius.

Mass—A measure of the amount of matter in a sample of any substance. Mass does not depend on the strength of a planet's gravitational force, as does weight.

Matter—Any substance. Matter has mass and occupies space.

Temperature—A measure of the average kinetic energy of all the elementary particles in a sample of matter.

Minutes are permitted to remain in the metric system for convenience or for historical reasons, even though they don't conform strictly to the rules. The minute, hour, and day, for example, are so customary that they're still defined in the metric system as 60 seconds, 60 minutes, and 24 hours—not as multiples of ten. For volume, the most common metric unit is not the cubic meter, which is generally too big to be useful in commerce, but the liter, which is one thousandth of a cubic meter. For even smaller volumes, the milliliter, one thousandth of a liter, is commonly used. And for large masses, the metric ton is often used instead of the kilogram. A metric ton (often spelled tonne in other countries) is 1,000 kilograms. Because a kilogram is about 2.2 pounds, a metric ton is about 2,200 pounds: ten percent heavier than an American ton of 2,000 pounds. Another often-used, non-standard metric unit is the hectare for land area. A hectare is 10,000 square meters and is equivalent to 0.4047 acre.

Converting between English and metric units

The problem of changing over a highly industrialized nation such as the United States to a new system of measurements is a substantial one. Once the metric system is in general use in the United States, its simplicity and convenience will be enjoyed, but the transition period, when both systems are in use, can be difficult. Nevertheless, will be easier than it seems. While the complete SI is intimidating because it covers every conceivable kind of scientific measurement over an enormous range of magnitudes, there are only a small number of units and prefixes that are used in everyday life.

See also Units and standards.

Mice

Mice are small fury mammals, usually living on the ground, with bright beady eyes, rounded ears, and long tails. Mice live all around the world, in almost every habitat, and are very important part of nature. They are typically vegetarians, often eating seeds and grain, but some species have developed much more comprehensive diets. Known for their high rates of reproduction, females are normally pregnant for three or four weeks and give birth to multiple young. In most species, the young are naked, blind, and helpless at birth. Mice are an important source of food for numerous animals and are preyed upon by a wide variety of predators, aging from owls to weasels. Mice also impact humans in a variety of ways.

Belonging to the Order Rodentia, mice, along with other types of rodents, are further classified in the suborder Myomoxpha. This is a huge suborder. In fact, more than one quarter of all mammal species on earth belong to the suborder Myomorpha, which includes five families: rats and mice (Muridae), dormice (Gliridae and Seleviniidae), jerboas (Dipodidae), and jumping mice and birch mice (Zapodidae). The family Muridae is the largest family, containing 1,082 species of mice, rats, voles, lemmings, hamsters and gerbils. While there are 14 subfamilies within this family, the vast majority of these species belong to four subfamilies: the New World rats and mice (Hesperomyinae), the Old World rats and mice (Murinae), gerbils (Gerbillinae), and voles and lemmings (Microtinae).

New World mice (Hesperomyinae)

Containing about 350 species, the subfamily of New World mice is the largest mammalian group. Members live in a wide range of habitats thriving in deserts, on mountains, in humid forests, and even on ice-bound plains. Geographically, they live as far north as the southern reaches of the North Pole and as far south as

Harvest mice on wheat.

Patagonia, which is the southern tip of South America. Most New World mice live on the ground, however some burrow into it, some live in semi-aquatic conditions, and some even live in trees. The Climbing mouse (*Rhipidomys venezuelae*), for instance, builds its nests in burrows beneath the roots of trees in the forests of South America but spends a lot of its life in the treetops.

Like most mice, New World mice are usually vegetarians, although some have adapted to eating small animals. For example, the northern grasshopper mouse, living in North America, is largely carnivorous. Dieting primarily on grasshoppers and scorpions, on occasion this mouse may even eat other mice.

Deer mice

A species of White-footed mice, the deer mouse (*Peromyscus maniculatus*) is the most common kind of New World mice, including around 65 subspecies. Their bodies range in size from 4.75-8.5 in (12-22 cm), and their tails measure between 3.25-7 in (8-18 cm).

Deer mice are probably the most abundant mammal in the western United States. These mice eat both plants and insects and are most active at night.

They are noted for their practice of gathering large quantities of food and hiding it in numerous locations to see them through times of bad weather. Since they do not hibernate, this practice is essential to their survival. Deer mice are quite fertile; they are able to bear young at seven weeks old and have litters of up to nine young after a pregnancy lasting three or four weeks.

Old World mice (Murinae)

Containing almost 400 different species, the subfamily of Old World mice includes mice and rats that are highly adaptable and tolerant of adverse natural environments. Oftentimes pests, these mice eat grains and crops, and can carry diseases. Three very interesting groups of Old World mice are the house mice, the wood mice, and spiny mice.

House mice

The most common species of Old World mice is the house mouse (*Mus*). A genus originating in southern Asia, the house mouse includes about 44 separate species; only one species is found in the United States. The body of the house mouse measures about 2.5-3.75 in (6-10 cm) long and is covered by brownish gray fur. Its tail, naked and scaly, typically measures about the same length as its body. Its ears and legs are fairly large.

One of the oldest known forms of domestic rodent pests, house mice have adapted their lives to human habitats. Often living in buildings and making nests behind paneling and beneath floorboards, house mice thrive in large cities and on farms. These mice are able to breed at three months old and have life spans of about four years. Typically, in a given year, a female house mouse can bear from four to six litters of four to eight young, although it is not unheard of for a litter to contain as many as 13 young. Like many other species of mice, the gestation period lasts three weeks and the young are born bald with their eyes shut. At about 13 days old, their eyes open, and fine hair covers their bodies. While the young initially start to feed on their own at around 17 days old, they nurse from their mothers until they are four weeks old. Interestingly, when a population of house mice grows too large for a given area, a form of natural birth control takes effect. Reproductive rates fall dramatically because adolescent females become infertile as their reproductive organs fail to mature or become inactive.

House mice live in family groups. The mice commonly groom each other, particularly on the backs of their necks where they are unable to groom themselves. Mutual grooming occurs daily in most mouse families. Within these family groups, the males have clearly defined ranks. These rankings are not indisputable, however. House mice fight and display threatening and submissive postures.

These social standings are directed at protecting the mice's territory, which the mice outline with their urine. Within the territory, the animals are able to live alone and build their nests, but they do not delineate their own smaller territories within the larger one. The house mouse territory provides the inhabitants with common escape holes and areas for urinating and defecating. The territory can be quite small as long as it provides the mice adequate food and shelter. In fact, the activities of the house mouse can be restricted to an area of only a few square yards. Every night, each mouse within the group typically investigates the entire territory to discover changes that have occurred during the day.

These mice are more active during the night, although they sometimes alternate between periods of rest and activity up to 20 times each day. Furthermore, they are able to move about in many different ways. Preferring not to go into the water, house mice are still able to swim, as well as to run, jump, and climb. Their sense of hearing is very good. They hear very high tones well, a useful ability when listening to other mice squeak, but are much less attuned to lower notes. Their sense of smell is also keen, enabling them to find food and know their territorial boundaries.

Because the many different subspecies have developed slightly different behaviors, they have been able to adapt to any place that man lives. Often, house mice live in hiding places near human food, even inside bags of grain. Because they live near man's own stores, these mice do not typically store their food. They gnaw their way into food storage containers, eating as much as they can stomach and spoiling even more. Although they prefer to eat grains and grain products, house mice can eat practically anything.

The most important European subspecies are the western house mouse (*Mus musculus domesticus*), found in northwestern Europe, and the northern house mouse (*Mus musculus musculus*), found in eastern, northeastern, and southeastern Europe. While these subspecies of house mice originated in Europe, they quickly spread as Europeans moved to other parts of the globe. The western house mouse lives almost exclusively in houses or other manmade structures, while the northern house mouse spends part of the year outside. Both subspecies are descended from wild subspecies.

Wood mice

Unlike the house mouse, some species of Old World mice live in fields and woods and rarely bother humans. One such species is the wood mouse (*Apodemus*). Wood mice are found as far south as Morocco reaching as far north as Iceland and are common throughout Europe and Scandinavia as well as Asia. Of the eleven species that have been identified, five live in Europe. Wood mice are similar in appearance to house mice but have bigger ears, longer hind legs, and their eyes protrude more noticeably. Their bodies range in size from 3-5 in (8-13 cm), and their tails are usually the same lengths as their bodies. Their soft hair comes in a variety of colors.

Nocturnal animals, wood mice live anywhere there is sufficient ground cover in which to hide from predators and to get food-particularly, on the edge of forests. Making their nests under tree roots, these mice leave their nests in the evenings and, in pairs, forage for seeds, berries, grubs, and other insects. If the weather is mild, these mice can breed rapidly, sometimes having four litters each year with an average of five young.

Spiny mice

Another interesting species of Old World mice in the spiny mouse (*Acomys*). As the name implies, their backs are covered with spiny, bristle-like hairs. These mice live throughout the dry environments of northern India and Africa; specifically, they live in deserts, prairies, and savannas. One species lives on the island of Crete in the Mediterranean Sea. They normally eat dried plants, small insects and spiders, and have even been discovered eating the dried remains of Egyptian mummies.

Like their fur, their tails are spiny. Notably, like lizards, their tails can be broken from their bodies rather easily. When a predator catches this mouse, it is often very surprised when it is left with only the animal's tail. Unlike lizards, however, the spiny mice can never grow tails to replace the ones they lose.

The breeding behavior of spiny mice and their maturity level at birth are significantly different from other species of mice. Spiny mice are pregnant for five or six weeks, rather than the three to four week period experienced by other mice During the birth of offspring, other female spiny mice in the group help with the delivery process by chewing through the umbilical cord and by licking the placentas from the newborns. Often, these "midwives" try to claim the young as their own. A few days later, however, the young are treated as the common children of the community, nursed by ever mother and accepted everywhere. Incredibly, the new mother is fertile again by the evening of the same day she delivers and is usually re-impregnated at this time. Unlike other mice, spiny mice are not naked, blind, and helpless at birth. Instead, they appear strong, covered with sparse hair, and their eyes are usually open. At three days old, they start to investigate their surroundings.

Mice and humans

House mice, as well as other species, have been linked to man for thousands of years. Their destruction of human food supplies and crops has been recorded in very early records. Importantly, these mice are also responsible for spreading a number of diseases, such as typhus, spotted fever, Salmonella food poisoning, and bubonic plague.

While many of their activities definitely have had a negative impact on humans, mice have also been provided a useful service. Ever since their importation to Europe from Japan in the mid-1900s, house mice, and some other species, have been used as laboratory animals for research in medicine and biology. In particular, mice are used to study human genetics, to test the effects of various drugs, and to follow the development of certain viruses. Furthermore, mice used in human pregnancy tests, and they help doctors better understand the way that cancer effects humans. Probably, the most commonly used species is the white mouse, an albino form of the house mouse.

Kathryn Snavely

Michelson-Morley experiment

In 1887 two American scientists, physicist Albert Michelson and physical chemist Edward Morley, performed an experiment that was designed to detect the motion of the Earth through a hypothetical medium known as the luminiferous ether which was thought to be present throughout space. They made their measurements with a very sensitive optical instrument now called a Michelson interferometer. Their observations showed no indication of movement through the predicted ether. This outcome was unexpected and has become one of the fundamental experimental results in support of the theory of special relativity, developed by Albert Einstein in 1905.

The luminiferous ether

During the 1800s scientists had become convinced that light was composed of waves, as opposed to a theory that light was made up of particles proposed more than a century earlier by Isaac Newton. They based their belief on experiments that demonstrated phenomena such as interference—the change in intensity caused by mixing two or more beams of light; and diffraction—the fact that beams of light do not always travel in straight lines.

But if light was a wave, what medium did it travel through? Earthquakes produce seismic waves that are transmitted by the Earth's crust and a clanging bell makes sound waves carried by air. Scientists were certain that light had to be transmitted by something, so it was hypothesized that there existed a luminiferous ether. The term luminiferous means light-bearing, but the word ether was not so specific. No substance could be associated with the ether, especially so in space where sunlight and starlight travel in what otherwise appears to be a vacuum. The ether was predicted, but had not been observed.

Scientists thought that the ether should be everywhere and that it must be stationary, at rest with respect to absolute space which, following Newton, was believed to exist independently of the objects in it. It was thought that by measuring the motion of the Earth relative to the ether it would be possible to observe the latter.

The Michelson interferometer

Designing an experiment that would detect the Earth's movement through the ether was a formidable task, requiring the comparison of the speed of light, which was already known to be about 186,300 miles per second (300,000 km/sec) and the speed of the Earth (almost 18 mi or 30 km per sec). Michelson, who excelled in the art and science of measurement, built an instrument to do the job.

He made use of the interference that occurs between light waves. Light waves are transverse waves, which means that they vibrate perpendicularly to the direction in which they travel. If two waves of light of a single color (monochromatic light) arrive at a screen with their crests and troughs aligned, they will interfere constructively, adding up to make higher crests and lower troughs. If, on the other hand, the waves arrive so that crests coincide with troughs, they will cancel with each other, leaving the screen in darkness.

In Michelson's apparatus monochromatic light from a source was sent toward a beam splitter—a partially silvered mirror—where half of the beam continued on to mirror #2 while the other half was reflected along a perpendicular path toward mirror #1. A compensating plate placed in path #1 assured that both beams passed through equal thicknesses of glass. Following reflections at the mirrors the beams returned to the beam splitter where they joined and travelled to the telescope. Because the two rays are not exactly parallel and the wavefronts are not exactly plane the observer would not see all light or all dark, but rather a set of interference fringes—alternating dark and light parallel lines.

With his interferometer Michelson would have been able to measure movement through the ether by noting the change in the position of the fringes as the apparatus was rotated. To understand this first think of yourself to be at rest with the interferometer. From the instrument's point of view, it is the ether that moves, creating an ether wind which would push against the light beams. If the Earth moves in the direction of path #2, then the ether wind will be felt in the opposite direction. Beam #2 will act like a sailboat sailing first against the wind and then with it. It will travel slower when it opposes the ether wind but faster when the wind is at its back. In contrast, Beam #1 travels perpendicular to the ether wind on both parts of its trip. Because the ether wind affects each beam by different amounts there is a difference in the times it takes the beams to travel along their respective paths. That difference shows up as a fringe pattern.

The sole presence of the fringe pattern, however, does not allow measurement of the Earth's motion. That is accomplished by rotating the entire instrument. As the two beams change their orientation with respect to the ether wind, their travel times change. That causes the fringes to move or shift from their initial position. By measuring the fringe shift as the interferometer rotated, it should have been possible to measure the Earth's velocity through a stationary luminiferous ether, or, from the laboratory perspective, the velocity of an ether wind across a stationary interferometer.

Michelson performed the experiment for the first time in Germany in 1881. Contrary to his expectations no fringe shift could be observed. He repeated the experiment in 1887 in the United States, this time in collaboration with Morley. They placed their optical elements on a granite slab, and the slab on a vat full of liquid mercury. They lengthened the path each beam had to travel, and took good care to control the temperature in their laboratory to avoid thermal distortions.

According to their calculations the Michelson interferometer should have registered a fringe shift of

about four-tenths (0.4) of a fringe. Instead, no fringe shift was observed. They were forced to conclude that their experiment had shown that the hypothesis of a stationary, luminiferous ether was not correct.

The null result

The Michelson-Morley experiment is a perfect example of a null experiment, one in which something that was expected to happen is not observed. The consequences of their observations for the development of physics were profound. Having proven that there could be no stationary ether, physicists tried to advance new theories that would save the ether concept. Michelson himself suggested that the ether might move, at least near the Earth. Others studied the possibility that rigid objects might actually contract as they travelled. But it was Einstein's theory of special relativity that finally explained their results.

The significance of the Michelson-Morley experiment was not assimilated by the scientific community until after Einstein presented his theory. In fact, when Michelson was awarded the Nobel Prize in physics in

1907, the first American to receive that honor, it was for his measurements of the standard meter using his interferometer. The ether wind experiment was not mentioned.

There has also been some controversy as to how the experiment affected the development of special relativity. Einstein commented that the experiment had only a negligible effect on the formulation of his theory. Clearly it was not a starting point for him. Yet the experiment has been repeated by others over many years, upholding the original results in every case. Even if special relativity did not spring directly from its results, the Michelson-Morley experiment has convinced many scientists of the accuracy of Einstein's theory and has remained one of the foundations upon which relativity stands.

See also Interference; Interferometry; Light; Relativity, special.

Further Reading:

Einstein, Albert. *Relativity: The Special and General Theory.* New York: Crown, 1961.

French, A.P. *Special Relativity.* New York: W.W. Norton, 1968.

Jenkins, F.A. and H.E. White. *Fundamentals of Optics.* New York: McGraw-Hill, 1976.

Physics Today. "Special Issue: Michelson-Morley Centennial." May 1987.

John Appel

Microburst see **Wind shear**

Microchip see **Integrated circuit**

Microclimate

Climate is the set of characteristic temperatures, humidities, sunshine, winds, and other weather conditions that prevail over large areas of space for long periods of time. Microclimate refers to a climate that holds over a very small area. Microclimates usually are slight modifications of the main background climate altered by features in the landscape. A forest creates a microclimate within the canopy of trees which is cooler, wetter, and has altered soil chemistry compared to the area outside the forest. The altered climate found within forests can support organisms that cannot survive in the surrounding grassland. Similarly a large city has altered wind flows due to the presence of tall buildings,

increased overall temperatures, and a very different type of ground cover than the surrounding plains. All these factors contribute to a microclimate characteristic of an urban area. Microclimates frequently support unique ecosystems. Mountain meadows, river valleys, tidal marshes, and crop lands have one or several microclimates which help determine the amount and type of organisms that thrives in these locations.

Microclimates are parts of a complex web of climates that exist on Earth. The general global climate of Earth can be thought of as a collection of many smaller scale climates that coexist like patches in a quilt. These subclimates are further divided into smaller scale climates each with its own distinctive features. For example the continent-wide climate of North America, called the microclimate, is distinctly different than that of South America. Within the North American macroclimate are several distinct mesoclimates which extend over distances much smaller than the continent. These include plains, mountains, and deserts. Making up each of these mesoclimates are smaller climate zones called local climates. Some distinct local climates are forests, croplands, and large cities. The smallest scale sub-climate is the microclimate defined as the climate which holds over a distance (in any direction) of less than 328 ft (100 m). Distinct microclimates include a small cornfield, a forest clearing, and the canyon formed by several tall city office buildings. Microclimates thus form the smallest building blocks of the overall global climate.

See also Weather.

Microorganisms

Microorganisms are organisms of microscopic dimensions, too small to be seen by the eye alone. To be viewed, microorganisms must be magnified by an optical or electron microscope. The most common types of microorganisms are viruses, bacteria, blue-green bacteria, some algae, some fungi, yeasts, and protozoans.

Viruses, bacteria, and blue-green bacteria are all prokaryotes, meaning that they do not have an organized cell nucleus separated from the protoplasm by a membrane-like envelope. Viruses are the simplest of the prokaryotic life forms, being little more than simple genetic material—either DNA (deoxyribonucleic acid) or RNA (ribonucleic acid)—plus associated proteins of the viral shell (called a capsid) that together comprise an infectious agent of cells. Viruses are not capable of independent reproduction. They reproduce by penetrating a host cell and diverting much of the metabolic and reproductive physiology of the cell to the reproduction of copies of the virus.

The largest kingdom of prokaryotes is the Monera, in which the genetic material is organized as a single strand of DNA, neither meiosis or mitosis occur, and reproduction is by asexual cellular division. Bacteria (a major division of the Monera) are characterized by rigid or semi-rigid cell walls, propagation by binary division of the cell, and a lack of mitosis. Blue-green bacteria or cyanobacteria (also in the Monera) use chlorophyll dispersed within the cytoplasm as the primary light-capturing pigment for photosynthesis.

Many microorganisms are eukaryotic organisms, having their nuclear material organized within a nucleus which is bounded by an envelope. Eukaryotes also have paired chromosomes of DNA, which can be seen microscopically during mitosis and meiosis, and a number of other discrete cellular organelles.

Protists are a major kingdom of eukaryotes that includes microscopic protozoans, some fungi, and some algae. Protists have flagellated spores, and mitochondria and plastids are often, but not always, present.

Protozoans are single-celled microorganisms which reproduce by binary fission and are often motile, usually using cilia or flagellae for propulsion; some protozoans are colonial.

Fungi are heterotrophic organisms with chitinous cell walls which lack flagella. Some fungi are unicellular microorganisms, but others are larger with thread-like hyphae forming a more complex mycelium, which can take the form of mushrooms in the most highly developed species. Algae are photosynthetic, nonvascular organisms, many of which are unicellular, or are found in colonies of several cells; they are therefore microscopic. Yeasts are a group of single-celled fungi that reproduce by budding or by cellular fission.

In summary, microorganisms comprise a wide range of diverse but unrelated groups of organisms, characterized only by their size. As a group, microorganisms are extremely important ecologically as primary producers, and as agents of decay of dead organisms and recycling of the nutrients contained in their biomass. Some species of microorganisms are also important as parasites and as other disease-causing agents in humans and other organisms.

See also Algae; Bacteria; Fungi; Protozoa; Virus; Yeast.

Microscopy

Microscopy is the science of producing and observing images of objects which can not be seen by the unaided eye. A microscope is an instrument which produces the image. The primary function of a microscope is to resolve, that is distinguish, two closely spaced objects as separate. The secondary function of a microscope is to magnify. Microscopy has developed into an exciting field with numerous applications in biology, geology, chemistry, physics, and technology.

The light microscope

The most common, inexpensive, and easy to use microscope is the light microscope which produces a magnified image of the object by bending and focusing light rays. The light microscope uses a variety of glass lenses to produce a magnified image which is focused before the eye. The magnifying properties of a converging lens, like that which is used in a typical magnifying glass or camera. Light from the object is bent, or refracted, as it passes through the lens producing an image which is inverted and magnified. In the simplest compound microscope, two converging lenses are used. The image from the first lens (objective) becomes the object for the second lens (eyepiece). The final image is much larger than either lens could produce independently. With a little effort, you can reproduce this effect yourself by using two magnifying glasses.

The wavelength of visible light ultimately limits the resolving power of the light microscope. Therefore, two objects which are separated by distances significantly less than about 0.4 micrometers (the smallest wavelength of visible light) can not be distinguished as separate. This is because the light microscope produces its images by reflecting from or transmitting visible light through a specimen. An analogy can be made to ocean waves at the beach, with wavelengths of a few meters. If two people were wading into the surf only a few inches apart (a separation much less than the wavelength of the ocean waves), it would be impossible to distinguish them as separate by analyzing the ocean waves which reflected from them. Despite these limitations, the resolution of the light microscope is sufficient to produce excellent images of many of the important cell structures and organelles, and consequently still has many applications, chiefly in biology.

History of light microscopy

Since the time of the Romans, it was realized that certain shapes of glass had properties which could mag-

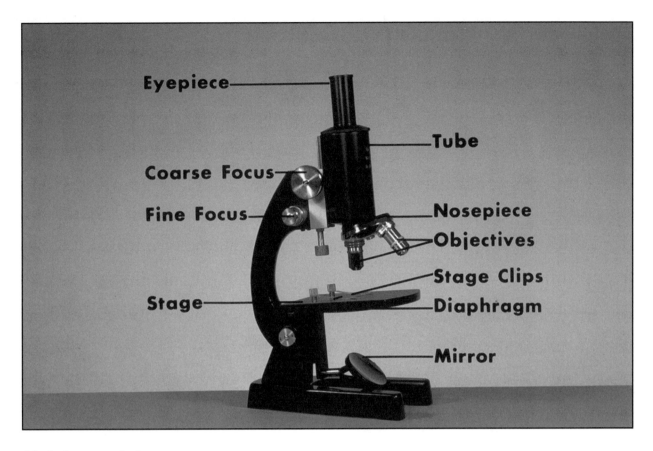

A typical compound microscope.

nify objects. By the year 1300, these early crude lenses were being used as corrective eyeglasses. It wasn't until the late 1500s, however, that the first compound microscopes were developed.

Robert Hooke (1635-1703) was the first to publish results on the microscopy of plants and animals. Using a simple two lens compound microscope, he was able to discern the cells in a thin section of cork. The most famous microbiologist was Antoni van Leeuwenhoek (1632-1723) who, using just a single lens microscope, was able to describe organisms and tissues, such as bacteria and red blood cells, which were previously not known to exist. In his lifetime, Leeuwenhoek built over 400 microscopes, each one specifically designed for one specimen only. The highest resolution he was able to achieve was about 2 micrometers.

By the mid-nineteenth century, significant improvements had been made in the light microscope design, mainly due to refinements in lens grinding techniques. However, most of these lens refinements were the result of trial and error rather than inspired through principles of physics. Ernst Abbé (1840-1905) was the first to apply physical principles to lens design. Combining glasses with different refracting powers into a single lens, he was able to reduce image distortion significantly. Despite these improvements, the ultimate resolution of the light microscope was still limited by the wavelength of light. To resolve finer detail, something with a smaller wavelength than light would have to be used.

ELECTRON MICROSCOPY

In the mid-1920s, Louis de Broglie (1892-1966) suggested that electrons, as well as other particles, should exhibit wave like properties similar to light. Experiments on electron beams a few years later confirmed de Broglie's hypothesis. Electrons behave like waves. Of importance to microscopy was the fact that the wavelength of electrons is typically much smaller than the wavelength of light. Therefore, the limitation imposed on the light microscope of 0.4 micrometers could be significantly reduced by using a beam of electrons to illuminate the specimen. This fact was exploited in the 1930s in the development of the electron microscope.

There are two types of electron microscope, the transmission electron microscope (TEM) and the scanning electron microscope (SEM). The TEM transmits electrons through an extremely thin sample. The

A scanning electron microscope at the Billancourt Centre, Boulogne, France. This system is used in the testing of Renault Sport's motor racing engines. The samples on screen are the fracture faces of components subjected to a tensile strength test.

electrons scatter as they collide with the atoms in the sample and form an image on a photographic film below the sample. This process is similar to a medical x ray where x rays (very short wavelength light) are transmitted through the body and form an image on photographic film behind the body. By contrast, the SEM reflects a narrow beam of electrons off the surface of a sample and detects the reflected electrons. To image a certain area of the sample, the electron beam is scanned in a back and forth motion parallel to the sample surface, similar to the process of mowing a square section of lawn. The chief differences between the two microscopes are that the TEM gives a two-dimensional picture of the interior of the sample while the SEM gives a three-dimensional picture of the surface of the sample. Images produced by SEM are familiar to the public, as in television commercials showing pollen grains or dust mites.

For the light microscope, light can be focused and bent using the refractive properties of glass lenses. To bend and focus beams of electrons, however, it is necessary to use magnetic fields. The magnetic lens which focuses the electrons works through the physical principle that a charged particle, such as an electron which has a negative charge, will experience a force when it is moving in a magnetic field. By positioning magnets properly along the electron beam, it is possible to bend the electrons in such a way as to produce a magnified image on a photographic film or a fluorescent screen. This same principle is used in a television set to focus electrons onto the television screen to give the appropriate images.

Electron microscopes are complex, expensive and to use them effectively requires extensive training. They are rarely found outside the research laboratory. Sample preparation can be extremely time consuming. For the TEM, the sample must be ground extremely thin, less than 0.1 micrometer, so that the electrons will make it through the sample. For the SEM, the sample is usually coated with a thin layer of gold to increase its ability to reflect electrons. Therefore, in electron microscopy, the specimen can't be living. Today, the best TEMs can produce images of the atoms in the interior of a sample. This is a factor of a 1,000 better than the best light microscopes. The SEM, on the other hand, can typically distinguish objects which are about 100 atoms in size.

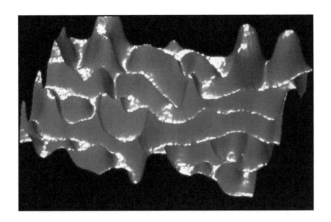

An atomic force micrograph of the surface of a thin copolymer film. The atomic force microscope (AFM) is capable of atomic-scale resolution, and works by drawing a very fine probe across the surface of the sample. The vertical motion of the probe is converted into electronic signals which are then processed to give the type of surface map seen here. The advantage the AFM has over the scanning tunneling microscope is that it works for samples that are not electrical conductors.

Scanning Tunneling Microscopy

In the early 1980s, a new technique in microscopy was developed which did not involve beams of electrons or light to produce an image. Instead, a small metal tip is scanned very close to the surface of a sample and a tiny electric current is measured as the tip passes over the atoms on the surface. The microscope which works in this manner is the scanning tunneling microscope (STM). When a metal tip is brought close to the sample surface, the electrons which surround the atoms on the surface can actually "tunnel through" the air gap and produce a current through the tip. This physical phenomenon is called tunneling and is one of the amazing results of quantum physics. If such phenomenon could occur with large objects, it would be possible for a baseball to tunnel through a brick wall with no damage to either. The current of electrons which tunnel through the air gap is very much dependent on the width of the gap and therefore the current will rise and fall in succession with the atoms on the surface. This current is then amplified and fed into a computer to produce a three dimensional image of the atoms on the surface.

Without the need for complicated magnetic lenses and electron beams, the STM is far less complex than the electron microscope. The tiny tunneling current can be simply amplified through electronic circuitry similar to that which is used in other electronic equipment, such as a stereo. In addition, the sample preparation is usually less tedious. Many samples can be imaged in air with essentially no preparation. For more sensitive samples which react with air, imaging is done in vacuum. A requirement for the STM is that the samples be electrically conducting, such as a metal.

Recent developments in microscopy

There have been numerous variations on the types of microscopy outlined so far. A sampling of these is: acoustic microscopy, which involves the reflection of sound waves off a specimen; x-ray microscopy, which involves the transmission of x rays through the specimen; near field optical microscopy, which involves shining light through a small opening smaller than the wavelength of light; and atomic force microscopy, which is similar to scanning tunneling microscopy but can be applied to materials which aren't electrically conducting, such as quartz.

One of the most amazing recent developments in microscopy involves the manipulation of individual atoms. Through a novel application of the STM, scientists at IBM were able to arrange individual atoms on a surface and spell out the letters "IBM." This has opened up new directions in microscopy, where the microscope is both an instrument with which to observe and to interact with microscopic objects. Future trends in microscopy will most likely probe features within the atom.

Further Reading:

Burgess, Jeremy, Marten, Michael, and Rosemary Taylor. *Microcosmos.* Cambridge: Cambridge University Press, 1987.

Eigler, D. M. and E. K. Schweizer. "Positioning Single Atoms with a Scanning Tunneling Microscope." *Nature* 344 (1990): 524-526.

Giancoli, Douglas. *Physics.* Englewood Cliffs, NJ: Prentice Hall, 1995.

Slayter, Elizabeth and Henry. *Light and Electron Microscopy.* Cambridge: Cambridge University Press, 1992.

Taylor, D., Michel Nederlof, Frederick Lanni, and Alan Waggoner. "The New Vision of Light Microscopy." *American Scientist* 80 (1992): 322-335.

Kurt Vandervoort

Microtechnology

Microtechnology is the use of compact, or very small, technical devices. Microtechnology includes microcomputer parts, space microdevices, microsurgery, and microelectronics. Technology is the application of inventions and discoveries to meet needs or obtain goals. The term micro, derived from the Greek word *mikros*, meaning small, is used to describe something that is unusually small. Microtechnology has the advantages of taking up less space, using less construction material, and costing less money. Initial manufacturing of such small components requires invention or reapplication of existing technology, a trained manufacturer, and precise manufacturing conditions. However, the resulting smaller equipment is less expensive to transport and store; this aspect of microtechnology makes it ideally suited for outer space use. Both microfilm and microfiche, which store information on film, are also examples of microtechnology; microfiche generally stores more than microfilm.

Microtechnology has emerged in various technological fields during the past 100 years. Advances in scientific knowledge and applications of that knowledge make microtechnology possible. Specific concepts and inventions have provided the necessary basis for microtechnology. These significant inventions include: the microscope, electricity, computers, and lasers. For example, microscopes allow technicians to view minute regions of computer microprocessors and other microdevice components. Microscopes also enable surgeons to view aspects of a patient's body at a resolution not possible for the naked human eye.

Computer microtechnology

Not long after the first computer was made, gradual improvements were made that increased computer functions and decreased computer size. Today's computers contain many microcomputer components—the major one being the microprocessor, a type of microchip. A microprocessor contains the entire computer central processing unit on a single chip.

Microchips come in a range of sizes and can be as small as 1 in^2 (6.45 cm^2). They are made of a slice of semiconducting material such as silicon or germanium and have specific electrical characteristics. The first microchips were made in the early 1960s, and can serve various functions within a computer. Some microchips are microprocessors; others can be memory or interface microchips. The microprocessor chip communicates with memory and interface chips within the computer through buses, or series of wires, that relay information.

Microcomputers are embedded in and control numerous modern devices such as automobiles, digital watches, telephones, and video cameras. The microelectronic circuits of these embedded computers are called integrated circuits. The miniature circuitry is "onboard" the chips.

Lasers

Computer microtechnology also utilizes laser technology. Lasers (the name is an acronym for light amplification by spectral emission radiation) are focused beams of light, amplified between opposing mirrors. The first laser was used in 1960 by the American physicist Theodore Maiman. Directed light has extraordinary specificity; a laser light can drill over 100 holes into the head of a pin. Lasers are used to guide missiles, align walls and ceilings of buildings under construction, print, and detect geophysical continental drift. All lasers have three major components: a light source, opposing mirrors that intensify the light beam, and an amplifying medium. Lasers are classified according to their amplifying medium and are generally of four types: semiconductor, solid state, gas, or dye. A laser beam can be directed through the ground and around bends. Laser light is used in communication since it can be conducted along glass fiberoptic cables, without considerable signal loss.

Laser microtechnology has many applications. Machines can use laser light to read or scan information. Bar code scanners in grocery stores routinely register product identification and cost with laser scanners. Lasers are also used to cut materials such as cloth and weld metals. In addition, lasers (particularly CO_2 lasers) are used in medicine. Lasers are used surgically and can shatter gall stones. Laser beams guide weapons, such as missiles, that contain laser designators that can detect and follow the laser light path. Some lasers are as small as a grain of sand.

Scientific and medical microtechnology

Several microtechnological applications exist in both science and medicine. Scientists use microscopes, micropipettes, microtomes, microelectrodes, and microcapsules in research. And surgeons use microscopes, micromanipulators, and microinstruments in microsurgery.

Scientists use microscopes to observe objects less than 100 µm, or 0.1 mm, in diameter. Scientists can also make thin slices of microscopic substances, including living material, with a microtome. Micropipettes are miniature pipettes used to inject substances into something else, such as a cell. Microelectrodes are electrodes that can measure an electrical charge across a cellular membrane; microelectrodes are also used to detect intracellular ionic flow that can signify other important cellular events. Microcapsules release their contents at set temperatures and pressures, and can be used in chemical, physical, and biochemical experiments to supply a substance at a set point.

In medical microsurgery, surgeons observe a patient's tissues through a microscope in order to make highly precise alterations to areas such as the eyes (cataract removal or corneal transplant), ears (middle ear bone replacement), larynx, blood vessels, cervix, fallopian tubes (obstruction removal), vas deferens (vasectomy reversal), and severed appendages and nerves. Microsurgery can be accomplished either with delicate surgical instruments held by the surgeon while viewing the surgical area under the microscope, or by a micromanipulator using microinstruments. A micromanipulator is a human-guided or programmed machine which manipulates microinstruments to perform surgical procedures. Lasers make a major contribution to medical microsurgery by virtue of their ability to make extremely precise surgical cuts. Laser surgery is also used to remove some skin lesions.

Space microtechnology

Any device sent into outer space must have certain characteristics. It must be able to withstand the stress of

KEY TERMS

Microchip—A very small piece of material containing an electrical circuit that can process or store information.

Microelectronics—Very small electronic circuitry.

Microprocessor—A microchip that houses a computer's entire central processing unit—the speed of which is limited by the conducting material comprising the chip.

Microsurgery—Surgery performed with visual assistance of a microscope that can also employ micromanipulation of microinstruments.

propulsion into space. It must also be able to utilize power in an efficient, non-wasteful, manner. And it must be able to manage thermal extremes. It is also very favorable for such devices to be as small and lightweight as possible and still function effectively. Several space microdevices have been created that meet these criteria. Miniature gas chromatographic ionization detectors, ion mobility spectrometers, x-ray diffraction, and fluorescence instruments are all in various stages of development. Each of these devices plays an important role in exobiology, the science of extraterrestrial environments that may support life.

A number of space microdevices have micromechanical functions; they either sense or respond to detected conditions such as the presence of a chemical or heat. Ionization detectors can identify chemical composition of a foreign sample. Model ionization detectors weigh only 1-2 g, and are sensitive enough to detect compounds at 10^{-14} mol/sec. A miniature "stable isotope laser diode spectrometer" has also been designed to determine sample ratios of carbon and oxygen isotopes. These advances in miniature space technology could help decrease payload (cargo not required for basic travel operations).

Further Reading:

Chester, A., V. Letokhov, and S. Martellucci, eds. *Laser Science and Technology*. New York: Plenum Press, 1987.

Cutts J, ed. *Advanced Microdevices and Space Sensors*. San Diego: The International Society for Optical Engineering, 1994.

Louise Dickerson

Microwave communication

Microwaves are radio signals with a very short wavelength. Microwave signals can be focused by antennas just as a searchlight concentrates light into a narrow beam. Signals are transmitted directly from a source to a receiver site. Reliable microwave signal range does not extend very far beyond the visible horizon.

If microwave signals were visible to the eye, cities would be seen to be crisscrossed by microwave transmissions carrying important signals. Any type of information that can move over telephone wires or coaxial cables can be transmitted over a microwave circuit as efficiently as through the wires and cables they supplement.

Microwaves and power

The ability to focus microwave signals into narrow beams results in very high antenna gain. Antenna gain increases the effective-radiated power of a microwave signal much as the reflector in a flashlight produces a tight beam of light powerful enough to illuminate distant objects. The most common microwave-antenna focuses the signal by reflecting it from a parabolically-curved reflecting surface sometimes called a dish.

High antenna gain means that microwave transmitters need not be extremely powerful to produce a strong signal. A transmitter rated at 10 watts or less, using an antenna that concentrates the signal toward its target, can produce a received signal as strong as if thousands of Watts were scattered in all directions.

Microwave transmitters

The lower-powered microwave signals used by communication transmitters are usually produced by solid-state devices. The Gunn diode is an example. When supplied with voltage from a well-regulated power supply these devices reliably produce a few watts of microwave signal.

Spatial diversity

A sharply-defined beam of microwave transmissions means that separate signals can use the same range of frequencies without mutual interference if the paths are carefully planned. Lower radio-frequency assignments can accommodate fewer users because longer-wavelength signals cannot be confined to a narrow beam. A relative immunity to interference allows each microwave signal to use a very wide bandwidth. Wider bandwidths are required when more information per second is transmitted.

A microwave communications tower in Munich, Germany.

It is common practice to locate microwave receivers and transmitters atop high buildings when hilltops or mountain peaks are not available. The higher the antennas are raised, the further will be the distance to the radio horizon. It takes many ground-based relay "hops" to carry a microwave signal across a continent. Since the 1960s the United States has been spanned by a network of microwave relay stations.

Satellites and microwaves

Earth satellites relaying microwave signals from the ground have increased the distance that can be covered in one hop. Microwave repeaters in a satellite in a stationary orbit 22,300 mi (35,881 km) above the earth is high enough to reach one third of the earth's surface. Microwave signals can be relayed by just one satellite repeater when that satellite is simultaneously above the horizon for both the earth-bound transmitter and the receiver.

Microwave propagation

Microwave signals usually travel from transmitter to receiver along nearly straight-line paths. There are occasional exceptions. The same atmospheric conditions that cause optical mirages can cause microwave-fading problems.

Microwave signals bend slightly when passing obliquely through layers of different air density. A microwave signal can be trapped beneath a temperature inversion, causing a strong signal to fade when the signal cannot reach a receiver atop a mountain peak. Atmospheric ducting can cause a microwave signal to follow the curvature of the earth so that it reaches far beyond the horizon. Radar signals at microwave frequencies may reveal the presence of surface ships at distances of hundreds of miles but be unable to display radar returns from aircraft in flight. This happens unpredictably but the problems usually persist for only short periods.

Microwave signals are reflected by flat surfaces. Plane reflectors may be used to bounce a microwave signal around a hill or a building that would otherwise block its path. Flat reflectors are often placed at the top of tall microwave-relay towers. Parabolic dish antennas at ground level face skyward, directed toward the reflectors that bounce their signals to the horizon.

A passive microwave reflector needs little maintenance and requires no power. Their principle drawback is that the strength of the microwave signal drops off as the inverse fourth power of the total distance when it has been reflected from a passive repeater, greatly increasing the path loss. Doubling the total distance reduces received-signal power by one sixteenth.

All wave-based phenomena interact strongly with objects having a size comparable to a wavelength. Raindrops and hailstones are similar in size to the wavelength of higher-frequency microwaves. A rainstorm can block microwave communication producing a condition called rain fade. Weather radar deliberately uses shorter-wavelength microwaves to increase interaction with rain.

Microwave path loss

Microwave communications systems must be carefully engineered if they are to provide reliable communications. Engineers can predict the signal loss in decibels (dB) for a given signal path. They are then able to specify the transmitter power, total antenna gain, and receiver sensitivity required for the circuit. Additional signal or gain can be specified to protect against most fades.

KEY TERMS

. . . .

Bandwidth—Range of frequencies available for a dedicated purpose.

Coaxial cables—Concentric wire and shield, used to carry complex signals.

Decibels—Logarithmically-based basis for power comparisons.

Ducting—Trapping a radio signal so it follows the earth's curvature.

Inversion—Condition when air temperature increases with added height.

Parabolic—Shape based on the parabola, a conic section from mathematics.

Passive reflector—Surface used to reflect a signal.

Propagation—Basis for the transmission of a signal.

Radar—Detection and location system using reflected microwaves.

Spatial diversity—Reduction of interference by maintaining physical separation.

As an example, suppose that a proposed path for a microwave relay system between a radio-station studio and a remote transmitter site is predicted to have a circuit loss of 110 dB. If the system design provides a safety cushion of 30 dB against the possibility of rain fade, the total gains and losses in the system must equal at least +140 dB. If the calculations fall short of this target by 10 dB, for example, the engineer can increase the power of the transmitter by a factor of 10, or increase the gain of one or both of the other antennas by 10 dB, or increase the receiver sensitivity, by 10 dB. Any combination of improvements that will add to 10 dB will provide the desired performance.

Microwave communication is nearly 100% reliable, in part because the circuits have been engineered to minimize fading and in part because computer-controlled networks often reroute signals through a different path before a fade becomes noticeable.

See also Antenna.

Further Reading:

ARRL, *The ARRL UHF/Microwave Experimenter's Manual*, Radio Society of Great Britain: American Radio Relay League, 1990.

ARRL. *The Satellite Experimenter's Handbook*, Radio Society of Great Britain: American Radio Relay League, 1990.

Hobson, Art. *Physics: Concepts and Connections*, Prentice-Hall, Inc., 1995.

Ostdiek, Vern J., and Donald J. Bord. *Inquiry Into Physics*. West Publishing Company, 1995.

RSGB. *Microwave Handbook. vol. 1-3*. Radio Society of Great Britain: American Radio Relay League, 1989, 1991, 1992.

Donald Beaty

Microwave radiation see **Electromagnetic spectrum**

Mid-ocean ridge see **Plate tectonics**

Midges see **True flies**

Migraine

Migraine, one of the most common headache conditions known to mankind, was first described during the Mesopotamian era, about 3000 B.C. Migraine is a familial disorder, sometimes accompanied by neurological disturbances, with attacks separated by pain-free interludes; some sufferers find that it is provoked by a particular stimulus, such as stress, loud noises, missed meals, or eating particular foods such as chocolate or red wine. Migraine is not a single medical entity, however, and symptom patterns are numerous and changeable. Migraine is a complex condition that is still poorly understood.

Clinical features

The clinical features of migraine have been divided into four distinct phases. The first phase is known as the *prodrome*. Symptoms develop slowly over a 24-hour period preceding the onset of the headache, and often include feelings of heightened or dulled perception, irritability or withdrawal, cravings for certain foods, and other features.

The second phase, known as the *aura*, features visual disturbances that may be described as flashing lights, shimmering zig-zag lines, spotty vision, and other disturbances in one or both eyes. There may be other sensory symptoms as well, such as pins and needles or numbness in the hands; all of these can be acutely distressing to the patient. This phase usually precedes the onset of headache by one hour or less.

Phase three consists of the headache itself, usually described as severe, often with a throbbing or pulsating quality. The pain may occur on one or both sides of the head, and may be accompanied by nausea and vomiting, and intolerance of light (photophobia), noise (phonophobia), or movement. This phase may last from 4-72 hours. During the final phase, called the *postdrome*, the patient often feels drained and washed-out; this feeling generally subsides within 24 hours.

Prevalence of the condition

It is estimated that at least one in eight adults suffers from migraine. This condition primarily affects young adults; although attacks may begin at any age, including childhood, the peak incidence is between ages 25-34 years. Women are two to three times more likely to be affected than men.

An outdated classification designated two types of migraine, classical and common, on the basis of the presence or absence of an aura. So-called classical migraine, preceded by an aura, accounts for approximately 15% of cases. Some 80% of migraine attacks occur without the aura phase; this type was previously designated as *common migraine*. Some patients may suffer both types of the disorder, at different times; others may experience an aura without the migraine.

Origins of the disorder

Migraine appears to involve changes in the patterns of blood circulation and neural signal transmission in the brain. In the 1930s, it was discovered that administration of the drug ergotamine reduced the pulsations of swollen cranial blood vessels, which often were associated with the pain of the headache. A vascular hypothesis for the origin of migraine was promoted for many years thereafter, postulating that the neurological symptoms (such as the visual and mood disturbances) were caused by constriction of the blood vessels, and that the headache itself was the result of dilation of these vessels, resulting in activation of pain-sensitive nerves nearby.

However, changes in blood flow resulting from vessel dilation and constriction are not observed in all migraine patients. In the early 1940s, a Harvard neuropsychologist named K.S. Lashley charted the development of his own migraine attacks, describing the advance of a luminous blind spot across his field of vision, and extrapolating the progress of the neurological disturbance on the underlying brain structures. He speculated that a wave of intense excitement was followed by a wave of complete inhibition in the neural

Phase 1 (The Prodrome): up to 24 hours prior to the headache
Roughly half of all migraine sufferers experience this stage, which is characterized by symptoms of heightened or dulled perception, irritability or withdrawal, and food cravings.

Phase 2 (The Aura): up to 1 hour prior to the headache
One out of five migraine sufferers experience this stage of visual disturbances. There may be flashing lights, shimmering zig-zag lines, and luminous blind spots, as well as non-visual sensations like numbness and pins and needles in the hands.

Phase 3 (The Headache): 4-72 hours long
Characterized by:
• Severe aching, often pulsating or throbbing pain on one or both sides of the head

• Intolerance of light (photophobia)

• Intolerance of noise (phonophobia)

• Nausea and vomiting

• Sensitivity to movement

• And less commonly, speech difficulties

Phase 4 (The Postdrome): up to 24 hours after the headache
Most migraine sufferers experience aching muscles and feel tired and drained after the headache, although some few go through a period of euphoria.

The phases of a typical migraine.

cells of the visual cortex, the region of the brain responsible for processing visual information. The electrical phenomenon known as spreading depression was soon verified by physiologists, and is an important part of the modern understanding of migraine development.

Currently, migraine development is partitioned into three phases. The first step is generation in the midbrain; for reasons not fully understood, normally functioning cells in this region begin sending abnormal electrical signals along their projections to other brain centers, including the visual cortex. The second step is activation of the blood vessels in the brain, wherein arteries may contract or dilate. The third step is activation of nerve cells that mediate the sensation of pain in the head and face. Some patients may experience only one of these three stages; this could explain individuals who experience only the aura, without the pain phase, for example.

Some evidence suggests a connection between migraine and levels of serotonin, a neurotransmitter found in the brain and numerous other cells and tissues. Migraine attacks have been correlated with falling levels of serotonin in the body. The connection has been strengthened by the observation that the drug sumatrip-

KEY TERMS

Aura—A phase that sometimes preceeds a migraine attack, characterized by visual disturbances such as spotty vision and flashing lights.

Visual cortex—The region of the brain responsible for processing visual information.

tan, which closely resembles serotonin chemically, is highly effective in treating migraine.

Further reading:

American Council on Headache Education, with Lynne M. Constantine and Suzanne Scott. *Migraine: The Complete Guide*. New York: Dell, 1994.
Raskin, Neil H. *Headache*. 2nd edition. New York: Churchill Livingstone Inc., 1988.
Sacks, Oliver. *Migraine*. Berkeley, CA: University of California Press, 1985.
Sandler, M., ed. *Migraine: A Spectrum of Ideas*. Oxford: Oxford University Press, 1990.

Susan Andrew

Migration

Migration is the act of moving from one place to another, and is often associated with seasonal movements of animals between their breeding territory and a wintering range. This activity is most readily observed in birds, but has been documented in many other animals as well, including insects, fish, whales, and other mammals. Migration is a complex behavior that involves timing, navigation and other survival skills.

Types of migration

The migration behaviors of different species of animals can be categorized as either complete, partial, differential, or irruptive. In complete migration, all of the members of a population will travel away from their breeding habitat at the end of that season, often to a wintering site hundreds or even thousands of kilometers away. The arctic tern (*Sterna paradisaea*) is an example of a complete migrant. Individuals of this species travel from the arctic to the antarctic and back again during the course of a year, a round-trip migration of more than 18,600 mi (30,000 km).

In other species, some individuals will remain at the breeding ground year round, while other members of the same species migrate away. These species are called partial migrants. American robins (*Turdus migratorius*), considered indicators of spring in some areas, are year-round residents in others.

Differential migration occurs when all the members of a population migrate, but not necessarily at the same time or for the same distance. The differences are often based on age or sex. Herring gulls (*Larus argentatus*), for example, migrate a shorter and shorter distance as they grow older. Male American kestrels (*Falco sparverius*) spend more time at their breeding grounds than do females, and when they do migrate, they do not travel as far.

Irruptive migration occurs in species which do not migrate at all during some years, but may do so during other years, when the winter is particularly cold or food particularly scarce. For example, some populations of blue jays (*Cyanocitta cristata*) are believed to migrate only when their winter food of acorns is scarce.

Directions of migration

Migration is usually thought of as a southward movement in autumn and a return northward in the spring. These migrations, termed latitudinal migrations, are the most common type, but there are several other directions in which migratory animals may travel. A mirror image of latitudinal migration, often called austral migration, occurs in the Southern Hemisphere. These migrations tend to be shorter than those in the Northern Hemisphere, mainly because of the scarcity of land in the cold regions of the Southern Hemisphere.

Some birds, such as prairie falcons (*Falco mexicanus*), travel east to west and back. These movements, called longitudinal migrations, are probably related to seasonal changes in the choice of prey and its location.

Elevational migration occurs in many animals that live on mountains. A short migration to lower elevations in winter will accomplish the same as a much longer southerly migration, since valleys have warmer climates than do mountaintops. A form of elevational migration also occurs in zooplankton, tiny animals which drift with the currents in the open ocean. In the summer, when tiny plants are abundant, the zooplankton live near the ocean surface, feeding on the plants. In the winter, they migrate 1,090 yd (1,000 m) deeper and do not feed at all.

Migration pathways

Migratory animals travel along the same general routes each year. Several common "flyways" are used by North American birds on their southward journey. The most commonly used path includes a 496-682 mi (800-1,100 m) flight across the Gulf of Mexico. In order to survive this arduous journey, birds must store extra energy in the form of fat. All along the migration route, but particularly before crossing a large expanse of water, birds will rest and eat, sometimes for days at a time. The recommencement of the journey will begin only when a certain amount of body fat is reached.

The requirement of stopover sites in addition to breeding and wintering sites makes migratory animals particularly susceptible to habitat loss, and thus many migrants are among our most endangered species.

Although most migrants travel at night, a few birds prefer daytime migrations. The pathways used by these birds tend to be less direct and slower than those of night migrants, primarily because of differences in feeding strategies. Night migrants can spend the day in one area, foraging for food and building up energy reserves for the night's non-stop flight. Daytime migrants must combine travel with foraging, and thus tend to keep to the shorelines, which are rich in insect life, capturing food during a slow but ever-southward journey.

Advantages of migration

Despite the dangers of long-distance travel, many different animals have developed migration strategies, presumably as a defense against the greater dangers of environmental uncertainty and competition. The breeding range of migratory animals is likely to cover a region whose environment becomes increasingly inhospitable after the breeding season is over (i.e. there is less food available in the winter), so it is advantageous to travel elsewhere. The wintering ranges will have food available year-round, but also many more animals competing for that food, as well as increased competition for shelter in which to raise their young. Hence the advantage of returning to the breeding grounds, where competition is less severe.

Navigation

Perhaps the most remarkable aspect of migration is the navigational skills employed by the animals. Birds such as the albatross (*Diomedea sp.*) and lesser golden plover (*Pluvialis dominica*) travel hundreds of miles over the featureless open ocean, yet unerringly home in on the same breeding grounds year after year. Salmon (*Oncorynchus* sp.) migrate upstream from the sea to the very same freshwater shallows in which they were hatched. Monarch butterflies (*Danas plexippus*) which began life in the United States or Canada travel to the same wintering grounds in southern California or Mexico that had been used by ancestors many generations removed.

How are these incredible feats of navigation accomplished? Different animals have been shown to use a diverse range of navigational aids, involving senses often much more acute than our own. Sight, for example, may be important for some animals' navigational skills, although it may often be secondary to other senses. Salmon can smell the water of their home rivers, and follow this scent all the way from the sea. Pigeons also sense wind-borne odors and may be able to organize the memories of the sources of these smells in a kind of internal map. It has been shown that many animals have the ability to sense the magnetic forces associated with the north and south poles, and thus have their own built-in compass. This magnetic sense, along with the sense of smell, are believed to be the most important factors involved in animal migration, but researchers are continually discovering new and unusual navigational systems throughout the animal kingdom.

Further Reading:
Baker, Robin, ed. *The Mystery of Migration.* New York: The Viking Press, 1981

KEY TERMS

Habitat—the place that an animal lives, which provides everything necessary for the animal's survival.

Navigation—the process of finding one's way to a known destination across unfamiliar terrain.

Halliday, Tim, ed. *Animal Behavior.* Univ. of Oklahoma Press, 1994
Long, Michael E. "Secrets of Animal Navigation." *National Geographic,* vol. 179, no. 6. June 1991.

David E. Fontes

Mildew

Mildews are whitish fungi that grow on moist surfaces. Some mildews are parasites growing on the surface of plant foliage or fruits. Other mildews grow on the moistened surfaces of materials made from plant or animal tissues, such as wood, paper, clothing, or leather.

The downy mildews are in the fungal family Peronosporaceae. These fungi can only exist as parasites, and under conditions favorable to their growth they can be important plant pathogens. Heavily infested leaves have whitish mycelium emerging through the small pores on their surface known as stomata, and through other exterior lesions. It is this downy mycelium that gives the fungus its common name. Various species are economically important, for example, *Plasmopara viticola* is a downy mildew of cultivated grapes (*Vitis vinifera*).

The powdery mildews are in the family of fungi known as the Erysiphaceae. These can be important parasites of grasses and other plants, especially under humid conditions. Severely infested plants can have a whitish or grayish bloom of mycelium and spores over much of their above-ground surfaces. One of the most important species is the powdery mildew of grasses (*Erysiphe graminis*), which affects a wide range of grasses grown as food for humans or as fodder for livestock.

When they are perceived to be pests, mildews are sometimes treated with a pesticide called a mildewcide.

Commonly used chemicals for this purpose include benzoic acid, formaldehyde, cresols, phenols, sulfur powder, and organic compounds containing mercury, lead, zinc, or copper. Infestations of mildews on books, walls, and other organic-rich surfaces can sometimes be treated by wiping with a dilute solution of domestic bleach (sodium hypochlorite).

See also Fungi; Fungicide.

Milkweed bug see **True bugs**

Milkweeds

Milkweeds are various species of perennial plants in the family Asclepiadaceae, a mostly tropical group that contains more than 1,800 species. Most species in this family are herbaceous, but others are woody climbers, shrubs, or small trees. The foliage and stems of milkweeds are often succulent, and when they are broken they weep a white, milky latex from which the common name of these plants is derived.

The most common milkweeds in North America are species in the genus *Asclepias* such as *A. syriaca*, the common milkweed. This species is the principal food of one of North America's best-known butterflies, the monarch or milkweed butterfly (*Danaus plexippus*). The monarch lays its eggs on *A. syriaca* and other species of milkweeds, and its larvae feed on their foliage. The monarch is a brightly orange-colored butterfly that flies slowly and might seem to be an easy prey for insect-eating birds and other predators. However, the adult and larval monarchs taste terrible because they contain chemicals obtained from the milkweeds while feeding. As a result, the monarch is avoided as food by most predators. An unrelated butterfly, the viceroy (*Limenitis archippus*), tastes fine but it is rarely eaten by most predators because it closely resembles the monarch in shape, color, and behavior. The milkweed-tainted monarch is the model in this system, while the viceroy is the mimic.

Some milkweeds have very attractive flowers and may be grown as ornamentals. The orange-colored flowers of the butterfly-weed (*A. tuberosa*) are a beautiful aspect of the taller-grass prairies of North America, and this species is sometimes grown in gardens.

The latex of milkweeds and other species in the family Asclepiadaceae can be used to make a natural rubber. During the World War II, when supplies of rubber from

Milkweed in seed.

Asia were not readily available in North America, research was undertaken to see whether this strategically important material could be obtained from milkweeds under cultivation. However, the yields of rubber were too small to make this enterprise worthwhile.

Some people like to gather the young, partially developed shoots or the seed pods of milkweeds in the late springtime before they have developed to the stage that they contain much of the milky latex. The shoots or pods are steamed, dressed with butter, and eaten as a tasty and nutritious vegetable.

Milky Way

On a clear, moonless night, away from the bright lights of the city, the Milky Way is visible—a fuzzy, milky band stretching across the sky. From the northern

A fish-eye lens view of the southern Milky Way from the constellation Sagittarius (left) through Scorpius, Centaurus, and Crux (the Southern Cross), to Carina (right). The Milky Way is intersected by dark lanes and clouds of dust, which obscure the stars beyond. The photo was taken from Ayers Rock, Australia.

hemisphere, the summer Milky Way passes through the constellations Scorpius and Sagittarius in the south and heads north through Aquila and Cygnus. The winter Milky Way slips between the hunting dogs, Canis Major and Minor, over the head of Orion the hunter, and through the feet of Gemini, the twins. The summer and winter Milky Way merge in the northern sky, passing through the constellations Cassiopeia and Perseus. The Milky Way is the plane of our galaxy, a vast spinning carousel of a few hundred billion stars. Our solar system is located about half way between the center and the edge of this 120,000-light-year diameter pancake shaped galactic disk. The "visible" Milky Way is simply the light from billions of faint stars blending into a fuzzy band across the sky.

History

In the minds of the ancient Greeks, the Milky Way clashed with the perfection expected in the heavens, and as such they thought it had to be an atmospheric phenomenon. The first hint of the true nature of the

Milky Way came in 1610 when Galileo examined it with his telescope. Galileo realized that the Milky Way was composed of an uncountable number of faint, individual stars.

In 1785 the musician turned astronomer William Herschel pioneered the technique of star counts in an attempt to deduce the structure of the Milky Way. Herschel pointed his telescope in various directions in the sky and counted the number of stars he could see in a standard size field of view. If he saw more stars in a given direction, Herschel assumed that the Milky Way extended farther in that direction. Herschel correctly concluded that the Milky Way was a disk shape, but he mistakenly concluded that we were at the center of that disk. The star counting technique he used was misleading. It didn't work because the galaxy is so vast that the interstellar dust—dust between the stars—blocks out light from the more distant stars, while we are at the center of the small part of the galaxy mapable by the star counting method, the galaxy extends beyond the region we can map. We must find beacons enough brighter than individual stars to be seen from the edges of the galaxy.

In 1917 Harlow Shapley mapped the extent of the galaxy by counting globular clusters rather than stars. Globular clusters are collections of roughly 100,000 stars. They can be seen from the distant reaches of the Milky Way. Just as Copernicus before him concluded that Earth is not the center of the solar system, Shapley proved that the solar system was not at the center of the galaxy. Since Shapley is time, astronomers have refined his technique and discovered new ways to deduce the size, structure, and contents of the Milky Way.

Structure of the Milky Way

The problem we face trying to deduce the structure of the Milky Way from our location within it is analogous to the problem faced by the Amazon Indians trying to map the rain forest while confined to its boundaries: it's simply too vast. To map the rain forest today we can simply fly over it in a plane; we cannot yet fly out of the galaxy in a spaceship to map its structure. We must find other methods.

Clues to the structure of our galaxy can be found by examining other galaxies similar to our own. The Milky Way has a disk structure with two spiral arms winding out from the center in the plane of the disk. The center, or nucleus, contains a small bulge. Surrounding this disk shape is a spherical halo composed of globular clusters similar to those used by Shapley to deduce our location within the Milky Way. "Similar Galaxies" have some overall structure.

We map the spiral arm structure of the Milky Way using ordinary optical light and looking for objects commonly found in spiral arms of other galaxies. To map the largest region possible we use bright objects. These objects, known as spiral arm tracers, include O and B spectral class stars, O and B associations, HII regions, and Cepheid variable stars. Astronomers put stars into different spectral classes. The O and B spectral classes are the two with the brightest and most massive stars. O and B associations are loose clumps of roughly a few dozen or so O and B stars. HII regions are clouds of ionized hydrogen surrounding very recently formed O or B stars. Cepheid variable stars vary in brightness in a particular way. The first member of this class was discovered in the constellation Cepheus, hence the name. These stars are one of the fundamental yardsticks used by astronomers to measure distances in the universe, so they can be used to find the distance to the spiral arm containing them. These spiral arm tracers allow us to map the spiral arm structure of the Milky Way. We can only map a small part, however,

as interstellar dust blocks the optical light from the more distant parts of the galaxy.

Astronomers use radio waves to map the far reaches of the Milky Way because the interstellar dust does not block radio waves as much as optical light. Spiral arms also contain interstellar gas composed mostly of hydrogen atoms. This interstellar gas is so thin (on average slightly less than one hydrogen atom per cubic centimeter of space) that it would be an excellent vacuum on Earth, but interstellar space is so vast that the interstellar gas still adds up to a lot of hydrogen atoms. These hydrogen atoms emit radio waves with a wavelength of 8 in (21 cm) that can penetrate the interstellar dust. The 21 cm radio waves allow us to map the spiral arm structure of even the distant parts of the Milky Way.

Using these and other techniques, astronomers have deduced the structure, size, and content of the Milky Way. The Milky Way consists of a fairly flat disk about 120,000 light years in diameter and 1,000 light years thick. (A light year is the distance light travels in one year, about 6 trillion miles.) The edge of the galaxy has a fuzzy rather than a sharp boundary, so the size estimates depend on what one calls the edge. This flat disk consists of a complex spiral pattern, rather than the two graceful arms found in some galaxies. In addition to the spiral arm tracers mentioned previously, the disk and spiral arms contain young stars of all spectral classes, galactic clusters composed of several hundred young stars, and interstellar clouds of gas, molecules and dust where new stars form. There is some recent evidence that the spiral arms do not begin at the center of the galaxy but at either end of a central bar structure like those found in barred spiral galaxies. The Sun and solar system are located on a spiral arm about 25,000 light years from the center.

The nucleus of the galaxy is surrounded by a nuclear bulge that is 12,000 light years in diameter and 10,000 light years thick. Surrounding this disk is a spherical halo, composed primarily of globular clusters. The halo may be as much as 300,000 light years in diameter and contains a considerable amount of unseen dark matter, perhaps as much as several times the amount of mass that we can see. The extent of the dark matter is difficult to determine because we can't see it and are not yet sure what it is. Some astronomers suggest that the dark matter portion of the halo may extend as far as half the distance to the Andromeda galaxy.

How many stars are there in the Milky Way? The spinning provides clues to the answer. The Milky Way spins because the individual stars in the galaxy are orbiting the center of the galaxy. Just as the Sun's gravity causes the planets to orbit the sun, the cumulative gravitational effect of the stars in the Milky Way cause the stars farther out to orbit the center of the Milky Way. The amount of gravitational force and hence the orbital properties depend on the mass. We can therefore study the orbital motions of the outer stars in the Milky Way to find the mass of the Milky Way. The mass of the Milky Way within a diameter of 120,000 light years is about 3 hundred billion times the mass of the Sun. Because the Sun is a fairly average star the Milky Way contains roughly 2 to 3 hundred billion stars. The orbital motions of the Sun are such that it moves around the center of the galaxy at about 220 km/s and takes about 250 million years to orbit the galactic nucleus once.

Formation of the Milky Way

The nucleus and halo of our galaxy contain older stars from the first batch to form. The globular clusters in the halo are anywhere from 10 to 17 billion years old and are among the oldest objects in the galaxy. These older stars are called population II stars. The disk and spiral arms consist of younger, second to third generation stars (population I) as well asinterstellar gas and dust. This difference in location between the older and younger stars in the Milky Way suggests something about the origin and evolution of the Milky Way. The older population II stars are distributed spherically in the halo, suggesting that when the galaxy first formed it had a spherical shape. The youngest stars are found in the flat disk, suggesting that the Milky Way has gradually flattened into a disk shape. Why? It is spinning. As the galaxy spins around, it flattens out.

But the history of the Milky Way may not be so simple. Detailed studies of the globular clusters in the halo and the different ages of stars in the halo and disk reveal some anomalies. For example, the contents of the halo do not always orbit in the same direction that the disk does. In addition, portions of the halo have very different ages. From this evidence, astronomers have concluded that the Milky Way may have formed as teh result of a merger of smaller systems such as globular clusters or dwarf elliptical galaxies.

Nucleus of the Milky Way

What is in the nucleus of the Milky Way? If we look with optical telescopes, we see nothing. The interstellar dust obscures the optical light. The center of the Milky Way does however contain very strong sources of radio waves, infrared light, and x rays. One such source, called Sagittarius A*, appears to lie at the precise center of the galaxy, the point about which the

---

KEY TERMS

· ·

Cepheid variable star—A type of star that varies in brightness as the star pulsates in size. Cephied variables are important distance yardsticks in establishing the distance to nearby galaxies.

Disk—The flat disk shaped part of the Milky Way galaxy that contains the spiral arms.

Galactic cluster—A cluster of roughly a few hundred young stars in a loose distribution. Also called an open cluster.

Galaxy—A large collection of stars and clusters of stars, containing anywhere from a few million to a few trillion stars.

Globular cluster—A cluster of roughly 100,000 older stars in a compact spherical distribution.

Halo—A spherical distribution of older stars and clusters of stars surrounding the nucleus and disk of our galaxy.

Light year—The distance light travels in one year, roughly 9.5 trillion kilometers or 6 trillion miles.

Milky Way—The galaxy in which we are located.

Nucleus—The central core of a galaxy.

Spiral arms—The regions where stars are concentrated that spiral out from the center of a spiral galaxy.

Spiral galaxy—A galaxy in which spiral arms wind outward from the nucleus.

---

entire system rotates. The vast energy omitted by Sagittarius A* comes from a region that is less than one light day in diameter (about the size of the solar system) compared to over 120,000 light years for the entire galaxy. There is more energy produced in a very small volume of space than we can easily explain. There is certainly not enough room in this volume to contain enough stars to explain the energy production. What produces so much energy in such a small region of space? Most astronomers think that there is a supermassive black hole with the mass of a million suns, in the core of the Milky Way. Black holes are so highly compressed that a supermassive black hole capable of explaining the energy output of the Milky Way's core would still have a small volume.

Quasars and other active galaxies also emit far more energy than can easily be explained from a small region in their nuclei. An active galaxy is a galaxy with at least 100 times the energy output of the Milky Way. Quasars are among the most energetic and distant types of active galaxy. These galaxies are also thought to contain supermassive black holes in the nucleus, even more energetic than the one in the nucleus of the Milky Way. The nucleus of the Milky Way may be a quieter version of the nucleus of an active galaxy or a quasar.

There are many mysteries concerning the Milky Way, including the nature of the energetic activity at its core, the unknown composition of the dark matter in the halo, and the uncertain process by which it formed.

See also Constellation; Galaxy.

Further Reading:

Bok, Bart J. and Priscilla F. Bok. *The Milky Way.* Cambridge, MA: Harvard University Press, 1981.

Binney, James. "The Evolution of Our Galaxy." Sky & Telescope 89, p20-26, March, 1995.

Trimble, Virginia and Samantha Parker. "Meet the Milky Way." *Sky & Telescope* 89, p26-33, January, 1995.

Van den Berg, Sidney and James E. Hesser. "How the Milky Way Formed." *Scientific American* p72-78, January, 1993.

Verschuur, Gerrit L. "Journey into the Galaxy." *Astronomy* p 33-39, January, 1993.

Verschuur, Gerrit L. "In the Beginning." *Astronomy* p 41-45, October, 1993.

Zeilik, Michael. *Astronomy: The Evolving Universe.* 7th ed. New York: Wiley, 1994. (Chapter 18).

Paul A. Heckert

Millet see **Grasses**

Millipedes

Millipedes are long, cylindrical, segmented, many-legged terrestrial arthropods in the Class Diplopoda, in total comprising about 10,000 species. The common name of these animals is derived from the Latin for "thousand legs," although most species actually have fewer than 200 legs, and some as few as about 60.

Millipedes have an elongate, almost cylindrical body form, with two short legs on each segment, except for the first three, anterior (head), segments, which do not have legs. Most species of millipedes have small, compound eyes, consisting of bundles of optical units known as simple eyes, or *ocelli*. Millipedes have a pair of large chewing mandibles at the head end, which they use to break up their food—usually decaying vegetation or the flesh of dead animals.

Millipedes are slow-moving, deliberate animals which usually live in damp and dark places, often under some sort of cover. Some species of millipedes feed on living plants, and when these animals are abundant they can causes significant damage. For example, *Oxidus gracilus*, a common millipede found in greenhouses, is sometimes considered to be a pest. A few species of millipedes are predators of other invertebrates.

When millipedes are disturbed, some species curl up into a tight spiral, with their head in the center. Some species also exude a foul, dark fluid from pores in the sides of their body when they are disturbed. This excretion can kill some types of insects when they are closely confined with these millipedes.

Millipedes have internal fertilization, with the male using specialized, modified legs on its seventh body segment to pass sperm to the female. Openings of the reproductive tracts of both sexes are located at the front of the body, between the second and third pairs of legs. Millipedes lay clutches of small, whitish eggs in damp places. The newly hatched millipedes have only three pairs of legs, with the other parts being added as the animals grow and molt.

The largest species of millipede in North America is *Narceus americanus*, a dark-brown animal with narrow, red, transverse rings on its body, occurs in moist coniferous forests of the west coast. This beautiful millipede can reach an impressive body length of 4 in (10 cm), while species of millipedes in the tropics can reach the length of a foot (30 cm).

See also Arthropods.

Mimicry

Mimicry may broadly be defined as imitation or copying of an action or image. In biological systems, mimicry specifically refers to the fascinating resemblance of an organism, called the "mimic," to another somewhat distantly related organism, called the "model." The set of mimic and model species involved is often referred to as a mimicry complex. Usually through escape from predation, the mimicry of a trait or traits helps the mimic to survive. This, coupled with the fact that the resemblance traits are genetically based, implies that mimicry complexes have been shaped by natural selection. There are two major types of mimicry,

This inoffensive beetle mimics a wasp.

Batesian and Müllerian, named after the naturalists that first theorized them upon their observations of butterflies. There are a few other types that are not as prevalent, such as aggressive mimicry.

Batesian mimicry

In 1862, H.W. Bates presented an hypothesis explaining the similar color patterns in several species sets of tropical butterflies in different families. His hypothesis was one of the early applications of Charles Darwin's theory of natural selection. Bates reasoned that an edible butterfly species that was susceptible to predation would evolve, due to selection by a bird predator, to look like an unpalatable, or distasteful model species. If the mimic was rarer than the model, then birds would encounter the distasteful model more frequently, and would learn to avoid all butterflies that looked like the distasteful ones. In fact, the relative rarity of the model was to Bates a prerequisite for such a phenomenon to evolve. As mimicry theory has progressed, mathematical models show that relative abundances of models and mimics, as well as relative palatability of the two species, will determine the outcome.

Müllerian mimicry

In the 1870s, Fritz Muller theorized a different type of mimicry. His idea, also based on sets of butterfly species, was that several species, all somewhat distasteful, would evolve to look like each other. Such an evolutionary strategy would in effect reduce predation on any of the species because the predator would learn to avoid a single color pattern, but since all of them had the same pattern, they would all be safe from predation. The rarer form, say species 1, would eventually converge to look like the more common form, species 2, as the individuals that looked too different from species 2 would be rapidly selected out by predators. Since species 2 was more common, the predator would have had more experience with it and would have had more opportunity to learn to avoid it than with species 1, the rare species. Individuals of species 1 that resembled species 2 would benefit from the predator's learned avoidance of species 2, and thus would proliferate. The species would evolve to share a similar pattern as relative frequencies shifted. If the two species were equal in abundance, Muller reasoned, it would not be possible to distinguish mimic from model, as both had converged on a common phenotype, or appearance.

Aggressive mimicry

A less common but equally fascinating type of mimicry involves not only a model and a mimic, but a "dupe" species that is tricked by the mimicry. In the previously noted types of mimicry, the dupe is the predator who is tricked out of a potential food source, but in aggressive mimicry, the word is especially appropriate as being duped as lethal. In aggressive mimicry, the mimic is a predator who imitates, usually in behavior, a model species in order to draw in a dupe, who then becomes prey. An example of this occurs in spiders of the family Mimetidae (mimic), who attempting to draw in spiders of other species (dupe) as prey items, produce vibrations on the webs of the dupe that mimic the prey items (model) of the dupe. When the dupe is tricked, and approaches what it thinks is food, the mimic attacks it and eats it. Bolus spiders are another type of aggressive mimic. They produce chemicals that mimic the sex pheromones of particular moth species. When male moths approach what they perceive to be a female in order to mate with her, they are caught by the bolus spider and become prey.

Further Reading:

Gilbert, L.E. "Coevolution and mimicry." In: Futuyma, D.J., and Slatkin, M., eds. *Coevolution*. Sinauer Associates, Inc., 1983.

Vane-Wright, R.I. "Mimicry and its unknown ecological consequences." In: Greenwood, P.H., ed. *The Evolving Biosphere*. pp 157-168. New York: Cambridge University Press, 1980.

Puja Batra

Mind see **Brain**

Minerals

In ordinary usage, minerals are the natural, non-living materials that compose rocks and are mined from Earth. Examples are metals, gemstones, clays and ores.

The scientific definition of a mineral is more limited. To be considered a mineral, a substance must be solid under ordinary conditions, thus excluding petroleum and liquid water. Minerals must be single, homogeneous (uniform) substances. Therefore quartz is a mineral, but rocks such as granite, which contain quartz mixed together with other minerals, are not considered minerals. Minerals must have definite chemical formulas, allowing only slight variations. Therefore, a sample of a particular mineral will have essentially the same composition no matter where it is from—Earth, the moon, or beyond. Minerals must be of nonbiological, or inorganic, origin, which excludes coal and peat. Finally, the atoms of which minerals are made must be arranged in orderly rows and stacks; that is, minerals must be made of crystals. Thus, to summarize the scientific definition, a mineral is a naturally occurring, inorganic, homogenous solid with a definite range of chemical composition and an ordered atomic arrangement.

With these restrictions, almost 4,000 different minerals are known, with several dozen new minerals identified each year. Every mineral possesses a combination of chemical composition and crystal structure that makes it unique, and by which it is classified (grouped with similar minerals) and identified. These minerals make up the solid Earth, the moon, and even meteorites. However, only 20 or so minerals compose the bulk of Earth's crust, that is, the part of the solid Earth accessible to human beings, extending from the surface downward to a maximum depth of about 55 mi (90 km). These minerals are often called the "rock-forming" minerals.

Chemical bonding and crystal structure

Mineralogists group minerals according to the chemical elements they contain. Elements are substances which cannot be broken down into simpler substances through chemical means. Over 100 of these are known, of which 88 occur naturally. However, most occur only in extremely small traces. Only 10 elements account for nearly 99% of the weight of Earth's crust. Oxygen is the most plentiful element, accounting for 49.2% of the weight of Earth's crust. Next is silicon, which accounts for 25.7% of its weight. Table 2 lists the 10 most abundant elements in Earth's crust. Most minerals are compounds; that is, they contain two or more elements. Only a few minerals, known as native elements, contain atoms of just a single element.

Chemical bonding

In molecules, elements are not merely mixed together, but are joined by chemical bonds. Chemical bonds in minerals are of four types: covalent, ionic, metallic, or Van der Waals, with covalent and ionic bonds most common. Two or more of these bond types can and do coexist in most minerals.

Covalent bonds are very strong bonds formed when atoms share electrons with neighboring atoms. Sulfur, and both of carbon's natural forms, graphite and diamond, are covalently-bonded minerals. So is quartz, which contains only silicon and oxygen.

Ionic bonds are strong bonds formed when electrons are transferred from one element to another. Since electrons carry a negative electrostatic charge, the element that acquires extra electrons becomes a negatively charged ion, an anion. The element that gave off the electron becomes a positively charged ion, a cation. The attraction between opposite charges binds anions and cations together in ionic compounds. Most metals (the elements iron, nickel, lead, aluminum, etc.) exist in nature as cations, rather than as electrically neutral atoms. Their mineral compounds are, therefore, usually ionic. This is true whether they are joined with one nonmetal, as in oxides (oxygen), or with two, as in sulfates (sulfur and oxygen) and carbonates (carbon and oxygen).

Metallic bonds are generally weaker than either covalent or ionic bonds, which explains why metallically bonded minerals (true metals), like silver, gold, and copper, can be worked — beaten into flat sheets, or drawn into thin wires. In metallic bonds, electrons move about the crystal constantly flowing between adjacent atoms, redistributing their charge. Because of this flow of electrons, true metals are also good electrical conductors.

Van der Waals bonds are very weak bonds formed by residual charges from the other types of chemical bonds. Graphite is probably the best example of the nature of Van der Waals bonds. The atoms in graphite's carbon layers are covalently bonded, but a weak residual charge attracts the layers to one another. Van der Waals bonds make graphite a very soft mineral, excellent for use in pencil lead.

Crystal structure

The faces and angles of natural crystals result from the orderly arrangements of the atoms and molecules that make up a crystal. The relation between crystal shape and microscopic structure was suggested in the seventeenth century by Robert Hooke and Christian Huygens. It was confirmed in the twentieth century with the development of x-ray diffraction, a technique that uses x-rays to examine the atomic structures of materials.

In modern terms, a solid substance is considered to be crystalline if its atoms or molecules are arranged in an orderly pattern that repeats at regular intervals. Therefore metals are crystalline, although the individual crystals making up a lump of gold are too small to see with the naked eye. By contrast, atoms making up glass do not have any orderly atomic arrangement. Therefore, glass, even it if is carved into the shape of a crystal, is not a crystalline material. Natural glasses such as obsidian (volcanic glass) are not technically minerals. Non-crystalline solids are called amorphous (without form).

Although there are thousands of different minerals, the shapes of their crystals can be described using just six basic geometric forms. These are called crystal systems. To determine what crystal system a mineral belongs to, it is nesessary to obtain a well-formed specimen, then observe the number and shape of the faces and the angles at which they meet. This task may be complicated by the fact that each crystal system includes several different forms, and a single crystal may combine several forms in its shape.

For example, consider the isometric system. This is the most symmetrical system, meaning that it has the greatest amount of "sameness" in its faces and angles. In fact, the basic geometric shape of the isometric system is a cube, having all sides of equal length and all angles equal to 90°. Halite crystals, which are cubic, are easily recognized as belonging to the isometric system. However, 15 forms are possible within the isometric system. Isometric mineral crystals include the octahedral (eight-sided) spinels, and the dodecahedral (12-sided) garnets. A single crystal combining several forms can look almost spherical.

Mineral groups

Naming mineral groups

Anions, because of their extra electrons, tend to be much larger than cations. Ionic crystals therefore are built mainly of stacks of anions, with the much smaller cations filling spaces between them. Minerals more closely resemble each other in structure or behavior if minerals with the same anions (rather than cations) are compared. That is why minerals are generally grouped according to their anions, even if the cations may be of

TABLE 1. REPRESENTATIVE MINERALS

Group and Constituent Elements	Mineral	Other Elements	Important or Representative Uses
NATIVE ELEMENTS	Graphite	carbon	PENCIL "lead", LUBRICANT
	Sulfur	sulfur	SULFURIC ACID, MATCH heads
	Silver	silver	PHOTOGRAPHY, JEWELRY
SILICATES Silicon and Oxygen	Asbestos	magnesium	FLAME-PROOF fabric
	Kaolinite	aluminum, hydrogen	clay for PORCELAIN, GLOSSY COATING for paper
	Muscovite (Mica)	potassium, aluminum, hydrogen	electric and heat INSULATION, decorative "GLITTER"
	Quartz sand	—	main ingredient in GLASS
	Talc	magnesium	COSMETICS
OXIDES Oxygen	Hematite	iron	ore of iron, IRON and STEEL
	Corundum	aluminum	GRINDING tools, Gems (ruby, sapphire)
SULFIDES Sulfur	Pyrite	iron	ore, source of SULFUR, "marcasite" JEWELRY
	Galena	lead	ore of LEAD
HALIDES Halogens	Halite	sodium, chlorine	TABLE SALT, source of sodium for LYE, improves workability of molten GLASS
SULFATES Sulfur and Oxygen	Gypsum	calcium, hydrogen	PLASTER
	Barite	barium	LUBRICANT for oil well drilling

REPRESENTATIVE MINERALS (cont'd)			
Group and Constituent Elements	Mineral	Other Elements	Important or Representative Uses
PHOSPHATES Phosphorus and Oxygen	Apatite	calcium, fluorine, hydrogen	source of phosphorus for FERTILIZER
CARBONATES Carbon and Oxygen	Trona	sodium, hydrogen	source ofsodium added to GLASS to improve workability melt
BORATES Boron and Oxygen	Borax	sodium, boron, hydrogen	CLEANSER, source of element BORON to improve heat resistance of GLASS

greater practical interest. For example, ore minerals are mined for the metals (cations) they contain, which can be changed from ions to neutral atoms of pure metal by a chemical process called smelting. Nevertheless, ore minerals (for example, oxides or sulfides) are grouped according to their non-metal elements.

Silicate minerals and the role of structure

Oxygen and silicon together make up almost three fourths of the mass of Earth's crust. The silicate minerals, a group containing silicon and oxygen atoms, are the most abundant minerals and are the major component of nearly every kind of rock. Silicate compounds make up over 90% of the weight of Earth's crust. Most silicate minerals contain other elements in their formulas; therefore, there is a great variety of silicate minerals. In some rocks such as granite, the different silicate minerals can be seen as the small interlocking crystals of various colors. In other rocks, the mineral grains may be too small to distinguish, but they are usually silicates.

Regardless of composition, all silicates have the same basic building unit, the silica tetrahedron. This consists of a silicon atom bound covalently to four oxygen atoms. The oxygen atoms occupy the corners of a geometrical shape called a tetrahedron. The silicon atom is at its center. The entire unit bears a negative electrical charge, enabling it to form compounds with cations.

Silica tetrahedra can join together by sharing oxygen atoms. The simplest result is two tetrahedra joined at one point or six tetrahedra forming a ring. Ribbons or sheets of silica tetrahedra can be millions of units long. If all four oxygen atoms are shared with neighbors, the tetrahedra form rigid networks that extend over the entire crystal. Such large silicates are inorganic polymers, large molecules built up of a great many similar small units. (The only other element known to form polymers is carbon, and carbon-based polymers are the basis of living things.)

The arrangements of tetrahedra affect the properties of the silicate minerals. Garnets are very dense and hard, because their tetrahedra stand alone, bound by strong ionic charge to nearby cations. Beryl forms long, six-sided crystals, which may be colored by traces of metal to form precious emeralds and aquamarines. On the atomic level, beryl contains rings of six tetrahedra, the rings stacked one upon the other with their holes aligned. In muscovite, the tetrahedra are arranged in sheets, with alternating layers of aluminum and potassium atoms between them. The result is flat, flaky crystals which can easily be separated by hand.

Non-silicate minerals

The so-called non-silicate minerals consist of a variety of different mineral groups each named for a particular anion. Only a few of these minerals contribute much volume to Earth's crust, but many of them are very important minerals for manufacturing and other industrial uses. Most mineralogists recognize 10 or so major non-silicate groups and a variable number of lesser groups. Table 1 lists several of the major non-silicate groups.

Native elements

A few minerals, called native elements, contain only one element. These include the so-called native metals, gold, silver and copper, which occur in lumps, veins, or flakes scattered in rocks. Diamond and graphite are both

TABLE 2. THE TEN MOST ABUNDANT ELEMENTS IN THE EARTH'S CRUST

Element	% weight of earth's crust
oxygen	49.2
silicon	25.7
aluminum	7.5
iron	4.7
calcium	3.4
sodium	2.6
potassium	2.4
magnesium	1.9
hydrogen	0.87
titanium	0.58

naturally occurring forms of pure carbon. Sulfur, a yellow non-metal, is sometimes found pure in underground deposits formed by hot springs. Although not common, these minerals are economically important.

Physical traits and mineral identification

Despite their great variety and complexity, an unknown mineral sample can often be identified by observing or testing for a few simple physical traits. A mineral's physical traits are a direct result of its chemical composition and crystal form. Therefore, if enough physical traits are recognized, any mineral can be identified. These traits include hardness, color, streak, luster, breakage or cleavage, specific gravity, and other properties. The results of tests are compared with tables of known minerals until a match is found.

Hardness

A mineral's hardness is defined as its ability to scratch another mineral. This is usually measured using a comparative scale devised about 200 years ago by Friedrich Mohs. The Mohs scale lists 10 common minerals, assigning to each a hardness from one (talc) to 10 (diamond). A mineral can scratch all those minerals having a lower Mohs hardness number. For example, calcite (hardness three) can scratch gypsum (hardness two) and talc (hardness one), but it cannot scratch fluorite (hardness four).

Color and streak

Although some minerals can be identified by their color, this property can be misleading because mineral color is often affected by traces of impurities. Streak, however, is a very reliable identifying feature. Streak refers to the color of the powder produced when one mineral is scratched by another, harder mineral. Fluorite, for example, comes in a great range of colors, yet its streak is always white.

Luster

Luster refers to a mineral's appearance when light reflects off its surface. There are various kinds of luster, all having descriptive names. Thus, metals have a metallic luster, quartz has a vitreous, or glassy luster, and chalk has a dull, or earthy luster.

Cleavage and fracture

Some minerals, when struck with force, will cleanly break parallel to planes of weakness in their atomic structure. This breakage is called cleavage. Muscovite cleaves in one direction only, producing thin flat sheets. Halite cleaves in three directions, all perpendicular to each other, forming cubes. A mineral's cleavage directions may reveal the crystal system to which it belongs.

However, most minerals fracture rather than cleave. Fracture is breakage that does not follow a flat surface. Some fracture surfaces are rough and uneven. Others show smooth, concentric depressions, called conchoidal fractures. Conchoidal fracture typically occurs in glasses, which are non-crystalline solids. However, it also occurs in many common crystalline minerals, for example garnet and quartz.

Specific gravity

Two minerals can look alike, yet a piece of one may be much heavier than an identical-sized piece of the other. The heavier one has a higher specific gravity.

When pure, each mineral has a predictable specific gravity. Therefore, this property is a very reliable clue to a mineral's identity. A mineral's specific gravity can be thought of as a ratio of its weight to that of an equal volume of water. For example, the specific gravity of gold is 19.3 (19.3 times that of water), while quartz is 2.65.

To determine a mineral's specific gravity, it is necessary to weigh a sample (using grams), then measure its volume (in cubic centimeters). The weight divided by volume is the density. To calculate specific gravity, divide the mineral's density by that of water. Since the density of water is one gram per cubic centimeter, specific gravity and density are equal (provided all measurements are made using the metric system.)

Other identifying properties

Some minerals have unusual properties that further aid identification. Fluorescent minerals viewed under ultraviolet light glow with various colors. Phosphorescent minerals glow in the dark after exposure to ordinary light. Triboluminescent minerals give off light when crushed or hit. Several minerals containing iron, nickel, or cobalt are magnetic. Over 100 minerals contain uranium, thorium, or other radioactive elements and are therefore radioactive. These are only a few of the unique properties that can be used to identify minerals. Finally, an experienced mineralogist will take into account the location in which an unknown mineral is found. The nature of the surrounding rocks and the presence of other minerals and elements all provide clues to help in identification.

Minerals and their uses

Everything that humankind consumes, uses, or produces has its origin in minerals. Minerals are the building materials of our technological civilization, and a single mineral may have many unrelated uses.

The mineral corundum provides a good example. Corundum is an extremely hard substance. Small bits of corundum are part of the rock called "emery" which has been used since ancient times as an abrasive, to cut and grind metal and stone. Pure corundum is still used for this purpose today. Another property of corundum is that it remains solid and stable at very high temperatures, well past the melting point of iron. Therefore, masses of small corundum crystals pressed together are shaped into "alumina" firebricks, crucibles, and other apparatus to use in furnaces. Corundum is also the basis of several gemstones.

Pure corundum is colorless. However, as is the case with many other minerals, trace amounts of metal in the

stone impart brilliant colors. Rubies are corundum colored red by traces of chromium. Sapphires come in shades of blue, yellow, green and violet; these varieties of corundum contain traces of iron, titanium or other elements.

Finally, corundum is indirectly a major source of aluminum metal. The ore of aluminum, called bauxite, is a mixture of several minerals containing aluminum together with oxygen and hydrogen. The first step in releasing the aluminum from the other elements is to convert the bauxite to corundum.

Table 1 lists a wide variety of familiar materials and the minerals that compose them. These and most other minerals will find even wider usage in the future as research in the field of materials science continues.

See also Anion; Crystal; Element, chemical; Industrial minerals; Metal; Mining; Ore; Precious metals; Van der Waals forces.

Further Reading:

Bates, Robert L. *The Challenge of Mineral Resources*. Hillside, New Jersey: Enslow Publishers, Inc., 1991.

Bates, Robert L. *Industrial Minerals: How They Are Found and Used*. Hillside, New Jersey: Enslow Publishers, Inc., 1988.

Hazen, Robert M. *The New Alchemists: Breaking Through the Barriers of High Pressure*. New York: Times Books (division of Random House), 1993.

Hochleitner, Rupert. *Minerals: Identifying, Classifying and Collecting Them*. (translated from the German by Kathleen Luft). Hauppage, New York: Barrons Educational Series, Inc. First English language edition, 1994.

Holden, Martin. *The Encyclopedia of Gemstones and Minerals*. New York: Facts On File, A Friedman Group Book, 1991.

Rocks and Minerals (magazine). Heldref Publications, 1319 Eighteenth Street, NW, Washington DC 20036. Official publication of the Eastern Federation of Minerological and Lapidary Societies and the Midwest Federation of Minerological and Geological Societies.

Ward, Fred. "Rubies and Sapphires." *National Geographic*. 180(4), Oct. 1991, pp. 100-125.

Sara G. B. Fishman

Minima see **Maxima and minima**

Mining

Mining is the process by which commercially valuable minerals are extracted from Earth's surface. Although many specific kinds of mining operations have been developed, they can all be classified into one of two major categories, surface and subsurface (or underground) mining. Mining activities are closely associated with a number of social, political, economic, and environmental issues.

History

Many metals occur in their native state or in readily accessible ores. Thus, the working of metals (metallurgy) actually dates much farther back than does the mining industry itself. Some of the earliest known mines were those developed by the Greeks in the sixth century B.C. As were mines for many centuries thereafter, these mines were worked by slaves and prisoners of war. By the time the Roman Empire reached its peak, it had established mining sites throughout the European continent, in the British Isles, and in parts of North Africa. Interestingly, some of the techniques used to shore up underground mines still in use today were introduced as far back as the Greek and Roman civilizations.

Exploration

Until the beginning of the twentieth century, the vast majority of mining was carried out in locations were ores were readily available. During the gold rush of 1848 in California and days of the 1890s in Alaska, for example, prospectors typically found the prize they were seeking in outcrops visible to the naked eye or by separating gold and silver nuggets from stream beds (prospecting).

Over time, of course, the more abundant, more readily accessible ore-beds had been exhausted. It became necessary for mining engineers to develop more sophisticated techniques for locating the site of potential mines. Today, a vast array of techniques is available for this purpose. For example, remote sensing provides a mechanism by which large stretches of land can be examined for potential ore locations. Various types of cameras (infrared, color, and thermal infrared, for example) carried aloft by satellites can photograph large land areas and suggest regions in which more detailed searches might be conducted.

These more detailed searches generally make use of geological, geophysical, or geochemical methods. Geological exploration of an area, for example, makes use of the fact that certain types of rock formation are likely to be associated with the presence of certain types of mineral beds. Geophysical techniques such as the use of gravimeters (which detect differences in the density of underlying rock) and seismographs (which report differences in the way shock waves travel through the ground) allow mining engineers to predict the structure of rock and the likelihood of mineral beds.

Surface mining

When an ore bed has been located relatively close to Earth's surface, it can be mined by surface techniques. Surface mining is generally a much preferred approach to mining such it is less expensive and safer than subsurface mining. In fact, about 90% of the rock and mineral resources mined in the United States and more than 60% of the nation's coal is produced by surface mining techniques. In terms of volume, coal min-

Earth movers strip mining for coal in West Virginia.

ing alone accounts for about half of all surface mining, extraction of sand, gravel, stone, and clay for another 35%, phosphate rock for about 5%, and all metallic ores, for about 13%.

Surface mining can be sub-divided into two large categories: open-pit mining (also called open-pit bench mining) and strip mining (also called open-pit strip mining). Open-pit mining is employed when an ore bed covers a very large area in three dimensions. Mining begins when scrapers remove any non-ore material, overburden, on top of the ore. Explosives are then used to blast apart the ore bed itself, and the fragments from the blasting are then hauled away in large trucks. As workers dig downward into the ore bed, they also expand the circular area in which they work. Over time, the open-pit mine develops the shape of a huge bowl with terraces running around its inside edge. The largest open-pit mine in the United States has a depth of more than 0.5 mile (0.8 km) and a diameter of 2.25 miles (3.6 km). Open-pit mining can continue until the richest part of the ore bed has been excavated.

Strip mining

When an ore bed covers a wide area in two dimensions, but is not very deep, strip mining is the preferred method of ore extraction. Strip mining begins as does open-pit mining, with scrapers and other machines removing any overburden above the ore deposit. This step involves the removal of two long parallel rows of material. As the second row is dug, the overburden removed is dumped into the first row. The ore exposed in the second row can then be extracted. When that step has been completed, machines can remove the overburden from a third parallel row, dumping the material extracted into the second row. This process can be continued as long as ore can profitably be removed. When mining has been completed, the land area is restored to something approaching its original condition, in which each row that has been dug up has been filled in with wastes from the next row. The land's appearance, however, is hardly what it was originally. Instead, it typically resembles a washboard with parallel rows of hills and valleys consisting of excavated soil.

Alluvial mining

Alluvial mining is another form of surface mining used to extract placer deposits. Placer deposits are collections of heavy minerals (such as gold and silver) that are intermixed with sand, gravel, and silt deposits along river, stream, and lake shores and banks. Sometimes these deposits can be removed mechanically, as early prospectors did, by agitating the metal-earth mixtures in simple pans. A more sophisticated and efficient way of separating useful placer minerals from the earthy materials with which they occur is a sluice box, a long, shallow box with wooden separators placed along its bottom. A sandy mixture taken from a river or lake is shaken in the sluice box, lighter materials are washed away, and heavier valuable minerals are left behind.

The general principles of surface mining have also been adapted for the mining of ocean bottoms. Scientists have known for some years that a number of valuable minerals occur on the ocean floor. Among these are manganese nodules that range in size from a fraction of an inch to a few inches in diameter. These nodules generally contain nickel, copper, cobalt, and other metals in addition to manganese and could be a valuable source of these minerals. So far, there have been relatively few commercial attempts to mine these nodules or other minerals on the ocean floor. One of the schemes that has been suggested, however, involves the use of very large buckets attached to cables that can be dragged across the ocean floor. The buckets can then be raised to the surface of the water and screened for the removal of the desired ore.

Subsurface mining

A number of important disadvantages are associated with the use of subsurface mining. The physical process of simply getting to an ore that may be hundreds or thousands of feet beneath Earth's surface is among the most obvious. Still, subsurface mining has long been practiced in every part of the world.

The exact technique to be used in subsurface mining depends on a number of factors, most important of which is the shape of the ore deposit and its general location in the surrounding rock. Sometimes a metalliferous ore (one containing a metal ore) can be reached by tunneling horizontally into the side of a hill or a mountain. In that case, the entry tunnel that leads to the ore deposit itself is called an adit. In other cases, the ore deposit may lie at some depth beneath a horizontal or gently sloping surface. In that case, a long vertical tunnel, called a shaft, must first be constructed.

The purpose of the adit or the shaft is to provide a passageway by which workers can get to the ore deposit. The first step in any form of subsurface mining, therefore, involves the preparation of a system by which workers can get into the deposit and by which the ore can be removed. This system consists of a variety of vertical, horizontal, and/or sloping tunnels. Horizontal tunnels in the system are known as levels, vertical tunnels extending downward from a level are called winzes, and vertical tunnels extending upward are called raises. The hollow areas produced by the removal of ore, in which mining is actually going on, are known as stopes.

An important phase of mine preparation is the strengthening of tunnels built into the earth. Some rock formations are especially fragile or porous, and tunnels must be reinforced with wooden timbers and ceilings and other structures to assure the safety of workers. In addition, ventilation shafts must be provided to allow workers a sufficient supply of air, which is otherwise totally absent within the mine.

Once all preparatory stages have been completed, the actual mining process can begin. Many different techniques and tools are used to remove ores from a mine. In many cases, the first step may be to blast apart a portion of the ore deposit with explosives. The broken pieces thus obtained are then collected in carts, railroad cars, or some other form of conveyance and taken to the mine opening. Wherever possible, the extraction process is carried out above a level so that the force of gravity can be used to move the ore from its bed into the cart or car.

Coal mining

Coal and a few other minerals are somewhat distinctive in that the beds in which they are located are often very compact and strong. Miners can remove very large sections of the desired mineral without too much fear of the mine's collapsing. A common technique that makes use of this approach is the room-and-pillar method. Large quantities of coal are removed while leaving behind columns of the mineral at regular intervals. The remaining columns act as supports to help hold up the ceiling of the coal mine. If conditions warrant, it may then be possible to remove the pillars themselves at the conclusion of mining operations.

Room-and-pillar operations are usually associated with coal mining, but other minerals can be excavated by the same process. Halite (sodium chloride) and sylvite (potassium chloride) are examples.

Other sub-surface techniques

Other techniques for the mining of sub-surface resources are also available. The removal of oil and natural gas by drilling into Earth's surface are well known examples. Such wells are possible because of the fact that oil and natural gas are commonly found in porous rocks beneath Earth's surface that are trapped at high pressure between nonporous strata. Tapping into the porous rock provides a release for the pressurized oil and natural gas.

In a technique broadly similar to oil drilling, certain water-soluble minerals can be removed from the earth by dissolving them with hot water that is piped into the ground under pressure. The minerals dissolve in the hot water and then are carried to the surface.

Yet another example of subsurface mining of a mineral is the Frasch process, used to mine sulfur. In the Frasch process, a system of pipes is sunk into a known deposit of sulfur at some depth under ground. Steam forced into one pipe melts the sulfur, which is then extracted in a liquid form through a second pipe.

Safety issues

Mining has traditionally been a very risky occupation. The most common cause of mine accidents is a failure in the mine itself. For example, a ceiling or walls collapse trapping workers beneath them. The mechanical equipment used in mines is another source of risk.

Workers may be injured in setting off explosives or in operating carts or cars.

Suffocation or poisoning are other causes of mine accidents. If ventilation systems are inadequate, miners will not be able to get the fresh air they need to survive. In some mines, toxic gases such as carbon monoxide exist naturally and, without protection of some kind, workers may be poisoned by them. Inhalation of coal dust or other harmful minerals can also result in death or serious injury. For many years, workers in asbestos mines, for example, were exposed to one of the most terrible of all carcinogenic agents, a fact of which they did not become aware for many years or decades.

Mine safety was poorly regulated in the United States for many years. The first state laws were passed in Pennsylvania, (1870), Illinois (1870), Ohio (1873), and Maryland (1876), although such laws were not always well enforced. The first federal law dealing with mine safety was passed in 1910. That law, the Organic Act of 1910, created the United States Bureau of Mines, one of whose responsibility it was to draft and enforce safety regulations. Over the past half century, safety conditions in most mines has improved dramatically. In the decade between 1975 and 1984, for example, there were only 11 mining disasters in which five or more lives were lost. The total number of deaths in these 11 incidents was 127. In comparison, in the decade before the Organic Act of 1910 was passed, there were 10 accidents in each of which no fewer than 100 workers were killed.

Environmental issues

Over the last three decades, the many environmental issues associated with mining have come under close scrutiny. In general, subsurface mining has fewer environmental issues associated with it than does surface mining. One problem with underground mining is that subsurface mines sometimes collapse, resulting in massive subsidence of land above them. Another problem is that waste materials produced during mining may be dissolved by underground water, producing water solutions that are deleterious to plant and animal life.

Surface mining has been more frequently associated with environmental degradation, at least partly because its effects are so visible. In many parts of the United States, vast areas of land have been denuded by strip mining. Often, it may take many years for vegetation to start regrowing once more and, even then, the land may never assume the appearance it had before mining began. Disruption of land by strip mining is also likely to increase the possibility of land erosion, resulting not only in the loss of soil itself, but also in the pollution of adjacent waterways.

KEY TERMS

Adit—A horizontal tunnel constructed to gain access to underground mineral deposits.

Level—A horizontal tunnel in a subsurface mine.

Overburden—Rocky material that must be removed in order to gain access to an ore or coal bed.

Panning—A manual device for separating metals and metallic ores from placer deposits on a small scale.

Placer—An ore deposit found along a river or stream.

Raise—Vertical tunnels extending upward from a level in a subsurface mine.

Room-and-pillar—A technique for mining certain kinds of minerals, especially coal, in which vertical shafts of the mineral are left in place to support the roof of the mine.

Shaft—A vertical tunnel constructed to gain access to underground mineral deposits.

Sluice box—A device used to separate metals and metallic ores from placer deposits.

Stope—Hollow areas produced by the removal of ore, in which mining is actually going on.

Subsidence—The sinking of a section of ground as the result, for example, of the collapse of an old underground mine.

Winze—Vertical tunnels extending downward from a level in a mine.

The United States Congress has considered a number of bills that would attempt to protect the environment from the worst abuses of surface mining. In 1977, for example, it adopted the Surface Mining Control and Reclamation Act. This act attempted to strike a balance among the needs of mining, agriculture, recreation, and other demands on the land. Among its provisions was the requirement that mining companies restore a mined area to a condition approximating that of its pre-mined appearance. The financial penalties assessed for noncompliance with this provision were, however, relatively modest. Companies have sometimes found that it was more profitable to ignore the restoration provisions of the act and to pay the fine that was eventually imposed.

See also Asbestos; Coal; Hydrocarbon; Metallurgy; Minerals; Ore; Stress, ecological.

An American mink (*Mustela vison*) in Flathead National Forest, in Montana.

Further Reading:

Brown, Maurice Russell, and Herbert Ralph Rice. *Mining Explained in Simple Terms*. Toronto: Northern Miner Press, 1968.

Stoches, Bohuslav. *Introduction to Mining*. London: Lange, Maxwell, and Springer, 1954.

Thomas, L. J. *An Introduction to Mining: Exploration, Feasibility, Extraction, Rock Mechanics*. Sydney: Hicks Smith & Sons, 1973.

David E. Newton

Mink

Minks are carnivores in the family Mustelidae, which also includes badgers, weasels, marten, and otters. Mink are closely related to the weasels and ermine, and are included in the same genus (*Mustela* spp.).

Mink have a long, compact body, with relatively short legs, webbed toes, and a long, bushy tail. Minks are larger and stoutes than other animals in the weasel group, and male minks are considerably larger than females, typically weighing about 4.4 lb (2 kg).

Minks are semiaquatic animals, and they have a highly varied diet, commonly feeding on small fish, aquatic and terrestrial invertebrates, amphibians, reptiles, small mammals, and birds. Minks are excellent swimmers, and can catch many types of aquatic prey. Minks are most active at dusk, night, and dawn. Their most usual habitat is riparian, that is, in the shrubby or forested habitats found in the vicinity of streams, rivers, and lakes. Mink also occur in the vicinity of marine habitats. Minks are solitary animals, except for groups consisting of a female and her recent young. The typical mink territory is several hectares in area.

The fur of minks is short, thick, soft, and lustrous, and is highly prized by the fur trade. Minks are extirpated or rare in many parts of their original range because of over-trapping for the fur trade. Today, most furs are obtained from mink that have been bred and raised on fur farms specifically for their pelts. Because of its superior pelage, the American mink is the preferred species for raising on fur farms. The natural color of wild minks is dark brown, but cultivated varieties are available in white, black, silver-blue, and blue pelages.

Species of minks

The American mink (*Mustela vison*) occurs throughout most of North America, except for parts of the arid southwest. These animals will live in the vicinity of a wide range of aquatic habitats. Mink make their dens in hollows in fallen logs and under stumps, and in burrows taken over from a muskrat or beaver.

The natural range of the Eurasian mink (*Mustela lutreola*) extends through much of central Europe, Ukraine, Belarus, and western Russia, with a disjunct population in France. This species has become widely extirpated from much of its natural range, through a combination of habitat changes and excessive trapping.

The recently extinct sea mink (*Mustela macrodon*) was a relatively large species that occurred along marine shores in parts of northeastern North America. This species was initially rare, and it was quickly made extinct by overexploitation for its fur. Studies of its skeletal materials that showed that the sea mink was a good species were not actually conducted until after this animal had become extinct. The sea mink was about twice the size of the American mink, with a relatively large skull, and other special characters. The species appears to have disappeared from New England in the 1860s or so, and the last known animal was killed on Campobello Island, New Brunswick, in 1894.

Further Reading:

Banfield, A.W.F. *The Mammals of Canada*. Toronto: University of Toronto Press, 1974.

Dunstone, N. *The Mink.* U.K.: Poyser Press,1993.

Grzimek, B. (ed.). *Grzimek's Encyclopedia of Mammals.* London: McGraw Hill, 1990.

Paradiso, J.L. (ed.). 1968. *Mammals of the World, 2nd ed.* Baltimore: John Hopkins Press, 1968.

Wilson, D.E. and D. Reeder (comp.). 1993. *Mammal Species of the World*. Washington, D.C.: Smithsonian Institution Press, 1993.

Bill Freedman

Minnows

Minnows are a diverse group of about 1,600 species of small exclusively freshwater fish in the family Cyprinidae. The most familiar of these fish are carp, minnows, tenche, and barbs. Species in the minnow family occur in Africa, Asia, Europe, and North America. In addition, some cultivated and game species have also been introduced to South America, New Guinea, Australia, New Zealand, and some other places. The greatest numbers of species of Cyprinidae occur in tropical Africa and in South and Southeast Asia.

Most species of minnow have a laterally compressed body, a terminal mouth, and relatively large, shiny scales. Minnows also have pharyngeal teeth in their throat, which are used to grind their food against a hard pad at the base of the skull. Male minnows are often smaller than females, and many species develop beautiful colors during the spawning season.

Most species of minnows are planktivorous, meaning they eat small crustaceans, insects, and other aquatic animals floating in the surface waters. Some of the larger species of minnow, such as carp, are omnivorous, eating both aquatic plants and animal matter.

Minnows are important in the food web of their freshwater ecosystems, because they are the food base for many species of predatory fish and other animals; minnows that are food for economically important sportfish are sometimes referred to as "forage" fish. Some North American species of minnows are also valuable as baitfish for sport fishing and are sold in large numbers for this purpose.

Some of the larger species in the Cyprinidae are cultivated as food in many parts of the world. The most important species in aquaculture is the common carp (*Cyprinus carpio*), along with the grass carp (*Ctenopharyngodon idella*), bighead carp (*Aristichtys nobilis*), and silver carp (*Hypophthalmichtys molitrix*). Enormous quantities of these fishes are grown in some parts of the world as food for humans, especially in Asia.

Several other species in the Cyprinidae are commonly kept as pets, either in indoor bowls or tanks, or in outdoor pools. The goldfish (*Carassius auratus*) is probably the world's most common pet fish. The koi is a golden-colored variety of the common carp that is often kept as a pet, especially in Japan. Many varieties of goldfish and koi have been developed by fish breeders. Some of these fish have bizarre shapes and behaviors, which would be totally maladaptive in wild fish, but are prized as unusual traits by many aficionados of these pet fish.

The minnow family in North America

About 200 species of fish in the minnow family are native to North America, with about 100 of them included in a single genus, *Notropis*, most of which are commonly called shiners. Minnows native to North America are all small species, while several larger, Eurasian species have been introduced to North America and now occur in self-sustaining populations.

The most widespread native species is the common or silver shiner (*Notropis cornutus*), which is virtually ubiquitous in many surface waters east of the Mississippi in the United States and is also widespread in eastern Canada. This species is important as a forage fish, and as a baitfish.

The pearl or northern dace (*Semotilus margarita*) is a widespread species that is especially important in brown-colored, boggy waters. The fallfish (*S. corporalis*) occurs in northeastern North America, and can grow as large as 18 in (45 cm), and is sometimes eaten by people.

The golden shiner (*Notemigonus crysoleucas*) occurs throughout the Great Lakes and Hudson Bay drainage, and is an important forage fish and common baitfish. The fathead minnow (*Pimephales promelas*) has a similar distribution and is also used as a baitfish.

The stoneroller (*Campostoma anomalum*) digests nutrients out of the copious quantities of mud that it ingests. The stoneroller has an enormously long intestine that coils 15 times around its air bladder.

In addition to the various native members of the minnow family, several species have been introduced to North America. The most familiar introduced species is the common carp (*Cyprinus carpio*). This fish is commonly cultivated as food in Europe and Asia, and it was released to many North American lakes in the hope of establishing a food resource that many immigrants would like to eat. Unfortunately, the common carp has caused some important ecological damage in many of the waterbodies where it has become established, resulting in the displacement of native species of fish and other animals and damage to aquatic vegetation.

The goldfish (*Carassius auratus*) has also been introduced to many ponds and lakes in North America, either deliberately as an ornamental fish, or more-or-less accidentally when unwanted pet goldfish were released into nearby ponds, or just flushed down a toilet. Like the common carp, alien populations of goldfish cause important ecological damage in many of the places where they have become well established.

See also Carp; Fish.

Further Reading:

Lee, D.S., C.R. Gilbert, C.H. Hocutt, R.E. Jenkins, D.E. McAllister, and J.R. Stauffer. *Atlas of North American Fishes*. Raleigh, NC: North Carolina State Museum of Natural History, 1980 (and updates).

O'Page, L. and Burr, B. *Field Guide to Freshwater Fishes of North America*. Boston, MA: Houghton Mifflin, 1991.

Winfield, I.J. and J.S. Nelson (eds.). *Cyprinid Fishes. Systematics, Biology, and Utilization*. New York: Chapman and Hall, 1991.

Bill Freedman

Minor planets (asteroids)

There are many hundreds of thousands of minor planets, or asteroids, within our solar system. They vary in size from a foot or so in diameter to a maximum of about 620 mi (1000 km). The majority of minor planets, the so-called main belt asteroids, circle the Sun in a region between the planets Jupiter and Mars. Many asteroid families have been identified, and there is a significant population of asteroids that travel along orbits which cross that of Earth.

The discovery of asteroids

The first asteroid was discovered serendipitously by the Italian astronomer Giuseppe Piazzi on the night

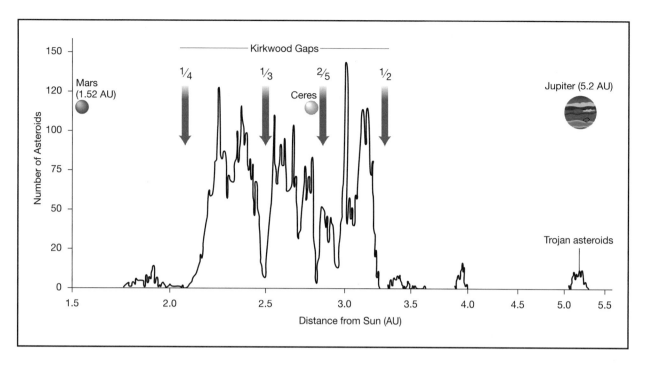

Figure 1.

of January 1, 1801. This asteroid, subsequently called Ceres after the Roman goddess of corn and harvests, has a diameter of 584 mi (940 km) and is the largest asteroid in our solar system. The next three largest asteroids, Pallas, Juno, and Vesta, were discovered in 1802, 1804, and 1807.

Astronomers have found that the number of asteroids increases dramatically with decreasing asteroid diameter; there is just one asteroid larger than 560 mi (900 km) across (Ceres), but there are three larger than 280 mi (450 km), 22 larger than 140 mi (225 km), and so on. The number of cataloged asteroids has grown dramatically since 1801, and it is estimated that some 100,000 minor planets larger than 0.62 mi (1 km) in diameter exist within our solar system. Despite their great numbers, however, the combined mass of all the asteroids is estimated to be just 0.04% of the mass of Earth.

The low collective mass of the asteroids within our solar system suggests that, rather than being the remnants of a disrupted planet, they are in fact leftover "building blocks" from the formation of the planets. Asteroid-like objects were among the first structures to form in our solar system some 4.6 billion years ago, and it has been suggested that the planets were formed through the collision and accretion of these primordial chunks of rock, or planetesimals. It has also been suggested that a planet did not form in the region presently occupied by the main belt asteroids because of the strong gravitational influence of Jupiter.

Main belt asteroids

Main belt asteroids revolve around the Sun on nearly circular orbits. It takes a main belt asteroid anywhere from 2.8-8.0 years to complete one circuit around its orbit.

Images obtained by NASA's space probe *Galileo* confirmed the long-held belief that asteroids are irregular shaped objects. The *Galileo* probe imaged the asteroid Gaspra in October 1991 and found it to be a highly cratered, 11.2 x 5.6 mi (18 x 9 km) sized rocky body. Likewise, when *Galileo* flew past the asteroid Ida in August 1993 it imaged an elongated, 31.2 x 9.3 mi (55 x 15 km) sized object sporting many scars and impact craters. The irregular shapes of these asteroids reflect an extensive history of collisions. Perhaps the most surprising of *Galileo's* discoveries during the Ida encounter, however, was the detection of a small 0.62 mi (1 km) sized moonlet in orbit about the asteroid.

The main belt region is not evenly populated with asteroids, and several zones have been found in which virtually no asteroids reside (Fig. 1).

The American astronomer Daniel Kirkwood first noticed these empty regions, or gaps, in 1866. Now called Kirkwood gaps, these asteroid-devoid zones are located near orbits for which the time to complete one

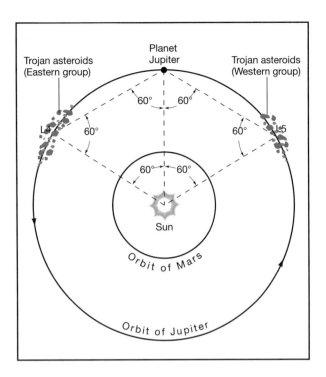

Figure 2.

circuit around the Sun is a simple fraction (e.g., 1/2, 2/3, 3/4, and so on) of Jupiter's orbital period. For example, given that Jupiter orbits the Sun once every 11.86 years, an asteroid belt gap would be expected at a distance of 3.3 astronomical units (AU) from the Sun, where any orbiting body would have a period of 5.93 years, one-half that of Jupiter. A gap is expected, and indeed one exists at 3.3 AU from the Sun. These Kirkwood gaps are produced by orbital resonance with Jupiter. When the orbital period of an asteroid is a simple fraction of Jupiter's, it will experience strong, frequently repeated tugs from Jupiter's gravitational field. Over time these periodic tugs will alter the asteroid's orbit, ultimately clearing out a gap at that particular distance from the sun. When no gravitational resonance exists, an asteroid's orbit tends to be stable.

Asteroids are classified according to their color and reflection spectra. An asteroid's color is determined by measuring how bright it appears through several specially constructed filters which pass only well-defined wavelengths of light. The color, indicated by a quantity called the color index, is essentially a measure of how well the asteroid reflects sunlight at different wavelengths. An indication of an asteroid's surface composition can be gleaned by measuring its reflection spectrum. Most asteroids are classified as C-type or S-type (Table 1). The C-type asteroids have a bluish color, and their reflection spectra indicate the presence of carbona-

ceous material at their surfaces. The S-type asteroids, on the other hand, are more reddish in color and their reflection spectra indicate that presence of surface silicate material. Other classifications include M-type, indicating the presence of surface metals, and R-type, indicating a deep, dark red color. Observations have revealed that the S-type asteroids tend to reside in the inner main belt, near the orbit of Mars. The C-type asteroids, in contrast, tend to reside toward the outer edge of the main belt nearer to Jupiter's orbit. The S-type asteroids are thought to be the primary source of stony and stony-iron meteorites, while the M-type asteroids are the most likely source of the iron meteorites.

Beyond the main belt

Not all asteroids reside in the main belt. The asteroid Hidalgo, discovered by American astronomer Walter Baade in 1920, for example, travels along an orbit which takes it from the inner edge of the main belt (2.0 AU from the Sun) to beyond the orbit of Saturn (9.7 AU). Likewise, the strange asteroid Chiron, discovered by Charles Kowal in 1977, moves along an orbit which brings it no closer than 8.5 AU to the Sun, but takes it all the way out to the orbit of Uranus (18.9 AU). Chiron is unusual because it occasionally shows cometlike behavior, emitting thin gases through evaporation from its surface.

The Trojan asteroids are an interesting group since they orbit the Sun at a distance of 5.2 AU—the same distance as the planet Jupiter. These asteroids move in a special way, and keep a near constant angle of 60° between themselves, Jupiter, and the Sun (Fig. 2).

This relative configuration of objects was shown to be gravitationally stable by the French mathematician Joseph Louis Lagrange in 1772, and the Trojans, with one group trailing and the other group leading Jupiter, occupy the so-called fourth and fifth Lagrange points. Several hundred Trojan asteroids have now been identified, the largest of which have diameters from 93-124 mi (150-200 km). The best studied Trojan asteroid, 624 Hektor, is unusual in that it appears to be nearly twice as long as it is wide. It has been suggested that 624 Hektor is in fact a binary asteroid, with the two components revolving around each other in near contact. (Several other asteroids have been found to be double.)

Several Earth-approaching asteroid groups have been discovered, and these have received considerable attention in recent times. This attention is warranted, since such asteroids will occasionally collide with Earth. Three main near-Earth asteroid (NEA) groups have been identified: the Aten group, the Apollo group, and the Amor group. The groups are distinguished

TABLE 1. PROPERTIES OF THE FIRST 20 ASTEROIDS TO BE DISCOVERED

Name	Classification	Orbital Period (yr)	Diameter (km)	Year of discovery
Ceres	C	4.60	940	1801
Pallas	C(?)	4.62	588	1802
Juno	S	4.36	248	1804
Vesta	U	3.63	576	1807
Astraea	S	4.13	120	1845
Hebe	S	3.78	204	1847
Iris	S	3.69	208	1847
Flora	S	3.27	162	1847
Metis	S	3.69	158	1848
Hygiea	C	5.55	430	1849
Parthenope	S	3.84	156	1850
Victoria	S	3.56	136	1850
Egeria	C	4.14	144	1850
Irene	S	4.16	150	1851
Eunomia	S	4.30	260	1851
Psyche	M	5.00	248	1852
Thetis	S	3.88	98	1852
Melpomene	S	3.48	162	1852
Fortuna	C	3.82	198	1852
Massalia	S	3.74	134	1852

TABLE 2. ESTIMATED NUMBER OF NEAR-EARTH ASTEROIDS IN THE SIZE RANGE FROM 10 METERS TO 10 KILOMETERS

Asteroid diameter (km)	Number of objects	Time between Earth Impacts (yr)	Impact energy (kilotons of TNT)
10	10	100 million	10 billion
1	1000	1 million	10 million
0.1	100,000	10,000	10,000
0.01	10,000,000	100	10

according to how closely the constituent asteroids approach Earth's orbit, and whether they make their closest approach near perihelion or aphelion. The Atens, for example, make their closest approach to Earth's orbit when they are at aphelion; the Amors, on the other hand, make their closest approach to Earth's orbit when they are near perihelion. Nearly 150 NEAs have been discovered, and the largest of these is about 5 mi (8 km) in diameter. No doubt many more NEAs await discovery.

TABLE 3. THE 10 LARGEST TERRESTRIAL IMPACT CRATERS

Crater name	Country	Diameter (km)	Age (million years)
Sudbury	Canada	200	1850
Chicxulub	Mexico	180	65
Acraman	Australia	160	570
Vredefort	South Africa	140	1970
Popigai	Russia	100	35
Manicouagan	Canada	100	212
Puchezh-Katunki	Russia	80	220
Kara	Russia	65	73
Siljan	Sweden	55	368
Charlevoix	Canada	54	357

Impact craters

Should a large NEA strike Earth, the consequences for humanity could be disastrous.

Fortunately, the average time between such collisions is long (Table 2), and a truly catastrophic collision, involving an asteroid larger than 6.2 mi (10 km), occurs on average once every 100 million years. A total of 130 impact craters have been identified on Earth's surface (Table 3), the largest of which is the Sudbury crater in Canada. The sizes of the known terrestrial craters vary from approximately 100 ft (30 m) in size to 200 mi (320 km) or more in diameter.

The last globally catastrophic collision between Earth and an asteroid probably took place 65 million years ago at the end of the Cretaceous period. It now seems reasonably likely that the extinction of many species, including the great dinosaur extinction which occurred at the Cretaceous-Tertiary boundary, was caused by the impact of a 6.2 mi (10 km) sized asteroid. The submerged remnants of the giant impact crater produced in this terminal Cretaceous collision were recently discovered on the coast of the Yucatan peninsula in Mexico. The crater, named Chicxulub (meaning horns of the devil), is approximately 112 mi (180 km) in diameter and has long been buried under coastal sediments.

See also Astroblemes; Meteors and meteorites.

Further Reading:

Beatty, J. Kelly. "Killer Crater in the Yucatan?" *Sky and Telescope* (July 1991): 38-40.
——. "Ida and Company." *Sky and Telescope* (January 1995): 20-23.
Cunningham, Clifford J. *Introduction to Asteroids*. Richmond, VA: Willman-Bell, 1988.
Grieve, Richard A. F. "Impact Cratering on the Earth." *Scientific American* (April 1990): 66-73.
Kowal, Charles T. *Asteroids: Their Nature and Utilization*. Chichester, England: Ellis Horwood, 1988.

KEY TERMS

. . . .

Color index—The difference in the brightness of an object when measured at two different wavelengths of light.

Cretaceous-Tertiary boundary—In geologic time, a period 65 million years ago separating the Cenozoic era from the Mesozoic era.

Perihelion—The point at which an object, in orbit about the Sun, is at its closest to the Sun.

Planetesimals—Asteroid-sized bodies that combined to form the planets.

Mint family

The mint family (Labiatae or Lamiaceae) is a large group of dicotyledonous plants occurring worldwide in all types of climates except in extreme arctic and antarctic conditions. There are about 3,000 species in the mint family and 200 genera. The most diverse groups are the genus *Salvia* with 500 species, *Hyptis* with 350 species, and *Scutellaria, Coleus, Plectranthus,* and *Stachys,* each with 200 species.

Some species in the mint family are economically important and are grown as herbs used to flavor foods and beverages or for the production of essential oils that are used as fragrances in perfumery. Some species are also grown as showy or fragrant ornamentals in gardens.

Biology of mints

Most species in the mint family are annuals or herb-like perennials, and a few species are shrubs. Most species of mints have aromatic glands and hairs on their stems and foliage, and when the leaves are crushed strongly scented vapors are released. The stems of mints are commonly four-sided in cross section, and most species have oppositely arranged leaves.

The flowers of mints are bilaterally symmetric. Because they are mostly pollinated by insects, mints have relatively brightly colored, nectar-rich flowers usually grouped into a larger inflorescence The lower, fused petals of the flower provide a platform for pollinators to land on called a lip (or in Latin, *labia,* from which the family name Labiatae is derived). Most species in the mint family have bisexual flowers, containing both male (staminate) and female (pistilate) organs. The fruits are small, one-seeded nutlets.

Native mints of North America

Many species in the mint family are native to natural plant communities of North America. Many additional species have been introduced from Eurasia and elsewhere, especially species that are grown in agriculture or horticulture, and some of these have escaped from gardens and become naturalized in appropriate habitats in North America.

Some of the more interesting and attractive groups of native species include the skullcaps (*Scutellaria* spp.), physostegias (*Physostegia* spp.), hemp-nettles (*Stachys* spp.), sages (*Salvia* spp.), horse-mints or bergamots(*Monarda* spp.), bugle-weeds (*Lycopus* spp.), and true mints (*Mentha* spp.).

Economic products obtained from mints

A number of herbs are derived from aromatic species in the mint family, sometimes as cultivars that have been selectively bred to enhance the aromatic qualities of the plants. The most commonly known of these herbs are derived from several herbaceous, perennial species in the genus *Mentha,* originally native to Eurasia

Basil (*Ocimum basilicum*).

but now cultivated widely in suitable, usually temperate climates. The common mint (*Mentha arvensis*), spearmint (*M. spicata*), and peppermint (*M. piperita*) are all used to flavor candies, chewing gum, toothpaste, and tea, and are sometimes used to prepare condiments to serve with meats and other foods. All of these species can be grown on heavy, wet soils that are unsuitable for most other crops. Peppermint is generally harvested in large-scale agriculture by mowing, its water content is partially dried, and the aromatic oils are extracted for use as flavorings and scents. Other species of mints are grown and harvested in similar ways.

The hoarhound (*Marrubium vulgare*) of Europe and Asia is another species used to flavor candies. Common sage (*Salvia officinalis*) is used to flavor foods, toothpaste, and mouthwash. Sweet marjoram (*Origanum majorana*) is used to flavor some types of cooked meats, stews, and other foods, as are basil (*Ocimum basilicum*), rosemary (*Rosmarinus officinalis*), summer savory (*Satureja hortensis*), thyme (*Thymus vulgaris*), hyssop (*Hysoppus officinalis*), clary (*Salvia sclarea*), and balm (*Melissa officinalis*).

Various species in the mint family contain aromatic essential oils that can be extracted and used to scent potpourri and other decorations or as fragrances in the mixing of perfumes. Lavender (*Lavandula officinalis*) is a Mediterranean shrub that is commonly used for these purposes. Lavender is an important ingredient of eau de cologne and lavender water, and it is commonly dried and put into small bags called sachets and used to scent clothing cupboards and drawers. Other species of the mint family from which essential oils are extracted include the pennyroyal (*Hedeoma pulegioides*), rosemary, sage, and thyme.

Catnip (*Nepeta cataria*) is a species that felines find intriguing, and they will contentedly smell this species and play with toys stuffed with its dry foliage.

Mints as ornamental plants

Some species in the mint family are commonly grown indoors or in gardens as leafy ornamentals. One of the more popular groups of foliage plants is the various species and varieties of coleus (*Coleus* spp.), bee-balm (*Monarda fistulosa*), bergamot (*Monarda didyma*), garden sage (*Salvia splendens*), and common sage (*Salvia officinalis*).

Many people cultivate their own herb gardens of various species in the mint family that are used as flavorings. This is done to ensure a continuous and fresh supply of these flavorful herbs for use in aromatic, epicurean cooking. Recently, people have also began to grow these plants indoors under artificial sources of light so that they will continue to have access to fresh edible mints during the winter.

Mints as weeds

Many species in the mint family are grown in gardens and in agriculture, and these have been transported around the world for cultivation in suitable climates. In some cases, these species have escaped from cultivation and have become minor weeds of agriculture, lawns, and disturbed areas. Examples of such weeds in North America include catnip, ground-ivy (*Glechoma hederacea*), heal-all (*Prunella vulgaris*), hemp-nettle

(*Galeopsis tetrahit*), henbit (*Lamium amplexicaule*), and motherwort (*Leonurus cardiaca*).

See also Herb.

Further Reading:

Hvass, E. *Plants That Serve and Feed Us*. New York: Hippocrene Books, 1975.
Klein, R. M. *The Green World. An Introduction to Plants and People*. New York: Harper and Row, 1987.
Woodland, D. W. *Contemporary Plant Systematics*. New Jersey: Prentice-Hall,1991.

Bill Freedman

Mirages see **Atmospheric optical phenomena**

Mirrors

Any reflective material can act as a mirror, because it will throw back enough light to form an image of its surroundings. The surface may be a plane, concave or convex. Planar or flat mirrors present a virtual image that reverses the object being reflected. Curved surfaces act more like lenses, without the aberrations to which glass lenses are prone. Nowadays such surfaces can be made from glass, metal, or plastic, often with a thin metal coating. Prisms can also act as mirrors.

Mirrors create a virtual image, which you can easily see in a hallway mirror, but they also produce a real image, which may not be detectable with diffuse lighting. If you place a single, bright filament bulb in front of a mirror, a reflection can be cast on a screen held between the two, a little above the bulb. The image of the bulb may seem to disappear once you remove the screen. If you keep looking at the space it once occupied and move away from the direct path of the light, however, you will be able to see the real image floating in that space.

Convex spherical mirrors, or fish-eyes, are used as rearview mirrors on cars or trucks. These form only a virtual image within the body of the mirror. A concave version is more common on magnifying makeup mirrors. Conic mirrors are parabolic or elliptic in shape, and will reflect perfect images from a certain distance only. Mirrors are also used as solar collectors and to focus military searchlights. In a Newtonian telescope, a conic mirror reflects an image backwards onto a retractable plane mirror, so the observer does not block any of the incoming light rays. Cassegrain telescopes are made from a pair of mirrors, one hyperbolic and the other paraboloid. The Cassegrain system provides a long focal length without taking up much space. Both these telescopes aid the detection of very distant stars.

In the age of the Hubble Telescope, the mirrors for such giant structures often use as much as 20,000 lb (9,000 kg) of a Pyrex-like glass called borosilicate. Such a vast stretch of material, 7 yd (6.5 m) across, cannot be ground normally. Surface irregularities could too easily develop. The material is melted and whirled in a huge circular furnace until it settles into shape. Afterwards the exterior is polished by a computer-programmed machine, to avoid human error as much as possible.

Mirrors have not changed structurally in thousands of years, since the ancient Egyptians used the first known metal hand mirrors. The so-called "True Mirror," which reflects a person's image without inverting it the way an ordinary looking-glass does, is actually made of two plane mirrors joined at a 90-degree angle to reflect a fused image. You can still make your own mirror for a small telescope by grinding two flat discs of glass together until the top piece becomes concave and the lower one convex. Both discs can then be finished separately with minute polishing.

See also Glass; Lens; Telescope.

Miscibility

Miscibility means how completely two or more liquids dissolve in each other. It is a qualitative rather than quantitative observation—miscible, partially miscible, not miscible. (To state exactly how miscible two liquids were, a scientist would use the larger concept of solubility, usually in a specific weight or volume per liter of solution.)

Two completely miscible liquids will form a homogeneous (uniform) solution in any amount. Water and ethyl alcohol, for example, are completely miscible whether the solution is 1% water and 99% ethyl alcohol, 50% of both, or 1% ethyl alcohol and 99% water. When first mixed, miscible liquids often show oily bands—called striations—in the bulk of the solution; these disappear when mixing is complete.

Like any other solubility phenomenon, miscibility depends on the forces of attraction between the molecules of the different liquids. The rule of thumb "like dissolves like" means that liquids with similar molecu-

lar structures—in particular similar polarity—will likely dissolve in each other. (Polarity means the extent to which partial positive and negative charges appear on a molecule, because of the type and arrangement of its component atoms.) Both water and ethyl alcohol have very polar hydroxyl groups (-OH) on their molecules, and therefore both undergo the strong intermolecular attraction known as "hydrogen bonding." Hexane, on the other hand, is not miscible with water because its molecular structure contains no polar groups of any kind that would be attracted to the water molecules.

See also Molecule; Qualitative Analysis; Quantitative Analysis; Solubility; Solution.

Missile see **Rockets and missiles**

Mistletoe

If you stand under a sprig of mistletoe at Christmas time, you might be kissed! It is interesting how a parasitic plant has come to represent such a romantic notion. Mistletoe belongs to the family *Viscaceae* and to the genus *Viscum, Phoradendron,* or *Arceuthobium.* Most commonly, mistletoe refers to either the Eurasian shrub *Viscum album* or one of the American species, such as *Phoradendron flavescens.* Mistletoe grows on the trunks and branches of a wide variety of trees. Mistletoe is an evergreen, and its stems have numerous branches. The plants have tough, oblong, green leaves, tiny flowers, and waxy, translucent, white berries with a viscous mesocarp (the portion of the berry between the skin and seed).

Mistletoe is considered to be a partial parasite or semi-parasite because it manufactures all of its carbohydrates through photosynthesis in its green leaves, but it depends on its host tree for water, minerals, and protein. There is one leafless flowering species of mistletoe of the genus *Arceuthobium* that is entirely parasitic and is damaging to conifers. A root-like structure (haustorium) of the mistletoe penetrates into the bark of the host tree and absorbs water, inorganic ions, sugars, amino acids, and hormones from the tree's xylem and phloem (inner and outer vascular parts of each stem). Dispersal of the seeds of these plants is primarily carried out by birds who eat the berries and fly to another tree, dropping the sticky berries onto the bark. Within days roots emerge from the germinating seed.

Mistletoe in Florida.

years ago mistletoe was used for a variety of ailments and conditions. Currently, the potential medicinal effects of mistletoe are being tested on laboratory animals. Some research is being done to see if certain extracts from mistletoe can destroy cancer cells. Along with some potentially beneficial substances, mistletoe contains toxic substances and therefore should not be eaten.

Christine Miner Minderovic

The tradition of kissing beneath the mistletoe is believed to come from a Norse legend in which Balder, the god of Peace, was killed with an arrow made of mistletoe. As the story goes, the gods bring Balder back to life by giving mistletoe to Freya, the goddess of Love, who makes the plant a symbol of love. Freya proclaimed that anyone who passed under mistletoe could be kissed. The Druids used mistletoe to welcome the new year and for religious rites and medicinal purposes, such as treating sterility and epilepsy. The French name for mistletoe, *herbe de la croix* (herb of the cross), comes from a legend describing how mistletoe was once a tree that was used to make Christ's cross. After Christ's death, mistletoe was cursed to never again grow from the earth and it was turned into a small parasite. Mistletoe was also associated with magical powers in some cultures, and is thought to have been the Golden Bough that opened the door to the Underworld for Sybil and for the hero Aeneas in Virgil's *Aenead*.

Each species of mistletoe has unique chemical properties and different medicinal possibilities. Hundreds of

Mites

Mites are tiny arthropods in the order Acari (or Acarina) which also includes the somewhat larger ticks. The Acari is in the class Arachnida which also encompasses the spiders and scorpions. Arachnids have four pairs of segmented legs, a body divided into a cephalothorax (that is, a united head and thorax), and abdomen, and they have a simple respiratory apparatus consisting of tracheae and/or book lungs. The Acari are a diverse group of at least 30,000 species, although the group is not yet well studied, and many additional species will undoubtedly be named.

Mites typically have small or minute bodies with roughly oval shapes and little differentiation of the cephalothorax and the unsegmented abdomen. Newly hatched mites are known as larvae, and they have only three pairs of legs. After the first molt the mite has four pairs of legs, and the animal is known as a nymph until the sexually mature adult stage is achieved.

Most species of mites are tiny creatures that live in organic debris of forests and grasslands where they feed on dead organic matter, fungal spores and hyphae, and plant matter. Many other species are predators of other mites and tiny insects such as springtails, or they are parasites of a wide range of animals. Terrestrial mites can be extremely abundant, and their populations may outnumber those of all other species of arthropods in many habitats. A few species of mites are aquatic, including some relatively large and attractive, bright-red or green-colored species known as water-mites commonly in the genus *Arrenurus*.

Some species of mites are important pests of agricultural plants. Certain species of spider mites or red mites (family Tetranychidae) are important pests of fruit trees grown in orchards, field crops, and greenhouses. Mite infestations may be managed by applying toxic chemicals such as pesticides, by reducing the

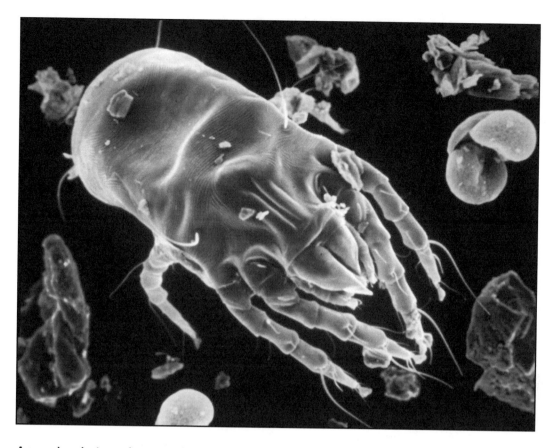

A scanning electron micrograph (SEM) of a dust mite.

amount of organic debris that is present in their habitat, or by encouraging species of mites that are predators of the injurious species.

Some mites physically affect domestic animals and humans. The chicken mite (*Dermanyssus gallinae*) is a serious, highly infectious, blood-sucking parasite of chickens and other fowl. The sheep scab mite (*Psoroptes ovis*) is a pest of sheep and other livestock. Scabies is an itchy skin condition caused by infestations of various species of itch or scab mites (family Sarcoptidae) that burrow into the skin. Many animals are afflicted by mange, a skin condition caused by species of mange mites (family Psoroptidae). Chiggers or harvest mites (family Trombiculidae) are another group of itch-causing skin parasites which can sometimes be vectors of human diseases in the tropics such as scrub typhus.

House-dust mites in the genus *Dermatophagoides* (family Acaridae) are common in homes and are an important cause of the allergies that many people develop to house dusts.

See also Arthropods.

Mitochondria see **Cell**

Mitosis

Mitosis is a process that sorts and evenly distributes a cell's genetic instructions to the nuclei of two daughter cells during cell division. Imagine dealing a deck of cards to two players so that the players' hands contain identical cards. In a similar way, mitosis distributes identical DNA instructions to new cells when the old cell divides.

Growth is based on cell division and mitosis. Some cells in the body—such as nerve and skeletal muscle cells—cannot divide, and they stay with us for life. But most tissues of the body grow and replace themselves by cell division. These cells go through a cell cycle from the time they are formed until the time when they divide. During the period of mitosis, the nucleus and cytoplasm divide to form two new cells. The rest of the cell cycle is known as interphase.

In the nucleus of a cell, DNA comprises a code carrying all the instructions that the cell needs to live. In the nuclei of eukaryotic cells, the DNA molecules, coiled like microscopic spaghetti, form compact, bulky structures called chromosomes. Under the light micro-

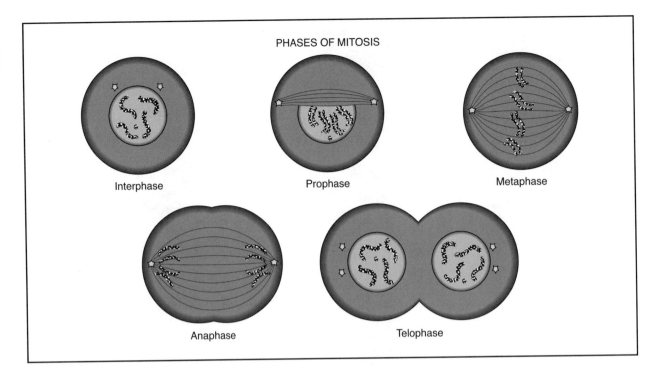

PHASES OF MITOSIS

Interphase

Prophase

Metaphase

Anaphase

Telophase

Figure 1. Stages of mitosis.

scope, chromosomes have the appearance of solid, flexible rods. Early microscopists applied the word chromosome, meaning "colored body," to structures that took up basic red or purple dyes in the nucleus of a dividing cell. Humans have 23 chromosomes, but other organisms, like the fruit fly, have as few as four, and others, such as the dog, as many as 39.

As chromosomes uncoil at the beginning of interphase, the thin threads of DNA, termed chromatin, become invisible to an observer looking through a light microscope. Each chromosome then makes a copy of itself, stringing together basic units available in the cytoplasm according to its own sequence. Now two identical DNA strands, called sister chromatids, are attached to each other by a structure known as a centromere. The DNA begins to twist and coil, curling more and more tightly.

At this point, the cell begins to assemble the scaffolding it needs for moving the chromosomes to opposite ends of the cell. In animal cells, the two centrioles—small cylinders containing tiny tubular elements—replicate. The cells of higher plants do not have centrioles.

Mitosis is a continuous process, but for convenience, scientists divide it into four stages: prophase, metaphase, anaphase, and telophase.

Prophase

The cell enters prophase as the long tangled DNA molecules, or chromatin, coil into the compact bodies of chromosomes. This coiling process is comparable to taking a thin strand 656 ft (200 m) long and coiling it into a cylinder 1 mm wide by 8 mm long. A structure called the kinetochore is formed on each chromatid at the outer face of the centromere region (See Figure 1). The nuclear membrane breaks down.

During prophase, the cells' cytoskeleton or structural framework made of the protein tubulin breaks down into subunits. From these subunits, a bridge of microtubules called the spindle apparatus forms between the two pairs of centrioles as they move apart. When the centrioles reach opposite ends of the cell, they extend microtubules in all directions. Like a boat moored to a dock with multiple lines, the centriole anchors itself to the cell membrane. This arrangement of microtubules—called an aster because of its star-like pattern—is thought to mechanically strengthen the spindle apparatus. Mitosis does not appear to depend upon the presence of centrioles, however. Destroying centrioles in animal cells with a laser beam does not prevent mitosis. Plant cells equipped with rigid cell walls, but neither centrioles nor asters, also grow by mitotic division.

As prophase continues, a set of microtubules grows from the kinetochore of each sister chromatid. The

KEY TERMS

Centromere—A constricted region of the chromosome joining two sister chromatids. The centromere is composed of highly repeated DNA sequences approximately 220 units in length.

Centriole—An arrangement of microtubules found in most animal cells and in cells of some lower plants and fungi.

Chromatin—The name given to loose tangle of DNA strands in the nuclei of cells during periods when they are not dividing. As a cell prepares to divide, chromatin strands condense into compact chromosomes.

Chromosomes—Structures in the eukaryotic cell nucleus consisting of heavily coiled DNA and proteins and carrying genetic information.

Cytokinesis—The physical division of the cytoplasm of a eukaryotic cell to form two daughter cells, each housing a newly formed nuclei.

Cytoskeleton—a network of assorted protein filaments attached to the cell membrane and to various organelles that makes up the framework for cell shape and movement.

DNA (deoxyribonucleic acid)—Strands of DNA, or deoxyribonucleic acid, are like long sentences of words composed of a four letter alphabet of nucleotide base pairs: A (adenine); T (thymine); G (guanine); and C (cytosine). The "words" contain the instructions for sequences of amino acids making up proteins.

Eukaryotic cells—Cells whose genetic material is carried on chromosomes inside a nucleus encased in a membrane. Eukaryotic cells also have organelles that perform specific metabolic tasks and are supported by a cytoskeleton which runs through the cytoplasm, giving the cell form and shape. In contrast, the more primitive prokaryotic cells are smaller than eukaryotes, and have no nucleus, distinct organelles, or cytoskeleton.

Kinetochore—A disk of protein bound to the centromere to which microtubules attach during mitosis, linking each chromatid to the spindle.

Microtubule—A hollow protein cylinder, about 25 nanometers in diameter, composed of subunits of the protein tubulin. Microtubules grow in length by the addition of tubulin subunits at the end and are shortened by their removal.

Nucleotide—The "letters" or basic units of DNA, containing a phosphate group, a 5-carbon sugar, and a ring-shaped nitrogenous base.

Spindle apparatus—An axis of microtubules formed between centrioles in animal cells that aids the equal distribution of chromosomes to new cells being formed.

microtubules extending from each chromatid become attached to opposite poles of the spindle.

Metaphase

In the second stage of mitosis, called metaphase, the pairs of sister chromatids line up in the center of the cell like couples taking their place on a dance floor. The centromeres of the chromosomes appear to be aligned within an imaginary plate midway between the centrioles and dissecting the cell at right angles to the spindle. Responding to some unknown cue, the centromeres divide in unison, freeing the sister chromatids to separate in the next phase.

Anaphase

As if following a neatly choreographed dance, the sister chromatids separate, rapidly moving toward the pole to which their microtubule is attached. The cell appears "stretched" as the spindle fibers slide past one another, elongating the spindle apparatus and further separating the poles. Shortening of the microtubules by removal of tubulin units pulls the chromosomes closer and closer to the pole. The movement of sister chromatids to opposite sides of the cell completes the equal division and distribution of genetic material.

Telophase

During telophase, or the "clean-up" stage of mitosis, the spindle apparatus is broken down, and the tubulin subunits stand ready to form the cytoskeleton of a new cell. The chromosomes, now clustered in two groups around the poles, uncoil into tangled threads again, and a new nuclear envelope forms around them. At this point, each new nucleus contains one copy of each chromosome. Mitosis is complete.

Cytokinesis

Cell division is not finished, however. During cytokinesis, the cytoplasm of a cell is physically divided to form two daughter cells housing the newly formed nuclei. In addition to dividing up the cytoplasm, cytokinesis distributes cellular organelles equally to the daughter cells. The binding of some molecules or organelles to the chromosomes or spindle microtubules ensures that each daughter cell will receive a fair share of cytoplasmic components.

A belt of microfilaments constricts the cell, pinching it in two. In plants, a cell plate forms, growing outward until it reaches the cell membrane and fuses with it. Cellulose is laid down on the new membranes, forming a strong new cell wall.

See also Chromosome; Deoxyribonucleic Acid Meiosis.

Further Reading:

Arms, Karen and Pamela S. Camp. *Biology*. 3rd ed. Philadelphia: Saunders College Publishing, 1987.

Beck, William S., Karel F. Liem, and George G. Simpson. *Life, an Introduction to Biology*. 3rd ed. New York: Harper Collins, 1991.

Raven, Peter H. and George B. Johnson. *Biology*, 3rd ed. St. Louis: Mosby Year Book, 1992.

Starr, Cecie and Ralph Taggart. *Biology, The Unity and Diversity of Life*. Belmont, CA: Wadsworth Publishing Company, 1992.

Elaine Friebele

Mitral valve see **Heart**

Mixture, chemical

A chemical mixture is a collection of molecules or atoms of different types. A mixture is distinguished from a pure substance, which has constant composition (is composed of a only one type of molecule or atom), and a unique set of physical properties (no matter how large or small a sample is observed). The properties of a mixture depend not only on the types of substances that compose it, but also on their relative amounts; the com-

position of a mixture is not constant. The separation of mixtures is big business, and separation science is a subdivision of chemistry.

Heterogeneous mixtures are non-uniform, with the components jumbled irregularly together; frequently the substances making up the mixture can be seen as bits of different textured or colored material. Homogeneous mixtures, on the other hand, look uniform. The molecules or atoms making up a homogeneous mixture are distributed evenly, all in the same phase. (Homogeneous mixtures can sometimes be mistaken for pure substances because of their uniform appearance.) Salt water solution is a homogeneous mixture, for example, but salt mixed with sand is a heterogeneous mixture.

Mixtures are separable into their component elements or compounds (at least theoretically) by purely physical processes. For example, if iron filings and sulfur powder are mixed together, they constitute a chemical mixture. This particular mixture is easy to separate by applying a magnet to draw out the iron—utilizing magnetic force is a physical process. If the iron filings and sulfur powder are heated, however, they undergo a chemical reaction to form a compound, iron sulfide, which does not respond to a magnet. Pure iron sulfide is homogeneous (uniform in appearance and properties), shows constant composition (a consistent ratio of iron to sulfur throughout any sample of it, large or small), consists of molecules all of one type, is no longer separable into two separate substances without another chemical reaction, and is thus no longer a mixture.

See also Compound, chemical; Element, chemical; Molecule.

Möbius strip

A Möbius strip is a twisted surface in space that is made by starting with a rectangular piece of paper, twisting one side through 180^0 (relative to the opposite side), and then joining it to the opposite side. That is, using the rectangle shown below, AC is joined to DB so

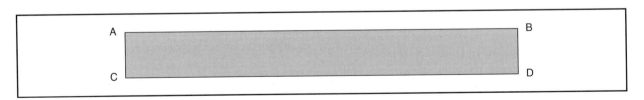

Figure 1.

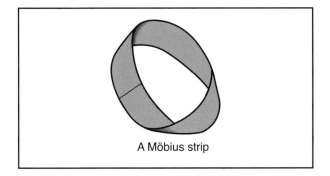

A Möbius strip

Figure 2.

Further Reading:

Richard Courant and Herbert Robbins. *What Is Mathematics?*, Oxford University Press, 1948.

Karl J. Smith. *The Nature of Modern Mathematics*, Wadsworth Publishing Company, 1973.

Roy Dubisch

that the point A coincides with the point D and the point C coincides with the point B.

It is a one-sided surface. That is, any point P on it can be joined to its opposite, Q (or to any other point) by a path that does not cross the edge of the surface. It is named after the 19th century mathematician, August Möbius.

If a Möbius strip is cut length-wise the result will be just one two sided surface. If cut again, the result will be two interconnected surfaces that, again, are two sided.

Mockingbirds and thrashers

Mockingbirds, thrashers, and catbirds are 31 species of medium-sized birds that are sometimes known as mimid thrushes, in the family Mimidae. This is an American family of birds, occurring widely from southern Argentina and Chile, through to southern Canada. The usual habitat of mimids is brushlands, forest edges, shrubby riparian areas, and recently disturbed forests.

Mimids range in body length from 7.9-11.8 in (20-30 cm), and are slender-bodied, with short, rounded

A curve-billed thrasher (*Toxostoma curvirostre*) perched near its nest in a cactus at the Arizona Sonora Desert Museum, Arizona.

wings, a long tail, and long legs. The beak is rather heavy and downward curving, and in some species is quite long and strongly decurved.

Mimids have a rather subdued plumage, with most species colored in brown or gray hues, often with a light throat or underparts, and sometimes with a spotted or streaked breast. Some species are solidly colored, while others have patterns, especially of white on the wings and tail. The sexes do not differ significantly in size or coloration.

Mimids feed on invertebrates, berries, and seeds. They forage on the ground, or in shrubs. Mimids are not social birds, and do not gather into flocks.

Mimids are highly territorial during the breeding season, sometimes attacking nearby dogs, cats, other birds, and even people who stray too close to their defended area. Mimids are loud, and delightfully versatile singers. Some species are excellent mimics, and incorporate aspects of the songs of other species into their own individualistic, highly varied renditions.

Mimids build their rather bulky, cup-shaped, grass-lined, twiggy nests in shrubs, or sometimes on the ground. Mimids lay 2-6 eggs, which are incubated by the female, although the male helps in rearing the young.

The best-known mimid in North America is the northern mockingbird (*Mimus polyglottos*), an acclaimed songster of shrubby and suburban habitats that breeds over most of the United States and Mexico, some Caribbean islands, and southern Canada.

The brown thrasher (*Toxostoma rufum*) is a common, rufous-backed bird with a white, spotted breast. This species occurs widely in temperate regions of eastern North America. The sage thrasher (*Oreoscoptes montanus*) is a common species of dry habitats in southwestern North America. Some other thrashers have considerably longer and more decurved beaks, especially the California thrasher (*Toxostoma redivivum*) and LeConte's thrasher (*T. lecontei*), both of which occur in the southwestern United States.

The catbird (*Dumetella carolinensis*) is a gray-bodied, black-capped bird, with rusty-brown under the tail coverts (that is, where the tail joins the body). This species breeds from southern Canada through most of the United States, and winters as far south as Panama. The catbird is named after its alarm call, which sounds remarkably like the mewing of a cat. The song is much more melodious.

Bill Freedman

Mode

The mode of a set of numbers is the number that occurs most frequently. There may be more than one mode. In the set (1,4,5,7), all four numbers are modes. But in the set (1,4,4,6), 4 is the only mode. The mode is one of the measures of central tendency, the others being the mean and the median.

See also Mean; Median.

Modular arithmetic

Modular arithmetic derives from the concept of congruence modulo m, written symbolically as

$a \equiv b \pmod{m}$

where a and b are any integers and m is a positive integer greater than 1. This means that a - b is divisible by m. For example,

$36 \equiv 16 \pmod{5}$

since 36-16 =20 is divisible by 5. Likewise 11 = 38 (mod 9) because 11-38 = -27 is divisible by 9.

The concept of congruence was first used by Carl Friedrich Gauss (1755-1855). Gauss was an outstanding mathematician as well as a master of astronomy, physics, geodesy, and statistics. He lived in Germany and for many years was director of the university observatory in Göttingen.

Many of the properties of equality are also true for congruences. For example, consider modulo 5. Since $5 \equiv 0 \pmod{5}$, $6 \equiv 1 \pmod{5}$, $7 \equiv 2 \pmod{5}$, etc., we need only consider the set {0,1,2,3,4}, called a *complete residue* set. Then, for example,

1+2 = 3, 3+4 = 2 [since $7 \equiv 2 \pmod{5}$], and 2×3 = 1 [since $6 \equiv 1 \pmod{5}$].

Indeed, we can produce tables for addition and multiplication. Where we note that not only do we have

a+b = b+a and a×b= b×a

for all a and b in the set {0,1,2,3,4} (addition and multiplication are commutative), but less obviously, we have associatively

a+(b+c) = (a+b)+c and a×(b×c)= (a×b)×c

and distributivity

a×(b+c)= a×b + a×c

again for all a, b, c in the set {0,1,2,3,4}. Furthermore, we have an additive identity, 0, such that a+0 =

0+a for all a in the set {0,1,2,3,4} and a multiplicative identity, 1, such that a×1 = 1×a for a in the set {1,2,3,4}. We can also see that we have both additive and multiplicative inverses. That is, for any a in {0,1,2,3,4} we have a b such that

a+b = b+a =0

and a c such that

a×c = c×a = 1

for any a in {1,2,3,4}. Specifically we have 1+4 = 0, 2+3 = 0, 3+2 = 0, and 4+1 = 0

and

1×1 = 1, 2×3 = 1, 3×2 = 1, and 4×4 = 1

A system in which an addition and a multiplication are defined and for which the commutative, associative, and distributive properties hold, where there exist identities for addition and multiplication, where every element has an additive inverse, and every non-zero element has a multiplicative inverse, is called a *field*. Other examples of fields are the set of rational numbers and the set of real numbers. Since the number of elements in our set (0,1,2,3,4} is finite, we have an example of finite field.

Do these results hold for an J complete residue set? Indeed they do *except:* for the existence of multiplicative inverses. Thus, if we consider the complete residue system mod 4 (0,1,2 ,3) we see that there is no multiplicative inverse for 2 since 2×0 = 0, 2×1 = 2, 2×2 = 0 [(because 4≡0 (mod 4)] and 2×3 = 2.

In order for multiplicative inverses to exist in a complete residue system mod m, it is necessary and sufficient for m to be a prime, or a number whose only divisors are 1 and m. Thus 2,3,5,7,11, and 13 are all primes but 4,6,8 and 9 are not.

The concept of congruence can be used to establish a rule for deciding whether a number is divisible by 9. A number is divisible by 9 if and only if the sum of its digits is divisible by 9. Thus, for example, 243,648 is divisible by 9 because 2+4+3+6+4+8 = 27 is divisible by 9 whereas 243,649 is not because 28 is not divisible by 9. A proof of this fact depends upon the fact that 10≡1 (mod 9).

Mohorovicic discontinuity see **Earth's interior**

Molarity see **Concentration**

Mold

A mold is the general term given to a coating or discoloration found on the surface of certain materials, produced by the growth of a fungus. Mold also refers to the causative organism itself.

Biology of molds

A mold is a microfungus (as opposed to the macro-fungi, such as mushrooms and toadstools) which feeds on dead organic materials. Taxonomically, the molds belong to a group of true fungi known as the *Ascomycotina*. The characteristics of the Ascomycotina are that their spores, that is their reproductive *propagules* (the fungal equivalent of seeds), are produced inside a structure called an *ascus* (plural *asci*). The spores are usually developed eight per ascus, but there are many asci per fruiting body (structures used by the fungus to produce and disperse the spores). A fruiting body of the Ascomycotina is properly referred to as an *ascomata*. Another characteristic of molds is their rapid growth once suitable conditions are encountered. They can easily produce a patch visible to the naked eye within one day.

The visible appearance of the mold can be of a soft, velvety pad or cottony mass of fungal tissue. If closely observed the mass can be seen to be made up of a dense aggregation of threads-like *mycelia* (singular, *mycelium*) of the fungus. Molds can be commonly found on dead and decaying organic material, including improperly stored food stuffs.

The type of mold can be identified by its color and the nature of the substrate on which it is growing. One common example is white bread mold, caused by various species of the genera *Mucor* and *Rhizobium*. Citrus fruits often have quite distinctive blue and green molds of *Penicillium*. Because of the damages this group can cause, they are an economically important group.

In common with the other fungi, the molds reproduce by means of microscopic spores. These tiny spores are easily spread by even weak air currents, and consequently very few places are free of spores due to the astronomical number of spores a single *ascomata* can produce. Once a spore has landed on a suitable food supply, it requires the correct atmospheric conditions, i.e., a damp atmosphere, to germinate and grow.

Some molds such as *Mucor* and its close relatives have a particularly effective method of a sexual reproduction. A stalked structure is produced, which is topped by a clear, spherical ball with a black disc, within which the spores are developed and held. The whole structure is known as a *sporangium* (plural, *sporangia*). Upon maturity the disc cracks open and releases the spores, which are spread far and wide by the wind. Some other molds, such as *Pilobolus*, fire their spores off like a gun and they land as a sticky mass up to 3 ft (1 m) away. Most of these never grow at all, but due to the vast number produced, up to 100,000 in some cases, this is not a problem for the fungus. As has already been mentioned, these fungi will grow on organic materials, including organic matter found within soil, so many types of molds are present in most places.

When sexual reproduction is carried out, each of the molds require a partner, as they are not capable of self-fertilization. This sexual process is carried out when two different breeding types grow together, and then swap haploid nuclei (containing only half the normal number of chromosomes), which then fuse to produce diploid *zygospores* (a thick-walled cell with a full number of chromosomes). These then germinate and grow into new colonies.

Effects of molds

The *Mucor* mold, when grown within a closed environment, has mycelia that are thickly covered with small droplets of water. These are, in fact, diluted solutions of secondary metabolites. Some of the products of mold metabolism have great importance.

Rhizopus produces fumaric acid, which can be used in the production of the drug cortisone. Other molds can produce alcohol, citric acid, oxalic acid, or a wide range of other chemicals. Some molds can cause fatal neural diseases in humans and other animals.

Moldy bread is nonpoisonous. Nevertheless, approximately one hundred million loaves of moldy bread are discarded annually in the United States. The molds typically cause spoilage rather than rendering the bread poisonous.

Some molds growing on food are believed to cause cancer, particularly of the liver. Another curious effect of mold is related to old, green wallpaper. In the nineteenth century, wallpaper of this color was prepared using compounds of arsenic, and when molds grow on this substrate they have been known to release arsenic gas.

The first poison to be isolated from a mold is aflatoxin. This and other poisonous substances produced by molds and other fungi are referred to as *mycotoxins*. Some mycotoxins are deadly to humans in tiny doses, others will only affect certain animals. Aflatoxin was first isolated in 1960 in Great Britain. It was produced by *Aspergillus flavus* that had been growing on peanuts. In that year, aflatoxin had been responsible for the death of 100,000 turkeys—a massive financial loss that led to the research that discovered aflatoxin. From the beginning of the 20th century scientists had tentatively linked a number of diseases with molds, but had not been able to isolate the compounds responsible. With the discovery of aflatoxin, scientists were able to provide proof of the undesirable effects of a mold.

Just because a particular mold can produce a mycotoxin does not mean it always will. For example, *Aspergillus flavus* has been safely used for many centuries in China in the production of various cheeses and soy sauce. *Aspergillus flavus* and related species are relatively common, and will grow on a wide variety of substrates, including various food-stuffs and animal feeds. However, the optimum conditions for vegetative growth are different from those required for the production of aflatoxin. The mycotoxin in this species is produced in largest quantities at high moisture levels and moderate temperatures on certain substrates. For a damaging amount of the toxin to accumulate, about ten days at these conditions may be required. Aflatoxin can be produced by *A. flavus* growing on peanuts. However, *A. flavus* will grow on cereal grains (such as wheat, corn, barley, etc.), but the mycotoxin is not produced on these growth media. Aflatoxin production is best prevented by using appropriate storage techniques.

Other molds can produce other mycotoxins, which can be just as problematical as aflatoxin. The term mycotoxin can also include substances responsible for the death of bacteria, although these compounds are normally referred to as antibiotics.

The molds do not only present humans with problems. Certain types of cheeses are ripened by mold fungi. Indeed, the molds responsible for this action have taken their names from the cheeses they affect. Camembert is ripened by *Penicillium camemberti*, and Roquefort is by *P. roqueforti*.

The *Pencillium* mold have another important use—the production of antibiotics. Two species have been used for the production of penicillin, the first antibiotic to be discovered: *Penicillium notatum* and *P. chrysogenum*. The *Penicillium* species can grow on different substrates, such as plants, cloth, leather, paper, wood, tree bark, cork, animal dung, carcasses, ink, syrup, seeds, and virtually any other item that is organic.

A characteristic that this mold does not share with many other species is its capacity to survive at low temperatures. Its growth rate is greatly reduced, but not to the extent of its competition, so as the temperature rises the *Penicillium* is able to rapidly grow over new areas. However, this period of initial growth can be slowed by the presence of other, competing microorganisms. Most molds will have been killed by the cold, but various bacteria may still be present. By releasing a chemical into the environment capable of destroying these bacteria, the competition is removed and growth of the *Penicillium* can carry on. This bacteria killing chemical is what we now recognize as penicillin.

The anti-bacterial qualities of penicillin were originally discovered by Sanford Fleming in 1929. By careful selection of the *Penicillium* cultures used, the yield of antibiotic has been increased many hundred fold since the first attempts of commercial scale production during the 1930s.

Other molds are used in various industrial processes. *Aspergillus terreus* is used to manufacture icatonic acid, which is used in plastics production. Other molds are used in the production of alcohol, a process that utilizes *Rhizopus*, which can metabolize starch into glucose. The *Rhizopus* species can then directly ferment the glucose to give alcohol, but they are not efficient in this process, and at this point brewers yeast (*Saccharomyces cerevisiae*) is usually added to ferment the glucose much quicker. Other molds are used in the manufacture of flavorings and chemical additives for food stuffs.

Cheese production has already been mentioned. It is interesting to note that in previous times cheese was merely left in a place where mold production was likely to occur. However, in modern production cheeses are inoculated with a pure culture of the mold (some past techniques involved adding a previously infected bit of cheese). Some of the mold varieties used in cheese production are domesticated, and are not found in the wild. In cheese production the cultures are frequently checked to ensure that no mutants have arisen, which could produce unpalatable flavors.

Some molds are important crop parasites of species such as corn and millet. A number of toxic molds grow on straw and are responsible for diseases of livestock, including facial excema in sheep, and slobber syndrome in various grazing animals. Some of the highly toxic chemicals are easy to identify and detect, others are not. Appropriate and sensible storage conditions, i.e., those not favoring the growth of fungi, are an adequate control measure in most cases. If mold is suspected then the use of anti fungal agents (*fungicides*) or destruction of the infected straw are the best options.

See also Fungi; Fungicide; Yeast.

KEY TERMS

Mycelium—The vegetative part of a fungus, a body of branching filaments.

Mycotoxin—A poisonous substance produced by a fungus.

Further Reading:

Arora, D., et al. *The Handbook of Applied Mycology*, vol. 1-5. Marcel Dekker Inc., 1991-92.

Carlile, M. J. and S. C. Watkinson. *The Fungi*. Academic Press, 1994.

Christensen, C. M. *Molds, Mushrooms and Mycotoxins*. University of Minnesota Press, 1975.

Hawksworth, D. L., B. C. Sutton, and G. C. Ainsworth. *Ainsworth and Bisby's Dictionary of the Fungi*, Commonwealth Agricultural Bureau, 1995.

Gordon Rutter

Mole

In chemistry, a mole is a certain number of particles, usually of atoms or molecules. Just as a dozen particles (abbreviated doz.) would be 12 of them, a mole of particles (abbreviated mol) is 6.022137×10^{23} of them. This number, usually shortened to 6.02×10^{23}, is known as Avogadro's number in honor of Count Amadeo Avogadro (1776-1856), an Italian professor of chemistry and physics at the University of Turin who was the first person to distinguish in a useful way between atoms and molecules. It is such a huge number (more than 600 billion trillion) because atoms and molecules are so incredibly tiny that we must have huge numbers of them before we can do anything useful with them.

A standard unit for counting numbers of particles is needed in chemistry, because atoms and molecules react with one another particle by particle. The amount of a chemical reaction—how much of the chemicals are used up or produced—is determined by the numbers of particles that are reacting. Weighing the chemicals wouldn't tell us anything very meaningful unless we knew how to translate those weights into actual numbers of atoms or molecules. For example, if one mole of substance A requires one mole of substance B to react with completely, we need to know how much of substance B to weigh out in order to have just the right amount, without any shortage or waste.

The mole is the translation factor between weights and numbers of particles. One mole of any substance weighs a number of grams that is equal to the atomic or molecular weight of that substance. Thus, if the atomic weights of iron and silver are 55.85 and 107.9, respectively, then 1.95 oz (55.85 g) of iron and 3.78 oz (107.9 g) of silver each contains 6.02×10^{23} atoms. Putting it the other way, a mole of iron (that is, 6.02×10^{23} atoms of iron) would weigh 1.95 oz (55.85 g), while a mole of silver would weigh 3.78 oz (107.9 g).

Iron and silver are elements, and are made up of atoms. Sodium chloride (table salt) and sucrose (cane sugar), on the other hand, are compounds, and are made up of molecules. Nevertheless, the mole still works: a mole of salt or sugar means $6.02 \times \zeta 10^{23}$ *molecules* of them. The molecular weights of salt and sugar are 58.45 and 342.3, respectively. Thus, 2.05 oz (58.45 g) of salt and 11.98 oz (342.3 g) of sugar contain the same number of molecules: 6.02×10^{23}.

Robert L. Wolke

Molecular biology

Molecular biology is an interdisciplinary approach of understanding biological functions and regulations at the level of molecules such as nucleic acids, proteins, carbohydrates, etc. A simple analogy is a car and its parts at the assembling industry or at the repair and maintenance work shop.

In 1945, William Astbury had coined the term "molecular biology" referring to the study of the chemical and physical structure of biological macromolecules (large sized molecules). There was and still is a strong belief that all forms of life have uniformity in biological processes. The pioneer findings in prokaryotes (a simple or primitive cell type, e.g., bacteria and blue green alga) are extended to eukaryotes (a complex or well developed cell type, e.g., animal and plant cells).

To understand molecular biology, the prerequisites are cell biology, genetics, biochemistry, organic chemistry, physics, and biophysical chemistry. Molecular biology deals with: (1) The physicochemical structure of macromolecules (nucleic acids, proteins, lipids, and carbohydrates) and their interactions. (2) Genetic materials—DNA (deoxyribonucleic acid) in most of the living forms or RNA (ribonucleic acid) in all plant viruses and in some animal viruses. (3) The central dogma, i.e., DNA is copied to make mRNA (messenger RNA) and mRNA is used as the template to make proteins. Formation of RNA is called transcription and formation of protein is called translation. Transcription and translation processes are regulated at various stages and the regulation steps are unique to prokaryotes and eukaryotes. The central dogma can be easily explained using this simple analogy: commander in chief (DNA) in an army gives the code message (mRNA) to the soldiers (transfer RNA). The soldiers translate the code message and carry out the actions on the field (ribosomal RNA, enzymes) to bring about the outcome or results (protein synthesis). (4) DNA regulation—determination of what type and amount of mRNA should be transcribed, which subsequently determines the type and amount of protein. This process is the bottom line for growth and morphogenesis. (5) DNA replication (making an exact copy of DNA) and DNA repair. (6) Mutations (sudden alterations in nitrogen containing bases of DNA), their effects, and the agents that cause mutations (e.g., ultrviolet rays and chemicals). (7) Mechanisms and rearrangement and exchange of genetic materials via small segments of DNA such as plasmids, transposable elements, insertion sequences, and transposons to obtain recombinant DNA (DNA with recombined or exchanged nitrogenous bases). (8) Genetic engineering—combination of biochemical, microbial, and molecular biological techniques to obtain desirable DNA sequence in larger quantity, which may be subsequently used to manufcture proteins in larger quantity (e.g. insulin production). (9) Viruses focusing on bacteriophages—lytic and lysogenic phages, viruses that infect bacterial cells reulting in the breaking of bacterial cells and symbiotic life along with bacteria, respectively. Molecular biology has thus found significant applications in the field of medicine, forensic science, and biomedical industries.

Molecular weight

Molecular weight is the sum of the atomic weights of the atoms in a molecule. A molecule can be viewed as an entity of one or more different atoms bound together by some kinds of mutual interactions. As an example, the molecular weight of water, H_2O, is calculated as $(2 \times 1.00797) + (1 \times 15.9994) = 18.0153$, where 1.00797 and 15.9994 are the atomic weights of hydrogen (H) and oxygen (O) atoms, respectively. In general, molecular weight can be determined by either chemical methods or mass spectrometry.

To know more about "molecular weights," one must first become familiar with the concept of "atomic weights." Because an element (e.g., carbon, oxygen, sulfur, etc.) often exists as a mixture of two or more (stable and unstable forms) natural isotopes that have the same number of protons but differ in the number of neutrons, atomic masses of these isotopes are slightly different from each other. In this case, atomic masses are averaged and the ratio of the resultant value to some standard is defined as the "atomic weight" of the element.

In 1961, the ^{12}C isotope of carbon was adopted as the atomic weight standard with a value of 12.00000 d, where d is dalton, the unit of mass for nuclides, named after the English chemist and physicist John Dalton (1766-1844). The dalton is, therefore, defined as exactly 1/12 of the mass of the neutral carbon (C) atom. According to this, the atomic weight of oxygen is 15.9994 ± 0.0001, and ± 0.0001 is due to natural variations in the isotopic composition of the oxygen element. For an oxygen molecule, O_2, the molecular weight is then given by $2 \times 15.9994 = 31.9988$, or 32 for all practical purposes. Strictly speaking, molecular weights are dimensionless, but in many cases, people do not distinguish them from molecular masses and use "gram/mole" as the unit.

Because molecules range in size from monatomic, diatomic, triatomic, to polyatomic, molecular weights can be as small as 4.0026 for gaseous helium (He), 2.0159 for hydrogen (H_2), and 44.01 for carbon dioxide (CO_2), or as large as several hundred thousand in proteins. For many macromolecules formed by polyreactions, for instance, a solution of polystyrene in benzene, the masses of the individual polymer molecules are distributed over a range of values. Thus, we have to use an average value to describe their molecular weight, and the easiest way to do that is simply to take the number average, i.e., $W_{average} = N\sum n_i w_i / \sum n_i$, where we add the products of each molecular weight (w_i) and the number of molecules (n_i) having that w_i, divide it by the total number of molecules in the solution and finally multiply it by the Avogadro Number N.

Depression of the melting point of a pure substance by adding a second compound and elevation of the boiling point of a liquid due to dissolving nonvolatile substances can be used to determine the molecular weight

KEY TERMS

. . . .

Avogadro Number N—The number of molecules present in one mole of whatever the compound is always equal to 6.0229×10^{23}. It was named for the Italian physicist Amedeo Avogadro.

Isotopes—Elements have the same number of protons (and of course, the same number of electrons) but differ in the number of neutrons. In other words, isotopes have different atomic weights or mass numbers.

Mass Number A—It is equal to the sum of the number of protons (i.e., the atomic number, given the symbol Z) and the number of neutrons in atoms.

Nuclides—It is used to describe the kind of matter involving nuclei with given values of mass number A and atomic number Z.

of the added compound or the dissolved substances. In the latter case, for instance, we have the temperature elevation $\Delta T = bm$, where m is the total molality (e.g., moles of solute per 1,000-gram solvent) of solutes and b is a constant characteristic of the solvent (e.g., 0.51 for H_2O and 2.6 for C_6H_6). As long as the weight ratio of solute to solvent is known, we can determine the molecular weight of the solute.

If we would like to obtain molecular weights directly and accurately, mass spectrometry is a good approach. Its principle can be explained in the following way: Molecules of interest are bombarded by energetic electrons, ionized, and broken up into many fragments of particular values of the charge-to-mass ratio, q/m. By applying an electrical potential and/or a magnetic field, ions are deflected according to their individual m/q values and either displayed on a photographic plate at different positions (an old method, also known as "mass spectrograph") or detected electronically. In other words, ions are differentiated because of the difference in their individual energy and angular spread as they travel. Of two ions either with the same charge or with the same mass, the lighter one or the one with greater charge will be deflected by the larger amount. By analyzing recorded mass spectra, information on the exact molecular weight and the structural units of the investigated molecules can be further derived.

Further Reading:

Morrison, R.T. and R.N. Boyd, *Organic Chemistry*, Allyn and Bacon, Inc., Boston, 1983.

Pauling, L., *General Chemistry*, Dover Publications, Inc., New York, 1970.

White, F.A. and G.M. Wood, *Mass Spectrometryl-Applications in Science and Engineering*, Wiley, New York, 1986.

Pang-Jen Kung

Molecule

It was not until knowledge about atoms and elements was gained that the make-up of the millions of different substances around us was understood. All the scientific knowledge we have today indicates that these different substances are made from only 92 different kinds of atoms that make up the naturally occurring elements.

These atoms are able to join together in millions of different combinations and arrangements to form all the substances in the universe. A molecule is formed when two or more of the same or different kinds of atoms join together. The newly formed substance is called a compound. Although the identity of the elements stays the same because the number of protons is the same, the physical and chemical properties of the compound are different from the properties of the elements from which they formed because the arrangement of the outermost electrons is different.

History

For centuries chemists and physicists believed that it was possible to transmute one element, such as lead, into another, such as gold. When the corpuscular theory of matter was developed and accepted (which could explain but not predict chemical changes in terms of transmutations), this belief was strengthened. By the middle of the eighteenth century, however, virtually all chemists and physicists believed that transmutations of matter into other kinds of matter were not possible. But lack of knowledge about the elements, the basic building blocks of all matter, hindered any real understanding of the nature of matter and the formation of new substances.

During the period between 1789 and 1803, Antoine-Laurent Lavoisier defined the elements as substances that could not be separated by fire or some other chemical means and John Dalton defined atoms as small, indestructible and invisible particles. These ideas cleared the way for understanding the makeup of all the substances in the universe. Dalton assumed that each kind of element had its own kind of atom, which was different from the atoms of all other elements. He also assumed that chemical elements kept their identity during all chemical reactions.

During the early nineteenth century, chemical experiments centered mainly around taking measurements of substances involved in chemical reactions both before and after the reaction. It was found that elements always reacted to form a new substance in the same ratio. If different ratios of the reacting substances were used, different substances were produced. Dalton's atomic theory went on to say that chemical compounds are the new substances that form when atoms combine with each other; that a specific compound always has the same kinds of atoms in the same ratio; and that chemical reactions do not involve a change in the atoms themselves but in the way they are arranged.

In 1809, French chemist Joseph-Louis Gay-Lussac and others began doing numerous experiments with gases by measuring the amounts of the gases that actually reacted. They found that two volumes of hydrogen reacted with one volume of oxygen to form two volumes of water, and that one volume of hydrogen gas reacted with one volume of chlorine gas to form two volumes of hydrogen chloride gas. In 1811, Amadeo Avogadro hypothesized that equal volumes of different gases, when at the same temperature and pressure, contained the same number of particles. These experimental results and theories eventually led to the determination of the number of atoms in the substances. The name molecule was later assigned to particles made up of more than one atom, which may be of the same or different atoms.

Formation

Of all the naturally occurring substances around us every day, there are only 92 that cannot be chemically changed to simpler substances. Two or three of these substances are so rare in nature that their natural occurrence is questionable. There are also 17 other known substances that are man-made in sophisticated instruments like cyclotrons. Together, these 109 pure substances are called elements. The atoms of the 92 naturally occurring elements are the building blocks for all of the substances in the universe.

When atoms join together in various combinations of kind and number, they form molecules. When molecules are made from two or more different kinds of atoms, the substances are called compounds. If molecules are made from only one kind of atom, the substances are elements. New combinations of the atoms produce new molecules and therefore different substances.

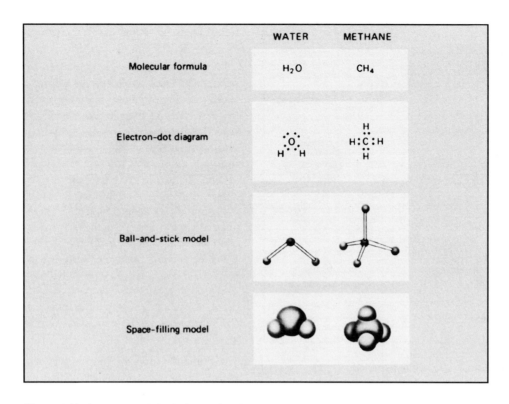

	WATER	METHANE
Molecular formula	H_2O	CH_4
Electron-dot diagram		
Ball-and-stick model		
Space-filling model		

Figure 1. Various ways of depicting molecules.

Special kinds of chemical formulas, called molecular formulas, are used to represent the kinds of atoms and the number of each kind of atom in a molecule. The simplest molecules are composed of just two atoms (usually a single atom is not referred to as a molecule), which may be the same or different. Oxygen gas (O_2), hydrogen gas (H_2), and nitrogen gas (N_2), are made up of molecules composed of just two atoms of oxygen, hydrogen, or nitrogen respectively. Since these substances are composed of only one kind of atom, they are elements. Carbon monoxide (CO) is a gas with molecules composed of one atom of carbon and one atom of oxygen and carbon dioxide (CO_2) is a gas with molecules composed of one atom of carbon and two atoms of oxygen. Water molecules (H_2O) are composed of one atom of oxygen and two atoms of hydrogen. These substances are compounds because the molecules that make it up have two kinds of atoms. Many molecules, especially those in living things such as sugar, fat, or protein molecules and molecules of DNA or RNA, are much larger and more complex.

It is possible for all the different substances in the universe to be produced from only 92 naturally occurring elements because there are endless ways to combine these 92 kinds of atoms, which are the building blocks for all molecules. The 26 letters of the alphabet can be compared to the 92 different kinds of atoms. Different words can be formed in many different ways: by using different letters, such as dog and dig and dodge and dug and dugout; or by using the same letters with different arrangements, such as dog and God and good; or mate and tame and meat, or met and meet and teem. Because of all these possibilities, the 26 letters of the alphabet form all the millions of words of the English language. Similarly, new substances form when different kinds or different numbers of atoms join, or when the same kinds of atoms join in different arrangements. And, just like the letters of the alphabet, the 92 naturally occurring elements form all the millions of different substances in the entire universe including all the various metals, plastics, materials for building, fabrics, all parts of all living things, etc. It is the kind, number, and arrangement of atoms within the molecule that determines what the substance is.

Characteristics

All molecules have a definite mass and size that are dependent on the atoms from which the molecule is made. The mass is equal to the sum of the masses of all the individual atoms in the molecular structure. The size is not only dependent on the atomic components of the molecule, but also on the arrangement of the atoms within the molecule and how tightly they are joined together.

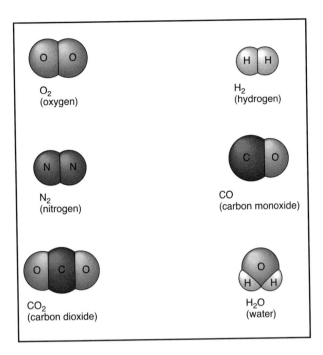

Figure 2. Models of various elements.

When atoms join other atoms to form molecules, the chemical and physical properties of the compounds are different from those of the elements from which they were formed. These include such things as color, hardness, conductivity, state (solid, liquid, gas), etc. When letters are used to form new words, such as dog, God and good from the letters g, o and d, the meanings of the new words cannot be discovered by observing or studying either the letters g, o and d, or the other words. The new words formed have new and different meanings. This is also true when new molecules form. The properties of the new substances cannot be found by studying the properties of the elements from which they formed or the properties of other similar molecules.

The molecular formula for sugar is $C_6H_{12}O_6$, which indicates that a sugar molecule is made up of six atoms of carbon, 12 atoms of hydrogen, and six atoms of oxygen. Carbon is an element that is black and often is found in powder form. It is well known as the major component of coal or the black that appears on burnt toast. Pure hydrogen is a the lightest gas known and pure oxygen is a gas present in the air and needed for living things to breathe and for fires to burn. When these three substances chemically combine in the ratio of $C_6H_{12}O_6$ to form sugar, which is a white, crystalline solid that has a sweet taste and is soluble in water, the properties of the sugar are unlike those of the pure elements from which it was formed. However, if sugar is reacted under extreme conditions (a chemical change), the original substances, carbon, hydrogen, and oxygen could be recovered.

Hydrogen and oxygen atoms can join to form water molecules. Once again, the properties of water (often used to extinguish fires) are completely different from the properties of oxygen gas (needed to support burning). These same two elements, hydrogen and oxygen, also form another common substance, hydrogen peroxide, with a molecular formula of H_2O_2. Hydrogen peroxide, in its undiluted form, can cause serious burns. When diluted, it is often used for bleaching and as an antiseptic in cleansing wounds. These properties are completely different from the properties of the elements from which it is made, hydrogen and oxygen, as well as from the similar molecule, water. You could not boil potatoes in H_2O_2 instead of H_2O without deadly effects. The properties of hydrogen peroxide differ greatly from those of hydrogen, oxygen, and water because each of the substances has its own specific number, kind, and arrangement of atoms.

While the molecular formula gives the basic information about what atoms are joined together and how many of each kind of atom, this formula does not give the whole story. The arrangement of the atoms within the molecule must also be considered since different arrangements of the same atoms within a molecule produce different substances. The molecular formulas for ethyl alcohol (formed from the fermentation of grains and fruits and present in all wines and liquors) and for methyl ether (sometimes used in refrigeration but not the same ether used as an anesthetic) are identical, C_2H_6O. However, the chemical properties are very different. This is because the atoms are arranged differently within the molecule. Molecular formulas cannot convey this information. Different kinds of formulas, called structural formulas, are needed to show molecular arrangements. In the case of ethyl alcohol, the oxygen atom is joined to a carbon atom and to a hydrogen atom. But in the case of methyl ether, the oxygen atom is joined to two carbon atoms. This different arrangement of atoms within the molecule is responsible for imparting different chemical properties to the compound. Thus, the new chemical properties are not only dependent on how many of each kind of atom have joined together, but on how these atoms are arranged within the molecule.

Much of the research in the field of chemistry today involves the formation of new substances by trying to change atoms within a molecule or the arrangement of the same atoms. This latter is a particularly important area when the arrangement of the atoms is changed from what is called a right-handed molecule to a left-handed molecule or vice-versa. Molecules such as

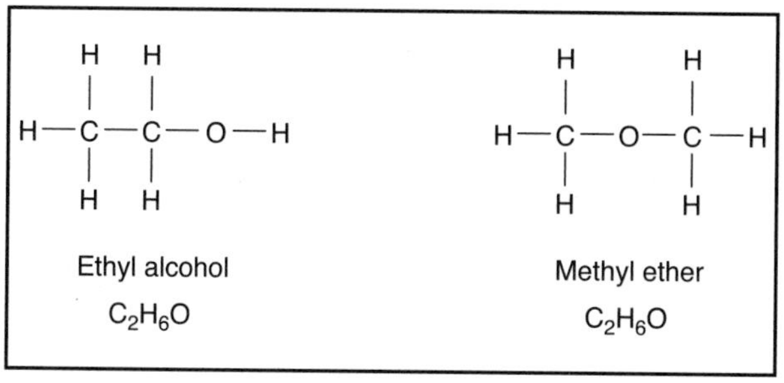

H   H
| |
H—C—C—O—H
| |
H   H

Ethyl alcohol
C_2H_6O

H   H
| |
H—C—O—C—H
| |
H   H

Methyl ether
C_2H_6O

Figure 3. Structural formulas help differentiate between substances that share identical molecular formulas, such as ethyl alcohol and methyl ether.

these behave as they do because of their shape, much like gloves fit either the right or the left hand because of their shape. Some of the current research on new fat-free commercial products, such as ice-cream or cooking oil, involves right- or left-handed versions of the original fat molecules. These mirror-images of the original molecules cannot be absorbed or used by the body because of the different shape of the molecule. Yet because they are often so similar, enough of the original properties of the fat remain intact to make it useful as a substitute. So far, the taste and their inability to withstand high temperatures in cooking are problematic.

Similarly, many powerful drugs in use today have both right- and left-handed versions. Most drugs contain both forms of the molecules because this mixture is cheaper and easier to produce. However, often only one version gives the desired effect while frequently the other produces unwanted side effects. Although it is chemically much more difficult and more expensive to produce drugs of only one "handedness," patients needing these drugs are finding the purer, single-handed version much easier to tolerate. Drug companies are beginning to pay attention and research is being done to produce drugs of only one "handedness" at a reasonable cost.

Molecular bonding

When compounds are formed, the identity of the atoms, which is associated with the number of protons in the nucleus, does not change. For example, oxygen atoms are still oxygen atoms whether they are part of oxygen gas molecules, water molecules, carbon dioxide molecules, etc., because the number of protons is unchanged.

But unlike mixtures, where two or more substances are mixed together but there is little or no interaction among the atoms of the various substances, there is interaction among the atoms within molecules. New compounds are formed when the atoms within the mol-

ecule form a chemical bond. These bonds are a sort of "glue" that hold the atoms together within the molecule. Bonds involve only the outermost electrons of the atoms, that is, those in the highest shell or energy level. It is this change in electron arrangements that is responsible for the new properties observed when compounds are formed. There are two major types of bonds, ionic and covalent.

An ionic bond forms when the outermost electrons are transferred from one atom to another. One atom loses one or more electrons and another atom gains these electrons. Sodium metal is a soft, shiny, and very reactive metal that is stored under kerosene to keep it from reacting with the oxygen in the air. Sodium atoms have only one electron at the highest energy level and would be more stable if they got rid of this electron. Chlorine is a very poisonous green gas involved in the purifying process of swimming pools and responsible for the characteristic smell around them. Chlorine has seven electrons at the highest energy level and would be much more stable with eight electrons at this level. When sodium and chlorine come in contact with each other, there is an instantaneous reaction. Neutral atoms of sodium metal give up one electron with their negative charge and form particles, called ions, with net charges of +1. Neutral atoms of chlorine gain negatively-charged electrons from sodium atoms and form particles, also called ions, with net charges of -1.

Throughout these changes, the number of protons and neutrons in the nucleus and all of the innermost electrons around the nucleus stay the same. Only an insignificant amount of the mass of the atom is associated with electrons, so the mass of the atom also stays essentially the same. However, a chemical change has occurred and the original properties of the atoms have changed because of the new arrangement of the electrons. The newly-formed sodium ion and the chloride ion are electrically attracted or bonded to each other because opposite charges attract each other. The substance formed is ordinary table salt which is a white, salty, crystalline solid, properties that are very different from the original elements of sodium and chlorine. The bond that formed is called an ionic bond and sodium chloride is called an ionic compound. An ionic bond is formed when the "glue" between atoms is the force of attraction between opposite charges. In fact, salt crystals are formed by the very neat and orderly arrangement of alternating sodium and chloride ions. Ionic bonds are most often formed between atoms of metals and atoms of non-metals.

Often, the outermost electrons of an atom are shared with the outermost electrons of another atom. Electrons move around the nucleus of an atom at very

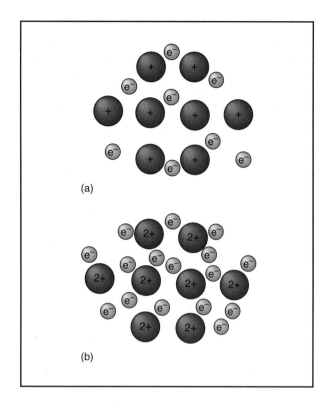

(a)

(b)

Figure 4. The electron sea model, (a) represents an alkali metal with one valence electron and (b) represents an alkaline earth metal with two valence electrons.

high speeds and, when electrons are shared between two atoms, the nuclei move so close together that the shared electrons spend part of their time near both nuclei simultaneously. This sharing of electrons by the nuclei of two atoms simultaneously is the "glue" that is holding them together within the molecule. This type of bond is called a covalent bond. Electrons that are shared can be contributed by either or both atoms involved in the bond formation.

Carbon atoms have four outermost electrons and need eight to be more stable. If one carbon atom shares each of its outermost electrons with a hydrogen atom, which needs only two electrons to become more stable, a molecule of methane is formed. The formula for the new substance formed is CH_4. Methane is often called marsh gas because it forms in swamps and marshes from the underwater decomposition of plant and animal material. It is widely distributed in nature and about 85% of natural gas is methane.

When things are shared, like sharing the sofa with a friend, they are not always shared equally. This is also true of electrons involved in covalent bonds. At times the electrons involved in bonding are shared equally between the nuclei of two atoms and the bond is called

a pure covalent bond. More often, however, the sharing is unequal and the electrons spend more time around the nucleus of one atom than of the other. The bond formed is called a polar covalent bond. Usually covalent bonds (both pure covalent and polar covalent) form when atoms of non-metallic elements bond to atoms of other non-metallic elements.

The "glue" or bonding that holds atoms of metals close to each other is usually referred to as a metallic bond. It is formed because the outermost electrons of the metal atoms form a sort of "sea" of electrons as they move freely around the nuclei of all the metal atoms in the crystal. These mobile electrons are responsible for the electrical and heat conductivity of the metals.

See also Atom; Chemical bond; Compound, chemical; Element, chemical; Formula, chemical; Formula, structural.

Further Reading:

William H. Brock, *The Norton History of Chemistry.* New York: W. W. Norton & Company, 1993.

Nicholas D. Tzimopoulos et al., *Modern Chemistry.* Austin: Holt Rinehart and Winston, 1990.

Martin Sherwood and Christine Sutton, *The Physical World.* New York: Oxford University Press, 1991.

David L. Heiserman, *Exploring Chemical Elements and their Compounds.* New York: Tab Books, 1992.

Stephen C. Stinson. "Chiral Drugs". *Chemical and Engineering News.* September 19, 1994.

Leona B. Bronstein

A mole rat (*Cryptomys hottentotus*) from southern Africa.

Mole-rats

Mole-rats are small, fossorial rodents, which means that they spend their entire lives underground in a sealed burrow system. Native to Africa, these little animals are found from the southernmost tip of the continent to about 10 degrees north of the equator. Mole-rats make up the family Bathyergidae, which includes 12 species in 5 genera (not to be confused with an unrelated family Spalacidae, containing a single genus that lives in eastern Europe and the eastern Mediterranean region). As a group, bathyergid mole-rats have the greatest diversity of both body size and social structure of any subterranean rodent. The species in three genera (*Bathyergus, Georychus,* and *Heliophobus*) are completely solitary. The species in the other two genera (*Cryptomys* and *Heterocephalus*) are social. The most social of all is also the smallest: weighing in at around 0.8 oz (23 g), the naked mole-rat (*Heterocephalus glaber*) lives in highly cooperative groups, sharing food, living quarters, and care of the young. At the other end of the spectrum is the solitary Cape dune mole-rat, in which adult males may weigh up to 63 oz (1,800 g).

Physical attributes

Mole-rats are well-adapted to life underground. Their eyes are much reduced, as is the visual center in the brain, suggesting that vision does not play much of a role in their dark, subterranean environment. In fact, it is not clear whether some mole-rat species can perceive light at all; most keep their eyes closed while going about their underground business, opening them only when alarmed. Their ears are also tiny, but their hearing is acute. Mole-rats communicate using a wide array of chirps, trills, and other vocalizations, as well as by drumming with their hind feet on the floor of the burrow. Their senses of smell and touch are also well developed, and are used to help identify and communicate with one another.

First-time viewers may find the mole-rat's appearance a bit odd: they have short limbs, cylindrically-shaped bodies, and very loose skin with numerous folds. Long hairs, called vibrissae, stand out from the skin of the head and body, providing sensory information. The incisor teeth protrude prominently from the mouth, and the lips close behind the teeth to keep out dust and soil. Some mole-rat species actually dig tunnels using their incisor teeth; other species dig using strong front legs armed with sturdy claws. Most mole-rats have short tails, but naked mole-rats have tails up to half of their body length, that are used to help guide the animal as it runs backwards along tunnels. Perhaps because of their tails, naked mole-rats can navigate as quickly and easily in the reverse direction as forward; if two animals meet in a tunnel, one of them may back up some distance before coming to a place it can turn around and face forward again.

Large, prominent teeth are also important in food-gathering, as mole-rats' primary food source is underground roots, tubers, and corms, which can be quite tough. Mole-rats occasionally eat above-ground shoots that are pulled underground from below; the animals almost never venture into the open air above. Tunnels used for food-collecting are dug up to the level where food is found; the main burrow system may lie several feet deeper in the earth. Collected food items are stored in a special food chamber, located off the main burrow.

Living environment

In addition to a food chamber, the burrow system also features chambers for nesting and for a communal toilet. In addition, mole-rats dig deep, blind-ended tunnels that they may use to escape enemies or to cool themselves; these tunnels may also function as drains in the event of flooding. Normally, the burrow system is not open to the surface, but rather is tightly sealed to provide protection against weather, extremes of temperature, and predators. Openings are necessary during tunnel excavation, in which a digging mole-rat loosens the soil with teeth or forelegs, pushes it beneath its body, and kicks it behind. When enough soil has accumulated in this way, the mole-rat backs up in the tunnel, pushing the soil behind it; the soil is directed out a side tunnel to the surface, where it is kicked out. With some species, the soil becomes compacted in being pushed on its way out, and may be seen emerging from the ground in a compacted core, like toothpaste being squeezed from the tube. With the naked mole-rat, the dry soil is vigorously ejected in a fine spray, creating the characteristic soil "volcanoes" that erupt at the excavation hole. An open hole, however, is an invitation to predators. Mole snakes have been observed to enter these excavation tunnels, and larger predators (herons, storks, skunks and weasels, for instance) may wait by a fresh opening for the digger to return with its next load of soil.

Social life

Little is known about courtship and mating in these animals, or about how new burrow systems become established. Individuals of solitary species will defend a territory, fighting viciously with any others it may encounter (perhaps under a rich food patch). Male-female pairs will tolerate each other in the same burrow for a day or so to accomplish mating, but they soon separate. The solitary female cares for the young until weaning, at about eight weeks; after this, antagonism and aggression build and the young finally disperse.

Biologists are especially interested in the highly social naked mole-rat, because they are one of the rare mammals that exhibits eusociality. Eusocial animals, such as many bees and wasps, live in colonies where only one or a very few individuals produce all the offspring, and the rest serve as sterile helpers; thus, we observe a division of labor. In naked mole-rats, one large female, known as the queen, is the only female to undergo reproductive cycling and produce offspring. In addition, a colony generally contains only 1-3 breeding males; reproduction in all other individuals is effectively suppressed, apparently by means of aggressive behavior and olfactory cues from the breeding adults, who appear to carefully sniff and monitor the physiological condition of the others. Nonreproductive adults carry out the tasks of tunnel digging and maintenance,

foraging for and storing food, and caring for the young, which of course are not their own. If the queen should die, violent fights may erupt as her successor asserts herself over her competitors. Ferocious defensive behavior has also been observed when the burrow systems of two separate colonies become linked by a common opening; mole-rats will fight to the death in defense of their home burrow.

Eusociality presents a problem to the evolutionary theory, which was recognized by Darwin. How could an animal evolve by means of natural selection (where organisms with particular traits survive and reproduce better than their competitors), if they forsake their own reproduction and devote themselves to helping others reproduce? How can a trait spread, if its bearer fails to produce offspring? Darwin's answer was that if an individual contributes enough to the reproduction of those who carry but do not express the trait, it can spread by natural selection. This explanation appears to work for naked mole-rats, where the nonreproductive workers help the queen produce offspring, who go on to recreate the same social structure at home or in another burrow. Evidently, this system suits them well; perhaps the group can collect more food than a single animal foraging alone. Perhaps the danger of traveling above ground means staying at home is more desirable than emigrating; suppressed reproduction may be necessary to keep colony numbers down and avoid starvation. It may be that their highly social population structure has enabled them to inhabit the hot, arid regions in Africa where the solitary species are not found.

Susan Andrew

Moles

Moles are small burrowing animals of the order Insectivora, mammals with teeth designed for crushing the outer shells of insects. The true moles and desmans (water-living moles) make up the family Talpidae, which inhabit most of North America and northern Eurasia. The similar golden moles of Africa, south of the Sahara, make up the family Chrysochloridae.

Moles vary from 1-3 in (24-75 mm) in length, plus a pink, naked tail that may be equally long, but is usually short. An adult male weighs more than 3.5 oz (100 g) and adult females less than that. A mole must eat its own weight in food each day or die, because its body has no fat preservation system.

The European mole (*Talpa europaea*).

Moles are thoroughly adapted for a life of digging. They have streamlined bodies, with nothing that might interfere with burrowing. Their front feet appear to come straight out of their bodies and are angled outward so that as they dig through soil, using first one hand, then the other, so that they appear to be swimming the breaststroke. Their flexible snouts are also used in digging, and their similarly tapered hind ends can easily move through soil. Unlike most mammals, whose hair lies toward the back of the body, a mole's fur can lie equally well in either direction as the animal moves in either direction. The fur is very soft.

Their functioning eyes reveal only light and dark. Instead they rely primarily on their senses of smell and touch. The surface of the muzzle is covered with thousands of tiny sensory organs that allow it to analyze even the most delicate touch. These organs, called Eimer's organs, identify food and digging sites. Their faces and forelimbs are also covered with special sensory hairs, called vibrissae.

The presence of moles is generally revealed by the presence of mounds of loosened soil called molehills. As they burrow, they toss the soil backward, and it eventually piles up on the surface. Surface burrows, which are visible from above, are dug in newly turned farmfields and very light soil, where the worms and other invertebrates the moles eat are near the top. Deep burrows, the digging of which produce molehills, are dug in heavier, drier soil where the invertebrates have moved downward to find moisture. These deep burrows may last many years and even many generations. They need to be rebuilt only if accidentally damaged. A mole marks a tunnel as its territory by giving off a strong odor from its scent gland. If the scent wears off and is not refreshed by the animal—perhaps because it has fallen prey to an owl—other animals may move into the burrow.

A mole's entire life centers around its burrow. Certain areas of a mole's burrow are used to store food, such as earthworms that have had their heads bitten off. In the center of the burrow is a nest lined with grasses and other dry material, such as scraps of paper hauled in from the surface. Every mole sleeps in its nest, but a female also raises her young in it until they have been weaned.

Moles breed in early spring, with two to eight little 2 inch (50 mm) young born in late spring. They are born blind, hairless, and red colored, weighing about

0.1 oz (3.5 g). They are out on their own by early fall. Though many die during their migration to find their own burrowing grounds, moles often live for six or seven years. They are capable of breeding when they are about a year old.

The nose of the strange star-nosed mole (*Condylura cristata*) of eastern North America is divided into 22 rubbery lobes, or tentacles, that make the black-furred animal look as if it has a pink flower on its nose. Each tentacle is covered with a large number of Eimer's organs. The star-nosed mole also has an unusual tail. Longer than most moles', it acts as a fat-storage organ during the breeding season. These are the only moles that lives in pairs, with the male helping to raise the young. Their fur is waterproof, which lets them dig into saturated soil, as well as swim in search of tiny crustaceans to eat.

The little American shrew-mole (*Neurotrichus gibbsii*) of the West Coast looks like a mole but has fur more like a shrew's, which doesn't change direction. This is the smallest American mole, averaging only 2.5-3 in (6-7 cm) in body length. Oddly enough, its closest relative lives straight across the Pacific in Japan. Shrew-moles, though they burrow like other moles, leave their shallow burrows to search for food among the litter on a forest floor.

The common, or eastern, American mole is *Scalopus aquaticus*. Despite its webbed back feet and its scientific name, the common American mole is not a water-living animal. It has the widest range of any American mole, from Mexico to New England to Florida. Other western moles of California include the broad-footed mole (*Scapanus latimanus*), the coast mole (*S. orarius*), and Townsend's mole (*S. townsendii*).

There are about 13 species of Old World moles, all in genus *Talpa*. The European mole (*T. europaea*) resides in most of Europe and over into central Russia. European moles have been known to turn their mole-hills into mountains, or at least "fortresses," by building quite large structures above ground. Fortresses are found only in areas that flood regularly.

Moles don't eat bulbs of flowering plants as many gardeners who have watched their flowers die believe. Instead, other creatures such as meadow mice move into mole burrows, from which they can reach those succulent plant parts. Moles are now generally left alone except on golf courses. Their very soft skins were often collected at the end of the nineteenth century for use in high-quality clothing.

Desmans

The two species of desmans make up a separate subfamily from the true moles. One (*Galemys pyrenaicus*) lives in the Pyrenees, the other (*Desmana moschata*) in Russia, both by fast-flowing rivers. Desmans are swimmers. They swim with the aid of a flattened, rudderlike tail, powerful legs, and long back feet. Their fingers and toes are also webbed.

Desmans are much larger than moles, sometimes reaching 16 in (41 cm) including their tails. Their long, flexible snouts contain nostrils that can be closed tightly against the water by special valves. Their ears can also be closed. Their fur is especially soft, and the Russian desman has long been killed for its marketable fur. Two or more desmans will share their burrows, located in the banks of a river.

Golden moles

The family of golden moles is made up of 17 species that live in Africa, south of the Sahara. They are not necessarily golden in color, though they do often have a colorful, lustrous sheen to their coats. They are tailless and, unlike true moles, blind. They are born with the remnants of useless eyes, which develop hairy coverings as they mature. The end of a golden mole's nose is leathery to aid in burrowing through the soil, though the primary digging is done by heavy, sharp claws.

Grant's desert golden mole (*Eremitalpa granti*) of the Namib Desert has only dry sand to dig through. Its meandering burrow collapses behind it as it continually digs. Only if rain has fallen recently does the burrow hold its shape for any length of time. Other golden moles live in moister places where their burrows hold their shape.

The large golden moles of South Africa (*Chrysospalax*) do not rely solely on ground invertebrates for food. They go to the surface at night to feed, hunting especially for giant worms. The surface may bring danger, however, and a golden mole that finds itself in danger may collapse dramatically, pretending to be dead. The Cape golden mole of Uganda (*Chrysochloris stuhlmanni*) lives at fairly high altitudes, up to 10,000 ft (3,050 m).

Further Reading:

Bailey, Jill. *Discovering Shrews, Moles & Voles.* New York: The Bookwright Press, 1989.

Caras, Roger A. *North American Mammals: Fur-Bearing Animals of the United States and Canada.* New York: Meredith Press, 1967.

Gorman, Martyn L., and R. David Stone. *The Natural History of Moles.* Ithaca, NY: Comstock Publishing Associates, 1990.

Jean F. Blashfield

Mollusks

Mollusks (phylum Mollusca) are the second largest group of invertebrates (the arthropods being the largest), with over 100,000 species. They are characterized by a head with sense organs and mouth, a muscular foot, a visceral hump containing the digestive and reproductive organs, and an envelope of tissue (the mantle) that usually secretes a hard, protective shell. Practically all of the shells found on beaches and prized by collectors belong to mollusks. Among the more familiar mollusks are snails, whelks, conchs, clams, mussels, scallops, oysters, squid, and octopuses. Less conspicuous, but also common, are chitons, cuttlefish, limpets, nudibranchs, and slugs.

The largest number of species of mollusks are in the class Gastropoda, which includes snails with a coiled shell, and others lacking a shell. The next largest group are the bivalves (class Bivalvia), the chitons (class Amphineura), and octopus and squid, (class Cephalopoda). The other classes of mollusks are the class Scaphopoda (consisting of a few species of small mollusks with a tapered, tubular shell) and the class Monoplacophora, a class once regarded as extinct, but now known to have a few living species restricted to the ocean depths.

Fossil shells recognizable as gastropods and bivalves are present in rocks from the Cambrian period, about 570 million years ago. Present classifications based on the evolutionary relationships of mollusks are derived from studies of embryonic development, comparative anatomy, and RNA nucleotide sequences. The findings suggest affinities of mollusks with sipunculid, annelid, and echiurid worms.

Mollusks provide a clear example of adaptive radiation. The gastropods and bivalves which were originally marine, subsequently radiated into fresh water habitats. Without much change in gross appearance, these animals developed physiological mechanisms to retain salts within their cells and prevent excessive swelling from water intake in fresh water. Several groups of freshwater snails then produced species adapted to life on land.

Gills adapted for the extraction of oxygen from water were transformed in land snails into lungs which extract oxygen from air, and the ammonia excretion typical of aquatic mollusks became uric acid excretion typical of birds and reptiles. A small squid, *Onycoteuthis,* moves so rapidly through the water that it often becomes airborne. It does not nest in trees, but it may help to explain why some authors ascribe to the squid *Loligo* a "parrot beak" and a "gizzard."

Restaurant menus often include bivalve mollusks (oysters on the half-shell, steamed mussels, fried clams), cephalopod mollusks (fried squid), or gastropod snails (escargots).

See also Bivalves; Chitons; Cuttlefish; Limpets; Octopus; Slugs; Snails; Squid.

Further Reading:

Abbott, R. T. *Seashells of North America.* New York: Western Publishing Company, 1968.
Florkin, M., and B. T. Scheer, eds. *Chemical Zoology*, Vol. VII, Mollusca. New York: Academic Press, 1972.
Morton, J. E. *Molluscs.* New York: Harper, 1960.

C.S. Hammen

Molybdenum see **Element, chemical**

Momentum

The momentum of an object is the mass of the object multiplied by the velocity of the object. The mass will often be measured in kilograms (kg) and the velocity, in meters per second (m/s), so the momentum will be measured in kilogram meters per second (kg m/s). Because velocity is a vector quantity, meaning that the direction is part of the quantity, momentum is also a vector. Just like the velocity, to completely specify the momentum of an object one must also give the direction.

A force multiplied by the length of time that the force acts is called the impulse. According to the impulse momentum theorem, the impulse acting on an object is equal to the change in the object's momentum. Notice the word change. The impulse is not equal to the object's momentum, but the amount the momentum changes. (This impulse momentum theorem is basically a disguised form of Newton's second law.) The force used to figure out the impulse here is the total sum of all the external forces acting on an object. Internal forces acting within an object don't count.

The consequences of this impulse momentum theorem are rather profound. If there are no external forces acting on an object, then the impulse (force times time) is zero. The change in momentum is also zero because it is equal to the force. Hence, if an object has no external forces acting on it, the momentum of the object can never change. This law is the law of conservation of momentum. There are no known exceptions to this fundamental law of physics. Like other conservation laws (such as conservation of energy), the law of conservation of momentum is a very powerful tool for understanding the universe around us.

Rockets provide a dramatic application of momentum conservation. Before launch, the rocket is sitting on the launch pad, so its momentum is zero. When the engines fire, the spent fuel is hurled out the back, by an internal, not external, force. The total momentum of the rocket and fuel must remain zero. The fuel has a negative momentum because it is spit out backwards. The rocket must therefore have an equal positive momentum, so the total will be zero. (Remember momentum is a vector; direction matters.) So, the rocket moves forward. The greater the momentum of the fuel spit out backwards, the greater the forward thrust of the rocket. You can test this yourself. Many toy stores sell plastic water rockets that use air pressure to push the water out the back. Try one of these rockets with water and with air only. The dramatic difference is because the water has more mass and therefore more momentum.

See also Mass; Newton's laws of motion; Velocity.

Monarch flycatchers

The monarch or old-world flycatchers are about four-hundred species of arboreal, insectivorous songbirds that make up the family Muscicapidae. There are three subfamilies in this group: the monarch and paradise flycatchers (*Monarchinae*), the fantails (*Rhipidurinae*), and the typical flycatchers (*Muscicapinae*). Some taxonomists consider these to be separate families, but they are treated as a single group here, referred to as muscicapid flycatchers.

Species in this group occur in Africa, Europe, Asia, and Australasia. Their usual habitats are forests, more-open woodlands, riparian zones, and some types of agricultural areas. Most species are tropical, but some migratory species occur in temperate regions.

Muscicapid flycatchers are small birds, with a typical body length of 4.7-5.5 in (12-14 cm), and rather short wings and legs. Their beak is strong and flattened, and broad at the base, so their gape is large. They have well-developed bristles at the base of their bill. These are known as rictal bristles, and are a common feature of birds that catch insects while flying.

Muscicapid flycatchers typically feed by pursuing and catching flying insects, using short, aerial sallies from a favorite, exposed perch. This type of feeding strategy is called, appropriately enough, "fly-catching."

Many species of muscicapid flycatchers have a rather subdued coloration of grays, black, and whites. Others, however, are quite brightly colored, with blues, reds, chestnuts, and other showy hues. The males of some species have elongated tail feathers, which can be several times longer than the body of the bird.

Muscicapid flycatchers are territorial. The males typically defend a breeding area by singing, even though the renditions of most species are relatively quiet and uninspired (only to the human ear, of course). They build a cup-shaped nest in a tree, or sometimes in a cavity, and lay 2-7 spotted eggs. Nest building and incubation may be carried out by both parents, or only by the female in many species. Both parents share the duties of rearing the young birds.

The pied flycatcher (*Ficedula hypoleuca*) is a widespread species in Europe and western Asia, migrating to Africa for the non-breeding season. Male pied flycatchers are striking, black-and-white birds, while the females are a more subdued gray.

The males of paradise flycatchers (*Terpsiphone* spp.) are attractive birds with very-long plumes extending from the center of their tail. The paradise flycatcher (*Terpsiphone paradisi*) occurs in South and Southeast Asia. This lovely bird has a black head with a crest, a white belly, a chestnut back, and two long, chestnut plumes extending from the tail. This species also occurs in a white-bodied, black-headed phase.

The male of the flame robin (*Petroica phoenicea*) of southeastern Australia and Tasmania is an extremely attractive, black-backed, red-bellied bird.

Fantails are active birds that have a pleasing habit of spreading the tail as a visual display. The friendly fantail (*Rhipidura albolimbata*) is a common, tame, inquisitive bird that occurs widely in montane forests of New Guinea.

Bill Freedman

Mongooses

Mongooses are African and Asian carnivores of the family Herpestidae. They are small, long, slender mammals, some of which are most widely known for their willingness to attack poisonous snakes and rats. In the past, members of the mongoose family have been included with the weasels, and sometimes the mongooses are included with civets and genets in the family Viverridae.

The largest mongoose is the white-tailed mongoose (Ichneumia albicauda) of southern Africa and Arabia. From head to tail, it is about 40 in (1 m) long and weighs about 9 lbs (4 kg). Two species of dwarf mongooses (Helogale) live in the savannas of the region around Ethiopia. They may be only a foot (30 cm) long, including the tail.

Mongooses tend to stand on their hind legs to survey their surroundings. They use their tails, which may be as thick at the base as their bodies, as balancing organs. The front arms hang loosely as they look around.

Although they are carnivores, many mongooses eat plants and fruit. Most, however, prefer meat in some variety, either insects, small reptiles, or small rodents and birds. They also eat birds' eggs when available, which they break by rolling them against rocks, usually backward between their legs. Marsh mongooses (Atilax paludinosus) of rivers in subsaharan Africa also break crab shells in the same way. One Asian species is so adept at eating crabs that it is called the crab-eating mongoose (Herpestes urva). Atilax will also eat crocodile eggs. Mongooses that kill snakes do so by wearing out the snake. They have great agility and energy and can keep going long after the snake is worn to exhaustion.

Most members of the mongoose family are solitary, living alone and usually hunting at night. Some, however, are quite colonial. Rarely would you see, for example, just one of the mongooses called meerkats standing alone. Instead, a whole row of these curious creatures will be standing on their hind legs, looking like 15-inch (38-cm)-high, furry, scraggly little men guarding the openings to their dens. The gray meerkat, also called the suricate (Suricata suricatta), lives in Namibia, Angola, and South Africa. It has very distinct rings around its eyes. In the same region is the red meerkat, or yellow mongoose (Cynctis penicillata). Sometimes the two species will share burrows. Meerkats have frequently been tamed and in captivity will eat a considerable amount of fruit.

Mongooses that live in colonies work together to defend themselves against a larger animal that may be attacking one of the group or trying to invade their den. Some of them, especially the banded mongoose (Mungos mungo) of most of subsaharan Africa, also hunt in packs. While looking for the beetles they like, they communicate with continuous low-pitched calls. The banded mongoose is somewhat thicker through its striped body than most mongooses. All mongooses leave scented trails from glands on the cheeks and around the anus.

Among the solitary mongooses, a dominant male chooses the females he wants to mate with. The mothers then raise the babies by themselves. There is usually only one young at a time, though some species produce up to four. Most offspring are born blind and just lightly furred after a gestation period that may vary from 6 to 17 weeks, depending on the species. Colony-living species, however, have a quite different child-care method. The care of the offspring are the joint responsibility of the adults, which take turns babysitting while other members of the pack are out feeding. Successful hunters bring food back to the babies and may take time to play with them before going off again. The number of litters a mongoose might have each year depends on the weather and the food supply.

Some mongoose species

The most common mongoose is the Small Indian mongoose (Herpestes javanicus). This animal is not only widespread in its own homeland, but it has been introduced in other places because of its skill at killing rats. It is now found in the West Indies and the Hawaiian Islands for that reason. The mongooses fondness for birds' eggs is one reason that they are often blamed for contributing to the extinction of many bird species in these islands. However, mongooses are probably only one of many reasons for the demise of species.

The Liberian mongoose (Liberiictis kuhni) was not discovered by the outside world until 1958. At that time it was a favorite food of native peoples in Liberia. It has not been seen often since, so it may be extinct.

There are four species (one each in four genera) of mongoose on the big island of Madagascar. They are in a separate subfamily because they have a slightly different ear structure than the African and Asian species. They are also probably the only mongooses that live in pairs. One species, the ring-tailed mongoose (Galidia elegans) is more comfortable in trees than on the ground, although it also swims. Two species have more definite lengthwise stripes on them than other mongooses. The Malagasy narrow-striped mongoose (Mungotictis decemlineata) and Malagasy broad-striped

Banded mongooses eating eggs they found and smashed against the rocks.

mongoose *(Galidictis fasciata)* are striped in black and beige. The Madagascan mongooses are not specifically known to be endangered, but since most mammals that live on the island are at least threatened, mongooses probably are, too.

Further Reading:

Hinton, H. E., and A. M. S. Dunn. *Mongooses: Their Natural History and Behaviour.* Berkeley, CA: University of California Press, 1967.

Knight, Linsay. *The Sierra Club Book of Small Mammals.* San Francisco: Sierra Club Books for Children, 1993.

Schreiber, A. et al. *Weasels, Civets, Mongooses and Their Relatives: An Action Plan for the conservation of Mustelids and Viverrids.* Island Press, 1989.

Jean F. Blashfield

Monitor lizards

Monitor lizards comprise about 24 living species of large lizards in the genus *Varanus*, family Varanidae. Monitors occur in tropical and sub-tropical regions of Africa, Asia, and Australia. Monitors are among the most advanced of the lizards, in terms of achieving an active, predacious lifestyle.

The largest species of monitor, and the world's largest lizard, is the very impressive Komodo dragon *(Varanus komodoensis)*, which can achieve a length of 9.8 ft (3 m) and a weight of 297.7 lbs (135 kg). The Komodo dragon is an endangered species, occurring only on a few, small Indonesian islands. An even larger monitor lizard known as *Megalania* was about twice as long as the Komodo dragon, and is known from fossils collected in Australia. The smallest species is the short-tailed monitor *(Varanus brevi-*

Komodo dragons (*Varanus komodoensis*) feeding on a goat carcass on Komodo Island, Indonesia.

cauda) of western Australia, only 7.9 in (20 cm) long and weighing 0.7 oz (20 g).

Biology of monitors

Monitors have a massive body and powerful legs. Most species have strong claws on their feet, and all but the largest monitors can climb well. The tail is long and powerful, usually about twice as long as the body, and can be used as a potent weapon. Monitors grow throughout their life, so the oldest individuals in a population are also generally the largest.

Monitors have a long, specialized tongue with a bifurcated tip that is highly sensitive to smell and taste. The tongue is extended to pick up scent trails, and is then retracted into the mouth where the scents are chemically analyzed using an organ on the roof of the mouth.

Monitors grow replacement teeth, located in the gaps between the mature teeth. Monitor lizards have at least 29 vertebrae above their hips. Nine of these are neck vertebrae, supporting the unusually long necks of these lizards. The powerful jaws are hinged in the middle, an adaptation for swallowing large prey. The head of monitors is tapered, and there are distinct ear holes.

Monitors are active predators, hunting during the day. They stalk a wide range of animals and eat carrion and eggs as well . Monitors ingest their prey whole if it is small enough, but they can also dismember large prey items so they can be swallowed.

Monitors, like all lizards, are poikilothermic or "cold-blooded", and are most energetic after they have been heated by the morning sun, since their muscles work much more efficiently and easily when they are warm. Monitors can run quickly to chase down prey.

When doing so they lift their body and tail clear off the ground.

Monitors also swim well, and often seek water as a refuge when threatened. They can walk underwater, and can use their tongue to smell underwater.

When threatened, monitors can be formidably aggressive animals. They can inflict painful bites and scratches, and the largest species are capable of killing a human. However, monitors can be readily tamed in captivity.

Species of monitors

The Nile monitor (*Varanus niloticus*) is a widespread, rather aquatic species found in Africa. The Bengal monitor (*V. bengalensis*) is widely distributed in southern Asia, occurring from Iran and Afghanistan, to Java in Indonesia. This species is a relatively terrestrial monitor, and in some parts of its range it may become dormant during periods of extended drought. The two-banded monitor (*V. salvator*) is a large, mainly aquatic species that can attain a length of almost 9.8 ft (3 m), and ranges from Bengal and Ceylon through southeast Asia. The giant monitor (*V. giganteus*) can reach a length of 7.9 ft (2.4 m), and is one of seventeen species of monitors that occur in Australia.

Perhaps the most impressive species of monitor, and the largest living lizard, is the Komodo dragon (*V. komodoensis*) of Komodo Island and a few other tiny islands east of Java in Indonesia. This powerful predator is capable of killing large animals, such as pigs, goats, or deer. The Komodo dragon has also been known to rarely kill inattentive or unlucky humans—it is certainly imprudent to fall asleep on the ground on the island of Komodo! The Komodo dragon feeds on carrion when it is available. The Komodo dragon is an endangered species, with a population of only a few thousand individuals. Fortunately, the Komodo dragon has been protected from hunting by the government of Indonesia. However, this remarkable animal is still significantly threatened by loss of its habitat, and by diminishment of its natural foods of deer and pigs by human hunters.

Monitors and people

Monitors are hunted in many places for their meat, skin, and eggs. A preparation of the fat of monitors is used in traditional Chinese medicine, and monitors may be hunted for this trade anywhere that they occur. All of these types of exploitation can reduce the populations of monitors, and many species are now endangered. Monitors are also threatened by losses of their natural habitat in many places. Some populations of the Indian monitor (*V. indicus*) have been decimated by poisoning caused by attempting to eat the cane toad (*Bufo marinus*). The cane toad excretes a very toxic chemical from large glands on the sides of its neck, which poisons native predators that attempt to eat the toad. The cane toad has been widely introduced in the tropics in misguided attempts to achieve a measure of biological control over some types of insects that are agricultural pests. Some species of predatory birds have also been decimated by the cane toad, and so likely have other species of monitors in addition to the Indian monitor.

See also Toad.

Further Reading:

Carroll, R.L. *Vertebrate Paleontology and Evolution*. New York: Freeman, 1988.
Grzimek, B. (ed.). *Grzimek's Animal Life Encyclopedia*. Vol. 6. *Reptiles*. New York: Van Nostrand-Reinhold, 1974.

Bill Freedman

Monkeys

Monkeys are tree-dwelling mammals that, along with prosimians, apes, and humans, make up the order Primata of the primates. The primate suborder Anthropoidea includes two different infraorders, the Platyrrhini, the New World monkeys, marmosets and tamarins, and the Catarrhini, the Old World monkeys, apes, and humans. The major division between New World and Old World monkeys, in addition to their distribution, is that the New World monkeys have three premolars and the Old World only two. Platyrrhini, literally translated means, "broad flat nose." New World monkeys have rounded nostrils that are set fairly far apart and face outward. The Old world monkeys, in contrast, have narrow nostrils with only a thin membrane between them, and they tend to face downward. Catarrhini, literally means "downward nose." Note that the term "New World monkey" includes the marmoset/ tamarin group as well as the species in family Cebidae. New World monkeys often have a prehensile, or grasping, tail while Old World monkeys lack a prehensile tail. Old World monkeys typically sleep sitting upright on narrow branches, and it is this group that usually has ischial callosities, which are hard, hairless pads on their posteriors. New World monkeys, on the other hand, tend to sleep stretched out on a branch, and lack these callosities.

A young female spider monkey (*Ateles geoffroyi*).

The Old World monkeys have a fully opposable thumb. This wide separation of the thumb from the rest of the fingers allows them to pick up small objects and to grasp tree branches firmly. The thumbs of the smaller New World monkeys are not fully opposable.

Primates such as gibbons, that swing by their arms (brachiate) to move among trees, have arms that are longer than their legs. Primates that leap from tree to tree, such as prosimians, have legs that are longer than their arms. Most monkeys fit in a third category of quadrapedal (four-footed) ground runners that have equal length arms and legs, which allows them to run along branches on all-fours.

Old World monkeys (family ceropithecidae) live in sub-Saharan Africa and in India and Southeast Asia, and include langurs, macaques, guenons, baboons, mandrills, colobus and leaf monkeys, and mangabeys. Most monkeys are forest dwellers but a few species, such as baboons, live in open grasslands or rocky highlands.

The only European monkey is the Babary "ape," which is actually a macaque monkey, *Macaca sylvanus*. Originally from the Atlas Mountains of North Africa, it has taken up residence on the island of Gibraltar, off southern Spain. Another macaque (*M. fuscata*) lives on the two main islands of Japan, at higher latitudes than any other monkey.

New World monkeys are found from southern Mexico to southern Brazil, and are grouped into two separate families. Marmosets and tamarins are in the family Callitrichidae, while the capuchins, titis, night monkeys (or douroucoulis), sakis, howlers, wooly monkeys, and spider monkeys are included in the family Cebidae. The cebid monkeys are sometimes referred to as "capuchin like monkeys" for lack of a better nonscientific term to separate them from the marmosets and tamarins.

Monkeys are social creatures that usually depend on their group to help educate infants, protect the members, and find mates. A group may be as small as three (a male, a female, and a single offspring) or as large as 200 individuals in some species. Such large groups contain several males, many females, and many young.

Male monkeys tend to be somewhat larger than females, and the males of many species have greatly enlarged canine teeth. Some species of monkeys exhibit distinct sexual dimorphism-different appearance for male and female, while others are similar.

It was long thought that Old World and New World monkeys had evolved separately and that their similarities were the result of their occupying similar habitats, a process called convergent evolution. However, more recent genetic studies have revealed that Old World and New World monkeys have evolved from a common Old World ancestor in Africa about 65 million years ago. The ancestors of the New World monkeys probably reached South America from Africa during the late Eocene, when the two continents were closer together than they are today. It has been postulated that the monkeys were carried on floating islands of fallen trees and debris across the ocean to South America where they established themselves in the rain forests and subsequently evolved into many different species.

A wheat field near Greeley, Colorado.

Further Reading:

Bromley, Lynn. *Monkeys, Apes and Other Primates.* Bellerophon Books, 1981.

Napier, J.R., P. H. *The Natural History of the Primates.* Cambridge, MA: The MIT Press, 1985.

Napier, Prue. *Monkeys and Apes: A Grosset All-Color Guide.* New York: Grosset & Dunlap, 1972.

Peterson, Dale. *The Deluge and the Ark: a Journey into Primate Worlds.* Boston: Houghton Mifflin, 1989.

Preston-Mafham, Rod and Ken. *Primates of the World.* New York: Facts on File, 1992.

Jean F. Blashfield

Monkfish see **Anglerfish**

Monoamine oxidase inhibitors (MAOIs) see **Antidepressants**

Monoculture

Monoculture refers to the practice of cultivating an agricultural species or tree under conditions where other species are absent or virtually absent. This is done in order to lessen the intensity of competition on growth of the desired crop species.

Selective breeding

The most extreme form of monoculture involves the cultivation of a single genotype of a crop species, to the exclusion of other genotypes and other species. (Note that a single genotype would mean that all of the crop plants are genetically uniform.) Genetic monocultures may be grown in cases where plant breeders have managed to develop uniform strains of plants that are optimally adapted for growth under certain environmental conditions. To practice this extreme type of monoculture, it must be possible to propagate the desired genotype using non-sexual means, such as cuttings, root grafts, or tillers. Seeds, in comparison, are genetically variable, although in intensive agriculture they may be derived from relatively narrow, inbred strains of variable species. Examples of agricultural species that can be propagated asexually and therefore can potentially be grown as genetic monocultures include: (1) sugarcane (*Saccharum officinarum*), which can be cultivated from rhizome cuttings, (2) bananas (*Musa sapientum*), which can be propagated from tillers, (3) tea (*Thea sinensis*), which can be grown from stem cuttings, (4) strawberries (*Fragaria x ananassa*), which can be cultivated using runners, and (5) apples (*Malus pumila*), cherries (*Prunus avium*), and other trees of the rose family, which can be propagated using root grafts.

Tightly controlled environment

Usually, monoculture is practiced as a component of an intensively managed system, in which many environmental factors are controlled to optimize growth conditions for the crop species. For example, to achieve a monoculture of an agricultural plant, only a particular species is actually planted. Other plant species are considered to be weeds, and attempts are made to remove them by hand weeding, manual cultivation, or through the use of a herbicide to which the desired crop species is tolerant, but the weeds are not. In addition, plants grown under monocultural conditions are usually spaced optimally in order to decrease the intensity of competition among individual crop plants. The system may also be fertilized with inorganic nutrients so that nutrient availability does not limit productivity. The monoculture may be irrigated to decrease the importance of water limitations, protected with insecticides against injurious insects, and treated with fungicides to reduce the incidence of diseases. All aspects of the monocultural system are designed toward the optimization of crop yield, to the degree that can be economically and ecologically achieved.

Managed environment

Monocultures in forestry are generally managed less rigorously, because of economic constraints on the intensity of management that can be usefully practiced. A rigorous attempt may be made to only cultivate a single species of tree under plantation conditions. However, smaller plant species may be tolerated in the plantation if they are judged to not excessively interfere with the growth of crop trees, and the system may not be fertilized, irrigated, or otherwise managed as intensively as often occurs in agriculture.

Bill Freedman

Monomer

A monomer is a molecule or compound, usually containing carbon, with a relatively low molecular weight and simple structure; monomers form the fundamental building blocks of polymers, synthetic resins, and elastomers. Thus, vinylidene chloride is the monomer from which polyvinylidene chloride is made, and styrene is the monomer from which polystyrene resins are produced.

One of the simplest monomers, ethylene, consists of two carbon atoms (represented by C) linked by a double bond, with two hydrogen atoms (represented by H) connected to each carbon.

$$CH_2=CH_2$$

In ethylene the carbon-hydrogen bonds are single covalent bonds, while the carbon-carbon bond is a double covalent bond. In the presence of heat, light, and an appropriate catalyst the ethylene molecule can be excited into a reactive state in which the carbon-carbon double bond is dissociated.

$$-CH_2-CH_2-$$

If two excited molecules come into contact, it is possible to link the ethylene molecules with single covalent bonds between molecules. When this process repeats itself, on the order of thousands of times, a chain is produced with a carbon backbone and a formula

$$H-(CH_2-CH_2)_n-H$$

The building unit or monomer in this case is ethylene. After n units of ethylene have been linked, the reaction may be terminated by the addition of a hydrogen to each end of the polyethylene chain. Such polymerizations are referred to as addition polymerization, in contrast to condensation polymerization in which molecules with diverse end groups react to give chains composed of units of varying size and chemical complexity. Nylon 66 is the condensation product of two monomers: adipic acid and hexamethylenediamine.

There are a number of other polymers formed by addition polymerization from compounds much like ethylene

$$CH_2=CRH$$

where R may be a halide, a benzene ring, etc. These are called vinyl compounds. Table 1 lists some of the frequently encountered vinyl monomers.

The dienes constitute another class of addition polymers. Dienes monomers have the following generic structure:

$$CH_2=CR-CH=CH_2$$

Table 2 lists some of the common diene monomers.

TABLE 1. SELECTED VINYL MONOMERS

Name	-R	Use of polymer
Ethylene	-H	Plastic
Vinyl chloride	-Cl	"Vinyl"
Propylene	$-CH_3$	Rope
Vinyl acetate	$-O-(CO)-CH_3$	Latex paints
Acrylonitrile	$-C \equiv N$	Orlon®
Styrene (vinyl benzene)	$-C_6H_5$	Drinking cups
Vinyl alcohol	-OH	Fiber

TABLE 2. SELECTED DIENE MONOMERS

Name	-R	Use of polymer
Butadiene	-H	Tires
Isoprene	$-CH_3$	Natural rubber
Chloroprene	-Cl	Neoprene

TABLE 3. SELECTED VINYLIDENE MONOMERS

Name	-R	-X	Use of polymer
Vinylidene fluoride	-H	-F	Plastic
Tetrafluoroethylene	-F	-F	Teflon®
Isobutene	-H	$-CH_3$	Elastomer

TABLE 4. COMMON COPOLYMERS

Name	Use of polymer
Ethylene-propylene-diene monomer (EPDM)	Elastomer
Styrene-butadiene-rubber (SBR)	Tire rubber
Acrylonitrile-butadiene-rubber (NBR)	Elastomer
Acrylonitrile-butadiene-styrene (ABS)	Plastic

The vinylidenes constitute yet another class of polymers. Vinylidenes have monomers with the following generic structure

$$CX_2 = CR_2$$

Table 3 lists some of the common vinylidene monomers.

When monomers of different kinds are united by addition polymerization, the product is known as a copolymer. Table 4 identifies some copolymers.

The *Polymer Handbook* (J. Brandrup and E.H. Immergut, Eds., 3rd. ed., Wiley Interscience, New York, 1990) lists hundreds of other monomers in commercial use. The number of polymers that can be produced synthetically from monomers would seem to be limited only by the imagination and ingenuity of the chemist.

See also Carbon; Polymer.

Mononucleosis see **Epstein-Barr virus**

Monosodium glutamate (MSG)

Monosodium glutamate (MSG), a compound represented by the formula $C_5H_8NNaO_4 \cdot H_2O$, is a sodium salt of the naturally occurring glutamic acid. Glutamic acid, first isolated in 1886, became an important industrial chemical when its sodium salt was found to enhance the flavor of certain foods. The elements that make up the MSG molecule can exist in two different forms, known as isomers, and only one form has the flavor enhancing effect. It is believed by some that MSG is responsible for a disease known as "Chinese Restaurant Syndrome." Subsequent studies however, have not established a direct link between MSG and this disease.

The identification of MSG began with the isolation of glutamic acid from a mass of wheat protein, called gluten, in 1886. The chemical structure of glutamic acid, a naturally occurring amino acid, was later identified in 1890. The flavor enhancing ability of MSG was discovered by the Japanese chemist Ikeda Kibunae (1864-1936). From a kelplike seaweed, which was traditionally used to add flavor to Japanese food, he isolated MSG and patented a method for its production in 1908. Commercial production of this flavor-enhancing agent soon followed and Japan's first major chemical industry was born.

In 1968, the safety of MSG came into question when a largely anecdotal report was published that suggested MSG caused a disease commonly referred to as "Chinese Restaurant Syndrome" (CRS). This disease was said to produce symptoms of burning, numbness, fever, and a tightness in the upper body. Although many subsequent studies failed to show any link between MSG and these symptoms, the safety of MSG as a food additive continues to be questioned by some.

The three methods for producing MSG that are most often employed are vegetable protein hydrolysis, microbial fermentation, and organic synthesis. Obtaining MSG by the hydrolysis of vegetable proteins is the oldest method of production. In this method, waste protein, such as wheat gluten and beet sugar molasses, is

KEY TERMS

Chinese Restaurant Syndrome (CRS)—A disease which involves symptoms of burning and numbness, believed to be caused by MSG in Oriental food.

Gluten—A mass of waste protein obtained from wheat or corn that is used as a raw material for producing MSG.

Hydrolysis—A chemical reaction that involves breaking down the structure of a protein by the addition of water.

Isomer—Chemical compounds that have identical formulas, but can be distinguished from each other by chemical or physical means.

Neutralization—A chemical reaction between an acid and a base that results in the formation of a salt and water.

placed in water and heated in the presence of an acid. Under these conditions, the peptide bonds—chemical bonds which connect the amino acids in the proteins—are broken. Each individual amino acid can then be isolated by a method known as crystallization. Glutamic acid crystals can be converted to the MSG by reacting them with sodium hydroxide. Another method of production requires the use of microorganisms that are capable of producing MSG. Bacteria such as *Micrococcus glutamicus* have the ability to convert some carbohydrates into amino acids. Glutamic acid is one of these amino acids, and it can be isolated, then converted to MSG by partial neutralization. MSG can also be produced synthetically by an organic reaction based on acrylate.

Characteristics of MSG

At room temperature, MSG ($C_5H_8NNaO_4 \cdot H_2O$) is a salt, which typically exists as a white, odorless crystalline powder that is soluble in water and alcohol. It does not have a melting point per se, but it decomposes when it is heated. When crystals of MSG are created in a water solution, they develop in the shape of rhombic prisms.

The molecules of MSG can exist in two different forms known as isomers. These isomers are chemically identical, but physically different because their molecular structures are dissimilar. In fact, the elements on the two MSG isomers, known as stereoisomers, are arranged in such a way that if they were placed next to each other, they would appear as mirror images. The isomers of MSG have different physiological effects, and only one of them, known as the L form, has flavor enhancing properties.

Although MSG is tasteless by itself, it is a flavor enhancer that can be used to improve the taste of meat, fish, fowl, vegetables, and soup. It is said to provide a unique flavor that is neither bitter, sour, sweet, or salty. Typically employed at concentrations between 0.2%-0.9%, it is used extensively by the food industry in canned, frozen, and dried foods and Oriental food. It has also been used, with sugar, to improve the palatability of bitter drugs.

Further Reading:

Filer, L. J. *Glutamic Acid: Advances in Biochemistry and Physiology.* Raven Press: New York. 1979.
Othmer, Kirk. *Encyclopedia of Chemical Technology.* Vol. 2. Wiley: New York. 1978.

Perry Romanowski

KEY TERMS

Albumen—The white of an egg.

Cloaca—The cavity into which the intestinal, genital, and urinary tracts open in vertebrates such as fish, reptiles, birds, and some primitive mammals.

Coracoid—A bone or cartilage projecting from the scapula toward the sternum.

Endothermic—An animal that uses its metabolism as a primary source of body heat and uses physiological mechanisms to hold its body temperature nearly constant.

Placenta—A vascular, membranous organ that develops in female mammals during pregnancy, lining the uterine wall and partially enveloping the fetus, to which it is attached by the umbilical cord. Following birth the placenta is expelled.

Vestige—A small, degenerate, or rudimentary organ or part existing in an organism as a usually nonfunctioning remnant of an organ or part fully developed and functional in a preceding generation or earlier developmental stage.

Monotremes

The order Monotremata ("one-holed creatures") is comprised of two families, Ornithorhynchidae, including the platypus, and Tachyglossidae, including the long- and short-beaked Spiny anteaters, or echidnas. Monotremes are found only in Australia, Tasmania, and New Guinea. Monotremes are a derivative of an early mammal stock but there is no direct evidence of what it might have been.

Monotremes are not closely related to marsupials or placental mammals, but rather they evolved from a distinct group of reptilian ancestors. Despite sharing some reptilian features, monotremes possess all the major mammalian characteristics: air breathing, endothermic, mammary glands, furred bodies, a single bone in the lower jaw, and three bones in the middle ear.

Monotremes have a reptilian-like shoulder girdle with distinct coracoid bones and a T-shaped interclavicle. Other reptilian-like skeletal features are present, including certain ribs and vertebral processes, as well as epipubic or "marsupium" bones. These bones are rudimentary and are analogous to those that support a pouch in present-day marsupials. However, it seems more likely that these bones are a vestige from reptilian

ancestors, associated with the attachment of strong abdominal muscles to support large hindquarters.

Unlike higher mammals with separate reproductive and excretory systems, monotremes have a cloaca, with only one external opening as in birds and reptiles. In male monotremes the penis is used only for the passage of sperm and not for urination as in other mammals. The overall pattern of reproduction is mammalian with a brief, vestigial period of development of the young in a soft-shelled egg. Once fertilized in the oviducts, the egg is covered with albumen and the tough, leathery shell forms. The egg is rounded, large-yolked, and compressible, rather than brittle like the eggs of birds. Echidnas develop a temporary pouch to incubate the egg and care for the young. The platypus does not develop a pouch and typically lays a single egg in a leaf nest. The mammae lack nipples, so the young lick milk from two lobules in the echidna's pouch or from the abdominal fur of the platypus. A three to six month period of maternal care is typical for monotremes.

Certain shrews and monotremes are the only groups of venomous mammals. In echidnas, the poison gland is present, but non-functional. Only the male platypus is capable of producing the venom and conveying it to a horny spur on the back of the ankle.

Delivered by a forceful jab of the hindlimbs, the venom is powerful enough to cause agonizing pain in humans and can kill a dog. Although the exact nature of the venom system is unknown, it may have originated as a defense against some long extinct predator. Today, dingoes occasionally prey on echidnas, but in historical terms, dingoes are relatively recent arrivals in Australia. Because echidnas are widely hunted for food and the platypus is quite sensitive to changes in its habitat, monotremes are considered vulnerable in status.

See also Anteaters.

Betsy A. Leonard

Monsoon

A monsoon is a seasonal change in the direction of the prevailing wind. This wind shift typically brings about a marked change in local weather. Monsoons are often associated with rainy seasons in the tropics (the areas of the Earth within 23.5° latitude of the equator) and the subtropics (areas between 23.5° and about 35° latitude, both north and south). In these areas, life is critically dependent on the monsoon rains. A weak monsoon rainy season may cause drought, crop failures, and hardship for people and wildlife. The central role that monsoons play in determining climates around the world has made their study a high priority for meteorologists.

Many parts of the world experience monsoons to some extent. Probably the most famous are the Asian monsoons, which include the distinctly different monsoons that affect India, north China, and Japan, and south China and southeast Asia. Monsoons also affect portions of central Africa, where their rain is critical to supporting life in the area south of the Sahara desert. Lesser monsoon circulations affect parts of the southwestern United States. These summer rainy periods bring much needed rain to the dry plateaus of Arizona and New Mexico.

General monsoon circulation

Monsoons, like most other winds, occur in response to the sun heating the atmosphere. In their simplest form, monsoons are caused by differences in solar heating between the oceans and continents, and they are most likely to form where a large continental land mass meets a major ocean basin. During the early summer, the increasing solar energy heats up the land surfaces fairly quickly. Water, on the other hand, heats much more slowly in response to the sun. This is one reason why we cool off by swimming in lakes during the summer—the water is still chilled from the recent winter and takes much of the summer to warm up. The enormous quantity of water in the oceans guarantees they will remain cooler than the nearby continents during the early summer. The relatively warm land surface will heat the air over it, causing it to rise, or convect. The convection of warm air produces an area of low pressure near the land surface. Meanwhile, the air over the cooler ocean will be more dense and tend to stay at the surface or sink downwards from aloft. Thus during the summer, oceanic air flows onshore toward the low pressure over land. This onshore flow is continually supplied by cooler oceanic air sinking from higher levels in the atmosphere. In the upper atmosphere, the rising continental air is drawn outward over the oceans to replace the sinking oceanic air, thus completing the cycle. In this way a large vertical circulation cell is set up, driven by solar heating. At the surface, the result is a constant wind flowing from sea to land.

The oceanic air moving onto the land is usually quite humid, due to its prolonged contact with the sea surface. As it flows on shore the moist marine air is pulled upward as part of the convecting half of the circulation cell. The rising air cools and eventually forms rain clouds. Rain clouds are especially likely when the continental areas have higher elevations (mountains, plateaus, etc.), because the humid sea air is forced upward over these barriers, causing widespread cloud formation and heavy rains. This is the reason why the summer monsoon forms the rainy season in many tropical areas.

In the late fall and early winter, the situation is reversed. Land surfaces cool off quickly in response to cooler weather, but the same property of water that makes it slow to absorb heat, called heat capacity, also causes it to cool slowly. As a result, continents are usually cooler than the oceans surrounding them during the winter. This sets up a new circulation in the reverse direction: air over the sea, now warmer than that over the land, rises and is replaced by winds flowing off the continent. The continental winds are supplied by cooler air sinking from aloft. At upper atmospheric levels the rising oceanic air moves over the land to replace the sinking continental air. Sinking air prevents the development of clouds and rain, so during the winter monsoon continental areas are typically very dry. This winter circulation causes a prevailing land to sea wind until it collapses with the coming of spring.

The Asian monsoons

While the thermal circulation described previously is a central part of monsoons, it is not sufficient to explain the world's most pronounced monsoons, those of Asia. Since they span such a huge area and affect over a billion people, the Asian monsoons have been studied for over a century to determine their causes and reasons for their variation. Although our understanding is not complete, it is clear that the monsoons of Asia are a complicated set of circulations, which combine the sun-driven winds with large scale circulations that span the entire planet. The extremely high mountains of the Himalayas also play a role in determining monsoon behavior.

An important factor in the development of the Asian monsoons is the existence of jet streams. These are great rivers of air, that ring the Earth at levels in the atmosphere ranging from 7-12 mi (12 to 20 km) above the surface. Jet streams are part of the global wind circulation, brought about by the large differences in temperature between the equator and the poles. Jet stream winds blow at several different latitudes, and play a major role in determining the weather beneath them. The monsoons of southern Asia are affected by two jet streams called the subtropical and the tropical jets. The subtropical jet is a permanent feature, flowing westerly (from west to east) at altitude of about 7 mi (12 km). It migrates over the year in response to the seasons, moving northward to higher latitudes in the summer and southward in the winter. It occasionally splits in two. The tropical jet is a weaker easterly (east to west) flow that forms near the equator at a height of nearly 12 mi (20 km). It is found only in the summer months.

The monsoon of India

The interplay of jet streams and monsoon winds is well illustrated in the Indian monsoon. During the early summer months, increased solar heating begins to heat the Indian subcontinent, which would tend to set up a monsoon circulation cell between southern Asia and the Indian Ocean. However, the subtropical jet stream occupies its winter position at about 30° north latitude, south of the Himalayan Mountains. As long as the subtropical jet blows over India, it inhibits the development of summer monsoon. As summer progresses, the subtropical jet slides northward. The extremely high Himalayas present an obstacle for the jet; it must "jump over" the mountains and reform over central Asia. When it finally does so, a summer monsoon cell develops, supported by the tropical jet stream overhead. The transition can be very fast—the Indian monsoon has a reputation for appearing suddenly as soon as the sub-

tropical jet is out of the way. The retarding effect of the subtropical jet delays the Indian monsoon by up to one month compared with the rest of Asia.

During the Indian summer monsoon, winds blow from the southwest, bringing moist air on shore. As the air is forced to rise over the foothills of the Himalayas, it causes constant and frequently heavy rains. The town of Cherrapunji, India, located on the Himalayan slopes, receives an annual rainfall of over 36 ft (11 m), making it one of the wettest places on Earth.

The summer monsoon ends as the highlands of Tibet begin to cool in the fall. The cooling atmosphere over Tibet allows the subtropical jet to reappear south of the Himalayas, bringing the rainy summer monsoon to an end. The circulation shifts to a winter monsoon cell, with sinking air over India and surface winds that blow out to sea. The resulting winter weather is dry.

The monsoons of South China and Japan

The monsoons of China and Japan are strongly affected by the huge land mass of Siberia. During the winter, the interior of Siberia becomes extremely cold. Cold air is dense, so a cold area of high pressure forms, where the air sinks from aloft. When it reaches the surface, the air spreads outward in all directions. The result is a dry winter monsoon that blows from the north through south China and southeast Asia. The same circulation affects northern China, Japan and Taiwan, where the prevailing wind is from the northwest. Although originally dry, the northwest winds pass over the sea and pick up moisture. When the winds arrive at the islands of Japan and Taiwan, they are forced up over the land. As a result, the western slopes of these islands experience a rainy winter monsoon.

During the summer, strong heating in the interior of Siberia sets up the summer circulation, giving south China, Indonesia, and southeast Asia humid southerly winds from the equator. Japan experiences winds from the south or southeast, which bring in moisture from the north Pacific Ocean.

When the monsoon fails

The importance of monsoons is demonstrated by the experience of the Sahel, a band of land on the southern fringe of the Sahara Desert. This area would also be arid if it were not for the seasonal monsoon, whose rains normally transform it to a grassland suitable for grazing livestock. The wetter southern Sahel can support agriculture, and many residents migrated to the area during the years of strong monsoons. Beginning in the late sixties, however, the annual monsoons began to

Further Reading:

Frater, Alexander, *Chasing the Monsoon*, New York: Alfred A. Knopf, 1991.

McCurry, Steve, *Monsoon*, New York: Thames and Hudson, 1984.

Meehi, Gerald A., "Coupled land-ocean-atmosphere processes and South Asian monsoon variability," *Science*, October 14, 1994, p. 263.

Navarra, John G., *Atmosphere, Weather and Climate*, Philadelphia: W.B. Saunders Co., 1979.

James Marti

KEY TERMS

Circulation cell—A circular path of air, in which warm air rises from the surface, moves to cooler areas, sinks back down to the surface, then moves back to near where it began. The air circulation sets up prevailing (constant) winds at the surface and aloft.

Convection—The rising of warm air from the surface of the Earth.

Heat capacity—The amount of heat required to raise the temperature of a substance; water has a high heat capacity, while land surfaces (soil, rock, etc.) and air have much lower heat capacities.

Jet stream—High speed winds that circulate around the Earth at altitudes of 7 to 12 mi (12 to 20 km) and affect weather patterns at the surface. Two important jet streams are the subtropical jet, flowing from west to east, and the weaker tropical jet, which flows from east to west.

Monsoon—A seasonal change in the direction of the prevailing wind, often associated with a rainy or a dry season.

Subtropics—Regions between 23.5 and about 35 degrees latitude, in both the northern and southern hemispheres, which surround the tropics.

Tropics—Regions of the Earth's surface lying within 23.5 degrees latitude of the equator.

fail. The pasture areas in the northern Sahel dried up, forcing nomadic herders and their livestock southward in search of pasture and water. The monsoon rains did not return until 1974. In the intervening six years, the area suffered devastating famines and loss of life, both human and animal, and placed extreme stress on the countries of central Africa.

Because of their tremendous effect on many tropical areas, atmospheric scientists continue to study the formation and variability of monsoons. Monsoon variations are still not entirely understood, making the prediction of the monsoon a distant goal. However, researchers have shown that monsoon are affected by El Niño, the changes in winds and sea water that occur in the tropical Pacific Ocean. Research continues into modeling monsoon circulations with complicated computer simulations.

See also Atmospheric circulation; Storm.

Moon

Earth's moon is a roughly spherical, rocky body orbiting the Earth at an average distance of 238,000 mi (382,942 km). Its diameter is about one-fourth Earth's diameter. Compared to moons of other planets, this is a large relative size. The diameters of other moons are a much smaller fraction of their planets' diameter.

The mass of the Moon is only about 1/80 the mass of the Earth, so the force of gravity is smaller. On the Moon the acceleration due to gravity is only one-sixth Earth's. You would, therefore, weigh one-sixth as much when standing on the Moon. The astronauts who landed there could leap high and long with very little effort because of the reduced gravitational force. This is why the Moon has no atmosphere. The escape velocity of the

The first footprint on the moon's surface, made by astronaut Neil A. Armstrong on July 20, 1969, shows the fineness of the lunar soil. The soil is produced when moon rock is weathered by impacting meteors, solar winds and extreme temperature changes. In many areas the soil appears to be a few meters thick.

A photo of the full moon taken from Apollo 17. The mare regions, which are relatively flat, appear as dark areas because they reflect less light. The highlands are lighter in color and have a more rugged surface than the mare. About 1/3 of the surface shown in this picture cannot be seen from the Earth.

Moon, which is related to the mass of the planet, is very low—about the same as the velocity due to collisional motion in an atmospheric gas mixture—so any atmosphere that might have once formed would have easily escaped the pull of the Moon's gravity.

We always see the same face of our Moon because it rotates on its axis at the same rate that it travels around the Earth—once every 29.5 days. This is no mere coincidence. The side of the Moon facing us is attracted more strongly by Earth's gravitational force than the opposite side. The force of gravity depends on the mass of the two interacting objects (here the Earth and the Moon) and the Moon has a mass asymmetry. There is more mass concentrated in the half of the Moon we see than in the other half. The effect is called "gravitational locking" and is a common occurrence in our solar system.

Phases and eclipses

As we observe the Moon from Earth, we see different phases of the Moon. We see these because, as the Moon orbits Earth, it comes between us and the Sun once a month at the time of a new Moon, and orbits Earth in very nearly the same plane that the Earth orbits the Sun. If the Moon's orbital plane had zero tilt off the Earth's orbital plane, we would see a total lunar eclipse every month.

There is actually about a 20° tilt, so we see total lunar eclipses only about seven times a year, when the Earth is directly between the Sun and the Moon. The Earth's shadow falls on the full Moon, and it slowly becomes dark and then bright again as it moves out of the Earth's shadow.

The lunar surface

Although surface features were observed as early as 1600 by Galileo, most of our knowledge of the surface is from spacecraft exploration.

In 1959 the Soviet Union sent the first spacecraft to orbit the Moon, sending back tantalizing photographs. American astronauts orbited the Moon in the 'Apollo 10' orbiter in 1968, followed by several lunar landings

A close-up of the back side of the moon taken from Apollo 13. The large mare area is Mare Moscoviense. The large crater on the horizon is IAU number 221.

by manned Apollo spacecraft from 1969 to 1972. These landed on the Moon six times during those years, providing copious data from the lunar surface. Apollo experimentation included soil-testing devices, cameras, seismometers, solar wind collectors, and rock collection. The Soviet Union also landed an unmanned craft during this time (1970), collecting additional data for analysis.

Moon rocks

Spacecraft experimentation found mostly igneous rock on the Moon (rock formed by cooling lava) but some sedimentary. The sedimentary rock was probably formed by falling debris after meteoritic impacts. The igneous rock in the marina is mostly basalt, but the highlands are mostly anorthosites. Both types form from cooling lava but under different conditions and at different cooling rates.

Radioactive dating of rocks brought back by the Apollo astronauts gives us the absolute age (the time since the rocks solidified) of the Apollo astronauts gives us the absolute age (the time since the rocks solidified)

of the highlands as 3.9 to 3.8 billion years, with the final lava flow around 3 billion years ago.

The Moon has no overall magnetic field. According to the currently-favored model of planetary magnetic fields (the dynamo model), this means either that the Moon probably has no molten core or that only a very small part of the core is molten. There is a weak magnetic field frozen in to the rocks, however, or the rocks have a north pole and a south pole, so it's possible that the Moon once had a magnetic field surrounding it.

Lunar origin

The fact that the oldest rocks on the Moon are about the same age as the oldest rocks found on Earth tells us that the two were formed around the same time. Rather than forming by gravitational clumping of matter in orbit around the Earth, however, our Moon is probably a captured asteroid. Studies of the differences in the compositions of the Earth and Moon indicate that, during the early stages of the Earth's formation, a large asteroid struck the Earth a glancing blow, and pieces of it, as well as pieces of Earth, flew back up to orbit the Earth in a ring-like system around the planet. Eventually, the force of gravity caused the fragments to coalesce and form our Moon. This is called the "ring ejection theory" of lunar origin.

See also Orbit; Spacecraft, manned; Satellite.

Mooneyes

The mooneye is a freshwater fish with very large eyes. Usually measuring between 16-21 in (40-51 cm) long, it has a deep, laterally thin body. Because it generally resembles a shad or herring, the mooneye has acquired such common names as toothed herring, big-eyed shad, or white shad. Mooneyes can be distinguished from shads and herrings by the presence of well-developed teeth on their jaws and tongues and by the absence of an adipose fin, which is a small, extra dorsal fin located well back on the fish's spine in front of its tail. The anal fin of a mooneye is moderately long with 23 to 33 rays, and its caudal, or tail, fin is well-developed. Its pelvic fins have 7-10 rays. Laterally, this fish has between 54 and 61 scales.

The mooneye belongs to the Order Osteroglossids, generally referred to as bonytongues. Within the Order, there are two Suborders: (1) Bonytongues (Osteoglossoidei) and (2) Featherbacks (Notopteroidea). The mooneye is classified in the latter suborder and in the family Hiodontidae. There are two species commonly accepted to be in this family, the *Hiodon tergisus* (mooneye) and the *Hiodon alasoides* (goldeye). A third species, the southern mooneye (*Hiodon selenops*), used to be considered a separate species, but scientists now think that it is identical to the common mooneye.

The two species can be differentiated by their eye coloring, dorsal fins, and the position of their ventral keels. As its name infers, the goldeye has gold-colored eyes. Furthermore, the mooneye has 11 to 12 rays comprising its dorsal fin. The same fin on the goldeye has only 9 or 10 rays. Finally, while both the mooneye and the goldeye have a fleshy keel on their belly, known as a ventral keel, its position on each fish is different. On the mooneye, the ventral keel does not extend in front of its pelvic fins; on the goldeye, it does.

The northernmost range of the mooneye extends northwest of the St. Lawrence River to the Hudson Bay and Manitoba. In the US, these fish live in Lake Champlain west to the Great Lakes, mostly in Lake Ontario and Lake Erie. In the Mississippi River, these fish occur as far south as Arkansas. The mooneye can also be found in the Mackenzie River system.

Mooneyes generally eat insects, but larger fish will eat mollusks and minnows if given the opportunity. They are abundant in their natural ranges, however, they are little known by fishermen. Although mooneyes are not considered to be gamefish, they will fight actively if hooked. Commercially, it is of negligible importance, its flesh being edible but not tasteful.

Moonrats see **Hedgehogs**

Moose

The moose (*Alces alces*), also known as elk in Europe, is a horse-sized, northern species of deer that occurs in the boreal and north-temperate forests of both North America and Eurasia. At one time the Eurasian and American moose were considered to be separate species, but these animals are fully interfertile and are now thought to be the same species. However, there are many geographically distinct subspecies of these animals.

Like other deer (family Cervidae), moose have cloven hooves, and are therefore in the mammalian order Artiodactyla. Moose are the largest animals in the deer family, weighing as much as 800 kg and standing as tall as 2 m. The largest moose occur in Alaska (*Alces alces gigas*). Moose are unusual-looking animals, with a long and large head, long legs, a short neck and tail, and a hump over their shoulders, which are taller than their hips. Moose convey a superficial appearance of ungainliness, but they can actually run swiftly and skillfully over difficult, uneven, and wet terrain. Moose are also good swimmers.

Moose are ruminants, meaning their stomachs are divided into four discrete chambers, which are concerned with particular, sequential aspects of digestion of the fibrous plant biomass that these animals feed upon. Moose ruminate, meaning they regurgitate and rechew forage that has spent some time fermenting in one of the chambers of the stomach.

Moose have large, shovel-shaped antlers, which are bony outgrowths of the frontal bones of their skull, a characteristic shared with other species in the deer family. The antlers of moose only develop on male animals. The antlers of the oldest, strongest males are especially large and wide (up to 7 ft, or 2m), and they have intri-

A moose feeding on pond vegetation in Baxter State Park, Maine.

cate outgrowths known as tines on their edge, which can number as many as forty. The antlers of moose are deciduous, meaning they are grown during the springtime and summer, for use in jousting with other males for access to females during the rutting season, and are later shed in the late autumn or early winter. While the antlers are growing, they are covered with densely vascularized tissue known as velvet, which dries once the antler growth is complete by the late summer. The dry velvet is removed by rubbing against trees and other solid objects, leaving only the bare antler bone exposed. Male moose also have a large dewlap hanging under their neck, sometimes called a bell.

During the autumn rutting season, fights between evenly matched bull moose can be dramatic contests, and can lead to death of one of the conbatants. Rarely, two bulls will lock their horns together so tightly that it causes the death of both animals. Bull moose are extremely aggressive during their rut, and at this time they are dangerous to humans.

Moose calves are born one or two at a time, and they are precocious, meaning that they are capable of standing and moving about with their mother soon after birth. The calves nurse for as long as a year, and moose can live for as many as 25 years. Moose are not very social animals, mostly coming together only for the purposes of breeding. In some regions with deep snow in the winter, moose may aggregate in dense stands of conifer trees, known as yards.

Moose feed on a wide variety of plants, and their diet varies seasonally. Most of the year moose feed by browsing on young shoots and foliage of woody shrubs and short trees. During the summer these animals prefer to eat herbaceous vegetation, including aquatic plants, which they seek while standing in the water, often feeding beneath the surface. At these times, individual moose can be approached rather closely (and carefully) by canoe, and can be taken totally by wide-eyed surprise when they lift their heads above water again, subsequently running away with enormous splashes.

The upper lip of the moose is unusually large and prehensile, and is adapted to feeding on woody plants. The long legs of moose make it easy for them to feed relatively easily in the canopy of shrubs and trees. However, this trait, in combination with their short neck, makes it difficult for these animals to feed on lower-growing, herbaceous vegetation. Therefore, when grazing on grasses and forbs, moose often must kneel

KEY TERMS

Browse—The twigs, foliage, and reproductive tissues of woody plants that are eaten by certain mammalian herbivores, such as moose and other deer.

Ruminant—Animals in the order Artiodactyla, having a four-chambered stomach, and that chew a pre-digested cud.

Rutting season—A period of sexual excitement in an animal, for example, in bull moose during the autumn.

Yard—A wintertime, forested habitat of certain species of deer, generally dominated by coniferous trees and having a relatively shallow accumulation of snow.

rather awkwardly. Moose diets are generally low in sodium, and these animals therefore crave salt. As a result, moose (and other deer) are sometimes seen along roadsides, eating vegetation that is relatively rich in sodium because of the use of road salt in winter.

Moose are hunted throughout their range, both for sport and as a source of wild meat and tough hides. Until rather recently, moose were overhunted over much of their range, and their populations were reduced to low levels. Now, however, the hunting of most moose populations is regulated, and are now much more stable.

In some regions of eastern North America, white-tailed deer (*Odocoileus virginianus*) have become quite abundant. This has largely happened because of activities of humans that create favorable habitat for the white-tailed deer, such as some types of forestry and the abandonment of agricultural lands. If moose also occur in places where white-tailed deer are abundant, they may suffer from a debilitating nematode parasite known as brainworm (*Parelaphostrongylus tenuis*). The deer population is resistant to this parasite, but the brainworm is abundant where the deer are common, and the moose population consequently suffers.

See also Deer.

Further Reading:

Banfield, A.W.F. *The Mammals of Canada.* Toronto: University of Toronto Press, 1974.

Grzimek, B. ed. *Grzimek's Encyclopedia of Mammals.* London: McGraw Hill, 1990.

Runtz, M.W.P. *Moose Country. Saga of the Woodland Moose.* Minocqua, WI: Northword Books, 1992.

Wilson, D.E. and D. Reeder (comp.). 1993. *Mammal Species of the World.* Washington, D.C.: Smithsonian Institution Press.

Bill Freedman

Mormyrid fish see **Elephant snout fish**

Morphine

Morphine, $C_{17}H_{19}NO_3+H_2O$, is a narcotic analgesic drug used primarily in medicine for its pain killing properties. Morphine was isolated from opium in 1805 and named for Morpheus, the Greek god of sleep, by the German chemist and pharmacist Friedrich W. Sertürner (1783-1841). Morphine is the principle and most active alkaloid obtained from the unripe seed capsules of the opium poppy, *Papaver somniferum*. There is evidence that morphine was ingested, in the form of opium, thousands of years B.C. Morphine can be synthesized in a laboratory but because it is difficult to do so, the medical industry relies on countries that produce opium such as India and Turkey for their morphine supply. The drug occurs as a white crystalline powder or colorless crystals and is available for legal medical use. Morphine and synthetically made morphine-like drugs are most often given to people who have pain caused by physical trauma, or those who have intense pain caused by diseases such as cancer.

Morphine has similar painkilling properties to endorphins and enkephalins, a group of amino acid compounds produced in the pituitary gland. The molecular structure of morphine is so much like that of endorphins that it is able to bind to and occupy specialized receptor sites located in various pain centers in the central nervous system. Morphine also alters the release of neurotransmitters. The perception of pain is thus changed and the emotional reaction to pain (fear of, or anticipation of pain) is also affected. Morphine also affects the bowel and causes constipation. One's pain threshold is elevated by morphine's ability to induce an extreme state of relaxation. Other effects of morphine include drowsiness, slowing of respiration, cough suppression, changes in the endocrine and autonomic nervous systems, nausea, and vomiting. The most serious side effect of morphine, as with other drugs derived from opium, is its addictiveness. For this reason, scientists have striven to synthesize drugs that mimic the painkilling attributes of morphine but do not have the same addictive properties. Two semisynthetic drugs that can be made from morphine are codeine, which is used for pain relief and cough suppression, and diacetylmorphine or heroin, an extremely potent and addictive drug.

Developed by the Bayer Company of Germany in 1898, heroin is obtained by treating morphine with acetic anhydride. Heroin, which is four to eight times as potent as morphine, was originally used as a cough suppressant and narcotic analgesic but proved to be even more addictive and have worse side effects than morphine and codeine. Although heroin is converted into morphine in the body, it acts on the brain faster than morphine. Heroin has greater lipid solubility and is able to cross the blood-brain barrier more easily. In the United States, heroin was sold over-the-counter as a cough suppressant until 1917. Because of its exceptional pain killing properties, heroin abuse has been a problem since it was discovered; however, addiction to heroin was not prevalent until after World War II. Today, the use and trafficking of heroin are a major problem throughout the world.

See also Addiction; Narcotic.

Further Reading:

Goodman and Gilman. *The Pharmacological Basis of Therapeutics*. 6th ed. New York: Macmillan, 1980.

Lewington, Anna. *Plants For People*. New York: Oxford University Press, 1990.

Mosquitoes

Mosquitoes belong to an order of insects called Diptera, which includes the common house fly. All together, the Diptera order, the flies, are responsible for carrying diseases to more than 50% of the world's population. Some 120,000 species of Dipteran flies have been catalogued, which includes more than 2,500 species of mosquitoes. More than 15,000 species of flies and 150 species of mosquitoes are found in North America.

Some species of mosquitos in the genera Anopheles, Aedes, and Culex are responsible for infecting human beings with diseases such as malaria, filariasis, and yellow fever. While pest flies carry diseases to humans and animals and cause a considerable loss to agricultural crops, their larvae also serve an important function in the process of decomposing dead plant and animal material, a role they share with many bacteria and fungi. Mosquito populations are a part of this process.

A mosquito withdraws its proboscis after feeding in Alpena, Michigan.

Characteristics

Mosquitoes have two pairs of wings, but their second pair of wings are reduced to short, peg-like structures called *halteres*. Mosquitoes have thin, long bodies and three pairs of extremely long legs. They have scales along the veins of their wings and long beak-like, sharp sucking mouth parts called a *proboscis*. These two features distinguish mosquitoes from other flies. Mosquitoes also have feathery or hairy antennae.

Female mosquitos are ready to mate within a few hours after reaching their adult stage, and males are ready usually within 24 hours. Mating usually occurs while the mosquitoes are in flight, but sometimes it occurs on the ground. The tone of the female wing beat attracts males, and they grab the females with their hind legs. Mating among mosquitoes is related to their swarming habits, which in some species, but not all, is the preliminary behavior to mating. Swarming usually occurs around sunset and near fences or other objects and can last from 10-30 minutes.

Mosquitoes feed on sweet nectar, fruit, and other sugary substances. The females of some of the species of mosquitoes also feed on blood which they need in order for their ovaries to mature and for their eggs to develop. The female blood meal can take place before or after she has mated. Female mosquitoes detect their blood hosts partly through the sense of smell and partly by sight. The distance over which a mosquito can detect a blood host can range from 20-90 ft (6-27 m). Research indicates that mosquitoes are attracted to hosts which are already under attack by other mosquitoes. Some adult male humans are more desirable to them than women or children. Human beings are not the only blood hosts that mosquitoes attack. This "vampire" of the insect world is known to feed on mammals, birds, lizards, fish, bats, and even caterpillars for its blood meal.

Life cycle

Mosquitoes have four stages to their life cycles beginning with the egg, then proceeding into a *larva* stage, followed by a *pupa* stage, and finally adulthood. Female mosquitoes deposit their eggs in a number of different environments depending on the particular species. While the larvae can only live in water, eggs are not always laid in water. Some species deposit their eggs in areas that may not be flooded for a number of years, but the eggs can survive for several years until the next flood. Other species deposit them separately on top of the water and others deposit them in groups on the water's surface. These are called "rafts."

When the eggs are first laid they are white in color, but they change to black or brown in a short time. Some mosquito eggs, such as the *Anopheles*, have a hull-like shape with extensions on either side, giving them the appearance of tiny rafts. Some mosquito eggs are able to trap air bubbles. From 30-500 eggs are laid at one time by females, depending on the species. Most hatch in two or three days into aquatic larva.

During the larva stage, they feed on plankton and move by wiggling, hence the name of "wiggler," which is applied to mosquito larvae. The larva life span varies again depending on the species. Some develop rapidly within days, while others may take months to develop. They also exhibit a variety of feeding habits, from scavenging dead food, bottom or surface feeding of plankton, to eating other living organisms. The next stage, the pupa which occurs just before maturity, takes place on the surface of the water, where the pupa breaks out of the larva shell. The transformation from larva to pupa takes only several minutes and occurs at the surface of the water. The pupa stage lasts from two to three days in the tropics to several weeks in cold climates.

As adult mosquitoes leave the pupal stage they swallow air which helps them expand their abdomen and wings. Among the various species there are different ratios of male and female births. The life span of mature mosquitoes ranges from a few days to over a month depending on the species and on the climate. Those living in hotter climates tend to have a shorter life span.

Malaria and yellow fever

Through her blood sucking, the female mosquito carries diseases like malaria and yellow fever to human beings. While it has been wiped out in some parts of the world, malaria is a disease that is still contracted in

---

KEY TERMS

Halteres—Shortened appendages in flies and mosquitoes at the rear of the thorax, where other insects have wings. Halteres help flies balance themselves.

Larva—The initial stage of a mosquito after it hatches from its egg.

Pupa—The stage of development of a mosquito after its larva stage and before its final adult stage.

---

many places of the world. The illness is characterized by periodic fever and chills in the victim. Malaria is caused by a protozoa that was first identified by English physician Ronald Ross (1857-1932) in 1898. Not all mosquitoes carry the protozoa that causes malaria, but those that do deposit a parasite in the bloodstream that is capable of destroying the person. There are effective drug treatments and preventions for malaria today, but those who have had the disease are susceptible to relapses. The main vector of the malarial parasite are species of Anopheles mosquito. Open control measures for the disease include spraying against adult flies and treating water sources where the larvae develop.

Yellow fever is another mosquito-born disease that causes jaundice in the victim, hence the name of the disease. The mosquito that carries the yellow fever virus to humans during its blood meal is *Aedes aegypti*. Jaundice causes a person to appear yellow in color, hence the name. While there is no exact treatment for yellow fever, most people recover and have an immunity to the disease for the rest of their lives. Immunization against the disease is available through vaccination, but the most effective method used to prevent yellow fever is through measures to control mosquito populations that transmit the disease to humans.

See also Malaria; Yellow fever.

Further Reading:

Arnett, Ross H. *American Insects*. New York: Van Nostrand Reinhold, 1985.

Imes, Rick. *The Practical Entomologist*. New York: Simon & Schuster, 1992.

Lane, Richard P., and Roger W. Crosskey. *Medical Insects and Arachnids*. London: Chapman and Hall, 1993.

"Mosquitoes Unlimited," *Natural History* (special issue; July 1991).

Vita Richman

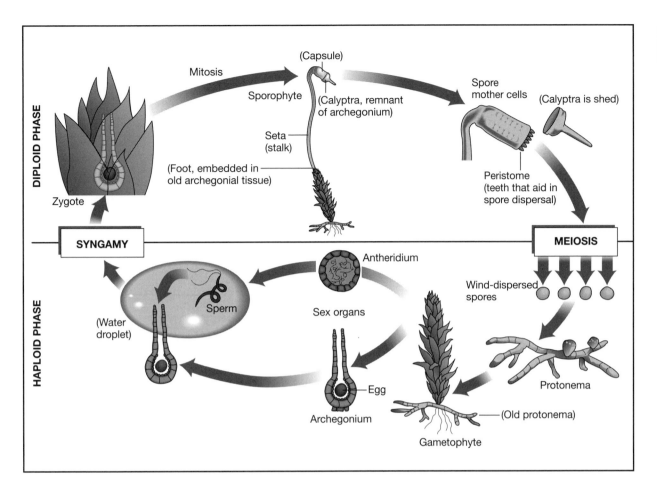

The life cycle of a generalized moss.

Moss

The mosses are the largest of the three classes in the plant phylum Bryophyta. The familiar small, green, and "leafy" moss plant is known as the gametophyte. This haploid multicellular phase is dominant in the moss life cycle. The mosses are the most broadly distributed of the three classes of bryophytes (which also includes liverworts and hornworts). There are more than 15,000 species of mosses worldwide. There are three subclasses of mosses: the true mosses (Bryideae), the peat mosses (Sphagnideae), and the granite mosses (Andreaeideae).

Bryophyte characteristics

Mosses share numerous features with the two other classes of bryophytes. They are more complex than algae yet simpler than the higher vascular plants. Like higher plants, bryophytes use chlorophyll-a, chlorophyll-b, and carotenoids as photosynthetic pigments. They store their food reserves as starch. They have cellulose in their cell walls, cell-produced rigid structures that are external to their plasma membrane. They form a cell plate, structures made of membranes representing the site of newly created cells, during cell division. Their spores, units capable of maturation, develop as a tetrad (a group of four cells) by meiosis, divisions of the cell nucleus that halve the number of chromosomes.

Two features of bryophytes tend to restrict them to moist environments, such as bogs and woodlands. First, unlike vascular plants, bryophytes lack a system with xylem and phloem for efficient transport of water and food. Second, the male sperm cells of bryophytes must swim through water to reach the female egg cells.

Bryophytes also differ from higher plants in that the sporophyte, their spore-producing diploid tissue, is nutritionally dependent on the dominant haploid gametophyte. In higher plants the gametophyte is dependent on the dominant sporophyte.

Moss characteristics

Mosses have several characteristics which distinguish them from other bryophytes. Only mosses have a multicellular rhizoid, a root-like subterranean tissue which absorbs water and nutrients from the soil. Liverworts and hornworts have single celled rhizoids. Only mosses have radial symmetry in that a cut down the long axis of an individual gives two similar halves. Only mosses and hornworts have stomata, cells specialized for photosynthetic gas exchange, on their sporophytes. Liverwort sporophytes lack stomata. In addition mosses do not have true leaves or stems. Their leaf-like structures are called phyllids. They are typically only one cell thick, although phyllids in some species are several cells thick.

Life cycle

A haploid moss spore germinates and gives rise to a protonema, a green multicellular tissue which superficially resembles a filamentous green alga. Under appropriate conditions, other moss cells can also be induced to form protonema. The protonema is typically subterranean and is rarely seen.

Buds form on the protonema producing the familiar "leafy" moss plant. Male and female reproductive organs typically grow near the tips of the "leafy" gametophyte. These are termed antheridia and archegonia, respectively. Most species are monoecious, in that antheridia and archegonia are on the same individual. Other species are dioecious in that antheridia and archegonia are on different individuals.

The archegonium is multicellular and produces a single immobile egg. The antheridium is also multicellular but it makes many motile sperm cells each with two flagella. A sperm cell swims through water to reach the archegonium. Then it travels down a tube in the archegonium to fertilize the egg and form a diploid zygote.

The zygote undergoes repeated cell division and elongates to become a multicellular sporophyte while still attached to the 'leafy' gametophyte. The thin stalk of the sporophyte is called the seta and the enlarged tip is called the capsule. The moss sporophyte is photosynthetic early in development, but later depends on the gametophyte for nutrition. Late in development, the sporophyte dries out and turns brown. Then the operculum (lid) comes off the capsule and haploid spores are released to the environment. The subclass of true mosses (Bryideae) are unique in having special peristome teeth inside the cap which regulate spore dispersal.

Habitat and ecology

Mosses are typically found in moist environments although most species can withstand prolonged periods of desiccation. In terrestrial ecosystems, mosses are important in preventing soil erosion. Numerous species of moss are found in fresh water but there are no salt water species.

Mosses are particularly prominent in the tropics, but they have a significant presence in the boreal forest, the woodlands of the temperate zones, and tundra regions. In the arctic tundra, mosses can constitute 50-90% of the ecosystem's biomass.

Evolution

The earliest known moss fossil is from the early Carboniferous period, about 320 million years ago. Mosses are not well-represented in the fossil record because their soft tissue is not well preserved. An examination of extant species indicates that bryophytes are a polyphyletic group. They appear to have evolved from more than one ancestral line.

Most botanists believe that mosses evolved from aquatic ancestors but there is debate about their evolutionary ancestry. It is commonly accepted by most botanists that mosses evolved from a simpler filamentous green alga. Although bryophytes appear intermediate in complexity between algae and vascular plants, they are unlikely to be an evolutionary "missing link" between these two groups.

Importance to humans

Compared to other groups of plants, mosses are not very economically important. However, *Sphagnum* moss has a long history of diverse uses and is certainly the moss of greatest importance to humans. In its natural habitat, Sphagnum selectively absorbs certain ions and secretes others. The bogs in which it grows become acidic and anaerobic over time, and the decomposition rate by bacteria is particularly slow in these bogs. Organisms buried in Sphagnum bogs remain well-preserved for a very long time.

Currently, the most common use of Sphagnum is by gardeners. They often mix dried Sphagnum (peat moss) with soil to improve the water-holding capacity of soil. The American white cedar grows in Sphagnum bogs. This tree has been used for a long time to make shingles for houses because its wood resists rotting. In the 1700s, most of America's white cedar came from Sphagnum bogs in the Pine Barrens of New Jersey. After all the standing trees were cut down, trees which were buried deep in the bogs for up to 1,000 years were dug up and used. These cedar trees had been preserved by the anaerobic and acidic environment created by Sphagnum moss. Cedar was mined from New Jersey's Sphagnum bogs until the 1850s.

Sphagnum has antiseptic properties and can hold up to 20 times its weight in water, much more than cotton. Sphagnum was used as a bandage for soldiers wounded in the Russo-Japanese War (1904-05) and World War I. By using Sphagnum for bandages, cotton could be saved for making gun powder.

Peat derived largely from Sphagnum is important as a fossil fuel, particularly in Scotland and Ireland. In Scotland Sphagnum also has an important role in the making of scotch whiskey. In the making of many scotches grains are steeped in water from a Sphagnum bog during the malting procedure. Later the wort, which derives from the malted grains, is boiled over a fire of burning Sphagnum peat. These uses of Sphagnum peat impart a characteristic flavor and aroma to scotch whiskey.

There are also several vernacular plant names in which the word moss is misused. Spanish moss is a flowering plant and relative of the pineapple. Reindeer moss is a lichen. Moss pink is a garden flower in the Phlox genus. Irish moss is a red alga. Club moss is a simple vascular plant.

Further Reading:

Greenaway, T. *Mosses and Liverworts.* Austin, TX: Raintree Steck-Verlag, 1992.

Margulis, Lynn, and Karlene V. Schwartz. *Five Kingdoms.* New York: W.H. Freeman, 1988.

Richardson, D.H.S. *The Biology of Mosses.* New York: Wiley, 1981.

Peter A. Ensminger

Moss animals

Moss animals, polyzoa, or ectoprocts (phylum Bryozoa) are some of the most abundant and widespread organisms in the animal kingdom. A considerable amount of confusion has surrounded the taxonomic arrangement of the moss animals. A similar, although not so diverse, group of animals known as entoprocts have now been distinguished in their own phylum, Entoprocta. The vast majority of moss animals are exclusively marine-dwelling species (class Gymnolaemata), with just a few of the more than 4,000 species described to date found in freshwater ecosystems (class Phylactolaemata). A third class, Stenolaemata, is also recognised, but contains relatively few living marine species. More than 500 species, however, have been recorded in fossil history.

This phylum is one of the largest of all animal taxonomic groups. Individually, moss animals are all tiny, often microscopic, animals that rarely measure more than 0.04 in (1 mm) in length. However, individual animals (or zooids, as they are known) congregate to form large encrusting colonies, which may reach more than 3.3 ft (1 m) in diameter. Most species live in shallow waters, although some have been recorded from a depth of 18,045 ft (5,500 m). Colonies may form on any hard surface that is continuously under water—rocks, shells, submerged timbers, seaweeds, etc.

Each animal is contained within its own body wall, which has just a single opening. A thin outer covering is secreted from the body wall to provide some support; there are no muscles within the body wall. The bulk of the body is taken up with the feeding and digestive system. There are no respiratory, circulatory, or excretory organs.

Moss animals vary widely in appearance: some are oval, while others are almost square or vase-shaped. The top of each animal is dominated by a special feeding structure known as the lophophore. Basically this consists of a crown of 8-100 ciliated tentacles which are used to create water currents for filter-feeding. The mouth opening lies within the circle of tentacles, but the anus is outside—an adaptation to prevent fouling of the tentacles with body wastes. When the animal is feeding, the lophophore is pushed out through the opening and the tentacles extended. The current created by the beating of tiny cilia sweeps a small water current down toward the base of the lophophore. Tiny food particles, mainly plankton, then enter the pharynx and pass through the digestive system to the stomach. Some species have a special lid that closes over the opening of the lophophore when the animals is not feeding.

Most bryozoans (including all freshwater species) are hermaphroditic—that is, each individual animal contains male and female reproductive organs. Reproductive patterns vary considerably across the phylum: some species release eggs and sperm simultaneously to the sea, with fertilization taking place outside the body. Others retain their eggs, which are fertilized by sperm borne in with the water column. Some species may be self-fertilizing. The resulting trocophore larvae are released from the body wall and disperse with the water currents. Most larvae are nonfeeding and settle within a few hours of having been released from the parent animal. When an individual larva settles, it may reproduce and spread by asexual means, forming identical zooids to the parent cell.

Mossbunker see **Herrings**

Mössbauer effect

Mössbauer effect is the recoil-free emission and resonant absorption of gamma (γ) rays from the nuclei of certain radioactive isotopes such as ^{57}Fe. These γ-rays, as emitted, do not lose energy from the recoil of the nuclei because the recoil momentum due to their emission or absorption is taken up by the whole bulky sample rather than by the emitting or absorbing nucleus itself. Under such conditions, the nuclei are bound rigidly in the lattice of a crystal, and the energy of recoil is negligible. Spectra based on Mössbauer effect have found numerous applications in studying the valence of an element in a chemical compound, the state of the irons and their electronic structure, as well as structural and magnetic properties of magnetic bulk and thin-film materials.

Mössbauer effect was first reported by Rudolph Mössbauer in 1958. Three years later, he won the Nobel Prize with his discovery. Since then, it is believed that nuclear γ-ray emission and absorption process can take place in recoil-free fashion. In reality, of course we have both recoil and recoil-free events. Mössbauer also utilized the Doppler (velocity) shift to modulate the γ-ray energy so that Mössbauer effect could be developed into a spectroscope for material characterization. The emission of γ-rays with natural or nearly natural line width allows for observing in the γ-ray spectra the interaction between the nucleus and its atom in solids and viscous liquids.

A radioactive parent or Co, Ta, serves as the primary source of the excited nuclear state of the iron isotope $^{57}Fe^*$. $^{57}Fe^*$ decays rapidly and emits a γ-ray that strikes another ^{57}Fe or of the absorber or of the sample to be studied) in its ground state. If the energy of the γ-ray matches the ^{57}Fe-$^{57}Fe^*$ energy separation, it will be absorbed via a resonant absorption process and ^{57}Fe is excited. Since we need to match the γ-ray frequency to the absorber energy levels, the energy of emitted γ-ray is modulated via the Doppler effect by oscillating the radioactive source. Therefore, absorption is observed as a function of relative velocities. The γ-radiation of interest is detected by a counter, and the data are processed by a multichannel analyzer in which each channel corresponds to a different velocity and a mechanism for synchronization is also installed. Certain elements and compounds have to be examined at cryogenic temperature such as -452° F (-269° C) to see the Mössbauer effect. The final results, or Mössbauer spectra, are usually plotted as curves of transmission (T) in % versus relative velocity and the transmitted intensity is a minimum at the velocity of exact resonance. These spectra consist of sharp lines due to recoil-free emission or absorption and of a featureless background due to recoil events and irrelevant radiation.

The transitions involved in the Mössbauer effect and the basic principle of Mössbauer spectroscopy, where the area enclosed by a dash box may be kept at cryogenic temperature.

In Mössbauer spectra, the resonance is shifted relative to the source frequency, generally called "isomer shift". Such a chemical shift is due to a difference in the s-electron density or the shielding of s-electrons between two cases. Therefore, a measure in the isomer shift provides us with the information on s-orbitals involved in the chemical bonding. In addition to the isomer shift, there are the second-order Doppler shift caused by temperature effects and the gravitational red shift caused by differences in the potential energy between the source and the absorber. Magnetic effects due to a net electron spin or an unpaired electron density, on the other hand, make the spectra often to be split into several lines. For a quadrupolar nucleus, under certain conditions or a change in the symmetry of the electron distribution, the energy of the nucleus exhibits a dependence on the nuclear orientation. This will then lead to the electric quadrupole splitting. When we look at Mössbauer spectra, the effect due to magnetic field and quadrupole splitting can be easily identified.

Based on the aforementioned mechanisms, Mössbauer spectroscopy has been applied successfully in all fields of natural science. For instance, Mössbauer effect study provides local information on both magnetism via

KEY TERMS

Doppler Effect—The phenomenon discovered by Austrian mathematician and physicist, C. Doppler (1803-1853) in which the apparent changes of frequency of sound waves or light waves vary with the velocity of the observer relative to the source; for instance, if they both are moving closer together, the observed frequency is higher than the emitted frequency.

Doppler Shift—The shift in frequency due to the Doppler effect.

Hyperfine Interaction—The magnetic interaction between the magnetic moment of a nucleus and the magnetic moment of an electron.

the hyperfine interaction and structure via the electric quadrupole interaction in ferromagnetic films. It evaluates electromagnetic moments of excited states. That the differences in chemical bonding due to the change in valence state lead to variations of the occupation of the conduction band and the magnetic exchange coupling also manifests in the Mössbauer spectra. When a small amount of impurities is introduced in order to improve the magnetic properties and chemical stability of the material, Mössbauer spectroscopy can help find at which crystallographic sites of the matrix material the impurity atoms are located. Since iron occurs in a variety of biologically important compounds or heme proteins, Mössbauer spectroscopy also has found use in molecular biology and clinical diagnosis.

Radioactivity; Spectroscopy.

Further Reading:

Cohen, R.L. ed. *Applications of Mössbauer Spectroscope.* New York: Academic, 1976.

Ellerbrock, R. D., A. Fuest, A. Schatz, W. Keune, and R.A. Brand, "Mössbauer Effect Study of Magnetism and Structure of fcc-like Fe(001) Films on Cu(001)," *Physics Review Letter* 74 (1995).

Li, F. J. Yang, D. Xue, and R. Zhou. "Mössbauer Study of the $(Fe_{1-x}Ni_x)_4N$ Compounds $(0 \le x \le 0.6)$." *Applied Physics Letter* 66 (1995).

Long, G.J., and J.G. Stevens, eds. *Industrial Applications of the Mössbauer Effect.* New York: Plenum Press, 1986.

Pang-Jen Kung

Moths

Moths, along with butterflies, belong to the order Lepidoptera, the second largest order of insects. They possess two pairs of wings covered with microscopic, overlapping scales having distinctive colors and patterns. The body and legs are covered with scales, or with long, hairlike bristles. The adult lepidopteran lacks mandibles (found in most other insects); it feeds on liquids, mostly nectar, by means of a long proboscis, which is coiled in a spiral under the head when not in use. The proboscis is extended by blood pressure and coiled by muscular action. In some instances, the adult moth does not feed and lacks the proboscis. The head of the adult insect bears a pair of large compound eyes with many facets, and usually also a pair of simple eyes or ocelli. The antennae are long and many-segmented. The lepidopteran life cycle has four stages: the egg; the larva (called caterpillar), which molts several times as it feeds and grows; the pupa, which is a non-feeding, quiescent stage; and the adult (or imago).

The larva is usually the most conspicuous stage in the life cycle. It feeds voraciously, usually on leaves, but in various cases by boring in stems, or fruit, or stored grain, or by chewing on fur, wool, or other material. Unlike the adult, the larva has strong mandibles and other mouth parts for cutting and chewing its food. The larva bears several pairs of simple eyes, but no compound eyes. Each of its three thoracic segments bears a pair of typical many-jointed walking legs, which become the legs of the adult. In addition, several of its ten abdominal segments bear a pair of soft, unsegmented, "prolegs" with hooklike processes which help in crawling and grasping. The larva of any given species undergoes a specific number of molts before transforming into pupa. The larval skin may be naked, or covered with long hairs, bristles, or spines. Also, many larvae have characteristic colored stripes or other distinctive patterns. The larval stage is frequently highly destructive to crops, fruit and shade trees, stored grain and flour, and other products.

Despite the fact that moths comprise the vast majority of the order Lepidoptera, adult moths are not as commonly seen as butterflies. This is because, while butterflies are active during the day, most moths are nocturnal, and spend the daylight hours resting on tree bark, among leaves, and in secluded areas. Many of them have wing colors and patterns which help to camouflage them in their natural surroundings. Easily recognizable differences between adult butterflies and moths make it easy to distinguish them from one another. For example, butterfly antennae are clubshaped at their tips, while moth

A cecropia moth (*Hyalophora cecropia*) in Royal Oak, Michigan. Adults of this species are seen increasingly in urban areas, and often during the day.

A cecropia moth larva (*Hyalophora cecropia*) in Royal Oak, Michigan.

antennae taper to a point and frequently are feathery. A moth's body is short and stout and much more hairy than the relatively slender body of the butterfly. A resting butterfly has its wings folded together over its back, while the wings of a moth at rest are spread out. Although some moths are brightly colored, the majority are rather drab. The pupa of a moth lives either in a silk cocoon, or, if naked, hidden under debris or rocks. In most butterflies, the pupa, called chrysalis, is naked and exposed. In flight, both moths and butterflies have the forewing and hind wing of each side coupled by a hooklike device. In size, as measured by the wing span, moths range from less than 0.8 in (25 mm) to over 12 in (30 cm). In a number of moth species, males and females differ in size, color, characteristics of the antennae and of the mouth parts, and other features.

Of the more than 50 families of moths, the following are particularly noteworthy. The family Tineidae includes the clothes moths, whose larvae feed on woolens, furs, and other textiles. Three major agricultural pests in the United States, the "Angoumois grain moth" (which destroys stored grain, especially corn), the potato tuber worm, and the pink bollworm (which damages the blossoms as well as the seed pods of the cotton plant) belong to the family Gelechiidae. Many of the common moths attracted to light at night are members of the family Tortricidae. The spruce budworm, which is a serious pest of pulpwood in North America, also is included in this family. Pyralidae is a large family, with over 1,100 North American species. The European corn borer (which bores into corn stems), and the sod webworm (a pest of turf grasses) are among the most destructive members of this family. Also included here is the wax moth, whose larvae live in beehives and feed on beeswax. In some species in this family, adult moths have a pair of "tympanic membranes" capable of detecting the ultrasonic squeaks of bats. One member of this family, the South American cactus moth *Cactoblastis cactorum* has been used successfully in biological control of the prickly pear cactus in Australia. The cactus itself, soon after its introduction into Australia from the Americas, reproduced prolifically and became a major pest on millions of acres of agricultural land. Introduction into Australia of the South American cactus moth, whose larvae feed exclusively on the prickly pear, has almost completely eliminated the host plant. Hawk moths and sphinx moths (family Sphingidae) are large, with a proboscis which is longer than the body when uncoiled. They are strong fliers. The larvae of the sphinx moth, called hornworms, are pests of tomato and tobacco plants. Another large family, with approximately 1,200 North American species, is Geometridae. The larvae of geometrid moths are the familiar inchworms, which move by a "looping" movement, rather than by crawling, since they lack the prolegs on all but two abdominal segments. Inchworms feed on leaves of fruit and shade trees and on vegetable plants, and can be highly destructive. Moths in the family Saturniidae are among the largest and most colorful, with wing spans up to 12 in (30 cm), and large "eyespots" or other markings on the wings. The family Lasciocampidae includes the "tent caterpillar" moths. Their larvae, which hatch from eggs in early spring, construct silken communal "tents" on branches of the crab apple and certain other trees. Their feeding activity almost totally defoliates the host tree. One of the most beneficial and interesting moths is the commercial silkworm moth, *Bombyx mori*, in the family Bombycidae. This moth, native to China, has been bred in captivity for thousands of years, and is the only example of an insect that has been completely "domesticated," as it no longer exists in the wild. The larvae of the silkworm moth are "fed" mulberry leaves. The long domestication has led to the

KEY TERMS

Compound eye—Photoreceptor organ composed of multiple, independent optical units, called ommatidia, each with its own lens, receptor cells, and field of view.

Mandible(s)—The first pair of feeding appendages in arthropods, typically short and unjointed, used for chewing, tearing, or grinding food.

Ocellus (pl. ocelli)—A simple light-sensitive organ with a single layer of pigment-covered receptor cells.

Proboscis—An elongate, non-rigid feeding tube of certain insects, used for fluid-feeding.

Tympanic membrane—Tightly stretched circular or oval patch on the integument of certain insects, which vibrates in response to sound, and provides stimulation to nerves connected to its inner surface.

degeneration of the larva's prolegs, and hence to its inability to climb trees. The source of commercial silk is the cocoon of the pupa. In order to obtain the silk, the pupae have to be destroyed by immersion in hot water, since allowing the adult moth to emerge from the cocoon would break the long, continuous silk thread. Noctuidae is a very large family, with over 3,000 North American species. Larvae of noctuid moths include such serious pests as cutworm and corn earworm. Cutworms are especially destructive of vegetable seedlings which they cut off just above the ground with their powerful mandibles. Tussock moths and gypsy moths belong to the family Lymantriidae. Tussock moth larvae cause extensive defoliation of Douglas fir forests in the Pacific Northwest, while the larvae of gypsy moths play a similar role in the destruction of deciduous trees in the Northeastern United States.

Many adult moths are instrumental in pollinating flowers in the course of their feeding. Female moths produce and release into the environment a hormone which attracts males for mating. (Such hormones, which exert their action outside the body of the organism are called "pheromones.") Many pheromones have been chemically analyzed, and a few of them are now produced in the laboratory. Such products are increasingly used as bait which is placed in traps to attract and kill harmful insects, and thus to control their populations. A number of moth species are known to undertake seasonal migrations over long distances.

Further Reading:

Borror, Donald J., and Richard E. White. *A Field Guide to Insects. America north of Mexico.* Peterson Field Guide Series. Boston: Houghton Mifflin, 1987.

Covell, C.V. *A Field Guide to the Moths of Eastern North America.* Peterson Field Guide Series. Boston: Houghton Mifflin, 1984.

Evans, H.E. *Insect Biology: A Textbook of Entomology.* Reading, MA: Addison-Wesley, 1984.

Holland, W.J. *The Moth Book. A guide to the Moths of North America.* New York: Dover, 1968.

Milne, L., and M. Milne. *Audobon Society Field Guide to North American Insects and Spiders.* New York: Knopf, 1980.

R.A. Virkar

Motion

The process by which something moves from one position to another is referred to as motion; that is, a changing position involving time, velocity and acceleration. Motions can be classified as linear or translational (motion along a straight line), rotational (motion about some axis), or curvilinear (a combination of linear and rotational). A detailed description of all aspects of motion is called kinematics and is a fundamental part of Mechanics.

The kinematical description of motion really began with Galileo. From observations Galileo introduced two concepts: velocity as the time rate of change of position and acceleration as the time rate of change of velocity. With velocity, acceleration, time and distance traveled (change of position) the complete kinematical description of motion was possible. Four algebraic equations resulted, each involving three variables and an initial position or velocity.

The position of an object must be given, or implied, relative to a frame of reference and its motion is then described relative to this frame. Within this frame, position, change of position, velocity, and acceleration require a magnitude (how much) and a direction, both being equally important for a complete description. Physical concepts having this nature are called vectors in contrast to scalar concepts which require only a magnitude for their description (for example, time and mass). Saying the mall is a 5 mi (8 km) drive may be true but doesn't guarantee one will find the mall. However, specifying 5 mi (8 km) north would give the mall's precise location. Magnitude and direction are equally important.

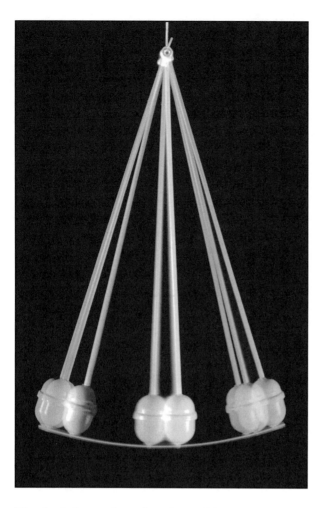

The simple harmonic motion of a pendulum.

In circular motion velocity is always parallel to the direction of motion and perpendicular to the radius of motion. The acceleration required to change the velocity's direction, called centripetal acceleration, is always perpendicular to the velocity and toward the center of motion. To change the velocity's magnitude an acceleration is required in the direction of the velocity. Hence, acceleration is required to change both magnitude and direction of velocity and are in different directions. This is applicable to curvilinear motion in general.

See also Acceleration; Newton's laws of motion; Velocity.

Motion pictures

Motion pictures, also called film, cinema or movies, are a series of images, recorded on strips of film, that create the illusion of continuous motion. A series of rapidly shown images appear to move because of a phenomena called the *persistence of vision*. The eye does not react instantly to changes in its field of vision. In fact, the eye continues to 'see' an image for 1/10- 1/20 of a second after it changes. So if a sequence of images can be shown at a rate of approximately 20 per second, it will appear as continuous motion to the eye. That is just what happens in a motion picture.

The invention of motion pictures

Many of the principles behind motion pictures were understood well before the invention of "the movies." In 1832, Simon Ritter von Stampfer of Vienna created the stroboscope. Images spinning on a disc were viewed through slits in a second disc. This displayed the images sequentially at a fast enough rate to simulate a couple seconds worth of motion. A primitive kind of slide projector called a magic lantern had been invented around 1640 in Rome by Athanasius Kircher. In 1853, these two inventions were combined by Austrian inventor and solider Franz von Uchatius (1811-1881), who used a magic lantern to cast stroboscopic images onto a wall. These were essentially cartoons, since they were animated drawings.

The invention of photography and improvement over the next several decades was another crucial ingredient. In 1877 photographer Eadweard Muybridge (1830-1904), working with an engineer, created a sequence of 24 images of a running horse, taken by 24 cameras. Soon these photographs were being projected by a device like the stroboscope. With Etienne Jules Marey's creation in 1882 of a camera that took bursts of sequential photographs, the basic building blocks for the creation of motion pictures had been invented. Inventor Thomas Edison (1847-1931), aware of these innovations, decided to create the visual equivalent of the phonograph: a camera and projection system that reproduced vision the way the phonograph he was working on reproduced sound.

Edison's assistant William Kennedy Dickson succeeded in 1889. He used a type of celluloid roll film developed for cameras, adding a series of perforations along the sides that held the film steady and moved it through a special camera. Once shot, the film was made into an endlessly running loop, and viewed through a magnifying glass. The device, called the kinetoscope, could only be viewed by one person at a time. It was not shown publicly until its patent came through in 1893.

Edison built a small motion picture studio in New Jersey, where his company created 50 ft (15 m) film loops. They were viewed at kinetoscope parlors at individual projectors. The first motion picture was of one of Edison's assistants sneezing. Soon they were filming acts from variety shows. Not realizing the potential of his invention, Edison had not taken out foreign patents on it. Soon it was being copied—and improved upon—in England, Germany, and France. Robert W. Paul (1869-1943) in England built a projector that made the film pause as each frame was shown. This made the frames show for longer than the space between them, lessening the flicker of earlier projectors.

In France, Auguste (1862-1954) and Louis Lumière (1864-1948), who manufactured photographic equipment, created their own projector and camera. They reduced Edison's 48 frames-per-second to 16, and called their projector the cinématographe, from the Greek word for movement (kinema) and drawing (grapheca). Paul and the Lumières projected their motion pictures onto a screen. This meant many people at once could watch a large image, and do so while seated. Not surprisingly, this motion picture experience proved more popular than Edison's kinetoscope. Edison unveiled his competing projector in April 1896, creating a tremendous stir. Photography itself was still relatively new; motion pictures were an experience no one had a comparison for. Short films of dancers and breaking waves were enough to fill audiences with amazement.

Though the basic machinery for motion pictures had been invented, the inventors realized that people would not be satisfied for long with the sheer novelty of the experience. Motion picture equipment was like a computer without any software. To make the invention useful, its software—namely interesting motion pictures—needed to be created.

French theater director and magician Georges Méliès (1861-1939) became the first true master of cinematic techniques during the 1890s. He filmed theater acts, but changed them to fit the motion picture format, arranging objects and backgrounds for the camera. He invented special effects, doing things like stopping the camera, changing the scenery and turning the camera back on. He discovered the fade in and fade out, wherein the scene gradually goes dark or comes up from darkness, and used them as a transition between scenes. Méliès used painted cut-outs and backdrops in his studio to enhance the fantasy effect created by his trick photography.

His A Trip to the Moon, (1902) became the first internationally successful motion picture, and the first science fiction film. In such work, Méliès showed how much the new medium could do beyond showing real events passing in front of a camera. Following his

example, others turned to telling stories with motion pictures, and they quickly became more sophisticated. The first Western, Edwin S. Porter's The Great Train Robbery, (1903) used a camera that moved with the action, rather than being fixed. It even included shots using a camera on a moving train. The popularity of these motion pictures spurred others to use similar techniques. Gradually the motion picture evolved its own visual language.

As the public began spending money to see films, motion picture distribution networks sprang up. Middlemen bought films and rented them to theaters that did not want to buy them outright. In 1907, over 100 distributors did business in the United States alone. A Pittsburgh firm created the nickelodeon when it began charging patrons five cents to watch a series of short motion pictures. The formula proved so successful that nickelodeons spread throughout the country. By 1908, motion pictures were becoming a large and rapidly changing business. A group of filmmaking studios and distributors, along with Edison, formed the Motion Pictures Patent Company to regulate copyrights, patents, and royalties. The group tried to take over the motion picture industry, but by 1910 of about 9,000 U.S. theaters, only half were licensed. These theaters used films by independent filmmakers and distributors.

The Patent Co. kept its actors anonymous to prevent them from becoming personally important and therefore able to command higher salaries. But an independent studio, the Independent Moving Picture Company, lured away a star, revealed that her name was Florence Lawrence, and gave her publicity. This started what became known as the star system, in which the primary actors were as, or more, important than whatever story was being told. Other stars followed, including Charlie Chaplin in the late 1910s. The importance of stars continues to this day. Some, such as Marilyn Monroe, have become mythic figures in modern culture.

By 1914 the Patent Co. collapsed as the more innovative independents grew. Motion pictures became longer and more ambitious. Film companies like Fox, Universal, Paramount, and MGM sprang up. Nickelodeons proved too small for the vast popularity of motion pictures, and were replaced by new theaters, some with thousands of seats and elaborate decor.

Sound joins the image

The ability to reproduce sound already existed in phonographs. Many tried unsuccessfully to link them to films. A workable system to join sound and motion pictures proved complex, and required a great deal of research money. American Telephone and Telegraph, the largest corporation in the U.S., worked on the problem through its Western Electric branch. A 1924 sound-on-a-disc system was at first rejected by the motion picture studios as too expensive. However, Warner Brothers, looking for an advantage over its rivals, finally accepted it anyway, investing millions of dollars in theaters and sound equipment.

The first motion picture with sound, *The Jazz Singer,* starring Al Jolson, became a huge hit. Warner Brothers instantly became one of the biggest forces in the motion picture industry. Its success forced rival studios to adapt sound. The cost of doing this, coming at the beginning of the Great Depression, left banks with a great deal of power in the film industry.

A rival sound system, developed by General Electric and the Radio Corporation of America, put the soundtrack on the film itself, running it in a track next to the images. Since the pictures and their soundtrack were linked on the film, they could never get out of synchronization. This system was also easier to set up. After intense competition and many lawsuits over patent rights, this system beat the sound-on-a-disc system.

Sound remained difficult to record during filming because the recording equipment was large and noisy. In the late 1940s, new magnetic recording techniques allowed sound to be recorded onto tape. This smaller, quieter system allowed sound to be recorded right on the film set.

Color comes to film

In the earliest days of motion pictures, color film had not yet been invented. Some films were colorized by hand, but that soon proved impractical. Color film first came out in the mid-1930s. It used three layers of colored film to reproduce the visual spectrum. Because color film was expensive and required precise control of lighting, black and white film remained the standard until the mid-1950s. Color and black-and-white were both used until the late 1960s, when color became the standard. This was partly because many films were sold for television broadcast after appearing in theaters, and black-and-white films were much harder to sell for television.

Later film history

In the 1920s and 1930s, motion pictures became a big business in the U.S., and most were produced like products on an assembly line. Often, Hollywood films did not have distinct personalities. They instead fit into genre types: western, musical, horror, gangster, and comedy. Exceptions, like Orson Welles' *Citizen Kane*

(1941), were rare. In Europe, motion pictures remained a smaller scale business that was also seen as an art. In 1925, the London Film Society was founded to promote motion pictures as an art form.

After World War II ended in 1945, the power of the Hollywood studios declined. Partly this came from a ruling by the U.S. Supreme Court that the studios had an illegal monopoly because they controlled the production, distribution, and showing of motion pictures. As a result, the studios were forced to sell their theaters. Foreign motion picture industries grew stronger, and started their own distribution systems, such as France's annual Cannes Film Festival. France, Italy, Sweden, and Japan all produced important and successful motion pictures.

Perhaps more than anything else, the rise of television changed the motion picture industry. People who could view visual entertainment at home for free were less likely to travel to a theater and pay money to see a film. The motion picture studios initially resisted the showing of their films on TV. By the mid-1950s, however, many studios were selling and renting their films to TV networks. To lure consumers to theaters, filmmakers began using technology to make seeing a film in a theater a more exciting experience.

One technology was Cinerama, popular in 1952, in which three separate projectors showed their images on a large, nearly semicircular screen. Six speakers provided stereo sound. Though initially popular, this medium required large theaters and expensive equipment. It proved economically unfeasible. CinemaScope, invented in the 1920s but not exploited until the 1950s, used special lenses to squeeze a wide-screen image onto normal 35 mm film. Another lens, put onto the projector, unsqueezed the image. The result was a wide-screen image that required theaters to invest less than $20,000. CinemaScope proved popular, and films like *A Star is Born* were made using it. The compression and decompression resulted in a blurry, grainy image, however. A better solution for wide screen was to use 70 mm film, as in MGM's "Oklahoma." After the success of this film, most major studios created a version of the 70mm process. Wide screen processes are still being developed, such as the OMNIMAX, which uses a special screen in the shape of a dome.

Equipment

Camera

In photography the exposure of film can be controlled by changing the amount of light entering the lens, or the amount of time the shutter remains open. The shutter speed in a motion picture camera is controlled by the fact that 24 frames must be shot per second. No exposure can be longer than 1/24th of a second. Motion picture cameras use a shutter that looks like a rotating propeller with two blades. The propeller can be made wider to decrease the percentage of time the lens is open, and thereby shorten exposures.

The pull-down mechanism, invented at the end of the 19th century, moves the film through the camera, holds it still in position for 1/24th of a second while the exposure is made, then moves the film to the next frame. It does this in perfect synchronization with the revolving shutter that exposes the film.

Early motion picture cameras were large and heavy. But by the mid-1950s, technology developed during World War II lead to smaller, lighter cameras that even allowed cinematographers to hold the smallest cameras. This freed the cameras from a tripod, allowing for more innovative camera work. For moving camera effects, cameras can be put on platforms that are attached to rubber wheels or steel rails like railroad tracks. They can also be raised and lowered on cranes.

Projector

At the end of the process, every motion picture goes through a projector. From the advent of sound until the mid-1970s projectors changed little. The system a projector uses for moving the film is similar to that used by a motion picture camera. A pull-down mechanism moves the film through the projector, while a rotating shutter only emits light while a frame is in position. The primary problem in making a projector was to provide a light source bright enough to enlarge a film frame enough to fill a theater screen-as much as 300,000 times-yet small enough to fit inside a projector.

The solution found to this problem, the carbon arc lamp, was used until the 1970s. These lamps used two carbon rods with a small gap between them. A strong electric current jumped the gap, creating a strong white light. These lamps needed constant adjustment, however, as well as a ventilation system. Most were replaced in the 1970s and 1980s by lamps using the inert gas xenon.

The projector also reads the soundtrack through a separate reader placed immediately after the lens. The soundtrack can be a magnetic strip or light pattern that runs along the side of the film. This light pattern, called optical sound, was the only system of sound reproduction until advances in magnetic tape recording in the 1950s. While soundtracks are now recorded and edited with magnetic tape or digitally, optical sound is often used on motion pictures because it can be printed right along with the images, and because so many theaters only have optical-sound equipment.

To record optical sound, sound waves are translated into electrical impulses, which in turn control a light beam that creates a photograph on a piece of film. When the optical soundtrack is played back, it passes before a lamp that projects its patterns onto a photoelectric cell. These intensities of light are converted into electrical impulses, then sound, which is amplified and sent to the speakers.

Producing a motion picture

Motion picture production has three primary stages: pre-production, production and post-production. Pre-production gets underway when financing is secured. It involves finishing a script, finalizing the cast and crew, deciding on how various shots will tell the story of the film, and figuring out locations. A detailed budget is created. Good pre-production work saves a great deal of time and money. It lays the groundwork for a smooth and efficient production.

In production, sets are built, locations are prepared and lit, and the actual filming takes place. Each aspect of film production can get intensely specialized. For example, there are many kinds of microphones, each with advantages and disadvantages. The sounds they pick up can be recorded onto many kinds of magnetic tape using a variety of tape recorders.

During filming, after optimal lighting has been determined, and other variables worked out, many shots are taken of each scene. To help quickly judge if shots were successful, a video image is often made simultaneously. It can be reviewed immediately, and decisions about how to change the next take of the scene can be made.

What happens when the filming is finished

The final phase of making a motion picture, post-production begins after the film footage has been shot, and results in the finished product. Post-production consists of editing, sound mixing, and special effects.

Editing is the process of putting camera shots together in a way that tells the story in an interesting manner. A camera shot is a piece of continuously shot film without a break in the action. Most motion-pictures consist of hundreds or thousands of such shots. Each shot may be filmed many times. The editor compares these shots and chooses one. Shots and soundtracks are compared and combined on editing tables that allow the comparison of as many as six film and sound tracks. Digital editing systems first came out in the 1980s.

Their use accelerated in the 1990s as computer technology rapidly improved. In digital editing a digital copy is made of all the shots for a motion picture. Using computers, editors can then try out various combinations of shots and edits. When a final version is selected, the editor can cut the actual pieces of film to create a motion picture that is put together just like the digital version.

Sound editing benefited from the explosion of recording technology associated with the music business. The advent of the multiple track magnetic recorder gave sound editors the ability to mix sounds together with a great deal of control and creativity. They could fade in a background sound like a rain storm in the same way that their counterpart in the music business might fade in a guitar solo. By the late 1970s, sound editors could use up to 16 separate tracks of sound, and each could have electronic effects added to it. In the 1980s, digital sound offered even more control.

Because the sound is initially recorded on a separate tape, it has to be synchronized with the film. An electronic timing pulse is used which controls the speed of the motors for the soundtrack and film mechanisms. Recording and editing the soundtrack can be almost as complex as filming the visuals. It has many components including dialogue, music, ambient sounds, and sound effects. The sound of a door slamming, for instance, is usually recorded separately in a sound studio, and may actually be the sound of a hammer striking a piece of metal.

Special effects

Special effects have always been one of the chief attractions of motion pictures. Special effects are generally created through animation, miniatures, or matte shots. Animation is any process whereby frames are shot individually. This can range from cartoons to sequences in which objects appear to move because the camera was stopped, the object was moved a little, and then another frame was taken. Computer-based special effects in which an object or face changes into another are also rendered one frame at a time.

Illusions of reality are created by paintings, miniatures, and false backgrounds. Miniatures are small models used for everything from the cities stepped on in Godzilla films to the space ships and buildings used in science fiction films. One of the most common special effects is a false background. In many motion pictures, the scenes of characters in a moving car are shot in a studio, using another film being projected onto a screen behind the action as a background. In older films, this projector was set behind a translucent screen and projected its images onto it from behind the action. This is called rear projection. The motion picture camera and the projector were synchronized so that a frame was projected just as the camera recorded a frame.

This system did not work well with color film. It proved difficult to keep the amount of light on the subject and the background the same, and to give them the same color. So a new system, called front projection, was invented. In front projection, the false background is projected at the same angle from which the camera is shooting. A one-way mirror is placed in front of the camera. The projected image reflects off the mirror onto the action. The camera 'sees' through the clear side of the mirror. Because the camera sees from the same angle as the projected image, the actors' shadows, cast onto the background, are blocked from view by their bodies.

Slow and fast motion are accomplished by changing the rate at which frames are shot. Because film is projected at 24 frames per second, anything shot at a greater rate appears slowed down when projected at 24 frames per second. Anything shot at a slower rate seems to move faster than normal when projected. These 'special effects' have applications to motion pictures and to science. They make it possible to watch a flower growing and opening in 20 seconds, or to watch an explosion that takes 10 seconds instead of one. Watching actions slowed down is often an advantage to those studying the behavior of people or animals.

The combination of computer technology with motion picture technology has given filmmakers the ability to create increasingly elaborate special effects. Animation and graphics can be created entirely by computer. These computer-generated images can then be combined with live-action footage through a process called analog image synthesis. Using a video camera, images on film are scanned into a computer. Once in the computer, the images can be easily manipulated, and then converted back into film. Films such as Steven Spielberg's *Jurassic Park* made extensive use of this technology to create the illusion of dinosaurs interacting with people onscreen.

A similar process called digital compositing uses the computer-scanning technique to manipulate live-action footage as well as animation. With it, a filmmaker can make it appear that an object or face changes into another. These effects are rendered one frame at a time. Computer technology has also advanced the area of puppetry, models, and miniatures. Miniature replicas are made of larger-than-life models. The two are then connected to a computer that plots their movements so that when the miniature is moved in a particular way, the full-size model moves in the same way. Innovations such as these ensure the continued development of motion picture technology.

See also Photography.

Further Reading:

Bernstein, Steven, *Film Production*. 2nd ed, Oxford, England: Focal Press, 1994.
Bordwell, David, and Kristin Thompson. *Film Art: An Introduction*. 4th ed. New York: Mcgraw-Hill, 1993.
Monaco, James, *How to Read a Film*. New York: Oxford University Press, 1977.
Stanley, Robert H., *The Celluloid Empire*. New York: Hastings House, Publishers, 1978.

Scott M. Lewis

Moundbuilders

The megapodes, or moundbuilders, are a fascinating group of birds found in Australia, New Guinea and its surrounding islands, eastern Indonesia, and the Philippines. Also known as "thermometer birds," scrubfowl, or brush turkeys, 22 species are recognized (seven genera) in the family Megapodiidae. A wide range of habitats are occupied by these species, ranging from semi-arid scrublands of Australia to tropical rain forests of Indonesia.

Megapodes are largely ground-dwelling birds, but many seek refuge in low branches if alarmed or threatened by predators. Most species feed on a wide range of insects, worms, snails, seeds and berries. With few exceptions, megapodes are dull colored birds: the plumage is generally dark brown and black or grey in appearance. All are about 20 in (50 cm) in total length, with large rounded wings and a medium-long tail. The legs and feet are sturdy, while the head is small. The head and neck of brush turkeys are bare apart from several coarse hairs.

One of the most unusual features of these birds is their habit of not incubating their eggs directly. Instead, they have devised a range of ingenious techniques which enables them to be free of the hazardous task of sitting on a clutch of eggs for several weeks at a time. All species of megapodes have evolved different means of overcoming this burden, but they all rely on the use of natural resources to heat and incubate their eggs. The scrubfowl (*Megacephalon*) display one of the simplest techniques: a nest site is carefully chosen and dug on a beach, often black volcanic ash or sandy soil exposed to the sun, where the female lays up to 30 eggs. When covered, the heat of the sand is sufficient to incubate the eggs and the parent birds have no further responsibility at the nest site. When the chicks hatch, they dig their own way out of the nest and quickly seek shelter in surrounding vegetation. Most can fly within 24 hours of emerging from the nest. Another simple manner of laying a clutch is seen in *M. freycinet*, which lives on islands off the Queensland coast in Australia and lays its eggs in simple cracks in exposed rocks, the sun's radiation being enough to incubate the eggs.

A far more complex ritual is practiced by forest-dwelling megapodes which may construct large mounds (measuring up to 33 in or 10 m in diameter and 16 ft or 5 m in height) of earth and vegetable material. Several pairs of birds may cooperate in the construction of such large incubating chambers. Once the mound has been constructed the male birds carefully monitor the inside temperature by probing the mound with their beaks. In addition to any solar radiation, as the vegetation decomposes in the warm, moist environment of the forest, it gives off heat, thereby providing ideal conditions for incubation. If the temperature is too high, the male removes some of the material and mixes the contents to allow air to circulate; similarly if it is too cool, additional materials may be added to the pile. The ideal temperature is thought to be in the region of 90-95°F (32-35°C). Only when the males are satisfied that the mound has reached a correct and stable temperature will the females begin to lay. Once they have done so, the males continue to monitor the daily temperature, until such time as the chicks emerge.

Megapodes and humans have always had a close relationship: although some adult birds are killed for food, it is their eggs that are the real treasure and these have been collected for food throughout history. While some species lay individual clutches of up to 30 eggs, others lay communally and often in very large numbers, particularly the maleo (*Macrocephalon maleo*), Moluccan megapode (*Eulipoa wallacei*), Polynesian megapode (*Megapodius pritchardii*) and the Melanesian megapode (*Megapodius eremita*). At some of these sites, tens of thousands of eggs may be laid each year. These offer ideal facilities for villagers to collect the eggs for food or trade purposes. While this exploitation was once carried out in a sustainable manner—many villages set strict quotas on the number of eggs that could be taken from individual mounds at a time—such practices have now largely disappeared. Continuing collection, as well as habitat loss and degradation from logging operations and agriculture which degrade the bird's habitat have, in many cases, now reduced local populations to the point that the harvest is no longer sustainable.

While human offtake and habitat loss have certainly played a major role in the demise of many species, many megapodes have also suffered as a result of ground predation. All of these species evolved in regions where the threat of ground predators was absent or very low. In recent decades, however, many species have been introduced by humans, particularly cats, dogs, rats and foxes, which have had a disastrous effect on many megapode populations. Introduction of feral predators is known to have decimated several populations in many Polynesian islands, leading to local extinctions. Other species, such as the Polynesian megapode on Niuafo'ou Island and the Tonga are also threatened by natural events, such as potential volcanic eruptions.

See also Extinction; Predator.

Mounds, earthen

Mounds are artificially constructed heaps or banks of earth built to contain sacred objects. Their basic construction is the same all over the world: a pit is dug and lined, and the sacred contents are deposited and covered with earth. Sometimes these objects are sprinkled with red ocher, a pigment used to make paint, perhaps as a way to revive the spirits thought to dwell within them.

If we were to go for a walk on an open plain in Illinois or Ohio and were to come across one of these "dirt piles," we probably would ignore it. But the archaeologist would be thrilled to find a sacred mound, for it might conceal vital clues to the ancient past of Native America: human and animal bones, weapons, ornaments, and mysterious clay figurines.

Some of the oldest and largest mounds in the world are found in America. The older North American mounds are cone-shaped and can reach heights of 70 ft (21 m) or more. Some of the more recent mounds are shaped like animals, people, or abstract forms and are therefore known as "effigy" mounds because they symbolize another object. No one knows what the effigy mounds were used for. Some archaeologists believe that they functioned as totem poles. As with totems, a few human bones were buried within the effigy mounds for their symbolic value. Found mostly in Wisconsin, Minnesota, Iowa, and Illinois, effigy mounds are shaped like deer, turtles, snakes, eagles, foxes, bears, birds, and human beings. Today the Great Serpent Mound winds along a river near a public park in Peebles, Ohio, for a distance of over 1 mi (1.6 km), its head recoiling as if to snatch into its hungry jaws a frog or other mysterious oval-shaped object. An enormous bird mound at Poverty Point, Louisiana, faces westward, its wings outstretched in a symbolic moment of flight.

Tens of thousands of mounds are found in the United States. Many more originally must have existed. Saint Louis was the location of so many sacred mounds that it was once known as Mound City; today just one of those mounds remains. A great number of mounds have been bulldozed into the ground, their contents either thoughtlessly pirated by treasure hunters or casually destroyed.

Most mounds were used for burials, but a significant number, built in the vicinity of the Mississippi River about 700 A.D. and later, were known as Temple Mounds. They looked like flat-topped pyramids crowned with wooden temples.

Who built the North American mounds? Archaeologists believe that they were the product of two ancient Native cultures: the Adena and the Hopewell.

Burial mounds

The Adena culture (c. 2800 B.C.-100 A.D.)

The Adena people probably were descended from archaic native Americans who inhabited parts of America in 3,000 B.C. Found primarily near Chillicothe, Ohio, but also located throughout north Kentucky, West Virginia, Indiana, and Pennsylvania, the Adena built conical mounds averaging 10-20 ft (3-6 m) in height. In the simplest form of Adena burial, the body was placed in a shallow pit lined with clay or bark and covered with layers of different-colored soils. As time went on, the Adena returned to the same burial mounds, added more burials on top of them, and covered them with fresh soil. This process went on for several generations until the mounds got to be enormous, some reaching heights of over 50 ft (15 m).

Some of the higher-ranking members of Adena society were given special burials. Their bodies were wrapped in cloth, sprinkled with red ocher, and placed in specially constructed thatch houses. Sometimes the burials were accompanied by grave goods—personal possessions such as weapons and tools, left there for use in the afterlife. The houses were then burned, and mounds were constructed over the charred remains.

The Hopewell culture (c. 2,300 B.C.-c. 400 A.D.)

Probably descended from the Adena tradition, the Hopewell culture originated in southern Illinois. Major Hopewell settlements are also found in Ohio, as well as New York, Ontario, Louisiana, Mississippi, Alabama, Tennessee, Georgia, and Florida.

Like Adena mounds, Hopewell mounds are conical, but some are also dome-shaped. They average 20-30 ft (6-9 m) high and are often found in clusters enclosed by artificially constructed ridges that may be circular, square, or octagonal. Mounds often were part of large social and religious complexes built on elevated areas, usually near a river valley. Because of their enormous size, their construction often required hundreds of workers, who laboriously scooped the earth with clamshell hoes and large animal bones and then carried it back to the mound in baskets and skin aprons. Many of these workers may have been women.

Most Hopewell were cremated, with burial usually reserved for higher-ranking members of society. When it came time for the funeral ceremony, the body was clothed in colorful garments covered with pearls, beer-teeth buttons, and other ornaments. Around the body were placed elaborate grave goods: cups made from giant sea snails; platform pipes decorated with birds of prey, beavers, cougars, toads, or bears; geometric or animal shapes carved out of mica (a silicon-containing mineral that divides into thin, partially transparent layers); panpipes; weapons; and many other objects. Wood carvings were deliberately broken, perhaps as a form of ceremonial sacrifice. Members of the deceased's family may also have been ritually sacrificed and buried at his side, to accompany him on his journey to the next world.

The Hopewell also continued the practice of placing bones in mortuaries known as charnel houses, some extending for more than 200 ft (61 m) and containing individual compartments. The houses were then burned, and a mound was constructed over the remains.

Temple mounds

Flat-topped pyramidal temple mounds are found in southern Mississippi, as well as Georgia, Oklahoma, Wisconsin, and probably beyond. Reaching 70-80 ft (21-24 m) in height, they were built in clusters, often around a central plaza. Many of them have log stairways or ramps leading up the sides to the temple, which was constructed of mud and thatch and may have housed an eternal flame.

The most famous temple mound complex is the Cahokia Mound site in southern Illinois. Covering more than 16 acres (6.4 ha), Cahokia Mound is larger than the largest pyramid in Egypt. It contains as many as 67 mounds. Monk's Mound, the largest of these at more than 50 ft (15 m) high, was the site of the temple that was probably was occupied by the ruling family. Its construction may have required more than 300 years of labor and more than 22 million cubic feet of earth.

Also at the Cahokia site is a mysterious structure known as Woodhenge. Similar to Stonehenge in construction, it consisted of a circle of red cedar posts that may have been used as a solar calendar by the priests to mark off specific astronomical events. These would have included the two annual equinoxes and the winter and summer solstices. The equinox is the point at which the center of the sun crosses the celestial equator and day and night are of equal length. The solstice is the point at which the sun is at its greatest distance form the celestial equator and appears to be farthest north or south in the sky. Knowledge of these events helped the priests to determine when to plant crops.

High-ranking members of society continued to be buried in the temple mounds with an elaborate accompaniment of grave goods, including a copper mask of the "long-nosed God," similar to that made by the ancient Maya. Most people, however, were buried in cemeteries outside the cities.

The decline of mound building

After 1400, mound building in North America came to a mysterious end. Flood, famine, or disease may have swept through the Native communities,

KEY TERMS

. . . .

Carbon 14—A radioactive isotope of carbon that decays at a uniform rate in living matter, used to determine the age of archaeological finds.

Charnel house—A building where dead bodies or bones are kept.

Effigy mound—A mound constructed to represent a living being or an abstract shape.

Exavation—The step-by-step removal of buried objects at an archaeological site.

Grave goods—Personal possessions, such as weapons and tools, buried with the deceased for use in the afterlife.

At the Cahokia site, researchers at the University of Southern Illinois at Edwardsville are using subsoil remote sensors. Linked to aboveground computers, the sensors relay electrical readings that determine the composition of the underground objects on the basis of their electrical properties.

Further Reading:

Jennings, Jesse D. *Prehistory of North America*. 3d ed. Mountain View, CA: Mayfield, 1989.

Mound Builders and Cliff Dwellers. Alexandria, VA: Time-Life Books, 1992.

Myron, Robert. *Mounds, Towns and Totems: Indians of North America*. Cleveland and New York: World Publishing Company, 1966.

Christine Molinari

claiming the lives of many of the mound builders. A widely accepted explanation holds that the decline in mound building was a reaction against a terrifying religious revival known as the Southern Death Cult. Its obsession with death is displayed in horrifying grave goods, including weeping masks, and skulls engraved with spiders, centipedes, and frightening figures that are a combination of humans, animals, and serpents.

Excavation techniques

Objects are removed from a mound in a systematic process of mapping and retrieval known as excavation. To begin excavating a mound, an archaeologist may dig a trench around the periphery and proceed to dig in pie-wedged sections, exposing each successive layer of burial. The area is sketched and photographed, and the location of each individual object recorded. Skeletal remains are examined for position (for example, extended or flexed) and for the direction of the burial along the cardinal points (north, south, east, or west).

After removal from the mound, objects are assigned a date according to one of several procedures, the most common of which is carbon-14 dating. Carbon-14 (or radiocarbon) is a radioactive isotope that is present in the atmosphere and absorbed into the tissues and bones of all living things. After death, carbon-14 is no longer absorbed but begins to decay to nitrogen at a fixed rate, or half-life, of approximately 5,730 years. Because carbon-14 decays at this fixed rate, an estimate of the age of an object can be made based on the rate of decay of its radiocarbon.

New methods of excavation are being developed to avoid disturbing the underground contents of mounds.

Mountain

A mountain is a large-scale topographic feature that is set apart from the local landscape by being much higher in elevation (topographic means having to do with the shape of the land surface).

Relative size of mountains

Mountains are taller than hills, but the distinction between hills and mountains is decided entirely by the people that live near them.

Thus, distinguishing mountains from smaller topographic features is partly a matter of perception, rather than of scientific measurement and comparison to a known standard. Absolute elevation above sea level does not make a high point into a mountain nearly so much as local relief does (relief is the difference between topographic high spots and low spots). In a landscape with thousands of feet or more of local relief, a feature several hundred feet tall would be considered an insignificant hill, whereas in Holland, it would be considered a mountain of the first order. Mountains of 4,000 ft (1,219 m), 10,000 ft (3,048 m), and 16,000 ft (4,877 m) may look vastly different on a map, but look equally large when observed in their local environment.

Duration of mountains

Mountains, like every other thing in the natural world, go through a life cycle. They rise, from a variety of reasons, and wear down over time, at various rates.

Although humans have always used mountains to represent eternity, individual mountains do not last very long in the powerfully erosive atmosphere of the earth. Mountains on the waterless worlds of Mars and the moon are billions of years old, but Earth's peaks begin to fracture and dissolve as soon as their rocks are exposed to air. The permanent part of a mountain range is not the shape taken by the rocks at the surface, but the huge folded shapes that the rocks were deformed into by the original orogenic event. (Orogeny is the process of mountain formation.)

Throughout their almost four-billion year history, the continents have been criss-crossed by many immense ranges of mountains. Most of the mountain ranges in the planet's history rose and wore away at different times, a long time ago. Where did these mountains go?

A range of mountains may persist for hundreds of millions of years, like the Appalachians. At several different times, the warped, folded rocks of the Appalachians were brought up out of the continent's basement and raised thousands of feet by tectonic forces. In order to stand for any considerable length of geologic time, a mountain range must experience continuous uplift. A tectonically quiet mountain range will wear down from erosion in a few million years. In North America's geologic past, for example, eroded particles from its mountains were carried by streams and dumped into the continent's inland seas, some of which were as large as the present-day Mediterranean. Those rivers and seas are gone from the continent, but the sediments that filled them remain, like dirt in a bathtub when the water is drained. The roots of all the mountain ranges that have ever stood in North America still exist, and much of the sand and clay into which the mountains were transformed still exists also, as rock or soil formations. This is true of all the continents of Earth.

Plate tectonics, the force that builds mountains

Orogeny is the process of mountain formation. Plate tectonics is the main force of nature responsible for orogeny. This continent-building process may be simply explained:

The Earth is covered with a thin, brittle crust. Below the crust is the mantle, a region where solid rock below a certain depth stretches like rubber.

The crust floats on top of Earth's mantle like the crust of grease that forms on top of a pot of chili or chicken broth in the refrigerator.

The Earth's crust has been broken into pieces, called plates.

The motion of a tireless heat engine that swirls and stirs within the earth's mantle, moves the plates.

Isostasy: The thicker parts of the continents float higher than the thinner parts, and any process that thickens the continental crust will bring about the uplift of the thickened portion. Continental crust "floats" in the mantle, and can be compared to the way an ice cube floats in water. An ice cube floats because it is lighter per unit volume than water—that is, ice is less dense than liquid water. The ice cube may weigh a few ounces, and rise a centimeter above the water's surface. An iceberg might weigh millions of tons, but float a hundred feet out of the water, because although it is vastly heavier than the ice cube, it is still less dense than water per unit volume—it floats. The more there is of it, the higher it floats. Similarly, any mass of continental crust, no matter how thick, is still less dense per unit volume than the mantle rock beneath it. Thus the edge of the continent begins rising to a higher elevation, and mountains begin to form.

Mountains are generated both at the edges of plates, and within plates. Other processes, such as sedimentation and erosion, modify the shape of the land that has been forged by plate tectonics.

Types of mountains

ISLAND ARCS. When the edge of a plate of Earth's crust runs over another plate, forcing the lower plate deep into Earth's elastic interior, a long, curved mountain chain of volcanos usually forms on the forward-moving edge of the upper plate. When this border between two plates forms in the middle of the ocean, the volcanic mountains form a string of islands, or archipelago, such as the Antilles and the Aleutians. This is called an island arc.

CONTINENTAL ARCS. When the upper plate is carrying a continent on its forward edge, a mountain chain, like the Cascades or the Andes, forms right on the forward edge. This edge, heavily populated with volcanos, is called a continental arc.

COLLISIONAL MOUNTAIN BELT. A continent or island arc runs into a continent, shattering and deforming the rocks of the collision area, and stacking up the pieces into a mountain range. This is how the Appalachians, Alps, and Himalayas were formed: the rocks of their continents were folded just as flat-lying cloth folds when pushed. Imagine how much taller your school would be if it were squeezed by bulldozers so it remained the same length east to west as it is now, but from north to south measured the width of a school bus. The result would be a tall wall of compressed material, and that is just what a collisional mountain belt is.

Collisional mountain belts are one of three types of boundary between plates of the earth's crust, along with mid-ocean ridges and inter-plate strike-slip faults. Mountains rise relatively quickly, over a few million years, such as the Appalachians did more than 200 million years ago. As these mountains begin to erode, the topography continually changes and develops. Hard rock layers influence the development of streams, because they resist erosion and form the ridgetops in the mountain range.

One special type of orogeny that can happen during a continental collision is the rise of ophiolite mountains. On rare occasions the crust beneath the ocean floor fractures along the tectonically active coast of a continent, and oceanic crust is thrust up over the shore and forms mountains. This spectacular form of plate-tectonic backfire is not supposed to happen, yet it does often enough to have its own name: obduction, meaning over- (ob-) -leading (-duction). A piece of oceanic crust, and the mantle rock beneath it, is heaved up onto the land to form mountains. The Taconic Mountains that rose in upstate New York 430 million years ago were an obducted ophiolite, as are the uplands around Troodos in Cyprus.

Fault block mountains: When a continent-sized "layer cake" of rock is pushed, the upper layers can be pushed more readily than the lower layers. The easy-to-push upper layers split from the deeper rocks, and a broad sheet of the upper crust, a few miles thick, begins to move across the continent. This thrust sheet floats on fluid pressure between the upper and lower sections of the crust. The horizontal split in the crust that separates the motionless lower crust from the floating upper layers is called a detachment fault in English, or a *decollement* in French.

Like a hydroplaning tractor trailer (viewed in very slow motion), the upper fault block glides until it runs into something. When the thrust sheet runs into something that resists its forward motion, the detachment fault turns into a ramp, leading up to the surface. The moving layer of upper crust is pushed up the ramp-like fault, and the front of the fault block rises out of the ground. The mountains thrown up where the thrust fault reaches the surface are one kind of fault block mountains. The mountains of Glacier National Park slid along a thrust fault over younger rocks, and out onto the Great Plains. Chief Mountain, a remarkable square mountain in Montana, moved to where it is now by sliding out onto the prairie on a thrust fault. The broad, flat fault block it belonged to, called a thrust sheet, has long since disappeared, leaving Chief Mountain standing alone.

Another kind of fault block mountains comes from stretching of Earth's crust. As the crust stretches, it pulls apart, making long faults that run perpendicular to the direction of pulling. These faults grow and connect with each other, isolating mountain-sized, wedge-shaped fault blocks. Some of these fault blocks begin slipping downward between more stable blocks that still rest on a firm foundation of deep rock. The stable blocks are called horsts, and the sinking blocks, that form valley floors, are called grabens.

MID-OCEAN RIDGE. The longest mountain chain on Earth, the mid-ocean ridge system is entirely under water. Twisting down the center of the Atlantic Ocean, it continues through the Indian and Pacific oceans. It is one of three types of boundary between plates of the crust, along with inter-plate strike-slip faults and collisional mountain belts. Along this ridge, lava continuously erupts, releasing heat from the planet's interior and extruding new strips of ocean floor.

STRATOVOLCANOS. Popocatepetl, Mt. Fuji, Vesuvius, and Mt. Ararat are all stratovolcanos. The prefix strato- refers to these mountains' characteristic layers, the result of alternately erupting ash and lava. Spectacularly tall and pointed, stratovolcanos may grow to an elevation of 2-3 mi (3.2-4.8 km) before collapsing. It is not certain that every stratovolcano collapses into a crater of superheated steam and molten rock. But the continents are dotted with the remains of these mountains' self-annihilations, some of whose like has not been witnessed in human history.

CINDER CONE. These volcanos build a pile of pyroclastic gravel and boulders (pyroclastic is derived from "fire"+"broken pieces") that forms a pointed or rounded cone. Because they are made of loose material, they quickly erode away unless further eruptions continue to build them.

SHIELD VOLCANOS. Often solitary volcanic mountains form as a volcano piles up rock above the ocean floor over millions of years. Hawaii, Bermuda, and the Canary Islands are shield volcanos. These islands, and others like them, are the work of hot spots (hot spot is a volcanically active site heated from below by a concentrated flow of heat out of the earth's mantle). Iceland is a hot spot that sits astride the mid-ocean ridge system. Shield volcanos also occur on continents, particularly in rift valleys where a continent is being ripped in two. Kilimanjaro is the classic example of a continental shield volcano. Olympus Mons on Mars is another classic shield volcano, and is the largest known mountain in the solar system.

VOLCANIC NECKS. In a cinder cone, lava rises through a vertical pipe before it erupts. The mountain resembles a huge pile of gravel. After an old cinder cone becomes extinct, the underground pipes that brought it lava from below solidify, and the pile of erupted material begins to wear away. Solid lava, usually a very hard rock, often fills the extinct volcano's vent. In a cinder cone, the solidified lava will resist the forces of erosion far longer than the ash, cinders, and other loose material of which the volcanic pile is made. Thus, as rain, wind, and frost scrub the soft exterior of the volcano away from the hard interior, a columnar mountain emerges. Shiprock, in New Mexico, and Devil's Tower, in Wyoming, are classic examples of these mountains, called volcanic necks.

EXPOSED PLUTONS. Plutons are masses of hard, visibly crystalline igneous rock that form deep in Earth's crust. Plutons rise through the earth's crust when they are molten, and freeze into solid rock far below the surface. Plutons can be as small as a highway roadcut, or as large as an entire mountain range. Mountains emerge from a landscape as erosive forces strip away the rocks that cover a pluton. A small pluton called a stock forms the granite core of Mount Ellsworth in southern Utah. The Sierra Nevada mountains are entirely made up of massed plutons, collectively called the Sierra Nevada batholith. The Yosemite Valley cuts into the solid granite interior of these mountains.

UNUSUAL VOLCANOS. A rare kind of mountain is the individual volcano with no known relationship to a volcanically active region. Solitary volcanos like these have erupted in tectonically quiet landscapes, such as east Texas of the Cretaceous period, and their cause remains a mystery.

Mesas are flat-topped mountains. They form when a solid sheet of hard rock sits on top of softer rock. The hard rock layer on top, called the "caprock," once covered a wide area. The caprock is cut up by the erosive action of streams. Where there is no more caprock, the softer rock beneath washes away relatively quickly. Mesas are left wherever a remnant of the caprock forms a roof over the softer rock below. A cuesta is a mesa that has been tilted, so the caprock forms a slope.

Inverted topography

When lava erupts from a volcano or fissure, it flows downhill like any other liquid, into low spots in the landscape. This is why a river valley makes a convenient path for a lava flow. When the lava has solidified in the lowest part of the valley, it may be harder than the rocks that form the valley's walls. So when

water again can flow through the valley, it flows around both sides of the lava flow. Eventually the lava flow has two valleys on either side of it, getting deeper every year. After thousands of years, a mesa will have been created, for the lava flow has become a caprock. This form of mesa is called inverted topography, because the low places become high places.

Outliers and monadnocks: Another term for a mountain made from a plateau worn by erosion is outlier. Not necessarily flat-topped, an outlier can be any hill or mountain left standing as the plateau with which it was once joined erodes farther and farther away. The Tepuis of Venezuela are outliers of a once-widespread plateau. A hard-rock mountain left standing after an entire mountain range has eroded away around it is a monadnock.

Weather effects of mountains

Mountains make a barrier for moving air. The wind pushes air, and clouds in the air, up the mountain slopes. The atmosphere is cooler at high elevations, and there is less of it: lower pressure makes it hard for lowland animals to get enough air to breathe. Dense masses of warm, moist air that move up and over a mountain swell as the air pressure confining them drops away. The air becomes colder in the same way as a pressurized spray can's contents become colder when the can's pressure drops rapidly. (The phrase that describes this phenomenon is adiabatic expansion.) Water that existed as a gas under the high pressure and temperature of the flatlands now condenses into cool droplets, and clouds form over the mountain. As the cloud continues to rise, droplets grow and grow, eventually becoming too heavy to float in the air. The clouds dump rain, and snow, on the mountain slopes. After topping the crest, however, the clouds may have no more moisture to rain on the other side of the mountain, which becomes arid. This rain shadow is best illustrated in the Sierra Nevada mountains of California, where tall redwood forests cover the ocean-facing side of the mountains, and Death Valley lies in the rain shadow.

Mountains' effect on evolution

Sometimes mountains can become refuges for species endangered by the drying climate, or other radical ecological change, in the surrounding lowlands. In this way mountains can influence a species' chances to live and prosper. Climatic "islands" like this may isolate one population from the rest of its species. Entire uncatalogued species of large animals have been found in the 1990s living in the mountains of southeast Asia. As generation succeeds generation, the genetic pattern that defines a population can change during its separation from the rest of its species. An isolated population may even become a species unto itself, unable to reproduce with the population from which it was once separated. This evolutionary phenomenon is called speciation, and mountain topography provides barriers between populations that have made speciation happen.

When the Grand Canyon was cut, speciation occurred in the squirrels that inhabit the high-altitude ponderosa pine forest of the southwest Colorado Plateau. The canyon's steep cliffs and desert terrain contained nothing for a squirrel to eat, so individual squirrels did not enter it. The squirrels stayed at home on the south rim or the north rim, and the populations ceased to interbreed with each other. The eventual result has been speciation: the north rim's Kaibab squirrel and the south rim's Abert squirrel have become separate species.

Mountains and humans

Transportation and communication are more difficult in mountains. Even today, mountain weather sometimes makes flying into mountains risky, and radio signals are blocked by the masses of stone. U.S. interstate highways close down due to snow, ice, and even rockfalls. The difficulty of operating in the mountainous countries of Afghanistan and Vietnam certainly affected the outcomes of the recent wars fought in those countries.

The thin, stony soil of mountain slopes possesses minimal value as farmland. Mountain meadows and forests provide a good pasture for grazing animals, however, and mountain people often practice pastoral agriculture. Herds of goats, cows, sheep, pigs, or llamas turn the upland vegetation directly into food and industrial products—wool, tallow, leather, and so on. But in order for farming and herding people to dwell in the mountains with any economic security, the population must remain low, to avoid using up all of the sparse resources.

Because of the difficulties mountains put in the way of in making a living at agriculture, mountain regions usually cannot support a prosperous agricultural tax base. People of mountain cultures, therefore, are used to being left alone by governments. These peoples' independent outlook is interchangeable around the world, whether they are Swiss, Papuan, Appalachian, or Jamaican Maroon. Language and customs from hundreds or thousands of years ago survive in remote mountains, preserved by the same geography that cut them off in the first place.

Unlike farmers, people of the world's industrial civilization can find in the mountains a great bounty of the resources they cannot live without. Geologic forma-

KEY TERMS

Collisional mountain belt—A mountain range that is built when two or more continents run into each other.

Fault block mountain—A mountain made of a mass of rock bounded by faults; that became a mountain as tectonic forces raised it up or lowered its surroundings.

Island arc—A string of volcanic mountains that emerge from the sea as islands.

Obduction—A geological "accident" wherein a piece of the oceanic crust gets put on top of the continental crust, as opposed to beneath it as usual.

Ore body—A geological formation in which an economically valuable mineral is concentrated.

Plate—One of the pieces into which Earth's crust is broken, which floats on top of the mantle, and is pushed around by tectonic forces.

Shield volcano—A broad, gently sloping volcanic mountain, often forming a solitary oceanic island, or located on land in a continental rift.

Stratovolcano—A large, steep-sided volcanic mountain, often located in an island chain (island arc) or on land in a series of volcanos along a tectonically active coast (continental arc).

Tectonic—Having to do with forces that fold and fracture the rocks of planets.

Thrust fault—A fault like a ramp, up which one fault block is pushed over another.

Thrust sheet—A slab of the crust that gets pushed up on top of a neighboring slab of crust.

Topography—The study of the shape of land surfaces. Also used to mean the shape of a land surface, as in "The topography of Switzerland is mountainous."

Uplift—An episode in the history of a region when tectonic forces lift the region's crust to a higher elevation.

Volcanic neck—A usually tall, steep mountain of lava rock that solidified in the volcano's throat, stopping up the volcano as it became extinct.

Volcano—A mountain that forms around a vent from which lava, ash, or other igneous rock is erupted.

tions of economically valuable minerals, called ore bodies, are left behind by the processes that make mountains. Mountain-building rearranges the formations that hold metal ores, coal, gemstones, asbestos, and other substances. These ore bodies come to rest near enough to the surface to be mined at a profit. Although many mining districts have been "mined out," this only means that the minerals that could be mined for a profit have been removed. The world's mountain ranges still contain vast amounts of economic minerals, out of sight under kilometers of rock. Present mining methods are too expensive to dig deep enough to process the great majority of them, however.

Broad, swift rivers drain mountains that receive large amounts of rain and snow. Dropping from the uplands, water rapidly accumulates kinetic energy (kinetic energy is the energy in a moving object). Hydroelectric power plants convert some of this energy into power, providing industries and cities with cheap, clean, and plentiful electric power. Mountainous Switzerland's hydroelectric power enabled it to become one of the world's leading industrial countries.

Further Reading:

Costello, D. *The Mountain World*. New York: Thomas Y. Crowell Company, 1975.

Crump, D., ed. *Mountain Worlds*. Washington, D.C.: The National Geographic Society, 1988.

George, U. "Tepuis—Venezuela's Islands in Time." *National Geographic* 175 (May 1989): 526-561.

Illustrated Atlas of the World. Chicago: Rand McNally & Company, 1992.

Mountain lion see **Cats**

Mousebirds

Mousebirds, or colies, are six species of nonmigratory birds of sub-Saharan Africa, making up the family Colidae. Their usual habitat is open brushlands, savannas, and forest edges.

Mousebirds are about 11-14 in (29-36 cm) long, at least one-half of which is made up of their long tail. This structure is composed of ten feathers of variable, but graduated length, the longest being in the center of the tail. Mousebirds have short, rounded wings, short legs, and stout feet with long toes and claws. If desired, all four of the toes can be directed forward, a rather unusual trait that can be utilized, for example, when the bird is

hanging from a twig as it forages. The beak is strong and somewhat hooked, and is useful for tearing the skin of tough fruits, allowing access to the edible interior.

The plumage of mousebirds is typically a subdued combination of grey or brown, with whitish and black markings. The legs are commonly red, and the head is conspicuously crested.

Mousebirds are gregarious animals, commonly roosting in tightly packed groups of as many as several dozen individuals. Mousebirds like to clamber and creep in trees as they forage, a habitat that undoubtedly contributed to the origin of their common name.

Mousebirds feed on fruits, seeds, tender plant shoots, and even leaves. Mousebirds are voracious feeders, and birds living in the vicinity of humans are sometimes regarded as local pests, because of significant damages they may cause to crops.

Mousebirds lay 2-4 eggs in a nest placed in a tree or shrub. Both parents share in the incubation of eggs, and in the care of their young. Sometimes several males help in the rearing of the same brood, and several females will occasionally lay eggs in the same nest, and share the incubation duties, sometimes brooding side-by-side.

The six species are: white-headed mousebird (*Colius leucocephalus*), chestnut-backed mousebird (*C. castanotus*), white-backed mousebird (*C. colius*), blue-naped mousebird (*C. macrourus*), bar-breasted mousebird (*C. striatus*), and red-faced mousebird (*C. indicus*).

Bill Freedman

MRI (magnetic resonance imaging) see **Nuclear magnetic resonance**

MSG see **Monosodium glutamate**

Mudfish see **Bowfin**

Mudflow see **Mass wasting**

Mudskippers see **Gobies**

Mulberry family (Moraceae)

The mulberry family occurs primarily in tropical and semi-tropical regions, and includes a wide variety of herbs, shrubs, and trees, characterized by a milky sap and reduced, unisexual flowers. This family includes 40 genera and 1,000 species, of which 500 species are members of the fig genus, *Ficus*. The Moraceae is a member of the order Urticales, class Magnoliopsida (the dicotyledons), division Magnoliophyta (flowering plants).

Flowers, fruits and leaves

Species of the mulberry family may be either monoecious or dioecious, depending on whether male and female flowers occur on the same plant (monoecious) or on separate plants (dioecious). Flowers of the Moraceae are in tightly packed groups, known as heads, spikes, catkins, or umbels. Fig flowers are produced inside a *synconium*, a hollow fleshy structure. The small flowers lack petals. Male flowers consist of four sepals, which are usually leaf-like appendages, and four stamens. Female flowers consist of four sepals and a pistil with a two-chambered ovary.

The fruit developed from a single female flower is either a fleshy drupe or a dry achene. The flowers fuse as they mature after fertilization, and a multiple fruit forms. The multiple fruit consists of small drupes or achenes grouped together in a single unit, and is usually round or oval shaped.

The best known fruit of the Moraceae is that of the common fig (*Ficus carica*), which has been cultivated for thousands of years. These cultivated figs develop without pollination, as this species does not produces male flowers. It is actually the synconium which is referred to as the fruit of the fig. In the case of fig varieties which are pollinated, the true fruit, an achene, develops inside the synconium. Figs are pollinated by wasps.

A wild form of the common fig, known as the *caprifig*, does produce male flowers. Pollen of the caprifig is sometimes used by fig breeders to fertilize female flowers of cultivated figs. In this process, known as *caprification*, a female gall wasp, carrying pollen from the caprifig, enters the synconium of a cultivated fig, where the pollinates the flowers, lay eggs, dies, and is absorbed by the synconium as the *fruit* develops. Figs produced by caprification are usually larger than cultivated fig fruits.

The fruits of some Moraceae, such as those from the jackfruit (*Artocarpus integra*), are very large, and can be up to 3 ft (1 m) long and weigh up to 99 lb (45 kg), although 44-55 lb (20-25 kg) is more common. Jackfruit leaves are much smaller than the fruits, usually 1.6 in (4 cm) or less.

Moraceae leaves occur in a variety of shapes and sizes. For example, breadfruit, (*Artocarpus communis*), has lobed leaves that reach 2 ft (61 cm) in length. The

Common fig (*Ficus carica*).

common fig also has deeply lobed leaves. Other species, such as the creeping fig (*Ficus pumila*), have cordate leaves that are much smaller, with entire margins. It is not unusual to find both lobed and unlobed leaves on the same plant, especially in mulberries (*Morus* spp.). Leaves can occur singly on the stem, on alternating sides. At the base of a young leaf's petiole is a pair of stipules, but these soon fall off and leave a small scar on the stem.

Species of the Maraceae may be evergreen, or they may have deciduous leaves that fall off at the end of the growing season.

Ecology, distribution and economic value

The family Moraceae was named after the mulberry, *Modus*. The red mulberry, (*Modus rubra*), is native to North America, where it occurs in moist woodlands. It produces a tasty, juicy fruit which is favored by birds, and although it is also good for people to eat, it is not economically important. The white mulberry, (*Modus alba*) is native to Asia. In China, leaves of the white mulberry are fed to cultivated silkworms, a type of moth larva. The white mulberry became naturalized in North America during unsuccessful attempts to establish a silk industry in colonial America. Unlike the native red mulberry, the white mulberry is somewhat weedy, and is often found around homes, in disturbed sites, along fencerows, and in moist, second-growth bottomlands. Fruits of the white mulberry may be white, pink, red, or deep purple. The dark purple fruits inspired the name (*Modus nigra*), although taxonomists have since determined this plant to only be a variety of *Modus alba*.

Similar in appearance to white mulberry, and also naturalized in the United States, is the ornamental shrub, paper mulberry (*Broussonetia papyrifera*), also

2412

native to Asia. This mulberry is shrubby, and may form thick colonies from root sprouts. Paper mulberry occurs around homes, fencerows, and disturbed sites. The bark of the paper mulberry is the source of tapa, a fiber used by Pacific islanders to make clothing.

The osage-orange, (*Maclura pomifera*), is a shrubby tree native to the Red River Valley of Texas, Oklahoma, and Arkansas. Like the mulberries, this species can propagate from root sprouts. The osage-orange is a thorny tree which bears a spherical, multiple fruit composed of achenes. The wood of this species is orange in color, and very strong. This wood was used by Native Americans to manufacture bows, and by early pioneers to make long-lasting fence posts and wagon wheels.

The genus *Artocarpus* includes the breadfruit and jackfruit, whose fruits are whose fruits are used in the Caribbean and South Pacific as food. As the name breadfruit implies, the fruit is starchy, when cooked similar in texture and taste to potatoes. Many tourists have eaten breadfruit while vacationing in the Caribbean, unaware that it wasn't potatoes. Breadfruit, native to parts of Asia and tropical Pacific islands, was to be brought to the Caribbean islands by Captain Bligh, of *Bounty* fame.

Species of the diverse fig genus, *Ficus*, take an assortment of forms. Some of the more unusual species include the strangler figs such as the banyan tree (*Ficus benghalensis*), which begins life as an epiphyte and sends down rope-like roots that eventually encircle and kill the host tree. A mature banyan trees is an impressive sight, with its large, spreading canopy, and numerous supporting trunks, often encircling a hollow cavity where the original host tree stood. The banyan tree is native to India, where it is considered sacred by Hindus. The bo tree, (*Ficus religiosa*), of India is believed to bring wealth and happiness to its owners. The bo tree is also considered sacred by Hindus, who believe their god Vishnu was born under one, and to Buddhists, who believe Gautama Buddha achieved nirvana while meditating under one of these trees.

Other important members of the fig genus are some popular horticultural species. The weeping fig, (*Ficus benjamina*), can be grown in pots into a small attractive tree with willowy branches and leaves. This species prefers bright light, moist soil, and a humid environment. The fiddleleaf fig, (*Ficus lyrata*), is a shrub with large leaves shaped like fiddles. The sap of the Indian rubber plant, (*Ficus elastica*), was once used to manufacture rubber. This species reaches tree proportions when cultivated as an ornamental in southern Florida.

KEY TERMS

Achene—A dry, indehiscent, one-seeded fruit, such as a sunflower "seed."

Cordate—Heart-shaped.

Naturalized—A non-native species which has become freely breeding beyond its natural range.

Synconium—The hollow, fleshy structure in figs which houses the flowers and is often incorrectly referred to as the fruit. The true fruit often has the achenes borne inside the synconium on the female flowers.

Unisexual—Flowers which bear either male or female reproductive organs.

Further Reading:

Duncan, W. H., and M. B. Duncan. *Trees of the Southeastern United States*. Athens, GA: University of Georgia Press, 1988.

Everett, T. H. *Living Trees of the World*. New York: Doubleday, 1968.

Godfrey, R. K. *Trees, Shrubs, and Woody Vines of Northern Florida and adjacent Georgia and Alabama*. Athens, GA: University of Georgia Press, 1988.

Mule see **Asses**

Multiple personality disorder

Multiple personality disorder (MPD) is a chronic and recurrent emotional illness. A person with MPD plays host to two or more personalities. Each identity has its own unique style of viewing and understanding the world and may have its own name. These distinct personalities periodically control that person's behavior as if several people were alternately sharing the same body. Because those diagnosed with multiple personality disorder often are not aware of the alternate personalities, called alters, inside themselves, they cannot account for blocks of time when these other identities control their memory, thinking, and behavior. In 1994 multiple personality disorder was renamed Disassociative Identity Disorder by the American Psychiatric Association.

History and incidence

Some psychologists and psychiatrists believe that instances of demon possession recorded over the centuries may have really been MPD, but the first complete account of a patient with multiple personality disorder was written in 1865. Four years later, French neurologist Pierre Janet discovered that a system of ideas split off from the main personality when he hypnotized his female patients. Soon afterward, William James, the father of American psychology, uncovered a similar phenomenon and termed the condition disassociation. In 1886, American author Robert Louis Stevenson popularized the disorder in his novel *The Strange Case of Dr. Jekyll and Mr. Hyde*. Although this work of fiction captured popular imagination, the concept of multiple personalities was rejected by Sigmund Freud and later by the behaviorists. The mental health community believed that the disorder was extremely rare if it existed at all.

Despite well-known movies such as *The Three Faces of Eve* and *Sibyl* which recounted the life stories of women with MPD, by the beginning of the last decade only about 200 cases had been documented in world psychiatric literature. Finally in 1980 the American Psychiatric Association officially recognized multiple personality disorder as a genuine emotional illness.

Today, MPD is a relatively popular diagnosis with 20,000 cases recorded between 1980 and 1990. Researchers currently believe that from 0.01-10% of the general population have this mental illness. MPD occurs from 3-9 times more frequently in women than in men. Some researchers believe that because men with MPD tend to act more violently than women, they are jailed rather than hospitalized and never diagnosed. Female MPD patients often have more identities than men, averaging 15 as opposed to males who average eight.

Because of the high number of MPD cases being diagnosed in the United States today, some professionals speculate that the diagnosis is culture-specific and caused by some unique characteristic of American society such as the high incidence of child abuse. Other experts, while not denying that MPD exists, believe that the high rate of MPD has been inflated by recent media attention focusing on criminal trials in which defendants use multiple personality disorder for the insanity defense. They also think that overly eager therapists may unknowingly encourage highly-suggestible patients to display symptoms during hypnosis. Experts who counter these assertions state that normal people cannot be taught, even under hypnosis, to imitate the measurable physical changes shown by those diagnosed with multiple personality disorder. They claim that in the past the condition was underreported, a situation now being corrected by a heightened awareness of the disease and its symptoms.

Causes of multiple personality disorder

Fifty-nine to ninety-eight percent of people diagnosed with multiple personality disorder were either physically or sexually abused as children. Many times when a young child is subjected to abuse, he or she spaces out or splits off from what is happening, becoming so detached that what is happening may seem more like a movie or television show than reality. This self-hypnotic state, called disassociation, is a defense mechanism which protects the child from thinking and from feeling overwhelmingly intense emotions. Disassociation walls these thoughts and emotions off so that the child is unaware of them. In effect, they become secrets, even from the child. According to the American Psychiatric Association, many MPD patients cannot remember much of their childhoods.

Not all children who are severely and repeatedly abused develop multiple personality disorder, but if the sexual or physical abuse is extreme and repeated disassociated clusters of thoughts and feelings may begin to take on lives of their own, especially when the child has no time or space in which to emotionally recover between abuses. Each cluster tends to have a common emotional theme such as anger, sadness, or fear. Eventually, as the walls of disassociation thicken, these clusters develop into full-blown personalities, each with its own memory and characteristics.

Some researchers believe that the reason why some abused children develop MPD may have a biological basis. Studies of how brain chemistry affects memory indicate that when an intensely traumatic experience occurs the brain's neurochemicals may be released in such large amounts that they influence the area of the brain responsible for memory to pigeonhole what is remembered into separate compartments. Depending on their individual brain chemistry, some human beings may be better able to disassociate than others. About a third of people with MPD have complex partial seizures of the right temporal lobe of the brain. Some researchers think that this form of epilepsy might also affect memory and be yet another cause for the disorder.

Although some studies show that the illness may be more common in first-generation relatives of MPD patients, there is no proof that the disorder is inherited.

Symptoms

A person diagnosed with multiple personality disorder can have as many as a 100 or as few as two separate personalities. (About half of the recently reported cases have 10 or fewer.) These different identities can resemble the main personality or they may be a different age, sex, race, or religion. Alters may resemble each other or be very unique. Each personality can have its own posture, set of gestures, and hairstyle, as well as a distinct way of dressing and talking. Some alters may speak in foreign languages or with an accent. Sometimes alternate personalities are not human, but are animals or imaginary creatures instead.

The process by which one of these personalities reveals itself and controls behavior is called switching. Most of the time the change is sudden and takes only seconds. Sometimes, however, it can take from hours or days. Switching is often triggered by something that happens in the patient's environment, but personalities can also come out under hypnosis or when the patient is given amyl nitrate (truth serum).

Sometimes the most powerful personality serves as the gatekeeper and tells the other weaker personalities when they may reveal themselves. Other times personalities fight each other for control. Most patients with MPD experience long periods during which the host personality, also called the main or core personality, remains in charge. During these times, their lives may appear normal.

When an alter dominates, however, chaos often reigns. Ninety-eight percent of people with MPD have some degree of amnesia when an alternate personality surfaces. When the host personality takes charge once again, the time spent under control of the alter is completely lost to memory. In some cases of MPD the host personality may remember confusing bits and pieces of the past. In some cases alters are aware of each other, while in others they are not.

Because alternate personalities are formed by childhood disassociation as a result of trauma, it is not surprising that 86% of people with MPD have one alter with a child's personality. Childhood and adolescent alters handle and act out emotions which the abused child could not such as rage or terror. Some act in very negative ways, avenging and persecuting the host personality to be self-destructive. Other alters, called internal self helpers, watch what is going on and give advice. Sometimes people with MPD describe these alters as seeing everything and feeling nothing. Other alternate personalities, however, act as friends.

One of the most baffling mysteries of multiple personality disorder is how alternate personalities can sometimes show very different biological characteristics from the host and from each other. Several personalities sharing one body may have different heart rates, blood pressures, body temperatures, pain tolerances, and eyesight abilities. Different alters may have unique reactions to medications. Sometimes a healthy host can

KEY TERMS

Alter—An alternate personality that has split off or disassociated from the main personality, usually after severe childhood trauma.

Disassociation—The separation of a thought process or emotion from conscious awareness.

Host—The main or core personality of a person with Multiple Personality Disorder, developing since the time of birth.

Hypnosis—A trance state during which people are highly vulnerable to the suggestions of others.

Personality—A group of characteristics that motivates behavior and set us apart from other individuals.

Trauma—An extremely severe emotional shock.

have alternate personalities with allergies and even asthma. An alter's blood glucose (sugar) may respond differently to insulin than the host's. Since studies done on people with such dramatically different alters have been small, no conclusions can be drawn and the puzzle remains to be solved.

Diagnosis and treatment

Most people with multiple personality disorder are diagnosed between the ages of 20 and 40. By that time they have been seeking help for their problems for an average of seven years and have usually been hospitalized several times. In some cases this happens because in addition to having multiple personality disorder, those who suffer from it are often anxious or depressed. In other cases, the rapid mood swings that occur when personalities switch can appear to be symptoms of bipolar illness, more commonly called manic depression. Finally, the voices of the personalities a person with MPD may report hearing are interpreted as the auditory hallucinations of schizophrenia.

Without treatment, MPD doesn't disappear by itself, although the rate of personality switching does seem to slow down in middle age. According to a 1993 study of 640 MPD patients, the most common treatment for MPD is long term psychotherapy twice a week. During these sessions, the therapist must develop a trusting relationship with the core personality and each of the alters. Once that is established, the emotional issues of each personality regarding the original child abuse are addressed. The host and alters are encouraged to communicate with each other in order to integrate or come together. Hypnosis is often a useful tool to accomplish this goal. At the same time, the therapist helps the patient to acknowledge and accept the physical or sexual abuse he or she endured as a child and to learn new coping skills so that disassociation is no longer necessary.

Usually this process takes place in the therapist's office.

About half of all people being treated for MPD require brief hospitalization, and only 5% are primarily or exclusively treated in psychiatric hospitals. According to the NIMH study, although sometimes mood altering medications such as tranquilizers or antidepressants are prescribed for MPD patients, they are often diagnosed as having anxiety or depression rather than the multiple personality disorder. The treatment of MPD lasts an average of four years.

Further Reading:

Braun, Bennett G. "Multiple Personality Disorder: An Overview." *The American Journal of Occupational Therapy* 44, No. 11 (1990): 971-976.

Cohen, Barry M., ed. *Multiple Personality Disorder from the Inside Out.* Baltimore: Sidran Press, 1991.

Curtin, Sharon Lynne. "Recognizing Multiple Personality Disorder." *Journal of Psychosocial Nursing* 31, No. 2 (1993): 29-33.

Putnam, Frank W. *Diagnosis and Treatment of Multiple Personality Disorder.* New York: Guilford Press, 1989.

Sizemore, Chris Costner. *A Mind of My Own: The Woman Who was Known as Eve Tells the Story of Her Triumph Over Multiple Personality Disorder.* New York: Morrow, 1989.

Weissberg, Michael P. *The First Sin of Ross Michael Carlson: A Psychiatrist's Personal Account of Murder, Multiple Personality Disorder, and Modern Justice.* New York: Delacorte Press, 1992.

Kay Marie Porterfield

Multiplication

Multiplication is often described as repeated addition. For example, the product 3×4 is equal to the sum, $4 + 4 + 4$, of three 4s. The law on which this is based is the distributive law — $a(b + c) = ab + ac$. In this instance, the law is applied to $4(1 + 1 + 1)$, which gives $4(1) + 4(1) + 4(1)$ or $4 + 4 + 4$.

When one or both of the multipliers are not natural numbers, the law still applies, $.4(1.2) = .4(1) + .4(.1)$ $.4(.1)$, but the terms of the sum are not simply "repeated," and other rules, such as the rules for placing the decimal point, are needed.

Of course one does not go all the way back to the distributive law every time he or she computes a product. In fact, much of the time in the early grades in school is devoted to building a multiplication table and memorizing it for subsequent use. In applying that table to products such as 12×23, however, one does make explicit use of the distributive law:

$$
\begin{array}{r}
12 \\
\times \quad 23 \\
\hline
36 \\
24 \\
\hline
276
\end{array}
$$

Here a is 12; b is 20; and c is 3.

In talking about multiplication, several terms are used. In 6×3, the entire expression, whether it is written as 6×3 or as 18, is called the "product." The 6 and the 3 are each called "multipliers," "factors," or occasionally "terms." The older words "multiplicand" (for the 6) and "multiplier" (for the 3), which made a distinction between the number which got multiplied and the number which did the multiplying have fallen into disuse. Now "multiplier" applies to either number.

Multiplication is symbolized in three ways: with an "$\times$," as in 6×3, with a centered dot, as in $6 \cdot 3$, and by writing the numbers next to each other, as in $5x$, $6(3)$, $(6)(3)$, or $(x + y)(x - y)$. This last way is usually preferred.

Multiplication is governed not only by the distributive law, which connects it with addition, but by laws which apply to multiplication alone. These laws appear in the table below.

Since arithmetic is done with natural numbers, some additional laws are needed to handle decimal fractions, common fractions, and other numbers which are not natural numbers:

Decimals: Multiply the decimal fractions as if they were natural numbers. Place the decimal point in the product so that the number of places in the product is the sum of the number of places in the multipliers. For example, $3.07 \times 5.2 = 15.964$.

Fractions: The numerator of the product is the product of the numerators; the denominator of the product is the product of the denominators. For example, $(3/7)(5/4) = 15/28$.

For all numbers a, b, and c	
ab is a unique number	the closure law
ab = ba	the commutative law
a(bc) = (ab)c	the associative law
a•1 = a	the multiplicative identity law
If ab = cb and b ≠ 0, then a = c	the cancellation law
From these laws one can derive three more useful laws:	
a•0 = 0	
If ab = 0, then a = 0, or b = 0, or both.	
The factors in a product many be combined in any order.	

Signed numbers: Multiply the numbers as if they had no signs. If one of the two factors has a minus sign, give the product a minus sign. If both factors have minus signs, write the product without a minus sign. For example, $(3x)(-2y) = -6xy$; $(-5)(-4) = 20$; $(-x)^2 = x^2$; and $(5x)(x) = 5x^2$.

Powers of the same base: To multiply two powers of the *same* base, add the exponents. For example $10^2 \cdot 10^3 = 10^5$, and $x^2 \cdot x = x^3$.

Monomials: To multiply two monomials, rearrange the factors. For example, $(3x^2y)(5xyz) = 15x^3y^2z$.

Polynomials: To multiply two polynomials multiply each term of one by each term of the other, combining like terms. For example, $(x + y)(x - y) = x^2 - xy + xy - y^2 = x^2 - y^2$.

Multiplication is the model for a variety of practical situations. In one we have a number, a, of groups with b things in each group. The product, ab, represents the total number. For example, seven egg cartons hold 7 × 12 eggs in all. In other situations we have "direct variation" or proportionality: y = kx. So many gallons of gasoline at so much per gallon calls for multiplication, as does computing distance as a function of rate and time, D = RT.

Unlike addition, in which a length plus a length is another length, and a length plus a weight, meaningless, the product of two quantities of the same type or of different types is frequently meaningful, and of a type different from both. For example, the product of two one-dimensional measures such as length becomes the two-dimensional measure, area. Multiplying a force, such as gravity, by a distance yields "work," which is a change in the amount of energy. Thus, while multiplication is closely tied to addition computationally, in appli-

cation it accommodates relationships of more complex dimensions.

While multiplication is ordinarily an operation between numbers, it can be an operation between other kinds of mathematical elements as well. Multiplication in the broader sense will obey many of the laws which ordinary multiplication does, but not necessarily all of them.

For example in "clock arithmetic" all the basic laws hold except for cancellation. In clock arithmetic, 3 × 4 = 3 × 8 because both leave the hands in the same position, but of course, 4 ≠ 8. In the multiplication of matrices, commutativity does not hold.

A particularly interesting extension of the idea of multiplication is in the Cartesian product of two sets. If A = {1, 2, 3}, and B = {x, y}, then A × B is the set {(1,x), (1,y), (2,x), (2,y), (3,x), (3,y)}, formed by pairing each element of A with each element of B. Because sets are sometimes used as the basis for arithmetic, Cartesian products form an important link between sets and ordinary multiplication.

See also Addition; Division.

KEY TERMS

Factor—A number used as a multiplier in a product.

Multiplier—One of two or more numbers combined by multiplication to form a product.

Multiplication—An operation related to addition by means of the distributive law.

Product—The result of multiplying two or more numbers.

Further Reading:

Dantzig, Tobias. *Number, the Language of Science.* Garden City, N.Y.: Doubleday and Co., 1954

Jourdain, Philip E. B. "The Nature of Mathematics" *The World of Mathematics,* James R. Newman, Editor. New York: Simon and Schuster, 1956

Klein, Felix, "Arithmetic," *Elementary Mathematics from an Advanced Standpoint,* New York, Dover, 1948

Smith, David Eugene and Ginsberg, Jekuthiel. "From Numbers to Numerals and from Numerals to Computation," *The World of Mathematics,* James R. Newman, Editor. New York: Simon and Schuster, 1956

J. Paul Moulton

Mummichog see **Killifish**

Mumps see **Childhood diseases**

Muon see **Subatomic particles**

Murre see **Auks**

Murrelet see **Auks**

Muscular dystrophy see **Neuromuscular diseases**

Muscular system

The muscular system is the body's network of tissues for both conscious and unconscious movement. Movement is generated through the contraction and relaxation of specific muscles. Some muscles, like those in the arms and legs, are involved in voluntary movements such as raising a hand or flexing the foot. Other muscles are involuntary and function without conscious effort. Voluntary muscles include skeletal muscles and total about 650 in the whole human body. Skeletal muscles are controlled by the somatic nervous system; whereas the autonomic nervous system controls involuntary muscles. Involuntary muscles include muscles that line internal organs. These smooth muscles are called visceral muscles, and they perform tasks not generally associated with voluntary activity throughout the body even when it is asleep. Smooth muscles control several automatic physiological responses such as pupil constriction when iris muscles contract in bright light and blood vessel dilation when smooth muscles around them relax, or lengthen. In addition to skeletal and smooth muscle which are considered voluntary and involuntary, respectively, cardiac muscle exists which is considered neither. Cardiac muscle is not under con-

scious control, and it can also function without external nervous system regulation.

Smooth muscles derive their name from their appearance when viewed in polarized light microscopy; in contrast to cardiac and skeletal muscles which have striations (appearance of parallel bands or lines), smooth muscle is unstriated. Striations result from the pattern of the myofilaments, actin and myosin, which line the myofibrils within each muscle cell. When many myofilaments align along the length of a muscle cell, light and dark regions create the striated appearance. This microscopic view of muscle reveals some hint of how muscles alter their shape to induce movement. Because muscle cells tend to be elongated, they are often called muscle fibers. Muscle cells are distinct from other cells in the body in shape, protein composition, and in the fact that they are multi-nucleated (have more than one nucleus per cell).

Skeletal muscles

Skeletal muscles are probably the must familiar type of muscle to people. Skeletal muscles are the ones that ache when someone goes for that first outdoor run in the spring after not running much during the winter. And skeletal muscles are heavily used when someone carries in the grocery bags. Exercise may increase muscle fiber size, but muscle fiber number generally remains constant. Skeletal muscles take up about 40% of the body's mass, or weight. They also use a great deal of oxygen and nutrients from the blood supply. Multiple levels of skeletal muscle tissue receive their own blood supplies.

Like all muscles, skeletal muscles can be studied at both a macroscopic and a microscopic level. At the macroscopic level, skeletal muscles usually originate at one point of attachment to a tendon and terminate at another tendon at the other end of an adjoining bone. Tendons are rich in the protein collagen which is arranged in a wavy way so that it can stretch out and provide additional length at the muscular-bone junction.

Skeletal muscles act in pairs where the flexing (shortening) of one muscle is balanced by a lengthening (relaxation) of its paired muscle or a group of muscles. These antagonistic (opposite) muscles can open and close joints such as the elbow or knee. Muscles which contract and cause a joint to close are called flexor muscles, and those which contract to cause a joint to stretch out are called extensors. Skeletal muscle which support the skull, backbone, and rib cage are called axial skeletal muscles; whereas, skeletal muscles of the limbs are called distal. These muscles attach to bones via strong, thick connective tissue called tendons. Several skeletal muscles work in a highly coordinated manner in activities such as locomotion, walking.

Skeletal muscles are organized into extrafusal and intrafusal fibers. Extrafusal fibers are the strong, outer layers of muscle. This type of muscle fiber is the most common. Intrafusal fibers which make up the central region of the muscle are weaker than extrafusal fibers. Skeletal muscles fibers are additionally characterized as "fast" or "slow" based on their activity patterns. Fast, also called "white," muscle fibers contract rapidly, have poor blood supply, operate anaerobically, and fatigue rapidly. Slow, also called "red," muscle fibers contract more slowly, have better blood supplies, operate aerobically, and do not fatigue as easily. Slow muscle fibers are used in movements which are sustained such as maintaining posture.

Skeletal muscles are enclosed in a dense sheath of connective tissue called the epimysium. Within the epimysium, muscles are sectioned into columns of muscle fiber bundles, called primary bundles or fasciculi, which are each covered by connective tissue called the perimysium. An average skeletal muscle may have 20 - 40 fasciculi which are further subdivided into several muscle fibers. Each muscle fiber (cell) is covered by connective tissue called endomysium. Both the epimysium and the perimysium contain blood and lymph vessels to supply the muscle with nutrients and oxygen and remove waste products, respectively. The endomysium has an extensive network of capillaries that supply individual muscle fibers. Individual muscle fibers vary in diameter from 10-60 micrometers and in length from a few millimeters to about 12 in (30 cm) in the sartorius muscle of the thigh.

At the microscopic level, a single muscle cell has several hundred nuclei and a striped appearance derived from the pattern of myofilaments. Long, cylindrical muscle fibers are formed from several myoblasts in fetal development. Multiple nuclei are important in muscle cells because of the tremendous amount of activity in muscle. The myofilaments, actin and myosin, overlap one another in a very specific arrangement. Myosin is a thick protein with two globular head regions. Each myosin filament is surrounded by six actin (thin) filaments. These filaments run longitudinally along the length of the cell in parallel. Multiple hexagonal arrays of actin and myosin exist in each skeletal muscle cell.

Each actin filament slides along adjacent myosin filaments with the help of other proteins and ions present in the cell. Tropomyosin and troponin are two proteins attached to the actin filaments that enable the globular heads on myosin to instantaneously attach to the myosin strands. The attachment and rapid release of this bond induces the sliding motion of these filaments which result in muscle contraction. In addition, calcium ions and ATP (cellular energy) are required by the muscle cell to process this reaction. Numerous mitochondria are present in muscle fibers to supply to extensive ATP required by the cell.

The system of myofilaments within muscle fibers are divided into units called sarcomeres. Each skeletal muscle cell has several myofibrils, long cylindrical columns of myofilaments. Each myofibril is composed of the myofilaments which interdigitate forming the striated sarcomere units. The thick myosin filaments of the sarcomere provide the dark, striped appearance in striated muscle, and the thin actin filaments provide the lighter sarcomere regions between the dark areas. A sarcomere can induce muscle contraction the way a paper towel roll holder can be pushed together before inserting it into a dispenser. The actin and myosin filaments slide over one another like the outer and inner layers of the roll holder. Muscle contraction creates an enlarged center region in the whole muscle. The flexing of a bicep makes this region anatomically visible. This large center is called the belly of the muscle.

Skeletal muscles function as the link between the somatic nervous system and the skeletal system. One does not move a skeletal muscle for the sake of moving the muscle unless one is a bodybuilder. Skeletal muscles are used to carry out instructions from the brain so that someone can accomplish something. For instance, someone decides that they would like a bite of cake. Unless the cake will come to the mouth by itself, the person needs to figure out some way to get that cake to their mouth. The brain tells the muscle to contract in the forearm allowing it to flex so that the hand is in position to get a forkful of cake. But the muscle alone cannot support the weight of a fork; it is the sturdy bones of the forearm that allow the muscles to complete the task of obtaining the cake. Hence, the skeletal and muscular systems work together as a lever system with joints acting as a fulcrum to carry out instructions from the nervous system.

The somatic nervous system controls skeletal muscle movement through motor neurons. Alpha motor neurons extend from the spinal cord and terminate on individual muscle fibers. The axon, or signal sending end, of the alpha neurons branch to innervate multiple muscle fibers. The nerve terminal forms a synapse, or junction, with the muscle to create a neuromuscular junction. The neurotransmitter, acetylcholine (Ach) is released from the axon terminal into the synapse. From the synapse, the Ach binds to receptors on the muscle surface which triggers events leading to muscle contraction. While alpha motor neurons innervate extra-fusal fibers, intrafusal fibers are innervated by gamma motor neurons.

Voluntary skeletal muscle movements are initiated by the motor cortex in the brain. Then signals travel down the spinal cord to the alpha motor neuron to result in contraction. However, not all movement of skeletal muscles is voluntary. Certain reflexes occur in response to dangerous stimuli, such as extreme heat. Reflexive skeletal muscular movement is controlled at the level of the spinal cord and does not require higher brain initiation. Reflexive movements are processed at this level to minimize the amount of time necessary to implement a response.

In addition to motor neuron activity in skeletal muscular activity, a number of sensory nerves carry information to the brain to regulate muscle tension and contraction to optimize muscle action. Muscles function at peak performance when they are not over-stretched or overcontracted. Sensory neurons within the muscle send feedback to the brain with regard to muscle length and state of contraction.

Cardiac muscles

Cardiac muscles, as is evident from their name, make up the muscular portion of the heart. While almost all cardiac muscle is confined to the heart, some of these cells extend for a short distance into cardiac vessels before tapering off completely. The heart muscle is also called the myocardium. The heart muscle is responsible for more than two billion beats in a lifetime. The myocardium has some properties similar to skeletal muscle tissue, but it is also unique. Like skeletal muscles, myocardium is striated; however, the cardiac muscle fibers are smaller and shorter than skeletal muscle fibers averaging 5-15 micrometers in diameter and 20-30 micrometers in length. In addition, cardiac muscles align lengthwise more than side-by-side compared to skeletal muscle fibers. The microscopic structure of cardiac muscle is also unique in that these cells are branched such that they can simultaneously communicate with multiple cardiac muscle fibers.

Cardiac muscle cells are surrounded by an endomysium like the skeletal muscle cells. But innervation of autonomic nerves to the heart do not form any special junction like that found in skeletal muscle. Instead, the branching structure and extensive interconnectedness of cardiac muscle fibers allows for stimulation of the heart to spread into neighboring myocardial cells; this does not require the individual fibers to be stimulated. Although external nervous stimuli can enhance or diminish cardiac muscle contraction, heart muscles can also contract spontaneously making them myogenic. Like skeletal muscle cells, cardiac muscle fibers can increase in size with physical conditioning, but they rarely increase in number.

Smooth muscles

Smooth muscle falls into two general categories, visceral smooth muscle and multi-unit smooth muscle. Visceral smooth muscle fibers line internal organs such as the intestines, stomach, and uterus. They also facilitate the movement of substances through tubular areas such as blood vessels and the small intestines. Multi-unit smooth muscles function in a highly localized way in areas such as the iris of the eye. Contrary to contractions in visceral smooth muscle, contractions in multi-unit smooth muscle fibers do not readily spread to neighboring muscle cells.

Smooth muscle is unstriated with innervations from both sympathetic (flight or fight) and parasympathetic (more relaxed) nerves of the autonomic nervous system. Smooth muscle appears unstriated under a polarized light microscope, because the myofilaments inside are less organized. Smooth muscle fibers contain actin and myosin myofilaments which are more haphazardly arranged than they are in skeletal muscles. The sympathetic neurotransmitter, Ach, and parasympathetic neurotransmitter, norepinephrine, activate this type of muscle tissue.

The concentric arrangement of some smooth muscle fibers enables them to control dilation and constriction in the intestines, blood vessels, and other areas. While innervation of these cells is not individual, excitation from one cell can spread to adjacent cells through nexuses which join neighbor cells. Smooth muscle cells have a small diameter of about 5-15 micrometers and are long, typically 15-500 micrometers. They are also wider in the center than at their ends. Gap junctions connect small bundles of cells which are, in turn, arranged in sheets.

Within hollow organs, such as the uterus, smooth muscle cells are arranged into two layers. The outer layer is usually arranged in a longitudinal fashion surrounding the inner layer which is arranged in a circular orientation. Many smooth muscles are regulated by hormones in addition to the neurotransmitters of the autonomic nervous system. In addition, contraction of some smooth muscles are myogenic or triggered by stretching as in the uterus and gastrointestinal tract.

Smooth muscle differs from skeletal and cardiac muscle in its energy utilization as well. Smooth muscles are not as dependent on oxygen availability as cardiac and skeletal muscles are. Smooth muscle uses glycolysis to generate much of its metabolic energy.

Disorders of the muscular system

Disorders of the muscular system can be due to genetic, hormonal, infectious, autoimmune, poisonous, or cancerous causes. But the most common problem associated with this system is injury from mis-use. Skeletal muscle sprains and tears cause excess blood to seep into the tissue in order to heal it. The remaining scar tissue leads to a slightly shorter muscle. Muscular impairment and cramping can result from a diminished blood supply. Cramping can be due to overexertion. Poor blood supply to the heart muscle causes chest pain called angina pectoris. And inadequate ionic supplies of calcium, sodium, or potassium can adversely effect most muscle cells.

Muscular system disorders related to the immune system include myasthenia gravis (MG) and tumors. MG is characterized by weak and easily fatigued skeletal muscles, one of the symptoms of which is droppy eyelids. MG is caused by antibodies that a person makes against their own Ach receptors; hence, MG is an autoimmune disease. The antibodies disturb normal Ach stimulation to contract skeletal muscles. Failure of the immune system to destroy cancerous cells in muscle can result in muscle tumors. Benign muscle tumors are called myomas; while malignant muscle tumors are called myosarcomas.

Contamination of muscle cells by infectious substances and drugs can also lead to muscular disorders. A Clostridium bacteria can cause muscle tetanus, which is a disease characterized by painful repeated muscular contractions. In addition, some types of gangrene are due to bacterial infections deep in a muscle. Gangrene is the decay of muscle tissue in varying degrees; it can involve small areas of a single muscle or entire organs. The poisonous substance, curare, blocks neuromuscular transmission in skeletal muscle causing paralysis. And large doses of prolonged alcohol consumption can cause muscle damage, as well.

The most common type of muscular genetic disorder is muscular dystrophy of which there are several kinds. Duchenne's muscular dystrophy is characterized by increasing muscular weakness and eventual death. Becker's muscular dystrophy is milder than Duchenne's, but both are X-linked recessive genetic disorders. Other types of muscular dystrophy are caused by a mutation which affects the muscle protein dystrophin which is absent in Duchenne's and altered in Becker's muscular dystrophies. Other genetic disorders

---

KEY TERMS

Cardiac muscle—Narrow, long, striated muscle tissue of the heart.

Skeletal muscle—Bundles of striated muscle cells which function in conjunction with the skeletal system as a lever system and for movements, in general.

Smooth muscle—Long, unstriated muscle cells which line internal organs and facilitate involuntary movements such as peristalsis.

Tendon—Collagen-rich connective tissue which bridges muscle and bone tissue.

(such as some cardiomyopathies) can affect various muscle tissues.

Further Reading:

Becker W. and D. Deamer, eds. "Cellular Motility and Contractility." *The World of the Cell*. 2nd ed. New York: The Benjamin/Cummings Publishing Company, Inc., 1991.

Rhoads R. and R. Pflanzer, eds. "The Motor System." and "Muscle." *Physiology*. New York: Saunders College Publishing. 1992.

Louise Dickerson

Muscle relaxants

Muscle relaxants are drugs that are administered to relax muscles. They are given to relieve the discomfort of muscle spasm or involuntary muscle contracture and also in cases of surgery to relax muscles and provide easier access for the surgeon. Some nonprescription drugs are available to combat painful contraction of the uterus during a woman's menstrual period.

Muscles can be divided into two classes, the voluntary or skeletal muscles and the involuntary or smooth muscles. The heart muscle, the myocardium, is a unique type of muscle that does not fit into either category. Skeletal muscles are those that are under voluntary control. The muscles that move the arms, that move the legs when you walk or run, or those that are involved in chewing are all skeletal muscles. They come into play only when you will them. Smooth muscles are those

CENTRALLY ACTING MUSCLE RELAXANTS AND THEIR ACTIONS

Drug Name (Trade Name)	Onset of action	Hours to peak concentration	Duration in hours
carisoprodol (Soma)	30 min.	4	4-6
chlorphensin carbamate (Maolate)	?	1-3	4-6
chlorzoxazone (Paraflax)	1 hour	3-4	3-4
cyclobenzaprine HCl (Flexeril)	1 hour	4-8	12-24
Metaxolone (Skelaxin)	1 hour	2	4-6
methocarbamol (Robaxin)	30 min.	1-2	?
orphenadrine (Banflex, Flexain, Marflex, Norflex, etc.)	1 hour	2	4-6

Note: The drug name is the generic name under which the drug is produced. The trade name is the name by which the drug is marketed by the pharmaceutical company that manufactures it.

that are not under conscious control. The muscles in the digestive organs are smooth muscles.

Usually it is the skeletal or striated muscles that will require therapy for painful spasm or will need to be relaxed to allow the surgeon to gain access to the abdomen easily. Muscle spasm may be associated with a trauma or may be brought on by multiple sclerosis, cerebral palsy, stroke, or an injury to the spinal cord. Severe cold, an interruption of blood supply to a muscle, or overexertion of the muscle also can lead to spasms. A muscle spasm actually is an increase in muscle tone brought on by an abnormality in motor control by the spinal nerves.

Skeletal muscles are controlled by large nerves in the spinal cord. The nerve cell or neuron is part of the spinal cord, but its projections, the axon and the many dendrites course outward to connect to muscle cells. The nerve axon is a sensory device that senses the muscle cells' current condition. The dendrites are motor fibers that deliver the instructions to change its state to the muscle fiber. The area at which the muscle and nerve connect is called the neuromuscular junction. It is here that the end releases a chemical called a neurotransmitter that crosses the microscopic space between the nerve and muscle and causes the desired response. Five such neurotransmitters have been described: acetylcholine, serotonin, norepinephrine, glycine, and gamma-amminobutyric acid or GABA. Of these, the

functions of three are known. Acetylcholine excites muscle activity and glycine and GABA inhibit it.

Muscle relaxants may act either peripherally, that is directly on the muscle, or centrally, in the spinal cord. Most such drugs act centrally, though how they perform their task is not understood. These drugs do not act directly on the muscle to relax it, they do not interfere with conduction along the nerve fiber, they do not stop the neurotransmitter from being released or crossing the nerve-muscle junction, and they do not alter the ability of the muscle to respond to the neurotransmitter. Somehow they act centrally to depress the central nervous system and may have a sedative effect.

The dosage of any muscle relaxing agent must be carefully tailored to achieve the desired result without overdosing the patient. Because these drugs have a sedative action the patient should be warned not to drive, operate machinery or perform any other task that requires wakefulness. An overdose of the drugs can put the patient to sleep and may well depress muscle function to the extent that the bladder will not contract normally and urine retention will occur. Also, some drugs will produce a change in the color of the urine of which the patient should be made aware.

The centrally acting muscle relaxants have an onset of action ranging from 30 minutes to an hour. They reach their maximum concentration in the blood between 1-8 hours, and their effects last for 4-24 hours. Dosages are designed to allow some overlap to maintain the desired blood concentration of the drug for maximum benefit (see table).

Only one drug is classified as a peripherally acting muscle relaxant. This agent, dantrolene sodium, acts directly on the muscle, so it has fewer side effects than do the centrally acting drugs. Dantrolene is marketed as Dantrium by its manufacturer. It is a slow-acting drug whose peak effect is not felt for some five hours after it has been taken. The peak effect of a single dose, however, does not constitute a therapeutic dose. The therapeutic effects of the drug may not be seen for up to a week or longer. The patient may be tempted to increase the dosage of the drug because it seems to have little effect in the beginning stages of therapy. Of course, this could be a critically unwise procedure that would be seen once the therapeutic dosage is built up.

Dantrolene seems to work directly on the muscle cell, affecting the sarcoplasmic reticulum within the cell. The sarcoplasmic reticulum in a muscle cell stores calcium. When the electrical signal through the nerve releases an excitatory neurotransmitter the sarcoplasmic reticulum releases calcium, which brings on the contraction of the muscle. Dantrolene seems to prevent the release of calcium, and thus short-circuits the muscle contraction.

Baclofen (marketed as Llorosal) is another muscle relaxant that acts on the spinal cord to lessen muscle spasms especially in patients with multiple sclerosis or spinal cord injuries. The chemical structure of baclofen is similar to that of the neurotransmitter GABA, which is an inhibitory chemical. Baclofen seems to inhibit neuron activity, which reduces muscle tone and reduces spasm. Its primary usage is in patients with spinal cord injury that has resulted in paralysis. The drug relaxes tightly flexed leg muscles, improves bowel and bladder control, and reduces muscle spasms both in number and severity. Baclofen builds up slowly and may require a month or two of therapy before the optimal dose is achieved. It does not have a high degree of sedative effect, so it may be preferable for many patients.

Another drug used to treat muscle spasms, diazepam, commonly known by its trade name, Valium, is a tranquilizer or antianxiety and anticonvulsant drug. Still, it has found a niche as a muscle relaxing drug in cases of acute, painful muscle spasm. Diazepam appears to work by enhancing the effects of the inhibitory neurotransmitter GABA. Only small doses of diazepam can be given as a muscle relaxant because of its sedative effects. For the patient who is not sensitive to the sedation often brought about by diazepam, the

KEY TERMS

Neuromuscular junction—The point at which a nerve ending intersects with a muscle cell. The nerve controls muscle movements.

Neurotransmitter—A chemical that is released from nerve ends to achieve a physiologic response, whether muscle contraction, speech, reflex action, or whatever.

Skeletal muscle—Also called voluntary or striated muscle, it is a muscle under conscious control by the individual. Striated muscles flex or extend the leg or arm, curl the fingers, move the jaw during chewing, and so forth.

Spasm—The uncontrolled tightening of a muscle to the point that it may become painful. A so-called Charlie horse is such a spasm.

Spinal nerve—A nerve fiber that rises from the spinal cord instead of directly from the brain. Spinal nerves control muscle movement without conscious thought from an individual.

drug can serve both to relieve muscle spasm and to relieve anxiety about that situation.

All muscle relaxing agents should be given with caution to anyone who is taking other drugs. The muscle relaxers will enhance the sedative effects of many other classes of drugs such as antihistamines, antidepressants, sedatives, other muscle relaxants, and tranquilizers.

In addition, they should not be suddenly discontinued. Stopping the drugs suddenly can lead to a return of symptoms to an even more painful degree. After the optimal clinical dosage is reached the physician will provide the drugs until the muscle spasm has passed and then wean the patient off the drug. In some cases, as in paraplegia, the drug may be given for years to maintain the patient's comfort.

See also Muscular system.

Further Reading:

Griffith, H. Winter. *Complete Guide to Prescription and Non-Prescription Drugs*. Los Angeles: The Body Press, 1991.
Zimmerman, David R. *Zimmerman's Complete Guide to Nonprescription Drugs*. Detroit: Visible Ink Press, 1993.

Larry Blaser

Mushrooms

Mushrooms are the fruiting bodies of certain species of higher fungi. The vegetative tissues of these fungi consists of immense lengths of microscopic, thread-like hyphae, and their aggregations known as mycelium, which grow in surface soils, organic debris, and in association with plant roots.

Strictly speaking, a mushroom is the sporulating or fruiting body of a fungus in the division Basidiomycetes, a large and diverse group of about 16,000 species, sometimes known as club fungi. Species of Basidiomycetes can be saprophytic, parasitic, or mycorrhizal in their ecology. Because of the relative complexity of their anatomy and breeding systems, the Basidiomycetes are considered to be the most evolutionarily advanced of the fungi. The mushrooms of these fungi are technically known as basidiocarps. These structures are formed of specialized mycelium, and are the spore-producing stage of development. The basidiocarp is a relatively short-lived stage of the life cycle, most of which is spent living as microscopic, thread-like hyphae, which ramify extensively through the growth substrate of the fungus.

However, in its common usage, the word mushroom is also used to refer to the spore-producing bodies of other types of fungi, in particular a few species in the division Ascomycetes or sac fungi, which includes the familiar, edible morels and truffles. Some of the non-Basidiomycetes species that develop "mushrooms" are also discussed in this entry.

Mushrooms have long been avidly sought-after as a tasty country food in many cultures, although some peoples, notably the Anglo-Saxons of Britain, have tended to disdain these foods. This has not been because of the flavor of mushrooms, but rather because some species are deadly poisonous, and these are not always easily distinguished from nontoxic and therefore edible species.

The mycophobia (that is, fear of fungus) common to some people and cultures can be illustrated in many ways, including the derivation of the word "toadstool," a commonly used name for mushrooms that have an erect stalk and a wide cap. "Tod" is the German word for death, and the deadly, poisonous nature of certain mushrooms may be the likely origin of the word toadstool. The etymology of toadstool is further compounded by the poisonous nature of toads. In any event, European folk tales refer to toadstools as places where poisonous toads sit on poisonous mushrooms in the forest, a myth perpetuated in whimsical drawings accompanying fairy takes and other stories intended for children.

Mushrooms have many fascinating properties, in addition to the extreme toxicity of some species. Mushrooms can sometimes grow extremely rapidly — in some cases, masses of mushrooms can seemingly appear overnight, under suitable environmental conditions, and usually following a heavy rainfall. Mushrooms may also have unusual shapes and growth patterns, for example, the concentric circles or "fairy rings" that some species develop in open places, such as fields and meadows. These and other interesting qualities were not easily explainable by naturalists in earlier times. As a result, mushrooms have acquired a supernatural reputation in some cultures, and are commonly associated with cold, dank, dangerous, or evil contexts. Many cultures have similarly regarded a few other creatures, such as snakes, bats, and spiders. Today, however, these various cultural prejudices are much less prevalent, because we have a greater scientific understanding of the biology and ecology of mushrooms and other unusual organisms.

Biology and ecology of mushroom-producing fungi

As was just noted, mushrooms are the fruiting bodies of certain types of fungi. Most of the biomass of these fungi consists of fine, thread-like hyphae, which grow extensively throughout the organic-rich substrate of their ecosystem. These fungi periodically develop spore-producing, reproductive structures known as mushrooms, under conditions of a favorable environment in terms of temperature and moisture, coupled with the accumulation of sufficient energy and nutrient reserves to support the reproductive effort. It may take years for these favorable circumstances to develop, and consequently mushroom populations in forests, prairies, fields, and other habitats can be highly variable in abundance.

Species of mushroom-producing fungi exploit various types of microhabitats. The most important of these are the surface soil and organic litter, large-dimension woody debris, mycorrhizae, and animal dung. These are discussed below:

(1) The hyphae of many species of fungus grow extensively through the soil and surface organic matter, such as the forest floor and the organic mat of prairies and savannas. These hyphae are the vegetative tissues of saprophytic fungi, which are an important component of the decomposer food web of their ecosystem.

(2) Many other species of fungi are saprophytes that grow in decaying wood, such as logs and branches lying on the forest floor, standing dead trees (these are known as "snags"), and rotting heartwood of living

trees. Some of these fungi become significant economic "pests," for example, by causing dry-rot of the wooden components of buildings.

(3) Many species of fungus grow in a close association with the roots of higher plants, in a mutualistic symbiosis known as a mycorrhiza. The mycorrhizal mutualism is very important to the nutrition of the plant, because of the greatly enhanced access to nutrients that is provided, particularly to phosphate.

(4) An additional habitat that may be exploited by mushroom-producing fungi includes piles of animals dung, especially the organic-rich manure of herbivores. These are known as coprophilous fungi.

Mushrooms of North America

Many species of mushrooms occur in the forests, prairies, fields, and towns and cities of North America. Obviously, it is not possible to deal with these in a comprehensive fashion. Some of the more widespread of the stranger species are briefly described here, while poisonous and edible ones are discussed in the following sections.

The largest mushroom to occur in North America are the giant puffballs (*Calvatia gigantea* and *C. booniana*). These species develop huge, ball-like mushrooms that can achieve a diameter of up to 19.5 in (50 cm).

The stinkhorn fungus (*Phallus inpudicus*) is a saprophyte that grows up out of the forest floor. This species is also sometimes known as the dog's-penis or devil's-penis, because of the anatomically-correct shape of the mushroom, and in the case of the latter name, it's terrible smell.

The artist's fungus (*Ganoderma applanatum*) is a large, semi-circular, relatively hard and corky mushroom that grows bracket-like out of the side of heart-rotted trees. The white surface of this fungus turns a darker brown when it is bruised. Consequently, the smooth, lower surface of the mushroom is sometimes used as a substrate to record messages and make drawings. The related sulphur shelf (*Laetiporus sulphureus*) also grows out of the side of heart-rotted trees, and is a bright yellow in color.

The scarlet elf cup (*Sarcoscypha coccinea*) is a lovely mushroom, with a deeply concave cup, that is white on the exterior, and a brilliant scarlet on the interior. This species occurs on rotting sticks and small logs in forests in the springtime.

The white worm coral (*Clavaria vermicularis*) occurs in clusters of erect, white, worm-like clubs

growing out of the forest floor, and is found during the summer and autumn.

The collared earthstar (*Geastrum triplex*) grows out of the forest floor. This species has a bulbous spore-case, surrounded by pointed, ray-like structures that give an overall appearance of a star-burst.

Poisonous mushrooms and drugs

Some species of mycorrhizal fungi develop mushrooms that are deadly poisonous. Perhaps the most famous, and most-rapidly killing species in this respect are the death or destroying angel (*Amanita virosa*) and the deathcap (*A. palloides*). There are other species of deadly mushrooms in the genus *Amanita*, and in the genera *Chlorophyllum* (green gill), *Cortinarius* (web-caps), *Galerina* (autumn skullcaps), *Gyromitra* (false morels), and *Lepiota* (parasol mushrooms). However, these are not, by any means, the only poisonous mushrooms that may be commonly encountered in wild habitats in North America. There are numerous other species of deadly mushrooms, which are never to be eaten.

A number of fungi are used as drugs, to induce hallucinations, feelings of well-being, and other pleasurable mental states. The fly agaric (*Amanita muscaria*) is a widespread species of Eurasia, North America, and Central America, and is a well-known poisonous mushroom. However, in smaller doses this species can induce a pleasant intoxication and hallucinations, and it has long been used by many cultures to induce these effects. This has been the case in Siberia, elsewhere in northeastern Asia, Central Asia, and India, where the drug is known by the indigenous name "soma." The fly agaric has also been used in northwestern Europe, where Viking warriors sometimes consumed this drug prior to battle and certain ceremonies, and were known as "berserkers," and in Central America, where the fungus was considered to be a food from the gods. In the famous children's story, *Alice in Wonderland,* Alice could change her size from very small to very large, by nibbling on a mushroom. This tale was undoubtedly influenced by the author's knowledge of the hallucinogenic properties of *Amanita muscaria*. It is well-known that prolonged or frequent use of this hallucinogen is damaging to the nervous system, and that large doses can be lethal, but this mushroom has nevertheless been important in many cultures, and is still routinely used for certain types of ceremonies.

Various species of American mushrooms known as psilocybin (*Psilocybe* spp.) are also hallucinogenic. These were used in religious ceremonies by some Amerindian cultures, for example, the Aztecs, who knew these mushrooms as teonanacatyl (especially using *P. mexicana*). However, these mushrooms are mostly used today as recreational drugs. Other mushroom-producing fungi which contain the same active ingredient, known as psilocybin, are species in the genera *Conocybe, Paneolus, Psathyrella,* and *Stropharia*.

A therapeutic drug is manufactured from the fruiting bodies of the ergot (*Claviceps purpurea*), which is a parasite on the flowering heads of certain grasses, especially rye (*Secale cereale*). The ergot fungus attacks the young fruits of the grasses, and then develops a bulbous, purplish structure. These are collected and used to make a medicine useful in treating low blood pressure, hemorrhages, and other maladies.

Edible mushrooms

The use of wild mushrooms as a food is an ancient practice. These fungi were undoubtedly well known to pre-historic, hunting and gathering cultures, as they are today to indigenous peoples who continue to live in natural forests. Once the identity of poisonous and edible mushrooms became fixed in cultural knowledge and tradition, the edible species, and sometimes those that could be used to induce non-lethal hallucinogens, were regularly gathered and utilized by people.

The tradition of the use of mushrooms as a country food continues today. The collection of edible mushrooms is an especially popular outdoor activity in much of Eurasia, where these foods can be very common in the spring and autumn in boreal and temperate forests. Mushroom collecting has been considerably less popular in Britain and North America. However, under the influence of immigrants from Europe and northern Asia, and the emerging popularity of natural history, more and more North Americans are actively seeking out these delicacies in wild habitats. This activity has been called "mushrooming," in parallel with the better-known sport of "birding."

Interestingly, most mushrooms are not a particularly nutritious food. They typically contain 90-95% water when fresh, the rest of their biomass being about 5% carbohydrate, 5% protein, and less-than 1% fat and minerals. The major benefit of eating mushrooms is their engaging, sometimes exquisite flavor, and in some cases their interesting texture.

The truffles are perhaps the most famous, and certainly the most expensive, of the edible mushrooms, being avidly sought-out for use in gourmet cooking, particularly in France. The best-known species of truffle is *Tuber melanosporum*, which is commonly mycorrhizal on species of oak, birch, and beech (*Quercus,*

Betula, and *Fagus* spp., respectively). Other Eurasian species of truffle include *Tuber aestivum* and *T. brumale,* while *T. gibbosum* occurs in conifer rain-forests of the west coast of North America. The spore-bearing mushrooms of truffles develop underground, and are commonly discovered using a specially trained, truffle-sniffing pig or dog.

The chanterelle (*Cantharellus cibarius*) is a yellow-to-orange mushroom of the floor of autumn forests, and is a delicious wild fungus. The king bolete (*Boletus edulis*) is another prized mushroom. The shaggy mane (*Coprinus comatus*) is delicious if picked when young. Puffballs can also be eaten, as long as their interior is still young and white-colored, and include the pear puffball (*Lycoperdon pyriforme*) and giant puffball (*Calvatia gigantea*). Other edible mushrooms include corn smut (*Ustilago maydis*), beefsteak (*Fistulina hepatica*), fried chicken mushroom (*Lyophyllum decastes*), fairy ring mushroom (*Marasmius oreades*), oyster fungus (*Pleurotus ostreatus*), and the morel (*Morchella esculenta*).

Some species of mushrooms have been brought into domestication, and are routinely grown on artificial media, to be harvested and sold as an agricultural product. Mushroom cultivation appears to have begun in England in the late eighteenth century, and it has become a major economic enterprise because of the rapidly increasing popularity of mushrooms as food.

The most commonly cultivated species of mushroom is the common meadow mushroom (*Agaricus campestris*; sometimes known as *A. bisporus*), which sustains a global economy exceeding $15 billion per year. This mushroom can be eaten fresh or dried for longer-term storage. This species is cultivated using an organic-rich medium, with the straw- and manure-rich cleanings of horse stables being a preferred material. The substrate must be sterilized, usually by a natural, high-temperature composting referred to as "sweating-out." This must be done before the substrate is inoculated with the *Agaricus*, to prevent the growth of other species of fungus, which may be pathogenic or more competitive than the desired species. The substrate is typically inoculated with "spawn," that is, masses of mycelium compressed into small briquettes, or with a laboratory culture of the *Agaricus*. The growth conditions should be dark or virtually so, as humid as possible, and the temperature kept constant at about 55-59° F (13-15° C). Mushroom farms may be developed in specially constructed, barn-like buildings, or in caves, worked-out mines, and cellars. Typically, the first mushroom "buttons" begin to appear about four weeks after inoculation and growth and proliferation of the

Agaricus mycelium, and the first harvests can be made after 7-8 weeks. The mushrooms can be continuously harvested for 4-6 months, after which the growth medium is considered to be "spent." However, this well-composted substrate can then be used as an excellent soil conditioner in gardens.

Other species of mushrooms are also cultivated, including the shiitake (*Cortinellus berkeleyanus*), a popular ingredient in oriental cooking. The shii-take mushroom is cultivated on rotting logs and is typically dried for storage.

A warning

Many people get great pleasure out of collecting and eating wild mushrooms. Many of the tastiest species are quite distinctive in shape and color and can be collected and eaten without any risk and with great pleasure. However, some species of edible mushrooms are rather similar to species that are deadly poisonous. When collecting wild mushrooms as food, it is always best to err on the side of certainty of identification and safety. The identification of some types of mushrooms is difficult, and there are no hard-and-fast rules for separating poisonous from edible species. This is the reason why there are numerous stories about experienced mushroom collectors who were poisoned by eating a misidentified fungus. Therefore, if you are not certain about the identity of a particular wild mushroom, do not consume it. If in doubt — throw it out!

See also Fungi, Fungicide.

Further Reading:

Atlas, R.M. and R. Bartha. *Microbial Ecology*. Menlo Park, CA: Benjamin-Cummings Pub. Co., 1987.
Klein, R.M. *The Green World. An Introduction to Plants and People*. New York: Harper and Row, 1987.
Lincoff, G.H. *The Audubon Society Field Guide to North American Mushrooms*. New York: Chanticleer Press, 1981.
McKnight, K.H. and V.B. McKnight. *A Field Guide to the Mushrooms of North America*. Boston, MA: Houghton Mifflin Co., 1987.
Raven, P.H., F.E. Evert, and H. Curtis. *Biology of Plants*. New York: Worth Publishers, 1976.
Sharma, O.P. *Textbook of Fungi*. New York: McGraw Hill, 1989.

Bill Freedman

Mushrooms, hallucinogenic see **Addiction**
Muskmelon see **Gourd family**

KEY TERMS

Hyphae (singular: hypha)—These are long, almost microscopic, tubular filaments of fungi.

Mutualism—An intimate relationship between two or more organisms that is beneficial to both.

Mycelium—This refers to thread- or mat-like aggregations of the fine fungal tissues known as hyphae.

Saprophyte—This refers to an organism that derives its energy by decomposing dead organic matter. Many species of mushroom-producing fungi live off the organic debris that is present in the mineral soil and, especially, the surface litter of leaves and woody debris on the forest floor.

Muskoxen

Muskoxen or muskox (*Ovibos moschatus*) are a species of large mammal in the family *Bovidae*, which also includes cattle, buffalo, antelope, sheep, and goats. The muskox is anatomically intermediate between sheep and cattle, and there has been taxonomic debate over which of these two groups the muskox should be more closely aligned with. As a result its genus, *Ovibos*, is a composite of the scientifically latinized words for sheep (*Ovis*) and cattle (*Bos*).

Muskoxen are arctic and subarctic animals of the Northern Hemisphere, historically occurring in both North America and Eurasia. However, muskox had been extirpated from Eurasia but have recently been re-introduced into Siberia from North American stock. For millennia up to about 8,000-10,000 years ago during and soon after the most recent of the Pleistocene glaciations, muskox were a component of a relatively diverse fauna of large animals of the northern regions. During that time, muskox and caribou ranged throughout much of the northern United States, Canada, Germany, France, Britain, Poland, Scandinavia, Ukraine, Belarus, and northern Russia, as did woolly rhinoceros, mastodon, mammoths, and other now-extinct large mammals. The reasons for the apparently simultaneous extinction of most of the species of this diverse mammalian fauna are not known. One popular hypothesis is that these species were overhunted by predatory humans; however, other environmental factors, perhaps associated with climate change, may also have been important. In some respects, muskox and caribou can be considered to be relics of this extraordinary ice-age fauna.

Muskoxen, when threatened, form a defensive circle.

Muskox are very large animals, with the biggest bulls measuring up to 7.5 ft (2.5 m) in body length, standing as tall as 4.5 ft (1.5 m) at the shoulder, and weighing as much as 1,433 lb (650 kg). Muskox have an extremely heavy pelage, consisting of coarse, dark brown, guard hairs, and an extremely soft and fine inner fleece that is virtually impenetrable to cold and moisture. Both sexes have horns that curve broadly downward and then up, but the bull's horns are especially massive, and meet at the forehead. The horns are keratinized, meaning that they are anatomically derived from fused hairs, rather than from the skull bones, as in deer (family Cervidae). Muskox have a superficially clumsy appearance, but when pressed they are nimble and fleet runners, even on very uneven and wet terrain.

Muskox are herding animals, sometimes occurring in groups of as many as 100 individuals, but more often they are found in herds of 10-15 or fewer. Usually these groups consist of mature bulls protecting their harem of mature cows, calves and immature offspring of various ages. As the young males mature and become potential competitors for females, they are driven from the herd by the dominant bull. The young bulls then form their own small herds; and as they age and grow stronger, the younger males challenge the dominant bull, eventually taking over the harem. Once driven off, the older bull muskoxen lead a solitary, wandering life.

When confronted by predators, muskox herds usually form into a tight defensive circle or line, with young calves protected in the center and mature animals on the periphery. This behavior provides a formidable barrier against natural predators such as wolves. However, humans armed with rifles can wipe out entire herds because the ring often does not break up, and animals do not flee as their partners are killed.

During the summer, muskox primarily graze on grasses, sedges, and forbs. During the winter, they mostly browse on woody shrubs; however in the high-arctic portions of their range, where shrubs are uncommon and vegetation is generally sparse, muskox must make do with lichens and any other vegetation that can be obtained. During winter muskox paw through the surface snow to obtain food. If the snow is very icy, the animals feed on plants on exposed ridges and plateaus, where snow cover is thinner. Muskox do not undertake extensive migrations, though they do move locally between winter and summer ranges.

During the nineteenth century, the muskoxen of northern North America were heavily hunted for their hides and meat, and their populations declined drastically. More recently, however, measures to conserve the species have allowed their populations to increase, and muskox are now expanding their range to re-occupy previously used habitat. This species is now sustainably hunted for subsistence and sport. There is even a small hunt conducted by Canadian Inuit to ship meat to southern markets, where muskox is considered to be an exotic food.

Further Reading:

Banfield, A.W.F. *The Mammals of Canada.* Toronto: University of Toronto Press, 1974.

Grzimek's Encyclopaedia of Mammals. Grzimek, B., ed. London: McGraw Hill, 1990.

Wilson, D. E. and D. Reeder. *Mammal Species of the World.* Washington: Smithsonian Institution Press, 1993.

Bill Freedman

Muskrat

The muskrat or musquash (*Ondatra zibethicus*) is a relatively large, amphibious rodent that is native to North America. The northern range of the muskrat reaches as far as the limits of the boreal forest from Alaska to Labrador and Newfoundland. The southern range of the muskrat extends through much of the United States as far south as northern Baha California, although not in the coastal plains of the southern states or coastal California. Muskrats have also been introduced in Europe, where it was hoped they would become a valuable source of fur.

Biology of muskrats

Muskrats can reach a body length of 12.6 in (32 cm), plus a long tail 11.8 in (30 cm) and a weight of about 3.3 lb (1.5 kg), although most animals are typically about 2.4 lb (1.1 kg) in weight. The waterproof fur (pelage) of muskrats is composed of a dense underfur, important for insulation, and a lager of longer, usually dark-brown, protective guard hairs.

Muskrats of both sexes have a pair of large glands near their anus, which enlarge during the breeding season, and produce a strongly scented chemical called musk, from which the common name of these animals is derived. Musk is used in the manufacture of per-

fumes, although it is not commonly harvested from muskrats for this purpose.

Muskrats are excellent swimmers, using their partially webbed feet which are fringed with stiff hairs that broaden the propulsive surface. The hairless, scaly tail is flattened, and is used as a rudder during swimming. Muskrats can remain submerged for as long as seventeen minutes, and they often do this to hide, when they feel threatened by a predator.

Muskrats mostly eat aquatic and riparian plants of various sorts, and they sometimes forage on land, occasionally in farmers' fields. Muskrats also eat mussels, fish, and other aquatic animals. Most feeding is done at night, dawn, or dusk, but muskrats are sometimes seen during the day.

Muskrats are found in marshes, swamps, and other types of static, open-water wetlands, where they build family houses made of mounds of piled-up reeds and cattails plastered with mud. These structures are typically more than one meter high and several meters broad. Into these mounds the muskrats construct a tunnel with an underwater access hole, leading to an internal den with a grassy bed. Muskrats also live along streams and rivers, where their dens are dug into earthen banks above the high-water level, with the access hole located under low-water and below the limit of freezing in winter. Muskrat houses and diggings are often destroyed during spring floods, and are not usually repaired; the muskrat will instead construct a new accommodation.

In optimal habitats such as reedy marshes, muskrat population densities can reach 85 animals per hectare. Sometimes, excessively large muskrat populations can degrade the local habitat, forcing a population crash until the vegetation recovers.

Muskrats are very fecund, and can produce several litters each year. They live in family units in mud lodges in territories, which they actively defend from incursions by other muskrats. During the spring, dominant females take possession of the best habitat and drive away younger females and males. Much strife occurs at this time, and some animals are killed during the fighting, and those that are driven away are often killed by predators.

Economic importance

Muskrats are widely trapped for their durable fur, which is prized for the manufacture of warm, fashionable coats and other garments. Where muskrats are abundant, trapping can have a significant economic impact, providing important employment for people liv-

A muskrat.

ing in rural environments. Millions of muskrats are trapped each year, and muskrats are one of the economically most important wild fur-bearing animals in North America. The best furs are obtained during winter, when the pelts are in prime condition. Some rural people also eat muskrats.

Muskrats are sometimes considered to be important pests, especially when they burrow into earthen dams, dikes, irrigation channels, and other structures. The burrows of muskrats weaken these constructed works, and can cause them to fail or erode. Muskrats are also regarded as pests in parts of their introduced range in Europe, where they are not well controlled by natural predators or disease.

The muskrat was introduced to Europe by Prince Colloredo-Mannsfield, who released five individuals in a pond on his estate near Prague, now in the Czech Republic, following a hunting expedition to Alaska. It is likely that all of the millions of muskrats in Europe and northern Asia are the descendants of these animals, which are actively controlled to decrease the damage they cause.

Bill Freedman

Mussels see **Bivalves**

KEY TERMS

. . . .

Musk—A strong-smelling secretion of the glands of some animals, generally associated with breeding and the marking of territories. Musk is produced by certain species of deer, cats, otter, the muskrat, and other animals. Musk is used to manufacture perfumes. Much of the modern usage involves synthesized musk.

Mustard family

The mustard family, or Brassicaceae, contains about 3,000 species of plants. These plants occur very widely on all continents except Antarctica and in a wide range of habitats from tundra and desert to forests of all types. Most species in the mustard family occur in the temperate zones, and many occur in the tundra of alpine or arctic environments.

The flowers of members of the Brassicaceae have four petals arranged in a cross-like pattern (the old name for this family was Cruciferae, referring to the cross of crucifixion). The flowers of mustards contain both female and male parts. There are six stamens, of which four have long filaments, and two have short filaments. The seeds of plants in this family are contained in a relatively long inflated structure called a silique or in a rounder flattened structure known as a silicle. When mature, the outer walls of the fruits fall away leaving an inner partition to which the seeds are loosely attached.

A few species of the mustard family are of major economic importance. These include the many varieties of the cabbage as well as rapeseed, radish, mustard, and others. Other species in this family are used in horticulture, and a few are considered to be important weeds.

The many varieties of the cabbage

The cabbage occurs in a remarkably wide range of cultivated varieties. Each of these varieties represents culturally selected variants of the basic species, the colewort (*Brassica oleracea*), originally native to Eurasia. Hybridization with some other species of *Brassica* was also likely important in the development of some of the domesticated varieties of the cabbage.

The most common variety in cultivation is the garden cabbage, a biennial plant that is harvested after the end of its first growing season and is eaten as a nutritious vegetable. This variety has been cultivated in the Mediterranean region for thousands of years. The fleshy leaves are aggregated into a head-like structure and are eaten raw or processed into cole slaw, sauerkraut, or some other dishes. The most common variety is green colored, but there is also a red variety known as red cabbage. The savoy cabbage is a less-common, more open-headed variety.

The curly kale is a leafy vegetable that does not form a compact head. Brussels sprouts look like tiny cabbages, but they develop in large numbers on the erect stem of this variety of cabbage. These sprouts can be harvested, and new ones will re-grow until the first hard frosts of autumn stop the regeneration. Kohlrabi is a starchy vegetable that develops as a short, inflated part of the above-ground stem. Kohlrabi can be green, white, or red in color. Cauliflower is a compact, white,

Market prize cabbage.

modified inflorescence. Broccoli is a more erect, green, modified inflorescence.

All of the varieties of cabbage are very nutritious foods, high in energy, vitamin C, iron and other minerals, roughage, and other useful qualities.

There are also some horticultural varieties of cabbage. These are valued for their multi-hued foliage of green, purple, and red. The colors of these plants last well into the early winter, so these horticultural cabbages can brighten gardens long after flowers have withered and the foliage of most species has been shed.

Other edible species

The turnip (*Brassica rapa*) is a biennial, cultivated plant. The starchy, yellowish, inflated root of this plant can be used as a food by people, or it may be fed to livestock. The swede (*Brassica napus*) produces an edible structure similar to that of the turnip.

Radish (*Raphanus sativus*) is a plant that develops an underground, starchy, bulb-like structure in the tissue region known as the hypocotyl, occurring between the true roots and the above-ground stem. The familiar radish that is eaten is this inflated hypocotyl. The most commonly grown variety is a round, red radish with a white interior, but white and black varieties of various shapes also occur.

The pungent root of horse radish (*Cochlearia armoracia*) is harvested and ground with vinegar to manufacture a delicious, sharp-tasting condiment, often served with meats.

Mustard is a yellow condiment prepared from the ground seeds of white mustard (*B. alba*). Sometimes the seeds of black mustard (*Brassica nigra*) are also used for this purpose.

The seeds of rapeseed (*Brassica napus*) contain up to 40% or more oil, which is extracted under pressure and used as an edible oil and for the preparation of margarine. The material left after the oil has been expressed is used as a nutritious fodder for livestock.

Several other species of mustards are utilized for their edible leaves. The pak-choi (*Brassica chinensis*), petsai (*B. pekinensis*), and false pak-choi (*B. parachinensis*) are important as cooked or steamed vegetables in the Orient. Watercress (*Nasturtium officinale*) is an annual aquatic plant whose tender, dark-green leaves are served as a steamed vegetable. Spinach (*Spinacia oleracea*) is another leafy, annual plant in which the raw or steamed foliage is eaten as a nutritious vegetable.

Weeds

A few species of the mustard family are considered to be important weeds. Agricultural weeds include various species of mustards in the genus *Brassica*, some of which are naturalized varieties of cultivated species. A few species are invasive into natural habitats, for example, the marsh cress (*Rorippa amphibia*), garlic-mustard (*Alliaria petiolata*), and dame's rocket (*Hesperis matronalis*). A few species are minor, aesthetic weeds of lawns and paths, for example, shepherd's purse (*Capsella bursa-pastoris*) and whitlow-grass (*Draba verna*).

Further Reading:

Hvass, E. *Plants That Serve and Feed Us.* New York: Hippocrene Books, 1975.

Klein, R. M. *The Green World. An Introduction to Plants and People.* New York: Harper and Row, 1987.

Woodland, D. W. *Contemporary Plant Systematics.* Englewood Cliffs, NJ: Prentice-Hall, 1991.

Bill Freedman

Mutagen

Mutagens are chemicals or physical factors (such as radiation) which increase the rate of mutation in the cells of bacteria, plants, and animals (including humans). Most mutagens are of natural origin and are not just a modern phenomenon: even dinosaurs were susceptible to mutagens. Mutagens can be found in the food we eat, the air we breath, or the ground we walk on. Very small doses of a mutagen usually have little effect while large doses of a mutatgen could be lethal. DNA in the nuclei of all cells encodes proteins which play important structural and functional (metabolic) roles in the cell. Mutagens typically disrupt the DNA of cells, causing changes in the proteins that the cell produces which can lead to abnormally fast growth (cancer), or even cell death. In rarer incidences mutagens can even cause protein changes which are beneficial to the cell.

History

The first mutagens to be identified were carcinogens, or cancer-causing substances. Early physicians detected tumors in patients more than 2,000 years before the discovery of chromosomes and DNA. In 500 B.C., the Greek Hippocrates named crab-shaped tumors cancer (meaning crab).

In England in 1775, Dr. Percivall Pott wrote a paper on the high incidence of scrotal cancer in chimney sweeps who were typically boys small enough to fit inside chimneys and clean out the soot. Pott suggested that chimney soot contained carcinogens which could cause the growth of the warts seen in scrotal cancer. Over a 150 years later, chimney soot was found to contain hydrocarbons capable of mutating DNA.

In France in the 1890s, Bordeaux wine workers showed an unusually high incidence of skin cancer on the back of the neck. These workers spend their days bending over in the fields picking grapes, so exposing the back of their necks to the sun. The ultraviolet (uv) radiation in natural sunlight was later identified as a mutagen.

Where mutagens exist

Mutagens can be found in foods, beverages, and drugs. Sometimes a substance is mutagenic because it is converted in the body into something harmful. Regulatory agencies are responsible for testing food and drugs to insure that the public is not unknowingly exposed to mutagens. However, some mutagen-containing substances are not tightly controlled. One such substance is found in the tobacco of cigars and cigarettes.

Some mutagens occur naturally, and some are synthetic. Cosmic rays from space are natural, but they are mutagenic. Some naturally occurring viruses are considered mutagenic since they can insert themselves into host DNA. Hydrogen and atomic bombs are manmade, and they emit harmful radiation. Radiation from nuclear bombs and gaseous particles from nitrogen mustard and acridine orange have been used destructively in war. On the other hand, some mutagens are used constructively to kill bacteria that could grow in human foods, such as the small doses of nitrites used to preserve some meat. Even though nitrites can be mutagenic, without the nitrites these meats could cause botulism; hence, the benefit outweighs the risk involved.

How mutagens work

Mutagens affect DNA in different ways. Some mutagens such as nitrogen mustard bind to a base and cause it to make a different amino acid. These mutagens cause point mutations, because they change the genetic code at one point, so changing a protein's amino acid sequence.

Mutagens such as acridine orange work by deleting or inserting one or more bases into the DNA molecule, so shifting the frame of the triplet code for an amino acid. Deletion and insertion mutations causing "frameshift" mutations can change a long string of amino acids, which can severely alter the structure and function of a protein product.

Normal cells recognize cues from their environment and respond with specific reactions, but cells impaired by a mutation do not behave or appear normal, and are said to be transformed.

Mutations in somatic (body) cells are not transferred to offspring. Mutated DNA can only be passed to the next generation if it is present in a germ cell such as spermatozoa and ova (eggs), each of which contribute half of the DNA of the new organism.

Types of mutagens

Chemical mutagens are classified as alkylating agents, cross-linking agents, and polycyclic aromatic hydrocarbons (PAHs). Alkylating agents act by adding molecular components to DNA bases, so altering the protein product. Cross-linking agents create covalent bonds with DNA bases, while PAHs are metabolized by the human body into other potentially mutagenic molecules.

Radiation is a potent mutagen, classified as Uv or ionizing radiation. Uv radiation causes covalent bonds to form between neighboring thymine bases in the DNA, so altering the DNA product at that location. Ionizing radiation includes the x rays, gamma rays, and subatomic particles. Ionizing radiation alters the way two strands of DNA interact. This high energy radiation passes through cells and tissues, cutting up any DNA in its path. Ionizing radiation can rearrange entire sections of the chromosomes, altering relatively long stretches of DNA.

Mutagens are often associated with specific cancers in humans. Aromatic amines are mutagens which can cause bladder cancer. Tobacco taken in the form of snuff contains mutagens which can cause nose tumors. Tobacco smoke contains mutagens such as PAHs and nitrosamine (a type of alkylating agent), as well as toxins such as carbon monoxide, cyanide, ammonia, arsenic, and radioactive polonium. Although tobacco products are legally and widely available, many physicians and government agencies warn about the health risks linking smoking with several types of cancer and heart disease.

In 1973, Bruce Ames introduced the most widely-used test to identify potential mutagens. Suspected mutagens are mixed with a defective strain of the bacteria *Salmonella*, which only grows if it is mutated. Substances which allow the *Salmonella* to grow are considered mutagenic.

Natural defense against mutagens

In addition to mutagen-induced DNA changes, spontaneous mutations occur in the dividing cells of the human body every day. The nuclei of the cells have repair enzymes which remove mutations and restore mutated DNA to its original form.

If these natural DNA repair mechanisms fail to keep up with the rate of mutation or the repair mechanisms themselves are defective, then disease can result. This latter case is seen in lung cancer due to cigarette smoking, where the nicotine in the smoke is thought to block an important repair process in the lungs.

See also Ames test; Cancer; Carcinogen; Cigarette smoke.

Further Reading:

Ruddon, Raymond. *Cancer Biology.* 2nd ed. New York: Oxford University Press, 1987.
Voet, Donald and Judith Voet. *Biochemistry.* New York: John Wiley & Sons, 1990.
Woodburn, John. *Cancer: The Search for Its Origins.* New York: Holt, Rinehart and Winston, Inc., 1964.

Louise H. Dickerson

Mutation

Mutation is a sudden change in DNA (deoxyribonucleic acid), the genetic material of life, that creates a change in an organism's appearance, behavior, or health. Organisms born with mutations can look very different from their parents. Albinos are an example of a mutation that eliminates skin pigment. Dwarfs are an example of a mutation that affects growth hormones. Mutations are usually harmful, but some may help an organism survive, by proving to be beneficial to the species. Useful mutations are the driving force behind evolution.

Errors in DNA

For many centuries, no explanation for the sudden appearance of mutations existed. Today we know that mutations are caused when the hereditary material of life is altered. Every cell contains DNA on threadlike structures called chromosomes. Stretches of DNA that code for specific proteins are known as genes. Human beings carry about 100,000 genes on their chromosomes. If the

DNA of a particular gene is altered, that gene will become defective. The protein for which it codes will also be missing or defective. Just one missing or abnormal protein can have an enormous effect on the entire body. Albinoism, for instance, is the result of one missing protein. This understanding of genetic inheritance is based upon experiments conducted by Thomas H. Morgan in 1910 with fruit fly mutations, and experiments conducted by George W. Beadle and Edward L. Tatum in the 1940s on bread mold mutations.

Errors in DNA take several forms. DNA itself is made up of subunits known as nucleotide bases. There are four kinds of bases: adenine, cytosine, guanine, and thymine. They are referred to by their initials: A, C, G, and T. DNA can be thought of as a code (the genetic code) written with these four letters. Mistakes in the genetic code occur when any of these nucleotide bases are out of place: either too few, too many, or the wrong kind. Mutation can be thought of as a kind of typographical error.

Let's say that a normal stretch of DNA looks like this: ATCTTTGGT.

Too many nucleotide bases—especially if the same pattern of bases repeat over and over—is a mistake: *ATCATCATC*TTTGGT.

Huntington's disease, a fatal disease which strikes people in their 40s or 50s and slowly disables their nervous system, occurs when a person inherits two copies of a mutated gene. One copy comes from the mother and one from the father. The Huntington's disease mutation is caused by a repeating triplet of bases in the gene.

The wrong bases in the wrong places is also an error: ATCTTT*CCA*.

Missing bases is another kind of error: ATCGGT.

Cystic fibrosis, a lethal disorder that clogs the lungs with mucus, occurs when a person inherits two copies of a mutated gene. In most cases, the mutation is the result of the absence of three thymine bases. Cystic fibrosis patients usually die before the age of 30.

Errors in all or part of a chromosome are also called mutations. Humans normally have 23 pairs of chromosomes. (Each pair of chromosomes is distinct under the microscope and scientists have numbered them for ease of identification.) An extra chromosome can have an enormous effect. Three copies of chromosome 21, for instance, results in Down's syndrome. People with Down's syndrome have a unique physical appearance and are developmentally disabled. If two chromosomes swap pieces, the result is known as a

A six-legged green frog.

translocation. A translocation between chromosome 9 and chromosome 22 leads to a certain type of leukemia.

Mutations that occur in an organism's egg or sperm cells are known as germinal mutations. Germinal mutations can be passed on to the organism's offspring. Mutations that occur in cells other than the sex cells are known as somatic mutations. They cannot be passed on. This is an important difference to keep in mind when discussing the causes of mutation. Some causes will affect only the somatic cells of the organism exposed. Other causes will affect the germ cells and will be passed on to many succeeding generations. In this manner, a mutation can become common in certain populations.

Causes of mutation

The opportunity for error exists every time a cell replicates. Almost always, DNA reproduces itself correctly. Yet if the genetic code is somehow altered—if part of it is missing, duplicated, or switched around—the result is a mutation. As might be expected, cells that divide many, many times in a lifetime are more at risk for errors than cells that divide less frequently. In humans, egg cells are fully formed when a baby girl is born and never divide. By contrast, sperm cells are constantly being produced. Indeed, the older a man is, the more frequently his sperm-producing cells have divided. By age 20, they will have divided 200 times. By age 45, about 770 times. This has led scientists to hypothesize that when a baby is born with a birth defect caused by an error in cell division, the father is the parent most likely to have contributed the gene with the mutation. Birth defects in this category include a type of dwarfism, Marfan syndrome, and a bony tissue disease known as myositis ossificans.

Uncontrolled cell growth, known as cancer, is also a kind of mutation. Cancer can be caused by environmental factors such as smoking. Repeated exposure to cigarette smoke may cause a somatic mutation in the lung cells that leads to lung cancer. Other environmental factors that are known to cause mutations include exposure to radiation, pesticides, asbestos, and some (now banned) food additives. Factors that cause mutations are known as mutagens. Those that cause cancer are known as carcinogens.

Scientists have found that carcinogens do their deadly work by engineering mutations in important genes. A gene known as p53, for instance, helps prevent the growth of tumors. Yet exposure to ultraviolet light and cigarette smoke can cause that gene to mutate. In its mutated form, the gene no longer prevents tumors. People with two copies of the mutated gene are likely to develop cancer. If mutated genes responsible for cancer are present in the egg or sperm cells, then a susceptibility to cancer may be passed on to future generations. This accounts for cancers that seem to run in families, and points to the existence of a germinal mutation.

Developing embryos and fetuses are especially at risk for mutation. Their cells divide very rapidly and become increasingly specialized for specific tasks. Pregnant women must be careful to avoid x rays, almost all medication, and even the extreme temperatures of hot tubs and saunas.

Mutation and evolution

We tend to think of mutation as the sudden appearance of a condition that has not existed before: a baby is born with webbed fingers, or with eyes of two different colors. Indeed, when Dutch botanist Hugo De Vries (1848-1935) coined the term in 1901, this is what he meant. The term is also used to describe genes that can lead to inherited diseases such as cystic fibrosis. It's less likely that we would call characteristics we take for granted—two eyes, ten fingers, hairless skin—mutations. Yet all those characteristics were once mutations too.

For every human trait, there was once a person in which the genetic mutation—the DNA for hairless skin or cystic fibrosis—first appeared. Certain traits—like hairless skin—must have occurred long ago because they are shared by all humans. Other traits occur only in certain populations of people. Cystic fibrosis, for instance, is most common in people of northern European descent. Sickle cell anemia, a serious blood disease, occurs frequently in people of African and Mediterranean ancestry. Tay-Sachs disease, a fatal disorder, is found primarily in Jews with eastern European ancestors. This suggests that the first person in whom such a mutation occurred came from that particular ethnic group. Not enough time has passed to allow that mutation to spread evenly across the population.

Another explanation is that the particular mutation proved to be a useful one for that population. We know, for example, that while two copies of the mutant sickle cell anemia gene causes illness, one copy confers a resistance to malaria. This would have been very useful to people living in the tropics where malaria is common. Scientists have hypothesized that some advantage must be conferred upon people with single copies of the cystic fibrosis gene or the Tay-Sachs disease gene.

KEY TERMS

Genome—The entire DNA of an organism.

Germinal mutation—A mutation in the germ cells (sperm or egg cells). This mutation can be passed on to succeeding generations.

Nucleotide base—One of the four chemical subunits of DNA: adenine, cytosine, guanine, and thymine.

Somatic mutation—A mutation in the body cells. This mutation cannot be passed on.

Translocation—A trade of chromosomal parts.

Over millions of years, advantageous mutations have allowed life to develop and diversify from primitive cells into the multitude of species on Earth today, including *Homo sapiens*. Indeed, human beings are the sum total of many, many mutations over the past three billion years. Evolution is led by mutation. If DNA replicated perfectly every time, without errors, only primitive cells would be found on Earth. Nothing would have changed in three billion years. Any mutations that allow an organism to survive and reproduce better than other members of its species are valuable. Mutations become especially important when an organism's environment is changing.

Animal and plant breeders use mutations to produce new or improved species of crops and livestock. Careful breeding in this manner has spawned all the different species of dogs and horses we know today. It has resulted in crops that are resistant to drought or insects or have a high yield per acre. Goldfish, yellow roses, and Concord grapes are all descendants of ancestors with specific mutations.

Much more will be known about human mutation when the human genome project is completed in 2005 A.D. The term "genome" refers to the sum total of an organism's DNA. The United States has committed to spending up to $3 billion over 15 years to identify all human genes and to catalogue every nucleotide base in the human genome. Knowing this will allow us to identify the genetic cause of mutations much more quickly.

See also Carcinogen; Chromosome; Deoxyribonucleic acid; Genetic disorders; Genetics; Human evolution; Mutagen.

Further Reading:

Angier, Natalie. "Genetic Mutations Tied to Father in Most Cases." *New York Times* (17 May 1994): B9.

——. "Researchers Trace the Primary Cause of Cystic Fibrosis to the Stone Age." *New York Times* (1 June 1994): A13.

Blakeslee, Sandra. "Genes Tell Story of Why Some Get Cancer While Others Don't." *New York Times* (17 May 1994): B6.

Lee, Thomas F. *The Human Genome Project*. New York: Plenum Press, 1991.

Pollack, Robert. *Signs of Life: The Language and Meanings of DNA*. Boston: Houghton Mifflin Company, 1994.

Wilcox, Frank H. *DNA: The Thread of Life*. Minneapolis: Lerner Publications Company, 1988.

Liz Marshall

Mutualism

Mutualism is a biological interaction that is beneficial to both parties. Most mutualisms are facultative, meaning the partners can successfully live apart. However, some mutualisms are so intimate that the interacting species can no longer live without each other; they have a mutually obligate interdependence. Many mutualisms are fascinating in their intricacies and reciprocal usefulness as is apparent in the examples described below.

Many species of angiosperm plants require the services of an animal vector to achieve pollination. The animal benefits in this mutualism from access to a source of food of nectar or pollen, while the plant benefits through having its gametes fertilized. Some pollination systems involve a remarkably tight co-evolution of the plant and animal species, with morphological and behavioral adaptations that make the mutualistic interaction more efficient and more interdependent. Some species of orchids, for example the genus *Ophrys*, have a floral structure and coloration that closely mimics that of the female of their pollinating species of wasp so that the plant becomes pollinated when the male wasp is tricked and attempts pseudo-copulations with its flowers. There are numerous other examples of similarly extraordinary co-adaptations of plant-animal pollination systems.

Another plant-insect mutualism involves a tropical ant (*Pseudomyrmex ferruginea*) and a shrub known as the bull's horn acacia (*Acacia cornigera*). This acacia has evolved hollow thorns that are used by the ants as protected nesting sites. In addition, the ants feed on protein-rich exudates at the tips of the leaflets of the acacia.

In return, the ants protect the acacia from competition with other plants by weeding the vicinity of their host of encroaching foliage. The ants also protect the acacia from many defoliators by killing herbivorous insects and attacking larger herbivores such as grazing mammals. Many other species of ants have developed mutualistic interactions with plant species. This fact is evidenced by the independent evolution of extrafloral nectaries by various families of plants. These organs exude nectar from leaves, stems, or branches, attracting ants that help to protect the plants from competition and herbivory.

A marine mutualism involves unicellular algae known as zooxanthellae and corals, a type of coelenterate animal. In this mutualism the coral provides the algae with shelter and inorganic nutrients, while the pigmented algae provide photosynthate. Sometimes this mutualism is upset by environmental stresses associated with unusually warm or cool water temperatures, a change in salinity, or excessive exposure to sunlight or shading. This leads to expulsion of the zooxanthellae by the coral, a phenomenon known as "bleaching," which may lead to death of the coral unless it can re-establish another algal mutualism.

Another interesting mutualism involves two animals, an African bird known as the honey guide (*Indicator indicator*) and a mammal known as the honey badger (*Melliovora capensis*). In this relationship the honey guide finds bee hives and then actively leads the honey badger to its discovery. The badger tears the hive apart with its strong claws and then feeds on the honey, while the bird feeds on the bee larvae and pupae.

See also Symbiosis.

Bill Freedman

Mycorrhiza

A "fungus root" or mycorrhiza (plural: mycorrhizae) is a fungus living in a mutually beneficial symbiosis (or mutualism) with the roots of a vascular plant. In this intimate relationship, the fungus benefits from access to energy-containing carbohydrates, proteins, and other organic nutrients excreted by, or contained in, the roots while the host plant benefits from an enhanced supply of inorganic nutrients, especially phosphorus.

The fungi carry out this function largely by increasing the rate of decomposition of organic matter in the immediate vicinity of the plant root, and by efficiently absorbing the inorganic nutrients that are liberated by this process. From the perspective of the plant, the most important of the mineral nutrients supplied by the fungus are compounds of phosphorus, and to a lesser degree, of nitrogen.

Mycorrhizae are a common type of mutualism; about 90% of the families of vascular plants live in this sort of beneficial relationship with fungi. Only a few economically important plant families do not develop mycorrhizae, among them the mustards (family Brassicaceae) and knotweeds (Polygonaceae).

Biology of mycorrhizae

A mycorrhiza is an intimate, biological relationship in which fungal hyphae integrate closely with the root tissues of a vascular plant. Plant roots that have an mycorrhizal fungus tend not to develop root hairs, relying heavily on the fungus to absorb nutrients and moisture from the soil. The fungal *hyphae* (root-like projections) are associated with the cortical cells of the root, and not with vascular tissues or the actively growing cells of the meristematic tissue at the tip of the root.

There are two basic types of mycorrhizae—endomycorrhizae and ectomycorrhizae. Endomycorrhizae are more common than ectomycorrhizae, although the latter type is more frequent in the economically important species of trees of temperate forests.

In ectomycorrhizae, the fungal hyphae form a diffuse veil or mantle around the outside of the plant root. The fungal biomass of a ectomycorrhiza typically comprises about 40% of the dry weight of the structure. The fungal hyphae penetrate the root to some degree, but they only occur in the spaces between the cortical and epidermal cells. Ectomycorrhizae occur in association with the roots of such tree species as pines (*Pinus* spp.), spruces (*Picea* spp.), willows (*Salix* spp.), oaks (*Quercus* spp.), and birches (*Betula* spp.). Under the influence of hormones secreted by the fungus, the plant roots tend to grow in a stubby, thickened, and much-branched fashion. Most of the species of fungi that are involved in ectomycorrhizae are Basidiomycetes, and a smaller number are Ascomycetes. Most forest mushrooms are the fruiting bodies of Basidiomycete fungi that are mycorrhizal with tree species.

In endomycorrhizae, the fungal hyphae mostly grow inside the plant root, and they penetrate and grow inside the cortical cells of the root. Many economically-important species of plants depend on endomycorrhizal fungi, including apple (*Pyrus malus*), strawberry (*Fragaria vesca*), tomato (*Lycopersicon esculentum*),

orchids (family Orchidaceae), and grasses (Poaceae). In fact, most of the important agricultural plants used by humans for food are endomycorrhizal. Although most conifers are ectomycorrhizal, a few species are endomycorrhizal, notably the redwoods (*Sequoia sempervirens*) and junipers (*Juniperus* spp.).

Importance of mycorrhizae

There is a great deal of evidence that clearly demonstrates the great importance of mycorrhizae to plant nutrition, especially in nutrient-poor soils. For example, many species of trees and shrubs can be grown in the greenhouse, but if these are then transplanted into an abandoned pasture, prairie, or some other non-forested habitat, they commonly fail to survive or grow well, and will exhibit signs of nutritional distress. This happens because the soils of those habitats do not have populations of appropriate species of mycorrhizal fungi to colonize the roots of the tree seedlings. If the seedlings are to do well in such habitats, they must be deliberately inoculated with an appropriate mycorrhizal fungus.

On the other hand, if the seedlings are transplanted into a recent clear-cut that was previously a forest dominated by the same or closely related species of trees (for example during post-harvest regeneration of the stand), they will generally do well. This happens because the clear-cut still has a population of mycorrhizal fungi that are suitable to inoculate the tree seedlings.

In some cases, plants will not do well in the absence of a mycorrhiza, even when they are growing in apparently fertile soil. In such a case, the mycorrhizal mutualism is said to be obligate. In most cases, however, plant species can survive in fertile soil in the absence of a mycorrhizal relationship with a fungus. In less fertile soil, however, these species may do very poorly without a mycorrhiza. In this case, the mutualism is said to be facultative.

When natural ecosystems are being converted into some sort of system that is managed for the benefits of people, it may be critically important to consider the mycorrhizal fungi on the site. In tropical forests, for example, almost all of the tree species depend on mycorrhizae to supply them with nutrients from the typically infertile soils on which these ecosystems develop. Moreover, the mycorrhizal fungi are critical to retaining nutrients within the forest biomass, and in preventing these chemicals from being washed away by the abundant tropical rains. If the forest is cleared and burned to develop new agricultural lands, much of the nutrient capital of the land is lost due to the reduction of grow-

KEY TERMS

. . . .

Cortex—The root cortex is a relatively soft tissue that occurs between the epidermis and the internal, vascular tissues.

Hyphae (singular: hypha)—These are tubular filaments of fungi, which in aggregate comprise the mycelium.

Root hair—These are tiny, tubular outgrowths of the root epidermis, mostly occurring behind the actively growing root tip, and used to increase surface area of the root to enhance the absorption of minerals and water from the soil.

ing biomass, including the destruction of much of the mycorrhizal fungi by the disturbance. Moreover, the fungi that do manage to survive are not necessarily appropriate symbionts for the species of grasses and other crops that farmers attempt to grow on the cleared land. Therefore, the conversion of the tropical forest, with its efficient recycling and use of the scarce nutrient resources, into a more open agricultural system with large losses of nutrient capital, often leads to a rapid degradation of the fertility of the site. This is a major reason why so many conversions of tropical forests into agriculture prove to be unsustainable.

Many mycorrhizal fungi in the Basiodiomycete group develop edible mushrooms, and these are gathered by many people for use in gourmet cooking. Perhaps the most famous of these mushrooms are the truffles, such as *Tuber melanosporum*, which is commonly mycorrhizal on species of oaks (*Quercus* spp.). The spore-bearing bodies of the truffle fungi develop underground, and must be found using specially trained, truffle-sniffing pigs or dogs. Mushroom collectors must be careful, however, because some mycorrhizal fungi develop fruiting bodies that are deadly poisonous, as is the case of the death or destroying angel (*Amanita virosa*).

Orchids (family Orchidaceae) are examples of plants that can only grow if they have an endomycorrhizal mutualism. Orchid seeds are tiny and dust-like, and they have virtually no stored energy to support the seedling when it germinates. The tiny orchid seedlings will only grow if they manage to become inoculated by an appropriate endomycorrhizal fungus. Until this fact was discovered by horticulturalists, orchids were extremely difficult to propagate and grow in greenhouses. Now, orchids are relatively easy to breed and cultivate.

Some species of vascular plants do not contain chlorophyll, and are incapable of photosynthesis. The whitish shoots of species such as the Indian pipe (*Monotropa uniflora*) depend entirely on their mycorrhizal fungus to supply the plant with organic nutrients needed for growth and reproduction. This is an unusual case in which the balanced, reciprocal dependence of the plant and fungal symbionts of a mycorrhiza have become unbalanced, to the degree that the plant is now parasitic on the fungus.

Further Reading:

Atlas, R.M. and R. Bartha. *Microbial Ecology.* Menlo Park, CA: Benjamin-Cummings Pub. Co., 1987.
Raven, P.H., F.E. Evert, and H. Curtis. *Biology of Plants.* New York: Worth Publishers, 1976.

Bill Freedman

Mycotoxin

Mycotoxins are toxic substances produced by molds and fungi, such as mushrooms. These toxic substances, known as secondary metabolites, are by-products of metabolism that are inessential to fungal growth. Although some mycotoxins can be used for medicinal purposes, most are poisonous if eaten in sufficient quantity.

Numerous mycotoxins have been studied and identified. Of particular interest are mycotoxins made by fungi that contaminate human foods or by poisonous mushrooms. Many grains, fruits, and vegetables can support fungal growth under certain conditions.

Agricultural attention to mycotoxins has focused on corn, nut, and fruit crops because of their susceptibility to mold growth and their importance in human diet. Climate conditions, including temperature and moisture can affect mold growth in harvested fields, with moister, warmer periods favoring growth. Mycotoxins serve as a defensive force for molds, because they can actually limit the role of competitive microorganisms in the vicinity. Although farm and food industries make every effort to eliminate mycotoxins because they can cause illness and devalue crops, mycotoxins cannot be completely removed, and small quantities of them continue to be present in many foods.

Many mycotoxins affect several target organs including the liver, which develops a toxicity. Mycotoxins harm their host by disrupting cellular activity. The phomopsons, a kind of mycotoxin, inhibit the normal activity of microtubule, essential structures inside cells which are required for cellular division. The Aspergillus family of fungi produce a very potent mycotoxin called aflatoxin. A number of aflatoxins have been isolated, with aflatoxin B (AFB) and aflatoxin G (AFG), an AFB derivative, occurring in greatest quantity. The aflatoxins bind to DNA in the cellular nucleus of the organism they attack, acting as a powerful, potentially fatal, mutagen. Other Aspergillus toxins which have been found in food include ochratoxin A (OA) and sterigmatocystin. OA is a mammalian carcinogen that causes renal disease in humans. Like many other naturally occurring mycotoxins, OA is found in a number of everyday foods. Varying levels of OA have been detected in beans, cereals, cocoa, coffee, corn, figs, flours, pork kidney, nuts, olives, peas, rice, sausage, and soy.

It would be difficult to find a food that does not contain myocotoxins. However, the fact that most foods contain very low, non-illness producing, levels of mycotoxins makes them perfectly safe to eat except for individuals with specific mycotoxic allergies. Mycotoxin levels in food vary according to location. In one study of sterigmatocystin in green coffee in the United States and Italy, twice as many samples from Italy tested positive for the presence of the mycotoxin. And even the U.S. samples that did test positive had levels below 5 ng/g, whereas the Italian samples averaged 1,200 ng/g.

Mycotoxins can be produced by the fungi that grow on the crop itself, the weeds surrounding the crop, or the soil in which the crop grows. *Alternia* fungi are natural soil inhabitants which produce several mycotoxins-alternariol and alternariol methyl ether (found on apples), and tenuazonic acid (found on tomatoes and in tomato paste). *Alternia* toxins are responsible for postharvest decay in these crops. Mycotoxin levels in foods are monitored and minimized by the food industry.

Although most mushrooms are harmless, poisonous mushrooms contain mycotoxins capable of attacking the human host with fatal consequences. The reaction times and symptoms vary according to mushroom. Some mycotoxins act immediatelly on the human host, with effects ranging from nausea, vomiting, hallucination, anxiety, muscle spasms, diarrhea, and hyperactivity or lethargy. The mycotoxins coprine, psilocybin/psilocin, muscarine, and ibotenic acid are all capable of causing these sudden symptoms. Other mycotoxins have more serious effects, are delayed in onset, and can be fatal. The delayed symptoms (which may persist up to 14 days after ingestion) include bloating, headache, severe vomiting, diarrhea, cramps, severe thirst, frequent urination, kidney pain, and death.

Potentially fatal mycotoxins that are classified as group A, B, and C poisons include monomethylhydrazine, the amatoxins, and orellanine.

The mode of action of mushroom-produced mycotoxins varies considerably. Alpha amanitin, amatoxin produced by some species of *Amanita*, is a class A poison which acts by inhibiting a critical nuclear polymerase that enables the cell to make protein. Once the function of this RNA polymerase is curtailed, basic life processes cease. Attempts to kill alpha amanitin with antibodies have proven to be even more harmful to patients than the poison itself. Most forms of mushroom poisoning can be treated with rapid lavage (induced vomiting) or medically approved ingestion of charcoal to absorb the toxin before it is absorbed into the stomach.

Although it may seem obvious that one would want to avoid toxic, or poisonous, mycotoxins, some cultures have historically sought out milder mycotoxins for their hallucinogenic properties. The class E poisons, psilocybin and psilocin, are found in many *Psilocybe* species such as *Psilocybe cubensis* known as "magic mushrooms" or "street mushrooms," these hallucinogens are similar in effect to, but less potent than, the psychedelic drug LSD. The Aztecs of South America used "sacred mushrooms" for religious rites, and other people from various cultures and times in history have experimented recreationally with mushrooms. While no treatment is required for these toxins, which wear off in about 6-10 hours, they can have extreme mood-altering effects and require avoidance of complex tasks such as driving. In addition, some people have had recurrent episodes of hallucinations from mushroom "tripping" years after use.

Further Reading:

Bray, G., and D. Ryan, eds. "Mycotoxins, Cancer, and Health." In *Mycotoxins, Cancer, and Health. Pennington Center Nutrition Series, vol 1*. Baton Rouge: Louisiana State University Press, 1991.

Speorke, D., and B. Rumack, eds. *Handbook of Mushroom Poisoning: Diagnosis and Treatment*. London: CRC Press, 1994.

Louise Dickerson

Mynah birds

Mynah or myna birds are species in the family Sturnidae, which also includes many species of starlings. The distinction between starlings and mynahs is not always clear, and these common names are sometimes used interchangeably. However, as considered here, the mynahs are tropical, Asian species, the most prominent of which are in the genus *Acridotheres* and *Gracula*.

The word mynah is derived from the Hindu word *maina*, itself derived from the Sanskrit word *madana*, both of which are names for the hill mynah.

Species of mynahs occur in forests, shrubby woodlands, and in urban and suburban habitats. Mynahs are medium-sized, stocky, robust birds, with a stout beak, strong legs, and a short tail. Their songs are innovative, raucous chatters made up of whistles, squeaks, and diverse, imitated sounds. Mynahs feed on a wide range of invertebrates and fruits. Mynahs nest in cavities in trees, and both sexes cooperate in feeding and raising the young birds.

The hill mynah

The hill mynah or talking mynah (*Gracula religiosa*) is native to secondary tropical forests and other wooded habitats in south and Southeast Asia. The hill mynah is perhaps the best-known species of mynah, and the species that learns to "talk" the best. (Actually, it only mimics human sounds, and has no idea about their context.)

The hill mynah has a glossy black body, a heavy orange-to-red bill, yellow legs and feet, and bare yellow skin behind the eyes, including an extended flap of skin known as a lappet, located behind the head. The hill mynah also has a white patch on the underwings, that is conspicuous when the bird is in flight. The hill mynah feeds only on fruit.

The hill mynah can be bred in captivity, and is an important species in the avian pet trade. This attractive cage-bird maintains a busy and noisy chatter, and can be easily trained to mimic human words and phrases.

The common mynah

The common or Indian mynah (*Acridotheres tristis*) is a native species of south Asia, from Afghanistan, Pakistan, and India, through to southwestern China and Indochina. However, humans have introduced this species far beyond its original, natural range, especially during the mid- to late-nineteenth century.

The common mynah has a dark-brown plumage, with a black head, throat, and upper breast, and a yellow beak, feet, and skin around the eye. A conspicuous white patch is visible under the wings when the bird is in flight.

The common mynah is a rather omnivorous bird, eating a wide range of invertebrates, fruits, and seeds.

When hunting for insects, the common mynah probes the ground with its closed bill, and then withdraws its beak while closely inspecting the hole, to see whether anything edible had been exposed.

The natural nesting sites of the common mynah are cavities in trees, either natural, or excavated by other species of birds, such as woodpeckers. However, in some of its introduced habitats where it lives in proximity to humans, the adaptable common mynah will also nest in holes in walls and buildings. Because the common mynah is a loosely colonial nester, large populations may breed in places where there are suitable nesting and foraging habitats.

The common mynah has been introduced to various places in the tropics beyond its natural range, including islands in the Indian, Pacific, and Atlantic Oceans. This species now occurs in Madagascar, South Africa, Australia, New Zealand, the Hawaiian Islands, Saint Helena, Mauritius, Fiji, Tahiti, the Marquesas, Singapore, Hong Kong, and many other non-native places. The common mynah was introduced to these places because it was believed that this bird would provide a useful service by eating pest species of insects that dwell in the soil, especially in orchards.

However, to say the least, these many introductions of the common mynah were severely misguided, and unfortunately this bird is often considered to be a pest in its novel habitats. The common mynah causes especially important damages in orchards of soft fruits and berries, such as bananas, papayas, guavas, pineapples, apples, and others. If common mynahs are abundant, they can cause enormous damages to these fruits by probing with their beaks, eating only a small quantity of the tissue, but greatly reducing its potential value in the marketplace.

Common mynahs are also considered pests where they develop large, communal roosts, which can involve dense aggregations of thousands of birds. These are considered nuisances because of the raucous noise, and the copious excrement that can accumulate.

Although the common mynah causes significant damages, it also provides some useful services. These birds do eat significant numbers of insect pests, although this benefit is generally considered to be far smaller than the damages that the common mynah causes. Also, the common mynah is one of the few non-human animals that can tolerate the harsh environments of tropical cities and towns. Just by being around, these birds provide a certain aesthetic benefit.

The common mynah is one of very few species that have greatly benefitted from the sorts of ecological changes that humans are causing on Earth. Because the

A mynah bird known to the locals as "Martin" on the island of Mauritius in the Indian Ocean.

common mynah is relatively well adapted to habitats that humans create, it has become a rather "successful" bird — a winner in a world that is becoming incredibly dominated by humans, and ecologically degraded their activities.

Other species of mynahs

The most diverse genus of mynahs is *Acridotheres*, a group that includes the common mynah. The white-vented or Javan mynah (*Acridotheres javanicus*) is native from east Pakistan to various of the islands of Indonesia. The bank mynah (*A. ginginianus*) is unusual, in that it excavates nesting cavities in earthen banks.

The crested mynah (*Acridotheres cristatellus*) is native to southern China and Taiwan. However, it has been introduced elsewhere, and is the only mynah to breed in North America. The crested mynah has been introduced to the city of Vancouver on the southwestern Pacific coast of Canada. Although its populations there have remained small, the crested mynah continues to breed in that area.

The Papuan or golden-faced mynah (*Mino dumontii*) and golden mynah (*M. anais*) are colorful, black-and-gold, fruit-eating species that occur widely on the island of New Guinea. The golden-crested mynah (*Ampeliceps coronatus*) is a glossy, black-bodied, yellow-headed species that occurs in south China and Indochina.

One of the world's rarest birds is the Bali or Rothschild's mynah (*Leucospar rothschildi*) of Bali. This species is a lovely, white-colored bird, with a black-colored mask, outer wing feathers, and base of tail. The Rothschild's mynah is a species of tropical forests, and it has become critically endangered because of the destruction of its habitat to extract valuable lumber, followed by conversion of the land into agricultural uses. Fewer than only fifty of these beautiful birds may still survive, most of them in a small, national park created largely to serve as habitat for their remnant population.

Further Reading:

Harrison, C.J.O. (ed.). *Bird Families of the World.* New York: H.N. Abrams Pubs., 1978.

Bill Freedman

Myopia see **Vision disorders**

Myrtle see **Sweet gale family**

Myrtle family

In both the New and Old Worlds many genera of the Myrtle family (Myrtaceae) unfurl their waxy, leathery leaves. Containing both trees and shrubs, this angiosperm family takes its name from the shrub *Myrtus*, which is found near the Mediterranean, in North Africa, and in South America.

Other well known genera from the Myrtaceae include ornamentals such as *Leptospermum* (Australian Tea Tree), *Eucalyptus*, *Verticordia* (feather flowers), and *Calliostemon* (bottle brush). Economically valuable taxa of the Myrtaceae also include *Eucalyptus* (timber, essential oils), *Pimenta* (allspice, pimento, bay rum), *Psidium* (guave), *Szygium* (cloves), and *Melaleuca* (timber). In fact, some of the tallest trees known from modern times were specimens of *Eucalyptus* estimated to have been over 350 ft (107 m) tall. If these reports are accurate, the eucalypts rival the redwoods (gymnosperms, Taxodiaceae) for the title of tallest trees. This could make *Eucalyptus* the tallest angiosperm, or flowering plant.

Broad taxonomy

In a broader taxonomic sense, the Myrtaceae is a dicot family in the class Rosidae, which also includes the rose and mallow families. The Myrtaceae falls into the order Mytrales, along with the families Lythraceae, Punicaceae (pomegranates), and Onagraceae (evening primroses).

An unusual and taxonomically useful trait found in the Myrtaceae involves the vascular system of the stem. In most dicotyledonous plants the food conducting cells of the vascular system, the sieve elements of the phloem, surround the water conducting cells, or xylem. In young stems there is usually another group of large cells which appear open in sections viewed under a light microscope. This group of cells is called the pith, inside the xylem. Unusually, some phloem occurs inside the pith in species of the Myrtaceae.

Species of the Myrtaceae are noted for leaf dimorphism: the leaves produced when the plants are young tend to be round and held closely to the branch, while leaves produced when the plants are mature are much longer and thinner. Whether juvenile or adult, the leaves of plants in the Myrtle family are opposite. Whenever a leaf is found on one side of the stem, another leaf is found on the opposite side.

Eucalyptus trees near Alice Springs, Australia.

The term myrtle, a common name for some species in the genus *Myrtus*, is also used as a common name for numerous other plants. These are not to be confused with species from the Myrtaceae. The best known plant called a myrtle, which is not a member of the Myrtaceae, may be the popular garden plant, crepe myrtle, (*Lagerstroemia indica*), of the Lythraceae or Loosestrife family.

The Myrtaceae is commonly subdivided into two subfamilies, the Leptospermoideae, which is distributed mostly in Asia and Africa, and the Myrtoideae, found in tropical America, Asia, Australia, and the Pacific. The myrtle family is best known from Australia. Many species in the genera *Eucalyptus*, *Calliostemon*, and *Verticordia*, among others, are found in Australia. However, many genera such as *Psidium* are present in the Americas, and *Myrtus* of the Mediterranean and Northern Africa. The genus *Eucalyptus* is probably the best known representative of the Myrtaceae.

Economic value

Species of the Myrtle family provide many valuable products, including timber (e.g. *Eucalyptus*), essential oils (e.g. allspice), and horticultural plants (e.g. ornamentals such as *Verticordia* and food plants such as *Psidium*, guava).

The various species of the Myrtaceae are sources of several valuable essential oils, produced by distillation from leaves. Many of the components of these oils are based on the isoprenoid unit, five carbon atoms linked together in a branched structure with a double bond between two of the carbon atoms involved in the branch point.

Eucalyptus oil includes eucalyptol, with the major component being 1,8-cineole, a modified monoterpenoid, along with hexanol and caproaldehyde. The composition of essential oils varies with the species from which they are distilled, giving each oil a unique character. *Eucalyptus risdoni* contains tasmanone, while *E. grandis* contains grandinol. One species of *Leptospermum* is used to produce a lemon-scented oil, including the compound leptospermone, and *Myrtus* yields the oil known as Eau d'Anges (literally, water of the angels).

Cloves and allspice also come from the Myrtaceae. Cloves, one of the best known spices from the Myrtle family, comes originally from the islands near Southeast Asia. The spice is composed of the whole, dried immature flower buds of the species *Szygium aromaticum*. Grown in Indonesia, Malaysia, and several African countries, the name for this popular spice comes from the Sanskrit *Katukaphelah*, which became the Greek *karyophyllon* and from there the English *clove*. The buds of this 38-49 ft (12-15 m) tree must be picked with very precise timing and sun-dried to avoid fermentation.

Cloves are a flavoring for mulled cider and ketchup, and for decoration in pomanders. Dried apples or oranges covered with cloves are valued for their pleasant scent. The scent of cloves was considered so pleasant that courtiers of Han Dynasty China chewed cloves to improve their breath before appearing in court. Cloves give their flavor and name to clove cigarettes, or *kretek* in Indonesia. They are made by mixing cloves with the tobacco.

Distilled clove oil was once used by dentists as an anaesthetic. Cloves were no longer used after some patients had adverse reactions. The principal component of this oil is eugenol, a complex alcohol based on the benzene ring, making it an aromatic chemical.

Allspice, or bay rum, also comes from the Myrtaceae. The spice is extracted from dried, unripe, pea-sized berries of the species *Pimenta dioica*, which are reddish brown in color. Unlike cloves, which are native to the Old World, the tall trees which produce these berries grow only in areas near their native climate of Central America and the West Indies. For this reason, the original producers had their business protected. Many other spices were eventually grown in places different than their origins, which hurt the economies of the original producing nations. Most worldwide production comes from the Caribbean—Jamaica, Haiti, Guatemala, and other nearby nations. The name comes from the Spanish *pimienta*, or black pepper. This confusion of names comes from the similar appearance of the pepper corns and the allspice berries. *Pimienta* also applies to the hot pepper, of the Solanaceae which also includes the tomato and the potato.

Allspice flavors a number of common foods including several liquors, such as Benedictine, pies, and ketchup. The principal active compound in allspice is eugenol, as in the case of cloves.

Many species from the Myrtle family have attractive glossy green leaves and colorful flowers making them popular horticultural plants. Many species are from arid regions, so the drought tolerance provides another valuable trait for horticulture. They are particularly valuable in regions with similar Mediterranean climates, such as southern California, where they remain bright and attractive during an otherwise bleak time of the year. Eucalypts make attractive street trees.

Their resilience has a negative side in the face of drought. The leathery leaves of Myrtaceous plants are rich in highly flammable hydrocarbons and present a fire hazard.

In their natural environments, this abundance of flammable oils acts to promote the survival and success of myrtaceous plants. Forest and brush fires occur normally during the dry times of the year in places where these species of the Myrtaceae live. The flammability of the myrtaceous plants feeds these fires. Species of *Eucalyptus* regenerate after these fires either from dormant buds or lignotubers, woody subterranean modified stems. Other species which might otherwise compete with Myrtaceous plants for resources such as water and sunlight are destroyed or damaged in the fires while Myrtaceous species, such as eucalypts, survive. Ironically, the ability to burn is actually a competitive advantage for these plants.

The Myrtle family provides a number of important timber species, including those of the genera *Eucalyptus* and *Melaleuca*. *Eucalyptus* provided the Australian aborigines the opportunity to make dishes and canoes. The roots of some species were used for food.

Species of *Eucalyptus* were first collected by expedition botanists travelling with Captain James Cook. The name *Eucalyptus* was created by botanist, David Nelson, on Cook's third voyage, from the Greek words for "well covered." The name came from complete covering of some parts of the flower bud by the operculum, or dome covering the make and female organs. The operculum sheds when the flower opens. The operculum is a ring of fused, hardened petals, as is found in the non-myrtaceous plant honeysuckle (*Lonicera*, Caprifoliaceae, soft petals). Species in the genus *Eucalyptus*, like the rest of the Myrtaceae, are woody perennials ranging in size from shrubs to tall trees.

The genus *Eucalyptus* is divided into six general types of eucalypts based on the appearance of the bark: the gums with their smooth outer bark resulting from annual shedding of the roughest outermost layer (*Eucalyptus apodophyolla*); the bloodwoods with tesselated bark, with the dead, outermost layer being composed of plates of short fibered material (*E. tesselaris*); the boxes, not to be confused with boxwood from the family possess short-fibered bark, which sticks to the outside of the tree after the outermost layer is dead, fading to a pleasant grey (*E. moluccana*), while the stringy barks also retain the outermost, dead layer of bark but take their name from its long fibered nature (*E. reducta*) peppermints; the ironbarks (*E. melanophloia*) are covered with a hard, furrowed bark which remains continuous after the outermost layer is dead. Finally, the minniritchi eucalypts have a partially detached outermost layer of bark which splits longitudinally to reveal the green inner bark (*E. orbifolia*). The ironbarks are known for the density and lasting quality of their wood. It is a particularly useful wood for heavy building and for railway ties.

Melaleuca, a genus known by the common name paperbark, yields ornamental timber. The various species of the genus include shrubs and trees which grow in swamps and marshes. The flowers resemble bottle brushes, showing the close relationship between this genus and *Calliostemon*. With the species of the genus *Leptospermum*, those of the genus *Melaleuca* share the common name tea-trees. It is from *Melaleuca*, not *Leptospermum*, that tea-tree oil is distilled.

Species of the genus *Melaleuca* were transferred to Florida for development purposes. People wanted to use the strong invasive roots of this tree to turn swampland into firm ground for building. However, in the swamps of Florida, *Melaleuca* has proven to be an invasive pest which has displaced many native species from the swamps. *Melaleuca* reproduces so quickly and so thickly that attempts to eliminate it from the swamps by cutting have met with little success. Efforts are being made to remove *Melaleuca* by introducing an insect which feeds on it. A similar phenomenon has occurred in New Caledonia, where when native trees have burned solid stands of *Melaleuca* replaced them.

Besides spices and timber, humans also use species of the Myrtaceae for food. The popular fruit guava is produced by species of several genera from the Myrtaceae. Pineapple guava grows on trees of the genus *Feijoa*, and strawberry guava comes from *Psidium littorale*, native to tropical America.

A number of species from the Myrtle family are used horticulturally or decoratively. Attractive flowers are produced by species such a *Leptospermum* and *Calliostemon*. Now grown in gardens around the world, species of *Calliostemon* were originally found growing in wet spots in Australia. Their bright flowers look like long round brushes, thus the common name for this

---

KEY TERMS

Essential oil—A mixture of hydrocarbons and organic heterocyclic compounds (secondary metabolites) produced by a plant species. The specific composition is also characteristic of a given species from which the essential oil is distilled. For example, distillation of allspice yields an oil composed principally of eugenol.

Eucalypt—A tree from a species of *Eucalyptus*.

Eugenol—The principal hydrocarbon compound in the scent and taste of the spices, cloves, and allspice.

Isoprenoid—A branched, five-carbon unit used by living organisms to produce a variety of compounds including the terpenoids, which are particularly abundant in the species of the Myrtaceae.

Pomander—From the French *pomme d'amber* (literally, apple of amber), originally a scented ball of amber or a scented apple. Usually an apple or orange scented by piercing the fresh fruit with cloves. When the fruit dries, the cloves remain in the fruit. They can then be used to scent household areas such as clothes closets.

---

genus, bottle brushes. Some species are unusual in that they are among the few plants in the world pollinated by birds instead of the wind or insects.

The flowers of *Leptospermum* resemble flattened roses, and the small dark green leaves resemble those of the herb rosemary. Before tea was available in Australia, the leaves of *Leptospermum* were used as a substitute for tea, which is made from the dried leaves of a species of *Camillia*. From this early use by European settlers, the genus *Leptospermum* derives the common name tea-trees. Young branches and dried seed pods of *Eucalyptus* are popular in floral arrangements. The young branches have the attractive round leaves tightly appressed to the stem and are characteristic of juvenile material from species of the Myrtaceae. The leaves are mottled with wax.

Further Reading

Bender, S. "Who Let Them In?" *Southern Living*, 1994, 52-54.

Burgess, T., Dell, B., and N. Malajczuk. "Variation in Mycorrhizal Development and Growth Stimulation by 20 *Pisolithus* Isolates Inoculated on to *Eucalyptus grandis*

W. Hill ex Maiden." *New Phytologist.* 127: 1994, 731-739.

Jones, M. and M. Sedgley. "Leaf Waxes and Postharvest Quality of *Eucalyptus* Foliage." *Journal of Horticultural Sciences.* 68(6) 1993: 939-946.

Swahn, J. O. *The Lore of Spices.* New York: Crescent 1991.

Douglas W. Darnowski

NADPH (nicotinamide adenine dinucleotide phosphate) see **Photosynthesis**

Nails see **Integumentary system**

Nanostructures see **Mesoscopic systems**

Nanotechnology

Nanotechnology is the technology of devices, including fabrication techniques, which are smaller than one micron in size. It involves the development of new electrical devices which depend on quantum effects which arise when the dimension of a structure is only a few atoms across. Since the techniques best suited for fabricating devices on the submicron scale originated in semiconductor processing technology for the production of integrated circuits, nanoscale devices are all based on semiconductors.

Nanofabrication techniques

Nanoscale devices are made using a combination of different fabrication steps. First is the growth stage, in which layers of different semiconductor material are grown on a substrate, providing structure in one dimension. Second is the lithography/pattern transfer stage, in which a pattern is imposed on a uniform layer, giving structure in the second and third dimensions. Repetition of these two stages results in the production of very complex, tridimensionally nanoscale semiconductor devices.

Growth stage

In the growth stage, each successive layer has a different composition in order to impose different electrical or optical characteristics on the carriers (electrons and holes). A variety of growth techniques can be used, with *molecular beam epitaxy* (MBE) and *metallo-organic chemical vapor deposition* (MOCVD) proving to be the most useful for nanostructures since they can be used to grow layers of a predetermined thickness to within a few atoms. In MBE, a gun fires a beam of molecules at a substrate upon which the semiconductor crystal is to be grown. As the atoms hit the surface, they adhere and take up positions in the ordered pattern of the crystal, and so a near perfect crystal can be grown one atomic layer at a time. The mixture of material in the beam is changed to give different layers, e.g. the introduction of aluminum to the growth of gallium arsenide will result in the production of a layer of aluminum gallium arsenide.

Lithography/pattern transfer stage

Epitaxial growth allows the formation of thin planes of differing materials in one dimension only. The two stage process of lithography and pattern transfer is used to form structures in the other two dimensions. In the lithography stage (see Figure 1), a film of radiation–sensitive material, alternately known as the resist, is laid on top of the semiconductor layer where the structure is going to be made, and a pattern is exposed on the resist using electrons, ions, or photons. The film is altered during the exposure step, thus allowing the resist to be chemically developed as a relief image. This image is then transferred to the semiconductor by doping, etching, growing, or lift–off as shown in Figure 1.

The exposure pattern can be written on the resist in a line by line manner using an electron or ion beam, or can be imprinted all at once, using a mask, much like spray painting a letter on a wall using a template. Exposure by writing the pattern with a beam is especially useful for making prototype structures, since it avoids the expense of making a new mask for each pattern; features as small as a few nm can be written this way. However, writing patterns one line at a time is time consuming and expensive when it comes to producing large quantities, so masks are used which allow the exposure

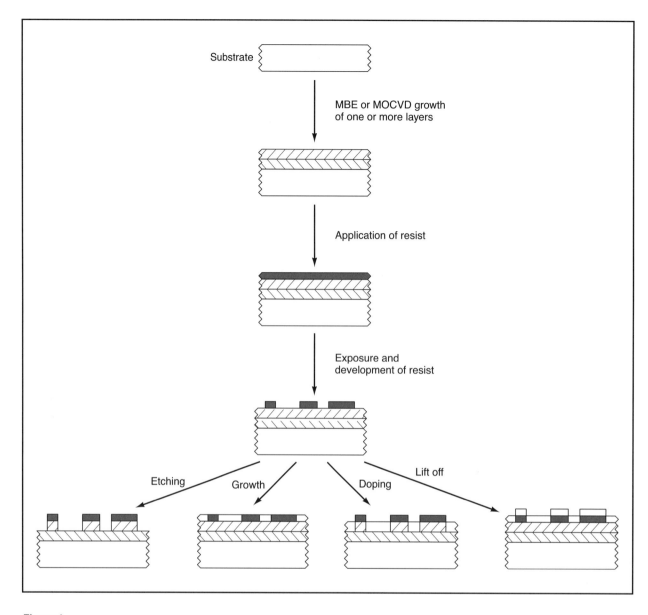

Substrate

MBE or MOCVD growth
of one or more layers

Application of resist

Exposure and
development of resist

Etching   Growth   Doping   Lift off

Figure 1.

of a number of chips simultaneously. Masks can be used with electron or ion beams or with photons. It is important to note that the wavelength of light for exposing a pattern has to be less than the smallest feature being exposed. Where nanoscale dimensions are involved, this necessitates the use of vacuum ultraviolet light or x rays. Penetration of the x rays into the semiconductor has to be avoided to prevent damage to the crystal, so wavelengths of 1.3 nm or 4.5 nm are preferred, since the polymeric resist exhibits an absorption depth of about 1 micron at these wavelengths.

The requirement on the wavelength of the x rays and the obvious need to have the x ray beam well directed necessitates the use of a well controlled x ray source, such as a synchrotron. Laser–based x ray sources are currently being considered as a less expensive alternative to the synchrotron.

Conventional nanoscale devices

In conventional semiconductors, the carrier velocity is limited to about 10^7 cm/sec, which results in limitations of current density and turn–on time, or frequency response. Because of the need for faster devices (it takes less time for a carrier to cross a smaller device) and the desire to squeeze more devices on to a single chip, e.g. a processor chip for computers, significant advances have been made since the 1970s in fabricating smaller devices.

It has been found that there are additional advantages to operating devices which are in the nanoscale regime. The carrier velocity limit of 10^7 cm/sec is set in large scale semiconductors by collisions with crystalline defects, phonons, etc. and can be characterized by a mean free path between collisions: the longer the mean free path, the fewer collisions and the higher the carrier velocity. It has been found that in nanoscale devices, the device itself can be considerably shorter than the mean free path, in which case a carrier injected at a high velocity, say 10^8 cm/sec, never suffers any collisions and therefore does not slow down. This phenomenon is termed ballistic transport and allows semiconductors to operate far faster than was possible before, reaching frequencies of 200 GHz.

There are severe complexities associated with the manufacturing of conventional nanoscale devices which appear to be major obstacles on the way to producing large quantities of these types of devices. This difficulty in manufacturing, coupled with the fact that ballistic transport devices perform best at low signal levels, in contrast to conventional electronics which operate well at high power levels, suggest that these new devices will not become widely available for use in computer chips in the near future.

Quantum effect nanoscale devices

According to the laws of quantum mechanics, free carriers in a metal or semiconductor can only take on specific values of energy which are defined by the crystal structure, i.e., the energy is quantized. However, for most practical purposes, there are so many closely-spaced energy levels that it appears that the carriers have a continuum of possible energies, except for the well-defined gaps characteristic of semiconductors. However, when the carrier is confined to a region where one or more of the dimensions reach the range of less than 100 nm, the quantum energy levels begin to spread out and the quantum nature becomes detectable. This reduction in size can take place in one, two or three dimensions, using the fabrication techniques discussed earlier, yielding structures known respectively as *superlattices*, *quantum wires*, and *quantum dots*.

When electrons are introduced into a semiconductor structure, they migrate to those positions where their energy is lowest, much like a pin–pong ball will come to rest in a dimple on a waffled surface. If the nanostructure is engineered correctly, then the electrons will

NANOTECHNOLOGY

KEY TERMS

Ballistic transport—Movement of a carrier through a semiconductor without collisions, resulting in extraordinary electrical properties.

Carriers—Charge carrying particles in semiconductors, electrons, and holes.

Epitaxy—The growth of crystalline layers of semiconducting materials in a layered structure.

Integrated circuits—Complex electronic circuits fabricated using multiple growth and lithography/pattern transfer stages to produce many miniature electronic elements on a monolithic device.

settle in the nanostructure itself and not in the adjacent layers. These carriers will then exhibit the quantum effects imposed on them by the nanostructure. The ability to engineer artificial atoms and molecules in semiconductors using nanofabrication techniques has resulted in a powerful new tool in creating novel semiconductor devices, e.g., quantum dots where the number of carriers trapped by the dot can be controlled by an external voltage.

It appears possible that nanoscale quantum effect devices may become widely used in complex electronic systems, e.g., a neural array of quantum dots spaced only a few 100 nm apart, but this will only take place after significant progress has been made in fabrication and tolerance.

See also Quantum mechanics; X rays.

Further Reading:

Nun, J. ed., *Gallium Arsenide Integrated Circuits: Design and Technology*, New York: Macmillan, 1988.
Physics Today, February 1990 Special edition on Nanoscale and Ultrafast Devices.
Physics Today, June 1993 Special edition on Optics of Nanostructures
Rungan, W.R. and Bean, K.E., *Semiconductor Integrated Circuit Processing Technologies*, Reading, PA: Addison Wesley, 1990.

Iain A. McIntyre

Naproxen see **Anti-inflammatory agents**

Narcissus plant see **Amaryllis family**

Narcotic

A narcotic is a substance that produces insensibility, or a stuporous state. The most notable characteristics of narcotics are their ability to decrease the perception of pain and alter the reaction to pain, and their extremely addictive properties. Narcotics often induce a state of euphoria or extreme well being. The word narcotic is derived from the Greek word *narké* (meaning *stupor*), and traditionally applies to drugs known as opiates. Recently, the word narcotic has been adopted to include non–opiate, addictive drugs such as cocaine and cannabis. Narcotics are primarily used in medicine as pain killers and are often called narcotic analgesics.

Opiates are compounds extracted from the milky latex contained in the unripe seed pods of the opium poppy *(Papaver somniferum)*. Opium, morphine, and codeine are the most important opiate alkaloids found in the opium poppy. Opium was used as folk medicine for hundreds, perhaps thousands of years. In the seventeenth century opium smoking led to major addiction problems. In the first decade of the nineteenth century, morphine was isolated from opium. About 20 years later, codeine, one–fifth as strong as morphine, was isolated from both opium and morphine. In 1898, heroin, an extremely potent and addictive derivative of morphine was isolated. The invention of the hypodermic needle during the mid–nineteenth century allowed opiates to be delivered directly into the blood stream, which increases the effects of these drugs. Synthetically produced drugs with morphine–like properties are called opioids. The terms narcotic, opiate, and opioid are frequently used interchangeably. Some common synthetically produced opioids include meperidine (its trade name is Demerol) and methadone, a drug often used to treat heroin addiction.

Scientists have discovered narcotic receptors in the brain, along with natural pain killing substances produced by the body called endorphins. Narcotics behave like endorphins and act on, or bind to, the receptors to produce their associated effects. Substances known as narcotic or opioid antagonists, are drugs that block the actions of narcotics and are used to reverse the side effects of narcotic abuse or an overdose. A new class of drugs, a mixture of opioids and opioid antagonists, has been developed so that patients can be relieved of pain without the addictive or other unpleasant side effects associated with narcotics. Most countries have strict laws regarding the production and use of narcotics because they are so addictive.

See also Addiction.

Natural fibers

Natural fibers may be of animal, vegetable, or mineral origin. Although the annual production of vegetable fibers outweighs that of animal or mineral fibers, all have long been useful to humans.

Animal fibers

Animal hair fibers consist of a protein known as *keratin*. It has a composition similar to human hair. Keratin proteins are actually crystalline copolymers of nylon, where the repeating units are amino acids. The fibrous proteins form crystals. They also crosslink through disulfide bonds present in the cystine amino acid.

Silks are partially crystalline protein fibers. Animal tendons consist of collagen, another fibrous protein with a complex hierarchical structure.

Wool

Wool forms the protective covering of sheep, screening them from heat and cold, and allowing them to maintain even body temperatures. The following are important characteristics of wool fibers. (1) They are 1 to 14 in (2.54 to 35.56 cm) or more in length, with diameters of 1/600th–1/3,000th in (.04 to .008 mm). (2) Their average chemical compositions are: carbon, 50%; hydrogen, 7%; oxygen, 22–25%; nitrogen, 16–17%; and sulphur, 3–4%. (3) They are extremely flexible and can be bent 20,000 times without breaking. (4) They are naturally resilient. (5) They are capable of trapping air and providing insulation. (6) They absorb up to 30% of their weight in moisture. (7) They are thermally stable, and begin to decompose only at 212°F (100°C).

Production of wool fabric

The conversion of wool fiber into fabric begins with the shearing of the sheep. In most of the United States, sheep shearing takes place in the spring. Professional shearers travel from place to place, where they are paid by the number of fleeces they shear. A good sheep shearer can shear 200 sheep per day.

Wool fleeces are sorted by hand according to their quality. The shoulder wool usually produces the best fiber, followed in order of quality by the side, neck, and back wool. After sorting, the wool is scoured to clean it and to prepare it for dyeing. After the wool has been dyed, it is carded to open the fibers. The fibers are then drawn into yarn, and any kinks present are removed by steam pressure. The yarn is next woven, examined, and burled to remove all knots and loose threads. In the fin-

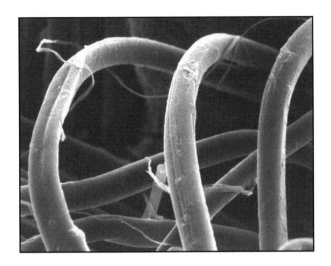

A scanning electron micrograph (SEM) of silk fibers from a kimono.

ishing process, the cloth is shrunk, washed and rinsed to remove all impurities and dirt picked up in the earlier operations. Then the cloth is dried and straightened to remove all wrinkles. Finally, the cloth is sheared to give it uniformity, and then moistened and passed through heated rollers for pressing.

Worsteds are produced in a similar process, but the wool fibers are twisted during processing to produce a smoother, harder surface. As a result, worsteds have harder surface finishes, greater durability, and sharper colorings than woolens.

Silk

Silk is a continuous protein filament spun by the silkworm to form its cocoon. The principle species used in commercial production is the mulberry silkworm, which is the larva of the silk moth, *Bombyx mori*. It belongs to the order Lepidoptera.

Silk and sericulture (the culturing of silk) probably began in China more than 4,000 years ago. The Chinese used silk for clothing, wall hangings, paintings, religious ornamentation, interior decoration, and to maintain religious records. Knowledge of the silkworm passed from China to Japan through Korea. The production of silk transformed the tiny, technologically backward Japanese islands into a world power.

Silk was also passed to Persia and Central Asia where it was encountered by the Greeks. Aristotle was the first Western writer to describe the silkworm. In 550 A.D., the Emperor Justinian acquired silkworm eggs and mulberry seeds, beginning the varieties of silkworms that supplied the Western world with silk for 1,400 years.

After World War II, the women's silk hosiery market, silk's single largest market, mostly was overtaken by nylon.

Properties

Silk fibers are smooth, translucent, rod–like filaments with occasional swellings along their length. The raw silk fiber actually consists of two filaments called fibroin bound by a soluble silk gum called *sericin*. Fibroin and sericin are made up of carbon, hydrogen, nitrogen, and oxygen.

Silk has several important qualities. (1) It is lower in density than wool, cotton, or rayon. (2) It is a poor conductor of heat and electricity. (3) It is capable of soaking up to 30% of its weight in moisture. (4) It is extremely strong, with a breaking strength as high as 65,000 psi. (5) It will stretch to as much as 20% of its length without breaking. (6) It is thermally stable; it is able to withstand temperatures as high as 284°F (140°C). (7) It becomes smooth, lustrous, and luxurious when processed. (8) It is remarkably resilient, and shows excellent wrinkle recovery.

Production of silk fabric

Sericulture requires scrupulous care and painstaking attention to detail. Breeder moths are first selected with great care. Eggs from the moths are repeatedly tested to ensure the quality of the larvae. The selected eggs are placed in cold storage until the early spring when they are incubated. After about a week, the eggs hatch into tiny silkworms. The worms are kept in clean conditions on trays of mulberry leaves. Young silkworms have voracious appetites, eating every couple of hours day and night for five weeks. To produce a pound of silk, one silkworm would have to eat 200 lb (90.8 kg) of mulberry leaves. In these first five weeks of life, the worms grow to 70 times their original size.

Once the silkworm's appetite has been sated, the worm is placed on a pile of straw or heather, where it begins spinning its cocoon. The silkworm first attaches itself to a twig. Then it begins spinning filaments of silk in an endless series of figure eights. This builds up walls within walls which are held together by gummy sericin that dries and hardens following exposure to air.

Without human intervention, the worm inside the cocoon would develop into a chrysalis and later into a moth. The moth would then burst the cocoon and break the one long strand of silk into many short ones. But sericulture destroys the worm inside the cocoon by stifling it with heat.

TABLE 1. SPECIALTY ANIMAL FIBERS

Animal fiber	Uses	Animal's natural or domesticated habitat
Alpaca	luxurious fabrics	Arequipa, Peru
Angora goat (Mohair)	carpets, upholstery, curtains, automobile cloth, clothing	Turkey, South Africa, southwestern United States
Angora rabbit	knitted sweaters, mittens, baby clothes	Turkey, Asia Minor
Beaver	textile use, hats	Europe, United States
Camel hair	overcoats, topcoats, sportswear, and sports hosiery	Chinese and Mongolian deserts
Cashmere goat	soft fibers for textiles	Tibet, China, Persia, Turkestan, Outer Mongolia
Chinchilla	fur	South American Andes
Fox	furs, scarves, muffs, jackets, coats, trimmings	all parts of the world
Guanaco	luxury fleece	Southern Argentina
Hare or jackrabbit	felt	United States; all parts of the world except Madagascar
Llama	textiles requiring impressive luster, warmth, and light weights	South America
Muskrat	fur	North America
Nutria	soft blends	South America
Opossum	trimming for cloth coats	Australia, southern United States, South America
Rabbit or coney	textile blends	Australia, domesticated all over the world
Raccoon	sportswear	United States
Vicuna	very soft cloth	Peru
Weasel family, including mink	furs for coats, trimmings, capes, etc.	Europe, Asia, United States

TABLE 2. SEED-HAIR FIBERS		
Fiber	*Uses*	*Place of Origin*
kapok	stuffing for mattresses, pillows, and furniture. life preservers	Africa, Southeast Asia
cotton	textiles, cordage	United States, Asia, Africa

The next step in sericulture is to unwind the cocoon. This process is called reeling. To produce uniform strands of raw silk for commercial use, filaments of five to 10 cocoons are combined into a single thread. To do this, the cocoons are first soaked in hot water. After the ends of the filaments have been located, the filaments are passed through porcelain guides where they are twisted into fibers of uniform length and regularity. Reeling may be done automatically or by hand.

Raw silk is wound into skeins. Thirty skeins constitute one book, which weighs around 4.3 lb (1.95 kg). Thirty books make a bale, which weighs 132.3 lb (60.06 kg). The bale is the basic unit of commercial transactions. About 900 lb (408.6 kg) of cocoons are required to produce one bale of raw silk.

Raw silk taken directly from the filature is too fine to be woven. It must first be made into a thicker and more substantial yarn in a process known as throwing. Throwing consists of: sorting the skeins according to quality; soaking selected skeins to remove the sericin; drying any skeins that have been soaked; rewinding the skeins onto bobbins; twisting the threads from two or more bobbins to form single strands; again twisting to produce a fine thread; and finally conditioning the highly twisted thread.

Specialty fibers from animals

In addition to wool and silk, a number of specialty fibers are also obtained from animals. In most cases, animal fibers are similar to each other. They grow in two principal coats: the shiny and stiff outer coat or hair; and the undergrowth or fur. Hair forms a protective shield around the animal's body against the elements; fur is closer to the skin and consists of shorter fibers than the hair that acts as insulation against heat or cold.

Fabrics containing specialty fibers are expensive because of the difficulties in obtaining the fibers, and the amount of processing required to prepare the fibers for use. Unlimited combinations of specialty fibers with wool are possible. Specialty fibers may be used to add softness or luster to fabrics. They also enhance the insulating properties of blended fabrics.

Vegetable fibers

Vegetable fibers were used by ancient man for fishing and trapping. Evidence exists that man made ropes and cords as early as 20,000 B.C. The Egyptians probably produced ropes and cords from reeds, grasses, and flax around 4000 B.C. They later produced matting from vegetable fibers, rushes, reeds, and papyrus grasses bound with flax string.

Vegetable fibers consist of *cellulose*, i.e., polysaccharides made up of anhydroglucose units joined by an oxygen linkage to form long molecular chains that are essentially linear, bound to lignin, and associated with various amounts of other materials.

Vegetable fibers are classified according to the part of the plant that they come from. The four groupings are: seed–hair fibers, leaf fibers, bast fibers, and miscellaneous fibers.

Seed–hair fibers

The first category of vegetable fiber is of seed–hair fibers, which includes: cotton, kapok, flosses obtained from seeds, seedpods, and the inner walls of fruit.

Cotton—history

Perhaps no other natural product has influenced the destiny of humankind as has cotton. It has clothed nations, enslaved men and women, monopolized labor, and given direction to entire industries.

The first historical mention of cotton was in the writings of Herodotus. Writing in 484 B.C., he described trees with fleece growing in them in India. Archeological discoveries have placed the use of cotton in India to 3000 B.C. or earlier. Cotton spread by trade to the Middle East, particularly Egypt, and later, in the seventh and eighth centuries, it was brought to Spain by the Moors.

TABLE 3. LEAF FIBERS

Fiber	Uses	Place of Origin
abaca	coarse sacks, coffee and sugar bags, floor coverings, webbing, industrial ropes, hoisting and drilling cables, nets, agricultural twines, hawsers and ships' cables, paper, tea bags	Philippines, Central America, Indonesia
sisal	coarse sacks, coffee and sugar bags, floor coverings, webbing, industrial ropes, hoisting and drilling cables, nets, agricultural twines, stuffing and upholstery materials, paper	Western Hemisphere, Africa, Asia, Oceania
henequen	coarse sacks, coffee and sugar bags, floor coverings, webbing, industrial ropes, hoisting and drilling cables, nets, agricultural twines, paper	Mexico
cantala	cordage	Philippines, Indonesia
istle	scrubbing and scraping brushes, brooms	Mexico
Mauritius	coarse sacks, coffee and sugar bags, floor coverings, webbing, cordage, paper	Brazil, island of Mauritius
phornium	cordage, paper	New Zealand
sansevieria	cigarette paper	Africa, Arabia, India, Sri Lanka
caroa	paper	Brazil
piassava	scrubbing and scraping brushes, brooms	Brazil
broomroot	scrubbing and scraping brushes, brooms	Mexico

New World explorers found cotton fabrics being manufactured in Peru, Mexico, and what is now the southwestern United States. Carbon 14 tests have dated the use of cotton in Peru as far back as 2500 B.C.

Europeans first planted cotton in the New World in Virginia, using seeds from the West Indies. The need to harvest cotton when the weather is perfectly dry meant at first that the European colonists had to spend long days working in the hot sun. They eventually circumvented their dislike for this labor by importing slaves to do the work for them.

In 1793 a young inventor named Eli Whitney developed the cotton gin, which allowed cotton seeds to be rapidly separated from the fiber mechanically. This single invention raised cotton exports from 400 bales a year in 1791 to 30,000 bales in 1800 and 180,000 bales in 1810. As a corollary, between 1790 and 1800, the slave population of the United States increased by 33%. By 1810 there were more than a million slaves in the Southern states; by 1860 the number had risen to more than 4 million.

Since the end of World War II, demand for cotton has been largely supplanted by one for synthetic fibers, particularly polyester and nylon. Incursions into the cotton market are due in part to the dwindling availability of land to raise cotton.

TABLE 4. BAST (SOFT) FIBERS		
Fiber	*Uses*	*Place of Origin*
flax	clothing, sacks and bags, canvas and sail-cloth, fabrics, string and yarns, cigarette paper	France, Belgium, Ireland, and Eastern Europe
hemp	clothing, sacks and bags, canvas and sail-cloth, fabrics, nets	People's Republic of China, Philippines, Brazil, Taiwan, Japan
jute	clothing, sacks and bags, canvas and sail-cloth, fabrics	India, Bangladesh, other Asian countries, Brazil
kenaf and roselle	clothing, sacks and bags, canvas and sail-cloth, fabrics, nets (kenaf)	People's Republic of China, former Soviet Union, Egypt, India, and Thailand (roselle)
urena	packaging	Brazil, Zaire
China jute	packaging	People's Republic of China, former Soviet Union, Japan, Korea, Argentina
sunn hemp	soft cordage	India

Cultivation and processing of cotton

Cotton cultivation requires a warm, humid climate and sandy soil. It takes from 80 to 110 days for planting and flowering; another 55 to 80 days are required for the flower to produce the cotton ball.

Today mechanical harvesters are used most often to gather cotton from the plants. A mechanical harvester can pick up to 650 lb (295.1 kg) per hour compared to the 15 lb (6.81 kg) that a hand picker can gather at the same time. Even so hand pickers are still sometimes preferred because mechanical harvesters tend to gather a great deal of waste matter along with the fiber.

After cotton has been harvested, the seeds must be removed. Essentially the same method devised by Whitney in 1793 is used. The seed cotton is fed into a gin consisting of a series of circular saws that separate the fiber from the seeds. The fiber is then compressed into bales weighing about 478 lb (217 kg). A second ginning separates out the short fibers leaving the more desirable longer fibers.

Turning the raw cotton into yarn requires many steps. First, any heavy impurities such as dirt or seeds are removed from the opened bales of cotton at the mill. Then the fibers are drawn into wide thin webs which are gathered into ropes or strands. The finer quality fibers are combed until all short lengths have been removed. Both combed and uncombed fibers are drawn and twisted to produce the finished yarn. Weaving the cotton fabric consists of interlacing lengthwise yarns with crosswise yarns to produce cotton cloth.

Leaf fibers

Leaf fibers come from the leaves of monocotyledonous plants. They are primarily used for cordage.

Bast fibers

Bast fibers come from the bast tissue or bark of plant stem. They are primarily used for textiles, thread, yarn, and twine.

Miscellaneous fibers

Miscellaneous fibers come from the sheathing leaf–stalks of palms, stem segments, stems, and fibrous husks. They are used primarily for brush and broom bristles, matting, and stuffing.

Mineral fibers

Table 6 lists the three principal natural fibers. But of the three fibers only asbestos is a true natural fiber. Glass and aluminum silicate fibers require human intervention in their processing, and might be better considered man–made fibers.

TABLE 5. MISCELLANEOUS VEGETABLE FIBERS

Fiber	Uses	Place of Origin
broom root	brooms, brushes	Mexico
crin vegetal	stuffing	North Africa
piassava	cordage, brushes	Brazil
coir	scrubbing and scraping brushes, brooms, door mats	Sri Lanka, India

TABLE 6. FIBERS OF MINERAL ORIGIN

Fiber	Uses	Place of Origin
asbestos	safety clothing, thermal insulation jacketing fabrics, barbecue mitts, commercial laundry and dry cleaning press covers, conveyor belts, dust filters, heating and ventilating ducts, electrical insulating tapes, yarns for electric wire insulation, fireproof draperies, fire-smothering blankets, brake linings	Canada, former Soviet Union
glass	composites, insulation, draperies, tire cord, filters	United States
aluminum silicate	packings and insulation for high temperatures	United States

Asbestos

Asbestos is a fibrous mineral mined from rock deposits. There are approximately 30 types of minerals in the asbestos group. Of the six that have commercial importance, only oneotile, a hydrated silicate of magnesium that contains small amounts of iron and aluminum, oxides, is used in fiber processing.

Asbestos probably formed prehistorically when hot waters containing carbon dioxide and dissolved salts under high pressure acted upon rock deposits of iron, magnesia, and silica.

The ancient Greeks knew of asbestos as early as the first century A.D.; the name comes from the Greek word for inconsumable. But asbestos did not find commercial use until it was used for packing and insulation when the steam engine was invented. Currently the world's leading suppliers of asbestos are Canada and the former Soviet Union.

Useful for heat protection, the most notable characteristic of asbestos is that it will not burn. It can be spun and woven into textiles. However, asbestos is a known carcinogen. It is highly toxic when inhaled as dust particles. The American Conference of Governmental Industrial Hygienists has established a maximum exposure level to chrysotile fibers. A worker may be exposed, without adverse effects, to 2 fibers/cc more than 5 microns long.

The first step in processing asbestos fibers is to separate the longer fibers—from 3/4–3/8 in (1.91–.94 cm)—from rock by pounding. The shorter fibers—up to 3/8 in (.94 cm) long—are separated from the rock by crushing and screening. The fibers are next graded according to length. Different grades of fibers are blended, combed, cleaned, and aligned in webs. The web is separated into ribbons or rope–like strands. (Slivers are formed into rolls or laps for electrical insulation). The strands are spun and twisted into yarns of various sizes, depending upon end use. Finally the yarns are woven into fabrics or plaited into braids using mechanical braiders.

See also Artificial fibers; Asbestos; Cellulose; Cotton; Silk cotton family.

Further Reading:

Lynch, Charles T. *Practical Handbook of Materials Science.* Boca Raton, Florida: CRC Press, Inc., 1989.

The New Encyclopedia of Textiles, Englewood Cliffs, N.J.: Prentice Hall, Inc., 1980.

Randall Frost

Natural gas

Natural gas is a mixture of hydrocarbons (molecules that contain only carbon and hydrogen) and gases (most notably methane, ethane, propane, and butane) which exists naturally in rocks beneath the surface of the earth. It is widely used as a heating source, and in some cases specific portions of the natural gas are used as starting materials in industrial processes. Natural gas is the product of the decaying of living matter over millions of years (as is also true for petroleum). Specific conditions (including low oxygen levels) are necessary for this to occur. The hydrocarbon gases are trapped in geological formations known as anticlines. Each of the major hydrocarbon components of natural gas is used as a fuel source.

Formation and composition of natural gas

Natural gas has its origins in decayed living matter, most likely as the result of the action of bacteria upon dead animal and plant material. In order for most bacteria to effectively break down organic matter to hydrocarbons, there must be low levels of oxygen present. This would mean that the decaying matter was buried (most likely under water) before it could be completely degraded to carbon dioxide and water. Conditions such as this are likely to have been met in coastal areas where sedimentary rocks and marine bacteria are com-

An offshore natural gas drilling platform.

mon. The actions of heat and pressure along with bacteria produced a mixture of hydrocarbons. The smaller molecules which exist as gases were then either trapped in porous rocks or in underground reservoirs where they formed sources of hydrocarbon fuels.

Natural gas, like petroleum, is a mixture of many organic substances. The most common substances in natural gas are summarized in the following table.

Other gases such as oxygen, argon, and carbon dioxide make up the rest of most natural gas sources. The exact composition of different sources of natural gas varies slightly, but in all cases, methane is by far the most common component, with other hydrocarbons also being very common. The largest sources of natural gas in the United States are found in Alaska, Texas, Oklahoma, western Pennsylvania, and Ohio. It is estimated that the supply of natural gas in this country may be sufficient to last for two centuries, although the more readily accessible sources have been used, meaning that

TABLE 1	
substance	*mole %*
methane (CH_4)	76
ethane (C_2H_6)	6
propane (C_3H_8)	4
butane (C_4H_{10})	2
nitrogen (N_2)	10

it will be more expensive to obtain natural gas in the future.

History of the discovery and use of natural gas

Natural gas is believed to have been first discovered and used by the Chinese, perhaps as early as 1000 B.C. Shallow stores of natural gas were released from just beneath the ground and piped short distances to be used as a fuel source. Natural gas could provide a continuous source of energy for flames. These "eternal fires" were found in temples and also used as attractions for visitors. In the 1800s, natural gas began to be piped short distances as a light source. With the discovery of oil in the 1860s natural gas was largely ignored as a fuel source. One of the early difficulties with natural gas was in transporting it from the source to other sites for use. The combination of electric lights and petroleum meant that containers of natural gas were used as heat sources for cooking in homes but for little else.

As the technology for piping gas from the source began to improve, it became possible to pipe natural gas over thousands of miles. This has meant that natural gas has become as convenient as petroleum and coal to use as a fuel source, and often with far less pollution. Natural gas burns with almost no byproducts except for carbon dioxide and water (as opposed to coal which often has large amounts of sulfur in it), and the heat released from the reaction (combustion of any of the hydrocarbon components of natural gas is an exothermic process). The combustion of methane, the most prevalent component of natural gas, is described by the reaction below:

$$CH_4 + O_2 \rightarrow CO_2 + H_2O + \text{heat energy}$$

Ethane is used less as fuel source than as a starting material for the production of ethylele (acetylene), which is used in welding.

Both butane and propane are relatively easy to liquefy and store. Liquefied propane and butane are used in disposable lighters and as camping fuels.

Liquefied natural gas

Since gases take up large amounts of space, they can be inconvenient to transport and store. The ability to liquefy the components of natural gas (either as a mixture or in isolation) has made natural gas much more practical as an energy source. The liquefaction of natural gas takes advantage of the different boiling points of methane, ethane, and other gases as a way of purifying each substance. A combination of refrigeration and increased pressure allows the individual gases to be stored and transported conveniently. At one time, the natural gas which often accompanied petroleum in the ground was simply burned off as a means of getting rid of it. Recently, however, this gas has been collected, liquefied and used along with the petroleum.

See also Gases, liquefaction of; Hydrocarbon.

KEY TERMS

Anticline—An upward fold in a geological formation that traps gases.

Combustion reaction—Reaction in which a substance is burned, usually as an energy source.

Exothermic reaction—A chemical process that releases heat (hydrocarbon combustion reactions are exothermic).

Fossil fuel—A substance or mixture of substances formed by the decaying of once living matter by bacteria.

Hydrocarbons—Molecules comprised solely of hydrogen and carbon atoms.

Further Readings:

Dichristine, Mariette, "Natural Gas Gets the Job Done," *Popular Science,* April 1991, p. 38.

Miller, William, "A Natural Selection (Natural Gas Vehicles)," *Industry Week*, September 7, 1992, p. 62.

Nulty, Peter, "Fill "er up with Natural Gas," *Fortune,* March 22, 1993, p. 21.

"Oil Company Discovers Gas Deposit Off Australia," *Wall Street Journal*, March 2, 1995, pp. C10, C12.

Vogel, Todd and Mimi Bluestone, "Gas Is Cooking Now," *Business Week,* October 24, 1988, p. 24.

Louis Gotlib

Natural numbers

The natural numbers are the ordinary numbers, 1, 2, 3, ... with which we count. Sometimes they are called "the counting numbers." They have been called "natural" because much of our experience from infancy deals with discrete objects such as fingers, balls, peanuts, etc. We quickly, if not naturally, learn to count them. The mathematician Kronecker is reported to have said, "God created the natural numbers; all the rest is the work of man."

The number zero is sometimes considered to be a natural number, but including zero introduces complications which one ordinarily wants to avoid. For instance, counting a group of objects is a process of putting them into one–to–one correspondence with the natural numbers. No one counts starting with zero, "0,1,2,3.." because then the last number used is no longer the number of objects in the group and the answer would be wrong.

Because there is some ambiguity about the meaning of "natural number," the terms "positive integers" (which do not include zero) and "non–negative integers" (which do) are often used instead. Experts in the foundations of mathematics would argue, however, that the natural numbers are different from the positive integers, although the difference is only in how the numbers are defined. For practical purposes, they are the same.

Ultimately all arithmetic is based upon the natural numbers. If one multiplies 1.72 by .047, for example, the multiplication is done with the natural numbers 172 and 47; then the result is converted to a decimal fraction by inserting a decimal point in the proper place—a process that is also done by counting. If one adds the fractions 1/3 and 2/7, the addition is not done directly, but only after converting the fractions to 7/21 and 6/21. Then the numerators are added, using natural–number arithmetic, and the denominators copied. Even computers and calculators reduce their complex and lightening–fast computations to simple steps involving only natural numbers.

Measurements, too, are based on the natural numbers. If one measures an object with a centimeter ruler, he or she relies on the numbers printed near the centimeter marks to count the centimeters, but the eye to count the millimeters. Whether the units are counted mechanically, electronically, or physically, it is still counting, and counting is done with the natural numbers.

The natural numbers can be defined formally by relating them to sets. Then zero is the number of elements in the empty set; 1 is the number of elements in the set containing the empty set; and so on. Another method is to base them on the Peano postulates. Here 2 is defined as the successor of 1; 3 the successor of 2; and so on. Then the postulates specify what properties 1 and its successors will have.

There is one branch of mathematics which concerns itself exclusively with the properties of natural numbers (including natural number–based modular arithmetic). This is the branch known as "number theory." Since the time of the ancient Greeks, mathematicians both amateur and professional have explored these properties for their own sake and for their supposed connections with the supernatural. And in recent times many practical uses, quite apart from counting and computation, have been found for the natural numbers and their special properties. These include check-digit systems, secret codes, and other uses.

See also Arithmetic; Fraction; Integers; Number theory.

Natural selection

While not the only agent of evolutionary change, natural selection is certainly the most important mechanism of adaptive evolutionary change in populations of organisms. Through the process of natural selection, individual organisms become better adapted to their local environment and thus acquire greater fitness, defined as an increase in reproductive success. If individual organisms vary in their ability to survive and reproduce, and those variations are inherited from parent to offspring, traits that are favored in the current biological conditions will spread in the population.

Historical background

Natural selection as a means for evolutionary change in living creatures was first proposed, simultaneously, by two British naturalists, Charles Robert Darwin (1809–1882) and Alfred Russell Wallace (1823–1913), in a joint paper presented to the Linnean Society in London in July 1858. It was a case of a simultaneous discovery, which are relatively rare in science. Since the early 1840s, Darwin had been at work compiling his book *On the Origin of Species by Means of Natural Selection*, laboriously presenting his theory and its ramifications; but he was stunned when in 1858 he received a letter from Wallace and a manuscript in which the young scientist detailed a strikingly similar theory. With some anxiety, Darwin contacted his friend, naturalist Sir Charles Lyell (1797–1875), who responded by arranging the joint announcement of Darwin's and Wallace's theory before the audience of the Linnean Society. The following year, Darwin published a condensed version of his book, ultimately establishing himself as the principal creator of the theory of natural selection.

A great deal of the material in the *Origin of Species* was inspired by Darwin's earlier travels aboard the HMS *Beagle*, on which he served as ship's naturalist during the years 1831–1836. The vessel circumnavigated the globe, with stops in Australia, although the voyage focused mainly on surveying the coast of South America, including the Galapagos Islands. The notebooks he produced during this time contained his detailed documentation of the great variety of living creatures he saw and his efforts to understand their sometimes curious features. He observed that marsupials, mammals who carry their young in a pouch, are almost entirely restricted to the Australian continent (although he could think of no environmental factor unique to Australia that could explain the need for pouches!). Specimens of mockingbirds and finches collected in different islands in the Galapagos were so distinct from one another that Darwin apparently came to doubt the fixity of species; after the *Beagle*'s return, he set about gathering evidence for evolutionary change and a mechanism to account for it.

Darwin did not develop his theory of natural selection, however, until some time after his return to London. Then, in the late 1830s, he engaged in the study of the writings of numerous philosophers and statisticians, including the economist T. R. Malthus. Malthus's *Essay on the Principle of Population* (1798) contained a critical idea that Darwin used in developing his argument, namely that uncontrolled growth of the human population must lead to famine and the ultimate elimination of a significant portion of the human race. Herein lies the foundation for Darwin's notion of the "struggle for existence" in a world in which all organisms are observed to produce many more offspring than are needed to maintain their numbers, and where superior variations would be preserved at the expense of less favorable alternatives.

Darwin was not the first to propose a theory suggesting that change in the forms of living things might have an environmental cause. One earlier proposal, put forward by the French naturalist Jean–Baptiste Lamarck (1744–1829), argued that organisms could improve themselves by their own efforts, and pass these improvements on to their offspring. This "inheritance of acquired characters" could explain, for example, the giraffe's long neck, which it would presumably develop by trying to reach leaves in high tree branches, stretching its neck to do so. Other early evolutionists expounded on the internal perfecting tendencies of living things, as if each somehow aspired toward an evolutionary goal. Darwin's contribution was different in that he proposed a testable theory that was based on the interactions between individuals, each engaged in the struggle to survive and reproduce in the local environment. Because there would never be enough food, nest sites, or mates for all progeny of all individuals produced, only the best competitors would survive and reproduce. The natural outcome of this struggle is that the features of the superior competitors become better represented in the population—not because of an internal "perfecting tendency," but because they provide greater fitness.

Fitness: measuring natural selection

The differential survival and reproduction of living organisms is measured as fitness, which is technically defined as the number of offspring produced that survive to maturity. Fitness is a relative concept; we are interested in the relative rate of increase of one genotype, the genetic constitution of an individual, over all the alternatives. Evolutionary biologists investigating the process of natural selection generally measure either the relative survival of individuals possessing some trait of interest, or the change in gene frequencies (the rate at which a gene increases in a population), between successive generations. Both measures are difficult to obtain, since they require documenting the survival of individuals and their offspring in the lab or in the field, and establishing a pattern of inheritance for the trait of interest. The process is further complicated since most observable traits—that is, most aspects of an organism's phenotype—are controlled by more than one gene. Individual genes may assort in different ways between generations; furthermore, they frequently interact to produce complicated effects. Sorting out the connection between phenotype and genotype is not usually an easy task, but it has been done for some traits in some organisms.

The traits that confer the greatest fitness will depend on the local environment, and what proves advantageous in one environment may be quite unsuitable in another. An example is sickle–cell anemia, a disease that, if left untreated, kills the affected individuals, who carry two sickle–cell genes. However, in populations where the disease malaria occurs, the sickle–cell trait will increase because heterozygotes—those with one sickle–cell and one normal gene—have increased resistance to malaria, and only mild anemia. Thus, natural selection produces genetic change in populations that may fluctuate or even reverse themselves, in accordance with local environmental conditions.

Evidence of natural selection

The use of the insecticide DDT provides a well–known example of natural selection in operation. When DDT is first sprayed on an area populated by insects, the population declines abruptly; the poison can remain effective on such populations for up to 10 years or more. The initial effectiveness then begins to diminish, so that increasingly greater applications are required to have the same impact. The reason is that DDT, a potent nerve poison, places a strong selective force on the insects; any that remain after the application of the pesticide are likely have some resistance to the poison, sometimes due to a single gene enabling the insects to detoxify it. Such a gene would quickly spread under a selective regime featuring repeated applications of the poison. What is more, once insects have evolved resistance to one insecticide, the time required to evolve resistance to others is reduced. It appears that once selection has honed the mechanisms of detoxification, those mechanisms are fairly easily appropriated for handling new toxins, allowing resistance to appear in one or two years instead of 10.

Directional selection

The evolution of pesticide resistance is an example of directional selection, wherein the selective agent (in this case DDT) applies force in one direction, producing a corresponding change (improved resistance) in the affected organisms. Directional selection is also evident in the efforts of human beings to produce desired traits in many kinds of domestic animals and plants. The many breeds of dogs, from dachshunds to German shepherds, are all descendants of a single, wolf–like ancestor, and are the products of careful selection and breeding for the unique characteristics favored by human breeders.

When selective change is brought about by human effort, it is known as artificial selection. By allowing only a selected minority of individuals to reproduce, breeders can produce new generations of organisms featuring particular traits, including greater milk production in dairy cows, greater oil content in corn, or a rainbow of colors in commercial flowers. The repeated artificial selection and breeding of individuals with the most extreme values of the desired traits may continue until all the available genetic variation has been exhausted, and no further selection is possible. It is likely that dairy breeders have encountered the limit for milk production in cattle—eventually, a cow's milk production will increase more slowly for a given increase in feed—but the limit has not yet been reached for corn oil content, which continues to increase under artificial selection.

Stabilizing and disruptive selection

Not all selective effects are directional, however. Selection can also produce results that are stabilizing or disruptive. Stabilizing selection occurs when significant changes in the traits of organisms are selected against. An example of this is birth weight in humans. Babies that are much heavier or lighter than average do not survive as well as those that are nearer the mean (average) weight.

On the other hand, selection is said to be disruptive if the extremes of some trait become favored over the intermediate values. Perhaps one of the more obvious examples of disruptive selection is sexual dimorphism, wherein males and females of the same species look noticeably different from each other. One sex may be larger, have bright, showy plumage or bear horns or some kind of ornament that the other lacks. The male peacock, for instance, has deep green and sapphire blue plumage and his enormous, fanning tail, while the female is a drab brown, with no elaborate tail.

Sexual dimorphism is considered to be the result of sexual selection, the process in which members of a species compete for access to mates. Sexual selection and natural selection may often operate in opposing directions, producing the two distinct sex phenotypes. Males, who are typically the primary contestants in the competition for mating partners, usually bear the ornaments such as showy plumage in spite of the potential costs of these ornaments, such as increased visibility to predators, and attacks from rival males. Females are less often involved in direct competition for mates, and they are not generally subject to the forces of sexual selection (although there are role reversals in a few species). Females are believed to play a critical role in the evolution of many elaborate male traits, however, because if the female preference has a genetic basis, female choice of particular males as mating partners will cause those male traits to spread in subsequent generations.

Frequency–dependent selection

Sometimes the fitness of a phenotype in some environment depends on how common (or rare) it is; this is known as frequency–dependent selection. Perhaps an animal enjoys an increased advantage if it conforms to the majority phenotype in the population; this occurs when, for example, predators learn to avoid distasteful butterfly prey, because the butterflies have evolved to advertise their noxious taste by conforming to a particular wing color and pattern. Butterflies that deviate too much from the "warning" pattern are not as easily recognized by their predators, and are eaten in greater numbers. Interestingly, frequency–dependent selection has enabled butterflies who are not distasteful to mimic the appearance of their noxious brethren and thus avoid the same predators. Conversely, a phenotype could be favored if it is rare, and its alternatives are in the majority. Many predators tend to form a "search image" of their prey, favoring the most common phenotypes, and ignoring the rarer phenotypes. Frequency–dependent selection provides an interesting case in which the gene frequency itself alters the selective environment in which the genotype exists.

At what level does natural selection operate?

Many people attribute the phrase "survival of the fittest" to Darwin, but in fact it originated from another naturalist/philosopher, Herbert Spencer (1820–1903). Recently, many recent evolutionary biologists have asked: Survival of the fittest what? At what organismal level is selection most powerful? What is the biological unit of natural selection—the species, the individual, or even the gene?

People sometimes say that organisms exhibit parental behavior or other traits "for the good of the species." In his 1962 book *Animal Dispersion in Relation to Social Behaviour*, behavioral biologist V. C. Wynne–Edwards proposed that animals would restrain their reproduction in times of resource shortages, so as to avoid extinguishing the local supply, and thus maintain the "balance of nature." However, Wynne–Edwards

was criticized because all such instances of apparent group–level selection can be explained by selection acting at the level of individual organisms. A mother cat who suckles her kittens is not doing so for the benefit of the species; her behavior has evolved because it enhances her kittens' fitness, and ultimately her own as well, since they carry her genes.

Under most conditions, group selection will not be very powerful, because the rate of change in gene frequencies when one individual replaces another in the population is greater than that occurring when one group replaces another group. The number of individuals present is generally greater than the number of groups present in the environment, and individual turnover is greater. In addition, it is difficult to imagine that individuals could evolve to sacrifice their reproduction for the good of the group; a more selfish alternative could easily invade and spread in such a group.

However, there are some possible exceptions; one of these is reduced virulence in parasites, who depend on the survival of their hosts for their own survival. The myxoma virus, introduced in Australia to control imported European rabbits (*Oryctolagus cuniculus*), at first caused the deaths of many individuals. However, within a few years, the mortality rate was much lower, partly because the rabbits became resistant to the pathogen, but also partly because the virus had evolved a lower virulence. The reduction in the virulence is thought to have been aided because the virus is transmitted by a mosquito, from one living rabbit to another. The less deadly viral strain is maintained in the rabbit host population because rabbits afflicted with the more virulent strain would die before passing on the virus. Thus, the viral genes for reduced virulence could spread by group selection. Of course, reduced virulence is also in the interest of every individual virus, if it is to persist in its host! We would not expect to observe evolution by group selection when individual selection is acting strongly in an opposing direction.

Some biologists, most notably Richard Dawkins (1941–), have argued that the gene itself is the true unit of selection. If one genetic alternative, or allele, provides its bearer with an adaptive advantage over some other individual who carries a different allele then the more beneficial allele will be replicated more times, as its bearer enjoys greater fitness. In his book *The Selfish Gene*, Dawkins argues that genes help to build the bodies that aid in their transmission; individual organisms are merely the "survival machines" that genes require to make more copies of themselves.

This argument has been criticized because natural selection cannot "see" the individual genes that reside

KEY TERMS

. . . .

Artificial selection—Selective breeding, carried out by humans, to produce desired genetic alterations in domestic animals and plants.

Fitness—The average number of offspring produced by individuals with a certain genotype, relative to that of individuals with a different genotype.

Gene frequency—The relative fraction of a particular gene in the population, compared to its alternatives.

Genome—The complete set of genes an individual carries.

Genotype—An exact description of the paired genetic alternatives possessed by an individual organism; also used to refer to such a pair at a single genetic locus.

Group selection—The replacement by natural selection of one or more groups of organisms in favor of other groups.

Natural selection—The differential survival and reproduction of organisms, producing evolutionary change in populations.

Phenotype—The outward manifestation of the genotype; the physical, morphological, and behavioral traits of an organism.

Sexual selection—The process of differential reproduction, either through competition between members of one sex for access to mates, or through choice by members of one sex for certain members of the other as mates.

in an organism's genome, but rather selects among phenotypes, the outward manifestation of all the genes that organisms possess. Some genetic combinations may confer very high fitness, but they may reside with genes having negative effects in the same individual. When an individual reproduces, its "bad" genes are replicated along with its "good" genes; if it fails to do so, even its most advantageous genes will not be transmitted into the next generation. Although the focus among most evolutionary biologists has been on selection at the level of the individual, this example raises the possibility that individual genes in genomes are under a kind of group selection. The success of single genes in being transmitted to subsequent generations will depend on their functioning well together, collectively building the best possible organism in a given environment.

See also Adaptation; Competition; Evolution; Genetics.

Further Reading:

Darwin, Charles R. *On the Origin of Species*. London: John Murray, 1859.

Dawkins, Richard. *The Selfish Gene*. Oxford: Oxford University Press, 1976.

Futuyma, Douglas J. *Evolutionary Biology*. 2nd ed. Sunderland, MA: Sinauer, 1986.

Gould, Stephen J. *The Panda's Thumb*. New York: Norton, 1982.

Harvey, Paul H., and M. D. Pagel. *The Comparative Method in Evolutionary Biology*. Oxford: Oxford University Press, 1991.

Kettlewell, H. B. D. *The Evolution of Melanism*. Oxford: Oxford University Press, 1973.

Mayr, Ernst. *The Growth of Biological Thought: Diversity, Evolution, and Inheritance*. Cambridge, MA: Harvard University Press, 1982.

Susan Andrew

Naturopathy see **Alternative medicine**

Nautical archaeology

Nautical archaeology is the branch of archaeology concerned with the excavation, identification, and study of the remains of sunken ships. The techniques used in nautical archaeology can be applied to the study of submerged ports, lost cities, sacrificial wells, and other underwater sites.

The ocean conceals a vast number of unexplored, and potentially valuable, archaeological sites. But the technology needed to explore these sites was not perfected until the mid–twentieth century. With the development of scuba gear, underwater transport, and other underwater devices, archaeologists have improved their ability to survey and retrieve objects underwater.

The artifacts—or archaeological finds—removed from the ocean have enriched our understanding of the history of boat building and navigation, as well as broadened our knowledge of everyday life on land. Because of the lower oxygen content of cold water, objects preserved in the ocean deteriorate much less rapidly than they do on land. A 1,000–year–old shipwreck still might contain the wooden implements and food used to cook the sailors' last meal, as well as the clothes they wore to dinner. The chances of finding such objects preserved on land would be extremely slim.

However, not all objects that sink into the ocean are preserved. If an object sinks near shore, it stands a chance of being shattered against the rocks or of being picked up by a curious diver. Even an object that sinks to depths of up to 50 ft (15 m) can be destroyed by the movement of large waves. In addition, organisms inhabiting the lower regions of the sea such as teredos (ship worms) can bore through the object. In a process known as encrustation, barnacles and coral can grow in a thick layer over the object, also causing it to deteriorate.

Techniques for underwater surveyance, retrieval, and analysis

Before objects can be removed from a shipwreck, the diver must map their precise location in relation both to the other objects and to the surrounding ocean terrain. Because the average diver can move through the water at a rate of only 0.5 mi/h (1 km/h), apparatus have been developed to speed up surveyance. A diver may ride in a hydrodynamic cradle, a flat metal one–diver "bobsled" with a window in front, which can be maneuvered to lower depths. A team of two divers may ride in a towvane, a top–shaped vessel with Plexiglas observation windows and hydrodynamic steering, similar to a diving bell. Or they may descend in a cubmarine, a small electrical battery–powered vessel steered by water jets that can submerge to depths of 164–197 ft (50–60 m).

At great ocean depths or in areas with poor visibility other devices may be employed. Sonar may be used to determine the location of large or encrusted objects by calculating the time it takes echoes to bounce off them. Underwater cameras may be towed by the boat to take pictures of a site in water with good visibility.

The method used to remove the objects will depend on their size and fragility. Ordinary objects may be brought up in plastic or net bags. Heavy objects may be lifted with chains and pulleys or with balloon–like air bags. These bags contain a small amount of compressed air that enables them to expand and rise to the surface as the water pressure decreases.

To determine the age of these objects, archaeologists had to develop new strategies. Although pottery phases and stratigraphy (the analysis of the origin, distribution, and succession of layers or strata of earth) can be used to date objects found on land, neither technique works reliably for objects found in the sea, where water may distort the shape of a jar or may carry away rocks

and silt from the scene of the wreck. Instead, archaeologists use anchors (and sometimes ship nails) to determine the age of a shipwreck. Like pottery, anchors were produced in different sizes and shapes and made of different kinds of materials (such as stone or iron) that conform to historical phases. Archaeologists use these features to assign the shipwreck a date.

The development of nautical archaeology

In the first century A.D., two large Roman ships sank to the bottom of Lake Nemi, southwest of Rome. Rumored to be carrying treasure, and lying at the relatively shallow depth of 49–75.5 ft (15–23 m), they were not entirely forgotten. In 1446, at the request of a church official, the noted Italian architect and theorist Leon Battista Alberti (1404–1472), assisted by divers, attempted to tow one of the ships to shore but succeeded only in raising a large statue. In 1556, a diver wearing a primitive diving apparatus consisting of a wooden "hood" and crystal face plate visited the site. He returned with a description of the ships, claiming that the decks were paved with red brick. In the late nineteenth century, the antiquities dealer Eliseo Borghi began to remove objects from the vessel and sell them at high prices to the Italian government, but the government soon halted Borghi's financial venture. It was not until 1928 that the Italian dictator Benito Mussolini, intrigued by rumors of the buried treasure, decided to raise the ships by draining the lake, partially by means of an old Roman overflow tunnel. Four years later, the water level had been lowered more than 70 ft (229.5 m), and the ships were raised, cleaned, and moved to a museum. No "treasure" was found, but the ships themselves were a spectacular find: they contained heated baths, private cabins, and paved mosaic decks. Both ships were destroyed during World War II.

The first large–scale salvage of a shipwreck was carried out by the Greek Navy in 1900. In about 80 B.C., a Roman vessel carrying a cargo of Greek amphorae (two–handled storage jars) sank to a depth of 60 m (197 ft) near the island of Antikythera, between Crete and southern Greece. Divers worked under extremely dangerous conditions to excavate the wreck. Laboring in storm–tossed seas, and able to remain submerged for only five minutes at a time, the divers nevertheless brought up a number of valuable objects. These included a statute by the Greek sculptor Lycippus and an early astronomical computer.

The first systematic archaeological excavation of a shipwreck was carried out in 1952 under the direction of Jacques–Yves Cousteau and Frédéric Dumas. The French team excavated a Roman amphora carrier that had sunk in the second century B.C. at Grand Congloué, near Marseilles. To assist in surveying the wreck, they decided to employ underwater photographic equipment. They also used a method known as an "airlift" to bring the amphorae to the surface. In this method, unbroken amphorae were filled with air, causing them to rise to the top of the water. To clear off debris from the wreck, the team used a vacuum pump attached to the ship.

The photojournalist Peter Throckmorton and the archaeologist George Bass employed underwater photography and precise methods of surveyance to excavate the Gelidonya wreck off the coast of Turkey. In about 1200 B.C., a trade vessel loaded with more than a ton of metal hit rocks and sank to the bottom of the sea on its journey to Phoenicia (modern–day Syria, Lebanon, and Israel). Explorers worked at a depth of 90 ft (27 m). They pinpointed the location of each object before bringing it to the surface. Heavy objects were raised with a winch and borne to the surface by air bags.

In 1961–64, Bass led the first excavation to be conducted completely underwater. Divers explored a wreck located off the coast of Turkey. Not far from the island of Yassi Ada, a seventh–century Byzantine amphora carrier lay buried in the sand, its wooden structure partially devoured by teredos. Rescuers excavated the ship by using bicycle spokes to keep the fragile wood from breaking off and drifting away until their work could be completed. To give them a better picture of the site, they built a metal scaffold overhead, complete with 16–foot–high (5 m) photographic towers. The undamaged part of the ship was salvaged and completely reassembled on land.

All of the wrecks discussed above were excavated in the Mediterranean Sea. Many wrecks have been excavated in other parts of the world—for example, China. In 1973 a shipwreck was discovered off the coast of Quanzhou in east China. Its cargo contained pottery and fragrant wood. Dated to 1277, the ship is one of the earliest examples of Chinese nautical design. Examination of the wreck brought to light a new fact about Chinese ship construction. Chinese ships were not flat–bottomed, as formerly believed, but rather V–shaped, with a keel that tapered inward.

Whole–ship retrieval

Early excavations succeeded in raising only the contents of shipwrecks or portions of the ships. Recent excavations have focused on raising the entire ship, with its contents intact.

One such project was carried out under the leadership of Anders Franzén, with the support of the Swedish government. In the seventeenth century, the Swedish king Gustavus II Adolph (ruled 1611–1632) decided to improve Sweden's military capability by building a powerful naval fleet. The pride of this fleet was the *Vasa*, an enormous 1,400–ton vessel that was set to depart on its first voyage from Stockholm Harbor. No sooner had it set out from port than it sank, within full view of the king.

Franzén believed that the ship lay at the bottom of the coldwater harbor in an excellent state of preservation. He made several attempts to locate the vessel—one with sonar—all of which failed. Then he made a lucky discovery. He came across a letter from the Swedish Parliament to the king that described the ship's exact location.

Various plans to raise the vessel were discussed. Rescuers decided that the safest plan would be to run cables through tunnels dug by divers beneath the ship. The divers would then swim through the tunnels with the cables and attach them to pontoons on either side of the ship. The pontoons would be filled with water until their decks were even with the water's surface. When the water was pumped out of the pontoons, the *Vasa* would begin to rise from the bottom of the harbor.

This plan was tried and it worked. The process was repeated several times, and the *Vasa* was pumped out of the water. A floating hall was built around it. Enshrined in the hall, and still containing its centuries–old cargo, the *Vasa* was floated to a museum site, where it remains on view today. Among the items found inside the ship were casks containing the sailors' original food and ale, implements for daily use, and twelve skeletons, many of them with their clothing still on, undisturbed down to the coins in their pockets.

In the 1980s, another remarkable vessel was raised from the sea. This time researchers worked to rescue a sixteenth–century naval vessel, the *Mary Rose*. In a tragedy strikingly similar to that which befell the *Vasa*, King Henry VIII watched from Southsea Castle as the pride of his fleet sank with its crew of 700 men on its way to battle France. The historian and archaeologist Alexander McKee believed that the *Mary Rose* was preserved in a deep bed of silt. He decided to raise the ship by attaching cables to a floating crane that lifted the ship out of the water. The ship was then continuously sprayed with water to keep it from drying out until it could be safely moved to shore. Medical equipment, pocket sundials, fishing gear, and leftover food from the ship broadened our knowledge of daily life in the sixteenth century.

Other uses of nautical archaeology

Techniques used in nautical archaeology have been applied to other kinds of underwater archaeology. Submerged ports and lost cities are also subjects of research. Excavated by the United States in 1960, the enormous Port of Caesarea was built by King Herod of Judaea in the first century B.C. to improve commerce with foreign merchants. Destroyed by an earthquake, the port still remains visible underwater. To construct the port, enormous stone blocks were lowered into the water to form a foundation for the five–mile–long pier (8 km) built on top, which included a large curved wall with towers and arched shelters for the merchants.

Destroyed by an earthquake in 1692, Port Royal was a flourishing center of commerce in the Caribbean. After the earthquake, the port sank to a distance of 65 ft (20 m) below sea level. A field school established to study the site has employed seventeenth–century maps to explore the submerged city and port.

The Maya are a Central American people who built an extensive civilization that flourished until the arrival of the Spaniards in the sixteenth century. The natural wells found in the limestone Yucatan Peninsula provided the Maya with a source of drinking water, but some wells were also the site of human sacrifice. In the early twentieth century, attracted by the prospect of finding treasure in the sacred wells, the American archaeologist Edward Herbert Thompson (1860–1935) purchased one of them for $70. To excavate the well he employed the highly unsystematic method of lifting objects out with a bucket. When this method proved unsatisfactory, Thompson dove down into the murky well with two Greek sponge divers, but the extremely low level of visibility thwarted any hope of finding the treasure. Thompson's mission did, however, bring to light a number of important archaeological finds—headdresses, wooden spears, and fabric—which would have otherwise perished had they been left to deteriorate on land.

More than half a century later, the National Institute of Anthropology and History made its own attempt to excavate the sacrificial well. This time, the water was chemically treated and filtered so that rescuers could see to a depth of 15.5 ft (5 m). The two-and-a-half-month excavation project produced other exciting finds. These included carved wooden stools, stone jaguars and serpents, and human remains.

Recent techniques of nautical excavation

To search for objects underwater, nautical archaeologists now employ robots and improved sonar tech-

nology. These methods were employed to excavate the *Titanic*, an "indestructible" ocean vessel than sank in 1912. To search for the *Titanic*, an American–French team employed three robots: Alvin, Angus, and Argo. Alvin was a midget submarine that could descend to the 13 ft (4 m) depth where the ship lay buried. The photographic craft Angus and the television camera craft Argo assisted in pinpointing the location of the *Titanic*.

During the *Titanic* mission, the French researchers used a new kind of sonar known as side–scanning sonar. Ordinary sonar surveys a narrow field that must be carefully mapped out in advance. Side–scanning sonar eliminates this drawback, by picking up signals at a diagonal.

See also Sonar.

Further Reading:

Lampton, Christopher. *Undersea Archaeology.* New York: Franklin Watts, 1988.

Throckmorton, Peter, ed. *The Sea Remembers: Shipwrecks and Archaeology from Homer's Greece to the Rediscovery of the Titanic.* London: Wiedenfeld & Nicolson, 1987.

Sunk! Exploring Underwater Archaeology. Minnesota: Runeston Press, 1994.

Christine Molinari

Nectar

Nectar is a sweet, pleasant–tasting liquid secreted by nectaries. These are specialized organs located inside flowers, and also outside. For example, the "glands" on leaf stalks of cherry (*Prunus*) and wattle (*Acacia*) trees are nectaries. The nectar produced inside flowers attracts crawling or flying insects, birds, or mammals. As a result of feeding on nectar, these visitors may transfer pollen from anther to stigma, within the same flower, or from one flower to another of the same species. Such pollen transfer ensures that fertilization takes place. The nectar produced by *Prunus* and *Acacia* nectaries attracts ants, which then protect the host plant from the leaf–eating larvae of other insects.

Nectar is sweet because of its large sugar concentration. Any or all of sucrose, maltose, glucose, and fructose may be present. Their proportions vary with species, as do their concentrations. For some species (e.g. hellebores, *Helleborus* spp.), the sugar present is entirely or almost entirely sucrose; for others (e.g. blue bells, *Campanula* spp.), the hexose sugars glucose and fructose are the major sugars present. Total sugar concentrations between 30% and 60% (by weight) are common. Nectar with relatively smaller sugar concentrations is preferred by insects, while larger concentrations are preferred by birds and mammals.

Amino acids are the most abundant of the other nutrients present in nectar. The relative proportions of amino acids versus sugars, and the acidity of nectar can change during the day. This may influence the timing of flower visits by specific nectar–seeking visitors, but the significance of these daily changes is not fully understood.

The production of nectar by nectaries occurs at precise stages of floral development, in flowers coinciding with pollen release, and with the stigmatic surface becoming receptive to pollen. Production is flexible—it stops if nectar is not removed, and resumes to compensate for nectar consumed by visitors. Floral structure can influence how the composition of nectar is controlled following production. Where the petals are fused to form a tube, the secreted nectar can be protected from a concentrating process that might otherwise come about through evaporation of water. This extends the period during which the nectar is most attractive to pollinators.

See also Flower; Pollination.

Negative

Negative is a term in mathematics that usually means "opposite." An electron's charge is called negative not because it is "below" but because it is opposite

that of a proton. A surface with negative curvature bulges in from the point of view of someone on one side of the surface but bulges out from the point of view of someone on the other side. A line with negative slope is downhill for someone moving to the right but uphill for someone moving to the left.

The term negative is most commonly applied to numbers. When negative is an adjective applied to a number or integer, the reference is to the opposite of a positive number. As a noun, negative is the opposite of any given number. Thus, –4, –3/5, and $-\sqrt{2}$ are all negative numbers, but the negative of –4 is +4. The integers, for example, are often defined as the natural numbers plus their negatives plus zero. Sometimes the word opposite is used to mean the same as the noun negative.

Technically, negative numbers are the opposites with respect to addition. If a is a positive number then $-a$ is a negative number because: $a + (-a) = 0$.

Allowing numbers and other mathematical elements to be negative as well as positive greatly expands the generality and usefulness of the mathematical systems of which they are a part. For example, if one owes a credit card company $150 and mistakenly sends $160 in payment, the company automatically subtracts the payment from the balance due, leaving –$10 as the balance due. It does not have to set up a separate column in its ledger or on its statements. A balance due of –$10 is mathematically equivalent to a credit of $10.

When the Fahrenheit temperature scale was developed, the starting point was chosen to be the coldest temperature which, at that time, could be achieved in the laboratory. This was the temperature of a mixture of equal weights of ice and salt. Because the scale could be extended downward through the use of negative numbers, it could be used to measure temperatures all the way down to absolute zero.

The idea of negative numbers is readily grasped, even by young children. They usually do not raise objection to extending a number line beyond zero. They play games that can leave a player "in the hole." Nevertheless, for centuries European mathematicians resisted using negative numbers. If solving an equation led to a negative root, it would be dismissed as without meaning.

In other parts of the world, however, negative numbers were used. The Chinese used two abaci, a black one for positive numbers and a red one for negative numbers, as early as two thousand years ago. Brahmagupta, the Indian mathematician who lived in the seventh century, not only acknowledged negative roots of quadratic equations, he gave rules for multiplying various combinations of positive and negative numbers. It was several centuries before Euopean mathematicians became aware of the work of Brahmagupta and others, and began to treat negative numbers as meaninful.

Negative numbers can be symbolized in several ways. The most common is to use a minus sign in front of the number. Occasionally the minus sign is placed behind the number, or the number is enclosed in parentheses. Children, playing a game, will often draw a circle around a number which is "in the hole." When a minus sign appears in front of a letter representing a number, as in $-x$, the number may be positive or negative depending on the value of x itself. To guarantee that a number is positive, one can put absolute value signs around it, for example $|-x|$. The absolute value sign can also guarantee a negative value, which is $-|x|$.

Nematodes see **Roundworms**

Neodymium see **Lanthanides**

Neon see **Rare gases**

Nephron see **Excretory system**

Neptune

Neptune is the eighth planet from the Sun and about four times the size of Earth. Astronomers consider Neptune to form with Uranus a subgroup of the Jovian planets (Jupiter, Saturn, Uranus, and Neptune). Neptune and Uranus are similar in size, mass, periods of their rotation, the overall features of their magnetic fields, and ring systems. However they differ in the structure of their atmospheres (perhaps the more conspicuous features of Neptune's clouds are caused by its significant internal energy source, which Uranus lacks), the orientations of their rotation axes, and in their satellite systems.

Neptune's large satellite Triton, which has a very thin nitrogen atmosphere with clouds, plumes, and haze, an extremely cold surface with nitrogen, methane, carbon monoxide, and carbon dioxide ices which interact with the atmosphere, and a fairly high mean density, make it seem more like Pluto than the other satellites of Neptune and those of Saturn and Uranus. Not enough is known about Pluto to explore these similarities; this probably awaits a successful flyby of the Pluto-Charon

system by the Pluto Fast Flyby mission early in the twenty–first century.

Discovery

Neptune was discovered in September, 1846, by Johann Galle in Berlin, Germany, on the first night of his search for a trans–Uranian planet which had produced previously unexplained perturbations of Uranus's orbit. These prompted Urbain Leverrier in France to calculate the predicted position of this undiscovered planet; he sent his calculations to Galle, who then discovered Neptune. However, there is evidence that Galileo Galilei had earlier fortuitously observed Neptune near Jupiter on December 28, 1612, and January 28, 1613, and J. Lalande also had observed it in 1795, but neither astronomer recognized Neptune as a trans–Saturnian (–Uranian) planet. Lassell discovered Neptune's largest satellite Triton several weeks later in 1846.

Characteristics

From Triton's 5.866 day period of revolution around Neptune and its 220,000 mi (354,300 km) mean distance from it, astronomers estimated Neptune's mass to be 17.14 Earth masses, according to Kepler's Thrid Law. From Neptune's mean radius of 15,290 mi (24,625 km), a mean density (mass divided by volume) of 1.64 grams/cm^3 was found. These values are similar to the ones found for Uranus. Uranus is slightly larger than Neptune, but Neptune is considerably more massive and denser than Uranus. Thus, Neptune is one of the Jovian planets, which are characterized by large sizes and masses but low mean densities (compared with the Earth). The last characteristic implies that Jovian planets have extremely thick atmospheres and are largely or mostly composed of gases.

Neptune is in a nearly circular orbit around the Sun at a 30.1 astronomical unit (a.u.) mean distance (4,500,000,000 km) from it, making it the most distant known Jovian planet (and probably the most distant known major planet, since recent findings indicate that the Pluto–Charon system is too small to be considered a major planet) from the Sun. Kepler's Third Law gives 165 years for Neptune's period of revolution around the Sun. Therefore, Neptune will not have made one complete revolution around the Sun since its discovery until 2011.

Observations from Earth

Our knowledge about Neptune came slowly before the 1989 *Voyager 2* flyby, due to its remoteness. Even when it is closest, telescopic observations show Nep-

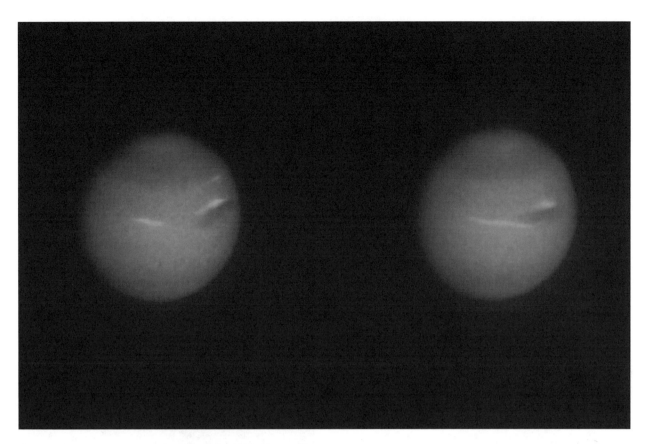

Two images of Neptune taken 53 hours apart. The images show surprisingly dynamic weather activity in Neptune's atmosphere. Because the planet receives less sunlight than any of the other gas giants (only 3% of the amount that Jupiter receives), scientists had expected less weather activity. *Voyager 2,* however, discovered winds blowing in excess of 1,100 miles per hour (1,900 kph) in a direction opposite Neptune's rotation. The winds are faster than those on any other planet, but because they are not turbulent, less energy is required to maintain their velocity.

tune as a small, featureless bluish–green disk of only 2.35" apparent diameter and 7.7 stellar magnitude. Spectroscopic observations showed that Neptune's color is produced by the absorption of sunlight by methane gas in its atmosphere; this is also true for Uranus. Observations of occultations (similar to eclipses) of stars by Neptune indicated that its atmosphere is mostly composed of molecular hydrogen and helium, which are also the main components of the other Jovian planets. These gases are inconspicuous in their visible spectra.

Soon after its discovery, it was found that Triton's orbit around Neptune is retrograde, meaning that, as seen from above Neptune's north pole, Triton revolves around Neptune clockwise instead of counterclockwise (direct motion). If one views the solar system from above the Sun's north pole, all the planets have direct (counterclockwise) revolutions around the Sun, and most of them have direct rotations; the exceptions are Venus, Uranus, and possibly Pluto. Infrared (at wave-

lengths longer than those of red light) observations of Triton since 1980 indicated the presence of an atmosphere containing methane, and the presence of nitrogen in solid or liquid form on its surface. However, its size and mass remained poorly known.

G.P. Kuiper discovered a second satellite, Nereid, in 1949. It is a small, faint (nineteenth magnitude) object in an orbit around Neptune that is distant (3,423,821 mi [385,513,400 km] mean distance) from it, very elliptical (eccentricity 0.756), and highly inclined (29° to Neptune's equator). A third satellite was suspected at about a 45,954 mi (74,000 km) distance from Neptune's center because of a simultaneous 8.1 second decrease in the brightness of a star observed simultaneously from two locations 4 mi (6 km) apart in May 1981. More will be said about this later.

From 1982, Neptune was suspected to have rings like the other Jovian planets. However, confirmation of suspected occultations of stars by rings of Neptune was not definite; occultations by possible rings were only observed sometimes. This led to the theory that Neptune had a set of incomplete arc rights which were maintained by gravitational perturbations from one or more "shepherd satellites" which were still undiscovered.

Efforts to determine Neptune's rotation period from Earth–based observations using spectroscopy to find it from Doppler shifts of spectral lines across Neptune's disk and searches for periodic brightness changes gave conflicting and almost always incorrect results.

Earth–based infrared observations of Neptune indicated by 1974 that, unlike Uranus, Neptune emits 2.4 times as much energy at infrared wavelengths as it receives from sunlight (insolation). This led to the inference that, like Jupiter and Saturn, Neptune has a significant internal heat source. This may be produced by continuing gravitational contraction or by the settling of denser materials to the center of a planet.

Results from the *Voyager 2* flyby

The *Voyager 2* spacecraft was launched from Earth in 1977, and then flew by Jupiter in July 1979, Saturn in August 1981, and Uranus in January 1986. Uranus accelerated *Voyager 2* toward a flyby of Neptune along a hyperbolic orbit in August 1989. The season on Neptune was late spring, nearly summer, in its southern hemisphere. The closest approach (29,240 km) to Neptune's center occurred at 3:56 Universal Time (U.T.) on August 25, 1989, about 4,900 km above the cloud tops of its north polar region. During *Voyager 2's* encounter with Neptune from June 5, 1989, to October 2, 1989, the observations it made greatly increased our knowledge about the Neptune system. The plane of Neptune's equator is tilted 29°.6 to the plane of its orbit around the Sun. *Voyager 2* flew by Triton at a minimum distance of 39,790 km on August 25, 1989 at about 9:10 U.T. It observed Triton continuously from about 6:00 U.T. to 12:00 U.T. on that date, and discovered much about Triton that will be discussed in detail in a separate section. The main discoveries *Voyager 2* made about Neptune, its rings, and its small satellites follow.

Neptune's magnetic field

Like the Earth and the other Jovian planets, Neptune has a strong magnetic field and a sizeable magnetosphere (the region of space where Neptune's magnetic field is dominant over the interplanetary field). *Voyager 2* did not find definite evidence for the existence of Neptune's magnetic field until eight days before its closest approach to Neptune, when radio and plasma wave observations of magnetospheric phenomena were

The size of Neptune's Great Dark Spot (top) compared to the size of the Earth (bottom). The Great Dark Spot is a huge storm of long duration in the planet's upper atmosphere. Its winds blow counterclockwise.

obtained. *Voyager 2* entered Neptune's magnetosphere about seven hours before its closest approach to Neptune and remained inside the magnetosphere for about three days. The center of Neptune's magnetic field is offset by 0.55 Neptune radius ($0.55N_R$) from Neptune's center, and its magnetic axis is tilted 47° with respect to Neptune's rotation axis (Neptune's magnetic poles are 47° from its poles of rotation). (See Figure 2)

In this way, Neptune's magnetic field is similar to that of Uranus (see Uranus), and is unlike the magnetic fields of the Earth, Jupiter, and Saturn, in which the offsets from the planets' centers and the tilts to their rotation axes are much smaller.

Voyager 2 also detected radiation belts of charged particles trapped in Neptune's magnetosphere. They include protons, electrons, charged molecular hydrogen, and charged heliumions. The particle density was

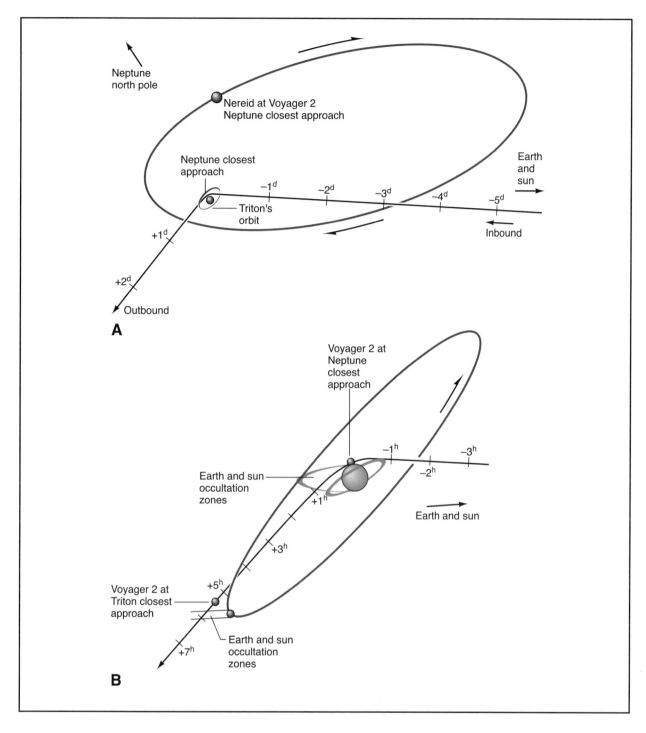

Figure 1. The *Voyager 2* trajectory through the Neptune system. (A) is a large view of the system showing the projected orbits of Nereid and Triton. Tick marks on the trajectory show *Voyager 2*'s position at one–day intervals. (B) is an enlarged view covering a 10–hour period that includes closest approaches to Neptune and Triton and passage through the Earth and solar shadows (occultation zones). Neptune's ring system is also indicated. Here tick marks along the trajectory are at one–hour intervals.

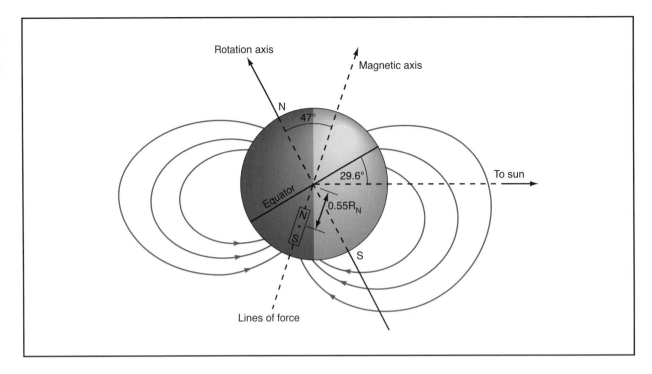

Figure 2. Diagram of the offset and tilted magnetic field of Neptune.

found to be even lower than that found in Uranus's magnetosphere. Neptune's rings and small nearby satellites affect the structure of the magnetosphere near Neptune. Triton affects the outer part of the magnetosphere; among other things, it is presumed to be the main source of the charged nitrogenions that are found there.

Neptune's rotation period

The tilt of Neptune's magnetic field to its rotation axis and the field's offset from Neptune's center cause fluctuations of its magnetic field that are associated with the rotation of Neptune's interior. From measurements of these fluctuations by *Voyager 2*, the rotation period of Neptune's interior of 16 hours, seven minutes was determined; this was the first reliable determination of Neptune's rotation period. The 12 hour to 21 hour rotation periods found for the atmospheric features observed by *Voyager 2* differ from the above value because of winds.

Atmospheric features

The *Voyager 2* images show that there are many more prominent features in Neptune's atmosphere in 1989 than were seen in Uranus's atmosphere in 1986: a Great Dark Spot at 20° South Latitude, a Small Dark Spot at 55° South Latitude which is encompassed by a circumpolar dark band from 45° South to 70° South Latitudes, another dark band from 6° North to 25° North Latitudes, and several elongated white clouds.

Except for their bluish color, *Voyager 2* images of Neptune seem more like those of Jupiter than Uranus.

The temperature at the aerosol layer in Neptune's atmosphere is about –346° F (–210° C), which is close to the temperature at the main cloud level in Uranus's atmosphere, and the effective temperatures of the atmospheres of both Uranus and Neptune were found to be close to this temperature. One would expect Neptune's visible troposphere and lower stratosphere to be about 59° F (15° C) colder than those of Uranus because of Neptune's greater distance form the Sun (30.1 a.u. vs. 19.2 a.u.); instead, the temperatures of these parts of the atmospheres of both planets are found to be about the same. Neptune's atmosphere seems to be considerably warmer than it would be if it received all or nearly all its heating from sunlight, as seems to be the case for Uranus. This is another indication that Neptune has a powerful internal heat source, unlike Uranus, which has at most a weak internal heat source (compatible with radioactivity in its interior) or none at all. *Voyager 2* infrared observations confirmed this; the emission to insolation ratio was found to be 2.6 from them instead of the value 2.4 found earlier. This internal heat source may be what drives the active features in Neptune's visible atmosphere, which are much less noticeable in Uranus's atmosphere.

Neptune's atmosphere was found to be similar to that of Uranus in that it seems to have little temperature change with latitude. This probably indicates enormous heat capacities for both atmospheres. Also Neptune has a hot (about 900° F [500° C]) ionosphere and an exosphere that consists mainly of a hydrogen thermal corona; both these atmospheric components seem similar to those of Uranus. However, Neptune's stronger gravity and slightly colder stratosphere cause much lower particle densities in Neptune's upper atmosphere than are found at the same heights above the cloud layers in Uranus's atmosphere.

Neptune's ring system

Voyager 2 confirmed the suspected existence of a ring system around Neptune, and moreover, that in at least one (the outermost) ring its particles show a noticeable concentration in a series of arcs, as had been hypothesized from the inconsistent results of Earth-based observations mentioned above. There are at least five rings around Neptune. The rings lie between 23,500 mi (38,000 km) and 39,000 mi (63,000 km) from Neptune's center, revolve directly around Neptune, are optically thinner and dustier (with much smaller average particle size) than Uranus's rings, are very dark with albedos (ratios of reflected to incident light) less than 0.07, and lie in or near the plane of Neptune's equator. Neptune's outer rings are closely associated with some of the six small satellites of Neptune discovered by *Voyager 2* (see below). The cause of the clumping of many of the particles in the Adams ring into the three compact arcs is still not definitely known. Gravitational perturbations by nearby satellites, especially by Galatea, are suspected of producing gravitational resonances which produce the arcs. The perturbed motions of ring particles can lead to collisions of them that may be the main source of the copious and extensive fine (micron–sized) dust observed in Neptune's rings. The plasma wave instruments on *Voyager 2* have detected a "halo" of dust around Neptune that extends far from the ring (equatorial) plane; it was detected even above Neptune's north polar region.

Like the case for Uranus's rings, the origin and evolution of Neptune's rings are unknown. Are they the result of earlier tidal disruption of other nearby satellites? Are they a transitory phenomenon, or will they persist for millions or billions of years? Comparison of the positions of the arcs in the Adams ring observed by *Voyager 2* in 1989 with their positions extrapolated back in time to 1984 and 1985 shows that they match the positions of three occultations of stars observed in those years. This indicates that the arcs in the Adams ring are stable over time intervals of at least five years.

Satellites

Voyager 2 discovered six more small satellites, which all have direct orbital motion around Neptune nearly in the plane of its equator and are all much closer to it than Triton. This brings the total number of known satellites of Neptune (excluding the vast number of ring particles) to eight. The four innermost satellites Naiad, Thalassa, Despina, and Galatea are within the ring system and must interact with it. Galatea's possible effect in producing and maintaining the arcs in the Adams ring has already been described; it orbits just 560 mi (900 km) inside that ring. Despina orbits Neptune about 434 mi (700 km) inside the Leverrier ring and may contribute to its stability, although arcs are not obvious in that ring.

All of Neptune's six innermost satellites are very dark, having albedos of 0.065 or less. Proteus, the largest and outermost of the newly discovered satellites, had details on its surface imaged. It is heavily cratered, with a 93 mi (150 km) diameter crater visible there. Proteus turns out to be somewhat larger than Nereid and has a mean radius of 130 mi (208 km); images of Proteus indicate it to be decidedly non–spherical. The images indicate also that Proteus is tidally locked to Neptune (that is, its rotation period equals its period of revolution around Neptune and keeps the same hemisphere always turned towards Neptune), as is Triton.

Larissa also was imaged with sufficient resolution for its surface to be studied in some detail. It is also decidedly non–spherical and dark. The sizes, shapes, albedos, and states of rotation of the four innermost newly discovered satellites are less definite. Nereid, Neptune's outermost satellite, was observed by *Voyager 2*, which determined its size (105 mi [170 km] radius) and albedo (0.15 to 0.20), which indicate that its surface seems more like those of Uranus's icy satellites Umbriel, Oberon, and the darker areas on Miranda than the surfaces of the six newly discovered satellites. Limited information was obtained from the probe's observations because Nereid was more than 2,800,000 mi (4,600,000 km) from *Voyager 2* at closest approach, and it give no definite information about Nereid's rotation period (it is probably not tidally locked to Neptune), pole position, or its mass. Finally, from the discovery observations of Larissa and its period of revolution around Neptune, it seems that Larissa was probably the satellite which produced the 8.1 second decrease of the brightness of a star in 1981 which was mentioned above.

Triton

Triton is the only satellite of Neptune whose mass could be determined from its gravitational perturbation

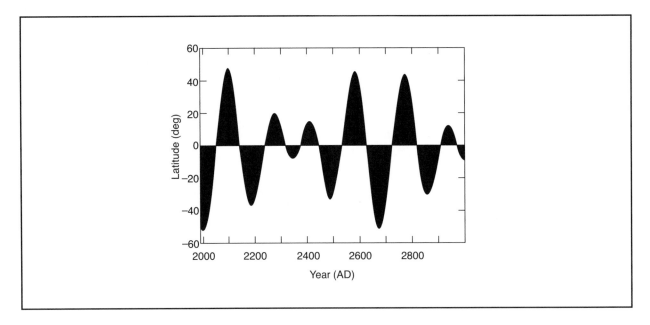

Figure 3. Graph of the latitude of the subsolar point on Triton from 1993 to 3000. This illustrates the complicated nature of the seasons on Triton.

of *Voyager 2's* hyperbolic flyby orbit. In addition to having its rotation tidally locked to its orbital revolution around Neptune, Triton's rotation axis is almost aligned (to within 1°) with the perpendicular to Neptune's orbital plane around the Sun. The fact that Triton's orbital plane around Neptune is tilted 23° to Neptune's equatorial plane and the nodes (the intersection points of Triton's orbit with Neptune's equator) process along the equator, making a 360° circuit around it in 688 years, causes the seasons on Triton to be much more complicated than they are on Neptune. A graph of the latitude of the subsolar point—the point directly below the sun—on Triton from the present to the year 3000 is shown in Figure 3.

The subsolar point was at about 45° South Latitude at the *Voyager 2* encounter, and since then has moved further south toward its farthest south value of 52° South Latitude.

The main discoveries that *Voyager 2* made about Triton are the following.

Triton's mass

Triton's mass was found to be $2.141.10^{22}$ kg (0.00358 Earth mass), and its radius 1352 km; from this, its mean density was found to be 2.07 grams/cm³. This makes Triton the densest satellite yet found beyond Jupiter, although Saturn's satellite Titan is considerably larger and more massive.

Triton's atmosphere

Triton has a thin atmosphere of mainly molecular nitrogen with a trace (.01%) of methane. Radio observations during the occultation of *Voyager 2* by Triton found a value of 1.5 Pascal for the atmospheric surface pressure (the pressure in the Earth's atmosphere about 75 mi [120 km] above sea level). Clouds are observed in the lower few miles of Triton's atmosphere, and haze is found as high as 31 (50 km) above its surface. Four mysterious plumes were observed to rise as high as eight km above the surface and then extend up to 93 mi (150 km) horizontally. The clouds and plumes showed the presence of winds in Triton's atmosphere. The mechanism which powers the plumes is uncertain; a "greenhouse" mechanism (which traps sunlight in a transparent solid nitrogen layer and then vaporizes some nitrogen), geothermal heat, and also "dust devils" in Triton's atmosphere have all been suggested.

Triton's surface

Triton's surface is very bright; its average albedo is about 0.8, while those for individual regions vary from 0.6 to nearly 1.0. Yellowish, pinkish, and peach–colored regions are seen on Triton's generally whitish background; these may show the presence of organic compounds produced by reactions of molecular nitrogen and methane in the presence of solar radiation, high energy electrons, or of cosmic rays. *Voyager 2* infrared observations gave a –391° F (–235° C) for Triton's surface, which varied very little across it. This is the coldest temperature observed for the surface of any solar system satellite or planet. Nitrogen and methane ice were both identified on the surface; at 1.5 Pascal atmospheric surface pressure, the atmosphere is in vapor equilibrium with nitrogen surface ice. Triton's surface has few craters (compared with the outer satellites of Saturn and Uranus), and it lacks craters larger than 19 mi (30 km) in diameter. The crater density is considerably lower than that on the most heavily cratered regions on Uranus's satellite Miranda. Many regions show evidence of resurfacing. Many darker streaks are seen on Triton's surface; they may be debris that has been deposited by earlier plumes. Part of Triton's surface, especially the western part of the equatorial region, shows a curious pattern somewhat resembling the skin of a cantaloupe, consisting of concentrations of pits and dimples crossed by ridges of possibly erupted viscous materials. This "cataloup" terrain is unique among the known surfaces of solar system bodies, and its origin is still unexplained.

Earth–based observations made in 1991 and 1992 made in near–infrared wavelengths with the United Kingdom Infrared Telescope Facility on Mauna Kea, Hawaii showed evidence of carbon monoxide and carbon dioxide ices on Triton's surface as well as those of nitrogen and methane. They confirmed the 391° F temperature of Triton's surface and found that there is less than 10% carbon monoxide ice dissolved in the nitrogen ice on Triton's surface.

This summarizes the present state of our knowledge about Triton. In size, mass, and mean density, Triton appears to be a larger and more massive variant of Pluto, since their mean densities are both nearly 2.1 grams/cm³. A plausible model for Triton's interior is one with a rocky core of about 621 mi (1,000 km) radius surrounded by a 217 mi (350 km) thick water ice mantle, above which there is a crust of nitrogen, methane, carbon monoxide, and carbon dioxide ices which is only a few miles thick.

Returning to Neptune, very little is now known about its interior except that its powerful internal energy source and strong magnetic field imply a field–generating region in Neptune's interior which extends through most of it, and that most of Neptune's interior is a fluid having a high internal temperature. Neptune's mean density indicates that it probably has a small rocky core surrounded by a hot fluid shell; this is surrounded by a second shell comprised of gaseous and icy water, ammonia and carbon compounds. Neptune's oblateness (polar flattening) of 0.0171 indicates that its interior is considerably denser than that of Uranus with

KEY TERMS

Doppler shift—The shift in wavelength of a spectroscopic line from its zero velocity wavelength to longer (redder) wavelengths if the source of the line is moving away from the observer or to shorter (bluer) wavelengths if the source is approaching the observer. It is used to measure velocity along the line of sight (radial velocity).

Precession—What happens when a turning moment (torque) is applied to a body with angular momentum. Instead of turning in the direction of the turning moment, the body's angular momentum will turn in a plane perpendicular to the one in which the turning moment acts.

Shepherd satellite—A planetary satellite whose gravitational perturbations on a particle tend to keep it in a stable orbit around the planet. The Pascal (Pa) is the metric unit of pressure (force per unit area). One Pascal is defined as a pressure of one Newton per square meter. The standard sea level atmospheric pressure on the Earth is 101,200 Pascals.

oblateness of 0.023. The precession of Triton's orbit gives some information about Neptune's internal structure. However, it is too far from Neptune (14.4 Neptune radii) for detailed mapping of Neptune's interior and gravity field. Accurate orbits are needed for the nearest newly discovered satellites and rings to do this; they are not yet available. Even if such orbits are determined, the information from them may not allow a unique model to be selected for Neptune's interior; this cannot yet be done for Uranus, where much more information about its close satellites and rings is available.

The Hubble Space Telescope observed Neptune in 1994 from Earth orbit and detected cloud features in its atmosphere which appeared to be different from those observed by *Voyager 2* in 1989. The main change noticed was that the Great and Small Dark Spots seemed to have disappeared by 1994. This indicates that these spots may be of much shorter duration than Jupiter's Great Red Spot, to which these large dark spots in Neptune's atmosphere have sometimes been compared.

Future Research

Observations of the Neptune system with the Hubble Space Telescope like the ones mentioned above should continue. But to answer most of the questions which *Voyager 2's* flyby has raised about the Neptune system, one must send spacecraft to Neptune. The next space mission to Neptune might be similar to the Cassini/Huygens mission to Saturn scheduled for launch in October 1997 and to arrive at Saturn in 2004. This two–spacecraft mission would put one spacecraft into orbit around Neptune, while the second spacecraft would go into a polar orbit around Triton, unlike the Huygens spacecraft, which is to enter Titan's atmosphere and possibly land on it.

See also Celestial mechanics; Kepler's laws; Jupiter; Planet; Pluto; Satellite; Saturn; Space probe; Solar system; Uranus.

Further Reading:

Beatty, J. Kelly, "Welcome to Neptune," *Sky and Telescope Magazine.* 78, No. 4 (1989): 358–359.

Beatty, J. Kelly. "Hubble's Worlds." *Sky and Telescope Magazine.* 89, No. 2,(1995): 25.

Chapman, Clark R., "Voyager at Neptune: Sorting Out the Early Results." *The Planetary Report.* 9, No. 6 (1989): 12–15.

"Galileo Saw Neptune." *Sky and Telescope Magazine.* 60, No. 5 (1980): 363.

Lunine, J.I., et. al. "Voyager at Triton." *Science.* 250, No. 386 (1990): 410–443.

Porco, Carolyn C., et. al. "Voyager 2 at Neptune." *The Planetary Report.* 12, No. 2, (1992): 4–23.

Stone, E.C., et. al. "The Voyager 2 Encounter with the Neptunian System." *Science.* 246 (1989): 1417–1500.

Stone, E.C., et al., "The Voyager Encounter with Neptune." *Journal of Geophysical Research* 96, Supplement, 18 (1991): 906–19, 268.

"Voyager's Last Picture Show," *Sky and Telescope Magazine.* 78, No. 5, (1989): 463–470.

Frederick R. West

Neptunium see **Element, transuranium**

Nerve growth factor

Nerve Growth Factor (NGF) is a polypeptide, a molecule composed of several amino acid units that has a protein–like behavior, but is not as complex as a protein in structure. NGF increases the growth of nerve cells, especially those in the peripheral nervous system, and directs the growth and orientation of nerve cell axons (processes which carry impulses away from the nerve cell body to adjoining dendrites). NGF is one of many growth factors found to be essential in cell divi-

sion (mitosis), and has been isolated from a variety of cells such as mouse salivary glands and developing nerve tissue. The behavior of NGF resembles that of polypeptide hormones such as insulin.

NGF has been studied most frequently in the development of the nervous system of embryos though surgical and chemical manipulation. Transplanting extra legs onto the backs of tadpoles has been found to cause the outgrowth of nerve fibers from the central nervous system to the leg. The chemical substance that directs the movement of the axons seems to react with receptors on the membrane of cells and causes a chain of metabolic events that stimulates the growth of the axons in a certain direction. Scientists have found a molecule that guides the growth of nerve cell axons in the visual retina of chick embryos. Injection of NGF into young mice or chickens causes the nerve cell bodies in sympathetic and sensory ganglia to enlarge, and seems to be essential for cell division (mitosis) in sympathetic nerve cells. If an antibody against NGF is injected into young mice, no sympathetic nervous system develops.

The study of NGF has applications in the treatment of injuries to the spinal cord, prevention of cognitive decline, and the treatment of certain brain diseases such as Alzheimer's. In experiments, animals that were deliberately injured to stimulate spinal injury victims were treated with collagen containing skin cells genetically modified to produce NGF. It was found that the experimental group of animals showed significant axon formation. The control animals did not show any signs of axon formation. This research could lead to the treatment of stroke and accident victims where there has been significant nervous system damage. Infusing NGF into the brains of aged rats with memory and learning impairments was found to increase their memory. The infused NGF seemed to prevent brain nerve cell death, and to stimulate the development of damaged neurons, which secrete acetylcholine, a brain chemical associated with memory. Researchers are also trying to find a way to introduce NGF into the brains of Alzheimer's disease patients, in an attempt to retard memory loss.

See also Alzheimer's disease; Memory; Nervous system; Neuron.

Nervous system

The nervous system coordinates behavior and helps to maintain the internal stability of animals. It may be as simple as the nerve net of Cnidarians or as complex as the centralized system of mammals. In all nervous systems the functional unit is the nerve cell or neuron, a cell specialized to transmit and receive a stimulus.

Evolution of invertebrate nervous systems

To survive, animals have to respond to changes in their internal and external environment. General responses are found in animals that have a simple nervous system and can only process information in a limited way. An example of this type of nervous system is found in the common freshwater *Hydra*, a cylinder-shaped inverebrate. It has a nerve net of neurons between the outer and inner layers of a sac–like body. The nerve net transmits impulses in all directions with no means of processing the information to make a specific response. In flatworms, such as planaria, there is a simple centralized nervous system. Here, neurons are organized into structures called ganglia which act to receive stimuli from the sensory structures and transmit them by way of a ladder–like arrangement of nerves to muscle cells. In this way, flatworms can make specific responses to stimuli, such as turning away from light, or curling up when touched. Higher invertebrates, such as annelids, arthropods, and mollusks, have a more complex nervous system with more highly developed sensory structures that allow the animals to receive, process, and respond to stimuli in a greater variety of ways. An example of this is the compound eyes of insects which send sensory information through nerve fibers to the ganglia in the head that serve as the brain. The information is then relayed to the other parts of the body through a nerve cord found on the ventral (lower) surface of the animal. The effectiveness of this arrangement is demonstrated by he rapid escape response of flies when attempts are made to kill them. In the octopus, a mollusk with well developed eyes and a central concentration of nerve cells, responses are highly specific, and the ability to learn how to perform complex tasks is evident.

Evolution of the vertebrate nervous system

The nervous system shows the greatest development in vertebrates. There is an increase in centralization with increasing elaboration of the brain with areas with specific functions. The central nervous system includes the brain and a dorsal (upper) spinal cord encased and protected by the skeletal system. The central nervous system is connected to the rest of the body through a peripheral nervous system that includes the nerves connecting the brain and spinal cord with receptors such as the ear and eyes and effectors such as the muscles in the body. In the evolution of vertebrates from fish to mammals, the most significant changes have occurred in the structure of the brain. Even in the earliest vertebrates, the brain had three divisions: the hindbrain, midbrain, and forebrain. In fish, the hindbrain is dominant and concerned mainly with motor reflexes. The largest section of the fish brain is the optic lobes in the midbrain, with the anterior of the brain (forebrain) composed of the olfactory lobes and the cerebrum. In the progression from fish to mammals, the hindbrain becomes less and less prominent, and the area of the brain used for receiving and integrating information becomes greater and greater as shown by an increase in the size and development of the cerebrum. The cerebrum is the part of the brain involved in learning voluntary movement as well as the interpretation of sensation. Birds and mammals have the largest brain mass relative to body size with the largest ratio found in man and porpoises. In man the brain weighs approximately 3 lb (1.4 kg) with the cerebrum making up 80% of the total brain mass.

Human nervous system—Central nervous system

In humans, centralization has reached the greatest degree of specialization. The brain and spinal cord are formed early in embryonic development. At the beginning of the third week of gestation, the embryo has already formed a neural plate on the dorsal surface which eventually folds together to form a hollow tube from which the brain and spinal cord develop. During this time the 100 billion neurons found in the brain are produced—the sum total of all the neurons that the brain will ever contain in an individual's lifetime. The brain is one of the largest organs in the body and consists of three main regions: the forebrain, midbrain, and hindbrain. The cerebrum, which is the most important area for neural processing, together with the thalamus and hypothalamus, forms the forebrain. In the midbrain are centers for the receipt and integration of several types of sensory information, such as seeing and hearing. The information is then sent on to specific areas in the cerebrum to be processed. The hindbrain consists of three parts: the medulla oblongata, the pons, and cerebellum, and it functions in maintaining homeostasis and coordinating movement. The pons and medulla of the hindbrain, together with the midbrain, form the brainstem, which is the location of reflex centers such as those that control heart beat rate and breathing rate. The other part of the central nervous system, the spinal cord, serves as a pathway for nerve tracts carrying impulses to and from the brain. It acts as the site for simple reflexes such as the familiar knee jerk. If a slice were made into the spinal cord, it would show a cord with a small central canal surrounded by an area of gray matter shaped like a butterfly surrounded by white matter. The gray matter is composed of large masses of cell bodies, dendrites and unmyelinated axons; the white matter is composed of bundles of axons that are called tracts, which send information to the brain or send information away from the brain.

Human nervous system—Peripheral nervous system

The central nervous system operates through the peripheral nervous system which is the "roadway" that links the central nervous system to the rest of the body. The nerves that carry information to the central nervous system from sensory receptors such as the eye are called sensory nerves or afferent nerves; those that carry impulses away from the central nervous system to effector organs such as the muscles are called motor nerves or efferent nerves. Commonly the fibers of sensory and motor neurons are bundled together to form mixed nerves. There are 12 pairs of cranial nerves that run to or from the brain, such as the optic and vagus nerves. There are 31 pairs of nerves called spinal nerves that originate from the spinal cord, such as the sciatic nerve and ulnar nerve, the nerve that is stimulated when you hit your elbow. Specific areas of the body are served by each of the spinal nerves. All sensory nerves enter the cord through a dorsal root, and all motor nerves exit through a ventral root. If the dorsal section of a root is destroyed, sensation from that area is also destroyed, but the muscles are still able to function. In the opposite situation, damage to the ventral root destroys muscle function, but sensory information is still processed.

There are two main divisions to the peripheral nervous system, the somatic and the autonomic. The somatic system involves the skeletal muscles and is considered voluntary since there is control over movement such as writing or throwing a ball. The cell bodies of the somatic system are in the central nervous system (CNS) with the axons running all the way to the skeletal muscles. The autonomic nervous system (ANS) affects internal organs and is considered involuntary since the processes such as heart beat rate and glandular secretions occur with usually little control on the part of the individual. The autonomic nervous system, in turn, is divided into two divisions, the parasympathetic and sympathetic. The parasympathetic system is most active in normal, restful situations and is dominant during quiet, relaxed periods. It acts to decrease the heartbeat and to stimulate the motility and secretions necessary for digestion. The sympathetic nervous system is most active during times of stress and arousal and is dominant when energy is required, when it increases the rate and strength of the contractions of the heart and inhibits the motility of the intestine. In addition to their effects, the two divisions of the ANS differ anatomically. The nerves of the parasympathetic system originate at the top and bottom of the central nervous system, while those of the sympathetic system emerge from the upper and central spinal cord. At the site of the effector organs, axons in the parasympathetic system release acetylcholine, while those in the sympathetic system release norepinephrine. Together with hormones, the autonomic system maintains homeostasis, the internal balance of the body.

Neuron

The functional unit of the nervous system is the neuron, a cell specialized to receive and transmit impulses. The types and functions of neurons found in organisms seem to be directed by several regulatory genes and by certain cues that occur during development. Once neurons mature, they lose the ability to divide. An exception is the olfactory neurons which are replaced every 60 days from stem cells resting beneath them, which ensures a supply as they wear out. Even though there are a variety of neurons, the essential structures are the same in each: a cell body containing the nucleus and two kinds of processes extending from it, the axon and dendrite. Axons transmit impulses away from the cell body to the dendrites of adjoining neurons. Some axons may be over 3 ft (1 m) in length, such as the sciatic nerve which runs from the spinal cord to the lower leg. The axons of the peripheral nerves are enclosed in a fatty (myelin) sheath formed from specialized cells called Schwann cells. The myelin sheath acts to insulate the axon, which helps to accelerate the transmission of a nerve impulse. Gaps along the sheath expose the axon fiber and are important in allowing nerve impulses to jump from one section of the axon to another. The speed at which nerve impulses travel depends on the diameter of the axon and the presence of the myelin sheath with some impulses from the large motor nerves to the leg muscles traveling as fast as 394 ft (120 m) per second. Damage to the sheath in multiple sclerosis patients causes impaired muscle control and other symptoms, an indication of the importance of the myelin sheath in the transmission of nerve impulses. Axons are bundled together and enclosed by connective tissue to form nerves. Dendrites are usually highly branched extensions of the cell body which receive impulses from axons. In some cases they may be very small, as seen in some of the neurons of the brain, or long, as is the sensory dendrite which runs from the foot to the spinal cord.

Nerve impulse

When a stimulus is strong enough, a nerve impulse is generated in an "all or none" response which means that a stimulus strong enough to generate a nerve impulse has been given. The stimulus triggers chemical and electrical changes in the neuron. Before an impulse is received, a resting neuron is polarized with different charges on either side of the cell membrane. The exterior of the cell is positively charged with a larger number of sodium ions present compared to the interior of the cell. The interior of the cell is negatively charged since it contains more potassium ions than the exterior of the cell. As a result of the differences in charges, an electrochemical difference of about −70 millivolts occurs. The sodium–potassium pump, a system which removes sodium ions from inside the cell and draws potassium ions back in, maintains the electrical balance of the resting cell. Since the cell has to do work to maintain the ion concentration, ATP molecules are used to provide the necessary energy. Once a nerve impulse is generated, the permeability of the cell membrane changes, sodium ions flow into, and potassium ions flow out of, the cell. The flow of ions causes a reversal in charges, with a positive charge now occurring on the interior of the cell and a negative charge on the exterior. The cell is said to be depolarized, resulting in an action potential causing the nerve impulse to move along the axon. As depolarization of the membrane proceeds along the nerve, a series of reactions start with the opening and closing of ion gates, which allow the potassium ions to flow back into the cell and sodium ions to move out of the cell. The nerve becomes polarized again since the charges are restored. Until a nerve becomes repolarized it cannot respond to a new stimulus; the time for recovery is called the refractory period and takes about 0.0004 of a second. The more intense the stimulus, the more frequent the firing of the neuron. When the impulse reaches the end of the axon, it causes the release of chemicals from small vesicles called neurotransmitters which diffuse across the synaptic gap, the small space between the axon and receptors in the dendrites. There is no physical contact between axons and dendrites (except in electrical transmission, usually found in invertebrates) which takes place through gap junctions.

The type of response by the receiving cell may be excitatory or inhibitory depending upon a number of factors including the type of neurotransmitters involved. All nerve impulses are the same whether they originate from the ear, heart, or stomach. How the impulse is interpreted is the job of the central nervous system. A blow to the head near the optic center of the brain produces the same results as though the impulse

KEY TERMS

Action Potential—A single nerve impulse caused by the reversal of the electric potential across a neuron membrane.

Axon—Thread–like structure extending from nerve cell bodies which carries impulses away from the cell body.

Dendrites—Branched structures of nerve cell bodies which receive impulses from axons and carry them to the nerve cell body.

Depolarization—Movement of ions across a cell membrane which removes an electric potential difference.

Ganglion—Cluster of nerve cell bodies. In vertebrates, found outside of the central nervous system and act as relay stations for impulses. In invertebrates, act as a "central" control.

Homeostasis—The internal stability of an organism.

Myelin—A multilayered membrane system of a Schwann cell that wraps around an axon. Made up of lipoproteins that act as insulators in speeding up the transmission of nerve impulses.

Nerve—Bundles of axons in a connective tissue sheath which follow a specific path.

Nerve impulse—A transient change in the electro–chemical nature of a neuron.

Neuron—Cell specialized to receive and transmit impulses; functional unit of the nervous system.

Neurotransmitter—A chemical released at the end of an axon which is picked up by receptors such as dendrites, muscles, or secretory cells.

Polarized—Two different charges on either side of a membrane caused by a difference in the distribution of charges; in resting nerve cells maintained by the sodium–potassium pump.

Reflex—A rapid response to a stimulus that involves a sensory and motor neuron and may involve an interneuron.

Refractory period—Recovery period for the neuron in which no new impulse can be generated; it cannot respond to a stimulus until it is repolarized.

Sodium–potassium pump—A special transport protein in the membrane of cells that moves sodium ions out and potassium ions into the cell against their concentration gradients.

Synapse—Space between axons and dendrites through which nerve impulses are transmitted by way of neurotransmitters.

had originated in the eyes. The neurons are the functional units of the nervous system through which coordination and control in organisms is executed.

See also Brain; Homeostasis; Neuron; Neurosurgery; Neurotransmitter; Reflex.

Further Reading:

BSCS Revision Team. *Biological Science: A Molecular Approach.* Lexington, MA: D.C. Heath & Co., 1990.

Campbell, Neil A. *Biology.* Menlo Park, CA: Benjamin/Cummings, Publishing Company, 1987.

Carey, Joseph, ed. *Brain Facts: A Primer on the Brain and the Nervous System.* Washington, D.C.: Society for Neuroscience, 1993.

Curtis, Helena, and N. Sue Barnes. *Biology.* 5th ed. New York: Worth Publishers, 1989.

Holtzman, Eric, and Alex B. Novikoff. *Cells and Organelles.* Philadelphia: Saunders College Publishing, 1984.

Kuffler, Stephen W., and John G. Nicholls. *From Neuron to Brain.* Sunderland, MA: Sinauer Associates, 1976.

Pine, Maya, ed. *Seeing, Hearing and Smelling The World.* Chevy Chase: Howard Hughes Medical Institute, 1995.

Purves, Dale. *Body and Brain: A Trophic Theory of Neural Connections.* Cambridge: Harvard University Press, 1988.

Raven, Peter H., and George B. Johnson. *Biology.* 3rd ed. St. Louis: Mosby Year Book, 1992.

Towle, Albert. *Modern Biology.* Austin, TX: Holt, Reinhart, and Winston, 1991.

Mary Finley

Neuroleptics see **Antipsychotic drugs**

Neuromuscular diseases

When humans are in good health, the nervous system and musculature work together so smoothly that there is little awareness of how efficiently this complicated biochemical machine functions. Neuromuscular diseases include a vast and bewildering array of related and unrelated disorders that have a certain similarity of symptoms in that both nerves and muscles are usually impaired. This term is usually applied to disorders of the motor unit and specifically excludes primary disorders of the central nervous system such as cerebral palsy.

The motor unit

The motor unit has four components: a motor neuron in the brain or spinal cord, its axon and related axons that comprise the peripheral nerve, the neuro-

muscular junction, and all the muscle fibers activated by the neuron. Like other cells, nerve and muscle cells have an external membrane that separates the inner fluids from those on the outside. The fluid on the inside is rich in potassium (K), magnesium (Mg), and phosphorus (P), whereas the fluid on the outside contains sodium (Na), calcium (Ca), and chloride (Cl). When all is quiet, the internal chemical composition of both nerve and muscle cells is remarkably constant and is called resting membrane potential. A primary reason for this constancy lies in the cells' ability to regulate the flow of sodium thanks to an enzyme in the membrane called Na+/K+ ATP–ase. Because the inside of the cell has less sodium than the outside, there is a negative potential (like a microscopic battery) of 70–90 mV. Under ordinary circumstances, the interior of the cell is 30 times richer in potassium than the extracellular fluid and the sodium concentration is 10–12 times greater on the outside of the cell. At rest, sodium tends to flow into cells and potassium oozes out.

When an impulse or current runs down a nerve and hits a muscle fiber, the action potential of the membrane is suddenly changed so that K moves out of the cell and the permeability to Na keeps increasing so that the inside may become positive by as much as 40 mV. In a fraction of a second, however, K moves back again and restores the cell membrane to normal. This process of movement of ions in and out of cells is known as action potential and is the basis for both the transmission of nerve impulses and muscular contractions.

This explains the biochemical processes involved, but anatomy also plays a role in movement. The critical spot is the synaptic cleft, the place where the nerve dips into the muscle. Here, the finely branched nerve fiber inserts into a microscopic bit of muscle tissue, and it is here that acetylcholine (ACh), the chemical responsible for the transmission of the nerve impulse, hooks onto the muscle fibers, stimulating them to contract. Enough calcium at the site makes the process go more smoothly, while magnesium slows the process. To keep ACh from accumulating in the cells, the enzyme cholinesterase destroys the excess.

To understand the physiological nature of muscle contractions, it is helpful to examine muscles microscopically. Muscle fibers have an outside membrane called the plasmalemma, an interior structure called a sarcolemma, transverse tubules across the fibers, and an inner network of muscle tissue called sarcoplasma. When a nerve impulse reaches the muscle, an action potential is set up and the current quickly travels in both directions from the motor end plate through the entire length of the muscle fiber. Now, and still inexplicably, the whole inside of the muscle tissue becomes involved as the current spreads and, aided by calcium, the contractile protein called actin causes the muscle component (myosin) to contract. An enzyme, ATP–ase, helps provide the energy needed for the muscular filaments to slide past each other. Relaxation occurs promptly when Ca flows into the muscle tissue and the cycle is completed. The muscle fiber is now ready to be stimulated again by a nerve impulse.

A constant need for ready energy exists because muscles must be able to respond on demand. Compounds such as creatine, phosphate, adenosine triphosphate (ATP), myoglobin, creatine kinase (CK), calcium, and a host of oxidative enzymes are all involved. Red musculature is usually more efficient than pale muscle because it contains more myoglobin and more oxidative enzymes. In any one motor unit, however, all the muscle fibers are the same type.

Muscles acquire about 90% of the energy they need from glycogen, a starchy compound that is synthesized and stored in the muscles. A small amount of glucose and some free fatty acids also provide energy both in vigorous exercise and at rest. Many enzymes, too many to name, take part in these energy reactions, and some neuromuscular diseases are caused by a failure of these enzymes to function properly.

Causes of neuromuscular dysfunction

When a single nerve impulse strikes a muscle it causes a "twitch", and ordinarily there is a brief refractory period of relaxation. If another impulse is received before relaxation is completed, the twitches can add up and cause a prolonged muscular spasm or tetany. Normally, muscles continue to function properly because the ACh that is transmitted down the nerve is enzymatically eliminated. Certain drugs such as neostigmine and physostigmine can block this action and paralyze a muscle. So can poisonous nerve gases and insecticides. In a neuromuscular disease called myasthenia gravis, antibodies can block the passage of ACh to the end plate creating a similar paralysis. Leg cramps at night, on the other hand, are due to sustained muscular contractions (200 per second). They can be relieved by quinine or diphenhydramine.

Paralysis can take place anytime there is a failure or interference in the transfer of biochemical impulses from nerve to muscle. On the other hand, hyperactivity of neuromuscular transmission can lead to minor twitches and cramps or to severe spasms as in tetanus (lockjaw) or amyotrophic lateral sclerosis (Lou Gehrig disease). There is still much to learn about both hyperactive and paralytic cases, but new research on DNA and immunology is proving helpful.

Abnormal levels of blood electrolytes such as sodium and potassium can also cause neuromuscular disturbances. When potassium is too high or too low, the muscles of the trunk, arms, and legs can be very weak, even to the point of paralysis. If the blood calcium is low (as in vitamin D deficiency or inadequate function of the parathyroid gland), twitching may occur. When blood calcium is too high, there may be profound weakness. Normal magnesium levels are also important to proper neuromuscular functioning.

Creatine is a nitrogenous organic acid that is normally present in muscle and other tissues. When muscle is injured creatine leaks out and can be measured in the blood as creatine kinase (CK). Blood levels of CK are increased when heart muscle is damaged, but also in muscle trauma, polymyositis, rapidly worsening cases of muscular dystrophy, vigorous exercise, or for no apparent reason.

The neuropathies: symptoms and clinical findings

Various types of diseases involve both the nerves and muscles. Some pathologic processes destroy nerves; others primarily attack muscles. Although the cause (or causes) of practically all of them still remains unknown, all are under intensive study.

Muscular dystrophy

This primary degenerative process, first described by Wilhelm Erb in 1891, affects the muscular fibers, not the nerves or end plates. In spite of extensive research, the cause has not yet been firmly established, although genetic factors are receiving strong consideration. A variety of types and classifications have been proposed, but all are based on age of onset, symptomatology, and rate of progression. One simple classification system includes: progressive muscular dystrophy or Duchenne type; facioscapulohumeral or Landouzy and Déjerine type; and limb–girdle dystrophies including distal muscular dystrophy, ocular myodystrophy, and myotonic dystrophy.

Progressive muscular dystrophy (Duchenne type) is the most important one of the group and the best studied. It accounts for almost 70% of all dystrophies, affects males five times more frequently than females, and almost always begins in the first five years of life. It is an inherited sex–linked recessive trait, and the abnormal gene is at the Xp21 locus. Its incidence is one in 3,600 in newborn males. Muscular weakness is noted first in the pelvis, shoulder girdle, and spine, and spreads peripherally to the extremities, especially to the legs. This weakness results in a waddling gait, an insecure stance on a wide base, and a lordotic (forward curved) posture. Weakness continues to spread all over the body, although some of the involved muscles appear to grow larger secondary to an invasion of muscle tissue by peculiar fat cells. This is especially evident in the calf muscles. Victims rarely survive to maturity.

Blood enzyme tests can detect the abnormalities associated with progressive muscular dystrophy early on, even before symptoms are clearly evident. Muscle tissue is rich in creatine and, when muscles are diseased, the creatine leaks into the blood and can be measured as creatine kinase (CK). The normal level of CK is about 160 IU/L, but an individual with Duchene muscular dystrophy may have CK levels as high as 15,000–35,000 IU/L. If the diagnosis is in doubt, genetic studies and muscle biopsy can also be done. The recent isolation of the Duchenne gene and the discovery that dystrophin is the abnormal encoded protein makes a precise molecular diagnosis possible. It also offers hope that the genetic basis for other dystrophies will be discovered soon.

Facioscapulohumeral muscular dystrophy or Landouzy–Déjerine dystrophy differs from the more common types in that it involves primarily the upper extremities, face muscles, and shoulder girdle. The condition starts later in life (usually by age 10) and may appear even in the elderly. Because it has a slower progress and longer duration, patients may develop irregular cardiac rhythms or even damage to the heart muscle. CK enzymes vary greatly, and electromyograms (EMGs) are not diagnostic. A muscle biopsy is the only way to confirm the presence of this condition. As in all other dystrophies, no satisfactory therapy is yet available.

Limb–girdle dystrophies also follow a slow course and often cause only slight disability. When the disease begins in the fingers and then spreads centrally toward the body, the term "distal" is employed. When paralysis starts in the eyelids and facial muscles, it is classed as "ocular." The causes of these conditions are obscure.

Although once considered rare, myotonic dystrophy is now being recognized with increasing frequency. It is an inheritable or familial condition that primarily affects young adults. The muscle groups of the hands, feet, and face ("taper mouth" is secondary to atrophy of face muscles) are most commonly involved. An individual with this condition may be easily able to shake hands but may have difficulty relaxing his grip. There are many accompanying glandular disturbances, changes in bones, and elevated blood cholesterol. Since so many body functions are affected by this disease, it

KEY TERMS

Acetylcholine (ACh)—A white crystalline chemical compound ($C_7H_{17}NO_3$) that transmits nerve impulses across intercellular gaps and activates muscular contraction.

Actin—A muscle protein, active with myosin, in muscle contraction.

Action potential—The change in the cell's current.

Cholinesterase—An enzyme that destroys acetylcholine and keeps it from accumulating at neuromuscular interfaces.

Creatine—A nitrogenous, organic acid found in the muscle tissue of many vertebrates. Blood levels increase when muscle is damaged.

Creatine kinase—A enzyme that is found and easily measured in blood and other tissues. It increases quantitatively when there is muscle destruction.

Dystrophin—An abnormal encoded protein isolated from the Duchenne gene at the Xp21 locus.

Glycogen—A starchy substance that is synthesized and stored in the muscles and a ready source of energy for muscular contraction.

Neuromuscular junction—Where the nerve fibers terminate in the muscle tissue.

Neuron—A nerve cell consisting of a nucleated portion from which there extrude smaller extensions called dendrites and longer processes called axons. Neurons may be either sensory or motor.

Plasmalemma—Outer sheath or membrane of muscle tissue.

Sarcolemma—Muscle tissue enclosed by muscle sheath and closely related to another substance called sarcoplasma.

is not surprising that death (from heart attacks) usually occurs before middle age.

The neuromyopathies

Neuromyopathies are similar to the dystrophies in that there is both nerve and muscular involvement, but there are also differences between the two categories. Some neuromyopathies start in childhood, while others begin later in life. Neuromyopathies involve more brain and spinal cord damage; causes can include infectious diseases, allergic conditions, immunologic problems, and toxic or traumatic injuries.

Amyotonia congenita of the Werdnig–Hoffmann type is the most prevalent condition in this group. In all types of amyotonia congenita, however, there is a failure of development or a degeneration of the motor neurons of the central nervous system or damage of the nerve pathways to the muscles. Since nerve activation of the muscles is diminished or lost completely, muscles atrophy. The condition is recognizable within the first few weeks of life. The child lies flaccid on his back with the head turned to one side, his cry is weak, and his reflexes are diminished or gone. In such severe cases, death occurs before the fifth year, but in some instances, a few years later. The condition is familial and affects both sexes equally. On biopsy the most striking microscopic characteristic of affected muscle tissue is the absence or loss of the development of "end plates," where the twig–like branches of the motor nerves dip into the muscle fibers. The motor nerves or axons also show some typical thickening. Several blood enzyme tests are available for differentiating neuromyopathy from dystrophy but, since neither condition can be effectively treated, the distinction has little therapeutic value.

Progressive muscular atrophy

Although there are several variations of this disorder, they all show wasting of the muscles ("atrophy") secondary to degeneration of the motor nerve system. The most common type is called amyotrophic lateral sclerosis and is popularly known as Lou Gehrig disease. Onset generally occurs between ages 40 and 70, but the disease can begin at other times in life. Although it may begin on one side it always becomes bilateral. It is always fatal (within two to five years after diagnosis), since it spreads upward to involve throat and other vital muscles.

See also Muscular system; Nervous system.

Further Reading:

Adams, Raymond D., and Maurice Victor. *Principles of Neurology.* New York: McGraw–Hill, 1989.

Klawans, Harold W. *Toscanni's Fumble and Other Tales of Clinical Neurology.* Chicago: Contemporary Books, 1988.

Joseph D. Wassersug

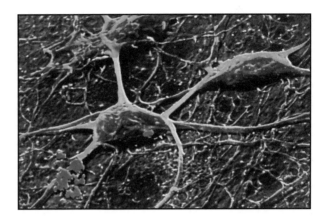

A scanning electron micrograph (SEM) of three neurons of the human cerebral cortex.

Neuron

Neurons are nerve cells (neurocytes), which, together with neuroglial cells, comprise the nervous tissue making up the nervous system. The neuron is the integral element of our five senses and of countless other physical, regulatory, and mental faculties, including memory and consciousness. A neuron consists of a nerve cell body (or soma), an elongated projection (axon), and short branching fibers (called dendrites). Neurons receive nerve signals (action potentials), integrate action potentials, and transmit these signals to other neurons or effector organs, such as muscles and glands. The structure and function of neurons is essentially the same in all animals, although the human nervous system is much more specialized and complicated than that of lower animals. Humans are born with a large, but finite, supply of neurons and those cells that are lost through aging, injury, or disease cannot be replaced.

Structure and function

Neurons exist in many shapes and sizes. Their structure, like that of other cells in the body or in nature, illustrates that structure often determines function. There are three basic structural and functional classifications of neurons.

Structural classification

The structural classification of a neurons depends upon the number of dendrites extending from the cell body. Multipolar neurons have several dendrites; the majority of neurons in the spinal chord and brain are multipolar. Bipolar neurons have only two processes: a single dendrite and an axon. Bipolar neurons are found

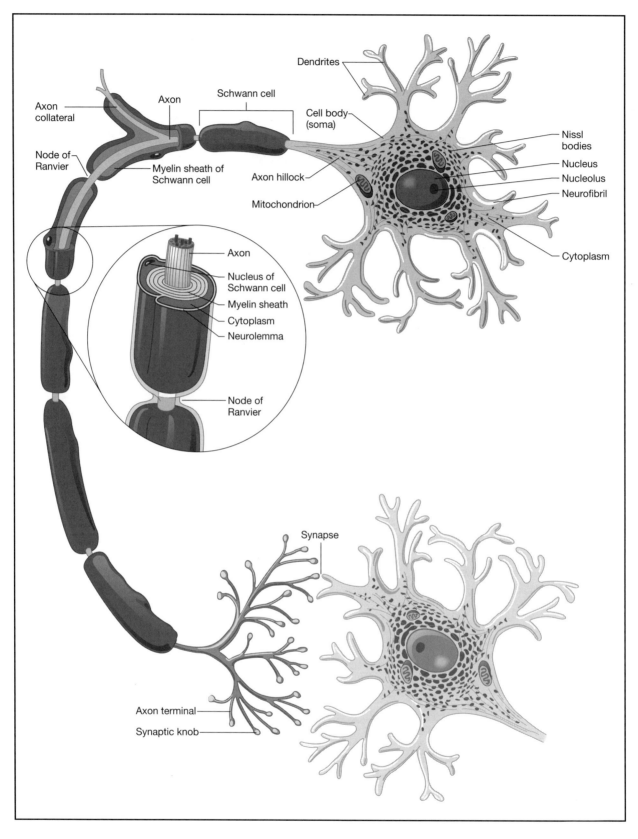

Axon
collateral

Axon

Schwann cell

Dendrites

Cell body
(soma)

Nissl
bodies

Nucleus

Nucleolus

Neurofibril

Node of
Ranvier

Myelin sheath of
Schwann cell

Axon hillock

Mitochondrion

Cytoplasm

Axon

Nucleus of
Schwann cell

Myelin sheath

Cytoplasm

Neurolemma

Node of
Ranvier

Synapse

Axon terminal

Synaptic knob

The features of a typical multipolar neuron.

in the sense organs—and in the retina of the eye and in olfactory cells. Unipolar neurons lack dendrites and have a single axon, and are also sensory neurons.

Nerve cell body

The nerve cell body contains a nucleus, a nucleolus, and cytoplasm containing the cell (such as mitochondria, endoplasmic reticulum, and so on). Unique to the nerve cell body are Nissl bodies, which are rough surfaced vesicles in the endoplasmic reticulum (cytoplasm located near the nucleus), and are involved with protein synthesis. Another characteristic structure of nerve cells are the neurofibrils, which are delicate threadlike structures that help to maintain the shape of the cell, and which transport substances between the cell body and the axon terminals. The plasma membrane around the cell separates the cytoplasm on the inside of the cell from the extracellular fluid on the outside. Cell membranes of neurons contain electrically gated channels, which when properly stimulated allow electrically charged particles (such as sodium and potassium ions) to pass across the barrier. This ionic exchange is the basis for the flow, or action potential, of the nerve impulse.

Axons

An axon is a single smooth projection arising out of the nerve cell body at a raised area called the axon hillock. Axons conduct nerve impulses away from the nerve cell body. Axons vary in length and diameter; some (such as those in the central nervous system) are very short, as small as 0.01 in (0.25 mm), while others (such as those in the peripheral nervous system) conduct impulses over long distances in the body, and can be 3 ft (1 m) long. The speed at which an impulse travels depends upon the diameter of the axon, with axons with large diameters (0.001 in/0.025 mm) conducting impulses more rapidly. Axons may have branches called axon collaterals. The main axon and its collaterals can split into smaller branches ending in small filaments called axon terminals. Axon terminals have knob–like swellings at the very end called synaptic knobs or end buttons. Each synaptic knob communicates with a dendrite or cell body of another neuron, the point of contact being a synapse. Under very high magnification, a very tiny space, the synaptic cleft or gap (about one millionth of an inch, or mm), can be detected between the synaptic knob and dendrite or cell body. Synaptic knobs contain hundreds of neurovesicles that contain a transmitter substance (or neurotransmitter). When a nerve impulse reaches the synaptic knob the neurotransmitter is ejected into the synaptic cleft and serves as a stimulus to the next adjacent neuron. The vast majority of all impulses transmitted occur at the synaptic gaps, although recent research indicates that chemical transmission can occur at other points along the axon. Many neurological diseases and psychiatric disorders result from a disturbance or alteration of synaptic activity. Drugs such as tranquilizers, anesthetics, nicotine, and caffeine target the synapse and can cause an alteration of impulse transmission.

Dendrites

Dendrites are so named because they resemble tiny trees (the Greek word for tree is *dendron*). The main function of a dendrite is to receive and integrate signals from neighboring neurons and conduct these signals to the nerve cell body. Dendrites are branched extensions of the cell's cytoplasm and contain all the normal cytoplasmic structures. A nerve cell's dendrites can branch out quite extensively, thus increasing the total surface area of the neuron and making more room to receive incoming signals from other nerves. A single neuron can receive signals from hundreds of other nerves. The dendrites in sensory neurons have specialized cells called receptors, which convert stimuli into electrical signals. Under the microscope, dendrites appear hairy; the little hairs or projections are called spines, and each spine is the site of a synapse, which is the point of communication between neurons.

Glial cells

One cannot discuss the neuron without mentioning glial cells or neuroglia. It was once thought that these cells simply held everything together (*gloios* means glue, in Greek), but we now know that neuroglia are highly specialized cells. For example, neuroglia are responsible for physical support, protection against infection (through phagocytosis), and the connection of nerve cells to blood vessels. The Schwann cell (or neurolemmocyte) is a common type of glial cell found in peripheral nerve axons. Schwann cells wrap "jelly roll style" around the axon, forming a whitish phospholipid (fatty) protective and insulating cover known as the myelin sheath. The myelin sheath of the axon of peripheral nerves has interruptions or exposed gaps known as the Nodes of Ranvier. Schwann cells also make up the neurolemma, a continuous sheath that covers both the myelin sheath and the axon at the Nodes of Ranvier. Action potentials traveling down the axon occur only at the Nodes of Ranvier, jumping rapidly from gap to gap (saltatory conduction), which conducts impulses significantly faster than in nonmyelinated nerves. The neurolemma is found only in peripheral nerve fibers and plays a crucial part in nerve fiber regeneration. Damaged axons will regenerate; damaged cell bodies will not. The myelinated sheaths of the axons of neuron in the brain and spinal cord (the central nervous system) are made from different glial cells (oligodendrocytes), which lack a neurolemma, so making the regeneration of their axons impossible. Multiple sclerosis is a serious demyelinating disease of the central nervous system. Not all axons are myelinated; the presence of myelin is one difference between white matter (which has myelinated axons) and gray matter (which does not).

Functional classification

Sensory neurons transduce physical stimuli, such as smell, light, or sound, into action potentials, which are then transmitted to the spinal cord or brain. Sensory neurons, which bring information into the central nervous system, are also referred to as afferent neurons. Motor neurons transmit nerve impulses away from the brain and spinal cord to muscles or glands and are also called efferent neurons. Interneurons transmit nerve impulses between sensory neurons and the motor neurons. Interneurons are responsible for receiving, relaying, integrating, and sending nerve impulses. Interneurons are found exclusively in the central nervous system and account for almost 99% of all the nerve cells in the body.

See also Nervous system; Neurotransmitter.

Further Reading:

Churchland, Patricia Smith. *Neurophilosophy*. Cambridge, MA: MIT Press, 1986.
Nathan, Peter. *The Nervous System*. New York: Oxford University Press, 1988.
Stevens, Leonard A. *Neurons: Building Blocks of the Brain*. New York: Thomas Y. Crowell, 1974.

Christine Miner Minderovic

Neurosurgery

Neurosurgery is surgery carried out on the central nervous system—the brain or spinal cord—or any peripheral nervous tissue.

Neurosurgery could be said to have begun in the early stages of man's evolution. Skulls of early man show signs of incision through the bone. Some skulls have as many as five openings cut into them. Probably at least some of this ritual was for magical purposes and some was medicinal, performed to release the spirits that were causing excruciating headaches or making an individual show signs of insanity, or to remove bone fragments resulting from trauma. This process is called trephination (less commonly, trepanation) and was a common procedure as early as the Neolithic period. Interestingly, this procedure was done in human settlements around the world. These clans or tribes had no contact with each other, yet they devised and practiced a similar procedure as a form of magic or medical therapy.

Trephining was done with a sharpened flint moved in rapid circular motions to cut through the bony skull. The procedure took about a half hour on a drugged patient. It is likely that early man had discovered the means to immobilize an individual so that the surgery could be carried out. Trephining was practiced as late as the mid–20th century among isolated peoples. Even cadavers were trephined to remove bone fragments which were then worn as amulets.

Needless to say, the survival rate of trephination was low. Skulls have been found, however, that show bone growth around the edges of the opening, indicating that the patient survived for a time after the procedure.

More often, skulls with trephined openings show the raw, incised edges of the operative area, indicating that the patient probably died during surgery or shortly thereafter. Infection was not understood, of course, and was a near certainty following surgery in such conditions.

It was not until late in the 19th century that further progress was made in the field of neurosurgery. In November, 1884, two British surgeons, Bennett and Godlee, operated to remove a brain tumor. Shortly thereafter, in 1888, Sir Victor Horsley removed a tumor from the spinal cord of one of his patients. That same year an American surgeon, W.W. Keen of Philadelphia, removed a meningioma, a hard, slow–growing tumor that grows on one of the membranes covering the brain. The year after that Keen tapped the ventricles of the brain, the small openings at the base of the brain in which fluid collects.

The development of the x ray provided a means for neurosurgeons to find tumors growing in the brain or bone splinters or other foreign objects. Still, it remained difficult to locate these growths precisely enough for surgical removal. The invention of stereotactic frames to provide precise guidance to underlying tumors helped to revolutionize surgery on the brain.

Current neurosurgery includes trephination along with other procedures to correct not only injury and disease of the central nervous system, but also to modify nerve supply to other areas of the body that may benefit from such surgery and to enhance the blood supply to the brain.

The neurosurgeon often is required to make rapid decisions as to whether surgery is needed and where to perform the operation when confronted with an individual with a significant injury of the head or spinal column. The escape of blood in or on the brain or spinal cord or a trauma that may render either of them susceptible to swelling often requires surgical correction. These delicate organs are confined within bony structures that provide no room for their enlargement. Swelling can build intolerable pressures as the brain or spinal cord is pressed against its protective bony vault.

The neurosurgeon's job

A surgeon who specializes in operating on the brain and other nervous tissue is a neurosurgeon. Usually this is very delicate, painstaking surgery that must be carried out within a restricted space. A slip of the knife, a misdirection of a probe, or other mistake can result in paralysis, loss of sight or hearing or balance, or other uncorrectable disorder. Probing deep within the brain requires an absolute certainty of the location of the lesion and how to approach it with minimal disturbance of the surrounding tissues. The neurosurgeon may be called upon to provide therapy in any of a number of traumatic situations or conditions.

Injury to the head or spinal column may result in swelling of the enclosed nervous tissues, may result in bleeding inside the skull which would place pressure on a localized area of the brain, or may involve bone fragments impinging on the brain or spinal cord as a result of a blow to the head or back. Certain congenital conditions such as hydrocephalus (excessive fluid on the brain) or spina bifida (a condition in which the spine has not closed around the spinal cord) frequently are treated by the neurosurgeon. Premature closure of the skull which will prevent the skull from expanding as the brain grows also requires surgery to separate the skull bones.

Tumor growth in the skull or spinal column also may require surgical correction. A benign (noncancerous) tumor in the brain usually is well defined and can be removed by very delicate surgery. A malignant (cancerous) tumor presents a much more challenging problem because it is not as clearly defined or as well contained as is the benign growth. Still, some areas of the brain remain unreachable by surgical tools and a growth in those areas cannot be removed. In that case the physician may resort to radiation therapy or the use of antitumor drugs.

The brain requires an especially copious blood supply. Large arteries in the side and back of the neck carry blood to the brain, but when these arteries become narrowed or blocked by fatty deposits (a condition called atherosclerosis), the blood supply to the brain may be reduced to an insufficient amount. In this case the physician may resort to a balloon catheter to clear the blockage. In this procedure, called angiography, the catheter is guided to the site of blockage, the tiny balloon on the end of the catheter is inflated to press the blockage out of the way, the balloon is deflated, and the catheter removed. In the event this procedure is not effective, however, the surgeon may need to operate on the blood vessels instead of the brain itself. A graft to bypass the blocked area may be called for or the vessel may be opened and the deposit removed (a procedure called endarterectomy) if the artery is accessible. In addition, an artery can balloon from the pressure of the blood within it. This is called an aneurism, and it forms at the site of a weak spot in the arterial wall. The swollen artery in itself may do no harm, but the weakened arterial wall can burst at any time, allowing the escape of blood into the brain. This is one form of stroke. If the artery is accessible the surgeon can remove the weak area and sew the ends of the artery together again. If the artery cannot be reached for surgical correction, some means can be taken to reinforce the arterial wall from within.

A so–called slipped disk or ruptured disk, damage to one of the cartilaginous disks between the vertebrae may form a protrubance into the spinal canal that impinges on the spinal cord. This may cause pain or even the inability to walk normally. Here again the neurosurgeon may need to take steps to remove the protrusion and in some cases fuse the vertebrae to prevent their flexing on the weakened disk.

In cases of intractable pain or involuntary movements that cannot be corrected, the surgeon may be called upon to interrupt the nerve supply to a given area. This function is more and more being taken over by medical therapy as physicians learn more about nerve functions and how to interrupt them medicinally, but the surgeon still provides a needed service.

Locating a tumor or area in which blood has been released inside the skull requires a rigorous diagnostic procedure. If the patient has had an accident such as a fall or automobile wreck in which he struck his head, the surgeon may be more aware of the possibility of the existence of a blood clot forming on the brain, bone fragments that may be impinging on the brain, or swelling of the brain. If the patient denies any accidental trauma to the head, but has had persistent and long-standing headaches, visual disturbances, dizziness, or other lingering symptoms, the surgeon is alerted to the possibility of an aneurism or other source of blood leakage or a developing tumor.

Diagnosis

The diagnosis of the source of a brain disorder has become infinitely more precise with the modern technology of computerized tomography (CT scan) or magnetic resonance imaging (MRI). Either of these scans can show serial views of the brain and the presence of a tumor or of excessive fluid build–up or intracranial bleeding. They also provide the means for precise measurement of depth of the growth and its angle from various landmarks on the skull. This enables the neurosurgeon to use a stereotactic frame to guide his instruments precisely to the site of the lesion.

The CT or MRI image shows a cross section of the brain at a certain level. Each exposure is slightly advanced from the previous one. In all, the images appear to be slices of the brain that show various details at each level. The computer control also allows the images to be combined to form a three–dimensional image so the physician can see the tumor or damaged area of the brain in relation to the complete structure. In this way he can decide whether the patient is a candidate for surgery or whether the tumor or other lesion is not accessible. The image also gives a good idea of whether the tumor is a cancerous lesion or is benign.

Stereotaxis

Stereotactic surgery is the use of a special frame that attaches to the skull and serves to guide the surgeon's instruments, electrodes, or cannulae precisely to a local area. The frame is called a stereoencephalotome, which combines the Greek words for solid, head, and to cut; thus, it is an instrument to cut through the solid head. In fact, the stereoencephalotome does no cutting. Instead, it is an instrument with a rounded frame that attaches to the patient's head and which can be used to guide instruments at precise angles into the brain.

Such an instrument was used as early as 1906 in experiments on animals. Animal brains were well studied and the landmarks of their skulls in relationship to underlying brain structures had been determined. Thus, the use of the stereoframe on an animal allowed the surgeon to place his instruments precisely in the brain. The human brain had not been studied as well, however, and it was not deemed possible to use the frame on a human patient. It remained for two American physicians to use x–ray images taken in the operating room to apply stereotactic surgery to a human patient in 1947. This work and that of others soon made available atlases of the human brain with precise measurements between points within the brain. By referring to such an atlas the surgeon can determine angles and distances through which the sterosurgical procedure must be carried out.

Once the surgeon has located the area of the brain he wishes to operate on, he places a stereotactic frame on the patient's head. Several types of frame can be used, each of which differs in its type of orientation. Some frames must be oriented with a trephined opening in the skull. Others are oriented by using landmarks on the skull such as the ear canals.

When the surgeon has placed the frame over the brain lesion he can position movable arms in the frame to guide electrodes or other instruments into the substance of the brain. This procedure often is used to guide hot or cold electrodes into a given area of the brain where the heat or cold can destroy a small bit of the brain tissue. This form of therapy is the last resort for patients who may be violent or exhibit dangerous mental symptoms. The destruction of the tissue that controls these dangerous characteristics may prevent the patient from hurting those around him.

KEY TERMS

· ·

Cannula (plural: cannulae)—A hollow tube inserted into an area of the body to drain fluid, guide an instrument, or provide a means to measure pressure or temperature.

Hyperkinesis—Excessive movement or motor activity. A syndrome that results from a brain lesion and leads to fidgeting, nervousness, constant movement, short attention span, and other symptoms in adolescence.

Neolithic period—The geological period that began approximately 12,000 years ago. It was during this period that man developed advanced stone tools and began to form farming societies.

Neuro- —Refers to the nervous system, including the brain, spinal cord, or the nerves leading to and from them.

In addition, tissue destruction can interrupt pain pathways to reduce pain from cancer or other lesions, which helps the patient to better cope with therapy. Certain diseases such as Parkinsonism or hyperkinesis, which involve involuntary movements or shaking can be helped by destroying a small area within the brain. Also this method can be used to remove a blockage of the drainage system of the brain, which in turn allows the build–up of cerebrospinal fluid and causes hydrocephalus. Removing the tumor blocking the drainage canal or implanting a tube through the canal to drain the fluid relieves the pressure within the skull. Of course, foreign bodies such as bullets also can be located and removed. Precisely focused radiation can be guided by stereoframes to converge on the site of a tumor and destroy it.

As physicians learn more about the brain and the precise location of various functions within it, the use of stereotactic surgery grows. The brain is the only organ that can study itself, and it continues to accumulate knowledge that serves its own best interest in times of illness or injury. With current technology scientists have begun the implantation of electrodes in the brain to allow the deaf to hear and the blind to see. The electrodes are threaded into the area of the brain that controls hearing or sight and then are connected through a computer to a light or sound receptor. Though this technique is in the beginning stages, progress in miniaturization of the hardware and the improved knowledge of brain structure and function are combining to make this field a promising venture for the near future.

See also Brain; Surgery.

Further Reading:

Snyder, D.P. "Repairing the Mind With Machines: The Supernormal Possibilities of Neural Prosthetics." *Omni*, 15 (September 1993):14.

Larry Blaser

Neurotransmitter

Neurotransmitters are chemical agents secreted at the end of axons that diffuse across the synaptic gap and transmit information to adjoining cells such as neurons, muscle cells, and glands by altering their electrical state or activity. There are many neurotransmitters with a variety of structures and functions; two of the principle ones are acetylcholine and norepinephrine. Since the neurotransmitters convey information, anything that affects their behavior affects the function of the organism.

Function of neurotransmitters

The neurotransmitters are stored in tiny sac–like structures called vesicles at the end of axons. When an impulse reaches the end of the axon, the vesicles release a neurotransmitter into the small space between the adjoining cells. Neurotransmitters diffuse across the synapse and bind to receptors in the receiving cell that are specific for the neurotransmitter. The kinds of reactions that occur in the receiving cell may vary. The cell may be excited and an action potential is set up and the impulse is transmitted; or the opposite effect may occur, and the cell will be inhibited from transmitting the impulse because it becomes hyperpolarized. Neurotransmitters function by changing the permeability of the cell membrane to various ions such as sodium and potassium. If an excess of sodium ions flows into the nerve cell, an impulse is generated. If an excess of potassium ions flows out, the impulse is inhibited. Sometimes the receiving cell receives a number of different messages at the same time, and they can cancel one another out. By their effects on the receiving cells, neurotransmitters coordinate behavior. The number and kind of neurotransmitter molecules received by the receptor cell, as well as the kind of receptor, determines whether the effect will be to stimulate or to inhibit. If neurotransmitters were allowed to operate over a long period of time, the results would be disastrous for the organism since there would be a constant overload of messages being sent. One way in which the problem is solved is through enzymes which break down the neurotransmitter very rapidly. One enzyme, acetylcholinesterase, can split one acetylcholine molecule every 40 microseconds. Many organic phosphates which are poisons operate by inhibiting acetylcholinesterase which leads to prolonged muscle contractions. Other neurotransmitters, such as norepinephrine and dopamine, are removed when they are taken up again by the vesicles in the axon endings after their release, or they are broken down by monamine oxidase.

Characteristics of neurotransmitters

The number of known neurotransmitters has increased tremendously over the past several years. One of the earliest ones studied was acetylcholine, the most common neurotransmitter found in both invertebrates and vertebrates. It is the stimulating agent for skeletal muscle cells, but is the inhibiting agent for heart muscle cells, which demonstrates that the action of a neurotransmitter is influenced by the target receptor cells. Norepinephrine, a catecholamine, is an example of a biogenic amine which is derived from the amino acid, tyrosine. It often works in an opposite way from acetylcholine in the autonomic nervous system and is also found in the cerebrum, cerebellum and spinal cord. Another catecholamine that is found in the brain is dopamine. It appears to be important in movement and regulating emotional responses. A widely distributed neurotransmitter, serotonin, is found in blood platelets, the lining of the digestive tract and the brain. It causes very powerful contractions of smooth muscle, and is associated with mood, attention, emotions, and sleep. LSD and mescaline, psychoactive drugs, mimic the structure and function of serotonin and other biogenic drugs to change the mental state of the user. One of the other amino acid derivatives, GABA (gamma-aminobutyric acid) is a major inhibitory transmitter in the central nervous system and it seems to play a role in Huntington's disease. In addition to the well known neurotransmitter, there are peptides such as the opioids involved in killing pain and causing sleepiness that act as neurotransmitters. Recently certain gases, nitric oxide and carbon monoxide, have been discovered to be released from neurons. Nitric oxide has been found to diffuse to the nerves of the digestive system and govern the relaxation required for the normal movements of digestion.

Neurotransmitters and disease

Interest in the neurotransmitter is based on evidence that knowledge of how they function provides insight into the cause of some diseases, the effects of certain substances, and the behavior of organisms. Myasthenia gravis, which is a disease characterized by weakness of muscles and fatigue, is caused by a disturbance in the action of acetylcholine on skeletal muscles and is now treated by drugs that enhance the effect of acetylcholine. The discovery that dopamine–containing neurons in the brain of Parkinson's disease victims degenerate, which results in the shuffling gait and trembling characteristic of the disease, led to the use of levodopa, a compound that replaces the dopamine.

Impairment of the dopamine system is also implicated in schizophrenia, a mental disease marked by disturbances in thinking and emotional reactions. Drugs, chlorpromazine and clozapine, that block dopamine receptors in the brain have been used to alleviate the symptoms and help patients return to a normal social setting. Depression, which afflicts about 3.5% of the population, is treated with antidepressants that affect norepinephrine and serotonin in the brain which helps to correct the abnormal excess or inhibition of signals that control mood, thoughts, pain, and other sensations. A new drug, fluoxetine, is a serotonin reuptake inhibitor which appears to establish the level of serotonin required to function at a normal level.

Alzheimer's disease, which affects an estimated four million Americans, is characterized by memory loss and the eventual inability for self–care. The disease seems to be caused by a loss of cells in the basal forebrain which secrete acetylcholine. Some experimental drugs to alleviate the symptoms have been developed, but presently there is no known treatment for the disease.

Neurotransmitters and drugs

The rise of drug addiction has directed attention to the role of neurotransmitters in attempting to understand how it happens and how it can be counteracted. Cocaine and crack are psychostimulants that affect neurons containing dopamine in the limbic and frontal cortex of the brain; when they are used they generate a feeling of confidence and feelings of power. However, when large amounts are taken, people "crash" and suffer from physical and emotional exhaustion as well as depression. Opiates such as heroin and morphine appear to mimic naturally–occurring peptide substances in the brain with opiate activity called endorphins. The endorphins act to kill pain and cause sleepiness.

It is believed that morphine and heroin combine with the endorphin receptors in the brain and reduce their production; as a result, the drugs are needed to replace the naturally produced endorphins and addiction may occur. Attempts to counteract the effects involve using drugs that mimic them, such as nalorphine, naloxone, and naltrexone. One of the depressant drugs in widest use, alcohol, is believed to cause its effects by interacting with the GABA receptor. Initially anxiety is controlled, but greater amounts reduce muscle control and delay reaction time due to impaired thinking.

Neurotransmitters' role in memory and learning

One of the most exciting areas of research is the attempt to find out how learning and memory take place. One of the earliest researchers who attempted to explain learning and memory as a function of cellular change was the Canadian psychologist, Donald O. Hebb. He maintained that repeated firing of axons results in metabolic changes in the presynaptic and post synaptic neurons.

Aplysia, a marine snail with only 20,000 relatively large neurons, has been used in studies to determine the biological basis of learning. A conditioned reflex in Apylsia has been shown to cause an increase in the release of a neurotransmitter that sets up a chain of reactions, one of which also increases the secretion of serotonin from a modulating neuron. In mammals, the hippocampus, part of the forebrain, stores long term memory for weeks before transferring it to the cerebral cortex. The transmitter used for long term potentiation is the amino acid, glutamate, which binds to receptors in the postsynaptic cell which allows calcium to flow in and set up the activation of other molecules known as kinases. A growing body of evidence implicates the role of dopamine as one of the most important chemicals that regulate cell activity involved in working memory. Studies done with aged monkeys shows that a deficiency in both dopamine and norepinephrine in the prefrontal cortex can induce a deficit in working memory. Injections of the deficient neurotransmitters restored memory function. Progress in deciphering the operation of the nervous system has helped to increase knowledge of the diverse role of the neurotransmitter.

See also Alzheimer's disease; Chemoreception; Memory; Nervous system; Neuron; Parkinson's disease; Schizophrenia.

Further Reading:

BSCS Revision Team. *Biological Science, A Molecular Approach*. Lexington, MA: D.C. Heath & Co., 1990.

Campbell, Neil A. *Biology*. Menlo Park, CA: Benjamin/Cummings, 1987.

Carey, Joseph, ed. *Brain Facts, A Primer on the Brain and the Nervous System*. Washington, D.C.: Society for Neuroscience, 1993.

Curtis, Helena, and N. Sue Barnes. *Biology*. 5th ed. New York: Worth Publishers, 1989.

KEY TERMS

. . . .

Action potential—A transient change in the electrical potential across a membrane which results in the generation of a nerve impulse.

Axon—Threadlike structures extending from neurons which carry impulses away from the cell body.

Catecholamine—Monoamines such as the neurotransmitters norepinephrine, serotonin, and dopamine that are synthesized from the amino acid, tyrosine, and have similar structures.

Conditioned reflex—A response in which one stimulus, the conditioned one, is associated with and elicits the same response as another stimulus, the unconditioned stimulus.

Dendrites—Branched structures of neurons which receive information from other cells.

Limbic system—Group of nuclei in the lower part of the forebrain involved in certain emotional and behavioral responses.

Monamine oxidase—An enzyme found in the brain and liver which breaks down catecholamines such as norepinephrine, serotonin and dopamine.

Synapse—Space between axons and dendrites through which neurotransmitters diffuse that initiate excitatory or inhibitory chemical or electrical changes.

Working memory—Memory that accesses and brings to mind information stored in long–term memory.

Fischbach, Gerald D. "Mind and Brain." *Scientific American* 3 (1992): 48–57.

Goldman–Rakic, Patricia S. "Working Memory and the Mind." *Scientific American* 3 (1992): 110–117.

Holtzman, Eric, and Alex B. Novikoff. *Cells and Organelles*. Philadelphia: Saunders College Publishing, 1984.

Kuffler, Stephen W., and John G. Nicholls. *From Neuron to Brain*. Sunderland, MA: Sinauer Associates, 1976.

LeDoux, Joseph E. "Emotion, Memory, and the Brain." *Scientific American* 6 (1994) : 50–57.

Purves, Dale. *Body and Brain, A Trophic Theory of Neural Connections*. Cambridge, MA: Harvard University Press, 1988.

Raven, Peter H., and George B. Johnson. *Biology*. 3rd ed. St. Louis: Mosby Year Book, 1992.

Mary Finley

Neutralization

In chemistry, the process in which an acid and a base react with each other to form a salt and water is known as neutralization. Just as a neutral color contains no vivid colors and a neutral person has no strong opinions, a neutralization reaction between an acidic and a basic (alkaline) solution lessens the acidic and basic properties of both solutions. Taking an antacid to settle a sour stomach, putting agricultural limestone on a garden or lawn, and mixing baking soda with vinegar are everyday examples of neutralization reactions.

History

As acids and bases are readily found in nature, neutralization reactions have been biological occurrences since ancient times. For instance, neutralization reactions involving carbonate and bicarbonate regulate the pH of our blood. However, fundamental understanding of neutralizations began with Svante Arrhenius (1859–1927) in 1884 and Johannes Brønsted (1879–1947) and Thomas Lowry (1874–1936) in 1923. These people first articulated the chemical properties of acids and bases and how the two substances react in water to form salts. Brønsted and Lowry defined acids as hydrogen proton donors and bases as hydrogen proton acceptors. The Brønsted-Lowry definition is best understood and most used by chemistry students. Gilbert Lewis's (1875–1946) definition of acids and bases, also published in 1923, is useful when substances do not contain or receive hydrogens.

Reactions

All neutralization reactions can be broadly summarized by the following equation:

acid + base → salt + water

Using a hydrogen ion to represent an acid and a hydroxide ion to represent a base, a neutralization reaction may also be expressed as

H^+	$+$	OH^-	$\rightarrow$	H_2O
hydrogen		hydroxide		water
ion		ion		molecule
ACID		BASE		

The formation of the salt is omitted in this generalized type of equation because the salt ions do not undergo a chemical change during a neutralization reaction.

Neutralization reactions usually take place in water. An example of a strong acid and a strong base reacting in water—indicated by (aq), meaning aqueous—is the reaction between two corrosive solutions, sodium hydroxide (NaOH) and hydrochloric acid (HCl), to form table salt (NaCl) and water. The table salt remains dissolved in the water and exists as ions of sodium (Na^+) and chloride (Cl^-).

$NaOH(aq)$	$+$	$HCl(aq)$	$\rightarrow$	$Na^+(aq)$	$+$	$Cl^-(aq)$	$+$	H_2O
sodium		hydrochloric		sodium		chloride		water
hydroxide		acid solution		ion		ion		solution
BASE		ACID			SALT			

Neutralization does not occur only in solution. Acidic and basic gases can undergo neutralization reactions, as in the reaction between the two corrosive gases ammonia (NH_3) and hydrogen chloride (HCl) to form the solid salt ammonium chloride (NH_4Cl).

$HCl(g)$	$+$	$NH_3(g)$	$\rightarrow$	$NH_4Cl(s)$
hydrogen		ammonia		ammonium
chloride gas		chloride gas		solid
ACID		BASE		SALT

Weak acids and bases will also undergo neutralization reactions. The reaction of the acetic acid (HAc) in vinegar with the sodium bicarbonate ($NaHCO_3$) in baking soda produces water, sodium ions (Na^+), acetate ions (Ac^-), and carbon dioxide gas (CO_2). The reaction between baking soda and acids in dough creates bubbles of carbon dioxide that make cakes and cookies rise and become fluffy.

HAc	$+$	$NaHCO_3$	$\rightarrow$	H_2O	$+$	Na^+	$+$	Ac^-	$+$	$CO_2(g)$
acetic		baking		water		sodium		acetate		carbon
acid		soda				ion		ion		dioxide
ACID		BASE				SALT				

Uses of neutralization

Neutralization of acidic water is an important step in reclaiming land that was once mined. Mine run–off renders water around the mine site acidic, and the acid must be neutralized with lime, or calcium oxide (CaO) acting as a base, before the area can be reclaimed. However, this procedure is expensive. Recent studies have shown that constructed wetlands—human–made shallow ponds containing water plants such as cattails—can be an effective and less costly method of neutralizing acid mine drainage.

Neutralization of soil is sometimes necessary in order to promote plant growth. The ability of plants to take nutrients from the soil into their roots is affected by the pH content of the surrounding soil particles. Acid rain can cause soil to become acidic. Some plants benefit from liming the soil. In the liming process, agricultural limestone—calcium carbonate ($CaCO_3$) that may also contain magnesium carbonate ($MgCO_3$)—neutralizes acid in the soil and provides nutrients to promote plant growth. Since liming can stimulate plant growth, it is important to also fertilize limed soil. This insures that all of the nutrients used by the plants for growth are maintained in the soil for the following year's growth. Soils may also become too basic, or alkaline, especially in areas where there is little precipitation. Substances that can act as acids—such as calcium sulfate, also called gypsum ($CaSO_4$), and sulfur (S_2)—can be applied to the soil for neutralization.

In areas where acid precipitation is a problem, neutralization reactions can damage limestone, marble, and plaster buildings and statues. These structures all are made of calcium carbonate ($CaCO_3$), a basic substance that is neutralized by acidic precipitation. These structures decay and become coated with a black substance that contains gypsum. Gypsum is the salt calcium sulfate ($CaSO_4$) that is formed when the sulfuric acid (H_2S) in acid rain reacts with the calcium carbonate ($CaCO_3$) in the building materials.

Acidic and basic hazardous wastes can often be safely disposed of using neutralization because the salts produced are usually non–hazardous and take up less space as solids than the liquid acids and bases.

An important application of neutralization reactions is in titration, which uses chemical reactions to determine the amount of a chemical substance existing in a sample of unknown purity. In a typical neutralization titration, a carefully measured amount of a known prepared solution of an acid is added to another solution containing an unknown amount of a base until the base has been neutralized. From the amount of acid needed to neutralize the base, the amount of base can be calculated. Alternately, a known amount of a prepared solution of a base can be added to an unknown acidic solution until it is neutralized, and this can establish the acid content. Most acidic or basic substances can be titrated. For example, a solution of sulfuric acid (H_2S) may be used to titrate water, sludge, sediment, or wastewater to determine its ammonia (NH_3) content. This helps establish the purity of the water. Another titration, known as the Kjeldahl titration, can be used to determine how much nitrogen (N_2) is in food, animal feeds, or blood, indicating the amount of protein present. Other elements that can be analyzed by using neutralization titrations include sulfur (S_2), carbon (C), chloride (Cl_2), fluoride (F_2), and phosphorus (P_2).

See also Acids and bases.

Further Reading:

Cardinall, Mario Emilio, Claudio Giomini and Giancarlo Marrosu. "More about the Extent of Acid–Base Reactions," *Journal of Chemical Education*. Vol. 68, no. 12, 1991, pp. 989–990.

KEY TERMS

Acid—A chemical substance that donates a hydrogen proton when it reacts with a base.

Acid precipitation—Rain, fog, sleet, or snow that has a lower pH than normal rain due to atmospheric pollutants; sometimes called acid rain.

Base—A substance that receives a hydrogen proton when it reacts with an acid.

Ion—An atom or combination of atoms that has a positive or negative charge.

pH—A logarithmic scale that expresses the concentration of hydrogen ions in a solution of water. A neutral solution with equivalent amounts of hydrogen and hydroxyl ions has a pH of 7.0 at room temperature. Acidic solutions have a pH of less than 7.0 and basic (alkaline) solutions have a pH of more than 7.0.

Salt—A solid that is made from a combination of positive and negative ions but has no net charge itself.

Titration—A process in which a carefully measured amount of a well-characterized chemical substance is added to a substance of unknown concentration until a complete reaction has occurred. Titrations are used for chemical analyses.

Kostiner, Edward. *Study Keys to Chemistry*. Barron's Educational Series, Inc., 1992.

Shakhashiri, Bassam Z. "Determination of the Neutralizing Capacity of Antacids." *Chemical Demonstrations: A Handbook for Teachers of Chemistry*. Vol. 3. Madison, WI: The University of Wisconsin Press, 1989.

Shakhashiri, Bassam Z. "Heat of Neutralization." *Chemical Demonstrations: A Handbook for Teachers of Chemistry*. Vol. 1. Madison, WI: The University of Wisconsin Press, 1983.

Summerlin, Lee R. "Milk of Magnesia versus Acid." *Chemical Demonstrations: A Handbook for Teachers of Chemistry*. Vol. 2. Washington D.C.: American Chemical Society, 1987.

Thompson, Ralph J. "The Extent of Acid–Base Reactions." *Journal of Chemical Education*. Vol. 67, no. 3, 1990, pp. 220–221.

Troeh, Fredrick R. and Louis M. Thompson. *Soils and Soil Fertility*, 5th edition. New York: Oxford University Press, Inc., 1993.

VanCleave, Janice Pratt. "Neutralization" and "Erupting volcano." *Chemistry for Every Kid: 101 Experiments That Really Work*. New York: John Wiley & Sons, Inc., 1989.

Catherine Hinga Haustein

Neutrino

Neutrinos are elusive subatomic particles that result from certain nuclear reactions. They escaped detection for 25 years after their existence was predicted. They have no charge and possibly no mass. Yet neutrinos have considerable energy and momentum. Neutrinos also barely interact with matter. They can penetrate nearly anything by sliding through the spaces between atoms. Because their interaction rate is so low, neutrinos produced in the core of the Sun fly directly out through the outer layers of the Sun, providing direct information on the Sun's core. Unfortunately, scientists are unable to find enough solar neutrinos, even after years of looking.

History

In the 1920s, physicists noticed some discrepancies in beta decay experiments. In beta decay, a neutron emits an electron, called a beta particle, and decays into a proton. In these experiments the total momentum and energy of the electron and proton after the decay was sometimes less than the initial momentum and energy of the neutron. Where did the missing momentum and energy go? According to fundamental laws of physics the total amounts of both momentum and energy must remain constant. Neither can just disappear.

In 1930, the Swiss physicist Wolfgang Pauli (1900-1958) wrote a letter addressed "Dear Radioactive Ladies and Gentlemen" to a meeting in Tübingen, Germany. He timidly suggested the idea of neutrinos as the particles that carry away the missing energy, but did not dare to publish the idea for another three years. Pauli originally called his suggested particle *neutron*, as neutrons had not been discovered in 1930. When neutrons were discovered the name "neutron" was taken, so Pauli's particle became the neutrino: the little neutral one.

Enrico Fermi's 1934 theory of beta decay used the neutrino hypothesis. This successful theory, still used for approximate calculations, was finally surpassed for very accurate calculations in the 1970s. But did neutrinos really exist? In the 1930s no experiments to detect them were possible or even imaginable.

In 1956, after a four-year search, F. Reines and C. L. Cowan finally succeeded in detecting neutrinos produced by the nuclear reactors at the Savannah River Reactor. By 1962, the particle accelerator at Brookhaven National Laboratory generated enough neutrinos to conduct an experiment on neutrinos. In several months, physicists observed a few dozen neutrino events. This first experiment showed that there are different types of neutrinos. Subsequent experiments revealed other properties of neutrinos.

Mass of neutrinos

Traditionally, we think neutrinos have zero mass, because experiments detect none. If neutrinos do have a mass, it must be less than about one hundred millionth the mass of the proton, the sensitivity limit of the experiments. Experiments conducted during late 1994 at Los Alamos National Laboratory hint at the possibility that neutrinos do have a very small, but nonzero, mass. Further experiments are needed to either confirm or refute this preliminary result.

A nonzero neutrino mass would have important astrophysical implications. Studies of the motions of galaxies show that there is a significant amount of dark matter in the universe. Perhaps as much as 90% of the mass of the universe is unseen. What comprises this dark matter? We don't know, but a nonzero neutrino mass could account for at least some of the dark matter in the universe.

Interactions with matter

Neutrinos have negligible interaction with matter. Consider an analogy. You cannot throw a basketball through a chain link fence. The ball is bigger than the holes in the fence. If your aim is perfect you might be able to throw a golf ball through the fence, but it is much more likely that it will hit one of the links in the fence. The golf ball is roughly the same size as the holes in the fence. A tiny ball bearing will easily pass through the fence and will only rarely hit one of the chain links in the fence. It is much smaller than the holes in the fence. Similarly, subatomic particles will pass through a barrier if they are smaller than the spaces between and within the atoms in the barrier. If they are larger, they are absorbed by the barrier. The size of a subatomic particle is expressed in terms of its cross sectional area. Technically the cross section of a subatomic particle does not mean exactly the same thing as for the balls in the example, but there is an effective cross section for determining the amount of interaction with matter. The cross section of a neutrino is incredibly small. It depends on the energy of the neutrino but will be roughly on the order of 10^{-40} square centimeters. In a beam of neutrinos passing through the center of the Earth, only one in a trillion will be blocked by the Earth. A slab of lead about 100 light years thick will only absorb roughly one third of the neutrinos striking it. This property makes neutrinos incredibly hard to find. They zip right through the detector.

KEY TERMS

Beta decay—The splitting of a neutron into a proton and an electron.

Beta particle—The electron produced by beta decay.

Cross section—A way of measuring the probability that a subatomic particle will interact with matter, roughly analogous to the cross sectional area.

Dark matter—The unseen mass in the universe with an unknown composition.

What SNU?

The small neutrino cross section makes it a useful probe of the Sun's interior. The energy producing nuclear reactions in the Sun's core also produce neutrinos. The energy takes a few million years to migrate to the Sun's surface; the neutrinos, zipping through the core at the speed of light, make it to the Earth in eight minutes. Neutrinos therefore probe what is going on in the Sun's core now rather than a few million years ago.

Raymond Davis has searched for solar neutrinos since 1967. His still operating experiment, using 293,265 lb (133 tons) of cleaning fluid at the bottom of a gold mine in Homestake, South Dakota, finds only one third the predicted number of neutrinos. The neutrino intensity is measured in Solar Neutrino Units (SNUs), leading astronomers to ask, "What SNU?" Davis's experiment can detect only the Sun's highest energy neutrinos. Two new experiments using 66,150 lb (30 tons) and 132,300 lb (60 tons) of an element called Gallium can detect more of the Sun's neutrinos. Initial results agree fairly well with the predictions. Continued study may soon resolve the solar neutrino problem.

See also Nuclear reactions; Subatomic particles; Star; Sun.

Further Reading:

Bahcall, John. "High Noon for Solar Neutrinos." *New Scientist* 135 (15 August 1992): 28–32.

Morrison, David, Sidney Wolff, and Andrew Fraknoi. *Abell's Exploration of the Universe.* 7th ed. Philadelphia: Saunders College Publishing, 1995.

Steinberger, J. "What do we Learn from Neutrinos?" *Science* 259 (26 March 1993): 1872–1876.

Taubes, Gary. "Neutrino Watchers go to Extremes." *Science* 263 (7 January 1994): 28–30.

Paul A. Heckert

Neutron

The structure of the atom can be pictured as a tiny solar system. At the center is the nucleus, which is surrounded by orbiting electrons. Inside the nucleus are two types of particles, neutrons (electrically neutral) and protons (positively charged). Under special experimental conditions, neutrons can be released from the nucleus. They are useful for creating new radioactive materials or for producing large amounts of nuclear energy.

The atom is so small that it would take several million of them to equal the size of the period at the end of this sentence. The nucleus is much smaller still, about 1/100,000 of an atom's size. Finally, neutrons and protons appear to be made up of three even smaller components called "quarks." Evidence for quarks comes from experiments done with very high energy particle accelerators.

Discovery

The neutron as a distinct, separate particle was discovered in 1932 by a British physicist, James Chadwick (1891–1974). He was using radiation emitted from radioactive radium to bombard various materials. When he irradiated the element beryllium, he found that a very penetrating particle was produced. It could go through an inch thickness of lead. Chadwick reasoned that the new particle must be electrically neutral, because all other radiation known at that time would have been stopped by the lead. Chadwick was awarded the 1935 Nobel Prize in physics for his discovery.

New radioactive materials

Enrico Fermi (1901–1954), a young Italian scientist, constructed a neutron source according to Chadwick's design, mixing radium and beryllium powder together in a small glass tube. Fermi's plan was to use this neutron source for making new radioactive materials. Together with his co-workers, he was successful in producing radioactive sodium, iron, copper, gold, and many other elements. Fermi received the 1938 Nobel Prize in physics for his work with neutrons.

Almost all elements found in nature can now be made radioactive. Radioactive potassium and phosphorus are used as tracers to measure how effectively plants take up fertilizer from soil. Radioactive iodine is applied in nuclear medicine to diagnose and treat thyroid problems. Radiation treatment for cancer therapy uses radioactive cobalt, which is made by irradiating ordinary cobalt with neutrons.

Nuclear energy production

When the element uranium is bombarded by neutrons, a unique reaction called fission takes place. The uranium nucleus breaks into two pieces, which fly apart with a large release of energy. In addition, several extra neutrons are emitted. These cause more uranium nuclei to split apart, which creates more energy and more neutrons in a so–called "chain reaction" process. In an atomic bomb, the chain reaction becomes an uncontrolled explosion. In a nuclear power plant, the chain reaction is maintained in a steady state by control rods which absorb extra neutrons.

See also Subatomic particles.

Neutron activation analysis

Neutron activation analysis is an analytical technique for determining the elements present in a material as well as the amount of each element in the sample. The technique is based on a well–known reaction from nuclear chemistry. When an element is bombarded with neutrons, some of the atoms of that element may capture neutrons and incorporate them into their nuclei. Those atoms that do so have the same atomic number (that is, are the same element) as the original target element, but have an atomic mass of one higher. Bombarding atoms of sodium–23 with neutrons, for example, converts them to atoms of sodium–24.

In most cases, the heavier atoms formed in this reaction are radioactive. They usually decay with the emission of a beta particle and a gamma ray. The energy associated with these decay schemes is characteristic of the radioactive isotope in question. For example, a gamma ray released in the decay of sodium–24 has an energy of 2.75 or 1.37 MeV.

In practice, nuclear activation analysis is carried out by placing the sample to be examined in a nuclear reactor. The neutrons available in the reactor bring about the n/ψ (neutron/gamma ray) reactions described above. The radioactive sample is then removed from the reactor and examined with a gamma ray spectrometer. This device measures the type and intensity of radiation released by the sample. These data can then be compared to standard tables to determine which elements and the amounts of each are present in the sample.

Neutron activation analysis is valuable as a non–destructive form of analysis. It can be used without fear of damaging or destroying the material being tested. It is also a very precise form of analysis, permitting the detection of very small quantities of an element. One application that illustrates these strengths is in the analysis of archaeological materials that are too fragile or too valuable to expose to other analytical techniques.

Neutron star

A neutron star is the dead remnant of a massive star. A massive star ends its life as a supernova, a catastrophic explosion that flings the star's outer layers into space, leaving only the core behind. If the mass of the core is between 1.4 and 2.5 times the mass of the Sun, it will become a neutron star, a solid mass of neutrons a hundred trillion times more dense than water. Neutron stars are tiny, about 32,810 ft (10 km) across, and they rotate very rapidly and have tremendously strong magnetic fields. Because they are massive and small, they also have intense gravitational fields. They are most easily observed in the radio and x ray portions of the spectrum, so they were not discovered until the late 1960s, when radio and x ray telescopes capable of detecting them began to become available.

The guest star

In 1054 A.D., astronomers in China noted the appearance of a "guest star" in the region of the sky we now call Taurus (the Bull). The new star was bright enough to be visible during the day, but faded within a few months. When we train our telescopes today on the place where this celestial interloper appeared, we see a spectacular cloud of gas, its filaments twisting and ragged. Its shape has led it to be called the Crab Nebula. The Crab is expanding, as if it had been flung violently outward from a central point.

When we observe the Crab with a radio telescope, something even stranger appears: there is an object at its center that flashes on and off like a strobe light, about 30 times per second. So regular are the flashes that they hardly seem to be a natural phenomenon. Indeed, Jocelyn Bell and Anthony Hewish, who discovered the first of these flashing objects, toyed with the idea of calling them LGM's—meaning Little Green Men! They eventually settled on the term *pulsar*, and today about 500 pulsars are known.

Almost a millennium ago, humans stared in wonder at a new, dazzling star. Today, there is a pulsar, seem-

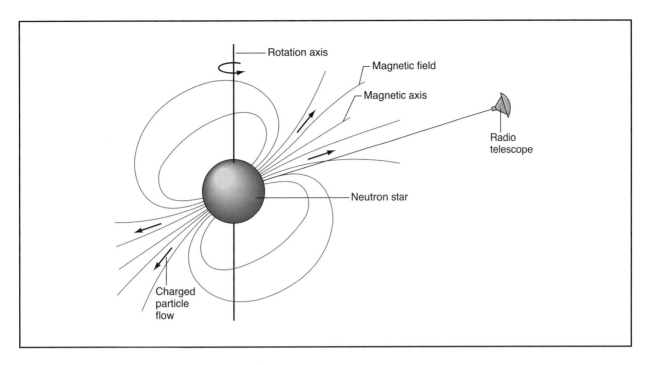

Figure 1. Illustration of the relationship between a neutron star's rotation axis and its magnetic axis.

ingly beaming pulses of radio radiation to us at precise intervals, and an angry–looking cloud of gas surrounding it. What has happened?

The origin of neutron stars

When a star that is between about three to eight times as massive as the Sun dies, it goes in spectacular fashion. The star's core temperature is in excess of half a billion degrees kelvin, and must remain this hot for thermonuclear fusion reactions involving its last reserves of fuel to take place.

Then the fuel runs out. No longer able to produce fusion reactions to sustain it, the star collapses. The core — a few million trillion trillion tons of it — falls in on itself, and in the ensuing cataclysm the star's outer layers are flung outward in a supernova explosion.

Your intuition might tell you that the collapsing core will keep falling, squeezing itself together until it becomes so dense that it can fall no farther. This is like when you crumple a sheet of paper into a ball. You can only squeeze it to a certain point, after which it is too tightly packed to reduce its size any further.

In the case of a collapsing star, a law of physics known as the Pauli Exclusion Principle describes this phenomenon. Atoms are composed of a nucleus surrounded by electrons. Electrons do not "orbit" the nuclei in the sense that planets orbit the Sun; rather, electrons exist in what are called "energy states," mean-

ing that they have only certain amounts of energy. The Pauli Exclusion Principle states that two identical electrons may not share the same energy state. It is therefore possible for the energy levels of an atom to become completely filled with electrons, in the same way that an auditorium can only hold as many people as it has seats. Matter with its energy levels filled like this is called *degenerate*.

The Pauli Exclusion Principle will come into play when the Sun dies and its core collapses. The carbon and oxygen atoms will become squeezed together until the atomic levels are filled and the whole core becomes a ball of degenerate matter. At this point, the resistance of the electrons to gravity, or *electron degeneracy pressure*, will halt the contraction. This ball of hot, degenerate, carbon and oxygen atoms is called a white dwarf, and it is the fate of the Sun.

If the collapsing core is between 1.4 and about 2.5 times the mass of the Sun, however, the gravity will be so strong that the electron degeneracy pressure will fail. Unable to resist the weight of their own gravity, the atoms will be crushed into a ball made mainly of neutrons about 32,810 ft (10 km) across. This object is called a neutron star.

Properties of neutron stars

With twice the mass of the Sun crammed into a space no larger than a small city, a neutron star is fantastically dense. A sugar–cube–sized piece of neutron star would weigh billions of tons.

Neutron stars rotate rapidly. This is because the original stellar core was rotating, and as it collapsed its rotation rate increased, in the same way figure skaters spin increasingly rapidly by drawing their extended arms in to their sides.

Neutron stars also have intense gravitational and magnetic fields. The gravity is strong because there is so much matter packed into so small a radius. If a friend dropped you onto a neutron star from, say, 50 million miles out, you would impact and explode with a blast larger than that of any current nuclear warhead. The magnetic field is strong because it is an intrinsic property of the neutron star's matter. When the original stellar core collapses, its magnetic field collapses with it and intensifies until it is a trillion times as strong as the Earth's.

Observing neutron stars

Many neutron stars look like the drawing in Figure 1. The neutron star's rotation axis is inclined with respect to its magnetic axis. (The same situation prevails on Earth.) The neutron star's rapid rotation and intense magnetic field cause radiation to be emitted in narrow beams from the magnetic poles. If the Earth happens to be in line with one of these beams, we will see a flash every time the neutron star rotates and carries the beam past us.

This is precisely what we see in the Crab Nebula. The rate of the flashes indicates the neutron star is spinning 30 times per second. (Compare that with the Sun's rotation period of about one month.) If a pulsar's beam never sweeps past our line of sight, however, we will never see it.

Some neutron stars are members of binary systems, in which they orbit another star. The intense gravity of the neutron star drags material off its companion. The material forms an *accretion disk* as it approaches the neutron star. In the process it becomes so hot that it begins to emit large amounts of x rays. Only a gravitational field as strong as one predicted to be associated with a neutron star could heat the infalling gas this much.

Even more spectacular are neutron stars that combine the above phenomena: the *binary pulsars*. In these systems we see pulses of x rays, as the powerful beams of high–energy radiation sweep past us.

Neutron stars have also provided the first direct evidence of planets outside the solar system. The pulsar PSR 1257+12 rotates 161 times per second—but its pulses are not evenly spaced, as are the ones from the

Crab. Observations made with the giant Arecibo radio telescope showed that some pulses arrive slightly too soon, others just a bit too late. This means something is tugging the pulsar back and forth slightly. Careful measurements showed that a pair of planets is responsible.

See also Pulsar; Star; Stellar evolution; Supernova.

Further Reading:

Bailyn, C. "Problems with Pulsars." *Mercury* (March–April 1991): 55.

Fienberg, R. T. "Pulsars, Planets, and Pathos." *Sky & Telescope* (May 1992): 493.

Hewish, A. "Pulsars After 20 Years." *Mercury* (January–February 1989): 12.

Jeffrey C. Hall

Newton's laws of motion

Earthly and heavenly motions were of great interest to Newton. Applying an acute sense for asking the right questions with reasoning, Newton formulated three laws which allowed a complete analysis (mathematical)

KEY TERMS

Binary pulsar—A pulsar in orbit around another star. The pulsar drags matter off its companion, heating it to the point that it emits x rays. These powerful beams of radiation sweep past our line of sight, producing flashes in the same way that single pulsars flash in the visible and radio.

Degeneracy pressure—The tendency of degenerate matter to resist further contraction under its own gravity. Neutron stars are prevented from being crushed into black holes by the degeneracy pressure of their tightly packed neutrons, which is sufficient to resist the neutron star's strong gravity.

Pulsar—A rapidly spinning neutron star with its magnetic axis inclined relative to its rotation axis. Radiation streams continuously from the pulsar along its magnetic axis, so if the magnetic axis passes through our line of sight as the pulsar rotates, we see a flash. The rate of the flashes reveals the rotation rate of the neutron star.

---

of dynamics, relating all aspects of motion to basic causes, force and mass. So great was Newton's work that it is referred to as the first revolution in Physics.

First law of motion

Galileo's observation that without friction a body would tend to move forever challenged Aristotle's notion that the natural state of motion on earth was one of rest. Galileo deduced that it was a property of matter to maintain its state of motion, a property he called inertia. Newton, grasping the meaning of inertia and recognizing that Aristotle's reference to what keeps a body in motion (outside influence) really should have been what changes a body's state of motion, set forth a first law of motion which states: A body at rest remains at rest or a body in constant motion remains in constant motion along a straight line unless acted on by an external influence, called force.

Examples of the first law

(1.) Why use seat belts? Riding in a car you and the car have the same motion. When the brakes are applied, the brakes stop the car. What stops you? Eventually the steering wheel, the dashboard, or the window unless they are replaced by a seat belt, which stops your body. When the accelerator is depressed with the car in gear the motor turns the wheels and the car moves forward. What moves you forward? As the car moves forward the seatback comes forward, contacts, you and pushes you forward.

(2.) While you are riding in the front passenger seat of a car, the driver suddenly turns left. What about you? You continue to move in a straight line until the door to your right, turning left, eventually runs into you. In the car it may appear to you that you slid outward and hit the door.

Second law of motion

The first law of motion concentrates on a state of constant motion but adds unless an outside influence, force, acts on it. Force produces a change in the state of motion (velocity describes a body's motion); that is, an acceleration. Newton found that the greater a body's mass the greater the force required to overcome its inertia and mass is taken as a quantitative measure of a body's inertia. He also found that applying equal force to two different masses, the ratio of their accelerations was inversely proportional to the ratio of their masses. Newton's Second Law of Motion is thus stated: A net force acting on a body produces an acceleration; the acceleration is inversely proportional to its mass and directly proportional to the net force and in the same direction.

This law can be put mathematically $F = ma$ where F is the net force, m is the mass, and a the acceleration. The second law is a cause–effect relationship. The net force acting on a body is determined from all forces acting and the resultant acceleration calculated (assuming a known mass). From the acceleration, velocity and distance traveled can be determined for any time.

Applications of the second law

(1.) Objects, when released, fall to the ground due to the earth's attraction. Newton's Universal Law of Gravity gave the force of attraction between two masses, m and M, as $F = GmM/R^2$ where G is the gravitational constant and R is the distance between mass centers. This force, weight, produces gravitational acceleration g, thus weight = GmM/R^2 = mg(2nd Law) giving g = GM/R^2. This relationship holds universally. For all objects at the earth's surface, g =32 ft/sec/sec or 9.0 m/sec/sec downward and on Jupiter 84 ft/sec/sec. Since the dropped object's mass does not appear, g is the same for all objects. Falling objects have their velocity changed downward at the rate of 32 ft/sec each second on earth. Falling from rest, at the end of one second the velocity is 32 ft/sec, after 2 seconds 64 ft/sec, after 3 seconds 96 ft/sec, etc.

For objects thrown upward, gravitational acceleration is still 32 ft/sec/sec downward. A ball thrown upward with an initial velocity of 80 ft/sec has a velocity after one second of 80–32= 48 ft/sec, after two seconds 48–32= 16 ft/sec, and after three seconds 16–32= −16 ft/sec (now downward), etc. At 2.5 seconds the ball had a zero velocity and after another 2.5 seconds it hits the ground with a velocity of 80 ft/sec downward. The up and down motion is symmetrical.

(2.) Friction, a force acting between two bodies in contact, is parallel to the surface and opposite the motion (or tendency to move). By the second law, giving a mass of one kilogram(kg) an acceleration of 1 m/sec/sec requires a force of one Newton(N). However, if friction were 3 N, a force of 4 N must be applied to give the same acceleration. The net force is 4N(applied by someone) minus 3N(friction) or 1N.

Free fall, example (1), assumed no friction. If there were atmospheric friction it would be directed upward since friction always opposes the motion. Air friction is proportional to the velocity; as the velocity increases the friction force (upward) becomes larger. The net force (weight minus friction) and the acceleration are less than due to gravity alone. Therefore, the velocity increases less rapidly, becoming constant when the friction force equals the weight of the falling object (net force=0). This velocity is called the terminal velocity. A greater weight requires a longer time for air friction to equal the weight, resulting in a larger terminal velocity.

(3.) A contemporary and friend of Newton, Halley, observed a comet in 1682 and suspected others had observed it many times before. Using Newton's new Mechanics (laws of motion and Universal Law of Gravity) Halley calculated that the comet would reappear at Christmas, 1758. Although Halley was dead, the comet reappeared at that time and became known as Halley's comet. This was a great triumph for Newtonian Mechanics.

Using Newton's Universal Law of Gravity (see example 1) in the second law results in a general solution (requiring calculus) in which details of the paths of motion (velocity, acceleration, period) are given in terms of G, M, and distance of separation.

While these results agreed with planetary motion known at the time there was now an explanation for differences in motions. These solutions were equally valid for applying to any systems body: earth's moon, Jupiter's moons, galaxies, truly universal.

(4.) Much of Newton's work involved rotational motion, particularly circular motion. The velocity's direction constantly changes, requiring a centripetal acceleration. This centripetal acceleration requires a net force, the centripetal force, acting toward the center of motion. Centripetal acceleration is given by a(central)=v^2/R where v is the velocity's magnitude and R is the radius of the motion. Hence, the centripetal force F(central) = mv^2/R, where m is the mass. These relationships hold for any case of circular motion and furnish the basis for "thrills" experienced on many amusement park rides such as ferris wheels, loop–the–loops, merry–go–rounds, and any other means for changing your direction rather suddenly. Some particular examples follow.

(a.) Newton asked himself why the moon did not fall to the earth like other objects. Falling with the same acceleration of gravity as bodies at the earth's surface, it would have hit the earth. With essentially uniform circular motion about the earth, the moon's centripetal acceleration and force must be due to earth's gravity. With gravitational force providing centripetal force, the centripetal acceleration is a(central) = GM/R^2 (acceleration of gravity in example 1 above). Since the moon is about 60 times further from the earth's center than the earth's surface, the acceleration of gravity of the moon is about .009 ft/sec/sec. In one second the moon would

fall about .06 inch but while doing this it is also moving away from the earth with the result that at the end of one second the moon is at the same distance from the earth, R.

(b.) With the gravitational force responsible for centripetal acceleration, equating the two acceleration expressions given above gives the magnitude of the velocity as v^2 = GM/R with the same symbol meanings. For the moon in (a) its velocity would be about 2,250 MPH. This relationship can be universally applied.

Long ago it was recognized that this analysis could be applied to artificial "moons" or satellites. If a satellite could be made to encircle the earth at about 200 mi it must be given a tangential velocity of about 18,000 mph and it would encircle the earth every 90 seconds; astronauts have done this many times since 1956, 300 years after Newton gave the means for predicting the necessary velocities.

It was asked: what velocity and height must a satellite have so that it remains stationary above the same point on the earth's surface; that is, have the same rotation period, one day, as the earth. Three such satellites, placed 120 degrees apart around the earth, could make instantaneous communication with all points on the earth's surface possible. From the fact that period squared is proportional to the cube of the radius and the above periods of the moon and satellite and the moon's distance, it is found that the communication satellite would have to be located 26,000 mi from earth's center or 22,000 mi above the surface. Its velocity must be about 6,800 mph. Many such satellites are now in space around the earth.

(c.) When a car rounds a curve what keeps it on the road? Going around a curve requires a centripetal force to furnish the centripetal acceleration, changing its direction. If there is not, the car continues in a straight line (first law) moving outward relative to the road. Friction, opposing outward motion, would be inward and the inward acceleration a(cent) =friction/mass = v^2/R. Each radius has a predictable velocity for which the car can make the curve. A caution must be added: when it is raining, friction is reduced and a lower velocity is needed to make the curve safely.

Third law of motion or law of action–reaction

Newton questioned the interacting force an outside agent exerted on another to change its state of motion. He concluded that this interaction was mutual so that when you exert a force on something you get the feeling the other is exerting a force on you. Newton's Third

Law of Motion states: When one body exerts a force on a second body, the second body exerts an equal and opposite force on the first body.

In the second law, only forces exerted on a body are important in determining its acceleration. The third law speaks about a pair of forces equal in magnitude and opposite in direction which are exerted on and by two different bodies. This law is useful in determining forces acting on an object by knowing forces it exerts. For example, a book sitting on a table has a net force of zero. Therefore, an upward force equal to its weight must be exerted by the table on the book. According to the third law the book exerts an equal force downward on the table. When two objects are in contact they exert equal and opposite forces on each other and these forces are perpendicular to the contacting surface.

Examples of the third law

(1.) What enables us to walk? To move forward parallel to the floor we must push backward on the floor with one foot. By the third law, the floor pushes forward, moving us forward. Then the process is repeated with the other foot, etc. This cannot occur unless there is friction between the foot and floor and on a frictionless surface we would not be able to walk.

(2.) How can airplanes fly at high altitudes and space crafts be propelled? High altitude airplanes utilize jet engines; that is, engines burn fuel at high temperatures and expel it backward. In expelling the burnt fuel a force is exerted backward on it and it exerts an equal forward force on the plane. The same analysis applies to space crafts.

(3.) A father takes his eight–year–old daughter to ice skate. The father and the girl stand at rest facing each other. The daughter pushes the father backwards. What happens? Whatever force the daughter exerts on her father he exerts in the opposite direction equally on her. Since the father has a larger mass his acceleration will be less than the daughter's. With the larger acceleration the daughter will move faster and travel farther in a given time.

Further Reading:

Corben, H.C. and Stehle, P. *Classical Mechanics*. New York: Dover, 1994.

Hagen, Robert M. and Trefil, James. *Science Matters*. New York: Doubleday, 1991.

Hewitt, Paul G. *Conceptual Physics*, 7th ed. New York: HarperCollins College Publishers, 1993.

Hobson, Art. *Physics Concepts and Connections*. Englewood Cliffs, NJ: Prentice Hall, 1995.

Kirkpatrick, Larry and Gerald Wheeler. *Physics: A World View*, 2nd ed. Chicago: Saunders, 1995.

KEY TERMS

. . . .

Centripetal acceleration—Produces a change in the direction of velocity and always perpendicular to the velocity vector. This, in turn is caused by a centripetal force.

Force—Influence exerted on an object by an outside agent which produces an acceleration changing the object's state of motion.

Inertia—Property of matter whereby any change in state of motion is opposed. Quantitatively measured by mass.

Teller, Edward, Teller, Wendy, and Talley, Wilson. *Conversations On The Dark Secrets Of Physics*. New York: Plenum Press, 1991.

Billy W. Sloope

Newts

Newts are lizard–shaped animals with a tail in the amphibian order Caudata (or Urodela), in the superfamily Salamandroidea, which also includes the salamanders. The distinction between newts and salamanders is not always obvious since both have a tail in the larval stage and the adult stage. However, newts do not have costal grooves on the sides of their body, they are less slippery than salamanders, they have a unique dentition on the roof of the mouth, and they tend to be more aquatic than salamanders.

Biology of newts

Like salamanders, newts have a complex life cycle, the stages of which are egg, larva, and adult. Some species of newts can be distinguished from salamanders in that the newts have two distinct adult stages.

In the case of the red–spotted newt (*Notophthalmus viridescens*) of North America, the red eft is the stage that occurs after transformation of the aquatic larva. The red eft is bright red or orange, and is a pre–reproductive adult stage. The red eft wanders widely in forests, sometimes for several years, and is most common on moist nights. Eventually, the red eft migrates to an aquatic habitat, changes to a yellowish color, develops a broad, adult tail fin, and becomes a sexually

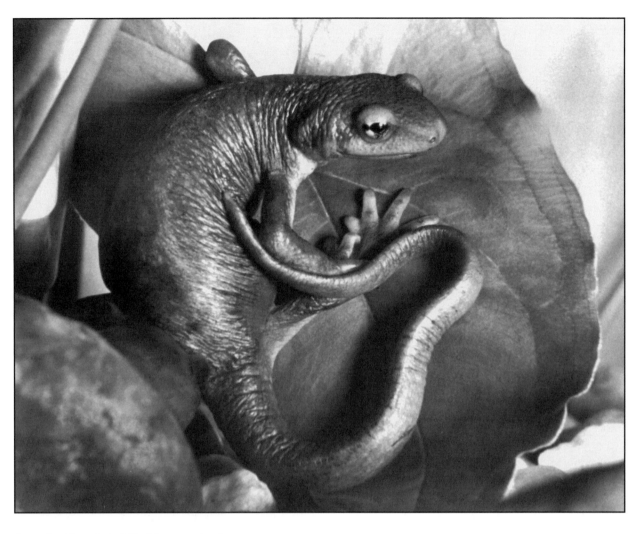

A rough-skinned newt (*Taricha granulosa*).

mature, breeding adult. The migration of red efts to water has been shown to be stimulated by the presence of the pituitary hormone prolactin.

Not all populations of red–spotted newts display this type of life cycle, for some coastal populations bypass the terrestrial red eft stage, and produce breeding adults directly from larvae. These adults may retain some larval characteristics, such as gills, which is an example at neoteny, or paedomorphosis.

Courtship in some species of newts involves elaborate aquatic displays by the male. These displays are designed to entice the female newt to pass over sperm–containing spermatophores that the male has previously deposited onto the surface of the sediment. If the male is successful, the female newt picks up the spermatophore with her cloacal lips and stores the spermatophore internally, which then fertilizes her

ova as they are laid singly on surfaces in the aquatic habitat.

The red eft stage of the red–spotted newt contains toxic, bad–tasting chemicals in its skin. As a result, many potential predators learn to avoid this animal, and will not eat red efts. The range of the red salamander (*Pseudotriton ruber*) overlaps part of the larger range of the red–spotted newt in the eastern United States. It appears that the superficially similar but non–toxic red salamander may be a mimic of the color of the red eft, taking advantage of the fact that many predators avoid this animal as food.

Newts have been shown to have a keen ability to find their way home to their natal or home pond. After they were displaced during an experiment, red–bellied newts (*Taricha rivularis*) studied in California proved to be capable of returning to their home stream within only one year, over a distance of up to eight kilometers (4.96 mi).

KEY TERMS

Complex life cycle—This is a life characterized by several radical transformations in anatomy, physiology, and ecology.

Metamorphosis—This refers to the great anatomical and physiological transformations that occur during the life of some animals.

Neoteny—The retention of juvenile characteristics in sexually mature adult animals.

Species of newts

Newts in the genus *Notophthalmus* are found in eastern North America, while species of *Taricha* are found in the west. The most common of the eastern newts is the red–spotted newt (*Notophthalmus viridescens*), which has a wide distribution in the eastern United States and southeastern Canada. The striped newt (*N. perstriatus*) occurs only in northern Florida, while the black–spotted newt (*N. meridionalis*) occurs on the Gulf coast of Texas and northern Mexico. The most widespread species of western newt is the rough–skinned newt (*Taricha granulosa*) of the coastal states and British Columbia. The California newt (*T. torosa*) occurs in coastal California and southern Oregon, while the red–bellied newt has a relatively restricted distribution in northern, coastal California.

The most common newts of temperate parts of Eurasia are animals in the genus *Triturus*, for example, the smooth newt (*Triturus vulgaris*), the crested newt (*T. cristatus*), and the alpine newt (*T. alpestris*). These newts do not have an eft stage, although the adults may spend some time on land. The mountain newts (*Euproctus* spp.) are another European group of newts.

Newts and people

Newts have little direct economic value, other than sometimes being kept as unusual pets. The value of newts derives from the fact that they are ecologically important in their natural communities and that they have an interesting biology.

Although little is known about the conservation status of newts, most species of newts in North America are not endangered. However, the amount and quality of their habitat in many places has declined greatly because of human influences, and this has caused local populations to decrease. Like so many other aspects of our natural, ecological heritage, it is important that the

population status of newts be monitored to ensure that they do not become endangered as a result of the activities of humans.

See also Salamanders.

Further Reading:

Bishop, S. C. *Handbook of Salamanders.* New York: Cornell University Press, 1994.

Duellman, W. E., and L. Trueb. *Biology of Amphibians.* New York: McGraw–Hill, 1986.

Goin, C. J., O. B. Goin, and G. R. Zug. *Introduction to Herpetology.* 3d ed. San Francisco: Freeman, 1978.

Halliday, T. R., and K. Adler. *The Encyclopedia of Reptiles and Amphibians.* New York: Facts on File, 1986.

Smith, H. M. *Amphibians of North America.* New York: Golden Press, 1978.

Bill Freedman.

New World monkeys

The New World monkeys of Central and South America belong to the family Cebidae and to the family Callitrichidae (the marmosets and tamarins). The Cebidae, or capuchin–like monkeys, are distinguished from the marmosets and tamarins by their possession of nails instead of claws on most fingers and toes, and three molars instead of two on either side of each jaw. Finally, cebids tend to give birth to one offspring at a time, while the marmosets and tamarins tend to have twins.

Cebid monkeys include capuchins (*Cebus*), night monkeys or douroucoulis (*Aotus*), titis (*Callicebus*), squirrel monkeys (*Saimiri*), sakis (*Pithecia*), bearded sakis (*Chiropotes*), uakaris (*Cacajao*), howler monkeys (*Alouatta*), spider monkeys (*Ateles*), the woolly spider monkey (*Brachyteles arachnoides*), and woolly monkeys (*Lagothrix*).

Cebid monkeys are all arboreal tree dwellers that feed on leaves, fruit, birds' eggs, tree frogs, and bark-dwelling insects and their larvae. The night monkey or douroucouli (Aotus trivirgatus) is the only nocturnal New World monkey; the rest are diurnal, or active during the day.

The cebid monkeys vary in size from the squirrel monkey (*S. sciureus*) with a body length of 10 inches (25 cm) plus a 15–inch (38 cm) tail, and a weight of about 1.5 pounds (0.68 kg) to the woolly spider monkey, or muriqui, which has a body length of 18 inches (46 cm), plus a 30–inch (75 cm) tail, and weighs about

35 pounds (17.5 kg). The males and females of most species of cebid monkeys are approximately the same size, but the two sexes often have different colorings, a phenomenon known as sexual dimorphism.

The larger species of cebid monkeys have a prehensile tail with a naked patch at the base which has fingerprint–like ridges for sensitive gripping. The smaller, more agile monkeys do not have a prehensile tail, but can nevertheless readily leap from branch to branch.

The group territories of different species of New World monkeys often overlap, and as many as five different species have been found living in one tree, usually at different levels. Some monkey groups have been known to establish long–lasting "friendships" with the social groups of a different monkey species.

The average gestation period of New World monkeys is about 145 days, which is about three weeks shorter than the gestation period of Old World monkeys, although some New World monkeys gestate as long as 225 days. The breasts of cebid monkeys are located near the armpits so that they can be reached by the young riding on the mother's back. Unlike humans, apes, and most Old World monkeys, female New World monkeys do not menstruate. In general, the smaller species are monogamous, living in family groups with only one male and one female, while the larger species tend to be polygamous with one male and a harem of several females.

Capuchins

The best known New World monkey (the one often known as the "organ grinder" monkey) is the capuchin (genus *Cebus*). This small monkey got its name from the dark patch of hair on the top of its head that resembles the hood worn by Capuchin monks. The four species of capuchins are also sometimes called ringtail monkeys because they carry their tails with the end curved into a circle.

Capuchins occur throughout Central and South America, from Honduras to southern Brazil. Capuchins live in open or closed forests, low–lying rain forests, or forested mountainsides. Capuchins eat a lot of fruit and often maraud through cultivated orchards; when an animal locates a good fruit tree, it makes loud whistling calls that draw the rest of its group to the food source.

Capuchins measure about 18 inches (45 cm) long, with a tail of the same length. The tail is only semi–prehensile, in that the monkey can wrap its tail around a branch to anchor itself, but the tail cannot support the animal's weight. Capuchins are intelligent monkeys with relatively large brains.

The black–capped capuchin (*C. apella*) of Columbia has a mat of dark fur standing up on its crown, often forming "horns," while the remainder of the body is grayish–brown. This monkey cracks nuts against the branches on which it sits.

Other species of capuchins lack the mat of hair on the head and have more variation in their body color. The white–fronted capuchin (*C. albifrons*) is found in an area from Ecuador to Columbia and even on the Pacific shores, where they eat oysters and crabs. This monkey is light tan in color with little variation in shading. The white–throated capuchin (*C. capucinus*) found from Central America to Ecuador is also primarily pale with a white face, but its fur grades into black down its back, on the crown on its head, and on its hands and feet. The weeper or wedge–capped capuchin (*C. nigrivittatus*) has a crown patch that makes a dark point above the eyes.

The capuchins congregate in large groups of up to 30 members, including several males, who often bond together. After a 180–day gestation period, a single infant is born. Females mature sexually at age four, males at seven or eight. These friendly, intelligent monkeys have been known to live in captivity for more than 40 years.

The night monkey

The douroucouli (*Aotus trivirgatus*), or night monkey, is the only nocturnal monkey. It has a round, fur–fringed face, no obvious external ears, and big eyes surmounted by white triangles of face fur. The fur is brown–gray with an orangeish tone on the chest and abdomen, but the color can vary considerably.

The night monkey measures about 14 inches (36 cm) long, plus a 12 inch (30 cm) tail and weighs slightly more than two pounds (1 kg). Night monkeys are found in forested regions from Panama to Argentina. These monkeys sleep in holes in hollow trees and eat fruits, leaves, and some insects. Unlike most monkeys, it does not use its fingers to remove foreign bodies from the fur of a monkey it is grooming; instead, it sorts through the fur with fingers and then removes the offending bits with its teeth. The eyes of the night monkey lack the reflective layer behind the retina that most nocturnal mammals have.

Male night monkeys are very aggressive, and family groups of parents with one or two young avoid contact with other groups. The males scare away other night monkeys by arching their backs, spitting, leaving scent on branches, and growling with a variety of sounds that are made more resonant by an inflatable sac on the throat. After a 133–day gestation period, the females produce usually one young, which is then carried by the father. The young become sexually mature at about two years.

Titis

There are three species of titis all in the genus *Callicebus*. The name titi derives from the Aymara language, meaning "little cat." Titis all have long hair, which makes them appear to be larger than they actually are. The three species of titi are small, measuring about 10 inches (25 cm) long, plus a tail that may be an additional 12 to 20 inches (30–50 cm), and weigh less than two pounds (about 0.08 kg).

Two species of titi, the white–handed titi (*C. torquatus*) and the dusky titi (*C. moloch*), occupy the same forested region of the upper Amazon. The dusky titi lives along rivers and in wet forests, while the white–handed titi lives on higher ground. The white–handed titi likes heights so much that it sleeps on the branches of the tall emergent trees that stand above the high canopy of the rain forest, several hundred feet above the forest floor.

The white–handed titi is primarily dark red in color, with a white neck band and light–colored hands. The white collar and "gloves" earn it the nickname "widow monkey" because its coloration matches the traditional apparel of a Brazilian widow. The dusky titi is gray, leaning toward reddish, with lighter areas. The third species, the masked titi (*C. personatus*) inhabits a small area in the coastal forests of southern Brazil. This species has black hands and feet and dark fur on its face.

Titis are very vocal monkeys, chattering away with many different types of sounds for long periods, especially early in the morning. They live in family groups, and much of the chatter is between different groups. When resting on a branch, titis sit with all four feet tightly together, ready to leap for a new branch in a single movement if danger threatens. Often, when two titis sit side by side, they entwine their tails. The single young is born quite helpless and must be carried for the first three months of its life. That task falls to the father except for the first two days of the infant's life. After it begins to get around the trees on its own, the young one is still guarded, protected, taught, and played with by the father.

Squirrel monkeys

There are two species of squirrel monkeys, the smallest of the New World monkeys. The common squirrel monkey (*Saimiri sciureus*) lives throughout most of South America's rain forest region. The red–backed squirrel monkey (*S. oerstedii*) occurs only in Panama and Costa Rica in the middle levels of the forest, where they eat primarily fruit, though they also use their narrow, sharply pointed teeth to devour small insects. Some authorities regard the red–backed squirrel monkey as a subspecies of the common squirrel monkey.

The common squirrel monkey is the species often kept as a pet. Its thick, short fur is gray, the chest is white, its legs are yellow, and it has white circles around its eyes, giving it a widow's peak above the nose. A large dark oval of bare skin encircles the nose and mouth on the muzzle.

Squirrel monkeys do not have a prehensile tail, and all swinging on branches is done with their arms, while their tails tend to rest curled over their shoulder. The tail is considerably longer than their 12–inch (30 cm) body.

Squirrel monkey groups vary from 20 animals up to 200 individuals. When such a large group takes over a tree, the other cebid species, even the larger ones, are overwhelmed and forced to leave. The large squirrel monkey social group has very complex social relationships among individuals and subgroups. Some subgroups consist only of males, who remain by themselves except during mating season. This precludes a male from taking care of its single offspring, unlike most of the species of New World monkeys. The mother monkey's female friends may help raise and care for an infant. A single infant squirrel monkey is born after a gestation period that varies from 152 to 172 days. It becomes independent at about a year and sexually matures at three years for females and five for males. Squirrel monkeys have been known to live almost 15 years.

In the 1960s, the red–backed squirrel monkey was imported into the United States by the thousands for use as pets. Capture for the pet trade together with the destruction of the rain forest has severely endangered the wild populations of this monkey. Today, the United States government has outlawed the importation of primates except for legitimate scientific purposes.

The saki family

The sakis, bearded sakis, and uakaris belong to the subfamily Pitheciinae and all have long shaggy hair. These monkeys of the Amazon basin and farther north eat primarily fruit and seeds. They bear one offspring, probably taken care of by the mother. The two species of sakis (*Pithecia*) have nostrils that are set farther apart than those of any other New World monkey. They differ from the two species of bearded sakis in several ways. The tail of the saki is as long as its 16–inch (40 cm) body length and is thick, bushy, somewhat baseball–bat shaped, and tapers to a pointed tip. The tail of the bearded saki is blunt at the tip. Sakis live in small family groups of only three or four individuals and prefer the lower reaches of the rain forest trees and may even venture onto the ground. The bearded saki stays wholly in the tree and prefers the upper layers, where a group of up to about 30 members stays in close touch. Sakis are known to eat birds and small mammals, something that the bearded sakis never do.

The male white–faced saki (*P. pithecia*) of the Guianas and northeastern Brazil has a stark white face set in a circular hood of long black hair and a triangle of black fur from between the eyes to the nose and mouth. The female and young of the white–faced monkey do not have white faces, rather, they are dark brown or black with some whitish fur around the face. The adult female has a line of white fur running from the eyes and around the mouth and has a reddish tone to the chest and abdomen.

The monk, or hairy saki (*P. monachus*), of the upper Amazon is colored very much like the female white–faced saki. The fur on its head curves forward as if forming a monk's hood that partially conceals the face.

Bearded sakis tend to look as if they have just come from a beauty salon. Their short, soft fur is very smooth, their full beards appear to be carefully trimmed, and poufs of longer fur above the eyes are smoothly bouffant. They have longer canine teeth than many monkeys which they use to break up tough fruit to reach the seeds inside.

The endangered black–bearded, or red–backed, bearded saki (*Chiropotes satanas*) lives between the Orinoco and Amazon rivers and has bare red skin patches on its face. The white–nosed bearded saki (C. albinasus) lives primarily south of the Amazon.

Uakaris are slightly larger than sakis but, unlike all other New World monkeys, have a very small tail. These monkeys live strictly along river banks. The red uakari (*Cacajao rubicundus*) is particularly ugly, with a vivid, naked, red face, and a bald head which is naked back to behind its ears, where a rust–colored coat of very long, shaggy fur begins. The bald uakari, also called the white uakari (*C. calvus*), has a similar appearance but has yellowish or silvery fur. Some authorities regard *C. rubicundus* as a subspecies of *C. Calvus*. The black–headed uakari (*C. melanocephalus*) has black fur on its head, and its arms, hands, and feet are also black, while its legs and tail are red. The yellow–brown body is not as raggedly shaggy as in the other uakaris. This species appears to be thriving in western Brazil but may be endangered in the rest of its range.

The name uakari (also spelled *ouakari*) was given to these animals by the Tupi people of the Amazon basin. The monkeys live at all levels in the rain forest and rarely descend to the ground. They are better at leaping between branches than many monkeys. The social groups may number up to 30 individuals. Female uakaris give birth to a single offspring every other year after a gestation of about 180 days.

Howler monkeys

The six species of howler monkeys in the subfamily Alouattinae possess a throat swelling with a special form of hyoid bone (the bone supporting the tongue muscles) that allows them to produce a deep, thundering roar which can be heard more than two miles away. Because of this throat swelling, their lower jaw juts forward more than in most other species of monkey. This jutting is not as noticeable as it might be, however, because the howlers are bearded. The throat is larger in the males than the females, and it is largest in the dominant male in a group of monkeys containing several males.

Howler monkeys are quite large, weighing up to 20 lbs (9 kg) and measuring 33 inches (91 cm) long, with an equally long and very strong prehensile tail, which is naked on the end third. Howler monkeys use their prehensile tails to attach themselves firmly to branches, and they may hang from their tails to keep their hands free while feeding on leaves. The mantled howler monkey (*A. palliata*) has to eat so many leaves to get the nourishment it needs that its intestines make up one–third of the volume of its body. The mantled monkey is found from southern Mexico south to Ecuador and has a black body with a gold mantle, or fringe, down the sides.

Howler monkey species vary primarily in their coloring. The Guatemalan or Mexican black howler monkey (*A. villosa*) is completely black, from the bare base to the tip of its tail. All the howlers have naked black faces, but the black–and–red howler (*A. belzebul*) has red hands and feet as well as tail tip. The red howler (*A. seniculus*) is bright copper. Only the black howler (*A. caraya*) has different forms of the males and females. The young of black howler monkeys are born golden–brown, and the males turn black as they mature. A howler group contains up to 20 monkeys, with two to four males and five to ten females in the group. A single young howler is born after a gestation of about 180 days. It clings to the mother's abdomen for the first several weeks until its tail matures enough for it to be able to cling to its mother's tail, when it moves around and rides her back, where it remains for a year or more.

Howler females reach maturity at about five years, and males at six to eight years.

The mantled, Guatemalan, or brown howler monkey (*A. fusca*) is an endangered species. Although some howlers live higher in the mountains, this lowland species is losing its habitat to logging, and individual animals are easily caught because their loud voices betray their location.

Spider monkeys and woolly monkeys

The subfamily Atelinae includes the spider monkeys, the woolly spider monkeys, and the woolly monkeys. These monkeys are as large as howler monkeys but thinner.

Spider monkeys (*Ateles*) are found in approximately the same range as the howler monkeys, though spider monkeys occur farther north in Mexico and extend south to Brazil. Howler monkeys may eat slightly immature fruit, while spider monkeys wait until it is truly ripe. The arms of spider monkeys are longer than their legs, giving them an ungainly spider–like appearance. Spider monkeys are extremely agile and can walk along branches, hang upside down, leap sideways, and even leap long distances downward. Spider monkeys are very adroit at swinging from branches by arm to arm movements, also called brachiation, an ability that requires special flexibility in the shoulders. Their tails are quite thick toward the base but slender and with a naked patch with ridges toward the tip which makes it quite sensitive.

The long tail is especially useful because, unlike many other monkeys, spider monkeys do not have an opposable thumb, meaning they are not very adept with their hands. Their skeletons show the remains of the thumb, and some individual animals have a slight protrusion where a thumb would be. Spiders live in large groups, though they often tend to break up into smaller family subgroups.

All spider monkeys have fairly long, shaggy fur, which is mostly dark brown or black. The fur on the head is brushed forward. The black–handed, or Geoffroy's spider monkey (*A. geoffroyi*) of Central America has golden, reddish, or bronze fur on its body and usually black hands and feet. The long–haired spider monkey (*A. belzebuth*) of the upper Amazon has chest and abdomen of a lighter color than the rest of its body. The brown–headed spider monkey (*A. fusciceps*) lives from Panama to Ecuador, between the ranges of the other two species.

In coastal parts of Brazil, the spider monkey's territory is taken over by the woolly spider monkey or muriqui (*Brachyteles arachnoides*). The woolly spider monkey is the heaviest monkey in Brazil, weighing 35 lbs (16 kg); it has the chunky body and thick fur of the woolly monkey but lacks a thumb. It is lighter brown in color than most of the relatives.

The woolly spider monkey's social groups, which used to number about 30 or 40, are now down to six to 20. Within a group's territory, the individuals separate by gender and can frequently be seen hugging each other. There may be only a few hundred woolly spider monkeys which have been reduced from half a million individuals when Europeans first arrived in South America. The large size and gentle nature of the woolly spider monkey makes them easy targets for hunting, and this species is now on the endangered species list.

The two species of woolly monkeys (*Lagothrix*) live in western South America, mostly at fairly high altitudes. Their thick fur makes the woolly monkeys look larger and stouter than they really are. The common woolly monkey (*L. lagothricha*), also known as Humboldt's monkey, is colored gray, black, or brown. The yellow–tailed or Hendee's woolly monkey (*L. flavicauda*) is deep red–brown with yellow fur along its tail and around its genitals. This monkey lives in a small mountainous area in northern Peru. The yellow–tailed woolly monkey was thought to be extinct from hunting for food and the pet trade, but a small wild population was rediscovered in the 1970s, and this species is now being bred in captivity.

Endangered New World monkeys

The Atlantic rain forest in Brazil has been called one of "the most devastated primate habitat in the world." Sixteen of the 21 primate species and subspecies that live in that ravaged Brazilian ecosystem are found nowhere else and will disappear along with their habitat. The human population of the region continues to put pressure on the forests, which are cut down for living space and firewood. The endangered woolly spider monkey has become the symbol of the conservationists in Brazil.

Other endangered species include the southern bearded saki (*Chiropotes satanas*), the yellow–tailed woolly monkey (*Lagothrix flavicauda*), and the Central American squirrel monkey (*Saimiri oerstedii*). As more and more of the rain forest is cleared, other New World monkeys could be added to the endangered species list.

Further Reading:

Knight, Linsay. *The Sierra Club Book of Small Mammals.* San Francisco: Sierra Club Books for Children, 1993.

Napier, J.R., and Napier, P.H.. *The Natural History of the Primates.* Cambridge, MA: The MIT Press, 1985.

Napier, Prue. *Monkeys and Apes: A Grosset All–Color Guide.* New York: Grosset & Dunlap, 1972.

Kerrod, Robin. *Mammals: Primates, Insect–Eaters and Baleen Whales.* Encyclopedia of the Animal World series. New York: Facts on File, 1988.

Peterson, Dale. *The Deluge and the Ark: A Journey into Primate Worlds.* Boston: Houghton Mifflin, 1989.

Preston-Mafham, Rod and Ken Preston-Mafham. *Primates of the World.* New York: Fact of File, 1992.

Jean F. Blashfield

Niche

The niche is an important ecological notion that considers the role that an organism or species plays in its community. Important aspects of the niche are environmental tolerance, use of resources, activities, and interactions with other organisms. Niche is an integrating concept because it considers organisms within the context of their biological tolerance of environmental extremes but is significantly modified by the influence of their interactions with other organisms, particularly through competition.

It must be understood that the niche is an abstract concept. Although niches cannot be seen or felt, ecologists can nevertheless understand their dimensions on the basis of environmental tolerances and opportunities as is discussed below.

The multidimensional niche

Species have limited abilities to tolerate extremes of environmental conditions. In other words, for all environmental factors there are upper and lower bounds of intensity that organisms can endure. For example, a particular species of plant or animal might be able to survive over an extended period of time within a zone of temperature bounded by certain high and low extremes. Extended exposures to hotter or colder temperatures cannot be tolerated, and the species will not occur in such environments. The boundaries of temperature tolerance can be represented as a component of the niche of the species in a single dimension—that of environmental temperature.

There are similar boundaries of tolerance for other environmental factors including climatic, chemical, and habitat variables, each of which can be similarly represented as a component of the larger niche in a single dimension. Conceptually, the niche of the species can be viewed as a multidimensional composite in which all of the boundaries of tolerance of diverse environmental influences are assembled into a single, multivariate factor. This is known as the fundamental niche, or the multidimensional zone (also known as a hypervolume) of environmental tolerance, in which an individual can potentially survive or in which a species can maintain viable populations.

However, in natural ecosystems species are rarely faced with habitat opportunities that are only defined by the boundaries of their tolerance of diverse environmental factors. The actual utilization of the fundamental niche is also significantly influenced by ecological interactions of various sorts. For example, other species may have similar tolerances of environmental factors. These species will seek to utilize some portion of the environmental opportunities that are available, resulting in the ecological interaction known as competition. Competition exerts a very important influence on the ability of species to optimally exploit their fundamental niche and on the structure of ecological communities. If species have very similar fundamental niches, then competition between them will be intense. In extreme cases this can cause one species to be eliminated from the community through a process known as competitive exclusion. More often, however, species are displaced by competition to particular zones within their fundamental niche.

Exploitation of the fundamental niche is also constrained by other ecological interactions such as predation, parasitism, and disease. All of these can restrict the opportunities for species to exploit their fundamental niche in an optimized fashion. Ecologists define the realized niche as the multidimensional hypervolume of environmental factors that species actually manage to exploit in nature in view of the powerful influences of competition, predation, parasitism, and disease.

Species must be present in the habitat in order to realize the benefits of some part of the range of their fundamental niche. If a location containing potentially suitable habitat cannot be colonized by a species, then it cannot utilize that part of its fundamental niche.

Realized niches are variable over time because they can respond to changes in the nature of ecological interactions. The introduction of a new, more capable competitor can eliminate an original species from its ecological community through competitive exclusion. A similar effect can be caused by introduced predators, parasites, and diseases. In contrast, the elimination of an important competitor, predator, parasite, or disease can release a species from a previously controlling influence, allowing it to expand the dimensions of its realized niche.

In general, the realized niche of species does not represent the environment conditions to which they are optimally adapted. The combined influences of diverse ecological interactions commonly relegate species to sub–optimal portions of their fundamental niche.

Ecological communities can be viewed as populations of various species that co–occur in space and time. Each species in the community maintains its populations by utilizing the opportunities available in its realized niche within the larger habitat. The number of species that can be maintained in the community and their relative abundance are determined by the diversity of niche opportunities, their stability over time, and the intensity of ecological interactions. The influences of these factors are optimized in old–growth tropical rain forests which maintain a greater diversity of species than any other terrestrial ecosystem. Among oceanic ecosystems, species diversity is greatest in coral reefs.

What is the niche of humans?

Humans also have fundamental and realized niches. Like other species, the fundamental niche of humans is bounded by their biological tolerance of extremes of environmental conditions.

However, unlike other species humans have developed an extraordinary ability to utilize technology to

KEY TERMS

Community—In ecology, a community is an assemblage of populations of different species that occur together in the same place and at the same time.

Competition—An ecological interaction between organisms of the same or different species associated with the need for mutually required resources that occur in supplies that are smaller than the potential demand.

Niche—The role that an individual or species plays in its community, including its activities, resource demands, and interactions with other organisms.

mitigate extremes of environmental conditions, allowing survival in otherwise inhospitable places. In this sense, humans have utilized technological innovations to greatly expand the boundaries of their realized niche. Humans can now sustain themselves in Antarctica, on mountain tops, in the driest deserts, in phenomenal densities in cities, and even in spacecraft.

Humans have also expanded the dimensions of their realized niche by managing the intensity of their interactions with other species. Humans control their own competitors, predators, parasites, and diseases, thereby reducing the constraints that these biological stressors exert on the realized, human niche. Humans also manage the ecological constraints of their mutualistic plants and animals such as agricultural cows, pigs, chickens, and plant crops.

The phenomenal expansion of their realized niche has allowed a great increase in the abundance of humans. For most of their evolutionary history, humans engaged in a hunting and gathering lifestyle, and their global population was probably a few million individuals. The first significant expansions of the realized human niche involved the domestication of fire and the development of primitive tools and agricultural methods, all of which allowed populations to increase. During the past several centuries of extraordinary technological development, populations of humans have grown especially quickly, and in 1995 almost six billion people were alive on Earth. This growth has been accomplished through expansion of the realized niche of industrial humans.

However, it must be understood that the remarkable technological expansions of the realized niche of humans require large and continual subsidies of energy, food, and other resources. These are needed in order to maintain the colonization of difficult environments and to continue the control of constraining ecological influences. If access to these resources is somehow diminished, then the ability of humans to colonize and manage their environment is diminished as well, or it collapses.

See also: Biodiversity, Competition, Symbiosis.

Further Reading:

Begon, M., Harper, J.L., and Townsend, C.R. *Ecology. Individuals, Populations and Communities*. 2nd ed. London: Blackwell Sci. Pub., 1990.

Ricklefs, R.E. *Ecology*. New York: W.H. Freeman and Co., 1990.

Bill Freedman

Neutrino see **Subatomic particles**

Nicotine

Nicotine (chemical formula $C_{10}H_{14}N_2$) is an alkaloid found primarily in leaves of the tobacco plant *(Nicotiana tabacum)*. Many societies throughout the world have prized nicotine for its mood–altering properties: It can produce either relaxation or arousal, depending on the user's state. Users commonly burn the leaves and inhale the smoke; some, however, may chew the leaves, while others either "snuff" finely ground leaves into their noses or place them between their cheeks and gums.

Nicotine is highly addictive. Nicotine addiction is also very difficult to break—only 20% of those who attempt to quit smoking are successful on their first try. To relieve the physical and psychological symptoms of nicotine withdrawal—restlessness, anxiety, irritability, difficulty in concentrating, and a craving for the drug—pharmaceutical companies now offer nicotine replacement systems. These systems deliver nicotine in a less addicting pattern that allows the dose to be gradually decreased and eventually eliminated. Even with nicotine replacement, however, successful quitting requires determination and psychological support.

Like most alkaloids, nicotine exerts its effects at receptors for chemicals that transmit nerve impulses. Specifically, nicotine acts at the nicotinic receptor class for the transmitter acetylcholine (the other class of acetylcholine receptor is the muscarinic, also named for

a compound—a mushroom derivative—that triggers only receptors of that class). Outside the brain, nicotinic receptors are found primarily in the sympathetic nervous system, while muscarinic receptors are found in the parasympathetic nervous system. Thus, nicotine use triggers sympathetic nervous system effects throughout the body.

These effects largely account for nicotine's unfavorable impact on the user's health. People pay a great deal of attention to the danger of lung cancer, which results when smokers inhale the tar from burning tobacco leaves. Yet fewer people die of lung cancer than from nicotine–induced heart attacks and strokes.

Among nicotine's effects on the body is constricting small arteries. This raises the blood pressure and makes the heart work harder, as does the faster heart rate that nicotine produces. Yet, because nicotine also constricts the arteries supplying the heart muscle, the organ receives less blood. When buildups of fatty plaque have already narrowed a person's heart arteries, this may be enough to trigger heart pain (angina) or an actual heart attack. At the same time, elevated blood pressure increases the risk of a stroke, with possible disability or death to follow.

Nicotine use can also worsen other circulatory problems, including poor circulation in the hands and feet and some men's difficulty in obtaining an erection.

See also Addiction; Cigarette smoke.

Nickel see **Element, chemical**

Nielsbohrium see **Element, transuranium**

Nighthawks see **Caprimulgids; Goatsuckers**

Nightshade

The family of plants known as nightshades is also known as the Solanacene. It is a large group of plants composed of more than 2,000 species and 75 different genera. Most nightshades are herbs, but some species are shrubs, vines, or trees. Most of the members of the nightshade family are native to parts of Central and South America, but about 100 nightshades can be found in North America.

Some species of nightshades are important sources of food, such as tomatoes, chili and bell peppers, pota-

A red missile pepper plant.

either fleshy like a tomato, or a dry fruit called a capsule, as in the tobacco plant.

Edible species of nightshades

The nightshade family supplies some important dietary staples. The tomato, potato, eggplant, and pepper all belong to this plant family, although they are each representative of different genera within the family. The botanical name of the tomato is *Lycopersicum esculentum*, the potato's is *Solanum tuberosum*, the eggplant is *Solanum melongena*, and peppers are named *Capsicum annuum, Capsicum frutescens longum, Capsicum fructescens conoides*: bell pepper, cayenne pepper, and chili pepper, respectively. With the exception of the potato, which is a tuber, the fruits of this group of plants are used as vegetables, for seasonings, sauces, and soups.

Tomato

The tomato is eaten in many countries around the world. This was not always the case, since the reputation of nightshades as poisonous plants preceded the introduction of tomatoes as food into diets in Europe and the United States. Native to Central America and Mexico, the tomato was cultivated and eaten by aboriginal inhabitants in those regions before the Spanish came to the Americas. It is referred to as a food in Italy as early as 1544. It is believed that the Italians may have gotten the tomato from the Turks, and it was known originally as the Moor's apple. After its introduction into France, the tomato became known as the love apple. The French later introduced the tomato into the New Orleans diet when they owned the Louisiana Territory. By 1597 it was being grown in England.

The reputation of the tomato as a nutritious and delicious food took a long time to gain acceptance. During the sixteenth century, some herbalists were writing that the tomato was a harmful food, but in Italy tomatoes were being dried in the sun and eaten without any ill effects. By the eighteenth century the tomato was being used in soups in England, Spain, and Portugal.

The tomato was introduced into the United States as a food around 1710, but did not become significant there until it was made into catsup in New Orleans in the latter part of the eighteenth century. Today tomatoes are a common element in American, Mexican, South American, European, and Asian diets. It is difficult to imagine a diet without pizza, spaghetti, salsa, or catsup. Besides its usefulness as fiber in the diet, the tomato is also an excellent source of vitamin C. Tomatoes come in a range of colors from red to yellow and, in size, from cherry tomatoes to large beefsteaks.

toes, and eggplant. A number of nightshade species have been used medicinally for thousands of years, and some species have narcotic and poisonous characteristics. Tobacco is a nightshade that has had a tremendous economic impact and has been a source of controversy since the early 1960s because of the link between smoking tobacco and several deadly diseases.

Other species in the nightshade family are grown as garden ornamentals. Well–known nightshade flowers include Browallia and Petunia, and the Chinese lantern is often found as an outdoor garden plant and sometimes as a potted house plant.

Some of the common characteristics of nightshades are alternating, simple leaves that are often hairy in texture and may have a strong odor. The size and shape of the leaves, however, vary greatly within the family. The flowers of these plants generally have a tubular shape, often with five petals attached, as in the petunia. The stamens of the flowers are connected at their base. When the ovary of the flower matures into a fruit, it is

A partially cut field of tobacco in southern Wisconsin.

Potato

The part of the potato plant, *Solanum tuberosum*, that is eaten is called a tuber. A tuber is a bud at the end of an underground stem, not a root, that becomes enlarged. Native to Peru and Chile, the potato had been eaten by the people living in that region for 7,000 years. The people of the Andes ate cooked tubers, and they also dried potatoes and ground them into flour. After the Americas were discovered by Europeans, potatoes were introduced into Europe and then later into North and Central America, where they had not been previously known by the native Americans who lived there. Many of the types that are common today were known by the Andean people, who also had blue, purple, and yellow varieties.

When the potato was first introduced into Europe, it was believed to cause diseases and to be toxic. In fact, there are toxins in the potato plant, but only in its leaves and flowers—not in the tuber. Potatoes became a dietary staple in Europe sometime during the eighteenth century. Its hardiness (it grows at high elevations in the Andes in a cold climate) helped to establish the potato as a crop that would help prevent famine.

Historically, the potato blight in Ireland during the mid–eighteenth century was the cause of a famine that led to mass emigration by poor Irish peasants to North America between 1846 and 1851. The destruction of the potato crop in Ireland, the staple for the mass of poor Irish, was caused by a fungus disease. Potatoes are also vulnerable to insect infestations.

Today various insecticides are used to control diseases that attack potato plants, and efforts have been made to produce a strain of potato that is resistant to disease. Experiments with hybrids is one avenue of research. More than 300 million tons of potatoes are produced around the world, with Russia, China, Poland, and the United States as the biggest producers of potatoes.

Eggplant and peppers

Sometime between 900 and 1200 A.D., the eggplant became popular in North Africa and Arabia. Thereafter it spread around the Mediterranean to Spain, Italy, Greece, and other countries. Spain introduced eggplant to the Americas, but today it is eaten mostly as a specialty dish, like eggplant parmigiana, ratatouille, and caponata, an eggplant relish. It is one of the important vegetables in the Japanese diet, and in India it is used in curry dishes or is pickled.

Nutritionally, the eggplant is primarily water with some carbohydrate, protein, mineral, and vitamin content. The fruit of the eggplant is considered a berry. In the seventeenth century its size and shape was somewhat different from its appearance today. Now it is cultivated for a gourd–like shape and the size is on the average about four inches in diameter and eight inches long. The skin is a thin, smooth, dark purple color. The plant of the eggplant is shrub–like and about 2–3 ft (.6 to .9 m) high. It has large gray, rough leaves and violet flowers.

Bell, cayenne, chili, and other varieties of peppers are used in various ways. Chili peppers are popular in Mexico and in the southwest United States. They are used as a seasoning, as cayenne, and a number of other varieties are also used to spice up dishes. Tabasco sauce and paprika are seasonings that come from varieties of pepper plants. Bell peppers are used both as a culinary addition to a dish, much like onions are used, and as a vegetable. Peppers are a good source of vitamin C. Albert von Szent–Gyorgyi received the Nobel Prize in 1937 for his discoveries regarding vitamin C and credits paprika peppers for helping him in his research.

Medicine

Henbane, Jimson weed, mandrake, and belladonna are the common names of nightshades that have medicinal uses. These plants contain alkaloids, substances that contain nitrogen, which can be isolated from the plant and used as drugs. The narcotic property of mandrake can produce sleep and may have been used as an anesthetic in ancient times. It is a small plant that has most of its leaves at the base. Its flowers are yellow–green in color, and it has a thick carrot–shaped root, the part that is used to produce medicine. While it is not used pharmaceutically anymore, some related plants are still a source of drugs.

Henbane has from 12 to 15 species, mostly native to the Mediterranean. Black henbane is the one that is used mainly for drugs, its principal alkaloid being hyoscyamine. It is a small annual or perennial with hairy, coarsely lobed leaves with an unpleasant odor. It is used as a pain reliever for spasms and as a sedative. Henbane is also sometimes used as an antidote to mercury poisoning and in the treatment of morphine addiction.

Jimson weed also contains the hyoscyamine alkaloid and can cause a temporary loss of vision, convulsions, dry skin, and dilated pupils. Some of its other common names are devil's apple, thorn apple, and stinkweed. Its botanical name is *Datura stramonium*. It grows profusely as a weed in this country. Like the henbane it has an unpleasant odor and coarsely lobed leaves with prickly capsules that contain its seeds. Its alkaloids are atropine, hyoscyamine, and scopolamine, and it is used medicinally in various treatments.

Belladonna, also called deadly nightshade, gets its name from its ability to dilate the pupils of the eyes. In the past women used belladonna for this purpose because they felt it made them more attractive. The word means "beautiful lady" in Italian. The plant is a medium–sized herb with long, dark green leaves and small purple flowers. The alkaloids in the plant come from the leaves and the root. Scopolamine and atropine are the main substances used from belladonna in medicine. They have been used as analgesics, anesthesia, and are especially useful in examining eyes. Atropine is also an antidote for some poisons.

Tobacco

A number of the nightshades that were used for medicine in the past became problematic because of adverse side effects, but they no longer stir the kind of controversy that tobacco has stirred in this country over the past several decades. Europeans discovered tobacco and the pleasures of smoking when they conquered the New World. The Spanish and the English colonists grew tobacco for export to their native countries as early as the seventeenth century. During the years of its early use it had the reputation to cure many diseases.

In its early use it was mainly smoked in pipes. In the eighteenth century snuff was a popular form of tobacco. Chewing tobacco was popular during the late nineteenth century, when cigars and cigarettes were also developed. There was some early opposition to smoking from religious leaders, and in places like China and the Near East, laws were passed to prohibit the importation of tobacco.

KEY TERMS

Alkaloid—Substances isolated from plants that contain nitrogen and can be used as drugs or poisons.

Capsule—A dried fruit as in the tobacco plant.

Dietary staple—An important food that is a mainstay of a person's diet.

Narcotic—A drug that depresses the central nervous system and is usually addictive.

Solanacene—Botanical term for nightshade plants.

Solanum tuberosum—Botanical name for the potato plant.

Toxin—A poisonous substance.

Tuber—A swollen bud of an underground stem, such as a potato.

Besides the growing of tobacco, its advertising has also become a major industry in this country. Tobacco manufacturers spend a larger percentage of their money in advertising than manufacturers of other products. Today in the United States there is much opposition to the type of advertising that takes place. Many opponents feel that the advertising is directed at young smokers who are the most vulnerable to smoking addiction.

While the United States is the leading producer of tobacco products, it is cultivated in many other parts of the world. The process of growing and curing tobacco before it is manufactured into cigarettes is a complex one and requires a considerable amount of hand labor. The plants are from 2 to 9 ft (.6 to 2.7 m) tall, with white, pink, or red flowers. The cultivated plants today have extremely large leaves.

The main areas of opposition to tobacco smoking are links to life–threatening illness such as heart disease and lung cancer. Once addicted to tobacco smoking, the smoker usually finds it difficult to stop because of physical dependence on nicotine, the harmful substance in tobacco. Nicotine acts on the nervous system as a stimulant. It increases the heart rate and narrows the blood vessels as well. People who try to stop smoking usually go through a series of withdrawal symptoms that can include irritability, restlessness, anxiety, and insomnia, which often make it difficult for the smoker to quit.

Further Reading:

Coffey, Timothy. *North American Wildflowers*. New York: Facts on File, 1993.

D'Arcy, W.G., ed. *Solanaceae: Biology and Systematics.* New York: Columbia University Press, 1985.

Gregerson, Jon. *The Good Earth.* Vancouver: Whitecap Books, 1992.

Heiser, Charles B., Jr. *The Fascinating World of the Nightshades.* New York: Dover Publications, 1987.

Westrich, LoLo. *California Herbal Remedies.* Houston: Gulf Publishing, 1989.

Vita Richman

Nightjars see **Caprimulgids; Goatsuckers**
Niobium see **Element, chemical**

Nitric acid

Nitric acid (HNO_3) is a colorless, liquid acid widely used in the manufacturing of explosives and fertilizers. When dissolved in water, molecules of nitric acid separate (or dissociate) into hydrogen ions (H^+) and nitrate ions (NO_3^-). The fact that nearly every nitric acid molecule dissociates is what makes nitric acid a strong acid. Nitric acid is often the starting material in the industrial production of nitrates for fertilizers.

Plants take up nitrogen from the soil in the form of ammonium ions (NH_4^+) and nitrate ions, and along with carbon containing molecules made during photosynthesis, these ions are used to synthesize amino acids, from which proteins are made. Within the past hundred years the demand for nitrogen fertilizers has grown dramatically as the need for fertilizers for agriculture has grown. The natural manner in which nitrates reach the soil involves the reaction of nitrogen gas and oxygen gas in the atmosphere to form nitrogen dioxide gas (NO_2), which then reacts with atmospheric water, making nitric acid, which provides a natural source of nitrates in water and soil.

During World War I, the Germans were very interested in using ammonium nitrate (NH_4NO_3), a salt of nitric acid, as an explosive. Many organic nitrates such as nitroglycerine and TNT are also highly explosive. Nitric acid is made by the reaction of ammonia with oxygen gas. The nitric acid which is produced can then be used to make a variety of compounds. This is a process that has allowed large amounts of fertilizers to be produced relatively inexpensively.

Nitric acid is also formed from the reaction of nitrogen oxides produced during the combustion (burning) of fossil fuels in automobile engines. These nitrogen oxides react with water in the atmosphere and form nitric acid, one cause of acid rain. High levels of nitrates in drinking water can contribute to the formation of nitrosamines, a group of carcinogenic (cancer causing) compounds.

See also Acids and bases; Explosives; Nitrogen cycle.

Nitrification

Nitrification is an aerobic microbial process by which specialized bacteria oxidize ammonium to nitrite and then to nitrate. Nitrification is a very important part of the nitrogen cycle, because for most plants nitrate is the preferred chemical form of nitrogen uptake from soil or water.

Nitrification is a two–step process. The first stage is the oxidation of ammonium (NH_4^+) to nitrite (NO_2^-), a function carried out by bacteria in the genus *Nitrosomonas*. The nitrite formed is rapidly oxidized to nitrate (NO_3^-) by bacteria in the genus *Nitrobacter*. Because nitrate and nitrite are much more mobile in soils than ammonium, nitrification can be viewed as a process that mobilizes nitrogen, making it more available for plant uptake but potentially allowing it to leach from the ecosystem. The latter is an undesirable attribute of nitrification because fixed nitrogen is an important component of the nutrient capital of ecosystems. In addition, large concentrations of nitrate or nitrite can pollute groundwater and surface waters.

Nitrification as a bacterial process

Nitrification is an autotrophic process during which bacteria couple energy release from the oxidation of ammonium with the biosynthesis of simple inorganic molecules such as carbon dioxide and water into organic compounds. Because chemical energy is being tapped by the bacteria, nitrification is known as a chemoautotrophic process rather than photoautotrophic, as when green plants utilize sunlight in their photosynthetic productivity.

Only a few types of aerobic bacteria are capable of performing the chemical reactions of nitrification. The first step in nitrification is the oxidation of ammonium to nitrite. This function is mostly carried out by bacteria in the genus *Nitrosomonas*, with lesser activity by the genera *Nitrosospira*, *Nitrosococcus*, and *Nitrosolobus*. The nitrite formed by these bacteria does not accumulate in soil because it is rapidly oxidized to nitrate. This stage is mostly accomplished by bacteria in the genus *Nitrobacter*, along with *Nitrosospira* and *Nitrosococcus*.

Environmental influences on nitrification

Any chemical reaction requires substrate molecules, which in the case of nitrification is ammonium. The most important natural source of this substrate is ammonium released from decaying organic matter through the microbial process of ammonification, during which this ion is produced as a waste product of the oxidation of various forms of organic nitrogen such as proteins. There are also inputs of ammonium from the atmosphere, both dissolved in precipitation and through the dry deposition of gas. The biological fixation of atmospheric dinitrogen (or nitrogen gas, N_2) into ammonia can be another important source of input, especially when legumes are cultivated in agriculture as well as in some natural ecosystems, for example, sites dominated by alders (*Alnus* spp.). Ammonium may also be added to agricultural soils in large quantities when inorganic fertilizers are used or when manure or sludges are spread on fields.

The genera of bacteria that are responsible for nitrification are highly sensitive to acidity, so this process does not occur at significant rates in acidic soil or water, especially in those with pH less than 5.5. Plants that grow in acidic habitats such as bogs and some forests must be capable of utilizing ammonium as their source of nitrogen nutrition because nitrate is not available in those habitats. Because *Nitrobacter* is somewhat more sensitive to acidity and some other stresses than *Nitrosomonas*, nitrite can accumulate under some conditions.

Interestingly, nitrification is a process that actually generates acidity, equivalent to two H^+ ions for every ion of NO_3^- produced by the oxidation of NH_4^+. However, the ammonification of organic nitrogen to ammonium consumes one H^+, as does the uptake of nitrate from soil by plant roots. Therefore, nitrification only acidifies soils if the ammonium substrate is added directly, for example through fertilization or by atmospheric deposition, or if the nitrate is not taken up by plants and leaches from the soil.

The nitrifying bacteria are also very sensitive to high temperatures. Their populations are substantially reduced by exposures to temperatures of 212° F (100° C), and they are virtually eliminated at temperatures hotter than 284° F (140° C). As a result, nitrifying bacteria are often uncommon after a ground fire. The rates of nitrification are correspondingly small, even if there is an abundant substrate of ammonium.

The rate of nitrification is known to decline during some ecological successions. This is probably caused by an increasing acidification of the ecosystem and perhaps also by the presence of organic chemicals that inhibit the nitrifying bacteria. Decreasing nitrification has been observed during the succession of abandoned pastures into old–field conifer forests in eastern North America as well as in conifer forest successions elsewhere. A potential benefit of decreasing nitrification during succession is that this causes the major form of soluble, inorganic nitrogen to become ammonium, an ion that is bound readily by soils and is not easily leached. However, nitrification does not always decrease during succession; it is known to increase when some abandoned farmlands develop into an angiosperm forest which tends not to acidify soils as much as most conifer forests.

Humans and nitrification

The use of nitrogen–containing fertilizers in agriculture has a strong influence on nitrification and on the nitrogen cycle more broadly. Rates of fertilization in intensive agricultural systems often exceed 500 kg of nitrogen per hectare per year. Much of the nitrogen addition occurs as ammonia or ammonium which is the substrate for nitrification, so this process can occur very rapidly, and nitrate may be present in large concentrations.

If soils with large nitrate concentrations become wet and anaerobic conditions develop, the rate of denitrification is greatly increased. Denitrification represents a loss of fixed nitrogen capital, and the emitted nitrous oxide (N_2O) may contribute to an enhancement of Earth's greenhouse effect.

If the availability of nitrate overwhelms the ability of the plant crop and soil microbes to assimilate this nutrient, some of the nitrate will leach from the site into groundwater and surface waters such as streams and rivers. This can contribute to the increased productivity of surface waters through eutrophication. In addition, large concentrations of nitrate in groundwater are of great concern for several reasons. Nitrate can react with amino compounds to form nitrosamines, which are poisonous and carcinogenic. Nitrate itself is not particularly toxic, but it can be chemically reduced in the gut of animals to form toxic nitrite. This reaction occurs especially rapidly in the relatively alkaline gut of infant humans, so they are especially sensitive to nitrite poisoning if they drink well waters with large concentrations of nitrate. Nitrite combines with hemoglobin in

KEY TERMS

. . . .

Ammonification—The microbial conversion of organic nitrogen to ammonium in soil or water.

Denitrification—The anaerobic, microbial reduction of nitrate to gaseous nitrous oxide (N_2O) or nitrogen gas (N_2) which are then emitted to the atmosphere.

Dinitrogen fixation (nitrogen fixation)—The conversion of atmospheric dinitrogen (i.e., N_2) to ammonia or an oxide of nitrogen. This process can occur inorganically at high temperature and/or pressure and biologically through action of the microbial enzyme, nitrogenase.

Leaching—The process of movement of dissolved substances in soil along with percolating water.

Nitrification—The process by which *Nitrosomonas* bacteria oxidize ammonium to nitrite which is then oxidized by *Nitrobacter* to nitrate.

the blood, forming a relatively stable complex that is therefore not available to transport oxygen and carbon dioxide and resulting in a toxic condition known as the "blue baby" syndrome. Cattle and sheep can also be poisoned by excessive exposures to nitrate, because nitrites are also readily formed by bacteria in their rumen.

See also Denitrification; Eutrophication; Fertilizers; Greenhouse effect; Nitrogen cycle; Nitrogen fixation.

Further Reading:

Atlas, R. M., and R. Bartha. *Microbial Ecology.* Menlo Park, CA: Benjamin/Cummings, 1987.
Freedman, B. *Environmental Ecology.* 2nd ed. San Diego: Academic Press, 1994.

Bill Freedman

Nitrogen

Nitrogen is the non–metallic chemical element of atomic number 7, with a symbol N, atomic weight 14.0067, specific gravity 0.96737 (compared to air),
melting point –410° F (–210° C), boiling point –384° F (–195.5° C).

Nitrogen is a non–metallic element located in group V of the periodic table. It has two stable isotopes: nitrogen–14, with an abundance of 99.634%, and nitrogen–15, with an abundance of 0.366%. At least five radioactive isotopes of the element have been prepared, with atomic weights of 12, 13, 16, 17, and 18.

Credit for the discovery of nitrogen is usually given to the Scottish physician Daniel Rutherford in 1772, although Henry Cavendish, Joseph Priestly, and Carl Scheele could also claim to have discovered the element at about the same time. Nitrogen was first identified as the product left behind when a substance was burned in a closed sample of air (which, of course, removed the oxygen component of air).

General properties

Nitrogen is a colorless, odorless, tasteless gas composed of diatomic molecules. Its molecules are represented by the formula N_2. The triple bond that holds the two nitrogen atoms together in a nitrogen molecule is very strong, and nitrogen is, therefore, a relatively unreactive element. When a substance burns in air, for example, it reacts with oxygen but, in most cases, not with the nitrogen that is also present in air. One important exception involves the combustion of magnesium in air, in which case both magnesium oxide and magnesium nitride are formed.

Nitrogen has a number of important industrial and commercial uses, as do many of its compounds. The most common of these compounds are those that contain nitrogen and hydrogen (some form of ammonia or its derivative compounds) or nitrogen, oxygen, and a third element, that is, the nitrates and nitrites.

Where it comes from

Nitrogen is the most abundant element in the atmosphere, making up about 78% by volume of the air that surrounds the Earth. The element is much less common in the Earth's crust, however, where it ranks 33rd (along with gallium). Scientists estimate that the average concentration of nitrogen in crustal rocks is about 19 parts per million, less than that of elements such as neodymium, lanthanum, yttrium, and scandium, but greater than that of well–known metals such as lithium, uranium, tungsten, silver, mercury, and platinum.

The most important naturally–occurring compounds of nitrogen are potassium nitrate (saltpeter), found primarily in India, and sodium nitrate (Chile saltpeter), found primarily in the desert regions of Chile and other South American nations. Nitrogen is also an essential component of the proteins found in all living organisms.

How nitrogen is obtained

Nitrogen is produced commercially almost exclusively from air, most commonly by the fractional distillation of liquid air. In this process, air is first cooled to a temperature below that of the boiling points of its major components, a temperature somewhat less than $-328°$ F $(-200°$ C). The liquid air is then allowed to warm up, allowing the lower–boiling–point nitrogen to evaporate from the mixture first. Nitrogen gas escaping from the liquid air is then captured, cooled, and then liquefied once more.

This process produces a high–quality product that generally contains less than 20 parts per million of oxygen. Both an "oxygen–free" form of nitrogen (containing less than two parts per million of oxygen) and an "ultrapure" nitrogen (containing less than 10 parts per million of argon) are also available commercially.

A number of methods are available for preparing nitrogen from its compounds in the laboratory on a small scale. For example, a hot aqueous solution of ammonium nitrite decomposes spontaneously to give elemental nitrogen and water. The heating of barium or sodium azide (NaN_3 or $Ba[N_3]_2$) also yields free nitrogen. In another approach, passing ammonia gas over a hot metallic oxide will result in the formation of free nitrogen, the free metal, and water. Yet another route is the reaction between ammonia and bromine, resulting in the formation of nitrogen and ammonium bromide.

How we use it

As more and more uses for the element have been found, the demand for nitrogen has increased dramatically over the past few decades. In 1988, for example, it was the second most widely produced chemical in the United States, with a production of 52.1 billion lbs (23.6 billion kg).

The most important applications of nitrogen depend on the element's inertness. For example, it is used as a blanketing atmosphere in metallurgical processes where the presence of oxygen would be harmful. In the processing of iron and steel, for example, a blanket of nitrogen placed above the metals prevents their reacting with oxygen, forming undesirable oxides in the final products.

The purging of tanks, pipes, and other kinds of containers with nitrogen can also prevent the possibility of fires. In the petroleum industry, for example, the processing of organic compounds in the presence of air creates the possibility of fires, a possibility that can be avoided by covering the reactants with pure nitrogen.

Nitrogen is also used in the production of electronic components. Assembly of computer chips and other electronic devices can take place with all materials submerged in a nitrogen atmosphere, preventing oxidation of any of the materials in use. Nitrogen is often used as a protective agent during the processing of foods so that decay (oxidation) does not occur.

Another critical use of nitrogen is in the production of ammonia by the Haber process, named after its inventor, the German chemist Fritz Haber. The Haber process involves the direct synthesis of ammonia from its elements, nitrogen and hydrogen. The two gases are combined at temperatures of 932–1,292° F (500–700° C) under a pressure of several hundred atmospheres over a catalyst such as finely divided nickel. One of the major uses of the ammonia produced by this method is in the production of synthetic fertilizers.

About a third of all nitrogen produced is used in its liquid form. For example, liquid nitrogen is used for quick–freezing foods and for preserving foods in transit. Materials can also be processed at the very low temperatures of liquid nitrogen in ways that they can not be handled at room temperature. For example, most forms of rubber are too soft and pliable for machining at room temperature. They can, however, first be cooled in liquid nitrogen and then handled in a much more rigid form.

Chemistry and compounds

Although molecular nitrogen is relatively inert, it will combine with a number of other elements at high temperatures. When it reacts with metals such as aluminum, magnesium, lithium, calcium, barium, strontium, and titanium, the products are known as nitrides. Lithium nitride (Li_3N), for example, is used to provide nitrogen in a variety of metallurgical operations.

Nitrogen and oxygen combine (again, at high temperatures) directly and indirectly to form a series of compounds that include nitrous oxide (or dinitrogen monoxide; N_2O), nitric oxide (or nitrogen monoxide; NO), dinitrogen trioxide (or nitrous anhydride; N_2O_3), nitrogen dioxide (NO_2), and dinitrogen pentoxide (or nitric anhydride; N_2O_5). Nitrogen and the halogens also react with each other to form a series of very unstable, explosive compounds that include nitrogen trifluoride (NF_3), nitrogen trichloride (NCl_3), and nitrogen triiodide (NI_3).

The most common compounds of nitrogen are those in which the element demonstrates oxidation numbers of 3–, 3+, or 5+. Ammonia (NH_3) and its compounds (ammonium compounds) are examples of the first of these, the nitrites (NO_2^-) are examples of the 3+ oxidation state, and the nitrates (NO_3^-) are examples of the 5+ oxidation state.

The process by which nitrogen is cycled through the environment, from plants to animals to the atmosphere and back to plants, is known as the nitrogen cycle. In that cycle, nitrogen gas in the atmosphere is converted ("fixed") to a combined form by the action of lightning, in which it is converted to an oxide of nitrogen, or by certain nitrogen–fixing bacteria in the soil, which change it into nitrates and nitrites. The combined nitrogen is then taken up by plants and used to form plant proteins.

Plant proteins are eaten by animals, who convert the proteins into animal proteins. When an animal dies, the proteins are returned to the soil, where denitrifying bacteria break down compounds of nitrogen and return nitrogen to the atmosphere in the form of an element.

Three compounds of nitrogen traditionally rank in the top 25 among those chemicals produced in the largest volume in the United States. They are ammonia (number five in 1988), nitric acid (number 12 in 1988), and ammonium nitrate (number 14 in 1988). All three of these compounds are extensively used in agriculture as synthetic fertilizers. More than 80% of the ammonia produced, for example, goes to the production of synthetic fertilizers.

In addition to its agricultural role, nitric acid is also an important raw material in the production of explosives. Trinitrotoluene (TNT), gunpowder, nitroglycerin, dynamite, and smokeless powder are all examples of the kind of explosives made from nitric acid. Slightly more than 5% of the nitric acid produced is also used in the synthesis of adipic acid and related compounds used in the manufacture of nylon.

Environmental issues

Some compounds of nitrogen have been implicated in a variety of environmental questions. For example, sodium nitrate and sodium nitrite have been used as food additives because of their ability to inhibit the growth of disease–causing microorganisms. The compounds are most widely used in preserving meats such as bacon, ham, sausage, hot dogs, and bologna, as well as some fish products.

However, questions have been raised about the possible effects of these additives on human health. Nitrites, for example, appear to decrease the ability of a young child's blood to carry oxygen. In addition, nitrites combine with organic compounds known as amines to form a family of toxic compounds known as

KEY TERMS

Fixation—The process by which elemental nitrogen in the atmosphere is converted to a compound, such as a nitrate or an ammonium compound.

Fractional distillation—A process by which two or more substances are separated from each other by allowing them to boil or evaporate at their own distinct boiling points.

Haber process—The chemical process by which nitrogen and hydrogen are combined with each other at high temperature and pressure over a catalyst to produce ammonia.

Isotopes—Two or more forms of an element that differ from each other in their atomic weights.

Nitrogen cycle—A series of chemical reactions by which elemental nitrogen in the atmosphere is converted to nitrates and ammonium compounds, those compounds are processed through the plant and animal world, and then are returned to the atmosphere as free nitrogen.

the nitrosoamines. These hazards have prompted some scientists and non–scientists alike to call for the ban of nitrates and nitrites as food additives.

Oxides of nitrogen are also involved in problems of air pollution. Although oxygen and nitrogen do not combine with each other at room temperature, they do react at elevated temperatures, such as those produced by an internal combustion engine. As a motor vehicle is operated, nitric oxide is constantly being produced. This oxide, however, readily reacts with oxygen in the air to form nitrogen dioxide, a reddish–brown toxic gas. The tan color that is sometimes associated with smog in urban areas is caused by the presence of nitrogen dioxide. Since nitrogen dioxide is harmful to humans and other animals at low concentrations and toxic at higher levels, its presence in polluted air is a serious environmental issue.

See also Element, chemical; Fertilizers; Gases, liquefaction of; Nitrogen cycle; Periodic table; Potassium nitrate.

Further Reading:

Brown, Theodore L., and H. Eugene LeMay, Jr. *Chemistry: The Central Science*, 3rd edition. Englewood Cliffs, NJ: Prentice–Hall, 1985.

Greenwood, N. N., and A. Earnshaw. *Chemistry of the Elements.* Oxford: Pergamon Press, 1990.

Hawley, Gessner G., ed. *The Condensed Chemical Dictionary*, 9th edition. New York: Van Nostrand Reinhold, 1977.

McGraw–Hill Encyclopedia of Science & Technology, 6th edition, Vol. 12. New York: McGraw–Hill Book Company, 1987.

Newton, David E. *The Chemical Elements.* New York: Franklin Watts, Inc., 1994.

Schroeder, Ronald W., "Nitrogen," in *Kirk–Othmer Encyclopedia of Chemical Technology,* Vol. 15. New York: John Wiley & Sons.

David E. Newton

Nitrogen cycle

Nitrogen is a critically important nutrient for organisms, being one of the most abundant elements in their tissues, and an integral component of many biochemicals, including amino acids, proteins, and nucleic acids.

The availability of biologically useful forms of nitrogen is a common limiting factor in the productivity of plants. This is especially true of plants growing in terrestrial and marine environments, and to a somewhat lesser degree in freshwater. Consequently, plants in many ecosystems will be more productive if the supply of available nitrogen is increased through fertilization. This is why fertilization is such a common practice in agriculture, and why nitrogen is by far the most commonly applied nutrient.

Most plants obtain their nitrogen by assimilating it from their environment, mostly as nitrate or ammonium dissolved in soil water that is taken up by roots, or as gaseous nitrogen oxides that are taken up by plant leaves from the atmosphere. However, some plants live in a symbiotic relationship with microorganisms that have the ability to fix atmospheric nitrogen (properly called dinitrogen) into ammonia, and these plants benefit greatly from access to an increased supply of nitrogen.

Almost all animals obtain the nitrogen they require by eating plants and assimilating the plant's organic forms of nitrogen, which are then broken down metabolically and used by the animal to synthesize their own necessary biochemicals. A few animals, however, can utilize inorganic sources of nitrogen. For example, ruminants such as the cow can utilize urea or ammonia, because microorganisms that live in their forestomachs can assimilate these inorganic chemicals and synthesize amino acids and proteins, which the cattle can then use.

Chemical forms of nitrogen

Nitrogen (N) can occur in many chemical forms in the environment. Organic nitrogen refers to a very diverse array of nitrogen–containing organic molecules, ranging from simple amino acids through proteins and nucleic acids, to large and complex molecules such as humic substances in soil and water. A smaller number of inorganic forms of nitrogen occur in the environment, but these are very important ecologically. The most prominent of the inorganic molecules of nitrogen are:

(1) Dinitrogen (N_2). Sometimes this molecule is less accurately called "nitrogen," although that term should properly be restricted to nitrogen atoms. Dinitrogen is a gas, and it is very unreactive because its two nitrogen atoms are held together by a relatively strong, triple bond. About 79% of the volume of Earth's atmosphere consists of dinitrogen, but because of its almost inert character few organisms can directly use this gas in their nutrition. As is explained below, N_2 must be "fixed" into other forms before it can be assimilated by most organisms.

(2) Nitrate (NO_3^-). This is a negatively charged ion (or anion), and is highly soluble in water. Nitrate is the preferred form of nitrogen nutrition for most species of plants. If nitrate is not assimilated by plants or microorganisms, it is readily leached from soils.

(3) Ammonia (NH_3) and ammonium (NH_4^+). Ammonia usually occurs as a gas, vapor, or liquid, while ammonium is a positively charged ion (or cation), formed by the addition of a hydrogen ion (H^+) to ammonia. Ammonium is soluble in water, although it is also electrochemically attracted to negatively charged surfaces associated with clays and organic matter in soil, and is therefore not as mobile as nitrate. Plants that are adapted to acidic soils can utilize ammonium as their source of nitrogen nutrition, although most species of non–acidic soils can only utilize nitrate.

(4) Nitric oxide (NO). This gas is emitted to the atmosphere mostly as a result of combustions. The NO of combustions is generated by two mechanisms: (a) oxidation of the organic nitrogen of the fuel of biomass, oil, or coal, and (b) combination of atmospheric dinitrogen with oxygen under conditions of high temperature and pressure, as occurs, for example, in the internal combustion engine of automobiles. NO is produced in large quantities by both of these reactions, and it is typically emitted into the atmosphere.

(5) Nitrogen dioxide (NO_2) and its products. In the atmosphere, emitted NO is oxidized to NO_2, which is therefore considered to be a secondary, non–emitted, gas. NO and NO_2 are often considered together, as NO_x.

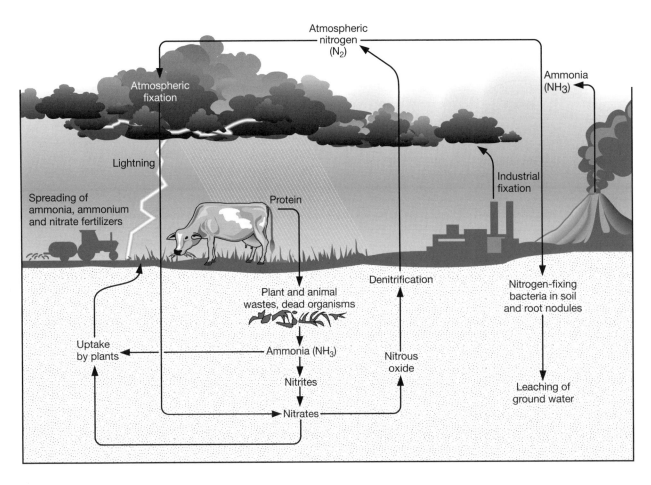

The nitrogen cycle.

In the atmosphere, gaseous NO_x may be directly taken in by plant foliage, or it may be oxidized to nitrate. The nitrate may combine with atmospheric cations, such as ammonium, to form an ammonium nitrate salt. Fine aerosols of ammonium nitrate particulates may directly deposit in ecosystems, or they may serve as condensation nuclei for the formation of ice crystals, which may eventually become snowflakes or raindrops that are delivered to ecosystems as precipitation. By these mechanisms, biologically useful forms of fixed nitrogen are deposited from the atmosphere. It should also be mentioned that atmospheric nitrate can also combine with hydrogen ion, and can occur as a dilute solution of nitric acid. This is the reason why nitrate derived from NO_x is such an important contributor to acidic precipitation (see entry on acid rain).

(6) Nitrous oxide (N_2O). The major source of atmospheric N_2O is denitrification occurring in wet, nitrate–rich soils. N_2O is a relatively unreactive and persistent gas in the atmosphere. However, N_2O is very slowly oxidized to NO_x gases under the influence of sunlight and atmospheric catalysts.

Depending upon environmental and biological conditions, all of these various organic and inorganic compounds containing nitrogen can be variously transformed. The diverse manners in which the movements and transformations of these chemicals occur is known as the nitrogen cycle.

Dinitrogen fixation

Atmospheric N_2 is very abundant, but this molecule is highly unreactive and cannot be assimilated by most organisms and used in their nutrition. To be useful to plants, dinitrogen must be "fixed" into inorganic forms that can be taken up by roots or leaves. Dinitrogen fixation can occur through non–biological processes. For example, during a lightning strike there is a brief occurrence of a very high temperature and high pressure, conditions that favor the combination of atmospheric N_2 and O_2 to form NO.

However, biological fixation of dinitrogen is typically more important. A few species of microorganisms can synthesize an enzyme, called nitrogenase, which is capable of catalytically breaking the triple bond of N_2, generating two molecules of ammonia for each molecule of dinitrogen that is reacted. Because the activation energy for this chemical reaction is rather high, it takes quite a lot of biological energy to fix atmospheric dinitrogen in this way, about 12–15 moles of adenosine triphosphate (ATP) per mole of dinitrogen that is converted. Despite the high energy costs, the dinitrogen fixation reaction is still very favorable ecologically, because access is gained to ammonia and ammonium, chemical forms of nitrogen that organisms can utilize for their nutrition. Because the nitrogenase enzyme is denatured by oxygen (O_2), the fixation reaction can only occur under anaerobic conditions, where oxygen is not present.

There are numerous species of free–living microorganisms that can fix atmospheric dinitrogen, including species of true bacteria, blue–green algae or bacteria, and actinomycetes. These microorganisms are most abundant in wet or moist environments, especially in situations where nutrients other than nitrate or ammonium are relatively abundant, for example, in rotting logs or other dead biomass, or in lakes that are well fertilized with phosphate from sewage. Such conditions are typically relatively deficient in available forms of nitrogen, and are commonly anoxic, creating obviously favorable opportunities for species of microorganisms that can utilize dinitrogen.

Some species of plants live in an intimate and mutually beneficial symbiosis with microorganisms that have the capability of fixing dinitrogen. The plants benefit from the symbiosis by having access to a dependable source of fixed nitrogen, while the microorganisms benefit from energy and habitat provided by the plant. The best known symbioses involve many species in the legume family (Fabaceae) and strains of a bacterium known as *Rhizobium japonicum*. Some plants in other families also have dinitrogen–fixing symbioses, for example, red alder (*Alnus rubra*) and certain actinomycetes, a type of microorganism. Many species of lichens, which consist of a symbiotic relationship between a fungus and a blue–green bacterium, can also fix dinitrogen.

Biological dinitrogen fixation is an ecologically important process, being ultimately responsible for most of the fixed nitrogen that occurs in the biomass of organisms and ecosystems. The only other significant sources of fixed nitrogen to ecosystems are atmospheric deposi-

tions of nitrate and ammonium with precipitation and dustfall, and the direct uptake of NO_x gases by plants.

Ammonification and nitrification

Ammonification is the process by which the organically bound nitrogen of microbial, plant, and animal biomass is recycled after their death. Ammonification is carried out by a diverse array of microorganisms that perform ecological decay services, and its product is ammonia or ammonium ion. Ammonium is a suitable source of nutrition for many species of plants, especially those living in acidic soils. However, most plants cannot utilize ammonium effectively, and they require nitrate as their essential source of nitrogen nutrition.

Nitrate is synthesized from ammonium by an important bacterial process known as nitrification. The first step in nitrification is the oxidation of ammonium to nitrite (NO_2^-), a function carried out by bacteria in the genus *Nitrosomonas*. Once formed, the nitrite is rapidly oxidized further to nitrate, by bacteria in the genus *Nitrobacter*. The bacteria responsible for nitrification are very sensitive to acidity, so this process does not occur at significant rates in acidic soil or water. This is the reason why plants of acidic habitats must be capable of utilizing ammonium as their source of nitrogen nutrition.

Denitrification

Denitrification is another bacterial process, carried out by a relatively wide range of species. In denitrification, nitrate is reduced to either nitrous oxide or dinitrogen, which is then emitted to the atmosphere. Denitrification occurs under conditions where oxygen is not present, and its rate is largest when concentrations of nitrate are large. Consequently, fertilized agricultural fields that are wet or flooded can have quite large rates of denitrification. In some respects, denitrification can be considered to be an opposite process to dinitrogen fixation. In fact, the global rates of dinitrogen fixation and denitrification are in an approximate balance, meaning that the total quantity of fixed nitrogen in Earth's ecosystems is neither increasing nor decreasing substantially over time.

Humans and the nitrogen cycle

One of the major influences of humans on the nitrogen cycle occurs through the use of nitrogen–containing fertilizers in agriculture. Under conditions in which agricultural plants have access to as much water as they require, their productivity is usually constrained by the rate at which they can obtain nitrogen in available forms, particularly nitrate, and sometimes ammonium. Under such conditions, farmers attempt to increase the availability of these nutrients, usually by applying fertilizers. In intensive agricultural systems, rates of fertilization often exceed 1,103 lb (500 kg) of N per hectare per year. This represents an enormously larger rate of nitrogen input than occurs naturally by atmospheric deposition and dinitrogen fixation, and it is also much larger than the rates in which ammonium and nitrate are made naturally available by ammonification and nitrification. Consequently, the ability of the crop and ecosystem to assimilate this much nitrogen input is satiated, and some of the input, especially nitrate, leaches from the site into groundwater and surface waters such as streams and rivers. This can cause a severe contamination of these waters in agricultural areas, which can lead to risks for human health through drinking nitrate–rich ground water, and contribute to increased productivity of surface waters through eutrophication. In addition, when soils with large nitrate concentrations become wet, the rate of denitrification is greatly increased. This represents a loss of fixed nitrogen capital, and the emitted nitrous oxide may contribute to an enhancement of Earth's greenhouse effect.

Humans also influence the nitrogen cycle by dumping sewage and other types of organic matter into waterbodies. There is a great deal of environmental damage associated with these practices, including lowered dissolved oxygen levels associated with microbial oxidation of the organic matter, and the presence of fecal pathogens and parasites. The accidental fertilization of waterbodies with large amounts of nitrogen contributes greatly to eutrophication.

Humans also affect the nitrogen cycle through the emissions of large quantities of NO_x gases to the atmosphere. The most important sources of emission are automobiles, power plants, home furnaces, and factories. The emitted NO_x is an important air pollutant, because it is critical in the photochemical oxidative reactions by which toxic ozone is formed, and because the NO_x is an important source of nitrate in acidic precipitation.

The nitrogen cycle is a critical biogeochemical process, and is the ultimate means of entry and exit of biologically available forms of nitrogen in ecosystems. However, there are many ways by which human activities can substantially change the rates of the processes in this cycle, causing a great deal of environmental damage. The key to sustainable management of the nitrogen cycle is the recognition of the minimum and maximum rates that represent a healthy degree of ecological function. Human influences must then be kept within those bounds of desirable rates of nitrogen cycling.

KEY TERMS

Ammonification—The microbial conversion of organic nitrogen to ammonium in soil or water.

Denitrification—The microbial oxidation of ammonium to nitrite, and then to nitrate.

Dinitrogen fixation (nitrogen fixation)—The conversion of atmospheric dinitrogen (N_2) to ammonia or an oxide of nitrogen. This process can occur inorganically at high temperature and/or pressure, and biologically through the action of the microbial enzyme, nitrogenase.

Leaching—The removal of dissolved substances in soil in percolating water.

Nitrification—The process by which *Nitrosomonas* bacteria oxidize ammonium to nitrite, which is then oxidized by *Nitrobacter* to nitrate.

Nitrogenase—The microbial enzyme that fixes dinitrogen, by cleaving its triple bond and forming ammonia.

Symbiosis—A biological relationship between two or more organisms that is mutually beneficial. The relationship is obligate, meaning that the partners cannot successfully live apart in nature.

See also Ammonification; Denitrification; Eutrophication; Fertilizers; Nitrogen; Nitrogen fixation.

Further Reading:

Freedman, B. *Environmental Ecology*. 2nd ed. San Diego: Academic Press, 1994.

Atlas, R. M., and R. Bartha. *Microbial Ecology*. Menlo Park, CA: Benjamin/Cummings, 1987.

Bill Freedman

Nitrogen fixation

Nitrogen fixation refers to the chemical conversion of nitrogen gas (dinitrogen, N_2) to some oxidized form, usually nitric oxide (NO) or ammonia (NH_3). Nitrogen fixation can occur through inorganic reactions or as a result of biological processes. Because the nitrogen atoms in dinitrogen are bound by a very strong triple bond, this gas is very stable and cannot be utilized as a source of nutrition by any but a few highly specialized microorganisms. These nitrogen–fixing microbes are critically important ecologically because nitrogen fixation is the ultimate source of the capital of available organic nitrogen in ecosystems.

It has been estimated that terrestrial ecosystems fix about 135 million metric tonnes of nitrogen/year (10^6 tonnes N/yr), and marine ecosystems 40 x 10^6 tonnes N/yr. The terrestrial fixation most commonly occurs in agroecosystems in which legumes are cultivated which fix an estimated 44 x 10^6 tonnes N/yr, while grasslands fix 45 x 10^6 tonnes N/yr, forests 40 x 10^6 tonnes N/yr, and all other terrestrial ecosystems 10 x 10^6 tonnes N/yr. Industrial fixation of nitrogen for the manufacturing of synthetic fertilizers contributed another 30 x 10^6 tonnes N/yr in the early 1980s, while fixation during combustion accounts for 19 x 10^6 tonnes N/yr. Because of increasing demands for nitrogen fertilizers for agriculture, it has been estimated that industrial fixation could increase to 100 x 10^6 tonnes N/yr by the year 2000.

Inorganic nitrogen fixation

Atmospheric dinitrogen can be fixed by inorganic reactions occurring in combustion, lightning strikes, and other circumstances involving high temperatures. Overall, naturally occurring non–biological fixation has been estimated to be equivalent to 10–20% of biological fixation of dinitrogen.

Nitrogen fixation is also associated with certain activities of humans. The internal combustion engines of automobiles burn fuels under conditions of very high temperature and pressure which favors the oxidation of nitrogen gas to nitric oxide, an important air pollutant and source of fixed nitrogen. The combustion of coal and other organic fuels also results in the formation of nitric oxide through both the fixation of nitrogen gas and the oxidation of the organic nitrogen of the fuel. Also, as noted previously, nitrogen gas is fixed industrially in enormous amounts to provide agricultural fertilizers. The industrial reaction is known as the Haber process, and it involves the use of hydrogen gas generated from the methane of natural gas to fix ammonium from dinitrogen.

Biological nitrogen fixation

Biological nitrogen fixation is accomplished through the catalytic action of an enzyme known as nitrogenase. Nitrogenase consists of two distinct proteins which contain molybdenum, iron, and sulfur. Because the nitrogenase proteins are denatured by exposure to oxygen (O_2), they can only operate in an anaerobic environment. Nitrogen fixation using nitrogenase requires rather large inputs of energy to drive the process, equivalent to about 150 calories of energy per mole of nitrogen gas that is fixed. Although nitrogen fixation is energetically expensive, it is nevertheless worthwhile for plants that grow in nitrogen–deficient habitats.

The nitrogenase enzyme can cleave other triple bonds in addition to that of dinitrogen gas, for example, that of acetylene. Most assays of nitrogen fixation rates take advantage of this fact, measuring nitrogenase activity through the rate at which ethylene is generated by the reaction of acetylene with this enzyme.

Only certain microorganisms can synthesize the nitrogenase enzyme. Some of these microbes are free–living in soils and water, while others occur in mutualisms with fungi or plants.

A large number of free–living bacteria of anaerobic environments have the ability to fix nitrogen, including the genus *Clostridium*. Fewer genera of aerobic bacteria have this ability. Free–living nitrogen fixation occurs most vigorously in habitats containing large quantities of carbon–rich organic debris such as rotting logs, heaps of sawdust, and compost piles.

Blue–green bacteria are free–living, photosynthetic microbes that fix nitrogen in aquatic habitats and moist soil, including the genera *Anabaena*, *Nostoc*, and *Calothrix*. Strains of these microbes also live in mutualisms with certain fungi in a symbiosis known as lichens which have an ability to fix nitrogen. *Anabaena* and *Nostoc* also occur in a mutualism with the floating aquatic fern *Azolla* which can be cultivated on the surface of rice paddies to fix nitrogen at a rate as great as 100–150 kg N/ha.yr, saving on the use of synthetic fertilizer.

Nitrogen–fixing bacteria can also occur in mutualisms with certain vascular plants. The best known of these associations are with species of legumes (order Leguminosae). About one–half of the world's 10,000 species of legumes occur in a nitrogen–fixing mutualism with bacteria in the genus *Rhizobium*. About 50 of these species are utilized in agriculture, for example, the food crops garden pea (*Pisum sativum*), broad bean (*Vicia faba*), and soybean (*Glycine max*), and the soil conditioners red clover (*Trifolium pratense*) and alfalfa (*Medicago sativa*). The strain of *Rhizobium* is specific to each legume species.

The *Rhizobium* occurs in specialized nodules on the roots of the legumes. These are developed when the soil–dwelling *Rhizobium* invades a root hair, stimulating the plant to form a nodule. Nodule development is

KEY TERMS

. . . .

Nitrogen fixation (dinitrogen fixation)—The conversion of atmospheric dinitrogen (i.e., N_2) to ammonia or an oxide of nitrogen. This process can occur inorganically at high temperature and pressure and biologically through action of the microbial enzyme, nitrogenase.

Nitrogenase—An enzyme synthesized by certain microorganisms that is capable of cleaving the triple bond of nitrogen gas generating ammonium, a biologically useful type of fixed nitrogen.

Mutualism—A relationship between two or more organisms that is mutually beneficial.

inhibited in acidic soils and if the concentrations of nitrate in soil are large. To protect the nitrogenase enzyme, the interior of the nodules is anaerobic. This is due in part to the presence of an oxygen–binding pigment known as leghaemoglobin which colors the nodule interior a dark red. The leghaemoglobin also serves as an oxygen carrier important for other aspects of bacterial metabolism, in this way performing a similar function as the haemoglobin of animals.

Several hundred species in other plant families also develop root nodules that can fix nitrogen. The best known of these are the woody plants known as alders (*Alnus* spp.), which develop nodules containing actinomycetes in the genus *Frankia*. Red alder (*Alnus rubra*) reaches tree–size, and its stands can fix hundreds of kilograms of nitrogen per year. Other non–leguminous plants that are known to fix nitrogen include the genera *Casuarina*, *Ceanothus*, *Myrica*, *Dryas*, and *Shepherdia*, variously associated with fungi, actinomycetes, or bacteria.

Some species of grasses occur in a relatively loose, non–obligate mutualism with nitrogen–fixing microorganisms. These associative symbioses include those of the crabgrass *Digitaria* with the bacterium *Spirillum* and that of another weedy grass, *Paspalum*, with *Azotobacter*. Although these nitrogen–fixing symbioses do not involve agriculturally important species of plants, they may nevertheless prove to be significant. Research is being conducted into the possibility of transferring the associative ability of nitrogen fixation of these species into grasses that are important in agriculture, such as corn (*Zea mays*) and wheat (*Triticum aestivum*). If this feat of bioengineering could be accomplished, it could lead to significant savings of nitrogen fertilizer which must be manufactured using non–renewable resources.

One last example of a nitrogen–fixing mutualism involves termites. These insects have a bacterium, *Enterobacter agglomerans,* in their gut that fixes nitrogen. This is important to termites because their diet of cellulose is highly deficient in nitrogen.

See also Legumes; Mutualism; Nitrogen cycle; Symbiosis.

Further Reading:

Atlas, R. M., and R. Bartha. *Microbial Ecology.* Menlo Park, CA; Benjamin/Cummings, 1987.
Freedman, B. *Environmental Ecology.* 2nd ed. San Diego: Academic Press, 1994.

Bill Freedman

Nobelium see **Element, transuranium**

Noble gases see **Rare gases**

Noddies see **Terns**

Noise pollution

Cars, trucks, lawn mowers, leaf blowers, chain saws, power drills, television, radio, video games, computers, . . . the list of noise makers in our modern life is almost endless, and our world keeps getting noisier. Noise—which can be defined as any unwanted sound— is one of the most common forms of pollution, one that can easily damage the hearing and general health of people and animals.

Noise and our hearing

The inner ear of humans (and other vertebrates) contains a snail–shaped structure called a cochlea that is lined with thousands of microscopic hairs. When sound vibrations enter the cochlea, they cause the tiny hairs to move back and forth. If strong vibrations blast into the cochlea, the hairs can be flattened and damaged. The damage usually results in some degree of hearing loss.

Sound is measured in decibels (dB). Zero dB represents the quietest sound that a healthy human can hear. One hundred dB equals a noise that is 10 billion times as intense as one dB. Brief exposure to more than 110 dB can damage ears immediately; prolonged exposure to more than 85 dB can damage ears gradually.

The most powerful sounds we encounter include jets taking off, loud amplified music, gun shots, and chain saws. Just one exposure to these sounds can damage our ears.

We also damage our ears if we are exposed to noises that are less loud, but that we hear more often. For example, office workers who daily endure noise from telephones and loud machines may lose some hearing over time. Workers in loud factories also experience hearing loss.

We can even hurt our hearing when we play. Motorboats, motorcycles, and snowmobiles all make loud noises likely to hurt our ears. Playing loud music on a personal stereo can also damage hearing. If someone near you can hear the music you are playing on your personal stereo, you are causing noise pollution for them and hearing loss for yourself.

Noise hurts more than our hearing. When we are exposed to loud noise, our bodies react as if we must flee danger. Our blood vessels narrow, our skin pales, our muscles tense—all evidence that our body senses danger. Because noise causes such signs of stress, many experts believe that noise can also make people irritable and confused. While such a situation might be acceptable for a short time, millions of people around the world live with noise every day and all night.

Who is affected

As many as 10 million Americans today have lost part of their hearing because of our noisy lives. People who work at airports seem especially at risk: One study showed that more than half the people working near runways suffered some hearing loss. People in other countries also suffer from noise pollution. For example, one scientist studied people who worked in a paper mill in India. Noise levels ranged between 80 and 100 dB all day. More than one–third of the workers showed some hearing loss. Germany alone calculates that its citizens and companies spend nearly four billion dollars a year correcting hearing problems.

Noise pollution can also affect animals. For example, sudden loud noises can wake animals that are hibernating. This, in turn, raises their metabolic rates and can cause them to consume fat reserves they need to survive through to spring.

Human noises can also interfere with other kinds of animal communication. This interference can inhibit an animal's ability to protect itself, to find food, and to live a normal life. For example, ships emit low–frequency sounds that interfere with whale communications. Other human noises can frighten whales away from their normal migration routes. In the desert, kangaroo rats (*Dipodomys* spp.) exposed to the roar of a dune buggy lose their ability to hear snakes approaching. Japanese quail (*Coturnix Coturnix Japonica*) have to call much louder than usual when they live in a noisy environment. Sooty terns (*Sterna fuscata*) abandoned their nests when jets flew overhead, creating sonic booms. Intense bursts of noise also caused condors (*Gymnogyps californianus*) to abandon their nests.

The federal government and noise

Because noise pollution causes so many problems, the United States government has passed laws to regulate noise. In 1987, for example, Congress passed the National Overflights Act. This law called for studies to determine the effect of air traffic over national parks. It also prohibited low–flying planes from flying over certain parts of Grand Canyon National Park.

Since 1972, when the Noise Control Act was passed, the Environmental Protection Agency (EPA) has been responsible for researching and regulating noise pollution in the United States. Between 1972 and 1981, EPA's Office of Noise Abatement and Control (ONAC) issued hundreds of reports about the severity of noise pollution in America, trained community leaders in ways to lessen the pollution, and recommended numerous regulations to reduce the impact. Its work was designed to educate communities and set uniform emission standards throughout the country. In 1982, however, ONAC was shut down as part of President Reagan's deficit reduction. The Noise Control Act was never repealed or amended, but it was no longer enforced at the federal level.

Protection from noise

Individuals can take many simple steps to protect themselves from the harmful effects of noise pollution. If people must be around loud sounds, they can protect their ears with ear plugs or ear protectors. They can muffle sound by using acoustic ceiling tiles, draperies, carpets, and sound–absorbing furniture in their homes, offices, and schools. They can also buy quieter models of machines and let store owners and manufacturers know that they prefer quieter products. Individuals can also help their communities investigate noise pollution and develop regulations to reduce the problem locally.

Some communities have enacted anti–noise ordinances. New York City issues fines to people who run excessively noisy air conditioners, to street construction crews whose equipment is too loud, and to impatient drivers who honk their horns. Police in Redondo Beach, California, can remove large speakers from cars if the music can be heard more than 50 feet (15.2m) away.

Communities can also reduce noise by locating freeways far from residential neighborhoods, by reducing the speed on freeways and other high–speed roads, by requiring developers to plant trees and shrubbery as sound mufflers, and by requiring people to build houses and other structures with materials that help absorb sound.

In Germany, roads are paved with materials that reduce sound, tires are manufactured to whine less, and lawn mowers and other equipment are designed to operate quietly. Australia also makes efforts to reduce noise. Manufacturers in some Australian states must label the noise level of products such as chain saws and lawn mowers. In Adelaide, police can also fine someone driving a noisy car.

As the human population continues to grow, the amount of noise in our world will also grow as we crowd together with gadgets, machines, and vehicles. To help ease the impact of this increasing amount of noise, some companies are developing a new technology called *anti–noise*. Anti–noise works by emitting a sound that exactly matches the noise. When the sound waves from the anti–noise device meet the sound waves from the noise, they cancel each other out. In such a case, no sound waves reach our ears; we do not hear the noise. Anti–noise can work as a kind of muffler on a noisy engine, or it can be built into headphones to silence all approaching noise. Even if we cannot eliminate noise pollution, we may be able to use anti–noise devices to escape some of the damage that noise can cause.

See also Hearing.

Further Reading:

Allman, William. "Good News About Noise." *U.S. News and World Report* (9 September 1991): 59.

Angus, Robert. "Raising a Ruckus About Noise: It Threatens Your Hearing and Your Health." *Omni* (February 1994): 18.

Bragdon, Clifford. *Noise Pollution: The Unquiet Crisis.* Philadelphia: University of Pennsylvania Press, 1970.

Browne, Malcolm. "Human Noises in Ocean Held to Threaten Marine Mammals." *New York Times* (19 October 1993).

Harris, Cyril. *Handbook of Noise Control.* New York: McGraw Hill, 1979.

Lee, David. "Breaking the Sound Barrier: The Rapidly Growing Air Tour Industry Is Generating Unacceptable Noise Levels in Some of Our Most Treasured National Parks." *National Parks* (July/August 1994): 24.

LeGro, Bill, and Doug Bruce. "Noise–proof Your Health." *Prevention* (January 1993): 50.

O'Brien, Bill. "Quest for Quiet." *Sierra* (July/August 1992): 41.

Raloff, Janet. "Dormant Noise Program's Silent Reverberations." *Science News* (17 August 1991): 100.

KEY TERMS

Anti–noise—Sound wave produced by a computer that matches the sound wave of an offending sound; when the two sound waves meet, the anti–noise cancels out the noise.

Cochlea—A snail–shaped structure in the inner ear that is lined with thousands of microscopic hairs.

Decibel—Measuring unit of sound volume, abbreviated dB.

Noise—Any unwanted, annoying, or disturbing sound; especially sound that can cause physical or psychological damage.

Shapiro, Sidney. "Rejoining the Battle Against Noise Pollution." *Issues in Science and Technology* (Spring 1993): 73.

Sundstrom, Eric, et al. "Office Noise, Satisfaction, and Performance." *Environment and Behavior* (March 1994): 195.

Toufexis, Anastasia. "Now Hear This—If You Can." *Time* (5 August 1991): 50.

Carolyn Duckworth

Non–Euclidean geometry

Non–Euclidean geometry refers to certain types of geometry which differ from plane and solid geometry which dominated the realm of mathematics for several centuries. There are other types of geometry which do not assume all of Euclid's postulates such as hyperbolic geometry, elliptic geometry, spherical geometry, descriptive geometry, differential geometry, geometric algebra, and multidimensional geometry. These geometries deal with more complex components of curves in space rather than the simple plane or solids used as the foundation for Euclid's geometry. The first five postulates of Euclidean geometry will be listed in order to better understand the changes that are made to make it non–Euclidean.

1.) A straight line can be drawn from any point to any point.

2.) A finite straight line can be produced continuously in a straight line.

3.) A circle may be described with any point as center and any distance as a radius.

4.) All right angles are equal to one another.

5.) If a transversal falls on two lines in such a way that the interior angles on one side of the transversal are less than two right angles, then the lines meet on the side on which the angles are less than two right angles.

A consistent logical system for which one of these postulates is modified in an essential way is non-Euclidean geometry. Although there are different types of Non-Euclidean geometry which do not use all of the postulates or make alterations of one or more of the postulates of Euclidean geometry, hyperbolic and elliptic are usually most closely associated with the term Non-Euclidean Geometry.

Hyperbolic geometry is based on changing Euclid's parallel postulate, which is also referred to as Euclid's Fifth postulate, the last of the five postulates of Euclidian Geometry. Euclid's parallel postulate may also be stated as one and only one parallel to a given line goes through a given point not on the line.

Elliptic geometry uses a modification of Postulate II. Postulate II allows for lines of infinite length, which are denied in Elliptic geometry, where only finite lines are assumed.

The history of non-Euclidean geometry

Euclid was thought to have instructed in Alexandria after Alexander the Great established centers of learning in the city around 300 B.C. Euclid was the mathematician who collected all of the definitions, postulates, and theorems that were available at that time, along with some of his insights and developments, and placed them in a logical order and completed what we now know as Euclid's Elements.

The influence of Greek geometry on the mathematics communities of the world was profound for in Greek geometry was contained the ideals of deductive thinking with its definitions, corollaries, and theorems which could establish beyond any reasonable doubt the truth or falseness of propositions. For an estimated 22 centuries, Euclidean geometry held its weight.

Despite the general acceptance of Euclidean geometry, there appeared to be a problem with the parallel postulate as to whether or not it really was a postulate or that it could be deduced from other definitions, propositions, or axioms. The history of these attempts to prove the parallel postulate lasted for nearly 20 centuries, and after numerous failures, gave rise to the establishment of Non-Euclidean geometry and the independence of the parallel postulate.

Several Greek scientists and mathematicians considered the parallel postulate after the appearance of Euclid's Elements, around 300 B.C. Aristotle's treatment of the parallel postulate was lost. However, it was the Arab scholars who appeared to have obtained some information on the last text and reported that Aristotle's treatment was different from that of Euclid since his definition depended on the distance between parallel lines. Proclus and Ptolemy also published some attempts to prove the parallel postulate.

Omar Khayyam provided extensive coverage on the proof of the parallel postulate or theory of parallels in his discussions on the difficulties of making valid proofs from Euclid's definitions and theorems. During the 13th century Husam al-Din al-Salar wrote a text on the parallel postulate in an attempt to improve on the development by Omar Khayyam.

The 18th century produced more sophisticated proofs and although not correct, produced developments that were later used in non-Euclidean geometry. The Italian mathematician, Girolamo Saccheri, in one of his proofs considered non-Euclidian concepts by making use of the acute-angle hypothesis on the intersection of two straight lines.

The attempt to solve this problem was made also by Farkas Bolyai, the father of Johann Bolyai, one of the founders of non-Euclidean geometry but his proof was also invalid. It is interesting to note that Johann's father cautioned his son not to get involved with the proof of the parallel postulate because of its complexity.

The founders of non-Euclidean geometry

The writings of Gauss showed that he too, first considered the usual attempts at trying to prove the parallel postulate. However, a few decades later, in his unpublished reports in his correspondence with fellow mathematicians such as W. Bolyai, Olbers, Schumacker, Gerling, Tartinus, and Bessel showed that Gauss was working on the rudiments of non-Euclidian geometry, the name he attributed to his mathematics of parallels. Gauss shared his thoughts on this topic and asked them not to disclose this information but Gauss never published them. It has been proposed by historians that Gauss was concerned that these concepts were too radical for acceptance by mathematicians at that time. And if this was the case, it probably was correct since the two founders of non-Euclidean geometry, Bolyai and Lobechevsky, received very little acceptance until after their deaths.

It was at the University of Kazan, in the Russian province of Kazakhstan, that Nicolai Ivanovitch Lobachevsky made his contributions in Non–Euclidean geometry. In his early days at the university, he did try to find a proof of the parallel postulate, but later changed direction. As early as 1826, he made use of the hypothesis of the acute angle already developed by Saccheri and Lambert in his lecture noting that two parallels to a given point can be drawn from a point where the sum of the angles of the triangle is less than two right angles. His works *On the Imaginary Geometry, New Principles of Geometry, With a Complete Theory of Parallels, Applications of the Imaginary Geometry to Certain Integrals and Geometrical Researches* are on the theory of parallel lines. He later completed his work in one French and two German publications. Lobachevsky developed his Pan-Geometry on the 28 propositions of Euclidean Geometry and the negation of the parallel postulate. He developed the concepts for non-Euclidean geometry by introducing two new figures—the Horocycle and the Horoscope. Using these two concepts and some transformation formulas, he developed his new geometry.

Although Lobachevsky continued throughout his career improving the development of non–Euclidean geometry, Johann Bolyai, the other mathematician given credit for its development apparently only spent slightly over a decade in his mathematical considerations. As indicated previously, Johann's father suggested that he not waste his time working on the complex problems of the parallel postulate. However, Johann and his friend Carl Szasz worked on the theory of parallels while students at the Royal College for Engineers at Vienna from 1817–1822. In 1823 Bolyai discovered the formula for the transformation which connected the angle of parallelism to the corresponding line. He continued with his development and sent his manuscript to his father who published it in 1832. The article was entitled "The Science of Absolute Space" in the Appendix of his father's book. Prior to its publication, Johann's father had sent the paper to Gauss for his consideration. It is reported that the paper originally sent in 1831 to Gauss was lost. Three months after the publication, the article was sent again to Gauss and in 1832 his father received his reply. Gauss indicated that he was impressed by the work but noted that he had been working on the same problem with similar results and was pleasantly surprised to have the development completed by his friend's son. Johann was deeply suspicious of this reply and apparently suspected Gauss of trying to take credit for his work. However, in this instance there was no problem, since Gauss had no publications on the topic and could not claim priority but Johann continued to be suspicious. After the publication of his work, Johann did very little significant

mathematical research. And even though he was interested in having his work published before Lobachevsky when he heard of Lobachevsky's contributions, he never completed the necessary research to report to the mathematical journals.

The most important conclusions of Bolyai's research in non–Euclidean geometry were the following: 1.) The definition of parallels and their properties independent of the Euclidian postulate. 2.) The circle and the sphere of infinite radius. The geometry of the sphere of infinite radius is identical with ordinary plane geometry. 3.) Spherical Trigonometry is independent of Euclid's Postulate. Direct demonstration of the formula. 4.) Plane trigonometry in non–Euclidean geometry. Applications to the calculation of areas and volumes. 5.) Problems which can be solved by elementary methods. Squaring the circle, on the hypothesis that the Fifth Postulate is false.

Elliptic non–Euclidean geometry

A later development following that of Bolyai's and Lobachevsky's Hyperbolic non–Euclidean geometry was that of Elliptic non–Euclidian geometry. The rudiments of elliptic non–Euclidean geometry were developed by Georg Friedrich Bernhard Riemann. His introduction to his foundations of spherical geometry apparently was used as the basis for his Elliptic Geometry which made use of the postulate that the sum of the angles of a triangle in space are greater than 180°. Based on the foundations that Riemann had introduced, Klein was able to further develop Elliptic non–Euclidean geometry and was actually the mathematician who defined this new field as Elliptic non–Euclidian geometry. Klein's Erlanger Program made a significant contribution in providing major distinguishing features among Parabolic (Euclidean geometry), Hyperbolic and Elliptic geometries.

Further Reading:

Krause, E.F. *Taxicab Geometry*. New York: Dover Publications, 1986.

Bonola, R. *Non–Euclidean Geometry*. New York: Dover Publications, 1911.

Golos, E.B. *Foundations of Euclidean and Non–Euclidean Geometry*. New York: Holt, Rinehart and Winston, 1968.

Greenberg, M.J. *Euclidean and Non–Euclidean Geometries*. San Francisco: W. H. Freeman and Co., 1974.

Rosenfeld, B.A. *A History of Non–Euclidean Geometry*. New York: Springer–Verlag, 1988.

Stillwell, J. *Mathematics and Its History*. New York: Springer–Verlag, 1989.

Trudeau, R.J. *The Non–Euclidean Revolution*. Boston: Birkhauser, 1987.

G.H. Miller

Nonmetal

A nonmetal is a chemical element that generally does not conduct heat or electricity very well, is usually a solid or a gas at normal temperatures, and (for solids) is difficult to reshape by pounding or beating. Nonmetals include elements such as carbon, sulfur, oxygen, and nitrogen. They are normally defined in contrast to metals, which are bright, shiny, solid elements (with one exception) that are good electrical and heat conductors. They are ductile, which means that pieces can be drawn into wires, and they are malleable, which means that they can be beaten into thin sheets. In chemical reactions, nonmetals usually react to make negatively-charged ions (anions) while metals usually react to make positively–charged ions (cations). Only about 20 elements are considered nonmetals, while the rest of them are considered metals. With the exception of hydrogen, all of the nonmetals are found in the right–hand side of the periodic table. In fact, many periodic tables have a bold line in a sort of stair–step shape in the right–hand side of the table. This bold line is the "border–line" between the metals and the nonmetals. Elements that are adjacent to the line share metal and nonmetal properties and are called metalloids or semi–metals.

There are some exceptions to the general properties of nonmetals. For example, carbon can conduct electricity, although it has all other nonmetal properties. Bromine is a liquid at normal temperatures, and it is the only liquid nonmetal. All of the elements that are gases at normal temperatures are nonmetals. All of the metals, on the other hand, are solids at normal temperatures except for mercury, which is a liquid. (The element gallium melts at 91–93° F [31–32° C], which is just above room temperature.)

See also Anion; Cation; Element, chemical; Metal; Periodic table.

Non–point source

Non–point sources refer to situations in which there are numerous relatively small sources of emission of gases, metals, pesticides, nutrients, or other substances into the environment. Collectively, these many sources can comprise a regional emission of large quantities of pollutants to the environment. However, this is different from point sources, in which there is a single, discrete source, such as a large smokestack or a sewage outfall.

For example, if the many buildings in a city are heated using individual furnaces that burn coal or oil, then each chimney will be a discrete source of emissions of sulfur dioxide, oxides of nitrogen, and particulates to the atmosphere. The urban air quality will also be influenced by numerous other relatively small sources of emissions, for example, those from automobiles, trucks, and buses. Although each chimney and tailpipe is, strictly speaking, a point source, their emissions rapidly coalesce to form a regional air pollution that affects the atmospheric environment throughout the city and its surroundings.

These diverse, non–point emissions can contribute to the occurrence of episodes of regionally degraded air quality, known as "smog." So–called reducing smogs are characterized by large concentrations of sulfur dioxide, particulates, and soot, and are common where large quantities of coal are burned in industry and used to heat homes and other buildings. Oxidizing smogs occur in sunny regions where there are large non–point emissions of hydrocarbons and oxides of nitrogen, chemicals that are precursors for the secondary formation of ozone. Non–point sources also contribute to the formation of acid rain, another regional environmental problem that is associated with emissions of sulfur dioxide and oxides of nitrogen.

Inputs of nutrients can affect aquatic ecosystems through a syndrome characterized by algal blooms, deoxygenation, and other symptoms of degraded water quality. The nutrient inputs can occur through large point sources such as municipal or industrial sewer pipes, or by more diverse non–point sources associated with agricultural fields and sewage disposal by individual homes.

Often, environmental degradation over large areas is caused by a combination of emissions of pollutants from both point–sources and non–point sources.

See also Point source.

Norepinephrine see **Neurotransmitter**

North America

The landmass occupied by the present–day countries of Canada, the United States, and the Republic of Mexico make up North America. Greenland (Kalaallit Nunaat), an island landmass to the northeast of Canada,

Non-point sources.

is also included in North America, for it has been attached to Canada for almost two billion years.

Plate tectonics is the main force of nature responsible for the geologic history of North America. Over ages of geologic time, the plates have come together to form the continents, including North America. Other processes, such as sedimentation and erosion, modify the shape of the land that has been forged by plate tectonics.

North American geologic history includes several types of mountain ranges as a result of plate tectonics. When the edge of a plate of earth's crust runs over another plate, forcing the lower plate deep into the earth's elastic interior, a long, curved mountain chain of volcanos usually forms on the forward–moving edge of the upper plate. When this border between two plates forms in the middle of the ocean, the volcanic mountains form a string of islands, or archipelago, such as the Antilles and the Aleutians. This phenomenon is called an island arc.

When the upper plate is carrying a continent on its forward edge, a mountain chain, like the Cascades, forms right on the forward edge. This edge, heavily populated with volcanos, is called a continental arc. The volcanic mountains on the plate border described above can run into a continent, shatter the collision area and stack up the pieces into a mountain range. This is how the Appalachians were formed. Imagine how high your school would reach if it were squeezed by bulldozers so it remained the same length east to west as it is now, but from north to south measured the width of a convenience store restroom. The result would be a tall wall of fractured rubble, and that is just what a collisional mountain belt is.

When a continent–sized "layer cake" of rock is pushed, the upper layers move more readily than the lower layers. The layers separate from each other, and the upper few miles of rock move on ahead, floating on fluid pressure between the upper and lower sections of the crust like a fully loaded tractor trailer gliding effortlessly along an icy road. The flat surface where moving

Mount Sopris in the Rocky Mountains near Aspen, Colorado.

layers of crust slide along the top of the layers beneath it is called a thrust fault, and the mountains that are heaved up where the thrust fault reaches the surface are one kind of fault block mountains. The mountains of Glacier National Park slid along the Lewis thrust fault over younger rocks, and out onto the Great Plains.

Another kind of fault block mountains comes from stretching of the earth's crust. A model of this kind of mountains could be made by compacting a six–inch thick layer of moist sand on top of a rubber (not rubberized) sheet. When the sheet stretches, mimicking the elastic properties of the lower crust, the sand will crack along lines perpendicular to the direction the sheet is being pulled. Some of the surface will remain the same height, and some blocks will slide down the sides of the blocks which remain stable. This is particularly noticeable if the top surface of the compacted sand has been dusted with powder. This is a model of the process that formed the mountains in the Basin and Range province.

Mountain ranges start being torn down by physical and chemical forces while they are still rising. North America has been criss–crossed by one immense range of mountains after another throughout its almost four–billion–year history.

A range of mountains may persist for hundreds of millions of years, like the Appalachians. On repeated occasions, the warped, folded rocks of the Appalachians were brought up out of the continent's basement and raised thousands of feet by tectonic forces. If mountains are not continuously uplifted, they are worn down by erosion in a few million years. In North America's geologic past, eroded particles from its mountains were carried by streams and dumped into the continent's inland seas, some of which were as large as the present–day Mediterranean. Those rivers and seas are gone from the continent, but the sediments that filled them remain, like dirt in a bathtub when the water is drained. The roots of all the mountain ranges that have ever stood in North America all still exist, and much of the sand and clay into which the mountains were transformed still exists also, as rock or soil formations.

Geologic history

North America in the Archean Eon

North America was not formed in one piece, or at one time, the way a cake is baked from batter. Various parts of it were formed all over the world, at various times over four billion years, and were brought together and assembled into one continent by the endless process of plate tectonics. What is now called North America began to form in the first two and one–half billion years of the earth's history, a period of time called the Archean Eon.

Some geologists speculate that the earth that created the oldest parts of North America barely resembled the middle–aged planet on which we live. The planet of four billion years ago had cooled enough to have a solid crust, and oceans of liquid water. But the crust may have included hundreds of small tectonic plates, moving perhaps 10 times faster than plates move today. These small plates, carrying what are now the most ancient rocks, scudded across the oceans of a frantic crazy–quilt planet. Active volcanos and rifts played a role in rock formation on the Archean Earth. The oldest regions in North America were formed in this hyperactive world. These regions are in Greenland, Labrador, Minnesota, and Wyoming.

The Earth changed over the next billion years. A sudden surge of continental construction created much of North America. Between three and four billion years ago, great basalt plateaus gradually built up under the oceans. As the planet cooled, the rock on the undersides of these plateaus changed from basalt to eclogite. Basalt floats on the earth's mantle, but the heavier eclogite sinks into it. All over the world, the eclogite tore away from the basalt plateaus and sank into the earth's hot mantle. Vast amounts of magma liquefied from the eclogite slabs as they sank into the hot mantle. This phenomenon is called partial melting, and it resembles what happens to cheese in a microwave oven. Solid cheese separates into melted fat and hard milk solids. The eclogite is the leftover solid cheese; the liquid magma is the melted fat. This magma rose through the basalt and formed 50% of what would become North America's continental crust. But in the Archean Eon, these pieces were still widely scattered on the planet.

In the late Archean Eon, the plates of Earth's crust may have continued to move at a relatively high speed. Evidence of these wild times can be found in the ancient core of North America. The scars of tectonic events appear as rock outcrops throughout the part of northern North America called the Canadian Shield. One example of this kind of scar, a greenstone belt, may be the mangled remains of ancient island arcs or rifts within continents. Gold and chromium are found in the greenstone belts, and deposits of copper, zinc, and nickel. Formations of iron ore also began to form in the Archean Eon, and fossils of microscopic cyanobacteria—the first life on Earth—are found imbedded in them.

North America in the Proterozoic Eon

North America's little Archean continents slammed together in a series of mountain–building collisions. The core of the modern continent was formed 1,850 million years ago when five of these collisions occurred at once around northeastern Canada. This unified piece of ancient continental crust, called a craton, lies exposed at the surface in the Canadian Shield, and forms a solid foundation under much of the rest of the continent.

In the two billion years of the Proterozoic Eon (2,500–570 million years ago), North America's geologic setting became more like the world as we know it. The cores of the modern continents were assembled, and the first collections of continents, or supercontinents, appeared. Life, however, was limited to bacteria and algae, and unbreatheable gases filled the atmosphere. Rampant erosion filled the rivers with mud and sand, because no land plants protected the earth's barren surface from the action of rain, wind, heat, and cold.

Sometimes tectonic stresses pulled the forming continents apart, creating cracks hundreds of miles or kilometers long in the crust. These cracks quickly filled with upwelling magma to form dikes of solid rock. There are so many of these dikes of black rock that they are collectively called dike swarms.

Rich accumulations of both rare and common metallic elements make Proterozoic rocks a significant source of mineral wealth for North America, as on other continents. Chromium, nickel, copper, tin, titanium, vanadium, and platinum ores are found together in the onion–like layers of crystallized igneous rocks called layered intrusions. Greenstone belts are mined for copper, lead, and zinc, each of which is mixed with sulfur to form a sulfide mineral. Sulfide minerals of lead and zinc are found in limestones formed in shallow seas, while mines in the ancient continental river and delta sediments uncover buried vanadium, copper, and uranium ores.

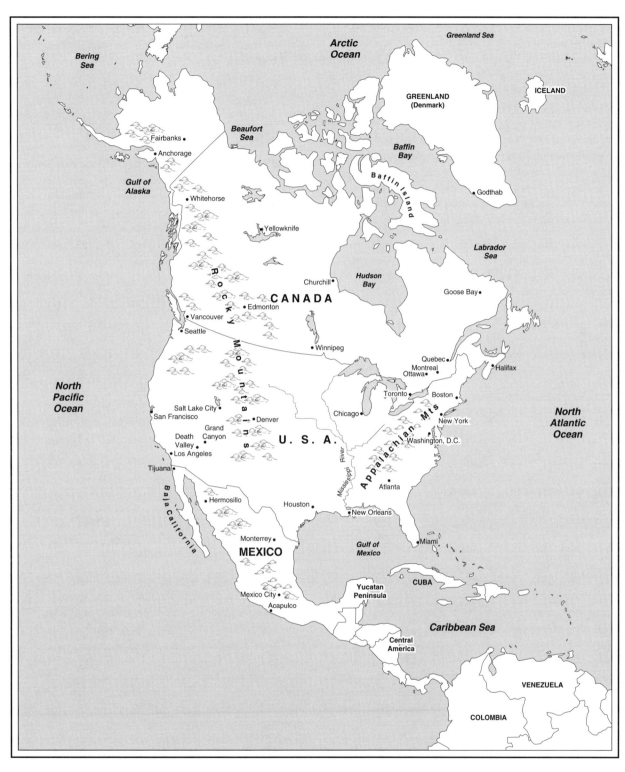

North America.

Most of the steel framework for buildings and machines and tools comes from the processing of a rich and peculiar legacy of the Precambrian environment. Volcanos under the seas of Archean and Proterozoic time erupted huge amounts of ferric iron (Fe^{2+}) into water filled with dissolved oxygen. The iron minerals that formed from the reaction of ferric iron and oxygen, hematite and iron hydroxides and sulfides, settled gently on the floors of lakes and quiet seas, season after season, for more than two billion years. The layers of iron minerals and chert formed amazing evenly striped rocks which have provided the world with its iron for more than a century. These banded iron formations are found in Greenland, Canada, and the Mesabi Range of Minnesota.

The banded iron formations disappear from the rock record at around 1.7 billion years ago, about the same time that oxides (minerals formed by reaction with oxygen) appeared abundantly in stream deposits. Some geologists theorize that previous to 1.7 billion years ago, oxygen was busy oxidizing iron in the sea to enter the atmosphere, and when the iron supply ran out, then the oxygen–rich atmosphere bubbled up out of the sea.

Like a continent–sized zipper, a huge rift opened from Kansas to Michigan's upper peninsula around 1,150 million years ago. Its tectonic activity shut down before tearing the continent in half, but left a trough 93 mi (150 km) wide filled with up to 10 mi (15 km) of stacked basalt lava flows and stream sediments. The rift is exposed today in the Keewenaw peninsula in upper Michigan. It once contained giant boulders of pure copper, some weighing several tons.

During the middle to late Proterozoic Eon, continental collisions attached new pieces of continental crust to North America's southern, eastern, and western borders. Between 30% and 40% of North America joined the continent in the Proterozoic. The crust underlying the continental United States east of Nevada joined the craton, as well as the crust underlying the Sierra Madre Occidental of Sonora, Chihuahua, and Durango in Mexico. The Mazatzal Mountains, whose roots outcrop in the Grand Canyon's inner gorge, rose in these mountain–building times in southern and central North America.

Phanerozoic time

North America experienced the sea washing over its boundaries many times during the three billion–plus years of its Archean and Proterozoic history. Life had flourished in the shallow tidewater. Algae, a long–term resident of North America, was joined later by worms and other soft–bodied animals. Little is known of early soft–bodied organisms, because they left no skeletons to become fossils. Only a handful of good fossils remain from the entire world's immense Precambrian rock record.

Then, about 570 million years ago, several unrelated lineages of shell–bearing sea animals appeared. This was the beginning of the Phanerozoic Eon of earth history, which has lasted from 570 million years ago to the present day. Vast seas covered much of North America in the early Phanerozoic, their shorelines changing from one million–year interval to the next. The seas teemed with creatures whose bones and shells we have come to know in the fossil record. These oceanic events are memorialized in the layers of stone each sea left behind, lying flat in the continent's heartland and folded and broken in the cordilleras. Geologists have surveyed the stacked sheets of stone left by ancient North American seas and have made maps of the deposits of each continental sea. The stacked layers are divided into sequences, each named for the sea that laid it down. Each sequence consisted of a slow and complex flooding of the continent. Sea level, mountain uplift, the growth of deltas, and other factors continually changed the shape of the continental sea.

Eastern and southern borders of North America

The eastern coast of North America was once part of an ancient "Ring of Fire" surrounding an ocean that has disappeared forever from the earth. From Greenland to Georgia, and through the Gulf coast states into Mexico, the collision of continents raised mountains comparable to the Himalayas and Alps of today. Several ranges were raised up on the eastern border of North America between 480–230 million years ago.

The Taconic mountains rose 480 million years ago, wrinkled under pressure like the hood of a wrecked car, from Maryland to the Gaspe Peninsula of Quebec. The compressed rocks from this mountain–building event are exposed in the Taconic Range of New York, and in eastern Pennsylvania. But by 410 million years ago the peaks that had towered over the East coast had been eroded away, and the sea washed over their exposed roots and covered them with level deposits of limestone. As these mountains wore down, the resulting sediment filled a shallow sea basin running from New York southward to Alabama, in layers up to 1,000 ft (300 m) thick.

Another collision about 450 million years ago created the Acadian mountain range, whose roots are exposed today in Newfoundland. These mountains began to be torn down by rain and wind, and by the time they had worn down to nothing, more than 63,000 cubic miles of sediment made from them had been dumped into the shallow continental sea between New York and Virginia—about the same amount of rock as the Sierra Nevada mountains of today. The bones of amphibians, the first land animals, are found in the rocks laid down by the streams of East Greenland.

The sleepless crust under North America's Pennsylvanian–age borders tossed and turned in complex ways. Three hundred million years ago, North America sat on the equator, its vast inland sea surrounded by rain forests whose fossilized remains are the coal deposits of the eastern United States. Small mountain ranges rose out of the sea that covered the center of the continent in Colorado, Oklahoma, and Texas. The Ouachitas stood in the Gulf coast states, the last great mountain range to stand there. In the eastern United States, the Allegheny mountain range stood where the Acadian and Taconic ranges had stood before.

The Ouachitas welded South America to the Gulf coast, at roughly the same time as the Alleghenies welded the East coast of North America to West Africa. The Ouachitas and Alleghenies stretched, unbroken, all the way around the eastern and southern coasts of North America. This joining of the world's continents formed Pangaea, the most recent supercontinent in geologic history. Pangaea's 150 million year history ended with the birth of the Atlantic Ocean and the separation of North and South America. As South America and Africa tore away from North America, Florida was left behind, attached to the intersection of the Allegheny and Ouachita mountains. Another legacy of this cracking of the earth's crust is the New Madrid fault, which runs through the North American Plate under the Mississippi valley.

Western border of North America

The tectonic story begun on the western border of North America around 340 million years ago continues in the present day. Land masses created far away from North America began to collide with the continent. Off the western coast, the tectonic forces began moving in a new direction, and a long quiet interval came to an end. These are some of the phenomena that resulted:

Around 340 million years ago, an offshore island arc, called the Antler Arc, struck the shores about where Nevada and Idaho now are (then the westernmost part of the continent), extending the shoreline of North America a hundred miles westward.

By 245 million years ago, the beginning of the age of dinosaurs, another island arc had run into the American west. The Golconda Arc added a Sumatra–sized piece of land to North America, and the continent bulged out to present–day northern California.

After the Golconda Arc piled onto the West Coast of that time, the crust broke beneath the continent's border, and the ocean's plate ran under North America's west coast like a speeding low–slung sport coupe might run under the rear bumper of a tractor–trailer. A continental arc was born around 230 million years ago in western North America, and its volcanos have been erupting frequently from the dawn of the age of dinosaurs (the Mesozoic Era) until today.

Several more island arcs struck western North America since the middle Jurassic period. The granite mountains of the Sierra Nevada are the roots of one of these island arcs. Landmasses created on the Pacific Plate have been scraped off it like the roof of the sports coupe mentioned earlier would be scraped off as it crammed itself under the rear bumper of a tractor-trailer. This mechanism is the origin of the west coast's ranges, the Cascades, and much of British Columbia and Alaska's southern coast.

A range of fault block mountains rose far inland as the continent was squeezed from west to east. The Sevier mountains stood west of the Cretaceous period's interior seaway, in what is now Montana, Idaho, Nevada, and Utah. The dinosaurs of that time (80–130 million years ago) left their tracks and remains in the mud and sand worn off these mountains.

In the same manner as large island chains were carried to North America on moving plates of oceanic crust, small pieces of land came to the coasts in this way as well. Numerous "exotic terrains," impacting on the western coasts during the Mesozoic and Cenozoic eras, added large areas now covered by British Columbia, Washington, Oregon, California, and Mexico. These little rafts of continental crust were formed far from their present location, for the fossils in them are of creatures that lived halfway around the world—but never in North America. A sizeable piece of continental crust—southern Mexico as far south as the Isthmus of Tehuantepec—joined northern Mexico between 180-140 million years ago.

Interior West

Starting 80 million years ago, new forces began to act on the inland west. Geologists do not know exactly what happened beneath the crust to cause these changes, but the features created on the surface by tectonic action underneath the crust are well known.

At the same time as the Sevier mountains ceased to rise, a similar range, facing the opposite direction, began to move upward. The earth's upper crust beneath the Rocky Mountain states was shoved westward in the Laramide orogeny, lifting the Rocky Mountains for the first time. These first modern Rocky Mountains drained the continent's last great shallow sea of inland North America as they rose. Huge mountains now stood in places where seas had rolled over Colorado, Wyoming, Utah, Idaho, Montana, and Alberta. In Mexico, the Laramide orogeny raised the Sierra Madre Occidental, and formed the mineral deposits that enrich Sonora, Chihuahua, Durango, and Zacatecas. In Colorado, Wyoming, and neighboring states, the Rocky Mountains began to erode away, and by 55 million years ago, the first Rockies had disappeared from the surface—the mountains' roots were buried in sediment from the eroded mountain tops. More recent uplift again exposed the Rockies, and Ice Age glaciers sculpted their tops into today's sharp peaks.

Twenty–five million years ago, after a quiet interlude, North America's western continental arc awoke, and its abundant volcanos again added new rock to the continent from British Columbia to Texas and down the mountainous spine of Mexico. The only area in the Southwest in which volcanos were uncommon was the Colorado Plateau, whose immunity to the tectonic forces around it is still a mystery. Around the borders of the Colorado Plateau's remarkably thick crust, one volcanic catastrophe after another covered the land. In this time the San Juan mountains were formed in Colorado. The Rocky Mountains began to slide westward and rose again on the thrust faults beneath them.

Ten million years ago, the Great Basin area of the United States was much shorter when measured east to west than it is today. It was then a mountainous highland. Some geologists propose that Nevada was an alpine plateau like Tibet is today—perhaps more than 10,000 ft (3,048 m) high. Starting then and continuing for five million years, this area began to be pulled apart. Long faults opened in the crust, and mountain–sized wedges slowly fell between ridges that were still standing on the unbroken basement rock miles below. Sediment from the erosion of these new ridges filled the valleys, enabling the valleys to become reservoirs of underground water, or aquifers. The low parts got so low that the area is indeed a basin; water does not flow out of it. Some geologists believe that the Basin and Range province stretches around the Colorado Plateau, into Texas, and extends down the Sierra Madre Occidental as far south as Oaxaca.

Another kind of pulling–apart of the continent happened in New Mexico's Rio Grande rift. As at the Keewenaw rift a billion years before, tectonic forces from beneath the earth's crust began pulling the surface apart just as east Africa is being pulled apart today. The

broad rift's mountainous walls eroded, and the sediment from that erosion piled up in the ever–widening valley. A new ocean was about to be formed in the southwest. Lava poured from fissures in the crust near Taos, New Mexico, filling the valley floor. Also like the Keewenaw rift, the Rio Grande rift stopped growing after a few million years, as the tectonic processes ceased pulling the continent apart. The modern Rio Grande was born as a consequence of this rift, and still runs through the rift valley.

A cataclysmic volcanic event happened in Oregon and Washington 17 million years ago. For an unknown reason, perhaps a disturbance deep in the earth's mantle, or a meteor impact, lava began pouring out of cracks in the earth. So much lava poured onto the surface at once that it ran from southeastern Oregon down the Columbia river valley to the Pacific Ocean. Huge cracks in the ground called fissures flooded broad areas with basalt lava over about 500,000 years. This flood of basalt is called the Columbia River plateau. A hot spot, or an upwelling of molten rock from the earth's mantle, appears to have caused the Columbia River plateau. As the North American plate moved westward between then and now, the hot spot stayed in one place, scorching holes in the earth's crust under Idaho and erupting the lava that makes the Snake River Plain a fertile farmland. This hot spot is assumed to be the heat source that powers the geysers of Yellowstone National Park.

Arctic region

In the early Jurassic period, 200 million years ago, the northernmost edge of North America tore away from the continent and began rotating counterclockwise. This part of the continent came to rest to the northwest of North America, forming the original piece of Alaska—its northernmost mountains, the Brooks Range. In the late Cretaceous period, the farthest part of this landmass from North America struck the edge of Siberia, and became the Chukotsk Peninsula. The remaining landmass of Alaska joined North America bit by bit, in the form of exotic terrains. The Aleutians, a classic island arc, formed in the Tertiary period. The about 40 active volcanos of the Aleutians have erupted numerous times in the 20th century, including several eruptions in the last decade from Mt. Augustine, Pavlov, Shishaldin, and Mt. Redoubt.

The Ice Age in North America

For reasons that are not yet fully understood, the earth periodically enters a time of planet–wide cooling. Large areas of the land and seas are covered in ice sheets thousands of feet thick, that remain unmelted for thousands or hundreds of thousands of years. Today, only Greenland and Antarctica lie beneath continent–sized glaciers. But in the very recent geologic past, North America's northern regions, including the entire landmass of Canada, were ground and polished by an oceanic amount of water frozen into a single mass of ice. This ice began to accumulate as the planet's weather cooled, and began to stay frozen all year round. As it built up higher and higher, it began to move out from the piled–high center, flowing while still solid.

Vast amounts of Canadian soil and rock, called glacial till, rode on the ice sheets as they moved, or surfed slowly before the front of the ice wall. Some of the richest farmland in the United States midwest and northeast arrived in its present location in this way—as well as boulders that must be removed from fields before plowing. In the unusual geographic conditions following the retreat of the ice sheets, barren soil lay on the landscape, no longer held down by the glacier. Windstorms moved tremendous amounts of this soil far from where the glacier left it, to settle out of the sky as a layer of fertile soil, called loess in German and English. Loess soils settled in the Mississippi and Missouri valleys, and also Washington, Oregon, Oklahoma, and Texas.

This continental glaciation happened seven times over the last 2.2 million years. Warm intervals, some of them hundreds of thousands of years long, stretched between these planetary deep–freezes. Geologists do not agree whether the ice will return or not. Even if the present day is in a warm period between glaciations, tens or hundreds of thousands of years may elapse before the next advance of the ice sheets.

Modern geologic events in North America

California lies between two different kinds of plate boundaries. To the south, the crust under California is growing; to the north it is shrinking. The part of California that sits on the Pacific plate between these two forces is moved northward in sudden increments of a few feet which are felt as earthquakes. A few feet at a time, in earthquakes that happen every few decades, the part of California west of the San Andreas fault will move northward along the coast.

Active faults also exist elsewhere in the United States, in the midwest and in South Carolina. The last sizeable earthquakes in these regions occurred more than a hundred years ago, and geologists assume that earthquakes will probably occur within the next hundred years. The Pacific Northwest and Alaska, sitting atop active tectonic environments, will certainly be shaken

KEY TERMS

Archean Eon—The period of time beginning at Earth's formation and ending two and one–half billion years ago.

Canadian shield—The oldest part of North America, made of rocks formed between 3.8 and 2.5 billion years ago, that underlies much of northern and eastern Canada.

Collisional mountain belt—A mountain range, like the Appalachians, caused by one continent running into another continent.

Continental arc—A volcanic mountain range, like the Cascades, that forms on the tectonically active edge of a continent, over a subduction zone.

Craton—A piece of a continent that has remained intact since the earth's earliest history, and which functions as a foundation, or basement, for more recent pieces of a continent.

Fault block mountains—A mountain range, like the Front Range of the Rocky Mountains, caused by horizontal forces that squeeze a continent, fracturing its crust and pushing blocks of crust up to form mountains. Also, a mountain range, like the Shoshone Range of Nevada, caused by horizontal forces that stretch a continent, fracturing the crust and causing some blocks of crust to sink down, leaving other blocks standing at high elevations above the valleys.

Glacial till—Soil, rocks, and other sediments deposited by glaciers that carry the sediments far from their point of origin.

Island arc—A volcanic mountain range, like the Aleutians, built on a tectonically active plate boundary in the sea, which appears as islands.

Plate tectonics—The interactions of the plates of Earth's crust, which float on top of the earth's mantle, and whose movements through geologic time have caused the major features of the continents.

Phanerozoic Eon—The period of time beginning 570 million years ago, in the rocks of which an abundant record of fossilized life exists.

Precambrian Era—The combined Archean and Proterozoic Eons, the first four billion years of Earth's history.

Proterozoic Eon—The period of time beginning two and one–half billion years ago and ending 570 million years ago.

by earthquakes for millions of years to come. The Great Basin, the western Rocky Mountains, and the United States northeast are all considered tectonically active enough for earthquakes to be considered possible.

North America's volcanic mountain ranges, the Cascades, and the relatively recent Mexican Volcanic Belt, have erupted often in the recent geologic past. These mountains will certainly continue to erupt in the near geologic future.

See also Hot spot; Magma; Plate Tectonics.

Further Reading:

Sullivan, W. *Landprints.* New York: The New York Times Book Co., Inc., 1984.

Stetter, J., ed. *Geology of the Great Basin.* University of Nevada Press, 1986.

Harris, D. and E. Kiver. *The Geologic Story of the National Parks and Monuments,* 4th ed. New York: John Wiley and Sons, 1985.

Colbert, E., ed. *Our Continent.* Washington, D.C.: The National Geographic Society, 1976.

Clinton Crowley

Northern parula see **Warblers**

No-see-ums see **True flies**

Nose see **Smell; Respiratory system**

Nova

Nova is a Latin word meaning new, and it describes the appearance of a seemingly "new star" in the sky, a brilliant object in a place where there was previously only a very faint star, or perhaps nothing at all.

A nova is a phenomenon that happens in a binary star system containing a white dwarf and a stable companion star. A white dwarf is the dead, collapsed core of a star that formerly was about the size of the Sun. When the Sun dies, it will become a white dwarf. Unlike the Sun, however, many stars exist in *binary* systems, where two stars orbit one another. In many binaries these stars may be separated by a distance much less than the distance from the Sun to the Earth.

Suppose we have a binary system with a white dwarf and a companion star that is expanding to become a red giant star. As the surface of the red giant star expands, it gets progressively closer to the white dwarf. Eventually, the surface of the giant may reach a critical point between the two stars where the gravity of the white dwarf is actually stronger than the giant's own gravity. If this happens, matter will begin streaming off the giant's surface and onto the white dwarf. This is like overfilling a bucket with water — eventually the water will overflow, and if there is an adjacent bucket, begin pouring into it. Likewise, the large star will begin to lose matter once its surface expands past its Roche lobe, the imaginary surface beyond which the giant star's gravity is no longer sufficient for it to retain its matter.

The white dwarf has tremendously strong gravity, because it is very massive and very small. Therefore, the companion star's matter, which is mostly hydrogen, is squashed into a dense, thin, hot layer on the white dwarf's surface. The more matter that streams onto the white dwarf, the hotter it gets, and eventually, thermonuclear fusion reactions begin. These reactions are just like those that occur in the center of a stable star like the Sun, converting the hydrogen to helium with an accompanying enormous release of energy. In a brief but violent cataclysm, the hydrogen on the white dwarf's surface burns away, and while it does so, the white dwarf brightens by as much as a factor of a million (15 magnitudes). This is a nova, and after reaching its peak brightness, it slowly fades over a period of weeks to months.

Because mass transfer in a binary system does not stop after a nova explosion, the white dwarf will start to reaccumulate matter. Novae therefore are recurrent, with the length of time between nova outbursts in a system depending on how fast the companion star is losing matter to the white dwarf. If the stream is just a trickle, it might be thousands of years until the next outburst. Other novae recur much more frequently. As a single star, the Sun is unlikely ever to become a nova after it dies. It may accrete enough matter just from the interstellar medium to become a nova, but such novae are extremely rare events due to the low rate of accretion of matter.

Novae should never be confused with supernovae, which are not just "big novae." Supernovae involve the explosion and destruction of a star or a white dwarf, while a nova is merely the conflagration of a surface layer of hydrogen on a white dwarf. Novae are much more common than supernovae, and they do not release nearly as much energy. Nevertheless, they are a good reason to be familiar with the sky: things do change up there, and you never know when you might look up and see a familiar constellation looking a bit different.

See also Binary star; Red giant star; Stellar evolution; Supernova; White dwarf.

Novocain

Novocain is the trademark name for procaine hydrochloride ($C_{12}H_{20}N_2O_2HCl$). It is used as a local anesthetic, particularly in dentistry, surgeries, and spinal anesthesia. A local anesthetic is a drug that temporarily blocks nerve conduction. Novocain is injected into tissue, a nerve trunk, or next to a nerve, or into the spinal canal. Like other local anesthetics, novocain prevents the initiation and conduction of nerve impulses by acting on the neuronal cell membrane. Nerve impulses are conducted by the exchange of sodium and potassium ions through the cell membrane. Novocain alters the permeability of the cell membrane to sodium ions, thus altering the polarity of the membrane and its ability to conduct a nerve impulse. As the anesthetic effect increases, the threshold for electrical stimulation increases and conduction of the nerve impulse decreases. Eventually, the nerve conduction is totally blocked.

Procaine hydrochloride was first synthesized by Einhorn in 1905 as a substitute for cocaine, the first local anesthetic. Cocaine, an alkaloid obtained from the leaves of the coca plant, *Erythroxylon coca*, is highly addictive and toxic. Procaine hydrochloride replaced cocaine as a local anesthetic because it is much less toxic, cheaper and easier to produce, and it is easier to sterilize. In contrast to cocaine, it is not addictive because it is less stimulating to the central nervous system.

Novocain is absorbed rapidly and begins to act within two to five minutes. The duration of the anesthetic effect usually lasts one to two hours, depending on the method of delivery, concentration of the solution, and the individual patient. Sometimes novocain is mixed with a drug called a vasoconstrictor. A vasoconstrictor constricts the blood vessels, reducing the flow of blood, which slows the rate of absorption so that the anesthetic effect lasts longer. Novocain is an odorless, white crystalline powder that is water soluble. It is available as a prepared solution as either pure or, depending on its intended use, mixed with other drugs.

See also Analgesia; Anesthesia.

Nuclear fission

Nuclear fission is a process in which the nucleus of an atom splits, usually into two pieces. This reaction was discovered when a target of uranium was bombarded by neutrons. Fission fragments were shown to fly apart with a large release of energy. The fission reaction was the basis of the atomic bomb, which was developed by the United States during World War II. After the war, controlled energy release from fission was applied to the development of nuclear reactors. Reactors are utilized for production of electricity at nuclear power plants, for propulsion of ships and submarines, and for the creation of radioactive isotopes used in medicine and industry.

History

The fission reaction was discovered in 1938 by two German scientists, Otto Hahn (1879–1968) and Fritz Strassmann. They had been doing a series of experiments in which they used neutrons to bombard various elements. If they bombarded copper, for example, a radioactive form of copper was produced. Other elements became radioactive in the same way. When uranium was bombarded with neutrons, however, an entirely different reaction seemed to occur. The uranium nucleus apparently underwent a major disruption.

The evidence for this supposed process came from chemical analysis. Hahn and Strassmann published a scientific paper showing that small amounts of barium (element 56) were produced when uranium (element 92) was bombarded with neutrons. It was very puzzling to them how a single neutron could transform element 92 into element 56.

Lise Meitner (1878–1968), a long–time colleague of Hahn who had left Germany due to Nazi persecution, suggested a helpful model for such a reaction. One can visualize the uranium nucleus to be like a liquid drop containing protons and neutrons. When an extra neutron enters, the drop begins to vibrate. If the vibration is violent enough, the drop can break into two pieces. Meitner named this process "fission" because it is similar to the process of cell division in biology. It takes only a small amount of energy to start the vibration which leads to a major breakup.

Scientists in the United States and elsewhere quickly confirmed the idea of uranium fission, using other experimental procedures. For example, a cloud chamber is a device in which vapor trails of moving nuclear particles can be seen and photographed. In one experiment, a thin sheet of uranium was placed inside a cloud chamber. When it was irradiated by neutrons, photographs showed a pair of tracks going in opposite directions from a common starting point in the uranium. Clearly, a nucleus had been photographed in the act of fission.

Another experimental procedure used a Geiger counter, which is a small, cylindrical tube that produces

The Davis-Besse Nuclear Power Plant on the shore of Lake Erie in Oak Harbor, Ohio.

electrical pulses when a radioactive particle passes through it. For this experiment, the inside of a modified Geiger tube was lined with a thin layer of uranium. When a neutron source was brought near it, large voltage pulses were observed, much larger than from ordinary radioactivity. When the neutron source was taken away, the large pulses stopped. A Geiger tube without the uranium lining did not generate large pulses. Evidently, the large pulses were due to uranium fission fragments. The size of the pulses showed that the fragments had a very large amount of energy.

To understand the high energy released in uranium fission, scientists made some theoretical calculations based on Albert Einstein's famous equation $E=mc^2$. The Einstein equation says that mass m can be converted ito energy E, and the conversion factor is a huge number, c, which is the velocity of light squared. One can calculate that the total mass of the fission products remaining at the end of the reaction is slightly less than the mass of the uranium atom plus neutron at the start. This decrease of mass, multiplied by c, shows numerically why the fission fragments are so energetic.

From uranium fission to chain reaction

Through fission, neutrons of low energy can trigger off a very large energy release. With the imminent threat of war in 1939, a number of scientists began to consider the possibility that a new and very powerful "atomic bomb" could be built from uranium. Also, they speculated that uranium perhaps could be harnessed to replace coal or oil as a fuel for industrial power plants.

Nuclear reactions in general are much more powerful than chemical reactions. A chemical change such as burning coal or even exploding TNT affects only the outer electrons of an atom. A nuclear process, on the other hand, causes changes among the protons and neutrons inside the nucleus. The energy of attraction between protons and neutrons is about a million times greater than the chemical binding energy between atoms. Therefore, a single fission bomb, using nuclear energy, might destroy a whole city. Alternatively, nuclear electric power plants theoretically could run for a whole year on just a few tons of fuel.

In order to release a substantial amount of energy, many millions of uranium nuclei must split apart. The fission process itself provides a mechanism for creating

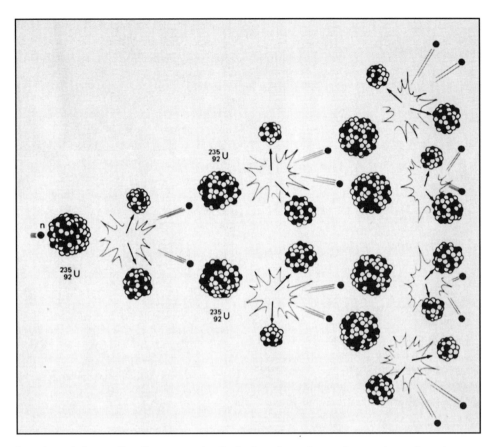

A nuclear chain reaction: the successive fissioning of ever-increasing numbers of uranium-235 atoms.

a so–called "chain reaction." In addition to the two main fragments, each fission event produces two or three extra neutrons. Some of these can enter nearby uranium nuclei and cause them in turn to fission, releasing more neutrons, which cause more fissions, and so forth. In a bomb explosion, neutrons have to increase very rapidly, in a fraction of a second. In a controlled reactor, however, the neutron population has to be kept in a steady state. Excess neutrons must be removed by some type of absorber material.

In 1942, the first nuclear reactor with a self–sustaining chain reaction was built in the United States. The principal designer was Enrico Fermi (1901–1954), an Italian physicist and the 1938 Nobel Prize winner in physics. He had emigrated to the United States to escape from Benito Mussolini's fascism. Fermi's reactor design had three main components: lumps of uranium (the fuel), blocks of carbon (the moderator, which slows down the neutrons), and control rods made of cadmium (an excellent neutron absorber). The reactor was built at the University of Chicago. When the pile of uranium and carbon blocks was about 10 ft (3 m) high and the cadmium control rods were pulled out far

enough, Geiger counters showed that a steady–state chain reaction had been successfully accomplished. The power output was only about 200 watts, but it was enough to verify the basic principle of reactor operation. The power level of the chain reaction could be varied by moving the control rods in or out.

The Manhattan Project, 1942–1945

General Leslie R. Groves was put in charge of the project to convert the chain reaction experiment into a usable military weapon. Three major laboratories were built under wartime conditions of urgency and secrecy. Oak Ridge, Tennessee, became the site for purifying and separating uranium into bomb–grade material. At Hanford, Washington, four large reactors were built to produce another possible bomb material, plutonium. At Los Alamos, New Mexico, the actual work of bomb design was started in 1943 under the leadership of the physicist J. Robert Oppenheimer (1904–1967).

The element uranium is a mixture of two isotopes, uranium–235 and uranium–238. Both isotopes have 92 protons in the nucleus, but uranium–238 has three addi-

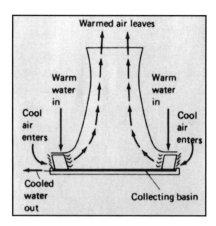

How a hyperbolic cooling tower
works.

tional neutrons. Both isotopes have 92 orbital electrons to balance the 92 protons, so their chemical properties are identical. When uranium is bombarded with neutrons, the two isotopes have differing nuclear reactions. A high percentage of the uranium–235 nuclei undergo fission, as described previously. The uranium–238, on the other hand, simply absorbs a neutron and is converted to the next heavier isotope, uranium–239. It is not possible to build a bomb out of natural uranium. The reason is that the chain reaction would be halted by uranium–238 because it removes neutrons without reproducing any new ones.

The fissionable isotope, uranium–235, constitutes only about 1% of natural uranium, while the non–fissionable neutron absorber, uranium–238, makes up the other 99%. To produce bomb–grade, fissionable uranium–235, it was necessary to build a large isotope separation facility. Since the plant would require much electricity, the site was chosen to be in the region of the Tennessee Valley Authority (TVA). The technology of large–scale isotope separation involved solving many difficult, unprecedented problems. By early 1945, the Oak Ridge Laboratory was able to produce kilogram amounts of uranium–235 purified to better than 95%.

An alternate possible fuel for a fission bomb is plutonium–239. Plutonium does not exist in nature but results from radioactive decay of uranium–239. Fermi's chain reaction experiment had shown that uranium–239 can be made in a reactor. However, to produce several hundred kilograms of plutonium required a large increase from the power level of Fermi's original experiment. Plutonium production reactors were constructed at Hanford, Washington, located near the Columbia river to provide needed cooling water. A difficult technical problem was how to separate plutonium from the

highly radioactive fuel rods after irradiation. This was accomplished by means of remote handling apparatus that was manipulated by technicians working behind thick protective glass windows.

With uranium–235 separation started at Oak Ridge and plutonium–239 production under way at Hanford, a third laboratory was set up at Los Alamos, New Mexico, to work on bomb design. In order to create an explosion, many nuclei would have to fission almost simultaneously. The key concept was to bring together several pieces of fissionable material into a so–called "critical mass." In one design, two pieces of uranium–235 were shot toward each other from opposite ends of a cylindrical tube. A second design used a spherical shell of plutonium–239, to be detonated by an "implosion" toward the center of the sphere.

The first atomic bomb was tested at an isolated desert location in New Mexico on July 16, 1945. President Truman then issued an ultimatum to Japan that a powerful new weapon could soon be used against them. On August 8, a single atomic bomb destroyed the city of Hiroshima with over 80,000 casualties. On August 11, a second bomb was dropped on Nagasaki with a similar result. The Japanese leaders surrendered three days later.

The decision to use the atomic bomb has been vigorously debated over the years. It brought a quick end to the war and avoided many casualties that a land invasion of Japan would have cost. However, the civilians who were killed by the bomb and the survivors who developed radiation sickness left an unforgettable legacy of fear. The horror of mass annihilation in a nuclear war is made vivid by the images of destruction at Hiroshima. The possibility of a ruthless dictator or a terrorist group getting nuclear weapons is a continuing threat to world peace.

Nuclear reactors for electric power production

The first nuclear reactor designed for producing electricity was put into operation in 1957 at Shippingsport, Pennsylvania. From 1960 to 1990, more than 100 nuclear power plants were built in the United States. These plants now generate about 20% of the nation's electric power. World–wide, there are over 400 nuclear power stations.

The most common reactor type is the pressurized water reactor (abbreviated PWR). The system operates like a coal–burning power plant, except that the firebox of the coal plant is replaced by a reactor. Nuclear energy from uranium is released in the two fission fragments. The fuel rod becomes very hot because of the cumulative energy of many fissioning nuclei. A typical reactor core contains hundreds of these fuel rods. Water is circulated through the core to remove the heat. The hot water is prevented from boiling by keeping the system under pressure.

The pressurized hot water goes to a heat exchanger where steam is produced. The steam then goes to a turbine, which has a series of fan blades that rotate rapidly when hit by the steam. The turbine is connected to the rotor of an electric generator. Its output goes to cross–country transmission lines that supply the electrical users in the region. The steam that made the turbine rotate is condensed back into water and is recycled to the heat exchanger. This method of generating electricity was developed for coal plants and is known to be very reliable.

Safety features at a nuclear power plant include automatic shutdown of the fission process by insertion of control rods, emergency water cooling for the core in case of pipeline breakage, and a concrete containment shell. It is impossible for a reactor to have a nuclear explosion because the fuel enrichment in a reactor is intentionally limited to about 3% uranium–235, while almost 100% pure uranium–235 is required for a bomb. The worst accident at a PWR would be a steam explosion, which could contaminate the inside of the containment shell.

The fuel in the reactor core consists of several tons of uranium. As the reactor is operated, the uranium content gradually decreases because of fission, and the radioactive waste products (the fission fragments) build up. After about a year of operation, the reactor must be shut down for refueling. The old fuel rods are pulled out and replaced. These fuel rods, which are very radioactive, are stored under water at the power plant site. After five to ten years, much of their radioactivity has decayed. Only those materials with a long radioactive lifetime remain, and eventually they will be stored in a suitable underground depository.

The controversy about nuclear power plants

There are vehement arguments for and against nuclear power. The various advantages and problems should be thoroughly aired so that the general public can evaluate for itself whether the benefits outweigh the risks. Additional electric power plants will be required in the future to supply a growing world population that desires a higher standard of living.

KEY TERMS

Chain reaction—An on–going process in which a neutron produced from fission enters a nearby nucleus, causes it to fission, and releases additional neutrons to continue the process.

Critical mass—The minimum amount of fissionable uranium or plutonium that is necessary to maintain a chain reaction.

Geiger counter—A small, cylindrical tube used to detect radioactivity, giving an output of voltage pulses when radiation passes through it.

Isotopes—Atoms of an element that have the same chemical properties but differ in mass due to a variation in the number of neutrons in the nucleus.

Plutonium—A man–made element that is created from uranium–238 by neutron bombardment and can be used as a material for fission energy.

Radioactive waste—The radioactive fragments produced by fission, which accumulate in the fuel rods of a nuclear reactor and eventually must be removed.

All methods of producing electricity have serious environmental impacts. The main objections to nuclear power plants are the fear of possible accidents, the unresolved problem of nuclear waste storage, and the possibility of plutonium diversion for weapons production by a terrorist group. The issue of waste storage becomes particularly emotional because leakage from a waste depository could contaminate ground water. Chemical dump sites have leaked in the past, so there is distrust of all hazardous wastes.

The main advantage of nuclear power plants is that they do not cause atmospheric pollution. No smokestacks are needed because nothing is being burned. France initiated a large–scale nuclear program after the Arab oil embargo in 1973 and has been able to reduce its acid rain and carbon dioxide emissions by more than 40%. Nuclear power plants do not contribute to the global warming problem. Shipments of fuel are minimal so the hazards of coal transportation and oil spills are avoided.

Environmentalists are divided in their opinions of nuclear power. It is widely viewed as a hazardous technology but there is growing concern about atmospheric pollution making nuclear power more acceptable.

Further Reading:

Graetzer, Hans G., and David L. Anderson. *The Discovery of Nuclear Fission: A Documentary History.* New York: Van Nostrand Reinhold, 1971. Reprint: Arno Press, 1981.

Graetzer, Hans G. and Larry M. Browning. *The Atomic Bomb: An Annotated Bibliography.* Pasadena: Salem Press, 1992.

Hafele, Wolf. "Energy from Nuclear Power," *Scientific American* 263: 136–144, September, 1990.

Kaku, Michio, and Jennifer Trainer. *Nuclear Power, Both Sides: The Best Arguments For and Against the Most Controversial Technology.* New York: W. W. Norton, 1982.

Murray, Raymond L. *Nuclear Energy*, 3rd ed. New York: Pergamon Press, 1988.

Wagner, Henry N., and Linda E. Ketchum. *Living with Radiation: The Risk, the Promise.* Baltimore: The Johns Hopkins University Press, 1989.

Wolfson, Richard. *Nuclear Choices: A Citizen's Guide to Nuclear Technology.* Cambridge, Mass.: MIT Press, 1991.

Hans G. Graetzer

Nuclear fusion

Nuclear fusion is the process by which two light atomic nuclei combine to form one heavier atomic nucleus. As an example, a proton (the nucleus of a hydrogen atom) and a neutron will, under the proper circumstances, combine to form a deuteron (the nucleus of an atom of "heavy hydrogen"). In general, the mass of the heavier product nucleus is less than the total mass of the two lighter nuclei.

When a proton and neutron combine, for example, the mass of the resulting deuteron is 0.00239 atomic mass unit less than the total mass of the proton and neutron combined. This "loss" of mass is expressed in the form of 2.23 MeV (million electron volts) of kinetic energy of the deuteron and other particles and as other forms of energy produced during the reaction. Nuclear fusion reactions are like nuclear fission reactions, therefore, in the respect that some quantity of mass is transformed into energy.

Some typical fusion reactions

The particles most commonly involved in nuclear fusion reactions include the proton, neutron, deuteron, a triton (a proton combined with two neutrons), a

helium–3 nucleus (two protons combined with a neutron), and a helium–4 nucleus (two protons combined with two neutrons). Except for the neutron, all of these particles carry at least one positive electrical charge. That means that fusion reactions always require very large amounts of energy in order to overcome the force of repulsion between two like–charged particles. For example, in order to fuse two protons with each other, enough energy must be provided to overcome the force of repulsion between the two positively charged particles.

Naturally occurring fusion reactions

As early as the 1930s, a number of physicists had considered the possibility that nuclear fusion reactions might be the mechanism by which energy is generated in the stars. Certainly no familiar type of chemical reaction, such as oxidation, could possibly explain the vast amounts of energy released by even the smallest star. In 1939, the German–American physicist Hans Bethe worked out the mathematics of energy generation in which a proton first fuses with a carbon atom to form a nitrogen atom. The reaction then continues through a series of five more steps, the net result of which is that four protons disappear and are replaced by one helium atom.

Bethe chose this sequence of reactions because it requires less energy than does the direct fusion of four protons and, thus, is more likely to take place in a star. Bethe was able to show that the total amount of energy released by this sequence of reactions was comparable to that which is actually observed in stars.

The Bethe "carbon–cycle" is by no means the only nuclear fusion reaction that one might conceive. A more direct approach, for example, would be one in which two protons fuse to form a deuteron. That deuteron could, then, fuse with a third proton to form a helium–3 nucleus. Finally, the helium–3 nucleus could fuse with a fourth proton to form a helium–4 nucleus. The net result of this sequence of reactions would be the combining of four protons (hydrogen nuclei) to form a single helium–4 nucleus. The only net difference between this reaction and Bethe's carbon cycle is the amount of energy involved in the overall set of reactions.

Thermonuclear reactions

The term "less energy" used to describe Bethe's choice of nuclear reactions is relative, however, since huge amounts of energy must be provided in order to bring about any kind of fusion reaction. In fact, the reason that fusion reactions can occur in stars is that the temperatures in their interiors are great enough to pro-

Tokamak 15, a nuclear fusion research reactor at the Kurchatov Institute, Moscow, Russia. The ring-shape of the reactor is the design most favored by nuclear fusion researchers. The ring contains a plasma mixture of deuterium and tritium at a temperature of up to 180 million° F (100 million° C). The tokamak is surrounded by powerful magnets that enclose the plasma with their fields and keep it away from the walls of the reactor vessel. At sufficiently high temperatures, the deuterium and tritium nuclei fuse, creating helium and energetic neutrons. It is these neutrons which carry the energy of the reactor.

vide the energy needed to bring about fusion. Since those temperatures generally amount to a few million degrees, fusion reactions are also known as thermonuclear (thermo = heat) reactions.

Fusion reactions on earth

The understanding that fusion reactions might be responsible for energy production in stars brought the accompanying realization that such reactions might be a very useful source of energy for human needs. Imagine

that it would be possible to build and operate a small "star" on the outskirts of your community that operated on nuclear fusion. That power plant would be able to supply all of the community's energy needs as far into the future as anyone could see.

The practical problems of building a fusion power plant are incredible, however, and scientists are still a long way from achieving that goal. A much simpler challenge, however, is to construct a "fusion power plant" that does not need to be controlled, that is, a fusion bomb.

Uncontrolled fusion power: The hydrogen bomb

Scientists who worked on the first fission ("atomic") bomb during World War II were aware of the potential for building an even more powerful bomb that operated on fusion principles. Here is how it would work.

The core of the fusion bomb would consist of a fission bomb, such as the one they were then developing. That core could then be surrounded by a casing filled with isotopes of hydrogen. Isotopes of hydrogen are various forms of hydrogen that all have a single proton in their nucleus, but may have zero, one, or two neutrons. The nuclei of the hydrogen isotopes are the proton, the deuteron, and the triton.

Imagine that a device such as the one described here could be exploded. In the first fraction of a second, the fission bomb would explode, releasing huge amounts of energy. In fact, the temperature at the heart of the fission bomb would reach a few millions degrees, the only way that humans know of for producing such high temperatures.

That temperature would not last very long, but in the microseconds that it did exist, it would provide the energy for fusion to begin to occur within the casing surrounding the fission bomb. Protons, deuterons, and tritons would begin fusing with each other, releasing more energy, and initiating other fusion reactions among other hydrogen isotopes. The original explosion of the fission bomb would have ignited a small star–like reaction in the casing surrounding it.

From a military standpoint, the fusion bomb had one powerful advantage over the fission bomb. For technical reasons, there is a limit to the size one can make a fission bomb. But there is no technical limit on the size of a fusion bomb. One simply makes the casing surrounding the fission bomb larger and larger, until there is no longer a way to lift the bomb into the air so that it can be dropped on an enemy.

On August 20, 1953, the Soviet Union announced the detonation of the world's first fusion bomb. It was about 1,000 times more powerful than was the fission bomb that had been dropped on Hiroshima less than a decade earlier. Since that date, both the Soviet Union (now Russia) and the United States have become proficient at manufacturing fusion bombs on an almost assembly–line schedule.

Peaceful applications of nuclear fusion

As research on fusion weapons was going on, attempts were also being made to develop peaceful uses for nuclear fusion. The concept of a "star" power plant just outside the city was never out of sight for a number of nuclear scientists.

The problems to be solved in controlling the nuclear fusion reaction have, however, been enormous. The most obvious challenge is simply to find a way to "hold" the nuclear fusion reaction in place as it occurs. One cannot build a machine made out of metal, plastic, glass, or any other common kind of material. At the temperatures at which fusion occurs, any one of these materials would vaporize instantly. So how does one contain the nuclear fusion reaction?

Traditionally, two general approaches have been developed to solve this problem: magnetic and inertial containment. To understand the first technique, imagine that a mixture of hydrogen isotopes has been heated to a very high temperature. At a sufficiently high temperature, the nature of the mixture begins to change. Atoms totally lose their electrons, and the mixture consists of a swirling mass of positively charged nuclei and electrons. Such a mixture is known as a plasma.

One way to control that plasma is with a magnetic field. One can design such a field so that a swirling hot mass of plasma within it can be held in any kind of a shape one chooses. The best known example of this approach is a doughnut–shaped Russian machine known as a tokamak. In the tokamak, two powerful electromagnets create fields that are so powerful that they can hold a hot plasma in place as readily as a person can hold an orange in his hand.

The technique, then, is to heat the hydrogen isotopes to higher and higher temperatures while containing them within a confined space by means of the magnetic fields. At some critical temperatures, nuclear fusion will begin to occur. At that point, the tokamak is producing energy by means of fusion while the fuel is being held in suspension by the magnetic field.

Inertial confinement

A second method for creating controlled nuclear fusion makes use of a laser beam or a beam of electrons or atoms. In this approach, hydrogen isotopes are suspended at the middle of the machine in tiny hollow glass spheres known as microballoons. The microballoons are then bombarded by the laser, electron, or atomic beam and caused to implode. During implosion, enough energy is produced to initiate fusion among the hydrogen isotopes within the pellet. The plasma thus produced is then confined and controlled by means of the external beam.

The production of useful nuclear fusion energy by either of these methods depends on three factors: temperature, containment time, and energy release. That is, it is first necessary to raise the temperature of the fuel (the hydrogen isotopes) to a temperature of about 100 million degrees. Then, it is necessary to keep the fuel suspended at that temperature long enough for fusion to begin. Finally, some method must be found for tapping off the energy produced by fusion.

A measure of the success of a machine in producing useful fusion energy is known as the Lawson confinement parameter, the product of the density of particles in the plasma and the time the particles are confined. That is, in order for controlled fusion to occur, particles in the plasma must be brought close together and they must be kept together for some critical period of time. All of this must take place, of course, at a temperature at which fusion can occur.

D–D and D–T reactions

The two nuclear reactions now most commonly used for power production purposes are designated as D–D and D–T reactions. The former stands for deuterium–deuterium and involves the combination of two deuterium nuclei to form a helium–3 nucleus and a free neutron. The second reaction stands for deuterium–tritium and involves the combination of a deuterium nucleus and a tritium nucleus to produce a helium–4 nucleus and a free neutron. The most common form of an inertial confinement machine, for example, uses a fuel that consists of equal parts of deuterium and tritium.

Hope for the future

Research on controlled fusion power has now been going on for a half century with somewhat disappointing results. Some experts believe that success may be "just around the corner," but others argue that the problems of an economically feasible fusion power plant may never be solved.

In recent years, scientists have begun to explore approaches to fusion power that depart from the more traditional magnetic and inertial confinement techniques. One such approach is called the PBFA process. In this machine, electric charge is allowed to accumulate in capacitors and then discharged in 40–nanosecond micropulses. Lithium ions are accelerated by means of these pulses and forced to collide with deuterium and tritium targets. Fusion among the lithium and hydrogen nuclei takes place, and energy is released. Thus far, however, the PBFA approach to nuclear fusion has been no more successful than has that of more traditional methods.

Cold fusion

The scientific world was astonished in March of 1989 when two electrochemists, Stanley Pons and Martin Fleischmann, reported that they had obtained evidence for the occurrence of nuclear fusion at room temperatures. During the electrolysis of heavy water (deuterium oxide), it appeared that the fusion of deuterons was made possible by the presence of palladium electrodes used in the reaction. If such an observation could have been confirmed by other scientists, it would have been truly revolutionary. It would have meant that energy could be obtained from fusion reactions at moderate temperatures.

The Pons–Fleischmann discovery was the subject of immediate and intense scrutiny by other scientists around the world. It soon became apparent, however, that evidence for cold fusion could not consistently be obtained by other researchers. A number of alternative explanations were developed by scientists for the fusion results that Pons and Fleischmann believed they had obtained. Today, some scientists are still convinced that Pons and Fleischmann had made a real and important breakthrough in the area of fusion research. Most researchers, however, attribute the results they reported to other events that occurred during the electrolysis of the heavy water.

Further Reading:

Cordey, J. Geoffrey, "Progress toward a Tokamak Fusion Reactor," *Physics Today*, January 1992, pp. 22–30.

Hogan, William J., "Energy from Inertial Fusion," *Physics Today*, September 1992, pp. 42–50.

Jensen, Torkil H., "Fusion—A Potential Power Source," *Journal of Chemical Education*, October 1994, pp. 820–823.

Peat, F. David. *Cold Fusion: The Making of a Scientific Controversy*. Chicago: Contemporary Books, 1989.

Rose, David J., and Melville Clark, Jr. *Plasmas and Controlled Fusion*. Cambridge, MA: M.I.T. Press, 1961.

KEY TERMS

....

Cold fusion—A form of fusion that some researchers believe can occur at or near room temperatures as the result of the combination of deuterons with palladium metal as a catalyst.

Deuteron—The nucleus of the deuterium atom, consisting of one proton combined with one neutron.

Isotopes—Two or more forms of the same element, whose atoms differ from each other in the number of neutrons contained in their nuclei.

Neutron—A subatomic particle with a mass of about one atomic mass unit and no electrical charge.

Nuclear fission—A nuclear reaction in which one large atomic nucleus breaks apart into at least two smaller particles.

Nucleus—The core of an atom consisting of one or more protons and, usually, one or more neutrons.

Plasma—A form of matter that consists of positively charged particles and electrons completely independent of each other.

Proton—A subatomic particle with a mass of about one atomic mass unit and a single positive charge.

Thermonuclear reaction—A nuclear reaction that takes place only at very high temperatures, usually of the order of a few million degrees.

U.S. Congress. Office of Technology Assessment. *Starpower: The U.S. and the International Quest for Fusion Energy*. Washington, D.C.: Office of Technology Assessment, 1987.

David E. Newton

Nuclear magnetic resonance

Nuclear magnetic resonance, NMR, is a process in which the nuclei of certain atoms absorb energy from a magnetic field that gyrates, or has a direction which rotates about some fixed axis. NMR provides a means of measuring nuclear properties using ordinary electro-magnetic fields rather than high–energy particles as in a particle accelerator. Its applications range from nuclear measurements to medical imaging.

History

NMR arose from theoretical work first published by the physicist I. I. Rabi in 1937. It was applied by Rabi in measurements of the magnetic moment of atomic nuclei. The method was later applied by physicists Louis Alvarez and Felix Bloch in 1940 to measure the magnetic moment of the neutron. Later it was used to measure atomic and molecular structure. Currently NMR has wide application in imaging of internal organs for medical diagnosis.

Physcial principles

The process on which NMR is based is essentially one in which the nucleus of an atom is caused to wobble, or precess, like a top. The wobble is maintained and increased, applying a force that varies at the same rate as the wobble itself.

Nuclear spin magnetic moment

Atomic nuclei possess nuclear spin, the angular momentum of the nucleus, which is due to rotation. Since nuclei contain an electric charge, in the form of protons, their rotation often produces an electric current which creates a magnetic field. Like an electromagnet, therefore, the nucleus has a magnetic moment.

Magnetic torque on a nucleus

When immersed in a magnetic field, a nucleus will experience a twisting force, or torque, which tends to line the spin axis of the nucleus up with the field, the same effect that causes two bar magnets to stick to each other in opposed directions. Because the nucleus is spinning, however, it will precess like a spinning top or gyroscope.

Nuclear orientation energy

The energy of the precessing nucleus depends on its orientation in the magnetic field. This energy can be increased by applying a rotating magnetic force to the nucleus. The force must rotate at a frequency known as the Larmor frequency, which is proportional to the applied magnetic field. This gyrating combination of fixed and rotating magnetic fields produces nuclear magnetic resonance.

Quantum effects

Since a nucleus is a system having atomic dimensions, quantum mechanical considerations limit its orientation energy in the magnetic field to certain specific values, which differ by multiples of the energy of a photon having the Larmor frequency. This is because the nucleus gains energy by absorbing photons—light quanta—from the rotating magnetic field.

Resonant frequency

The resonant frequency of a nucleus in NMR depends on three factors: the distribution of mass and charge in the nucleus, and the magnetic field. Thus even if two atoms have identical nuclei, they may have different resonant frequencies if they are located within different external fields. This may be the case, for example, if they occur within different chemical compounds, the motion of the electrons with a molecule will contribute to the total magnetic nuclei.

Uses of NMR

Applications of NMR are based on its ability to measure nuclear properties of atoms within a sample of material. All NMR applications use three: (1) a strong magnetic field; (2) a radio frequency signal generator to provide a rotating field; and (3) a detector to observe the resonance. The detector is an induction coil which picks up the electric signal from the precessing nuclei.

Nuclear magnetic moments

The magnetic moment of an atomic nucleus is one of the determining factors of the Larmor frequency. Thus NMR can be used to get information about nuclear magnetic moments.

Chemical analysis

The Larmor frequency is dependent on the magnetic field at the location of the nucleus, which depends on the influence of nearby atoms. Thus the NMR frequency depends on the chemical structure of the molecules in a sample of material. NMR is therefore a useful tool for chemical analysis.

Medical applications

The largest area of application of NMR is in medical diagnosis. In this area, the technology is usually referred to as magnetic resonance imaging (MRI). The principle of MRI is identical to that of the use of NMR in chemical analysis. Essentially, the different materials in the body resonate at different frequencies depending on their chemical compositions. Position information is

KEY TERMS

. . . .

Angular Momentum—Rotational momentum; resistance to change in rotation rate.

Atomic Nucleus—The small, dense, central portion of an atom.

Gyration—Motion similar to that of a gyroscope; the precession of rotation axis.

Induction—The process in which a changing magnetic field causes electric current.

Magnetic Moment—The strength of a magnetized object.

Oscillation—A smooth vibrational motion or change.

Precession—A systematic change in the direction of a rotation axis.

Resonance—The enhancement of the response of a system to a force, when that force is applied at a particular frequency known as the resonant frequency.

obtained by using an external magnetic field which varies with position, so that resonance at a particular frequency with a given substance, such as fatty tissue, will occur only at a particular position or set of positions within the body. The resonant response is then analyzed and displayed using a computer.

Further Reading:

Naeye, Robert. "Magnetic Field Goal." *Discover* (June 1995): 128.

Pake, George E. "Nuclear Magnetic Resonance in Bulk Matter." *Physics Today* (October 1993): 46.

Ramsey, Norman F. "Early Magnetic Resonance Experiments: Roots and Offshoots." *Physics Today* (October 1993): 40.

Reiman, Arnold L. *Physics, Vol. III: Modern Physics.* New York: Harper Row, 1973.

Slichter, Charles P. *Principles of Magnetic Resonance.* New York: Harper Row, 1963.

Nuclear medicine

Nuclear medicine is a medical specialty that uses radioactive materials, called radionuclides, to help diagnose and treat a wide variety of diseases, and for biomedical research. The development of nuclear medicine reflects the advances in the fields of nuclear physics, nuclear chemistry, and, later, molecular biology. While there was considerable research in the nuclear sciences during the first part of the 20th century, it was not until the 1930s and 1940s, when radioactive substances were made readily available by nuclear reactors and cyclotrons, that nuclear medicine evolved into a separate specialty.

Nuclear medicine procedures are an important diagnostic tool, and are performed in hospitals and many outpatient facilities all over the world. A nuclear medicine team commonly consists of a nuclear medicine physician, a nuclear medicine technologist, a nuclear medicine physicist, and a radiopharmacist. Nuclear medicine procedures sometimes detect the presence of disease rather than provide a specific diagnosis, and are frequently performed together with other medical imaging modalities such as x ray, CT, MRI, and ultrasonography. In some cases, a disease may be detected before an organ function is altered or symptoms appear. Early detection prompts early treatment.

Radionuclides and radiopharmaceuticals

A nuclear medicine procedure always requires the use of a radionuclide. Radionuclides, by virtue of their natural tendency to achieve stability, decay or disintegrate at a constant rate. Each radionuclide has its own distinct method of decay and rate of decay, or half–life. During disintegration, radionuclides emit electromagnetic radiation (photons), which can be detected, localized, and quantitated by sophisticated radiation detectors. Most frequently, the radionuclide is chemically bound to a stable molecule or compound chosen for its ability to localize in a specific organ system. The combination of the radionuclide bound to a molecule or compound is known as a radiopharmaceutical. The foundation of radionuclide or radiopharmaceutical use is based on the tracer principle, invented by the Hungarian chemist Georg von Hevesy (1885–1966) in 1912. Hevesy demonstrated that radioactive nuclides had chemical properties that were identical to those of their nonradioactive, or stable, form, and therefore could be used to "trace" various biochemical and physiological behaviors in the body and thereby obtain diagnostic information.

Typically, the radiopharmaceutical is injected intravenously (in a vein), but some studies require inhalation (as a radioactive gas), or ingestion. The distribution of the radiopharmaceutical in the body or organ can reveal the normal or altered state of blood flow, capillary permeability, tissue metabolism, or specific function of an organ system. For example, if the physiology of an organ system or area of an organ is changed for reasons such as a tumor, absence of blood flow, duct blockage, or disease process, the way in which the radiopharmaceutical is incorporated will reflect any alteration. Nuclear medicine procedures can show structural as well as functional changes.

Radiopharmaceuticals are also chosen for their particular radioactive properties such as half–life, type of radiation emitted during decay, photon energy, cost, and availability. Today, ^{99m}technetium (^{99m}Tc), a daughter product of ^{99}Molybdenum (^{99}Mo), is the most commonly used radionuclide for nuclear medicine procedures and for making radiopharmaceuticals. Technetium is considered ideal because it gives a low radiation dose to the patient, has a low energy (140keV), most of its decay emissions are gamma–rays, has a short half–life (six hours), is inexpensive and easily obtained, and combines easily with many compounds.

Instrumentation

Unlike an x–ray procedure, where an image is obtained by an x–ray beam (generated by a machine) that passes through the body, a nuclear medicine image occurs when the radioactive decay occurring within the body is detected and recorded externally. Nuclear medicine images are most often obtained by a machine called a scintillation camera or gamma camera, invented in 1958 by the American physicist Hal Anger. The images or pictures are often called scans, which is a word left over from the time when nuclear medicine images were obtained by scintillating detector machines called rectilinear scanners. Whether using a scanner or camera, the physics of radiation detection are the same. A scintillation or gamma camera is made of many components. This machine is capable of detecting radiation and converting the detected events into electrical impulses. The radiation detector is made of a material, most commonly a sodium iodide crystal, that emits a flash of light or scintillation when hit by ionizing radiation or gamma rays. The detector is fitted with a collimator, a device that directs the path of the gamma rays to the crystal. The light flashes are converted into electrical impulses, which are then amplified, sorted, and counted. These counted events, or quantitative information, reflect the amount or distribution of the radioactive material used in a given procedure. Most gamma cameras are equipped with computers to process the information collected, to store the information, and to produce an image of the organ of interest. The resulting picture is usually seen as a two–dimensional image on a black and white or color television monitor. Some common nuclear medicine imaging procedures include

lung, thyroid, liver, spleen, biliary system, heart, kidney, brain, and bone scans.

Treatment and nonimaging procedures.

Nonimaging nuclear medicine exams such as radioimmunoassay studies require mixing serum with radioactive tracers to detect the presence of a certain hormone, chemical, or therapeutic drug. In other nonimaging studies the patient is given a radiopharmaceutical, and after a certain amount of time, samples of blood or urine are obtained and tested. Occasionally, a large amount of a radioactive substance is given to a patient to produce a biologic effect. For example, the therapeutic treatment for Grave's disease, a hyperactive condition of the thyroid gland, requires a high dose of radioactive iodine (^{131}I)—enough to destroy thyroid tissue. Radioactive iodine is often used to treat or detect thyroid conditions because the thyroid naturally organifies, or "traps," iodine—one's thyroid cannot tell the difference between stable or radioactive iodine. When radioactive iodine is ingested, the thyroid, depending on its physiological state, absorbs a certain amount, temporarily making the thyroid radioactive.

Recent Developments in Nuclear Medicine

Advances in monoclonal antibody research, radiopharmaceuticals, and computer technology have allowed nuclear medicine practitioners to probe deeper into the workings of the human body. Tumor–specific antibodies have been labeled or mixed with radiopharmaceuticals and administered to patients for both localizing and treating various types of tumors.

Conventional planar studies do not give detailed information about the depth of an abnormality seen on an image. The tomographic (tomos is the Greek word for slice) principle has been applied to nuclear medicine procedures enabling the physician to see regions of an organ in slices or layers. Two tomographic methods in nuclear medicine are single proton emission computerized tomography (SPECT) and positron emission tomography (PET). Like conventional images, tomographic images show how a radiopharmaceutical is distributed within an organ. Areas of normal, increased, or decreased distribution can be seen, thus revealing areas of altered biochemical and physiological function. When a tomographic study is obtained, the gamma camera detector circles the body and obtains multiple two dimensional images at various angles. The images are reconstructed by a special computer program and an organ can be visualized, in slices or layers, from top to

KEY TERMS

Blood–brain barrier—A selective impermeability of the capillaries of the brain which allows some substances to enter the brain while preventing others.

Disintegration—Spontaneous nuclear transformation characterized by the emission of energy and/or mass from the nucleus.

Gamma ray—Electromagnetic radiation originating from the nucleus of an atom.

Half–life—The time taken for a group of atoms to decay to half their original number.

Ionizing radiation—Any electromagnetic or particulate radiation capable of direct or indirect ion production in its passage through matter.

Monoclonal antibody—An antibody made in a laboratory, derived from a single clone, so that each hybrid cell produces the same antibody.

Nuclide—Any nucleus plus its orbital electrons.

Photon—The quantum or particle of light.

Positron—A type of beta particle with a positive charge.

Radionuclide—Radioactive or unstable nuclide.

bottom, front to back, and left to right. Viewing organs in slices eliminates interference from areas overlying a possible abnormality.

Single photon emission computed tomography (SPECT) studies are most often used for cardiac imaging and brain imaging, although the tomographic technology can be helpful for viewing other organs as well. SPECT studies use conventional radionuclides such as ^{99m}technetium and ^{123}Iodine. PET studies use only positron emitting radionculides such as ^{11}Carbon, and ^{18}Fluorine. PET imaging units commonly have two detectors to take advantage of the nature of positron decay. When a positron (a positively charged Beta particle) is emitted from the nucleus, it collides with an electron and is annihilated. The annihilation produces two gamma rays that travel in opposite directions (180°), each with the characteristics energy of 511 keV. With two photons or gamma rays traveling in opposite directions and two detector heads, the quantitave data and localization information is increased. The radionuclides used for PET are very short lived and therefore a cyclotron must be on site. Cyclotrons and PET equipment is very expensive, so there are few institutions that

perform these tests. Their clinical use is consequently very limited. The focus of PET is biochemical rather than structural and is used most often for exploring neurochemical phenomena in the brain. PET can help distinguish one form of dementia from another, test for psychiatric drug effectiveness, and demonstrate regional metabolic differences between certain psychiatric disorders. PET and SPECT imaging procedures are used to study the areas of the brain affected by strokes, epilepsy, and Parkinson's disease. Newer SPECT radiopharmaceuticals, because of their ability to cross the blood–brain barrier, have made it possible to study brain function and metabolism. Since assessing brain function is important to both physical medicine and behavioral medicine, SPECT may very well move these studies into the clinical setting.

Further Reading

Grigg, E.R.N. *The Trail of Invisible Light for X–Strahlen to Radiobiology.* Springfield, Il.: Charles C. Thomas, 1965.

Spencer, Richard P. *New Procedures in Nuclear Medicine.* Florida: CRC Press, Inc. 1989.

Stimac, Gary K. *Introduction to Diagnostic Imaging.* W.B. Saunders Co. Harcourt, Brace, Jovanovich, 1992.

Christine Miner Minderovic

Nuclear physics see **Physics**

Nuclear power

Nuclear power is any method of doing work that makes use of nuclear fission or fusion reactions. In its broadest sense, the term refers to both the uncontrolled release of energy, as in fission or fusion weapons, and to the controlled release of energy, as in a nuclear power plant. Most commonly, however, the expression nuclear power is reserved for the latter of these two instances.

The world's first exposure to nuclear power came with the detonation of two fission ("atomic") bombs over Hiroshima and Nagasaki, Japan, events that brought World War II to a conclusion. A number of scientists and laypersons perceived an optimistic aspect of these terrible events. They hoped that the power of nuclear energy could be harnessed to do much of the work that all human societies face. Those hopes have been realized to only a modest degree, however. Some serious problems associated with the use of nuclear power have never been satisfactorily solved and, after three decades of progress in the development of controlled nuclear power, interest in this energy source has leveled off and, in many nations, declined.

The nuclear power plant

A nuclear power plant is a system in which energy released by fission reactions is captured and used for the generation of electricity. Every such plant contains four fundamental elements: the reactor, coolant system, electrical power generating unit, and the safety system.

The source of energy in a nuclear reactor is a fission reaction in which neutrons collide with nuclei of uranium–235 or plutonium–239 (the fuel), causing them to split apart. The products of any fission reaction include not only huge amounts of energy, but also waste products, known as fission products, and additional neutrons. A constant and reliable flow of neutrons is insured in the reactor by means of a moderator, which slows down the speed of neutrons, and control rods, which control the number of neutrons available in the reactor and, hence, the rate at which fission can occur.

Energy produced in the reactor is carried away by means of a coolant, a fluid such as water, liquid sodium, or carbon dioxide gas. The fluid absorbs heat from the reactor and then begins to boil itself or to cause water in a secondary system to boil. Steam produced in either of these ways is then piped into the electrical generating unit where it turns the blades of a turbine. The turbine, in turn, powers a generator that produces electrical energy.

The high cost of constructing a modern nuclear power plant reflects in part the enormous range of safety features needed to protect against various possible mishaps. Some of those features are incorporated into the reactor core itself. For example, all of the fuel in a reactor is sealed in a protective coating made of a zirconium alloy. The protective coating, called a cladding, helps retain heat and radioactivity within the fuel, preventing it from escaping into the plant itself.

Every nuclear plant is also required to have an elaborate safety system to protect against the most serious potential problem of all, loss of coolant. If such an accident were to occur, the reactor core might well melt down, releasing radioactive materials to the rest of the plant and, perhaps, to the outside environment. To prevent such an accident from happening, the pipes carrying the coolant are required to be very thick and strong. In addition, back–up supplies of the coolant must be available to replace losses in case of a leak.

On another level, the whole plant itself is required to be encased within a dome–shaped containment struc-

ture. The containment structure is designed to prevent the release of radioactive materials in case of an accident within the reactor core.

Another safety feature is a system of high–efficiency filters through which all air leaving the building must pass. These filters are designed to trap microscopic particles of radioactive materials that might otherwise be vented to the atmosphere. Other specialized devices and systems have also been developed for dealing with other kinds of accidents in various parts of the power plant.

Types of nuclear power plants

Nuclear power plants differ from each other primarily in the methods they use for transferring heat produced in the reactor to the electricity generating unit. Perhaps the simplest design of all is the boiling water reactor plant (BWR) in which coolant water surrounding the reactor is allowed to boil and form steam. That steam is then piped directly to turbines, whose spinning drives the electrical generator. A very different type of plant is one that was popular in Great Britain for many years, one that used carbon dioxide as a coolant. In this type of plant, carbon dioxide gas passes through the reactor core, absorbs heat produced by fission reactions, and is piped into a secondary system. There the heated carbon dioxide gas gives up its energy to water, which begins to boil and change to steam. That steam is then used to power the turbine and generator.

Safety concerns

In spite of all the systems developed by nuclear engineers, the general public has long had serious concerns about the use of such plants as sources of electrical power. Those concerns vary considerably from nation to nation. In France, for example, more than half of all that country's electrical power now comes from nuclear power plants. The initial enthusiasm for nuclear power in the United States in the 1960s and 1970s soon faded, and no nuclear power plants have been constructed in this country in more than a decade.

One concern about nuclear power plants, of course, is an echo of the world's first exposure to nuclear power, the atomic bomb blasts. Many people fear that a nuclear power plant may go out of control and explode like a nuclear weapon. And, in spite of experts' insistence that such an event is impossible, a few major disasters have instigated the fear of nuclear power plants exploding. By far the most serious of those disasters was the explosion that occurred at the Chernobyl Nuclear Power Plant near Kiev in the Ukraine in 1986.

On April 16, of that year, one of the four power-generating units in the Chernobyl complex exploded, blowing the top off the containment building. Hundreds of thousands of nearby residents were exposed to lethal or damaging levels of radiation and were removed from the area. Radioactive clouds released by the explosion were detected as far away as western Europe. More than a decade later, the remains of the Chernobyl reactor remain far too radioactive for anyone to spend more than a few minutes in the area.

Critics also worry about the amount of radioactivity released by nuclear power plants on a day-to-day basis. This concern is probably of less importance than is the possibility of a major disaster. Studies have shown that nuclear power plants are so well shielded that the amount of radiation to which nearby residents are exposed is no more than that of a person living many miles away.

In any case, safety concerns in the United States have been serious enough to essentially bring the construction of new plants to a halt in the last decade. Licensing procedures are now so complex and so expensive that few industries are interested in working their way through the bureaucratic maze to construct new plants.

Nuclear waste management

Perhaps the single most troubling issue for the nuclear power industry is waste management. After a period of time, the fuel rods in a reactor are no longer able to sustain a chain reaction and must be removed. These rods are still highly radioactive, however, and present a serious threat to human life and the environment. Techniques must be developed for the destruction and/or storage of these wastes.

Nuclear wastes can be classified into two general categories, low-level wastes and high-level wastes. The former consist of materials that release a relatively modest level of radiation and/or that will soon decay to a level where they no longer present a threat to humans and the environment. Storing these materials in underground or underwater reservoirs for a few years or in some other system is usually a satisfactory way of handling these materials.

High-level wastes are a different matter. The materials that make up these wastes are intensely radioactive and are likely to remain so for thousands of years. Short-term methods of storage are unsatisfactory because containers leak and break open long before the wastes are safe.

For more than two decades, the United States government has been attempting to develop a plan for the storage of high-level nuclear wastes. At one time, the plan was to bury the wastes in a salt mine near Lyons, Kansas. Objections from residents of the area and other concerned citizens made that plan infeasible. More recently, the government decided to construct a huge crypt in the middle of Yucca Mountain in Nevada for the burial of high-level wastes. Again, complaints by residents of Nevada and other citizens have delayed placing that plan into operation. The government insists, however, that Yucca Mountain will eventually become the long-term storage site for the nation's high-level radioactive wastes. Until that site is actually put into operation, however, those wastes are in "temporary" storage at nuclear power sites throughout the United States.

History

The first nuclear reactor was built during World War II as part of the Manhattan Project to build an atomic bomb. The reactor was constructed under the direction of Enrico Fermi in a large room beneath the squash courts at the University of Chicago. It was built as the first concrete test of existing theories of nuclear fission.

Until the day on December 2, 1942, when the reactor was first put into operation, scientists had relied entirely on mathematical calculations to determine the effectiveness of nuclear fission as an energy source. It goes without saying that the scientists who constructed the first reactor were taking an extraordinary chance.

That reactor consisted of alternating layers of uranium and uranium oxide with graphite as a moderator. Cadmium control rods were used to control the concentration of neutrons in the reactor. Since the various parts of the reactor were constructed by piling materials on top of each other, the unit was at first known as an atomic "pile." The moment at which Fermi directed the control rods to be withdrawn occurred at 3:45 p.m. on December 2, 1945, and that date can legitimately be regarded as the beginning of the age of controlled nuclear power in human history.

Nuclear fusion power

Many scientists believe that the ultimate solution to the world's energy problems may be in the harnessing of nuclear fusion. A fusion reaction is one in which two small nuclei combine with each other to form one larger nucleus. As an example, two hydrogen nuclei may combine with each other to form the nucleus of an atom known as deuterium, or heavy hydrogen.

KEY TERMS

. . . .

Cladding—A material that covers the fuel elements in a nuclear reactor in order to prevent the loss of heat and radioactive materials from the fuel.

Coolant—Any material used in a nuclear power plant to transfer the heat produced in the reactor core to another unit in which electricity is generated.

Containment—Any system developed for preventing the release of radioactive materials from a nuclear power plant to the outside world.

Generator—A device for converting kinetic energy (the energy of movement) into electrical energy.

Neutron—A subatomic particle that carries no electrical charge and that has a mass of zero.

Nuclear fission—A reaction in which a larger atomic nucleus breaks apart into two roughly equal, smaller nuclei.

Nuclear fusion—A reaction in which two small nuclei combine with each other to form one larger nucleus.

Nuclear pile—The name given to the earliest form of a nuclear reactor.

Turbine—A device consisting of a series of baffles mounted on a wheel around a central shaft used to convert the energy of a moving fluid into the energy of mechanical rotation.

Many scientists now believe that fusion reactions are responsible for the production of energy in stars. They hypothesize that four hydrogen atoms fuse with each other in a series of reactions to form a single helium atom. An important byproduct of these fusion reactions is the release of an enormous amount of energy. In fact, gram–for–gram, a fusion reaction releases many times more energy than does a fission reaction.

The world was introduced to the concept of fusion reactions in the 1950s when the Soviet Union and the United States exploded the first fusion ("hydrogen") bombs. The energy released in the explosion of each such bomb was more than 1,000 times greater than the energy released in the explosion of a single fission bomb.

As with fission, scientists and non–scientists alike expressed hope that fusion reactions could someday be harnessed as a source of energy for everyday needs. This line of research has been much less successful, however, than research on fission power plants. In essence, the problem has been to find a way of containing the very high temperatures produced (a few million degrees Celsius) when fusion occurs. Optimistic reports of progress on a fusion power plant appear in the press from time to time, but some authorities now doubt that fusion power will ever be an economic reality.

Further Reading:

Controlled Nuclear Chain Reactions: The First Fifty Years. La Grange Park, IL: American Nuclear Society, 1992.

Glasstone, Samuel, and Alexander Sesonske. *Nuclear Reactor Engineering*, 4th edition, 2 vols. New York: Chapman and Hall, 1994.

McGraw–Hill Encyclopedia of Science & Technology, 6th edition. New York: McGraw–Hill Book Company, 1987.

Okrent, David. *Nuclear Reactor Safety: On the History of the Regulatory Process.* Madison, WI: University of Wisconsin Press, 1981.

David E. Newton

Nuclear reactor

A nuclear reactor is a device by which energy is produced as the result of a nuclear reaction, either fission or fusion. At the present time, all commercially available nuclear reactors make use of fission reactions, in which the nuclei of large atoms such as uranium (the fuel) are broken apart into smaller nuclei, with the release of energy. It is theoretically possible to construct reactors that operate on the principle of nuclear fusion, in which small nuclei are combined with each other with the release of energy. But after a half century of research on fusion reactors, no practicable device has yet been developed.

Theory of fission reactors

When neutrons strike the nucleus of a large atom, they cause that nucleus to split apart into two roughly equal pieces known as fission products. In that process, additional neutrons and very large amounts of energy are also released. Only three isotopes are known to be fissionable, uranium–235, uranium–233, and plutonium–239. Of these, only the first, uranium–235, occurs naturally. Plutonium–239 is produced synthetically when nuclei of uranium–238 are struck by neutrons and transformed into plutonium. Since uranium–238 always occurs along with uranium–235 in a nuclear reactor, plutonium–239 is produced as a byproduct in all commercial reactors now in operation. As a result, it has become as important in the production of nuclear power as uranium–235. Uranium–233 can also be produced synthetically by the bombardment of thorium with neutrons. Thus far, however, this isotope has not been put to practical use in nuclear reactors.

Nuclear fission is a promising source of energy for two reasons. First, the amount of energy released during fission is very large compared to that obtained from conventional energy sources. For example, the fissioning of a single uranium–235 nucleus results in the release of about 200 million electron volts of energy. In comparison, the oxidation of a single carbon atom (as it occurs in the burning of coal or oil) releases about four electron volts of energy. When the different masses of carbon and uranium atoms are taken into consideration, the fission reaction still produces about 2.5 million times more energy than does the oxidation reaction.

Second, the release of neutrons during fission makes it possible for a rapid and continuous repetition of the reaction. Suppose that a single neutron strikes a one gram block of uranium–235. The fission of one uranium nucleus in that block releases, on an average, about two to three more neutrons. Each of those neutrons, then, is available for the fission of three more uranium nuclei. In the next stage, about nine neutrons (three from each of three fissioned uranium nuclei) are released. As long as more neutrons are being released, the fission of uranium nuclei can continue.

A reaction of this type that continues on its own once under way is known as a chain reaction. During a nuclear chain reaction, many billions of uranium nuclei may fission in less than a second. Enormous amounts of energy are released in a very short time, a fact that becomes visible with the explosion of a nuclear weapon.

Arranging for the uncontrolled, large–scale release of energy produced during nuclear fission is a relatively simple task. Fission (atomic) bombs are essentially devices in which a chain reaction is initiated and then allowed to continue on its own. The problems of designing a system by which fission energy is released at a constant and useable rate, however, are much more difficult.

Reactor core

The heart of any nuclear reactor is the core, which contains the fuel, a moderator, and control rods. The fuel used in some reactors consists of uranium oxide, enriched with about 3–4 % of uranium–235. In other reactors, the fuel consists of an alloy made of uranium

and plutonium–239. In either case, the amount of fissionable material is actually only a small part of the entire fuel assembly.

The fuel elements in a reactor core consist of cylindrical pellets about 0.6 in (1.5 cm) thick and 0.4 in (1.0 cm) in diameter. These pellets are stacked one on top of another in a hollow cylindrical tube known as the fuel rod and then inserted into the reactor core. Fuel rods tend to be about 12 ft (3.7 m) long and about 0.5 in (1.3 cm) in diameter. They are arranged in a grid pattern containing more than 200 rods each at the center of the reactor. The materials that fuel these pellets are made of must be replaced on a regular basis as the proportion of fissionable nuclei within them decreases.

Moderators

A nuclear reactor containing only fuel elements would be unusable because a chain reaction could probably not be sustained within it. The reason is that nuclear fission occurs best with neutrons that move at relatively modest speeds, called thermal neutrons. But the neutrons released from fission reactions tend to be moving very rapidly, at about 1/15 the speed of light. In order to maintain a chain reaction, therefore, it is necessary to introduce some material that will slow down the neutrons released during fission. Such a material is known as a moderator.

The most common moderators are substances of low atomic weight such as heavy water (deuterium oxide) or graphite. Hydrides (binary compounds containing hydrogen), hydrocarbons, and beryllium and beryllium oxide have also been used as moderators in certain specialized kinds of reactors.

Control rods

A chain reaction could easily be sustained in a reactor containing fuel elements and a moderator. In fact, the reaction might occur so quickly that the reactor would explode. In order to prevent such a disaster, the reactor core also contains control rods. Control rods are solid cylinders of metal constructed of some material that has an ability to absorb neutrons. One of the metals most commonly used in the manufacture of control rods is cadmium.

The purpose of control rods is to maintain the ratio of neutrons used up in fission compared to neutrons produced during fission at about 1:1. In such a case, for every one new neutron that is used up in causing a fission reaction, one new neutron becomes available to bring about the next fission reaction.

The problem is that the actual ratio of neutrons produced to neutrons used up in a fission reaction is closer to 2:1 or 3:1. That is, neutrons are produced so rapidly that the chain reaction goes very quickly and is soon out of control. By correctly positioning control rods in the reactor core, however, many of the excess neutrons produced by fission can be removed from the core and the reaction can be kept under control.

The control rods are, in a sense, the dial by which the rate of fission is maintained within the core. When the rods are inserted completely into the core, most neutrons released during fission are absorbed, and no chain reaction occurs. As the rods are slowly removed from the core, the rate at which fission occurs increases. At some point, the position of the control rods is such that the 1:1 ratio of produced to used up neutrons is achieved. At that point, the chain reaction goes forward, releasing energy, but under precise control of human operators.

Reactor types

In most cases, the purpose of a nuclear reactor is to capture the energy released from fission reactions and put it to some useful service. For example, the heat generated by a nuclear reactor in a nuclear power plant is used to boil water and make steam, which can then be used to generate electricity. The way that heat is removed from a reactor core is the basis for defining a number of different reactor types.

For example, one of the earliest types of nuclear reactors is the boiling water reactor (BWR) in which the reactor core is surrounded by ordinary water. As the reactor operates, the water is heated, begins to boil, and changes to steam. The steam produced is piped out of the reactor vessel and delivered (usually) to a turbine and generator, where electrical power is produced.

Another type of reactor is the pressurized water reactor (PWR). In a PWR, coolant water surrounding the reactor core is kept under high pressure, preventing it from boiling. This water is piped out of the reactor vessel into a second building where it is used to heat a secondary set of pipes also containing ordinary water. The water in the secondary system is allowed to boil, and the steam formed is then transferred to a turbine and generator, as in the BWR.

Some efforts have been made to design nuclear reactors in which liquid metals are used as heat transfer agents. Liquid sodium is the metal most often suggested. Liquid sodium has many attractive properties as a heat transfer agent, but it has one serious drawback. It reacts violently with water and great care must be taken, therefore, to make sure that the two materials do not come into contact with each other.

At one time, there was also some enthusiasm for the use of gases as heat transfer agents. A group of reactors built in Great Britain, for example, were designed to use carbon dioxide to move heat from the reactor to the power generating station. Gas reactors have, however, not experienced much popularity in other nations.

Applications

At the end of World War II, great hopes were expressed for the use of nuclear reactors as a way of providing power for many human energy needs. For example, some optimists envisioned the use of small nuclear reactors as power sources in airplanes, ships, and automobiles. These hopes have been realized to only a limited extent. Nuclear powered submarines, for example, have become a practical reality. But other forms of transportation seldom make use of this source of energy.

Instead, the vast majority of nuclear reactors in use today are employed in nuclear power plants where they supply the energy needed to manufacture electrical energy. In a power reactor, energy released within the reactor core is transferred by a coolant to an external building in which are housed a turbine and generator. Steam obtained from water boiled by reactor heat energy is used to drive the turbine and generator, thereby producing electrical energy.

Reactors with other functions are also in use. For example, a breeder reactor is one in which new reactor fuel is manufactured. By far the most common material in any kind of nuclear reactor is uranium–238. This isotope of uranium does not undergo fission and does not, therefore, make any direct contribution to the production of energy. But the vast numbers of neutrons produced in the reactor core do react with uranium–238 in a different way, producing plutonium–239 as a product. This plutonium–239 can then be removed from the reactor core and used as a fuel in other reactors. Reactors whose primary function it is to generate plutonium–239 are known as breeder reactors.

Research reactors may have one or both of two functions. First, such reactors are often built simply to test new design concepts for the nuclear reactor. When the test of the design element has been completed, the primary purpose of the reactor has been accomplished.

Second, research reactors can also be used to take advantage of the various forms of radiation released during fission reactions. These forms of radiation can

KEY TERMS

. . . .

Chain reaction—Any reaction in which one of the products formed is the same as the material needed to begin the reaction.

Electron volt—A unit for measuring energy. An electron volt is the energy gained or lost by an electron as it passes through a potential difference of one volt.

Generator—A device for converting kinetic energy (the energy of movement) into electrical energy.

Isotopes—Forms of an element that have the same number of protons, but different numbers of neutrons.

Neutron—A subatomic particle that carries no electrical charge and that has a mass of zero.

Nuclear fission—A reaction in which a larger atomic nucleus breaks apart into two roughly equal smaller nuclei.

Nuclear fusion—A reaction in which two small nuclei combine with each other to from one larger nucleus.

Turbine—A device consisting of a series of baffles mounted on a wheel around a central shaft used to convert the energy of a moving fluid into the energy of mechanical rotation.

be used to bombard a variety of materials to study the effects of the radiation on the materials.

See also Generator; Nuclear fission; Nuclear fusion; Nuclear reactor; Nuclear power; Radioactivity; Turbine; Uranium.

Further Reading

Croall, C., and S. Sempler. *Nuclear Power for Beginners.* New York: State Mutual Books, 1990.

Ebinger, Charles K. *Nuclear Power: The Promise of New Technologies.* Washington, D.C.: CSI Studies, 1991.

Jones, P. M., ed. *Nuclear Power: Policy and Prospects.* New York: John Wiley & Sons, 1987.

McGraw–Hill Encyclopedia of Science & Technology, vol. 7, 6th edition. New York: McGraw–Hill Book Company.

Nuclear Power, Nuclear Fuel Cycle and Waste Management, Part C: Status and Trends, 1993. Lanham, MD: UNIPUB, 1993.

The Way Things Work, vol. 2. New York: Simon and Schuster, 1971.

David E. Newton

Nuclear survey methods see **Subsurface detection**

Nuclear waste see **Radioactive waste**

Nuclear weapons

Nuclear weapons are explosive devices, bombs, or warheads that release nuclear energy. Their extraordinary destructive power comes from the core of the atom, the nucleus. One type of nuclear weapon, the atom bomb, uses the energy released when nuclei of heavy elements like uranium–239 or plutonium, split apart. A second even more powerful type of nuclear weapon, the hydrogen bomb, uses the energy released when nuclei of light elements, types of hydrogen atoms, are forced together, or fused.

Nuclear devices have been fashioned into weapons of many shapes with many purposes. Nuclear bombs can be dropped from airplanes; warheads can be delivered by missiles launched from land, air or sea; artillery shells can be fired from cannon; mines can be placed in land and sea. Some nuclear weapons are small enough to destroy only a portion of a battlefield. Others are large enough to destroy entire cities and more.

Nuclear weapons can be thousands or even millions of times more destructive than conventional chemical explosives. Unlike chemical explosives, nuclear weapons have no peacetime uses. They are designed and built for use by the military of nations like the United States, France, Great Britain, China, India, Pakistan, Russia and several other former Soviet Republics. Israel is also believed to have them. Iran and Korea are interested in building them. Since nuclear weapons were invented and built during World War II, they have been used only twice, both times against the Japanese by the United States.

Development of nuclear weapons

Albert Einstein did not know it at the time, but when he published his special theory of relativity in 1905 he provided the world with the basic information needed to build nuclear weapons. Einstein said that the amount of matter, or mass, of a body or an object is associated with a specific amount of energy. The exact amount of energy in a body equals its mass multiplied by the square of the speed of light. The speed of light, 186,282 miles per second, is such a large figure that a small piece of matter contains a vast amount of energy. A baseball–size sample of uranium–235, for example, can explode with as much energy as 20,000 tons of TNT, a conventional chemical explosive used for comparison. One pound of explosive material in a nuclear weapon is approximately 100,000 times as powerful as one pound of TNT.

As World War II approached, two German chemists, Fritz Strassmann and Otto Hahn, pointed a stream of neutrons at a sample of uranium and succeeded in splitting the nuclei of uranium atoms. This splitting of nuclei is called nuclear fission. It was explained by physicists Lise Meitner from Austria and Otto Frisch from Great Britain. The energy released through nuclear fission was the source of power for the first atomic bomb built in the United States by a large team of scientists lead by physicist Robert J. Oppenheimer. This highly secret research and development program was called The Manhattan Project.

The first atomic bomb was detonated in Alamogordo, New Mexico, on July 16, 1945. Three weeks later, on August 6, a bomber named *Enola Gay* dropped a four–ton atomic bomb containing 12 lbs (5.4 kg) of uranium–235 on the Japanese city of Hiroshima. Seventy thousand people died as a direct result of the blast. Within two months, nearly twice that many were dead. Three days after the first explosion, a bomb containing several pounds of plutonium was dropped on Nagasaki. Thirty thousand people died in the seconds following the explosion. The Japanese surrendered the next day, ending World War II.

The first nuclear weapons were atomic or A–bombs. They depended on the energy produced by nuclear fission for their destructive power. However, scientists like physicist Edward Teller knew even before the first atomic bomb exploded that the fission weapons could be used to create an even more powerful explosive, now called a Thermonuclear, Hydrogen, or H–bomb. This weapon gets it power from the energy released when atoms of special forms of hydrogen called deuterium or tritium are forced together, a process called nuclear fusion. Starting a nuclear fusion reaction is even more complicated than setting off an atomic bomb. It requires such heat and force to initiate it, that the atomic bomb is used as a detonator to explode the fusion bomb.

The United States tested the first hydrogen bomb on November 1, 1952. It exploded with the force of millions of tons of TNT. Just nine months later, the Soviet Union tested a similar device.

For the next 40 years, the United States with its allies and the former Soviet Union with it allies raced to build more nuclear weapons. The end of the cold war in the early 1990s led to a significant decrease in the numbers of nuclear weapons in the world.

How nuclear weapons work

Conventional, chemical explosives get their power from the rapid rearrangement of chemical bonds, the links between atoms made by sharing electrons. In chemical explosives, atoms dissociate from other atoms and form new associations, but the atoms themselves do not change. Nuclear weapons are based on an entirely different principle. They derive their explosive power from changes in the structure of the atom itself, specifically in the core of the atom, the nucleus.

Atomic bombs use the energy released when nuclei of heavy elements split apart or fission. Uranium and plutonium are the two elements that can be used as fuel for this type of weapon. When nuclei of these atoms are struck with rapidly moving neutrons, they are broken into two nearly equal size pieces. They also release more neutrons, which split more nuclei. If enough atomic nuclei split they will release enough neutrons to ensure that all the nuclei of all the atoms in a sample will be split. This is called a chain reaction. When it is uncontrolled, enormous amounts of energy are released in a fraction of a second. This release of energy is the power behind the atomic bomb.

Uranium and plutonium are called fissile materials because they can support a fission chain reaction if enough material is concentrated in one place. Too small a sample would not generate enough neutrons to keep the fission process going. A one pound sample of uranium–235, a sample about the size of a ping–pong ball, is not large enough to support a chain reaction. The atomic bombs used in World War II proved that 12 or so pounds of fissile material, larger than a ping–pong ball but still small enough to fit into your hand, is enough to maintain a chain reaction. The smallest amount of material that can support a chain reaction is called the critical mass.

The instant enough bomb material is gathered together into a critical mass, it starts a chain reaction and explodes. This means that the fissile material cannot be stored in a critical mass until the instant it is meant to explode. Therefore, the sample of uranium or plutonium in an atomic bomb is either separated in two pieces or packaged in a way that keeps it below its critical mass. To set the bomb off, the two separated pieces of bomb material are rammed together to create a critical mass. One design for creating a critical mass involves firing a subcritical mass "bullet" of bomb material into a subcritical mass "target" of bomb material. Together, the "bullet" and the "target," create a critical mass that starts a chain reaction leading to a nuclear explosion.

A different design was used to detonate the bomb dropped on Nagasaki. Plutonium was stored in one large but subcritical mass. It was compressed into a critical mass by means of carefully and symmetrically placed chemical explosive. When the chemical explosive surrounding the subcritical piece of fissile material exploded, the blast forced the bomb material into a density that reached critical mass. In either type of design, once the critical mass is reached, the explosion follows in a millionth of a second and the temperature in the bomb center reaches millions of degrees.

In order for nuclear fission to occur, a bomb must use heavy atoms for fuel. Heavy atoms have many subatomic particles, neutrons, and protons in their nuclei. When the heavy nuclei split apart they release energy. Another more powerful type of nuclear weapon uses forms of hydrogen as fuel. Hydrogen has few subatomic particles in its nuclei and is called a light element. Instead of splitting atoms apart, these atomic nuclei are forced together, a process called nuclear fusion. Energy is released when hydrogen nuclei fuse to create helium. The sun also generates energy by fusing hydrogen into helium.

Because hydrogen is lighter than uranium, more hydrogen atoms fit into a sample of the same weight. Even though one fusion reaction releases less energy than one fission reaction, more hydrogen than uranium atoms can be packed into a nuclear weapon so fusion weapons produces bigger explosions than fission weapons of the same size. Fusion only occurs at temperatures of millions of degrees. On Earth only an atomic bomb can create such temperature instantaneously. That is why atomic bombs are used as detonators for hydrogen fusion bombs.

By 1954, a new feature had been added to the hydrogen bomb to create an even more dangerous weapon. Like earlier hydrogen bombs, this weapon was detonated with the explosion of an atomic or fission weapon. This raised temperatures enough to cause the hydrogen atoms in the bomb to fuse and explode like a regular hydrogen bomb. The designers also enclosed this new bomb in a shell of uranium–238. Neutrons released from the fusion of hydrogen caused the uranium–238 in the surrounding jacket to undergo fission which added to the power of the blast. This new device was, in effect, a fission–fusion–fission bomb. The second fission reaction did not create a second chain reac-

tion, however. All of this took place within a fraction of a second.

The power or "yield" of nuclear weapons is expressed in terms of how much TNT would be required to equal the blast. So much TNT would be required to equal a nuclear explosion that the units kilotons (thousands of tons) and megatons (millions of tons) of TNT are used to describe the blasts.

Effects of nuclear weapons

Nuclear weapons produce two important effects that are also produced by conventional chemical explosives. They release heat and generate shock waves, pressure fronts of compressed air that smash objects in their paths. The heat released in a nuclear explosion creates a sphere of burning, glowing gas that can range from hundreds of feet to miles in diameter, depending on the power of the bomb. This fireball emits a flash of heat that travels outward from the site of the explosion or ground zero, the area directly under the explosion. This heat can cause second degree burns to bare human flesh miles away from the blast site if the bomb is large enough. Although this heat can start fires, it seems that much of the fire damage in Hiroshima and Nagasaki following the nuclear explosions resulted from damaged electrical, fuel, gas, and other systems following physical damage caused by the shock or blast wave that accompanied the explosion.

The shock wave produced when a nuclear weapon explodes creates a front of moving air more powerful than any produced by a natural storm. Destructive winds follow the front of displaced air, causing more damage to objects in their path. Many nuclear weapons are designed to be detonated high above their targets to take advantage of this shock effect. The more powerful the bomb, the higher in the sky it will be detonated. The nuclear bombs dropped on Japan exploded between 1,500 and 2,000 feet (458–610 m) above their targets. A large bomb with the power of 10,000,000 tons (10 megatons) of TNT is capable of destroying most houses within a distance of more than 10 miles from the blast site.

Unlike conventional explosives, nuclear devices can release significant amounts of radioactivity and pulses of electromagnetic energy. Radioactivity, or penetrating radiation, is the release of subatomic particles from unstable atomic nuclei. Besides the greater power of nuclear weapons, radiation is the one feature that most distinguishes chemical from nuclear explosions. Radiation can kill outright in very high doses and cause illness, including cancer, at lower doses. The initial burst of radiation during a nuclear explosion is made up of gamma rays (or x rays) and neutrons. The energy of this radiation is so high that the particles and waves can often penetrate buildings. Later, a second type of radiation contaminates the explosion site and often enters the atmosphere where it can travel thousands of miles before falling back to earth. This type of radiation is called radioactive fallout. Radioactive fallout could contaminate the Earth and poison living things for years following a nuclear war.

Fission bombs and fission–fusion–fission bombs produce more fallout than hydrogen bombs because the fusion of hydrogen atoms generates less radioactive byproducts than does fission of uranium or plutonium.

Electromagnetic pulses are like giant "power surges." They can destroy most electronic circuits ranging from those in your toaster to the controls of sophisticated airplanes.

The effects of fires and destruction following a nuclear war might even change the climate of the planet. In 1983, a group of scientists including Carl Sagan published the "nuclear winter" theory that suggested that particles of smoke, dust and other debris produced by fires caused by many nuclear explosions would block the Sun's rays from reaching the surface of the earth. This, in turn, would reduce temperatures to below freezing, damage the protective ozone layer that blocks the sun's cancer–causing ultraviolet rays, and change wind patterns and ocean currents. These climatic changes, according to the theory, would destroy crops and lead to the death of many more animals and humans than were killed outright by nuclear explosions. Some people have challenged these predictions, but others, including some United States government agencies, support them.

Nuclear weapons today

Today nuclear weapons are built in many sizes and shapes not available in the 1940s and 1950s. They are designed for use against many different types of military and civilian targets. Some weapons are less powerful than 1,000 tons of TNT, while others have the explosive force of millions of tons of TNT. Small nuclear shells can be fired from cannons. Nuclear warheads mounted on missiles can be launched from land–based silos, ships, submarines, trains, and large wheeled vehicles. Several warheads can be fitted into one missile. These MIRVs or multiple independent reentry vehicles can release 10 or so individual nuclear warheads as well as decoys far above their targets making it difficult for the enemy to intercept them.

Even the ability of nuclear weapons to release radioactivity has been exploited to create different types of weapons. "Clean bombs" are weapons designed to produce as little radioactive fallout as possible. A hydrogen bomb without a uranium jacket would produce relatively little radioactive contamination, for example. A "dirty bomb" could just as easily be built with materials that contribute to radioactive fallout. Such weapons could also be detonated near the earth's surface to increase the amount of material that could contribute to radioactive fallout. "Neutron" bombs have been designed to shower battle fields with deadly neutrons that can penetrate buildings and armored vehicles without destroying them. Any people exposed to the neutrons, however, would die.

The United States and Russia signed a Strategic Arms Reduction Treaty in 1993 to eliminate two thirds of their nuclear warheads in 10 years. By 1995, nearly 2,500 nuclear warheads had been removed from bombers and missiles in the two countries, according to U.S. government officials. Although thousands of nuclear weapons still remain in the hands of many different governments, recent diplomatic trends have helped to lower the number of nuclear weapons in the world.

In May 1995, more than 170 members of the United Nations agreed to permanently extend the Nuclear Non–Proliferation Treaty first signed in 1960. Under terms of the treaty, the five major countries with nuclear weapons—the United States, Britain, France, Russia, and China—agreed to commit themselves to eliminating their arsenals as an "ultimate" goal. The other 165 nations agree not to acquire nuclear weapons. Israel, which is believed to possess nuclear weapons, did not sign the treaty. Two other nuclear powers, India and Pakistan, refused to renounce nuclear weapons until they can be convinced their nations are safe without them.

Further Reading:

Miller, Richard L. *Under the Cloud, The Decades of Nuclear Testing.* New York: The Free Press, 1986.

Pringle, Laurence. *Nuclear War, From Hiroshima to Nuclear Winter.* Hillside, NJ: Enslow Publishers, Inc., 1985.

Stephenson, Michael and Roger Hearn. *The Nuclear Casebook.* London: Frederick Muller Limited, 1983.

Sternglass, Ernest J. *Secret Fallout, Low–Level Radiation from Hiroshima to Three Mile Island.* New York: McGraw–Hill Company, 1981.

Walmer, Max. *An Illustrated Guide to Strategic Weapons.* New York: Prentice Hall Press, 1988.

Dean Allen Haycock

KEY TERMS

Atomic bomb—An explosive weapon which uses uranium–235 or plutonium as fuel. Its tremendous destructive power is produced by energy released from the "splitting of atoms" or nuclear fission. Also called A–bomb, atom bomb, or fission bomb.

Hydrogen bomb—An nuclear explosive weapon which uses hydrogen isotopes as fuel and an atom bomb as a detonator. More powerful than an atom bomb, the Hydrogen bomb derives its destructive power from energy released when nuclei of hydrogen are forced together to form helium nuclei in a process called nuclear fusion. Also called H–bomb or Thermonuclear bomb.

Isotope—One of two or more atoms having the same number of protons but a different number of neutrons in their atomic nuclei. Uranium–235 and Uranium–238 are isotopes of uranium. Deuterium and tritium are isotopes of hydrogen. Isotopes have the same number of protons (atomic number) but a different number of neutrons.

Nuclear fission—"Splitting the atom." A nuclear reaction in which an atomic nucleus splits into fragments with the release of energy, including radioactivity.

Nuclear fusion—A nuclear reaction in which an atomic nucleus combines with another nucleus and releases energy.

Nuclear weapon—A bomb or other explosive that derives it explosive force from the release of nuclear energy.

Plutonium—A heavy, rare natural element that undergoes fission in a nuclear bomb. It is produced artificially by bombarding uranium-238 with neutrons. The addition of one neutron to the nucleus of uranium-238 changes it into plutonium-239 which is called "weapons grade plutonium," the most efficient form for making weapons.

Radioactivity—Spontaneous release of subatomic particles or gamma rays by unstable atoms as their nuclei decay.

Radioisotope—A type of atom or isotope, such as strontium–90, that exhibits radioactivity.

TNT—trinitrotoluene, a conventional chemical high explosive.

Uranium—A heavy natural element found in nature. More than 99% of natural uranium is a form called U–238. Only U–235 readily undergoes fission and it must be purified from the other form.

Nucleic acid

Two nucleic acids, DNA (deoxyribonucleic acid) and RNA (ribonucleic acid), are found in living things which serve to store, translate, and pass on the genetic information of an organism to the next generation. Nucleic acids are universal to all life, in eukaryotic and prokaryotic cells, as well as in viruses. The mitochondria of eukaryotic cells also contain some DNA, known as mitochondrial DNA.

Nucleic acids have a special physical structure that lets them be the information chemicals of living things. DNA and RNA are both giant molecules consisting of long chains of small, repeating chemical units called nucleotides joined together like the box cars of a train. Each nucleotide unit carries a single piece of information, corresponding to an individual letter in a word; when nucleotides are strung together in long chains, the nucleic acids contain messages corresponding to words and sentences. The information in the genes (lengths of nucleic acid) in the nucleus is translated by cells into polypeptides and proteins in the cytoplasm. The cell then can read these "words" and know what to do.

Proteins are important because they make up cell structure and because they function as enzymes, which are catalysts which control the various biochemical pathways in cell metabolism.

There are important differences between the two nucleic acids. DNA has two long chains, or strands, of nucleotides that mirror each other and which are arranged in a double helix format. RNA has a single strand. Furthermore, the four bases of the nucleotides of DNA are adenine, cytosine, guanine, and thymine, while those of RNA lack thymine, which is substituted by uracil. The DNA, copies of which are found in every cell of the body, represents the permanent copy of an organism's entire genetic information, which is passed on to the next generation. The RNA is never more than a temporary copy of a small fraction of the information. There are three types of RNA: messenger RNA (mRNA), transfer RNA (tRNA), and ribosomal RNA (rRNA). DNA serves as the master set of blueprints for all of an organism's functions, and RNA acts as the specialist that interprets a small portion of these instructions for use in the cells and tissues of the organism. In short, living organisms use the nucleic acid DNA to preserve their biological information and the nucleic acid RNA to access it.

See also Chromosome; Deoxyribonucleic acid; Gene; Genetics; Ribonucleic acid.

Nucleon

Nucleon is a generic word for the heavy particles that make up the atomic nucleus: the protons and neutrons. It is like the generic word *fruit*, used to include apples, oranges, and many others, except that the class of nucleons contains only two members.

The *nucleon number* of a nucleus is just another term for mass number; it is simply the total number of nucleons in the nucleus. In the symbol for a particular kind of nucleus, the nucleon number or mass number is written to the upper left of the symbol of the element. For example, the symbol for a nucleus of carbon–14, the isotope of carbon that contains six protons (because all carbon nuclei do) plus eight neutrons for a total of 14 nucleons, is ^{14}C.

The use of the ending *–on* for the names of sub-atomic particles began with *electron*, a word that was coined in 1891 by the Irish physicist George J. Stoney (1826–1911) by modifying the word *electric* to come up with a name for the basic unit of electricity. This was six years before J. J. Thomson (1856–1940) actually measured the electron as a particle.

After Ernest Rutherford (1871–1937) discovered the atomic nucleus in 1911, he proposed the name *proton* for the very lightest of all nuclei: the nucleus of the ordinary hydrogen atom. *Proto–* is Greek for *first*. In 1932, when James Chadwick (1891–1974) discovered another particle in the nucleus that was very similar to the positive proton except that it was electrically neutral, it was natural for him to call it a *neutron*. It was then equally natural to call both nuclear particles *nucleons*, especially when nuclear theory began to treat the proton and the neutron as two different states of the same fundamental particle.

Nucleons are no longer thought to be the ultimate nuclear particles, however. Current theory says that each proton and neutron is made up of a trio of fundamental particles called *quarks*—particles that are thought to be the truly basic entities in nuclear matter. The proton is thought to consist of two quarks of charge +2/3 each (called *up* quarks) and one quark of charge –1/3 (called *down* quarks). The charge of the whole proton, which is +1, is the sum of the charges of its quarks: two times +2/3 and one times –1/3 make +3/3 or +1. The neutron, on the other hand, consists of one *up* quark of charge +2/3 and two *down* quarks of charge –1/3 each. The neutron's net charge of zero comes from the charges of its quarks: one times +2/3 and two times –1/3 make zero.

See also Subatomic particles.

Nucleus, cellular

The nucleus is a large membrane–bound cell organelle which houses the chromosomes and which occupies roughly 10% of the volume of all eukaryotic cells. The nucleus is separated from the rest of the cell and the cytoplasm by a double membrane known as the nuclear envelope. The outer layer of the nuclear membrane is studded with small openings called nuclear pores, which allow for the controlled movement of selected molecules in and out of the nucleus. Most of a eukaryotic cell's DNA is found in the chromosomes of the nucleus, while a very small amount of DNA is present in the mitochondria. All plant and animal cells with a nucleus and known as eukaryotic cells, (meaning "true nucleus") while bacterial cells which lack a nucleus are known as prokaryotic cells.

Nuclear structures

The DNA–containing nucleus has been described as a balloon filled with thick solution with a fibrous mesh which holds the DNA in place and which moves molecules about.

The major components of the nucleus include the chromosomes, the nucleolus, the nucleoplasm, and the nuclear cortex. Chromosomes are made of DNA; the nucleolus manufactures ribosomal components; and the nucleoplasm is the fluid and filaments inside the nucleus. The nuclear cortex is a dense area on the inner face of the nucleus, which tethers the chromosomes in place when the cell is not undergoing division.

Not all cells have a nucleus. Bacterial cells lack a nucleus and so do the red blood cells of mammals. Red blood cells (or corpuses) need to be flexible enough to get into tiny capillaries to deliver oxygen and nutrients to the cells. Some cells have more than one nucleus (multinucleated), for example, nutrient–providing cells in the garden pea plant and lilies both have some multi–nucleated, nutrient–providing cells. The long, tube–like skeletal muscle cells in vertebrates are also multinucleated.

Nuclear functions

The nucleus is the core of a eukaryotic cell. Its primary function is to separate events inside from the cytoplasm outside. This separation of space and time supports the careful choreography of the detailed molecular dance happening inside the nucleus.

A non–dividing nucleus (in a state) "resting," is actually making the molecules which allow the rest of the cell to function. One of the most important events taking place in the nucleus is transcription, which is the transfer of the instructions on the DNA to the RNA. DNA is a stable store of genetic information, which must be transcribed (via RNA molecules) to construct the proteins coded in its blueprint.

Messenger RNA makes a "mirror image" copy of a stretch of the DNA molecule and then moves RNA out of the nucleus through the nuclear pores into the cytoplasm. There the RNA locates the ribosomes where it consumes the protein products with the help of transfer RNA molecules.

Prior to cell division, the nucleus replicates itself so that the two new cells will each contain genetic information. Several nuclear enzymes coordinate the replication of DNA. During cell division, the nuclear envelope breaks down, and equal copies of DNA and cytoplasm are partitioned into two daughter cells. After division, the nuclear envelopes reform in each daughter cell around its own copy of DNA. This fundamental sequence of events allows for the continuation of eukaryotic life during embryonic development and cellular regeneration throughout life.

See also Cell; Chromosome; Deoxyribonucleic acid; Ribonucleic acid.

Further Reading:

Agutter P.S. *Between Nucleus and Cytoplasm.* New York: Chapman and Hall, 1991.

Alberts, B., et al. *Molecular Biology of the Cell.* 3rd ed. New York: Garland Publishing, 1994.

Becker, W., and D. Deamer. *The World of the Cell.* 2nd ed. New York: Benjamin/Cummings, 1990.

Louise H. Dickerson

Nucleus, atomic see **Atom**

A numbat (*Myrmecobius fasciatus*).

Numbat

Sole members of the family Myrmecobiidae, numbat is the aborigine name for these small marsupial mammals, otherwise known as banded anteaters. They are slightly larger than rats and weigh about one lb (.454 kg). Considered one of the most attractive marsupials, their general color varies from grayish–brown to reddish–brown, broken by several prominent white bars across the back and rump. A white–bordered dark stripe passes from the base of each ear through the eye to the snout. Tail length is about 7 inches (17.7 cm.) and when it is erect and fluffed it looks like a bottle brush.

Active only in the daytime and living in shrub woodland and eucalyptus forests, numbats search fallen branches and logs for termites which they pick up with their slender, cylindrical 4 in (10 cm) tongue. Since ants, grit, and soil are swallowed, it is believed that these are taken accidentally. Although numbats do not chew their food, their small and widely spaced teeth number between 50 and 52, the largest number of teeth found in any marsupial. Numbats use hollow logs for shelter throughout the year and may dig burrows in the ground to take refuge from the cold. They are solitary for most of the year except when young are present. Generally four young are born between January and May, attaching themselves to the nipples of the female who lacks the typical pouch.

More widespread in the past, numbats now occur only in the southwest portion of Western Australia. Destruction of their habitat for agriculture and predation by foxes has contributed to most of their decline. Despite stabilization of their habitat, numbat populations are currently small and scattered. Because they are considered rare and endangered, breeding colonies have been established with the hope of returning animals to the wild.

See also Anteaters; Marsupials.

Number theory

Number theory is the study of natural, or counting numbers, including prime numbers. Number theory is important because the simple sequence of counting numbers from one to infinity conceals many relationships beneath its surface.

Prime and composite numbers

One of the most important distinctions in number theory is between prime and composite numbers. Prime numbers can only be divided evenly (with nothing left over) by 1 and themselves. Prime numbers include 2, 3, 5, 7, 11, 13, 17, and so on to infinity. The number 1 is not considered a prime. All primes are odd numbers except for 2, because any even number can be divided evenly by 2.

A composite number can be divided, or factored, into two or more prime numbers in addition to 1 and itself. Ten is a composite number because it can be divided by 2, 5, 1, and itself. The numbers 2 and 5 are the prime factors of 10. Any whole number that is not a prime is a composite.

One difference between prime and composite numbers is that it takes relatively little time to determine if a number is prime, but far longer to determine the prime factors of a composite number, especially if the composite is very large (100 digits or more). This discrepancy in computation time is important in developing computer security systems.

Prime numbers do not occur in a predictable way. There are sequences of primes which can be partially described in a formula, but sooner or later the formula breaks down. One formula, invented by Marin Mersenne (1588–1648) is $2^p - 1$, where p is a prime number. Although this formula generates many primes, it also misses many primes. Another formula, invented by Leonhard Euler (1707–1783), generates prime numbers regularly for the series of consecutive numbers from 0 to 15 and then stops. The formula is $x^2 + x + 17$, in which x is any number from 0 to 15.

Famous formulas in number theory

Number theory is full of famous formulas that illustrate the relationships between whole numbers from 1 to infinity. Some of these formulas are very complicated, but the most famous ones are very simple, for example, the theorem by Fermat below that proves if a number is prime.

Fermat's theorem

Pierre de Fermat (1601–1665) is one of the most famous number theoreticians in history, but mathematics was only his hobby. He was a judge in France, and he published very little during his life. He did correspond extensively with many leading intellectuals of his day, and his mathematical innovations were presented to these pen pals in his letters.

One of Fermat's many theorems provides a quick way of finding out if a number is prime. Say n is any whole number, and p is any prime number. Raise n to the power of p, and then subtract n from the result. If p is really a prime number, then the result can be divided evenly by p. If anything is left over after the division, then the number p is not prime. A shorter way of putting this formula is this: $n^p - n$ can be divided evenly by p.

Here is a simple illustration of Fermat's theorem. Let n = 8 and p = 3. If Fermat's theorem is right, then $8^3 - 8$ must be divisible by 3. Multiply 8 by itself three times (8 x 8 x 8): the product is 512. Subtract 8 from 512: the result is 504. Divide 504 by 3: the result is 168. Fermat's theorem works for any whole numbers that meet the conditions of the formula.

Gauss and congruence

Karl Friedrich Gauss (1777–1855) has been called the "Prince of Mathematicians" for his many contributions to pure and applied mathematics. He was born to poor parents in Germany. His high intelligence was noticed early and nurtured by his mother and uncle, but his father never encouraged Gauss in his education.

One of Gauss's most important contributions to number theory involved the invention of the idea of congruence (or agreement) in numbers and the use of what he called "modulos" or small measures or sets of numbers. In effect, his theory of congruence allows people to break up the infinite series of whole numbers into smaller, more manageable chunks of numbers and perform computations upon them. This arrangement makes the everyday arithmetic involved in such things as telling time much easier to program into computers.

Gauss said that if one number is subtracted from another ($a - b$), and the remainder of the subtraction can be divided by another number, *m*, then *a* and *b* are congruent to each other by the number *m*. Gauss's formula is as follows: *a* is congruent to *b* modulo *c*. For example, 720 − 480 = 240. The remainder, 240, can be divided by 60, 20, 10, and other numbers. However, for our purposes, we will only focus on 60. Using Gauss's expression, 720 is congruent to 480 by modulo 60. That is, both 720 and 480 are related to a third number (the remainder after 480 is subtracted from 720), which can be multiplied by 60.

In an abstract sense, this computation is related to such everyday arithmetic functions as telling the time of day on a digital watch. When the watch tells the time, it does not say "240 minutes past noon." It says "4 o'clock" or "4:00." To express the time of day, the digital watch uses several kinds of modulos (or small measures) which have been used for centuries: 60 minutes in an hour, 12 hours in the a.m. or p.m. of a day, and so on. If the watch says it is 4:00 in the afternoon, then, from one frame of reference, it has subtracted 480 minutes from the 720 minute period between 12 noon to midnight. What remains is 240 minutes past noon. That is, 720 − 480 = 240. The remainder, 240, can be divided evenly by the modulo 60 (and by other numbers which we will ignore).

When we tell the time everyday, however, we do not use Gauss's terminology. Our clocks are already divided into modulos and we simply note the hour and how many minutes come before or after the hour. The importance of Gauss's congruence theory is that he created the formulas that allowed an immense variety of arithmetic actions to be performed based on different sets of numbers.

Famous problems in number theory

Number theory is an immensely rich area and it is defined by the important problems that it tries to solve. Sometimes a problem was considered solved, but years later the solution was found to be flawed. One important challenge in number theory has been trying to find a formula that will describe all the prime numbers. To date, that problem has not been solved. Two of the most famous problems in number theory involve Fermat.

Fermat's failed prime number formula

Many mathematicians, including Mersenne and Euler, have tried to find a formula that will define all the prime numbers. No one has ever succeeded.

Fermat had one of the most famous failures. He thought that if he squared 2 and then raised the square of 2 to a higher power, which he labeled n (a whole number), then the results would be nothing but primes. His formula looks like this: $_2 2^n + 1 = $ a prime number. This formula appeared to work until Leonhard Euler proved it wrong. Euler found that if 5 is substituted for n in the formula $_2 2n + 1$, the resulting number is 4,294,967,297, which can be divided equally by 641 and 6,700,417.

Fermat's last theorem

Fermat wrote his famous "Last Theorem" in the margin of a book some time in the late 1630s. He said that the equation $x^n + y^n = z^n$ has no solutions in whole numbers if n is greater than 2. Mathematicians have been trying to prove or disprove this theorem for centuries. Princeton University professor Andrew J. Wiles apparently had proved it correct but later flaws were found in his proof. By late 1994 Wiles thought the flaws had been solved. Wiles announced in June 1992 that he had proved Fermat right. However, it will take several years before other mathematicians will be able to verify Wiles's proof.

Current applications

Number theory was labeled the "Queen of Mathematics" by Gauss. For many years it was thought to be without many practical applications. That situation has changed significantly in the twentieth century with the rise of computers.

Prime and composite numbers play an important role in modern cryptography or coding systems. Huge volumes of confidential information (credit card numbers, bank account numbers) and large amounts of money are transferred electronically around the world every day, all of which must kept secret. One of the important applications of number theory is keeping secrets.

Using Fermat's theorem, a computer can quickly compute if a number–even a large number–is prime. However, once a computer finds out that a number is not prime, it then takes a long time to find out what its factors are, especially if the number is a large composite (say 120 digits long). It can take years on a supercomputer to find the prime factors of large composite numbers.

This time gap between finding out if a number is prime and factoring the primes in a composite number is useful to cryptographers. To create a security system, they invent numerical codes for the letters and characters of a message. Then they use an encoding algorithm (a series of steps to solve a problem) to turn a message into a long number. If the message is more than a cer-

KEY TERMS

. . . .

Algorithm—A set of steps for solving a problem.

Composite number—A number that can be divided into two or more prime numbers in addition to 1 and itself.

Congruence—The relationship between two numbers if they have the same remainder when they are divided by a number.

Cryptography—The study of creating and breaking secret codes.

Factors—Numbers that are multiplied with other numbers to equal a product. In the multiplication of 2 x 2 = 4, each 2 is a factor. Also, factors are the numbers that result when numbers are divided. For example, 10 and 10 are factors of 100.

Modulo—A number by which two other numbers can be divided to give the same remainder.

Prime numbers—Numbers that can only be divided evenly by 1 and themselves.

Product—The result of multiplying two or more numbers. Six multiplied by 7 gives the product of 42.

Set—A group of units or numbers.

Whole numbers—The positive integers: 1, 2, 3, 4...

Computer cryptography systems are only one application of number theory. Other formulas of number theory allow computer programs to find out many years in advance what days of the week will fall on what dates of the month, so that people can find out well in advance what day of the week Christmas or the Fourth of July will occur. Many computers have preinstalled internal programs that tell users when they last modified a file down to the second, minute, hour, day of the week, and date of the month. These programs work thanks to the formulas of number theorists.

Further Reading:

Davenport, Harold. *The Higher Arithmetic: An Introduction to the Theory of Numbers.* 6th edition. Cambridge: Cambridge University Press, 1992.

Dunham, William. *The Mathematical Universe.* New York: John Wiley and Sons, 1994.

"Finessing Fermat, Again: The Wily Proof may Finally Be Finished." *Scientific American* 272.2 (February 1995): 16.

Peterson Ivars, *The Mathematical Tourist: Snapshots of Modern Mathematics.* New York: W.H. Freeman and Company, 1988.

Spencer, Donald D. *Exploring Number Theory with Microcomputers.* Ormond Beach, FL: Camelot Publishing Company, 1989.

Patrick Moore

tain length, say 100 characters, then the cryptography program breaks the message into blocks of 100 characters. Once the message is translated into a number, the program multiplies the number of an encoded message by a certain prime (which could be a 100 digit number) and by a composite number. The composite number is the product of two prime numbers, which have been randomly selected and which must be in both the encoding algorithm of the sender and the decoding algorithm of the receiver. The prime numbers making up the composite number are usually quite long (100 digits and longer). When the message is transmitted from the sender to the receiver, some of the numbers are made public, but the primes that make up the composite number are kept secret. They are only known by the decoding algorithm of the authorized person who receives the message. Anyone who is eavesdropping on the transmission will see a lot of numbers, but without the prime numbers from the encoding and decoding programs, it is impossible to decode the message in any reasonable time.

Numeration systems

Numeration systems are structured methods or procedures for counting in order to determine the total units in a collection. Numeration systems consist of counting bases (base 2, base 5, base 10, base 20, etc.) and some form of representation. This representation might be as primitive as the hand signals used in aborigine cultures and in the trading pits of stock exchanges, or it could be written on paper or inscribed magnetically in an electronic medium like a computer diskette.

Why numeration systems exist

Numeration systems exist for three reasons: to identify, to order, and to tally.

Numeration systems are used to identify people and property, because they preserve confidentiality, increase security, and minimize errors caused when there are many people with the same name or many identical objects in the same production run in a factory assembly line. There are thousands of people named "John Jones," and even if John Jones uses his middle initial, he can still be confused with another John Jones with the same initial. Thus numeration systems are developed for credit cards, social security cards, bank accounts, serial numbers for products, and other reasons. These identification numbers might be very long to defeat a criminal who is randomly guessing at numbers in order to steal from someone's bank account or credit card account.

Numeration systems also define a person or unit's order in a series, for example, to determine who crosses a finish line in a race in first, second, or third place. Numbers that define order are known as the ordinal numbers (first, second, etc.) and contrast with the cardinal numbers (one, two, three, etc.) which express a tally or total of units.

Finally, numeration systems are used to tally or total; to find out how many items or units are involved in a calculation involving addition, subtraction, multiplication, or division.

History

No one knows exactly when ordered numeration systems began, but counting has been around for tens of thousands of years. A notched baboon bone dating back 35,000 years was found in Africa and was apparently used for counting. In the 1930s, a wolf bone was found in Czechoslovakia with 57 notches in several patterns of regular intervals. The bone was dated as 30,000 years old and is assumed to be a hunter's record of his kills.

The earliest recorded numbering systems go back at least 3000 B.C., when Sumerians in Mesopotamia were using a numbering system for recording business transactions, and Egyptians and people in ancient India were also using numbering systems around the same time. The decimal or base 10 numbering system goes back to at least 1800 B.C., and decimal systems were common in European and Indian cultures from at least 1000 B.C.

One of the most important innovations in western culture was the development of the Hindu–Arabic notation system (1, 2, 3, ... 9), which is the international standard today. The Hindu–Arabic system had been around for at least 2,000 years before the Europeans heard about it, and it has many important innovations. One of these was the place–holding concept of zero. Although the concept of zero as a null place holder had appeared in many cultures in different forms, the first actual written zero as we know it today appeared in

India in 876 A.D. The Hindu–Arabic system was brought into Europe in the tenth century with Gerbert of Aurillac (945–1003), and it slowly and steadily began to replace Roman numerals (I, II, III, IV...) in Europe, especially in business transactions and mathematics. By the sixteenth century, Europe was well versed in the far simpler and more economical Hindu–Arabic system of notation, though Roman Numerals were still used, and are even used today.

Numeration systems continue to be invented to this day, especially when companies develop systems of serial numbers to identify new products. The binary (base 2), octal (base 8), and hexadecimal (or base 16) numbering systems used in computers were extensively developed in the late 1950s for processing electronic signals in computers.

The bases of numeration systems

The base of a numeration system is its frame of reference or the starting point on which it grounds its counting method. Although any numeration system must be abstract, the basic concept of number makes more sense to people if it has some obvious, immediate reference point in human experience. For that reason, many bases of numeration systems are founded upon the most obvious and immediate things in a person's visual field: a person's arms, hands, fingers, and toes. Common bases of numeration systems are the two arms of a person (base 2 system), the fingers of one hand (base 5 system), the fingers of both hands (base 10 system), or the total of all a person's fingers and toes (base 20 system). There are many other bases for numeration systems (base 4, base 7, base 8, base 16, etc.), but only a few will be discussed here.

Base 2

Although most base 2 numeration systems have now been replaced by decimal (or base 10) systems, the base 2 system was one of the most common numeration systems in ancient times. In a base 2 system, to indicate a number like three or four, the person says "two-and-one" or "two-and-two." The number 10 is indicated with "two-and-two-and-two-and-two-and-two."

However, as a person counts to higher and higher numbers in a base 2 system, it becomes harder and harder to remember one's place in the long string of twos. Thus, as cultures grew more complex and needed to count to higher numbers, base 2 systems became obsolete.

Base 10 or decimal

The base 10 or decimal system has now spread throughout the world and is the most commonly used numeration system today. The digits to the left and right of the decimal point are named according to their distance from the decimal. The first ten numbers, in their order of distance from the left of the decimal point are:

one = 1

tens = 10

hundreds = 100

thousands = 1,000

ten thousands = 10,000

hundred thousands = 100,000

millions = 1,000,000

ten millions = 10,000,000

hundred millions = 100,000,000

billions = 1,000,000,000

These numbers continue indefinitely. To the right of the decimal point the numbers are one tenth, one hundredth, one thousandth, one ten–thousandth, one hundred–thousandth, one millionth, and so on.

Base 60

The base 60 system seems very strange to Western readers. From long habit, we are accustomed to the decimal system, and it is easy to understand numbering systems based on two (arms), five (fingers), ten (fingers on both hands), and so on. However, the base 60 system survives in our time–measuring system of 60 seconds to a minute and 60 minutes to an hour. It also survives in angle measurement and in navigational systems that measure longitude and latitude: 60 seconds equal one minute of arc, 60 minutes equal one degree of arc, and 360 degrees of arc equal an entire circle.

The base 60 system began with the Sumerians in Mesopotamia around 3000 B.C. No one knows how it got started, though scholars speculate that it had something to do with the 60 to 1 ratio between the weights of the Sumerian measurement system. Others speculate that it was the result of the combining of a base 6 and base 10 numbering system. A rational explanation for using 60 as a base is that 60 can be divided evenly by 2, 3, 4, 5, and 6, which simplifies many computations.

Place–value systems

A place–value system assigns a certain value to the spatial location of a number in a series. For example, in the decimal system, a number's position relative to others in a series defines its category as being in the tens, hundreds, thousands, ten–thousands, and so on. In the number 1,234, the "4" occupies the slot representing zero through 9, the "3" occupies the slot representing 10 through 99, the "2" occupies the slot representing 100 through 999, and the "1" occupies the slot representing 1000 through 9999.

Place value systems are important because they make common arithmetic functions much more efficient. If people are to manipulate spatial symbols readily, they need a method that is simple, consistent, and symmetrical so that numbers can be lined up visually and quickly grouped at a glance according to their value. Without the place values of the decimal system, simple arithmetic functions of addition, subtraction, multiplication, and division are enormously difficult because they are intimidating, time–consuming, overly complicated, and prone to error.

The Roman numeral system (I, II, III, IV, ...) lacks an efficient way to represent place, and it makes simple arithmetic functions very difficult to perform for most people. Compare below the simple process of adding 17, 38, and 3 in Roman numerals and Hindu–Arabic numerals.

XVII	17
XXXVIII	38
III	3
LVIII	58

Most people who are familiar with Hindu–Arabic numbers find that adding the Roman numerals on the left is baffling.

Although place–value systems make it easier for people to do arithmetic, they also help computers perform electronic computations at blinding speeds. A common place–value system used in computers is the binary number system, which is a base 2 system. The binary system has two values: "0" and "1." These values correspond with the signals "high" and "low" in the electronic circuits of computers. Because these numbers are so simple, computers can process them electronically up to a trillion times per second, depending on the speed of the computer.

In the binary system, each place from right to left is valued at 2 times the place to its right. Thus the first place can be zero or one, the second place to the left is valued at two, the third place to the left is valued at

KEY TERMS

· ·

Arc—The continuous path described by a curved line.

Base—The foundation or reference point upon which a counting system is built.

Hindu–Arabic numbers—Although commonly called "Arabic" numerals, the numbering system represented as 1, 2, 3, 4 … 9 represents a combination of innovations from Arabic and Hindu (or Indian) cultures.

Latitude—The lines that run east and west on a map which are used to measure the distance north and south of the equator.

Longitude—The lines on a map that run perpendicular to the equator which are used to measure distances east and west.

Mesopotamia—The area in the ancient Middle East between the Tigris and Euphrates rivers, which is now in Iraq.

Place-value—The location of a number relative to others in a sequence. In the decimal system the number 3 in the series 2,300 occupies the hundreds place.

Roman numerals—The numbering system developed during the Roman Empire: I, II, III, IV, V, and so on.

four, the fourth place to the left is valued at eight, and so on. The following list indicates the binary values of the first ten numbers of a decimal system:

decimal		binary
0	=	0
1	=	1
2	=	10
3	=	11
4	=	100
5	=	101
6	=	110
7	=	111
8	=	1000
9	=	1001
10	=	1010

For example, the decimal number 3 above has two 1s in its binary format. The 1 on the right in the binary format is equal to 1, because its place value can only be 1 or 0. But the 1 on the left in the binary format (for the decimal number 3) occupies the place that is valued at 2

in the binary system. Consider another example: look at the decimal number 10 as it is formatted in the binary system: 1010. The fourth number (1) from the right occupies the place valued at 8; the 0 in the third place means it is valued at zero; the 1 in the second place from the right means it is valued at 2; and the 0 in the right–most place means zero. Thus, in the binary place–value system, $8 + 0 + 2 + 0 = 10$.

Although this system seems cumbersome to people who are used to the decimal notation system, it is perfectly suited for the ways that computers manipulate electric currents to process large quantities of data at very fast rates.

Further Reading:

Barrow, John D. *Pi in the Sky: Counting, Thinking, and Being.* Oxford: Oxford University Press, 1992.

Boyer, Carl B. *A History of Mathematics.* Princeton, New Jersey: Princeton University Press, 1985.

Hogben, Lancelot. *Mathematics for the Million: How to Master the Magic of Numbers.* New York: W. W. Norton, 1983.

Swetz, Frank J. *Capitalism & Arithmetic: The New Math of the 15th Century.* LaSalle, IL: Open Court Press, 1987.

Patrick Moore

Nuclear reactions

Simply put, nuclear reactions are interactions involving collisions between atomic nuclei. Such reactions are the source of the energy generated by nuclear power plants and delivered by nuclear weapons. They are also the source of the energy which enables stars to shine and so are at the heart of stellar astrophysics.

There are two fundamentally different, indeed virtually opposite, ways in which nuclear reactions generate energy. If two light atomic nuclei combine to form a heavier nucleus, the mass of the product nucleus is usually less than the mass of the nuclei from which it was assembled. The mass that apparently disappears emerges as energy in accordance with the famous formula of Albert Einstein; $E=mc^2$. While the amount of mass lost during this reaction is very tiny, the speed of light (c) is a very large number which appears squared in the formula. The result is that a small amount of mass yields a very large amount of energy. The combining of two nuclei to form a more massive nucleus is called nuclear fusion. The lighter the initial products, the more energy that is liberated during the fusion process. Thus the fusion of hydrogen into helium results in the largest fraction of the initial mass (about 0.007 or 0.7%) being converted to energy of any fusion reaction. The fusion of helium into carbon yields significantly less energy, and even less is produced from the fusion of heavier nuclei.

If a massive nucleus such as uranium is split, the mass of the pieces is less than the mass of the initial nucleus. Again, this mass difference appears as energy, as it does in fusion of the light elements. This process of obtaining energy by breaking up heavy elements is called fission. Fission is the energy source for the atomic bomb and modern nuclear power plants. During fission heavy elements such as uranium, thorium, and plutonium are broken up to produce energy and some additional nuclear particles which, in turn, are used to break up more of the massive nuclei. If not controlled, the process, called a chain reaction, yields a bomb. If controlled, fission can yield energy to generate electric power. The majority of the energy released appears as heat which is transported away from the reactor by a heat exchanger where it is used to produce steam. The steam is then utilized in much the same way as in a coal–fired power plant to spin turbines which run electric generators.

Important as fission processes have been for the development of atomic energy on earth, they play virtually no role in stellar astrophysics. Stars derive their energy from nuclear fusion. It is a common misconception that the hydrogen bomb and controlled thermonuclear fusion projects produce energy in the same manner as the Sun. This is not strictly true. There are certain variants of hydrogen called isotopes, specifically deuterium and tritium, which undergo nuclear fusion more readily than ordinary hydrogen. These isotopes are rare to non–existent in stars, but are used in "hydrogen" bombs and most controlled thermonuclear fusion projects.

The possibility of nuclear reactions seemed distant during the first quarter of the twentieth century. Although the idea that nuclear reactions could provide the energy to power the stars was put forth by Sir Arthur Stanley Eddington in 1926, the specific processes were suggested by Hans Bethe just before the outbreak of World War II. The first actual demonstration of nuclear fusion on a grand scale took place in the detonation of the first "hydrogen" nuclear device in 1954. Since then there has been a considerable effort to harness the processes of the fusion bomb so that they could be restrained to produce electric power in a controllable manner. While all these efforts have revolved around the utilization of the heavier isotopes of hydrogen, the Sun manages to "control" the nuclear fusion of hydrogen by producing the power required to oppose the crushing forces of its self gravity and flood the solar system with light.

The vast majority of stars obtain the energy to oppose gravity and shine at the same time from the fusion of hydrogen into helium. There are two main processes which combine four atoms of hydrogen to yield one atom of helium and a considerable amount of energy. In stars like the Sun the fusion cycle that combines the four hydrogen nuclei is called the proton–proton cycle. The first step in this cycle combines two protons, or hydrogen nuclei, to form the isotope of hydrogen called deuterium, which quickly collides with an additional proton to yield a light isotope of helium known as helium three (^{3}He). When two of these light helium (3He) nuclei collide they form the normal isotope of helium (^{4}He) and two protons. Since repeating the sequence twice requires six protons and the last step generates two, the net change is four hydrogen to one helium and substantial amounts of energy. Stars more massive than the Sun also derive their energy by combining four hydrogen nuclei to form one helium, but they utilize carbon, nitrogen, and oxygen in a complex series of fusion events. These additional elements act as nuclear catalysts as their number is neither increased or decreased by the cycle. They also give the cycle its name: the CNO cycle.

When stars completely use their supply of hydrogen they evolve to a phase where the helium produced from the hydrogen fusion itself undergoes nuclear fusion. Here two helium nuclei collide and form an isotope of beryllium which is inherently unstable and decays almost immediately back to the original two helium nuclei. If the beryllium nucleus is hit by a third helium nucleus during the brief time that it exists, it may form carbon and liberate a significant amount of energy. Since helium nuclei were known historically as alpha-particles, the entire process is called the triple-alpha process.

In massive stars the exhaustion of helium as fuel will lead to the nuclear fusion of carbon. When the carbon is used up, other reactions can occur. The successive use of more massive nuclei as nuclear fuel is less efficient as the mass of the fusing elements approaches iron. Without nuclear fuel to supply heat to the star, the gravitational forces of the star's mass cause the star to collapse. The collapse provides enough energy to allow nuclear fusion to run beyond iron, making more massive elements, but robs energy from the collapsing star in the process, because fusion reactions involving iron require more energy from their surroundings than they produce. This process of creating the elements found in the periodic table is called nucleosynthesis. The details of the terminal collapse are complicated, but lead to a final explosion where much of the matter in the star is hurled into space in an event called a supernova. This titanic collapse leading to a terminal explosion is the source of all elements in the universe more massive than iron.

George W. Collins, II

Nut

A nut is a type of fruit. Like all fruits, a nut develops from the ovary of a mature, fertilized flower. A nut is thick, dry, hard, and partly or entirely enclosed by a husk. A nut is indehiscent, in that it does not open along a naturally occurring seam, and remains closed even when fully mature.

A nut is a simple fruit, in that it is derived from the pistil of a single flower. Although a nut contains only one seed, the flower from which it develops has a compound ovary, with many ovules (immature and unfertilized seeds). Following fertilization, the other ovules of the flower undergo spontaneous abortion and die.

Familiar nuts include acorns, hickory nuts, walnuts, and beechnuts. The word 'nut' is also used mistakenly to refer to the seeds or fruits of some other plants. Thus, pine nuts and peanuts are really seeds and not nuts. Brazil nuts and coconuts are really a different type of fruit, technically referred to as a drupe, and not nuts.

Most nuts have a large concentration of protein, and are an important food source for wildlife. Humans often eat nuts as well. Formerly, Native Americans would leach out the astringent tannins from acorns so they could be eaten. North Americans once prized the nuts of the American chestnut *(Castanea dentata)* as a food. However, these trees have been decimated by an introduced fungus, known as the Chestnut blight. Now, nuts of the sweet chestnut tree *(Cadtomea sakua)* are occasionally served instead.

See also Fruits.

Peter A. Ensminger

Nuthatches

Nuthatches are small, short–tailed, large–headed birds in the family Sittidae in the order Passeriformes, the perching birds. There are 25 species of nuthatches, occurring on all continents except South America, Africa, or Antarctica.

Most species of nuthatches are forest birds which clamber over the bark of trees seeking insects, spiders, and arthropod eggs. Nuthatches can climb in any direction—including head–first down tree trunks, and even clamber upside–down beneath large limbs. The preferred food is arthropods, but when these are not abundant (during autumn, winter, and spring), nuthatches eat fruits and seeds, including the relatively large nuts of trees such as beech, oak, hazel, and chestnut. The edible matter of hard fruits such as acorns and hazelnuts can be rather difficult to extricate from their protective tissues. Some species of nuthatches accomplish this task by wedging the nut into a woody crevice and then hammering it open using their relatively stout beak. Hence the origin of their common name, nuthatch.

Two species of nuthatch, the brown–headed nuthatch of North America *(Sitta pusilla)* and the orange–winged sittella *(Neositta chrysoptera)* of Australia, are known to manipulate small twigs with their beaks for use in drawing insects within reach from deep in bark crevices or rotted wood. These are rare examples of the use of tools by birds.

Nuthatches are not gregarious, although during winter they will sometimes flock with other small forest birds, such as chickadees, tits, and kinglets. Presumably, this is done for reasons of safety, because flocks of small birds have a better chance of detecting predators early.

Nuthatches defend territories, and are non–colonial breeders. The typical nuthatches (genus *Sitta*) nest in deep crevices or cavities in trees. The cavities may be natural, or the nuthatch may excavate it in soft, rotted wood. Most nuthatch species will also use an aban-

A white-breasted nuthatch (*Sitta carolinensis*) at Kensington Metropark, Michigan. Nuthatches are often seen on the trunks of trees pointing downward in search of insects and larvae.

doned cavity previously excavated by another species, such as a woodpecker, and they may also use nestboxes. If the entrance to a cavity is too large, Eurasian species of nuthatches will make the hole smaller, and safer, by plastering its edges with mud. North American nuthatches do not do this.

Nuthatches have their greatest species diversity in central Asia, where there are 13 species, of which 12 are in the genus *Sitta*. There are four species of nuthatches in North America. The red–breasted nuthatch (*Sitta canadensis*) breeds widely in northern coniferous and mixed wood forests. This species is non–migratory, generally remaining in the same locale during winter. The red–breasted nuthatch usually excavates its own nest cavity in rotted wood of dead trees or stumps, and it smears the edge of the entrance hole with conifer pitch, although the reason for this behavior is not known. The white–breasted nuthatch (*S. carolinensis*) is a widespread resident of broadleaf and mixed wood forests. The brown–headed nuthatch occurs in southeastern pine forests, and the pygmy nuthatch (*S. pygmaeus*) inhabits pine forests of the west.

See also Arthropods; Conifer.

Bill Freedman

Nutmeg

The nutmeg family, Myristicaceae, order Magnoliales, consists of evergreen trees of the tropical rain forests. The genus *Myristica* includes about 120 species, the best known of which is the nutmeg tree (*Myristica fragrans*).

The nutmeg tree is native to the Moluccas, a group of islands in eastern Indonesia, also known as the Spice Islands. However, nutmeg is now cultivated in much of southern Asia, the West Indies, and Brazil. The nutmeg tree is the source of nutmeg and mace, two valuable spices that have been the objects of secret trading, theft, monopolies, and violent battles. Other *Myristica* species, such as *M. argentea, M. malabarica,* and *M. fatua,* are rather similar to *M. fragrans.* However, their fruit does not have the characteristic, intense aroma or flavor, and these species are only used for local medicinal purposes, as food additives, or for adulteration of more–valuable nutmeg or mace. .

Myristica fragrans can reach a height of 60 ft (20 m) and has leathery, somewhat aromatic leaves that grow to about 6 in (15 cm) long. This dioecious (male and female flowers occur on separate plants) tree has small, unscented, yellow flowers that superficially resemble those of lily–of–the–valley. Plantations cultivate mostly female trees, but intersperse them with male trees. When the tree is about eight years old, it bears its first crop of fruit, and it can continue to bear fruit up to the age of 80–100 years.

The tough, yellowish, one–seeded fruit (known as a drupe) is about 2 in (5 cm) in diameter and has a peach–like shape. When ripe, the fleshy outer covering of the fruit splits open, revealing its oval seed (the nutmeg), which is wrapped in a bright, red–orange, lacy covering called an aril (the mace).

After the fruit is picked, the outer covering is removed. The aril is taken off the seed, flattened into strips, dried, and sold either as whole strips or finely ground. The seeds are air–dried for several weeks, or sometimes, more rapidly over a fire. The nutmeg kernel is removed from the seed coat or husk, and is then dipped in lime to prevent insect infestation and seed germination. Nutmeg is sold either whole or ground up.

The nutmeg tree flowers and bears fruit year-round. The trees are harvested two to three times per year, with an annual average of 500 fruits (nutmegs) per tree. About 400 lb (180 kg) are needed to produce 1 lb (0.5 kg) of mace.

The inferior, or damaged fruits are made into oil of mace or nutmeg butter, and sold to industries for the manufacturing of soap, perfume, flavoring for candy, gum, soft drinks, and condiments. Nutmeg is often used in rich foods and sauces (for example, in eggnog and custard), and baked goods. Mace has a similar flavor to nutmeg, but is much more subtle, and is used in baked goods, sauces, soups, and meat dishes.

Nutmeg has been used medicinally for its sedative properties. An alkaloid–like substance called myristicin is a psychotropic, which in excessive doses can cause hallucinations, disorientation, and convulsions.

Christine Miner Minderovic

Nutria see **Beavers**

Nutrient deficiency diseases

Nutrient deficiency diseases occur when there is an absence of nutrients which are essential for growth and health. Lack of food leading to either malnutrition or starvation gives rise to these diseases. Another cause for a deficiency disease may be due to a structural or biological imbalance in the individual's metabolic system.

There are more than 50 known nutrients in food. Nutrients enable body tissues to grow and maintain themselves. They contribute to the energy requirements of the individual organism and they regulate the processes of the body. Carbohydrates, fats, and proteins provide the body with energy. The energy producing component of food is measured in calories. Aside from the water and fiber content of food, which are also important for their role in nutrition, the nutrients that serve functions other than energy production can be classified into four different groups: vitamins, fats, proteins, and minerals. All are necessary for proper body function and survival.

Early vitamin deficiency diseases

Casimir Funk (1884–1967), born in Warsaw, Poland. Originated the word vitamin in 1912, spelling it as vitamine, because he thought they were part of a group of organic compounds containing nitrogen, called amines. The final –e was later dropped in 1920 at the suggestion of the English nutritionist Jack Cecil Drummond who pointed out that these trace–like substances found only in food and essential for good health were not always amines. By 1914 Funk theorized that beriberi, scurvy, and pellagra were caused by a vitamin deficiency.

Scurvy

Scurvy is one of the oldest vitamin deficiency diseases recorded and the first one to be cured by adding a vitamin to the diet. Scurvy was a common malady of sailors of the age of exploration of the New World. It has been recorded that Vasco da Gama was supposed to have lost half of his crew to scurvy in his journey around the Cape of Good Hope at the end of the 15th century and Richard Hawkins reported that he lost 10,000 sailors from the disease a century later.

The main symptom of scurvy is hemorrhaging. Hemorrhage marks appear as spots under the skin or bruises, given the medical terms of petechiae and ecchymoses. The gums are swollen and usually become infected (gingivitis). Bleeding can take place in the membranes covering the large bones as well as in the membranes of the heart and brain. Wounds heal slowly and the bleeding in or around vital organs can be fatal. The disease is slow to develop and is manifested early by fatigue, irritability, and depression.

In 1747 a British naval physician, James Lind, in a response to a an outbreak of scurvy conducted a controlled experiment. He took 12 of the sailors who had developed scurvy and divided them up into six groups and gave each pair different medicines such as nutmeg, cider, seawater, and vinegar, while others were given lemons or oranges. The two men given the oranges and lemons both completely recovered in about a week after the experiment.

His *Treatise of the Scurvy* published in 1753 is the first example of a controlled clinical trial experiment. In his treatise, Lind gave a thorough review of other authors who had written on scurvy along with a careful clinical description of the condition. It was not until the end of the 18th century that the British navy finally had its sailors drink a daily portion of lime or lemon juice to prevent scurvy.

Vitamin C (ascorbic acid) is necessary for collagen formation, which is the protein component of connective tissue, strong blood vessels, healthy skin and gums, formation of red blood cells, wound healing, and the absorption of iron. In addition to scurvy, other scurvy–like conditions can develop from a deficiency of vitamin C, such as adult acne, easy bruising, sore gums, and hemorrhages around bones. Good sources for vitamin C are citrus fruit, broccoli, strawberries, cantaloupe, and other fruits and vegetables.

Beriberi

Discovering the causes for beriberi became part of the history of discovering vitamins. Christian Eijkman (1858–1930) was a Dutch physician who was a member of a government commission sent to the East Indies in the 1880s to study the disease beriberi, which was prevalent in southeast Asia, where the main diet is comprised of unenriched rice and wheat.

There are three forms of this disease: infantile beriberi, wet beriberi, and dry beriberi. Infantile beriberi occurs when a mother who breast feeds her child is lacking vitamin B₁ thiamine. The mother who nurses the child may not manifest the disease, but the deficiency occurs through the breast feeding and the child usually dies after the fifth month. In the childhood and adult versions of the disease there is a preliminary condition of fatigue, loss of appetite, and a numb tingling feeling in the legs. This condition can then lead to either wet or dry beriberi.

In wet beriberi there is an accumulation of fluid throughout the body and a rapid heart rate that can lead to sudden death. In dry beriberi there is no fluid swelling, but there is a loss of sensation and a weakness in the legs. The patient first needs to walk with the aid of a stick and then becomes bedridden and easy prey to an infectious disease.

In Eijkman's laboratory he noticed that some of the fowl he was experimenting with developed paralysis and polyneuritis, as in the dry form of beriberi. The director of the hospital forbade Eijkman from feeding these birds with table scraps which consisted mainly of polished rice. He therefore began to feed them with whole rice, after which he noticed that they regained their movement and there was no recurrence of paralysis.

The idea that the birds had some form of beriberi was rejected by Eijkman's colleagues. His explanation for the cure was that the polished rice had some toxin in it which the unpolished rice did not have. This explanation was rejected by a fellow researcher, Gerrit Grijns (1865–1944), who also stayed on to study the disease after the commission had already left. He found that when the chickens were taken off the rice diet completely and feed with meat instead, they did not develop the characteristic paralysis, but if the meat were overcooked, then the condition would reappear. In 1901 Grijns showed that beriberi could be cured by putting the rice polishings back into the rice.

Vitamin B₁ (thiamine) prevents the disease or symptoms of beriberi. Food sources for this vitamin are meats, wheat germ, whole grain and enriched bread, legumes, peanuts, peanut butter, and nuts.

Pellagra

Pellagra is a vitamin deficiency disease associated with poverty. The symptoms of pellagra are referred to as the "three D's"—diarrhea, dermatitis, and dementia and if disease is not treated it may lead to death. Gaspar

Casal (c. 1691–1759) was the first to publish a thorough explanation of pellagra in 1762 after his death. He studied and wrote about the disease which he observed in a region of Spain where it was called "mal de la rosa," because of the reddened dermatitis which appeared around the back of the neck. Even though the belief of his time was the disease was caused by an infection, Casal believed origins were from inadequate nutrition.

The popular belief that pellagra was caused by infection lasted from the 16th century to the early 20th century until Joseph Goldberger (1881–1929) a member of the United States Public Health Service studied the high numbers of cases in the southern United States. Goldberger established that pellagra was caused by an insufficient amount of niacin (vitamin B₃) also known as nicotinic acid and the active form of niacin that the body uses called niacinamide.

Rickets

Rickets is a bone disease deficiency caused by a lack of vitamin D, called the "sunshine" vitamin because it is the only vitamin that can be produced by the effects of sunlight on the skin. It was a common disease of infants and children, but since all milk and infant formulas have vitamin D added to them, it is rarely seen today. In rickets, legs will become bowed by the weight of the body and the wrists and ankles are thickened. The teeth are badly affected and take a longer time to come in. All the bones are affected by not having sufficient calcium and phosphorous for their growth and development. Lack of exposure to sunlight, which helps to produce Vitamin D, is a major cause for childhood rickets. Crowded slum conditions in areas where there was little or no sunlight were responsible for its appearance in the earlier stages of the industrial revolution.

An adult version of rickets caused by a deficiency of Vitamin D, calcium, and phosphorous is called osteomalacia. The bones become soft and deformed and there is rheumatic pain. The disease is observed in the Middle East and Asia more so than in western countries. The way to prevent rickets and other bone diseases such as osteoporosis is a combination of calcium, phosphorous, and vitamin D.

Other vitamin deficiency diseases

Night blindness or the difficulty of seeing in dim light is caused by a deficiency in vitamin A which helps in the formation of visual purple needed by the eyes for night vision. The deficiency can also cause glare blindness when the eye is either exposed to too much light or a sudden change in the amount of light when entering a darkened room. Another eye disease caused by vitamin

A deficiency is xerophthalmia which can lead to blindness. This condition affects the cells of the cornea, other eye tissues, and the tear ducts, which stop secreting.

Vitamin A deficiency can create a number of adverse skin conditions, problems with tasting and smelling, and it may also cause difficulties with the reproductive system.

Vitamin E and K deficiencies are rare. Vitamin E protects against substances that oxidize quickly and vitamin K promotes normal blood clotting. Vitamin B_{12} (cobalamin) provides protection against pernicious anemia and mental disturbances. Vitamin B_6 can also protect against anemia as well as dermatitis, irritability, and convulsions.

Mineral deficiency diseases

There are about 25 mineral elements in the body usually appearing in the form of simple salts. Those which appear in large amounts are called macro minerals while those that are in small or trace amounts are micro minerals. Some that are essential are calcium, phosphorous, cobalt, copper, fluorine, iodine, iron, sodium, chromium, and tin. Aluminum, lead, and mercury are not as essential.

Goiter

Iodine is necessary for the proper functioning of the thyroid gland which controls the body's basal metabolism rate through its production of two hormones, thyroxine, and triiodinethyronine. Without a sufficient amount of iodine in the diet the gland begins to enlarge its cells in its efforts to produce the hormone, thus producing a goiter, which is a swelling around the neck. Certain regions lack iodine in the soil which leads to cretinism, the physical and mental development of an infant passed on from the lack of iodine in the mother's diet.

Protein (amino acid) deficiencies

Proteins are needed in the body for amino acids. Proteins are broken down in the digestive system to form amino acids which are then absorbed by the rest of the body to form new proteins in the form of vital body tissues such as muscle, connective tissue, and skin. There are two types of protein, fibrous and globular proteins. Fibrous protein is insoluble and goes into making the structural tissues of the body. Globular protein forms amino acids that become enzymes and hormones and other vital parts of cellular functioning within the body.

Adults rarely suffer from protein deficiency diseases unless there is an impairment in the intestinal tract, but in countries plagued by insufficient food children will develop protein deficiency diseases that lead to very high mortality rates.

Marasmus and kwashiorkor

A specific wasting away disease caused by protein deficiency in third world countries that lack adequate food supplies is called kwashiorkor. It is a word which describes the condition of an infant who has to be weaned away after a year to make room for the next baby. The weaning food, which is mainly sugar and water or a starchy gruel lacks protein or has a poor quality of protein. The weaning diet for these young children leads to other nutrient deficiency diseases as well.

Symptoms of kwashiorkor are apathy, muscular wasting, and edema. Both the hair and the skin lose their pigmentation. The skin becomes scaly and there is diarrhea and anemia, and permanent blindness can result from this condition. Marasmus is another condition of a wasting away of the body tissues from the lack of calories as well as protein in the diet. In marasmus the child is fretful rather than apathetic and is skinny rather than swollen with edema. Aside from contrasting symptoms between the two diseases, there may be converging symptoms which would be described as marasmic kwashiorkor.

There is a wide variation of deficiencies between energy and protein deficient diseases as in the cases described by marasmus and kwashiorkor. The term protein–energy malnutrition (PEM) is used to describe those differences. PEM is the result of poverty as well inadequate information on diet. In some countries there is the mistaken belief that the child should not be given high protein food, which is served to the father, while the child drinks the fluid the meat was cooked in.

In cases of severe PEM it is necessary to hospitalize the child and to administer antibiotics to prevent infections which accompany the condition. Diets rich in protein should be continued after hospitalization, using skimmed milk powder for an energy basis. Legumes (beans) and fish meal are also good sources for protein. Social and political problems have to be managed to allow relief workers to help and to provide an ongoing source of food preparations that can be consumed for adequate nourishment by those in need.

Treatment and prevention

The amounts of most nutrients, especially vitamins, needed to both prevent and treat deficiency diseases are small. The average intake of 1mg of vitamin B_1 is sufficient to prevent a deficiency disease of that vitamin, while 10mg of B_1 could cure an advanced case of someone about to die of beriberi. Although small doses of vitamins cure deficiencies, large doses of some vitamins such as A and D can be harmful since these two vitamins are already stored by the liver. Vitamins A and D are fat soluble vitamins and can accumulate to the point of becoming toxic. Most other vitamins are water soluble and are excreted in the urine throughout the day.

Diet and supplements

Most nutritionists insist on a well–balanced diet consisting of the major food substances as an effective and economical way of obtaining nutrients for health. On the other hand, advocates of health food stores maintain that the FDA's required daily allowances (RDAs) for nutrients are much too low and that cultivation of much of our food supply and its preparation robs our diet of much of its nutrient value.

The American Dietetic Association (ADA) recommends that nutrient needs should come from a variety of foods taken from different dietary sources rather than self–prescribed vitamin supplementation. In order to avoid either the problem of nutrient deficiencies or excesses they recommend that physicians or licensed dieticians should be the source of prescribing supplementation.

The ADA, however, does make allowances for supplement usage under the following conditions: Iron supplements may be required by women when there is excessive menstrual bleeding. Pregnant and breast-feeding women need supplements, especially iron, folic acid, and calcium. People who are dieting and are therefore are on very low calorie diets may require supplementation if they are not getting the right amount of the nutrients they need. Vegetarians may need boosts of vitamin B–12, calcium, iron, and zinc. Newborns are sometimes given vitamin K to prevent abnormal bleeding. Those people who have diagonsised disorders or diseases or are being treated with medications which affects the absorption or metabolism of the nutrient may require supplementation.

Recent research on vitamins A and C

Research using 22,000 physicians under the supervision of the Department of Medicine at Harvard is studying the long–term effects of beta carotene (vitamin A) in lowering the incidence of cancer and boosting resistance to infection. It is also being studied in the treatment of AIDS. Beta carotene is a safer version of vitamin A than the preformed oil form called retinol. It is found in carrots, sweet potatoes, broccoli, spinach,

collards, turnip greens, kale, and many other vegetables that.

Vitamin C, also known as ascorbic acid, is used as a supplement by more people than any other supplement. Its popularity is due to the work of the two–time Nobel laureate, Linus Pauling who maintained that vitamin C was effective in preventing and lessening the effect of colds and in the treatment of cancer. Pauling's vitamin C program called for megadoses that far exceeded the government's RDA recommendations. Pauling recommended a daily dose of between 2,000 and 9,000 milligrams. The National Research Council recommends 60 mg for adult daily and 100mg for smokers.

The discovery of micro nutrition was made in the early twentieth century as a result of finding the cure for certain diseases, the nutrient deficiency diseases such as scurvy, beriberi, and pellagra. The new dimensions of fully understanding and using our knowledge of nutrients remain to be established from the ongoing research in this area of nutritional science.

See also Malnutrition; Nutrients; Nutrition.

Further Reading:

Eschleman, Marian M. *Nutrition & Diet Therapy*. New York: Lippincott, 1991.

Guthrie, Helen A. *Introductory Nutrition*. Boston: Mosby College Publishing, 1989.

Hendler, Sheldon S. *The Doctor's Vitamin and Mineral Encyclopedia*. New York: Simon and Schuster, 1990.

Williams, Sue R. *Nutrition and Diet Therapy*. Boston: Mosby College Publishing, 1989.

Yudkin, John. *The Penguin Encyclopedia of Nutrition*. New York: Viking, 1985.

Jordan P. Richman

Nutrients

Nutrients are any chemicals that are required for life. Nutrients can be of two basic types: (1) inorganic substances absorbed by autotrophic organisms such as plants and certain microorganisms for use in their synthetic reactions and metabolism; or (2) biomass ingested as nourishment by animals and heterotrophic microorganisms.

Plants absorb a wide range of mineral nutrients, which they utilize in their photosynthetic reactions and other metabolic processes to manufacture all of the biochemicals that they require for growth and reproduction. Some nutrients are required by plants in relatively large quantities. These are called macronutrients and include compounds of the following elements: carbon, hydrogen, oxygen, nitrogen, phosphorus, potassium, calcium, magnesium, and sulfur. Of these, carbon is required in the largest quantity, typically making up about one–half of the dry weight of plant tissues, while hydrogen, oxygen, nitrogen, and calcium occur in concentrations of one to several percent. Phosphorus, potassium, magnesium, and sulfur typically account for 0.1% to 1% of the dry weight of plants. Micronutrients are required by plants in much smaller quantities and include metals such as copper, iron, and zinc.

Animals must eat plants or other animals to obtain virtually all of their nutrients. After ingestion, animals typically digest their food and thereby break it down into relatively simple biochemicals and inorganic chemicals, which are then absorbed through the gut and used in the animal's metabolism. The largest nutritional need of animals is for energy to support their respiration

and growth, and sources of fixed energy such as plant or animal biomass are ingested for this purpose. There are also a few micronutrients that animals require in small quantities, but they cannot synthesize. These include biochemicals called vitamins, which must be ingested with food. Some animals can also utilize mineral forms of certain nutrients, which they may take directly from the inorganic environment without eating biomass. For example, many large grazing mammals will utilize salt licks when they are available, because these animals crave sodium, which is not usually present in sufficiently large concentrations in the plants that they eat.

Appropriate nutrition for all organisms is a matter of both quantity and balance. For good nutritional health, all of the essential inorganic and organic nutrients must be available, but they must be obtainable in an appropriate balance. A severe shortage of even a micronutrient required in trace quantities can result in severe metabolic dysfunctions, and even death of organisms.

See also Nutrition; Vitamin.

Nutrition

Nutrition is the means by which organisms obtain and use nutrients. Nutrition is also the determination of the kinds and quantities of substances (nutrients) needed by organisms to sustain life. Some organisms such as plants require only a supply of light, water, and a few other molecules and ions in order to thrive, and are known as autotrophs, or self nourishers, for they literally build their own molecules and capture energy in the process. There are a few other non–plant autotrophic organisms in the deep oceans near geothermal vents that are able to build their own nutrients without using sunlight.

While green plants get the energy they need directly from sunlight, animals must get the energy that they need for life functions from plants.

The major types of molecules found in organisms are water, carbohydrates, proteins, lipids, and nucleic acids.

Proteins are large molecules built from different combinations of large numbers of amino acids. Of the 20 different amino acids that make up our body's proteins, we can build 12 from other foods, but there are eight amino acids that humans also need and which they cannot make, called essential amino acids. One of the

A healthy diet includes a variety of foods.

eight essential amino acids (methionine) is found in corn but not in beans, and two others (lysine and tryptophan) are found in beans but in only small amounts in corn. Therefore, the combination of beans and corn, found in many Mexican foods, supplies a balance of the essential amino acids.

The present focus is primarily on human nutrition. The base of the U. S. Department of Agriculture Food Guide pyramid, the part with the greatest volume, consists of the cereal foods: bread, pasta, and rice. Data from around the world indicate that people whose diets have a large proportion of these foods tend to be healthier. This food group, mostly carbohydrates, should provide most of the energy needed. The recommendations are given in servings. A serving varies from food to food, but is in the range of 1–2 oz (30–60 g) per serving. Depending on physical size, age, gender, and activity, six to 11 servings per day are recommended from the cereal group.

The second level of the food pyramid consists of fruits and vegetables. These are especially important in supplying micronutrients. Micronutrients are elements that help regulate physiological pathways. A second benefit derived from this group comes from indigestible fiber, which is correlated with better functioning and health of the large intestine. Five to nine servings a day are suggested from this group.

The third level of the pyramid consisting of proteins in the form of meats, eggs, beans, nuts, and milk products is smaller than the first and second levels to emphasize that the percentage of these foods should be smaller in comparison to the total intake. The major function of proteins is to repair or build new tissue and to supply enzymes and hormones.

At the tip of the pyramid are the lipids, representing a small volume, demonstrating that fats and oils should be consumed in small quantities for optimum health.

MINERALS AND TRACE ELEMENTS

Micronutrients are subdivided according to the quantities needed in the human diet. If more than 100 milligrams per day of an element is needed, it is classed as a mineral. The seven essential minerals are calcium, magnesium, phosphorus, sodium, potassium, sulfur, and chlorine. Substances that are essential but needed in amounts of less than 100 mg per day are called trace elements. These are iron, copper, iodine, manganese, zinc, molybdenum, selenium, and chromium. There are likely others (such as boron) that are yet to be identified.

Calcium and phosphorus are both used structurally to form bones and teeth. Lesser known but vital functions of calcium include its uses as an enzyme activator and as a regulator of nerve and muscle activity. Phosphorus is also a component of nucleotide molecules that are structural components of the nucleic acids, DNA and RNA, and of the energy transfer molecules such as ATP, NAD, and FAD.

Magnesium is found in bones too, but, more importantly, it is needed in adequate amounts to work with calcium in regulating nerve and muscle activity. In fact, an early symptom of magnesium shortage can be irregular heart action. Sodium is necessary for the proper functioning of the nerves and muscles. Sodium is more concentrated in the fluids outside of the cells than the intraocular fluids. Sodium is more often consumed in excess because it is easy to enhance the flavors of foods by adding table salt (sodium chloride). Potassium ions are most concentrated in the fluid inside cells. There is evidence that high blood pressure can be prevented or controlled by increasing one's intake of potassium. Chloride functions as an electrolyte balance for the sodium and other positive ions in cell and tissue fluids and is necessary for the salivary enzyme ptyalin to help digest starch. Sulfur is a component of three amino acids and is part of the enzyme molecules active in the oxidation of fatty acids.

These minerals must be in their ionic form so as to be soluble and absorbable. Many minerals are often chelated, that is, attached to a larger organic particle such as an amino acid, or anions such as gluconate, lactate, or citrate to be properly observed. Some trace elements function in cooperation with an enzyme or a vitamin molecule to bring about physiological responses.

More and more, people are choosing foods for their vitamin or mineral content, because the foods provide specific nutrients that may otherwise be missing. Adding daily supplements of vitamins C, E, and A (or its precursor beta carotene) to diets may promote good health and fight disease.

See also Amino acid; Carbohydrate; Lipid; Nutrients; Proteins; Vitamin.

Further Reading:

Begley, S. "The End of Antibiotics." *Newsweek* (28 March 1994): 47–51.

Chandra, R. K. "Effect of Vitamin and Trace–Element Supplementation on Immune Responses and Infection in Elderly Subjects." *Lancet* 340 (1992): 1124–1127.

KEY TERMS

. . . .

Anion—A particle such as an atom or molecule which has more electrons than protons. It has a negative charge.

ATP—Adenosine triphosphate, the universal energy molecule.

Carbohydrates—Compounds that contain carbon, hydrogen, and oxygen. The ratio of carbon to oxygen is about one to one. Examples are sugar, starch, and cellulose.

Electrolyte—Any solution containing negative and positive ions.

FAD—Flavin–Adenine Dinucleotide.

Geothermal vent—An opening in the sea floor occurring between crustal plates. Hot hydrogen sulfide bubbles up through these and supports unusual forms of life.

Gluconate, lactate, etc.—These terms refer to the anionic components of organic salts. For example, a positive potassium ion can be balanced in an electrolyte with a gluconate anion. If the liquid part were to be evaporated, the residue would be crystalline, potassium gluconate salt.

Life processes—Term referring to activities such as metabolism, cell division, excretion, and movement.

Lipids—Molecules in this group are made of the same elements as carbohydrates, but in lipids there is much more carbon than oxygen. Examples are fats, oils, and cholesterol.

NAD—Nicotinamide–Adenine Dinucleotide.

Nucleic acids—This is a generic term including both RNA (ribonucleic acid) and DNA (deoxyribonucleic acid). The DNA encodes genetic information and the RNA molecules use it to direct protein building.

Nucleotide—Molecular units that make up the nucleic acids. Each is composed of a nitrogen base, a sugar, and a phosphate group.

Oxidation—A biochemical process which is part of metabolism. It involves the steady but relatively slow release of energy from food molecules for cell activity.

Proteins—Large molecules built from long chains of smaller molecules, the amino acids. Nitrogen is an element in protein in addition to the carbon, hydrogen, and oxygen found in major food molecules. The tough flexible parts of an animal such as skin, cartilage, and muscle are mostly protein.

Eng, M., et al. "Isomeric Trans Fatty Acids in the U. S. Diet." *Journal of American College of Nutrition* 9 (1990): 471–486.

Greenberg, R. E., et al. "A Clinical Trial of Antioxidant Vitamins to Prevent Colorectal Adenoma." *The New England Journal of Medicine* 331 (1994): 141–147.

Horiba, N. "A Pilot Study of Japanese Green Tea as a Medicament: Antibacterial and Bactericidal Effects." *Journal of Endodontics* 17 (1991): 122–124.

Murray, M. *The Healing Power of Herbs.* Rocklin, CA: Prima Publishing, 1992.

Richardson, J. S. "Free Radicals in the Genesis of Alzheimer's Disease." *Annals of the New York Academy of Science* (24 September 1993): 73–76.

Rimm, E. B., et al. "Vitamin E Consumption and the Risk of Coronary Heart Disease in Men." *New England Journal of Medicine* 328 (1993): 1450–1455.

Yeusheng, Z., et al. "A Major Inducer of Anticarcinogenic Protective Enzymes from Broccoli: Isolation and Elucidation of Structure." *Proceedings: National Academy of Science* 89 (1992): 2399–2403.

Chester VanderZee

Nux vomica tree

The nux vomica tree (*Strychnos nux–vomica*) is a species in the tropical family Loganiaceae. The range of the nux vomica in cultivation extends from Sri Lanka, India, southern China, southeast Asia, and northern Australia.

The nux vomica grows as tall as 49.2 ft (15 m). The nux vomica has roundish, opposite leaves and attractive white flowers. The roughly spherical fruits of the nux vomica are large hard–rinded berries that contain three to eight round, flattened, grayish seeds. These seeds are covered with silky hairs, are known as strychnine nuts, and are hard and extremely bitter in taste. The seeds of the nux vomica contain several alkaloids that are useful for some purposes, particularly strychnine, and to a lesser extent brucine.

The alkaloids are extracted from ground strychnine nuts by boiling with alcohol and acetic acid. Lactose is then added to the extract, and the result is known as strychnine extract.

In very small doses, strychnine has been used as a tonic and stimulant and to treat some nervous and digestive disorders. However, strychnine is a virulent poison and must be used with great care. Symptoms of acute strychnine poisoning include painful cramps, convulsion, and eventually paralysis, often leading to death by incapacitation of the respiratory system.

Strychnine is sometimes used as a rodenticide to control rats, mice, and other rodent pests of agriculture and human residences. In this use, strychnine could be considered to be a natural, organic pesticide. However, strychnine is still an extremely toxic chemical which can cause significant non–target damages during its routine use. This could occur, for example, if poisoned rodents are scavenged by raptorial birds or mammalian predators which are then secondarily poisoned. As such, the use of strychnine as a pesticide or as a medicine for humans must be carefully managed and controlled.

Bill Freedman

Nylon see **Artificial fibers; Polymer**

Oaks

Oaks (*Quercus* spp.), members of the Beech family (Fagacea), are trees and shrubs having simple, alternate leaves found throughout the world. Characterized by their strong, complex wood, wind–pollinated flowers, fruits called acorns, and their ability to live for centuries, oaks have played an important role in temperate landscapes. Of the 500 species in the genus *Quercus*, approximately 90 are found in the United States and Canada, with another 112 species in Mexico. Another member of the Beech family that is closely related to the oaks is the tanoak (*L. densiflorus*), which is found in California and is the only representative of this Asian genus found in North America. It has flowers similar to the chinkapin (*Castanopsis*) and bears acorns like the oaks, thus making it a possible evolutionary link between the two genera.

Evolution

The *Quercus* genus is quite old, being one of the early angiosperms of the Miocene epoch (26 –12 million years ago). Over time, oaks have divided into two main lineages, with an intermediate subgenus for less genetically distinct species. The red oaks (*Erythrobalanus*) are characterized by pointed leaves with bristles or spines that can be either lobed or unlobed. The acorns have a hairy inner shell and mature in two years (except for California live oaks, *Q. agrifolia* which mature in one year) on the twigs of the first year's growth. The smooth bark is dark gray, black or brown, with reddish brown wood. The white oak (*Leucobalanus*) leaves are rounded and smooth but can also be lobed or unlobed. Acorns mature in one year and have a smooth inner shell. The wood is light brown or yellow and the bark is scaly or rough brown to light gray. The leaves of the intermediate oaks (*Protobalanus*) are unlobed, although some may have green spines or teeth. The inner shell of the acorns can be

either smooth or hairy, but does not mature until the second year. The bark can be either scaly or rough, with a wide color range. The wood is generally light brown and not as commercially valuable as that in the other oak families.

Biology and ecology

Found in a wide variety of habitats, oaks prefer loamy, well drained soils. The roots are quite extensive, reaching out at least three times the height of the tree and down as deep as 15–40 ft (4.6–12.2 m), depending on site conditions.

There are both evergreen and deciduous species. Each leaf of the evergreen oaks falls after one to two years, but there is no synchronous leaf loss. New leaves form during either the first spring growth or a smaller secondary flush of growth which can occur when conditions are favorable. Deciduous oaks follow the typical pattern of fall leaf loss in response to decreased daylight, winter dormancy, and spring flush of new leaves and flowers.

Oaks vary in size from small shrubby species to trees with majestic dimensions. The tallest oak, reaching up 123 ft (37.5 m), with a circumference of 21.6 ft (6.6 m) and a canopy spread over 83.6 ft (25.5 m) is a black oak found in Warrensville Heights, Ohio. Other oaks notable for their size are: the Wye live oak (*Q. virginiana*) in Maryland standing 91.8 ft (28 m) tall; a 106.6-ft (32.5 m) tall coast live oak (*Q. agrifolia*) in Chiles Va Mey, California, and a northern red oak (*Q.rubra*) in Ashford, Connecticut, standing 77 ft (23.5 m) tall and spreading 105 ft (32 m).

Relying primarily on wind pollination, massive quantities of pollen are produced in the male flowers (25–100 per catkins) each spring. The female flowers tucked inconspicuously in the nodes of axial twigs mature a little later, avoiding self–pollination. Either single or clusters of two to three acorns begin forming. Most trees begin acorn production after 20 years. Crop production varies yearly according to numerous factors, but an individual tree can produce over 5,000 nuts in a good year. Of these, roughly 25% are likely to be infested with weevils, making them inedible and unviable.

Because of their huge investment in acorn production, oaks play a critical role in supporting wildlife and maintaining regional biodiversity. Many migratory species of birds and bats roost or nest in them, in addition to using the food resource. In California, it is estimated that over 5,000 species of insects, more than 80 species of reptiles and amphibians, 150 species of birds, and over 60 species of mammals rely upon oaks for some part of their lifecycle. Acorn or mast production is such a significant element of most oak ecosystems that crop failure can be life threatening for many species.

Diseases

Oaks are subject to infection by numerous pathogens, most of which do little more than temporary harm to the tree. The exceptions are root–related diseases caused by various fungi. Oak wilt, caused by *Endoconidiphora fagacearum* has become a serious problem in the eastern and central United States. Oak root rot or honey fungus (*Armellaria* spp.) and avocado root rot (*Phytophthora* spp.) are more problematic in the western region. Most oaks are resistant unless environmental stresses weaken the tree to the point that the fungus can proliferate. Little can be done to save a severely infected oak.

Distribution

Because of their widespread distribution, oaks play an significant ecological role in many forest communities. Of the 90 forest type covers described in the United States and Canada, oaks are an important element in 64. and include both evergreen and deciduous species. Some of the more important species in North America include the northern red oak (*Q. rubra*), the black oak (*Q. velutina*), and the white oak (*Q. alba*) in the east. The coast live oak (*Q. agrifolia*), the gambel oak (*Q. gambelii*), and the wayleaf oak (*Q. undulata*) are most widespread in the western region.

Most species are limited to either the eastern or western regions of the continent, with chinkapin oak (*Q. muehlenbergii*) and shin oak (*Q. havardii*) the only species to bridge the gap through the prairies. Due to the spread of development pressures and conversion of rangeland into housing and commercial uses, there are now several species of oaks facing serious decline. Of these, the Oglethorpe oak (*Q. oglethorpensis*) in Georgia, the valley oak (*Q. lobata*), blue oak (*Q. douglasii*), and Englemann oak (*Q. engelmanii*) in California and several species with limited ranges in Texas, New Mexico, and Arizona are considered either rare, threatened or endangered.

Contributing to this problem is the lack of regeneration of many oak species. For a wide variety of reasons, including changes in understory vegetation, soil compaction, damage by grazing animals, changes in fire frequency and associated forest species, natural recruitment of new trees is limited in many areas. Mixed age stands are not as common as single age stands in many areas. More intensive management to provide light openings, reduce soil compaction, and eliminate competitive species is slowly beginning to turn this trend around. Prescribed burning to restore a more natural fire ecology is being done in many areas. The thick bark of oaks is particularly adapted to withstand forest fires and they can resprout from the root crown if the tree is burned.

Historic importance

The name *Quercus* comes from the Celtic, *quer* meaning "fine," and *cuez* meaning "tree." Historically, the Celtic religion as well as that of other cultures venerated old oak trees, using them as a focus for spiritual rituals. The Druids believed the oak to be a sacred tree, the symbol of their religion, and potent source of wisdom. The ancient Greeks believed the rustling leaves of a sacred oak to be oracles from Zeus. In Allonville, France, an oak 44.3 ft (13.5 m) in circumference was consecrated as a Roman Catholic church in 1696 and the chapel built into the canopy can hold five to 10 worshipers. Since many oaks live for over 300 years, their longevity and durability became the subject of literary metaphors and the trees serve as reminders of many historic events. The oldest documented oak lived for 950 years in Switzerland.

When William Penn landed in 1682, the Holly Halls white oak stood tall near Elkton, Maryland. Recently threatened by development, it has been afforded protection by the city and still remains. A bur oak (*Q. macrocarpa*), known as the Council Oak, standing in Sioux City, Iowa shaded Lewis and Clark as they met with the natives. Longfellow's famous poem "Evangeline" includes reference to a live oak (*Q. virginiana*) still standing as a historic landmark in St. Martinville, Louisiana. The Jack London Oak (*Q. agrifolia*) was planted near the Oakland (California) City Hall after the author died. The oak tree first visited by Spanish explorer Vizcaino in 1602 and the site of the first mass held by Father Serra in Monterey, California, in 1770 finally died and was replaced by a monument in

1896. The Oak of Peace still standing in Glendale, California, was the site of the meeting between General Andres Pico and Colonel John C. Fremont that ended the War with Mexico in 1847. Species of oak are the state trees of Connecticut, Georgia, Illinois, Iowa, Maryland, New Jersey, and the District of Columbia.

Economic importance

Because they are widespread and generally large, oaks have been used in numerous ways. The leaves, flowers, and bark were used by indigenous peoples in both Europe and North America for making medicinal drinks used to cure fevers, stop vomiting, and control diarrhea. Tannins extracted from the bark were used both for dying and tanning hides. The chestnut oak (*Q. prinus*) was logged to virtual extinction due to the high quality tannin it provided for the tanning industry.

Acorns

In addition to the wildlife reliant on acorns as a food source, many indigenous peoples also utilized this resource. Acorns provided a staple food supply for many Native Americans, especially in California. A valuable source of nutrients, acorns are high in fat, carbohydrates, some protein, and vitamins A, C, and E. Preparations included leaching the bitter tannins by grinding the inner nut into flour, immersing this in running water, and then making either gruel or bread. Each oak species tastes different and certain species, such as California black oak (*Q. kelloggii*) were preferred, due to their lower tannin content. Acorns remain viable for several months following ripening and can be stored in granaries for years. Considered a sign of fertility by Nordic and Native American peoples, acorns were used symbolically in many ceremonies.

Wood

The structural characteristics of the wood make oak one of the most versatile hardwoods, valued by many industries. The strength of oak wood is a result of the inner structure of vessels and fibers. The ring porous nature of the woody tissue results from uneven vessel growth. During the spring and summer, large vessels and fibers grow, followed by smaller vessels as the season progresses. In deciduous species, the vessels are almost non–existent and during the fall and winter are replaced by fibers. This provides distinct growth rings and adds to the structural integrity of the wood. It also provides a distinctive grain pattern when planed into thick planks for panelling and cabinetry.

In red oaks, the vessels remain open over time, allowing fluid conduction to continue. These species are used in making railroad timbers and furniture. The vessels of the white oaks become gummed up with tyloses and are more valuable for barrel staves and flooring. Casks made of oak are in high demand for fermenting wine in France and many other countries. Many of the early sailing ships used oak timbers for hulls and ribs. A famous example is *Old Ironsides*, a U.S. Navy frigate whose restoration used many large timbers of live oak (*Q. virginiana*). The destruction of the English oak (*Q. robur*) forests in Europe to construct the navies of the 1600s was one of the many economic incentives for colonizing the New World with its untouched expanses of hardwood forests.

The cork oak (*Q. suber*) is another commercially valuable species found throughout the Mediterranean region. The thick bark composed mostly of cork cells can be harvested every 10 years in early summer to provide sheets of soft, smooth cork useful in many ways. The cork cells capture air inside as they dry, making the material extremely resilient and buoyant. Cork has been used to manufacture floats, handles, stoppers, and as insulation, since it is a poor conductor of heat and sound.

Probably the most common worldwide use of oak is as fuel. Oak burns very hot, providing up to 23 million BTU per cord. Charcoal made of oak was extremely important to small local industries during the nineteenth century. Most hardwood forests are managed for fuel wood harvesting or lumber, with oaks considered the most valuable species.

Ecological significance

In addition to ecological and aesthetic landscape value, another important role of oaks is in maintaining watershed integrity. The sometimes deep, always extensive root system of oaks stabilizes slopes, limits erosion, and allows groundwater recharge. The wide canopies dissipate the rainfall and prevent surface erosion, while allowing slow saturation into the soil. The ability of oaks and other trees to reduce air pollution and trap airborne particulates is well documented. Noise abatement and temperature modulation in urban areas is also provided by the large, dense oaks. These important contributions of oaks to the sustainability and livability of our landscapes are vital. Careful examination of the role played by oaks in maintaining watershed integrity and preservation efforts on a bioregional scale are needed to ensure that the oak woodlands endure into the future.

See also Beech family.

Further Reading:
Altman, Nathaniel. *Sacred Trees.* San Francisco: Sierra Club Books, 1992.

Lewington, Richard, and David Streeter. *The Natural History of the Oak Tree*. New York: Dorling Kindersley, 1993.

Miller, Howard, and S. Lamb. *Oaks of North America*. Happy Camp, CA: Naturegraph Publishers, 1985.

Rosi Dagit

Oats see **Grasses**

Obesity see **Eating disorders**

Obsession

The main concern of psychiatrists and therapists who treat people with obsessions is the role they play in a mental illness called obsessive–compulsive disorder (OCD). Obsessions need to be distinguished from compulsions in order to understand how they interconnect with compulsive behavior and reinforce this debilitating illness.

In psychiatric literature, obsessions are defined as disruptive thoughts and impulses that cause the sufferer a great deal of distress. These thoughts can then lead to compulsive behavior, such as the ritualistic washing of hands, to relieve the anxiety that the obsessional thoughts create. The obsessions come first, then compulsive behavior follows. Obsessions often take the form of thoughts about becoming contaminated, engaging in unwanted sexual acts, about committing a violent act, or doubts about having performed an act, such as locking the door when leaving the house.

Obsessive–compulsive disorder (OCD)

Obsessive–compulsive disorder is classified as an anxiety disorder. Other anxiety disorders are panic attacks, agoraphobia (the fear of public places), phobias (fear of specific objects or situations), and certain stress disorders. This illness becomes increasingly more difficult to the patient and family, because it tends to consume more and more of the individual's time and energy. While a person who is suffering from an obsession is aware of how irrational or senseless the fear is, he or she is overwhelmed by the need to perform ritualistic behavior in order to relieve the anxiety connected with the obsession.

People who suffer from OCD may have obsessions but no compulsions to act on them. The obsessive thoughts, nevertheless, consume a great deal of time and energy. Someone who is very religious and has sex-ual obsessions that violate the person's personal beliefs may become extremely distressed when the thoughts become all–consuming.

Obsessive–compulsive personality disorder

People with personality traits, like being a perfectionist or rigidly controlling, may not have OCD, but may have obsessive–compulsive personality disorder. In this illness the patient may spend excessive amounts of energy on details and lose perspective about the overall goals of a task or job. Obsessive personalities tend to be rigid and unreasonable about how things must be done. They tend also to be workaholics, forgoing the pleasures of leisure–time activities over work. They are often inflexible, unaffectionate, lack generosity, or may tend to hoard objects that are worthless and have no sentimental value to them.

Like obsessive–compulsive disorder, it can be time–consuming, but it does not carry with it specific obsessions or compulsions. The obsessive behavior arises more from generalized attitudes about perfectionism than from a specific concern about contamination or obsessive thoughts of a specific nature. The obsessive personality may be able to function quite successfully in a work environment but makes everyone else miserable by demanding the same excessive standards of perfection.

Treatments for obsessive–compulsive illnesses

The problem for treatment of obsessive–compulsive illnesses must follow careful diagnosis of the specific nature of the disorder.

The methods used to treat these illnesses include a careful physical and psychological evaluation, medications, and therapies.

In behavior therapy, the patient is encouraged to control behavior, which the therapist feels can be accomplished with direction. The patient is also made to understand that thoughts cannot be controlled, but that when compulsive behavior is changed gradually through behavior modification methods, obsessive thoughts will diminish. In this therapy patients are exposed to the fears that produce anxiety in them, called flooding, and gradually learn to deal with their fears.

Cognitive therapists feel it is important for OCD patients to learn to think differently in order to improve their condition. Most professionals who treat obsessive–compulsive illnesses feel that a combination of

KEY TERMS

Anxiety disorder—An illness in which anxiety plays a role.

Behavior therapy—A therapeutic program that emphasizes changing behavior.

Cognitive therapy—A therapeutic program that emphasizes changing a patient's thinking.

Compulsive behavior—Behavior that is driven by an obsession.

Flooding—Exposing a person with an obsession to his or her fears as a way of helping him or her face and overcome them.

Obsessive–compulsive disorder—A mental illness in which a person is driven to compulsive behavior to relieve the anxiety of an obsession.

Obsessive–compulsive personality disorder—The preoccupation with minor details to the exclusion of larger issues; exhibiting overcontrolling and perfectionistic attitudes.

therapy and medication is helpful. Some antidepressants, like Anafranil (clomipramine) and Prozac (fluoxetine), are prescribed to help alleviate the condition.

See also Anxiety; Compulsion.

Further Reading:

Amchin, Jess. *Psychiatric Diagnosis: A Biopsychosocial Approach Using DSM–III–R*. Washington, D.C.: Psychiatric Press, 1991.

Baer, Lee. *Getting Control*. Boston: Little, Brown, 1991.

Green, Stephen A. *Feel Good Again*. Mt. Vernon, NY: Consumers Union, 1990.

Jamison, Kay Redfield. *Touched with Fire*. New York: Free Press, 1993.

Neziroglu, Fugen, and Jose A. Yaryura–Tobias. *Over and Over Again*. Lexington, MA: D. C. Heath, 1991.

Vita Richman

Ocean

Oceans are large bodies of saltwater that surround the Earth's continents and occupy the basins between them. Ocean basins are the part of the seafloor that lies beyond the margins of the continents, generally in water deeper than 600 ft (183 m). Therefore, an ocean is both larger in area and deeper than a sea.

Origin of ocean water

As the earth formed in a cloud of gas and dust more than 4.5 billion years ago, a huge amount of lighter elements, including hydrogen (H) and oxygen (O), became trapped inside the planet as the gases condensed and formed molten rock. Materials of different densities separated out; in the young planet's molten interior, heavy elements sank and light elements rose. Gases rose through thousands of miles of molten and melting rock, to erupt on the surface through volcanos and fissures.

Within the planet and above the surface, oxygen combined with hydrogen to form water (H_2O). Enormous quantities of water—enough to fill oceans if it were liquid—shrouded the globe as an incredibly dense atmosphere of water vapor. Near the top of the atmosphere, where heat could be lost to outer space, water vapor condensed to liquid and fell back into the water vapor layer below, cooling the layer. This atmospheric cooling process continued until the first raindrops fell to the young Earth's surface and flashed into steam. This was the beginning of a fantastic rainstorm, reminiscent of the poetic stories of creation, in which the world's oceans fell out of the sky.

Many geologists believe this process may have happened several times, because planetoids (rocks the size of moons or asteroids) were still colliding with the early earth until about 3.9 billion years ago. Monstrous planetoid impacts would have vaporized all the water on the planet's surface. The earth has been changed so much by plate tectonics that no vestige of its original appearance remains. Unlike Earth, the faces of the moon, Mars, and Mercury bear the marks of the turbulent earliest history of the solar system. Hellas Basin on Mars and Caloris Basin on Mercury are the scars of planet–shattering impacts. One of these giant craters can be seen from anywhere on Earth: the moon's large round dark "eye," called Mare Imbrium.

Lithospheric plates and the origin of the seafloor

The oceanic plates beneath the ocean waters and above the earth's mantle are made up of igneous rock, formed from the magma, or molten rock, at mid–oceanic ridges. If you think of the plates as the skin of the earth, then the mid–oceanic ridge system is a 38,000–mile–long (64,000 km) cut in that skin. This cut bleeds lava, and never heals, because as soon as a "scab" of solidified lava develops over it, the two sides are pulled apart—allowing more molten rock to ooze forth into the ocean water. In this way, plates of oceanic crust are formed; one long thin section at a time bonds to the most–recently–made edges.

Hydrologic cycle

It may be that most of the water on Earth today has been cycling between the oceans, the land, and the Earth's atmosphere for more than four billion years. However, small amounts of "new" water escape the planet's interior, from volcanoes, even today.

Weather effects of ocean waters

Water possesses the unusual property of being able to absorb a large amount of heat energy before its temperature changes. It follows that water must lose a large amount of heat energy before it cools noticeably. The net result of this phenomenon is that water, more than air or earth, tends to remain at the temperature at which it is already. Water is not given to sudden, wild extremes of temperature. Therefore water has a strong moderating effect on climates. Where there is water, there are more moderate temperatures. A "maritime" (meaning "ocean–like") climate means a moist climate that rarely experiences temperature extremes.

Nearly all coasts experience this maritime effect, but it is especially apparent along coasts where there are large–scale oceanic currents. The moderating effects of the Gulf Stream are a good example. Caribbean sunshine warms the waters of the Gulf Stream in the tropics. This warm water then flows up the east coast of the United States and finally crosses the Atlantic to the coast of Western Europe. This warm current is why England's climate is so much warmer than areas at about the same latitude in North America. However, when the Gulf Stream is diverted southward, Western Europe experiences extreme cold—the last such event, in the 17th century, is known as the "Little Ice Age."

Opening and closing of ocean basins

Oceans, like most natural phenomena, exist across a span of time called a "life cycle." For a new ocean to be born, the earth's crust beneath an ocean or a continent must be torn, or rifted, apart.

An ocean basin ceases to exist because its lithosphere gets entirely subducted (that is what usually happens) or obducted (rare and localized). An ocean basin no longer grows when its mid–oceanic ridge gets pulled

---

KEY TERMS

Continental shelf—That part of the continental margin that is covered with relatively shallow water; continental shelves average about 50 mi (80 km) wide and 420 ft (128 m) deep.

Maritime climate—A moist climate that is neither too hot nor too cold, caused by the moderating effect of water on temperatures.

Pelagic sediment—Sediment that exists in the open ocean, away from land.

Pillow lava—The form that basaltic lava takes when it is erupted deep under water.

Trenches—The deep, trough–like depressions in the ocean floor that oceanic crust descends into when it is destroyed.

Turbidity currents—Dense, fast–moving currents of mud and water that surge down the continental slope at great speed.

---

down into a subduction zone, or gets crammed into a mountain range on the side of a continent. If it is not growing any larger in area, then it can not replace the area it loses to subduction and obduction. Eventually the processes of subduction and obduction put all the oceanic crust of the dying ocean basin either under bordering continents (by subduction) or on top of the bordering continents (obduction). This life cycle of an ocean basin is the same no matter how long it takes or how large the ocean gets to be.

What happens to the water in the dying ocean? Remember, this process takes tens of millions of years. The water flows gradually into other oceans as the basin shrinks, and also departs through evaporation and precipitation.

See also Abyssal plain; Coast and beach; Continental shelf; Coral reef; Hydrologic cycle; Hydrothermal vents; Ocean basin; Ocean zones; Oceanography; Saltwater; Sea level; Seamounts; Tides.

Further Reading:

Borgese, E., Ed. *Ocean Frontiers.* New York; Harry N. Abrams Inc., 1992.
Brower, K. *Realms of the Sea.* Washington D.C.; National Geographic Society, 1991.
Carson, R. *The Sea Around Us.* New York, Oxford University Press, 1989.

Clinton Crowley

Ocean basin

Ocean basins are that part of the Earth's surface that extends seaward from the continental margins, ranging from an average water depth of about 6,500 ft (2,000 m) down into the deepest trenches. The ocean basins constitute one of the two major topographic features of the Earth's surface, the other being the continents. Ocean basins cover about 70% of the total sea area and about half of the planet's total surface area.

In contrast to the landforms of the continents so familiar to humans—features such as mountains, plateaus, hills, and rivers—the various topographic features of the ocean basins, the "oceanscape," are still not well understood by scientists. Some authorities claim that scientists know more about the surface of the Moon than they do about the ocean basins here on Earth. This situation exists because the ocean basins are thousands of meters below the water's surface, and they can be explored only with remote measuring equipment or, rarely, in special research submarines known as submersibles.

Among the things we do know about the ocean basins is that the familiar landscapes of continents are mirrored, and generally magnified, by comparable features in the ocean basin. The largest underwater mountains, for example, are higher than those on the continents, and underwater plains are flatter and more extensive than those on continents.

The basins of Earth's four oceans, the Atlantic, Pacific, Indian, and Arctic, differ from each other in many respects. Yet, they all contain certain common features that include oceanic ridges, trenches, and fracture zones and cracks, abyssal plains and hills, seamounts and guyots.

Oceanic ridges

Some of the most impressive topographic features of the ocean basins are the enormous mountain ranges, or oceanic ridges, that cover the ocean floor. The Mid–Atlantic Ridge, for example, begins at the tip of Greenland, runs down the center of the Atlantic Ocean between the Americas on the west and Africa on the east, and ends at the southern tip of the African continent. At that point, it continues around the eastern edge of Africa, where it becomes the Mid–Indian Ridge.

The Mid–Indian Ridge then divides along the center of the Indian Ocean basin, with a second arc curving away south of the Australian continent. As that ridge continues eastward from Australia, it eventually heads northward on the floor of the Pacific Ocean, along the western coastline of South and Central America. In this region, the ridge is known as the East Pacific Ridge. Because of all these interconnections, some scientists say that a single oceanic ridge encircles Earth, one that stretches a total of more than 40,000 mi (65,000 km).

In most locations, the oceanic ridges are 6,500 ft (2,000 m) or more below the surface of the oceans. In a few places, however, they actually extend above sea level and form islands. Iceland, the Azores, and Tristan de Cunha are examples of such islands.

Running along the middle of an oceanic ridge, there is often a deep crevice known as a rift, or median valley. This central rift can plunge as far as 6,500 ft (2,000 m) below the top of the ridge that surrounds it. According to the theory of plate tectonics, ocean ridges are formed when molten rock, or magma, escapes from the Earth's interior to form the lithospheric plates (which include the seafloor) of the Earth, a process known as seafloor spreading. Rifts may be the specific parts of the ridges where the magma escapes.

Trenches

Trenches are long, narrow, canyon–like structures, most often found adjacent to a continental margin. They occur much more commonly in the Pacific than in any of the other oceans. The deepest trench on Earth is the Marianas trench, which runs from the coast of Japan south and then west toward the Philippine Islands. Its deepest spot is 36,152 feet (11,022 meters) below sea level and it runs a distance of about 1,580 miles (2,550 kilometers). The longest trench is located along the coast of Peru and Chile. Its total length is 3,700 miles (5,900 kilometers) and it has a maximum depth of 26,420 feet (8,055 meters).

Earthquakes and volcanic activity are commonly associated with trenches. In fact, the trenches that encircle the Pacific Ocean are sometimes called the Ring of Fire because of the volcanic activity located there. According to the plate tectonic theory, trenches form at sites where one lithospheric plate is forced beneath another, or subducted, as a result of seafloor spreading elsewhere. Friction between the two plates is responsible for the associated earthquakes and volcanic activity.

Fracture zones

Further evidence of seismic activity in the ocean basins is the presence of fracture zones. These are regions where, along numerous faults, sections of the ocean floor slide past each other, relieving tension created by seafloor spreading at the ocean ridges. Ocean crust in a fracture zone looks like it has been sliced up by a giant knife. The faults usually cut across ocean ridges, often nearly at right angles to the ridge. A map of the North Atlantic Ocean basin, for example, shows the Mid–Atlantic Ridge traveling from north to south across the middle of the basin, with dozens of fracture zones cutting across the ridge from east to west.

Some of the largest fracture zones are located along the eastern edge of the Pacific Ocean. The Clipperton And Clarion Fracture Zones, for example, originate along the western coast of Mexico and extend up to 3,300 mi (5,300 km) to the west. At their maximum, these zones may be almost 30 mi (50 km) wide and 10,500 ft (3,150 m) deep.

Abyssal plains and hills

Abyssal plains are relatively flat areas of the ocean basin with slopes of less than one part in a thousand. They tend to be found at depths of 13,000–16,000 ft (4000–5000 m). Oceanographers believe that abyssal plains are so flat because they are covered with sediments that have been washed off the surface of the continents for thousands of years. On the abyssal plains, these layers of sediment have now covered up any irregularities that may exist in rock of the ocean floor beneath them.

Abyssal plains found in the Atlantic and Indian Ocean tend to be more extensive than those in the Pacific Ocean. One reason for this phenomenon is that the majority of the world's largest rivers empty into either the Atlantic or the Indian Oceans, providing both ocean basins with an endless supply of the sediments from which abyssal plains are made.

Abyssal hills are irregular structures on the ocean floor that average about 825 ft (250 m) in height. They often occur over very wide stretches of the ocean floor and are especially common in the Pacific Ocean. Abyssal hills are probably just smaller versions of the volcanic features known as seamounts.

Volcanic cones

Largely unseen by human eyes, the ocean basins are alive with volcanic activity. Magma flows upward from the mantle to the ocean bottom not only through rifts, but also through numerous volcanoes and other openings in the ocean floor. Seamounts are submarine volcanoes and can either be active or extinct. Guyots are extinct volcanoes that were once above sea level, but have since subsided below the surface. As they subsided, wave or current action eroded the top of the volcano to a flat surface.

KEY TERMS

Fracture zone—Faults in the ocean floor that form at nearly right angles to the ocean's major ridges.

Guyot—An extinct, submarine volcano with a flat top.

Ridge—Very long underwater mountain ranges created as a byproduct of seafloor spreading.

Rift—A crevice that runs down the middle of a ridge.

Seafloor spreading—The plate tectonic process whereby new oceanic crust is created at ridges.

Subduction—The plate tectonic process whereby a lithospheric plate is destroyed when it plunges beneath an adjacent plate.

Seamounts and guyots typically rise about 0.6 mile (1 km) above the ocean floor. One of the largest known seamounts is Great Meteor Seamount. It extends to a height of more than 1,300 ft (4,000 m) above the ocean floor in the northeastern part of the Atlantic Ocean.

See also Abyssal plain; Continental shelf; Hydrothermal vents; Magma; Ocean; Oceanography; Plate tectonics; Volcano.

Further Reading:

Golden, Fred, Stephen Hart, Gina Maranto, and Bryce Walker. *How Things Work: Oceans.* Alexandria, VA: Time–Life Books, 1991.

David E. Newton

Oceanography

Oceanography, the study of the oceans, is a combination of the sciences of biology, chemistry, physics and meteorology.

Ancient explorers of the ocean were sailors and fishermen, who learned about marine biology by observing the sea life and discovering when it was most plentiful. They observed the effects of wind, currents and tides, and learned how to use them to their advantage, or to avoid them. These early humans discovered that salt could be retrieved from seaweed and grasses.

Polynesians combined what they knew about the weather, winds, and currents to investigate the Pacific Ocean, while the Phoenicians, Greeks, and Arabs explored the Mediterranean Sea. The early Greeks in general and Heroditus (495–428 B.C.) in particular believed that the world was round. Heroditus performed studies of the Mediterranean which helped sailors of his time. He was able to take depth measurements of the sea floor by using the fathom as a unit of measure, which was the length of a man's outstretched arms. Today the fathom has been standardized to measure 6 ft (1.8 m) in length.

Aristotle (384–322 B.C.) also studied marine life. One of his contemporaries, a geographer by the name of Poseidarius, studied the tides and their relationship to the phases of the moon.

Pliny (23–79 A.D.) was a Roman naturalist who discovered, by studying marine biology, that some organisms had medicinal uses. One of his predecessors, Seneca (4 B.C.–65 A.D.) predicted that interest in the oceans would fade and "a huge land would be revealed." We know, of course, that this prediction came true with the discovery of North America. A period of about 1,000 years followed when no new studies were done until the fifteenth century. Christopher Columbus performed oceanographic studies on his voyages.

Captain James Cook, the explorer, was one of the first scientists to study the oceans' natural history. A surge in scientific studies took place in the seventeenth century during which scientists tried for the fist time to combine the scientific method with sailors' knowledge.

U.S. navy lieutenant Matthew Fontaine Maury (1806–1873) is considered the "father" of modern oceanography. It was during the nineteenth century that the name was given to the science.

In December 1872 the British ship HMS *Challenger* began a four–year journey, which lasted until May of 1876. This was the first major study done from a purely scientific viewpoint, and since that time significant strides have been made. The advent of submersible vehicles allowed for first–hand study of the ocean floor and the water above it. In 1900 Prince Albert of Monaco established two institutes to study oceanography.

Even though the study of the oceans has entered the technological age, there is much we still do not know. Oceanographers of the 1990s use satellites to study changes in salt levels, temperature, currents, biological studies, and transportation of sediments. As scientists develop new technologies, the future will open new doors to the study of oceanography.

See also Ocean.

Ocean sunfish

The ocean sunfish (*Mola mola*), also called the headfish, is so named because of its unique shape: it looks as if it is all head and no body.

The ocean sunfish is a very large species that lives in tropical and temperate waters. The ocean sunfish has a flattened, oval body that may measure 11 ft (3.5 m) in length and weigh as much as 2,000 lbs (1,000 kg). In contrast to its huge size, it has a vertebrae column of only 0.5 in (12 mm) in length. The body is oval and has a thick leathery skin. Most ocean sunfish are gray, olive brown, sometimes nearly black, with light undersides.

The ocean sunfish has a snout which protrudes out beyond a small mouth, which consists of both an upper and lower jaw. The jaws are toothed and are joined to form a single, sharp–edged beak.

The fins of the ocean sunfish are distinctive: there is a single long dorsal fin extending from the top and an equally long anal fin. The body ends abruptly with a low tail fin, and a rounded and wavy tail. The pointed–tailed sunfish (*Mola lanceolata*), has a tail drawn out into a point in the middle. The oblong–shaped sunfish (*Ranzania truncata*) has a tail with a more rounded margin. These two species are smaller than the *Mola mola*, with the *Ranzania truncata* seldom exceeding 2 ft (60 cm).

The young of ocean sunfish are a relatively normal fish shape compared to the shape of the adult. A captured female sunfish had approximately 300 million eggs in its ovaries. The larvae of the sunfish are about 0.10 in (2.5 mm) long and similar in shape to conventional fish. The shape soon changes with the growth of both the anal and dorsal fins, and the body becomes covered with spines. This coat of spines is then lost until there are only five spines left. These five long spines shorten until they are lost completely. After this stage the bulky, disc–like, body begins to form. The young ocean sunfish is then about 0.5 in (12 mm) long.

In order to steer its way through the ocean, the ocean sunfish waves both the anal and dorsal fins in unison from side to side. These fins add a twisting motion as they wave. The small, continuously flapping, pectoral fins are thought to only act as stabilizers, having no effect on the propulsion or steering of the animal. The tail is used as a rudder. Steering is accomplished by the use of the gills. The sunfish steers itself by squirting a strong jet of water out of one gill opening or the other, or out of its mouth. The food of the ocean sunfish consists of plankton, jellyfish, shellfish, crustaceans, squid, and small fish, so speed is not essential.

The life of ocean sunfish is very simple and does not require much intelligence, and its brain is smaller than its spinal cord.

The ocean sunfish has frustrated harpooners for many years. When pierced by a harpoon, a sunfish makes no attempt to take evasive action, but rather makes sounds described as sighing, groaning or grunting. Theses sounds are made by grinding their throat teeth together and may or may not indicate distress. No evasive action is necessary because the ocean sunfish has about 2–3 in (5–7.5 cm) of gristle under its tough skin. Harpooners have been known to try dozens of times before piercing this skin. Indeed, it has even been said to be bullet–proof.

Often ocean sunfish are seen sunning themselves on the ocean surface, most often during calm weather. At times, the ocean sunfish may go down to a depth of about 650 ft (200 m). The sunfish is most often seen singly or in pairs, but at certain times of the year they may come together in schools of a dozen or more. Basking in the sun by sunfish has often been disputed. Some believe that sunfish seen at or near the surface must either be dead or dying. A biologist has investigated this phenomenon and concluded that ocean sunfish in this position are, for the most part, sick or dying. Other underwater investigations have shown that the ocean sunfish, when at rest, goes to a darker color and when it begins to swim the color changes to a very light shade.

Ocean thermal energy conversion see
Alternative energy sources

Ocean trench see **Plate tectonics**

Ocean zones

Ocean zones are layers within the seas that contain distinctive plant and animal life. They are sometimes referred to as ocean layers or environmental zones. A system of zonation frequently used by oceanographers grew out of suggestions made by Joel Hedgpeth in 1957. According to that system, the ocean environment is first divided into two broad categories, known as realms, the *benthic realm*, consisting of the seafloor; and the *pelagic realm*, which consists of the ocean waters. Each of these realms is then subdivided into separate zones according to the depth of the water,

which strongly influences the types of plant and animal life they contain.

Water depth vs. light penetration

The single most important factor in distinguishing vertical subdivisions of the benthic and pelagic realms is the availability of solar energy. Sunlight obviously cannot penetrate beyond a certain depth in the ocean. Some organisms have, however, evolved to cope with the absence of sunlight at great depths. Plants require sunlight to carry on photosynthesis, the process that converts carbon dioxide, water, and other nutrients to simple carbohydrates, providing food for themselves and for higher organisms. Below a depth of about 650 ft (200 m) insufficient sunlight penetrates to allow photosynthesis to occur. The interval from the surface to 650 ft (200 m) is therefore known as the *euphotic* ("eu–" = good, "photo–" = light) *zone*.

From the standpoint of living organisms, the euphotic zone is probably the most important of all oceanic zones since it is the only place in which any significant amount of photosynthesis takes place. By some estimates, about two–thirds of all the photosynthetic activity that occurs on the Earth (on land and in the water) takes place within the euphotic zone.

From 650–3,000 ft (200–1,000 m), the layer known as the *dysphotic* ("dys–" = bad; "–photic" = light) *zone*, light is very dim (about 1% penetrates) and photosynthesis rarely occurs. Below this depth, down to the deepest parts of the ocean, it is perpetual night. This layer is called the *aphotic* ("a–" = without; "–photic" = light) *zone*. At one time, scientists thought that very little life existed within the aphotic zone. However, they now know that a variety of efficient and interesting organisms can be found living on the deepest parts of the ocean floor. (Some classifications include the dysphotic zone with the aphotic zone and refer to the euphotic zone simply as the photic zone.)

The benthic realm

The benthic realm extends from the shoreline to the deepest parts of the ocean floor. The section of the shoreline above the high tide line is known as the supralittoral, supratidal, or "splash," zone. It is actually covered by water only during the highest tides of the year. The next lower region of the shoreline, between high and low tide, is referred to as the littoral, or intertidal, zone. The portion of the seafloor below low water, extending outward to the edge of the continental shelf, is the sublittoral, or subtidal, zone. Typically, the base of the sublittoral zone corresponds to the base of the euphotic zone. (Some classifications use the term littoral to refer to the entire shore zone, from the supratidal to subtidal zones of the continental shelf.)

The floor of the continental slope, extending from a depth of about 650–13,200 ft (200–4,000 m), is defined as the bathyal zone. The bathyal zone includes all of the dysphotic zone and the upper aphotic zone, so it is a dark and foreboding place. The abyssal plains, flat, nearly featureless expanses of ocean floor at depths ranging from 13,200–20,000 ft (4,000–6,000 m), occupy the abyssal zone. Finally, the deepest parts of the ocean bottom, within the ocean trenches, are defined as the hadal zone.

The benthic realm is an especially rich environment for living organisms. Scientists now believe that up to 98% of all marine species (not individuals, but species) are found in or near the ocean floor. Some of these are fish or shellfish swimming just above the ocean floor, but most are organisms that burrow in the sand or mud, bore into or are attached to rocks, live in shells, or simply move about on the ocean floor.

In the deeper parts of the ocean floor, below the euphotic zone, no herbivores (plant eaters) can survive. However, the "rain" of dead organic matter from above still supports thriving bottom communities.

The pelagic realm

Scientists often separate the pelagic realm into two regions, or divisions. The portion of the ocean that overlies the continental shelf, to a maximum depth of about 650 ft (200 m), is known as the neritic, or coastal, division. The portion outward from the continental shelf is classified as the oceanic division.

Epipelagic zone

It is in the epipelagic zone, from the surface to 650 ft (200 m) (corresponding to the euphotic zone), that phytoplankton (algae and microscopic plants) live. They are the primary producers of the ocean, the lowest level on the oceanic food web. Using the process of photosynthesis, they convert carbon dioxide, water, and other nutrients to the simple carbohydrates, providing food for themselves and for higher organisms.

On the next level upward in the pelagic food web are the primary consumers, the zooplankton (microscopic animals). They feed on phytoplankton and, in turn, become food for larger animals (secondary consumers) such as sardines, herring, tuna, bonito, and other kinds of fish and swimming mammals. At the top of this food web are the ultimate consumers, the toothed whales. (A baleen whale's diet consists mostly of plankton).

Mesopelagic zone

The dysphotic zone of the pelagic realm, from a depth of about 650–3,000 ft (200–1,000 m), is known as the mesopelagic zone. In the mesopelagic zone, a number of organisms survive by spending daylight hours within this zone and then rising toward the surface during evening hours. In this way, they can feed off the phytoplankton and zooplankton available near and on the surface of the water while avoiding predators during the day. The most common organisms found in the mesopelagic zone are small fish, squid, and simple shellfish.

A number of inhabitants of the deeper dysphotic zone have evolved some interesting adaptations for living in this twilight world. They often have very large eyes, capable of detecting light only 1% as intense as that visible to the human eye. A majority also have light–producing organs that give off a phosphorescence that makes them glow in the dark.

Bathypelagic, abyssopelagic, and hadalpelagic zones

Organisms found in the aphotic zones of the pelagic realm, the bathypelagic zone (about 3,000–13,000 ft [1,000–4,000 m]), the abyssopelagic zone (about 13,000–20,000 ft [4,000–6,000 m]), and the hadalpelagic zone (below 20,000 ft [6,000 m]), have evolved some bizarre adaptations for survival in their lightless environment. In these regions, pressures may exceed 500 atmospheres—500 times that of atmospheric pressure, or the equivalent of several tons per square inch—and temperatures never get much warmer than about 3° C (37° F). Organisms within these zones generally prey on each other and have developed special features such as expandable mouths, large and very sharp teeth, and special strategies for hunting or luring prey.

Recent discoveries

As oceanographers extend their studies to the deepest parts of the oceans, they continually encounter surprises in the kinds of marine life found there. One of the most interesting of these surprises was the discovery of deep sea vents found near the Galapagos Islands in 1977. These vents are located in regions where molten rock lies just below the surface of the seafloor, producing underwater hot springs. Volcanic "chimneys" form when the escaping super–heated water deposits dissolved minerals and gases upon coming in contact with the cold ocean water. The vents are surrounded by intriguing communities of organisms never seen before the 1977 discovery.

The basis for these non–photosynthesis based communities are bacteria that obtain energy from the oxidation of hydrogen sulfide escaping from the vents—a process called *chemosynthesis*. These bacteria (primary producers) are then used as foods by tube worms, huge clams, and mussels, and other organisms (primary consumers) living around the vents. These communities live in total isolation from photosynthetic–based communities (all other biological communities are photosynthesis based), and may provide clues to the nature of early life on Earth. Later studies have shown that hydrothermal vent communities exist in other parts of the ocean depths as well.

See also Continental shelf; Hydrothermal vents; Ocean; Photic zone.

Further Reading:
Golden, Fred, Stephen Hart, Gina Maranto, and Bryce Walker. *How Things Work: Oceans.* Alexandria, VA: Time–Life Books, 1991.

David E. Newton

Ocelot see **Cats**

Octet rule see **Chemical bond**

Octopus

The octopus is an invertebrate in the class Mollusca (the molluscs), which also includes snails, clams, and squid. Octopuses are cephalopod molluscs which are generally considered to be the most advanced members of the class.

There are about 220 species of octopus found in every ocean of the world, ranging in size from the North Atlantic octopus (measuring 2 in/5.1 cm across) to the Pacific octopus (measuring 30 ft/9 m across).

The octopus has no hard, protective shell; instead, its body is covered by the soft mantle. The body of the octopus is rounded, like a cranium, and positioned, apparently, "above" the octopus's eyes, which makes it look like a "head." The eyes are one of the octopus's most striking features, and are among the most physically advanced eyes of all invertebrates, comparable in complexity to human eyes, which also work in a similar way.

The octopus has eight legs, lined with double rows of suction cups, that encircle its parrotlike beak. These cups are powerful; it requires 6 oz (170 g) of force to remove a single attached cup, so the combined suction power of dozens of suckers makes a very secure grip. The octopus attaches the suction cups by placing them on the surface it wishes to cling to, and then tightening the tiny muscles at the top of each sucker, resulting in a vacuum effect.

Each of the octopus's skin cells contains a packet of pigment (red, yellow, blue, brown, and black) surrounded by muscles that, when contracted, can balloon the packet to many times its original size. When this happens, the entire octopus changes color faster than any other animal. The colors seem to be associated with moods: a frightened octopus will turn stark white, an angry one, fiery red. A contented octopus usually is the color that will camouflage it with its surroundings. The skin can also change texture, becoming smooth, spiny, or lumpy as the octopus wishes.

The octopus distracts attackers by squirting out a jet of sepia, or ink, through its siphon. The resulting ink cloud is similar in size to the octopus, which immediately turns pale as it shoots out the ink. The octopus quickly flees, swimming backward via powerful jets of water sprayed through its siphon. Predators of the octopus include orcas, dolphins, sharks, groupers, moray eels, seals, and the Atlantic halibut.

Although the octopus has a dangerous reputation, it is, in fact, a shy creature that prefers to be left alone, even by other octopuses. Attacks on human swimmers usually happen when the octopus has been tormented and bites its attacker. The hard beak can inflict deep wounds, and the blue–ringed octopus of Australian waters injects potentially fatal venom with its bite. The beak is used normally to subdue prey, such as fish, other molluscs, and crabs. When an octopus catches a fish, the octopus kills it quickly by biting the fish's backbone just behind the head. Single–shelled molluscs cannot be pulled apart by the octopus's strong suckers, so the octopus drills a hole in the shell with its radula, or rasping tongue, which is typical of all molluscs. Once the mollusc shell is breached, the octopus injects venom that kills the snail and makes it semi–liquid.

Octopuses prefer to live alone and come together only during the mating season. Copulation consists of the male slipping the tip of one of its arms into the female's mantle; this arm has a groove running along its length down which pass packets of sperm. In some species, the sperm are contained in the tip of an arm, which breaks off inside the female.

After mating, the female octopus retires to a small cave, where she lays several thousand eggs. She weaves them into strings, which she attaches to the roof of the cave. As the eggs develop, she keeps them clean by blowing jets of water on them and running her arms through them. The young octopuses that hatch are tiny replicas of their parents.

Every octopus has two optical glands (so named because they sit upon the optical nerves) which shut off the octopus's desire to eat once it has mated. This means that once a male or female octopus has reproduced, it will soon die, whether in the wild or in captivity.

F. C. Nicholson

Ohm see **Units and standards**

Ohm's law

Ohm's law is a relationship between the voltage across an electric circuit, the electrical resistance in the circuit, and the current in the circuit. This law is named after its discoverer, Georg Simon Ohm. Ohm found that for most electric circuits, the voltage across the circuit was equal to the current flowing through the circuit times the electrical resistance of the circuit. For the same voltage, a circuit with a low resistance will have a higher current than a circuit with a higher resistance.

The voltage, properly called the potential difference, is measured in volts, and the current in amperes (amps). The resistance is therefore in volts per ampere, which is defined as ohms.

It is important to understand that Ohm's law is not a fundamental law that always applies, such as the law of gravity. Rather it is an empirical law that has been found by experiment to work fairly well most of the time. There are times, however, usually in extreme cases, when Ohm's law breaks down. For example, if an extremely high voltage is applied across a circuit, Ohm's law will not predict the correct value for the current. Even though Ohm's law does not always apply it works for most everyday situations and is therefore very useful.

For example, why will a short circuit blow a fuse or circuit breaker? When a short circuit occurs, most of the electrical resistance in the circuit is bypassed. In effect, a new circuit with a very low resistance is created. So, according to Ohm's law if the resistance is very low the current must be very high. Fuses and circuit breakers are designed to protect the circuit by blowing when the current becomes too high. Hence, the short circuit will produce a current high enough to blow the fuse. As another application, electronic devices often have resistors placed in the circuit to increase the resistance and therefore limit the current.

Oilbird see **Caprimulgids**

Oil drilling

Oil is a fossil fuel found largely in vast underground deposits from which it must be extracted. Oil and its byproducts did not have any real economic importance until the middle of the 19th century when it began to assume its present role as the basis of a major international industry. Today, oil is produced on every continent but Antarctica and has become so valuable that it is sometimes called "black gold." Despite increasingly sophisticated methods of locating possible deposits and improved extraction techniques, oil is still obtained by drilling.

History

Oil or petroleum was known in the ancient world and had several uses. Usually found when it bubbled up to the earth's surface at what is called an "oil seep," it was used primarily as a lubricant, for caulking ships, and for jointing masonry. The Chinese knew and used oil as far back as the 3rd century B.C., and when the Italian explorer, Marco Polo (c. 1254–1324), visited the Baku region on the Caspian Sea in what is now Russia, he saw a fire in a temple that was kept burning by natural gas. Deposits of oil are always accompanied by reservoirs of petroleum gas also called natural gas.

Interest in obtaining oil did not occur until a 19th century discovery was made. In the 1840s, Scottish chemist James Young (1811–1883) experimented with "rock oil" or shale impregnated with oil and found that he could distill what came to be called kerosene from it. This first byproduct of oil was considered by its discoverers to have excellent illuminating properties and was put to use in lamps. Since candles or lamps were the only source of artificial lighting at this time, kerosene for lamp–lighting was seen as a potentially major market. This economic incentive spurred individuals to seek a larger, regular source of oil beyond what was available at known oil seeps, and thus the logic of drilling for oil became apparent. It also was very obvious that the best place to drill for oil was at or near an oil seep. In fact, spewing oil had been a sometimes embarrassing byproduct of drilling for water. Now it would be welcome.

In the United States, one of the best known oil seeps was at Titusville, Pennsylvania, and it was there that an American entrepreneur, George H. Bissell, directed his attention. He hired a former railway conductor, Edwin L. Drake (1819–1880), to drill there for oil, and on August 27, 1859, this first oil well to be drilled struck paydirt at a depth of only 70 ft (21 m). The oil industry had begun. It would be a minor industry for some time however, since the only product of crude oil that was thought to be useful was kerosene. The remainder was simply thrown away. Fifty years later however, with the invention of the internal combustion engine and with greater knowledge of the nature and varied applications of petroleum, the real oil industry we know today was born in earnest. This market would prove to be international in scope and have seemingly limitless potential, so drilling for oil became a very serious and sometimes very rewarding undertaking.

Obtaining oil from beneath the earth can be reduced to two fundamentals: Knowing where to drill and being able to get down to the deposit. The earth itself offers several clues as to the presence of oil, and besides the oil seeps themselves, certain types of sedimentary rock are known giveaways. Where there are no such obvious geological signs, seismographic methods are used to survey subterranean deposits. This modern method uses sound waves that bounce off underground rocks and provide information about subsurface geol-

ogy. Other even more sophisticated methods of mapping the earth's subsurface involve magnetic and gravity surveys. Magnetic surveys locate sedimentary basins where oil may exist by measuring the small differences in the earth's magnetic field that exist because of the different type of rocks found there. For example, sedimentary rocks are nearly nonmagnetic. Gravity surveys concentrate on the place–to–place variations in the earth's gravity, and sedimentary rocks are known to have their own gravity signature. Despite all of today's highly sophisticated scientific methods for locating potential oil deposits, there is still no guarantee that oil will always be found where everything indicates it ought to be. The proof is always in the drilling. Drilling techniques therefore become equally important to prospecting.

Whether drilling for water or oil, drilling technology has a similar early history. The ancient Chinese practiced the simplest form of penetrating below the earth with a system called the *percussion method*. This is essentially like using a hammer since it repeatedly raises and drops a heavy tool. This impact drilling was used to drill the first oil well in Pennsylvania, and it employed a chisel–like bit that was suspended from a cable to a lever on the surface. The up–and–down motion of the lever pounded the bit into the bottom of the hole and slowly chipped away pieces of rock. This was a slow process since it had to be stopped periodically so the rock chips could be removed. For this method to work, the hole also had to be free of liquids, and it was this "dry" drilling that usually resulted in the "gushers" we often think of as a successful oil well strike. A great deal of oil was often lost before these gushers could be capped and brought under control.

Today, almost all oil wells are drilled by the rotary method. This method best resembles a power drill or dentist's drill as opposed to the percussion method's pile–driving system. The rotary drill was first developed in Europe in the 1930s and soon replaced the percussion or cable–tool system. Instead of a heavy weight at the end of a cable trying to punch a hole in the ground, a rotating bit is attached to a length of pipe and gradually bores its way down into the earth. The piping is supported vertically above the hole by a derrick. These towers were first made of wood but now are built of steel. The taller the derrick, the more sections of pipe it can handle and the fewer stops it has to make. As the bit goes deeper, more lengths of heavier pipe are added at the top, forcing the bit to dig deeper. The rotary bit itself is shaped like a doughnut with teeth and is spun by a motor. One of the great advantages of the rotary method is that the hole must be kept full of liquid while drilling in order to keep the cutting head cool. This weighted fluid or chemical mixture is simply called "mud" and serves two other important purposes. It carries crushed rock to the surface (making for continuous drilling until the bit wears out), and it prevents "gushers" by the corking action of its own weight and density. Modern oil wells also have blow–out preventers that make gushers a thing of the past. These are heavy, rubber–tipped pistons that can be hydraulically closed to totally seal off a well.

A variation of the rotary method of drilling is turbo–drilling in which a fluid–powered turbine is placed at the bottom of the bore hole and just above the bit. This method is very efficient since the turbine drives the bit which is right next to it rather than thousands of feet above it. Further, energy is not wasted spinning the drill pipe all the way down the hole. Compared to the well depths of the 1920s (about 8,200 ft or 2,500 m), today's drills can reach down more than 30,00 ft (9,400 m).

When first drilled, the oil in many wells is usually driven upwards by the pressure of underground natural gas, and well–head valves are used to regulate its flow. As the gas pressure eventually drops, it is often necessary to pump oil from the well using the commonly seen rocking–arm device. Finally, if there is still enough good quality oil down below, wells can be pressurized with water, mud, or compressed gases to force much of it to the surface. However, as oil wells eventually dried up and the hunt for new reservoirs became increasingly more rewarding, new techniques were devised to reach oil buried in deposits deep beneath the sea.

Marine or offshore drilling began in 1894 when jetties were built from the California shore to tap the Santa Barbara oilfield. By the 1920s, fixed offshore drilling rigs were built in the Caspian Sea, and mobile drilling barges began to appear off the United States Gulf Coast. Although today's offshore drilling techniques are basically the same as those on land, the crews and the equipment need a stable platform that sits above the water and waves. These structures must hold everything from the derrick and rotary motors to living quarters for the crew, and engineers are faced with designing them to withstand the fierce, open–ocean storms that regularly occur. Once a semi–submersible rig has tapped a well, production platforms are installed. These are enormous, man–made structures that are attached to the sea bottom, and from which up to thirty separate wells are sometimes tapped using a method called *directional drilling*. Oil well drilling is a difficult, dirty, and dangerous job, but it becomes increasingly lucrative and strategically more important as today's reservoirs are used up.

See also Hydrocarbon; Natural gas; Oil spills.

KEY TERMS

Blow–out preventer—A hydraulically–operated device made of heavy, rubber–tipped pistons that prevents a surge of oil from gushing up out of the well as it is being drilled.

Derrick—The steel tower on a drilling rig or platform that is tall enough to store at least three lengths of 30–ft (9 m) drill pipe.

Directional drilling—The drilling of a number of wells at slightly different angles from a single production platform.

Drilling mud—A chemical liquid that cools and lubricates the drill bit and acts as a cap to keep the oil from gushing up.

Gusher—An uncontrolled burst of oil high into the air that often caused damage and wasted oil.

Production platform—A large structure of either steel or concrete that is anchored to the sea bed or floats on the sea above an oil well and contains all of the necessary equipment.

Rotary drilling—A drilling system in which the drill bit rotates and cuts into rock.

Further Reading:

Brantly, John Edward. *History of Oil Well Drilling,* Houston: Book Division, Gulf Publishing Co., 1971.
Lynch, Michael. *How Oil Rigs Are Made,* New York: Facts On File, 1985.
Williams, Trevor I. *The Triumph of Invention: A History of Man's Technological Genius,* London: Macdonald Orbis, 1987.

Leonard C. Bruno

Oil spills

Petroleum is a critically important natural resource. However, petroleum is often mined in places that are far away from the regions where most of its consumption occurs. Petroleum must therefore be transported in large quantities, mostly by oceanic tankers, barges on inland waters, and overland pipelines. Any of these transportation systems can cause pollution through accidental spills of oil, by operational discharges associated with cleaning of the storage tanks of tankers, or during unloading at refineries. Some accidental oil spills have been spectacular in their magnitude and ecological damages, involving losses of huge quantities of petroleum from wrecked supertankers or offshore platform facilities.

In addition, chronic oil pollution is caused by relatively frequent discharges of hydrocarbon–laden waste waters from petroleum refineries and in urban runoff. Although each of these spills typically involve relatively small quantities of material, the spills occur rather frequently, so in total, large amounts of oil are spilled in this way.

Characteristics of petroleum

Petroleum is a naturally occurring mixture of organic chemicals, most of which are hydrocarbons (that is, containing only hydrogen and carbon atoms). Petroleum is synthesized from biomass by complex, anaerobic reactions occurring at high pressure and temperature over long periods of time deep in sedimentary geological formations. Petroleum can occur as natural gas, as a liquid known as crude oil, or as a semi–solid tar or asphalt in oil sands and shales. There are hundreds of molecular species in petroleum, ranging from gaseous methane with only 16 g/mole, to very complex substances weighing more than 20 thousand g/mole.

Petroleum mined at different places differs in its physical and chemical characteristics. Some crude oils are very thick and viscous, others are light and volatile. The lighter petroleums evaporate relatively quickly when they are spilled into the environment, although they leave residues of relatively heavy molecular species that are more persistent in terrestrial or aquatic habitats, and therefore cause longer–lasting damage.

Oil pollution

The total spillage of petroleum into the oceans through human activities is estimated to range from about 0.7–1.7 million tons (0.6–1.5 million tonnes) per year, equivalent to less than 0.1% of the quantity of petroleum transported by tankers. In comparison, the production of hydrocarbons by marine plankton is about 28.7 million tons (26 million tonnes)/year. Although these "natural" hydrocarbons contribute to background concentrations in the oceans, they are well dispersed and are not associated with ecological damage or pollution. In addition, natural oil seeps contribute about 6–13% of the total petroleum input to the oceans, sometimes causing local damage.

The largest and most damaging events of oil pollution involve spills of petroleum or heavy bunker fuel from disabled oceanic tankers or drilling platforms, from barges or ships on inland waters, or from blowouts of wells or broken pipelines on land. Sometimes damage is also caused by the relatively frequent spills and operational discharges associated with coastal refineries and urban runoff. Large quantities of oil are also spilled when tankers clean out the petroleum residues from their huge storage compartments, often discharging the oily bilge washings directly into the ocean.

Some examples of disastrous oil spills include the following accidents involving oceanic supertankers: (1) the *Torrey Canyon*, which ran aground in 1967 off southern England, spilling about 129 thousand tons (117 thousand tonnes) of crude oil; (2) the *Metula*, which wrecked in 1973 in the Strait of Magellan and spilled 58 thousand tons (53 thousand tonnes) of petroleum; (3) the *Amoco Cadiz*, which went aground in the English Channel in 1978, spilling 253 thousand tons (230 thousand tonnes) of crude oil; (4) the *Exxon Valdez*, which ran onto a reef in Prince William Sound in southern Alaska in 1989 and discharged 39 thousand tons (35 thousand tonnes) of petroleum; and (5) the *Braer*, which spilled 93 thousand tons (84 thousand tonnes) of crude oil off the Shetland Islands of Scotland in 1993.

Some huge oil spills have also occurred from offshore platforms. In 1979 the *IXTOC–I* exploration well had an uncontrolled blowout that spilled more than 551 thousand tons (500 thousand tonnes) of petroleum into the Gulf of Mexico. Smaller spills include one that occurred in 1969 off Santa Barbara in southern California, when about 11 thousand tons (10 thousand tonnes) were discharged, and the Ekofisk blowout in 1977 in the North Sea off Norway, which totalled 33 thousand tons (30 thousand tonnes) of crude oil.

Large quantities of petroleum have also been spilled during warfare. Because petroleum and its refined products are critically important economic and industrial commodities, enemies have commonly targeted tankers and other petroleum–related facilities during wars. For example, German submarines sank 42 tankers off the east coast of the United States during the Second World War, causing a total spillage of about 460–thousand tons (417 thousand tonnes) of petroleum and refined products. There were 314 attacks on oil tankers during the Iran–Iraq War of 1981–1987, 70% of them by Iraqi forces. The largest individual spill during that war occurred when Iraq damaged five tankers and three production wells at the offshore *Nowruz* complex, resulting in the spillage of more than 287 thousand tons (260 thousand tonnes) of petroleum into the Persian Gulf.

The largest–ever spill of petroleum into the marine environment occurred during the brief Gulf War of 1991. In that incident Iraqi forces deliberately released an estimated 0.6–2.2 million tons (0.5–2 million tonnes) of petroleum into the Persian Gulf from several tankers and an offshore tanker–loading facility known as the *Sea Island Terminal*. An additional, extraordinarily large spill of petroleum to the land and atmosphere also occurred as a result of the Gulf War, when more than 700 production wells in Kuwait were sabotaged and ignited by Iraqi forces in January, 1991. The total spillage of crude oil was an enormous 46 to 138 million tons (42 to 126 million tonnes). Much of the spilled petroleum burned in spectacular atmospheric conflagrations, while additional, massive quantities accumulated locally as lakes of oil, which eventually contained 5.5 to 23 million tons (5 to 21 million tonnes) of crude oil. Enormous quantities of petroleum vapors were also dispersed to the atmosphere. About one–half of the blowouts were capped by May, and the last one in November, 1991.

After oil is spilled into the environment, it dissipates in a number of ways. Spreading refers to the process by which spilled petroleum moves and disperses itself over the surface of water. The resulting slick can then be transported by currents and winds. The rate and degree of spreading are affected by viscosity of the oil, wind speed, and turbulence of the water surface. Evaporation is important in the initial reductions of volume of oil spillages, especially of relatively light and volatile hydrocarbon fractions. Evaporation typically accounts for almost 100% of spilled gasoline at sea, 30–50% of spilled petroleum, but only 10% of bunker fuel. Solubilization occurs when some fractions of the spilled oil dissolve into the water column, causing a contamination of subsurface waters in the vicinity of the oil spill. For example, beneath a petroleum slick in the North Sea the concentration of hydrocarbons in water was 4 g/m^3 (ppm), compared with about 1 mg/m^3 (ppb) in uncontaminated seawater. Lighter hydrocarbon fractions of petroleum are much more soluble in water than heavier ones, and aromatics are much more soluble than alkanes. (Aromatic hydrocarbons such as benzene and naphthalene have an unsaturated ring structure, while alkanes such as octane have a linear structure.) In addition, some of the spilled hydrocarbons are slowly oxidized by ultraviolet radiation and microorganisms into simpler compounds, ultimately to carbon dioxide and water.

The combined influences of solubilization, evaporation, and oxidation are known as weathering. Weathering preferentially removes the lighter hydrocarbon fractions, leaving a residual material made up of rela-

tively heavy hydrocarbons. Over the shorter term in aquatic environments, this residuum forms a stable water–in–oil emulsion known as "mousse," which is the material that usually impacts shorelines after offshore spills. The mousse combines with sediment particles on the shore to form sticky patties of oil and sand, which eventually form asphaltic lumps.

At sea, weathering of the mousse eventually results in the formation of a dense, semi–solid, asphaltic residuum known as "tar balls." In the vicinity of frequently travelled tanker routes world–wide, tar balls can be commonly found floating offshore and on beaches. Tar balls are especially common in places where the oceanic circulation resembles a surface vortex. A well known example of this phenomenon is the oceanic gyre known as the Sargasso Sea, famed for its accumulations of natural debris such as floating seaweeds, as well as human debris, including tar balls.

Ecological damages of oil spills

Even small oil spills can cause important damages in ecologically sensitive environments. For example, a small discharge of oily bilge washings from the tanker *Stylis* during a routine cleaning of its petroleum–storage compartments caused the deaths of about 30 thousand seabirds, because the oil was spilled in a place where the birds were abundant. This is a regrettably common occurrence—that is, relatively small, even operational spillages of petroleum cause large ecological damages, especially to seabirds and marine mammals.

Studies made after large oceanic spills have shown that the ecological damages can be intense. After the *Torrey Canyon* spill in 1967 hundreds of kilometers of the coasts of southern England and the Brittany region of France were polluted by oily mousse. The oil pollution caused severe ecological damages, due to the physical and toxic effects of fouling of organisms with petroleum residues. Those direct ecological damages were made much worse by some of the cleanup methods, because of the highly toxic detergents and dispersants that were used. As with many oil spills, seabirds were among the most tragic victims of the *Torrey Canyon* incident. This accident caused the deaths of at least 30 thousand birds, causing a substantial decrease in their breeding populations in subsequent years.

The damages caused by detergents and dispersants during the cleanup of shorelines polluted by the *Torrey Canyon* spill were an important lesson. Subsequent cleanups of oil spills involved a much more judicial use of less toxic chemicals. In addition, their use became largely restricted to offshore locations and places of high value for industrial or recreational purposes, rather than natural habitats.

In 1978, the *Amoco Cadiz* was wrecked in the same general area as the *Torrey Canyon*. Great ecological damages were also caused by this accident. However, they were less intense than those caused by the *Torrey Canyon* because less–toxic detergents and dispersants were used during the cleanup, in much smaller quantities, and only in high–value places such as harbors.

The most damaging oil spill ever to occur in North American waters was the *Exxon Valdez* accident of 1989. More than most tanker accidents, this one was very preventable, because it involved an intoxicated captain who had given temporary command of the supertanker to an unqualified and inexperienced subordinate, who quickly erred in his navigation and ran the ship aground onto a well known reef. The spilled oil affected about 1,179 mi (1,900 km) of shoreline of Prince William Sound and its vicinity, causing especially great ecological damages in tidal and subtidal habitats. Large numbers of sea mammals and birds were also affected in offshore waters. An estimated five to 10 thousand sea otters (*Enhydra lutris*) were present in Prince William Sound, and at least one thousand of these charismatic mammals were killed by oiling. About 36 thousand dead seabirds of various species were collected from beaches and other places, but the actual number of killed birds was probably in the range of 100–300 thousand birds. At least 153 bald eagles (*Haliaeetus leucocephalus*) died from poisoning when they scavenged the poisonous carcasses of oiled seabirds.

Great efforts were expended in cleaning up the oiled shorelines, almost entirely using manual and physical methods, rather than dispersants and detergents. In total, about 11 thousand people participated in the cleanup, and about $2.5 billion was spent by the ship owners and $154 million by the U.S. federal government. This was by far the most expensive cleanup that has ever been undertaken for an oil spill. Within a year of the spill, the combined effects of the cleanup and winter storms had removed most of the residues of the *Exxon Valdez* spill from the environment. However, there has been a lingering controversy about the longer–term ecological damages that were caused, including effects on the regionally important fisheries for herring and salmon.

See also Petroleum; Water pollution.

Further Reading:

Freedman, B. *Environmental Ecology*, 2nd ed. San Diego: Academic Press, 1994.

KEY TERMS

. . . .

Bilge washings—Hydrocarbon-contaminated water that results from cleaning of the petroleum–holding compartments of a tanker, and may then be discharged to the environment.

Bunker fuel—A relatively viscous, liquid hydrocarbon mixture, also known as bunker–C fuel oil, that remains after lighter hydrocarbons are distilled from petroleum during refining. Bunker C is used as a fuel by oil–fired generating stations, heating plants, and ships.

Detergent—A chemical used as a cleaning agent because it encourages the formation of an oil-in-water emulsion.

Dispersant—A chemical agent that reduces the surface tension of liquid hydrocarbons, encouraging the formation of an oil–in–water emulsion. This reduces the volume of residual oil on shorelines or the water surface after a spill.

Mousse—A water–in–oil emulsion that is formed by turbulence of the surface water after a petroleum spill to the aquatic environment.

Petroleum—A naturally occurring, liquid mixture of hydrocarbons that is mined and refined for energy and the manufacturing of chemicals, especially plastics. Also known as crude oil.

GESAMP. *Impact of Oil and Related Chemicals and Wastes in the Marine Environment. Joint Group of Experts on the Scientific Aspects of Marine Pollution (GESAMP)*, Report 50, London: International Marine Organization, 1993.

Bill Freedman

Okapi see **Giraffes and okapi**

Old-growth forests

Old–growth forests are natural ecosystems that are dominated by large, old trees, usually of a mixed species composition, and with all ages present in the community. Old–growth forests also contain many scattered, dead trees, both standing and lying on the forest floor. Old–growth forests in the tropics are threatened by conversion to agriculture and by other disturbances, while old–growth forests in the temperate zone are mostly threatened by forestry. Losses of these old–growth ecosystems are the most important of the modern threats to biodiversity, because of the extinctions that are caused. The special values of old–growth forests are best preserved through the designation of large, landscape–scale, ecological reserves.

Properties of old–growth forests

Old–growth forests are an end–of–succession, climax ecosystem. Old–growth forests are dominated by trees of great age, but occurring within a mixed–species community with an uneven–aged population structure (that is, all tree ages are represented in the community). The physical structure of old–growth forests is very complex, and includes multiple layers and gaps of foliage within the canopy, great variations of tree sizes, and many large, standing dead trees (these are called "snags") and dead logs lying on the forest floor. In some ecological contexts the term "old–growth forest" might also be used to refer to senescent stands of shorter–lived species of trees, such as cherry, birch, or poplar. However, the usual interpretation is that an old–growth forest is a terminal–succession or climax ecosystem, with the broad features described above climax.

For old–growth forests to develop, a very long time must pass between events of disturbance that are severe enough to cause a stand–level mortality of dominant trees. Therefore, old–growth forests occur in places or regions where fire, hurricanes, and other catastrophic disturbances are rare. These circumstances are especially frequent in places receiving a great deal of rainfall throughout the year. Consequently, many of the best examples of old–growth forests are tropical and temperate rain forests.

Species dependent on old–growth forests

Old–growth forests provide a habitat with particular ecological characteristics. These features are not present or as well developed in mature forests that are younger than old–growth forests. Some wildlife species require these specific qualities of old–growth habitats, and they therefore need extensive areas of old–growth forest as all or a major part of their range. Some well–known, North American examples of species considered to be substantially dependent on old–growth forests are birds such as the northern spotted owl (*Strix occidentalis caurina*), marbled murrelet (*Brachyramphus marmoratus*), and red–cockaded woodpecker (*Picoides borealis*), and mammals such as marten (*Martes americana*) and fisher

(*M. pennanti*). Some species of plants may also require or be much more abundant in old–growth forests than in younger, mature forests. Examples include Pacific yew (*Taxus brevifolia*) and various species of lichens occurring in old–growth Douglas–fir (*Pseudotsuga menziesii*) forests of western North America.

A critical habitat requirement for many of the species of old–growth forests is the presence of large trees with dead tops, and large snags and logs lying on the forest floor. These habitat features are absent or uncommon in younger natural forests, and in intensively–managed, second–growth forests created through forestry. Snags and living but heart–rotted trees are especially important to woodpeckers, which excavate nesting cavities that may later be used by the many secondary species that cannot excavate their own hollows.

The northern spotted owl is a non–migratory bird of the northwestern United States and southwestern Canada that requires large tracts of old–growth, moist–to–wet, conifer forest as its habitat. Each breeding pair of northern spotted owls requires more than about 600 ha of old–growth forest, and each breeding population needs at least 20 pairs to be viable. However, old–growth forests in this region are extremely valuable as a natural resource that can be exploited by humans for profit, and this ecosystem type has been greatly reduced in area and fragmented by logging. Consequently, populations of this bird have been reduced, and the northern spotted owl has been recognized as a "threatened" species in the United States. Under the U.S. Endangered Species Act, designation under this status requires that a management plan must be developed to protect the threatened species. Because the northern spotted owl is jeopardized by the logging of old–growth forests, the plans for its protection have resulted in the withdrawal from forestry usage of large areas of valuable forest that could otherwise be profitably exploited. The strategy to protect the spotted owl would preserve large ecological reserves of old–growth forest as its essential habitat (as well as for other species dependent on this type of habitat). However, at the same time that the owl is protected, important, shorter–term, economic opportunities are lost to the forest industry because there is less high–value, old–growth timber available for exploitation.

The red–cockaded woodpecker also has a requirement for old–growth forests, in this case certain types of pine forests (especially loblolly pine, *Pinus taeda*) in the southeastern United States, in which this bird excavates nesting cavities in large, living trees that have fungal heart rot. The red–cockaded woodpecker breeds in small colonies, and it has a complex social system, involving non–breeding adult birds that assist breeders in the rearing of their broods. Old–growth pine forests that satisfy the habitat needs of red–cockaded woodpeckers have been greatly diminished and fragmented by conversions to agriculture, forestry plantations, and residential lands. This has reduced the populations of red–cockaded woodpeckers, which are further threatened by natural disturbances such as wildfire and hurricanes. Unlike the spotted owl, the endangered red–cockaded woodpecker is somewhat tolerant of a limited intensity of disturbances of its habitat. There is some evidence that trees can be safely harvested from stands in which this species breeds, as long as its nesting colonies are protected by buffers (that is, by surrounding unharvested strips wider than about 2,625 ft (800 m), and sufficient foraging habitat remains available. However, there is not yet enough scientific evidence to support this sort of an integrated management strategy for forestry and red–cockaded woodpeckers. Until this controversy is resolved, the ecologically prudent strategy for preservation of the red–cockaded woodpecker requires setting aside large ecological reserves of its natural habitat.

Compared with the temperate–forest examples described above, enormously larger numbers of species are dependent on old–growth tropical forests. Because wildfire and other catastrophic disturbance are uncommon in the humid tropics, this climatic regime usually favors the development of old–growth rain forests. This ecosystem supports an extraordinary richness of species of plants, animals, and microorganisms that are utterly dependent on this type of forest. Because of the enormous numbers of species supported under relatively benign climatic conditions in old–growth tropical rainforests, ecologists consider this biome to represent the acme of development of terrestrial ecosystems. Regrettably, tropical forests of all types are being rapidly lost through conversions to agriculture and other disturbances. Many of the endemic species of tropical forests have become extinct, and most of the others are becoming increasingly endangered.

Dead wood

As was noted previously, important habitat requirements of many species of wildlife relate to the numbers of dead trees in the forest, occurring as standing snags or as logs lying on the ground. These features are especially critical to some birds, which use the deadwood for nesting in excavated or natural cavities, as perches for hunting, resting, and singing, and as a substrate on which to forage for their food of insects and spiders. For example, a study in the northwestern United States found that up to 45% of the species of breeding birds

are cavity nesters. These include various species of woodpeckers that actually excavate cavities, as well as other species that are secondary users of those cavities, or that use natural hollows.

Unfortunately, modern forestry does not accommodate this habitat feature very well. Because forestry plantations usually have very few snags or other types of deadwood, cavity–dependent species of wildlife are at risk in these highly managed, secondary forests. As a result, forestry–related degradation of the habitat of these animals has become an important environmental issue in many areas. This concern is especially relevant to old–growth forests, because deadwood is such an important characteristic of this type of ecosystem. For example, as many as six woodpecker species can co–occur along with other cavity–dependent species in old–growth forests of the Pacific northwest of the United States. It may be possible to accommodate most of these species, while still practicing forestry, if an appropriate system of integrated management can be developed. One study done in that region suggested that about 70% of the woodpecker population could be maintained in selectively harvested old–growth forests, as long as at least four snags remained per hectare on harvested sites.

Controversy over use

Because of their great quantities of large–dimension timber of desired species of trees, old–growth forests are a very valuable natural resource. However, old–growth forests are rarely managed by foresters as a renewable, natural resource. Usually, these forests are "mined" by harvesting, followed by a conversion of the site to a younger, second–growth forest, which is only allowed to develop into a middle–aged forest before it is harvested in turn. This management strategy is pursued because old–growth forests sustain little or no net production of new biomass, since the growth by living trees is approximately balanced by the deaths of other trees through senescence, disease, or accident. Because the primary objective of forestry is to optimize the productivity of tree biomass, it is economically preferable to harvest the secondary forests soon after their productivity starts to decrease. However, this occurs long before they become old–growth forests.

Because of this forestry practice, old–growth forests have been greatly fragmented and diminished in area. Consequently, threats of further losses of this natural ecosystem engender great controversy. To conserve some of the important characteristics of old–growth temperate forests, including some of their dependent species, so–called "new forestry" harvesting systems are being encouraged in some areas. Compared with clear–cutting

KEY TERMS

Clear-cutting—A method of forest harvesting by which all trees of commercial size are removed from the site. Usually the trees are de-limbed, and the branches and foliage are left on the site as slash while the stem is removed as a commercial product.

Community—In ecology, a community is an assemblage of populations of different species that occur together in the same place and at the same time.

Old-growth forest—A late-successional forest, characterized by great age, uneven-aged population structure, domination by long-lived species, and complex physical structure, including multiple layers in the canopy, large trees, and many large snags and dead logs.

Plantation—A tract of land on which trees have been planted and tended, often as a single-species population.

Selection-cutting—A method of forest harvesting in which only trees of a desired species and size class are removed. This method leaves many trees standing, and relies on natural regeneration to replace the harvested trees.

Succession—A process that occurs after disturbance, and that involves the progressive replacement of earlier species and communities with others. In the absence of further disturbance succession culminates in an old-growth of climax community that is determined by climate, soil, and the nature of the participating species.

and plantation establishment, these new systems are relatively "soft" in terms of the intensity of the disturbance that is caused, and the physical integrity of the forest remains substantially intact after the harvest. For example, a system being encouraged in the old-growth forests of western North America is selection-cutting with some degree of snag retention, followed by natural regeneration of trees instead of planting.

However, even the new forestry practices cause substantial changes in the character of the forest. If the societal objective in some areas is to preserve the special, natural values of old-growth forests, this can only be done by setting aside large, landscape-scale, reserves in which commercial forestry is not practiced. Only natural ecological dynamics and disturbances are allowed

to occur in those ecological reserves. The landscape perspective is important to the preservation of old-growth forests, because particular stands of this ecosystem cannot be preserved forever, since they are inevitably subject to the effects of unpredictable, catastrophic disturbances and/or environmental changes. However, if the ecological reserve is large enough, these stand-level dynamics can be accommodated, because a continuum of stands within the natural, old-growth successional dynamic can be sustained over the longer term.

Old-growth forests are a unique type of natural ecosystem, with great intrinsic value. If old-growth forests are to always be a component of Earth's natural biodiversity, then human societies will have to preserve them in large ecological reserves, even if this means that there will be some short-term economic losses.

See also Acid rain; Biodiversity; Climax (ecological); Forests; Forestry; Rain forest; Slash-and-burn agriculture; Sustainable development.

Further Reading:

Freedman, B. *Environmental Ecology, 2nd ed.* Academic Press, San Diego, CA., 1994.

Gillis, A.M. The new forestry. An ecosystem approach to land management. *BioScience*, 1990, 40: 558–562.

Hansen, A.J., Spies, T.A., Swanson, F.J., and Ohmann, J.L. Conserving biodiversity in managed forests. *BioScience*, 1991, 41: 382-392.

Maser, C. *The Redesigned Forest.* Stoddart Pub. Co., Toronto, Ont., 1990.

Wildlife and Vegetation of Unmanaged Douglas-fir Forests. U.S. Department of Agriculture, Forest Service, Gen. Tech. Rep. PNW–285. Pacific Northwest Forest and Range Experiment Station, Portland, OR., 1991.

Bill Freedman

Olefin see **Alkyl group**

Olive family

The Olives family is a family of flowering plants known to botanists as the Oleaceae. The Oleaceae have about 25 genera and over 500 species. Most species are native to temperate and tropical regions of the Northern Hemisphere. The best known trees of this family are olive and ash, while the most familiar shrubs are privet, lilac, and golden bell, all popular ornamental plants.

Characteristics of the olive family

The flowers of most species have radial symmetry, in that any longitudinal section through the center of the flower would divide it into two identical halves. The flowers of some species are bisexual, in which both male and female organs are present. The flowers of other species are unisexual, in that they have male organs or female organs, but not both. The flowers of most species have four sepals (the typically green, leaf–like parts which constitute the outermost whorl of flowers) and four petals (the typically pigmented, leaf–like parts which are interior to the sepals, but exterior to the sexual organs). Most species have flowers with two stamens (male organs) and one pistil (female organ). The pistils of most species contain four ovules, which develop into seeds after fertilization.

The fruit of some species, such as the ash, is a samara, or a dry, one–seeded fruit which is indehiscent (lacks a suture), and has wing–like structures to facilitate dispersal by the wind. The fruit of other species, such as the olive, is a drupe, or a fruit with a fleshy outer layer and a hard inner layer containing one seed. The fruit of other species is a berry, a fruit that is fleshy throughout and has one or more seeds.

Some species, such as ash, have seasonally deciduous leaves, which fall off in the autumn after they become non–functional. Other species, such as olive, have persistent leaves, in that there are always some leaves attached to the tree, even when they are no longer functional. In most species in this family, the leaves arise opposite to one another on the stem. The leaves of some species, such as lilac and golden bell, are simple in that they consist of a single blade. The leaves of other species, such as ashes, are compound, and are composed of many separate leaflets.

Important species

The olive tree (*Olea europea*) is the best known and most economically important species in this family. This Mediterranean native produces olives and olive oil. Italy and Greece are the major producers of these products. However, olive trees are now cultivated throughout the world, including southern California, South America, and Australia. Olive trees cannot withstand cold winter temperatures.

Olive trees probably originated in Greece, and were later introduced to Italy and elsewhere in the Mediterranean region. Olive oil was well known to the peoples of the Middle East several millennia ago. The Old Testament of the Bible mentions the use of olive oil as an ointment, food, and for burning in lamps. Olive trees are especially well–known in Italy and Greece, where olives and olive oil have been used in the cuisine for thousands of years.

The olive tree has persistent leaves, blooms in the spring, and produces mature fruits in the late autumn or winter. The unripe fruits are green and bitter, while ripe fruits are purple to black in color. The bitterness of the green, unripe fruits can be removed by soaking them in a solution which is alkaline (high pH) or is saturated with salt. Once the bitterness has been removed, green olives are typically pickled in a salt solution for later eating.

Olive oil is made from the ripe, purple fruits. Olive oil has a relatively high percentage of unsaturated fatty acids, and is purportedly healthier than many other vegetable oils. It consists of about 80% oleic acid and 10% palmitic acid. "Extra virgin" olive oil is considered the best, and is prepared by extraction without the use of chemical solvents. "Pure" olive oil is extracted with the use of chemical solvents, and this process removes some of the color and flavor that is so characteristic of extra virgin olive oil.

Olive trees are slow-growing, but can live one thousand years or more. The trunks of mature trees have a very characteristic, gnarled appearance. Olive trees are not used as timber, but the wood has a fine grain and has been traditionally used to make hand–carved implements.

There are about 65 trees and shrubs in the ash (*fraxinus*) genus. All species are native to the Northern Hemisphere, and about 18 are native to North America. The leaves of all ash species arise opposite to one another on the stem, and with one exception (*Fraxinus anomala*), are pinnately compound, in that they consist of numerous small leaflets which arise from a central stalk.

The white ash (*Fraxinus americana*) is the tallest and most important of the American ashes. It grows throughout the angiosperm forests of eastern North America, and has a characteristic long, straight trunk and leaves which turn yellow or purple in the autumn. The wood of white ash is flexible and light, and is used to make baseball bats and furniture.

Lilac (*Syringa vulgare*) is native to southeastern Europe, but is widely cultivated throughout the United States and much of southern Canada as an ornamental, flowering shrub. Lilac shrubs produce large, branched inflorescences, referred to as panicles, in early spring. The flowers are purple or white, and have a characteristic aroma. Lilac has escaped form cultivation and become naturalized in parts of temperate North America. This naturalized, European native is the state flower of New Hampshire.

KEY TERMS

Bisexual—Refers to a flower with functional male and female organs.

Drupe—A fruit which has a fleshy outer layer, and a hard inner layer which encloses a single seed.

Pistil—The female reproductive organ of a flower, which contains ovules that develop into seeds after fertilization by pollen.

Sepal—The external whorl of a flower, which is typically leaf–like and green.

Stamen—The male reproductive organ of a flower, which produces pollen.

Unisexual—Refers to a flower which has male or female organs, but not both.

Unsaturated—Refers to an organic molecule which has at least one double or triple bond between carbon atoms.

Privet (*Ligustrum vulgare*) is also a shrub native to Europe. It can take substantial abuse, and so has become the most widely planted hedge plant in the United States. Privet produces flowers in May, and blue–black berries in summer which are eaten by birds. Birds disperse the seeds within the berries, and have thereby naturalized privet through much of the United States.

Golden bell (*Forsythia viridissima* and several other species of *Forsythia*) is a cultivated shrub which is native to China. Golden bell has twigs which are yellow–brown in color, and it produces brilliant, yellow flowers in early spring. Like privet, it is a popular hedge plant.

Further Reading:

Audubon Society and Staff. *Familiar Trees of North America: Eastern Region.* New York: Knopf, 1987.
Audubon Society and Staff. *Familiar Trees of North America: Western Region.* New York: Knopf, 1987.
Heywood, V.H. *Flowering Plants of the World.* Oxford University Press, 1993.
Johnson, H. *Encyclopedia of Trees.* Random House, 1990.

Peter A. Ensminger

Omnivore

An omnivore is any animal that is a generalist feeder, consuming a wide variety of foods that can include both animal and plant matter. Because they have attributes of both carnivores and herbivores, omnivores have relatively diverse linkages within ecological food webs.

Some examples of omnivorous animals are pig and bear, both of which will eat a remarkably wide range of plant and animal products. Most wild populations of these animals are primarily herbivorous, eating a wide variety of plant products, depending on their seasonal and geographic availability. However, both of these animals are also opportunistic meat eaters. If meat can be readily attained through predation or scavenging, these animals will eagerly avail themselves of this food.

Interestingly, humans are the most omnivorous of all animals. Only a limited number of plant and animals species, about 100, are actually consumed by humans in relatively large quantities. However, products of additional thousands of plant and animal species are consumed as victuals by humans, as long as the food is nutritious and there is access to the resource. In a few cases, humans even consume some foods that are potentially extremely poisonous, usually for cultural reasons, or because in small amounts the toxin may act as a hallucinogen. One extreme case is the consumption by Japanese (especially men) of flesh of a puffer fish known as fugu (*Spheroides rubripes*) in sushi restaurants. This meal is prepared with exquisite care by highly skilled chefs, who must excise a small gland containing an extremely toxic biochemical called saxitoxin. If this preparation is not accomplished properly, then the meal will be quickly lethal to the patron. Because of this danger, the eating of fugu is considered to be an act of great bravado, for which the consumer gains respect in the eyes of his peers. This deliberate exposure to such an extraordinarily toxic food is symptomatic of the remarkable omnivory displayed by humans.

See also Carnivore; Food chain/web; Herbivore.

Bill Freedman

Onager see **Asses**

One–to–one correspondence

In mathematics, one–to–one correspondence refers to a situation in which the members of one set (call it A) can be evenly matched with the members of a second set (call it B). Evenly matched means that each member of A is paired with one and only one member of B, each member of B is paired with one and only one member of A, and none of the members from either set are left unpaired. The result is that every member of A is paired with exactly one member of B, and every member of B is paired with exactly one member of A. In terms of ordered pairs (a,b), where a is a member of A and b is a member of B, no two ordered pairs created by this matching process have the same first element and no two have the same second element. When this type of matching can be shown to exist, mathematicians say that "a one–to–one correspondence exists between the sets A and B."

Any two sets for which a one–to–one correspondence exists have the same cardinality, that is they have the same number of members. On the other hand, a one–to–one correspondence can be shown to exist between any two sets that have the same cardinality, as can easily be seen for finite sets (sets with a specific number of members). For example, given the sets A = {1,2,3,4,5} and B = {2,4,6,8,10} a one–to–one correspondence can be established by associating the first members of each set, then the second members, then the third, and so on until each member of A is associated with a member of B. Since the two sets have the same number of members no member of either set will be left unpaired. In addition, because the two sets have the same number of members, there is no need to pair one member of A with two different members of B, or vice versa. Thus, a one–to–one correspondence exists. Another method of establishing a one–to–one correspondence between A and B is to define a one–to–one function. For example, using the same sets A and B, the function that associates each member of A with a member in B that is twice as big is such a function. This type of function is called a one–to–one function because it is reversible. In mathematical terminology, its inverse is also a function. It could just as well be defined so it maps each member of B onto a unique member of A by associating with each member of B that member of A that is half its value.

One–to–one functions are particularly useful in determining whether a one–to–one correspondence exists between infinite sets (sets with so many members that there is always another one). For example, let X be the set of all positive integers, X = {1,2,3,4,5,...}, (the three dots are intended to indicate that the listing goes on forever), and let Y be the set of odd positive integers Y = {1,3,5,7,9,...}. At first glance, it might be thought that the set of odd positive integers has half as many members as the set of all positive integers. However, every odd positive integer, call it y, can be associated with a unique positive integer, call it x, by the function

TABLE 1. ONE-TO-ONE CORRESPONDENCE

Positive Integers $\rightarrow$	Odd Positive Intergers $\rightarrow$	Positive Intergers
x	$y = 2x - 1$	$x = \dfrac{y+1}{2}$
1	1	1
2	3	2
3	5	3
4	7	4
5	9	5

$f(x) = y = (2x-1)$. On the other hand, every positive integer can be associated with a unique odd positive integer using the inverse function, namely $x=(1/2)(y+1)$ (see Table 1).

The function f is a one-to-one function and so a one-to-one correspondence exists between the set of positive integers and the set of odd positive integers, that is, there are just as many odd positive integers as there are positive integers all together. Carrying this notion further, the German mathematician, George Cantor, showed that it is also possible to find a one-to-one correspondence between the integers and the rational numbers (numbers that can be expressed as the ratio of two whole numbers), but that it is not possible to find a one-to-one correspondence between the integers and the real numbers (the real numbers are all of the integers plus all the decimals, both repeating and nonrepeating). In fact, he showed that there are orders of infinity, and invented the transfinite numbers to describe them.

Further Reading:

Buxton, Laurie. *Mathematics for Everyone*. New York: Schocken Books, 1985.
Gowar, Norman. *An Invitation to Mathematics*. New York: Oxford University Press, 1979.
McKeague, Charles P. *Intermediate Algebra*, 5th ed. Fort Worth: Saunders College Publishing, 1995.
Moore, A. W. "A Brief History of Infinity." *Scientific American* 272 (4): 112–116 (1995).
Silverman, Richard A. *Essential Calculus With Applications*. New York: Dover, 1989.

J. R. Maddocks

Onion see **Lily family**

Opah

Opahs (*Lampris guttatus*) *are* a bony ray–fin oceanic fish, with a world–wide distribution, in the Family Lamprididae of the Order Lampridiformes. Opahs are known only from specimens found stranded on the beach or captured accidentally by commercial travelers because these fish live at depths of 325–1,300 ft (100–400 m). Little is known of their life habits, but they are very fast swimmers and feed on fish and squid. Opahs reach sizes of up to 25 ft (7.8 m) long and weigh up tp 110 lbs (50 kg). Their body is compressed from side to side but deep from back to belly, with fins that are more or less sickle–shaped. The color of opahs is remarkably brilliant: they have bright red fins, a deep blue back, shading to pinkish on the belly, with round milk–white spots on the sides. Opahs are also known as moonfish.

Ophioroids see **Brittle star**

Opiate see **Narcotic**

Opossums

The American or common opossum (*Didelphis marsupialis*) is the only member of the order Marsupialia to occur naturally in North America. The American opossum occurs from southern Ontario through to most of South America. The only other member of its genus is *D. azarae*, which occurs through much of South America. However, other genera and species of the family Didelphidae, the New World Opossums, occur in Central and South America.

The usual habitat of both species of opossums is brushy or forested, ranging from an open to a full canopy. However, the common opossum will also feed in fields and other open habitats, as long as they are close to trees. Opossums are solitary animals, coming together only to mate. Northern animals remain active throughout the winter, although they often suffer from frost–bite, which can cause them to lose parts of their ears and the tips of their tail.

Opossums can have a body length as great as 18 in (50 cm), plus a tail of up to 21 in (54 cm). Their pelage consists of a dense underfur, which is variably colored black, brown, red, grey, or white, with scattered, white–tipped guard hairs. The head is light–colored, often with three dark lines extending backward from the snout. The tail is almost naked and prehensile.

Female opossums have a deep, fur–lined, abdominal pouch (or marsupium), usually containing 13 nipples. The young are born in an early stage of development. Although recently born young are tiny (approximately bee–sized) and virtually helpless, they are able to use their partially developed forelegs to slowly crawl to their mother's pouch, where they suckle and grow until they can move about independently of their parent. As many as 25 babies may be born, but no more than 13 can be accommodated by the number of teats in the marsupium, and usually only about seven to eight babies survive to the point where they can leave the pouch. The weaned young are often carried on their mother's back for some time, until they become fully independent.

Opossums can climb well, and are both terrestrial and arboreal in their habits. They usually spend the day denning in a cavity in rocks, a hollow log, or some other shelter, emerging at night to feed. Opossums are omnivorous in their diet, feeding on a wide range of plant and animal matter, including insects, mice, birds, and frogs that they hunt, as well as carrion.

When struck by a human or other potential predator, a common opossum will often roll onto its back or side and feign death, a behavior known as "playing possum." This may be an involuntary act, possibly induced by a shock–like reaction, and is usually performed with a gaping mouth, a lolling tongue, and closed eyes. This might seem to be a dangerous response to a potentially lethal confrontation, but many predators will not attack a seemingly dead animal.

The fur of opossums killed in the early winter is dense and is sought after by hunters. The common opossum is also eaten in some places, with roasted "possum and taters" considered a delicacy in parts of the southern United States. Opossums can be trapped or hunted at night with hounds and lights. Fortunately, the opossum is quite fecund and has managed to maintain its abundance in spite of rather intense hunting pressures. In fact, the opossum has even expanded its range considerably to the north during the past century.

See also Marsupials; Phalangers.

Bill Freedman

Opportunistic species

Opportunistic species of animals or plants are adapted to exploit newly available habitats or resources and are typically found in unpredictable, transient, and variable environments. For example, clear–cut forests create well–lit open areas which are colonized rapidly by the windbone seeds of opportunistic species of plants, many of which are regarded as weeds by farmers and gardners. Besides producing easily dispersed seeds, opportunistic species characteristically have a rapid growth rate, quickly establishing themselves in the new environment. Opportunistic species also have other characteristics: they reproduce early, have a small body size, and produce large numbers of seeds or offspring, a strategy known to ecologists as r–selection. Opportunistic species are most prominent during the early stages of ecological succession, when species that are more competitive in the long run are not very abundant. Opportunistic species have a great ability to alter their growth rate, physiology, or behavior to better suit the environmental conditions with which they are faced. Usually, this opportunistic response is accomplished without changes in the genotype, in which case it is known as phenotypic plasticity.

Environmental resources and opportunities

To be successful in the evolutionary sense, all organisms must grow and reproduce successfully, and to accomplish these functions they have particular requirements for environmental resources. Plants, for example, need access to an appropriate supply of sunlight, water, and inorganic nutrients such as carbon dioxide, nitrate, phosphate, calcium, and about 20 other chemicals. Similarly, animals require a suitable habitat, replete with the appropriate foods to eat and places for shelter to complete their life cycle. The requirements of organisms for resources must be satisfied within an appropriate ecological context, for example, in terms of the temperature regime, or the types of diseases, parasites, or predators that are present.

In some ecological situations, the availability of resources is highly constrained, and this poses severe limitations to the growth and reproduction of organisms. However, some species are genetically adapted to surviving under these sorts of difficult circumstances. Their adaptive syndrome is referred to as competitive if access to resources is limited by the presence of other species with similar needs (an interaction that ecologists refer to as competition). In other cases, the availability of resources may be lacking because of infertile soil, excessively cold or hot temperatures, pollution, or some other type of non–living stressor, in which case the adaptive syndrome is called stress tolerant.

In contrast, certain ecological situations are characterized by a relatively great abundance of resources. This is often the circumstance, for example, after a mature, highly competitive plant community, growing on a fertile site, is subject to a severe disturbance. Because the disturbance kills many mature plants, the biological demand for resources is greatly decreased, so that competition is no longer very important and resources are freely available. The adaptive syndrome exhibited by species that take advantage of this temporary circumstance is referred to as ruderal. Ruderal species are highly opportunistic, in that they are adapted to taking advantage of temporary conditions of a great availability of resources.

The broad characteristics of ruderal species can be illustrated by considering the general features of plants that exhibit this strategy. Ruderal plants are usually herbaceous, small, short–lived, and highly fecund. Ruderal plants devote a large proportion of their productivity to the development of a great number of seeds, which may be long–lived in soil, or are readily dispersed over long distances. Moreover, ruderal plants have a relatively great potential for phenotypically plastic responses to variations of resource availability. Clearly, the ruderal strategy is highly opportunistic, and has evolved to allow rapid and vigorous colonizations of fertile habitats soon after disturbance, while competition is a weak interaction in the recovering ecosystem.

Opportunistic species in novel circumstances

Sometimes, species that are not particularly prominent in their native habitat become important pests when

KEY TERMS

. . . .

Genotype—The genetic constitution of an organism.

Phenotype —The actual, biological expression in an individual organism of its genetically based information, as influenced by environmental conditions.

Phenotypic plasticity—The variable degree of expression of genetically based biological potential, in terms of growth form, biochemistry, behavior, etc., depending on environmental circumstances.

Ruderal—Refers to a plant that occurs on recently disturbed sites, until the intensification of competition–related stresses associated with succession eliminates it from the community.

they are introduced by humans into a new habitat. In such cases, these organisms are opportunistically responding to a novel ecological circumstance that enhances their access to resources. This response is made possible because the species are no longer constrained by the specifically adapted herbivores, predators, or diseases that occur in their native habitat, a situation that is referred to as ecological release. Most of the important species of weeds in agriculture have opportunistically responded to favorable circumstances in the new environments to which they have been introduced, as have invasive animal pests, such as rats and mice.

Of course, there are limitations to the ecological success of opportunistic species. In stable environments, where disturbance is infrequent, there are few circumstances that are favorable to opportunistic species, and they will be rare in the biota. Such conditions are common, for example, in old–growth forests and other climax ecosystems. However, many human activities result in extensive disturbances of natural ecosystems. As a result, opportunistic species are faring much better today than they did prior to the global environmental changes that are being caused by humans.

See also Adaptation; Stress, ecological; Succession.

Further Reading:

Barbour, M .G., J. H. Burk, and W. D. Pitts. *Terrestrial Plant Ecology*. 2nd edition. Don Mills, Canada: Benjamin/Cummings, 1987.

Freedman, B. *Environmental Ecology*. 2nd edition. San Diego: Academic Press, 1994.

Bill Freedman

Optical data storage

Almost from the invention of the laser, researchers were considering the possibilities of optical data storage. Throughout the 1960s and 1970s, a number of companies were at work on optical data storage systems, held back in large part by the cost and performance level of available lasers. In 1982, Sony Corp. revolutionized the music industry with the introduction of the compact disc (CD). CD–ROM systems for computers quickly followed, expanding the capability of desktop computing. More recently, writable optical disks have been developed, and considerable ground has been gained in holographic data storage technology.

Optical data storage refers to any method of storing data using light. The most common method is optical disk, which offers a data density considerably higher than magnetic methods. There are three types of optical disks: ROM, or read only memory; WORM, or write once, read many times; and MO, or magneto optical disk, a disk which, like magnetic computer disks, can be repeatedly written on and repeatedly erased.

For ROM systems, information is recorded on a master disk by pulsed laser. The laser beam is varied or modulated, such that digital data is encoded in the pulses. The beam heats up and distorts a thermally sensitive layer on the master disk, recording a bit of data as a depression in the surface. The depressions are submicron in size, separated by grooves spaced 1.6 microns apart.

Once the master disk is created, copies can be produced quickly and cheaply (the cost of a CD is estimated at less than $1). Injection molded polycarbonate replicas made from the master disk are coated with aluminum to increase reflectivity, then sealed in protective plastic.

The data retrieval system consists of a low power (3 mW), continuous wave diode laser, a series of optics to focus and circularize the beam before it reaches the CD, more optics to check that the beam is reading the proper area of CD at the correct location, and a detector to decode the signal. The disk spins, and the read head containing the laser and optics scans across it. The beam is reflected from the depressions on the optical disk, and the detector reads variations in the intensity and polarization of the light. These variations are decoded and converted to an electrical signal. In the case of a music CD, the electrical signal is transmitted to a speaker, the speaker diaphragm vibrates, and the result is music.

CDs are capable of carrying prodigious amounts of information, over 600 megabytes on a single disk. In addition to the music and film formats, CD–ROMs bring extensive databases to the desktop computer, and the average user's fingertips. World atlases, encyclopedias, and comprehensive periodical indexes are just a few of the CD–ROM products available.

Write once, read many, or WORM systems, are a bit more complicated than ROM systems. Though they have essentially the same optical system for data retrieval, for writing operations they require a more powerful laser and a modified storage disk.

Writable WORM disks are made of different material than consumer CD–ROMs. Typically, a thermally sensitive film is sandwiched between layers of glass or plastic. During the write phase, digital data is converted into an optical signal by varying or modulating a laser beam. The laser puts out about 30 mW of power, since it has to be capable of distorting the write layer. The tightly focused, modulated beam shines through the transparent glass or plastic and hits the thermally sensitive layer, heating it to create distortions that represent bits of data. These distortions are usually either bumps, depressions, or variations in opacity in the material that will make changes in the reflectivity of the surface. To read the disk, the laser/read assembly is scanned over the surface at lower power, and a detector reads and decodes variations in the surface reflectivity to obtain the original signal.

Once recorded, the data cannot be rewritten, and short of destruction of the disk, cannot be erased. WORM disks are being used for archival purposes or in documentation–intensive applications such as insurance, banking, or government.

Magneto–optical disks (MODs) are rewritable, and operate differently than either ROM or WORM disks. Data is not recorded as distortions of a thermally sensitive layer within the disk. Rather, it is written using combined magnetic and optical techniques. Digital data consisting of 1s and 0s is encoded in the optical signal from the laser in the usual manner. Unlike the ROM or WORM disks, however, the MOD write layer is magnetically sensitive.

On a microscopic level, magnetic materials are made up of tiny regions known as domains. Each domain acts like a small magnet. In non–magnetic material, the magnetic poles of the domains are randomly aligned. In magnetic material, the poles tend to align in the same direction, creating the macroscopic magnetic poles and field of the magnet. In paramagnetic material, the poles of the domains are flexible, and

can be preferentially aligned by an external magnet so that the material becomes magnetic.

Returning to the MOD system, the modulated laser beam heats up a small spot of the magnetic write layer to its Curie temperature, the temperature at which magnetic material can become paramagnetic. The magnetic pole of the domain is then aligned by an external magnet located on the read/write head. As soon as the laser moves on, the spot cools down and the domain remains preferentially aligned. To record a binary "1," the magnetic pole of the external magnet is oriented upward, forcing the domain's north pole to point upward. To write a binary "0," the external magnet's magnetic field is reversed, and the domain's north pole points downward.

The MOD is erased by orienting the external magnet's north pole downward and scanning the laser across the disk with uniform beam intensity, recording 0's over the whole disk. The MOD is read by scanning a laser over the spinning disk and evaluating the effect of the magnetic pole orientations on the reflected light.

Other avenues of rewritable disk technology have been developed. One type uses differences in the reflectivity of a material in its crystalline and amorphous, or non–crystalline state, to record data. The laser heats up a tiny bit of surface and the material there crystallizes, standing for a binary "1." Bits of surface still in the amorphous state stand for a binary "0." To read, the laser is scanned over the surface, and the detector decodes the signal from variations in the reflectivity. To erase, the laser is scanned in a continuous wave, to heat the material up just enough to return to the amorphous "0" state.

The optical data storage capacity curve is going up exponentially, and experts predict storage capabilities of 2.6 gigabytes within a year. Optical disk data density is driven by the minimum spot size of the tightly focused laser beam writing the data. The spot size is directly proportional to the wavelength of the laser. The shorter the wavelength, the smaller the spot, and the more data that can fit on the disk. Diode lasers currently used in optical disk systems emit in the red region of the spectrum (780 nm). Devices that emit in the green (532 nm) and the blue regions have been developed. Researchers are working to increase lifetime, output power, and reliability to be on a par with the currently used CD lasers. Those improvements will follow shortly, and it is simply a matter of time before even higher density optical disks are available.

The biggest advantage of optical data storage is the quantity of data that can be recorded. With MODs, desktop computers can have the storage capabilities of a mainframe. There are at present, however, some draw-

Higgins, Thomas V. "Technologies Merge to Create High–Density Data Storage." *Laser Focus World* (August 1993): 57–65.

Lenth, Bill. "Optical Storage: A Growing Mass Market for Lasers." *Laser Focus World* (December 1994): 87–91.

Kristin Lewotsky

Optical emission spectrometry see **Spectroscopy**

Optic nerve see **Eye; Vision**

Orange tree see **Citrus trees**

KEY TERMS

Curie Temperature—The temperature at which magnetic domains become randomized.

Digital data—Data that is encoded in binary form, as a series of 1s and 0s.

Magnetic domain—Microscopic regions of a magnetic material which behave as miniature magnets and control the material's behavior. If they are preferentially oriented, the material is magnetic; if they are randomly oriented, the material is non–magnetic.

Modulation—Variation, especially of optical signals.

Paramagnetic—A material whose magnetic domains are random, and can be oriented by an external magnetic field.

backs to the technology. Optical disk systems are significantly slower than conventional magnetic storage systems. Researchers are presently working on ways to consolidate and lighten the somewhat cumbersome optical systems required for read/write operations, allowing quicker operation.

Other methods of optical data storage are being explored, particularly holographic data storage. A hologram is simply an image recorded using optical phase information that makes it appear three–dimensional. A pattern of 1s and 0s can be recorded as easily as a picture, and more quickly than the corresponding number of 1s and 0s can be sequentially stored. Though groups have demonstrated the feasibility of this approach, the development of a rewritable material capable of recording holograms and offering long term storage stability is still in its early stages. Significant electronic development is required as well. For the time being, optical disk technology seems to be securely in the forefront.

Despite minor drawbacks, optical data techniques are the technology of the future for data storage. The potential for great strides forward in performance clearly exists. If progress continues at its present clip, magnetic drives may just go the way of vinyl records, and the year 2000 may find us all complaining about our puny 1 gigabyte hard drives.

See also: Hologram.

Further Reading:

Carlin, Donald B. "Optical Recording Drives Diode–Laser Technology." *Laser Focus World* (July 1992): 77–84.

Orang–utan

Orang–utans are large, long–haired, red apes (*Pongo pygmaeus*) that inhabit the lowland primary forests of Borneo and a small area in the mountainous region of northwest Sumatra. Formerly their distribution extended throughout the tropical rain forests of Asia, but these apes are now endangered primarily due to the clearing of these forests for timber and agriculture. Orang–utans are related to the other great apes of Africa—the gorilla and the chimpanzee. In the Malay language, orang–utan means "man of the woods."

Physical characteristics and habits

Orang–utans are sexually dimorphic, where the adult males are about twice the size of the females. The height of the male is about 54 in (137 cm), it weighs 130–200 lb (60–90 kg), and has an arm span of 7–8 ft (2.1–2.4 m). The long, coarse, typically reddish brown coat ranges from bright orange in juveniles to maroon or dark brown in some adults. The fur is especially long and shaggy over the shoulders where it may reach up to 18 in (45.7 cm). Orang–utans lack the strong brow ridges found in chimpanzees and gorillas and have a dish–shaped face which is hairless and usually black; young animals have pinkish skin on the muzzle and around the eyes. As the males mature, they develop deep throat pouches which extend under the arms and over the shoulder. Cheek flanges made of fatty tissue are present in both species. Male orang–utans from Borneo have huge cheek flaps, resembling horse blinders while males from Sumatra have long, oval faces with cheek flanges that extend sideways and a well–defined moustache and beard.

Orang–utans are largely arboreal and spend only 15% of their time on the ground. Although these apes tend to be slow moving and cautious, their very long arms and hooked hands and feet provide an effective means of moving rapidly through the forest. Orang–utans are versatile climbers, using modified overarm brachiation as a secondary mode of locomotion. Leaping or jumping over any distance is uncommon. Orang–utans use their flexible joints and powerful hands and feet to distribute their weight over several small branches, any one of which would not support them. When a gap in the canopy is encountered, they use their weight to swing trees back and forth until the distance can be bridged. Most orang–utans will occasionally descend from the trees to the forest floor, though the practice is most common among adult males. Once on the ground, orang–utans walk quadrupedally using a form of knuckle–walking with the weight carried on the bunched fists rather than on the knuckles. It is doubtful that these animals ever walk in a bipedal fashion because the extension of the hip promotes an accompanying extension of the knee, causing a stiff–legged gait. Also, the foot is in an inverted position and bears the weight of the body on the outer border of the foot.

At night, orang–utans sleep in nests high above the ground; the structure of the forest dictates whether they choose higher or lower supports. Large nests are usually located below small ones; however, most nests are built in the middle level of the forest. Orang–utans show a preference for nesting in locations that afford good visibility, and they change nest location each night. During the day, less elaborate nests are built for rest and protection against heavy rainfall. Just as humans use umbrellas, orang–utans have been observed holding leafy branches over their heads to shield them from rain.

Diet

Orang–utans spend an average of one–third of their day foraging for food. They exhibit a bimodal feeding strategy, meaning they feed most actively in the morning and late afternoon, and rest during the middle of the day. Orang–utans prefer to eat fruits just before ripening, especially the tropical spiny–skinned, pulpy durian. As much as 60% of all food eaten is fruit. Other items of the diet include young leaves, shoots, lianas, bark, flowers, wood pith, mineral–rich soil, and small amounts of ants, bees, honey, and wasp galls. Small foods, such as berries and leaf shoots, are picked directly with their lips or fingers. Large fruits are held in the hands. Water is not obtained from streams, but from succulent vegetation and what can be collected from tree holes. Using a hand to dip the water, orang–utans drink droplets falling from their hairy wrists.

Communication

Orang–utans are the least vocal of the great apes, but they do maintain an effective communication system. Their most dramatic vocalization is the long call, given only by fully adult males. The call has been likened to the sound produced by large volumes of water roaring through steel pipes. The precise functions of the long call are not known. The call certainly serves to space out adult males in territories. It probably also serves several other functions, including a territorial warning to drive away other males, a sexual display to attract receptive females, and a social signal to inform the community of the location of the dominant male. Males show a tendency to call in bad weather, when another male is visible or calling, when close to sexually receptive females, and as part of the copulatory process. In both the Bornean and Sumatran forests, calls are audible up to 1.2 mi (2 km) from the source.

Other vocalizations include a variety of grunts, squeaks, moans, barks, and screams. Alarmed and agitated individuals produce "kissing" and "gluck-gluck-gluck" sounds that seem to indicate increasing levels of annoyance. These noises are often accompanied by aggressive physical displays such as shaking and breaking branches. Males use their huge size and other secondary sexual characteristics during intimidation displays. They inflate their throat sacs and elevate the hair on their shoulders and arms to make themselves look larger. When threatening, individuals open their mouths wide to show their teeth, and when fearful, they extend their prehensile lips.

Behavior and reproduction

Orang–utans are considerably more solitary than the other apes. Adult males interact with other orang–utans only to fight over responsive females and mate. The most common social units are with the mother and her offspring, subadult males, and various small groupings of adolescents of both sexes. Orang–utans are long lived (around 50 years) and have long intervals between births. Females mature at about 10 years and remain fertile until about 30 years of age. Although there is no visible evidence of estrus, when a female is pregnant, her swollen, white genitalia are readily observable. Gestation lasts 264 days. The young orang–utan is totally dependent on its mother for food, protection, and transportation during its first year. The young are weaned at about three years and begin to climb and forage for their own food at age four. At six or seven years old, orang–utans reach sexual maturity and establish their independence.

KEY TERMS

Arboreal—Living in trees.

Brachiate—To swing by the arms from branch to branch.

Dimorphic—Having two distinct forms.

Durian—The tree and fruit of *Durio zibethinus*, a plant cultivated in Indonesia, the Philippines, Malaysia, and Thailand. The fruit is 6–8 in (15–20 cm) in diameter and has a hard external husk covered with coarse spines. Inside, five oval compartments are filled with sweet, custard–like pulp.

Flange—A protruding rim, edge, rib, or collar.

Genitalia—The reproductive organs, especially the external sex organs.

Gestation—The period of carrying developing offspring in the uterus after conception; pregnancy.

Prehensile—Adapted for seizing or holding, especially by wrapping around an object.

Succulent—Having thick, fleshy leaves or stems that conserve moisture.

Conservation of orang–utans

For thousands of years, the orang–utan has been the victim of human exploitation. Early humans found it an abundant source of food and hunted it to the point of extinction in some areas. More recently in Borneo, it served as a substitute for humans in head hunting rites. In the 1960s, the population was further decimated by the collection of young animals for zoos and the pet trade. Despite legal protection by the governments of Malaysia and Indonesia, the capture of young orang–utans has not yet been completely halted.

Today the greatest threat to this species is habitat destruction and disruption. Rain forest is rapidly being logged and cleared for agricultural development and mining on Borneo, leaving only patches of suitable habitat. The orang–utan is very sensitive to human intrusion and, as a consequence, suffers a further reduction of an already low rate of reproduction. For this reason, research on how it responds to alteration of its habitat, especially selective logging, is necessary. Several protected reserves for this species have been designated in Sumatra and Borneo, but these reserves must be managed effectively and remaining habitat must be preserved for the orang–utan to escape extinction.

See also Apes; Primates.

Further Reading:

Book of Mammals, vol. 2. Washington, D.C.: National Geographic Society, 1981.

Burton, Maurice, ed. *The New Larousse Encyclopedia of Animal Life*. New York: Bonanza Books, 1984.

Cox, James A. *The Endangered Ones*. New York: Crown Publishers, 1975.

Galdikas, Biruté M. F. "My Life With Orangutans." *International Wildlife* (Mar–Apr 1990): 34–41.

Macdonald, David, ed. *The Encyclopedia of Mammals*. New York: Facts on File, 1984.

Napier, J. R., et. al. *The Natural History of the Primates*. Cambridge, MA: The MIT Press, 1985.

Romer, Alfred S. *The Vertebrate Story*. Chicago: The University of Chicago Press, 1959.

Tuttle, Russel H. *Apes Of The World: Their Social Behavior, Communication, Mentality, and Ecology*. New Jersey: Noyes Publications, 1986.

Betsy A. Leonard

Orbit

An orbit is the path followed by a celestial body moving in a gravitational field. When a single object, such as a planet, is moving freely in a gravitational field of a massive body, such as a star, the orbit is in the shape of a conic section, that is, elliptical, parabolic, or hyperbolic. Most orbits are elliptical.

The exact path and position of an object in space can be determined by taking into account seven orbital elements. These elements deal with the mathematical relationships between the two bodies. To determine the orbit of a celestial body, it must be observed and precise measurements taken at least three times. However, at least 20 precise observations, covering at least one full revolution, are needed for accurate orbital elements to be determined. If two bodies that move in elliptical orbits around their common center of mass (for example, the Sun and Jupiter) were alone in an otherwise empty universe, we would expect that their orbits would remain constant. However, the solar system consists of the Sun, eight major planets, and an enormous number of much smaller bodies all orbiting around the solar system's center of mass. The masses of these objects all influence the orbits of each other in small and large ways.

Perturbation theory

The Sun's gravitational attraction is the main force acting on each planet, but there are much weaker gravitational forces between the planets, which produce perturbations of their elliptical orbits; these make small changes in a planet's orbital elements with time. The planets which perturb the Earth's orbit most are Venus, Jupiter, and Saturn. These planets and the Sun also perturb the Moon's orbit around the Earth–Moon system's center of mass. The use of mathematical series for the orbital elements as functions of time can accurately describe perturbations of the orbits of solar system bodies for limited time intervals. For longer intervals, the series must be recalculated.

Today, astronomers use high–speed computers to figure orbits in multiple body systems such as the solar system. The computer can be programmed to make allowances for the important perturbations on all the orbits of the member bodies. Such calculations have now been made for the Sun and the major planets over time intervals of up to several tens of millions of years.

As accurately as these calculations can be made, however, the behavior of celestial bodies over long periods of time cannot always be determined. For example, the perturbation method has so far been unable to determine the stability either of the orbits of individual bodies or of the solar system as a whole for the estimated age of the solar system. Studies of the evolution of the Earth–Moon system indicate that the Moon's orbit may become unstable, which will make it possible for the Moon to escape into an independent orbit around the Sun. Recent astronomers have also used the theory of chaos to explain irregular orbits.

The orbits of artificial satellites of the Earth or other bodies with atmospheres whose orbits come close to their surfaces are very complicated. The orbits of these satellites are influenced by atmospheric drag, which tends to bring the satellite down into the lower atmosphere, where it is either vaporized by atmospheric friction or falls to the planet's surface. In addition, the shape of Earth and many other bodies is not perfectly spherical. The bulge that forms at the equator, due to the planet's spinning motion, causes a stronger gravitational attraction. When the satellite passes by the equator, it may be slowed enough to pull it to earth.

Types of orbits

A synchronous orbit around a celestial body is a nearly circular orbit in which the body's period of revolution equals its rotation period. This way, the same hemisphere of the satellite is always facing the object of its orbit. This orbit is called a geosynchronous orbit for the Earth where, with its sidereal rotation period of 23 hours 56 minutes 4 seconds, the geosynchronous orbit is 21,480 miles (35,800 km) above the equator on the

---

KEY TERMS

Drag—A frictional force on a moving body that is produced by a fluid (air, water, etc.) through which the body moves. Drag slows the body and dissipates its energy of motion (kinetic energy).

Earth's surface. A satellite in a synchronous orbit will seem to remain fixed above the same place on the body's equator. But perturbations will cause synchronous satellites to drift away from this fixed place above the body's equator. Thus, frequent corrections to their orbits are needed to keep geosynchronous satellites in their assigned places. They are very useful for communications and making global meteorological observations. Hence, the vicinity of the geosynchronous orbit is now crowded with artificial satellites.

The Space Age has greatly increased the importance of hyperbolic orbits. The orbits of spacecraft flybys past planets, their satellites, and other solar system bodies are hyperbolae. Other recent flybys have been made past Comet Halley in March 1986 by three spacecraft, and past the asteroids 951 Gaspra in October 1991 and 243 Ida in August 1993; both flybys were made by the Galileo spacecraft enroute to Jupiter. Although accurate masses could not be found for these small bodies from the hyperbolic flyby orbits, all of them were extensively imaged.

Orbits of double and multiple stars

The orbits of double stars, where the sizes of the orbits have been determined, provide the only information we have about the masses of stars other than the Sun. Close double stars will become decidedly non–spherical because of tidal distortion and/or rapid rotation, which produces effects analogous to those described above for close artificial planetary satellites. Also, such stars often have gas streaming from their tidal and equatorial bulges, which can transfer mass from one star to the other, or can even eject it completely out of the system. Such effects are suspected to be present in close double stars where their period of revolution is found to be changing.

Multiple stars with three (triple) or more (multiple) members have very complicated orbits for their member stars, and require many perturbing effects to be considered. The investigation of the orbits of double and multiple stars is important for solving many problems in astrophysics, stellar structure, and stellar evolution.

See also Celestial mechanics; Geocentric theory; Heliocentric theory; Kepler's laws; Moon; Planet; Satellite; Solar system; Star; Sun.

Frederick West

Orbitals, atomic see **Quantum mechanics**

Orchid family

The many species of orchids comprise one of the largest families of flowering plants, the Orchidaceae, which contains about 1,000 genera, and about 20,000 species. Orchids have a worldwide distribution, and they occur in a wide variety of habitats, although their greatest diversity of species is in tropical rain forests. The most species–rich genera of orchids are *Dendrobium* and *Bulbophyllus*, each with about 1,500 species, and *Pleurothallis*, with 1,000 species.

Species of orchids can have very unusual morphological traits and ecological relationships, especially with their species of pollinating insects. For these reasons, along with the great beauty of their flowers, orchids hold a special place in the hearts of botanists, ecologists, and horticulturalists. However, appreciation of the intrinsic value of orchids extends far beyond the scientists who work with these plants—few people fail to be enthralled by the loveliness of orchid flowers.

Biology and ecology of orchids

Orchids are herbaceous perennials, meaning their above–ground tissues die back periodically, for example, at the end of the growing season. However, the plants are long–lived, and are perennated by their underground rhizome or corm, from which new shoots emerge.

Orchids exploit two broad types of habitats—terrestrial and epiphytic. Terrestrial orchids have their perennating tissues in the surface substrate of the ground, such as the soil or organic floor of a forest, or the surface sediment or peat of a wet meadow. In contrast, epiphytic orchids use taller plants as a platform upon which to grow within the canopy. Epiphytic orchids do not obtain any of their moisture or nutrients from their host—they only use the tree as a physical substrate upon which to grow, perched on a branch, or as a climbing plant, similar to a vine.

Orchid leaves are usually arranged alternately on their stem, or are basal around the flowering stalk. In a few species the leaves are reduced to small scales, and photosynthesis is mostly carried out by the green stem. Orchid leaves are simple, have non–toothed margins, are usually strap–shaped or linear, have a longitudinally parallel venation, and sheath to their base (that is, they lack a petiole).

The flowers of orchids are strongly zygomorphic, and are perfect, containing both female and male reproductive structures. The flowers may be borne singly or as a group (or inflorescence). There are three sepals which may be green or colorful and petal–like, and there are three petals. The two lateral petals are known as wings and are mirror images of each other, while the central petal is highly modified as a so–called lip (or labellum). The lip generally serves as a landing platform for pollinating insects. The lip commonly has a nectar–bearing sac or spur, which is usually brightly colored and pleasantly odorous and is intended to attract insect pollinators. There are one or two stamens, which are largely united with the stigma and style to develop a composite structure, known as the column. The anthers produce one to eight large pollen masses, known as pollinia. The pistil is composed of three united carpels and contains numerous ovules, usually numbering in the thousands. During its development, the flower of many orchids twists 180° on its supporting stalk, so that the mature flower is actually presented upside–down. The seeds of orchids are very numerous within the ripe capsule. The seeds are tiny and dust–like, contain almost no energy reserves, and are dispersed by the wind.

Pollination is usually by an insect, which is attracted by a combination of the bright color of the flower, a fragrant aroma, and nectar. Some species of orchids have tightly co–evolved with one or a few species of pollinating insects, so now the two species are highly dependent on each other. In the case of the bee orchid (*Ophrys apifera*, and related species of *Ophrys*), the floral structure and coloration mimics the shape and color of the female of their pollinating species of wasp or bee. In addition, the orchid produces chemicals that closely mimic the sex–pheromones of their pollinator wasp and therefore further help to attract the males. The orchid becomes pollinated when the male wasp is tricked and attempts to copulate with the orchid flowers.

Almost all species of orchids develop a mutualistic symbiosis (that is, a mutually beneficial relationship) with a fungus, an alliance that is known as a mycorrhiza. This relationship is beneficial to the fungus, which gains access to some of the energy fixed by the orchid during photosynthesis. The mycorrhiza is extremely important to the orchid, because it greatly enhances the rate at which nutrients, especially phosphate, can be extracted from the environment. The mycorrhiza may also allow the orchid to utilize the energy and nutrition of organic matter in its growth substrate, which can be absorbed by the mycorrhizal fungus. Orchid seeds are very tiny and have few energy reserves, and their seedlings rarely survive for long if they do not develop a mycorrhiza soon after germination.

In a few specialized cases, saprophytic species of orchids rely entirely on their mycorrhizal fungus to provide them with organic nutrition, which is obtained by tapping into the decomposer food web of the forest floor. In these cases, the saprophytic orchid can be considered to be parasitic on its mycorrhizal fungus.

Native orchids in North America

Hundreds of species of orchids are native to natural habitats of North America. A few of the more prominent species are described below.

Species of lady–slipper orchids grow on the surface of the ground, in open forests, prairies, and wetlands such as bogs and fens. Lady–slipper orchids have one or several large, showy flowers. The lip is greatly inflated (this is the "lady's slipper"), with the margins of its orifice inrolled. A nectar–seeking, pollinating insect, usually a bee, passes through this orifice into the chamber of the lip, and is then drawn to the vicinity of the stigmatic surface by nectar, odor, and a visual trail of dots known as nectar guides. If the insect is carrying a pollinium from another lady–slipper flower, it is deposited to the receptive stigmatic surface, and then another pollinium is picked up, commonly on the forehead of the bee, which then exits through another hole. World–wide, there are about 50 species of lady–slipper orchids. The stemless lady–slipper (*Cypripedium acaule*) is a widespread species in North America, with solitary flowers that are a lovely pink and sometimes white. The yellow lady–slipper (*C. calceolus*) occurs in calcium–rich, moist forests and wetlands and has a solitary, bright–yellow flower. The showy lady–slipper (*C. reginae*) is relatively tall, reaching 15.8 in (40 cm) in height, and has one to three large, pink and white flowers. The white lady–slipper (*C. candidum*) occurs in calcium–rich wetlands and prairies and has a single white flower.

There are about 50 species of orchis orchids. These plants have large, showy flowers which are white or white and pink in color. North American species include the showy orchis (*Orchis spectabilis*), which occurs in rich woods in eastern North America, while the round–leaved orchis (*O. rotundifolia*) occurs in the west.

There are about 450 species of *Platanthera* orchis. These orchids have their relatively small but quite beautiful flowers arranged in a spiral fashion along an erect stalk. Some wide–ranging, white–flowered species in North America include the small woodland orchis (*Platanthera clavellata*) and the tall white orchis (*P. dilatata*). The yellow fringeless orchis (*P. integra*) has yellow flowers. The long–bracted orchis (*P. viridis*) and pale–green orchis (*P. flava*) have greenish flowers. The crested orchis (*P. cristata*) has orange flowers, and the purple fringed orchis (*P. psycodes*) has purple flowers.

The grass–pink orchid (*Calopogon pulchellus*) is a pink–flowered species that occurs widely in acidic wetlands, especially bogs. The dragon's–mouth or arethusa (*Arethusa bulbosa*) produces a single pink flower, and is also a species of acidic wetlands. The rose pogonia or snake–mouth (*Pogonia ophioglossoides*) also develops a single pink flower, as does the calypso or fairy–slipper (*Calypso bulbosa*).

Ladies' tresses develop their relatively small but lovely flowers in a spiral along an erect stem. Most species have white or white–yellow flowers. Some widespread examples include the nodding ladies' tresses (*Spiranthes cernua*) and slender ladies' tresses (*S. gracilis*).

Coral–roots are saprophytic orchids of forests. These plants lack chlorophyll and depend on nutrition available from the decomposer food web of the forest floor to supply their nutrition. These plants and their flowers are reddish purple in color. The most widespread species is the spotted coral–root (*Corallorhiza maculata*).

The helleborine (*Epipactus helleborine*) is a species native to Eurasia that has become widely naturalized in North America. This green–flowered orchid is a common weed in many cities.

Orchids and humans

Many people have a deep regard for the beauty of orchids, and wild plants are actively sought out for viewing during their flowering period. Hiking and other types of back–country explorations are an increasingly popular recreational activity. These out–of–doors ventures are greatly enhanced by the presence of flowering orchids, in much the same way that sightings of charismatic animals, such as bears, deer, and eagles, can make a day very special.

Because orchids are so renowned for the beauty of their flowers, they are commonly cultivated in greenhouses, homes, and, in warm and humid climates, in outdoor gardens. The most popular genera of horticultural orchids are *Catteleya*, *Cymbidium*, *Dendrobium*, *Epidendrum*, and *Vanda*, all of which are species native to tropical forests.

In addition to cultivating these beautiful plants for their aesthetic value in homes and gardens, orchids are also grown in great numbers for the cut–flower industry. These orchids are grown to provide flowers for pleasing displays in vases in hotels, offices, meetings, and other commercial places and functions, and to manufacture into corsages for social events such as weddings and formal dances.

Horticulturalists have invested tremendous amounts of time and money to develop reliable methods of breeding and propagating orchids. Although breeders have long been skilled at achieving hybrid crosses between species and even between genera of orchids, for some time they experienced few successes in establishing and growing seedlings after germinating the dust–like seeds of these plants. However, this horticultural barrier was substantially overcome by the discovery of the critical importance of the mycorrhizal relationships of orchids. Inoculation with an appropriate mycorrhizal fungus is now an integral component of the methodology used to cultivate orchid seedlings, and successful establishment of seedlings can now be routinely achieved. In addition, dependable methods have also been worked out for the propagation of orchids using tissue culture and other non–sexual means of establishing new plants.

Considering these great advances of orchid horticulture, it is highly regrettable that so many of these plants continue to be collected from wild natural habitats. Many species of wild orchids have become critically endangered by excessive, often illegal collection of plants for the horticultural trade. Unfortunately, orchid rustling can be a rather profitable endeavor, especially for rare species, which are enthusiastically sought after by unscrupulous aficionados and collectors of these charismatic plants. Considering the endangered status of so many species of orchids, it is important that their wild populations be left undisturbed in their natural habitats and horticulture be limited to the propagation of plants that are already in cultivation.

The only food obtained from the orchid family is a flavoring substance known as vanilla, which is extracted from the ripe, seed–bearing fruits, or "beans," of the vanilla orchid (*Vanilla fragrans*), a climbing orchid native to the West Indies and Mexico. Vanilla was used by the Aztecs as a flavoring for chocolate. Today, vanilla is mostly obtained from plants grown in plantations, but this relatively expensive natural product is increasingly

---

KEY TERMS

Co–evolution—This is the intrinsically linked evolution of two or more species, as a result of a close ecological relationship such as pollination, predation, herbivory, or mutualism.

Epiphyte—A non–parasitic plant that grows on another plant.

Mutualism—An intimate relationship between two or more organisms that is beneficial to both.

Saprophyte—In the botanical sense, this is a plant that lacks chlorophyll and depends on its mycorrhizal fungus to tap into energy available in the decomposer food web of the forest floor.

Perfect—In the botanical sense, this refers to flowers that are bisexual, containing both male and female reproductive parts.

Symbiosis—A biological relationship, in which different species interact in some meaningful way.

Zygomorphic (or irregular)—This refers to flowers that are bilaterally symmetric, that is, a vertical, longitudinal section of the flower yields two sections that are mirror images of each other.

---

being replaced by a synthetic vanilla, manufactured from a substance obtained from oil of cloves.

See also Mycorrhiza.

Further Reading:

Arditti, J. *Fundamentals of Orchid Biology*. New York: Wiley, 1992.

Correll, D. *Native Orchids of North America: North of Mexico*. Stanford, CA: Stanford University Press, 1950.

Cullen, J., ed. *The Orchid Book. A Guide to the Identification of Cultivated Orchid Species*. Cambridge, U.K: Cambridge University Press, 1992.

Dressler, R. L. *The Orchids. Natural History and Classification*. Cambridge, MA: Harvard University Press, 1990.

Luer, C. A. *The Native Orchids of the United States and Canada, Excluding Florida*. New York: New York Botanical Garden, 1975.

Bill Freedman

TABLE 1. ORDINAL NUMBERS

Cardinal	Ordinal	Ordinal symbol
one	first	1st
two	second	2nd or 2d
three	third	3rd or 3d
four	fourth	4th
...	...	...
twenty	twentieth	20th
twenty-one	twenty-first	21st
...	...	...
one hundred	one hundredth	100th
one hundred one	one hundred first	101st
...	...	...

Ordinal number

The number 8 can be used in three ways: to tell "how many," to tell "where" in a ranking, and to name someone or something. The girl with the number 8 on her baseball uniform, who is 8th in the batting order, playing on a team that scores 8 runs, is using the same number in each of these ways. When she is 8th in the batting order, she is using the number as an ordinal number. An ordinal number is one which is used to indicate where in an ordered list someone or something occurs. A number used to tell how many is a "cardinal number." A number which is used to name something is neither a cardinal nor an ordinal number.

The ordinal name of a number differs somewhat from the cardinal name. In most instances the cardinal name can be converted into the ordinal name by adding "th." Thus the cardinal number one thousand becomes the ordinal number one thousandth; four becomes fourth; and so on. In the case of 1, 2, and 3, however completely different names are used:

The clear distinction between cardinal and ordinal forms of 1 and 2 arises from the way in which the events or things they describe differ. A runner who comes in first comes in ahead of anyone else, and that is what is most notable about the event, not that one runner has crossed the line. Likewise, someone coming in second "follows," and that, too, is something which can be noted without consciously counting the two runners. By the time the third runner comes along, counting becomes a helpful if not necessary aid in determining his or her position. The similarity between "three" and "third" (and the Latin roots from which they come) reflects this. Beyond 3, counting is almost essential, and the cardinal and ordinal forms are almost the same.

The ordinal name of a number is used in some instances where no ranking is intended or where the ranking is vestigial. The names given to the denominators of common fractions are ordinal names although they signify the number of uniform parts into which each unit is cut. Thus three-fifths indicates that each unit has been divided into five equal parts, and the fraction represents three of them. However, when the fraction is written with numerals, 3/5, both numerator and denominator are written in the cardinal form.

On the other hand there are times when the cardinal form of a number is used in an ordinal sense. In counting a group of objects one is putting them into one–to–one correspondence with the numbers 1, 2, 3, . . . in order. That is why the counting process works. Nevertheless one counts, "one, two, three, . . . ," not, "first, second, third . . . ."

Mathematicians who work with infinity have extended the concept of ordinal number to apply to certain classes of infinite numbers as well.

Ore

Ore is metalliferous rock that can be mined and processed at a profit. Although a broader definition includes nonmetallic rocks like rock salt and gypsum, most geologists classify these materials as industrial rocks and minerals.

History

Gold, silver, and copper artifacts left by prehistoric tribes and ancient civilizations attest to an interest in ores extending back to earliest times. Indeed, human history is divided into chalcolithic (copper–stone), bronze, iron, and atomic (uranium) ages based on the use of metals. In spite of this, little was known about the origin of ore until relatively recent times. Greek philosophers believed that metallic veins were living things with roots at depths and near–surface branches of different metals. Astrologers contended that gold, silver, iron, and mercury were formed under the influence of the Sun, Moon, Mars, and Mercury.

The first major break from this line of thinking came in 1556 with the publication of *De Re Metallica* by a German physician writing under the Latinized pen name of Georgius Agricola. Agricola's keen observations and naturalistic explanations marked a departure from the speculations of the ancients. His work remains a Renaissance Age classic, and Agricola is recognized as the father of economic geology.

Major advances in the study of ore deposits were made following the discovery and development of the many great metal–bearing veins in the western United States. An outgrowth of this period was a belief that ores are related to emanations given off by cooling igneous rocks. Although still considered a process of great significance, sedimentary and metamorphic processes are also recognized as important.

Formation of ore

A cubic mile of average rock contains approximately one trillion dollars worth of metal; yet no one is mining ordinary rock. The expense involved in processing ordinary rock is just too great. Fortunately, ore provides a less expensive option. Ore is formed by geologic processes which concentrate metals to tens or even thousands of times their average crustal abundances. Even then, a mine may not prove profitable unless a host of other geologic and nongeologic conditions are met.

Geologic factors include the deposit's size, depth, and amenability to processing. Small amounts of arsenic, for example, may poison the deal through the added expense of its removal. Higher amounts could mean a profitable arsenic mine. Profitability also ties the definition of ore to a host of nongeologic conditions including demand for the metal, geographic location of

the deposit, local labor conditions, local energy costs, governmental regulations, and many other economic factors.

Besides metals, ore commonly contains minerals of no particular value. Gold, for example, occurs in veins composed mostly of quartz. Although not of economic value, gangue minerals can yield valuable information on the origin of the deposit. Quartz, for example, reveals the temperature at which the ore formed, information that could be useful in directing the search for more gold along the vein. In addition, it is doubtful that the gold mineralization would have been noticed had not quartz caught the eye of a geologist who knew that precious metals sometimes occur in veins of quartz.

Ore deposits are relatively rare and tend to be distributed in an irregular fashion around the globe, but there is nothing unusual about the manner in which they form. They develop, in fact, from the same geologic processes that form ordinary igneous, sedimentary, and metamorphic rocks.

Igneous ore deposits

Igneous rocks form from the solidification of molten rock called magma. Magmas also contain dissolved gases, and partly solidified magmas contain mineral grains, some metalliferous. As magma solidifies, metallic elements usually remain widely dispersed, but igneous processes can cause their concentration. In rare cases, dense metallic minerals settle to form metal–rich layers at the bottom of the magma chamber. Metal may also separate from the magma if the sulfur content rises to the point where a sulfur–rich magma forms, separates, and sinks. Many metals are naturally attracted to sulfur, and they separate with the new magma. These processes are thought to have formed some chromium, nickel, and platinum–rich layers within igneous rock, but a related process forms a wider variety of ores.

Hydrothermal ore deposits

As magmas solidify, water and other gaseous constituents tend to be concentrated in the decreasing amount of molten rock. At some point these constituents may literally boil off, penetrate the surrounding rock, and condense to a hot, water–rich fluid. These igneous emanations are termed hydrothermal fluids. They are mobile and capable of dissolving metals from rock through which they pass. They tend to lose the metals they carry and form ore deposits when they encounter a favorable location. Favorable spots include rock fractures or openings along faults were hydrothermal fluids form veins. Other sites include sedimentary rocks like limestone or gypsum. Hydrothermal fluids can chemically react with these rocks to deposit ore. Alternatively, the hydrothermal fluid may simply mix with groundwater, causing the fluid's temperature and composition to change and ore to be deposited.

Hydrothermal fluids need not be igneous emanations, but groundwater heated by a nearby mass of magma. Hydrothermal waters may reach the surface in hot springs and geysers, as at Yellowstone National Park. Water sampling and drilling at locations similar to Yellowstone has shown that ore minerals are being deposited at depth.

Sedimentary ore deposits

Sedimentary processes form ore either through the selective removal of nonmetallic components or by concentration of metallic minerals. Rock at the earth's surface is subjected to weathering and leaching, the process that turns rock into soil. Aluminum resists being leached, and bauxite, the ore of aluminum, is actually an aluminum–rich soil. Bauxite forms in the humid tropics from intense and prolonged weathering of aluminum–bearing rocks. The concentration of heavy metallic grains forms placer ores. Placer gold, for example, accumulates along streams were currents are too weak to carry the heavy flakes of gold but strong enough to winnow away ordinary rock fragments. Some entire beds of marine sedimentary rocks contain enough metal to be considered ore. Examples include sedimentary beds rich in iron, manganese, and even lead, zinc, and copper. For some, hydrothermal fluids issued from submarine hot springs may have been involved. Others may simply have been deposited directly from metal–rich ocean water.

Metamorphic ore deposits

Metamorphic rocks are formed from heat and fluids near cooling magma (contact metamorphism) and by high temperatures and pressures deep with the crust (regional metamorphism). Although rock metamorphism certainly plays an important role in ore deposition, most of the resulting deposits are classified as hydrothermal. Relatively few ore deposits actually form in regionally metamorphosed rocks, but regional metamorphism drives water and other volatile components from the rock to form hydrothermal fluids responsible for ore deposits elsewhere. Contact metamorphic rocks contain a wide variety of ore deposits, but because hot fluids are commonly involved, they are generally considered to be part of the hydrothermal realm.

Mineral exploration

Mineral exploration has not always been a science. Since ancient times, prospectors relying heavily on luck and persistence have successfully discovered ore deposits of all descriptions. The ancient Romans worked every deposit of significance within the bounds of their empire, and it is said in Mexico that if gold and silver ore was at the surface, the Conquistadors found it. This testament to the Spanish obsession with precious metals has led some to conclude that nothing is left to discover, but that does not discourage the modern exploration geologists. They prefer to say that if ore was not at the surface, the Spanish did not find it. And so the search for metal continues in a scientific way with significant discoveries continuing to be made.

Successful mining companies use a systematic approach based upon knowledge gained from the study of previously discovered and developed ore deposits. It allows them to pinpoint likely areas for more intense exploration, and to find even hidden deposits from telltale surface geochemical and geophysical indications, or even through remote sensing from aircraft and satellites. The final exploratory phase involves actual drilling and sampling of the suspected deposit. Only then can the final assessment of economic factors be made and the exploration target classified either as ore or just interestingly mineralized rock, perhaps a future ore if economic conditions change.

Mining and processing

Mining removes ore in the least costly manner available. Surface pits are preferred, but the shape of many vein deposits require mining via underground shafts and tunnels. It is likely that mines of the future may simply inject chemicals or even bacteria to dissolve the metal of interest, allowing it to be pumped to the surface. Uranium mining is already done by chemical leaching. Once above ground, the ore is typically crushed, pulverized, and then upgraded during a process called beneficiation. Beneficiation separates metal and gangue into concentrates and waste material called tailings. The exact beneficiation technique depends on the type of ore being processed and it is usually done at the mine site to avoid transportation costs. Concentrates are generally sent to a smelter for further separation of metals.

Environmental considerations

Ore deposits supply much of the raw material on which modern industrial society is based. "If you can't grow it, it has to be mined," say mining geologists about

KEY TERMS

· ·

Gangue — The valueless component of ore, commonly quartz and calcite.

Hydrothermal fluid — Hot water–rich fluid capable of transporting metals in solution.

Igneous — Formed by solidification of molten rock called magma.

Industrial rocks and minerals — Rocks of economic value exclusive of metallic ores, mineral fuels, and gems.

Metamorphic — Formed by deformation and/or recrystallization of preexisting rocks.

Ore — Rock, usually metallic, that can be mined and processed at a profit.

Sedimentary — Formed by accumulation of sediment, mostly commonly by deposition from water.

extraction of metals from ever lower grade deposits. Industry, government, and universities are constantly developing new exploration techniques and more efficient recovery methods.

See also Industrial minerals; Metal; Minerals; Mining; Precious metals.

Further Reading:

Craig, James, David Vaughan, and Brian Skinner. *Resources of the Earth.* Englewood Cliffs, New Jersey: Prentice Hall, 1988.
Evans, Anthony. *Ore Geology and Industrial Minerals: An Introduction.* Boston: Blackwell Scientific Publications, 1993.
Kesler, Stephen. *Mineral Resources, Economics and the Environment.* New York: MacMillian College Publishing Company, Inc., 1994.

Eric R. Swanson

the materials consumers use. In addition, much of what is grown would not be possible without metals. Platinum, for example, is used as a catalyst in the chemical reaction that produces nitrogen for fertilizer, and metals are used in the production of pesticides, petroleum, and plows. But the winning of metal has not come without a cost. Mining has historically been a dangerous business and one prone to environmental problems. Mining, beneficiation, and smelting have led to the introduction of unacceptable levels of metals into lakes, streams, and ground water. It has injected dust into the atmosphere and spread metals and acid rain across the land. Subsurface mining has caused surface subsidence problems now plaguing some old mining towns. Mines are an economic necessity and actually occupy only slightly more United States land area than airports. A clean environment is also a necessity for health and quality of life. Although problems from mining's early days remain, modern mining methods are considerably safer and have a much less negative environmental impact. Pollution control during the mining and processing of ore, and land reclamation after mine closure are now being considered as one of the economic factors in determining if mineralized rock is indeed ore.

Future developments

Unlike products from the forest and farm, ores are a nonrenewable resource. The economic survival of industrial societies is linked to the discovery of new supplies of metals and to improved technology for the

Organ

An organ is a functional structure of multicellular organisms which consists of a group of several different tissues. Many multicellular organisms have individual cells grouped together into tissues, a group of many associated cells with similar function; tissues grouped together into organs, a group of tissues interacting so as to form a functional unit; and organs grouped together into organ systems, a group of closely interacting organs.

Animals, plants, and fungi often have many different organs whose different functions are integrated, enabling multicellular organisms to maintain, grow, and reproduce. The organization of cells into tissues and organs presumably leads to a higher level of physiological integration and efficiency. In general, plants and fungi have fewer organs than animals. Moreover, the bodies of plants and fungi are not always as easily divided into discrete organs as are the bodies of animals.

Some examples of organs in animals are the stomach, heart, and lungs. The structure and function of the stomach are described here as an example. The stomach is an expanded region of the digestive system which is connected to the esophagus at the anterior end, and to the small intestine at the posterior end. The stomach stores and breaks down food before it passes through the pyloric valve, a special valve at the posterior end, and then into the small intestine, another organ. Glands in the stomach wall secrete special chemicals and enzymes which are responsible for the partial digestion of food.

Some examples of organs in plants are the leaf, stem, and root. Leaves are among the most prominent plant organs, so they are described here. A leaf is an outgrowth of a stem. Leaves have three main physiological functions: photosynthesis, the biological conversion of light into chemical energy; transpiration, the evaporative movement of water out of the plant; and cellular respiration, the breakdown of foods and synthesis of high energy compounds.

Some examples of organs in fungi are haustoria (absorbing organs) and the sexual organs. The sexual organs of basidiomycete mushrooms are the best known fungal organs, so they are described here. In typical basidiomycete mushrooms, the fungal body develops into a morphologically complex organ called a basidiocarp. The basidiocarp is composed of sterile cells called psueudoparenchyma, and fertile club-shaped cells, called basidia. The basidia arise from the underside of the fleshy gills of a mushroom and each bears four haploid spores. These spores are shed from the gills, germinate, and eventually fuse with another sexually compatible individual.

See also Tissue.

Organic compound see **Compound, chemical**

Organic farming

Organic agriculture refers to systems in which crops are grown using natural methods of maintaining fertility of the soil, and methods of pest control other than the use of synthetic pesticides. Compared with conventional agriculture systems that intensively use manufactured fertilizers and pesticides, much smaller environmental costs and damages are associated with the practices of organic systems. However, yields tend to be smaller in organic agriculture than are obtained using more intensively managed systems. Overall, the balance of these considerations (that is, environmental damages and yield) suggest that compared with more intensive agriculture, organic agricultural systems are much more sustainable of soil quality, ecological integrity, and energy and material resources.

Organic methods of maintaining soil tilth and fertility

Soil fertility is a function of two major characteristics: the tilth of the soil, and the ability of the soil to supply essential nutrients.

Tilth refers to the physical structure of soil, and is strongly influenced by the concentration of humified organic matter. In soils with good tilth the ability to hold water is great, so that excessively rapid drainage is avoided and rainwater can be used more effectively by growing plants. The organic matter also helps to bind nutrients, thereby preventing them from being lost by leaching, and releasing them slowly for more efficient uptake by growing plants. In addition, soils with good tilth have their sand–sized and smaller inorganic particles loosely aggregated into lumpy structures, which improves soil aeration and eases the growth and penetration of plant roots.

Typically, soil tilth becomes badly degraded in conventional, intensively managed agricultural systems, because soil organic matter is progressively lost through plowing and decomposition, while inputs with plant debris are relatively small. Compaction by heavy vehicles also helps to degrade soil tilth. In contrast, a major goal of organic agriculture is to maintain or increase the concentration of organic matter in soil, using methods that are described below, in regard to nutrients.

Plants require more than 20 nutrients for proper growth. Some of these nutrients are obtained primarily from soils, especially compounds of nitrogen, phosphorus, potassium, calcium, magnesium, and sulfur. These nutrients are primarily taken up by plants as inorganic compounds. For example, nitrogen is mostly assimilated from soil as nitrate or ammonium, while phosphorus is taken up as phosphate. In natural ecosystems, these inorganic compounds are steadily recycled by microorganisms from dead organic matter such as plant litter. The microorganisms have the ability to metabolize complex, organic forms of nutrients and convert them to simple, inorganic forms, such as the ones just listed. As they perform this function, the microorganisms gain access to the fixed energy and nutrients of dead biomass that they require for their own growth and reproduction. Therefore, soil fertility in natural ecosystems is largely associated with organic matter, from which inorganic nutrients are slowly released from their complex, organic forms. These are then efficiently taken up by plants, so that little of these precious nutrients is lost to ground or surface waters or to the atmosphere.

However, in intensively managed agricultural systems, inorganic nutrients are usually added directly, in the form of manufactured fertilizers of various sorts. Synthetic inorganic fertilizers are manufactured industrially from raw materials and energy. For example, rock phosphate mined in Florida or elsewhere is manufactured into super– and triple–superphosphate fertilizers. Inorganic nitrogen fertilizers such as urea and ammonium nitrate are commonly manufactured by combining atmospheric dinitrogen with hydrogen obtained from methane (natural gas). Inorganic potassium is obtained from potash, a mined material rich in that chemical, while calcium and magnesium are obtained from limestone (calcium carbonate) and dolomite (calcium, magnesium carbonate). Sulfur fertilizers are manufactured from elemental sulfur or sulfuric acid obtained from sour natural gas or from air–pollution control at metal smelters. The manufacturing of all of these fertilizers has large costs in terms of energy and depletion of non–renewable material resources.

Often, the rates of fertilization in intensively managed agriculture are intended to satiate the needs of crop plants for these chemicals, so their productivity will not be limited by nutrient availability. However, excessive rates of fertilization have environmental costs. These include the contamination of ground water with nitrate, eutrophication of surface waters caused by nutrient inputs, especially phosphate, acidification of soils because of the nitrification of ammonium to nitrate, large emissions of nitrous oxide and other nitrogen gases to the atmosphere, with implications for acid rain and Earth's greenhouse effect, and the need to use herbicides to control the weeds that also flourish under these artificially rich conditions.

In contrast, organic methods of maintaining site fertility focus on soil organic matter. Much action is expended on maintaining or increasing the amounts of organic matter in soil, because this is the reservoir from which inorganic nutrients are slowly made available to growing crop plants. Organic matter is also critical to soil tilth, as was previously described. Organic farmers add nutrient–containing organic matter to their soils in three major ways:

(1) As dung and urine of animals, which contains both organic matter and large concentrations of nutrients. However, care must be taken to avoid the contamination of surface and ground waters with pathogenic bacteria. This method of organic fertilization also causes local air pollution with ammonia and distasteful smells.

(2) As green manure, or growing or recently harvested plant material that is directly incorporated into the soil, usually by plowing. The most fertile green manures are biomass of plants in the legume family, such as alfalfa or clovers, because these have a symbiosis with a bacterium that can fix atmospheric dinitrogen (N_2) into biologically useful nitrogen. Consequently, legume–derived green manures are a commonly used organic means of fertilization with nitrogen.

(3) As compost, or partially decomposed and humified organic material. Composting is an aerobic process by which microorganisms aided by soil animals break down and metabolize organic material, eventually forming complex, large molecular–weight materials known as humic substances. These are resistant to further decay, and are very useful as a soil conditioner, and to a lesser degree as an organic fertilizer.

It is important to understand that growing plants take up the same, simple, inorganic forms of nutrients (for example, nitrate, ammonium, or phosphate) from soil, regardless of whether these are supplied by organic or manufactured fertilizers. The important difference between fertilization using organic or synthetic materials is in the role of ecological processes versus manufacturing. Organic methods rely more heavily on renewable sources of energy and materials, rather than nonrenewable materials and fossil fuels. Overall, the longer–term environmental implications of maintaining soil tilth and fertility using organic methods are much softer than those associated with conventional, intensive agriculture.

Organic methods of managing pests

In agriculture, pests are any organisms that significantly interfere with the productivity of crop plants or animals. This can occur when insects eat foliage or stored produce, when bacteria or fungi cause plant or animal diseases, or when weeds interfere excessively with the growth of crop plants. In conventional agriculture, these negative influences of pests are usually managed using various types of pesticides, such as insecticides, herbicides, and fungicides. On the shorter term, these methods can be effective in reducing the influence of pests on agricultural productivity. However, important environmental damages are associated with the use of pesticides.

Organic farmers do not use synthetic, manufactured pesticides to manage their pest problems. Rather, reliance is placed on other methods of pest management, the most important of which are:

(1) The use of varieties of crop species that are resistant to pests and diseases. If the crop species has genetically based variations of tolerance to the pest or disease, then resistant varieties can be developed using standard breeding techniques;

(2) Atacking the pest biologically, by introducing or enhancing populations of its natural predators, parasites, or diseases;

(3) Changing other ecological conditions to make the habitat less suitable for the pest. Depending on the

pest, this may be possible by growing plants in mixed cultures rather than in monocultures; by rotating crops or by using a fallow period so that pest populations do not build up in particular fields; by managing the over-wintering microhabitat of certain pests; by using mechanical methods of weed control such as hand–pulling or shallow plowing; and by other means. Obviously, use of these techniques requires knowledge of the ecological requirements and vulnerabilities of important pest species.

(4) Undertaking careful monitoring of the abundance of pests, so that specific control strategies are only used when required. Note that this may include the use of certain pesticides, but these must be based on a natural product. For example, an insecticide based on the bacterium *Bacillus thuringiensis* or B.t. may be acceptable, as may one based on pyrethrum, a chemical extracted from several species of plants related to the daisy. However, synthetic analogues of these, such as genetically engineered B.t. or synthesized pyrethroids are not considered acceptable in organic agriculture.

Note that many of these pest–control practices are important components of a system known as integrated pest management. However, in that system pesticides are often used as a last resort, when other methods do not work effectively enough. In organic agriculture, pesticides are not used (other than the "natural" ones just referred to).

In addition, organic farmers, and the consumers of the goods that they produce, must be relatively tolerant of some of the damages and lower yields that pests cause. Consumers, for example, must be satisfied with apples that have some degree of blemishing associated with scab, a fungal-caused problem that does not affect the nutritional quality or safety of the apple, but that has become associated with poor aesthetics. In conventional agriculture, this particular cosmetic damage is managed through the use of pesticides, in order to supply consumers with apples of an aesthetic quality that they have become conditioned to expect.

Use of antibiotics and growth regulating hormones

In some types of intensive culture of agricultural livestock, animals are kept together under very crowded conditions, often inside large buildings in a poorly ventilated and smelly environment, and often continuously exposed to their manure and urine. Under these sorts of conditions animals are highly vulnerable to developing infections of various sorts, which ultimately cause reductions of growth, and may result in death. To manage this problem, intensive agriculture typically relies

on antibiotics. These may be given to animals when they are actually sick, or added continuously to their food as a prophylactic treatment. Ultimately, humans are exposed to small residues of antibiotics in products of these animals that they consume. It has not been scientifically established that this exposure poses an unacceptable risk to humans, potentially occurring, for example, through the evolution of resistant varieties of antibiotic–resistant pathogens. Nevertheless, there is controversy about the antibiotic contamination of foodstuffs from intensive agriculture.

Organic farmers might also use antibiotics to treat an infection in a particular sick animal, but they do not continuously add those chemicals to the food that is fed to livestock. In addition, many organic farmers attempt to keep their animals under more open and sanitary conditions than are often conventionally used to intensively rear livestock under dense, industrial conditions. Animals that are relatively free of the stresses of crowding and constant exposures to manure are more resistant to diseases, and have less of a need of antibiotics.

In addition, some industrial systems of raising livestock use synthetic growth hormones, such as bovine growth hormone, to increase the productivity of their animals, or of animal products such as milk. Inevitably, these hormones persist in trace contaminations in the animal products that humans consume. Although no risk to humans has been convincingly demonstrated from these exposures, there is controversy about the potential effects. Organic farmers do not use synthetic growth hormones to enhance the productivity of their livestock.

Organic and non–organic foods

Many people believe that organically grown foods are safer or more nutritious than the same foods grown using conventional agricultural systems. In large part, these beliefs are influenced by the occurrence of trace contaminations of non–organic foods with pesticides, antibiotics, or growth hormones. Although this topic is highly controversial, it is important to understand that scientific studies have not yet convincingly demonstrated that organically grown foods are indeed safer or more nutritious than conventional agricultural produce.

From the environmental perspective, the most important differences between food grown by organic and conventional methods is in the resulting environmental effects of the agricultural systems. Organic agricultural systems result in less use of non–renewable resources of energy and materials, in better health of the agricultural ecosystem, and in enhanced sustainability of the agricultural enterprise.

KEY TERMS

Humus—Amorphous, partially decomposed organic matter. Humus is an important and persistent type of soil organic matter, and it is very important in soil tilth and fertility.

Nutrient—Any chemical that is required for life. The most important nutrients that plants obtain from soil are compounds of nitrogen, phosphorus, potassium, calcium, magnesium, and sulfur.

Organic matter—Any biomass of plants or animals, living or dead. The most important form of organic matter in soils is dead, occurring as humic substances.

Tilth—The physical structure of soil, closely associated with the concentration of humified organic matter. Tilth is important in water– and nutrient–holding capacity of soil, and is generally beneficial to plant growth

Why isn't organic agriculture more popular?

The environmental damages and resource use associated with organic agriculture are much less than those of conventional agricultural systems. However, yields tend to be smaller, and the organically grown produce is often relatively expensive to the consumer. Overall, the balance of these two considerations suggests that society receives a positive net benefit from the use of organic agricultural systems.

However, organic agricultural systems will not become more widely adopted unless a number of socioeconomic conditions change. First, larger numbers of consumers will have to be willing to pay the somewhat higher costs of organically grown food, and they will have to modify some of their perceptions about the aesthetic qualities of certain foods. Second, vested agricultural interests in big–business, government, and universities will have to become more sympathetic to the goals and softer environmental effects of organic agriculture. These institutions will have to support more research into organic agriculture, and promote the use of those systems. Lastly, it will be necessary that the practitioners of intensive agricultural systems be made to more directly and sensibly deal with the environmental damages that are associated with their activities, especially the use of manufactured pesticides and fertilizers.

See also Crop rotation; Fertilizers; Fungicide; Herbicides; Integrated pest management; Pesticides.

Further Reading:
Carroll, R.C., J.H. Vandermeer, and P.M. Rossett. *Agroecology.* New York: McGraw-Hill, 1990.
Conford, P. (ed.). *A Future for the Land: Organic Practices From a Global Perspective.* London: Green Books, 1992.
Soule, J.D. and J.K. Piper. *Farming in Nature's Image: An Ecological Approach to Agriculture.* Island Press, 1992.

Bill Freedman

Organism

An organism is any individual living entity. Organisms range in size and complexity from microorganisms to multicellular plants and animals. Modern biologists classify Earth's organisms into five kingdoms on the basis of common patterns of the design of life, that is, in their cellular and sub–cellular organization, metabolism, reproduction, and behavior. Listed in order of their earliest appearance in the fossil record of life, these kingdoms are:

(1) Monera or prokaryotic microorganisms, which do not have their genetic material organized within a bounded organelle called a nucleus, along with other distinctive characteristics. Earth's simplest organisms occur in this group, in particular viruses, which consist of little more than a proteinaceous shell containing nucleic acids. Viruses are incapable of reproduction without parasitizing the metabolism of an unrelated host cell. Other major groups of monerans are blue–green bacteria and true bacteria.

(2) Protista are a diverse group of microorganisms, containing the simplest of the eukaryotic organisms, which have an organized nucleus, one or more flagellae, and generally contain mitochondria and plastids. The most representative group is the protozoans, but some flagellated fungi and algae are placed within this group.

(3) Fungi are a diverse group of non–flagellated, unicellular or multicellular organisms, ranging in complexity from single–celled yeasts, through multicellular but microscopic fungi growing as a thread–like mycelium, to relatively complex fungi that develop large mushrooms as their reproductive structures.

(4) Plantae, or green plants, utilize solar radiation trapped by chlorophyll or other pigments to fix simple mineral nutrients into energy–rich biochemicals in a metabolic process called photosynthesis. Organisms in

this diverse group range from unicellular algae, through multicellular but non–vascular algae, liverworts, and mosses, to vascular plants such as ferns, conifers, and flowering plants.

(5) Animalia, or multicellular animals, are heterotrophic organisms that are capable of movement, often in response to sensory stimuli, and with other distinctive characteristics. Animals range in size and complexity from small sponges and arthropods to large vertebrates weighing tons.

All of Earth's organisms are related to varying degrees, sharing certain commonalities of physiology and other functions. Moreover, it is clear that some of Earth's distinctive organisms have a relatively ancient lineage that extends far back into the geological past, while other organisms are enormously more complex in biological organization than others. However, the modern, evolutionary interpretation of life suggests that none of Earth's organisms are "higher" or more "primitive" than any others, and that none have greater intrinsic value. Evolution has not occurred as a progression of types of organisms that represents a logical, directed succession from simple organisms (such as viruses and bacteria) to much more complex organisms (such as birds and mammals). Earth's diversity of living organisms utilizes body and metabolic plans of varying complexity, but all species represent successful adaptations to the planet's habitable environments.

See also Animal; Bacteria; Fungi; Microorganisms; Plant; Protozoa; Virus.

Bill Freedman

Oribi see **Dwarf antelopes**

Origin of life

No one knows how life originated on Earth. Most scientists believe life began three to four billion years ago when the Earth's atmosphere and landscape were very different from today. Numerous experiments performed over the past 50 years suggest that many important ingredients of life including amino acids and components of nucleic acids, genetic materials, may have formed under conditions that existed on Earth billions of years ago. A recent popular scientific theory about the origin of life suggests that RNA, a nucleic acid related to DNA, played a crucial role.

Background of the origin of life

There are many theories about the origin of life. The Earth is approximately 4.6 billion years old. Fossils of microorganisms similar to blue–green algae are present in three billion year–old rocks. This suggests that life evolved sometime in the first billion years after the Earth was formed. Algae–like plants are more complex that even simpler life forms such as bacteria. It is likely, therefore, that the oldest living things we have found evolved from less complex ancestors.

Several facts support the theory that life evolved from a simple ancestor during the first billion years of Earth's history. First, all living things are made of chemicals rich in the same type of organic, or carbon–containing, compounds. Second, the same 20 amino acids make up the proteins present in all living things. And third, all living things have their genetic blueprint encoded in nucleic acids, DNA or RNA. These nucleic acids contain the instructions for building proteins from amino acids. One class of proteins, called enzymes, in turn, acts as essential chemical tools for making and regulating nucleic acids and for controlling other functions that are essential to maintaining life. Enzymes are chemicals that greatly increase the speed of a chemical reaction. Nearly all enzymes are proteins; RNA can act as an enzyme in a few instances.

Besides acting as enzymes, proteins also provide structure for cells and help them obtain nutrients, functions without which cells could not exist. These two types of molecules, nucleic acids and proteins, are so widespread and so essential to life that many scientists assume they, or closely related compounds, were present in the first life forms on Earth.

Theories on the origin of life

For most of human history, people believed that small creatures such as insects, amphibians, and mice appeared by "spontaneous generation" in the folds of old clothes and in piles garbage and refuse. The Italian physician Francesco Redi challenged this belief in 1668 when he proved that maggots came from eggs laid by flies, not from the decaying matter in which they were found.

One of the most elegant series of experiments that helped to disprove spontaneous generation was designed and conducted by the French microbiologist Louis Pasteur in 1860s. Pasteur sterilized two containers, both containing a broth rich in nutrients. He exposed one container directly to the air. He exposed the second container to the air but he added a trap, a downward loop in the connecting tube, to it. Air could still reach the broth in the second container through the tube, but dust and other particles which might contaminate the broth fell into the trap. Bacteria and mold quickly grew in the first container and made its broth cloudy and rank. The broth in the second container, however, remained clear and sterile. This suggested that the microorganisms in the first container did not arise spontaneously but instead were introduced by dust and contaminates which were prevented from getting into the second container by its trap.

Although Redi, Pasteur, and other scientists disproved spontaneous generation as a believable explanation for the origin of life, they also raised a new, and difficult, question: if organisms can arise only from other organisms, then how did the first organism arise?

Charles Darwin, who, with Alfred Russell Wallace discovered the theory of natural selection, suggested privately that life could have formed first in "some warm little pond" rich in minerals and chemicals and exposed to electricity, light, and heat. Darwin believed that once the first living thing appeared, all other creatures that have ever lived could have evolved from it. Many of the laboratory experiments designed to shed light on the origin of life have been variations of the "warm little pond" Darwin described.

A second important piece in early explanations of the origin of life was provided by the Soviet scientist, Aleksandr Oparin and the British scientist J. B. S. Haldane. Oparin and Haldane suggested in the 1920s that the Earth's atmosphere billions of years ago was very different from its atmosphere today. We breathe 78% nitrogen and 21% oxygen. (The remaining 1% is a mixture of 11 other gases.) This is an oxidizing atmosphere. Oparin noted that in unprotected environments, oxygen interferes with the formation of organic compounds necessary for life by oxidizing hydrogen atoms (taking them to form compounds) from other compounds which need them to create life. Oparin reasoned that the atmosphere present when life began on Earth was a reducing atmosphere, one that contained little or no oxygen, but was full of gases that could provide hydrogen atoms to compounds needed to create life for the first time.

Instead of nitrogen and oxygen, Oparin and Haldane suggested that the early, reducing, atmosphere consisted of hydrogen, water vapor, ammonia, methane, and other hydrocarbons (molecules made of carbon and hydrogen atoms). This mix of gases could readily provide hydrogen for chemical reactions. The early atmosphere contained little or no oxygen, according to the two scientists.

Energy for rearranging atoms and molecules into organic forms that promoted the formation of life on the young Earth came from the heat of volcanoes, sunlight, and lightning, according to this theory. This model of the world when life first formed became popular with scientists after a graduate student named Stanley Miller at the University of Chicago designed an experiment to test it in 1953. Miller filled a closed glass container with the gases Oparin and Haldane said were likely to have been in the atmosphere billions of years ago. In the bottom of the container he placed a reservoir of water and above it, an electrical spark crackled all during the experiment. After one week, Miller found that amino acids and other organic chemicals had formed from the gases and water in his model of the early Earth which was a version of Darwin's "warm little pond."

In the years since Miller reported his results, other researchers have repeated them and gone on to find more amino acids and even components of nucleic acids, the molecules that encode the genetic information of organisms. Work influenced by these experiments led many scientists to believe that the concentration of organic molecules in the nutrient–laden, warm "ponds" (which may have been tidal pools, puddles, or lakes billions of years ago) increased over time and eventually formed themselves into carbohydrates, lipids, proteins, and the building blocks of nucleic acids. Energy was supplied by electricity or ultraviolet radiation. The assembly of more complex compounds from simpler ones may have occurred on oily drops floating in the pond or on clay or mineral surfaces.

Some scientists believe that the young Earth was too violent a place for life to have developed on the surface. They say meteors showered the earth then just as they did the moon. Deep–sea vents, holes in the Earth's crust under the oceans, are more likely places for the evolution of life according to this view. The hot water and minerals that pour from the vents may have provided a place for life to get its start, if these scientists are correct.

Scientists today believe that the early atmosphere may not have been as strongly reducing as the one proposed by Oparin and Haldane and used in Miller's experiment. Volcanoes probably added carbon monoxide, carbon dioxide, and nitrogen to the early atmosphere. It may even have contained traces of oxygen. Nevertheless, more recent experiments like Miller's, but using a less reducing atmosphere have produced the formation of organic compounds just like Miller found, although less organic material was detected. All 20 of the amino acids found in living cells have been created in the laboratory under conditions designed to mimic the experimenter's idea of what the Earth was like billions of years ago.

Amino acids are linked together in cells by specific enzymes to form proteins. When this happens, a hydrogen molecule and a hydroxyl group (OH) are removed from the amino acids which then link up. The hydrogen and OH group also link up to form a water molecule. Without enzymes, amino acids will not link up in this way, or as a biochemist would describe it, the polymerization reaction will not proceed in water. If this is true, then how, before life began and cells existed, could amino acids join together to form proteins? One possibility is that amino acids may have linked together on hot sand, clay, or even rock. Laboratory experiments have shown that amino acids and other organic building blocks of larger molecules, called polymers, can join together when dilute solutions of them are dripped onto warm sand, clay, or rock. The larger molecules formed in this way have been named proteinoids. It is easy to imagine Darwin's "warm little pond" complete with amino acids splashing onto some nearby hot volcanic rock. Clay and iron pyrite (fool's gold) have properties that might have made them good "platforms" for the formation of larger molecules from smaller building blocks billions of years ago.

Proteinoids can cluster together into droplets that separate and may protect their components from the surroundings. In this way the droplets are like cells but they can not reproduce. These droplets are called *microspheres*. When fats, called lipids, are present, the droplets that form are even more like cells. A mixture of linked amino acids called polypeptides, sugars called polysaccharides, and nucleic acids are then shaken and they also form into droplets called coacervates. All of these droplets are called protobionts and may represent a stage in the development of life.

The formation of amino acids and other organic compounds is still presumed to have been a necessary step in the formation of life, but another step in the process must have happened soon after. Self–replicating molecules would have to form by this time in order for life to continue. Scientists presume these self–replicating molecules were like today's nucleic acids.

Once molecules that could replicate were formed, evolution would account for future development of life on Earth. The molecules best adapted to the environment would have duplicated themselves more efficiently and more often than competing molecules. Eventually, primitive cells appeared, and perhaps coacervates or other protobionts played a role at this stage in the development of life. Once cells became established in the early "warm little pond," evolution (the adaptation of species over time to a changing environment through natural selection) eventually led to all life forms that have ever existed on Earth.

The "RNA world" and the origin of life

Living cells today typically store genetic information in DNA. The information is transferred to RNA. RNA forms proteins by translating the information dictated by DNA. The proteins perform basic cell functions necessary to maintain life and reproduce. The odds that the components of this complex sequence of events, DNA to RNA to protein, evolved at the same time are poor. Some scientists propose that RNA appeared on Earth before DNA. This view was straightened by the discovery that some forms of RNA called *ribozymes* can act like biological catalysts and speed biological reactions enough to make them useful to cells. In other words, some RNA can act like non–protein enzymes. These scientists suggest that RNA was capable of ordering the sequence of amino acids, forming proteins, and replicating itself in a type of "RNA world." RNA in this world was more important than DNA.

Scientists who favor the "RNA world" suggest that RNA could self–replicate even before DNA and protein enzymes had evolved. Single–stranded RNA might have been able to assume a shape that allowed it to line up amino acids in specific sequences to create specific protein molecules, according to recent conjectures. RNA molecules that happened to cause amino acids to link up to form a protein that could help the RNA molecule replicate or survive would have an advantage over other RNA molecules in the "RNA world." At this point, molecular evolution and natural selection would take over in furthering the development of life. The RNA that produced useful protein enzymes would survive better than those that did not.

Critics of the "RNA world" say that the evidence that RNA could have self–replicated is weak. Instead they suggest that other organic molecules, not nucleic acids, were the first self–replicating molecules that served to store genetic information. These simple hereditary systems were later replaced by nucleic acids in the course of evolution, according to this scheme.

Panspermia

Radio astronomers have found that organic molecules, which might have played an important role in the formation of life, are present in dust clouds in outer space and in meteors that have fallen to earth. This provides further evidence that chemicals important for the development of life may have been present on the Earth billions of years ago. The presence of complex organic

KEY TERMS

Coacervates—A cluster of polysaccharides, nucleic acids and polypeptides formed when a solution of these molecules is shaken. Coacervates are a type of protobiont.

Organic compound—A molecule containing carbon atoms.

Protobiont—Cell–like aggregates of organic molecules capable of maintaining a separate environment slightly different from their surroundings. Protobionts are not capable of reproduction but may have been one step toward the formation of life on Earth.

compounds outside our solar system suggests that the formation of chemical compounds important for life may be more likely than we once thought.

Their presence in outer space also suggests to a few scientists that life never originated on this planet. Instead, they believe life originated somewhere in outer space and arrived on Earth. Many researchers discount this hypothesis because they feel radiation and the extremes of temperature in space would kill any living organism before it could reach Earth. This suggestion also suffers from the drawback that it merely shifts from Earth to another, undefined place in the universe.

A theory known as *panspermia* suggests that organic precursors to life arrived on earth in meteors. Once here, the organic compounds arranged themselves into molecules that eventually led to the development of life. This theory simplifies the problem of explaining the origin of life by suggesting that the formation of simple organic compounds did not have to take place on Earth. The development of life from those compounds remains to be satisfactorily explained in this and all other theories about the origin of life.

See also Amino acid; Chemical evolution; Deoxyribonucleic acid; Enzyme; Evolution; Natural selection; Nucleic acid; Proteins; Ribonucleic acid.

Further Reading:

Crick, Francis. *Life Itself, Its Origin and Nature.* New York: Simon and Schuster, 1981.
Mellersh, Anthony. "The Origin of Life." *Natural History* (6 June 1994): 10–12.
Orgel, Leslie E. "The Origin of Life." *Scientific American* (October 1994): 77–83.

Dean Allen Haycock

Orioles

The true or forest orioles include 28 species of medium–sized birds that make up the family Oriolidae. These birds occur in Africa, Europe, Asia, Southeast Asia, the Philippines, New Guinea, and Australia. Their usual habitats are forests, open woodlands, and savannas. Most species are tropical, but some migratory species occur in temperate regions.

Orioles are jay–sized birds with long, pointed wings, and a strong, pointed, slightly down–curved bill, which may be colored red, blue, or black. Male orioles are bright–colored birds, commonly yellow with black patterns on the wing, tail, and head. Females have a more subdued coloration. The family name, Oriolidae, is derived from the Latin word *aureus*, meaning golden, and refers to the bright–yellow base color of the golden oriole of southern Europe (see below).

Orioles tend to skulk in dense cover in wooded areas, and are not easily seen. Orioles have a melodious, if somewhat quiet song, and louder, harsher, call notes. Courting includes spectacular, closely coordinated pursuits of the female by the male through the tree canopy. The pendulous, tightly woven, cup–shaped nest of orioles is constructed by the female in a forked branch of a tree, and contains two to five eggs. The female does most or all of the incubation, but is fed by the male during her confinement. Both parents rear the young. The figbirds (*Sphecotheres* spp.) of Australasia construct much looser nests of twigs.

Orioles mostly feed on invertebrates in the tree canopy. Unlike most other birds, orioles will feed on hairy caterpillars, which can sometimes be quite abundant. However, these insect larvae are rubbed and beaten by orioles against a branch, to remove many of the hairs before the prey is eaten. Orioles also eat small fruits when they are available.

Species of true orioles

The golden oriole (*Oriolus oriolus*) is a relatively abundant and well–known species of forests and wooded parks and gardens of temperate Europe and western Asia. This species winters in Africa, Madagascar, India, and Sri Lanka. The attractive male has bright–yellow plumage, with a black tail and upper wings, and a black mask. The female is a lime green color. The golden oriole is bold and pugnacious in the vicinity of its arboreal nest, attacking and driving off potential predators such as crows and small hawks.

The black–headed oriole (*Oriolus xanthornis*) is another relatively common and widespread species, occurring in forests in south and southeast Asia. The black–naped oriole occurs from India to southern China and southeast Asia, as far as the Philippines. The yellow oriole (*O. flavocinctus*) and olive–backed oriole (*O. sagittatus*) are greenish–yellow Australian species. The black–and–crimson oriole (*O. cruentus*) of Malaya, Borneo, Sumatra, and Bali is mostly black–colored, with dark, crimson patches on the breast and on the wings.

The yellow figbird, or bananabird (*Sphecotheres viridis*), occurs in various types of forests in northern Australia. This greenish and yellow species commonly nests in the immediate vicinity of a nest of the drongo (*Chilbea bracteata*) or helmeted friar bird (*Philemon yorki*), both of which are aggressive species that drive away predators, but do not bother other songbirds.

The Asian fairy–bluebird or blue–backed fairy bluebird (*Irena puella*) occurs in lowland rainforests from India to Borneo and Sumatra in southeast Asia. The male fairy–bluebird is a very attractive bird, with a bright blue back, and a black face and breast. The female is a more uniformly and subtly–colored blue. This species is placed by some avian taxonomists in the family Irenidae, which also contains the leafbirds.

Some species of medium–sized birds of the Americas are also commonly known as orioles. However, these orioles are various species of medium–sized birds in the blackbird family (Icteridae), which also includes blackbirds, grackles, cowbirds, meadowlarks, and the bobolink. For example, the northern oriole (*Icterus galbula*; the eastern race is known as the Baltimore oriole) is a common songbird of open forests in North America, where it builds its characteristic, pendulous nests, often in elm trees.

See also Blackbirds.

Further Reading:

Harrison, C. J. O. (ed.). *Bird Families of the World*. New York: H.N. Abrams Pubs., 1978.

Bill Freedman

Orlon see **Artificial fibers; Polymer**

Orthopedics

Orthopedics is the branch of medicine that specializes in diseases and injuries of bones. Humans have had to contend with broken bones or malformed bones since prehistory. Early weapons were the type to strike prey or an adversary. A strong man wielding a club or stone axe could splinter bones or disjoint a shoulder or leg. Of course, these injuries probably were frequently lethal, especially if the skin was broken and infection set in. Those that healed may well have left the victim with a deformed arm or joint that was permanently out of alignment.

Physicians eventually developed ways to treat broken bones, however, as evidenced by ancient Egyptian hieroglyphics depicting injured limbs wrapped and braced to heal normally. As wars were waged on a larger scale and weaponry became more efficient and deadly, fractures and other bone injuries became more prominent.

Physicians developed simple prosthetics to replace for example, a lower leg that was amputated as the result of a wound. A hand was replaced by a cup that fit over the wrist and had a hook attached.

The term orthopedics was coined by a French physician, Nicholas Andre, who published a book in 1741 on the prevention and correction of musculoskeletal deformities in children. He united the Greek term orthos, meaning straight, with paedeia, the rearing of children. The term orthopaedics remained in use, though the specialty has broadened much beyond the care of children. Andre's illustration at the beginning of his book, that of a strong post to which is tied a growing but crooked sapling, remains the symbol of orthopedic societies today.

Early orthopedics concentrated on the correction of such childhood conditions as scoliosis (curved back), paralysis as with poliomyelitis, tuberculosis of the bone, and congenital defects such as clubfoot or deformed hip. Gradually orthopedists included fractures, dislocations, and trauma to the spine and skeleton within their specialty.

Bone is a living and functioning part of the body. A broken bone will generate new growth to repair the fracture and fill in any areas from which bone is removed. Therefore, a bone that is congenitally deformed (from birth) can be manipulated, cut, braced, or otherwise treated to provide a normal form. A broken bone held in alignment will heal and no physical deformity will result.

For decades orthopedics was a physical specialty. The physician provided therapy to manipulate bones and joints to restore alignment, and then applied casts or braces to maintain the structure until it healed. Fractures of the hip, among other injuries, were considered to be untreatable and they were ignored. The patient was made as comfortable as possible to allow the fracture to heal and then he had to adjust his lifestyle to account for difficulty in walking or inability to bend, or other handicaps remaining from healing of the deformed joint.

In the 1930s a special nail was developed to hold bone fragments together to allow them to heal better. A few years later a metal device was invented to replace the head of a femur (thigh bone) that formed part of the hip joint and that often would not heal after being fractured. Later a total hip joint was invented and it continues to be revised and improved to allow the patient maximum use and flexibility of the leg.

Currently the orthopedic specialist continues to apply physical methods to align fractures and restore a disrupted joint. Braces and casts still are used to hold injured bones in place to allow them to heal. Now, however, the physician can take x rays to be certain that the bones are aligned properly for healing to take place. X rays also can be taken during the healing process to ascertain that the alignment has not changed and that healing is occurring apace.

Bones that are crushed and have little chance of healing can be helped by transplanting bits of bone from other locations in the body to fill areas from which bone splinters were removed. The operating room in which an orthopedic procedure is to take place resembles a woodworking shop. The physician needs drills, screwdrivers, screws, staples, nails, chisels, and other tools to work the bone and connect pieces with each other.

Deformities of virtually any bone can be corrected. Even facial bones that are malformed can be reshaped or replaced to provide a normal face or to correct defects in the oral cavity. Bone transplants from one individual to another are commonplace. The patient who loses a limb from a disease such as cancer can have a normal–appearing prosthesis fitted and can be taught to use it to attain a near–normal lifestyle.

Many orthopedic surgical procedures no longer require an open incision to fully expose the joint. Now flexible orthoscopes can be inserted into a joint, such as the knee, and can be manipulated through the joint to locate and identify the nature of the injury. The orthoscope, or endoscope, has a light to illuminate the interior of the joint. The physician can look through one end of the scope or he can watch a television monitor to which is attached a tiny TV camera on the endoscope. Once the injury is identified the physician can fit the end of the endoscope with a variety of tools such as scissors, clamps, scalpels, and so on to remove a growth, or cut the ragged end of a torn ligament and sew the structures back together. This kind of surgery is

considered outpatient surgery for which the patient reports to the hospital or clinic in the morning and is home by evening. Physical therapy often is required after surgery to restore flexibility and strength to the joint and prevent muscle mass loss.

Orthopedists often specialize in areas such as sports medicine, pediatric deformities, facial surgery, hand surgery, and so forth. Each specialty requires training and education specific for that specialty. Each has unique problems and requirements.

See also Skeletal system.

Oryx

The oryx (*Oryx gazella*) is a species of antelope in the family Bovidae. Oryx are native to a rather wide range, extending from the Middle East through much of Africa. There are eight recognized subspecies of oryx, which vary greatly in body and horn shape, and in habitat requirements. In some taxonomic treatments, some of the subspecies are treated as distinct species.

Mature oryx weigh 221–463 lbs (100–210 kg), have a body length of 5–7.9 ft (1.6–2.4 m), and a tail length of 19–35 in (45–90 cm). Both male and female oryx have long horns, which, depending on the subspecies, vary in shape from spear– to bow–shaped. The legs of oryx are rather long and slender, the neck rather short, the eyes small, and the ears fairly short and pointed. The round tail ends in a black tassel of longer hairs. The basic body color varies from greys and browns to cream in the case of the Arabian oryx. In addition, there are striking dark–brown or black markings on the body.

Oryx are loosely social animals, occurring in herds of several to as many as 60 animals. During the breeding season, male oryx fight over access to females. Oryx bear single young, after a gestation period of about nine months. Oryx browse on shrubs and graze on grasses and forbs. Although they drink when water is available, oryx are capable of going long periods without having access to drinking water, for as long as several months in the case of the desert subspecies of oryx. Like some other mammals of dry habitats, oryx are efficient at preventing water loss from their lungs and other moist surfaces, and they have very concentrated urine. These adaptations allow the water produced by normal metabolism to satisfy most of the requirements for water.

The Arabian oryx (*Oryx gazella leucoryx*) of the Arabian Peninsula and the scimitar–horned oryx (*O. g. dammah*) of the Sahara are both desert animals. Unfortunately, these subspecies have been over–hunted to endangerment. During the 1950s and 1960s the Arabian oryx was close to extinction, but it has since been bred in captivity and protected more rigorously in its native habitats. The wild populations of Arabian oryx have been supplemented by releases of captive–reared animals, and although still rare and endangered, this subspecies has become more abundant in parts of its former range.

Most subspecies of oryx utilize semi–desert, steppe, and savanna habitats, as is the case of the South African oryx or gemsbok (*Oryx gazella gazella*), and the East African oryx or beisa oryx (*O. g. beisa*). Although populations of both of these oryx have been greatly depleted by over–hunting and loss of habitat, they are still fairly abundant animals in some parts of their range.

See also Antelopes and gazelles.

Bill Freedman

Oscillations

An oscillation is a particular kind of motion in which an object repeats the same movement over and over. It is easy to see that a child on a swing and the pendulum on a grandfather clock both oscillate when they move back and forth along an arc. A small weight hanging from a rubber band or a spring can also oscillate if pulled slightly to start its motion, but this repeated motion is now linear (along a straight line). On a larger scale, you can notice oscillations when bungee jumpers fall to the end of their cords, are pulled back up, fall again, etc. Actually, oscillations are all around us, even in the pages of this book.

Anything, no matter how large or small, can oscillate if there is some point where the object is in stable equilibrium. Stable equilibrium means that an object always wants to return to that position. Suppose you placed a marble at the exact center inside a very smooth bowl. If you tap the marble slightly to move it a small distance, it rolls back towards the center, overshoots, rolls back, overshoots, etc. The marble is oscillating as it continues to return to center of the bowl, its point of stable equilibrium. If you think of the marble and the bowl as a "unit," you can see that the "unit" stays together even though the marble is oscillating (unless you tap the marble so hard that it flies out of the bowl). This is the reason for using the term stable.

On the other hand, what if you turned the bowl over and tried the same experiment by placing the marble on top at the center. You might succeed in balancing the marble for a short time, but eventually you will touch the table or a breeze will move the marble a small amount and it will fall. When this happens, the "unit" of marble and bowl comes apart and no oscillation can happen. In this case, the center of the bowl would be a point of unstable equilibrium, since you can balance the marble there, but the marble cannot return to that point when disturbed to keep the "unit" from disintegrating.

For the motion of a child on a swing, the bottom of the arc (when the swing hangs straight down) is the point of stable equilibrium. The point of stable equilibrium for a weight on the rubber band is the location at which the weight would hang if it was very slowly lowered. In either case, an oscillation occurs when the object (child or weight) is moved away from stable equilibrium. If we pull the swing back some distance the child will move toward the bottom of the arc. At the instant the swing is at the point of stable equilibrium, the child is moving the fastest since as the swing proceeds up the arc on the other side, it slows down. The higher the swing was when the motion was started, the faster the child moves at the bottom. The swing overshoots stable equilibrium and the child rises to the same distance on this side of the bottom as on the starting side. For a brief instant the swing will stop before the swing begins to retrace its path, traveling in the other direction.

This simple example demonstrates several properties shared by all oscillations: 1) The point of stable equilibrium is the center of the oscillating motion since the object moves the same distance on either side. That distance is called the amplitude of the oscillation. 2) At either end of the motion, the object stops briefly (slowest location) while the fastest location is when the object is just passing through the point of stable equilibrium. 3) The energy that an object has when it is oscillating is related to the amplitude. The larger the amplitude, the larger the energy.

Oscillations also have two very specific properties regarding time. Every oscillation takes a certain amount of time before the motion begins to repeat itself. Since the motion repeats, we really only need to worry about what happens in one cycle, or repetition of the oscillation. If we pick any point in the motion and follow the object until it has returned to that same point ready to repeat, then the oscillation has completed one cycle. The amount of time that it took to complete one cycle is called the period, and every cycle will take the same amount of time. Suppose for the child on a swing we pick the point at the bottom of the arc. When the swing

KEY TERMS

Cycle—One repetition of an oscillation as an object travels from any point (in a certain direction) back to the same point and begins to move again in the original direction.

Equilibrium—The condition when all the influences (forces) trying to move an object are balanced, at least for an instant.

Frequency—The number of cycles of an oscillating motion which occur per second. For example, if the period for one cycle is 0.5 second, then the frequency is (1 cycle)/(0.5 second) = 2 cycles per second = 2 Hertz.

Period—The amount of time it takes for one cycle of an oscillating motion.

moves through that position, we start a timer. The child will swing up, stop, swing back down through the bottom (but traveling in the other direction), swing up, stop, and swing back through our point. Now the child has returned to our starting point and the motion is about to repeat, so we stop our timer. The curious thing is that even when the amplitude is changed, the period stays the same. This is because even though the child moves faster when pulled higher to start the motion, the swing also has farther to travel to complete a cycle.

The other time property is called the frequency, which tells how often the motion repeats. This really gives the same information as the period since if it takes 0.5 second for 1 cycle, then the frequency will be (1 cycle)/(0.5 second) = 2 cycles per second. Often a unit called the Hertz (Hz) is used to represent a cycle per second. The cycles per second should sound familiar because the magnitude, or amplitude, of the electrical current in most households oscillates at 60 cycles per second. The time properties of an oscillation are very important since they control how best to add energy to the motion.

The child on a swing, weight on a spring, and bungee jumper on an elastic cord are all types of oscillations which we can see with our eyes. However, if you kick a rock (disturb it) and it does not disintegrate, then the atoms within the rock must be in stable equilibrium. The atoms within the rock are therefore capable of oscillating. Small oscillations are actually occurring all the time in every seemingly solid substance, including the rock and this page. We cannot see this motion, but we do feel it. The larger the amplitude of those

small oscillations of the atoms, the hotter the object, and that is something we can detect directly.

James J. Carroll

Oscilloscope

An oscilloscope is an instrument that provides a graphical display of electrical signals. It presents a considerable amount of information about the operation of a circuit almost instantly, and the visual nature of the display provides insights that tables of numbers do not offer. Oscilloscopes are extremely useful for monitoring and diagnosing electrical circuits or devices. Though it can plot an electrical signal versus another signal, the most common oscilloscope display mode shows the behavior of an electrical signal as a function of time. The signal amplitude, or voltage, is displayed on the vertical axis of the screen, while the horizontal axis represents the time sweep. Electrical phenomena often happen faster than can been seen with the eye. At the same time they are generally oscillatory, or cyclical, and can be displayed as a motionless trace on a fast graphing device such as an oscilloscope.

Unlike other types of electrical meters, oscilloscopes show changes in voltage and circuit behavior instantly, and when power to a circuit is removed, the oscilloscope display response is immediate. Thus, an engineer or electrician diagnosing a system can observe such rapid, and potentially damaging phenomena as transients, or voltage surges. This is a significant benefit of the oscilloscope.

Oscilloscopes use a cathode ray tube, or an electron gun, to display data. Electrons are produced by the filament of the tube and focused into a tight beam. Two pairs of electrostatic deflection plates, vertically oriented and horizontally oriented, control the beam and direct it toward the phosphor coated screen. When the electron beam impacts a section of the phosphor screen, it causes the material to glow, thus emitting light and conveying information. If the vertical pair of deflection plates are connected to an amplified voltage and the horizontal pair are connected to a "clock," the beam deflection will map the voltage as a function of time. The electron beam is swept across the screen, creating the circuit trace.

The oscilloscope can be adjusted for maximum usefulness of display. In the time–sweep mode, the instrument can be adjusted to show multiple cycles on

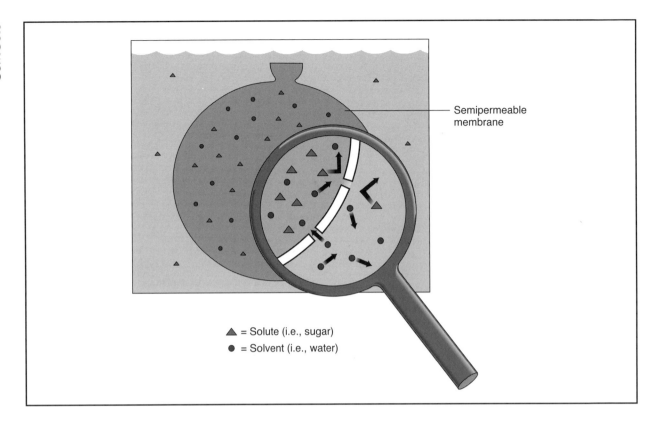

= Solute (i.e., sugar)
= Solvent (i.e., water)

Figure 1. Random collisions with semipermeable membrane.

the screen, or just one. The vertical scale can be adjusted to match the amplitude of the signal being studied. A scope can be set up to "trigger" or begin to display a signal under certain conditions, for example, a rising signal or a falling signal. It can also be connected to two circuits at once, displaying both traces. Some oscilloscopes have memory, and can continue to display a given signal for a given time. Sampling oscilloscopes are useful for very high frequency applications.

See also Electric circuit.

Osmium see **Element, chemical**

Osmosis

Osmosis is the movement of solvent, such as water, through a barrier from a less concentrated solution into a more concentrated solution. It occurs when two solutions are separated by a semipermeable membrane which allows only the solvent to pass through. Osmosis plays a major role in the chemistry of living things and also has applications in medicine and technology.

Osmosis was first described in 1748 by J. A. Nollet. He placed a solution of "spirits of wine" (ethyl alcohol and water) in a bottle and sealed it with a piece of pig's bladder. The bladder, like most biological membranes, was semipermeable. Upon immersion of the bottle in a larger container of pure water, the bladder swelled, and eventually burst, as water moved into it from outside. Nollet concluded that the solution exerted a kind of pressure, now called osmotic pressure. Later work by H. Dutrochet (1826) and J. H. van't Hoff (1885) led to mathematical formulas describing osmosis as a physical property of solutions.

Although osmosis moves solvent in one direction, its cause is the random motions of molecules in all directions. The driving force is the difference in concentration of solute on either side of the membrane. Suppose that two solutions, one more concentrated and the other more dilute, are separated by a semipermeable membrane.

On the dilute side, almost all of the molecules hitting the membrane at any moment are solvent, and can pass through. But on the concentrated side, more of the "hits" are from solute particles, which cannot pass through. Therefore, at any moment, more molecules enter the concentrated side than leave it. As a result, the

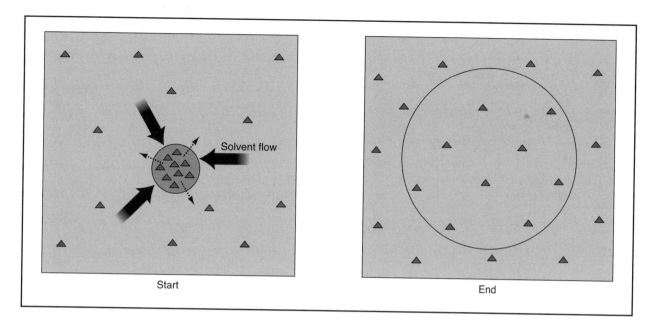

Figure 2. Osmosis equalizes concentration.

volume of the concentrated side grows. But change in volume also changes the concentration. As the trapped solute particles spread over a larger volume, they become more dilute. The other side, which shrinks, becomes more concentrated. The process continues until both sides reach equal concentration.

Osmotic pressure

As osmosis proceeds, pressure builds up on the side of the membrane where volume has increased. Ultimately, the pressure prevents more water from entering, so osmosis stops. The osmotic pressure of a solution is the pressure needed to prevent osmosis into the solution. It is measured in comparison with pure solvent. The osmotic pressure is directly related to the different heights of the liquid on either side of the membrane when no more change in volume occurs. Osmotic pressure depends on the temperature and the original concentration of solute. Interestingly, it does not depend on what is dissolved. Two solutions of different solutes, for example alcohol and sugar, will each have the same osmotic pressure, provided they have the same concentration. Osmotic pressure is therefore a colligative property of solutions, one which depends only on the concentration of dissolved particles, not on their chemical identity.

Osmosis in living organisms

Living cells may be thought of as microscopically small bags of solutions contained within semipermeable membranes. For the cell to survive, the concentration of solutes within the cell must stay within a safe range.

A cell placed in a solution more concentrated than itself (a hypertonic solution) will shrink due to loss of water, and may die of dehydration. A familiar example is a carrot placed in salty water. Within a few hours the carrot will become limp and soft because its cells have shrivelled. A cell placed in a solution more dilute than itself (a hypotonic solution) will expand as water enters it. Under such conditions the cell may burst.

Organisms have various methods for keeping their cell solute concentrations within safe levels. Some live only in surroundings that are isotonic (have the same solute concentration as their own cells). For example, jellyfish which live in salt water have much higher cell solute concentrations than do fresh water creatures. Other animals continually replace lost water and solutes by drinking and eating, and remove the excess water and solutes through excretion of urine. Plant cells are protected from bursting by the rigid cell wall which surrounds the cell membrane. As water enters, the cell expands until it pushes up tight against its cell wall. The cell wall pushes back with an equal pressure, so no more water can enter.

Osmosis contributes to the movement of water through plants. Solute concentrations increase going from soil to root cells to leaf cells, and the resulting differences of osmotic pressure help to draw water upward. Osmosis also controls the evaporation of water ing or agriculture. Salt can be removed by placing the seawater in contact with a semipermeable membrane, then subjecting it to pressures greater than 60 atmospheres. Under these conditions, reverse osmosis occurs, pushing the water molecules out of the seawater into a reservoir of pure water.

See also Concentration; Desalination; Membrane; Osmosis (cellular); Solution.

Further Reading:

Galston, Arthur W. *Green Wisdom.* New York: Basic Books, 1981.
Gross, Cynthia S. *The New Biotechnology: Putting Microbes to Work.* Minneapolis: Lerner Publications, 1988.
Margulis, Lynn, and Dorion Sagan. *The Microcosmos Coloring Book.* Boston: Harcourt Brace Jovanovich, 1988.
Tocci, Salvatore. *Biology Projects for Young Scientists.* New York: Franklin Watts, 1987.
Uehling, M. D. "Salt Water on Tap." *Popular Science* 238 (April 1991): 82–85.

Sara G. B. Fishman

from leaves by regulating the size of the openings (stomata) in the leaves' surfaces.

Applications of osmosis

Preserving food

For thousands of years, perishable foods such as fish, olives, and vegetables have been preserved in salt or brine. The high salt concentration is hypertonic to bacteria cells, and kills them by dehydration before they can cause the food to spoil. Preserving fruit in sugar (jams, jellies) works on the same principle.

Artificial kidneys

Victims of kidney disease rely upon artificial kidney machines to remove waste products from their blood. Such machines use a process called dialysis, which is similar to osmosis. The difference is that the dialyzing membrane permits not just water, but also salts and other small molecules dissolved in the blood to pass through. These move out into a surrounding tank of distilled water. The red blood cells are too large to pass through the dialyzing membrane, so they return to the patient's body.

Desalination by reverse osmosis

Oceans hold about 97% of the Earth's water supply, but their high salt content makes them unsafe for drink-

Osmosis (cellular)

Osmosis is the movement of water across a membrane which is selectively permeable. In osmosis, water moves across a membrane from a region with low solute concentration to a region with high solute concentration. Thus, osmosis tends to equalize the solute concentrations in two separate membrane–enclosed regions.

In living cells, water moves by osmosis across membranes between cells or between membrane-enclosed compartments within an individual cell. All biological membranes are considered selectively permeable since they are highly permeable to water but much less permeable to other substances, such as ions, proteins, and other solutes dissolved in the cell. Osmosis is a passive process, in that it requires no expenditure of cellular energy.

Osmotic pressure is the pressure exerted by dissolved solutes in a solution of water. The stronger the concentration of the dissolved solutes, the greater the movement of water up the concentration gradient, and the greater the osmotic pressure. The significance of osmosis in biology is illustrated by two examples below.

Osmosis in red blood cells

Mammalian red blood cells have a biconcave (doughnut–like) shape. If red blood cells are placed in a 0.3 M NaCl solution, there is little net osmotic movement of water, the size and shape of the cells stay the same; the NaCl solution is isotonic to the cell. If red blood cells are placed in a solution with a lower solute concentration than is found in the cells, water moves into the cells by osmosis, causing the cells to swell; such a solution is hypotonic to the cells. When red blood cells are placed in pure water, water rapidly enters the cells by osmosis and causes the cells to burst, a phenomenon known as hemolysis. If the red blood cells are placed in a solution with a higher solute concentration, water moves out of the cell by osmosis, the cell becomes smaller and crenated in shape; such a solution is hypertonic to the cells.

These observations have several important practical implications. First, hospitals must store red blood cells in a plasma solution which has the correct proportions of salts and proteins. The plasma solution is made to be slightly hypertonic to the red cells so that the integrity of the cells is preserved and hemolysis is prevented. Second, when doctors inject a drug intravenously into a patient, the drug is suspended in a saline solution which is slightly hypertonic to red blood cells. Intravenous injection of a drug in pure water will cause some of the patient's red blood cells to hemolyze because water is hypotonic to the red blood cells.

Osmosis in plant cells

Plant cells are surrounded by rigid cellulose walls, (unlike animal cells), but plant cells still take in water by osmosis when placed in pure water. However, plant cells do not burst because their cellulose cell walls limit how much water can move in. The cell walls exert pressure, called turgor pressure, as the cells take up water. Turgor pressure is analogous to the air pressure of an inflated tire. These physical forces can be described by a simple mathematical equation: $\psi = P + \pi$ (2) where ψ ("Psi") is the water potential, a measure of the overall tendency of water to move into a cell; P is the pressure potential, a measure of the turgor pressure exerted by the cell walls; and π is the osmotic potential (see above). Water always moves from regions of higher ψ to areas of lower ψ. Animal cells do not have cellulose cell walls, so P = 0 and $\psi = \pi$ for these cells.

The significance of osmosis to plant function is best appreciated by describing its role in the regulation of guard cells. Guard cells are specialized cells scat-

tered across the surface of plant leaves. Each pair of guard cells surround a special pore, termed a stoma (plural stomata) and control its opening. Guard cells have a special arrangement of microfibrils in their walls, so that when the guard cells swell the stomata open. When the stomata of a plant leaf are open, this increases photosynthetic gas exchange and movement of water out of the plant by transpiration.

In many plants, certain environmental stimuli, such as sunlight, stimulate the guard cells to take up potassium from surrounding cells. This causes their osmotic potential (π) to decrease and water moves in by osmosis. Thus, the guard cells swell, the stomata open, and the rate of gas exchange through the stomata increases. This increases the rate of photosynthesis and plant growth.

Other environmental cues, such as water shortage, cause plants to transmit chemical signals to the guard cells, causing them to release potassium, which increases their osmotic potential, and to lose water by osmosis. This causes the guard cells to shrink, so closing the stomata, and decreasing the rate of water transpiration through the stomata. This reduces water loss and prevents wilting of the plant.

Plants rely upon other environmental signals to regulate the osmotic movement of water into their guard cells and the opening of the stomata, so that the advantage of increased photosynthesis is balanced against the disadvantage of increased water loss.

See also Diffusion; Transpiration.

Further Reading:

Salisbury, F. B., and C. W. Ross. *Plant Physiology.* Belmont, CA: Wadsworth Publishing Company, 1992.

Peter A. Ensminger

Ossification

Ossification is the process of the synthesis of bone from cartilage. There are two types of ossification—intramembranous and endochondral ossification. Bone may be synthesized by intramembranous ossification, endochondral ossification, or a combination of the two.

Intramembranous ossification is the transformation of the mesenchyme, cells of an embryo into bone. During early development of vertebrate animals, the embryo consists of three primary cell layers: ectoderm on the outside, mesoderm in the middle, and endoderm on the inside. Mesenchyme cells constitute part of the embryo's mesoderm and develop into connective tissue such as bone and blood. The bones of the skull derive directly from mesenchyme cells by intramembranous ossification.

Endochondral ossification is the gradual replacement of cartilage by bone during development. This process is responsible for formation of most of the skeleton of vertebrate animals. In this process, actively dividing bone–forming cells (osteoblasts) arise in regions of cartilage called ossification centers. The osteoblasts then develop into osteocytes, which are mature bone cells embedded in the calcified (hardened) part of the bone known as the matrix.

Most bones arise from a combination of intramembranous and endochondral ossification. In this process, mesenchyme cells develop into chondroblasts and increase in number by cell division. Then, the chondroblasts enlarge and excrete a matrix which hardens due to presence of inorganic minerals. Then, chambers form within the matrix and osteoblasts and blood–forming cells enter these chambers. The osteoblasts then secrete minerals to form the bone matrix.

Mature hardened bone is living tissue consisting of an organic component and a mineral component. The organic part mainly consists of proteins such as collagen fibers, an extracellular matrix, and fibroblasts, which have the living cells that produce the collagen and matrix. The mineral part of bone, which is made of hydroxyapatite and calcium carbonate, and gives bones their strength and rigidity. During the life of an individual, osteoblasts continually secrete minerals while osteoclasts continually reabsorb the minerals. Bedridden hospital patients and astronauts often show loss of bone because reabsorption by osteoclasts exceeds synthesis by osteoblasts. Bones become more brittle as a person ages because the mineral part of the bones decreases.

See also Collagen; Osteoporosis; Skeletal system.

Peter A. Ensimger

Osteoporosis

Osteoporosis is a condition in which bone mass, and therefore bone strength, is decreased. This results in a greatly increased risk of fracture. Primary osteoporosis is osteoporosis which occurs due to normal, predictable changes within the body during the aging process. Secondary osteoporosis occurs as a result of some other specific disease process which produces osteoporosis as one of its symptoms.

The basics of bone formation

To understand osteoporosis, it is helpful to understand the basics of bone formation. Bone is formed on a protein base (collagen) by the deposition of minerals, particularly calcium. This laying down of bone is carried out by specialized cells called osteoblasts. The formation of new bone occurs most effectively along lines of stress/weight that are experienced by the bone.

Other cells, osteoclasts, are responsible for resorbing (taking up) bone. These cells actually digest already-formed bone.

This active resorption–formation cycle within bone occurs throughout life, so that old bone is always being replaced by new bone. When the resorption phase is accelerated, or the formation phase is slowed, less calcified bone exists. This is the state which results in the weakened bone structure present in osteoporosis.

Why osteoporosis occurs

A decrease in the rate of bone mineralization is a predictable effect of aging. For example, in infancy, the turnover rate of calcium in bone is 100%; by adulthood, this turnover rate falls to only 18% per year.

Women are particularly prone to osteoporosis because of several factors. Women have less bone mass than men to begin with, so the threshold level at which osteoporosis may cause fractures is reached more quickly. It is believed that the bone formation phase is encouraged in some way by the presence of estrogen. In women, estrogen production drops off drastically following menopause (the cessation of the menstrual period). This change in the chemical environment within the bodies of older women apparently results in a decrease in the bone formation phase. With bone resorption continuing at its normal pace, but without the normal pace of bone replacement occurring, bone mass decreases.

Because the pattern of bone formation occurs in response to weight/stresses borne by the bone, disuse osteoporosis occurs in individuals who are on bed rest for prolonged periods of time, as well as in individuals experiencing the relative weightlessness of space flight.

Other causes of osteoporosis include many diseases which alter the hormonal/chemical environment of the body, including thyroid disease, disease of the parathyroid (a gland responsible for calcium levels within the body), gastrointestinal diseases (which can alter the ability of the body to absorb calcium in the diet), diseases which decrease the amount of estrogen produced, and certain liver diseases.

Alcohol and some drugs can also affect calcium levels in the body, thus producing osteoporosis. Some of these drugs include thyroid medications, steroid preparations, anti–seizure medications, and certain chemotherapy (anti–cancer) agents.

Congenital diseases (diseases present at birth) of connective tissue (a group of tissues of the body which includes bone) can cause abnormalities of bone structure, and therefore osteoporosis. Such diseases include osteogenesis imperfecta (brittle bone disease) and Marfan's syndrome.

Symptoms of osteoporosis

Symptoms of osteoporosis occur primarily due to the results of bone fractures. The most common locations for such fractures are those bones which should normally have the highest turnover rate of resorption–formation. The wrist is one such location,

and a characteristic fracture of the wrist due to osteoporosis is known as a Colle's fracture.

The vertebrae normally also have a high bone turnover rate, and osteoporosis frequently manifests itself by compression fractures of the vertebrae. These fractures can occur after seemingly normal activity, including sneezing or bending/twisting to pick up a relatively light object. This can be asymptomatic for the patient, or can result in back pain. Either way, the patient's vertebrae are compressed down on themselves, and the patient actually loses height. The hunchback appearance of many elderly women (sometimes referred to as dowager's or widow's hump) is due to this effect of osteoporosis on the vertebrae.

The hip (specifically the bone called the femur) is another extremely common location for an osteoporotic fracture. In fact, while it was initially thought that an individual falling resulted in a broken femur, it now believed that some femur fractures occur somewhat spontaneously, and the already broken hip then causes the individual to fall.

Diagnosis

Ideally, diagnosis of osteoporosis should be made prior to the occurrence of symptom–causing fractures. Various radiologic techniques are available to measure the density (solidity) of bone, and include x–ray and CT (computed tomography) examinations of the spine, femur, and wrist bones.

In the case of osteoporosis which is not due to normal aging, but is secondary to another disease process, other laboratory examination may be necessary. Calcium blood level, thyroid, liver, and parathyroid function may need to be evaluated. Other diseases which cause secondary osteoporosis (such as gastrointestinal disease) are usually evident due to other symptomatology.

Treatment

Treatment of secondary osteoporosis varies depending on the actual disease process which has produced the osteoporosis, and may include adjustments to thyroid medication, dietary supplementation with calcium or vitamin D (which is involved in the ability of the intestine to absorb calcium in the diet), or other treatment of the primary disease.

Treatment of primary osteoporosis in the elderly involves adequate intake of calcium and vitamin D, as well as regular exercise. Exercise is helpful both to strengthen muscle and to increase weight–bearing activity (remember that bone formation occurs most

KEY TERMS

Estrogen—A hormone present in both males and females. It is present in greatly larger quantities in females, however, and is responsible for many of those physical characteristics which appear during female sexual maturation.

Fracture—A break in a bone.

Menopause—The time in a woman's life when the chemical environment of her body changes, resulting in decreased estrogen production (among other things) and the cessation of her menstrual period.

Osteoblasts—Those cells which are responsible for the building of new bone.

Osteoclasts—Those cells which are responsible for the taking up/digestion of old bone.

effectively along lines of stress and weight–bearing). Bone loss can be decreased in elderly women by estrogen replacement therapy, ideally beginning during the first years of menopause.

Unfortunately, the majority of treatment for osteoporosis occurs in the form of treatment of the fractures resulting from the disease, and includes pain medications and heat for vertebral compressions, simple casts for uncomplicated fractures, or hip replacement surgery for more complicated hip fractures.

The importance of osteoporosis in terms of the misery it causes and its economic impact is underscored by these statistics. About one–third of all women over the age of 70 experience hip fracture. Of those elderly people who fracture a hip, about 15% die of complications secondary to that hip fracture. A large percentage of those who survive are unable to return to their previous level of activity, and many times a hip fracture precipitates a move from self–care to a supervised living situation or nursing home. The yearly cost of osteoporotic injury in the United States is greater than $10 billion.

See also Skeletal system.

Further Reading:

Andreoli, Thomas E., et al. *Cecil Essentials of Medicine.* Philadelphia: W. B. Saunders Company, 1993.
Berkow, Robert, and Andrew J. Fletcher. *The Merck Manual of Diagnosis and Therapy.* Rahway, NJ: Merck Research Laboratories, 1992.

Ganong, William F. *Review of Medical Physiology.* Norwalk, CT: Appleton & Lange, 1993.

Rosalyn Carson–DeWitt

Ossicles see Ear

Ostriches see **Flightless birds**

Otters

Otters are small to medium–sized mammals with long bodies, flattened heads, broad muzzles, and long stiff whiskers. Their tails are strong, long, flattened, and somewhat tapered. Otters have short legs and webbed toes; they are adapted well to a semi–aquatic existence and are skilled swimmers. The outer fur of otters is short, very dense, and highly water resistant. They also have a layer of soft underfur which traps an insulating layer of air and helps them stay warm while in the water. Otters are carnivores and have teeth that are adapted either to eating fish or to crushing the shells of various crustaceans, depending on species and diet. The ears of otters are small and can close (with the help of special muscles), while their hearing is good. Their eyes are small but their sight is good due to special lenses that help them see clearly underwater. Male otters are usually 28% larger than females.

Otters are members of the weasel family, called Mustelidae. There are five subfamilies within this family: weasels, minks, and polecats (Mustelinae); skunks (Mephitinae); badgers (Melinae); honey badgers (Mellivorinae); and otters (Lutrinae). The Lutrinae subfamily includes six genera: sea otters, river otters, clawless otters, giant otters and two genera of small–clawed otters, and some 18 species, with 63 subspecies.

Diet

Otters can be separated into two groups on the basis of their diet. The first group, which includes river otters and giant otters among others, specializes in eating fish. These species have sharp teeth that are useful in catching and gripping their slippery prey. The second group, which includes the small clawed otters and sea otters, specializes in eating invertebrates, such as shellfish. These otters have blunted teeth useful in breaking shells. However, otters are highly adaptive, and neither group solely eats just one type of prey.

Play

Otters are extremely playful. Anyone who visits a zoo can see otters sliding down embankments and flipping about in the water. Otters typically twist and turn as they swim, sometimes on their backs and sometimes on their sides. Having seemingly unlimited energy, otters often slide down muddy banks over and over again with no apparent motive other than sheer enjoyment.

There is some disagreement about how much time otters spend in play in the wild. Some think that play in the wild is limited to teaching the young the fighting and hunting skills that they will need to survive, and that sliding activity is simply a way for otters to move quickly. Others think that otters play extensively in the wild for pure enjoyment as well as for more practical reasons.

Sea otter

Sea otters (*Enhydra lutris*) measure up to 4 ft (1.3 m) long with a 12–in (30.5–cm) tail. Sea otters are common on rocky coastlines and islands on both sides of the North Pacific Ocean from Japan north to the Aleutian Islands and south to the coast of California.

Sea otters spend almost all of their lives at sea and are the only mustelids able to do so. While they are in the water, they usually lie on their backs, grooming themselves, feeding their young, resting, or eating. Sea otters come to land to breed or when the weather is bad, for while they are skilled swimmers, they are slow and clumsy on land. When sea otters swim, they use their tail and hind feet, tucking their front feet under their chests. Their webbed hind feet, resembling those of sea lions, are much bigger than the hind feet of other otters. The tail is shorter than that of other otters, as are the fingers, which have small, rectractile claws.

The thick reddish to deep black fur, which is soft and silky in texture, serves to insulate sea otters from the cool water. Sea otters do not have an excess layer of fat for insulation, like many other aquatic mammals. They rely on a layer of air in their fur to protect them from the cold, and they keep their fur aerated by rubbing it with their feet to squeeze the water out. They contort themselves and wriggle around until the fur on even the most hard–to–reach parts of their bodies is aerated. Also, sea otters tend to blow on their coats to increase the amount of trapped air.

Sea otters feed on clams, mussels, and other crustaceans. To break open these hard shells, they use rocks, which they bring up from the sea bed, as tools. As a sea otter lies on its back, it places the stone on its chest and beats the prey against it, thereby cracking the shell and exposing the meat inside. At twilight, sea otters move into kelp beds to sleep, tangling themselves in the vegetation so that they do not drift out to sea.

Sea otters breed every two years. The female bears one pup after a gestation period of eight to nine months. The newborn pup is well developed, having all of its teeth and open eyes. The mother carries and nurses her offspring on her stomach while swimming on her back.

River otters

There are 11 species of river otter, including the Eurasian river otter (*Lutra lutra*), the North American river otter (*Lutra canadensis*), the southern river otter (*Lutra provocax*), and the smooth otter (*Lutra perspicillata*). Often confused with European mink, the river otter is heavier, with a broader face and a tail which is stout at the base, becoming flatter and more tapered toward the end. River otters are most prevalent in Eurasia and North America, although a few species are found in Central and South America, as well as in limited areas of Africa and Southeast Asia.

River otters usually live near rivers, although some species live near flooded areas, lakes, brackish water, and on coastal islands. When the food supply runs low, river otters will move away from their native waters to hunt. They prefer to move via water but will travel on land if they must. These otters usually hunt at night, often staying underwater for up to eight minutes at a time. Normally, the adults hunt alone, but mothers will hunt with their young for a significant period of time after they are born. Traveling long distances during a single night's hunt, they conceal themselves in the day in reeds and other vegetation before hunting again the next night. In a few days, these otters return to their home waters. During the winter, river otters slip through cracks in ice to hunt, sometimes surfacing through the hole to breathe. River otters eat fish, muskrats, and aquatic birds.

The female river otters bear their young in burrows between April and June. Born with their eyes closed, the young nurse for about four months, opening their eyes about one month after birth. They usually grow to adult size in two years.

Grooming is very important to river otters. However, unlike many other mammals, river otters do not nibble their coats looking for insects. Instead, like sea otters, they tend to groom themselves with the goal of drying out their fur to keep it waterproof. They do this by rolling and squirming on dry land or rubbing against trees or plants.

Clawless otters

There are three species of clawless otter in the genus *Aonyx*—two are found in Africa and one is found in Asia. Otters in this genus differ from river otters and the giant otter in having much smaller claws and in having webbing on their feet that is either entirely absent or that does not extend to the ends of their toes. The Asian small–clawed otter (*Aonyx cinerea*) is the world's smallest otter, measuring just 25.6–35.5 in (65–90 cm) and weighing about 11 lb (5 kg). This species lives in small streams, rice paddies, and coastal mangrove swamps from the Philippines through Indonesia, southeast Asia, and southern China westward to southern India. It is a very social animal, and lives in groups of up to 15 individuals. Its diet consists primarily of fish, molluscs, and crabs.

Two other species of clawless otter—the Cape clawless otter (*Aonyx capensis*) and the Congo clawless otter (*A. congica*)—are found in Africa. The Cape clawless otter of sub–Saharan Africa lives in swamps, rivers, streams, estuaries, and lakes. This species has no webbing on its forefeet, enabling it to use its fingers freely to probe mud and gravel for prey. Its diet includes crabs, molluscs, frogs, and fish. The head and body of the Cape clawless otter measures 28.4–35.9 in (72–91 cm) and its tail is 15.8–28 in (40–71 cm) long. The male is larger than the female.

The Congo clawless otter, found in west and central equatorial Africa, is not as well known as the closely related Cape clawless otter. It is similar in size and color to *A. capensis*, but is distinguished from it by silver tips on the fur of the head and neck, and by dark patches of fur between the eyes and nostrils. Of all the otters, this species is least adapted to an aquatic environment. It prefers swampy habitats such as marshes and lake margins, where it preys upon frogs, crabs, earthworms, and fish. The Congo clawless otter has shorter, thinner (less insulating) fur than other otters. Its forefeet are unwebbed, hairless, and clawless—all adaptations for searching for its food in mud, gravel, or other debris.

Giant otter

The giant otter (*Pteronura brasiliensis*) of Brazil is the largest otter species; it measures up to 7 ft (2.1 m) long, including its tail, and can weigh more than 50 lb (23 kg). Like other otters, it has webbed hind feet and a large flat tail suited for swimming. Giant otters hunt in groups of 20 or more during the morning and at twilight. Having a diet similar to the river otter, giant otters consume their prey by holding it in their forepaws and consuming it head first. These otters live in dens dug in riverbanks, and have one or two offspring each year.

Human impact on otters

Otters have been hunted by humans for centuries for their soft, thick fur and because of competition for fish due to the predatory habits of otters. Trade in otter fur was once very active, but the hunting of otters for their fur has declined in recent years, due both to the decline in otter populations (especially certain species of river otter) and the passage of laws protecting otters. The best otter pelts are reportedly from the North American river otter, specifically from otters living in Labrador.

Otters, being fairly intelligent animals, have occasionally been trained. Otters catch and retrieve fish in Sweden and China, and in India, tame, muzzled otters have been used to drive fish into nets.

Further Reading:

Chanin, Paul. *The Natural History of Otters.* New York: Facts on File Publications, 1985.
Grzimek, H. C. Bernard, ed. *Grzimek's Animal Life Encyclopedia.* New York: Van Nostrand Reinhold, 1993.
The Illustrated Encyclopedia of Wildlife. London: Grey Castle Press, 1991.
MacMillan Illustrated Animal Encyclopedia. New York: MacMillan, 1992.
Mason, C. F., and S. M. Macdonald. *Otters: Ecology and Conservation.* London: Cambridge University Press, 1986.

Kathryn Snavely

Otter shrews

Otter shrews are small otter–like aquatic mammals in the superfamily Tenrecoidea, family Potamogalidae, with silvery fur. The three species of otter shrews belong to the order Insectivora, and all live in west and central Africa near the equator.

The Potamogalidae family includes two genera—*Micropotamogale* and *Potamogale*. These genera contain a total of three distinctive species of otter shrew—the giant African otter shrew (*Potamogale velox*), the small African otter shrew (*Micropotamogale lamottei*), and the Ruwenzori otter shrew (*M. ruwenzorii*).

Giant African otter shrews, one of the largest insectivores, are the most common type of otter shrew. These otter shrews have a head and body length of 11.4–13.8 in (29–35 cm) and a tail measuring 9.7–13.8 in (24.5–29 cm). They have small eyes and ears and flattened muzzles with white whiskers. Flaps covering their nostrils act as valves when the animal is submerged, but their feet are not webbed.

Giant African otter shrews are insectivores, and have several adaptations for an aquatic life. For example, their elongated bodies and powerful compressed tails resemble those of common otters. These adaptations make otter shrews skilled and rapid swimmers. Further, because of their preference for living near water, they commonly feed on freshwater crabs, fish, and amphibians. Although giant otter shrews are somewhat clumsy on land, they can move rapidly.

Giant otter shrews are found in the rain forest zone of central Africa including Zaire, Angola, Cameroon, and Gabon, at altitudes up to 1,800 ft (549 m). They inhabit wetlands from muddy bogs to clear mountain streams. These otter shrews dig tunnels in stream banks which they enter from below the water level. In the daytime, otter shrews take shelter in their burrows, and in the late afternoon, they come out to feed and play.

The two species of dwarf African otter shrew in the genus *Micropotamogale* are about half as large as the giant African otter shrew. The small African otter shrew (also called the Nimba otter shrew), which lives in West Africa, has a head and body length of about 6 in (15 cm) and a tail measuring around 4.3 in (11 cm). Its feet are not webbed. Ruwenzori otter shrews have larger bodies than small African otter shrews and their tails are longer and more powerful. Their feet are also larger and are webbed. These otter shrews live in the Ruwenzori Mountains in Zaire and Uganda.

Dwarf African otter shrews are the rarest species. They are found in Guinea, Liberia, and the Ivory Coast. These small otter shrews prefer to live near shallow water, such as in swampy areas with a lot of undergrowth or small pools of water. Like the giant African otter shrew, dwarf otter shrews eat fish, freshwater crabs and insects, and they are most active at night.

The small African otter shrew is considered endangered by IUCN—The World Conservation Union. Some portions of its habitat have already been devastated by mining activities and other areas are threatened.

See also Shrews.

Outcrop

When weathering and erosion expose part of a rock layer or formation, an outcrop appears. An outcrop is the exposed rock, so named because the exposed rock "crops out." Outcrops provide opportunities for field geologists to sample the local geology—photograph it, hold, touch, climb, hammer, map, sniff, lick, chew, and carry it home. Classes often visit outcrops to see illustrations of the principles of geology that were introduced in lecture. You often can see geologists or students identifying rocks in roadcuts, outcrops along the road where highway construction exposed the rocks.

Mountainous regions, where any loosened Earth material swiftly washes away, contain some of the best outcrops because a greater percentage of the rock formation lies exposed. Rocks crop out especially well across steep slopes, above the tree line (elevation above which trees cannot grow), and on land scraped free of soil by bulldozer–like glaciers. Sediment collects and plants grow in flatter areas, obscuring the rocks. In some areas soil and sediment may completely cover all the underlying rock, such as in the southeastern United States. However, in the desert southwest, the opposite is often the case. Outcrops cut the cost of mapping for geologists. The greater expense of geologic mapping in an outcrop–free area results from high–priced drilling to sample the rocks hidden below the surface.

See also Erosion; Weathering.

Ova see **Reproductive system; Sexual reproduction**

Oval window see **Ear**

Ovaries see **Reproductive system**

Ovary (plant) see **Flower**

Ovenbirds

Ovenbirds are 200 species of birds that compose the rather large family Furnariidae, occurring from southern Mexico through Central and all of South America. Ovenbirds occur in a wide variety of habitats, ranging from mature tropical forests to semi–desert, and from coastal lowlands to alpine tundra. In other words, the ovenbird family is very rich in species, and these birds successfully exploit almost all of the habitable ecosystems within their major range.

Many species of ovenbirds build a characteristic, dome–shaped nest of clay, which resembles an old–style, wood–fired bakers' oven, and is the basis of the common name of this group of birds. Depending on the species, the nest can be located on a horizontal branch of a tree, on a post, or on the ground. The nest is constructed of mud, with plant fibers mixed in for greater strength. These materials are carried in the bill. The dome is about 12 in (30 cm) in diameter, can weigh about 9 lb (4 kg), and is kiln–like in shape, with a deep, narrow entrance. There is an inner, walled–off, nesting chamber, lined with grasses. Although old nests physically last for several years, ovenbirds construct a new structure for each brood.

Some species of ovenbirds nest in an underground burrow or in a tree cavity. The rufous–fronted thornbird (*Phacellodomus rufifrons*) builds bulky, communal nests out of thorny twigs in trees, with each pair having a separate entrance and nesting cavity.

Ovenbirds are small, plainly colored, olive green or brown birds, with a lighter, often streaked belly. Most species have a light–colored throat and a white line over the eye. A few species have very long tail feathers, as much as several times the length of the body. The sexes do not differ in size or coloration.

Ovenbirds are insectivorous, eating a wide diversity of invertebrates. Depending on the species, these may be gleaned from the ground, rocks, woody debris, foliage, or other microhabitats. Some coastal species of *Cinclodes* even forage in the intertidal zone at low tide, a unique strategy among the passerine, or perching birds.

Five eggs are typically laid, and are incubated by both parents, which also share the raising of the young birds.

One of the most widespread and familiar species is the red ovenbird or baker (*Furnarius rufus*). The nest of this species is commonly built on the top of a post. The pair sings duets, while sitting on the top of their oven.

A species of ground–inhabiting wood warbler (family Parulidae) of North America builds a dome-topped nest, and is also commonly known as an ovenbird (*Seiurus aurocapillus*). However, this species is not related to the true ovenbirds, of the family Furnariidae.

Bill Freedman

Oviparous

Oviparous is a zoological term that refers to animals that lay eggs which then hatch externally.

Oviparous animals may fertilize their eggs either externally or internally. External fertilization involves the passage of the sperm to the ova through an ambient medium, usually water. For example, frogs achieve external fertilization of their eggs during amplexus, when the male deposits sperm over the eggs as they are laid by the female. External fertilization in many aquatic invertebrates is less well controlled; for example, in the case of many marine invertebrates which shed immense numbers of gametes to the water more or less simultaneously, with ova and sperm meeting somewhat by chance. All animals that fertilize their eggs externally are oviparous.

In cases of internal fertilization, male animals somehow pass their sperm into the female. For example, male salamanders deposit a sperm packet, or spermatophore, onto the bottom of their breeding pond and then induce an egg–bearing (or gravid) female to walk over it. The female picks up the spermatophore with the somewhat prehensile lips of her cloaca, and retains it inside of her body where the eggs become fertilized. These fertilized eggs are later laid and develop externally, representing oviparity.

Many species of fish, most species of lizards and snakes, all species of crocodilians and birds, and even certain primitive mammals such as the platypus and echidnas achieve internal fertilization of their eggs through copulation. If the eggs are then laid to develop externally, the process represents oviparity.

Ovoviviparity involves retaining of the fertilized eggs in the body of the female until they hatch, so that "live" young are born.

See also Ovoviviparous; Viviparity.

Ovoviviparous

Ovoviviparous is a zoological term that refers to animals that produce eggs but retain them inside the female body until hatching occurs, so that "live" offspring are born. The egg–hatching strategy of ovoviviparity occurs in a rather wide diversity of animals, including certain insects, fish, lizards, and snakes. However, ovoviviparity is much less common than the external development of fertilized eggs (that is, oviparity).

Ovoviviparous insects do not provide oxygen or nourishment to their developing eggs; they merely provide a safe brooding chamber for development. However, species of ovoviviparous fish, lizards, and snakes appear to provide some nutrition and oxygen to their developing progeny within the oviduct (although most nutrition is provided by the yolk of the eggs). Moreover, in these species the eggshell is greatly reduced in thickness and is essentially reduced to a membrane. Because some nutrition is provided to the developing egg and larva and the eggshell is essentially absent, the cases of ovoviviparity in fish, lizards, and snakes are considered by some zoologists to represent true live birth, or viviparity.

There are many cases of ovoviviparity, but only a few vertebrate cases will be used here to illustrate the syndrome. The guppy (*Lebistes reticulatus*) is a small, freshwater fish that is native to the West Indies and northern South America, and is commonly kept as a pet in aquaria. The guppy is internally fertilized, and the eggs are retained in the oviduct of the female where they hatch and develop, so that live young are born.

Similarly, the garter snake (*Thamnophis sirtalis*) is a common and widespread species in North America. This species achieves internal fertilization by copulation, incubates the eggs within the oviduct of the female, and gives birth to live young in the late summer. At birth, the young snakes are enclosed in an amniotic sac from which they quickly escape and then slither away to lead an independent life.

An extremely unusual case that may represent a border–line case of ovoviviparity involves a very rare (and possibly extinct) species of Australian frog. The gastric–brooding frog (*Rheobatrachus silus*) is thought to fertilize its eggs externally (fertilization has never been observed by scientists), but the female then swallows the eggs and retains them in her stomach. There the eggs hatch and develop over about a 37–day period, to be "born" as small froglets through the female's mouth, almost identical in morphology to the adult, except for size. In this case, the fertilized eggs develop, hatch, pass through their larval stage (that is, the tadpole stage), and metamorphose into a froglet, which is "born" through the mouth. While she is brooding eggs, the female does not eat, and she suppresses the production of stomach acids and digestive enzymes so as to not digest her progeny. The extraordinary case of the gastric–brooding frog may represent the only known case of an externally fertilized, ovoviviparous species (unless the definition of ovoviviparity is restricted to cases in which the eggs are brooded within the reproductive tract of the female).

See also Oviparous; Viviparity.

Bill Freedman

Owls

Owls comprise two closely related families in the avian order Strigiformes—the barn owls, or Tytonidae, and the typical owls, or Strigidae. Owls are relatively large birds, with a big head and short neck, a hooked beak, talons adapted to seize prey, and soft, dense plumage adapted for swift yet almost silent flight. Owls have large eyes located on the front of their face but almost fixed in their sockets, so that the entire head must be rotated or bobbed for the gaze to be shifted and for distance to be visually gauged.

Owls have excellent hearing and very large ears, although these are covered by feathers and are not readily seen. The ears are placed asymmetrically on the head to aid in detecting the location of distant, weakly noisy prey. The sense of hearing is probably also aided by the facial disk of owls, which helps to focus sound waves onto the ears. The sense of hearing of owls is so acute that the nocturnally hunting species can accurately strike its prey in total darkness, following the squeaks and rustling sounds created by a small mammal in motion.

The sex of an owl is not easy to distinguish, although typically, female owls are larger than males. Owls begin to incubate their eggs as they are laid, which means that hatching is sequential, and different–sized young are in the nest at the same time. During years in which prey is relatively abundant, all of the young will have enough to eat and may survive. In leaner years, however, only the largest young may be fed adequately.

Most owls are nocturnal predators, mostly feeding on small mammals and birds, but sometimes on small reptiles, frogs, larger insects, and earthworms. A few specialized owls feed on fish. Owls are known to change their food preference, depending on local or seasonal availability. Most owls do not digest the fur, feathers, or bones of their prey, and they regurgitate these items as pellets, which can be collected at roosts and examined to learn about the feeding habits of these birds.

Barn owls

The barn owls are a distinctive–looking group, with a characteristic facial disk of stiff, white feathers, dark eyes, long legs, and other features that distinguish them from typical owls. All barn owls are nocturnal predators, mostly of small mammals. There are nine species of barn owls (genus *Tyto*) and two species of closely related grass owls (genus *Phodilus*).

The most familiar species is the barn owl (*Tyto alba*). The barn owl is one of the most widely distributed species of birds, occurring on all continents but Antarctica, and with about 30 races described, many of which are endemic to particular oceanic islands. The barn owl is the only representative of this family in the Americas, occurring uncommonly through most of the United States and in much of Central and South America. The barn owl roosts in cavities in trees and in barns and abandoned buildings, and it hunts at dusk and at night over marshes, prairies, fields, and farmyards.

Typical owls

There are about 120 species of typical owls. Most species are brownish colored with dark streaks and other patterns, which helps the birds blend with the environment when roosting in trees or flying in dim light. Most typical owls have distinct facial disks. Many species have feathered "ear" tufts, which are important for determining another owl's silhouette and are used by owls in species recognition. Also important for recognition are the distinctive hoots and other calls of these birds. Most typical owls have a brilliant yellow iris, and they have excellent vision in the dark. These birds also have extraordinary hearing, which is important for detecting and capturing prey.

Typical owls occur worldwide, in almost all habitats where their usual prey of small mammals, birds, lizards, snakes, and larger insects and other invertebrates can be found. Most species occur in forests, but others breed in desert, tundra, prairie, or savanna habitats. These birds are solitary nesters, and because they are high–level predators they maintain relatively large territories, generally hundreds of hectares in area. Territories are established mostly using species–specific vocalizations, although more direct conflicts also sometimes occur. Northern species of owls are migratory, moving south as deepening snow makes it difficult for them to find and catch small mammals.

Larger owls tend to eat bigger prey than smaller owls. The eagle owl (*Bubo bubo*) of northern Eurasia has a body up to 26 in (67 cm) long and weighs as much as 9 lb (4 kg) or more, and is a formidable predator that feeds on animals as large as ducks, hares, other birds of prey, porcupines, foxes, and even small deer. In contrast, the tiny, 5 in (13 cm) elf owl (*Micrathene whitneyi*) of the southwestern United States and western

Mexico mostly eats insects and arachnids, including scorpions. Some species of owls are rather specialized feeders. The fish–owls of Africa and Asia, such as the tawny fish–owl (*Ketupa flavipes*) of south China and southeast Asia, mostly catch fish at or very near the water surface.

There are 17 species of typical owls breeding in North America. The largest species is the great horned owl (*Bubo virginianus*), with a body length of about 20 in (50 cm). This is a widespread and relatively common species that occurs almost everywhere but the northern tundra, feeding on prey as large as hare, skunks, and porcupines. The smallest species of owl in North America is the previously mentioned elf owl.

The screech owl (*Otus asio*) is a relatively familiar species in woodlands of temperate regions. This 8 in (20 cm) long species occurs in several color phases— grey, red, and brown—and it nests in cavities and sometimes nestboxes.

The snowy owl (*Nyctea scandiaca*) breeds in the tundra of North America and Eurasia. However, this species wanders much farther to the south during winter, when the small mammals it eats are difficult to obtain in the Arctic. The snowy owl is a whitish–colored bird that nests on the ground, feeds during the day, and is relatively tame, often allowing people to approach rather closely.

The burrowing owl (*Speotyto cunicularia*) is a species that inhabits grasslands and prairies in southwestern North America and southern Florida. This species hunts during the day, and often hovers distinctively while foraging. In the prairies, these owls typically roost and nest in the burrows of black–tailed prairie dogs (*Cynomys ludovicianus*).

The spotted owl (*Strix occidentalis*) is a rare species of coastal, usually old–growth, forests of southwestern North America and parts of Mexico. This northern subspecies (*S. o. caurina*) is listed as "threatened" under the U.S. Endangered Species Act. Because the habitat of the spotted owl is being diminished by logging of the old–growth forests of Washington, Oregon, and California, plans have been developed for the longer–term protection of this bird. These plans require the protection of large tracts of old–growth, conifer–dominated forest to ensure that sufficient areas of suitable habitat are available to support a viable population of these owls.

Importance of owls

Owls that feed in agricultural areas provide benefits to humans by killing large numbers of small rodents which might otherwise eat crops in the field or in storage. Owls are also widely sought by bird watchers, who highly value sightings of these elusive and mysterious–looking predators. Bird watchers and other naturalists spend a great deal of money for transportation and birding paraphernalia to engage in their pursuit of owls and other birds.

Owls are rarely viewed as pests. In rare instances, they may kill some gamebirds, such as grouse or pheasant, and gamekeepers have killed owls and other birds of prey for this reason. However, owls are not true pests, and enlightened game managers no longer kill these birds.

Owls are, however, threatened by other activities of humans. They are exposed to toxic chemicals in forestry and agriculture, and this has taken a toll on some species of owls. Burrowing owls, for example, have been poisoned by exposure to the insecticide carbofuran, which is used to control epidemic populations of grasshoppers in prairie agriculture.

More important, however, have been the effects of habitat loss on owls. The impact of urban, industrial, and agricultural development on the environment degrades the habitat of owls and other species, causing large reductions in their populations and even their disappearance from some locations. In North America, this type of effect on owls is best illustrated by the case of the spotted owl, which is threatened by logging in its habitat of old–growth conifer forests. In this particular case, the owls can only be protected by setting aside large areas of suitable habitat as ecological reserves. This strategy is costly for the forest industry, because it results in large amounts of valuable timber being protected from exploitation. However, this must be done if spotted owls and their associated species are to sustain their populations in their natural habitat.

Further Reading:
Burton, J.A., ed. *Owls of the World. Their Evolution, Structure, and Ecology.* London: Peter Lowe, 1992.
Harrison, C. J. O., ed. *Bird Families of the World.* New York: H. N. Abrams, 1978.
Hume, R. *Owls of the World.* Limpsfield, England: Dragon's World, 1991.
Voous, K. H. *Owls of the Northern Hemisphere.* New York: Harper Collins, 1990.

Bill Freedman

Ovulation see **Menstrual cycle; Reproductive system**

Oxalic acid

Oxalic acid is the more common name of ethanedioic acid. The name ethanedioic acid communicates that the molecule has two carbon atoms (as in ethane) and two acid groups (COOH). It has the chemical formula $C_2H_2O_4$ and the structure of the molecule is shown below:

It is a white solid used in removal of certain kinds of stains, in removing calcium ions from solutions, and in tanning leather. It occurs naturally and is toxic. The potassium and calcium salts of oxalic acid are found naturally in cabbage, spinach, and rhubarb leaves, and are also found in the bark of some species of eucalyptus trees. The metabolism of sugar by many species of mold results in the production of oxalic acid. Ingestion of large amounts can cause kidney damage, convulsions, and death.

The most common uses of oxalic acid are in tanning leather and removing rust and ink stains. In stain removal, it acts as a reducing agent (a substance that donates electrons to other substances) and is relied on by most dry cleaners for this purpose. Iron rust stains contain iron in its oxidized form (Fe III); the oxalic acid reduces it to its colorless reduced form (Fe II). Oxalic acid is also used to clean metals in many industries and is also used in the purification of glycerol (glycerin).

Few people ingest toxic amounts of oxalic acid directly. However, if a child or pet swallows antifreeze (which typically contains ethylene glycol and has a sweet taste), enzymes in the body will metabolize the ethylene glycol to oxalic acid, which is the reason antifreeze is toxic.

In many industrial processes oxalic acid is used to remove calcium ions from solutions. The reaction of calcium ions with oxalic acid produces an insoluble solid, calcium oxalate.

Oxidation see **Oxidation-reduction reaction**

Oxidation–reduction reaction

Oxidation–reduction reactions, also known as redox reactions, are chemical processes in which electrons are transferred from one atom, ion or molecule to another. Explosions, fires, batteries, and even our own bodies are powered by oxidation–reduction reactions. When iron rusts or colored paper bleaches in the sun, oxidation–reduction has taken place.

Oxidation–reduction reactions can be thought of as a combination of two processes: oxidation, in which electrons are lost, and reduction, in which electrons are gained. The two processes cannot occur independently of each other. A mnemonic device used by chemists to help keep things straight is "LEO says 'GER'," which stands for Loss of Electrons, Oxidation. Gain of Electrons, Reduction.

The driving force of oxidation–reduction reactions is the transfer of electrons. Although it is sometimes difficult to remember what happens to electrons during oxidation and what happens during reduction, a look at familiar processes can help keep this straight. Some of the first oxidation–reduction reactions understood by chemists were those involving oxygen. Oxygen, the most plentiful element on earth, combines readily with numerous other elements. When combined with other elements in a compound or molecule, oxygen frequently is an electron "hog." It takes electrons away from many other elements and this oxidizes them. The oxygen takes the negatively charged electrons and becomes a negatively charged ion. The oxygen has been reduced, somewhat like taking in negative thoughts will reduce a person's positive attitude. An example of this is the reaction between oxygen in the air and iron. The iron metal becomes positively charged and the oxygen becomes negatively charged. The two charged ions now attract each other and hang around together in the form of iron oxide, or rust.

History

Probably the earliest human use of oxidation-reduction reactions occurred 7,500–4,500 years ago in the Copper/Bronze Age. Copper ores were heated in the presence of carbon to produce copper metal. In this process, the copper in the ore was reduced to copper metal and the carbon was oxidized to carbon dioxide. This same process was applied to iron ores during the Iron Age, which occurred 4,500–3,500 years ago.

The use of oxidation–reduction reactions has long been a part of pottery making. Differences in color in the clay or glaze can be produced when firing pottery under oxidizing conditions when lots of oxygen is present or under low oxygen reducing conditions, such as with a partially closed kiln or a fire with green leaves on it. Clay containing iron will be orange–red if fired under oxidizing conditions due to the presence of red

iron oxide and black in reducing conditions when black iron oxide—in which the iron has a lower oxidation number—forms. Among the people who have historically used oxidizing and reducing fire conditions are the Native Americans in the southwestern United States and the Greeks in the Early Bronze Age.

Another historic use of oxidation–reduction reactions is in explosives, substances that burn—are oxidized—so rapidly that they cause huge amounts of pressure. Gunpowder, thought to be the first explosive used, originated in China as early as 960 A.D. It appeared in Europe around the 13th century. Eighteen forty–six was a banner year for explosives—nitrocellulose and nitroglycerin were both developed that year. TNT (trinitrotolmene) saw widespread use in World War I. Since 1955, a commonly used cheap and powerful explosive has been a mixture of ammonium nitrate and fuel oil. This was used to bomb the Federal Building in Oklahoma City in 1995, and its use may be curtailed in the future.

Fireworks, a colorful and bright form of oxidation–reduction reactions, are believed to have first been used in China in the sixth century.

An important step in the understanding of oxidation–reduction reactions was the discovery of oxygen. Joseph Priestley (1733–1804) was the first scientist on record to prepare oxygen in the laboratory. This historic reaction was also an oxidation–reduction reaction. Priestly heated mercury oxide and formed elemental mercury and oxygen. In this reaction, mercury was reduced and the oxide ion was oxidized. Antoine Lavoisier (1743–1794) recognized that when substances are burned, they combine with oxygen. He even figured out that our bodies burn food and give off carbon dioxide as we produce energy. Tragically, the life of this great chemist was ended prematurely when he was beheaded during the French Revolution.

Oxidation numbers

Oxidation numbers, sometimes called oxidation states, help chemists keep track of the numbers of electrons that surround each atom in a chemical reaction, and how they change in oxidation–reduction reactions. When an atom gains an electron (is reduced), its oxidation number is increased by one. There are some simple rules for assigning oxidation numbers to elements in chemical compounds. These rules are:

1. The oxidation number of an element, having neither gained nor lost any of its electrons, is zero. For example, the oxidation number of pure copper, Cu, is

zero, as is the oxidation number of each oxygen atom in a molecule of oxygen, O_2.

2. The oxidation number of an elemental ion is the same as its charge. An ion of copper with a plus two charge, Cu^{2+}, has an oxidation number of plus two. A fluoride ion, $F-$, has an oxidation number of minus one.

3. Some elements almost always form compounds in which they have a particular oxidation number. Aluminum always forms a plus three ion and therefore exists in the plus three oxidation state in compounds. Sodium and other alkali metals almost always form a plus one ion; its oxidation state is plus one. Hydrogen can form compounds in which the hydrogen atom has an oxidation number of either plus one or minus one. When the hydrogen has an oxidation number of plus one, it is written on the left hand side of the chemical formula. If its oxidation number is minus one, it is written on the right hand side. Oxygen usually has a minus two oxidation number. Chlorine and other halogens usually take on a minus one charge. Other elements are not so predictable. Nitrogen can have oxidation numbers of +5,+4,+3, +2,+1, and −3.

4. The sum of the oxidation numbers in a neutral molecule or compound is zero. Table salt, with the chemical formula of sodium chloride, is made up of two ions, a positively charged sodium ion and a negatively charged chloride ion. A water molecule consists of two hydrogen atoms, each having an oxidation number of plus one, and an oxygen atom with an oxidation number of minus two.

It is often easier to follow oxidation–reduction reactions if they are split into two half reactions. One–half reaction indicates what is happening to the chemical substances and electrons in the oxidation portion of the reaction. The other half–reaction does the same for the reduction portion. The complete reaction is the sum of the two half reactions.

A useful tool for chemists is a table of standard reduction potentials. This table lists common half reactions, and assigns each a numerical value that indicates how easily the reduction reaction proceeds—that is, how eagerly electrons are accepted. A high standard reduction potential value indicates that the substance is easily reduced. A low standard reduction potential indicates that the substance is easily oxidized—it prefers to lose electrons. In general, a substance will oxidize something that has a lower reduction potential than it has. The halogens, chemical elements found in group 17 of the Periodic table, are strong oxidizing agents because their atoms readily accept negative ions. The alkali metals such as sodium, found on the left side of the Periodic table in group 1, are strong reducing agents because their atoms readily give up an electron, becoming positive ions. The arbitrary zero point for standard reduction potentials has been designated as this reaction:

$$2H^+ + 2 \text{ electrons} \rightarrow H_2$$

This reaction has been assigned a potential of 0.000 volts under standard conditions. The standard reduction potential for fluorine gas is 2.+890 volts while that for sodium metal is −2.714 volts.

Examples of oxidation–reduction reactions

Combustion

Let us look at an oxidation–reduction more chemically as we examine what happened to the Hindenburg in 1937. The *Hindenburg* was a dirigible filled with hydrogen, which gave it the lift it needed to keep afloat. The *Hindenburg* was a luxurious mode of transportation complete with a dining room and 25 private rooms. However, its first voyage, from Germany to the United States, ended tragically with the destruction of the airship and the loss of 36 lives because of the explosive combination of hydrogen and oxygen illustrated by this equation. The oxidation numbers of each element are indicated below the chemical formulas:

hydrogen	+	oxygen	$\rightarrow$	water
$2H_2$	+	O_2	$\rightarrow$	H_2O
0		0		+1 (H) −2 (O)

Hydrogen underwent a loss of electrons; it was oxidized. Oxygen underwent a gain of electrons; it was reduced. In terms of half reactions, the oxidation half reaction shows what happens to the hydrogen:

$$H_2 \rightarrow 2H^+ + 2 \text{ electrons}$$

while the reduction half reaction illustrates what happens to the oxygen:

$$O_2 + 2 \text{ electrons} \rightarrow O^{2-}$$

Hydrogen and oxygen combined once again to produce a fireball in the sky in 1986. This time, the space shuttle *Challenger* was destroyed by the explosion and all seven crew members aboard were killed. Cold temperatures before the launch fatigued the O–rings that sealed the *Challenger*'s booster tanks containing 500,000 gallons of liquid hydrogen and oxygen. The controlled combination of hydrogen and oxygen was intended to provide power needed to launch the *Challenger* just as the combustion of gasoline provides power to a car. A spark ignited the two liquids and set off a massive uncontrolled oxidation-reduction reaction.

Oxidation–reduction reactions are often accompanied by release of heat and sometimes, flame. Combustion reactions are oxidation-reduction reactions that occur when oxygen oxidizes another material. For example, burning carbon in a lump of coal produces carbon dioxide. The reaction can be illustrated as:

$$C \quad + \quad O_2 \quad \rightarrow \quad CO_2$$
carbon   oxygen   carbon dioxide

In this reaction, carbon is oxidized, going from an oxidation number of 0 to +4. The oxygen is reduced from an oxidation number of 0 to –2. A similar reaction occurs when hydrocarbon fuel is burned.

Corrosion

Corrosion reactions also involve oxidation of substances by oxygen. However, these reactions are limited to the oxidation of metals, do not give off the light associated with combustion, and usually occur when moisture is present. Corrosion occurs most rapidly when metals are strained and bent; the metals rapidly oxidize in the strained regions. Corrosion can be inhibited by covering metal surfaces with paint or metals which are less easily oxidized. An example is the plating of iron with chromium on nickel. In some cases, more easily oxidized metals are used to coat or come in contact with the metal that is being protected. Then these will react more readily with the oxygen. An example is galvanizing: coating iron with zinc. Some substances such as aluminum quickly form an oxide coating in areas that are exposed, but this coating is inert to oxygen and this prevents further corrosion. That is why aluminum does not "rust."

Biological processes

Photosynthesis consists of a series of oxidation-reduction reactions which begin when carbon in carbon dioxide is reduced and electrons are passed to molecules in the plant. When living things break down molecules of food to produce energy, carbon dioxide, and water, oxidation–reduction has taken place in the form of cellular respiration. As in photosynthesis, a series of chemical reactions are necessary to complete cellular respiration. Another important biological process, the nitrogen cycle, is composed of a series of oxidation and reduction reactions. Bacteria take nitrogen from the air and reduce it to ammonia and nitrates, nutrients that plants use to make proteins, nucleic acids, and other nitrogen–containing molecules needed for their metabolism. Other bacteria in soil convert nitrates back into nitrogen gas. Many of the oxidation–reduction reactions that occur in living organisms are regulated by enzymes.

Current and future uses

Dangerous as they may be, oxidation–reductions are used all the time. Burning, bleaching, batteries, met-

allurgy, and photography all rely on oxidation–reduction reactions. An important application of oxidation–reduction reactions is in electrochemical cells. (These types of cells should not be confused with biological cells. The word cell comes from *cella*, Latin for chamber or small room.) In an electrochemical cell, the oxidation reaction is physically separated from the reduction reaction, and the electrons pass between the two reactions through a conductor. Oxidation occurs at the anode and reduction occurs at the cathode. Electrochemical cells can produce electricity or consume it. Batteries and dry cells are commonly used electrochemical cells that produce electricity. The battery for your car is probably a 12 volt battery, made from a combination of six cells producing two volts each.

Cells that use electricity can be used to deposit metals onto surfaces in a process known as electroplating. Electroplating can be used to make jewelry, mirrors, and shiny surfaces resistant to abrasion, tarnishing and corrosion. Metal salts in a solution called the plating bath are reduced to metal at the cathode of the electrochemical cell.

Oxidation–reduction reactions are widely used to produce chemicals that are used in manufacturing. The chemical that is produced in the most volume in the United States is sulfuric acid. It is made by oxidizing sulfur with oxygen to produce sulfur trioxide (SO_3). This is dissolved in water to give sulfuric acid, H_2SO_4.

Not all important oxidation–reduction reactions involve oxygen. A commonly produced chemical that does not contain oxygen is ammonia. To produce ammonia, NH_3, by an oxidation–reduction reaction, nitrogen and hydrogen are combined together under pressure at 932° F (500° C) with a catalyst. The nitrogen is oxidized and the hydrogen is reduced. The resulting ammonia can then be used to make fertilizers, dyes, explosives, cleaning solutions, and polymers.

Hydrogen acts as a reducing agent in many manufacturing processes. It can be used to make shortening from vegetable oils in a process known as hydrogenation. It can even reduce ions of metals such as silver and tungsten to pure metals.

Oxidation–reduction reactions are an important component of chemical analysis. Potassium permangante and cerium (IV) solutions can be used as strong oxidizing agents in the analysis of iron, tin, peroxide, vanadium, molybdenum, titanium, and uranium. Potassium dichromate is an oxidizing agent used in the analysis of organic materials in water and wastewater.

Oxidation–reduction reactions can be used for bleaching materials and sanitizing water. Sodium hypochlorite is used in solution as a liquid laundry bleach and as a solid component of dishwasher powders and cleansers. Calcium hypochlorite is often used for swimming pool sanitation. The hypochlorites kill bacteria in water by oxidizing them. Ozone is a powerful oxidizing agent that can also be used to purify water. The ozone destroys bacteria and organic pollutants. Water that has been sanitized by ozone is free of the unpleasant taste, smell, and byproducts associated with chlorinated water.

Metals are rarely found free in nature, but occur in ores. The metals are in their oxidized form in the ores and must be reduced to the metals (oxidation number zero) in order to be used. Some metals are easily reduced. For example, mercury can be produced from a mercury sulfide ore simply by heating it in air. Iron is produced from ore by heating with coke (impure carbon) and oxygen. The coke reduces the iron in the ore. Other metals are more difficult to reduce and are only obtained after electrons are pumped into their ores using electricity. Aluminum is such a metal. As long as oxygen is around, corrosion will act to reverse the reduction of the metals achieved in metallurgy. Metals that are most resistant to corrosion are those with high standard reduction potentials such as gold and platinum.

Oxidation–reduction reactions are responsible for food spoilage. The main source of oxidation is oxygen from the air. Preservatives that are added to foods are often reducing agents.

Oxidation reactions are important in many reactions that keep our bodies going. But oxidation has also been blamed for aging, cancer, hardening of the arteries, and rheumatoid arthritis. Research is being done to evaluate the benefits of antioxidants in foods and dietary supplements. Antioxidants are natural reducing agents such as fat soluble vitamin E and vitamin C (ascorbic acid). These substances might inhibit damaging byproducts of oxidation reactions that can occur in the human body after exposure to some toxic chemicals. One concern that scientists studying antioxidants have is that substances do not always act the same way in the human body that they do outside of it. For example, vitamin C is a reducing agent. If lemon juice is squirted on a cut apple, the vitamin C in the juice will prevent the browning of the apple that is caused by oxidation of the apple by the air. However, Vitamin C might act as an oxidizing agent in the body.

The reaction can be harnessed as a source of energy. When hydrogen and oxygen are carefully fed into an electrochemical cell called a fuel cell, the oxidation–reduction reaction can be used to provide electrical power, for example, for space craft. The only byproduct

KEY TERMS

Combustion—An oxidation reduction reaction involving oxidation by oxygen accompanied by light, heat, and often by flame.

Corrosion—A reaction in which a metal is oxidized and oxygen is reduced, usually in the presence of moisture.

Disproportionation—An oxidation-reduction reaction in which the same chemical species is oxidized and reduced.

Electrochemical cell—A device in which an oxidation reaction is physically separated from a reduction reaction in a way that allows electrons to flow between them.

Half reaction—The isolated oxidation or reduction reaction that is a part of a complete oxidation–reduction reaction.

Oxidant (oxidizing agent)—A chemical substance which oxidizes materials by removing electrons from them.

Oxidation—A process in which a chemical substances loses electrons and undergoes an increase in oxidation number.

Reductant (reducing agent)—A chemical substance which reduces materials by donating electrons to them.

Reduction—A process in which a chemical substance gains Electrons and undergoes a decrease in oxidation number.

of the reaction between hydrogen and oxygen is non–polluting water. Another application of the hydrogen/oxygen reaction is to use hydrogen combustion to power vehicles. Currently, hydrogen is produced from water using electricity and it takes more energy to make the hydrogen than is obtained from its combustion. In the future, hydrogen might be made using solar energy and would provide a non–polluting fuel.

The natural ability of algae and other water plants to oxidize harmful materials in sewage has been used in sewage lagoons, also known as oxidation pond systems. Small volumes of raw sewage can be treated simply by directing the sewage into shallow ponds containing algae and other water vegetation. In Belgium, nitrates are removed from wastewater by bacteria that reduce the nitrates to nitrogen which can be safely released into the atmosphere.

See also Antioxidants; Combustion; Cell, electrochemical; Electron; Hydrogenation; Nitrogen cycle; Oxidation state; Oxygen; Photosynthesis.

Further Reading:

Atkins, P.W. and J. A. Beran. *General Chemistry,* 2nd edition. New York: Scientific American Books, 1992, page 102–117.

"Explosion on the Lady Delta" (video). Films for the Humanities and Sciences, P.O. Box 2053, Princeton, NJ 08453–2053.

Halliwell, Barry. "Antioxidants: Sense or Speculation?," *Nutrition Today,* Vol. 29, No. 6, November/December 1994, pages 15–19.

Kostiner, Edward. *Study Keys to Chemistry*, Theme 17 "Oxidation–Reduction Reactions and Electrochemistry." Barron's Educational Series, Inc, 1992.

Lowe, James N. *Worlds of Chemistry*, Chapter 8. New York: McGraw Hill Book Company, 1989.

Raven, Peter H. and George B. Johnson. "Oxidation–Reduction: The Flow of Energy in Living Things" and "The Nitrogen Cycle," *Biology,* 3rd Edition. Dubuque, Iowa: Wm. C. Brown Publishers, 1992, pages 138–139, 490–491.

Catherine Hinga Haustein

Oxidation state

The oxidation state of an atom is a description of how many electrons it has lost or gained from its original state. Each type of atom has a certain number of electrons (which varies from atom to atom) in its elemental form. When an atom forms a bond or otherwise interacts with another atom, it is possible that it will lose or gain an electron. If an atom is electronegative, it is more likely to take an electron away from another atom. If it is electropositive, it holds its own electrons weakly and is more likely to lose an electron when it interacts with another atomic species.

The oxidation number of an atom refers to the number of electrons it has lost or gained. Electrons are assigned a negative charge, so by convention if an atom has gained an electron, its oxidation number is reduced. For example, if an atom gains an electron, it has an oxidation number of –1. For this reason, an atom which receives an electron is described as having been "reduced." If an atom loses an electron, its oxidation number rises, and it is described as having been "oxidized." In an oxidation–reduction reaction, two atomic species interact so that one is reduced and one is oxidized.

An atom can be oxidized or reduced when a bond is formed. In a chemical bond, electrons are shared by two atoms. However, there is often one atom which is more electronegative than the other, and so holds electrons more tightly than the other. For this reason, one atom takes on a partial positive charge, and the other becomes partially negative. A bond such as this is called an ionic bond. In a very ionic bond, the electrons belong almost entirely to one atom. That atom has a new oxidation state of –1, and the atom which has "lost" its electron has an oxidation state of +1.

See also Atom; Electron; Oxidation–reduction reaction.

Oxidizing agent see **Oxidation-reduction reaction**

Oxpeckers see **Starlings**

Oxygen

Oxygen is a non–metallic element of atomic number 16. Its symbol is O, the atomic weight is 15.9994, the specific gravity is 1.10535 (compared to air), the melting point is 360° F (–218° C), and the boiling point is 360° F (–218° C).

Oxygen is a non–metal in group VIA of the Periodic table. Its three stable isotopes have atomic weights of 16, 17, and 18. The first is by far the most abundant, constituting 99.763 percent of all oxygen atoms occurring in nature. Oxygen–17 makes up an additional 0.037 percent, and oxygen–18, 0.200 percent of all oxygen atoms. A number of radioactive isotopes of the element have also been prepared, the most widely used commercially being oxygen–15, which decays by the emission of a positron with a half life of 122 seconds.

Oxygen was discovered independently by the Swedish chemist Carl Scheele and the English chemist Joseph Priestley in the period 1773–1774. The element was given its name by the French chemist Antoine Laurent Lavoisier in 1777. Its name comes from the French word for "acid–former," reflecting Lavoisier's incorrect belief that all acids contain oxygen.

General properties

Oxygen is a colorless, odorless, tasteless gas that is slightly soluble (1.2 in [3.08 cubic centimeters] per 39.4

in [100 cubic centimeters of water] at room temperature. It is considerably more soluble in some organic solvents, such as ethyl alcohol, carbon tetrachloride, and benzene. Oxygen is less soluble in sea water than in pure water, although still soluble enough to support the survival of marine organisms.

Oxygen exists in three allotropic forms, monatomic oxygen (O), diatomic oxygen (O_2), and triatomic oxygen (O_3). The first of these is sometimes called nascent oxygen, and the last is more commonly known as ozone. Under most circumstances in nature, the diatomic form of oxygen predominates. In the upper part of the stratosphere, however, solar energy causes the breakdown of the diatomic form into the monatomic form, which may then recombine with diatomic molecules to form ozone. The presence of ozone in the Earth's atmosphere is critical for the survival of life on Earth since that allotrope has a tendency to absorb ultraviolet radiation that would otherwise be harmful or even fatal to both plant and animal life on the planet's surface.

Some scientists are now concerned about the possible depletion of the ozone layer in the upper stratosphere. There is strong evidence that certain synthetic chemicals, such as the Freons and compounds known as the chlorofluorocarbons (CFCs) may be causing destruction of ozone molecules in the atmosphere. The most widely accepted theory says that solar radiation causes such chemicals to break apart, releasing a free chlorine atom to the stratosphere. That chlorine atom then reacts with ozone molecules, converting them into diatomic oxygen molecules. One of the disturbing aspects of this theory is that it suggests that a single chlorine atom can cause the decomposition of many thousands of ozone molecules.

The environmental hazard posed by this series of reactions is that the level of ultraviolet radiation reaching the Earth would be expected to increase as more and more ozone molecules are destroyed. Ultraviolet radiation has been implicated in a number of biological problems for plants, animals, and humans, including an increase in skin cancer and in eye problems. In response to this threat, most of the world's nations have agreed to reduce the amount of Freons, CFCs, and other ozone–depleting chemicals produced and sold each year.

Where it comes from

Oxygen is the most abundant element on the Earth's surface. It makes up 20.948% of the atmosphere by volume and 45.5% of the lithosphere by weight. It occurs both as the free element (in the atmosphere) and in the combined form (in the lithosphere and hydrosphere). Its most common and best known compound is probably water. Water contains 88.9% oxygen, by weight.

In the lithosphere, oxygen occurs in a wide variety of compounds, such as the oxides, silicates, carbonates, phosphates, sulfates, and a variety of more complex compounds.

Nearly all of the oxygen found on Earth today is produced by biological activity. During the process of photosynthesis, carbon dioxide and water react in the presence of chlorophyll to produce carbohydrates and oxygen. Scientists believe that oxygen was essentially absent from the Earth's atmosphere when the planet was first created. As life developed on Earth and photosynthesis became more common, the rate of production increased until the present concentration of oxygen in the atmosphere, the oceans, and the crustal rocks was reached about 580 million years ago.

Oxygen can be prepared on a small scale by the decomposition of oxygen–containing compounds. In the laboratory, for example, it can be produced by heating potassium chlorate with manganese dioxide as a catalyst or by the gentle warming of mercury(II) oxide. The element can also be produced by the electrolysis of water. When an electrical current is passed through water to which a small amount of inorganic acid has been added, water molecules break apart to form hydrogen gas and oxygen gas. Although this method is relatively simple to employ, the cost of energy needed to carry out the reaction is usually prohibitively high for commercial applications.

By far the most important method of producing oxygen commercially is by the fractional distillation of liquid air. A sample of air is first cooled below the boiling point of most gases that make up air, a temperature of less than $-328°$ F ($-200°$ C). The liquid air is then allowed to evaporate. At a temperature of $-320°$ F ($-195.8°$ C), nitrogen begins to boil off. When most of the nitrogen is gone, argon and neon also boil off, leaving an impure form of oxygen behind. The oxygen is impure because small amounts of krypton, xenon, and other gases may remain in the liquid form. In order to further purify the oxygen, the process of cooling, liquefying, and evaporation may be repeated.

Oxygen is commonly stored and transported in its liquid form, a form also known as LOX. LOX containers have the general appearance of very large vacuum bottles consisting of a double–walled container with a vacuum between the two walls. The element can also be stored and transported less easily in gaseous form in steel–walled containers 4 ft (1.2 m) high and 9 in (23 cm) in diameter. In many instances, oxygen is manufactured at the location where it will be used. The process of fractional distillation described above is sufficiently simple and inexpensive that many industries can provide their own oxygen–production facilities.

How we use it

Oxygen has so many commercial, industrial, and other uses that it consistently ranks among the top five chemicals in volume of production in the United States. In 1988, for example, 37.1 billion lbs (16.8 billion kg) of the element were manufactured in the United States.

The uses to which oxygen is put can be classified into four major categories: metallurgy, rocketry, chemical synthesis, and medicine. In the processing of iron ore in a blast furnace, for example, oxygen is used to convert coke (carbon) to carbon monoxide. The carbon monoxide, in turn, reduces iron oxides to pure iron metal. Oxygen is then used in a second step of iron processing in the Bessemer converter, open hearth, or basic oxygen process method of converting pig iron to steel. In this step, the oxygen is used to react with the excess carbon, silicon, and metals remaining in the pig iron that must be removed in order to produce steel.

Another metallurgical application of oxygen is in torches used for welding and cutting. The two most common torches make use of the reaction between oxygen and hydrogen (the oxyhydrogen torch) or between oxygen and acetylene (the oxyacetylene torch). Both kinds of torches produce temperatures in the range of 5,432° F (3,000° C) or more and can, therefore, be used to cut through or weld the great majority of metallic materials.

Oxygen, in the form of LOX, is widely used as the oxidizing agent in many kinds of rockets and missiles. As an example, the huge external fuel tank required to lift the space shuttle into space holds 145,000 gal (550,000 l) of liquid oxygen and 390,000 gal (1,500,000 l) hydrogen. When these two elements react in the shuttle's main engines, they provide a maximum thrust of 512,000 pounds.

The chemical industry uses vast amounts of oxygen every year in a variety of chemical synthesis reactions. One of the most important of these is the cracking of hydrocarbons by oxygen. Under most circumstances, heating a hydrocarbon with oxygen results in combustion, with carbon dioxide and water as the main products. However, if the rate at which oxygen is fed into a hydrocarbon mixture is carefully controlled, the hydrocarbon is "cracked," or broken apart to produce other products, such as acetylene, ethylene, and propylene.

Various types of synthetic fuels can also be manufactured with oxygen as one of the main reactants. Producer gas, as an example, is manufactured by passing oxygen at a controlled rate through a bed of hot coal or coke. The majority of carbon dioxide produced in this reaction is reduced to carbon monoxide so that the final product (the producer gas) consists primarily of carbon monoxide and hydrogen.

Perhaps the best known medical application of oxygen is in oxygen therapy, where patients who are having trouble breathing are given doses of pure or nearly pure oxygen. Some common instances in which oxygen therapy is used include surgical procedures, following heart attacks, and during infectious diseases. In each case, providing a person with pure oxygen reduces the stress on his or her heart and lungs and speeds the rate of recovery.

Pure oxygen or air enriched with oxygen may also be provided in environments where breathing may be difficult. Aircraft that fly at high altitudes, of course, are always provided with supplies of oxygen in case of any problems with the ship's normal air supply. Deep–sea divers also carry with them or have pumped to them supplies of air that are enriched with oxygen.

Some water purification and sewage treatment plants use oxygen. The gas is pumped through water to increase the rate at which naturally occurring bacteria break down organic waste materials. A similar process has been found to reduce the rate at which eutrophication takes place in lakes and ponds and, in some cases, to actually reverse that process.

Finally, oxygen is essential to all animal life on Earth. A person can survive a few days or weeks without food or water, but no more than a few minutes without oxygen. In the absence of oxygen, energy–generating chemical reactions taking place within cells would come to an end, and a person would die.

Chemistry and compounds

Oxygen is one of the most active of all chemical elements. The oxygen–oxygen bond in diatomic oxygen is relatively strong, but once broken, the atomic oxygen formed (O) reacts readily with the vast majority of elements. The noble gases and noble metals are the most important exceptions, although oxy compounds of most of these elements are also known and can be prepared by indirect methods.

The reaction between oxygen and another element generally results in the formation of a binary compound known as an oxide. The reaction itself is known as oxidation. For example, the oxidation reaction between oxygen and sodium produces sodium oxide. In many cases, an element may form more than one oxide. Copper, as an example, forms both copper(I) (cuprous) oxide and copper(II) (cupric) oxide. Nitrogen forms five oxides: nitrous oxide (N_2O), nitric oxide (NO), dinitrogen trioxide (N_2O_3), nitrogen dioxide (NO_2), and dinitrogen pentoxide (N_2O_5).

Perhaps the most important of all oxides is water, by far the most abundant compound on the planet. Water is composed of two hydrogen atoms bonded to a single oxygen atom by means of a strong covalent bond.

In many cases, the reaction between oxygen and another element is highly exothermic. One of the best known of such reactions is the one that takes place between carbon and oxygen, to form (usually) carbon dioxide and carbon monoxide. It is this reaction, which takes place when coal burns, that was responsible to a significant extent for the development of huge new energy sources during the Industrial Revolution that transformed human society.

Oxygen also reacts with a number of compounds. For example, hydrocarbons react with oxygen at high temperatures to form (primarily) carbon dioxide and water vapor. Oxidation that takes place very rapidly, usually at high temperatures, is known as combustion. The combustion of hydrocarbons in petroleum and natural gas has been another major source of energy in human civilization over the past 200 years.

Some forms of oxidation occur more slowly, without the production of noticeable heat or light. When plants and animals die, for example, the organic materials of which they are made slowly react with oxygen in the atmosphere. This form of oxidation is known as decay. The decay of organic matter is a highly complex chemical phenomenon, with a large variety of chemical products formed in the reaction.

Inorganic materials also react slowly with oxygen. When iron and certain other metals are exposed to oxygen (in the presence of water), they form oxides. The best known of all metallic oxides is probably rust, a hydrated form of iron(III) (ferric) oxide with the general formula $Fe_2O_3 \cdot nH_2O$. The rusting of bridges, buildings, motor vehicles, tools, fences, and other structures is a major economic problem throughout the world. A number of techniques, such as galvanizing, tinning, painting, and enameling are used to reduce or prevent the rusting of materials.

See also Element, chemical; Gases, liquefaction of; Nonmetal; Ozone; Periodic table; Photosynthesis; Respirator.

KEY TERMS

Allotrope—One of two or more forms of an element.

Combustion—A form of oxidation that occurs so rapidly that noticeable heat and light are produced.

Cracking—The process by which large hydrocarbon molecules are broken down into smaller components.

Electrolysis—The process by which an electrical current is used to break a compound apart into its components.

Isotopes—Two or more forms of the same element that differ from each other in their atomic weights.

Lithosphere—The solid portion of the Earth, especially the outer crustal region.

LOX—An abbreviation commonly used for liquid oxygen.

Metallurgy—The science and technology that deals with the winning of metals from their ores and their conversion into forms that have practical value.

Nascent oxygen—An allotrope of oxygen whose molecules each contain a single oxygen atom.

Ozone—An allotrope of oxygen that consists of three atoms per molecule.

Producer gas—A synthetic fuel that consists primarily of carbon monoxide and hydrogen gases.

Ultraviolet radiation—A form of electromagnetic radiation that is part of solar radiation, with wavelengths in the range from about 100 to 4,000 Å.

Further Reading:

Brescia, Frank, Stanley Mehlman, Frank C. Pellegrini, and Seymour Stambler. *Chemistry: A Modern Introduction*, 2nd edition. Philadelphia: W. B. Saunders Company, 1978, Chapter 19.

Greenwood, N. N., and A. Earnshaw. *Chemistry of the Elements*. Oxford: Pergamon Press, 1990, Chapter 14.

Hawley, Gessner G. *The Condensed Chemical Dictionary*. New York: Van Nostrand Reinhold Company, 9th edition, 1977.

McGraw–Hill Encyclopedia of Science & Technology, 6th edition. New York: McGraw–Hill Book Company, 1987, volume 12, pages 604—608.

Newton, David E. *The Chemical Elements*. New York: Franklin Watts, 1994.

Sawyer, Donald T. *Oxygen Chemistry*. New York: Oxford University Press, 1991.

David E. Newton

Oystercatchers

Oystercatchers are six rather similar–looking species of oceanic shorebirds that comprise the family Haematopodidae. Oystercatchers occur widely on sub-arctic, temperate, and tropical seacoasts, on all of the continents except Antarctica.

Oystercatchers are relatively large shorebirds, with a body length of 15–21 in (40–53 cm). They have pointed wings, a short tail, short but heavy legs, and three–toed feet. Their most distinctive feature is their long, blunt, knife–like (that is, vertically flattened), red or orange beak. This unique bill is used as a hammer and in a wedge–like fashion to twist open the shells of reluctant bivalves upon which oystercatchers feed. Oystercatchers also eat crustaceans, polychaete worms, and other intertidal and shoreline invertebrates.

There are two major types of color patterns among species of oystercatchers. These birds can either be all black, or black above and white–bellied. The sexes do not differ in size or coloration.

Oystercatchers are strong, direct fliers. They typically occur on sandy or rocky beaches. Oystercatchers are wary birds, and when they detect a potential danger they repeatedly utter a loud, clear, piping sound as a call note.

Oystercatchers build their crude scrape–nests on remote, open beaches, or sometimes in fields and meadows near the coast. They lay two to four eggs, which are incubated by both parents, which also share the care of the young birds. Parent oystercatchers put on very convincing broken–wing displays to lure predators away from their nest or babies. Young oystercatchers are able to follow their parents soon after birth, and are able to fly and feed themselves after about five weeks.

All species of oystercatchers are in the genus *Haematopus*. Two species occur in North America. The American oystercatcher (*H. palliatus*) is a black-backed, white–bellied species that occurs on mudflats and sandy beaches of the southeastern states and western Mexico. The black oystercatcher (*H. bachmani*) is an all–black species that tends to occur on rocky beaches.

The most widespread species of oystercatcher in Eurasia (*H. ostralegus*) is sometimes known as the sea–pie or mussel–pecker, and is a black and white species. The sooty oystercatcher (*H. fuliginosus*) of Australia is an all–black species.

Bill Freedman

Oysters see **Bivalves**

Ozone

Ozone (O_3) is a bluish, relatively dense (1.6 times as heavy as air) gas, and a strong oxidant. Ozone occurs naturally in relatively large concentrations in the stratosphere, a layer of the upper atmosphere higher than about 3.8–10.7 mi (8–17 km), depending on season and location. Ozone also occurs in the lower atmosphere (or troposphere), where it is by far the most damaging of the photochemical air pollutants. Where these chemicals are abundant, they are known as an oxidizing or Los Angeles–type smog. This condition develops in sunny places where there are large emissions of hydrocarbons and oxides of nitrogen from automobiles and industry, especially where atmospheric temperature inversions are common.

Photochemical air pollutants are secondary chemicals, which means that they are not emitted, but are synthesized from primary, emitted pollutants during complex photochemical reactions occurring in a sunny atmosphere. In addition to ozone, important photochemical air pollutants include peroxy acetyl nitrate (PAN), hydrogen peroxide (H_2O_2), and aldehydes. These secondary gases are the ingredients of oxidizing smogs that are harmful to people and vegetation exposed to this type of pollution.

Most countries have set standards for ground–level concentrations of ozone, with a view to avoiding damage to vegetation and discomfort to humans. Up to 1979 the standard for the maximum, one–hour average concentration of O_3 was 80 ppb (parts per billion) in the United States. However, in that year the standard was raised to 120 ppb, because 80 ppb was being so frequently exceeded in many places. In a practical sense the original ozone standard could not be enforced, so it was increased. However, large regions of the U.S. cannot even meet the criterion of 120 ppb, especially in the southwestern states.

In the vicinity of Los Angeles the maximum one–hour concentration of ozone can exceed 500 ppb, and it is typically greater than 100 ppb for at least 15 days per year. In other cities in North America the annual maximum one–hour concentration is typically 150–250 ppb, and it is typically 90–180 ppb in London, England.

Humans and other animals are sensitive to ozone. This gas irritates and damages exposed membranes of the respiratory system and eyes. Ozone can also induce asthma. Sensitive people are affected at concentrations that commonly occur during oxidizing smogs.

Ozone causes substantial damage to both agricultural and wild plants in many places, causing a distinctive, acute injury that reduces the photosynthetic area of foliage. Most plants are acutely injured by a two to four hour exposure to 200–300 ppb ozone, while longer–term exposures to about 100 ppb cause yield decreases, even in the absence of acute injuries. However, some species are relatively sensitive to ozone. In one experiment in the laboratory, tobacco was acutely injured by exposures to only 50–60 ppb for two to three hours, and spinach by 60–80 ppb for one to two hours. Sensitive species of conifers can be injured by 80 ppb over a 12–hour exposure.

An important field study conducted at various sites throughout the United States involved the exposure of crop plants to either ambient air at each site, or to a typical "background" ozone concentration of 25 ppb. Symptoms of acute ozone injuries were observed at all five of the study sites, although the damages were more frequent and severe in the southwest. On average, it was estimated that exposures to ambient ozone concentrations caused yield decreases of about 53–56% in lettuce, 14–17% in peanut, 10% in soybean, and 7% in turnip. Overall, it has been estimated that ozone causes crop losses equivalent to 2–4% of the potential yield in the U.S., with an economic value of billions of dollars.

Trees can also be damaged by ozone, as has been well documented for conifer forests along the western slopes of the Sierra Nevada and San Bernardino Mountains of southern California. In this case, ozone–polluted air is transported eastward from the vicinity of Los Angeles to the mountains, where forests are damaged. The most sensitive species of tree is ponderosa pine (*Pinus ponderosa*), the naturally dominant species in these forests. Other species of conifers are less sensitive to ozone, and these replace the ponderosa pine when it is killed by the air pollution. The smog damage was first noticed during the 1950s, but the actual cause was not attributed to ozone until 1963. The ozone injuries to pine are diagnostic, characterized initially by a pale–green mottling of foliage, then a tissue death that spreads from the leaf tip, premature loss of foliage, and

KEY TERMS

Acute toxicity—A poisonous effect, produced by one or several shorter–term exposures to a toxic chemical, and causing observable anatomical damages, and ultimately death.

Inversion—An atmospheric condition in which air temperature increases with increasing altitude, instead of the usual decrease. The occurrence of a temperature inversion causes stable atmospheric conditions beneath, which can result in an accumulation of air pollutants if emissions continue during the inversion event.

Photochemical—Refers to an enhancement of the rate of a chemical reaction by particular wavelengths of electromagnetic radiation.

Photochemical smog—Air pollution caused by complex reactions involving emitted chemicals, chemicals formed secondarily in the atmosphere, and sunlight.

Smog—Refers to an atmospheric condition with poor visibility and large concentrations of air pollutants.

ultimately death of the tree. Ozone–stressed trees are also vulnerable to secondary damages caused by bark beetles and fungal pathogens, which often kill weakened trees.

See also Air pollution; Atmosphere, composition and structure of; Chlorofluorocarbons; Oxygen; Ozone layer depletion; Smog.

Further Reading

Freedman, B. *Environmental Ecology*, 2nd ed. San Diego: Academic Press, 1994.
MacKenzie, J.J. and M.T. El–Ashry (eds.). *Air Pollution's Toll on Forests and Crops*. Yale University Press, New Haven, CT: 1989.

Bill Freedman

Ozone layer depletion

Ozone is a natural constituent that occurs in relatively large concentrations in the upper–atmospheric layer known as the stratosphere, occurring higher than

5–10.6 mi (8–17 km) in altitude and extending to about 31 mi (50 km). Stratospheric ozone is very important to life on the surface of Earth, because this gas absorbs much of the incoming solar ultraviolet radiation, and thereby shields organisms from its deleterious effects. Since the mid–1980s there has been evidence that concentrations of stratospheric ozone are being diminished as a result of complex photochemical reactions involving chlorofluorocarbons (CFCs). These persistent chemicals are synthesized by humans, used for various purposes, and then emitted to the lower atmosphere, from where they eventually reach the stratosphere and deplete ozone.

Stratospheric ozone

Typically, stratospheric ozone (O_3) concentrations are about 0.2–0.4 ppm (parts per million), compared with about 0.03 ppm in unpolluted situations close to ground level in the troposphere. Stratospheric ozone concentrations are also measured in Dobson units (DU). A Dobson unit is equivalent to the amount of ozone that, if accumulated from the entire thickness of the atmosphere and spread evenly over the surface of the Earth at a pressure of one atmosphere and a temperature of about 68°F (20°C), would occupy a thickness of 10 μm (0.01 mm). Typically, stratospheric zone occurs at a concentration of about 350 DU, equivalent to a layer of only 0.1 in (3.5 mm) of that gas at a pressure of one atmosphere at sea level.

Stratospheric ozone is formed and consumed naturally by photochemical reactions involving ultraviolet radiation (indicated as UV in the reaction equations below) and atoms or molecules of oxygen, as follows: $O_2 + UV \rightarrow O + O(1)\ O + O + M \rightarrow O_2 + M(2)\ O + O_2 + M \rightarrow O_3 + M(3)\ O_3 + UV \rightarrow O_2 + O(4) \rightarrow O_3 + Cl \rightarrow O_2 + ClO(5)$ where M is some energy–accepting chemical. To review: molecular oxygen (O_2) interacts with ultraviolet radiation and splits into oxygen atoms (O) (reaction 1), which either recombine to form O_2 (reaction 2), or combine with O_2 to form O_3 (reaction 3). Once formed, the ozone can be consumed by various reactions, including a photodissociation involving ultraviolet radiation (reaction 4), or reactions with trace gases such as nitric oxide (NO), nitrogen dioxide (NO_2), and nitrous oxide (N_2O), or with simple molecules or ions of chlorine (reaction 5), bromine, and fluorine. At any time, the formation and consumption of ozone proceed simultaneously. The actual concentration of ozone is a net function of the rates of reactions by which it is formed, and the rates of the reactions that consume this gas.

Rates of ozone formation are largest over the equatorial regions of Earth, because solar radiation averages most intensely over those latitudes. However, stratospheric winds carry tropical ozone to polar latitudes, where it tends to accumulate. On average, ozone concentrations average about 450 DU over subpolar regions, and 250 DU over the tropics. However, ozone concentrations can be as large as 600 DU during the wintertime maximum over the Antarctic.

Human activities have resulted in large increases in emissions to the atmosphere of some of the ozone consuming substances or their precursors. As a result, there are concerns about potential changes in the dynamic equilibria among the stratospheric ozone reactions, which could result in decreases in ozone concentration.

The first concerns about depletion of stratospheric ozone were raised in the 1960s. At that time, a number of scientists suggested that emissions of water vapor and various other chemicals from high–flying military jets and rockets might cause a consumption of stratospheric ozone. These discussions intensified during the early 1970s, when there were proposals to develop fleets of supersonic aircraft flying in the stratosphere (mostly for economic reasons, this capital–expensive commercial venture did not materialize). Some scientists additionally suggested that emissions of oxides of nitrogen from vehicles and agricultural practices might also have some effect on the ozone layer, as could emissions associated with launchings of space shuttles and other spacecraft.

The first suggestions of actual depletions of the ozone layer are from evidence that, since about the mid–to–late 1970s, there have been large decreases in the concentrations of stratospheric ozone at polar latitudes during the period of late winter to early springtime. These term used to describe these phenomena is ozone "holes." These seasonal occurrences are most noticeable over the Antarctic, where the ozone holes develop between September and November when the stratosphere is intensely cold, but sunlight is once again intense following the end of the winter (the polar winter occurs in perpetual solar darkness). The first truly convincing evidence of ozone holes was obtained over Antarctica in 1984, when the average ozone concentration in October was found to be 180 DU, compared with 300 DU in the early 1970s. In 1987, springtime stratospheric ozone over Antarctica was only 120 DU. These sorts of observations stimulated a re–examination of earlier data from satellites and other observation systems, which suggested that the ozone holes had existed since at least the 1970s.

The antarctic ozone holes typically develop at altitudes of 7.4–16 mi (12 to 25 km). The average decreases in springtime stratospheric ozone concentrations over Antarctica have been 30–40%. However, in some years the ozone holes are more intense than this. For example, during October 1987 the average decrease of stratospheric ozone over the Antarctic was 50%, and it was 95% in the most intensely depleted zone of the lower stratosphere, at 9–12 mi (15–20 km).

The immediate cause of the depletions of stratospheric ozone is believed to involve atoms of chlorine or simple compounds such as chlorine monoxide (ClO). However, these chemicals are thought to have an indirect origin through human activities, especially the emission of CFCs to the atmosphere. Once formed in the stratosphere by the degradation of a CFC molecule, a single chlorine atom is capable of destroying as many as 100,000 ozone molecules before it is removed from the upper atmosphere.

The occurrence of seasonal ozone holes is restricted to high–latitude regions, especially over Antarctica, and to a lesser degree over the Arctic. However, concentrations of stratospheric ozone can also be affected at lower latitudes, although the ozone depletion is relatively small. This happens during the late springtime, when the normal lower–latitude ozone concentrations are diluted by ozone–depleted polar air that becomes widely dispersed as the ozone holes break up and dissipate. One study estimated that seasonal concentrations of stratospheric ozone over mid–latitudes of the Southern Hemisphere may have decreased by 3–8% during the 1980s.

The importance of stratospheric ozone

Stratospheric ozone is biologically important because it selectively absorbs much of the incoming solar electromagnetic radiation within the ultraviolet (UV) range. Ozone is very effective within the so–called UV–C wavelength range of 200–280 nm, somewhat less so in the UV–B range of 280–320 nm, and it is rather ineffective in absorbing UV–A at 320–400 nm. However, UV–A is not very damaging to organisms. Although UV–C is extremely damaging, virtually none of this radiation penetrates through Earth's upper atmosphere. Therefore, the greatest anxiety in terms of biological damages caused by ultraviolet radiation concerns the relatively variable exposures to UV–B, which are directly influenced by concentrations of stratospheric ozone. Note, however, that fluxes of UV–B to Earth's surface are also related to certain conditions in the troposphere, such as the thickness of cloud cover, concentrations of particulates and certain chemicals, and changes in the angle of the sun, which influences the thickness of atmosphere that must be penetrated before the surface is reached.

Because ozone selectively absorbs these deleterious wavelengths of solar radiation, it serves as an ultraviolet shield. As such, stratospheric ozone helps to protect humans and other organisms on Earth's surface from some of the harmful effects of exposure to this high–energy electromagnetic radiation. In fact, without the protective action of the stratospheric ozone layer, it is likely that terrestrial life would not be possible on Earth, and that oceanic life would be restricted to relatively greater depths than those at which it can now comfortably occur.

If not intercepted, ultraviolet radiation is capable of damaging genetic material. The genetic materials deoxyribonucleic acid (DNA) and ribonucleic acid (RNA) and many proteins and other biochemicals are effective absorbers of ultraviolet radiation. DNA and RNA are especially efficient at absorbing wavelengths shorter than 320 nm, but these important chemicals are damaged by this absorption. Damages caused to genetic materials could result in an increased incidence of skin cancers. Basal carcinomas account for about 75% of human skin cancers, and squamous cell carcinomas about 20%. These are both serious diseases, but they can usually be successfully treated if detected early enough. The other skin cancer is malignant melanoma, a deadly disease that accounts for about 5% of total skin carcinomas, and which is often quickly fatal after it is diagnosed.

It is well known that people living in relatively sunny places have increased risks of all of these skin cancers, and that individual behaviours that increase exposures to UV–B also carry higher risks of developing these diseases (for example, sunbathing, or occupation exposures related to working outdoors, such as in agriculture, fishing, or construction). Compared with white–skinned people, individuals with relatively dark skin are much more tolerant of exposure to UV–B, because they are protected by the skin pigment, melanin. Within skin–color types, there are well established, statistical relationships between exposures to UV–B and risks of developing skin cancers, most notably malignant melanoma. Using these sorts of data, predictions have been made of increased rates of skin cancers that could be expected to result from increased exposures to UV–B caused by depletions of stratospheric ozone. For example, the U. S. Environmental Protection Agency has suggested that a 1% decrease in stratospheric ozone could result in a 2% increase in exposure to UV–B, and a 3–6% increase in skin cancers. In fact, many countries have reported increased incidences of all skin cancers. Usually this phenomenon is mostly attributed to human behaviors that influence exposure to UV–B, such as sunbathing. However, increased exposures related to depletions of stratospheric ozone may also be important.

Other human–health effects of ultraviolet exposure include increased risks of developing cataracts and other damages to the cornea such as snowblindness, damage to the retina, a suppressed immune system, sunburns of exposed skin, skin allergies, and an accelerated aging of the skin.

Of course, domestic and wild animals are subject to the same sorts of increased risks of diseases and damages associated with increased UV–B exposure as are humans. Unlike humans, however, these animals cannot wear chemical sunscreens, hats, or other protective clothing to diminish those risks.

Other potential ecological damages associated with increased ultraviolet exposures include decreases of plant productivity in regions stressed by UV–B radiation, caused in part by the degradation of photosynthetic pigments. All terrestrial plants are at risk, as are plants occurring in shallow waters. The most exposed plants occur at high altitude, for example in alpine tundra, or at high latitude, such as polar seas and tundras. However, few data are now available that allow a general evaluation of the importance of these potential decreases in plant productivity.

In addition, some stratospheric ozone makes its way to the lower atmosphere, where it contributes to ozone pollution there. Ozone is an important pollutant in the lower troposphere because it damages agricultural and wild plants, weakens synthetic materials, and causes discomfort to humans (see entry on ozone). During events of great turbulence in the upper atmosphere, such as thunderstorms, stratospheric ozone may enter the troposphere. Usually this only affects the upper troposphere, although observations have been made of stratospheric ozone reaching ground level for short intervals of time. On average, stratospheric incursions account for about 18% of the ozone in the troposphere, while photochemical reactions within the lower atmosphere itself account for the remaining 82% of tropospheric ozone.

Stratosphere and chlorofluorocarbons

Chlorofluorocarbons (CFCs) are compounds that contain atoms of carbon, chlorine, and fluorine (see entry on CFCs). CFCs are very stable chemicals, and they are easily liquified and gasified, non–flammable, and of low toxicity. CFCs have had many industrial uses, especially in refrigeration, as propellants in aerosol sprays, as blowing agents used to manufacture synthetic foams and insulation, as cleaning agents for

KEY TERMS

. . . .

Electromagnetic radiation—The energy of photons, having properties of both particles and waves. The major wavelength bands are, from short to long: cosmic, ultraviolet, visible or "light," infrared, and radio. Solar electromagnetic radiation is emitted by the Sun, and is the major external source of energy to the Earth.

Ozone holes—Decreased concentrations of stratospheric ozone, occurring at high latitudes during the early springtime. Ozone holes are most apparent over Antarctica, where they develop under intensely cold conditions during September and November, allowing a greater penetration of deleterious solar ultraviolet radiation to Earth's surface.

Stratosphere—A layer of the upper atmosphere above an altitude of 5–10.6 mi (8–17 km) and extending to about 31 mi (50 km), depending on season and latitude. Within the stratosphere, air temperature changes little with altitude, and there are few convective air currents.

Troposphere—The lower atmosphere, occurring below the stratosphere. Conditions in the troposphere are relatively turbulent and moist, and temperature tends to decrease with increasing altitude.

electronic components, as carrier gases for sterilants of medical instruments, and as dry–cleaning fluids. After most of these uses, CFCs are emitted to the lower atmosphere, where they are very persistent. The CFCs slowly penetrate into the stratosphere, where exposures to highly energetic, short–wave solar radiation are intense, causing the CFCs to degrade. This releases chlorine and fluorine atoms, which are then available to consume ozone molecules in secondary reactions. It has been estimated that CFCs account for at least 80% of the depletion of stratospheric ozone.

As a result of widespread awareness and concerns about the role of CFCs in the depletion of stratospheric ozone, the uses and emissions of these chemicals are being rapidly diminished. Some uses are already widely banned, for example, the use of CFCs as propellants in aerosol spray cans. A conference sponsored by the United Nations Environment Programme in 1987 resulted in the so–called *Montreal Protocol*, which was subsequently revised and made more stringent in 1990, when it called for a complete phaseout of global CFC use by the year 2000. However, some important users of CFCs have committed to earlier phaseouts of the use of CFCs, some by 1997. Although there has been a relatively rapid and effective international response to CFC emissions, the problem of CFC–caused depletions of stratospheric ozone will not be so quickly abated. This is because these chemicals are very persistent in the environment, so that CFCs already present will also be around for many decades. Moreover, there will continue to be substantial emissions of CFCs for years after their manufacture and uses are banned, because of continued atmospheric releases from older CFC–containing equipment and products that are already in use.

See also Atmosphere, composition and structure of; Chlorofluorocarbons; Greenhouse effect; Ozone.

Further Reading:

Benedick, R. E. *Ozone Diplomacy: New Directions in Safeguarding the Planet.* Washington, DC: World Wildlife Fund, 1991.

Clark, S. L. *Protecting the Ozone Layer: What You Can Do.* New York: Environmental Information Exchange, 1988.

Lyman, F. "As the Ozone Thins, the Plot Thickens." *Amicus Journal* 13 (Summer 1991): 20–28, 30.

Zurer, P. S. "Ozone Depletion's Recurring Surprises Challenge Atmospheric Scientists." *Chemical and Engineering News* (24 May 1993): 8–18.

Bill Freedman

Pacemaker

The heart is a unique organ that must function continuously to pump blood supplying oxygen to the body. It speeds up during special times of need, as when an individual is running or doing stressful work. It slows at night or during sleep when the demand for blood decreases.

This tiny pump, about the size of a fist, squeezes approximately 2.5 fl oz (75 ml) of blood out into the body with each beat. At a normal heart rhythm, this adds up to about 10 pt (5 l) of blood each minute. The heart pumps 2,500 gal (9500 l) of blood each day, and more than 100 million gal (400 million l) of blood in a lifetime. Every heartbeat must be regulated in time and intensity.

The heart muscle is driven by an internal pacemaker, a small nodule of tissue lodged in the right atrium (upper chamber), called the sinoatrial (SA) node. It generates a small electrical signal that travels through special fibers in the heart to stimulate a timed, sequential contraction of the heart muscle called the sinus rhythm.

The SA node may function irregularly over time or even stop functioning, which will interfere with the performance of the heart. There are other electrically active tissues that will issue regulatory signals if the SA node stops generating an electrical current. The heartbeat will slow considerably under guidance of the next layer of tissue. An abnormally slow heartbeat is called bradycardia. The heartbeat may also become irregular, developing an arrhythmia. On the other hand, the SA node may become overactive, causing the heart to race at an abnormally high speed, a condition called tachycardia.

To correct problems of rhythm disturbance or SA node malfunction, cardiologists often use a pacemaker, an electrical device implanted in the shoulder or abdomen of the patient with a wire leading to the heart. This mechanical pacemaker generates the electrical sig-

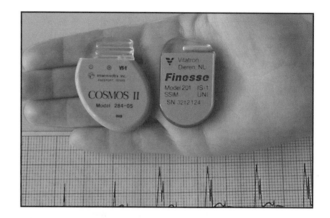

Pacemakers like these are usually implanted under the skin below the collarbone and connected to the heart by a wire inserted into a major vein in the neck and guided down into the heart.

nal which regulates the heart's functions. The rate of heartbeat, which is set when the pacemaker is implanted, can be changed if necessary without surgery. Modern pacemakers are available to correct virtually any form of arrhythmia.

The first pacemaker, the result of long, arduous research, was used in a patient in 1958. The pacemaker device was not implanted, but its wire was connected to the patient's heart. The pacemaker itself was so large that it had to be carted around in a grocery store cart. While it was a solution to the patient's arrhythmia, it was hardly practical. Fortunately, pacemakers were soon miniaturized.

The pacemaker was designed to regulate every single heartbeat. It took over the function of the SA node; from the time of implantation, the patient's heartbeat was directed by the pacemaker at a preset speed (usually about 70-72 beats per minute). Thus the patient's capacity for exercise was limited because no matter what conditions he was under, his heart maintained the same rate of beating. It would not speed up to provide additional oxygen needed by the tissues when the patient exercised. Since then, however, a great deal of progress has been made.

Current models of pacemakers monitor the heart to determine the heart rate and do not interfere with the heart function unless the heart rate drops below a predetermined speed (usually 66 to 68 beats per minute). Only then will the pacemaker deliver an electrical signal to drive the heart until the pacemaker determines that the SA node is again on track. The mechanical device then ceases its signals and returns to monitoring the heart rate. This is called demand pacing.

Current pacemakers weigh less than an ounce (25 g), are about the size of a quarter, and pace the upper and lower chamber as needed.

Some patients are at risk of a form of arrhythmia called fibrillation, which is a completely uncoordinated, quivering, nonfunctional heartbeat. If not corrected quickly, fibrillation can cause death. Since 1985, pacemakers have been available to monitor the speed of the heart and deliver an appropriate electrical shock to the heart muscle if it begins to fibrillate. The device can deliver a low-level pacing shock, an intermediate shock, or a jolting, defibrillating shock if necessary.

Surgeons prefer to implant pacemakers in the shoulder because the procedure can be carried out under local anesthetic. The wire from the pacemaker is inserted into one of the large veins in the shoulder and fed down into the heart, through the right atrium and into the ventricle where it is attached to the heart muscle. If the wire cannot be fed through veins that are too small or diseased, the pacemaker can be implanted in the abdomen.

Doctors must see patients with pacemakers frequently to check the battery power and make sure the circuitry is intact. Leads may become disconnected, the wire may break, or scarring may form around the electrode, all of which can render the pacemaker useless. Patients should avoid sources of electromagnetic radiation, including security scanning devices at airports and diagnostic tests using magnetic resonance imaging (MRI), both of which can turn off the pacemaker. Some states prohibit a person from driving an automobile for a period of time after he has received a pacemaker if he has previously experienced unconsciousness as a result of arrhythmia.

See also Circulatory system; Heart.

Further Reading:
Doebele, J. "A better mousetrap." *Forbes.* 154 (October 1994): 238+.
Farley, Dixie. "Implanted defibrillators and pacemakers: A gentler jolt and tickle for trembling hearts." *FDA Consumer* 28 (April, 1994): 10-14.

Larry Blaser

PAH see **Polycyclic aromatic hydrocarbons**

Pain

Pain, in its most basic form, can be described as an unpleasant physical sensation resulting from a variety of outside stimuli, from a pin prick to a serious burn. However, pain is a complex experience that eludes simple definitions. Not only does the central nervous system play a crucial role in the experience of pain, but psychological factors can also affect how an individual perceives pain. Most pain results from the intense stimulation of nerve endings beneath the skin that serve as the body's alarm system for detecting injury. For the majority of people, such pain is immediate and intense. However, in certain situations, the feeling of pain may be delayed or may fail to occur altogether (as sometimes happens with soldiers in the midst of battle). Another baffling aspect of pain is its persistence after the source of pain is gone, such as phantom limb pain that continues even after the injured limb has been amputated. Although people usually seek to avoid pain, some people, called sadomasochists, can derive pleasure from pain.

The physical origins of pain

Despite the advances made in the study of pain over the past 50 years and the evolution of several pain theories—such as the specificity, pattern, and gate-control theories—many questions remain about the physiological and psychological components of this enigmatic but common experience. Most scientists agree, however, that the physiology of pain is a complex biochemical process that begins with pain receptors on nerve fibers that lie beneath the skin. An outside stimulus, such as intense heat, a cut, or even an exceptionally strong handshake, causes biochemicals on the nerve endings to produce a series of electrical nerve impulses. These impulses pass a "pain message" through the spinal cord to the brain's thalamus, which is located on top of the brain stem and processes the signals to the cerebral cortex. It is the cerebral cortex that interprets the feeling of pain and produces the appropriate reaction, such as pulling the hand away from a hot surface.

A number of biochemicals are involved in the experience of pain. Prostaglandins are biochemicals that are released where the injury occurs. These prostaglandins increase blood circulation in the injured area in order to battle infection and promote healing by increasing the supply of white blood cells, antibodies, and oxygen. Prostaglandins also work in concert with other biochemicals, like bradykinin, to increase nerve ending sensitivity and transmit electrical impulses to the brain. The speed at which these electrical impulses travel will vary according to the type of pain. For example, a pin prick may cause only a slight pain, but the impulse it triggers travels at the astonishing rate of 98 ft/sec (30 m/sec). In contrast, the pain impulse of a slight burn or ache travels at approximately 6.5 ft/sec (2 m/sec). As a result, some types of pain may cause immediate flinching whereas other kinds of pain produce a delayed response.

As scientists continue to study pain, they are uncovering more detailed information concerning its physiological intricacies. For example, they have identified certain receptors in the brain's neurons—called the NMDA receptors—that may amplify pain messages in the spinal cord, causing an individual to feel pain after touching an area that has been burned. Scientists are also locating with increased precision the areas of the brain that process pain information. One study has indicated that three specific structures in the cerebral cortex interpret pain messages, including where the pain is located. One structure, the anterior cingulate gyrus (which is thought to control emotions), may also play a crucial role in an individual's response to pain. Another group of researchers have found that a complex network of nerves in the brain may control the various responses that different people will have to the identical amount of pain.

Types of pain

Pain occurs in various degrees, from dull and aching to piercing and intense. Acute pain is usually associated with tissue injury and, for the most part, occurs for only a short amount of time. Chronic pain, however, persists for long periods of time, even years after the injury that originally caused the pain has gone away. For example, severe burns can create scar tissue that can continue to cause excruciating discomfort. Certain disorders, such as arthritis or cancer, may also cause persistent pain. In the case of phantom limb pain, an individual may continue to perceive pain in an arm or leg that has been amputated as though the appendage was still there. The precise cause of phantom limb pain is unknown. One theory is that the nerve endings remaining after the amputation continue to process the electrical pain impulses. Other theories focus on the firing of spinal cord neurons and the intricate neuronal circuitry of the brain.

Specific types of pain include causalgia (caused by severe burning that injures the nerve fibers under the skin) and neuralgia (caused by factors like viral infections and nerve degeneration that damages peripheral nerves). Headaches are the most common of all pain and may be chronic or acute in nature. Vascular headaches, like migraines, are caused by the constriction and dilation of the blood vessels in the area around the brain. Tension headaches have their origin in muscular contractions and are usually associated with psychological factors such as stress and depression. Traction or inflammatory headaches, which account for approximately 2% of all headaches, are caused by diseases.

Psychological factors in the individual experience of pain

The psychology of pain is a complex area of study. Although pain is universal in that every human being experiences it in one form or another, individual feelings of and responses to pain vary greatly. Each individual has a unique pain threshold (the point at which they first begin to experience pain) and tolerance to pain. Cultural heritage, tension, emotions, fears, and expectations all play a role in the experience of pain.

For example, in certain cultures specific rites and rituals may involve a pain that is readily accepted by the people within that particular society. Scientists believe that people in these cultures experience that

KEY TERMS

Anterior cingulate gyrus—A part of the brain that may play a critical role in controlling emotions and response to pain.

Biochemicals—The biological or physiological chemicals of living organisms.

Bradykinin—A biochemical present in the blood that acts as a vasodilator (which causes the dilation of blood vessels).

Causalgia—A type of pain caused by severe burning of the skin.

Central nervous system—The brain and spinal cord components of the nervous system that control the activities of internal organs, movements, perceptions, thoughts, and emotions.

Cerebral Cortex—The external gray matter surrounding the brain and made up of layers of nerve cells and fibers; it is thought to process sensory information and impulses.

Endorphins—Biochemicals produced by the brain that act as opiates and reduce pain.

Neuralgia—Severe throbbing or stabbing pain that originates in the nerve fibers.

Neurons—Nervous system unit that includes the nerve cell, dendrites, and axons.

NMDA receptors—Specific neuron receptors that strengthen neural connections and may play a role in pain perception.

Prostaglandins—A biochemical substance, present in many tissues, that plays an important role in healing injured areas and relaying pain messages to the brain.

Thalamus—A structure at the top of the brain stem that acts as the primary relay station for biochemical messages from the spinal cord to the brain.

emotional states may also cause biochemical changes that lower the amount of endorphins (naturally occurring opiates) produced by the brain.

Pain control

Pain control is achieved primarily through the use of drugs or through psychological approaches. Anesthetic and opiate drugs block pain signals to the brain or inhibit certain chemicals involved in the electrical pain impulses. Aspirin, the most widely used form of pharmaceutical pain control, works on the injured tissue itself by blocking the synthesis of prostaglandins, thus reducing the amount of pain impulses received by the pain receptors.

Psychological approaches to reduce pain by increasing an individual's pain threshold and tolerance were largely developed for chronic pain sufferers, but may also work in cases of acute pain. One such method involves focusing the attention on something other than the pain, such as a past pleasant experience, music, or even a complex mathematical problem. Relaxation and meditation techniques are used to reduce stress and muscle tension that may increase feelings of pain. Exercise can also help reduce pain because it causes the brain to produce more endorphins.

See also Analgesia; Anesthesia.

Further Reading:

Ackerman, Diane. *A Natural History of the Senses.* New York: Vintage Books, 1991.

Barinaga, Marcia. "Playing Telephone With the Body's Message of Pain." Science 258 (1992): 1085.

Benton, Myron. "The Mystery of Pain Thresholds." *Cosmopolitan* (April 1989): 122-123.

Melzack, Ronald and Patrick D. Wall. *The Challenge of Pain.* New York: Basic Books, 1983.

Poppy, John. "It's All in Your Head?" *Esquire* (April 1990): 85-89.

Toure, Halima. *Pain.* New York: Impact Books, 1981.

David Petechuk

pain to a far lesser degree than others from different cultures would if they underwent the same experience. In such cases, the ability to focus on other aspects of the ritual, such as its social or religious ramifications, may act as a psychological sedative that helps the individual better tolerate the pain or, perhaps, feel no pain at all. The expectation of pain also determines how much pain is felt. Two people, for example, may go to the dentist; the person who has greater anxiety about the experience is likely to feel a greater amount of pain. Tension and

Paleobotany

Paleobotany is the study of the plant life of the geological past. Paleobotany is mostly pursued through the study of fossils, or impressions of plant parts that have been preserved in sedimentary rocks, coal, or other geological deposits. The most ancient plant fossils are older

Fossilized *Alethopteris*, a seed fern from the Pennsylvanian period.

than one billion years, as is the case of microscopic impressions of Precambrian algae. There are also much younger fossils, as is the case of pollen in recently deposited lake sediments.

The primary goals of paleobotany are to discover the earliest appearances of various groups of plants, and to understand the evolutionary relationships among these taxa. Other objectives of paleobotany include the use of knowledge about fossil plants to infer the likely characteristics of their environment, including the type of climatic conditions under which they grew. Paleobotanists are also interested in the nature of the communities of fossil plants, and the species of animals with which they may have lived. Sometimes paleobotanical knowledge can be used for more practical purposes, such as assisting in the discovery of underground reserves of fossil fuels.

Paleobotanists commonly collect and identify microscopic spores, pollen, and bits of larger tissues. They also may identify larger, macroscopic plant remains such as leaves and even fossil tree trunks. Often, only the major plant group to which these plant parts belong, such as order or family, can be identified. In the case of more recent plant fossils that represent species that are still extant (not extinct), the remains may even be identifiable down to genus or species. Sometimes, the age of samples is known quite accurately. Paleobotanical studies of some recent lake sediments have shown that sometimes sediment layers develop that are annual accumulations. The total number of layers can be subreacted from the current year to determine an age for the sequence or any layer within.

Palynology (the study of fossil spores and pollen) is an important subdiscipline of paleobotany, and can be used to illustrate the nature of paleobotanical research in general. Palynologists search samples of lake sediment or bog peat of known age, carefully identifying and counting the microscopic pollen. Identification serves to place each specimen into whatever fossil group it belongs, down to the most specific level possible, which is often to the species.

From the assemblages of fossil pollen, palynologists make inferences about the types of forests or other plant communities that may have occurred in the local environment. These interpretations must be made carefully, however, because species are not represented in the pollen record in ways that directly reflect their abundance as mature plants. For example, pollen of wind-pollinated species is relatively abundant in lake sediments, whereas species that are insect pollinated are not well represented. For example, palynological studies of lake sediment might indicate that about 15,000 years ago the local environment around a particular lake in Minnesota used to support species that are now typical of northern tundra, while 10,000 years ago the vegetation was a boreal forest of spruces and fir.

More recently, the pollen assemblage may be dominated by species such as oaks, maples, basswood, chestnut, and other species of trees from more temperate climates. Combining these sorts of observations and knowledge of the present, climatically-influenced distributions of these species, palynologists can come to insightful conclusions about both the historical plant communities and past climates that occurred after the most recent glaciation ended in the region in which the lake occurs.

See also Fossil and fossilization.

Bill Freedman

Paleomagnetism

Paleomagnetism is the study of ancient magnetism in rocks. The phenomenon was first discovered by the French physicist Achilles Delesse in 1849. Delesse observed that certain magnetic minerals in rocks were lined up along the Earth's magnetic field, just as if they were tiny compasses that had been set in place in the rocks. A related discovery that was even more startling was made by the French physicist Bernard Brunhes in 1906. Brunhes observed that the magnetic minerals in some rocks are oriented in exactly the reverse position that would be expected if they were simply tiny compasses. That is, some of these minerals were oriented with their north poles pointing to the Earth's north magnetic pole, and their south poles to the Earth's south magnetic poles.

The magnetization of minerals in rocks

The phenomena observed by Delesse and Brunhes can be explained because of the fact that certain common iron-containing minerals are affected by any magnetic field, including that of the Earth. Two of the most important of these minerals are the oxides of iron, magnetite (Fe_3O_4) and hematite (Fe_2O_3). When these minerals occur in molten rock, their atoms are free to move in such a way as to align themselves with the Earth's magnetic field. When the rocks cool, the minerals are then frozen in position, oriented along the Earth's magnetic north-south axis.

Magnetic minerals found in rocks today, however, are not necessarily oriented along the Earth's present magnetic north-south axis. They may have shifted slightly in a vertical direction (their inclination or dip) or in a horizontal direction (their declination). The deviation of a mineral's orientation to the present magnetic field is of value in determining changes in the Earth's structure in the past.

For example, a magnetic mineral originally laid down along the equator would have an inclination of 0°, while one laid down at one or the other of the poles would have an inclination of 90°. Suppose one finds a rock lying at 40° north latitude with minerals that have an inclination of 0°. Then, one might conclude that this rock originally was laid down along the equator and, by some means, it was transported northward by a distance of 40° of latitude.

Magnetization of minerals

Minerals can be magnetized and oriented with the Earth's magnetic field in a variety of ways. One of these methods was described above. Igneous rocks are formed when molten rock escapes from beneath the Earth's surface and cools sufficiently to form new rocky material. As long as the original rock is molten, minerals are too hot to hold a magnetic field or to stay in a permanent position. As the rock cools, however, it reaches a point where it can retain a magnetic field and assume a fixed position. At this point, the minerals are frozen into place as compass-like indicators of the direction of the Earth's magnetic field.

Magnetic minerals can also be found in sedimentary rocks. As sand, silt, clay, and other such materials are moved from place to place by wind, water, waves, and other forces, the magnetic minerals are constantly reoriented. However, when these materials finally settle out and form permanent accumulations, the minerals orient themselves with the Earth's magnetic axis as they settle. Therefore, these sediments, which may eventually become sedimentary rocks, preserve the orientation of the Earth's magnetic field just as igneous rocks do.

Magnetization of minerals also occurs within rocky material during the chemical changes that result from metamorphism, or exposure to highly elevated temperature and pressures, which produces metamorphic rocks. Again, freedom of movement allows the minerals to become magnetized along the Earth's existing magnetic lines of force.

The study of the orientation of magnetic minerals laid down in the past is, however, further complicated by the fact that more than one episode of magnetization may have affected a sample. For example, an igneous rock might be worn away by erosion and then redeposited as a sedimentary rock. Then this sedimentary rock may be metamorphosed to produce a metamorphic rock, and then this rock may be exposed to another episode of metamorphism. Each of the metamorphic episodes has the potential to reorient the original sediments, or it may leave them relatively undisturbed. As you can see, recognizing the changes in the magnetic materials that occurred over millions of years within such a rock might be difficult.

Measurement of paleomagnetism

The study of paleomagnetism was born in the 1940s when the British physicist Patrick M. S. Blackett invented a device for measuring the very small amount of magnetic fields associated with magnetic minerals. The astatic magnetometer consisted of a number of tiny magnets suspended on a thin fiber. The magnetometer was rotated around a sample and the amount of magnetism measured by changes in the fiber.

Today, two other devices are more commonly used to study paleomagnetic materials: the spinner magnetometer and the cryogenic magnetometer. Each of these devices represents a significant improvement in the ability of a researcher to detect and measure the magnetic field associated with a mineral.

Applications of paleomagnetism

The results of paleomagnetic studies over the past four decades have had a revolutionary influence on our understanding of Earth history. The most significant single finding is that the orientation of magnetic minerals in rocks is often very much out of phase with the Earth's present magnetic field. At least two possible explanations for this phenomenon are possible and, in fact, have been proposed by scientists.

First, the Earth's magnetic field itself may have changed over time. In such a case, one might argue that magnetic minerals are lying in exactly the same location that they have always been, and the differences in their orientation are caused by the movement of the magnetic poles, not the minerals.

Second, one might argue instead that the Earth's magnetic field has been constant throughout history, and variations in the orientation of magnetic minerals have been caused by the movement of the minerals themselves. Since the minerals are now—and have for a long time been—frozen into the rocks, this theory would suggest that it is the rocks themselves that are moving across the Earth's surface.

In fact, scientists now know that both of these explanations are correct; the Earth's magnetic poles have wandered from place to place over time *and* the rocks in which magnetic minerals are found have traveled across the Earth's surface. We now have evidence that the polarity of the Earth's magnetic field has shifted (the north pole changing to the south pole, and vice versa) at least 171 times in the past 76 millions years. These reversals of polarity take place rather slowly, over a period of 5,000-10,000 years. They then remain fixed for a period of up to a million years.

In addition to these dramatic reversals of polarity, the Earth's magnetic poles also appear to have wandered extensively across the top and the bottom of the globe. About 300 million years ago, for example, the north magnetic pole was located in the eastern region of Siberia. It then traveled northward to the northern coast of Siberia, along to the coastline to Alaska, and then northward to its present location.

Paleomagnetism and plate tectonic theory

Even when the effect of reversal and change of location of the Earth's magnetic poles are taken into consideration, deviations of magnetic minerals in rocks from true north are still observed. In some cases, this deviation is very great. Since the 1960s, scientists have believed that the reason for these variations is that large chunks of the Earth's surface have moved significant distances across the planet's face over millions of years.

The theory of plate tectonics says that the Earth's crust and upper mantle, or lithosphere, consists of about a dozen large segments, known as plates, that are about 60 miles (100 kilometers) thick and thousands of miles wide. These plates slide back and forth on top of a lower layer of material known as the asthenosphere. The plates collide with each other head on, slide back

---

KEY TERMS

....

Compass—A device for detecting the presence and direction of a magnetic field.

Declination—The vertical deviation of a compass needle from true magnetic north.

Inclination—The horizontal deviation of a compass needle from true magnetic north.

Magnetic field—The region in space in which a magnetic force can be felt.

Magnetic pole—A space in which magnetic force appears to be concentrated. The two opposing magnetic poles are designated as the north and south poles of a magnetic.

---

and forth against each other, and pull apart from each other. Significant geological events, such as volcanoes and earthquakes, are produced.

One of the strongest pieces of evidence for plate tectonics has been paleomagnetism. Evidence has shown, for example, that some rocks in Alaska have magnetic minerals oriented in such a way that they must have been laid down at or near the equator. The fact that they are now at 70° north latitude suggests strongly that the plate on which they are riding must have migrated a very long distance during Earth history.

Paleomagnetism can also be used to match up land masses that are now separated from each other, but which must once have been joined. For example, the orientation of magnetic minerals along the eastern coast of South America very closely matches that of similar minerals on the western coast of Africa. This correlation, taken with other evidence, provides strong support for the notion that South America and Africa were once joined together as a single land mass.

One of the most remarkable successes of paleomagnetism has been in the study of sea floor spreading. Mid-oceanic ridge-rift systems are areas in the oceans where the edges of two plates, and any continents that may be on them, are being forced away from each other by currents in the underlying asthenosphere. Magma from the asthenosphere is pushed up from below the rift to fill in the void created by spreading and to create new ocean floor.

Strong evidence for this theory has come from the study of paleomagnetism on either side of these rifts. Magnetometers dragged by survey ships sailing above the rifts have found that the patterns of orientation of magnetic minerals on either side of a rift are mirror images of each other. Patterns of high and low intensity and specific inclination and declination running parallel to the rift on one side are exactly matched by similar patterns on the opposite side. This pattern could exist only if new rock were being formed simultaneously on either side of the rift, as suggested by the above theory.

Further Reading:

Butler, Robert F. *Paleomagnetism.* Boston: Blackwell Scientific Publications, 1992.

David E. Newton

Paleontology

Paleontology is the study of ancient animal life and how it developed. It is divided into two subdisciplines, invertebrate paleontology and vertebrate paleontology. Paleontologists use two lines of evidence to learn about ancient animals. One is to examine animals that live today, and the other is to study fossils. The study of modern animals includes looking at the earliest stages of development and the way growth occurs (embryology), and comparing different organisms to see how they are related evolutionarily (cladistics). The fossils that

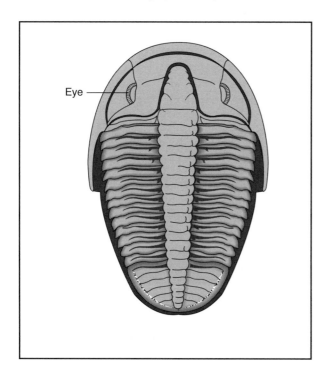

Figure 1. Trilobite.

paleontologists study may be the actual remains of the organisms, or simply traces the animals have left (tracks or burrows left in fine sediments). Paleontology lies at the boundary of the life sciences and the earth sciences. It is thus useful for dating sediments, reconstructing ancient environments, and testing models of plate tectonics, as well as understanding how modern animals are related to one another.

Invertebrate paleontology

An invertebrate is essentially a multicellular animal that lacks a spinal column encased in vertebrae and a distinct skull. There are about 30 phyla, or groups, of invertebrates, and roughly 20 of these have been preserved as fossils. Still other phyla probably existed, but are not represented in the fossil record because the animals' soft bodies were not preserved. Only one invertebrate phylum is known to have become extinct—the Archaeocyathida. These organisms, which were superficially similar to sponges, did not survive past the Middle Cambrian period (530 million years ago).

The different body plans of invertebrates most likely evolved during the Precambrian, between 1,000 and 700 million years ago. There was an "explosion" of invertebrate evolution in the Lower Cambrian (beginning about 570 million years ago), which lasted perhaps only 10 million years. During this time the different phyla, including those existing today, developed. Meanwhile, the glaciers from a Proterozoic ice age were melting, raising sea levels above the continental shelves. This gave invertebrates more places to live. There are no fossils showing how the first invertebrates evolved; they just suddenly appear in the fossil record. This may be because they were evolving so quickly, and because they developed hard shells, allowing them to be preserved. Many organisms from this period were preserved in the Burgess Shale formation (530 million years ago) in British Columbia, Canada.

The sponges (phylum Porifera) appeared in the Middle Cambrian. The bodies of these "lower" invertebrates are neither symmetrical nor differentiated into tissues. Sponges are less evolutionarily advanced than members of the phylum Cnidaria, which includes jellyfish, corals, and sea anemones. These two phyla may have arisen directly and independently from the protists (simple one-celled organisms such as bacteria, algae, etc).

The appearance of bilateral symmetry (two halves which are mirror images of each other) was an important evolutionary breakthrough. The most primitive bilaterally symmetrical animals are the flatworms (phylum Platyhelminthes). Platyhelminthes gave rise to the

Researchers cleaning dinosaur fossils in a paleontology laboratory in Esperaza, France. The fossils arrive encased in a protective plaster cast and with some of the original surrounding rock still attached. They are cleaned thoroughly and treated with stabilizing chemicals before being studied or classified.

coelomates, which have a coelom, or internal body cavity. The coelomates split into two evolutionary lines, the protostomes (molluscs, annelids, and arthropods) and the deuterostomes (echinoderms and chordates). A few phyla, such as the phylum Bryozoa, are intermediate between the two lines. Of the nearly 20,000 species of bryozoans known, only 3500 are still living.

The molluscs are a very diverse group of invertebrates. They include snails, chitons, and cephalopods (squids and octopuses). Recent studies of invertebrate genetic material has shown that molluscs and annelids (segmented worms) probably evolved from arthropods. *Neopilina*, which was discovered in 1957, is a modern, "primitive mollusc." It is similar to what the first molluscs are believed to have looked like. One of the main reasons molluscs have evolved so many different forms is that they have diverse methods of eating and of avoiding being eaten.

The arthropods ("jointed foot") are the most successful group of organisms ever. They include centipedes, insects, crustaceans, horseshoe crabs, spiders, scorpions, and the extinct trilobites and eurypterids.

Arthropods evolved 630 million years ago. The trilobites lived for 350 million years, from the Lower Cambrian to the Late Permian, and developed into over 1500 genera (Fig. 1). They had compound eyes with thin, biconvex lenses made of calcite. The last of the trilobites died out at the end of the Permian. The eurypterids were ancient water-scorpions (Fig. 2). Most eurypterids were less than 7.9 in (20 cm) long, but some giant forms grew nearly 6.5 ft (2 m) long, making them the largest arthropods ever.

Insects colonized the land just after plants did, about 410 million years ago. Cockroaches and dragonflies appeared over 300 million years ago, and for the next 100 million years, insects were the only animals that could fly. The chelicerates (spiders, mites, scorpions, horseshoe crabs, and eurypterids) evolved in the Cambrian.

The echinoderms (phylum Echinodermata) include starfish, sea-urchins, sea cucumbers, and crinoids. A great many of these organisms were fossilized because they have skeletons made of calcite plates. The greatest number of different genera of echinoderms lived during

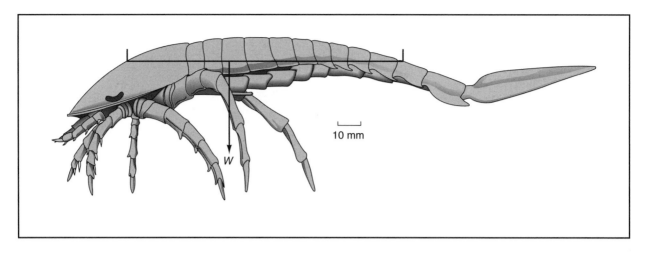

Figure 2. Eurypterid.

the Carboniferous (360-286 million years ago). The embryology of modern echinoderms suggests that they are related to the chordates. Modern echinoderm larvae have a ciliated band that runs along both sides of their bodies. The "dipleurula theory" suggests that ancient adult echinoderms had this band also, and that in the ancestors of the chordates, it fused along the back to form the beginnings of the dorsal nerve. Pikaia, a worm-like creature found in the Burgess Shale, is the oldest known chordate (Fig. 3). It lived in the Middle Cambrian (about 530 million years ago.

Vertebrates are a subphylum of the Chordata (chordates). Lower vertebrates have a notochord, which is a flexible cartilage rod that runs along their backs; this is replaced in higher vertebrates with a vertebral column. Vertebrates are also called craniate chordates because they are the only animals with a distinct cranium (skull). The oldest known vertebrate remains date from

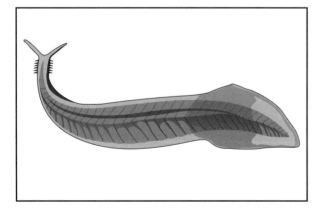

Figure 3. *Pikaia*, the world's first known chordate; found at Burgess Shale.

the Upper Cambrian and Lower Ordovician (around 505 million years ago).

The first vertebrates were fishes. They evolved primarily during the Devonian (408-360 million years ago). The earliest fishes did not have jaws. Unlike modern jawless fishes (hagfishes and lampreys), the extinct forms were heavily armored and had pairs of fins (Fig. 4). Jaws may have evolved from gill arches near the head, but there are no transition fossils which show this. Rays and sharks, which have skeletons of cartilage instead of bone, are the most ancient living fishes with jaws. Bony fishes, such as coelacanths and the ancestors of most modern fresh and saltwater fishes, probably evolved early in the Devonian. Coelacanths were believed to be extinct until a living one was discovered in 1938 in the Indian Ocean (Fig. 5). Fishes thrived until the Late Devonian (360 million years ago), when a mass extinction wiped out 76% of fish families.

The amphibians were the first vertebrates to leave the seas for dry land. They evolved from fishes about 360 million years ago. One of the challenges to living on land is that animals must be able to support their own weight rather than simply allowing water to support them. The lobed fins of the bony fishes already contained the major bones that became the limbs of the early tetrapods ("four feet"); many of these bones are still used in our own limbs today.

The earliest-known amphibian was the Ichthyostega (Fig. 6). It and other early tetrapods probably ate invertebrates such as cockroaches and spiders, as well as little fishes. The diadectomorphs appear to have been somewhat transitional between amphibians and reptiles. They belong to a category of amphibians called reptiliomorphs (as opposed to the batrachomorphs, or "true" amphibians).

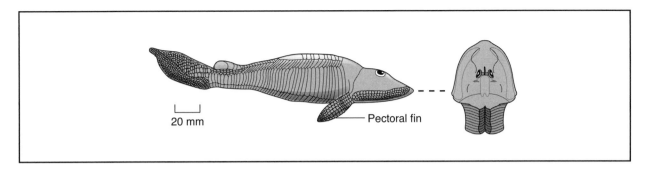

Figure 4. An ancient jawless fish, *Hemicyclaspis*.

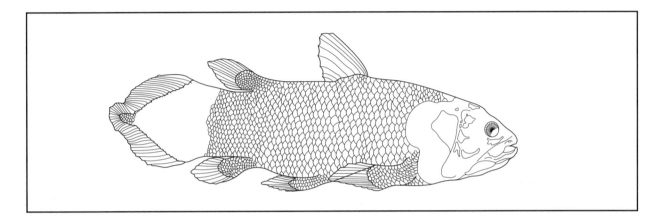

Figure 5. The coelacanth *Latimeria*.

The first reptiles, which were about the size of small lizards, emerged about 300 million years ago. They had a crucial advantage over amphibians in that their eggs could hatch on land, freeing them from spending part of their lives in the water. Among these early reptiles were the ancestors of modern birds and mammals. The pelycosaurs were the most varied of the Early Permian reptiles. Some had tall, skin-covered "sails" that may have helped regulate their body temperature (Fig. 7). The main herbivores in the Late Permian were the dicynodonts, and the main carnivores were the gorgonopsians such as *Arctognathus*. *Arctognathus* had huge canines and could open its jaws 90°. The ancestors of the crocodilians arose in the late Triassic. *Terrestrisuchus* was small (1.64 ft (0.5 m) long), probably ate insects and small reptiles, and may have walked bipedally on its long hind legs. Unlike its descendants, it did not live in the water.

Triassic oceans were filled with placodonts, nothosaurs, and ichthyosaurs (Fig. 8). Placodonts had heavy teeth which were probably used to crush the hard shells of molluscs. Nothosaurs had pointed teeth in their small heads, and may have eaten fish. Ichthyosaurs ("fish lizards") were shaped somewhat like giant porpoises with long, narrow jaws. They grew up to (15 m) long in the Late Triassic, but were smaller during the Jurassic and Cretaceous. Plesiosaurs, along with ichthyosaurs, ruled the Jurassic and Cretaceous seas. Plesiosaurs were probably related to nothosaurs (Fig. 9). Their paddles, however, were flat and like an airplane wing in cross-section, so that these animals may have moved through the water by "flying," the way penguins and sea turtles do.

The largest mass extinction of all time occurred at the end of the Permian (248-238 million years ago). All

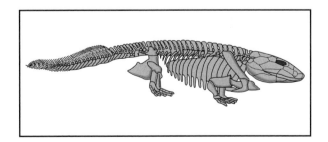

Figure 6. *Ichthyostega*.

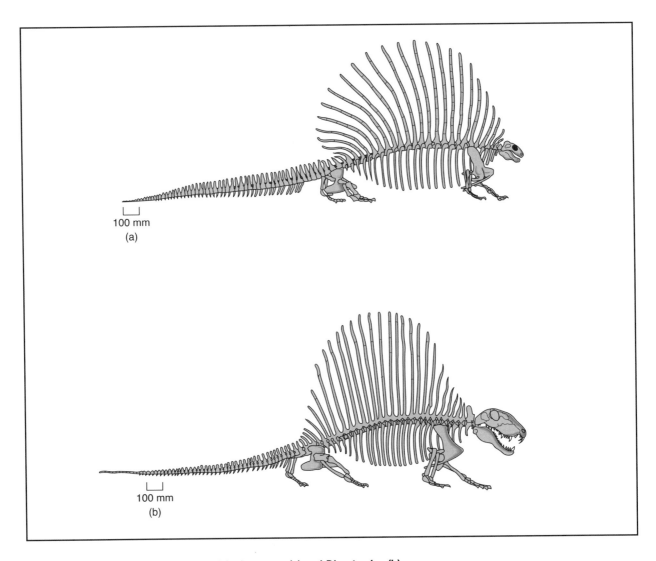

100 mm
(a)

100 mm
(b)

Figure 7. Two advanced pelycosaurs: *Edaphosaurus* (a) and *Dimetrodon* (b).

but about 10 tetrapod families died out, as well as 96% of marine species.

The dinosaurs ("terrible lizards") arose in the Late Triassic (230 million years ago). The earliest dinosaurs walked upright on two legs and were carnivorous. Dinosaurs are divided into two groups, the Saurischia and the Ornithischia, based on their hips. The saurischians had "lizard hips" and the ornithischians had "bird hips." The lizard hips arose first; Triassic dinosaurs were saurischians. While saurischians included both carnivores (meat eaters) and herbivores (plant eaters), all of the ornithischians were herbivores. The carnivorous saurischians are known as the theropods. They included the Late Jurassic *Allosaurus* and Late Cretaceous *Tyrannosaurus*, which probably was the largest carnivore ever to walk the earth. *Brachiosaurus* was a herbivorous saurischian. This sauropod had a long neck and short, thick legs like an elephant's, which were

designed for bearing its enormous weight. There were two kinds of bird-hipped dinosaurs, the Late Cretaceous Cerapoda and the Late Jurassic Thyreophora. The former included hadrosaurs (duck-billed dinosaurs) and ceratopsians ("horned faces"), and the latter included ankylosaurs and stegosaurs.

One of the major debates among paleontologists is whether or not dinosaurs were warm-blooded. Some scientists suggest that a four-chambered heart would have been necessary to pump blood up the long necks of the sauropods to their brains. Mammals and birds, which are warm-blooded, have four-chambered hearts, but so do the cold-blooded crocodilians. The debate has not been conclusively resolved.

There are two main models that attempt to explain the success of the dinosaurs. According to one, dinosaurs out-competed the mammal-like reptiles over

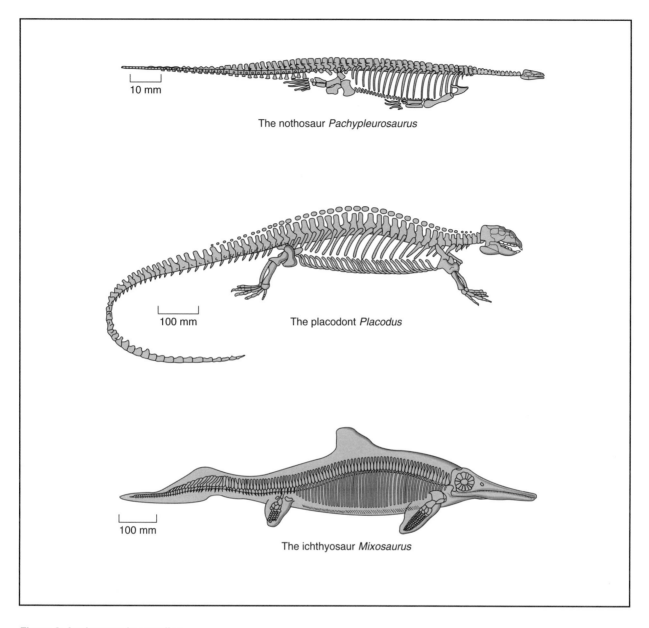

The nothosaur *Pachypleurosaurus*

The placodont *Placodus*

The ichthyosaur *Mixosaurus*

Figure 8. Ancient marine reptiles.

a long period of time due to superior adaptations such as upright walking. The other model, which is supported by fossil evidence, says that the dinosaurs took advantage of openings created by two mass extinctions. By the end of the Triassic, dinosaurs had taken over the land. They were dominant for 165 million years, from the Late Triassic until their extinction at the Cretaceous-Tertiary (K-T) boundary some 65 million years ago. This massive extinction may have taken place in only a week or lasted for tens of thousands of years—this has not been determined yet, but further study may provide an answer. One prominent theory for the cause of this event is that a meteorite hit the earth 65 million years ago, creating a cloud of dust which obscured the sun and prevented photosynthesis for several months. This set off a chain reaction which culminated in the death of many life forms on earth.

The pterosaurs ("winged reptiles") were closely related to the dinosaurs, and lived at the same time (Fig. 10). They had short bodies with long necks, and pointed jaws. They ranged from the pigeon-sized *Eudimorphodon* to the largest of all flying creatures, *Quetzalcoatlus*, which is believed to have had a wing span of up to 49 ft (15 m). Thanks to some well-preserved

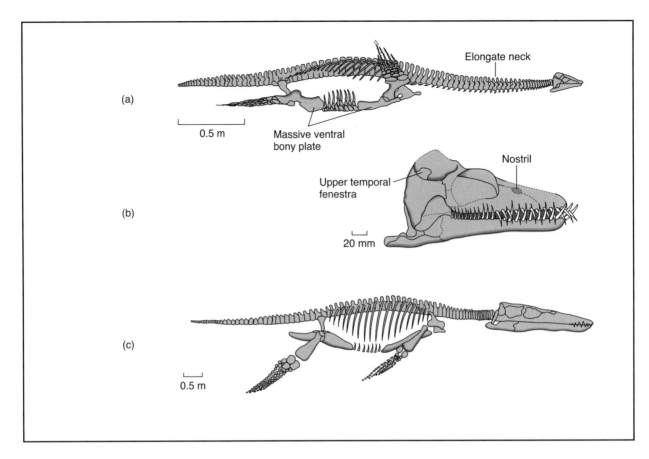

Figure 9. Late Jurassic plesiosaurs: *Cryptoclidus* (a & b) and *Liopleurodon* (c).

pterosaurs, we know they had hair, and were therefore possibly warm-blooded.

Birds evolved from the theropod dinosaurs. The first bird, *Archaeopteryx,* lived in the Late Jurassic (150 million years ago) (Fig. 11).This small, magpie-sized bird had sharp teeth on both jaws, and feathers. The presence of teeth, claws on the fingers, and its bony tail are reptilian characteristics, whereas the feathers and "wishbone" (fused collarbones) are bird characteristics.

The ancestors of mammals were mammal-like reptiles called cynodonts. Cynodonts arose in the Late Permian (about 245 million years ago). Some were dog-sized carnivores, and others were herbivores. One way the transition to mammals can be seen is in the manner in which the jaws are joined. Mammals have a new joint not present in reptile jaws which allows for the side-to-side action of chewing. The earliest true mammals appeared in the Late Triassic (230 million years ago). One was the tiny, shrew-like *Megazostrodon.* Because of its size and the fact that it had pointed teeth, it was probably an insectivore. Mammals radiated widely in the Paleocene Epoch (66-58 million years ago), taking advantage of the openings left by the

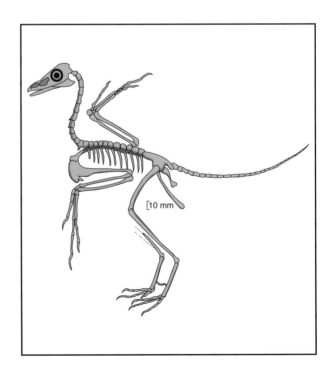

Figure 11. The first bird, *Archaeopteryx.*

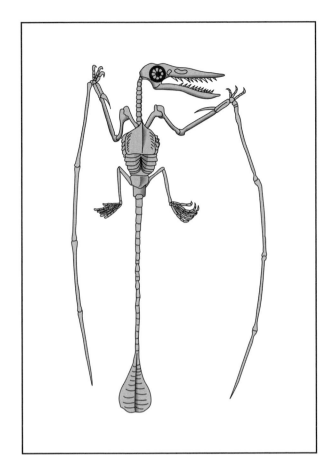

Figure 10. The pterosaur *Ramphorhynchus gemming.*

KEY TERMS

Cladistics—The study of evolutionary relationships between organisms based on analysis of the similarities and differences of their physical traits, that is, based on evolutionary divergence.

Coelom—An internal body cavity in which the digestive organs are suspended.

Embryology—The study of the development and early growth of living organisms.

Extinction—The condition in which all members of a group of organisms have ceased to exist.

Invertebrate—A multicellular animal that lacks a spinal column encased in vertebrae and a distinct skull.

Notochord—A flexible cartilage rod that runs along the back in chordates.

Phylum—A taxonomic division of animals, one level below kingdom in the taxonomic hierarchy (plural: phyla).

Vertebrate—An animal with either a notochord or bony spinal column and a distinct skull.

Palladium see **Element, chemical**

dinosaurs when they died out. The mammals were intelligent and took care of their young for an extended period of time, which probably gave them an edge over other animals. Mammals now appear in many very different forms, including the orders Insectivora (shrews), Carnivora (cats, dogs, seals), Chiroptera (bats), Cetacea (whales), Proboscidea (elephants), Tubulidentata (aardvarks), and Primates.

See also Dinosaurs; Mammals; Primates; Vertebrates.

Further Reading:

Benton, Michael J. *Vertebrate Palaeontology.* London: Uniwin Hyman, 1990.

Chaline, Jean. *Paleontology of Vertebrates.* New York: Springer-Verlag, 1990.

Enay, R. *Palaeontology of Invertebrates.* New York: Springer-Verlag, 1993.

Gould, Stephen Jay. *Wonderful Life. The Burgess Shale and the Nature of History.* New York: W.W. Norton & Company, 1989.

Kathryn M. C. Evans

Palms

The palm family is an ancient group of plants dating from at least the late Mesozoic Era, about 85 million years ago. Palms are flowering plants. Flowering plants have been subdivided into two major groups: the monocotyledons which bear only one seed leaf (cotyledon) and the dicotyledons which bear two seed leaves. Palms are among the most diverse of the families of monocotyledons, surpassed in numbers of genera and species only by the orchid, grass and lily families. The palm family contains about 212 genera and 2,800 species. Palmae is the old scientific name for the palm family and is still occasionally used.

Distribution

Palms are widely distributed throughout moist tropical and subtropical regions of the world. They can be found in steamy rain forests, deserts, mangrove swamps, and high mountain thickets. Palms are uncom-

Coconut palms in Florida.

mon in hot, dry regions, however, occurring only where there is a constant source of underground water. The distribution of palms in the tropics is uneven. The greatest diversity of palms is in the eastern tropics of Indo-Malaysia, the Guianas, and Brazil. Africa has relatively few palms with only 16 genera and 116 species; there are fewer palms in all of Africa than on the island of Singapore. The low diversity of palms in Africa is attributed to the dryness of much of the continent.

Palm species are also unequally distributed taxonomically among genera. A small number of genera contain a disproportionately large percentage of palm species. The genus *Calamus* is the largest with about 400 species in the Old World tropics. In the New World, *Chamaedorea* is a large genus with about 100 species in southern Mexico, Central America and northern South America. The average number of species per genus is relatively small at 13 and more than half of all the genera have 5 or fewer species. Seventy-three of the 212 genera of palms consist of only one species that is geographically restricted to a small area, often on an island. The palm floras of the New and Old Worlds are on the whole quite dissimilar.

Very few palms occur in temperate regions. In Europe, for example, there are only two native palms: the dwarf fan-palm (*Chamaerops humilis*), which is found in dry sandy and rocky places along parts of the Mediterranean coast, reaching the latitude 44°N, and the Cretan palm (*Phoenix theophrasti*), which is an extremely rare palm found only on the eastern side of Crete. In the Himalayas at 32°N, the palm *Trachycarpus* reaches an altitude of 7,875 ft (2,400 m) where snow lasts from November to March. In North America, the genus *Serenoa*, which includes the palmettoes of the southeastern states, reaches 30°N. The scarcity of palms

in temperate regions where frosts occur is likely related to their mode of growth. Palms generally have only one growing point which is at the tip of the stem or trunk. If this single bud is killed, then the palm dies. It appears that in the vast majority of palms, the growing tip is highly sensitive to frost and that few species have been able to overcome this sensitivity.

Structure

Palms are mostly unbranched shrubs or trees, and are the main tree family within the monocotyledons. Typically the solitary erect stem is crowned by large, persistent leaves that are sheathing at the base. The leaves of *Raphia fainifera* are the largest of any flowering plant, sometimes reaching more than 65 ft (20 m). Palm leaves are occasionally simple, but usually they are dissected into a fan shape (palmate) or feather shape with many distinct segments that run perpendicular to the main axis of the leaf (pinnately compound). The stem may be very short, so as to appear virtually absent, to 164 ft (50 m) in height. Not all palms have single stems or trunks. Some palms have clustered stems that arise from buds at the base of the initial stem, for example, *phoenix*. A few unusual species, such as *Chrysalidocarpus madagascariensis*, have some individuals with solitary straight trunks and other individuals with clustered trunks. Some palms are climbing vines, such as the rattans.

The trunk of palms is very different from the trunk of the conifer or dicotyledonous trees that dominate temperate regions. Conifers, such as pines, spruces, and hemlocks, and dicotyledenous trees, such as maples, oaks, and elms, increase the width of their trunk as they grow by a process called secondary growth. During this process, a ring of specialized cells under the bark of the tree produces new wood toward the center of the tree and other kinds of specialized conducting tissues toward the bark side. Secondary growth is absent in palms. Instead, when a seed germinates, the seedling first grows into an inverted cone whose width matches the full width of the trunk to be grown. Only after this radial growth is completed does the seedling begin to grow vertically, maintaining its width. If a nail is driven into a conifer or dicotylenous tree's trunk, the tree will grow around it eventually completely embedding the nail within the trunk. A nail driven into the trunk of a palm will remain where driven and not become embedded within the trunk.

Palm flowers are occasionally bisexual, but usually they are unisexual. When unisexual, the flowers of each sex may be on the same plant or, as in humans, only one sex is found per individual. The flowers are small and are generally borne on large, many-branched stems (inflorescences) that are located within the crown or just below it. Flower parts are normally in threes. The pollination biology of palms is not well studied, nevertheless, both wind and insect pollination are common in the family.

Palm fruits are berries, which are simple, fleshy fruits that contain one or more seeds, or drupes, which are simple, fleshy fruits that contain one seed that is surrounded by a bony pit, a stone fruit. The largest fruit in the world comes from the double coconut palm (*Lodoicea sechellarum*) and weighs up to 40 lb (18.2 kg).

Economic uses

Within the tropics, the palms rank second in economic importance after the grasses. Palms are used for food, oil, fiber, and as ornamentals.

Food

Dates are the fruit of the date palm (*Phoenix dactylifera*) and have been in cultivation for at least 8,000 years. Most dates are grown in Asia Minor and North Africa with an annual production of 2,000,000 metric tons. In the United States dates are grown in Arizona and California. Dates contain 70% carbohydrate but little protein (2%) or fat (2.5%). They have long been an important source of nourishment for nomadic tribes of the Arab world. Dates are usually eaten fresh but can be made into paste. Dates are sometimes mixed with a variety of milk products which increases the protein content. Muslims consider the date palm to be the "tree of life" because according to their tradition the tree was made from the dust left over after Adam was created.

Coconuts are the fruit of the coconut palm (*Cocos nucifera*). About 30 billion coconuts are produced each year, mostly in the Philippines, Indonesia, Sri Lanka, Malaysia, and Mexico. Although coconuts are an important food for some Pacific maritime societies and are sold in markets throughout the world, most of the annual harvest is used for the production of coconut oil, which will be discussed later.

Sago or sago starch is an important source of carbohydrate for many people of the tropics, from Thailand to New Guinea. Sago is derived from the pith (central portion of the trunk) of the sago palm (*Metroxylon sagu*), which grows in freshwater swamps that are otherwise useless for cultivated crops. Sago is readily extracted from the trunks and has the added advantage that it can be stored virtually pest-free. The one disadvantage is that sago has little protein. Sago is also

extracted from several other species in the genera *Arenga* and *Caryota*.

The sap of a variety of palms, including *Borassus* and *Caryota*, is fermented to produce palm wine, also called palm toddy. When fermented palm sap is distilled, the liquor known as arrack is produced.

In Southeast Asia, the betel nut, which in fact is the seed of the betel palm (*Areca catechu*), is commonly used for its mildly narcotic effect. The betel nut is chewed with a leaf of a local pepper plant and this in combination with a bit of lime makes the mouth and saliva red. With constant use, the teeth of betel addicts turn black. It has been estimated that a tenth of the world population chews betel nuts.

Oil

A number of palms are major sources of edible oils that are refined into cooking oil, margarine, and shortening. Palm oils are also used in the manufacture of candles, soaps, lubricating greases, and stabilizers in plastic and rubber compounds. The African oil palm (*Elaeis guineensis*) is the single most important oil-producing palm, having recently surpassed the coconut. The African oil palm is a sun-loving species that grows naturally in a 155 mi (250 km) wide strip along the coast of western Africa from Senegal to Angola, but is now planted throughout much of the tropics. The fruits of the oil palm are 23% oil by weight and most of the oil is in the outer husk which surrounds the inner stone. The yields from plantations are enormous with one hectare yielding as much as 5 tons of crude palm oil per year. The oil is collected by digesting the fruit to a pulp which is then centrifuged or pressed to separate the oil. The American oil palm (*E. oleifera*) is native to Central America and northern South America where it is extensively utilized. The American oil palm is better adapted to wet habitats than the African oil palm and the two species have been interbred to improve plantation stock.

The coconut palm is thought to be native to Polynesia, but it has been propagated and cultivated throughout the tropics for so long that its origin is uncertain. Coconut palms were until recently the major source of palm oil. The majority of the annual coconut harvest goes toward the production of oil. Coconut oil is derived from copra, which is the white flesh inside the seed (coconuts bought in a grocery store have had their large outer husk removed). One coconut tree may yield 198 lbs (90 kg) of copra a year and 9-11 gals (35-40 l) of oil. Coconut oil is especially suited for the manufacture of fast-lathering soaps and is also used as a hardening agent in a number of seemingly unrelated products such as cosmetics, margarine and rubber. Coconut meat is of course widely used in baking, cooking, and candy making.

Fiber

Palms produce a variety of useful fibers. Shells of the coconut are covered by tough fibers which are collected by soaking the shells in salt water to loosen the fibers. The fibers, called coir, are then beaten, washed and combed out. Coir is used as stuffing and woven into mats. Raphia fiber is obtained from the genus *Raphia* by stripping the surface of young leaves. The best-known fiber palms are the rattans which belong to the large genus *Calamus*. Rattans are interesting palms in that they are climbers and often vine-like. Unlike many climbers which use roots to attach themselves to their host or twining behavior to grip onto a stem, the rattans are scramblers that hoist themselves up leaf by leaf as the spiny stem hangs like a rope down to the roots. The hanging stems of many species of rattan are cleaned and split for use. Rattan is widely used for canework such as basketry.

Ornamentals

Palms are a symbol of the tropics and many have been selected and grown for their beauty. The royal palm (*Roystonea regia*) is a tall, elegant palm that is commonly planted along streets and boulevards in cities throughout the tropics and subtropics, including the southern United States. The sentinel palm of southern California (*Washingtonia filifera*) is also widely planted as an ornamental. Perhaps the most beautiful of all palms is the lipstick or sealing wax palm (*Cyrostachys renda*), which is native to peninsular Malaysia, southern Thailand, Borneo, and Sumatra. The sheathing leaf bases and petioles are brilliant red—a rare color for non-flower tissue in plants. Unfortunately this much coveted palm grows poorly outside of its native range.

Many of the palms have multiple uses, such as the coconut. Throughout the tropics a large number of palm species are used locally and intensively. Many of these species are now threatened. As was noted previously, a large proportion of palm species occupy small, geographically restricted areas and so local intense usage of these can have a devastating impact on their population size and survival, as can land clearance. One of the most destructive practices is the local harvesting of trees for palm hearts, which are the tasty shoot tips and associated tissue. The shoot tip is the only growing point on a palm stem and so its removal causes the death of the tree, or in branched species the stem. Increased awareness of this problem and of conservation of palms in

KEY TERMS

. . . .

Fiber—A generic term for a variety of strands of plant cells that consist of specialized long, thick-walled cells, technically called fiber cells, or other conducting or strengthening cells.

general is necessary to ensure the biodiversity of these attractive and economically important plants.

Further Reading:

Bateman, G. *Flowering Plants of the World*. Oxford: Oxford University Press, 1978.
Stewart, L. *A Guide to Palms and Cycads of the World*. London: Cassell Publishers, 1994.

Les C. Cwynar

Palynology see **Dating techniques; Pollen analysis**

Pancreas see **Digestive system**

Pandas

The common name "panda" applies to two different species: the familiar and well-loved giant panda and the lesser-known red panda. Scientists originally thought the two species were closely related because of similarities in their behavior, diet, anatomy, and distribution. Despite these shared features, however, researchers have now determined that the two species are not related as closely as was previously thought.

Giant pandas

Despite the popularity of the giant panda, the familiarity of its image to most people around the world, and its status as an endangered species, much is still unknown about the species' biology. Researchers studying the animals in the Chinese mountain preserves where many of the remaining pandas live are hoping to correct this, and to increase the chances of saving the species from extinction.

Giant pandas (*Ailuropoda melanoleuca*) are large, heavily-set animals with distinctive coloration: white fur with black or brownish-black patches on their legs,

A giant panda in China.

to portions of north-central Sichuan Province and southern Gansu Province, and the Qinling Mountains of Shaanxi Province in China.

Giant pandas are descended from the same ancestor as are animals like dogs, cats, bears, and raccoons, and so are placed in the order Carnivora (carnivores) within the class Mammalia (mammals), even though they have lost most of their meat-eating habit. The question remains as to whether giant pandas are more closely related to the bear family (Ursidae) or the raccoon family (Procyonidae) within the order Carnivora.

The first westerner to describe the giant panda was Pere Armand David, a French missionary living in China, in 1869. He called the panda a bear, based on its bear-like appearance. The next year scientists in Europe examined skeletons and concluded that giant pandas resembled red pandas (which were classified in the raccoon family) more than they did bears. For over a century, scientists argued about what to call the giant panda, with experts endorsing each of the possibilities.

Many aspects of the panda's skeletal structure and behavior support the idea that it is not a bear. An especially important piece of evidence is the presence in the giant panda of a special "sixth digit" which acts as an opposable thumb. This "thumb", which is an extension bone in the panda's wrist, serves the same purpose as a human thumb: it allows giant pandas to grasp bamboo shoots and efficiently strip off the leaves. The red panda also has such a "thumb", although it is less well-developed. Other aspects of panda biology which bears do not possess include: well-developed molar teeth, vegetarianism, and non-hibernation in winter.

Recently-developed molecular biology techniques have allowed scientists to create a "family tree" (called a phylogenetic tree) of the relationships between bears, pandas, and raccoons. Giant pandas are shown to be more closely related to bears than to raccoons, and are now placed in the bear family. Red pandas are placed in the raccoon family, although there are some questions about this relationship as well (see below).

Reproduction

Giant pandas are territorial throughout the year, with males and females maintaining separate feeding territories. During the breeding season (March to May in the wild), males increase their territory size to overlap the territories of several females, with whom they attempt to mate. Gestation is usually five months long, and 1-2 young are born (although only one is ever raised by the mother). The young are 3.15-4.55 oz (9-130 g) and 5.85-6.6 in (15-17 cm) at birth, and are blind and helpless. They are first covered with only

shoulders, ears, and around the eyes. Fully-grown giant pandas measure 4-5 ft (1.2-1.5 m) from nose to rump and weigh 156-350 lb (75-160 kg). The major habitat of giant pandas is sub-alpine spruce-fir-bamboo forests, at altitudes of 8,200-11,500 ft (2,500-3,500 m) above sea level. Adults are solitary, except females with offspring, and live in tree holes, small caves or crevices in rocks. Although their diet consists largely of bamboo stems and leaves, pandas also eat other plant material (such as irises, crocuses, vines, grasses, and tree bark) as well as some meat. To obtain sufficient nutrients from their fibrous foods, pandas spend 10-14 hours per day eating up to 80 lbs (36 kg) of bamboo.

Evolution and classification

Fossils of giant pandas dating to the middle to late Pleistocene era (about 600,000 years ago) have been found throughout central and southern China. This suggests that the prehistoric range of giant pandas was much greater than the present range, which is restricted sparse white fur, but the characteristic black patches appear within two weeks. At two months, the cub weighs 6.6- 11 lb (3- kg), its eyes open and it begins to crawl, although its hind limbs will not yet support it. At six months, the cub is weaned (stops suckling), although it may not leave its mother until she becomes pregnant again six months later.

After leaving their mothers, young female pandas are thought to migrate some distance and form a territory in a different area than their mother. This behavior reduces inbreeding in panda populations. Pandas become sexually mature at 6-7 years of age, and probably live to about age 15 in the wild. The small number of young produced per female per year, plus the relatively late age of sexual maturity, combine to cause low giant panda population growth rates. This, in turn, makes giant panda populations particularly susceptible to extinction.

Conservation and captive breeding

In 1984 the U.S. Fish and Wildlife Service listed the giant panda as an endangered species, restricting importation of giant pandas into the United States. Illegal international trade in giant pandas is controlled under the Convention on International Trade in Endangered Species of Wild Fauna and Flora (CITES). The total giant panda population in the wild is now thought to be between 1,000 and 1,200 individuals, most of which probably live in the 13 forest reserves established for pandas in China. The two major direct threats to the pandas are habitat loss and poaching.

Because the giant panda lives in only particular types of sub-alpine forest, destruction of this habitat by human deforestation means that giant pandas living there have no other place to go. It is estimated that suitable giant panda habitat has been halved in the last 20 years. The Chinese government is attempting to combat this problem with a 10-year plan to relocate logging operations in panda habitats, to create 14 new reserves and to expand the existing reserves.

Although pandas are protected under the law as an endangered species, poaching still occurs. Panda pelts sell for more than $10,000 in Hong Kong, Taiwan and Japan. The Chinese government has set sentences for convicted poachers of life imprisonment or even death, and these stiff sentences may begin to deter poachers.

Pandas have been kept in western zoos since the 1930's, and in Chinese zoos since the 1950's. The first giant panda birth in captivity was recorded at the Beijing Zoo in 1963, and several other successes followed. The first captive birth outside China occurred in 1980 at the Mexico City Zoo. The Chinese government presented a pair of pandas, Hsing-Hsing and Ling-Ling, to the National Zoo in Washington, D.C. in 1972. For 20 years, the pair attracted visitors from around the country, although they never succeeded in raising young. Ling-Ling died in 1992, at age 23. To date, captive births outside of China have been few, although researchers in many countries are trying to develop successful breeding programs.

Red pandas

Red pandas (*Ailurus fulgens*) are small, raccoon-like mammals with striking coloration. Their coats are reddish to dark chestnut on their backs and darker on their legs and bellies, with striped tails, white on the faces and the fronts of the ears, and red or brown stripes from the outside corners of the eyes to the corners of the mouth. Adult red pandas are 20-24 in (50-60 cm) long, with bushy 11-19 in (28-49 cm) tails, and weigh 7-10 lb (3-4.5 kg). They are native to Asian conifer-bamboo forests, at altitudes of 4,900-13,000 ft (1,500-4,000 m). Red pandas are nocturnal: they forage for food on the ground at night, and sleep in trees during the day. Like giant pandas, red pandas eat mainly bamboo (although they eat only the leaves, not the stems), and they supplement their diet with grasses, fruits, and some small animals such as insects.

Red pandas are thought to be mainly solitary and territorial, with the territory of a male overlapping the territories of several females in the breeding season. One or two young are born in mid-May to mid-July after a three to five month gestation period. Females give birth in tree holes and rear the young alone. The young are weaned at five months, and become sexually mature at 18-20 months of age.

Like giant pandas, red pandas are classified in the order Carnivora within the class Mammalia. Within this order, the red pandas are usually placed in the raccoon family with their closest relatives, the raccoons, coatis, and olingos. However, the World Conservation Union (the IUCN) places the red panda in its own family, the Ailuridae, mainly because the red pandas are found only in the Old World, while all other members of the Procyonidae are found only in the New World.

Red pandas are found over a much wider range than giant pandas, although this is still a relatively small area. They are found in the Himalayas, from Nepal to Sichuan and Tibet. At present some researchers estimate the Nepalese population size of red pandas to be 300, although other workers argue that this estimate is too low. Population sizes in other areas of the red panda's range are unknown but are thought to be declining. The IUCN classifies the red panda as threatened.

KEY TERMS

. . . .

Bamboo—Tropical grass with tough woody stem from which fronds sprout.

Inbreeding—Breeding between closely-related individuals, undesirable because of increased chance of recessive traits or birth defects appearing in the offspring.

Phylogenetic tree—A diagram showing the evolutionary relationships between groups of organisms.

Procyonidae—A family in the order Carnivora, including the olingos, ringtails, coatis, kinkajou, red panda, and raccoons.

Ursidae—A family in the order Carnivora, including all types of bears and the giant panda.

Like giant pandas, red pandas are affected by habitat destruction and poaching. Deforestation removes not only their food supply, but also the trees in which they nest. Red panda habitat is protected in the system of Chinese reserves designed for the giant panda, but the situation in other parts of the panda's range is unclear. Red pandas are hunted for their fur and, in places, for their meat. CITES has reduced the illegal trade in red pandas, although animal dealers may get around the convention by falsely stating that their animals originated in captive breeding programs. Red panda captive breeding programs are relatively successful, with five breeding programs world-wide.

Further Reading:

Glatston, Angela. *The Red Panda, Olingos, Coatis, Raccoons, and their Relatives.* Gland, Switzerland: IUCN, 1994.

Jing, Zhu and Li Yangwen. *The Giant Panda.* Beijing: Science Press, distributed by Van Nostrand Reinhold Co., 1980.

McClung, R.M. *Lili: A Giant Panda of Sichuan.* New York: Morrow, 1988.

O'Brien, Stephen J. "The Ancestry of the Giant Panda." *Scientific American* 257, no. 5 (1987): 102-107.

Schaller, G.B. *The Last Panda.* Chicago: University of Chicago Press, 1993.

Wenshi, P. "New Hope for China's Giant Pandas." *National Geographic* 187, no. 2 (1995): 100-115.

Amy Kenyon-Campbell

Pangaea see **Continental drift; Plate tectonics**

Pangolins

Pangolins, also called scaly anteaters, are subsaharan African and Asian mammals that have horny scales covering the upper parts of their bodies. All seven species belong to one genus, *Manis,* making up the order Pholidota. The overlapping brown, gold, olive or purplish scales serve to protect the animal from predators. Pangolins feed on ants, termites, and other insects; they use their long, narrow tongues to probe insect nests and extract their prey. The name *pangolin* comes from a Malay word that means "rolling over."

The family name, Manidae, means "scaled animals." The pangolin's scales grow out of the animal's skin. They are regularly shed and replaced both as the animal grows and throughout its life, which may be 10 or more years. The back edges of the scales are sharp. If frightened, a pangolin can curl up in a very tight ball, with only the sharp edges of its scales exposed. In this condition it is safe from all predators except the larger cats and hyenas. The Asian species have several hairs growing from the base of each scale; the African species have hair only on their exposed surfaces.

The largest pangolin is the giant pangolin (M. gigantea) of Africa. It may reach a total length of more than 5 ft (1.5 m), of which about half is scale-covered tail. Its amazing tongue is almost as long as its body. This tongue can be 27 in (69 cm) long, though probably only half that length is extended beyond its sheath and into ant nests. The tongue is anchored to an attachment point on the animal's pelvis and is kept sticky by a huge salivary gland located in the chest. The thousands of ants the animal traps on its tongue are not chewed but deposited directly into a muscular, thick-walled stomach that grinds them up; the pangolin has no teeth or chewing muscles. Like the South American anteaters, the pangolin has powerful front limbs with massive claws that can tear apart termite nests. The Cape pangolin *(M. temmincki)* burrows underground during the day and hunts for termites at night.

The giant pangolin and the other ground-dwelling species have difficulty walking on the ground because of the massive claws on their forefeet. They can tuck the claws up and walk slowly on the side of the forefeet, but if they are in a hurry, pangolins generally rise up on their hindfeet and run two-legged, using the tail for balance.

The smallest pangolin is the long-tailed pangolin *(M. tetradactyla),* also of Africa. It is about 30 in (76 cm) from head to tail. Unlike the giant pangolin, which is a ground-dwelling animal, the long-tailed pangolin lives high in the canopy of trees. These animals also eat

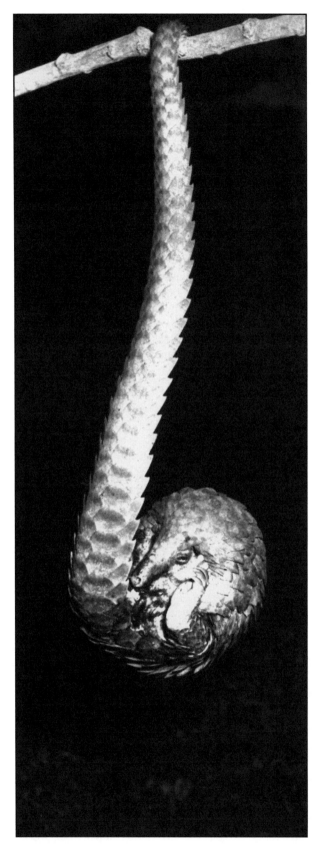

A pangolin.

termites and ants, but they target the species that build hanging nests. The long-tailed pangolin's tail contains more vertebrae, or spinal bones, than any other mammal. The 46 or 47 bones make the tail flexible enough to wrap around tree branches and let the animal hang upside down or curl up tightly in a little ball while it sleeps. The very tip of the tail is bare, making it more sensitive.

The three Asian species are the Chinese pangolin *(M. pentadactyla),* the Indian pangolin *(M. crasicaudata),* and the Malayan pangolin *(M. javanica).* Not a great deal is known about these animals, but they are equally comfortable on the ground and in trees.

Pangolins generally lead solitary lives except when mating. After a gestation period of about 18 weeks, the female gives birth to usually a single offspring. It is born with soft scales that quickly harden. The infant clings to its mother's back or tail as she moves about feeding. If threatened by harm, the mother can safely curl up around her infant until the danger passes.

Although no pangolin is currently known to be seriously endangered, all of them are suffering from habitat reduction. In Africa, pangolins are hunted for their meat and scales. In some Asian countries pangolin scales are believed to have medicinal value, leading to indiscriminate killing of these animals.

Further Reading:

Kerrod, Robin. *Mammals: Primates, Insect-Eaters and Baleen Whales.* New York: Facts on File, 1988.

Jean Blashfield Black

Pansy see **Violet family**

Panther see **Cats**

Papaya

The papaya or pawpaw (*Carica papaya*) is a tropical tree originally native to the Americas, probably Mexico. This species is easily cultivated, produces large, edible fruits, and now is distributed worldwide to suitable climates where it is grown for subsistence and commercial agriculture. The papaya has large deeply incised, sometimes compound leaves that sprout near the top of the plant. This plant does not develop true woody tissues because it is a giant, soft-stemmed, perennial herb that grows to be as much as 32.8 ft (10 m) tall. Individual plants generally die after about four years.

The papaya is dioecious, that is unisexual, for male and female flowers are borne by separate plants. The flowers are yellow and sweet-smelling and open at night to attract moths, the pollinators of the papaya.

The economically important fruits of the papaya are large, yellow-green or reddish, melon-like, multi-seeded berries each weighing as much as 22 lb (10 kg). The fruits of the papaya emerge from the stem of the plant in a phenomenon known as cauliflory. The papaya bears fruit year-round.

The flesh of the papaya fruit is orange-yellow and edible. Papaya fruits can be eaten fresh, boiled, preserved, or reduced to a juice. Other products can be created from the milky latex of the papaya including a base for chewing gum and an extract containing the enzyme papain. Papain is used to tenderize tough meats by predigesting some of their proteins.

Paper

Paper was probably first produced from bamboo and rag fibers about 2,000 years ago. By the eighth century, papermaking technology had spread to the Middle East. By the middle of the twelfth century, the Moors had transplanted the technology to Spain, from where it spread throughout Europe. Rags continued to be the chief source of paper fibers until the introduction of papermaking machinery in the early 1800s, when it became possible to obtain papermaking fibers from wood.

Hand-made and machine-made papers both consist of tiny cellulosic fibers pressed together in a thin sheet. Each of these fibers is a tiny tube, about 100 times as long as it is wide. Today, most fibers come from wood, though in earlier times, the source was more likely to have been rags of linen or cotton. The length of wood fibers from conifers is about 1/8 to 1/4 inch, and from hardwoods, about 1/25 inch. Other vegetable fibers are much longer. Cotton fibers, for example, may be one or more inches in length, with diameters of 1/50 inch. The source material is reduced to a slurry of fibers that floats freely in water, and many of the fibers will have been broken or cut when making the pulp. When the water is removed, the fibers form a thin layer of pulp which eventually becomes paper.

Hand-made paper

Rags to be made into paper are first sorted, and any unsuitable ones are discarded. Seams are opened, and nonfabric materials, such as buttons, are removed. The rags are chopped into small pieces and then cleaned by boiling them in strong cleansing solutions. Next, they are rinsed and beaten while damp until all of the threads have disintegrated and the fibers float freely in water. This is the paper pulp.

The very dilute pulp is next sent to the vat where the paper will actually be made. A rectangular mold containing wires running at right angles to each other is used to make a film of the pulp. Traditional molds have thin, closely spaced parallel wires running across the mold at the surface. These are attached to thick, widely spaced wires beneath them that run in the opposite direction. Paper formed on this type of mold typically reveals a ladderlike pattern when held up to the light, and is known as laid paper. Woven paper is formed on a mold of plain woven wire screening. Thin wire forming a design may be attached to the mold's surface wires to produce a watermark in the finished paper. A rectangular frame, called the deckle, is placed over the mold to convert the mold into a sort of tray.

The papermaker then dips the mold with the deckle attached into the vat of dilute pulp and draws up a small amount of pulp on the surface of the wire. The mold is then shaken and tilted until most of the water has drained through the wire. The deckle is removed, and additional water is allowed to drain off. A second worker takes the mold and transfers the film of pulp to a piece of damp felt, laying a second piece of felt across the top.

This process continues until a stack of alternating wet paper and felt has built up. The stack is placed in a press to eliminate any residual water. Then the paper and felt are separated, and the paper is pressed by itself and hung up to dry. When dry, the paper sheets are dipped in a tub containing size (essentially gelatin or very dilute glue) and dried again. This gives the paper a harder and less absorbent finish than it would otherwise have had.

All paper was made by hand until the early nineteenth century. Artists use most of the handmade paper consumed today, though hand printers can still be found who believe it the finest printing surface available.

Machine-made paper

Hardly any paper for book printing is made from rags today. Wood now is the main ingredient of paper pulp, though the better papers contain cotton fiber, and the best are made entirely of cotton. The fibers are converted into pulp by chemical and/or mechanical means.

Chemical pulp starts with logs that have had their bark peeled off and that have been reduced to chips. The wood chips are boiled in strong caustic solutions that dissolve away parts of the wood that are not cellulose, such as lignin and resin, and leave the cellulose fibers more or less free. There are two chief processes for producing chemical pulp: the kraft process, and the sulfite process. The kraft process uses the wood of either deciduous (e.g., poplar) or coniferous trees (e.g., spruce, fir, and hemlock) and produces a very strong paper. The sulfite process is less widely used and employs only coniferous wood and an acid solution in paper manufacture.

Mechanical pulp is mostly made by stone-grinding peeled logs in a stream of water so that the wood is broken up into fibers. Spruce, balsam, and hemlock are the woods considered best suited for pulping by this process. The ground wood contains all of the constituents of the original wood, including those that would have been eliminated as impurities in chemical pulp manufacturing. Mechanical pulp is mainly used for newsprint because paper made from mechanical pulp quickly discolors and becomes brittle. It also tends to be weak. A superior, stronger form of mechanical pulp is called thermomechanical pulp. It is made from wood chips treated by steam under high pressure. Mechanical pulp is sometimes added to chemical pulp for making low cost book papers. A paper containing no mechanical pulp is called a free sheet.

Before the pulp can be made into paper, it is necessary to mechanically beat or refine it. It is also usually bleached with chlorine and calcium hypochlorite. Unbleached kraft pulp is used for grocery bags and heavy wrapping paper. Other materials may also be added to the pulp depending on the type of paper to be made. For book paper, fillers such as white clay and titanium oxide may be added to provide opaqueness and extra whiteness. Size may be added for stiffness and smoothness. Dyes are added for tinted papers. The specific combination of pulp and additives used to produce a particular type of paper is called the furnish for that paper. With better grades of paper, care is taken to produce a furnish that is chemically neutral (pH 7 on the acid-base scale). For a paper to have long life, it must be acid-free.

The machine that converts the pulp into paper is called a fourdrinier machine, after Henry and Sealy Fourdrinier who financed its development in England in the early 1800s. The fourdrinier machine takes pulp that is still 99% water and converts it into a continuous web of paper containing only a small amount of moisture.

Pulp is continuously fed into the fourdrinier machine on the surface of a moving endless belt of fine mesh screening, usually made of nylon. Deckle straps prevent the liquid pulp from slopping over the sides. The screening is shaken from side to side as it moves forward to help drain the water. Suction boxes below the screening pull more water through, as a wire-mesh-covered cylinder presses on the web of pulp from above. The cylinder may be covered with a plain wire cloth to impart a wove effect, or with wire in a ladder pattern to produce a laid effect. To produce a watermark, the papermaker attaches a wire design to the cylinder.

The now very soggy paper is placed on an endless belt of wool felt that carries it between a series of rollers that squeeze more water from it. It then passes over a series of very large, steam-heated, cast-iron drums that complete the drying process. During drying, the web is held tightly against the hot drums by endless belts of fabric.

After the paper has dried, it is usually run through a series of highly polished metal (calendar) rollers that further compact it and smooth its surface. The calendar rolls are arranged in pairs; each pair rolls at a different speed; this effectively polishes the paper. A variety of calendared finishes can be obtained, ranging from antique (softest and dullest), through eggshell, vellum, machine finish, to English finish (hardest and shiniest available without further treatment).

Further treatment may include supercalendaring, surface sizing, or coating. Supercalendaring is a polishing process similar to the calendaring process but done on a separate machine. The final finish of coated papers are brushed or rolled on in liquid form. The finish may be matte or glossy. Most papers include size in the furnish, but additional sizing may be added to the surface by running the paper through a vat of sizing material to provide a harder finish after the paper is made. The paper may be coated with fine clay. The clay is adhered to the surface of the paper with adhesives. The paper is then supercalendared with extremely smooth rollers. Dull coated papers are made with clays that finish dull, and are less calendared. Other papers are gloss coated. Papers may be coated on one or both sides.

Machine-made paper has a pronounced grain, as evidenced by its tendency to tear and fold preferentially in one direction. This is because the cellulose fibers tend to align themselves in the direction of travel as the pulp is laid down on the wire. Shaking does not completely achieve random alignment. In reeled paper, the grain always runs lengthwise. In sheet paper, the grain may run either the long way or the short way, depending on how it was cut from the reel.

Like most fabrics, paper has a right and wrong side. The bottom of the web (called the wire side) next to the screening at the wet end of the fourdrinier machine is slightly rougher than the top (or felt) side. If only one side of the paper is to be used, the smoother side is usually chosen. Paper made on a twin-wire fourdrinier machine has either two felt sides or two wire sides; this is because two webs of pulp are laid down simultaneously and pressed together as the paper is dried and finished. One-sided paper is more expensive than ordinary two-sided paper.

Paper categories

Paper is available in a wide variety of weights, colors, textures, and finishes for a multitude of purposes. Book papers are intended for book and journal printing. Almost all bookpapers are surface-sized for offset lithography. The sizing resists penetration by the water and ink used in offset printing. Book papers are mainly made from Kraft pulp, sometimes with machine pulp added. Text papers are available in many colors and textures for use in advertising leaflets, endpapers, etc. They are also sized for offset printing. Cover papers are used for heavier papers, and are chiefly used for covers for pamphlets, journals, and paperback books. Newsprint is made for printing newspapers, advertising catalogs, inexpensive paperbacks, and other items that will probably only be read once if at all, and then thrown away. It is made from machine pulp, usually with some chemical pulp added for strength. Bond is made mainly for office use and ranges in quality from top-grade papers made from 100% rag pulp to low-grade stocks consisting largely of machine pulp.

Paper weights

Paper varies in thickness and weight. Both measurements are used to calibrate stock. At the paper mill, the thickness of a sheet is measured in thousands of an inch (mils). For the purposes of bookmaking, this number is converted into pages per inch. Book papers may vary from 200 to nearly 1000 pages per inch, but the commonly used 50-pound machine-finished papers generally run about 500 to 550 pages per inch, each leaf counting as two pages. That corresponds to an average thickness of about 1/250 inch (4 mils) for the thickness of one sheet of 50-pound machine-finished paper.

Paper is sold by weight. Different grades of the same type of paper are distinguished by the weight of some standard quantity of that paper. For most of the

world, the standard quantity is one sheet of paper per one square meter in area. In the U.S., the system of basis weights is used to compare the weights of papers. The standard quantity is one ream, or 500 sheets, but the standard sheet size varies from one category of paper to another. For book papers, the standard sheet measures 25 by 38 in (64 by 97 cm). For cover stocks, the standard size is only 20 by 26 in (51 by 66 cm), so a 50-pound cover paper is nearly twice as heavy as a 50-pound book paper. For bond papers, the standard size is 17 by 22 in (43 by 56 cm), so a 20-pound bond is approximately equal to a 50-pound book paper.

In Europe, the metric A series of stock sizes is based on a standard sheet of paper, rectangular in shape (841 mm by 1189 mm) and one meter in area. This is called size A0. Cutting this sheet in half produces size A1; cutting the A1 sheet in half produces size A2, and so on down to size A5, which is 1/32 the area of A0. In this sizing system, all of the sheets have the same shape: the ratio of the short side to the long side is identical throughout the series of sizes.

Further Reading:

The Chicago Manual of Style, Chicago: The University of Chicago Press, 1982.

KEY TERMS

Calendar rolls—Highly polished metal rollers used to compact paper after it has dried.

Furnish—Specific combination of pulp and other ingredients used to make a particular kind of paper.

Fourdrinier machine—The machine that forms paper from pulp, named after the English family that financed its development in the early 1800s.

Kraft process—A process in which sodium sulfate is reduced by heating with carbonaceous matter in a furnace to form sodium sulfide, which is then used in a water solution with sodium hydroxide as a cooking liquor. The wood pulp is then cooked under pressure and at high temperatures. The kraft process, also known as the sulfate process, has a less corrosive influence on iron and steel than the sulfite process.

Sulfite process—A process in which sulfur dioxide is passed through calcium carbonate to form calcium bisulfite in an excess of sulphurous acid as the cooking liquor. The wood pulp is then cooked under pressure at high temperatures.

Hunter, Dard. *Papermaking: The History and Technique of an Ancient Craft,* New York: Dover Publications, Inc., 1974.

Lee, Marshall. *Bookmaking,* New York: R. R. Bowker Company, 1979.

Shannon, Faith. *The Art and Craft of Paper*, San Francisco: Chronicle Books, 1994.

Randall Frost

Papyrus see **Sedges**

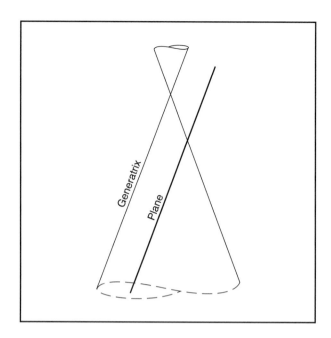

Figure 1.

Parabola

A parabola is the open curve formed by the intersection of a plane and a right circular cone. It occurs when the plane is parallel to one of the generatrices of the cone (Figure 1).

A parabola can also be defined as the set of points which are equidistant from a fixed point (the "focus") and a fixed line (the "directrix") (Figure 2).

A third definition is the set of points (x,y) on the coordinate plane which satisfy an equation of the form $y = x^2$, or, more usefully, $4ky = x^2$. Other forms of equation are possible, but these are the simplest.

The "axis" of a parabola is the line which passes through the focus and is perpendicular to the directrix. The "vertex" is the point where the axis crosses the parabola. The "latus rectum" is the chord passing through the focus and perpendicular to the axis. Its length is four times the distance from the focus to the vertex.

When a parabola is described by the equation $4ky = x^2$, the vertex is at the origin; the focus is at (o,k); the axis is the y-axis; the directrix is the line $y = -k$.

In spite of the infinitude of cones—from skinny ones to fat ones—which yield parabolas, all parabolas are geometrically similar. If one has two parabolas, one of them can always be enlarged, as with a photographic enlarger, so that it exactly matches the other. This can be shown algebraically with an example. If $y = x^2$ and $y = 3x^2$ are two parabolas, the transformation $x = 3x$ $y = 3y$ which enlarges a figure to three times its original size, transforms $y = x^2$ into $3y = (3x)^2$, which can be simplified to $y = 3x^2$.

This reflects the fact that all parabolas have the same eccentricity, namely 1. The eccentricity of a conic section is the ratio of the distances point-to-focus divided by point-to-directrix, which is the same for all the points on the conic section. Since, for a parabola, these two distances are always equal, their ratio is always 1.

A parabola can be thought of as a kind of limiting shape for an ellipse, as its eccentricity approaches 1. Many of the properties of ellipses are shared, with slight modifications, by parabolas. One such property is the way in which a line intersects it. In the case of an ellipse, any line which intersects it and is not simply tangent to it, intersects it in two points. So, surprisingly, does a line intersecting a parabola, with one exception. A line which is parallel to the parabola's axis will intersect in a single point, but if it misses being parallel by any amount, however small, it will intersect the parabola a second time. The parabola continues to widen as it leaves the vertex, but it does so in this curious way.

A parabola's shape is responsible for another curious property. If one draws a tangent to a parabola at any point P, a line FP from the focus to P, and a line XP parallel to the axis, will make equal angles with the tangent. In Figure 3, $\angle$ FPA $=\angle$ XPB. This means that a ray of light parallel to the axis of a parabola would be reflected (if the parabola were reflective) through the focus, or a ray of light, originating at the focus, would be reflected along a line parallel to the axis.

A parabola, being an open curve, does not enclose an area. If one draws a chord between two points on the parabola, however, the parabolic segment formed does

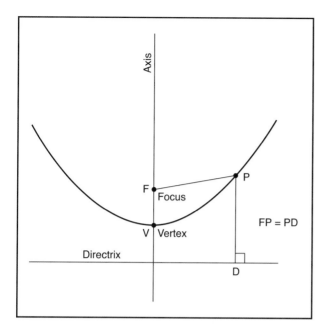

Figure 2.

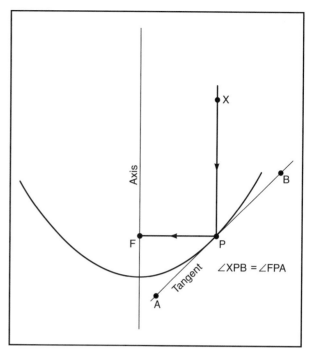

Figure 3.

have an area, and this area is given by a remarkable formula discovered by Archimedes in the third century B.C. In Figure 4, M is the midpoint of the chord AB. C is the point where a line through M and parallel to the axis intersects the parabola. The area of the parabolic segment is 4/3 times the area of triangle ABC. For example, the area of the parabola $y = x^2$ and the line $y = 9$ is $(4/3)(6 \times 9/2)$ or 36. What is particularly remarkable about this formula is that it does not involve the number π as the formulas for the areas of circles and ellipses do.

Drawing parabolas

Unlike ellipses, parabolas do not lend themselves to simple mechanical drawing aids. The ones occasionally described in texts work crudely. Templates are hard to find. The two best methods for drawing parabolas both involve locating points on the parabola and connecting those points either by eye, or with the help of a draftsman's french curve.

The equation of $4ky = x^2$ or $y = x^2/4k$ can be used to plot points on graph paper. The parameter K, which represents the distance from the focus to the vertex, should be chosen to make the parabola appropriately "sharp" or broad. A table of ordered paris (x,y) will help in point plotting. Enough points should be plotted, especially near the vertex where the curvature of the parabola changes most rapidly, that a smooth, accurate curve can be sketched.

Uses

Parabolas show up in a variety of places. The path of a bomb dropped from an airplane is a section of a parabola. The cables of a well-designed suspension bridge follow a parabolic curve. The surface of the water in a bowl which is rotating on a turntable will assume the shape of a parabola rotated around its axis. The area of a circle is a parabolic function of its radius. In fact, the graphs of all polynomial functions $y=ax^2 +bx + c$, of degree two are parabolic in shape.

Perhaps the most interesting application of a parabola is in the design of mirrors for astronomical telescopes. The rays of light from a star, a galaxy, or even such a nearby celestial object as a planet are essentially parallel. The reflective property of a parabola sends a ray which is parallel to the parabola's axis through the focus. Therefore, if one grinds a mirror with its surface in the shape of a parabola rotated around its axis and if one tilts such a mirror so that its axis points at a star, all the light from that star which strikes the mirror will be concentrated at the mirror's focus.

Of course, such a mirror can be pointed at only one star at a time. Even so, the mirror will reflect rays from nearby stars through their own "foci" which are near the real focus. It will bring into focus not only the one star at which it is pointed, but also the stars in the area around the star.

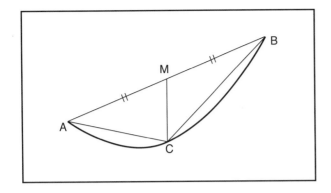

Figure 4.

The process can be reversed. If the light source is placed at the focus, instead of concentrating the rays, the reflector will act to send them out in a bundle, parallel to the axis of the reflector. The large searchlights used during air raids in World War II were designed with parabolic reflectors.

Parabolic reflectors are used in other devices as well. Radar antennas, the "dishes" used to pick up satellite television signals, and the reflectors used to concentrate sound from distant sources are all parabolic.

Further Reading:

Eves, Howard. *An Introduction to the History of Mathematics.* New York: Holt, Rinehart and Winston, 1976.

Finney, Thomas, Demana, and Waits. *Calculus: Graphical, Numerical, Algebraic.* Reading, Mass.: Addison Wesley Publishing Co., 1994.

Hilbert, D. and S. Cohn-Vossen. *Geometry and the Imagination.* New York: Chelsea Publishing Co. 1952.

Zwikker, C. *The Advanced Geometry of Plane Curves and Their Applications.* New York: Dover Publications, Inc., 1963.

J. Paul Moulton

Paradisaeas see **Birds of paradise**

Paradise widowbird see **Weaver finches**

Paraffins see **Alkyl group**

Parakeets see **Parrots**

Parallax

How far away is a star? When we see a star as a small point of light in the sky we have no direct easy way to measure its distance. Astronomers must use very indirect methods to measure the distances to stars and other astronomical objects. Measuring a star's parallax is a way to find its distance. This method takes advantage of the apparent shift in position of a nearby star as it is observed from different positions as the Earth orbits the Sun. Because the parallax effect depends upon the Earth's motion about the Sun, it is often referred to as the heliocentric parallax.

How parallax works

To understand how parallax works, hold your thumb in front of your face. Alternately open and close each eye and notice how your thumb appears to move back and forth with respect to the background wall. Now move your thumb closer to your face and notice how this effect increases as the distance between your eyes and thumb decreases. This apparent motion (you didn't really move your thumb) is called the parallax. The brain subconsciously uses information from both eyes to estimate distances. Because the distance estimates require observation from two points, people who have lost an eye will lack this depth perception. A parallax is any apparent shift in the position of an object caused by a change in the observation position.

As the Earth orbits the Sun, astronomers can observe a nearby star at six-month intervals with the Earth on opposite sides of the Sun. The nearby star appears to move with respect to the more distant background stars. Note that the star (like your thumb) is not really moving. The parallax effect is an apparent motion caused by the motion of the observation point (either to the other eye or to the opposite side of the Sun). The closer the star, the larger will be its apparent motion. This parallax, when combined with the principles of geometry and trigonometry, can be used to find the distance to stars that are relatively close. Closer stars will have a larger parallax.

Astronomers measure the parallax in the form of an angle. For even nearby stars these angles are quite small. The closest star to the Sun, Proxima Centauri, has a parallax angle of less than 1 second of arc. A second of arc is 1/3600th of a degree (1°=60 minutes of arc=3600 seconds of arc, 1 minute of arc=60 seconds of arc). At a distance of 3 mi (5 km), a quarter will have an angular diameter of roughly 1 second of arc. Measuring such small angles is obviously difficult, but astronomers have managed to overcome the difficulties, detecting parallax for the first time in 1838.

The parallax angle is defined as one half of the apparent angular motion of the star as the Earth orbits from one side of the Sun to the opposite side. This definition is the same as the apparent motion that would be observed if the two observation points were the Sun and Earth. Once this angle is measured, the distance between the Sun and the star is the Earth-Sun distance divided by the tangent of the parallax angle.

To simplify this calculation astronomers use a distance unit called a *parsec* (short for *parallax-second*). A parsec is the distance to a star that has a parallax angle of exactly one second of arc. One parsec is 206,265 times the distance between the Earth and Sun, 3.086×10^{13} kilometers, or 3.26 light years. The distance to a star in parsecs is then simply 1 divided by the parallax angle measured in seconds of arc.

Parallax measurements

In the sixteenth century, Copernicus proposed that the Earth and planets orbited the Sun. At the time one of the arguments proposed against the Copernican view was that there should be a heliocentric parallax if the Sun was indeed the center of the solar system. At the time no such parallaxes had been observed. Copernicus countered rather simply by stating that the stars were much farther away than anyone had ever imagined, so the parallax was too small to observe. When astronomers finally managed to measure a parallax, it turned out that Copernicus was right.

Astronomers did not succeed in measuring a parallax angle until 1838, when three astronomers working independently measured the parallaxes of three different stars. Friedrich Bessel in Germany, Thomas Henderson in South Africa, and Friedrich Struve in Russia measured the parallaxes of the stars 61 Cygni, Alpha Centauri, and Vega, respectively.

From the ground, astronomers are now able to measure accurately parallaxes for only about 1,000 stars that are within 20 parsecs of the Sun. This ground based limit requires measuring parallax angles that are as small as 1/20th of a second of arc. The quarter mentioned above is now 62 mi (100 km) away. For greater distances astronomers must use even more indirect methods that build on the distances found by parallax measurements. Improving the accuracy of parallax

KEY TERMS

. . . .

Heliocentric parallax—The parallax caused by the Earth Orbiting the Sun.

Light year—The distance light travels in one year, roughly 9.5 trillion kilometers or 6 trillion miles.

Parallax—An apparent change in position of an object caused by a change the observation position.

Parsec—The distance at which a star will have a parallax angle of one second of arc, 3.26 light years.

Second of Arc—An angular measurement, 1/3600th of a degree.

measurements will also improve the accuracy of the indirect methods that depend on parallaxes.

The Earth's atmosphere limits the accuracy of parallax measurements from the ground, by limiting the resolution (sharpness) of a stellar image. Sharper images, and therefore more accurate parallax measurements, require getting above the Earth's atmosphere. In 1989, the European Space Agency launched the Hipparcos satellite, with the mission of measuring the parallaxes of roughly 120,000 stars. The newly repaired Hubble Space Telescope is also capable of measuring parallaxes far more accurately than they can be measured from the ground. When the new accurate parallax measurements from these space missions become available, we will have accurate distance measurements to a much larger sample of stars. Accurate distances will both help us attain more accurate measurements of the fundamental properties of stars, therefore increasing our understanding of stellar structure, and improve the accuracy of our cosmic distance scales.

Further Reading:

Marschall, Laurence, A., Steven J. Ratcliff, and Thomas J. Balonek. "Parallax You Can See." *Sky & Telescope* 84, (December 1992): 626-29.

Morrison, David, Sidney Wolff, and Andrew Fraknoi. *Abell's Exploration of the Universe.* 7th ed. Philadelphia: Saunders College Publishing, 1995.

Zeilik, Michael. *Astronomy: The Evolving Universe.* 7th ed. New York: Wiley, 1994.

Zeilik, Michael, Stephen Gregory, and Elske Smith. *Introductory Astronomy and Astrophysics.* Philadelphia: Saunders, 1992.

Paul A. Heckert

Parallel

Two or more lines (or planes) are said to be parallel if they lie in the same plane (or space) and have no point in common, no matter how far they are extended.

Parallelogram

A parallelogram is a plane figure of four sides whose opposite sides are parallel. A *rhombus* is a parallelogram with all four sides of equal length; a *rectangle* is a parallelogram whose adjacent sides are perpendicular; and a *square* is a parallelogram whose adjacent sides are both perpendicular and equal in length.

The area of a parallelogram is equal to the length of its *base* times the length of its *altitude*.

See also Parallel; Perpendicular.

Parasites

A parasite is an organism that depends on another organism, known as a host, for food and shelter. The parasite usually gains all the benefits of this relationship, while the host may suffer from various diseases and discomforts, or show no signs of the infection. The life cycle of a typical parasite usually includes several developmental stages and morphological changes as the parasite lives and moves through the environment and one or more hosts. Parasites that remain on a host's body surface to feed are called ectoparasites, while those that live inside a host's body are called endoparasites. Parasitism is a highly successful biological adaptation. There are more known parasitic species than nonparasitic ones, and parasites affect just about every form of life, including most all animals, plants and even bacteria.

The study of parasites

Parasitology is the study of parasites and their relationships with host organisms. Throughout history people have coped with over 100 types of parasites affecting humans. Parasites have not, however, been systematically studied until the last few centuries. With his invention of the microscope in the late 1600s, Anton von Leeuwenhoek was perhaps the first to observe microscopic parasites. As Westerners began to travel and work more often in tropical parts of the world,

medical researchers had to study and treat a variety of new infections, many of which were caused by parasites. By the early 1900s, parasitology had developed as a specialized field of study.

Typically, a parasitic infection does not directly kill a host, though the drain on the organism's resources can affect its growth, reproductive capability and survival, leading to premature death. Parasites, and the diseases they cause and transmit, have been responsible for tremendous human suffering and loss of life throughout history. Though the majority of parasitic infections occur within tropical regions and among low-income populations, most all regions of the world sustain parasitic species, and all humans are susceptible to infection.

Though many species of viruses, bacteria, and fungi exhibit parasitic behavior and can be transmitted by parasites, scientists usually study them separately as infectious diseases. Types of organisms that are studied by parasitologists include species of protozoa, helminths or worms, and arthropods.

Protozoa

Protozoa are one-celled organisms that are capable of carrying out most of the same physiological functions as multicellular organisms by using highly developed organelles within their cell. Many of the over 45,000 species of known protozoa are parasitic. As parasites of humans, this group of organisms has historically been the cause of more suffering and death than any other category of disease causing organisms.

Intestinal protozoa are common throughout the world and particularly in areas where food and water sources are subject to contamination from animal and human waste. Typically, protozoa that infect their host through water or food do so while in an inactive state, called a cyst, where they have encased themselves in a protective outer membrane and are released through the digestive tract of a previous host. Once inside the host, they develop into a mature form that feeds and reproduces.

Amebic dysentery is one of the more common diseases that often afflicts travelers who visit tropical and sub-tropical regions. This condition, characterized by diarrhea, vomiting and weakness, is caused by a protozoan known as *Entamoeba histolytica*.

Another protozoan that causes severe diarrhea, but is also found in more temperate regions, is *Giardia lamblia*. Among Leeuwenhoek's discoveries was *G. lamblia*, which is a now well publicized parasite that can infect hikers who drink untreated water in the back country.

Other types of parasitic protozoa infect the blood or tissues of their hosts. These protozoa are typically transmitted through another organism, called a vector, that carries the parasite before it enters the final host. Often the vector is an invertebrate, such as an insect, that itself feeds on the host and passes the protozoan on through the bite wound. Some of the most infamous of these protozoa are members of the geneses *Plasmodium*, that cause malaria; *Trypanosoma*, that cause African sleeping sickness; and *Leishmania*, which leads to a number of debilitating and disfiguring diseases.

Helminths

Helminths are worm-like organisms of which several classes of parasites are found including nematodes (roundworms), cestodes (tapeworms), and trematodes (flukes). Leeches, of the phylum Annelid, are also helminths and considered as ectoparasitic, attaching themselves to the outside skin of their hosts.

Nematodes (roundworms)

Nematodes, or roundworms, have an estimated 80,000 species that are known to be parasitic. The general morphology of these worms is consistent with their name; they are usually long and cylindrical in shape.

One of the most infamous nematodes is *Trichinella spiralis*, a parasite that lives its larval stage encysted in the muscle tissue of animals, including swine, and make their way into the intestinal tissue of humans who happen to digest infected, undercooked pork.

The largest parasitic roundworm, common among humans living in tropical developing countries, is *Ascaris lumbricoides*. This roundworm can grow up to 14 in (35 cm) in length within the small intestine of its host.

One roundworm, *Enterobius vermicularis*, or pinworm, actually thrives in more temperate climates. This relatively small roundworm is not limited to humans living in relative poverty, but is known to infect the well-off just as easily.

Adult worms of *Wuchereria bancrofti* live in the blood and lymph of the host. Elephantiasis, characterized by extreme enlargement of a host's extremities, is the rare but dramatic result of the host body's defensive reaction to the presence of the worms.

Known to dog owners *Dirofilaria immitus*, or heartworm infection, if left untreated, can kill a dog as the worms infect the heart tissues and eventually weaken the cardiac muscles to the point of failure.

Cestodes (tapeworms)

Cestodes, or tapeworms, are a class of worms characterized by their flat, segmented bodies. The segments are called proglottides and hold both male and female reproductive organs, allowing self-fertilization. Proglottides that contain fertilized eggs break off or dissolve, passing the eggs out of the host. Adult tapeworms typically reside in the intestinal tract of vertebrates, attaching themselves to the mucosal lining with hooks or suckers on their scolex, or head. They do not possess a digestive tract, or alimentary canal, of their own, but absorb nutrients through their tegument, or skin, from partially digested food as it passes through the host.

Common tapeworms that frequent humans are *Taenia saginata*, *Taenia solium* and *Diphllobothrium latum*. These parasites use intermediate hosts—cattle, swine and fish respectively. Many parasites infect an intermediate host organism while in a developmental form, but they do not grow to maturity until they have been transmitted to the final or definitive host. In the *Taenia* species, the eggs are passed into cattle or swine through infected soil. They develop into an intermediary stage, called a cysticercus, that embeds in the muscle and connective tissue of the animal. Infected animals that are processed for meat but improperly cooked still harbor the parasite and pass the cysticerci on when consumed by humans. The cysticeri develop into adult tapeworms that attach to the intestinal lining of the host. The cysticerci of *T. solium* can, themselves, cause medical complications. Instead of developing immediately into adult tapeworms, these cysticerci can migrate to any organ of the body, commonly ending up in the muscles or brain. A serious infection in the brain can lead to mental complications, including seizures and personality changes.

Trematodes (flukes)

Trematodes, or flukes, are another class of helminths that have parasitic species. Adult flukes are typically flat, oval-shaped worms that have a layer of muscles just below the tegument, or skin, that allow the worm to expand and contract its shape and, thus, move its body. Flukes usually have an oral sucker on their anterior end, sometimes ringed with hooks, that is used to attach themselves to the host's tissues.

The life cycle of a typical trematode begins when eggs, that are passed out of a previous host's digestive tract, find themselves in fresh water. The ciliated larval form, called miracidia, emerge from the eggs and swim until they find the appropriate species of their intermediate host: usually a snail. The miracidia penetrate the snail and change into another form, called sporocysts. The sporocysts undergo further changes resulting in yet another form of the parasite called cercariae, which burrow out of the snail and pass into the water again. A cercaria has a flagella-like tail that helps it swim through the water in search of its final host, typically a mammal or avian species. The cercariae make contact with the skin of a host and burrow in. Host animals may also become infected with flukes by ingesting meat, usually fish or crustaceans, that are harboring the cercariae in an encysted form, called metacercaria, within their tissues. In either form, once inside the final host the parasite moves through tissues or the blood to the desired organ, often the intestine or liver, where it matures into a reproducing adult, starting the cycle again.

Clonorchis sinensis, a fluke common in the Far East, is a trematode that uses fish as one of its intermediate hosts and fish-eating mammals, including humans, as a final host. The adult *C. sinensis* flukes eventually make their way through the bile ducts to the liver of the host.

Another fluke that uses both a snail and a second intermediate host is *Paragonimus westermani*. Freshwater crabs and crayfish can harbor *P. westermani* metacercaria that, in turn, may be consumed. The adult of this parasite makes its way into the lungs of its host.

Some of the most infamous flukes are species of the genus *Schistosoma* that cause the often fatal schistosomiasis. The cercariae of these flukes infect human hosts directly by burrowing into the skin of a person wading or swimming in infected water. One species, *S. mansoni,* enters the blood stream as an immature worm and can be carried through various organs, including the lungs and heart, before maturing in the liver.

Arthropods

Arthropods are organisms characterized by exoskeletons and segmented bodies such as crustaceans, insects and arachnids. They are the most diverse and widely distributed animals on the planet. Many arthropod species serve as carriers of bacterial and viral diseases, as intermediate hosts for protozoan and helminth parasites, and as parasites themselves.

Insects

Certain insect species are the carriers of some of humanity's most dreaded diseases, including malaria, typhus, and plague. As consumers of agricultural crops and parasites of our livestock, insects are also humankind's number one competitor for resources.

Mosquitoes, are the most notorious carriers, or vectors, of disease and parasites. Female mosquitoes rely on warm-blooded hosts to serve as a blood meal to nourish their eggs. During the process of penetrating a host's skin with their long, sucking mouth parts, saliva from the mosquito is transferred into the bite area. Any viral, protozoan or helminth infections carried in the biting mosquito can be transferred directly into the blood stream of its host. Among these are malaria, yellow fever, *W. bancrofti* (filariasis and elephantiasis) and *D. immitis* (heartworm).

Flies also harbor diseases that can be transmitted to humans and other mammals when they bite to obtain a blood meal for themselves. For example, black flies can carry river blindness, sandflies can carry leishmaniasis and kala-azar, and tsetse flies, found mainly in Africa, carry the trypanosomes that cause sleeping sickness. Livestock, such as horses and cattle, can be infected with a variety of bot flies and warbles that can infest and feed on the skin, throat, nasal passages and stomachs of their hosts.

Fleas and lice are two of the most common and irritating parasitic insects of humans and our livestock. Lice commonly live among the hairs of their hosts, feeding on blood. Some species are carriers of the epidemic inducing typhus fever. Fleas usually infest birds and mammals, and can feed on humans when they are transferred from pets or livestock. Fleas are known to carry a variety of devastating diseases, including the plague.

Arachnids

Another prominent class of arthropods that contains parasitic species is the arachnids. Though this group is more commonly known for spiders and scorpions, its parasitic members include ticks and mites.

Mites are very small arachnids that infest both plants and animals. One common type is chiggers, which live in grasses and, as larva, grab onto passing animals and attach themselves to the skin, often leading to irritating rashes or bite wounds. Scabies are another mite that causes mange in some mammals by burrowing into the skin and producing severe scabs, lesions and loss of hair.

Ticks also live their adult lives among grasses and short shrubs. They are typically larger than mites, and it is the adult female that attaches itself to an animal host for a blood meal. Tick bites themselves can be painful and irritating. More importantly, ticks can carry a number of diseases that affect humans. The most common of these include Rocky Mountain spotted fever, Colorado tick fever, and the latest occurrence of tick-borne infections: Lyme disease.

KEY TERMS
. . . .

Arthropod—A phylum of organisms characterized by exoskeletons and segmented bodies.

Cestodes—A class of worms characterized by flat, segmented bodies, commonly known as tapeworms.

Definitive host—The organism in which a parasite reaches sexual maturity.

Helminths—Term to define various phyla of worm-like animals.

Intermediate host—An organism infected by a parasite while the parasite is in a developmental form, but does not sexually mature.

Nematodes—Characterized by long, cylindrical bodies, commonly known as roundworms.

Protozoa—One-celled organisms.

Trematodes—A class of worms characterized by flat, oval-shaped bodies, commonly known as flukes.

Vector—Any agent, living or otherwise, that carries and transmits parasites and diseases.

Control of parasites

Most parasitic infections can be treated by use of medical and surgical procedures. The best manner of controlling infection, though, is prevention. Scientists have developed and continue to test a number of drugs that can be taken as a barrier, or prophylaxis, to certain parasites. Other measures of control include improving sanitary conditions of water and food sources, proper cooking techniques, education about personal hygiene, and control of intermediate and vector host organisms.

See also Arachnids; Arthropods; Dysentery; Flatworms; Fleas; Flies; Lice; Malaria; Mites; Protozoa; Roundworms; Strepsiptera; Tongue worms.

Further Reading:

Brown, Harold, and Franklin Neva. *Basic Clinical Parasitology.* Norwalk, CT: Appleton-Century-Crofts, 1983.

Jaenike, John. "Behind-the-scenes Role of Parasites." *Natural History* June 1994: 46-48.

Moore, Janice. "The Behavior of Parasitized Animals." *BioScience* (Feburary 1995): 89-96.

Noble, Elmer, and Glenn Noble. *Parasitology: The Biology of Animal Parasites.* Philadelphia: Lea and Febiger, 1989.

Schmidt, Gerald, and Larry Roberts. *Foundations of Parasitology.* St. Louis: Times Mirror/Mosby College Publishing, 1989.

Tilton, Buck. "Don't Drink the Water." *Backpacker* (Feburary 1994): 50-55.

Warren, Kenneth, and John Bowers, eds. *Parasitology: A Global Perspective.* New York: Springer-Verlag, 1983.

Jeffrey R. Corney

Parathyroid glands see **Endocrine system**

Parity

Parity is both an operation and an intrinsic property used to describe particles and their wavefunctions (mathematical representations of one or more particles) in quantum mechanics (a branch of physics focusing on particles smaller than an atomic nucleus).

The parity operation is a combination of a left-right trade (mirror reflection) with a top-bottom switch. This combination is also called a spatial inversion. How objects behave under a parity operation defines their intrinsic parity. All microscopic particles have an intrinsic parity that helps us tell them apart. An object or group of objects that is the same before and after a parity operation is called parity invariant. A parity invariant object has 'even' or '+1' intrinsic parity. If the parity of an object changes due to a parity operation, it has 'odd' or '-1' intrinsic parity.

Even though people do not obey reflection symmetry (their right and left sides are different), scientists believed that the laws of physics were parity invariant. In 1956 a Chinese-American scientist named Tsung Dao Lee figured out that the idea of parity invariance had not been tested in relation to one of the fundamental forces of physics, the weak force (responsible for spontaneous decays of some microscopic particles). This prompted Lee and a colleague, Chen Ning Yang, to think of a clever experiment to test the parity invariance of the weak force. Later in 1956 Dr. Chien-Shiung Wu carried out this difficult experiment using a radioactive (spontaneously decaying) element called Cobalt. Wu observed the direction of electrons (smallest naturally-occurring charged particles) coming out of the Cobalt due to its radioactive decay. She found that the electrons did not come out the way she expected. Thus this experiment was not parity invariant. Since it tested the weak force, this meant the weak force was not parity invariant either. This result was so important that Yang and Lee won the 1957 Nobel Prize in physics for it. Now we know when we see parity invariance the weak force is the culprit. All other fundamental forces are parity invariant.

Parity is often studied along with charge conjugation. Charge conjugation changes a particle into its opposite, or antiparticle, by changing the sign of its electric charge. Even though parity is not conserved by itself, it was thought that the combination of parity(P) and charge conjugation was conserved. In 1964, however, physicists J. H. Christenson, J. W. Cronin, V. L. Fitch, and R. Turlay discovered that CP conservation is not obeyed by studying the decays of particles called Kaons. Scientists know that the laws of nature must obey conservation of the combination of parity, charge conjugation, and time symmetry(T), because of the way they are formulated. This is called CPT symmetry. Since we know CP symmetry is not conserved, it follows that time symmetry must not hold, so that total combination, CPT, can be conserved. Physicists are looking for experimental evidence to disprove CPT conservation. If they find it, we may have to rethink the laws of physics.

Lesley Smith

Parkinson's disease

Parkinson's disease or Parkinsonism is named for the English physician James Parkinson. His description of the various manifestations of the disease was published in 1817, in a work entitled "An Essay on the Shaking Palsy." He used the terms "shaking palsy" or "paralysis agitans" to describe a group of related symptoms, which he carefully observed and recorded. It is now known that this neurological disorder is caused by damage to certain areas of the brain. The main symptoms of the disease are tremor while at rest and abnormal movements of the arms and legs while standing or walking. These are accompanied by a number of other symptoms, including speech problems, a stiff, bent-over position, insomnia, and constipation.

All related disorders are attributed to a malfunction of the basal ganglia (which contain a rich array of neurotransmitters and receptors controlling muscular movements) and of the substantia nigra (where dopamine is produced). Dopamine is one of the brain chemicals involved in the control of physical movement, and Parkinsonism is characterized by dopamine depletion. Secondary Parkinsonism, in which symptoms are of a passing nature, is due to temporary dopamine depletions induced most commonly by antipsychotic drugs.

Cause

The basal ganglia control movements of the muscles, muscle tone, balance, coordination of groups of muscles that oppose each other, and the change of state necessary for muscles to go from rest to motion. Control from this section of the brain also enables some muscles to remain at rest while others are in action. In a healthy state, signals pass from the motor cortex of the brain to the reticular formation and spinal cord and then to the various muscles that are to undergo contraction. At the same time, other signals follow a different pathway through the basal ganglia, where the nerve signal is dampened (subdued or toned down) so that the resulting contraction does not become jerky (too sudden or quick). Dopamine, found in the basal ganglia, is the neurotransmitter responsible for the dampening effect of the motor signal. If the dampening effect should become too strong, then another neurotransmitter, acetylcholine, counteracts the effects of the dopamine, thus maintaining a balance in the force of the signals sent to the muscle.

In Parkinson's disease, degeneration of the basal ganglia, along with damage to the dopamine-producing cells of the substantia nigra, hampers the proper functioning of the nerve pathway that controls movements of the muscles. The muscles become excessively tense, a condition that gives rise to tremor and a rigid joint action. The movements of the body also begin to slow down as a result of this malfunction. Drug treatments are designed to increase the level of dopamine or inhibit the release of acetylcholine, which counteracts dopamine.

Damage to the basal ganglia may be caused by an environmental factor, such as an unknown toxic chemical. Another supposition is that an early viral infection causes the degeneration. Parkinsonism may follow encephalitis or other forms of brain injury. As yet no definite link has been made with genetic factors as a major cause of the disease. The disease is not contagious, and while it generally affects older people, there are also cases of juvenile Parkinsonism. Cases involving younger people who had used street drugs of unknown composition and developed full-blown symptoms of the disease as a result have been reported. Some of these cases were favorably treated with implantations of dopamine-producing tissues from fetal brain cells.

Incidence and symptoms

In the United States there are about 1.5 million people who suffer from Parkinson's disease (1 person in 100 over the age 60), and each year 60,000 new cases are reported. The elderly are most vulnerable to the condition, with men showing a greater tendency toward the disease than women. In about 15% of cases, symptoms of the disease begin to show when patients are in their 40s, but the majority of cases occur somewhat later, between the ages of 50 and 70. Those who smoke seem to show a lower incidence of the disorder. While there is no cure for the disease and the factors responsible for the brain damage are not fully understood, the mechanism of brain-cell deterioration and the brain chemicals involved has been carefully studied.

At the beginning of the illness, one side of the body may begin to exhibit symptoms. Eventually, however, the disorder spreads to both sides of the body. At first there are signs of difficulty in walking and other basic movements of the body, such as turning, rising from a seated position, standing, and sitting down. These movements seem labored and become difficult to perform. Body movements slow down, and they are executed very carefully with much deliberation. The muscles at rest are so tense that they become rigid. Simple facial movements become difficult to execute because of this rigidity of muscle tone. The face begins to look like a mask. Walking movements become altered. Instead of the natural arm swing, the arms hang limply at the side. The patient shuffles while walking, and sideways turns of the head are replaced by whole body movements.

Tremor is one of the characteristic signs of Parkinsonism, but not all patients actually display that symptom. While it is immediately obvious and recognizable, tremor is not necessarily more of a disability than the other symptoms of the disorder. Tremor occurs while the patient is at rest and is reflected mostly in the hands, in spasms entailing a rolling motion of various fingers. Other parts of the body may also be involved in the tremor, notably the lips and the head. While the Parkinson's patient is involved in some task, the tremor may relent for a short period of time.

Some patients undergo a general decline of mental ability (dementia). They begin to forget recent events, get lost in a known neighborhood, or fail to comprehend what is going on about them. The skin becomes excessively oily, a condition known as seborrhea, particularly in the areas of the face and scalp. Blood pressure may also begin to fluctuate over a wide range, and these fluctuations create further difficulties in treatment. Toward the later stages of the disease, when all of these symptoms are present, some patients become totally helpless.

Diagnosis

Only a postmortem examination provides conclusive evidence of Parkinsonism, while a live clinical neurological examination may present difficulties in diagnosis. Certain symptoms readily show the presence of the disease, such as tremor, slow body movements, and the inability to perform joint motor activities. There are, however, other conditions that can be mistaken for Parkinsonism because they are also characterized by the tremor syndrome and certain other symptoms.

While the exact cause of Parkinsonism can only be determined at autopsy, a clinical diagnosis when the patient is still alive allows doctors to prescribe the most effective treatment. The physician begins a diagnosis with the patient's general medical history along with a careful examination. In the absence of certain symptoms of the disease, an experienced physician may be able to exclude Parkinson's disease and search for other causes of neurological impairment, such as tumors of the brain, especially in the cerebellum which controls balance. A CAT scan is used to determine the presence or absence of brain tumors. The appearance of tremor is carefully studied to determine whether or not it qualifies as a symptom of Parkinsonism. New diagnostic methods allow physicians to target the affected brain areas precisely. An analysis of cerebrospinal fluid along with magnetic resonance imaging (MRI) can reveal damage to areas of the brain like the substantia nigra. An increase in lipid (fat) oxidation in the substantia nigra suggests that free radicals are damaging nerve cells producing dopamine. If that is the case, antioxidants and scavengers that destroy free radicals may improve the symptoms.

Treatment

There are organizations that can give families help in learning how to manage the illness in its early stages. Exercise is important along with special aids to help movement. Drug therapy is important in later stages of the disease when symptoms become debilitating if left untreated. The drug treatment is complex because dosages have to be carefully regulated and different combinations of drugs have to be used.

Despite certain severe side effects, the drug levodopa (l-dopa) is currently used as the most effective medication in the treatment of Parkinson's disease. Some of the adverse side effects are disorders of the digestive system, hemorrhage, disturbances in heart

KEY TERMS

. . . .

Basal ganglia—Groups of nerve cells located within the white matter of each cerebral hemisphere. They are important for coordinating signals along the motor pathways of the central nervous system.

CAT scan—Computerized axial tomographic scanning, also called CT scanning, which uses diagnostic x rays and a computer to give cross-sectional images at different angles of the brain and other parts of the body.

Dementia—Impairment of mental functioning due to illness or aging.

Dopamine—Neurotransmitter essential for proper movement functions of the body.

Levodopa (l-dopa)—Precursor to dopamine, used as drug for Parkinson's disease because, unlike dopamine, it can cross the brain blood barrier.

MRI—Magnetic resonance imaging, a non-x-ray imaging technique used to diagnose the brain and other parts of the body.

Substantia nigra—A layer of deeply pigmented nerve cells in the brain containing dopamine-producing cells.

Tremor—Involuntary shaking movements of the hands while at rest produced in Parkinson's disease by a lack of dopamine.

rhythm, depression, confusion, possible psychotic reactions, and delirious episodes. The extent of these reactions appears to be dependent on the amount of medication used. In some patients the mask-like facial expression gives way to distorted facial expressions, and other unusual body movements may result from the use of the drug.

A combination drug called Sinemet composed of levodopa and carbidopa (a drug that alleviates levodopa's side effects) is given in careful dosages often requiring changes in the amount taken. Patients respond differently to this combination drug. Some will be able to take it hourly, others just three times daily.

For all of its adverse side effects, l-dopa has helped many sufferers from Parkinsonism to deal with their illness. Other drugs, which are not as effective but do have fewer side effects, are sometimes used for milder cases of Parkinson's disease. Two such drugs are

bromocriptine and amantadine. Anticholinergic drugs are used to deal with tremor. These drugs can be used alone or in combination with l-dopa. Sometimes they are used to help diagnose a questionable condition. They are not noted for providing important long-term relief.

In order to replace the dopamine in 100 Parkinson's disease patients, Swedish and American doctors have used brain cells from fetal brains for brain implantation. Although the results of this experimental procedure were highly favorable, there has been resistance against this form of treatment because the brain cells were taken from aborted fetuses. Adrenal tissue that produces dopamine is now being used for experimental purposes instead.

Another newer experimental treatment that has shown success in restoring movement for some younger Parkinsonism patients is a brain operation that excises certain portions of the affected area of the brain. While symptoms were dramatically relieved, the outcome of the treatment is still being studied.

Further Reading:

Dauphin, Sue. *Parkinson's Disease: the Mystery, the Search, and the Promise.* Tequesta, Florida: Pixel Press, 1992.

Duvoisin, Roger. *Parkinson's Disease: a Guide for Patient and Family.* New York: Raven Press, 1991.

Lang, A. E. "Motor disorders symptomatology." In *Neurology in clinical practice,* edited by W. G. Bradley, et al. Boston: Butterworth-Heinemann, 1991, pp. 315-316.

Jordan P. Richman

Parotias see **Birds of paradise**

Parrots

Parrots, macaws, lories, parakeets, and related birds, known collectively as psittacids, are 328 living species of birds that make up the family Psittacidae. The psittacids and the cockatoos (family Cacatuidae) are the only families in the order Psittaciformes.

Species of psittacids occur in Central and South America, Africa, Madagascar, South and Southeast Asia, New Guinea, Australia, and New Zealand. The greatest richness of species occurs in Australasia and South America. No native species of the parrot family now breed in North America, although one previously abundant species, the Carolina parakeet, is recently extinct.

The endangered hooded parakeet (*Psephotus dissimilis*).

Parrots are arboreal birds, living in and around trees. Most species breed in forests, ranging from temperate to tropical, but other species occur in savannas and other relatively open, treed habitats.

Parrots and their allies are beautifully colored birds, and they are also quite intelligent and personable. These birds are very interesting and vital components of their ecosystems, and sightings of psittacids are highly sought-after by bird-watchers and field ornithologists. Several species are also commonly kept as pets.

Biology of parrots

Parrots range in body length from 3-40 in (8-102 cm). Their head is relatively large, the neck is short, the body is chunky, and their wings are long and usually rounded. Some species have a short tail, but in others the tail is quite long. Parrots have short, strong legs and feet, with long claws, and the toes arranged in a zygo-dactyl manner, that is, with two pointing forward, and two backward.

Parrots and their allies are highly adapted to living in trees. Both the feet and beak are very dexterous, and are used as aids to climbing. The feet are also used to hold and maneuver food and other objects, as are the beak and tongue. No other birds have the dexterity of parrots.

The bill and the large, muscular tongue of parrots are highly distinctive. The upper mandible is down curved and strongly hooked, and the lower mandible fits neatly into the shell of the upper when the beak is closed. The upper mandible is attached to the skull by a flexible joint, which allows relatively free-ranging, up-and-down movement. The nostrils are contained in a specialized, fleshy, enlarged structure known as a cere, present at the top of the upper mandible, where it joins the face. Like many other species of seed-eating birds, parrots have a well-developed crop, an esophageal pouch in which hard seeds are kept for softening, and a gizzard where the seeds are ground with particles of inorganic grit and small stones.

Almost all of the psittacids are rather attractive, brightly colored birds. The most frequent base color of the plumage is green, but this is commonly offset by bold patterns of bright red, yellow, blue, violet, white, or black. The sexes are similarly colored in most species.

Parrots and their allies are highly social birds, commonly occurring in noisily chattering, shrieking, squawking, or whistling family groups and larger flocks. Some of the smaller species in semi-arid habitats can occur in huge colonies; flocks of budgerigar (*Melopsittacus undulatus*) in Australia can contain more than one-million individuals. The social psittacids forage in groups, mostly for fleshy fruits and seeds. Some species forage in fruit orchards, where they may cause significant damages. Flocks of psittacids are wary and wily, and are usually difficult to approach closely.

Psittacids fly quickly and directly, using rapid wingbeats, but they tire quickly and do not usually fly very far. Most species are sedentary, spending the entire year in and around their breeding territory. However, species living in arid and semi-arid habitats often wander widely in search of food, which can vary greatly among years depending on the amounts and timing of the rains.

Psittacids are mostly vegetarian birds. Many species are frugivorous, eating fruit as the major component of their diet. Others also eat seeds, buds, and other plant matter. A few species also eat insects, and the kea (*Nestor notabilis*) of New Zealand is known to eat sheep carrion. (This has led to erroneous beliefs that the kea also kills healthy sheep. The kea may, however, finish off sheep that are virtually dead.). Most species of psittacids will habitually hold their food in their feet as they eat. The beak is used to crack seeds and nuts—captive individuals of hyacinthine macaws *(Prosciger aterrimus)* are even able to crack the hard shell of Brazil nuts.

Parrots have a monogamous breeding system, in which the male and female are faithful to each other, sometimes for life. The nest is usually located in a hollow in a tree. That cavity may have been developed naturally through decay, or it may have previously been excavated by another species of bird, such as a woodpecker. A few species will also nest in hollows in rock piles, earthen banks, or similar places. The clutch size ranges from 1-12, with larger species laying fewer eggs. Both sexes incubate the eggs, and they share in the feeding and rearing of the babies. Young parrots are fed by regurgitation.

Parrots are relatively long-lived birds. In captivity, individuals of some of the larger species have lived for more than 80 years.

Species of parrots

The parrots and their allies in the family Psittacidae include a wide range of groups of species. The systematics of psittacids is not totally agreed upon, but there appear to be 6-8 subfamilies, some of which may eventually be segregated into separate families after additional research is completed. The major groups of parrots are described below.

The "typical" parrots are a heterogenous group that contains most species of psittacids, and comprises the subfamily Psittacinae. These range in size from the tiny hanging parrots *(Loriculus spp.)*, only 3-3.5 in (8-9 cm) long, to the largest parrots, the macaws, which can reach a body length of more than 3 ft (1 m). Typical parrots occur throughout almost all of the range of the parrot family, including all of the native species of the Americas. A few prominent examples are the scarlet macaw *(Ara macao)*, hyacinthine macaw, and green or common amazon *(Amazona amazonica)* of tropical forests in South America, the African grey parrot *(Psittacus erithacus)* and you-you *(Poicephalus senegalus)* of tropical rainforests in Africa, and the eclectus or red-sided parrot *(Eclectus roratus)* of tropical rainforests and eucalyptus forests of Australasia. This latter species is unusual in its sexual dimorphism, with the male having an all-green body with red wing-patches, and the female a red body with blue on the belly and wings.

The lories and lorikeets are about 60 species of often long-tailed species that make up the subfamily Loriinae, native from Southeast Asia through Australasia. These birds have a brush-tipped tongue, useful for feeding on nectar and pollen. The lories and lorikeets also eat fruits, seeds, and invertebrates. The rainbow lorikeet *(Trichoglossus haematodus)* breeds in diverse types of forest in Australia, New Guinea, and nearby islands.

The long-tailed parrots are species in the subfamily Polytelitinae. The most familiar species to most people is the cockatiel *(Nymphicus hollandicus)* of Australia, which can be bred in captivity and is commonly kept as a pet.

The fig-parrots or lorilets are five species in the subfamily Opopsittinae. These are small-bodied, large-headed, short-tailed, fruit- and seed-eating birds of tropical forests. The double-eyed fig-parrot *(Psittaculirostria diophthalma)* occurs in Australia and New Guinea.

The broad-tailed parrots are 29 species of Australasia and New Zealand that make up the subfamily Platycercinae. The most familiar species is also the smallest in this group, the budgerigar *(Melopsittacus undulatus)* of Australia, which is one of the world's most popular cage-birds. The rosellas (Platycercus) are larger birds, and are also sometimes kept as pets.

The pygmy parrots are six species of tiny birds that comprise the subfamily Micropsittinae. These birds occur in tropical forests of New Guinea and nearby islands.

The kea *(Nestor notabilis)* and kaka *(Nestor notabilis)* of New Zealand are the only members of the subfamily Nestorinae. These are both relatively omnivorous species of montane regions, which include relatively large quantities of animal foods in their diet.

The owl parrot or kakapo *(Strigops habroptilus)* is the only member of the subfamily Strigopinae. The kakapo is a nocturnal, ground-living species that only occurs in high-elevation heathlands of New Zealand. This species cannot fly, although it can glide from higher to lower places, but must later walk back up. The continued survival of this unusual species is severely threatened by introduced predators, such as dogs.

The cockatoos are large birds with mobile crests, occurring in Australasia and parts of Southeast Asia. These are in the family Cacatuidae, and are not members of the Psittacidae, although they are very similar animals.

Parrots in North America

No native species of parrots breed in North America. The only native species known to have bred in

North America was the once-abundant, Carolina parakeet *(Conuropsis carolinensis)*. Regrettably, this native species is now extinct, with the last sightings of the species occurring in Florida as late as 1920. The original range of the Carolina parakeet was the southeastern United States, although it sometimes wandered as far north as New York and elsewhere near the Great Lakes. The Carolina parakeet was brightly colored bird, with a lime-green body, a yellow head, and peach-colored feathers about the face.

The Carolina parakeet lived mostly in mature bottomland and swamp forests, where it foraged for fruits and roosted communally. Although Carolina parakeets were sometimes killed for their colorful feathers, they were not highly valuable in this sense. This native species became extinct because it was considered to be a pest of agriculture, as a result of damages that flocks caused while feeding in fruit orchards and grain fields. The Carolina parakeet was relentlessly persecuted by farmers because of these damages. Unfortunately, the species was an easy mark for extinction because it nested and fed communally, and because these birds tended to aggregate around their wounded colleagues, so that entire flocks could be easily wiped out by hunters.

The red-crowned parrot *(Amazona viridigenalist)* is a native, breeding species in northeastern Mexico, and is an occasional visitor to the valley of the Rio Grande River in southern Texas. In addition, the thick-billed parrot *(Rhynchopsitta pachyrhyncha)* has been a rare visitor to montane pine forests in Arizona. However, there have been no sightings of these species for several decades.

A number of species in the parrot family have been introduced to North America, and several of these have established locally breeding feral populations, especially in southern Florida. These alien parrots include the budgerigar, native to Australia, and the canary-winged parakeet *(Brotogeris versicolorus)*, native to South America. A few other escaped species have also nested in south Florida, including the monk parakeet *(Myiopsitta monachus)* of Argentina, and the red-crowned parrot *(Amazona viridigenalis)* of Mexico.

Parrots and people

At least 15 species in the parrot family have recently become extinct, all as a result of human influences. The greatest threats to rare and endangered psittacids are to species occurring in naturally small populations, for example, those endemic to islands or to unusually restricted, continental habitats. These species are mostly put at risk by habitat losses associated with the conversion of their natural ecosystems into agricultural, urban, or forestry land-uses. In addition, rare species of psittacids have great value in the illicit pet trade, and illegal trapping can further endanger their already small populations.

In certain cases, members of the parrot family are considered to be serious agricultural pests. This happens when locally abundant populations destroy fruits in orchards, or eat large quantities of ripe grain. These species are sometimes persecuted to reduce those damages.

Psittacids are economically beneficial in some places, because bird-watchers and other tourists come to see these animals, either in their natural habitat, or in aviaries or theme parks. For example, feeding stations for wild psittacids are maintained in several places in Australia, as tourist attractions. One place in Queensland draws thousands of rainbow lorikeets *(Trichoglossus haematodus)* and scaly-breasted lorikeets *(T. chlorolepidotus)* to daily feedings, and is a renowned attraction for tourists. In other places, theme parks have developed around world-class collections of tame or caged parrots, for example, Parrot World in Florida.

Numerous species of psittacids are kept as pets. Their attraction includes their beautiful plumage, interesting behavior, tameness if they are raised from a young age, and the fact that some species can be trained to imitate human speech. The parrots whose natural calls are rasping and harsh tend to be the most proficient mimics of human words.

The most abundant psittacids in captivity are the budgerigar, cockatiel, peach-faced lovebird *(Agapornis roseicollis)*, masked lovebird *(A. personata)*, green amazon, and African grey parrot. Many other species are also kept as pets, but less commonly. These birds sometimes escape from their cages, or are deliberately released in attempts to establish breeding populations, mostly for aesthetic reasons.

Further Reading:

Alderton, D. *The Atlas of Parrots.* TFH, Neptune City, NJ, 1991.

Alderton, D. *Parrots.*, New York, New York: Hodder, 1992.

Ehrlich, P.R., D.S. Dobkin, D. Wheye. *Birds in Jeopardy.* Stanford, California: Stanford University Press, 1992.

Forshaw, J.M. *Parrots of the World*, 3rd ed. Minneapolis, MN: Avian Pubs., 1989.

Freedman, B. *Environmental Ecology*, 2nd ed. Academic Press, San Diego, 1995.

Harrison, C.J.O., ed. *Bird Families of the World.* New York, New York: H.N. Abrams Pubs., 1978.

Long, J.K.. *Introduced Birds of the World.* New York, New York: Universe Books, 1981.

Pasquier, R., ed. *Conservation of New World Parrots.* Washington, D.C.: Smithsonian Press, 1981.

KEY TERMS

. . . .

Feral—This refers to a non-native species that is able to maintain a viable, breeding population in a place that is not part of its natural range, but to which it has been introduced by humans.

Frugivore—An animal the subsists largely or entirely on fruit.

Sexual dimorphism—The occurrence of marked differences in coloration, size, or shape between males and females of the same species.

Sparks, J. and A. Soper. *Parrots: A Natural History*. New York, New York: Sterling Pub. Co., 1990.

Bill Freedman

Parsley see **Carrot family**
Parsnip see **Carrot family**

Parthenogenesis

Parthenogenesis in animals refers to reproduction in which a new individual genetically identical to the parent develops from an unfertilized egg. The analogous event in plants, which results in seed formation without fertilization, is called agamospermy. Parthenogenesis is viewed as an aberration of sexual reproduction because animals that reproduce by parthenogenesis evolved from organisms that once reproduced sexually. In sexual reproduction female sex cells (ova) must be fertilized by male sex cells (typically sperm), for development to occur.

Types of parthenogenic organisms

The term parthenogenesis was first used in 1849 by the biologist Richard Owens. Although most animals reproduce sexually, some species of vertebrates and invertebrates reproduce by parthenogenesis. Of these species the most frequently studied are fish, reptiles and insects. Parthenogenetic animals are classified as either facultative or obligate. Facultative parthenogens (usually invertebrates) can reproduce either parthenogenetically or sexually at all times, whereas obligate parthenogens are animals in which individuals of at least one generation reproduce by parthenogenesis.

Obligate parthenogens may be further subdivided into either constant parthenogens or cyclical parthenogens. All generations of species showing constant parthenogenesis reproduce by parthenogenetic methods, and are typically composed of only females. Examples of these organisms include species of lizards, minnows, and brine shrimp. Cyclical parthenogens, such as aphids, alternate parthenogenetic generations with a sexual generation. In the summer months aphids reproduce by parthenogenesis, but the onset of the fall acts as a signal for new offspring to develop into males which then mate with available females (sexual reproduction) producing fertilized eggs that hatch in the spring.

Cellular mechanisms

Parthenogens, unlike sexually reproducing animals, are faced with the unique problem of how to maintain a complete set of chromosomes. Chromosomes are cellular structures composed of DNA and protein that contain the genetic information cells need to function properly. In animals which reproduce sexually, reduction division (meiosis) occurs in cells destined to become eggs or sperm. Meiosis is the process where the chromosome content of a dividing cell is divided and reduced, producing egg or sperm cells with only half the normal number of chromosomes. When an egg is fertilized the chromosomes from the sperm are injected into the egg so restoring the fertilized egg's chromosome number to that of the parents body cells. Fertilization does not occur in parthenogenetic animals, which have developed special mechanisms to insure that a full set of chromosomes are passed on to the next generation.

The cellular mechanisms by which parthenogenetic animals maintain a full set of chromosomes are known as apomixis and automixis. Each mechanism either alters or suppresses meiosis. Apomictic parthenogens are those in which meiosis is completely suppressed whereas automictic parthenogens are those in which the early stages of meiosis occur but the event is altered so that no chromosome division results.

Sexual vs. non-sexual reproduction

Most organisms reproduce sexually because there is a competitive advantage in producing offspring with genetic contributions from two individuals rather than one. The genetic recombination which occurs during meiosis and on fertilization allows new gene combinations to come together in the next generation. Organisms with new gene combinations are more variable and offer more options for selection pressures to select the best adaptations for the environmental conditions, for example making use of different food resources or being more resistant to pathogens.

Parthenogenetic animals receive all of their genes from one parent and therefore no new gene combinations are created. It may seem that this method of reproduction would put species that use it at a competitive disadvantage to sexually reproducing animals but it may be advantageous in some cases. To reproduce, a sexually reproducing organism must first find a mate and then combine gametes with this mate. This process requires a great deal of time, energy and it may well result in no offspring. Parthenogenic organisms do not experience this cost of reproduction and therefore usually can reproduce sooner after birth and produce more offspring. Animals which live in environments that are hospitable for only a short time period are often parthenogenic because mating would take time that these organisms don't have; these animals need to produce large numbers of offspring to compensate for the low survival rate of the offspring. Minnows found in the southwestern United States living in rivers that dry to the point where only puddles remain, demonstrate parthenogenetic reproduction so eliminating the need for a suitable mate to be present in a given puddle. Another advantage of parthenogenetic reproduction is that most offspring are unlikely to survive the dry months, regardless of whether or not sexual recombination occurs. Therefore organisms which produce a greater quantity of offspring are more likely to have one survive to the next generation.

Parthenogenesis may also be advantageous in stable environments with ample food resources. These environments favor organisms with the ability to reproduce quickly allowing their offspring to consume the food resources before others do. This is the reason why certain cyclical parthenogens are so successful. For example, aphids reproduce parthenogenetically in the summer to exploit the abundant leaves which they feed upon. In the fall aphids produce fertilized eggs which may endure fluctuating environmental conditions when dormant during the winter or limited food supplies when they hatch in the spring.

See also Asexual reproduction; Chromosome; Fertilization; Sexual reproduction.

Further Reading:

Catton, Chris, and James Gray. *Sex In Nature*. New York: Facts on File, 1985.

Colinvaux, Paul. *Ecology*. New York: John Wiley & Sons, 1986.

Hughes, Roger. *A Functional Biology of Clonal Animals*. London: Chapman and Hall, 1989.

Suomalainen, Esko, Anssi Suara, and Juhani Lokki. *Cytology and Evolution in Parthenogenesis*. Boca Raton, FL: CRC Press, 1987.

Steven MacKenzie

KEY TERMS

Agamospermy—Seed development that occurs from an egg cell of a plant without it first being fertilized.

Apomixis—Egg production without meiosis that results in the egg retaining a complete set of chromosomes.

Automixis—Egg production in which meiosis is altered so that the egg retains a complete set of chromosomes.

Chromosomes—Cellular structures composed of DNA and protein that carry genetic information.

Constant parthenogens—Animals that always reproduce parthenogenetically.

Cyclical parthenogens—Obligate parthenogens that alternate sexually reproductive generations with parthenogenic generations.

Facultative parthenogens—Animals with the potential to reproduce parthenogenetically or sexually at all times.

Fertilization—Process where a male sex cell unites with an egg to form a recombinant egg.

Meiosis—Cell division which produces sex cells with only half the chromosome number as the parent.

Obligate parthenogens—Animals in which individuals of at least one generation reproduce parthenogenetically.

Recombination—Process where genes from two individuals are contributed to an offspring.

Sex cells—Cells which contribute genes to new offspring.

Particle accelerator see **Accelerators**

Particle accelerator see **Accelerators**

Particle detectors

Particle detectors are instruments designed for the detection and measurement of sub-atomic particles such as those emitted by radioactive materials, produced by particle accelerators or observed in cosmic rays. They include electrons, protons, neutrons, alpha particles, gamma rays and numerous mesons and baryons. Most

The End Station A experimental hall at the Stanford Linear Accelerator Center (SLAC) in California contains three giant particle spectrometers which detect particles of various energies and angles of scatter. The particles are created when electrons from SLAC's 1.8 mile (3 km) long linear accelerator collide with a target in front of the spectrometers. The large spectrometer dominating the picture is about 98 ft (30 m) long and weighs 550 tons (500 metric tons); a man below it can be used for size comparison. A smaller, circular spectrometer is to its left, and the third, even larger, is mostly hidden by the central one. Experiments at End Station A in 1968-72 confirmed the existence of quarks.

detectors utilize in some way the ionization produced when these particles interact with matter.

Geiger counter

The Geiger counter is one of the oldest and simplest of the many particle detectors. The counter was developed in the early part of the 20th century by Hans Geiger and Wilhelm Muller, shortly after the discovery of radioactivity. A schematic diagram of a Geiger counter is shown in (Figure 1). A wire electrode runs along the center line of a cylinder having conducting walls. The tube is usually filled with a monatomic gas such as argon at a pressure of about 0.1 atmosphere. A high voltage , slightly less than that required to produce a discharge in the gas, is applied between the walls and the central electrode. A rapidly moving charged particle which gets into the tube will ionize some of the gas molecules in the tube, triggering a discharge. The result of each ionizing event is an electrical pulse which can be amplified to activate ear phones or a loud speaker,

making the counter useful in searches for radioactive minerals or in surveys to check for radioactive contamination. The counter provides very little information about the particles which trigger it because the signal from it is the same size no matter how it is triggered. However, one can learn quite a bit about the source of radiation by inserting various amounts of shielding between source and counter to see how the radiation is attenuated.

Scintillation detector

Scintillation counters are made from materials which emit light when charged particles move through them. To detect these events and to gain information about the radiation, some means of detecting the light must be used. One of the first scintillation detectors was a glass screen coated with zinc sulfide. This sort of detector was used by Ernest Rutherford in the early versions of his classic experiment in which he discovered

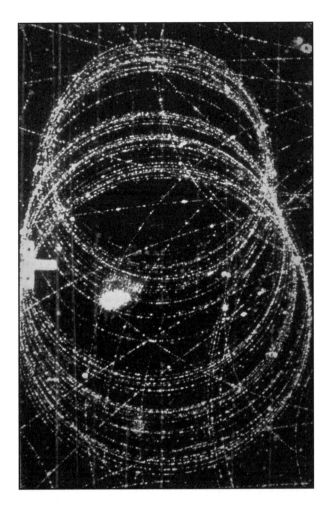

An electron in a magnetic field spirals some 36 times at a cloud chamber at the Lawrence Berkeley Laboratory in California. The track of the electron, which starts at the bottom of the picture, is some 33 ft (10 m) long. Its spiral becomes tighter half way up the picture because the electron loses energy by radiating a photon. The small irregularities in the spacing between the loops are due to scattering when the electron is deflected slightly by collisions with atoms in the chamber's gas.

the nucleus of the atom by scattering alpha particles from heavy atoms such as gold. The scattered alpha particles hit the scintillating screen and the small flashes produced were observed by experimenters in a darkened room using only the human eye.

The modern scintillation counter usually uses what is called a photo multiplier tube to detect the light. Light incident on the photocathode of such a tube is converted into an electrical signal and amplified millions of times after which it can be sent to appropriate counters. Physicists working at particle accelerators often use transparent plastic materials like Lucite or plexiglass to which are added materials to make them scintillate. These plastic scintillators can be cut to con-

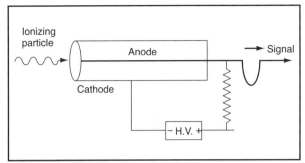

Figure 1. Schematic diagram of the Geiger counter.

venient shapes, mounted on a photomultipler tube and placed in particle beams to provide a very fast signal when charged particles pass through them.

A very useful scintillation detector, particularly for the measurement of gamma rays, utilizes a transparent crystal of NaI (sodium iodide) mounted on a photomultiplier tube. These crystals are particularly useful because charged particles produce in them an amount of light which is directly proportional to their energy over a fairly wide range. A schematic diagram of a gamma ray scintillation spectrometer is shown in Figure 2. Gamma rays have no charge and thus no detector is sensitive to them directly. Fortunately, gamma rays interact with matter and produce charged particles—usually electrons. For the measurement of gamma ray energies, the two most important interactions are the photoelectric effect and the Compton effect. These two processes can combine to produce energetic electrons in the crystal which scintillates to produce an amount of light directly proportional to the gamma ray energy. These light pulses are converted to electrical pulses in the photomultiplier tube. These are amplified and sent to a pulseheight analyzer which sorts out the pulses and displays a pulse height spectrum. A particular gamma ray shows up as a fairly sharp peak in this pulse height distribution.

Solid state detectors

Similar results with much improved energy resolution, the sharpness of the peaks in the pulse height distribution, can be obtained using solid state detectors made from semi-conducting materials such as silicon or germanium. When properly constructed, the electrical charges released in the material by the passage of charged particles can be collected directly producing a short electrical pulse which can be amplified and analyzed. Germanium detectors made for use with gamma rays can have peaks in the pulse height distribution almost 100 times narrower than the peaks from a sodium iodide detector. To obtain this improved resolu-

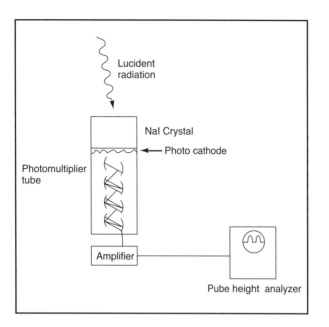

Figure 2. A gamma ray scintillation spectrometer.

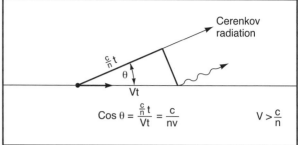

$$Cos\ \theta = \frac{\frac{c}{n}t}{Vt} = \frac{c}{nv} \qquad V > \frac{c}{n}$$

Figure 3. Cerenkov radiation.

tion these detectors must be cooled to the temperature of liquid nitrogen 77K (-196°C).

Smaller solid state detectors, usually made from silicon, are also used for measuring the energy of alpha particles, beta rays (electrons) from radioactive materials and X rays.

Neutron detectors

Since neutrons are uncharged, their detection must depend on an interaction with matter which produces energetic charged particles. There are several nuclear reactions initiated by neutrons which result in charged particles. One of the most useful for slow neutrons is the reaction in which a neutron is incident on a boron nucleus. This reaction produces a lithium nucleus and an alpha particle, both of which are rapidly moving. Note that it is the boron isotope of mass 10, with a natural abundance of about 20%, that is required for this reaction and that the alpha particle is simply the nucleus of the helium atom. The boron is usually incorporated in the gas molecule BF_3 (boron trifluoride) which can be used as the gas in a proportional counter, which is much like a Geiger counter. The difference is simply that the voltages used are lower so that the discharge does not spread disruptively along the whole central electrode with the result that the electrical signal coming from the tube is proportional to the number of ions produced. The signals are much smaller than from a Geiger tube and require more amplification but the signal produced by the lithium nucleus and alpha particle, both of which are heavily ionizing, is relatively large and easily distin-

guishable. For fast neutrons, the probability of this boron reaction becomes very low so that other methods are required. A useful technique is to use a proportional counter filled with hydrogen. Fast neutrons colliding with the protons in hydrogen produce energetic protons which produce a signal from the counter.

Cerenkov detectors

When a charged particle moves through a transparent material with a velocity v, greater than the velocity of light in that material, it radiates light in the forward direction at an angle whose cosine is equal to c/vn, where n is the index of refraction of the material. This light is called Cerenkov radiation and can be detected with photomultiplier tubes as was the case with scintillation detectors (Figure 3). It is named after the Russian physicist Pavel Cerenkov who discovered it in 1934. The special theory of relativity limits particle velocities to values less than c, the velocity of light in a vacuum. Cerenkov detectors can be of two types. A threshold detector merely detects the fact that light is emitted and indicates that the velocity of the particle passing through it is greater than c/n. Other more complicated detectors can actually determine the velocity v by measuring the angle at which light is emitted.

Cloud chambers and bubble chambers

A cloud chamber utilizes an enclosed volume of clean air saturated with water vapor. If this volume of air is enclosed in a cylinder with a piston and the volume is suddenly expanded, the temperature of the air falls causing the mixture to become supersaturated. If a charged particle passes through the volume at this time the vapor tends to condense on the ions produced, leaving a trail of water droplets on the path of the charged particle. With proper illumination and timing these trails can be photographed. If a magnetic field is applied, the radius of curvature of these tracks can be measured and this information, combined with the density of droplets along the trail can be used to measure the energy of the particle. The cloud chamber was first used by C.T.R. Wilson around the turn of the century and was useful in the early days of nuclear physics but suffered from several disadvantages such as the long time required to recycle and the low density of air. In 1932 Carl D. Anderson discovered the positron, the antiparticle of the electron while using a cloud chamber to observe cosmic rays.

A rather similar device called the bubble chamber was developed using liquids rather than a gas. Liquefied gases such as hydrogen, xenon, and helium have been used. Pressure is applied to the liquid to keep it a liquid above its normal boiling point at atmospheric pressure. If the pressure is suddenly reduced the liquid is superheated but will not boil spontaneously, at least for a short time. In order to boil, the liquid must have small irregularities on which bubbles of vapor form and they can be provided in the bubble chamber by the ions left by charged particles passing through the chamber. Thus tiny bubbles form along the tracks of particles passing through the chamber just after the pressure has been reduced. The bubbles grow very quickly but if the tracks are photographed at just the right time after expansion they are revealed as a thin trail of tiny bubbles. Bubble chambers work very well with particle accelerators that are pulsed. The expansion of the chamber can be timed so that particles from the accelerator pass through just after the chamber is expanded. As with the cloud chamber, application of a magnetic field permits measurement of the curvature of the tracks and when this information is combined with the density of bubbles along the track the energy, momentum, charge (sign) and mass of the particle can be determined. The bubble chamber was invented in 1953 by the American Physicist Donald Glaser who used a small glass device containing about 30 cubic centimeters of diethyl ether. The use and size of bubble chambers grew during the following decades culminating in the discovery of the omega minus particle in the 80 in (203 cm) bubble chamber at Brookhaven National Laboratory in 1964 and the construction of the 3168 gal (12,000 l) "Gargamelle" chamber at the CERN laboratory in Geneva Switzerland in the early 1970s. In recognition of the great importance of this device to particle physics research, Glaser was awarded the Nobel Prize for physics in 1961.

Wire chambers

In many nuclear and particle physics experiments, beam lines are constructed along which secondary particles of interest, produced by an accelerator, are maintained in a beam by a series of focusing and bending magnets. Wire chambers are used along these beam lines to actually track individual particles as they move along the beam line. The chambers are similar in a general way to the Geiger counter since they are gas counters. Instead of one wire the chambers have many parallel wires spaced at distances of a few millimeters. The position of charged particles passing through the chamber can be measured with uncertainties even less than the wire spacing, using fast timing circuits. These chamber measurements facilitate identification of the particle and the measurement of its momentum.

Large layered detectors

The ultimate in particle detectors are probably those being used and constructed at large national and international laboratories such as Fermilab in Illinois and CERN in Geneva, Switzerland. At these locations colliding beam accelerators have been built which produce collisions of fundamental particles, such as electrons and positrons at CERN, and protons and anti-protons at Fermilab. At various points around these large circular accelerators the counter rotating beams cross, and head on collisions can take place making large amounts of energy available for the production of other particles. Huge detectors costing millions of dollars and requiring hundreds of physicists to run them, are constructed surrounding these collision points. At Fermilab, two of these large devices, one called CDF and the other DZero, have recently reconstructed events, produced in these collisions, which provide strong evidence for the existence of the long sought top quark. To do this the detectors are designed to detect as many of the millions of particles produced in these collisions as possible. At DZero about 400,000 proton-anti-proton collisions occur per second. The detectors, weighing thousands of tons, are constructed in layers and almost completely surround the collision points. They utilize most of the detection techniques discussed above including scintillators, solid state detectors and devices similar to wire chambers which provide much improved performance. These are called silicon microstrip detectors. They are made up of closely spaced strips of silicon detectors which give very fast position measurements of particles accurate to about 0.01 mm. The thousands of individual detectors and detector systems are connected to computers which help select the very special events that might involve the top quark from the millions that do not.

Further Reading:

Blatt, Frank J. *Modern Physics*. McGraw Hill, 1992.
Das, Ashok and Thomas Ferbel. *Introduction to Nuclear and Particle Physics*. John Wiley, 1994.
Knoll, Glen F. *Radiation Detection and Measurement*, 2nd edition. John Wiley and Sons Inc., 1989.

KEY TERMS

Anti-proton—The anti-particle of the proton. Identical to the proton except that its charge is opposite in sign.

Gamma rays—Energetic electromagnetic radiation emitted by radioactive nuclei, produced by particle accelerators and present also in cosmic rays.

Mesons and baryons—Sub-atomic particles, usually with very short lifetimes, believed to be composed of quarks in various combinations.

Omega minus particle—A short lived baryon believed to be made up of three quarks called "strange" quarks.

Photomultiplier tube—An electronic tube, sensitive to very small amounts of light. The tube converts a light signal into an electrical signal of useful size.

Positron—The anti-particle of the electron. Identical to the electron except that its charge is opposite in sign.

Quarks—Fundamental fractionally charged particles believed to combine in various ways to form the mesons and baryons. Six quarks are believed to exist but ordinary matter is made up of only two—the so called up and down quarks which in various combinations make up the neutron and proton.

Litke, Alan M. and Andreas S. Schwarz. "The Silicon Microstrip Detector." *Scientific American* (May, 1995): 76.

Taylor, John R. and Chris D. Zafirates. *Modern Physics for Scientists and Engineers*. Prentice Hall Inc., 1991.

Robert L. Stearns

Particle physics see **Physics**

Particles, subatomic see **Subatomic particles**

Partridges

Partridges are species of fowl in the family Phasianidae, which also includes the pheasants, chickens, peafowl, francolins, and quail. Partridges occur naturally in Eurasia, but they have been introduced as game birds to other places as well, including North America.

Partridges are medium-sized, stocky birds with short, rounded wings, a short tail, and a short, stout bill, in which the upper mandible overhangs the tip of the lower. The legs are short and stout, and the feet are strong and armed with sharp claws, useful for digging and scratching while foraging for food on the ground.

Partridges eat a wide variety of seeds, fruits, leaves, and buds, as well as invertebrates, which are captured on the ground. The chicks mostly eat arthropods, switching to a diet richer in plant foods after much of their initial growth has been completed.

Partridges build their nests in a concealed place on the ground, and they may lay as many as 15 eggs. These are incubated only by the female, which also has the sole responsibility for raising the chicks. Baby partridges are precocious, and can walk, run after their mother, and feed themselves soon after hatching. Partridges sexually mature at an age of about one year. During the non-breeding season, partridges assemble into flocks, which forage and roost together.

Like most other species in their family, partridges are gamebirds, and are hunted as food and for sport. As a result, partridges are economically important, but they are also vulnerable to over-hunting, which can severely reduce the sizes of their populations. It is critical that these birds be conserved by careful regulation of hunting-related predation, as well as by management and preservation of their necessary habitat.

The Hungarian, European, or grey partridge (*Perdix perdix*) is a wide-ranging species that is native from the British Isles, through Europe and Russia, to Mongolia. However, this species has been introduced as a gamebird well beyond its natural range. The grey partridge is now an established species in North America, occurring in various places from southern Canada to the northern and middle United States.

The chukar (*Alectoris chukar*) is native to mountainous habitats of Europe and Asia. This species has been introduced as a gamebird to drier, open mountain habitats in southwestern Canada and the northwestern United States.

Sometimes, species of grouse and ptarmigan are locally known by the common name partridge—for example, the ruffed grouse (*Bonasa umbellus*) of North America. However, these birds are in a quite different family, the Tetraonidae.

See also Pheasants; Peafowl; Quail.

Bill Freedman

Partridges.

Pascal's triangle

Pascal's triangle is a well known set of numbers aligned in the shape of a pyramid. The numbers represent the binomial coefficients. Binomial coefficients represent the number of subsets of a given size. The numbers in Pascal's triangle are also the coefficients of the expansion of $(a+b)^n$, $(a+b)$ raised to the n-th power. So for n equals to three, the expansion is $(a+b)*(a+b)*(a+b)$ which equals $(a^2+2ab+b^2)*(a+b)$ which equals $(a^3 + 3ab^2 + 3ba^2 + b^3)$. The coefficients are 1,3,3,1. These are listed in the third row of Pascal's triangle.

History

Pascal's triangle was also known as the Figurate Triangle, the Combinatorial Triangle, and the Binomial Triangle. The triangle was first given the name, "Pascal's triangle," by a mathematician named Montmort in 1708. Montmort wrote the numbers in the form below known as the combinatorial triangle.

1 1 1 1 1 1 2 3 4 1 3 6 1 4 1

The combination of numbers that form Pascal's triangle were well known before Pascal, but he was the first one to organize all the information together in his treatise, 'The Arithmetical Triangle.' The numbers originally arose from Hindu studies of combinatorics and binomial numbers, and the Greek's study of figurate numbers. The Chinese also wrote about the binomial numbers in 'Precious Mirror of the Four Elements' in 1303. The figurate numbers were known over 500 years before Christ. There are square and triangular figurate numbers. The first four of each are shown below.

The Triangular numbers:

1   3   6   10

The Square numbers:

1   4   9   16

Additional square and triangular numbers are formed by increasing the size of each respectively. Actually, figurate numbers can be formed from any polygon. Another set of figurate numbers could be formed using the pentagon, a polygon with five sides. The figurate numbers were studied heavily to learn about counting numbers and arrangements. For example, if a woman was asked to determine which of two sacks of gold coins was worth more, she would probably have to count the coins. To count the coins, the best approach would be to stack the coins into short stacks of a given number. Then the number of stacks could be counted. Counting numbers, looking at the patterns and studying the ways objects could be arranged led to the numbers in Pascal's Triangle. The study of combining or arranging objects by various rules to create new arrangements of objects is called Combinatorics, an important branch of mathematics. Pascal's triangle in its current form is shown below. It is the same as the above combinatorial triangle rotated 45 degrees clockwise.

$(A+B)^0$ 1
$(A+B)^1$ 1   1
$(A+B)^2$ 1   2   1
$(A+B)^3$ 1   3   3   1
$(A+B)^4$ 1   4   6   4   1
$(A+B)^5$ 1   5   10   10   5   1

Pascal's Triangle

Each new row in Pascal's triangle is solved by taking the top two numbers and adding them together to get the number below.

The triangle always starts with the number one and has ones on the outside. Another way to calculate the numbers is Pascal's Triangle is to calculate the binomial coefficients, written C(r;c). A formula for the binomial coefficients is r! divided by c!*(r-c)!. The variable r represents the row and c, the column, of Pascal's Triangle. The exclamation point represents the factorial. The factorial of a number is that number times every integer number less than it until the number one is reached. So 4! would be equal to 4*3*2*1 or 24.

Binomial numbers or coefficients

Binomial coefficients are written C(r;c) and represent "the number of combinations of r things taken c at a time." The numbers in Pascal's Triangle are simply the binomial coefficients. The importance of binomial coefficients comes from a question that arises in every day life. An example is a how to take three books from a shelf two at a time. The first two books alone would be one way to take two books from a set of three. The other ways would be to take books two and three or books one and three. This gives three ways to take two books from a set of three. For larger arrangements, listing the number of combinations can be nearly impossible. So instead, the binomial coefficient can be found instead. For the above three books taken two at a time, all that needs to be found in the binomial coefficient C(3,2), which is the third row and second column of Pascal's triangle, or three.

Pascal

Blaise Pascal (1623-1662), a founder of the theory of probability, developed the earliest known calculating machine that could perform the carrying process in addition. The machine, finished in 1642, could add numbers mechanically using interlocking dials. Machines like these eventually led to the first punch card machines and computers. Pascal had a great influence on people like Leibniz and Newton. His father was also a mathematician, and made sure Blaise had the best education possible by introducing him to the Martin Mersenne's "Academy" at the age of fourteen. The academy was one of the best places to study mathematics at the time, and his father was one of the founders. When Pascal was young, he was introduced to the work done in combinatorics and the binomial numbers. His paper compiling the work of the Chinese, Hindus and Greeks would later cause his name to be permanently attached to the combinatorial triangle forever.

Probability theory

A number of unsolved problems in Pascal's days encouraged the formation of probability theory. The Gambler's Ruin and the Problem of Point are two examples of such problems.

The Gambler's Ruin was a problem Pascal challenged the great mathematician, Pierre de Fermat, to solve. The problem, according to one explanation, was determining what the chances of winning were for each of two men playing a game with two dice. When an eleven was thrown on the dice by the one man, a point would be scored. When the second man threw a fourteen on the dice, he would score a point. The points only counted if the opponent's score was zero. Otherwise, the point scored by one of the men would be subtracted from his opponent's score. So one of the men would always have a score of zero throughout the game. The game was one won when one man gained twelve points. Pascal asked, what was the probability of each man winning? Binomial coefficients can be used to answer the question.

The Problem of Points was also a game about probabilities. The question was determining how a game's winnings should be divided if the game was ended prematurely. Questions about games like these stirred the development of probability theory, and the need to understand binomial numbers completely.

Further Reading:

Banks, J. Houston. *Elements of Mathematics.* Allyn and Bacon, 1961.
Dickson, Leonard Eugene. *History of the Theory of Numbers.* G. E. Stechert, 1934.

KEY TERMS

Binomial Numbers or coefficients—Numbers which stand for the number of subsets of equal size within a larger set.

Combinatorics—The branch of mathematics concerned with the study of combining objects (arranging) by various rules to create new arrangements of objects.

Pascal, Blaise—Blaise Pascal (1623-1662), a well known mathematician, was a founder of the theory of probability. The combinatorial triangle was given his name when he published a paper compiling the previous work done by the Hindus, Chinese and Greeks.

Pascal's Triangle—A set of numbers arranged in a triangle. Each number represents a binomial coefficient.

Probability theory—The study of statistics and the chance for a set of outcomes.

Edwards, A. W. F. *Pascal's Arithmetical Triangle*. Charles Griffin, 1987.

Richardson, William. *Finite Mathematics*. Harper and Row, 1968.

Sondheimer, Eric, and Alan Rogerson. *Numbers and Infinity*. Cambridge University Press, 1981.

Ronald Walpole and Raymond Myers. *Probability and Statistics for Engineers and Scientists*. Macmillan Publishers Company, 1989.

David Gorsich

Passion flower

Species of passion vines (*Passiflora* spp.; family Passifloraceae) that twine upward in tropical, subtropical, and some temperate regions of the world. They occur most often in wet forests, though some species may occur in drier, more open places. These vines have glossy leaves shaped like rounded human hands, and their flowers are often sweetly scented and packed with a ring of colorful filaments. The tendrils of passion vines hold the flexible, immature parts of the plants in place as they grow over and across other plants and physical obstacles.

The genus *Passiflora*, the best known group in the family Passifloraceae, also includes genera such as *Ade-nia* and *Basananthe*, both principally known from Africa. The plant families related most closely to the Passifloraceae are the Turneraceae, (watermelons, cucumbers), and Begoniaceae (begonias).

Humans have long valued passion flowers for their beauty, cultivating them in greenhouses and gardens, and as annual plants in temperate zone gardens. Most species are not hardy and need extra protection in temperate regions, with a notable exception being *Passiflora incarnate*, the maypop. This vine occurs naturally in the southern and middle states along the Atlantic coast of the United States. Its egg-shaped fruits follow fertilization of the white or purple flowers, and were once eaten by Native Americans and used medicinally as a sedative and anti-inflammatory.

The passion fruit flavor in prepared foods usually comes from the fruit of *Passiflora edulis*. Other notable fruits produced by species of *Passiflora* include the football-sized granadilla, from *P. quadrangularis*. Popular ornamental species include *P. caerula*, with its sky-blue flowers; *P. alato-caerula* , a blue-purple flowered hybrid; and *P. mollissima*, the banana passion flower, so named for the shape of its fruit.

The passion flower was used by Catholic missionaries in the Americas to teach about the crucifixion of Christ. It is the events of Christ's "passion," or suffering, which were said to be represented in the parts of the flower: three stigmas or female receptive parts for the three nails used in the crucifixion, the five anthers for Christ's five wounds, the spiky corona for the crown of thorns, and the five petals and five sepals for the ten faithful apostles (the twelve apostles minus Peter and Judas). Additional interpretations are sometimes given to other parts of the plant, such as the identification of the rounded leaves with the hands of those who crucified Christ.

Pathology see **Disease**

Pawpaw see **Laurel family**

PBB see **Polybrominated biphenyls**

PCB see **Polychlorinated biphenyls**

Peafowl

The peafowl are three large, and extraordinarily beautiful species of fowl in the family Phasianidae, which also includes the pheasants, chickens, partridges, francolins, and quail. Species of peafowl are native to

A peacock (*Pavo cristatus*).

Asia and Africa. However, these gorgeous creatures have been kept in captivity as ornamental birds for several thousand years, and they are now found in zoos and aviaries in many parts of the world.

Peafowl are the largest of the species in the Phasianidae. These birds can weigh about 11 lb (5 kg), and can be as long as 6.5 ft (2 m), including the tail. Their most distinctive character is the very large, spreadable tail or "train" of the male bird, also known as a peacock. Other distinctive characteristics of peafowl include their long neck, a heavy, hooked bill, a crest on the top of the head, and long, strong legs and feet.

Peafowl are animals of tropical forests. They forage on the ground during the day, and roost in a tree for protection at night. Peafowl are omnivorous, eating a wide range of fruits, seeds, and buds, as well as diverse invertebrates gleaned from the forest floor.

During much of the year, peafowl live in small groups. However, they split up into pairs during the breeding season. Peacocks have spectacular courtship displays, the highlight of which is the spreading of the train to impress the female, or peahen. The train is at least two times longer than the body of the peacock, and it is spread into a more-than semi-circular fan (about 210° of spread). The expanded train is greenish in color, and is punctuated by a large number of eye-like, iridescent spots at the end of each of the approximately 100 tail feathers. The peacock also has several distinctive, startling, harsh, discordant screams and wails that it utters during the courting season and during displays of its fan.

Once it has secured a mate, the peacock builds a nest, usually in a thicket. The female lays a clutch of about ten eggs, which she alone broods. The peahen also takes care of the chicks.

The blue or common peafowl (*Pavo cristatus*) is a native bird of India and Sri Lanka. Small populations of feral birds have also been established in various places beyond the native range, for example, in Australia. The head, neck, and breast are an iridescent blue in this species. The blue peafowl is the most abundant peafowl in captivity. White and black varieties of this species also exist in domestic collections.

The green peafowl (*Pavo muticus*) is native to Indochina and Java. This species has a green head, neck, and breast. This species is also kept in captivity.

The Congo peafowl (*Afropavo congensis*) is a very rare, little-known species of tropical forests of Zaire. The discovery of this species in 1936 created a sensation, because it could scarcely be believed that such a large, beautiful bird had not been seen by naturalists prior to that time.

See also Pheasants; Partridges; Quail.

Bill Freedman

Peanut see **Legumes**

Peanut worms

Peanut worms are a group of over 300 species of worms, classified as a separate Phylum Sipunculida (Phylum Sipuncula, by some authors), called Sipunculids or Sipunculans in English. They have a simple tubular shape, with "a rube within a tube" body plan and the internal organs inside a body cavity (coelom), that is lined by a fine epithelium called peritoneum. They are non-segmented and bilaterally symmetrical; some specialists include the Sipunculids among the Protostomes, with most worms, arthropods, and molluscs. Their earliest appearance on earth dates back to the Paleozoic Middle Devonian deposes. The Sipunculids are exclusively marine and usually lead a sedentary life on the bottom of the sea. Some, like *Sipunculus*, bury in sand and mud. Others are rock-boring like *Phascolosoma* and *Parasipidosiphon* in the Antilles, and *Cloeosiphon* in the Indian Ocean near the Maldive Islands. They are common in tropical reef limestone; in Hawaii up to 700 Sipunculids were counted on one square meter of coral rock. The mechanism of rock boring is not known. Although mucus is found in burrows, Sipunculids do not build true tubes like other marine worms.

Sipunculids have no known economic value, but their importance for the interpretation of the history of life on earth and of the relationships of different invertebrate groups should not be underestimated. They also contribute to the ecological balance in their respective habitats.

The body of a peanut worm is relatively simple, divided into an anterior narrow section called the introvert, and a larger posterior trunk. The introvert is not a proboscis: it can be retracted into the anterior end of the trunk; it represents the head and the anterior part of the worms's body. The mouth, surrounded by an oral disc, is found at the outer tip of the introvert and it is covered by a scalloped fringe, lobes, tentacles, or tentacular lobes, some with grooves lined with cilia. On the outside the introvert may be covered with spines, tubercles, or other small projections. The eversion (extrusion) of this structure is due to the muscle contraction of the body wall and the increased pressure of the fluid in the body cavity (coelom) occurring when feeding. The exact mode of feeding varies with species: some depend on ciliary movement to create currents which bring small particles into the mouth. Dead organic matter (detritus) may be trapped in mucus when the tentacles are placed upon it. Some Sipunculids are carnivores and ingest small animals and microorganisms from the substrate. A Sipunculid found in the North Sea, *Golfingia procera*, is a predator on an annelid worm of the genus *Aphrodite* (known as a seamouse): it penetrates its body and sucks out the contents. The introvert invaginates (folding inward so that an outer wall becomes an inner wall), and the ingested food passes into the esophagus, the anterior part of the digestive system which in Sipunculids is U-shaped. The long intestine descends to the posterior end of the trunk and then ascends anteriorly in a twisting spiral. The rectum is short and opens through the anus, usually located at the anterior part of the trunk. There is no blood-vascular system and no gas-exchange organs, but the coelomic fluid contains corpuscles with hemerythrin, a respiratory pigment, like human hemoglobin, but containing copper. It serves to carry oxygen to various parts of the body as the corpuscles move around. Excretion of waste products of metabolism is accomplished by a pair of large sac-like metanephridia, which may be compared in function to our kidneys. These open at the level of the anal opening anteriorly and ventrally. Particulate waste products are picked up by clusters of cells located on the peritoneum and capped by a ciliated cell, called "fixed urns." Some of these "urns" become detached and float in the body fluid in the coelom and help pick up waste products that are to be removed by the metanephridia.

The nervous system resembles that of the annelid worms, but it is not segmented. The "brain" is the dorsal ganglion, an accumulation of nerve cells located over the esophagus, which extend into a single ventral nerve cord.

Sensory cells are abundant especially at the end of the introvert. In some species these may be specialized as chemoreceptors that respond to chemical stimuli, or as a pair of pigmented ocelli, primitive light receptors, located in the brain, or better said, dorsal ganglion.

In peanut worms the sexes are separate, male or female. Respective sex cells form from certain parts of the lining of the body cavity, where retractor muscles of the body wall arise. They are shed into the body cavity (coelom) where they mature into sperms or eggs. These leave the body through the excretory channels of the metanephridia. When males shed sperms into the sea water, the nearby females are stimulated to shed mature eggs, which are fertilized externally. The fertilized eggs begin to divide by spiral cleavage, like in some annelids and molluscs. The development may be direct, into a young adult, or, first, a free swimming larva worm that drops to the bottom. This metamorphosis may take one day as in *Golfingia* or a month, as in *Sipunculus*. Asexual reproduction by constriction and separation of the posterior end of the trunk occurs in a few Sipunculids.

Sophie Jakowska

Pear see **Rose family**

Peas see **Legumes**

A javelina (*Tayassu tajacu*), or collared peccary, at the Aransas National Wildlife Refuge, Texas. Note the irregular collar (which is yellowish in color) running from shoulder to shoulder.

Peccaries

Peccaries are wild pigs (order Artiodactyla, family Tayassuidae) of the New World which are relatives of the wild pigs of the Old World. Peccaries are the only pigs native to the New World pigs, all other pigs in North and South America are formerly domestic animals that have escaped and become feral. Taxonomists recognize three species of peccaries: the collared peccary *(Tayassu tajacu)* of the southwestern United States and Mexico; the white-lipped peccary *(T. pecari),* which inhabits plains, forests, valleys, and deserts throughout most of northern South America; and the tagua or chaco *(Catagonus wagneri),* which was thought to be extinct, but living specimens were found in 1975 in the arid Gran Chaco region of South America in Paraguay, Argentina, Bolivia, and Brazil.

Peccaries are even-toed hoofed animals that are sometimes called javelinas (javelins) because their tusks look like javelins or spears. Peccaries have a musk gland on the back near the rump that gives off a very powerful odor, resulting in the alternate common name of musk hog.

The tagua is the largest peccary, reaching as much as 80 lbs (36 kg) and a shoulder height of about 43 in (1 m), almost twice the size of the collared peccary. It has a large head that seems out of proportion to its body. The white-lipped peccary's stiff hair is dark reddish brown and the white on it is actually on the sides on its jaws, not on its lips. It is about 3 ft (1 m) long and weighs about 66 lbs (30 kg). The collared peccary is grizzled gray with a whitish, collar-shaped stripe of fur on the neck. Adults have a faint black stripe on their backs, which is more visible in young animals. The males and females of all species are the same size.

From the side, a peccary's head looks triangular with a round, flat snout making one corner of the triangle. The snout is used for rooting out their food of bulbs and tender shoots as well as prickly pear cactus, a particular favorite. The long legs have tiny, hoofed feet with four toes on the front and three on the back. Peccaries do not run much except when in danger, and even walking is kept at a minimum, with the animals preferring a quiet life of lazing during the day and leisurely feeding at twilight and dawn.

Peccaries live in groups that may number more than 100 animals and depend on the group for defense. The collared peccary tends to live in smaller groups, usually numbering less than 10 members. A closely packed group of angry, squealing animals with large, jutting canine teeth like tusks does not present an inviting target for jaguars and other big cats. As the group moves, the members mark their territory with their musk glands.

Males and females in the group mate at any time, but the young, usually twins, are generally born in summer after a gestation period that lasts about 115 days for the collared peccary and up to 160 days for the white-lipped peccary. The newborn peccaries can move almost immediately, and they will stay with the mother for several months.

Peccaries serve as a tasty food source for the people that live near them. In some parts of the United States, the collared peccary has come to be regarded as a game animal, and is the target of organized hunting parties. If hounded by hunters, peccaries are apt to turn and try to attack. Hunting and loss of habitat has brought the numbers of these New World pigs down to very low levels, and these animals are now protected in a number of reserves and parks throughout South and Central America.

Further Reading:

Burton, John A., and Bruce Pearson. *The Collins Guide to the Rare Mammals of the World.* London: William Collins Sons & Co., 1987.

Stidworthy, John. *Mammals: The Large Plant-Eaters.* Encyclopedia of the Animal World. New York: Facts On File, 1988.

Jean F. Blashfield

Peeps see **Sandpipers**

Pelicans

Pelicans are large coastal birds belonging to order Pelecaniformes, along with gannets, tropicbirds, darters, frigatebirds, and cormorants. All of them have throat pouches to one extent or another, but only the pelicans' are so big. They eat nothing but fish, and the pouch is a handy device for catching their food.

The pelican has perhaps the most unusual bill in the bird world. It is quite long—18 in (46 cm) in some

A brown pelican (*Pelecanus occidentalis*) at the Everglades National Park, Florida. Unlike the American white pelican, the brown is nonmigratory, preferring saltwater habitats year round.

birds—with the top part, or mandible, flat, narrow, and quite stiff. The bottom part has a solid upper edge surrounding a pouch of skin that can stretch almost endlessly to hold great quantities of fish. This soft, flexible tissue extends down onto the neck. The birds do not fly back to their nests with food in the pouch. They would not be able to keep their balance in flight. Instead, it serves as a net to catch fish. Up to 2 gal (7.6 l) of water can be taken in and then forced out through the closed mandibles, leaving the captured fish behind. They are then swallowed.

The famed diving brown pelican (*P. occidentalis*) is the only one that actually dives into the water to fish. The other pelicans skim the surface as they fly or settle on the waves to fish. Some even work in colonies to "herd" the fish together.

Pelicans are amazing fliers, with the ability to cover hundreds of miles a day, taking advantage of rising warm air currents to carry them without wing motion. However, as soon as they spot fish below them, they can descend to just over the ocean, where they flap their wings with a slow, strong beat until they are ready to dive into the water. Most large water birds such as cranes, herons, and storks fly with their necks outstretched in front of them. Pelicans, on the other hand, fly with their heads curved back against their bodies.

Although all seven species of pelicans are in the same genus, those seven divide into two groups by their coloring and where they nest. Four species of all white birds nest on the ground in large flocks, or colonies. These include the American white *(Pelecanus erythrorhynchos)*, which is the largest pelican; the European white *(P. onocrotalus)*; the Australian *(P. conspicillatus)*; and the Dalmatian *(P. crispus)*. The other three are primarily brown and they nest in trees. These include the brown pelican so prominent in Florida waters; the pink-backed pelican *(P. rufescens)*, which is pinkish-gray on its head and neck; and the gray or spot-billed pelican *(P. philippensis)*. The latter has a row of spots the length of both sides of its bill.

As breeding season approaches, the pelicans' bills and the naked patches on their heads often change color. In addition, they may molt, with the new feathers being different colors and indicating that it is mating time. At nesting time, the male gathers the materials, which are put into place by the female. The female lays usually only one or two chalky white eggs that hatch after an incubation of about four weeks.

Young pelicans hatch out with black or white skin and flipperlike wings. They quickly grow a soft layer of down. They are very noisy, hissing and squealing almost continuously, but as they grow these birds become silent. Although more than one egg may be laid, the first bird hatched-is usually the strongest, and takes over the nest and forces the smaller, weaker ones out. It then grows very rapidly, demanding the efforts of both parents to bring home enough food. The young reaches into the parents' pouches to get fish, which they regurgitate. The offspring does not leave home until it has eaten enough to develop a layer of fat on its body to support its needs until it learns to dive for its own food. The young become sexually mature at three or four years. Pelicans in the wild can live to be about 20 to 25 years old. In captivity, they may live much longer.

The eastern white pelican of eastern Europe and Africa is about the same size as the American white but with a longer wingspan. Overlapping its range in Europe is the range of the rare Dalmatian pelican, which can be distinguished from it by its gray bill and bright orange pouch. Overlapping the eastern white's African range south of the Sahara is the range of the pink-backed pelican, which has been described as "dowdy" because its colors are so muted.

The American pelicans

The brown pelican has light brown or gray, white-edged feathers on its body. The back of its neck has a lengthwise band of reddish feathers, and its head is crowned with yellow feathers. Its bill is gray instead of the yellow of many pelicans. It dives directly into the water for its fish, sometimes from great heights. Brown pelicans live along the seacoasts of Florida, the Gulf, California, and northern Mexico. They often nest on mangrove islands, perched on the outermost branches of the trees.

Another population, called the Peruvian brown pelican, lives along the coast of Peru where it feeds in the Humboldt Current. It is quite a bit larger than the north American bird, with a body length of 5 ft (152 cm) as compared to 45 in (114 cm). Ornithologists are still debating whether or not it is a separate species *(P. thagus)* from the North American pelican.

The large American white pelican weighs up to 20 lbs (9 kg) and has a wingspan of almost 10 ft (3 m). It looks all white until seen in flight, when its black flight feathers show. It is a freshwater bird, nesting on inland lakes, in central Canada and the northern central states. It spends the winter along the seaside, especially in Florida, the Gulf of Mexico, and Texas. It feeds by floating and dipping its pouch into the water. During the breeding season, the American white pelican develops a temporary hornlike growth on the upper mandible. It also grows longish plumes on its head.

Brown pelicans were seriously endangered in the late 1960s and early '70s because the pesticide DDT had gotten into their eggs, which could not develop normally. After the use of DDT in the United States was banned, these birds gradually began to recover. Although this problem has occurred recently, pelicans have been in danger before. About 1900, they were being killed for their long flight feathers, which fashion decreed for women's hats. Bird lovers persuaded President Theodore Roosevelt to declare Pelican Island, near Cape Canaveral, Florida, as the nation's first national wildlife refuge in 1903. Today there are more than 400 national refuges in the United States.

Further Reading:
Cook and Schreiber. *Wonders of the Pelican World*. New York: Dodd, Mead & Co., 1985.

Sanford, William R., and Green, Carl R. *The Pelicans.* Wildlife Habits and Habitats series. Mankato, MN: Crestwood House, 1987.

Stone, Lynn. *The Pelican.* A Dillon Remarkable Animals Book. Minneapolis: Dillon Press, 1990.

Jean F. Blashfield

Penguins

The penguin is a primitive, flightless bird highly specialized for marine life. Measuring one to three feet tall, most species look very similar. Generally speaking, the penguin is dark-blue or dark-gray on top with a white belly. Some penguins, however, have crests on their heads and/or patches of color on their heads and throats. Its legs are set wide apart and its wings are used as flippers. Most species of penguin live and breed on the continent of Antarctica, on islands near the continent, or on the southern coasts of South America, Australia, South Africa, or New Zealand. Four northern species inhabit the western coast of South America, as far north as the Galapagos Islands off of Ecuador.

Penguins have very unusual and distinct characteristics, thus, their relationship to other orders of birds is not fully understood. In fact, scientists dispute whether penguins should have their own superorder or even subclass. However, it is generally agreed that penguins belong to the Order Sphenisciformes and the family Spheniscidae. There are six genera of penguins within this family and from 16 to 18 species.

Modification of marine life and harsh environment

This bird has made numerous adaptations to life in harsh, marine conditions. Its legs, effectively used as oars, are set wide apart and connected rather far back on its body, which is long and rounded. Short, glossy feathers cover its body to form a dense fur-like matting, which is waterproof and helps keep the bird warm.

Although all of the bones needed for flight are present in its wings, they are tightly bound to each other by ligaments and are shortened and flattened. Given these adaptations, its wings have become unfoldable flippers or paddles used in swimming. The muscles in its chest, which are used to move its wings, are proportionately quite large, extending from its neck to the lower portion of its abdomen. The penguin uses its triangular tail for steering in the water.

Locomotion

Having legs located far back on their bodies makes it necessary for penguins to walk upright when on land. While some of the smaller species are fairly coordinated, the larger ones—like the Emperor penguin—are particularly clumsy on land. Penguins do not always have to walk, however. On steep icy slopes, penguins go from location to location by sliding on their bellies, using their feet to steer and their flippers to steady themselves.

Underwater, penguins can move very swiftly; their normal speed is between 3-6 mph (4.8-9.6 km/h), although they can move faster for short bursts. They have three basic modes of transporting themselves in the sea. The first form, called underwater flight, is a quick trip to the water for feeding or to avoid a predator, such as a sea lion. The second form, known as porpoising, is used by the penguin for longer distances. In this form, the penguin alternates between swimming deep in the water and leaping out of the surface. It is thought that the penguin increases its speed by reducing water resistance when swimming this way; also, this type of swimming allows the bird to catch a quick breath of air without stopping. The final form of swimming is the duck-style—head and tail erect— which the penguin assumes just before going ashore to orient itself.

Penguins occasionally dive great distances on their quests for food, which consists primarily of fish and crustaceans. For example, Emperor penguins reportedly can dive 850 ft (259 m) below the water's surface and remain there for approximately 18 minutes without breathing.

Social behavior

Penguins are very social animals; they travel, feed, breed, nest, and winter in large groups. Furthermore, they even have a species-specific form of vocal communication. On several Antarctic and sub-Antarctic islands, colonies number in the millions. For example, there are up to two million royal penguins that congre-

A gentoo penguin with its chick.

gate on the Macquarie Island, 750 mi (1,207 km) south-west of New Zealand. Furthermore, there are 10 million birds living on one of the South Sandwich Islands, which are located north of Antarctica.

There are several potential reasons for penguins' highly social behavior. First, mature penguins tend to return to the area where they were born to breed. Second, they are safer from predators—which include skuas, sharks, killer whales, and especially leopard seals—in large groups. Third, they learn about the location of food from each other. Fourth, group living provides better care and protection for their young and protection against the cold.

Within the social structure, there are two levels: the family and the breeding group. Within the family, which consists of the parents and usually two children, the young are cared for and defended against other penguins. Within the breeding group, defenses are used against the skua and vocal communication causes the birds to breed at about the same time.

Nesting

Though penguins spend the majority of their time in the water or on the coastline, their nesting colonies are often located miles away from the water. Penguins tend to mate with their partner from the prior year's breeding season. The males stake out the territory, which could only be a few square yards. Nests are made in a wide variety of locations, including in rock crevices or burrows, in the open with stick and grass, or on a bare patch of ground.

Usually all but the two largest species—the Emperor and the King penguins—lay two eggs. The two large species lay only one. The Emperor penguin endures the worst breeding conditions of any bird in the world. After the female lays her egg during the dark Antarctic winter, she returns to the water to feed and regain her strength; while she is gone, the male incubates the egg on top of his feet. During this 64 day period, when the temperature can dip below 40° F (4° C), the male huddles with other males to stay warm and eats nothing but snow. When the chick is born, he feeds it with a milky substance he regurgitates. Both Emperor and King penguins have their young in the winter, so that they will become independent in the summer when food is abundant. Newborns of all species are born covered with a thick layer of brown or gray down. This down molts into feathers that look like those of the adult when the bird is a juvenile.

Maintaining body temperature

When a penguin dives into the Antarctic Ocean, it is greeted by a water temperature that is forty degrees below its own temperature. (A person without a wet suit can live about ten minutes in water that cold.) Thus, penguins have adapted certain mechanisms to keep themselves warm. First, each penguin has a 0.7-1.1 in (2-3 cm) thick layer of fat and thick, waterproof plumage to insulate itself. Further, when in the water, the penguin is much more active than when on land. Thus, its metabolism increases, producing more metabolic heat.

The coldest weather species—the Emperor penguin—has made additional adaptations for surviving the most extreme cold. The Emperor has the largest body of any species, measuring about 3 ft (1 m) tall and weighing 88 lbs (40 kg); thus, compared to birds with smaller bodies, it has relatively less surface area exposed to the cold compared with its weight. It also has the most fat of any species and can live for two to four months during the winter without eating. The Emperor has more extensive feather cover than other species, including feathers on its bill and feet, except the toes. Its flippers are shorter and feet are smaller than its relatives, reducing their exposure to the cold. In fact, the Emperor penguin has made so many adaptations that it no longer needs to find solid land for any phase of its life and can live on ice alone.

This heat insulation is very effective, sometimes too effective. The problem with the insulation is that penguins are always in danger of overheating. This is especially true when they are fighting or running during the warmest months of the year—December, January, and February.

Further Reading:

Davis, Lloyd S. and John T. Darby. *Penguin Biology.* New York: Academic Press, Inc., 1990.

Grzimek, H.C. Bernard, Dr., ed. *Grzimek's Animal Life Encyclopedia.* New York: Van Nostrand Reinhold Company, 1993.

MacMillan Illustrated Animal Encyclopedia. New York: MacMillan Publishing Company, 1992.

Miller-Schwartze, Dietland. *The Behavior of Penguins: Adapted to Ice and Tropics.* Albany: State University of New York Press, 1984.

Pearl, Mary Corliss, Ph.D. Consultant. *The Illustrated Encyclopedia of Wildlife.* London: Grey Castle Press, 1991.

The New Larousse Encyclopedia of Animal Life. New York: Bonanza Books, 1987.

Kathryn Snavely

Peninsula

A peninsula is a piece of land surrounded by water on three sides and joined to a larger body of land by an isthmus, or neck. A peninsula is a topographic high spot; a dry land range of hills or mountains created during the formation of the Earth's crust. It is left visible when the low areas on both sides either subside and become submerged, or when the water level rises and floods the valleys. The coast of Maine and the Chesapeake Bay are excellent examples of shorelines of submergence. The Delmarva Peninsula, which forms the eastern section of the Chesapeake Bay, formed millions of years ago as the Susquehanna River eroded a river valley which was subsequently swamped when the sea level rose.

Because of their segregation from the primary body of land to which they are connected, peninsulas provide their inhabitants with relative isolation. During continental wars, peninsulas can be defended at the narrow isthmus. During peacetime, invasion by immigration tends to pass by because they lie off the main routes of travel. Thus, peninsulas can provide havens where humans and animals of ancient decent may still be found quite unadulterated. Examples are the Cornish and Welsh in peninsulas in western England; Australian aborigines of the Cape York Peninsula; and non Indo-European speaking people of the Indian peninsula.

During wars involving oceanic invasion, however, peninsulas are often targeted as the gateway to the continent. Two examples are the occupation of the Gallipoli Peninsula by Britain, from which they invaded Turkey during World War I, and the United States World War II entry into Europe through Italy's Calabrian Peninsula and France's Conetin Peninsula.

Because of this vulnerability, small peninsulas are often politically different from their mainland continent. For example, the Florida Peninsula for many years belonged to Spain. Conversely, large peninsulas often

A rocky peninsula in Acadia National Park, Maine.

become independent from their continental neighbors—like the peninsulas of Sweden and Italy.

The world's largest peninsulas are Arabia—1,254,000 sq mi (2,017,686 km); Southern India—800,000 sq mi (1,287,200 km), Alaska—580,000 sq mi (933,220 km), Labrador—502,000 sq mi (807,718 km), Scandinavia—309,000 sq mi (497,181 km), and the Iberian Peninsula—225,000 sq mi (339,525 km).

Marie L. Thompson

Penis see **Reproductive system**

Pentyl group

Pentyl is the name given to the portion of an organic molecule that is derived from pentane and has the molecular structure $-CH_2CH_2CH_2CH_2CH_3$. The pentyl group is one of the alkyl groups defined by dropping the -ane ending from the parent compound and replacing it with -yl. The pentyl group is derived from pentane ($HCH_2CH_2CH_2CH_2CH_3$) by removing one of the end hydrogens. The parent compound consists of five carbon atoms connected by single bonds (C-C) and each carbon atom is connected to a variable number of hydrogen atoms (C-H). The number of C-H bonds formed is dependent on the carbon atom's chain position, with each of the five carbon atoms having a total of four bonds. The name pentane is derived from the Greek work, *pente*, which means five. There are three other similar five carbon atom containing alkyl groups. The isopentyl group has the molecular structure of $-CH_2CH_2CH(CH_3)_2$ and is identified as a pentyl derivative that has a methyl group ($-CH_3$) branching from the end of a chain of four carbon atoms. The neopentyl group is a chain of three carbon atoms with two methyl groups attached to the end carbon atom and is represented by $-CH_2C(CH_3)_3$. Similarly, the tert-pentyl group, $-C(CH_3)_2CH_2CH_3$ is a five carbon atom alkyl group that has two carbon atoms bonded to the attaching carbon atom. Pentane is a low boiling liquid that is found in natural gas and crude oil. It can be obtained by liquefying the vapors formed from heating crude oil. Pentane and the similar five carbon atom compound, isopentane,

KEY TERMS

. . . .

Isopentyl group—an alkyl group with the molecular structure of $-CH_2CH_2CH(CH_3)_2$ and is identified as the pentyl derivative that has a methyl group ($-CH_3$) branching from the end of a chain of four carbon atoms.

Neopentyl group—a chain of three carbon atoms with two methyl groups attached to the end carbon atom and is represented by $-CH_2C(CH_3)_3$.

Pentane—the compound whose molecular structure is $CH_3CH_2CH_2CH_2CH_3$ and consists of five carbon atoms connected by single bonds (C-C) and each carbon atom is connected to enough hydrogen atoms (C-H) to have a total of four bonds each.

Pentyl group—the name given to the portion of an organic molecule that is derived from pentane and has the molecular structure - $CH_2CH_2CH_2CH_2CH_3$.

Tert-pentyl group—an alkyl group with the molecular structure of $-C(CH_3)_2CH_2CH_3$ and is identified as the five carbon atom alkyl group that has two carbon atoms bonded to the attaching carbon atom.

are both the components of gasoline. Pentane has an octane number of 62 and 93 is the octane number for isopentane. Pentane when mixed with red dye is used as the fluid in thermometers that measure very cold temperatures.

Pentyl or five carbon atom alkyl groups are also referred to as amyl groups. The term amyl is derived from the Latin word for starch, *amylum*, and is used because the five carbon atom amyl alcohols were first isolated from fermentation products. Amyl or pentyl alcohols consist of a chain of five carbon atoms with a hydroxyl group (-OH) connected to one of the carbon atoms. Each carbon atom is also connected to enough atoms resulting in each carbon atom having a total of four bonds. If the hydroxyl group is connected to the first carbon atom, the compound is called n-amyl alcohol or 1-pentanol. Sec-amyl alcohol or 2-pentanol has the hydroxyl group connected to the second carbon atom and 3-pentanol has the -OH connected to the third carbon atom. Amyl alcohols are used in the manufacture of lubricants, fragrances, flavors, solvents, and other important chemicals. For example, n-amyl alcohol is industrially converted into zinc diamyldithiophosphate and zinc diamyldithiocarbamate compounds,

which are additives of grease and motor oil since they slow the wear and deterioration of metal parts. Amyl alcohol can also be converted to amyl bromide an important chemical in the photographic industry. It can be chemically converted into the cyclic ester, octalactone. Octalactone is a synthetic coconut flavor additive of various foods and is an ingredient found in many floral smelling perfumes. Amyl salicylate, another compound prepared from amyl alcohol, is used extensively in the manufacture of perfumed soaps.

The compounds prepared from amyl alcohols are not the only commercially important compounds that contain a pentyl group. Amyl mercaptan has a thiol group (-SH) connected to a chain of five carbon atoms. Amyl mercaptan is also commonly referred to as "Pentalarm" which is added to natural gas to give it a skunk-like smell. Natural gas has no odor and without the addition of amyl mercaptan, a gas leak would be undetectable.

See also Alkyl group.

Further Reading:

Arctander, S. *Perfume and Flavor Materials of Natural Origin* New Jersey: Arctander, Elizabeth, 1960.
Kirk-Othmer, *Encyclopedia of Chemical Technology* Amyl Alcohols, Volume 2, page 709, Hydrocarbons, Volume 13, page 812, New York: John Wiley and Sons, 1991.
McMurry, J. *Organic Chemistry California*: Pacific Grove, California: Brooks/Cole Publishing Company, 1992.

Andrew Poss

Peony

The peony is an attractive flower, much beloved of gardeners. It is in the family Paeonaceae, though in the past it was in the family Ranunculaceae with other flowers such as the buttercup.

The generic name is Paeonia and there are some 50 species in this group.

The name peony comes from Paeon, a physician in Greek mythology. His teacher was jealous of his skills as a healer and intended to murder him. The gods took pity and Pluto turned him into a flower to save him from this fate. With this start it is not surprising that there is a wealth of folklore attached to these species. The plant is alleged to relieve headaches, cure convulsions, prevent nightmares, and if placed by the door of a house it will also keep all those inside safe from evil spirits. A truly miraculous and versatile plant indeed.

There are many species of peony scattered throughout the Northern Hemisphere. No wild species are native to the eastern United States, though *P. brownii* and *P. californica* are found in the western United States.

The flower color ranges from white through yellow, pink, and red to purple. Flower size is variable from 1-10 in (2.5-25.4 cm) in diameter and they are usually produced in the early spring for six to eight weeks. A couple of the larger species (such as *P. lutes*) will occasionally produce flowers in the fall as well.

The majority of species are hardy shrubs up to 5 ft (1.5 m) tall. Some of the tree growth forms will reach 10 ft (3 m). All are quite long lived—an age of 50 years is not uncommon.

All peonies are beautiful and easy to grow. They will grow outdoors in Canada and all of the United States, although they will not thrive in subtropical sections of the southern states. Peonies do not like shade or poor drainage soils and they have very few problems with disease or pests. Many hybrids are produced, both naturally and artificially.

Pepper

Pepper, one of the world's most important spices, comes from the fruit (peppercorns) of a flowering shrub, in the genus *Piper*, family Piperceaea. The pepper plant originates from India, which is still the world's largest producer of pepper. The plant grows in hot, humid regions such as India, Indonesia, Malaysia, and Brazil. The United States is the world's largest importer of pepper. At the time when Europeans were searching for new sea routes to the East, in search of spices, pepper was worth its weight in gold and was often exchanged instead of money. When a sea route around Africa's Cape of Good Hope was discovered, the price of pepper in Europe dropped dramatically.

Piper nigrum (black pepper) is the best known and most used species of pepper. This plant is a woody vine, mostly cultivated in plantations. Thick, glossy-green, ovate leaves grow alternately on the stem, opposite spikes of delicate flowers that grow in clusters. The berries that follow are the pungent fruit, or peppercorns. Black pepper is a perennial, and yields fruit when about three years old. It reaches full maturity, and produces a full crop, at seven to eight years old, and can continue to bear fruit for 20 years.

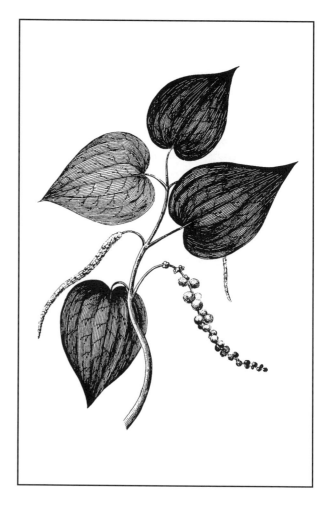

An illustration of black pepper (*Piper nigru*).

The peppercorns may be harvested at different stages of ripeness. Green peppercorns are picked before they are fully ripe, and are used fresh, pickled, or carefully dried, to retain their color. Black peppercorns, having the strongest flavor, are obtained by drying the immature, green berries in the sun until they are wrinkled and black. Berries left on the plant to fully ripen are red. The red peppercorns are soaked and peeled, producing white peppercorns. Pepper is used to flavor foods, and is considered to be a digestive stimulant.

Other species of peppers, such as *P. longum*, *P. cubeba*, and *P. guineense*, produce peppercorns that are used locally for medicinal purposes, or are made into oleoresins, essential oils, or used as an adulterant of black pepper. Berries of pepper trees from the genus *Schinus*, family Euphorbiaceae, are not true peppers, but are often combined with true peppercorns for their color, rather than their flavor. *Schinu terebinthifolius* is the source of pink peppercorns, but must be used sparingly, because they are toxic if eaten in large quantity.

Betel leaf (*P. betel*) chewing, practiced by the Malays of Malaysia and Indonesia, is as popular as cigarette smoking in that region. Chewing the leaves aids digestion, decreases perspiration, and increases physical endurance.

Pepper, chili see **Nightshade**

Peptide linkage

Proteins are made up of amino acids, which are joined by peptide linkages. Although there are only 20 different naturally occurring amino acids, various combinations of these form the thousands of proteins used in metabolism.

All amino acids have a similar structure. There is a central carbon atom, called the -carbon ("alpha-carbon") and this is bonded to an amino group on one side and a carboxyl group on the other. Also bonded to the -carbon is a side chain which is one of 20 different chemical groups and is what gives the different amino acids their unique identity and function. However, the backbone of an amino acid consists solely of the-carbon, the amino group, and the carboxyl group, and this is the same for all amino acids.

The amino group consists of a nitrogen atom bonded to two hydrogen atoms: H-N-H. The carboxyl group is a carbon bonded to an alcohol group (-OH) and double-bonded to an oxygen. This structure, O=C-OH, is called a carboxylic acid group.

Proteins are constructed from amino acids which are assembled by the formation of peptide bonds. The amino group of one amino acid bonds with the carboxyl group of another, eliminating one water molecule (HOH). The bond between the two amino acids consists of a nitrogen with one hydrogen bonded to a carbon with a double-bonded oxygen: H-N-C=O.

This simple structure, the peptide bond, is the basis to all of the enzymes and other proteins which make life possible.

See also Amino acid; Proteins.

Percent

Percent is a device for expressing hundredths. Thus P% stands for $P \times 0.01$. For example, 6% is equal to six hundredths (6×0.01, or 0.06) and 7.2% is equal to 7.2×0.01, or 0.072. As shown by these examples, to change from a percent to a number, we divide the percent figure by 100. Conversely, to convert hundredths to percent, we multiply the number by 100.

Perception

Human perception is the active reception and coordination of information received through our sensory systems in order to make sense of the environment and to behave effectively within it. In contrast with the direct and immediate sensations actually received and transmitted, perception is the transformation of that information into nerve cell activity that is transferred to the brain where further processing occurs. Our perceptual systems do not passively receive stimuli from the world, instead they actively select, organize, interpret, and sometimes distort sensory information. The real world then may not be the same as the one we perceive. Broadly, perception can be said to be the study of the human organism's relation to the physical world.

Perceptual systems

Human beings possess five basic perceptual systems. The basic orientation system informs us of the position of the body in relation to the environment through receptors sensitive to gravity, such as those in the vestibular mechanism in the inner ear. The haptic or tactual system responds to pressure and temperature sensations using the skin, muscles, and joints. The haptic system uses the kinesthetic sense (information from the muscles), and the proprioceptive sense (information from the skeletal joints). The auditory perceptual system allows us to locate the sources of sounds, and to recognize organized sound structures such as speech and melodies. What is often called the savory system combines the senses of taste and smell which are intimately related. They both respond primarily to chemical aspects of the environment. The visual system responds to light received through the eye, or more precisely, the light sensitive cells of the retina. Fully functioning visual systems perceive color, distance, depth, motion, and form.

While perception involves information coming in from all of the sense modalities, psychologists have tended to focus on visual perception. This is because many aspects of visual perception are not easily explained by sensory processes alone, they seem instead to involve more higher-level brain processing than for instance, taste, or scent perception. For the same reasons this entry emphasizes visual perception.

Historical background

Perception is studied by philosophers, physiologists, physicians, and psychologists. Physiologists and physicians focus primarily on sensation and the underlying physical processes connected to perception. Systematic thought about perception began with ancient Greek philosophers who were interested primarily in the sources and validity of human knowledge. This still active branch of philosophy, known as epistemology, explores whether a real physical world exists independent of our experience of it, and whether our perceptions are an accurate reflection of that world. Epistemologists also question whether we are born with certain innate forms of knowledge, or whether all knowledge is learned through experience.

The systematic examination of mental organizations of physical sensations falls largely within the domain of psychology. In contrast with philosophers, psychologists use scientific methods to investigate perceptual questions. Many of the questions raised by philosophers are reflected in the larger issues that are still investigated by psychologists today. These issues include how our perceptions are formed from the interaction of the physical environment and our sense organs, the accuracy of our perceptual systems in perceiving the world, and what, if any, aspects of perception reflect innate properties of the brain versus being learned through experience.

Classical perceptual phenomena

Many aspects of perception are, quite simply, amazing, often denying easy explanation based on stimulation of the sensory systems alone. The perceptual phenomena discussed below have historically been the subject of much research and they pose a continuing challenge to researchers and theoreticians in perception.

Constancy

One of the most striking aspects of perception is constancy. Constancy refers to how our perception of objects remains the same despite changes in their image on the retina. Constancy is seen in the perception of a number of different properties of objects such as size, shape, color, and orientation. We will discuss only size and shape constancies.

Size constancy refers to perceiving familiar objects as approximately the same size regardless of their distance from the observer. Thus, for example, a person's size does not appear to expand or contract as they come toward you or move away, even though their image on the retina does become larger and smaller based on their distance.

Shape constancy refers to an object's shape being perceived as remaining the same despite being viewed from different perspectives with different shapes being projected onto the retina. A circular shape such as a pie on a table for example, is still perceived as circular even when you sit down at the table and perceive it from the side. This is despite the fact that circles viewed from the side produce not circular but elliptical images on the retina.

Perceptual constancy is one of the hallmarks of the field of perception, for it strongly indicates that visual perception involves more than the direct registration of the retinal image in the brain. Without perceptual constancy the world would be perceived as a booming blur of chaotic confusion in which the sizes, shapes, and colors of objects would be constantly shifting. Thus it can be seen that perceptual constancy serves an important adaptive function.

Despite constancy's great importance and prevalence across much of visual perception, there still no widely agreed upon explanation of it. There is, however, great agreement that constancy is based in part on the observer using appropriate contextual cues in the environment. For example in size constancy it seems that in most instances we use estimates of detected distance based on various cues (for instance, haze, and a smoothing of textured surfaces such as grass are indicators of distance) to estimate an object's true size. And it seems that without cues enabling an accurate estimation of distance from an object, the perceived constancy of size ceases. For example, if one is extremely distant from objects without many intermediate visual cues enabling an accurate assessment of that distance, their perceived size would decrease. This is evident when looking at the world from a very high mountain top, or from a very tall building. From this distance, houses, cars, trees, and people below look very small, as if they were in miniature.

Perception of motion

The perception of motion has been the subject of much research. The mystery lies in how perceived movement cannot be accounted for by the movement of an object's image across the retina. If that were so, movement of the observer, or eye movement would lead to perceived object movement. For example, when riding a bike the rest of the world would be perceived as moving. Another phenomenon of motion perception that cannot be fully explained by sensory processes involves saccades which are rapid directed eye movements. Because the eye sees detail only in a small area in the center of the eye called the fovea, in order to obtain detailed information from any object or scene, the eye must perform saccades so that the fovea receives enough information. Yet the images of stationary objects do not appear to move even when their retinal image moves due to saccades.

Evidence suggests motion perception can be partially explained by our apparently automatic use of numerous specific spatial and sequential relations between stimuli. Perceived motion then depends on such factors as the change in angular direction of the object from the observer, and the relation of the object in motion to the field in which it is perceived. For example, as an object moves through space it systematically covers and uncovers the background through which it is moving. Thus if a lion is running toward you across an open grassy plain, the grass will appear to be blocked out at the lion's leading edges as he moves toward you, and the grass that was not visible behind him will become visible as he gets closer.

In addition to contextual environmental factors, specific visual receptor cells that detect different types of movement such as up and down have been discovered. Despite this knowledge, many questions about the exact mechanisms of motion perception remain unanswered.

Form perception

Form perception is what enables us to identify objects and distinguish them from each other. Rather than a loose grouping of apparently separate stimuli, we see the world as organized with interrelated objects having definite shapes and forms. And as with many other perceptual phenomena, the light projected onto the retina from objects cannot account for our visual perception of the world. It seems perceiving form involves certain organizational principles, many of which were discovered by the Gestalt school of psychology. These rules or principles illustrate our tendency to organize and group separate elements of the visual world.

In the figure-ground rule, Gestalt psychologists found that when looking at unfamiliar scenes, familiar or consistent shapes tend to stand out as figures, and unfamiliar or undifferentiated shapes are perceived as the background. So, when looking at an abstract painting in which there are very few clearly defined forms, those forms that appear familiar, or that are repeated, will tend to be perceived as standing out from the rest of the painting which is then perceived as the background for those forms.

Gestalt psychologists also described a number of perceptual grouping principles. They found that when we perceive various stimuli we tend to group them according to their similarity, or according to their closeness to one another. Another principle, that of good configuration, is a very general organizing tendency that incorporates a number of figural characteristics. These include a tendency toward closure or perceiving a whole figure when there are actually gaps in its contour, and continuation in form where smooth continuous contours tend to be perceived over uneven or irregular contours.

The perception of form can be said to result, in part, from characteristics of the nervous system, as well as learning and experience. Yet there is no single theory of form perception that can fully account for the ability to perceive form. Nor is there a general principle that can pull together the many different types of form perception.

Depth perception

This entails perceiving the three-dimensionality of the world and objects. This clearly involves more than the nature of images sent to the retina since the retina has a two dimensional surface and images projected onto it are two-dimensional.

In the 1800s researchers discovered that our binocular vision greatly aids depth perception. Binocular vision refers to having two eyes that are at slight distances from one another, so that each receives a slightly different perspective of the object or scene being focussed upon. It seems that these small differences in perspective greatly aid depth perception. The ears also use the slight differences in time between stimulation received to locate the source of sounds.

In addition, most environments have common patterns corresponding with varying distances that provide visual clues about space and depth. Such clues include blocking of a far object by a near one, increasing haze with increasing distance, perspective, and shadow.

In sum, binocular vision and environmental cues can account for many aspects of depth perception. In addition, based on research with animals and human infants too young to have had experience with depth perception, it appears that humans and various species of animals are born with some innate visual mechanism to perceive depth.

Illusions

Illusions are misperceptions of stimuli, where what is perceived does not correspond to the actual dimensions or qualities of the physical stimulus. Geometrical illusions usually involve the misperception of the direction or size of parts of figures.

The mechanisms that produce many types of illusions are as yet not understood, but they seem to involve the misapplication of perceptual phenomena like constancy. Illusions are natural, occurring regularly and following regular rules. Illusions should not be confused with hallucinations which are responses in the absence of any external stimulus, or with delusions which are basically mistaken beliefs.

Innate and learned

A theme running throughout the study of perception since the time of the ancient Greeks has been whether perceptual processes are learned or innate. Innate means existent or potential at birth due to genetic factors. Learned means that the ability is based on remembered past experience with similar or relevant stimuli.

One way to test these ideas is to examine humans or animals who from birth had no visual experience, and thus no opportunities for visual learning, and to test them when their sight is restored. Perceptual functions are then tested to see which, if any, are intact. This was done with human beings born blind because of cataracts before surgical methods were developed to safely remove them. Cataracts are a disease of the eye in which the crystalline lens or its capsule are or become opaque. It was found that after their cataracts were removed they were normally responsive to changes in color and light, but they were unable to tell when a figure was present, or to discriminate between simple shapes. It took a period of two to three months before they were able to perform these tasks with ease.

Along the same lines, research with animals deprived of visual experience from as close to birth as possible, finds that even without visual experience, some of the animals can perceive visual depth cues. Research also finds that animals raised without opportunities to see (for example if reared in the dark) sustain long-lasting deficits in their perceptual abilities. Indeed, such deprivation can even affect the weight and biochemistry of their brains.

Studies with human infants find that at even one or two days of age, they are able to perform detailed visual discriminations, and they show preferences for visually complex or novel stimuli. While this line of research cannot prove the ability is not learned, it does lend support to these abilities being present at birth in some form.

In sum, it seems that while some fundamental visual perceptual abilities are innate, visual experience is necessary to maintain and further develop them.

Broad theoretical approaches

Over the last century a number of theories have been proposed to account for perception. Each theory, however, has encountered difficulties in accounting for some of the above-discussed phenomena of perception. And most perception researchers today do not adhere to one theory, instead they believe those aspects of the theories that have some experimental support, or that seem most logical and sound.

Classical theory

What is sometimes referred to as classical theory is usually associated with Hermann von Helmholtz who believed perception results from a process of unconscious inference about what the stimulus affecting the sense organs is most likely to be. He thought these unconscious inferences are formed by past experiences and learning, and they are unconscious because people are clearly not aware of making them.

Gestalt theory

Probably the most well-known theory of perception, Gestalt theory, developed partly as a reaction against the view that perception could be broken into simpler elements and that it was the result of learned mental associations between simple sensations. This view, the basis of Helmholtz's theory, was also put forth without the process of unconscious inference by such famous psychologists as W. Wundt and E.B. Titchener. Gestalt theory, founded by K. Koffka, W. Köhler, and M. Wertheimer, argued that while simple sensations could be seen as making up organized perceptions, our nervous system is primed to perceive the organization of sensory stimuli over the individual sensory elements themselves. The process of organization is basic to perception, and the common saying "the whole is greater than the sum of its parts" illustrates this important concept.

Moreover, while Gestalt theorists believe learning may play a role in perception, perceptual organization results from innate organizing processes in the brain itself. To Gestaltists then, studying perception was in effect studying the brain.

Psychophysical or direct theory

This theory as put forth by J. J. Gibson holds that perception may be fully explained by the properties of the stimulation we receive from the world interacting with our sensory capabilities. Characteristics of scenes and events in the physical world may give sufficient information for the nervous system to be able to specify them. Thus, there is no need to posit unconscious mechanisms of inference as put forth by the Helmholtzian theory, or higher order organizations of stimuli as proposed by Gestalt theory.

Modern sensory physiology

This theory proposed by E. Hering and E. Mach believes the structure of the nervous system may fully explain at least some perceptual constancies as well as depth perception. E. Hering also proposed that there may be visual receptor cells organized into certain functional patterns that provide color sensation. And in fact these functionally patterned receptor cells have been found. These findings have strongly influenced current views of color perception, and the study of perception and sensation in general. It is still unknown however whether similarly organized receptor cells may exist for, or contribute to, perceptual phenomena such as the constancies and illusions. But their demonstrated existence may indicate that many perceived qualities of the physical world are based on such specific sensory mechanisms.

Current research/future developments

Some of the more recent theoretical and research developments fall within the areas of emotion, neuropsychology, ecological psychology, and artificial intelligence.

Emotion

Reflecting a trend across psychology as a whole, there has been a renewed and increased interest in how emotion influences perception and attention. This research investigates such questions as how emotion influences the focus and duration of attention, how quickly the emotional meaning of various stimuli can be processed, and whether individuals attend to positive and negative stimuli in different ways. Unlike most past research on perception this evolving area often researches socially meaningful perceptual stimuli, such as the perception of emotion in facial expressions and in vocal tones.

Neuropsychology

Neuropsychologists study changes in thinking due to brain injury, and use brain imaging techniques such as magnetic resonance imaging (MRI) and positron emission tomography (PET) scans, to examine the activity of the brain while performing high-level mental tasks such as problem-solving. A number of their findings have challenged explanations of perception based on behavioral studies. And improvements in brain imaging techniques hold the promise of shedding even more light on the neural basis of perception.

Ecological psychology

Ecological psychology attempts to specify the unchanging and limiting aspects of perceptual stimuli in the environment. They also stress how the nature of perceptual stimuli supports perception. This approach is most closely associated with the psychologist J.J. Gibson.

Artificial intelligence

This is an interdisciplinary field combining research and theory from cognitive psychology and computer sciences. It focuses on the development of artificial systems, such as computers, that show thinking processes similar to humans. This approach believes that for a complete explanation of perception it is necessary to divide it into three levels of analysis: 1) hardware, or its physiological aspects, 2) algorithms for operation, or what the processes of perceiving are, and 3) the theory of the task to be performed, or what are the qualities of our environment that enable perception. It is hoped that these divisions will serve as an important intellectual tool and aid our understanding of perception.

In sum, perception is a field ripe with unanswered questions that continues to fascinate researchers who may greatly benefit from new technologies and new perspectives. Indeed, recent technological advances in the measurement of eye movements (saccades) have made their study much easier for researchers interested in changes in the focus of visual attention.

See also Hearing; Smell; Taste; Touch; Vision.

Further Reading:

Masin, S.C., ed. *Foundations of Perceptual Theory.* New York: Elvesier Science, Inc., 1993.

Niedenthal, P.M. and S. Kitayama, eds. *The Heart's Eye: Emotional Influences in Perception and Attention.* New York: Academic Press, 1994.

Ono, T., ed. *Brain Mechanisms of Perception and Memory: From Neuron to Behavior.* New York: Oxford University Press, 1993.

KEY TERMS

. . . .

Constancy—A striking aspect of perception, constancy refers to how our perception of properties of objects such as size, shape, and color, remains the same despite changes in their image on the retina.

Delusions—Mistaken beliefs.

Fovea—Small area in the center of the eye that perceives detail.

Gestalt theory of perception—Holding that organization is basic to perception, discovered many rules of organization used in perceiving form.

Hallucinations—Responses in the absence of any external stimulus.

Illusions—Naturally occurring misperceptions of stimuli that follow regular rules.

Retina—An extremely light-sensitive layer of cells at the back part of the eyeball. The image formed by the lens on the retina is carried to the brain by the optic nerve.

Saccade—Rapid directed eye movement, often used to obtain detailed information about an object or scene.

Schiffman, H.R. *Sensation and Perception: An Integrated Approach*, 3rd ed. New York: John Wiley & Sons, 1990.
Sekular, R. and R. Blake. *Perception*, 3rd ed. New York: John Wiley & Sons, 1993.

Marie Doorey

Perch

Perch belong to the class Osteicthyes, whose members have a skeleton of bone rather than cartilage. Bony fish comprise the largest group of vertebrates living today, both in the number of individuals (millions) and in the number of species (about 30,000). Perch occur in both fresh water and sea water throughout the entire world. Perch live at depths in the oceans as great as 7 mi (11.5 km) and in mountain streams or lakes as much as 3 mi (5 km) above sea level.

Perch belong to Order Perciformes in the sub-class Actinapterygii, the ray-finned fish, whose fins are sup-ported by jointed rays, and which have large eyes, no internal nostrils, and a swim bladder. The Order Perciformes is the largest order of fishes, with 150 families, 1367 genera, and 7791 species. Members of this order usually bear spines on their fins, have scales with serrated edges, and a tail fin with 17 rays. The Perciformes are the most diverse of all fish orders and are dominant forms in both marine habits (75% of the species) and freshwater habits (25% of the species). Members of the order Perciformes include swordfish, tuna, mackerel, gobies, blennies, mullets, cichlids, and remoras. Two suborders (Percoidei and Gobioidei) include well over half of all species of perch. The Percoidei is the largest suborder with about 3524 species, many of which are desirable as human food-fishes, including striped bass, bluefish, snappers, barracudas, sunfishes, and perches. The family Percidae, with 9 genera and 146 species, includes all of the freshwater perches found in the northern hemisphere. Ninety percent of these species occur in North America east of the Rocky Mountains and most of these are darters. The Order Perciformes is characterized by two dorsal fins, one or two anal spines, and pelvic fins on the ventral, anterior trunk, with the base of the pelvic fin located forward of the pectoral fin. The vertebrae of perch number between 32-50; the largest species is the Walleye measuring some 90 cm (3 ft).

The genus *Perca* has three species: *Perca fluviatilis,* a Eurasian species, the yellow perch, *Perca flavescens* of North America, and *Perca shrenki* of Asia. All three species are generalized forms that probably represent the ancestral type from which the other species were derived.

The Old World counterpart of the yellow perch is the European perch, *Perca fluviatilis*. The two species are extremely similar and are separable only by minor differences; consequently, the classification of these two forms as two species or a single species is controversial.

The yellow perch is the preferred freshwater fish of many commercial fisheries in the United States. In the Great Lakes region of the United States and Canada commercial fisheries take between 5,000 and 10,000 tons of yellow perch per year from Lake Erie. This tonnage fluctuates from year to year due to fish population changes and to economic factors involved in delivering the catch to consumers. In Europe, perch are more popular as a sport fish than a commercial fish. Perch are very popular sport fish in Finland and in land-locked countries such as Switzerland. They are less popular in Great Britain and other countries with a significant salmon fishery.

See also Bony fishes.

Further Reading:

Craig, J. F. *The Biology of Perch and Related Fish*. London: Croom Helm, 1987.

Lauder, G. V., and K. F. Liem. "The Evolution and Interrelationships of the Actinopterygian Fishes." *Bull. Mus. Comp. Zool.* 150, No. 3 (1983): 96-197.

Nelson, J. S. *Fishes of the World*. 2nd ed. New York: Wiley, 1984.

ers, were found by computers. The largest of these, 756,839 yields a perfect number of 227,832 digits.

At the present time no odd perfect numbers are known. It is suspected that none exist and this hypothesis has been tested by computers up to 10^{300} but, of course, this does not constitute a proof that none exist.

The terminology of "perfect" goes back to the Greeks of Euclids time who loved to personify numbers. Thus if the sum of the divisors was less than the number, the number was called deficient. If the sum was greater than the number it was called abundant.

Further Reading:

Burton, David. *Elementary Number Theory (Third Edition)*. C. Brown Publishers, 1994.

Rosen, G. Kenneth. *Elementary Number Theory and Its Applications. (Third Edition)*. Addison-Wesley, 1993.

Roy Dubish

Perfect numbers

A perfect number is a whole number which is equal to the sum of its divisors including 1 by excluding the number itself. Thus 6 is a perfect number because 1 + 2 + 3 = 6. Likewise 28 is a perfect number because 1 + 2 + 3 + 4 + 7 + 14 = 28.

Leonard Euler (1707-1783), a mathematician born in Switzerland but who worked in Germany and Russia, proved that every even perfect number is of the form $2^{p-1} (2^p -1)$ where p is a prime and $2^p -1$ is also a prime, called a Mersenne prime in honor of Mersenne (1588-1648), a Franciscan friar who often served as an intermediary in the correspondence between the most prominent mathematicians of his time. For example, if p = 2, a prime, then $2^{p-1} = 2^2 -1 = 4$—1 = 3 is also a prime and $2^{p-1}(2^p -1) = 2 \times 3 = 6$ which, as we have seen is indeed a perfect number. If p = 3, the next prime, then $2^p -1 = 2^3 -1 = 8-1 = 7$ is again a prime. This gives us $2^2 \times 7 = 4 \times 7 = 28$ which, as we have seen, is also a perfect number. The first case where p is a prime but $2^p -1$ is not occurs when p = 11. Here we have $2^{11} -1 = 2048-1 = 23 \times 89$.

The search for even perfect numbers, then, is the same as the search for Mersenne primes. At the present time 32 are known corresponding to p = 2, 3, 7, 13,..., 756,839 where the last one, as well as some of the oth-

Periodic functions

A periodic function is a function whose values repeat at regular intervals. Given an interval of length t, and a function f, if the value of the function at x+t is equal to the value of the function at x then f is a periodic function. In standard function notation this is written f(x+t) = f(x) (read "f of x plus t equals f of x"). The shortest length t for which the function repeats is called the period of the function. The number of times a function repeats itself within a fixed space or time is called its frequency. The maximum value of the function is called the amplitude of the function. When the graphs of two functions having the same period and frequency repeat at different values of the independent variable (x), they are said to be phase shifted or out of phase, and the difference is called the phase angle.

A function may be represented by a graph, which is a picture of how the value of the function (dependent variable) changes when the independent variable changes. Some of the more common periodic functions include the sawtooth, the square wave, and the trigonometric functions (sine, cosine, and tangent) (see Figure 1).

Many natural phenomena can be understood in terms of the repeating patterns of waves. For instance, sound travels in waves, energy travels on the surface of liquids in the form of waves, light behaves like a wave,

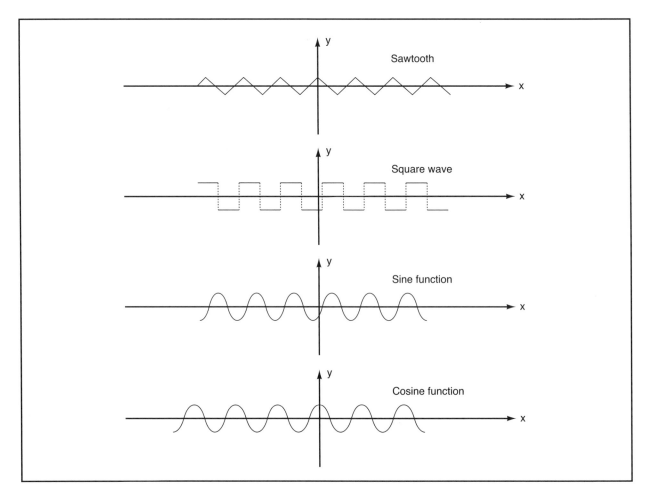

Figure 1.

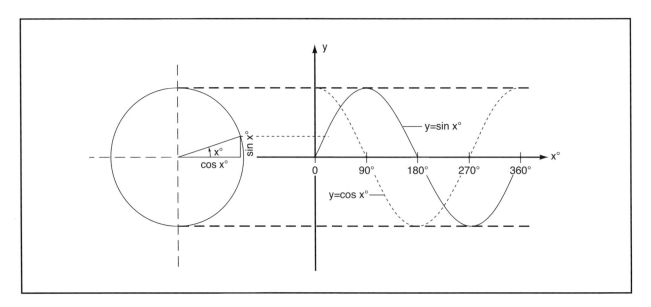

Figure 2.

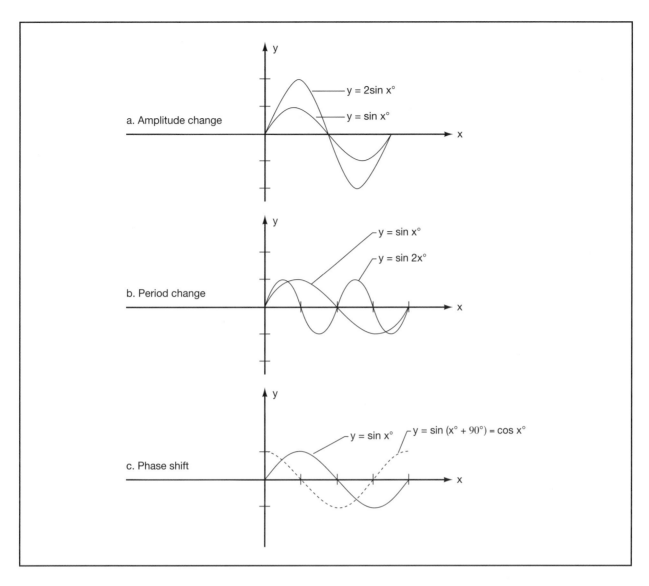

Figure 3.

radio signals travel as waves, and alternating current electricity behaves like a wave. All of these phenomena are described by periodic functions, sometimes called wave functions. The sine and cosine functions derive from the lengths of adjacent sides of a right triangle (sides that meet to form a 90° angle), and describe how the lengths of these sides change when the hypotenuse (the side of a right triangle that is opposite the 90° angle), taken to be the radius of a circle with a length of 1 unit, is rotated through 360°. Because the hypotenuse can be rotated a full 360° as many times as desired, the length of each side will repeat itself as the hypotenuse is rotated twice, then three times, then four times, and so on. The sine function (f(x) = sin x) describes how the length of the vertical side changes and the cosine func-

tion (f(x) = cos x) describes how the length of the horizontal side changes (see Figure 2).

It is interesting to see how the graphs of these functions change when the amplitude, period, and phase are changed (see Figure 3).

For both functions, the amplitude is changed by changing the radius of the circle, and the period is adjusted by multiplying the angle of rotation by a constant before determining the length of either side. Adding the value of a fixed angle to the angle of rotation before determining the length of a side, adjusts the phase. In general form, then, these functions are written f(x) = A sin (Bx + C), or f(x) = A cos (Bx + C) where x is the angle of rotation, A determines the amplitude, B determines the period, and C determines the phase.

With physical phenomena, it is often the case that the independent variable of interest is time. The period (t), then, has units of seconds, and the frequency (ω) is the inverse (1/t) of the period. The wavelength (λ) is the distance the wave travels in the time (t) that it takes to complete one period, and depends on the velocity with which the wave travels. Radio waves, for instance, travel at the speed of light (300,000 km/s). If your favorite radio station is 98.7 FM, then you can calculate the wavelength of the radio waves it broadcasts, since the call number corresponds to the frequency of the broadcast waves in MHZ (1 Hz is the equivalent of 1 cycle/s). The wavelength is given by the formula $\lambda = v/\omega$, where v is the velocity of the wave. The station at 98.7 on the FM dial is broadcasting radio waves that are approximately 9.8 ft (3 m) long.

Further Reading:

Abbot, P. and M. E. Wardle. *Teach Yourself Trigonometry.* Lincolnwood, IL: NTC Publishing, 1992.

McKeague, Charles P. *Trigonometry.* 3rd ed. Fort Worth, TX: Saunders College Publishing, 1994.

Pierce, John R. *Almost All About Waves.* Cambridge, MA: MIT Press, 1981.

Swokowski, Earl W. *Pre Calculus, Functions, and Graphs.* Boston: PWS-KENT Publishing, 1990.

J. R. Maddocks

Periodic table

The arrangement of the chemical elements into periods (horizontal rows) and groups (vertical columns) is called the periodic table. The elements in the table are represented by symbols (one, two, or three letters) in individual squares. Above each chemical symbol appears the atomic number of the element. These whole numbers are the number of protons present in the nucleus of that element. Below the element symbol appears the atomic weight which is the average weight of all the isotopes of that element. The elements are arranged in order of increasing atomic numbers. Elements of the same group are found to have similar chemical properties. The ultimate effectiveness of the periodic table is that it takes 111 individual elements and arranges them so that information about a given element is known merely by where it is found in the periodic table. The discovery that the elements could be arranged in a periodic table was made by the Russian chemist Dmitri Ivanovitch Mendeleev (1834-1907). Since its discovery in 1869 the periodic table has guided chemical research including the discovery of new elements. This ability to lead scientific inquiry over a 130 year span has contributed to the periodic table being considered one of the greatest scientific constructs. The magnitude of the scientific time span over which the periodic table has guided research is more strikingly illustrated when it is considered that it has been used from a time prior to the discovery of the light bulb till a time past the launching of the space shuttle.

Construction of the table

The discovery of the individual elements was a necessary prerequisite for the construction of the periodic table. The first pure elements have been known since the time of the Ancient Greeks who used the metallic elements gold, silver, tin, copper, lead, and mercury. The first individual credited with the discovery of an element was Hennig Brand, a German scientist who discovered the element phosphorous in 1649. There were 63 known elements in 1869, the year Mendeleev created the periodic table.

Dmitri Ivanovitch Mendeleev (1834-1907) was born in Siberia and studied chemistry at St. Petersburg Institute in Russia. He went on to become a science teacher and later a lecturer and researcher at the University of St. Petersburg. It was through his experience as a teacher that Mendeleev realized that a classification system of the known elements was needed. Earlier attempts were made at ordering the known elements,

The periodic table (Figure 1).

but they suffered from either being too simplistic or led to inconsistencies that limited their usefulness.

With the purpose of assembling the 63 known elements into an ordered system Mendeleev wrote the elements names on flash cards. The flash cards also contained the atomic weight, specific gravity, as well as other known chemical data for that element. By arranging the cards so that elements having similar chemical properties would lie under each other, the first periodic table was formed.

Mendeleev's predictions

Mendeleev came to believe in his periodic table to such a degree that he changed the atomic weights of known elements so that they fit where they "belonged" in his table. He did this with no experimental evidence, only his belief in his table. In one such case he changed the atomic weight of beryllium (Be) from 14 (which placed it in group 15 above Nitrogen) to 9. This placed it in group 2 above magnesium with which it was more closely related chemically. Even more daring Mendeleev predicted the properties of undiscovered elements. Based on gaps in the periodic table Mendeleev deduced that in these gaps belonged elements yet to be discovered. Based on other elements in the same group he predicted the existence of eka-aluminum, eka-boron, and eka-silicon (later to be named gallium, scandium, and germanium). Mendeleev predicted the atomic weight of each element along with compounds they each should form. Within fifteen years of Mendeleev's predictions these elements were discovered, and their properties were found to closely match his predictions. These fulfilled predictions went a long way to convincing any remaining doubters of the infallibility of the periodic table.

Another change Mendeleev made based on chemical analogy and intuition was placing iodine after tellurium, even though the atomic weight of iodine was less than tellurium. This anomaly along with the difficulty of where to place the inner transition metals were problems that would soon be definitively solved. At the time of the periodic tables construction little was known of atomic structure. With further scientific discoveries such as the existence of protons and the existence of electronic shells, these mysteries were explained and placed into there current places in the periodic table.

Refinement in the measurements of atomic weight, the ordering of the elements based on atomic number rather than atomic weights, and the discovery of new elements have led to the continuing evolution of the periodic table. But since Mendeleev's time the periodic table has remained basically unchanged, providing testament to the power of his original insight.

Layout of the periodic table

The first step in being able to use the information contained in the periodic table is to understand how it is arranged. Most periodic tables are similar to one another but to lessen confusion the periodic table shown in Figure 1 will be used. One of the first things that stands out is that the table is composed of metals, nonmetals, and metalloids.

The metallic elements are familiar to us all through our everyday lives. From experience we know that metals are hard, conduct heat and electricity very well (think about electrical wires and pots and pans), and can be formed into many different shapes that once formed retain their shape. The only metal that is not a solid is mercury which exists as a liquid and is often used in thermometers. The non-metal elements familiar to us include the atmospheric gases nitrogen and oxygen. But other important non-metals, especially for the maintenance of life, are carbon, hydrogen, sulfur, and phosphorus. Most nonmetals are either gases or solids and are poor conductors of heat and electricity.

The placement of metals and non-metals in the table, it should be noticed, is not random. The non-metals all occur on the right hand side of the table, while the metals occur on the left hand side. Moving across the table from metals to non-metals we encounter the metalloids which include boron, silicone, germanium, arsenic, antimony, tellurium, and astatine. The properties of mettaloids fall in-between those of metals and nonmetals. A mettaloid which should be familiar is silicon, the major material of which computer memory chips are made.

The periods of the table are numbered on the left hand side from 1 - 7. The first group contains 2 elements (hydrogen and helium) the 2nd period and 3rd period contain 8 elements, while the 4th and 5th periods contain 18 elements respectively.

The numbering of groups (the vertical columns) follows a couple different conventions both of which you should be familiar with. In the one system, commonly used in North America, Roman numerals, and letters are used to denote the various groups. The alternate system, devised by the International Union of Pure and Applied Chemistry Convention (IUPAC—the same group responsible for certifying atomic weights and element names), numbers the groups from 1 through 18. The IUPAC system is the system to which most countries are turning and this is the system used in this text.

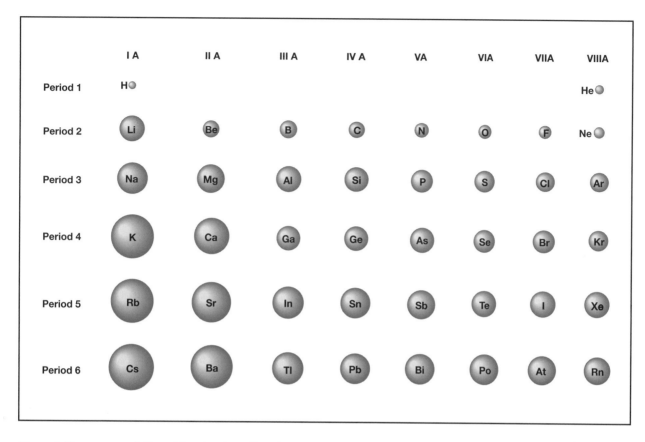

Figure 2. Size representation of the atomic radii of the main-group elements.

The alternative system numbering will be shown in parenthesis when applicable.

In both systems the various groups in the periodic table are placed into families which consist of groups of related elements. These families are given the same name in each system. Groups 1 and 2 (IA, IIA) are called the main group metals. Group 1 individually is referred to as the alkali metals while group 2 is called the alkaline earth metals. The Group 1 and 2 metals are both very reactive and readily form positive charged atoms (called cations) by losing electrons. Group 1 metals lose 1 electron to become +1 cations and Group 2 metals can lose two electrons to become +2 cations.

Groups 3 through 12 (refer to table to see alternate numberings) are referred to as the Transition metals. The Transition metal family, unlike the main group 1 and 2 metals, form cations of differing charge (many transition metal compounds are colored). Groups 13 through 18 (lllA-VlllA) are called the main group nonmetals. The inner transition metal family is comprised of lanthanides and actinides, neither of which are numbered in either system.

As briefly explained before, each box along with the symbol for the element represents an individual ele-

ment. Each element is characterized by a unique atomic number (the number that appears above the elemental symbol) which denotes the number of protons in the nucleus of that atom. One can see that the number of protons determines the element. If an atom has 6 protons in its nucleus it is a carbon atom, while 34 protons determine a selenium atom. Protons each carry a charge of +1, while electrons carry a charge of -1. Therefore, neutral elements must have equal numbers of protons and electrons.

Also contained in each box is a number that is written below each elemental symbol. This number is the atomic weight, it is the average atomic weight for a given element. It is an average because not all atoms of a given element weigh the same. While all atoms of the same element must have the same number of protons, as mentioned above, they can differ in the number of neutrons they contain in the nucleus. Neutrons, as there name implies, are neutral particles found in the nucleus that help to stabilize the nucleus in which all the protons of like positive charge are found also. Some elements have only one form, such as sodium. All sodium atoms consist of 11 protons and 12 neutrons. Atoms containing the same number of protons (and therefore the same element) but different numbers of neutrons are referred to as isotopes. For example, there are 2 isotopes of carbon. Carbon-12 has 6 protons and 6 neutrons in its nucleus and a natural abundance of 98.889%, while carbon-13 has 6 protons and 7 neutrons with a natural abundance of 1.111%. By averaging the atomic weight of each isotope of carbon, the average atomic weight of 12.01 amu (1 amu = 1.66×10^{-27} kilogram) is calculated and appears under carbon in the periodic table. It is important to note that isotopes of the same element are in most instances chemically indistinguishable.

Electronic structure

At this point it should be clear what makes one element different from another (differing numbers of protons), but what makes them similar? What allowed Mendeleev to arrange the elements into a periodic table whereby elements with similar chemistry were placed one under the other?

The last piece of atomic sub-structure needed to fully explain the arrangement of the elements of the periodic table is the electron configuration. It is the arrangement of the electrons around the nucleus that determines the degree and type of reactivity an element will exhibit. At the time that Mendeleev assembled the periodic table, electrons as well as the sub-atomic structure of the atom were yet to be discovered. Their discovery revealed the underlying principles upon which the periodic table is based.

Elements that appear in the same group have the same valence shell electron configuration. The valence shell is the outer-most shell of an atom. Shell and period are terms that are equivalent, both are used to represent energy levels of electrons within an atom. The higher the period the higher the energy of the electrons contained there. By this reasoning it is easy to see that the valence electrons in potassium (K) must be of higher energy than the valence electrons in sodium (Na). It is the electrons in the valence shell that are involved in chemical reactions. Electrons below the valence shell are considered core electrons and are not important when determining reactivity. To be able to fully use the table, subshells need to be briefly explained.

As just explained the shell is merely the period that an element is found in. Oxygen is in period 2 or shell 2, while sulfur is in shell 3. Each of the families of elements belong to a particular subshell. We won't go into detail on the physical meaning of subshells, we only need to know that the valence electrons of the main group metals (groups 1 and 2) are in the s subshell. The valence electrons of the main group non-metals (groups

13 through 18) are in the p subshells, the transition metal electrons are in the d subshells, while the inner transition metals are the f subshells. The energy of the subshells increases, within the same shell, from s, then p, then d, and finally f.

The s subshell can hold 2 electrons, the p subshells hold 6 electrons, the d subshells hold 10 electrons, and the f subshells hold 14 electrons. There can only be 2 electrons per subshell, therefore there is only 1 s subshell, 3 p subshells, 5 d subshells, and 7 f subshells.

To illustrate how these electronic properties are relevant to the periodic table lets look at the first 3 elements of group 16, oxygen, sulfur, and selenium. Each of these elements has a valence shell electron configuration of s^2p^4. So although they are each in different periods their electronic structure is the same and we expect them to have similar chemistry. We are all familiar with the compound water which has the formula H_2O. Likewise there are the compounds H_2S and H_2Se. In a similar fashion, if one is told that the group 15 element nitrogen, with the valence shell electronic configuration s^2p^3, forms the compound NH_3 (called ammonia), can you infer the formula of the compound that forms between phosphorus and hydrogen? By analogy to NH_3 we expect the compound to have the formula PH_3. It is by this same type of reasoning that Mendeleev predicted the existence of the unknown elements.

Group 18 in the periodic table, called the noble gases, are all very unreactive elements. They do not easily combine, if at all, with other elements. This indicates that there is some special stability to the electron configuration s^2p^6 which the noble gases possess. When an element has the full shell configuration s^2p^6 it is referred to as having an octet. Much of the reactivity of the elements can be described as an attempt to achieve an octet.

In the ionic compound sodium chloride (NaCl) we find a positively charged sodium atom (Na^+) and a negatively charged chlorine atom (Cl^-). If we look at the valence shell electron configuration of each ion we can see that a chlorine atom, by gaining an extra electron, goes from a s^2p^5 (group 17) configuration to the stable s^2p^6 (group 18) configuration of the chloride ion. The chloride ion is referred to as being isoelectronic (having the same electronic configuration) as argon. The sodium atom (s^1) can lose an electron to become a sodium cation with the stable s^2p^6 configuration, making it isoelectronic with neon.

Other trends

There are general reactivity trends that are useful to know. Metals and non-metals usually combine to form ionic compounds with the metal giving up an electron to become positively charged and the non-metal element gaining an electron to become negatively charged. Non-metals usually combine with one another to form covalent bonds in which the electrons are not fully transferred but are shared between the two elements. Examples of this are molecular oxygen O_2, molecular chlorine Cl_2, ammonia NH_3, and carbon dioxide CO_2.

The degree of metallic character of an element can be estimated by that element's location in the periodic table. Metallic character decreases moving from left to right across a period. This is clearly demonstrated in each of the first six periods where each period starts off with metallic elements, but ends with non-metallic elements. Metallic character is also found to increase moving down a group. This trend is most clearly demonstrated by groups 14-16, although it is true for the other groups as well (i.e., cesium is more metallic than sodium) Each of the groups 14-17 begins with a non-metal followed closely by a metalloid and eventually a metallic element.

Another trend that the periodic table orders is size. The atomic radii (the scientific term for the size of an atom) of the elements increases going down a group, while it decreases going across a period. See Figure 2.

In the periodic table, the last naturally occurring element is uranium (element 92). Uranium is a radioactive element. Radioactive elements are unstable and breakdown to form lighter elements and in the process give off energy. All of the elements that occur past uranium are manmade, and are referred to collectively as the transuranium elements.

Recent and future research

While the general form of the periodic table has withstood the test of time and should change very little in the future, alterations of the periodic table have been and continue to be made. One area that could see minor changes is the atomic weights. In the future more accurate ways to measure the weights of atoms may be invented. The magnitude of these changes though would be exceedingly small.

The largest area of change in the periodic table will come from the man-made creation of new chemical elements. Every element past uranium in the periodic table has been made by scientists in high energy particle accelerators. The first transuranium element made was element 93, discovered by E. M. Macmillan and P. H. Abelam at the University of California at Berkeley in 1940. The two discoverers of this element named it neptunium.

The discovery of elements 95 and 96 caused a dilemma. It was thought that these new elements should be placed after actinium (element 89) in the d-block transition metal family. Glenn T. Seaborg, Nobel Prize winner in 1951 for the discovery of plutonium as well as nine other transuranium elements, felt that they should be placed under the lanthanides in a new group as part of the inner transition metal family. Further experimentation showed that they did belong in the inner transition metal family. The discovery of elements 104-111, which belong in the transition metals family, proved that the proposed groupings were correct.

Unlike most of the naturally occurring elements which can be handled and studied, the transuranium elements are all radioactive and breakdown incredibly fast. The synthesis and detection of transuranium elements takes great technical expertise. In addition the experimental machinery needed to do this work is extremely expensive as well as complicated, therefore only a few research centers in the world are involved in this area of study.

The transuranium elements are synthesized by colliding accelerated charged particles with heavy atoms (i.e., curium and lead). In certain collisions the nuclei of the accelerated charged particles and the stationary heavy atoms will fuse to produce a new transuranium element. The lifetimes of these new elements is so short that they often breakdown into other elements within fractions of a second and are detected only by their breakdown products, referred to as daughter elements.

The last elements known to date are 110 and 111, both were made in late 1994 by an international team of scientists. These scientists did this research at GSI, a research center for heavy ion research in Darmstadt, Germany. Element 110 was made by colliding nickel atoms with an isotope of lead. Researchers in Russia have plans to make a different isotope of element 110 by colliding sulfur atoms with plutonium atoms.

Based on theoretical calculations some researchers believe that not all transurannium elements will be so unstable. Already different isotopes of element 106 have been made that are stable for up 33 times longer than the original isotope discovered in 1974 (even at 33 times longer lifetime it only is stable for a maximum of thirty seconds). It is theorized that some isotopes of the yet to be made transuranium elements should be stable for very long periods of time, allowing them to be studied chemically. Many exciting discoveries remain to be uncovered concerning the creation of new elements, and with the periodic table as a guide their place is already awaiting them.

Names of the elements

The naming and symbol of the elements in the periodic table is an interesting story itself. Many of the element symbols are derived from the elemental name such hydrogen (H), oxygen (O), chlorine (Cl), and calcium (Ca). Other element symbols seem to bear no relationship to their name such as sodium (Na), tin (Sn), and lead (Pb). These elemental symbols all derive from the Latin name of the element: natrium, stannum, and plumbum. Many of the elements have been named by their discoverer and this convention holds today.

The element phosphorus was named by its discoverer for the property that it glows when exposed to air. Phosphorous in Greek means "I bear light." From the names of the elements such as francium, americium, europium, berkelium and californium it is clear that geographic locations were used to name them. Still other elements have been named to honor people. In this category falls element 101, mendelevium, named to honor the discoverer of the periodic table. Others in this category include einsteinium and nobelium, named after Albert Einstein and Alfred Nobel.

At this time to name an element a researcher or team of researchers must be certified by IUPAC as the discoverers of that element, at which time they are free to name the compound. Currently elements 104-109 are subject to a naming controversy. In the Periodic Table elements 104-109 appear under temporary names. The proposed names of these elements by IUPAC are in order dubnium, joliotium, rutherfordium, bohrium, hahnium, and meiterium. These names are provisional and will probably be subject to change.

A particular controversy among these involves element 106 which researchers at Berkeley were credited with discovering by IUPAC. Following historical convention the Berkeley researchers were free to name the element. They chose to name it seaborgium, after Glenn T. Seaborg who contributed to the element's discovery. But IUPAC ignored the recommendations of the discoverers and suggested the name rutherfordium for element 106. The controversy has yet to be resolved, although the name seaborgium is recognized as the official name in the United States. A vote of the IUPAC Council is scheduled for August 1995 to resolve the issue.

As a final testament to the great respect with which the periodic table is held, it is instructive to hear Glenn T. Seaborg talk about the significance of having his name assigned to element 106: "A thousand years from now, seaborgium will still be in the periodic table, whereas the twentieth-century Nobel Prize-winners will seem a very small part of history... This honor will last as long as civilization."

KEY TERMS

Anion—A negative ion (i.e., Cl⁻)

Atomic number—The number of protons in the nucleus of an atom. The number that appears over the element symbol in the periodic table.

Atomic weight—The average weight of all isotopes of a given element, expressed in amu (1amu = 1.66×10^{-27} kilogram).

Cation—A positive ion (i.e., Na⁺).

Covalent bond—A bond formed by the sharing of electrons between atoms.

Electron—Subatomic particle of -1 charge found outside of nucleus.

Electron configuration—The arrangement of electrons in subshells in an atom.

Element—A pure substance that can not be changed chemically into a simpler substance.

Family—A set of groups characterized by the same subshell.

Group—A vertical column of the periodic table that contains elements possessing the same electronic configuration.

Ionic bond—A bond formed between anions and cations.

Isotope—Atoms with the same number of protons but differing numbers of neutrons.

Neutron—A subatomic particle with no electric charge.

Nucleus—Small core at the center of atoms that contain the protons and neutrons.

Octet (noble gas configuration)—The stable electron configuration found with group 18 elements, also referred to as the closed shell configuration.

Period—Horizontal rows of the periodic table.

Proton—Subatomic particle of +1 charge.

Shell—Energy level within an atom. The period of an element determines the shell number.

Subshell—Further energy levels found within a given shell. Elements in the same family share the same subshell.

Transuranium—Term given to all the manmade elements of greater atomic number than 92.

See also Atom; Atomic number; Atomic weight; Element, chemical; Elements, families of; Subatomic particles; Valence.

Further Reading:

Brock, William H. *The Norton History of Chemistry.* New York: W.W. Norton & Company Inc., 1992.

Hoffmann, Roald and Torrence, Vivian. *Chemistry Imagined Reflections on Science.* Washington: Smithsonian Institutional Press, 1993.

Naeye, Robert. "An Island of Stability." *Discover.* (August 1994): 15.

Roberts, Royston M. *Serendipity Accidental Discoveries in Science.* New York: John wiley & Sons Inc., 1989.

Michael G. Roepel

Permutations see **Combinatorics**

Perpendicular

Perpendicular is a term describing two lines or planes in a plane or three lines or planes in space that meet so that all angles formed are the maximum possible. This results in what is termed a 90° angle between lines or planes. Sometimes the term *orthogonal* is used with the same meaning, although orthogonal is also used outside of geometry; perpendicular is not.

Illustration

The angle (θ) between the horizontal (L_H) and the vertical (L_V) lines and planes (P_H) and (P_V) is 90°. The two lines or two planes are perpendicular as shown in Figure 1.

Drawing, construction

The way to construct a line perpendicular to any given line (L) at any given point (P) is illustrated in Figure 2.

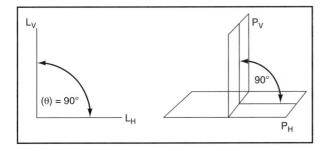

Figure 1.

The arm of this crane is perpendicular to its support.

First measure equal distances both to the left (L_L) and to the right (L_R) of point P with a compass. Then find the intercept X of those equal lengths (L_L and L_R). The line that connects point P to intercept X is perpendicular to the original line L.

Analogies

Nature and the home surroundings are filled with perpendicular lines. Like trees grow perpendicular to the surface plane of the soil in which they were planted, most creatures "great or small" are perpendicular to ground in walking position. Towers (with the exception of Pisa's slanted tower in Italy) stand perpendicular to the plain ground, as perfect walls are perpendicular to the floor in buildings.

Jeanette Vass

Persimmon tree see **Ebony**

Pertussis see **Whooping cough**

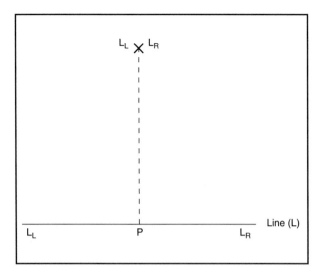

Figure 2.

Pesticides

A pesticide is any substance that is used by humans to gain some advantage in their continuous struggle with various types of pests. In the sense used here, a pest is any plant, animal, or microorganism that is considered to be undesirable, from the human perspective. As such, pests include: (1) microorganisms and other pathogens that cause diseases, (2) insects that are the vectors of disease-causing pathogens, (3) weeds that compete with crop plants for water and nutrients, and (4) the many types of fungi, insects, mites, rodents, and even birds that cause losses of the economic values of crop plants and/or domestic animals. The abundance and impact of almost all of these pests can be managed through the judicious use of pesticides.

Consequently, there are some very important benefits of the use of pesticides, including: (1) increased yields of food and fibre crops, because they can be protected from diseases, competition from weeds, defoliation by insects, and parasitism by nematodes; (2) prevention of spoilage of stored foods; and (3) prevention of illnesses and saving of the lives of humans and domestic animals through the control of certain diseases.

However, the considerable benefits of pesticide use are partly offset by important damages that are caused. In some cases, humans have been poisoned by accidental exposures to toxic pesticides. More commonly, however, ecological damages may be caused by pesticide use, sometimes resulting in the deaths of large numbers of wildlife.

In this entry, the nature of pesticides and their uses will be described, followed by several cases of environmental damages that have been caused by their use.

Classification of pesticides by target

Pesticides can be catalogued according to the pest that is their intended target, as follows: (1) insecticides are used to kill insects that defoliate plants, or that are the vectors (that is, means of transmission) of deadly diseases of humans, such as malaria, yellow fever, plague, and typhus; (2) herbicides are used to kill weeds, in order to release desired crop plants from the deleterious effects of competition, and thereby increase the yield of agricultural harvests; (3) fungicides are used to protect agricultural plants from fungal pathogens, which in some cases can cause complete failures of crops; (4) acaricides are used to kill mites, which are pests in agriculture, and ticks, which can carry encephalitis and other debilitating diseases of humans and domestic animals; (5) molluscicides are used against snails and slugs, which can be important pests of agriculture. In some aquatic systems, molluscs are the vector of human diseases, such as schistosomiasis; (6) nematicides are used to kill nematodes, which are important parasites of the roots of some crop species; (7) rodenticides are used to control rats, mice, gophers, and other rodent pests of human habitation and agriculture; (8) avicides are used to kill birds, which can sometimes depredate agricultural fields; (9) preservatives are used to protect wood and fabrics from decay-causing organisms, especially fungi; and (10) antibiotics are used to treat bacterial infections of humans and domestic animals.

Uses of pesticides

The most important uses of pesticides are to prevent diseases of humans, and to increase yields in agriculture and forestry. These major usages are described below.

Human health

In some parts of the world, insects and ticks are important vectors in the transmission of deadly diseases of humans. The most important of these diseases and their arthropod vectors are: (1) malaria, which is caused by the protozoan *Plasmodium*, and spread to humans by mosquitoes in the genus *Anopheles*; (2) yellow fever and similar viral diseases such as encephalitis, also spread by mosquitoes; (3) trypanosomiasis or sleeping sickness, caused by the protozoan *Trypanosoma* and spread by the tsetse fly *Glossina*; (4) plague or black death, caused by the bacterium *Pasteurella pestis* and transmitted to people by the flea *Xenopsylla cheops*, a

The great horned owl preys on the tern

The tern feeds on small fish

The bald eagle and peregrine falcon prey on ducks

Precipitation

Insect sprayer

Pesticide contaminated species are harvested by humans

Due to pesticide contaminantion fewer ducklings will hatch

Aquatic contamination

Zooplankton become contaminated

Large predatory fish feed on smaller fish

Ducks become contaminated from feeding on plants and small fish

Small fish feed on plants and plankton

Plants take up contaminants through their roots

The path of pesticides through the environment.

parasite of rats that lives in association with humans; and (5) typhoid fever, caused by the bacterium *Rickettsia prowazeki*, and transmitted to humans by the body louse *Pediculus humanus*.

The incidences of these diseases can be greatly reduced by using pesticides to reduce the abundance of their vectors. For example, the populations of mosquito vectors can be reduced by applying an insecticide to

their aquatic breeding habitat, or by applying a persistent insecticide to the walls and ceilings of buildings, where these insects tend to rest. Insecticides have been quite successfully used to achieve reductions of the incidence of malaria in the tropics. However, in some regions this disease is re-emerging, because mosquitoes have evolved tolerance to some of the commonly used insecticides, and because the *Plasmodium* parasite has become tolerant of drugs.

Agriculture

Modern, technological agriculture uses pesticides in large amounts to control weeds, arthropod pests, and plant diseases, all of which can cause important losses of crops. In agriculture, arthropod pests are regarded as competitors with humans for a common food resource. In severe cases defoliation by arthropods can cause complete failures of agricultural yield, as is the case of acute infestations of locusts. More usually, however, defoliation only reduces crop yields, although this can be economically important. In some cases, insects might only cause trivial damages in terms of reduced yield, but the cosmetic damages that are caused can reduce the economic value of some crops. For example, larvae of codling moth (*Carpocapsa pomonella*) consume little of the apple fruit that they infest, but the aesthetic damages that they cause can render the produce unusable for human consumption.

Weeds are considered to be any plants that interfere with the productivity of crop plants, by competing for limited supplies of light, water, and nutrients. To reduce the effects of weeds on crop productivity, fields may be sprayed with a herbicide that is toxic to the weeds, but not to the crop plant. For example, the herbicide 2,4-D is toxic to many angiosperm (that is, broad-leaved) weeds, but not to members of the grass family. Consequently, fields of maize, wheat, barley, rice, and other agricultural grasses are often treated with herbicides such as 2,4-D to achieve reductions of weed populations.

Pesticides can also be used to control some important diseases of agricultural plants. For example, some major fungal diseases of crop plants can be managed with fungicides, including late blight of potato (caused by *Phytophthora infestans*), apple scab (*Venturia inequalis*), and *Pythium*-caused seed-rot, damping-off, and root-rot of many agricultural species.

Forestry

In forestry, pesticides are mostly used for the reduction of weeds in plantations, and to control defoliation by epidemic populations of insects. Most herbicide use in forestry is intended to release desired conifer species from the deleterious effects of competition with broad-leaved herbs and shrubs. Insecticide use is mostly aimed to controlling insect infestations that can kill trees over large areas, particularly spruce budworm (*Choristoneura fumiferana*) and gypsy moth (*Lymantria dispar*). In almost all regions, the quantities of pesticide used in forestry are much smaller than in agriculture.

Other uses

Large quantities of pesticides are also used in homes, and in urban areas more generally. For example, large quantities of insecticides are used to kill insects such as cockroaches and termites in homes, and rodenticides are used to kill rats and mice. To cultivate aesthetically pleasing, grassy lawns, broad-leaved weeds are controlled using herbicides, and insecticides may be used to kill pest insects and nematodes. Golf courses are especially intense users of pesticides, especially on putting greens where the quality of the lawn must be very consistent. On a per-unit area basis, the use of pesticides on golf-course putting greens exceeds that of almost any usages in agriculture.

Quantities used

The global use of all pesticides is about 2.5-2.9 million tons per year (this total includes "conventional" pesticides such as insecticides, herbicides, and fungicides, as well as preservatives and disinfectants). In the early-1990s, the value of these chemicals ran about $20 billion dollars in the United States.

The United States uses more pesticides than any other country, as much as one-third of global use. In 1989, the domestic use of conventional pesticides in the U.S. was about 500 million kg. Domestic U.S. production of pesticides was 591 million kg, imports were 90 million kg, and exports 180 million kg. Another 455 million kg of preservatives and disinfectants were used in the U.S. in 1989.

Herbicides accounted for about 61% of the total quantity of pesticides used in the U.S., insecticides 21%, fungicides 10%, and all others 7%. The ten most commonly used pesticides in the U.S. in recently years are: alachlor (a herbicide, 45 million kg), atrazine (herbicide, 45 million kg), 2,4-D (herbicide, 24 million kg), butylate (herbicide, 20 million kg), metolachlor (herbicide, 20 million kg), trifluralin (herbicide, 14 million kg), cynazine (herbicide, 9.2 million kg), malathion (insecticide, 6.9 million kg), metribuzin (herbicide, 6.0 million kg), and carbaryl (insecticide, 5.6 million kg).

Chemical classification of pesticides

Pesticides can also be classified according to the similarities of their chemical structures. The most important groups of pesticides are the following:

Inorganic pesticides

Inorganic pesticides are based on toxic elements, especially compounds of arsenic, copper, lead, and mercury. For example, Bordeaux mixture is a complex pesticide with several copper-based active ingredients, and used as a fungicide for fruit and vegetable crops. Various arsenicals are used as non-selective herbicides and soil sterilants, and sometimes as insecticides.

Organic pesticides

Organic pesticides are a very diverse group of chemicals. Some active ingredients are produced naturally by plants, but most organic pesticides have been synthesized by chemists. Prominent classes of organic pesticides are:

(a) Natural organic pesticides that are extracted from plants, such as insecticides based on the alkaloid nicotine, which is extracted from tobacco and often applied as the salt nicotine sulfate. Another naturally derived insecticide is pyrethrum, a complex of chemicals extracted from a species of marigold (*Chrysanthemum cinerariaefolium*), related to the daisy.

(b) Synthetic organo-metallic fungicides such as the organomercurials, including phenylmercuric acetate and methylmercury.

(c) Phenols used as fungicides in the preservation of wood, for example pentachlorophenol.

(d) Chlorinated hydrocarbons, such as the insecticides DDT, DDD, dieldrin, and methoxychlor. DDE is a related non-insecticidal chemical, but it is an important metabolic-breakdown product of DDT. Residues of DDT and its chemical relatives are persistent in the environment, typically having a half-life of about 10 years in soil. Their persistence, and their selective partitioning into lipids such as animal fats, has caused a general bioaccumulation of chlorinated hydrocarbons, especially in predatory birds and mammals at the top of ecological food webs. The chlorophenoxy acid herbicides, such as 2,4-D and 2,4,5-T, are much less persistent, and are selective for broadleaved weeds.

(e) Organophosphorus pesticides are a diverse group of chemicals, most of which are used as insecticides or nematicides. Most of these chemicals have a high acute toxicity to arthropods but a short environmental persistence. Some organophosphate insecticides are very toxic to non-target organisms such as fish, birds, and mammals. Some prominent examples of organophosphate insecticides are fenitrothion, malathion, parathion, and phosphamidon. Glyphosate, an important organophosphorus herbicide, is not very toxic to animals.

(f) Carbamate pesticides generally have a high acute toxicity to arthropods, but a moderate environmental persistence. Important examples of carbamate pesticides are aminocarb, carbofuran, and carbaryl.

(g) Triazine herbicides are mostly used in corn monoculture. Examples are atrazine, hexazinone, and simazine.

(h) Synthetic pyrethroids are mostly used as insecticides in agriculture. Most synthetic pyrethroids are highly toxic to fish and invertebrates, of variable toxicity to mammals, and of relatively low toxicity to birds. Prominent examples are cypermethrin, deltamethrin, permethrin, synthetic pyrethrum and pyrethrins, and tetramethrin.

Biological pesticides

Biological pesticides are based on bacteria, fungi, and viruses that are toxic to pests. The most widely used biological insecticide is manufactured from spores of the bacterium *Bacillus thuringiensis*, or B.t. Formulations based on B.t. are relatively specific against leaf-eating moths and biting flies, such as blackflies and mosquitoes. Consequently, the non-target effects of B.t. are smaller than that of many other insecticides.

Toxicity to humans

Unfortunately, the use of pesticides results in some toxic exposures to humans. Each year, an estimated one-million pesticide poisonings occur globally, resulting in 20 thousand fatalities. However, even though less-developed countries account for about 20% of global pesticide use, they sustain about 1/2 of the human poisonings. This occurs because these countries generally have greater illiteracy, relatively lax enforcement of regulations regarding pesticide use, and inadequate availabilities of protective equipment and washing facilities for pesticide users. There have been a few incidents of widespread toxicity to humans, as occurred at Bhopal, India in 1984, where more than 2800 people were killed and more than 20 thousand seriously injured by an accidental emission (about 40 tonnes) of poisonous methyl isocyanate vapor, a chemical used to manufacture an agricultural insecticide.

Environmental effects of pesticide use

The intended result of any pesticide application is to reduce the abundance of a pest species to below an economically acceptable level. In some situations this objective can be selectively attained, without causing important non-target damages. For example, the careful use of a rodenticide in the home can result in a selective kill of rats and mice, while minimizing (but never eliminating) risks to non-target mammals, such as cats, dogs, and children. However, during most uses of pesticides in agriculture and forestry, exposures are complex and not very well controlled. Consequently, whenever a pesticide is broadcast sprayed over a field or forest, many non-target organisms are exposed to the chemical on the treated site. In addition, some of the sprayed pesticide invariably drifts away from its intended site of deposition, so that off-site, non-target organisms and ecosystems are exposed.

One ecologically important problem is a widespread environmental contamination with persistent pesticides, including the occurrence of chemical residues in wildlife, in well-waters, in foods, and even in humans. Ecological damages have included the poisoning of wildlife by some pesticides, and the disruption of ecological processes such as productivity and nutrient cycling. The ecological importance of damages caused to non-target organisms depends partly on their role in maintaining the integrity and functioning of their ecosystem. From the human perspective, however, the importance of non-target effects of pesticides is also influenced by specific economic and aesthetic considerations.

Many of the worst cases of environmental damages caused by pesticides were associated with the use of relatively persistent chemicals such as DDT; most modern pesticide usage generally involves less-persistent chemicals. However, the global use of pesticides is expanding in scale and intensity, and although a great deal is known about some of the environmental consequences of this technological activity, not all of the potential ecological effects are understood.

Perhaps the best known examples of ecological damages caused by pesticide use concern the effects of DDT and related organochlorine insecticides on birds, marine mammals, and other wildlife. For example, these chemicals are known to accumulate to large concentrations in predatory birds, affecting their reproduction, and sometimes killing adults. There have been widely publicized collapses of populations on local and/or regional scales of peregrine falcon, bald eagle, brown pelican, western grebe, and other predatory birds. The detrimental effects on birds and other wildlife, along with the discovery of widespread occurrences of chlorinated hydrocarbons in human tissues, led to the banning of the use of DDT in most industrialized countries in the early 1970s. However, mostly because they are so effective in controlling the arthropod vectors of human diseases, DDT and related insecticides are still manufactured and used in many tropical countries.

Some of the pesticides that replaced DDT and its organochlorine relatives also cause damages to wildlife. For example, carbofuran, a commonly used agricultural

KEY TERMS

Active ingredient—Within a pesticidal formulation, the particular chemical that actually causes toxicity to the pest. The formulation also contains nonpesticidal chemicals, the so-called inert ingredients. These are used to dilute the active ingredient, to improve its spread or adherence on foliar surfaces, and to otherwise increase the efficacy of the formulation.

Acute toxicity—A poisonous effect caused by a single, short-term exposure to a toxic chemical, and resulting in biochemical or anatomical damages, or even death of the organism.

Drift—The off-site occurrence or deposition of a pesticide spray.

Nontarget effects—Effects on organisms other than the intended pest target of pesticide spraying.

Pest—An organism that is considered to be undesirable, from the perspective of humans.

Persistence—The length of time that a pesticide occurs in a component of the environment; for example, in soil. Persistence can be influenced by the rate of chemical breakdown, and by mass-transport processes such as volatilization, erosion of pesticide-containing particles, or the flushing of water in streams or ponds.

Residues—The quantity of a pesticide that remains in the environment after application. Residues disappear at various rates, depending on their persistence.

insecticide, has killed thousands of waterfowl and other birds that feed in treated fields. Similarly, use of the insecticides phosphamidon and fenitrothion to kill spruce budworm in forests in New Brunswick, Canada, has killed an untold number of bird species.

These and other environmental effects of pesticide use are highly regrettable consequences of the broadcast spraying of these toxic chemicals in order to cope with problems of pest management. Similarly effective alternatives to most uses of pesticides have not yet been discovered for most pest-control problems, although this is a vigorously active field of research. Researchers are becoming increasingly successful in the discovery of pest-specific methods of control that cause little non-target damage, and in developing effective methods of integrated pest management that do not rely solely on pesticides. So far, however, not all pest problems can be dealt with in these ways, and our society will continue to use pesticides to prevent diseases of humans and domestic animals, and to protect agricultural and forestry crops from weeds, diseases, and other losses caused by economically important pests.

See also Biomagnification; DDT; Fungicide; Herbicides; Integrated pest management; Organic farming.

Further Reading:

Briggs, S. A. *Basic Guide to Pesticides: Their Characteristics and Hazards.* Washington, D.C.: Taylor & Francis, 1992.

Freedman, B. *Environmental Ecology.* 2nd ed. San Diego: Academic Press, 1994.

Hayes, W. J. and E. R. Laws (eds.). *Handbook of Pesticide Toxicology.* San Diego: Academic Press, 1991.

Pimentel, D., et al. "Environmental and Economic Costs of Pesticide Use." *Bioscience* 41 (1992): 402-409.

Bill Freedman

Pests

Pests are any organisms that are considered, from the perspective of humans, to be undesirable in some ecological context. For example, pests could be insects that compete with humans for some common resource, such as agricultural production or timber. Other pests might be associated with diseases of humans, livestock, or agricultural plants. Pests could also be unwanted weeds that compete with desired agricultural plants for necessary resources. Or pests may merely have aesthetics that are viewed as undesirable, as is the case of weeds in lawns.

When pests are abundant enough to cause damages that are considered to be unacceptable, the abundance of the pests may be managed in some way. For example, if wolves are considered to be an important predator of livestock or wild ungulates, they may be killed by shooting them or by using poisons. The most important reason for plowing in agriculture is to reduce the abundance of weeds. Often pesticides are used, for example to protect crops and livestock from diseases and depredations by fungi, insects, mites, nematodes, and rodents, to protect crop plants from competition with weeds, or to protect humans against the insect vectors of disease-causing pathogens. There are substantial benefits to humans of the use of most pest-management strategies.

It is important to understand, however, that the very species that are considered to be pests may have desirable attributes in other contexts, or their values may at least be neutral. Therefore, whether an organism is viewed as a pest is entirely a matter of judgement, and the criteria generally focus on the needs and perspectives of humans is an anthropocentric viewpoint.

The notion of contextually varying merits of organisms can be illustrated by considering the case of plant pests, or so-called weeds. Weeds can be defined as any plant that interferes with the productivity of a desired crop plant, or with some other human purpose. Weeds can severely decrease the productivity of crop plants by competing with them for light, water, nutrients, and more broadly, space. Many studies in agriculture and forestry have demonstrated that weeds can significantly reduce the production of crops. For example, on unweeded plots in Illinois there was an average reduction of yield of corn of 81%, and a 51% decrease was observed in Minnesota. Weeds can also reduce the yields of wheat and barley, typically by 25-50%. Weeds similarly cause decreased yields of other agricultural plants, and they can also be important in forestry, where they may interfere with the growth of desired species of trees.

However, sometimes a particular species is a weed, and sometimes it is not. Consider, for example, the case of the red raspberry (*Rubus strigosus*). This species is considered to be an important weed in forestry in parts of North America, because it can quickly overtop young conifer plants and interfere with their growth. This reduces the length of time it takes until the next crop of trees is large enough to harvest from the site. Because its competition with conifers can be interpreted in terms of substantial economic damages, the red raspberry is considered to be an important silvicultural weed, and its abundance may be managed using herbicides or manual weeding treatments. However, this same species can produce tasty fruits in large quantities on the same site on which it is regarded, from the forestry perspective, to be a pest. The raspberry fruits can be beneficial as food to humans and to wild animals. The lush growth of red raspberry also helps to quickly restore improved aesthetics to recently harvested forests, and the plant helps to reduce erosion and nutrient leaching from disturbed sites. In any event, the red raspberry has intrinsic value, regardless of any perceptions of its worth by humans. There are many other examples that demonstrate the fact that pests are only considered as such in certain contexts, and from certain perspectives.

See also Herbicides; Pesticides.

Southern giant petrels (*Macronectes giganteus*).

Petal see **Flower**

Petrels and shearwaters

Petrels and shearwaters are wide-ranging oceanic birds with a characteristic tubenose and other specialized features which equip them well for a life spent mostly at sea. Found throughout the world, these long-lived colonial nesting seabirds include some 79 species in four families, all in the Order Procelliformes. These seabirds show a great range in body size from the giant petrel, with a 6 ft (2 m) wing span to the robin-sized diving petrel; however, they are all fairly uniform in color, either all dark, or dark and light. The sexes are externally alike. While several species are globally endangered and a number of others quite rare, a majority are numerous and thriving.

Distribution

Most petrels and shearwaters nest on isolated islands in the southern oceans, some as far south as Antarctica. Several species, however, breed in Hawaii, northwestern United States (including Alaska), Maine, and Canada. These birds frequently range far from their birthplaces, covering thousands of miles in an endless search for food. The greater shearwater, for example, nests on the Tristan da Cunha islands in the South Atlantic Ocean but may be found in the North Atlantic coast from Florida to Newfoundland during the northern summer. Other species may spend months circumnavigating the Pacific.

Life History

Breeding in these seabirds occurs when an individual reaches sexual maturity, usually between three and seven years. After an elaborate courtship and mating, a single white egg is laid, usually in a burrow or crevice, although some of the larger members of this group lay eggs on bare ground. Adult birds show long term fidelity to their mates, and to their nest sites.

Incubation time varies from about 40 days in the smaller petrels to about 55 days or more in the larger species. Both sexes incubate and care for the chick, which is fed a regurgitated mixture of rich stomach oil and fishy remains. Importantly, chicks can store large deposits of fat between feedings which may be at intervals from several days to a week.

Chicks take their first flights when they reach 46 to 100 days old. These chicks spend their first year at sea before returning back to land to socialize and to investigate future nesting sites. Petrels and shearwaters can live relatively long lives, reaching into their upper twenties.

Adaptations

Birds which spend most of their life flying over vast windy stretches of ocean must have a variety of ways of dealing with the stresses and demands of such an existence, and petrels and shearwaters are remarkable in their adaptations. Most species have longish narrow wings designed for gliding and soaring, while some of the smaller diving petrels have short stubby wings which work well in the underwater pursuit of fish. To watch these graceful birds "shearing" the wavetops with their stiff-winged, seemingly effortless flight is to witness a true natural wonder.

Characteristic tubular nostrils located on top of the bill serve as a means to expel excess salt from their large salt glands, located internally near the eye sockets. These salt glands allow these birds to drink seawater without any harmful effects since their kidneys cannot produce a concentrated urine. The horny structure of the exterior nostrils protects the internal nasal passageways from the irritating salt spray and also serves as an opening to their very efficient olfactory organs. Petrels and shearwaters have an excellent sense of smell which they use to find food, burrows, and other birds.

These seabirds have oily waterproof feathers and a dense undercoat of insulating down. Their webbed feet not only help them swim but are also used, especially by the storm petrels, to patter upon the ocean's surface in search of floating bits of food.

The strong bills have a food-grabbing hook on the end, and the typical dark, or dark and light plumage helps them blend in to a monochromatic landscape.

The Petrels and Shearwaters have a characteristic musky odor arising from their stomach oils, which are used as a food for the young, as a defensive weapon (squirted when needed), and as additional waterproofing for their feathers.

Food

Some shearwaters and petrels dive to catch fish while other species feed on the surface of the ocean

KEY TERMS

Down—Short but springy and spread-out underfeathers in a bird which act as insulation by trapping dead air.

Macroplankton—Larger, visible members of the free-swimming and floating organisms found in the surface waters of oceans such as shrimp, jellyfish, and copepods.

where they pick up crustaceans, macroplankton, squid, and even garbage from ships. Giant petrels eat the young and eggs of other birds, and one may find a variety of Procelliformes feasting on the remains of a dead whale or seal.

Conservation

The introduction of "exotic" mammals, such as rats, pigs, dogs, and cats onto islands used by breeding seabirds has led to the large scale decimation of entire colonies. The dark-rumped petrel, for example, is now restricted to small remnant colonies on just four islands in the Galapagos islands of Ecuador, and less than four islands in Hawaii.

Further Reading:
Dorst, Jean. *The Life of Birds.* Vol. 2. New York: Columbia University Press, 1974.
Ehrlich, Paul, et al. *The Birder's Handbook.* New York: Simon and Shuster, 1988.
Harrison, Peter. *Seabirds: An Identification Guide.* Boston: Houghton Mifflin Co., 1983.
Terres, John. *The Audubon Encyclopedia of Birds.* New York: Knopf, 1980.
Wareham, John. *The Petrels: Their Ecology and Breeding Systems.* San Diego: Academic Press, 1990.
Welty, Joel Carl. *The Life of Birds.* 3rd. ed. New York: Saunders College Publishing, 1982.

Peter Salmansohn

Petroglyphs and pictographs

In archaeology, petroglyphs and pictographs are terms used to describe forms of "rock art." Petroglyph refers to a rock carving or etching, while the term pictograph is commonly applied to a rock painting. Typically, these features are found on the vertical or over-hanging surfaces of large boulders and are sometimes associated with nearby settlements. However, they are often found isolated a great distance from living areas. Although both types of rock art can be traced back to early prehistoric times, their occurrence in historic contexts are not uncommon. In fact, many traditional aboriginal cultures in Africa and Australia still practice the art of rock painting.

Origin and manufacture

Some of the oldest known rock art features are pictographs in France and Spain, cave paintings made by the Cro-Magnon culture of early humans have been dated to more than 30,000 years old. Protected from rain and sunlight in deep, underground passages, these features have withstood the ravages of time. Most of these colorful images are of animals such as deer and antelope, and are strikingly detailed and life-like.

When humans migrated into North America some 12,000 years ago the practice of creating rock art was brought with them. As time progressed and people spread out across the Western Hemisphere so did the use of rock art. Eventually, nearly all of the more than 200 distinct Native American tribes in North America used some form of rock art in ceremony. Interestingly, many of the artistic elements or patterns used in petroglyphs and pictographs are very similar among these many diverse groups.

From historic cultures that continue to create rock art, we have learned that petroglyphs were made by using a hand-held stone as a chisel or hammer to etch designs into boulders.

Pictographs, however, were considerably more complex to make because of the materials required for paint. Red pigments, which generally comprise the most common color found in rock paintings, were made from ground iron oxides obtained from the minerals hematite or magnetite. Talc, gypsum, or lime was used to make white, charcoal or graphite were employed for black, and copper ores were sometimes used for greens and blues.

These minerals were ground into fine powders then mixed with a resin, such as pine pitch. An oil base was sometimes added by grinding certain seeds or extracted from animal fat. Paints were applied either by fingers or with brushes made from the shredded end of stick, animal fur, or fibrous plant leaves.

Current research

Although pictographs and petroglyphs have withstood hundreds, perhaps thousands of years of exposure, modern pollutants and vandalism, coupled with natural elements, have accelerated their destruction. Recently, scientists have used microscopic mineral sampling to measure the types of chemical elements found in pictograph pigments. Additionally, studies have included the use of diversional watersheds, shelters, and application of protective adhesives to prevent rock art erosion. The continuing study of chemical compositions and rates of panel decay could one day lead to the discovery of a proper means by which to preserve these features indefinitely.

Petroleum

Petroleum is a term that includes a wide variety of liquid hydrocarbons. Many scientists also include natural gas in their definition of petroleum. The most familiar types of petroleum are tar, oil, and natural gas. Petroleum forms through the accumulation, burial, and transformation of organic material, such as the remains of plants and animals, by chemical reactions over long periods of time. After petroleum has been generated, it migrates upward through the Earth, seeping out at the surface of the Earth if it is not trapped below the surface. Petroleum accumulates when it migrates into a porous rock called a reservoir that has a non-porous seal or cap rock that prevents the oil from migrating further. To fully understand how petroleum forms and accumulates requires considerable knowledge of geology, including sedimentary rocks, geological structures (faults and domes, for example), and forms of life that have been fossilized or transformed into petroleum throughout the Earth's long history.

Tremendous petroleum reserves have been produced from areas all over the world. In the United States, the states of Alaska, California, Louisiana, Michigan, Oklahoma, Texas, and Wyoming are among the most important sources of petroleum. Other countries that produce great amounts of petroleum include Saudi Arabia, Iran, Iraq, Kuwait, Algeria, Libya, Nigeria, Indonesia, the former Soviet Union, Mexico, and Venezuela.

Petroleum products have been in use for many years. Primitive man might have used torches made from pieces of wood dipped in oil for lighting as early as 20,000 B.C. At around 5000 B.C., the Chinese apparently found oil when they were digging underground. Wide-

The 799 mile long Trans-Alaska Pipeline is capable of transporting over 1.2 million barrels of oil per day.

spread use of petroleum probably began in the Middle East by the Mesopotamians, perhaps by 3000 B.C., and probably in other areas where oil seeps were visible at the surface of the Earth. Exploration for petroleum in the United States began in 1853, when George Bissell, a lawyer, recognized the potential use of oil as a source of lamp fuel. Bissell also recognized that boring or drilling into the Earth, as was done to recover salt, might provide access to greater supplies of petroleum than surface seeps. In 1857, Bissell hired Edwin Drake, often called "Colonel" Drake despite having worked as a railroad conductor, to begin drilling the first successful oil well, in Titusville, Pennsylvania. The well was drilled in 1859. Once the usefulness of oil as a fuel was widely recognized, exploration for oil increased. By 1885, oil was discovered in Sumatra, Indonesia. The famous "gusher" in the Spindletop field in eastern Texas was drilled in 1901. The discoveries of giant oil fields in the Middle East began in 1908 when the company now known as British Petroleum drilled a well in Persia (now Iran). During World Wars I and II, oil became a critical factor in the ability to successfully wage war.

Currently, petroleum is among our most important natural resources. We use gasoline, jet fuel, and diesel fuel to run cars, trucks, aircraft, ships, and other vehicles. Home heat sources include oil, natural gas, and electricity, which in many areas is generated by burning natural gas. Petroleum and petroleum-based chemicals are important in manufacturing plastic, wax, fertilizers, lubricants, and many other goods. Thus, petroleum is an important part of many human activities.

Types of petroleum

Petroleum, including liquid oil and natural gas, consists of substances known as hydrocarbons. Hydro-carbons, as their name suggests, comprise hydrogen and carbon, with small amounts of impurities such as nitrogen, oxygen, and sulfur. The molecules of hydrocarbons can be as simple as that of methane, which consists of a carbon atom surrounded by 4 hydrogen atoms, abbreviated as CH_4. More complex hydrocarbons, such as naphthenes, include rings of hydrogen and carbon atoms linked together. Differences in the number of hydrogen and carbon atoms in molecules as well as their molecular structure (carbon atoms arranged in a ring structure, chain, or tetrahedron, for example) produce numerous types of petroleum.

Different types of petroleum can be used in different ways. Jet fuel differs from the gasoline that automobiles consume, for example. Refineries separate different petroleum products by heating petroleum to the point that heavy hydrocarbon molecules separate from lighter hydrocarbons so that each product can be used for a specific purpose. Refining reduces the waste associated with using limited supplies of more expensive petroleum products in cases in which a cheaper, more plentiful type of petroleum would suffice. Thus, tar or asphalt, the dense, nearly solid hydrocarbons, can be used for road surfaces and roofing materials, waxy substances called paraffins can be used to make candles and other products, and less dense, liquid hydrocarbons can be used for engine fuels.

Sources of petroleum

Petroleum is typically found beneath the surface of the Earth in accumulations known as fields. Fields can contain oil, gas, tar, water, and other substances, but oil, gas, and water are the most common. In order for a field to form, there must be some sort of structure to trap the petroleum, a seal on the trap that prohibits leakage of the petroleum, and a reservoir rock that has adequate pore space, or void space, to hold the petroleum. To find these features together in an area in which petroleum has been generated by chemical reactions affecting organic remains requires many coincidences of timing of natural processes.

Petroleum generation occurs over long periods of time, millions of years. In order for petroleum generation to occur, organic matter such as dead plants or animals must accumulate in large quantities. The organic matter can be deposited along with sediments and later buried as more sediments accumulate on top. The sediments and organic material that accumulate are called source rock. After burial, chemical activity in the absence of oxygen allows the organic material in the source rock to change into petroleum without the organic matter simply rotting. A good petroleum source rock is a sedimentary rock such as shale or limestone that contains between 1% and 5% organic carbon. Rich source rocks occur in many environments, including lakes, deep areas of the seas and oceans, and swamps. The source rocks must be buried deep enough below the surface of the Earth to heat up the organic material, but not so deep that the rocks metamorphose or that the organic material changes to graphite or materials other than hydrocarbons. Temperatures less than 300° F (150° C) are typical for petroleum generation.

Once a source rock generates and expels petroleum, the petroleum migrates from the source rock to a rock that can store the petroleum. A rock capable of storing petroleum in its pore spaces, the void spaces between the grains of sediment in a rock, is known as a reservoir rock. Rocks that have sufficient pore space through which petroleum can move include sandstone, limestone, and rocks that have many fractures. A good reservoir rock might have pore space that exceeds 30% of the rock volume. Poor quality reservoir rocks have less than 10% void space capable of storing petroleum. Rocks that lack pore space tend to lack permeability, the property of rock that allows fluid to pass through the pore spaces of the rock. With very few pores, it is not likely that the pores are connected and less likely that fluid will flow through the rock than in a rock with larger or more abundant pore spaces. Highly porous rocks tend to have better permeability because the greater number of pores and larger pore sizes tend to allow fluids to move through the reservoir more easily. The property of permeability is critical to producing petroleum: If fluids can not migrate through a reservoir rock to a petroleum production well, the well will not produce much petroleum and the money spent to drill the well has been wasted.

In order for a reservoir to contain petroleum, the reservoir must be shaped and sealed like a container. Good petroleum reservoirs are sealed by a less porous and permeable rock known as a seal or cap rock. The seal prevents the petroleum from migrating further. Rocks like shale and salt provide excellent seals for reservoir rocks because they do not allow fluids to pass through them easily. Seal-forming rocks tend to be made of small particles of sediment that fit closely together so that pore spaces are small and poorly connected. The permeability of a seal must be virtually zero in order to retain petroleum in a reservoir rock for millions to hundreds of millions of years, the time span between formation of petroleum to the discovery and production of many petroleum fields. Likewise, the seal must not be subject to forces within the Earth that might cause fractures or other breaks in the seal to form.

Reservoir rocks and seals work together to form a trap for petroleum. Typical traps for petroleum include hills shaped like upside-down bowls below the surface of the Earth, known as anticlines, or traps formed by faults. Abrupt changes in rock type can form good traps, such as sandstone deposits next to shale deposits, especially if a sand deposit is encased in a rock that is sufficiently rich in organic matter to act as a petroleum source and endowed with the properties of a good seal.

An important aspect of the formation of petroleum accumulations is timing. The reservoir must have been deposited prior to petroleum migrating from the source rock to the reservoir rock. The seal and trap must have been developed prior to petroleum accumulating in the reservoir, or else the petroleum would have migrated farther. The source rock must have been exposed to the appropriate temperature and pressure conditions over long periods of time to change the organic matter to petroleum. The necessary coincidence of several conditions is difficult to achieve in nature.

Petroleum exploration and production

Petroleum exploration and production activities are performed primarily by geologists, geophysicists, and engineers. Geologists look for areas of the Earth where sediments accumulate. They then examine the area of interest more closely to determine whether or not source rocks and reservoir rocks exist there. They examine the rocks at the surface of the Earth and information from wells drilled in the area. Geologists also examine satellite images of large or remote areas to evaluate the rocks more quickly.

Geophysicists examine seismic data, data derived from recording waves of energy introduced into the rock layers of the Earth through dynamite explosions or other means, to determine the shape of the rock layers beneath the surface and whether or not traps such as faults or anticlines exist.

Once the geologist or geophysicist has gathered evidence of potential for a petroleum accumulation, called a prospect, an engineer assists in determining how to drill a well or multiple wells to assess the prospect. Drilling a well to explore for petroleum can cost as little as $100,000 and as much as $30,000,000 or more, depending on how deep the well must be drilled, what types of rocks are present, and how remote the well location is. Thus, the scientists must evaluate how much the well might cost, how big the prospect might be, and how likely the scientific predictions are to be correct. In general, approximately 15% of exploration wells are successful.

Once a successful exploration well has been drilled, the oil and/or gas flow are pumped to the surface of the Earth through the well. At the surface, the petroleum either moves through a pipeline or is stored in a tank or on a ship until it can be sold.

Petroleum reserves

Estimates of the amount of recoverable oil and natural gas in the United States are 112.6 billion barrels of oil and 1,073.8 trillion cubic feet of natural gas. Worldwide estimates of recoverable oil and natural gas are 1 trillion barrels of oil and 5 quadrillion cubic feet of natural gas. These worldwide reserves are expected to supply 45 years of fuel at current production rates with expected increases in demand. However, such estimates do not take into account reserves added through new discoveries or through the development of new technology that would allow more oil and natural gas to be recovered from existing oil and natural gas fields.

Daily consumption of oil in the United States exceeds 17 million barrels of oil per day, of which approximately 7 million barrels are in the form of gasoline for vehicles. Over half the petroleum consumed in the United States is imported from other countries. (Assuming oil costs $20 per barrel and we import 8.5 million barrels per day, over one billion dollars per week are spent on oil imports). While the United States has tremendous reserves of petroleum, the undiscovered fields that remain tend to be smaller than the fields currently producing petroleum outside of the United States. Thus, less expensive foreign reserves are imported to the United States. When foreign petroleum increases in price, more exploration occurs in the United States as it becomes more profitable to drill wells in order to exploit smaller reservoirs.

Current research

Current research in petroleum includes many different activities. Within companies that explore for and produce petroleum, scientists and engineers try to determine where they should explore for petroleum, how they might recover more petroleum from a given field, and what types of tools can be lowered into wells in order to enhance our understanding of whether or not that individual well might have penetrated an oil or gas field. They also examine more fundamental aspects of how the Earth behaves, such as how rocks form and what forms of life have existed at various times in the Earth's history. The United States Geological Survey continues to evaluate petroleum reserves and new technology to produce oil and gas. The federal government operates several facilities called Strategic Petroleum

KEY TERMS

Barrel—A unit of volume typically used for oil. A barrel contains 42 gal (160 l).

Field—An accumulation of oil or natural gas (or both) that can be produced, usually for a profit.

Hydrocarbon—Compound made from atoms of hydrogen and carbon. Methane (CH_4) and propane (C_3H_8) are simple, gaseous hydrocarbons. Oil can vary from tar to very light liquid hydrocarbon to natural gas.

Natural gas—Gaseous hydrocarbon.

Oil—Liquid hydrocarbon.

Petroleum—Substances made of hydrogen and carbon compounds ("hydrocarbons"), typically also containing impurities such as nitrogen, sulfur, and oxygen.

Reservoir rock—A rock that has sufficient pore space and connection between pores to allow oil or gas to be stored in the rock and to flow out of the rock. Sandstones and limestones can be excellent reservoir rocks.

Seal—Rock made of fine particles and having little pore space or connection between pores that prevents fluids from leaking out of a reservoir rock. Shale and salt provide some of the best seals for petroleum reservoirs.

Sedimentary rock—Rock made up of grains of preexisting rock or organic matter, or rocks that precipitate from water. Sandstone and limestone are common sedimentary rocks.

Source rock—Sedimentary rock containing sufficient organic matter (1/2% to 5% organic carbon from organic matter in a source rock is typical) to generate petroleum.

Trap—A structure in which petroleum can accumulate and be stored. Anticlines (dome-shaped structures below the surface of the Earth) can form good traps. Traps can also form along faults and in areas where rock types change rapidly.

Reserves that store large quantities of petroleum for use in times of supply crisis.

Petroleum exploration specialists are using a type of geophysical data known as three-dimensional seismic data to study the structures and rock types below the surface of the Earth in order to determine where exploration wells might successfully produce petroleum. Geochemists are assessing the results of studies of the chemistry of the surface of the Earth and whether or not these results can improve the predictions of scientists prior to drilling expensive exploratory wells.

Significant recent discoveries of petroleum have been made in many areas of the world: Algeria, Brazil, China, Egypt, Indonesia, the Ivory Coast, Malaysia, Papua New Guinea, Thailand, the United Kingdom, and Vietnam, among others. In the United States, the Gulf of Mexico, Gulf Coast states, California, and Alaska continue to attract the interest of explorationists.

See also Air pollution; Fossil and fossilization; Hydrocarbon; Internal combustion engine; Natural gas; Oil drilling; Oil spills; Plastics.

Further Reading:
Horn, M.K. "Oil and Gas." *Geotimes*, v. 40, n. 2, 1995.
Oil and Gas Journal, weekly journal published by PennWell.
Yergin, Daniel. *The Prize.* New York: Simon and Schuster, 1991.

Gretchen M. Gillis

Peyote see **Addiction; Cactus**

pH

pH is a numerical measure of the acidity or alkalinity of a solution. The pH scale was developed by Sorensen in 1909 and is generally presented as ranging from 0-14, although there are no theoretical limits on the range of the scale (there are substances with negative pH's and with pH's greater than 14, although for most substances the range of 0-14 suffices). A solution with a pH of less than 7 is acidic and a solution with a pH of greater than 7 is basic (alkaline). The midpoint of the scale, 7, is neutral. The lower the pH of a solution, the more acidic the solution is and the higher the pH, the more basic it is. The pH symbol is an abbreviation for the expression "potential of hydrogen." or "power of hydrogen." Mathematically, pH is defined by the equation: $pH = - \log [H_3O^+]$, or $- \log [H^+]$. Where H^+ represents a hydrogen ion or a proton, and H_3O+ represents the hydronium ion. It can be thought of as a water molecule with a proton attached. The square brackets mean "the concentration of, in moles per liter." Thus, $[H_3O^+]$ means "the concentration of hydronium ions is moles per liter.

TABLE		
Substance	*Approximate pH*	*H_3O^+*
battery acid (sulfuric acid)	0	1M
lemon juice	2	1×10^{-2}M
vinegar	2.5	3×10^{-3}M
coffee	5	1×10^{-5}M
distilled water	7	1×10^{-7}M
borax	9	1×10^{-9}M
household ammonia solution	11	1×10^{-11}M
1M NaOH (sodium hydroxide, lye)	14	1×10^{-14}M

The chart above lists some common substances and their approximate pH's. Notice the pH does not have to be a whole number and that a difference of .3 pH units can means twice the acidity (or concentration of hydronium ions).

The pH of solutions may be measured electronically with a pH meter (better pH meters can measure to .001 pH units) or by using acid base indicators, chemicals which change color in solutions of different pH.

See also Acids and bases.

Phainopepla see **Waxwings**

Phalangers

Phalangers are a small group of arboreal mammals belonging to the family *Phalangeridae*, of which 14 species are recognized in three genera. Phalangers, more commonly known as possums and cuscuses, are marsupials but with a vague resemblance to some monkeys. Indeed many early European explorers thought that they were monkeys. These species occur in Australia, New Guinea and adjacent islands west to Sulawesi (Indonesia) and east to the Solomon Islands. New Guinea is thought to be the main center for evolution of these species with eight species represented. In addition to their natural range, some species have been introduced, such as the brushtail possum (*Trichosurus vulpecula*) to New Zealand (for their valuable fur) and the common cuscus (*Phalanger orientalis*) to the Solomon Islands.

Phalangers are short, compact animals with thickly furred bodies. A wide range of colors occur from the predominantly reddish-brown fur of the common cuscus to the pure white coat with dark spots of the spotted cuscus (*Spilocuscus maculatus*) and the strikingly marked black spotted cuscus (*S. rufoniger*), the largest of all phalangers with a black back, orange-russet limbs, white underside and russet and white head. In most species the short ears are concealed by the thick fur. Their limbs are adapted to climbing, with sharp, curved claws for climbing and clawless, but opposable, first hind toes which assist with grasping small branches. They also have a strong prehensile tail, which is usually bare towards the tip. Phalangers are most active at night—their large, forward-pointing eyes enable them to receive sufficient light to guide them through the tangle of branches and leaves in the forest canopy. A wide range of food items are taken, including young leaves, buds, shoots, fruit and occasionally insects, birds eggs and small lizards.

Little is known about the social behavior of many of these species. Phalangers are probably capable of breeding throughout the year, but apart from when females are receptive to breeding, they all appear to be solitary animals, occupying a range of 7.5-20 acres (3-8 ha), depending on food, shelter and population density. In the wild, phalangers are relatively long-lived animals, with some living up to 13 years of age.

Possums and cuscuses are well-known to humans—possums, in particular, for the economic damage they cause in timber plantations, as well as for their crop-raiding habits. In New Zealand, the damage caused to native vegetation has also been significant, as most of these trees evolved in the absence of foliage-feeding animals and are therefore unable to produce enough toxins to repel attack. It is also thought that the common brushtail may spread tuberculosis, which has led to a major eradication scheme of this species in New Zealand.

As they rarely come down to the ground, possums and cuscuses have few natural predators, apart from large birds of prey and snakes. Human activities are thought to have had a major impact, at least on certain species, through habitat destruction which, in certain cases, is made worse by hunting pressure. Although the precise conservation status of most species is still uncertain, at least one species, the Woodlark island cuscus (*Phalanger lullulae*) which is confined to Woodlark island and Alcester island in Papua New Guinea is known to be in serious trouble. A species of lowland rain forest cuscus, it is only known from eight specimens—four collected in 1894 and another four from 1953. Almost nothing is known about the ecology of this cuscus, which is now thought to be threatened as a result of deforestation and overhunting within its restricted range. Another species about which very little is known is the scaly-tailed possum (*Wyulda squamicaudata*)—the only species in its genus—known from northwestern Australia. In New Guinea, most species of cuscus are hunted for their meat and prized fur which is worn at special ceremonies. It is essential that appropriate conservation measures are taken to protect the native habitat of all of these species and to fully evaluate the extent of threats facing them from habitat loss and hunting.

See also Marsupials.

Phalaropes see **Sandpipers; Shore birds**

Pharynx see **Digestive system; Respiratory system**

Pheasants

Pheasants are large species of fowl in the family Phasianidae, which also includes the partridges, peafowl, francolins, and quail. The greatest diversity of pheasants occurs in Asia, but native species also occur in Africa and Europe. In addition, many species of pheasants have been widely introduced as gamebirds beyond their natural range. Pheasants are also kept as handsome showbirds in zoos, parks, and private aviaries.

Male pheasants, or cocks, are beautifully colored birds, with a distinctive, long tail that approximately doubles the length of the animal. Their body can be colored in hues and patterns of yellow, orange, golden, red, blue, green, black, or white. Female pheasants, or hens, have a much more subdued and cryptic coloration. Pheasants also have a long neck, a strong beak that is hooked at the tip, and strong legs and feet for scratching in the forest floor to find their foods of fruits, seeds, and invertebrates.

Pheasants are mostly terrestrial birds, foraging widely over the forest floor for food. At night, however, most species roost in trees for safety.

Cock pheasants are strongly territorial during the breeding season. They defend their territory by making loud screeches, cackles, crowings, and squawks. Cock

A male ring-necked pheasant (*Phasianus colchicus*) on Pelee Island, Ontario.

pheasants will also fight each other when necessary, using a sharp spur on the back of their leg as a potentially lethal weapon. Cock pheasants mount spectacular displays to impress potential mates, including elaborate struttings with their colorful finery displayed to its best vantage, with the tail spread widely in some species.

Pheasants are polygynous, meaning a single male will mate with as many females as possible. Competition for mates is very intense in polygynous species, and this commonly leads to the evolution of seemingly bizarre traits in male birds, which are intended to impress the females, as in the pheasants. Some of these traits may even be maladaptive in terms of everyday life, for example, by making male birds more vulnerable to being killed by predators. However, the traits are highly favorable in terms of sexual selection, and this is why they can persist in the population.

Most species of pheasants nest on the ground, but some do so in trees. Female pheasants build the nest, incubate the eggs, and care for the chicks. Pheasant babies are precocious, meaning they can leave the nest soon after birth, following their hen and foraging for themselves. The family group stays in close contact by frequently clucking and peeping at each other. The chicks develop quickly, and develop flight feathers and can fly long before they reach adult size.

Species of pheasants

By far, the most familiar pheasant to the largest number of people is the red jungle fowl (*Gallus gallus*), a wild species of tropical forests of South and Southeastern Asia. However, domesticated varieties of this bird are commonly known as the chicken. This bird has been domesticated for thousands of years, and today an estimated 10-11 billion occur in captivity in agriculture.

In fact, the chicken may be the world's most abundant bird, albeit mostly in cultivation.

Other than the chicken, the most familiar species of pheasant is the ring-necked or versicolor pheasant (*Phasianus colchicus*), a species native to Europe and Asia. This species has been introduced as a gamebird to many places beyond its natural range. For example, feral populations of ring-necked pheasants occur in many places in temperate regions of North America, as well as in Australia, Africa, and elsewhere. The ring-necked pheasant is now the world's most widely distributed gamebird.

The Japanese pheasant (*Phasianus versicolor*) is native to Japan, but has been introduced to Europe and elsewhere as a gamebird.

The Lady Amherst's pheasant (*Chrysolophus amherstiae*) is native to Tibet and Burma. This species has a white and black extensible neck cape, consisting of a ruff of long feathers on the back of the head, that during courtship displays can be extended into an almost semicircular, downward-hanging fan. The golden pheasant (*C. pictus*) has a similar neck cape, but it is colored gold and black. Both of these birds maintain small, feral populations in England and in other places where they have been successfully introduced.

Many people consider the most spectacular species of pheasant to be the argus pheasant (*Argusianus argus*) of peninsular Malaya, Borneo, and Sumatra. In this species, the tail is more than twice as long as the body proper, and can be fanned widely in the manner of a peafowl.

Pheasants and people

Some species of pheasants are extremely important economically. The most valuable species, of course, is the domestic chicken. Billions of individuals of this species are eaten each year by people around the world, as are even larger numbers of chicken eggs.

Other species of pheasants are important as game birds, and are hunted as a source of wild meat, or for sport. However, pheasants can easily be overhunted, so it is important to conserve their populations. In some places, pheasants are raised in captivity and then released to penned or unpenned areas, where people pay a fee to hunt the birds.

Pheasants are also of great aesthetic importance. Various species are kept in captivity in zoos, parks, and private aviaries. This is mostly done for the pure joy and educational value of having such lovely creatures in plain view.

KEY TERMS

Feral—This refers to a non-native, often domesticated species that is able to maintain a viable, breeding population in a place that is not part of its natural range, but to which it has been introduced by humans.

Polygyny—A breeding system in which a male will attempt to breed with as many females as possible. In birds, the female of a polygynous species usually incubates the eggs and raises the babies.

Sexual selection—This is a type of natural selection in which anatomical or behavioral traits may be favored because they confer some advantage in courtship or another aspect of breeding. For example, the bright coloration, long tail, and elaborate displays of male pheasants have resulted from sexual selection by females, who apparently favor extreme expressions of these traits.

Unfortunately, many species of pheasants are becoming increasingly scarce and even endangered in their native habitats. This is largely happening because of local overhunting of the birds, in combination with losses of natural habitat due to the harvesting of trees for valuable timber, and often the subsequent conversion of the land into agricultural and residential uses.

The increasing endangerment of so many beautiful species of pheasants is highly regrettable. This problem is only one facet of the general threat posed by human activities to Earth's legacy of biodiversity, and it must be effectively dealt with if species of pheasants are to always live in their wild, natural habitats.

Further Reading:

Beebe, W. *Monograph of the Pheasants.* New York: Dover Publications, 1991.

Delacour, J. *The Pheasants of the World, 2nd ed.* London: Beech Publishing House, 1977.

Harrison, A.D. (ed.). *Bird Families of the World.* New York: Abrams Pub., 1978.

Hill, D. and P. Robertson. *The Pheasant. Ecology, Management, and Conservation.* London: Blackwell, Sci. Pub., 1988.

Howman, K. *The Pheasants of the World.* Blackie, WA: Hancock House, 1993.

Long, J.L. *Introduced Birds of the World.* New York: Universe Books, 1981.

Bill Freedman

Phenyl group

A phenyl group is the functional group C_6H_5. It is the portion of an organic molecule that is derived from a benzene molecule, C_6H_6, by removal of a hydrogen atom. The term phenyl is used when a benzene ring is connected to a chain of six or more carbon atoms. If there are fewer than six carbon atoms in the chain, the compound is named as a substituted benzene. The phenyl group can be abbreviated in chemical structures as -Ph or sometimes as the Greek letter phi, -ϕ.

Benzene is a cyclic compound containing six carbon atoms and six hydrogen atoms. The molecular formula for benzene, C_6H_6, was determined soon after it was isolated by Michael Faraday in 1825 from the oily deposits removed from London's gas pipes. Later in 1834, benzene was found by Mitscherlich to be the product obtained from various chemical reactions involving gum benzoin, a fragrant medicinal ointment. In the manuscript describing his experiments, Mitscherlich suggested the compound be called benzin. Liebig, who edited the paper, renamed the compound benzol based on the German word for oil, *öl.* English and French chemists eventually changed the *-ol* ending to *-ene*, resulting in the name benzene. The reasoning was that the *-ol* suffix indicates an alcohol group whereas the *-ene* is used for compounds that contain double bonds. The term pheno, based on the Greek word, *phainein,* meaning "to shine" was proposed by Auguste Laurent in 1837.

This suggestion was never accepted, but it resulted in the term phenyl being commonly used when referring to the -C_6H_5 group. During the early 19th century, benzene was well established in a number of industrial processes, but its chemical structure had not been determined. August Kekulé in 1858 had developed the theory, which later proved true, that carbon atoms could be connected by bonds to form chains like those that make up alkanes. He then directed his attention to the structure of benzene. As the story goes, in 1865, Kekulé was writing at his desk one night and could not concentrate on the problem. He started to gaze into the fire in his fire place, when he eventually fell asleep. August had a dream of carbon atoms dancing before him, slowly forming chains and the chains turning into snakes. One snake's head

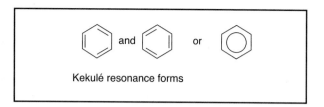

Kekulé resonance forms

Figure 1.

grabbed its own tail and formed a ring. Kekulé quickly woke up and spent the rest of the night developing his proposal that carbon atoms can be connected in a manner that forms rings. He combined this idea with the molecular formula for benzene, C_6H_6, and suggested the structure, shown in Figure 1. Kekulé also knew that benzene does not undergo the same types of reactions as simple chains of carbon and hydrogen atoms and that it has a greater chemical stability. In 1872, he proposed that the double bonds in benzene are not situated between any two carbon atoms but move around the ring. The best way to represent benzene is by what are called the Kekulé resonance forms or a hexagon with a circle in it.

In the left-hand representations, the benzene molecule is drawn as a hexagon with alternating single and double bonds. This is a shorthand method of drawing compounds used by chemists. A carbon atom is represented by an intersection of two straight lines or at the end of a line and the correct number of hydrogen atoms to give each carbon atom four bonds is implied but not drawn. The two equivalent Kekulé resonance forms indicate that the bond between any two carbon atoms in benzene is a combination of a single bond and a double bond. The hexagon with a circle means that the "real" structure for benzene is a combination of the two Kekulé resonance forms. This combined bond form is called resonance. The use of hexagon with a circle to represent benzene, was first suggested by Johannes Thiele in 1899. Today, it is the representation most preferred by chemists. Benzene and other cyclic compounds that have alternating single and double bonds which oscillate, such as naphthalene and anthracene, are called aromatic hydrocarbons.

Those compounds that have a chain of carbon atoms connected to a phenyl group are called arenes. Arenes are named by two different methods depending on the length and complexity of the carbon atom chain. If the chain of carbon atoms contains six or fewer carbon atoms, then the arene is named as a benzene ring with the appropriate alkyl group. For example, a benzene ring connected to a chain of two carbon atoms is named ethylbenzene. However, if the carbon atom

chain is longer than six carbon atoms or is rather complex, then the arene is designated as a phenyl group attached to the alkane chain. The compound, 3-phenyloctane, consists of a chain of eight carbon atoms with the third carbon atom bonded to a benzene ring. No matter what the length of the carbon atom chains; if the compound contains two or more benzene rings, it is named as a phenyl-alkane. A central carbon atom bonded to two benzene rings and to two hydrogen atoms would be called diphenylmethane.

The phenyl group is an important structural unit in many natural and synthetic or man made chemicals. It is an integral part of the molecular framework of many drugs, herbicides, dyes, plastics, perfumes, and food flavorings. Phenylephrine is used in the treatment of asthma, as well as in conjunction with various anesthetics to increase their time of activity. The melon flavored compound 2-phenyl propionaldehyde contains a benzene ring in its molecular framework. Phenylethyl alcohol is used routinely in the perfume industry because of it's rose fragrance. Various pesticides such as the phenylureas and phenylcarbamates contain phenyl rings and many of the preparations of indigo dye, a dye used in making blue jeans, use phenyl containing compounds such as N-phenylglycine.

See also Benzene.

Further Reading:

Fieser, L.F. and M. Fieser, *Advanced Organic Chemistry.* New York: Reinhold Publishing Co, 1961.

Kirk-Othmer, *Encyclopedia of Chemical Technology.* Ketones, Volume 4, page 73, New York: John Wiley and Sons, 1991.

McMurry, J. *Organic Chemistry.* Pacific Grove, CA: Brooks/Cole Publishing Company, 1992.

Partington, J.R. *A History of Chemistry, Vol 4.* London: Macmillan & Co., 1964.

Andrew Poss